The
SANDERS
Price Guide to
AUTOGRAPHS

Fifth Edition

In Memoriam: George Sanders (February 11, 1924—August 26, 1998)

The
SANDERS
Price Guide to
AUTOGRAPHS

Fifth Edition

THE WORLD'S LEADING AUTOGRAPH PRICING AUTHORITY

FOUNDED BY GEORGE SANDERS 1924-1998

Helen Sanders and Ralph Roberts

The Leading Autograph Reference Publisher ™

Publisher: Ralph Roberts
Vice-President/Publishing: Pat Roberts
Director of Autograph References
    and Chairperson of Advisory Board: Helen Sanders

Cover Design: Rochus Kofler
Executive Editor: Pat Roberts
Editors: Helen Sanders, Pat Roberts, Ralph Roberts, Gayle Graham

Interior Design and Electronic Page Assembly: **WorldComm**®

Printed in the United States of America

10 9 8 7 6 5 4 3 2 1
Fifth Edition

Trade Paper version: ISBN 1-57090-091-4

Limited Hardback version: ISBN 1-57090-094-9

Library of Congress Catalog Card Number: 99-64709

 While every effort has been made to ensure the accuracy of the information in this book, the authors and publisher accept no responsibility for inaccuracries or omissions, and the authors and publisher will in no event be liable for any loss of profit or any other damage, including but not limited to special, incidental, consequential, or any other damages. Be sure to read Chapter 20 "How to Use This Price Guide" in this book for how our pricing works and how to use those prices.

The opinions expressed in this book are solely those of the authors and are not necessarily those of Alexander Books.

Trademarks
Names of products mentioned in this book known to be or that are suspected of being trademarks or service marks are capitalized. Use of a product or service name in this book should not be regarded as affecting the validity of any trademark or service mark.

Alexander Books—a division of Creativity, Inc.—is a full-service publisher located at 65 Macedonia Road, Alexander NC 28701. Phone (828) 252-9515 or (828) 255-8719 fax or e-mail **sales@abooks.com**. Dealer inquiries welcome.

Internet web sites: **http://www.autograph-book.com** and **http://www.abooks.com**

Contents

Section 1: Information

Section 2: Ralph's Stuff

Section 4: Autograph Organizations

16 I.A.C.C. / I.A.D.A. by Stephen Koschal — 211

17 The Manuscript Society by David R. Smith — 213

18 P.A.D.A. — 215

19 THE U.A.C.C. (Universal Autograph Collectors Club) by Bob Erickson — 217

Section 5: Prices

20 How to Use This Price Guide — 221

21 Prices — 233

Section 6: Facsimiles

22 Facsimiles 637

Section 7: Autograph Dealers

23 Autograph Dealers 690

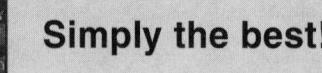

Preface

by Helen Doolittle Sanders

Prior to that fateful day in the last week of August, 1998 George and I sat down to discuss the upcoming edition of this book you now hold in your hand. Just as we had discussed the previous editions... their faults... their redemptions.... What improvements could be made and how... We also gave ourselves a little pat on the back and said, "By golly, we did it!" Good, bad or indifferent. Four editions already and this will be the fifth. We did it!

Nobody else even wanted to try. Remembering back ten to fifteen years or so, we tried desperately to encourage someone to write a price guide. After all, there were price guides for every collectible imaginable; Wedgwood Plates, Royal Doulton China, Coins, Stamps, Guns, Hummel Figurines, First Edition Books, Art and even prices for Collectible Lunch Boxes were available but nowhere could you get a clue as to the value of an autograph, signed letter, autographed photo or document. Nothing!

Who knew more at that time about this subject than the First Lady of Autographs—Mary Benjamin (see Chapter 7). But she was not interested. In fact, Mrs. Benjamin was rather opposed to having any such thing published. The love of history, the search, and the ultimate joy of acquisition— that is what mattered to her. And now I look back many years to the time we were in her New York City office on Madison Ave as she held up a document saying to George, "George, I think you should have this!" To which George replied, "how much is it, Mary?" Mary answered, "Six hundred dollars."

How many times since then did we laugh about not buying this very important piece of American History, signed by both George Washington and Thomas Jefferson, in pristine condition for $600? Perhaps she was right. Perhaps we collectors were better off emotionally and ethically before the commercialization of what was once a simple hobby?

Suggested for this monumental price guide task, of course, were Charles Hamilton, who was far too busy, and two other highly respected dealers, who I think, in hindsight, were probably insulted at the suggestion, no matter how competently they could have put together such a guide.

It was only by accident that Ralph Roberts—in February, 1986—had made an appointment to come over and interview George regarding a subject totally unrelated to autographs. On seeing the framed items decorating our walls he innocently asked about a price guide. "Who does the price guide?" To which we replied that there was none. Because he had just written and published a book about auctions, he was a bit surprised and remarked about the things displayed on the walls. "How do you arrive at a value for them? You know, for insurance, or if you wanted to sell them?"

At that time, back in the mid 1980s, we had no reply except to say that no one wanted to do such a book and that it be virtually impossible anyway because of the time and research required and that certainly the database for such a project would be impossible as well. (Keep in mind the limitations of a 1980s computer.) Ralph, however, being a computer genius, said he would write a program to handle the data. And so he did! For the first edition of this price guide he had to write eight versions of them to get it to work.

No, Ralph was not an autograph collector at that time. I did not think he had to be an autograph collector to write computer programs, format, typeset and distribute a book on autographs, although after 14 years, he has gained a great deal of expertise in the field and is now a very knowledgeable collector. There is no doubt he is smarter than all of us. Let's face the truth here: there would be no price guide were it not for the persistence of Ralph Roberts and his ability to computerize the price guide; thus making possible an otherwise impossible task.

The program used in the production of this book is, of course, *copyrighted*. The copyrighted database was devel-

George and Helen Sanders during a visit to the offices of Alexander Books in 1997.

oped after hours, weeks, months and years of research, and contains millions of items. It was not just randomly plucked out of some list. From our extensive database, we have selected those names that we believe our readers are most interested in. It was carefully selected research followed by a one-at-a-time computer entry. It is very consoling, having now completed as many editions as we have, to know that tucked in amongst the thousands of names are some that are not even real people. These were added for additional protection in the event that someone would want to scan the database for commercial use, which would, consequently, have made all of our hard work fruitless. Like mapmakers put false or obscure towns on their maps for protection, we have done the equivalent.

This book and our others, which have preceded it, is a labor of love for a hobby that was ignored for many years. It was written for those who had an interest but had nowhere to go for help. It is, after all, just a guide for you to use in order to make your own decisions. It is not perfect but it is honest. If shoes are going to be filled because of the absence of George Sanders, I suggest it is the individual collector who is going to fill them with his or her questions and with his or her individual honesty in each collecting quest.

George and Helen Sanders

It has taken from the time of George's sudden death to now, August, 1999, to update prices, add additional names, comments, dates and useful information. During this sad time of vulnerability it is indeed unfortunate that advantage was taken by one of our competitors to so hurriedly produce a temporary substitute for our book.

George's shoes are still under my bed after 50 years of loving companionship. No one can ever fill them. And for the lucky ones of you who had the opportunity to have meaningful conversations with him over the years or were fortunate enough to have him set you on the right road to collecting autographs, please go ahead and miss him just a little bit and I shall go ahead and do what I have always done in regards to this book.... give you the names, prices and information to the best of my ability.

I HOPE, IN THE NEAR FUTURE, GOD WILLING, TO BE ABLE TO TELL YOU ABOUT THE **REAL** GEORGE SANDERS. AUTOGRAPHS WERE ONLY A PART OF HIS MOST AMAZING LIFE!

autographically yours,

George Sanders

Helen Paolette Sanders

About This Price Guide

by Ralph Roberts, coauthor and publisher

This is our <u>eighth</u> autograph price guide over the last twelve years. We invented autograph price guides and have done more of them than anyone else in the world. Our first two were published by the Wallace-Homestead Book Company of Radnor, Pennsylvania—owned by Capital Cities/ ABC at that time and now by Krause Publications of Iola, Wisconsin. These were **The Price Guide to Autographs** 1st and 2nd editions, and were released in 1988 and 1991 respectively. Our third price guide, **The 1994 Sanders Price Guide to Sports Autographs**, was published by Scott Publishing—the famous stamp guide people—in 1994. The fourth book (and the 3rd edition of general prices) was **The 1994-95 Sanders Price Guide to Autographs**, the first published by Alexander Books of Alexander, North Carolina—our current publisher—who also published the **1995-1996 Sanders Price Guide to**

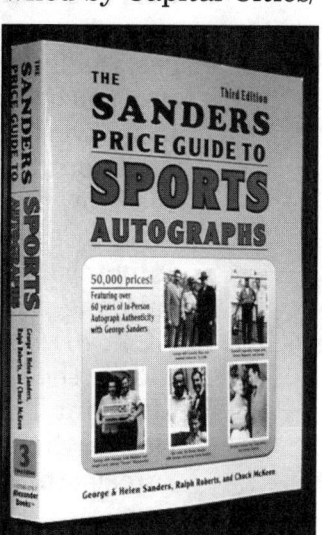

Sanders Sports, 3rd Edition

Sports Autographs (the 2nd edition of our sports price guide). The sixth price guide was **The Sanders Price Guide to Autographs** (4th edition) and the seventh was issued in December, 1998, being the 3rd edition of the sports price guide; currently available. You now hold in your hands: **The Sanders Price Guide to Autographs** (5th edition).

We have various other autograph-related books in the works and continue in our staunch commitment of bringing you the very *best* autograph reference library available anywhere!

The autograph field has grown dramatically in the last few years, just as our efforts in compiling the best price guides in the hobby have also expanded severalfold. This price guide reaches new heights of completeness with the most names and prices of any autograph price guide ever published. That's the goal we strive for with every new edition.

One important item you should know is that this book—even though it has more names and more prices than you've ever had in one convenient place before—*has everthing except sports-related names and prices*. All sports-related names and materials are to be found in our sports price guide, **The Sanders Price Guide to Sports Autographs**. We simply have too many names and prices to put everything into one volume. So, yes, you'll need both books, but these two volumes together now give you over *a thousand* pages of the best information available in the world of autographs.

To order any of our price guides, simply call or fax 1-800-472-0438, or access **www.autograph-book.com** for secure Visa/MasterCard ordering, or send a check for $29.45 (includes $4.50 shipping and handling in the U.S. only—overseas inquire as to shipping) to Alexander Books, 65 Macedonia Road, Alexander NC 28701 USA. Or order through any bookstore. We are distributed in the U.S. by Ingram, Baker & Taylor, Quality Books, and Midpoint Trade books. In Canada, our distributor is Hushion House. Our e-mail address is **sales@abooks.com**.

Ralph Roberts
August, 1999

Right: George Sanders gets an autograph from Baseball Hall of Fame pitcher Bob Feller. George's 60 years of collecting experience, and the almost equal time of Helen Sanders, contribute greatly to making the Sanders autograph price guides the world's leading authority on the value of signatures.

Acknowledgments

These are the splendid men and women (in alphabetical order) who have made the interesting hobby of autograph collecting one of the most rewarding experiences of our lives. They are, in varying degrees, responsible for the happiness and financial gains that make this never-ending pursuit such a truly exciting undertaking. In most cases this list includes personal friends, acquaintances, competitors, suppliers, members of the media, family members, and, most importantly, learned advisors. Not one forger or spin doctor is included.

Jon Allan
Bob Allen (*Antique Week*)
Allan Abrams (Toledo *Blade*)
Tim Anderson
Russell Atwood, *Arts & Entertainment*
Al Avalon, Hawaii
Jack L. Bacon
Edward Baig (*Business Week*)
Arbe Barais
Catherine Barnes
Robert F. Batchelder
David M. Beach (contributor, financial prices)
Chris Bell, Midpoint
Mary A. Benjamin
Saimi Rote Bergmann (The Repository, Canton, OH)
Jim Berland
Barbara Bigham (*Autograph Times*, Phoenix, AZ)
Norman Boas
Warren Boroson

(Hackensack *Sunday Record*)
Harvey Brandwein
Fremont Brown, Asheville
Brenda Burch (WLOS-TV, Asheville, NC)
Walter Burks
Carol Cain (Mobile Alabama *Register*)
Dr. Ronald R. Caldwell
Paul Carr
John E. Carter
Dwight Chapin (San Francisco *Examiner*)
John Crudele (New York *Post* Syndicate)
Duane Dancer (KLIF, Dallas)
Roy and Mies Deeley (England)
John Denos, actor/producer
Suzanne Dolezal (Detroit *Free Press*)
Amy Dunkin (*BusinessWeek*)
Sophie Dupre (England)

Carla Eaton
Robert "Bob" Eaton
Tom Eisaman
Bob Erickson (Pres., UACC)
Nancy Fraser, Midpoint
    Trade Books
Clifford O. Feingold, D.D.S.
Phillip Fiorini (*USA Today*)
Cathy & Roger E. Gilchrist
Bud Glick
Anita Gold, syndicated
    columnist
Cy Gold, Ace Enterprises
Miegan & Chandler Gordon
Dr. Greg Glance
Marilyn Greenwald (*Boys
    Life* magazine)
Gil and Karen Griggs
Jim Hagar
Diane Hamilton
Donn Harmon
Gary Hendershott
Stephen Hisler
Jeanne Hoyt
Jaime Hubbard, *Financial
    Post*, Toronto
A. Bruce Hunt III
Christopher C. Jaeckel
Lloyd Jassin, world's finest
    copyright attorney!
Betty, Susan & Greg
    Johnson
Eric Kampmann, Midpoint
    Trade Books
Eileen Keiter
Sandy Kenyon, KQNA,
    Arizona
Kristin & Michael Kern
    (Oregon)
Susan and Peter Kerville
    (Australia)
Carol King (Asheville, NC)
Stephen Koschal (IACC/DA)
Pierce A. Koslosky, Jr.
Gail Kump, Midpoint

John La Barber
John Laurence (Florida)
Kenneth R. Laurence
    (Florida)
Gary & Connie Lawrence (IL)
Alan Levi
Stephen Levy
Jerry D. Litzel (Ames, Iowa)
James Lowe
David H. Lowenherz
George S. Lowry
Bill Luetge
Joe and Scott Lusk (TN)
Bill Maloney (Software
    Solutions, Asheville NC)
Cathy Marshall (CNN News)
Emma & J.L. Mashburn
Dr. Michael J. & Patrice
    Masters
Frank & Ruth Ann Matthews
Rebecca May *curiocity for
    kids*
Ann McCutchan (Gannett
    News Service)
Pam & Chuck McKeen
Beth McLeod (South Palm
    Beach *County Living*)
Harold P. Merry
C.J. Middendorf (San Diego,
    CA)
Bonni J. Miller (*Goldmine*
    magazine)
George Robert Minkoff
Michael Minor
Stuart J. Morrissey
Howard S. Mott
Matthew Mrowicki and the
    CACC
J.B. Muns
Harry Nadley, Phila.
Donn Noble
William J. Novick
Karen & James Oleson
Nancy Page
Basil "Bill" Panagopulos

Beverly Parkhurst, Dallas
Jerry E. Patterson
Louise Pennisi
Cordelia & Tom Platt
Robert L. Polk
Talmage Powell
Angelica Giesser & Udo
    Prager (Germany)
ProComm Studio Services
    (Arden, N.C.)
Stephen S. Raab
Larry Rafferty
Celeste & Ray Rast
Diana J. Rendell
Annette Reynolds, Baton
    Rouge *State-Times*
Tracy & John Reznikoff
Brian Riba
Stanley J. Richmond
Pat Roberts
Hinda Rose (England)
Sheila & Rhodes T. Rumsey
Bill Safka
Joseph R. Sakmyster
Rebecca & Stephen G.
    Sanders
Dana and George M.
    "Sandy" Sanders
Richard Saunders
Todd Savage, Chicago
    Tribune
Harris Schaller, UACC
David Schulson
Gemma Sica
Ann & Louis Sica, Jr.
Kaye & Merv Slotnick
James Smalldon
Pat & Jim Smith (Wells,
    Maine)
Dr. Lewis C. Sommerville
William W. Stanhope
Christophe Stickel
Jim Stingl, Milwaukee
    Journal/Sentinel
Jim Stinson

Gerard A.J. Stodolski
Georgia Terry
Bob Tollett
E.N. Treverton
Louis Trotter
Wallace Turner (New York
    Times)
Larry Vrzalik
Susan Sanders Wadopian
Joan, Erin & Lael Wadopian
Joel Sanders Wadopian
John Waggoner (*USA
    Today*)
Dewey Webb (Phoenix,
    Arizona *New Times*)
Daniel Weinberg
Bob Wieselman, UpTime
    Computers, Asheville
Michelle and Tom Williams
John Wilson (England)
Al Wittnebert (Treasurer,
    UACC)
Chris Wloszczyna (*USA
    Today*)
Jaye Wright (*Florida Today*)
Dr. Ellis "Bill" Zussman
    (Wisconsin)

autographically yours,

Geor G. Sanders

Helen Doolittle Sanders

Ralph Roberts

Helen Sanders: An Appreciation

by Ralph Roberts

There were one or two who said—both unkindly and <u>untruthfully</u>—that there would be no more Sanders price guides after the unfortunate passing of George Sanders in August, 1998. Those people were wrong. We got the sports autograph guide out in December, 1998. This book you hold in your hand went to press in August, 1999. More follow.

Yes, George contributed much to these books—his was the personality that served as our spokesperson, a task he was exceptionally good at and which served us very well. He contributed his encyclopedic knowledge of the autograph field to help us stay on the straight and narrow, maintaining our integrity and putting out the most honest guides possible. He wrote the occasional chapter in readable but uniquely stylistic prose that sang ever so sweetly of his love of autographs. He importuned other autograph experts to contribute their valued wisdom.

And me? I wrote some. I created the computer techniques and databases that makes this price guide possible. I hammer out the editorial consistency of the books. I design the format and do the typesetting. I act as publisher and make sure the books sell after they reach print.

But Helen Sanders, of course, <u>does all the real work</u>—not George and I. We never did, it was Helen. <u>She does the prices</u>! That's the most Gargantuan task. Month after month, year after year of arduous, painstaking garnering of information from scores of dealers and many other sources. Endless hours of analyzing trends, studying anomalies, totaling figures, finding a true average; a statistical mean but one infused with Helen's professional judgement that accurately will become a guide for the value of a particular signature. No one else has the knowlege nor the million-plus item database accumulated over fourteen years to match her. She is truly the Queen of Prices.

The
SANDERS
Price Guide to
AUTOGRAPHS

Fifth Edition

Section 1:

INFORMATION

*Being an illuminating collection of informative
articles by carefully selected experts on the collection and perservation of autographs, and including
chapters on the joy and magic of autograph collecting, an extensive chapter about signed magazine
covers, rare and unusal presidential material, military signatures, First Day Covers, as well as an
inspiration tribute to the late and great autograph
dealer Mary Benjamin.*

George Sanders never missed the chance for an in-person autograph. Here he happily retreives his pen from the immoratal comic Danny Kaye after getting the comedian's signature. George and his wife Helen's encyclopedic knowledge of the autograph field is the firm foundation on which The Sanders Price Guides are based, but we never stop learning about this wonderful hobby to better serve our readers.

Chapter 1

The Joy and Magic of Autograph Collecting

by Ralph Roberts

For me, it all started on February 13th, 1986—as I write this, that's almost exactly thirteen years ago. The number '13' has turned out to be quite lucky for me, and for of you, the legion of autograph collectors that have come to depend on these price guides. (And for that, we thank you!)

I was doing freelance interviews in those long ago days for a local weekly newspaper, eking out a meager but adequate living as a freelance writer. That paper—the *Carolina Sun*—has regrettably long since set, although Bill Taylor, its most excellent editor, now prints our own paper, the *Alexander News*. [For a free copy, e-mail me at ralph@abooks.com or drop a note to me at 65 Macedonia Road, Alexander NC 28701 USA.] Anyway, someone had suggest an interview of this reputedly interesting old geezer who went along the roads of our beautiful mountain area picking up trash.

It sounded like a neat little human-interest angle piece, Bill and I both agreed—this elderly gentleman who cared enough to police up the beer cans and fast food wrappers so carelessly discarded by those too-plentiful insensitive yahoo defilers of Mother Nature. I was immediately for doing the story but Bill's opinion was important as he authorized the $40 or so check I would get for my time. (Thanks, Bill!)

The supposedly-to-be short interview turned out to be much more! The guy who answered the door at the substantial brick home (I checked the address twice just to make sure) was not "some old geezer." He was friendly, educated, and quickly proved himself to be obviously knowledgeable about the world.

"What this?" I asked, after being ushered into the living room and peering at a framed letter on the wall.

"Abraham Lincoln," George Sanders said. "An original letter in his hand."

"And this one," I said, suddenly impressed, "Why, it's Robert E. Lee!"

"North and South," he agreed pleasantly, humoring a small town, small paper reporter. After all, he had interviewed kings and presidents, movie stars, and more of the high and mighty of this world than most of us ever read about much less hobnob with in person. What's more; he had gotten their autographs!

Still, he was nice to me and willing to help me get a good interview. Looking back on it now, I suspect—having done so many from my side of the notepad—he was kindly helping me structure a good interview.

We sat down and, with his lovely wife Helen, a firm friendship seemed to instantly develop. George Sanders had been in movies, served as Director General of Broadcasting in New Zealand, and done a thousand other fascinating things, as had Helen. I was in interviewer's Heaven.

"Why am I interviewing you about trash?" I asked.

"Beats me," he said.

That first interview turned out to be wide-ranging always coming back to his and Helen's lifetime love, autographs. They had thousands upon thousands of them. In my head, all the many books to be written were suddenly appearing. Here was a treasure trove of information.

[I believe this will be our 13th book overall

For years, George and Helen traded autographs from their home above a scenic North Carolina mountain lake. A drawing of the house by artist Lee Pantas became part of their logo.

with the Sanders, Sanders, Roberts byline—there's that lucky number again!]

"Have you ever thought about doing an autograph price guide?" I asked after the article came out, and they saw I could string words together without tripping over my word processor.

"We would need a little help," Helen said.

With no little effort, we went on to put together the world's first comprehensive autograph price guide, and it was the very well-received first edition of this book. [**The Price Guide to Autographs**, published by Wallace-Homestead, 1988.]

My mutual endeavors with George and Helen continued to expand in the past 13 years. We sadly lost George last year but Helen and I roll on with several other projects underway.

This chapter, as in the first edition, has an interview I did of George. We've carefully updated it to reflect the current autograph market.

By the way, up until shortly before his death, George still picked up trash along the road for both exercise and simply to keep a beautiful area unsullied. He won several civic awards for his efforts.

Maybe, one day, I'll get around to doing that article about trash, but probably not. There's just too much else about George to write first.

Why Collect Autographs?

There are—according to the late nationally recognized autograph expert and leading author in the field, Charles Hamilton—over 2,000,000 people who now collect autographs and manuscripts with more than 20,000 newcomers joining the hobby each year. Hamilton wrote that a few years ago, we can assume those numbers have and continue to increase dramatically.

Autographs have a thrill and magic about them even greater than stamps. More and more collectors are happily discovering this. Demand for quality reference books on this fascinating and profitable pursuit is widespread.

Stamp collecting, up until this series of references, had one huge advantage over autographs and manuscripts—the *Scott*

Catalogue (*Scott Standard Postage Stamp Catalogue*, Amos Press, Sidney, Ohio). This bible of stamp collectors has gone through close to *150* editions! Each new edition published is guaranteed many tens of thousands of "automatic" sales from collectors and dealers who dare not be without the most current "standard" pricing information. Overall, Scott's has now sold in the millions of copies!

[By the way, speaking of Scott's, we had the thrill of that company publishing the first edition of our Sanders Price Guide to Sports Autographs... Thanks, Stu Morrissey!]

A similar price guide for autographs and manuscripts had long been needed. This book was not just a good idea, it was already *wanted* by thousands of autograph and manuscript collectors who would, as stamp collectors do Scott's, automatically order every new edition. There was simply nor yet is any other comprehensive standard pricing guide in the field. We have enjoyed great success and we certainly owe it to all of you out there, our beloved readership. Thanks for your support!

The fact of life for the millions of us who currently collect autographs, and for those newcomers constantly joining this exciting hobby and profession, is that a guideline is needed; something to go by other than dealers' asking prices. *That* needs no amplification as to reality and as to who has the advantage if you have no such guide. A bit better is digging through auction prices realized on similar material, but that calls for a lot of time and expense.

So, whether wanting to buy *or* sell, **The Sanders Price Guide to Autographs** is invaluable to you! We get bigger and better with every new edition. In one convenient place is more information on the collecting and pricing of autographs than has ever been offered! We sincerely hope that it will benefit you for years to come.

What's It Worth?

That old document or letter you've just found may be worth thousands of dollars, <u>or practically nothing</u>.

How do you know?

Babe Ruth (above, autographing baseballs—right, closeup of a Ruth signed horsehide) is reputed to have signed as many as 10,000 baseballs a year. Yet, today, authentic versions of these scribbled upon orbs from the Sultan of Swat are rare and valuable—$4,500 on average. Which brings us again to a point we must make: you'll not find that price in this book. All sports-related prices are in **The Sanders Price Guide to Sports Autographs**, 3rd edition, published in December, 1998 also by Alexander Books for $24.95 plus $4 s&h. Order it via our secure web site at **http://autograph-book.com** or e-mail **sales@abooks.com** or call **1-800-472-0438** (voice & fax) or just use snail mail to Alexander Books, 65 Macedonia Road, Alexander NC 28701 USA. Or just tell your local bookstore,"get it, please."

tion—the signatures of Methodist and Episcopal bishops. Also one could gather letters of Civil War soldiers, or doughboys in War World I, using a unified and interesting theme to make the whole worth more than the part.

Although a person who holds autographs and manuscripts merely for their investment potential misses out on much of the magic enjoyed by the true collector, typically prices continue to increase. Hamilton, in his book, gives the example of the refugees who left Nazi Germany at the onset of World War II. The lucky few who did manage to escape were stripped of all their jewels, family estates, paintings and cash. They were passed by the border guards, in many cases, with only a handful of worthless old family papers.

If Marshal Goering, an avid autograph collector, had realized the untold millions of marks that left the Third Reich as rare letters of Martin Luther, Voltaire, Beethoven, Napoleon, and others, he might personally have insisted on serving as a customs agent. Those fortunate people who got their assets out in this manner, were able to sell them and start afresh in the New World.

The advice that Hamilton and George Sanders gave in starting an autograph collection of your own is not to specialize too much, but rather to gather five or six different collections at the same time. Experts liken this to the same way that a stock investor will diversify his portfolio.

One example given of diversification is what would have happened if you had started collecting thirty years ago in the categories of science, music, World War I, Napoleon, and American Western autographs. Except for World War I, in which prices have declined, the collection would have held its value. Plus, due to dramatic increases in music and science, the overall worth would be considerably more than your original outlay.

Another important advantage of diversification is that you can afford to wait on "safe" buys, avoiding premium prices. Since you are collecting a number of different categories, the opportunities for lower prices will be greater. Additionally, the wider selection of material will probably be more interesting to your friends. Researching into several fields will also keep each fresher and more exciting to you.

The true rewards of autograph and manuscript collection come not from financial gain but through the romance of holding true written history. The aura that seems to glow from a paper that George Washington touched and wrote upon, a check signed by Orville Wright, an autographed first edition of Mark Twain's, Napoleon's signature, a letter from Theodore Roosevelt—all these and many others can warm you over the flame of our mutual heritage, the Family of Man. As can, equally, the heart touching letter of a Civil War soldier, little more than a boy, to his sister back home. All these and more are the attractions of owning and having these bits of history.

Certainly some caution is usually in order, and you really need all the references you can get. Take the photograph of film goddess-legend Greta "I vant to be alone" Garbo opposite. A

Typical "signed" movie star photograph of the 20s and 30s. If it's white, it's not real!

signed picture of her from the late 20s or early 30s, as this one appears to be, would certainly bring about $10,000 at auction. Yet, I picked it up in an antique mall in Tennessee the other day for a mere $20! Did I think I had a true find? Nah, but I got it specifically to use as an example in the book.

Not only is the Garbo signature probably not authentic, it is not even on the photograph. What they did back in those low tech days (and it was pretty slick) was have the star (or *someone*) sign the *negative* of his or her photograph. Black ink on the film became white on the print. In that manner, the studio could print thousands upon thousands of photographs with which to answer the entreaties of adoring fans.

Store up all such tips as the one above that you can find. They will save you much money and aggravation, and make your hobby all the more enjoyable.

Practicalities

One of the best ways we could think of to give an introduction to the true joy and magic of collecting autographs is by reprinting the interview with George included below. Both the beginner and the advanced collector will find many helpful tips.

Being the person *answering* the questions was certainly a novel experience for noted autograph collector, and coauthor of these autograph references, George Sanders. During more than 40 years interviewing hundreds of notable people, he was usually on the receiving side of the microphone.

Harry S. Truman, John F. Kennedy, Martin Luther King, Lyndon Johnson, Jack Nicklaus, Clark Gable, Marilyn Monroe, Richard Nixon, John Wayne, Bob Hope, Ty Cobb, James Dean, Ronald Reagan—these are only a few of the movers and shakers who gave him exclusive interviews for his nationally syndicated radio and television talk-shows and companion newspaper columns known as *Sanders Meanders*.

As a broadcast newsman, a columnist—and an actor himself in over 20 motion pictures and on television as well, appearing in *December Bride* and *Wild Bill Hickok*—it was only natural that he started collecting signatures of the celebrities with whom he came in daily contact. His personal collection at the time of this interview was well over 20,000 pieces, all kept track of by a home-based computer controlled by his wife, Helen.

Retired from broadcasting since 1977, Sanders devoted himself fulltime to autograph and manuscript collecting literally up until he passed away in August, 1998. He earned the lasting respect of dealers and fellow collectors around the world. This updated interview was originally conducted by me and took place in his home when we first met in 1986.

Interview of George Sanders

Sanders: For 40 years I have been tremendously interested in collecting historical documents, letters, manuscripts, signed photographs and just plain signatures of the men and women who have made and *are* making history. It has taken years, but I'm now able to buy intelligently and with some expertise. My investment is large and I've learned to protect that investment with considerable research and meaningful study. This is certainly not a hobby for the uninformed.

I've watched autograph material rise in cost from a point where one could acquire choice Presidential letters and documents for a hundred dollars to today's market where the same type of material is priced anywhere from $2,000 to $10,000. That's quite a financial jump in just the past 30 years.

Roberts: How do you find new autograph pieces for your collection?

Sanders: Helen and I have been shopping all over the United States and the World. In 1984 we searched throughout Europe for six weeks and found marvelous letters written by Dr. Sigmund Freud, Charles Darwin, Renoir, Dickens and some outstanding Winston Churchill material. While walking around London with a friend, we visited a stamp shop. We asked if they had any covers (envelopes) with franking signatures on them. The very proper English gentleman pushed some early stamped envelopes across the glass counter and they just happened to be pieces signed by Charles Dickens.

The stamp dealer was selling them for quite reasonable

prices because the old used stamps on them weren't very important to stamp collectors and that's all he cared about. This sort of thing happens quite frequently. The autograph collector receives a big bargain because stamp dealers or auction houses simply don't grasp the value of autograph items.

[**Editor's note**: This condition, however, is rapidly changing due in large part to our autograph price guides, we modestly point out. Sorry.]

I once bought a President James Polk free frank at a stamp auction

George—in 1996—proofs the 4th edition of **The Sanders Price Guide to Autographs** at Alexander Books. Helen and Ralph both share and carry his sense of perfection and attention to detail in putting together these price guides.

for a mere $35! It is a $750 item, but obviously *not* in the philatelic world.

Roberts: Do you specialize in anything?

Sanders: Yes, I have the collection divided topically. I'd say the primary portion of my entire collection is in U. S. Presidents, The Arts, Science, Industry, Heads of State, Civil War, Celebrities and Military Leaders. Included in the collection are association pieces such as assassins, First Ladies, Cabinet members and advisors. I shall continue to buy good presidential material whenever a really fine value appears.

Those other divisions? The Arts? The artistic side of autographs. Lumped together are artists, composers and sculptors. Civil War? Just Civil War material, exclusively, which is separate from Military Leaders which includes those people from ALL eras of history. A collection of important Heads of State and Royalty, men and women of Science, plus a general collection of Celebrities who do not necessarily fit into a specific category.

Another collection which should be mentioned is Vintage Theatrical and Motion Picture Stars—probably one of the finest in the country today.

My personal collection of modern entertainers is quite extensive because I knew so many film and TV personalities during my 15 years in Hollywood. When I first started, as a serious collector, my collection was amassed on the basis of all the notable people I was interviewing on the air. Helen and I kept guest books just as Carol Burnett did, with one page for each celebrity. In those 35 years as a disc jockey, TV host, gossip columnist, commercial announcer, TV news anchorman and finally, broadcasting executive, we were able to acquire hundreds of important signatures at no financial cost whatsoever. It also provided us with an excellent collection of authentic in-person autographs second to none with which we are able to make truly accurate assessments against the current barrage of autopens, facsimiles, secretarials and the ever-dreadful forgeries that so undermine the material of serious collectors.

There was so much of value in that collection of genuine in-person signatures that part of it was sold to a dealer for $200,000 in 1983.

[**Author's note**: later auctions brought even more. I was privileged to personally see and handle much of this collection over the years. It was truly *awesome* as well as being an intensive education in autographs that money could not have bought.]

With 20,000 pieces currently in my collection it is necessary to keep the really expensive autograph pieces in bank vaults. Such items as the personal letters to me from several presidents and the many items John F. Kennedy signed for me in person are, literally, money in the bank.

Roberts: What about the authenticity of a piece, and how do you tell if it's worth the money?

Sanders: Well, I have probably as fine a library of autograph-related books as anyone for use in private research, where I can carefully check out facsimile or forged material. Plus, I have the very good fortune to personally know such knowledgeable autograph experts and/or dealers as Mary Benjamin, Paul Richards, Robert Batchelder, and many others. I must also include the former autograph auction whiz and authority, Charles Hamilton, who gave our hobby the publicity impetus it needed from the 1950s to the present day. His many books on the subject are oft-consulted tomes and necessary for any serious collector to own.

[**Editor's note**: We were honored to have the late, great Charles Hamilton supply the foreword for both the third and fourth editions of this book.]

My mentor for decades has been a very fine lady, Mary Benjamin, whose gentle persuasion lifted my philographic tastes from the mundane contemporary material I was gathering for free, to the valuable historic pieces I now treasure. She's the daughter of Walter R. Benjamin, founder of the oldest auto-graph-selling firm in America. Miss Benjamin is one of my dearest friends and I'm able to consult with her anytime. In recent years, I find myself consulting her learned nephew and business colleague, Christopher "Kit" Jaeckel, who is always pleasant and informative. Like myself, a former TV news an-chorman, Kit has been of great assistance to my collection.

But to more fully answer your question, one way to authen-ticate material is through personal knowledge of the historically important people one wishes to collect.

Many of the persons I knew and interviewed are now vintage and I have copies of their handwriting in my own collection. I know what their in-person handwriting is really like. Their in-person signatures on photographs, books, and in guest books are extremely worthwhile in comparing with other material of theirs being offered by dealers or private collectors. I have the *real thing* so there is little chance that I can't identify nor be unable to know whether an item written in my lifetime is valid or not.

However, it takes years of study to sense what is autopen and what is not. What is a secretarial signature and what is not. And the hazards of identification of engraving, woodcuts, or rubber stamps are rather formidable. Naturally, I'm afraid I annoy many trusting souls who offer autographed photos of stars like Clark Gable, Carole Lombard, Greta Garbo, Jean Harlow, Humphrey Bogart, Laurel & Hardy, Charles Chaplin, John

Richard Nixon signs a book for George. His vocation of broadcaster allowed George access to celebrities and that incredible experience with thousands of in-person autographs is one of the firm foundations these price guides rest upon. It is our privilege to preserve and present this knowledge for your use.

Wayne, Fatty Arbuckle and the like which I frequently (and reluctantly) determine to be bogus.

This is not a hobby for the lazy scholar. Just as you recognize the fact that no two handcrafted antiques are exactly alike, so, too, you have to realize that no two letters are alike. If Jack Kennedy wrote a letter in longhand, he surely didn't write any two alike. His handwriting has great variants, as did his signature, but with careful study and the use of books containing facsimiles of Kennedy's hand, one becomes familiar with these differences.

Roberts: This may be a bad way to phrase it, but what is *hot* right now?

Sanders: It depends on the age of the collector. If you are an adult with money to invest, I suggest that U.S. Presidents are always a best buy and U.S. Vice Presidents are also a fine investment. Classical music composers, world-famous artists, and exceptional authors are always an excellent place to invest large sums of money. To the young, to teenagers, there's a very good market for rock artists. However, it is a bit on the fad side and probably such items will not appreciate, let alone hold their present value. Such contemporary show business material is always chancy but certainly great fun for the youthful collector. Remember that artist Andy Warhol said, "We'll all be famous for about 15 minutes," and that's not sufficient time to become a worthwhile autograph item.

For example: the big band leaders of the 1930s, 1940s and 50s were extremely popular when I was a kid. Let's take the Dorsey Brothers, Russ Morgan, Ted Weems, Stan Kenton and many, many others. Who remembers? Glenn Miller, who was killed in a World War II air crash, is still valuable, but most of his contemporaries are selling for very modest prices. Duke Ellington is valuable but it's his contribution as a composer rather than as a bandleader that placed him on a U. S. postage stamp and into autograph collections.

As to my thoughts regarding Rock artists, I'd say the Beatles and Elvis Pressley will probably retain their good value because they were the first super stars in their musical field. The untimely death of Lennon and of Elvis added value—there are no more signatures of theirs to acquire in person or by mail. Currently, Bruce Springsteen, Madonna, Mick Jagger, and Michael Jackson seem to be retaining their value with some minor appreciation.

The first of anything is usually valuable. Take inventors. Thomas Edison, Eli Whitney, Cyrus McCormick, Samuel Colt, the Wright Brothers and Alexander Graham Bell, are all expensive items. They have never waned in collector interest. In other words, the historic or celebrated people who did something before anyone else thought to do it, seem to be forever collectible and increase considerably in value.

Roberts: What about World War I autographs? I have read

that they were expensive between the two World Wars, but have dropped now?

Sanders: I'm pleased you asked about that period of history. For some reason World War I has lost considerable interest. Only General John Pershing, because he was the Commander of the American Expeditionary Force, plus the French field marshals, Foch and Joffre, are sought after. Some of the Germans, Ludendorff, von Hindenburg, Ernst Udet, von Richthofen and a few others are worthy of investment. Even theatrical stars of that era, such as Elsie Janis, Douglas Fairbanks, Sr. and most obviously, Sir Harry Lauder, have lost value in recent years.

Colonial and Revolutionary War material is a specialty in itself. Such material has retained its considerable value very well. It's truly *American*, and if you're wise, you'll collect Red, White & Blue American material. However, good colonial pieces are not for an anemic autograph budget.

U. S. Presidential items will never be bargain-priced. You can specialize in almost any one president and your investment will grow annually. Most autograph experts, with possibly the exception of Charles Hamilton, try to steer clear of any conversation that deals with the aspects of investment profits. As for me, I simply wouldn't be interested in nurturing a hobby that didn't show considerable appreciation. Rare autographs are too expensive to be treated like a recreational novelty. These are not toys; they are expensive pieces of world or U.S. history. If there will never be any worthwhile gain financially then why invest big money in them?

What I have just said is diametrically opposed to what a great many autograph dealers want to hear or read. But, I ask you, why should anyone invest $3,000 in a Sigmund Freud letter and learn 20 years later that it's only worth $1,000? I would like to think that Dr. Freud was important enough in the field of psychiatry and that I had taken good enough care in the area of proper preservation of that letter, that it would, in 20 years or even less, be worth far more than my original investment. The 1987 stock market crash seriously diminished many types of investments, but as of this moment autograph prices have either risen or stabilized. Need I say more?

A stupid purchase in autographs is just like a stupid buy in anything else. Think long and hard before you purchase! In other words, autograph collecting is not for the impulse buyer.

Roberts: What about association pieces written by people who are not famous?

Sanders: One of the things that started my interest in the Civil War was that my wife's great grandfather, Elkanah Doolittle, was an officer, second-in-command of the 20th Connecticut Volunteers, which since we now live in the South, we don't enthusiastically discuss. In any case, he was a respected officer who somehow managed to survive four years of combat duty and ultimately die of old age.

His letters had been handed down from generation to generation and no one in the Doolittle family had ever done any research on them. Years ago, at Radio Station KRKD in Los Angeles, I had leisure time between broadcasts to work on his numerous letters written from 1861 to 1865. Doolittle was an educated man and his letters were a joy to read and re-read. What was important about his letters was that he had a genuine sense of the history he was living and wrote about important generals he met and served under. He obviously did not like nor vote for Lincoln but vividly described Lincoln's review of the Connecticut troops and even referred to the immortal president as that "great ape in the White House", which was the first time I had seen that expression used by a Union officer.

Yes, I find most association pieces extremely important because they preserve the fringe activities surrounding an important historical personage or event.

If someone should discover a letter written by former Secretary of the Interior Albert Fall in President Harding's Cabinet, who was proven guilty of accepting bribes in the Teapot Dome scandal of the 1920s, in which he wrote, "Well, I'm an old man now and I don't mind admitting that I was a thief, but I don't know why Harding was covered-up. He certainly shared our guilt!" Suddenly we're talking about a $1,000 or more letter. Few people recall Fall's name at this point in time, but it would be the fact that he was pointing an accusing finger at Harding that would make such a letter highly valuable.

Filed away upstairs I have a letter from an obscure American. I don't know much about its author, but it is a three page missive written about the Russians from his vantage point as a foreign service officer in Moscow and St. Petersburg in 1850. It is almost uncanny because you would think it was written a few weeks ago giving an American's view of Russian behavior—their secretiveness, their connivances, their mistrust of outsiders before Gorbachev and perestroika. A letter like this, with that studied description of what was going on inside and out of the Czar's court, is not only exciting to read but has valuable content for scholars to consider.

Obviously, there are various facets of autograph collecting. That term in itself is a misnomer. Autograph collecting is the act of requesting a celebrity to place his or her signature in your autograph book, or on a menu, or in a book written by or about that celebrity. That's in-person autograph collecting. Many collectors of such signatures mail cards, photographs, typescripts, books, bookplates, and so forth, to the celebrity whose autograph they want. This latter group of collectors, unfortunately, often receive secretarial signatures, autopen junk or just downright forgeries. Frequently they invest more in postage costs and address lists than the signature of the celebrity in question was ever worth. That is the sad, tedious side of autograph collecting.

Manuscript collecting is expensive and worthwhile, with scholars being the prime acquisitors. They know what they want and will all too frequently invest fortunes in their respective collections. It is not an area for the novice.

Whatever your specialty is within this hobby, one must do his homework. If I didn't force myself to go outside and walk in the beautiful North Carolina woods that surround the lovely lake in front of our home, I could happily spend easily eight to ten hours a day with my collections, sometimes without leaving my desk. It is that exciting. I care that much about it and heartily encourage others interested in history, sports, entertainment, science, the arts or celebrities in general to join with all the world's autograph buffs and share in a hobby that has many benefits for the soul as well as the pocketbook.

The Great Garbo

After this interview, Helen Sanders made an incredible find in the world of autographs, a *stack* of Greta Garbo letters! These fascinating and exceedingly rare letters are intimate windows into the private life of a public cult goddess but privately mysterious person. Along with extensive other Garbo-related material, they are currently being assembled into book form by Helen and Ralph Roberts. At the September 1987 Herman Darvick auction, just one of these Garbo letters sold for $6,600 including the 10 per cent auctioneer's commission. The value today would be appreciably more.

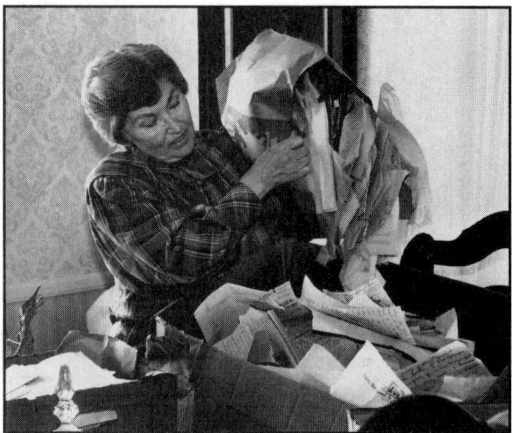

Helen Sanders empties one of the many, many boxes of old letters she searched through while finding the incredible treasure trove of Greta Garbo love letters. Her sheer persistence rescued these wonderful letters from trush dump oblivion and preserved them. One of the true triumphs in autograph collecting history.

These letters give us a fascinating window into the soul of one of this century's most mysterious women.

Wishing <u>You</u>, Joy and Magic

Yes, the joy and magic of autograph collecting is always there! We hope something similar to Helen's victory happens for you in our mutually-loved, fantastic hobby. Your dreams *can* come true, but not without a little work and study on your part. To recognize a *find*, you need to be armed with *knowledge*. Our books help but, regardless, learn all you can. Good luck!

Chapter 2

Collecting People on Magazine Covers

by Helen Sanders and Ralph Roberts

To the dedicated seeker of authentic autographs there can be no more genuine thrill than to receive a favorite celebrity's "in person" signature. Failing that, access to a known version of that signature obtained in person by a trusted expert can be worth its weight in gold. That, of course, is one of the valuable features of the **Sanders price guides** that no competitor has hope of matching.

As a professional broadcaster, interviewer, newspaper and magazine columnist, actor, master of ceremonies for countless banquets and long-time radio and television broadcasting executive in the United States and New Zealand, author George Sanders had the great good fortune of meeting, shaking hands and swapping yarns with a goodly portion of the greatest names in the last six decades of the 20th century! He hobnobbed with the great and near-great, with celebrities of the moment; with politicians, movie stars, and sports legends; with business leaders, singers of melodious songs, and inventors of note; with famous clergy, brave military heroes, and high-flying aviators. The list goes on and on. Thousands of luminaries that he met and *got their autographs*!

As his wife and partner for almost 50 years, Helen Sanders toted cameras, microphones, tape recorders and the always present leather bound autograph guest books. It was a lifetime of good fun kibitzing with celebrities while garnering one of the premier autograph collections of all time.

On the following pages are many examples of photo opportunities that clearly illustrate how most celebrities are usually cooperative and generally delighted to pose and oblige polite collectors with their coveted autographs.

While this book is very much a memorial to George Sanders—who passed away just before its publication—the photographs that follow are far more than just a celebration of his life. George undisputedly—thanks to the luck and glory of his profession as broadcaster and journalist and always an autograph collector over almost 60 years of this most interesting century—amassed more *documented* in-person autographs than any other person in history. We have literally thousands of glossy 8x10 photographs of George with about every celebrity you can think of to prove this fact. They all signed for him and were glad to do it. This incredible experience and expertise of his in the collection of *authentic* signatures began these autograph

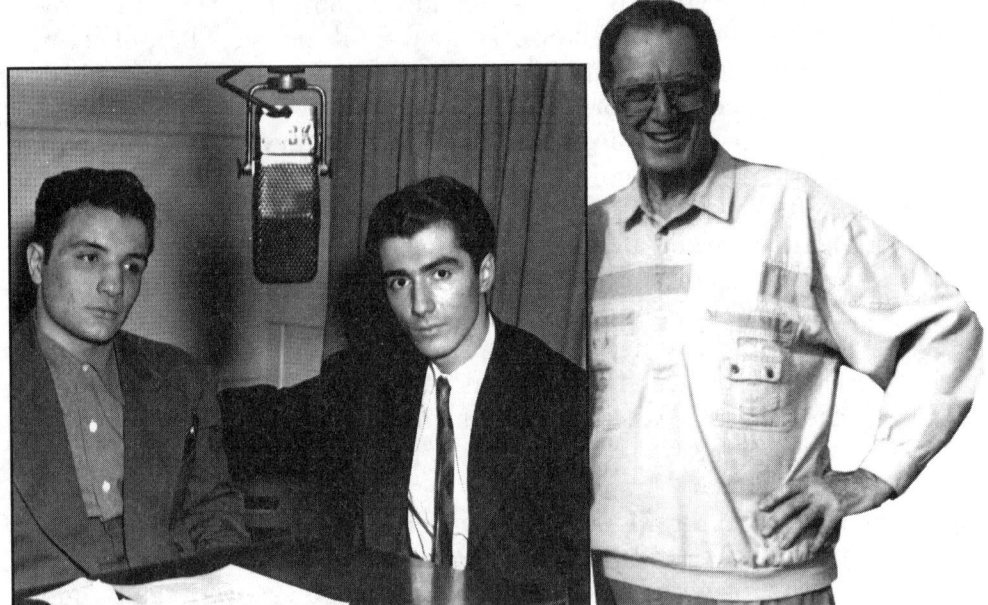

George Sanders (above)—interviewing boxing legend Jake "Ragin' Bull" La Motta in 1939—at age 15, was already a veteran broadcaster, having begun as a child actor on WXYZ in Detroit. To the right, age 74, in 1998—he still had his looks and was still doing commercials. His was an incredible life!

price guides 10 years ago, and will continue them for many years to come. George Sanders has left behind a vast legacy of autographic information that continues to benefit the thousands of collectors and dealers using the **Sanders Price Guides to Autographs**.

Having a vast array of autographic resources after he retired from broadcasting—photographs with celebrities, in-person signatures, and much more—George had great fun in putting together specialty collections. We continue to publish these because they offer a fantastic resource *for you*, as well, being chock full of authentic in-person autograph facsimiles.

In the previous edition of this book (the fourth edition), we featured George's "Philography Meets Philately" collection. This is autographs by persons who have appeared on postage stamps, most fascinatingly combining the hobbies of autograph collecting and stamp collecting. That collection is so extensive that we have published it now as a separate facsimile reference book, entitled not surprisingly **Philography Meets Philately** (Autograph House, 96 pages, 6x9 inches, ISBN 1-56664-149-7, $9.95. Call 1-800-472-0438 to order or e-mail **sales@abooks.com**).

The collection featured in this chapter consists of people pictured with George Sanders who have also appeared on major magazine covers. In this case, mostly *Time* and *Newsweek* with a few from *Life* and *People*. We present you with the photograph of the celebrity with George and, wherever possible, also a facsimile of that person's signature.

We do not show the covers themselves (although they are in George's collection) because of copyright legalities. These magazine publishers would be all too happy to allow us to reproduce the covers but—the price to reproduce as many covers as we wanted being prohibitive—we rather quickly devised an alternative. Instead, we tell you the date of the cover in the collection.

As to the covers, while someone like Richard Nixon or Lyndon Johnson might have appeared on dozens of covers, we include only the date of the actual cover in George's collection's binders.

We hope you find this collection both fascinating and useful.

Photograph Credits

We wish to thank some of the world's most talented photographers, who opened their respective lenses and expended countless old-fashioned flashbulbs so they might capture so many memorable moments for us in company of celebrities.

These professional photographers include Julius "Bud" Clauss from University of Detroit days, the late Carl Vermilya (KPTV-Channel 12, Portland, Oregon), John A. Boyer (Los Angeles), Photo-Art Commercial Studios of Portland, Oregon, Irving L. Antler (Hollywood), Frank Parr (Portland, Ore.), Rothschild Photos (Los Angeles), William Fraker (R.K.O., Paramount Pictures in Hollywood), Sam J. Cole (Monrovia, California), Coy Watson (Los Angeles), Alva Gregory (Paramount Pictures publicist), Davis Photos (Azusa, California), Dick Farris (Portland, Oregon), O'Brien Photos (Altadena, California), Helen Doolittle Sanders and Bruce Luzader of Portland, Oregon.

1968 Presidential nominee and former Vice President of the United States Hubert Humphrey with George and a *Time* magazine cover Humphrey signed.

People on Covers

On the following pages are photographs of George Sanders with a wide range of celebrities, all of whom have appeared on major magazine covers. We include the date of their appearance and in most cases also a facsimile of the famous person's autograph. All of these photographs are from the private collection of Helen Sanders.

Above, jazz immortal Louis "Satchmo" Armstrong with George. Armstrong appeared on the cover of TIME February 21, 1949. Right, dancing great Fred Astaire shares an outdoor moment with George. Astaire and fellow dancer Gene Kelly hoofed their way across the cover of NEWSWEEK on May, 31, 1976.

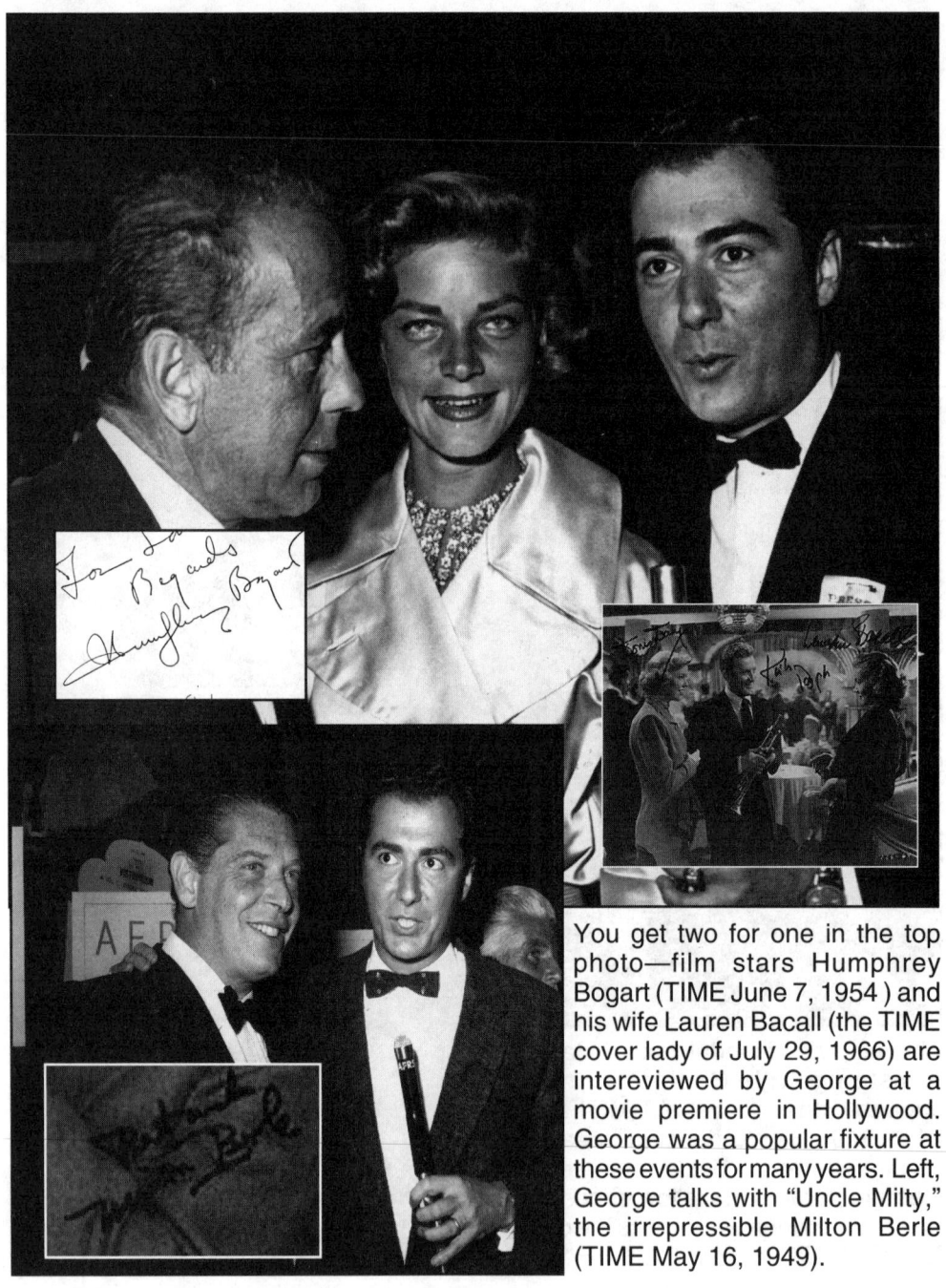

You get two for one in the top photo—film stars Humphrey Bogart (TIME June 7, 1954) and his wife Lauren Bacall (the TIME cover lady of July 29, 1966) are intereviewed by George at a movie premiere in Hollywood. George was a popular fixture at these events for many years. Left, George talks with "Uncle Milty," the irrepressible Milton Berle (TIME May 16, 1949).

To the immediate right, George with actress Shirley Booth (TIME August 10, 1953). Far right, "the Man in Black," the great country music legend Johnny Cash (LIFE November 21, 1969). Below, Governor of California Pat Brown (TIME September 15, 1958) examines a

bumper stick on a 1957 Chevolet. Pat Brown was Governor Jerry Brown's father. The sticker was for an event that George was helping to promote. Wish we had that Chevy, huh?

Above left, head circled, famous newsman Walter Cronkite (TIME October 14, 1966) works a news conference with George Sanders, head circled right. Cronkite went on to become the CBS evening news anchor for many years. Left, George interviews famous heart surgeon (now in his nineties) Dr. Michael DeBakey (TIME May 28, 1965). And below, German Bishop Dibelius (TIME April 6, 1953) answers a few questions for a news program on which George was a regular contributor.

George Sanders (head circled left) watches Queen Elizabeth II of England (TIME May 3, 1976) on a royal visit to New Zealand in the 1970s. At this time, George was Acting Director General of Radio New Zealand and, in fact, all of that country's broadcasting operations. Right, Duke Ellington (TIME August 20, 1956) in the 1930s instructs a very young George in some of the finer aspects of music. George grew up in Detroit, Michigan, and worked during his teen years as a radio interviewer.

Above, actor Henry Fonda (who appeared on the cover of TIME February 16, 1970 with his son Peter and daugher Jane as "the Flying Fondas") discusses his latest movie with George. Left, John Kenneth Galbraith (who graced the cover of SATURDAY REVIEW April 20, 1968) graciously signs for Sanders.

Arizona's Senator Barry Goldwater, statesman and 1964 presidential candidate (TIME June 14, 1963), signs for George Sanders above at a news event which George was covering. Far right, the renowned expert in the game of bridge, Charles Goren (TIME September 29, 1958) gives George a quick lesson in the finer points of the pasttime. Near right, Hotelman Conrad Hilton (TIME December 12, 1949) pauses for a chat live on George's mike.

James R. "Jimmy" Hoffa (TIME August 31, 1959) was a famous but ill-fated labor leader. Reputed to have been murdered, his body has never been found. He was the subject of a recent feature movie. Above, he meets with George at an airport in the 1960s. Hoffa was president of the Teamsters Union and has now been followed in that post by his son, also named James Hoffa. Left, the well-known actor William Holden (TIME February 27, 1956) poses with George at a gala affair in Hollywood.

Above, George (sitting right) attentively covers a news conference by Vice President Hubert Humphrey (TIME April 1, 1966). Right, President Lyndon Baines Johnson (NEWSWEEK April 22, 1968) works the crowd in his downhome folksy style followed by newsman Sanders.

Estes Kefauver

Above center, one of the funniest men ever Danny Kaye (TIME March 11, 1946) returns a pen to a happy George Sanders, who has just garnered yet another great autograph! Kaye was a huge Hollywood star in the 1940s and went on to television fame in the 50s. Left, former Vice presidential candidate and senator Estes Kefauver (TIME March 24, 1952 with George.

Ethel Kennedy (TIME April 15, 1969), the wife of Robert F. Kennedy, is interviewed by Sanders in the early seventies in Oregon. Nice sideburns, George!

Above, George with President John F. Kennedy (TIME July 11, 1960). Below
George interviews Attorney General Robert F. Kennedy (TIME October 10, 1960).

Above, George shares a moment with the great civil rights leader Martin Luther King (TIME March 19, 1965). Right, vice presidential candidate (with Nixon in 1960), senator, and ambassador to South Vietnam, Henry Cabot Lodge (TIME September 26, 1960) elucidates for the ever-present Sanders microphone.

George with country music great, the melodious "coalminer's daughter," Loretta Lynn (PEOPLE June 5, 1978).

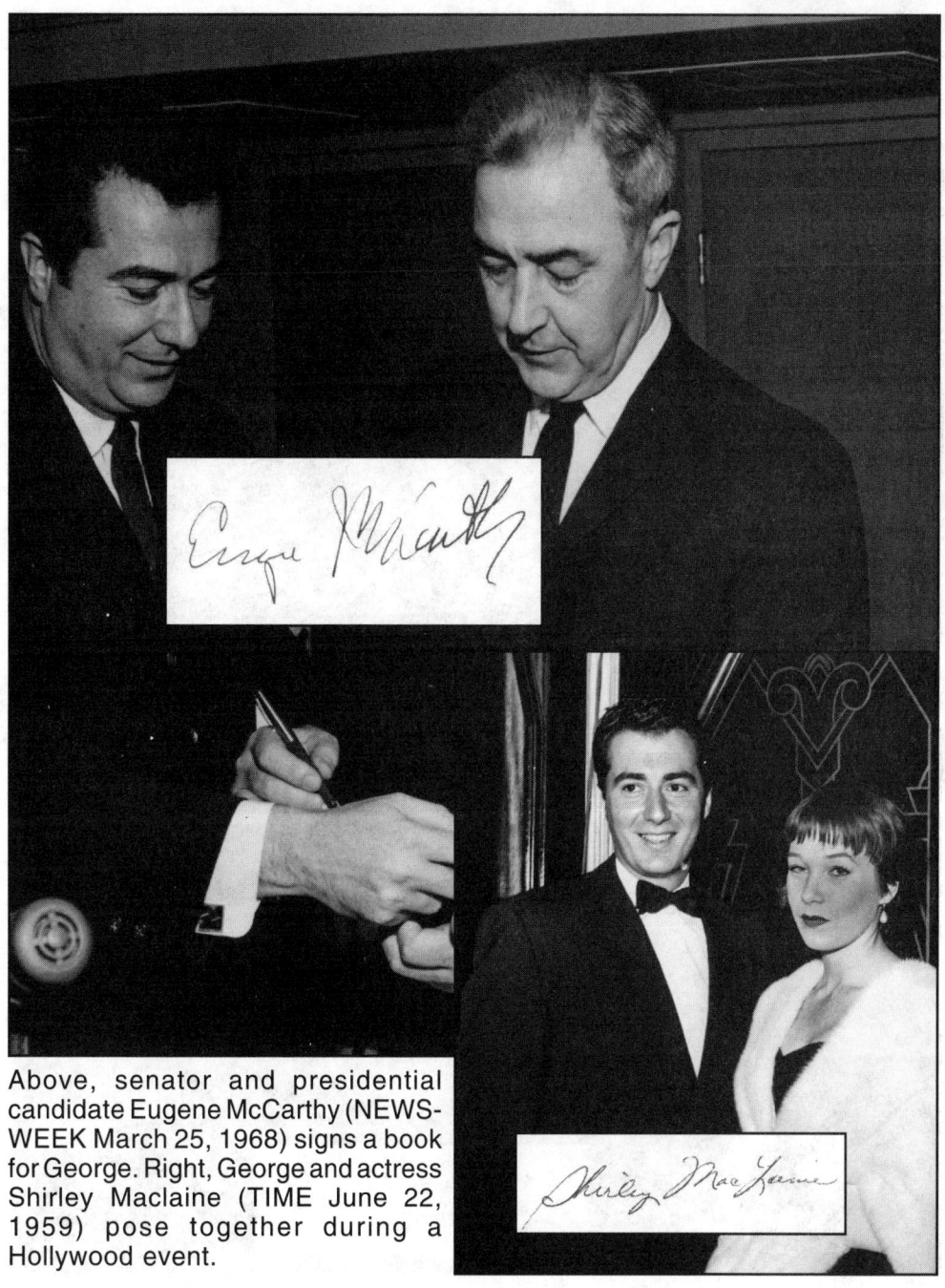

Above, senator and presidential candidate Eugene McCarthy (NEWS-WEEK March 25, 1968) signs a book for George. Right, George and actress Shirley Maclaine (TIME June 22, 1959) pose together during a Hollywood event.

Above, left, labor leader George Meany (TIME September 6, 1961) expounds for George Sanders. Below, Oregon's maverick senator Wayne Morse (TIME January 17, 1955) discusses the politics of the Northwest with journalist Sanders.

George with Oregon senator Richard L. Neuberger who appeared on the same
TIME January 17, 1955 cover as did his colleague Senator Morse (facing page).

President Richard Nixon (TIME October 31, 1960) and George Sanders were friends of many years standing. Facing page, Nixon signs one of his books for George. Above, a very young George, a very young Nixon, and George's father (George R. Sanders, Sr.) converse in Southern California sometime in the late 1940s. Right, Nixon while Vice President talks with George.

Four of the top disc jockeys of the early 1950s. Second from left is Jack Paar (TIME August 18, 1958) and far right is young George Sanders, who was a disc jockey before moving into news. That's Gene Autry on the cover of the magazine. Paar, of course, went on to become the first king of late night television.

George Sanders (standing a little close there, aren't you, George?) with music legend Dolly Parton (PLAYBOY October, 1978). And just to save you some time looking for that issue, no, she was not nude in it!

George greets famous Illinois senator Charles Percy (TIME September 18, 1964), ready to interview him for KWJJ, Portland, Oregon.

A signed photograph of George with Bishop James Pike (TIME November 11, 1966) and two of George's three children—son Sandy and daughter Susan.

Recently assassinated Israeli leader Yitzhak Rabin (TIME December 2, 1974) graciously signs his autograph for George.

Above, Vice President Nelson Rockefeller (TIME May 22, 1964) addresses a news conference covered by George Sanders (far right above). Left, George (unusually far left for a change) listens to Secretary of State Dean Rusk (TIME February 4, 1966).

George swaps some jokes with comedian Mort Sahl (TIME August 15, 1960).

George listens to the Chairman of the Board, Frank Sinatra (TIME August 29, 1955) while working as a newsman at the premiere of the movie THE JOKER IS WILD.

Young George Sanders in 1951 receives a national disc jockey award from no less than a scantily clad Elizabeth Taylor (TIME August 22, 1949). Wow!

Above, Georgia's Senator Herman Talmadge (TIME October 15, 1956) is interviewed by Sanders. Below, George shakes hands with President Harry Truman (TIME April 23, 1951), who he worked for in the White House. Facing page, George gets a book signed by Truman.

This is a very interesting photograph, the last one George put in his "People on Covers" collection, but he had not finished captioning it. The gentleman on the left is baseball immortal and Hall of Famer Ted Williams (TIME April 10, 1950). We <u>think</u> the guy in the middle is Los Angeles Mayor Sam Yorty (TIME September 2, 1966). At least that cover is there but he looks like (as Helen says) he's had a bad smog day. That's definitely George on the right.

Chapter 3

Internet Auctions

by Stuart Lutz

Editor's Note: *The explosion of the internet and the worldwide web has dramatically altered the way things are bought and sold. This is no less true in the autograph world. We're all—so it seems—rushing to get online. You'll certainly be able to bid on this book regularly in such online auctions as eBay and Amazon.com. But, like any auction venue, the internet requires knowledge about what you are doing. Heed the following advice from autograph expert Stuart Lutz. It could make your online experiences much more enjoyable. See you on eBay!*

One recent winter night in New Hampshire, I decided to check out the eBay web site for kicks. Often, I randomly type in the names of various historical figures to see what is available for sale. On this particular evening, I entered the name of my favorite writer, Mark Twain. A number of items came up, some of which were not autographs. I was intrigued by a signed Twain book that was, at $500, a veritable bargain. Intrigued, I rushed the mouse to the button and clicked on it, hoping I had found a real bargain.

Alas, I was disappointed to learn it was one of his many facsimile "signed" books with the inscription *"This is the authorized edition of my works Mark Twain."* I knew immediately it was not genuine, for two years ago, I coauthored an article in *Autograph Collector* about the holograph of Mark Twain and I specifically included a copy of this facsimile so collectors could be wary of this tricky piece. Many novices believe that this particular piece is authentic, for the signature and handwriting genuinely resemble Twain's powerful and frenzied script. The seller on eBay was also fooled by it, so I sent him a gentle message stating that it most likely was a printed facsimile that was not authentic. To further my case to him, I e-mailed him the *Autograph Collector* web site with my Twain article, hoping he would see it himself and

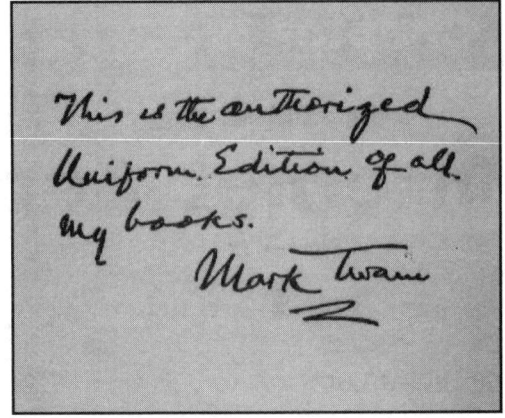

A printed facsimile of Mark Twain's handwriting, not a genuine autograph!

decide to pull the non-genuine piece. I have an AOL account, as did the seller, so I requested a return receipt and I knew the seller saw my message shortly before the end of the sale. The next day, the book, which might be worth a few dollars, sold in excess of $700. I was left with a moral dilemm: should I e-mail the winner of the piece that he bought a non-genuine piece? In the end, I decided not to, for I did not want to deal with an angry seller and a possible lawsuit. After all, let the buyer beware, but I will pass on this piece of advice to you: BEWARE OF INTERNET AUCTIONS!

I have recently seen so many examples of non-genuine material offered that I will just choose a couple as examples. One man was selling a Babe Ruth signature complete with a certificate of authenticity, commonly abbreviated on-line as COA. When I saw the image of the Ruth "signature," I was pleasantly surprised to see that Ruth's name was spelled correctly. If my 85-year-old grandmother had used a pink Sharpie marker in the midst of the great 1906 Frisco quake, she could have created a better forgery. Perplexed, I asked the enthusiastic seller who "authenticated" this, and he wrote back that some forensic agency guaranteed it was authentic.

In another example, a seller offered an Abraham Lincoln piece "signed in the late 1860s." Since Lincoln was shot in April

1865, it is highly doubtful that he would have signed a great deal of material in the late 1860s. The chance of this particularly bad forgery however, being signed in the late 1860s or even the late 1960s was very high and I had little doubt of the seller's claim as to its signing period. BEWARE OF INTERNET AUCTIONS!

The number of outright forged George Washingtons, Abraham Lincolns, Robert E. Lees and Greta Garbos offered for sale in on-line auctions is staggering. The same is true for the secretarially signed Marilyn Monroe signed photographs and the Ulysses S. Grant "signed" *Memoirs* [which were not released until after his death]. I cringe even harder every time I see a bid next to one of these spurious pieces.

I cannot condemn the online auctions as a whole, for I have found some veritable bargains and been extremely pleased with just about all of my carefully screened purchases. For example, I bought a 1907 letter with an extremely early reference to college basketball for $2.00. I have found some hard-to-find Bob Dylan posters at a very reasonable prices. I have acquired books for half of the Barnes and Noble price. All of my purchase transactions have been prompt and I have yet to be stiffed by a seller who cashed my check and did not send me my material. So there are certainly bargains for an experienced collector.

When the last edition of **The Sanders Price Guide to Autographs** was released, no one had ever heard of the host of companies that have online auctions, including eBay, Yahoo!, AuctionUniverse, Amazon.com, and CollectIt! Internet auctions are the greatest change in the autograph field in the past five years, yet they are also the most potentially disturbing. The reason is simple: Internet auctions cut out the experienced dealer, allowing anyone and everyone to sell to the public. Many of these so-called "Internet autograph peddlers" wouldn't know **The Sanders Price Guide to Autographs** if it fell on them and strongly suspect that Charles Hamilton is the guy on the ten dollar bill.

I do want to make an important differentiation when I speak of "Internet Auctions." Many reputable autograph dealers have online bidding forms on their own web sites so a client can easily bid in their current auctions. Likewise, a number of well-known

A land grant signed by Zachary Taylor's secretary. Although this eBay seller responsibly listed this one as signed by Taylor's secretary, many novice sellers do represent secretarially-signed Presidential land grants as authentic. [NOTE: Jackson was the last President to authentically sign land grants.]

autograph dealers sell their material on eBay using their real names. These are NOT the people I warn you against because they are experienced and accountable. I am specifically warning you against the unaccountable, novice dealers who sell on general online auction sites like eBay and Yahoo!.

Consider what the autograph field was like in ancient times before the rise of the Internet, say five years ago. A person would pick up an autograph at a garage sale or an estate sale. Since they often did not know if it was authentic or not, they would send either copies or the original to a dealer, who would then tell the owner if it was authentic, autopen, printed, or secretarial. If it turned out to be non-genuine for any reason, the dealer would return it to the owner, and that would be the end of the piece.

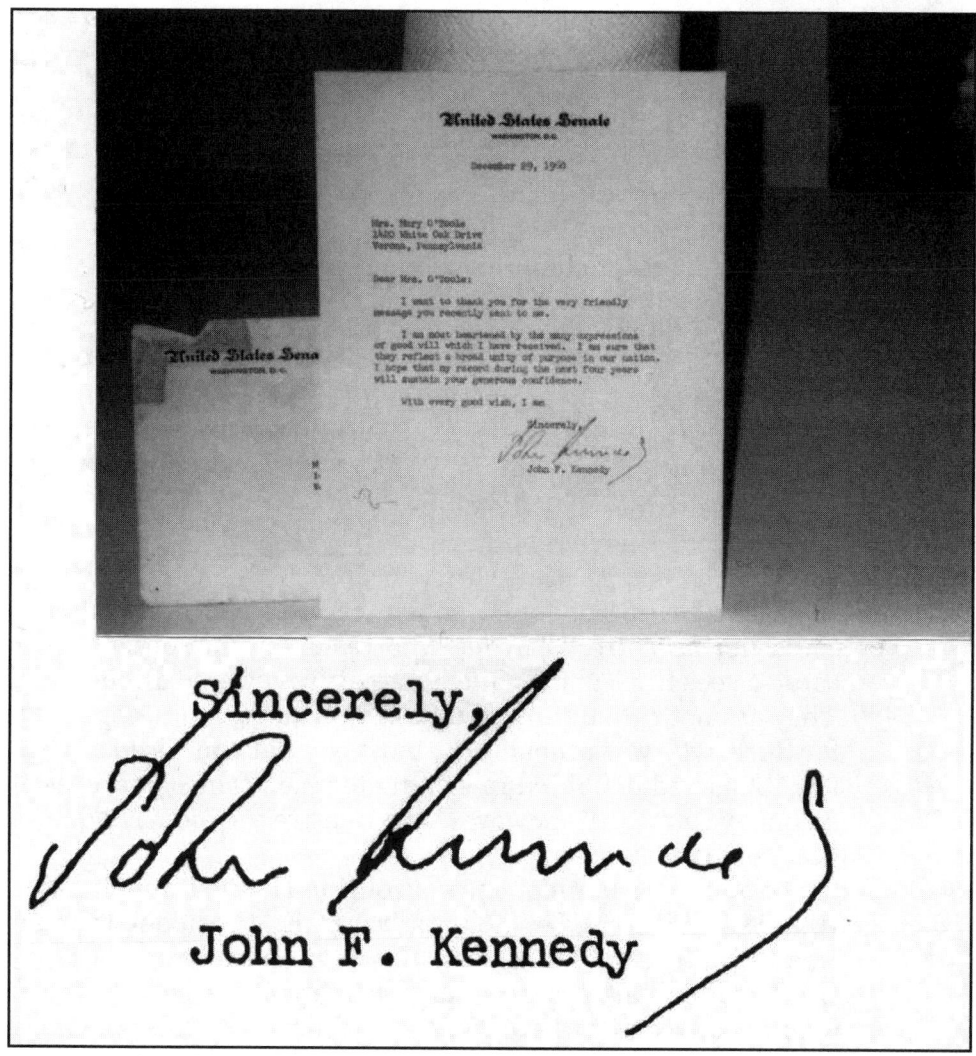

A John F. Kennedy typed letter signed with an autopen pattern that has been well-known in the autograph field for nearly 40 years.

Today, that is no longer true. By cutting out the experienced dealer, Internet auction prices are lower, but buying is far chancier. I have seen more autopen and secretarial signatures sold online as guaranteed genuine than I care to remember. Unfortunately, innocent customers are getting suckered. In one of my favorite Internet excuses, a book with a forged George Washington signature was offered on eBay [with a COA, of course!]. The seller wrote that he could have chosen to sell this wonderful piece through Christie's or Sotheby's, but magnanimously decided to sell it directly to the public through the magic of eBay. The truth is any auction house or knowledgeable dealer would have laughed at them for bringing in such counterfeit material.

A Presidential document with a printed-on signature of Lyndon Baines Johnson, represented on eBay as authentic by the seller.

Another concern is the number of pieces I have seen advertised with exaggerated rarity, such as Babe Ruth or John Kennedy clipped signatures rated by the seller as "rare." Anyone who reads an auction or dealer catalog sees Ruth and Kennedy signatures offered all the time. They are not rare by any stretch of the imagination, especially for Ruth, who was probably the most popular American alive in the 1920s and delighted in signing for kids. The signatures of Kennedy and Ruth, however, are relatively expensive due to great demand.

In another example, I saw a routine Harry Truman letter from 1959 advertised on eBay as "rare." Ex-President Truman was a prolific correspondent and is extremely common in routine letters. There are truly rare Truman pieces, such as Presidential handwritten letters and anything from his ten week Vice Presidency or relating to his failed haberdashery shop in the 1920s. It's just that post-Presidential letters with routine content are everywhere, and this seller was clearly misleading buyers, intentionally or not.

The rise of Internet auctions should be of great alarm to experienced dealers, and not because they are getting cut out of the selling process. Imagine if you bought the Mark Twain book I described earlier for $700. You treasure it dearly for five years, but then decide you need to sell it to pay for something else. So you call up an autograph dealer, expecting to make a small profit in the intervening five years. When the dealer tells you that it is close to worthless, there is no place to turn since very, very few Internet dealers offer any type of lifetime money-back guarantee that all experienced dealers routinely have. So you decide to eat your $700, but it is the last time you will ever buy an autograph. Next time, you decide you are better off putting $700 in a mutual fund or another type of collectible.

Additionally, in the past, dealers have had an informal theft hotline, where if a collection was stolen from either a dealer or a collector, all dealers would be notified to look for particular pieces. With the ease of Internet auctions, stolen autographs can be quickly sold with little chance of recovery.

Dealers have a critical obligation in this matter. If they see obvious autopenned, secretarial or facsimile material offered for sale on the Internet, it is their obligation to make the seller aware of this. When I tell sellers about non-genuine material, I often state that the autopen or secretarial pattern they have for sale can be found in Charles Hamilton's *American Autographs* or some other autograph reference book. Many times at shows, if someone is displaying an obvious forgery or autopen, dealers will discreetly say something to the seller. Why should it be any different on the Internet? It is far better for the entire business to act now than to have an angry horde of suckered people in five years swearing that they will never buy another signature in their lifetime.

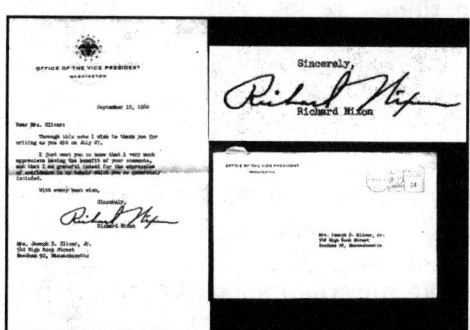

A Richard Nixon letter signed with an autopen. This familiar Nixon pattern has been reproduced a number of times in various autograph books and sadly, the seller did not do the most basic research on his or her material. Though the seller guarantees this piece for life, it does not make it any more genuine and it sold for over $300.00.

Rules for Internet Auctions

Here are six basic rules to follow when bidding for autographs on Internet auctions:

1. There are a number of truly experienced dealers who sell autographs on eBay, Yahoo! and AuctionUniverse because they can reach an enormous audience quickly and cheaply. If you feel comfortable enough buying from that dealer's fixed price or mail bid auction, you probably will feel comfortable enough buying from his or her Internet auction that is hosted on a general auction web site such as AuctionUniverse or eBay.

2. Many sellers claim to be members of the Universal Autograph Collectors Club, the Manuscript Society or the International Autograph Dealers Alliance—all fine organizations that have greatly helped the autograph collecting community. Affiliation with these groups, however, means nothing online unless the seller is willing to give you a lifetime guarantee for the full purchase price if the piece is ever found to be non-authentic. Demand this before bidding.

3. Never purchase anything that does not have a scanned image or the offer of a scanned image (such as the seller faxing you a copy). But even then, things are not so clear-cut. For example, a high-quality color photograph of an authentic, signed photograph can easily fool experienced dealers, and a scanned image of this non-genuine piece would be very deceptive.

4. COA means absolutely nothing. Anyone can offer a certificate. I cannot believe the number of John F. Kennedy autopen patterns that have been offered for sale as genuine, complete with a COA.

5. Ask yourself this before sending a check: What is your maximum financial threshold for losing money? Are you willing to send $100 to a complete, unaccountable stranger who might cash your check and not send you your material?

6. If the price is too good to be true... need I finish the cliché?

Best of luck collecting, and please, please, <u>please</u>, keep your guard up when bidding online. I want you to be a long-term autograph collector, not a short term sucker angry at the autograph market.

Stuart Lutz may be contacted via e-mail at **StuartKL@aol.com**.

Chapter 4

Hail to the Chief

Collecting the Presidents of the United States

by Michael Minor and Larry F. Vrzalik

Collecting presidential autographs is an interesting and exciting quest as well as a journey through the history of the United States. Although assembling a complete collection of presidential autographs is costly and fraught with perils, the end result is well worth the effort. A handful of certain presidents will cost as much as all of the others.

In general terms, all other factors being equal, the most expensive presidential autographs are Washington, Jefferson, John Adams and Lincoln. Although signatures (on small cards or cut from letters or documents) are the least expensive format they can, in certain instances, be among the most difficult to assemble. "Cut" signatures of Washington, Jefferson, John Adams and Lincoln, and some of the other early presidents, are quite scarce in comparison to their letters or documents. The answer is obvious—in their day few people collected autographs; however, when collectors did write and request a presidential autograph, the president responded in most instances with a full autograph letter signed!

Also, most people had the great good sense not to clip a presidential signature off a document or letter. Thus, it is far easier, albeit more costly, to find a complete Washington or Lincoln letter than a cut signature. Nevertheless, with patience, a collection of presidential signatures can be assembled and if properly and archivally matted with portraits or engravings such a collection can be very handsome, dramatic and even spectacularly presented. What could be more impressive than to have the walls of a library or other great room lined with a complete collection of presidential signatures matted with their portraits!

The ultimate presidential item is a fine content presidential Autograph Letter Signed—a letter written by a president as president and entirely in his handwriting, followed by letters or documents signed while in office. Generally speaking presidential A.Ls.S. are the most costly, particularly if they have good or historic content. Ironically, presidential A.Ls.S. of modern presidents, or A.Ls.S. of any date, are, with few exceptions, infinitely rarer than those of earlier presidents such as Washington and Lincoln. The reason, of course, is because Washington and Lincoln hand wrote most of their letters. However, after the invention of the typewriter, handwritten presidential letters became more and more scarce. For this reason, a routine presidential A.L.S. of Bill Clinton would be worth as much and probably more than a routine Washington presidential A.L.S.

Several of our presidents were generals and military heroes before becoming president. Their military date letters

Third person presidential ALS (Autograph Letter Signed) of Thomas Jefferson evidencing his idiosyncrasy of not beginning his sentences with capital letters.

Very rare full signature of Zachary Taylor on pay voucher as a young army officer. Perhaps unique.

Conclusion of a typical Taylor ALS. Note the signature of "Z. Taylor."

PRESIDENTIAL AUTOGRAPHS　87

are usually more desirable and valuable than their later presidential letters. Among this group is Washington, Jackson, Grant and Eisenhower.

Presidential documents are another area of collecting. There are many types of presidential documents which include the land grant, ships papers or "sea letters," seal authorizations, military appointments, civil appointments, particularly postmaster appointments, pardons and executive orders. The most common types of presidential documents are land grants and military commissions. Land grants through the first term of Andrew Jackson were personally signed by the president, but secretarially signed thereafter.

Some presidential documents contain the signatures of two presidents because the co-signing cabinet officer later became president. These documents are highly desirable. Some of the combinations are: Washington and Jefferson, Jefferson and Madison, Madison and Monroe, Monroe and J.Q. Adams, Jackson and Van Buren, Polk and Buchanan, Pierce and Jefferson Davis (as Secretary of War), Theodore Roosevelt and Taft, Wilson and Franklin D. Roosevelt (as Assistant Secretary of the Navy), Harding and Hoover, and Coolidge and Hoover.

Another exciting area of collecting is presidential signed photographs, although a complete collection is impossible to assemble as the first photographs were not made until the 1840s. The first president to be photographed was John Quincy Adams in old age, although no signed photograph of him is known to exist. However, there are signed 8vo engravings of him. There is also reputedly a signed engraving of Washington. Andrew Jackson was photographed shortly before his death in 1845 but there are no signed photographs of him. The earliest president of whom signed photographs in the technical sense are known is Martin Van Buren in old age. There are no known SP's of W. H. Harrison, Tyler, Polk, or Taylor. There are signed photographs of Pierce and every succeeding president. As one might suspect, signed photographs of the early presidents are rare and costly. Those of Lincoln are the most expensive. A nice signed photograph of

SPIEGEL GROVE, FREMONT, O.

2 JULY, 1889.

The friends who have sent telegraphic messages, letters, floral tributes and newspaper articles, tokens of their regard for Mrs. Hayes, and of sympathy with me and my family, are so numerous that I can not, by the use of the pen alone, within the time it ought to be done, suitably express to all of them my gratitude and thanks.

I therefore beg them to excuse me for sending in this form my assurance of the fullest appreciation of their kindness, and of my lasting and heartfelt obligation to each of them.

My Dear Sir:

I beg you to receive my grateful thanks for your Expressions of Sympathy & Condolence—

Sincerely

Rutherford B. Hayes

Mr. A. S. Solomons

Above, printed acknowledgement of sympathy letter on the death of his wife, Lucy, on the bottom of which President Rutherford B. Hayes has written an ALS. Right is a rare full signature of Hayes.

with pleasure

Rutherford Birchard Hayes

> EXECUTIVE MANSION.
> WASHINGTON
>
> *Sir: The bearer, Mr Lewis is a very deserving patriot. I will be much gratified if you can properly give him Employment – RBHayes*
>
> *1879*

Executive Mansion card on which Rutherford B. Hayes has written an ALS. Hayes is the first president of whom this type card is available.

Lincoln and his son, which he signed "A Lincoln and son" sold for over $100,000.00 several years ago.

The signed photographs of some of the later 19th century presidents are inexplicably rare and costly, e.g., Benjamin Harrison and Arthur. Of the 20th century presidents JFK is quite rare in authentically signed SP's, as most are secretarially or autopen signed. Nevertheless, a collection of presidential signed photographs is worth far more than its weight in gold but is not for the faint hearted or the impatient.

Signed Executive Mansion or White House cards are another area of collecting. Again, a complete collection is not possible but they make an extremely attractive and desirable collection. This format was introduced by U. S. Grant of whom only one example is known. Practically speaking, they are theoretically obtainable for every president from and after Rutherford B. Hayes. These attractive cards are approximately 2.50 x 3.50 and have either "Executive Mansion, Washington" or "The White House, Washington," embossed on them in blue. Theodore Roosevelt changed the official name of the presidential residence from the "Executive Mansion" to "The White House" in 1901. Truman is scarce but obtainable in this foremat. Starting with Eisenhower they become increasingly rare. No authentically signed JFK, LBJ or Clinton White House cards are known to the authors. Those for the other presidents, starting with Nixon, are extremely rare. Starting with Carter, White House cards have a vignette of the White House superimposed on the body of the card. The Carter cards have a green vignette. Reagan continued this custom but changed the vignette color to blue, as they have remained.

Another attractive and highly collectible presidential item is the signed White House vignette which was introduced by Chester Arthur; however, they are not obtainable for all the presidents following Arthur. Nevertheless, they make an attractive assemblage.

Some collectors specialize in presidential letters on certain topics, e.g. health, religion, finances, etc. Such collections make fascinating reading.

Another interesting area of specialization is collecting presidential bank checks. While bank checks of Washington, Jefferson and Lincoln are obtainable, they are rare and expensive; however, for some of the later presidents, e.g., LBJ, they are unobtainable. Still, such a collection is highly interesting and gives great insight into our Chief Executives.

Good content presidential letters of any date— pre or post presidential, are desirable. Personally we would prefer having a letter of good or historic content of non-presidential date than a presidential ALS sending an autograph!

Not all presidents were good letter writers. And, like everyone, not all presidents were good spellers or had legible handwriting. It was Grover Cleveland who said "it takes a poor mind to only be able to think of one way to spell a word!" Jackson and Truman are well known for their inventive spelling.

In our opinion the best letter writers of the presidential series, in chronological order, were: Washington, whose letters are not only beautifully written but beautifully phrased; John Adams, who could and often did write scathing and highly opinionated letters about the burning issues of the day; Jefferson, although they were a bit formal and stilted; Jackson, who was a notoriously poor speller, but wrote pithy and interesting letters; W. H. Harrison, who could but usually did not write interesting letters; Tyler, Fillmore and Lincoln, whose letters are usually short but often beautifully phrased; Andrew Johnson, Cleveland, Theodore Roosevelt, Taft, Wilson, FDR, Truman, Reagan, Bush and Clinton.

Harding's letters, like his speeches, were known for their rambling but flowery tenor. "His speeches left the impression of pompous phrases moving over the landscape in search of an idea. Sometimes these meandering words would actually capture a straggling thought and bear it triumphantly, a prisoner in their midst, until it died of servitude and overwork"—former Wilson Secretary of the Treasury, William Gibbs McAdoo.

In terms of presidential letters, Truman is in a category by himself. His letter to music critic Paul Hume, who had written an unfavorable review of Margaret's debut as a professional singer, is perhaps the most controversial letter ever written by a sitting president. In much more graphic detail Truman told the critic if he ever met him he would give him a black eye and a bloody nose and "...you'll need a supporter below!" Truman began his letter to Hume by telling him he had read his "lousy review" in the newspaper, and went on to tell Hume that he was an "eight ulcer man on a four ulcer job," and then quite colorfully commented on his ancestry. The country was divided between being aghast that a president would stoop to writing such a shocking letter to being supportive of a father defending his daughter. Critics coined the slogan "To err is Truman!" Truman never apologized nor showed any discernible sign of remorse.

HERBERT HOOVER

The Waldorf-Astoria Towers
New York, New York   10022
March 22, 1964

My dear President Moses:

I have not forgotten.

And if I am not able to be present at the inaugural ceremony on April twenty-second I shall send a message, as you suggest.

Yours faithfully,

The Honorable Robert Moses
President
New York World's Fair 1964-1965
World's Fair, New York   11380

One of Hoover's last letters, signed shortly before his death.

Rare full signature of Franklin Delano Roosevelt.

THE WHITE HOUSE

WASHINGTON.
AUG
31
12 M
1935
D. C.

Mr. William T. Marshall
Hotel Willard
Washington, D.C.

Illegal presidential free frank of F.D.R. on a White House envelope. F.D.R. did not have the franking privilege as president. Only a few are known to exist.

I recall with understanding the occasions of which you write and assure you that it is heart-warming to receive word from service associations.

Again many thanks for your kind offer, and with best wishes,

Sincerely,

Rare signature of Eisenhower as "Ike Eisenhower."

Another interesting area of collecting, and one in which the coauthor, Michael Minor, collects, is "Presidential Rarities or Oddities," some of which are illustrated in this chapter.

In terms of penmanship, perhaps Washington had the most attractive handwriting. Lincoln's penmanship was plain and usually legible although, with the stress of war many of his presidential notes and directives are difficult to decipher. Jefferson's handwriting is tiny and characterized by his idiosyncrasy of not making capital letters. His signature is so much larger than his handwriting that, at first glance, it appears to have been written by another. John Quincy Adams wrote a plain but attractive hand which changed little through out his life. Taylor's writing was bold, plain and attractive. He preferred a broad nibbed pen which made his letters quite distinctive and attractive. Truman, LBJ, Ford, Carter, Reagan and Clinton all wrote or write legible and attractive hands.

John F. Kennedy's handwriting is almost undecipherable and his signature varied the most. He has the distinction of having the worst handwriting of all the presidents. Martin Van Buren is a close second and worthy of 'honorable mention' in the "Hall of Fame of Illegible Handwriting" is George Bush.

The two fanciest or most florid signatures of all the presidents are those of James K. Polk and James Buchanan. Attractive, too, are the signatures of Washington, Jefferson, John Adams, Taylor, Taft and Wilson.

Another area of collecting is that of books signed by the presidents. These include presidential memoirs and other books owned or authored by the presidents. Not all our presidents have written their memoirs, particularly many of the 19th century ones. Most of the 20th century presidents have. Some of the presidents, e.g., Wilson, Hoover, Nixon, Ford and Carter have written a number of books, all of which are desirable to find signed. Another category of books are those owned by a president and from their personal library. Such books are extremely rare, expensive, and highly desirable in several instances—Washington, Jefferson and Lincoln. Books from Jefferson's library incorporate a code used by Jefferson incorporating letters from words in which he encoded his initials.

LINCOLN DAY RALLY

Honorable

Richard M. Nixon

Speaker

Washington Hilton Hotel — International Ballroom

THURSDAY, FEBRUARY 10, 1966

8:30 p.m.   Admission $1

AUDITORIUM SEATING   *LINCOLN DAY RALLY*   *AUDITORIUM SEATING*

Rare in-person full signature of Nixon. Nixon never used his middle name or initial in his signature. Probably written in full at the request of a shrewd collector.

Many presidents had their own personalized book plates, e.g., Washington and many others wrote their names inside their books, or both. Books from Buchanan's library are quite desirable because he bequeathed his library to his favorite niece, Harriet Lane, who was his White House hostess, and who wrote her name "Harriet Lane Johnston" below Buchanan's signature, further authenticating the volume. As a point of interest, the autographic material of Harriet Lane, one of our youngest, loveliest and most popular First Ladies, is much scarcer than the material of her presidential uncle. It was for the lovely young Harriet Lane that the popular pre-civil war ballad "Listen to the Mockingbird" was written and dedicated.

FDR collected bibelots, or miniature books, which he bequeathed to his children along with his famous stamp collection. The remainder of Roosevelt's vast library is housed in his presidential library at Hyde Park, New York. The FDR bibelots are all signed, usually on the first free blank end paper, or inside the front cover. Beneath his signature he usually wrote "Hyde Park"—however, inside those bibelots he obtained during his presidency he wrote "The White House" below his signature.

There are many presidential book rarities as well as many

Rare, early signature of Jimmy Carter signed as "J.E. Carter, Jr."

easily obtainable volumes, e.g., most of those authored and signed by Hoover, Nixon, Carter and Ford. However, in 1912 Hoover and his wife translated an early mining treatise Agricola's *De Re Metallica*, first published in 1556. These rare volumes also contain Hoover's scarce early signature "H.C. Hoover." As a member of the Warren Commission, Gerald Ford wrote a book about Lee Harvey Oswald entitled *Portrait of the Assassin*. Signed copies are quite rare.

The young JFK wrote a memorial tribute to his brother who was killed in WWII entitled *We Remember Joe,* and his master's thesis *Why England Slept*. Later, when he was in the Senate, he also authored the Pulitzer Prize winning book *Profiles in Courage*. All three volumes are scarce and highly desirable. Most copies of *Profiles in Courage* bear secretarial inscriptions. Rare and probably unobtainable is a privately printed memorial tribute Theodore Roosevelt wrote after the death in childbirth of his first wife, Alice Lee, in which he wrote "...the light has gone out of my life forever..." He gave his infant daughter, Alice, into the care of his sister and went west. The rest, as they say, is history!

Collecting presidential material is an educational, stimulating and exciting pursuit. We highly recommend it to you.

Michael Minor and Larry F. Vrzalik are leading autograph experts and partners in Lone Star Autographs in the the great state of Texas. They may be reached at 1-972-932-6050.

Chapter 5

Military Autographs of the 20th Century

by Terry Patton

F ew events in history have more impact and attract more interest than armed conflict. Consequently, the men and women who plan, lead, and fight these campaigns become historically significant people, for better or worse.

World War II, the culmination of the conflict which began in 1914, is undoubtedly the most influential event of the past 100 years and will continue to impact the structure of the political process throughout the world well into the next century.

The opportunity to own actual pages of history from this tumultuous time offers great collecting potential. Imagine holding a letter signed by General Patton in 1944 at his peak of glory, a signature of Winston Churchill during the dark days of 1940, or a document signed by Field Marshall Rommel, the Desert Fox.

The vast amount of material available inspires such areas of collectibility as U.S. Generals, Medal of Honor winners, world leaders, or signatures of those who fought for the defeated powers. Yes, they had their heroes, too! This latter category is the fastest growing segment in the field of military signatures, especially those of Germans. These would include aviation (top aces), generals and field marshalls, and holders of the Knights Cross, German's highest military award whose signed photos were avidly collected at the time by young would-be heroes.

Documents such as performance evaluations, combat reports, and award recommendations provide excellent collectible value as they can be thoroughly researched and are often written and signed by well known people such as Rommel.

Actual award certificates for decorations such as the Iron Cross offer an interesting collecting field. These documents were usually signed by the commanding officer and are named to the individual recipient, giving his rank, military unit and date of the award. It is, therefore, possible to research the precise battle or activity and where it occurred when the man won his decoration.

Currently among the most sought-after subjects are the German flying aces of WWI and WWII. During the war, German pilots were kept in combat almost continuously, allowing them to achieve very high levels of "kills." Erich Hartmann holds the record at 352 downed planes! Anything signed by these pilots, be it photos, letters, or official documents is in great demand.

Two of America's top generals in World II—Dwight D. Eisenhower (hand on hip with signature superimposed), Commander-in-Chief (at the time) of Allied Forces in North Africa, and General George C. Marshall, U.S. Army Chief of Staff.

When acquiring any military signatures, especially on photos, it is imperative that you deal with a knowledgeable and reputable source. There are forgeries as well as facsimile signatures that are very difficult to defeat. The safest place to obtain authentic material is from a dealer specializing in this area. There are a number of reputable dealers both in the United States and abroad who will gladly assist you in what to look for and what to avoid. When choosing someone to deal with, ask questions regarding their experience, references, and return policies.

Auction houses and collectible shows can also be good sources for material. Be sure the auction house offers a return privilege as you will most likely be bidding by mail or telephone on an auction lot that you will not have a chance to examine until you receive it. Collectible shows can be very lucrative—and very

Above, signed photograph of Erich Hartmann, German air ace with 352 planes shot down. Right, a postcard signed by Field Marshall Rommel, the legendary Desert Fox. Both signatures are in high demand by collectors.

China's Generalissimo Chiang Kai-Shek, President Franklin D. Roosevelt, and British leader Winston Churchill confer during World War II with facsimiles.

treacherous. In most cases, you will have to rely on your own knowledge and expertise with little or no recourse. Therefore, as with any collecting specialty, there is no substitute for knowledge. Study your subject before investing. After all, the full satisfaction in owning a particular signature comes with learning about all the events surrounding it.

It doesn't take a fortune to get started collecting military signatures. Prices range from $25 for postwar signed photographs of Knights Cross holders to many thousands of dollars for historically significant documents.

Don't be surprised when you enter this field of collecting to find yourself "catching the fever" and wanting to learn as much as possible about this eventful period—and acquiring your own page of history.

Terry Patton, owner of PATTON Militeria Collectibles, has more than 15 years as a full-time dealer specializing in German signatures and documents. Contact Terry at 770-529-0307.

Chapter 6

Autographed First Day Covers Combining Philography with Philatelics

by Thomas B. Eisaman

Editor's Note: *The melding of philography (autograph collecting) with stamp collecting was of great interest to George Sanders. Some of you will recall his lengthy chapter in the fourth edition of this book. Thomas Eisaman—a leading expert in this fast growing area of collecting—continues our coverage of the subject.*

Collecting United States First Day Issues is an integral and interesting part of *philately* (stamp collecting). It is as old as the hobby itself. This is an area of specialty that also appeals to the knowledgeable autograph collector. To put it simply the collecting of autographed First Day Covers and Event Covers are the HOTTEST area in the *philographic* (autograph collecting) arena. This area offers the collector an opportunity to draw two fields together, thus creating a unified market that is forever increasing in popularity and value.

With the growing number of single stamps issued by the postal service there is a myriad of avenues for the collector to consider when combining philately with philography. This takes under consideration the new contemporary issues such as the "American Classic Films," "Cartoon Classics," "Rock and Roll," and "Country Western Singers," not to mention the classic issues released after WWII.

Many of these issues can be obtained at a dollar amount far below the cost of a color photograph. In addition, there are many photographs available that are not approved by the celebrity. Therefore, many celebrities refuse to sign them. Celebrities that we have had contact with enjoy signing postal issues, as a matter of fact they prefer to sign them in many cases.

Another factor to consider is the storage of your collection, many collectors like to display framed signed photographs throughout their homes, however, just how much wall space does one have available? First Day covers can be placed into an album for safe keeping or displayed in a matted format with an approved photograph.

Philography, on the other hand, is no stranger to philatelics, as a matter of fact, these two fields merged with American history during the Revolutionary War in the form of Free Frank letters generated from officers in the government. The franking privilege continued as our young nation matured in the form of political franking privileges. This privilege created one of the most overlooked categories in philographics today, but that is another topic that will be covered at a later date.

First Day Covers

Over the last eighty years, philatelic covers or First Day Covers, which include Event Covers, began to emerge. It has been documented that on September 1, 1923, George W. Lynn placed the first two cent Harding stamp to an envelope and canceled each item on the first day of issue. Thus creating our nation's first "First Day Issue" envelope.

As early as 1929, A.C. Roessler is credited with placing a design or cachet on the left hand side of a postage envelope tying the design or theme to the stamp, thus creating the first *cachet* First Day Cover. It is also known that individuals, such as Dr. E.P. Cressler, have been credited with combining the philographic signature of the Postmaster in a designated area with the first day cancellation. This documents some of the first autographs on covers as we know them today and proves that the industry was alive and flourishing back then.

This procedure was also very popular with Event Covers which were first used to commemorate a specific theme within the field of aviation in the early 1920s. It is know that our first air mail pilots were required to sign limited numbers of phila-

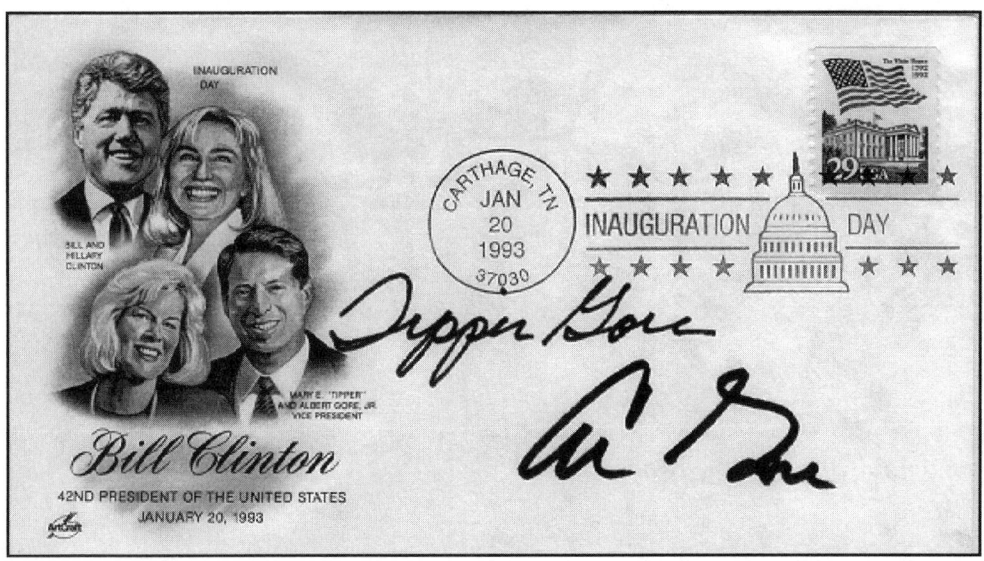

A potential matchup for the 2000 presidential election is Al Gore vs. George W. Bush, Jr.—son of former president George Bush. Above is a First Day Cover (actually an "Inaugural Portrait Cachet") signed by Vice-president Al Gore and his wife, Tipper. Note the postmark of Carthage, TN—Gore's hometown. Below is a First Day Cover issued in honor of Texas statehood, signed by now Texas governor George W. Bush, Jr. Both of these FDCs may be considered Event Covers.

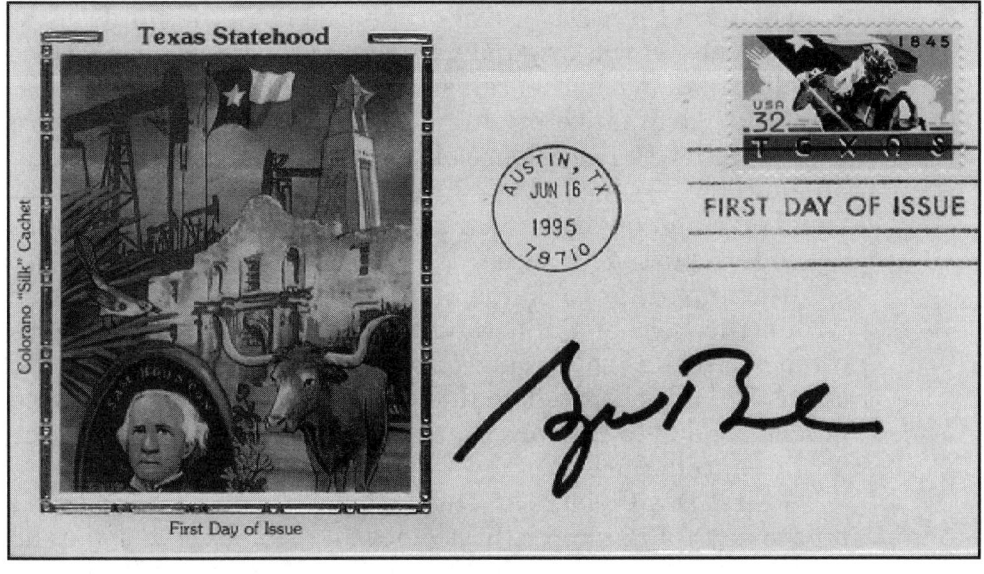

Well know anchorman on NBC News with Chet Huntley and later co-anchor of ABC's "This Week" (1981-1997) signed this FDC honoring the freedom of speech.

telic material upon delivery. This takes under consideration individuals such as Earl Ovington, Basil Rowe and Charles A. Lindbergh, not to mention Amelia Earhart's early flights.

The term First Day Cover originated from the words "first day of issue." It was originally used in a machine cancel format which began with the release of the .03 cent Northwest Territory Ordinance on July 13, 1937. Hand cancels were introduced with the release of the Washington Irving Stamp on January 29, 1940. This gave definition to the term First Day Issue and opened a window of opportunity to collectors of modern postage stamps.

It is important to define and document a First Day Cover within the field of Philography. Collectors and dealers have often overlooked the proper terminology in defining a specific cover. This has created confusion and an imbalance in price guidelines due to the rarity factor of a specific stamp, cover or postal cancellation.

A First Day Cover is an envelope bearing a stamp canceled on the day that stamp is first placed on sale. It is a philatelic

FDCs signed by two military heroes. Above, Robert Morgan, hero pilot of the "Memphis Belle" in WWII has signed a FDC honoring General Hap Arnold. Morgan lives near the authors of this book and was honored a few years ago with an exciting movie about his exploits. His plane is on permanent display in Memphis. Below, a FDC honoring the military's successful campaign during Desert Storm. The FDC is appropriately signed by General Colin Powell, who was our top ranking soldier.

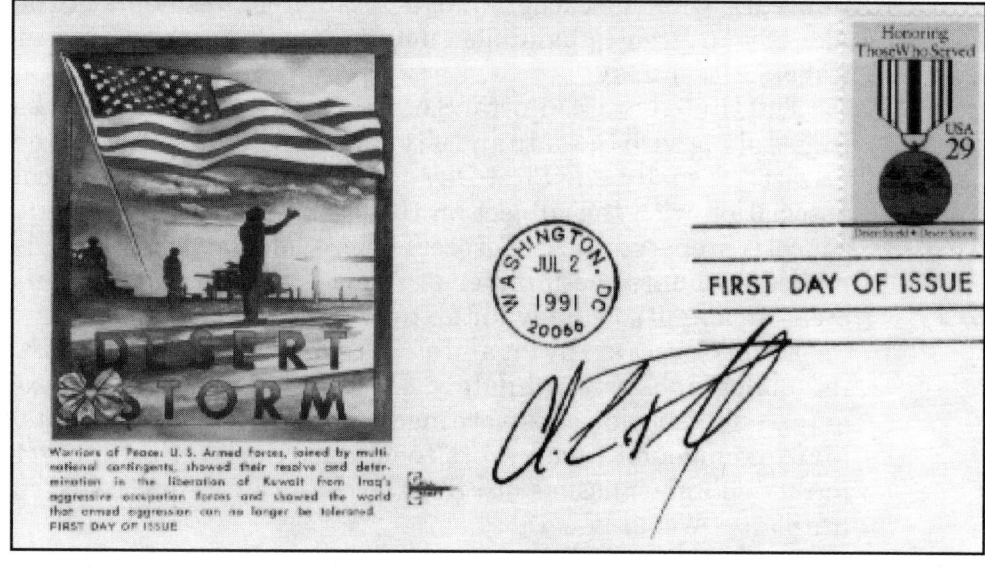

Cartoonist Dave Graue—who draws "Alley Oop"—not only signed this FDC honoring comic strips, he also did a sketch of our favorite caveman!

presentation of when, where, and why the stamp was issued. Please keep in mind that the United States Postal Service cannot celebrate a famed person until they have been dead for ten years, with the exception of assassinated presidents or the like of martyred individuals such as Martin Luther King or Robert F. Kennedy.

The United States Postal Service announces a stamp to be issued along with the date and city from which the stamp will be released. Usually, the First Day city is chosen for its historical association with the subject on the stamp. The first day issue cancel is prepared and the process begins for that day only. This procedure limits the number of items that are canceled thus creating a limited supply for an overwhelming demand.

Event Covers are by far and away the cornerstone of combining philography with philately. During the war years for example only generic issues were made available for special events. Many commemorative events took place during this era, yet most well known issues of First Day Issues were not released until after World War II.

Those of us who grew up watching Annette Funicello on "The Mickey Mouse Club" still love her! This FDC signed by the First Lady of Mouse Ears is therefore highly desirable. Below, is a FDC signed by a more current celebrity, Jay Leno of the "Tonight Show" on NBC. Leno has added a quick self-portrait in addition to his sig.

Creative artists and cachet manufacturers were able to design Event Covers using rubber stamps for the first airmail flown by Earl Ovington. They also used designs documenting that "Lindbergh Flies the Mail Again" in 1928. The stamp used could be as simple as a generic American Flag stamp of the era. Other designs included commemorative events such as the return of MacArthur to Corregidor to the launch of Gemini, Apollo and STS space missions on through Inaugural issues of contemporary Presidents or Vice Presidents.

There are literally thousands of avenues for the advanced stamp collector and just as many for the philographer both advanced or novice. One is only limited by his or her own imagination and knowledge in a specific subject. In this chapter, please find some nice examples.

Categories to Consider Collecting

- Presidents - Vice Presidents
- Presidential First Ladies
- Senators & Members of Congress
- Foreign Political
- John F. Kennedy Relations to Family
- Watergate-Nixon Cabinet
- Supreme Court Justices
- Civil Rights
- Authors
- Famous Attorneys
- Miscellaneous Celebrities
- Journalists, Commentators & Broadcasters
- Medal of Freedom Recipients
- Artists
- Cartoon Artists
- Actresses
- Actors
- Comedians
- Producers & Directors
- Composers
- Playwrights
- Conductors
- Big Band Era
- Rock & Roll Music
- Country Western Music
- Jazz Music
- Opera
- Science & Technology
- V-2 Rocket Team
- Inventors & Explorers
- Medical Doctors
- Nobel Laureates
- Aviation (Early Air Mail) Astronauts- Mercury, Gemini, Apollo & STS Military- Army, Navy, Air Force & Marine Military Aviation
- Congressional Medal of Honor Recipients

(Sports categories will be covered later)

Thomas B. Eisaman is Portfolio Director for the Historical Document Society. He may be contacted at P.O. Box 160991, Miami FL 33116. Or telephone 1-800-237-7340.

Chapter 7

Mary Benjamin

(1905-1998)

by Al Wittnebert

Editor's Note: *Last year was not a totally happy one for the autograph hobby—we lost both George Sanders (a founder of this price guide) and that most regal and widely beloved queen of autograph dealers, Mary A. Benjamin. With the passing a bit earlier of autograph legend Charles Hamilton, we have now lost the three people who did the most during the 20th century for the autograph hobby and who most deserve the credit for its flourishing state today. We shall miss them! Below is Al Wittnebert's tribute to Mary. It was originally published in the Mar.-Apr. issue of the UACC's* Pen and Quill, *and we reproduce it here by the author's kind permission.*

It was with great sadness that I learned longtime autograph scholar and dealer Mary Benjamin had passed away at age 93. In a time when a great many autograph dealers have neither the time nor the inclination to learn their trade, and are more interested in making money than in acquiring knowledge, Mary and her company stood proud as an example of what an autograph dealer should be, could be, and can be.

Mary took over her father's business—the prestigious Walter R. Benjamin Autographs, Inc.—in 1940. Having worked with and learned from her father for thirteen years prior to her taking over the oldest and most respected dealership in the world, Mary went on to establish herself as a respected professional and pioneer in this new field.

Walter Benjamin started his business back in 1887 when

he purchased and saved countless historic documents from being destroyed. In 1907, when he found that the United States Customs Service had sold 140 tons of old documents to a junk dealer, he persuaded the man to let him go through the refuse, and ended up paying 25 cents each for thousands of documents signed by American Presidents.

Following her father's lead, Mary saved thousands of questionnaires filled out by prominent Americans for the *Dictionary of American Biography*. Her photographic memory and knowledge of history served her well, and before long she attracted many who brought her their treasures. Mail came to her from all

Mary Benjamin examines an autograph collection in 1946 as depicted in this old photograph from the *Saturday Evening Post*.

In Memoriam: Mary A. Benjamin (1905-1998)

over the country, sometimes addressed simply to "The Autograph Lady."

Mary also had the distinction of giving back knowledge and education to her customers by issuing *The Collector,* which as most of us know is a combination catalogue and informational newsletter. This unique publication demonstrated—and continues to demonstrate—the commitment and innovation that made Mary who she was. *The Collector* always made a point of providing information to the collector which proved useful in a complex field.

In 1946, she published *Autographs: A Key to Collecting.* This was one of the first publications of its kind, and with numerous reprints it is still one of the best reference books on the subject ever written. She was married to the Columbia professor Harold G. Henderson, and although his special area of expertise was Japanese art, the two spent many hours reading old manuscripts together and discussing history. Following his death, Mary moved the firm to the town of Hunter, near Albany, and remained active in the business until 1995. Walter R. Benjamin Autographs is now operated by her nephew Christopher Jaeckel, who became her assistant in 1971.

Mary Benjamin was a good teacher and role model, opening the door for women in this field: a recent study found that 40% of all autograph dealerships are either run by women or have women partners. She was a loyal member of both the UACC (Universal Autograph Collectors Club) and the Manuscript Society, and supported each organization with advertising in their respective journals.

The autograph community mourns the passing of Mary Benjamin; with that passing comes a challenge to all of us to rededicate ourselves to learning the complexities of the hobby we love.

Al Wittnebert is a longtime autograph collector and dealer. He currently serves as Treasurer of the UACC and is a Life member of that fine organization. He operates Al Wittnebert's Autographs in Florida and may be contacted at P.O. Box 1392, Mt. Dora FL 32756 or call (352)383-1958. Al's web site is **www.sign-here.com**.

The
SANDERS
Price Guide to
AUTOGRAPHS

Fifth Edition

Section 2:

Ralph's Stuff

Being a compendium of three useful chapters about practical pursuits; to wit preservation of your valuable pieces of paper, framing and matting, and detecting autopens and forgeries.

Helen Sanders and Ralph Roberts—coauthors and editors of the **Sanders price guides**—with the award they received in January, 1999 for having the bestselling book in Amazon.com's autograph category, the 4th edition of **The Sanders Price Guide to Autographs**.

HOLLYWOOD, 1950: George R. Sanders, Sr. and Grace Sanders (George's parents), cowboy star Roy Rogers, and a youthful Helen and George Sanders. George and Helen's long tenure in Hollywood in the broadcasting and entertainment business garnered them a wealth of autograph knowledge that the Sanders guides pass along to you, our readers.

Chapter 8

Paper and Its Enemies

The Care and Preservation of Autographs and Other Manuscripts

by Ralph Roberts

Old documents, letters, manuscripts, and autographed items of all sorts sing of magic; of wondrous times long gone yet recorded for the ages on paper. We, as collectors, possess these documents briefly in the grand scope of eternal time, cherish them, and—it is hoped—fulfill our custodial duty to ourselves and posterity by preserving and passing along these fragile paper legacies.

This chapter describes the basics of properly caring for and storing your paper treasures.

Paper and Its Enemies

Paper was invented in China about 100 A.D., spreading to Europe over the next few hundred years via merchants traveling and trading along the Silk Route. The manufacture of paper spread rapidly into Europe and was readily available by the time Johannes Gutenberg invented printing with movable type on printing presses in the 15th century.

The raw materials for paper—vegetable fibers—were far more plentiful than the ages older writing media such as parchment (treated animal skins) or the papyrus (split reeds) of the ancient Egyptians. Literacy boomed, then exploded with the arrival in general usage of the printing press. Books, tracts, pamphlets, chapbooks, business contracts, education documents, newspapers, magazines, and so forth and so forth—all of these and more have been printed and printed and printed in the ensuing centuries. Hundreds of billions pieces of paper, a good many millions—the crux of our hobby here—*signed*!

For hundreds of years, paper has been both plentiful and cheap, and thus the medium of choice for written records. But the delicate nature of paper means that many environmental factors cause it to deteriorate.

Here are the leading enemies of paper:

Acids Acids are public enemy number one to paper, yet are used extensively in its manufacture.

Inks Some inks contain chemicals that can cause discoloration or even deterioration of paper.

Air Exposure to the atmosphere is not helpful to the life of paper. Sulfur dioxide in industrial areas, for example, might combine with the tiny amounts of iron or copper in some papers. This produces sulfuric acid, causing the paper to turn brittle or even decompose.

Moisture Being fibrous, paper absorbs water, expanding and breaking apart its basic structure. Protect paper from moisture in amounts small and large, including water vapor (i.e. high humidity).

Light Ultraviolet light (sunlight) causes organic matter, which paper is, to decompose, and the ink on it to fade. Filtering out ultraviolet with special glass or plastic is good, but only absolute darkness truly preserves.

Temperature High temperatures (80 degrees or more) combined with low humidity cause paper to totally dry out and become brittle.

Dust Sharp edges of dust particles scour paper. Once embedded, they cannot be removed without damage. Plus fungus spores exist in dust and can cause discoloration and other harmful effects.

Insects Silverfish, termites, cockroaches, and other insects find paper tasty.

Humans	Mere careless handling of paper shortens its life. Sweat and skin oils, tape and other adhesives, rusting paper clips—all are ways in which we damage paper.

So, let's look at some specific tips for protecting paper from its many enemies.

Some Tips for Older Documents

Prior to the early 19th century, most paper was made from linen and cotton rags. It is actually more durable and, potentially, longer lasting than the paper of the last two hundred years, although modern "acid-free" papers are getting very good.

Older documents, however, do suffer from being folded. Before the invention of the file cabinet, papers were usually tied up in bundles with string or ribbon for storage. The English government often used red ribbon (tape) instead of string, thus coining the term "red tape" as applied to bureaucratic paperwork.

It is not uncommon to find such bundles still tied and folded in this manner. Should you acquire one of these, immediately unfold each piece and place them between two pieces of acid-free paper and onto a flat surface for gradual unwrinkling. A weight, such as a book, may be placed on top as long as it does not come in contact with the document. All paper clips, pins, ribbons, and so forth should be removed. Wax seals, if intact (which is rare) should be left in place.

Acid

Many pieces of paper carry the seeds of their own destruction deep within—acid! Dealers and librarians can tell horror stories of manuscript collections preserved in folders or framed in which the paper degenerated, or was left with stains and other damage.

Beginning in the 19th century, new and improved methods of papermaking came about. Wood fibers were "pulped" via chemical means and turned into paper. Wood, as the raw ingredient of paper, was and still is cheap and plentiful.

Unfortunately, acid occurs naturally in wood. One look at an old "pulp" magazine from the 1930s—pages yellowed, tattered, and crumbling—can immediately show you how this internal destructive process works. Or last year's newspaper, for that matter—as yellow as the journalism some tabloids contain.

As a rule of thumb, the higher the wood pulp content of the paper, the greater the acid content. Newsprint, the cheapest kind of paper, has the most pulp content. Even newspapers, pulp magazines, and old comic books (also with a high pulp content) can be preserved, though. In fact, a good collectible comic book store can be of great benefit to the collector. The better ones carry such preservation materials as acetate or Mylar® bags and sleeves, deacidification aids from sprays to deacidification sashes (a kind of ribbon placed between pages that leaches acid from paper). These latter actually remove acid from paper, dramatically increasing its life. For valuable pieces on cheap paper, these can be a very worthwhile investment.

The specification of "acetate or Mylar®" above is important. Many plastics will allow the migration of acid or other harmful chemicals into paper. Acetate is a "clean" plastic that protects paper, as does the trademarked polyester film, Mylar®.

The mistake some collectors make is to put a newspaper clipping in the same folder with a valuable collectible such as an autograph piece. Even though the autograph might be on good paper, the acid in the newsprint can quickly stain, even ruin the valuable document. Put such items in an acetate or Mylar® holder, and protect it from contact with other paper!

Plastic folders are also available at most office supply stores, as well as those specializing in stamp or photography supplies. More specialized products, such as those made of Mylar®, are to be found at serious comic book stores, and autograph or stamp dealers. Even if designed for comic books, stamps, or photographs, these are fine for any collectible paper that fits into them. Always ask for acid free material—it is truly worth the extra money.

If you are unable to find Mylar® products locally, call Bill Cole Enterprises, Inc. at (781) 986-2653, or visit their extensive internet website at **http://www.neponset.com/bcemylar/index.htm**. Ask for their catalog, it's a good introduction to the types of preservation materials currently available in an affordable price range.

Bill Cole Enterprises manufactures and sells the R-Kival™ brand of Mylar® sheet and magazine protectors. You'll want to check out their acid-free backing boards also.

Paper collectors in general certainly can learn a lot about preservation from stamp collectors and from comic book fans. Stamps are usually more delicate and likely to fade than many other documents. Check out the preservation aids in stamp stores. The same goes for comic stores. The Mylar® sleeves used for comic books along with their acid-free backing boards are perfect for autographed items!

Buying plastic folders already punched for a three-ring binder makes your storage problems easier. Just be sure and try to use archival quality such as Mylar® whenever possible You can have a notebook or notebooks for each category of your collection: Civil War, Presidential, the various Sports categories, Vintage Movie Stars, Entertainers, or however your collection logically divides.

If you have a manuscript of several pages, remove all paper clips and staples and discard them. These will rust and discolor the paper. The general rule here is to let nothing but the protective archival quality material come in contact with the piece. Engravings, newspaper clippings, even photographs (which are sometimes still coated with chemicals) should all be stored in a separate sleeve or folder.

In All Humidity

Acid is not the only enemy of paper, so too is humidity. Excessive humidity, such as storing papers in a basement or garage, can lead to mold. Some areas, such as the Southeastern U.S., are especially hazardous to the collectors of books, stamps, and autographs. If you have this problem, the purchase of a dehumidifier for the room autographs are stored in, is a very wise investment.

You may also place small packets of silica gel (the stuff that is packed with new cameras and radios) inside binders, etc. These soak up water vapor from the air, but must be replaced after a period of time. The relative humidity should never be more than 70 percent, and about 50 is the best.

Heat and low humidity, as mentioned already, are just as much of a problem, causing paper to become brittle. A good rule of thumb is to keep your collection as comfortable as yourself temperature wise.

In the Harsh Light of Day

Another enemy is light, especially the ultraviolet laden destructiveness of direct sunlight. If you display an autographed document or any other piece of collectible paper in a frame, ultraviolet shields are available which will protect them, both from the sun and artificial light sources such as fluorescent tubes.

For most of your collection, a closet shelf or closed file cabinet works. Keeping paper in absolute darkness is always good.

Dust Unto Dust

Dust can also be harmful. The shelves where you keep your collection should be kept clean. The same for filing cabinets, if those are used. Dust can carry particles of various chemicals that deteriorate paper.

In general, there is nothing wrong with taking a piece out of its storage place for an occasional airing, just as stamp collectors air stamps. In fact, air circulating around paper is usually beneficial assuming the air is clean. No piece should be sealed up too tightly.

Which brings us to a very important point, what is the use of having a collection if you can't occasionally look at it and show off your rare pieces to others? Don't hide it away all the time!

Danger! Humans Present

Paper can deteriorate or be defaced easily if care is not taken. In past years, collectors often would take a pencil and write the source and purchase price of a letter or other document directly on it. Many thousands of pieces now have such markings on

Above (from the author's personal collection), detail of an original leaf (page) from *Biblia Sacra, Quid In Haec Editione A Theologis Lovaniensibus Praestitum Sit...* (*The Holy Bible, Prepared by the Theologians of Louvain*) Printed at Antwerp, the Netherlands, by Christopher Plantin in 1583. This wonderful paper is over 415 years old! Except for some minor spots caused by moisture (called *foxing*), it is as flexible as the day it was made. A true treasure to be preserved for future generations.

them, or dealers' prices and comments such as "very rare," and so forth.

Whatever you do, *do not* attempt to erase these penciled notes. They don't injure the paper and may be of considerable importance in establishing provenance. The handwriting of many old-time dealers and collectors are recognizable by experts and collectors who have handled large numbers of manuscripts, thus helping to prove authenticity.

Now, however, *nothing* should be written on a collectible item. Nor should other paper (unless absolutely known to be acid-free) come in contact with it. So records for your collection need to be kept physically separate in some manner.

Prevention is Preservation

Places with big bucks—such as the Library of Congress and the National Archives—are using and developing wonderful high tech methods of preserving our paper heritage. Yet, we collectors can do the most simply through exercising care in the handling of collectible paper items.

The basic rules we've covered here are easy enough.

1. Don't make acid in the paper worse by putting it in contact with other paper or plastic other than Mylar® or other acid-free types.

2. Remove any paper clips or staples.

3. Keep it clean by not exposing paper to harmful dust.

4. Protect paper from ultraviolet light.

5. Handle pieces carefully to avoid perspiration or skin oils getting on valuable pieces. A pair of white lab gloves is a good idea.

6. Give your collection a nice dark place to live in—not too humid or hot.

7. Love and enjoy it, for that's the true reason to collect.

Ralph Roberts is the author of over 80 books and thousands of articles, and is both coauthor and publisher of the Sanders price guides. An avid collector of paper documents—both autographed and otherwise—he has addressed manuscript preservation in several books and many articles. Ralph's e-mail address is **ralph@abooks.com**.

Chapter 9

Basics of Matting and Framing

by Ralph Roberts

As we saw in my previous chapter in this book—"Paper and Its Enemies"—*light* is an avowed and deadly enemy of autographs. The simple fact of life is that light causes ink on paper to fade. Ultraviolet shields, nonreflective glass, and the like can decrease this fading action, but nothing except total darkness forever will completely guard against light's harm.

So a really rare and valuable autograph—such as a Shoeless Joe Jackson (infamous member of the "Black Sox" baseball team which threw the World Series, see **The Sanders Price Guide to Sports Autographs** for current value)—should not be framed and displayed. Keep it in some secure place— a place protected both from thieves and light. A better choice for display might be a favorite actor, actress, football player, or whatever your interest runs to in current celebrities.

If you do frame and hang a piece (and they can look quite awesome in your living room, den, office, or wherever), *never* place it where direct sunlight has a chance of hitting. Reflected daylight is also dangerous, causing fading, as is fluorescent lighting. Ultraviolet shields or special UV glass will help protect against the worst of light damage.

This chapter is meant as an overview of matting and framing (with the emphasis on matting), not to serve as a step by step guide. It gives you an introduction and presents resources you'll find invaluable as you proceed in learning this most satisfying and profitable pursuit. We'll see here how simple it all is!

Matting and framing—placing the autograph with pieces of cardboard-like material (called *matboard*) to artistically set off the item and then placing it in a frame (usually covering the piece with glass)—does take a modicum of skill, tools, and materials. This craft, if you collect and/or sell a lot of autographs is well worth learning and will *quickly* pay for itself. Professional framers charge ~~exorbitant~~ *er*... professional prices. Doing your own matting and framing saves lots of money and is a very rewarding accomplishment. Also it is quite smart to mat and frame an attractive piece, thus enhancing its value should you ever decide to sell as well as protecting it. Many galleries demand that items be matted and framed before they will even consider displaying them for sale, even on consignment.

Still, for the occasional piece, most people take it to a framing shop. When you entrust an autograph document or letter or signed photograph to a framer, some precautions are in order. First, (at least for the most valuable pieces) you should insist that the matting board used should be "museum board," i.e. acid-free. The thickness of board chosen should be one which will keep the autograph from touching the glass of the frame, and also allow for some air circulation.

Explain vigorously to the framer that masking tape, or any other kind of tape with acidic content *should never* be used, nor should the autograph be pasted down in any manner, not even to prevent wrinkling or buckling. Most framers—being professionals—will and should be even more adamant about protecting from acid damage than you. The framer, also, must not be allowed to cut or trim the piece in any way. Engravings or photographs framed with the autograph, must not be allowed to touch it either (since harmful chemicals or acids could be transferred).

Matting

To *mat* a piece of artwork, photograph, or other autographed item is to place a border of matboard around the item. Matting does several things for you. A properly chosen color complements and enhances the presentation of the piece, making it more striking to the eye of the beholder. Matting also protects

Simple matting—a piece of art or an autographed item is placed on a backing board as above. A hole large enough to show the piece as you would like is cut into some matboard that is the same size as the backing board. The three components (mat, art piece, backing board) are placed together into a frame. (Art courtesy of Alto's EZ Mat, Inc.)

the piece by not allowing it to come into contact with the glass in the item's frame. Should water condense on the back of the glass, the mat protects your valuable treasure from direct contact with moisture.

Learning How to Mat

The process of matting is, indeed, relatively easy once someone shows you how it's done. The figure at the left of this paragraph details the simple process and the component parts of a completed mat. This example is called a *single mat* since only one piece of matboard is used. If another matboard of a different color had been placed behind the first with a hole slightly smaller—resulting in a colored border around the artwork—we would call it a *double mat*. Three mats are a _triple_, and a very brave person in the framing and matting class I took while writing this chapter, did a *fiver*! That's five sheets of matboard with varying size center holes, which formed a very striking and interesting framing of the artwork. However, not to despair—the most common matting is double matting, which most likely will fill your needs in a nice elegant manner.

Learning matting and framing is easier if you have some support and ready resources to find answers to your questions, especially when you run up against a problem during the actual process of measuring or cutting a mat.

Following are the two resources which have helped me the most in mastering matting and framing.

The first involves taking a class on the subject. You may have to do a little research to find such a class, but it will be worth your effort. A good starting point are local art supply stores. Often these stores will occasionally offer classes, or at least know who does in your area.

Here in my home state of North Carolina, we are blessed with a strong community college system. These local technical colleges—such as Asheville-Buncombe in my end of the state—offer adult extension classes in the evenings. For practically no money, you can learn scores of things from French to creative writing to all sorts of artsy and crafty things. The class I took on framing and matting was a 10-week course (every Thursday evening from 6:30 to 9 p.m.) with tons of "hands on" experience. For this, I paid the lordly tuition sum of $35.00. Not bad. Supplies, of course, are extra, but we get a student discounts on mats, frames, and so forth, and this is all for our own projects, so we are saved bunches of money!

In fact, you might want to check out the supplier we used—Presto in Hendersonville, North Carolina. They carry an extensive selection of everything you need in the way of frames and matboards and related items. Their web site and online catalog is **www.framingsupplies.com**. Or call 1-800-334-9060. I am assured that they will be delighted to mail you a catalog.

Racks full of the wide stock of matboard you can order at **www.framingsupplies.com**.

Our instructors at A-B Tech were two very nice ladies—Peggy Hester and Sheryl Cordell. Both are professionals in framing and matting, and very well-versed in the field. Many of the tips that follow in this overview chapter, they have imparted in class. I hope you will be as lucky as I've been in finding a good, solid local class.

But, even if you don't find local help, literally a world of knowledge is right at your finger tips—the internet! One of the best is **www.altosezmat.com**—sponsored by Alto's EZ Mat, Inc. In my opinion, Alto manufactures the best, easiest to use, and most economical to purchase mat cutting system going. On their web site, Alto presents mat cutting systems, books on matting and framing, training videos, and a lot of great articles full of techniques that will make your own projects simple to do yet give a highly professional-looking result!

Matboard Colors and Textures

Back to matboard. Matboard, itself, is a special kind of paperboard (fine cardboard of sorts) which is specifically designed for mounting artwork. Matboard is available in an awesomely wide range of colors and surface textures, and with white, black or colored cores. Looking at a portion of the list of colors offered by matboard manufacturer Crescent—for example—we find such colors as Cameo Rose, Dawn Gray, Newport Blue, Congo Green, Pompeian Red, Oak Brown, Raven Black, Peach, Kelly Green, Pastel Pink, Ivory, Baltic Blue, Boulder Brown, Redwood, and scores more.

Selecting the color or combination of colors that most strikingly sets off your item is not as daunting as the above list of colors may, at first glance, suggest. Crescent and other manufacturers offer "swatch" kits much as do paint and wallpaper manufacturers. In the case of mats, these are usually quite inexpensive and yet indispensable to the matting and framing maven. (Which you will quickly become—really, 'tis easy!) The prices of these kits run from six or seven dollars for simple swatches up to the mid-twenties or so for corner samples.

To use these samples of colors, simply hold them up against your piece to be matted, decide on the best color or color combination, and order those mats. The name of the color and its order number will be on the back of the swatch. You'll develop some favorite colors also, and keep those all the time.

Four methods of selecting colors may be used. They are:

Monochromatic—two shades of the same color such as light blue and dark blue. This is usually the <u>safest</u>.

Complementary—Colors which are opposite on the color wheel such as blue and orange (color wheels may be obtained at most art supply stores).

Analogous—Colors adjacent on the color wheel (this type of color selection requires the most caution and the most knowledge about how colors work in general).

Neutral—Such colors as brown, black, and gray that work with almost anything.

Years ago all mats were either white or off-white—a rather boring state of affairs. Modern matboards offer almost infinite combinations of colors and textures.

But don't go totally hog-wild (as we say up here in the Carolina mountains). Just because vivid colors are available, keep in mind your end goal in going to the trouble and expense of matting and framing your piece in the first place—that is, to complement and enhance the autographed item or other artwork, not to overpower it!

Again—referring back to the four methods of choosing color and color combinations on the previous page—there are accepted rules in selecting color. Don't try to imagine or guess at the result. Nothing beats actually holding those swatches up to the piece to be matted. Another method of obtaining swatch samples, is to keep scraps from previous matting jobs.

In addition to color there is also something called *value* in matting. Value here refers to color instead of autograph pricing and is the relationship between light and dark. Samuel and Alto Albright—writing in their most useful and highly recommended little book *Alto's Introduction to Matting* ($9.95 from **www.altosezmat.com**)—state that the safest choice is for the color value to be close to the medium overall value of the artwork. Otherwise—if the mat colors are too light or too dark in relation to the piece—the artwork respectively will appear to jump out of the mat or be overpowered by a dark mat. To get the medium overall value, Alto suggests that you match the mat value with the value of the predominant colors in the piece.

Alto sums up mat color quite well, and I quote by permission:

"Usually the color of the mat will be either a tint or a shade. A tint is a color with white added to make it a lighter value. A shade is a color grayed to make it a darker value. Colors high in saturation (not tinted or shaded) will tend to dominate an artwork and are better used as an accent or liner rather than the main top mat..."

Finally on color. We autograph collectors quite often find ourselves framing pieces without any color other than a black and white signature or a letter written in ink or even a black and white signed photograph. Don't put color around such as these; a better framing effect is achieved by using neutral colors such as black, brown, and the many grays. Crescent, for example, makes a matboard called Photo Gray that works exceptionally well with black and white photographs. I like to use an off-white as the main board and the Photo Gray as the liner in a double mat (I'll show you how to do a double mat shortly).

Types of Matboard

As we saw earlier, matboard is a special kind of paperboard specifically designed for mounting artwork or, in our case as autograph collectors and dealers, autographed items. Because matboard *comes in direct contact* with the item being matted and framed, it should be of the proper quality for the art being matted. You would not want to use el cheapo matboard to mat a Robert E. Lee or Abraham Lincoln letter, nor would it be useful to use very expensive archival or museum board to mount a two-dollar signature from someone of fleeting fame.

Choose properly but do not stint for the truly expensive pieces—you are matting and framing not just for yourself but for future generations. Do all you can to discharge your stewardship and preserve the items for the ages.

Here is a quick overview detailing the types of matboard (thanks to Alto's EZ Mat):

Standard Matboard: Made of wood pulp, which has acid content. Like it old newspaper, it will eventually turn yellow due to acid-burn. Use only for works of temporary value.

Neutralized Matboard: Made of buffered wood pulp, it is non-acidic but not acid free. Eventually the buffer will become acidic. Use for craft projects, student work, presentations or posters. After several years this type may yellow and may need to be replaced.

100% Alpha Cellulose: Made from wood fibers that have had all potentially acidic materials chemically removed. This type of matboard is acid-free and meets the Library of Congress standards for MUSEUM QUALITY matboard. Use for fine art and signed prints.

100% Rag Board: Made from cotton fibers, this type of matboard contains no wood. It is acid-free and buffered to prevent acidity after long exposure to the atmosphere. It meets the Library of Congress standards for MUSEUM QUALITY matboard. Use for fine art, signed prints and needleart.

Nonbuffered 100% Rag Board: This is a special rag board made without buffering agents. Use it for certain types of photographs (albumen, dye transfer and chromogenic prints) and textiles (silk and wool) because buffering in regular rag board could react to the acidic dyes used in these processes and fabrics, altering their colors.

We can sum up which type of matboard you should use for a given project this way: The common "standard" matboard purchased in art supply stores (unless you specifically ask) is probably acidic and not appropriate for any piece that has monetary or sentimental value. The matboard manufacturer Crescent (which we already mentioned) offers a very wide range of matboards that have acid-free cores and backing papers (the backing papers determine the color of the board. As we've already mentioned, a great place with great prices for Crescent matboards is Presto—whose site is on the worldwide web at **www.framingsupplies.com**, or call 1-800-334-9060 and ask for their catalog. It includes frames also and is very handy.

Another source for Crescent matboard and a staggering array of other artistic supplies is one of my favorite catalogs, Dick Blick Art Materials. Call 1-800-621-8293 for a catalog. Check out their very attractive and informative web site at **www.dickblick.com**. Both Presto and Dick Blick carry Alto and other mat cutting equipment such as Logan.

Higher quality or *acid-neutralized* matboard, 100% rag board and 100% alpha cellulose board are all non-acidic. These latter two types of matboard both meet the Library

From the **www.dickblick.com** web site.

of Congress standard for *museum quality* board. Of course, you'll find that a non-acidic matboard is somewhat more expensive than standard, with museum board being top of the line. Yet the difference in cost is surprisingly not all that much, maybe two or three dollars for a large sheet. I personally recommend choosing a good acid-free board. Remember, your framed piece will be hanging around on your wall, then someone else's wall, then someone else's wall for decades to come. Do it right, huh?

There are, of course, many other brands of matboard besides Cresent. You might check with your local art supply store to see what brands and qualities of matboard they carry.

Tools for Matting

Like any other seemingly complicated pursuit, matting and framing suddenly becomes absurdly simple when you have the right tools and know the techniques. Matting is quite inexpensive to get into—there is very little initial investment required. Following are the basic tools needed for cutting mats (framing, we'll discuss later in the chapter, but that tool list is equally minimal as well).

Utility knife with retractable blade: X-Acto® makes a wide range of these. They look like the knives used to open boxes at your local grocery or hardware store. In fact, any of those would work find. You use the utility knife to cut matboard and backing board to the proper size for matting and framing.

Emery board (or fine sandpaper): Emery board is just like that used to smooth fingernails after cutting. It serves exactly the same function in mat cutting; i.e. removing any rough edges.

Double-faced tape: Used to hold your mat construction together. You want acid-free tape and Scotch® has it.

Kneaded eraser: Available at any art supply store, this eraser removes dirt and other smudges from matboard and artwork before framing without damaging the mat or art.

Calculator: A great help in figuring out the dimensions so that you know where to cut.

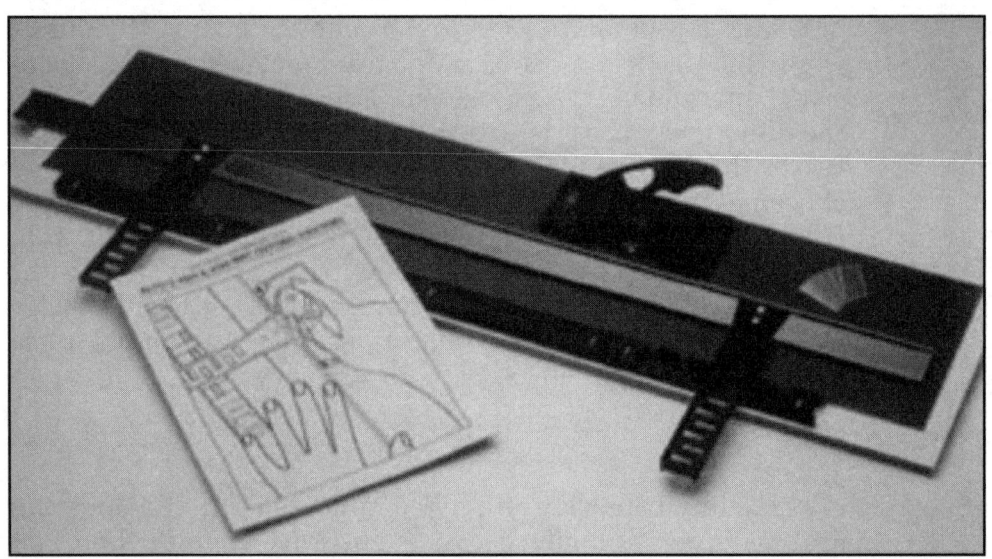

Alto Model 4501 mat cutter.

A wooden or metal ruler: any old yardstick will do, but a nice metal one from an art supply store is easier to use and more accurate. Cost is only seven or eight dollars or so.

Mat Cutter: The only expensive item needed is the mat cutter itself. This device lets you cut nice, professional beveled edges for the window through which artwork is displayed. I recommend highly Alto's Model 4501 at $129.95 retail. There are cheaper mat cutters and a host of more expensive ones, but this is the one I've found best for us more casual matters. Visit Alto's website at **www.altosezmat.com** for more details or to order.

Double Matting—A Practical Exercise

Finally for our introduction to matting, let's do a practical exercise. At least, it's practical for me because I'm winding up with a framed piece on my wall.

I have a cover from the 4th edition of **The Sanders Price Guide to Autographs**, which came out in October, 1996. I saved it for the past several years, meaning to frame it for the wall of my office. Now's the time to do it, as the 5th comes out.

We are going to double-mat the cover because for the type of matting you'll be doing (i.e. of autographed items) double-matting will probably be what you choose ninety percent of the time. To review, placing a second matboard of a different color behind the first with a hole slightly smaller—resulting in a colored border around the artwork—is called a *double mat*. This border—assuming you chose the proper colors for the inner and outer mats and that this color combo peacefully coexists with the artwork or other piece being matted—can pleasingly and strikingly set off the matted and framed item.

Again, as Peggy and Sherry drummed into us during the matting and framing course I took at A-B Tech: art (and that applies to autographed items) simply looks better matted. There are exceptions, so my favorite matting ladies said, such as oils, acrylics and some needlework. In general, however, mats pull out the colors in the art and enhance it. Laying swatches on top gives you an excellent idea of the final look.

Another general tip: don't ever assume a piece is exactly square (or exactly a rectangle). Measure horizontal and vertical dimensions at both ends. Usually, unless there is a very obvious reason not to, you'll be able to mat items by cutting normal square or rectangle holes.

There are a lot of considerations about the final look you want for pieces, such as formal, casual, contemporary, Victorian, and so forth. All this is beyond the scope of this basic introductory article. I suggest you use the Alto's EZ Mat site as a starting point after you've learned matting basics. Then you can research and employ more sophisticated techniques.

Now, back to our simple double-matting exercise. The first step is to do some measurements and calculations. An important rule of thumb, by the way, is to *measure twice and cut once*. Like in carpentry or sewing, you'll waste a lot less material if you know exactly the dimensions needed for each component part. Plan it out first!

In my case, I took the cover I want to mat and measured the part of it that I want to show in the finished frame; i.e. the area to be displayed. In planning out the finished look, I had decided that a margin of about two inches of matboard around the cover would look good. Your own margins should be something on this order. Too narrow of an outer mat and you get a "ribbon" like look which is not attractive. The inner mat (the border) of a double mat, of course, should be narrow, something on the order of a quarter inch.

As to colors, I selected an off-white for the front mat and a nice gold for the inner mat—the latter color goes well with the blues and purples in the cover of the 4th edition. By the way, since I designed the cover of the 4th and typeset the book as well as being coauthor and publisher, a framed copy of the cover on the wall has more than a little meaning for me. I even took my trusty Sharpie and autographed it.

photos of matting example by Teresa Woods & Pat Roberts

The author uses a steel ruler and pencil to measure and mark where the first piece of matboard is to be cut. Always mark on the *back* of the board.

Now, the trick in matting is knowing where to cut. My basic mat construction is four pieces (from back to front) a piece of quarter inch foam core backing board (buy it the same place as you get matboards), the cover, the inner matboard (gold), and the front mat (off-white). Some people (Alto, for example) also recommend a board to mount the art on, but I just use the backing board and save one piece.

To determine the outer dimensions of the three boards (all the same except for the inner mat which can be smaller) I took the measurements of the area to be shown (16.25 x 9 inches for the front, back, and spine of the book cover), added a quarter inch for portion that will be showing of the gold inner mat, then hit a minor snag that required a pause for thinking. Normally, one would just add two inches all the way around for the front mat margin, but if I did that, the overall

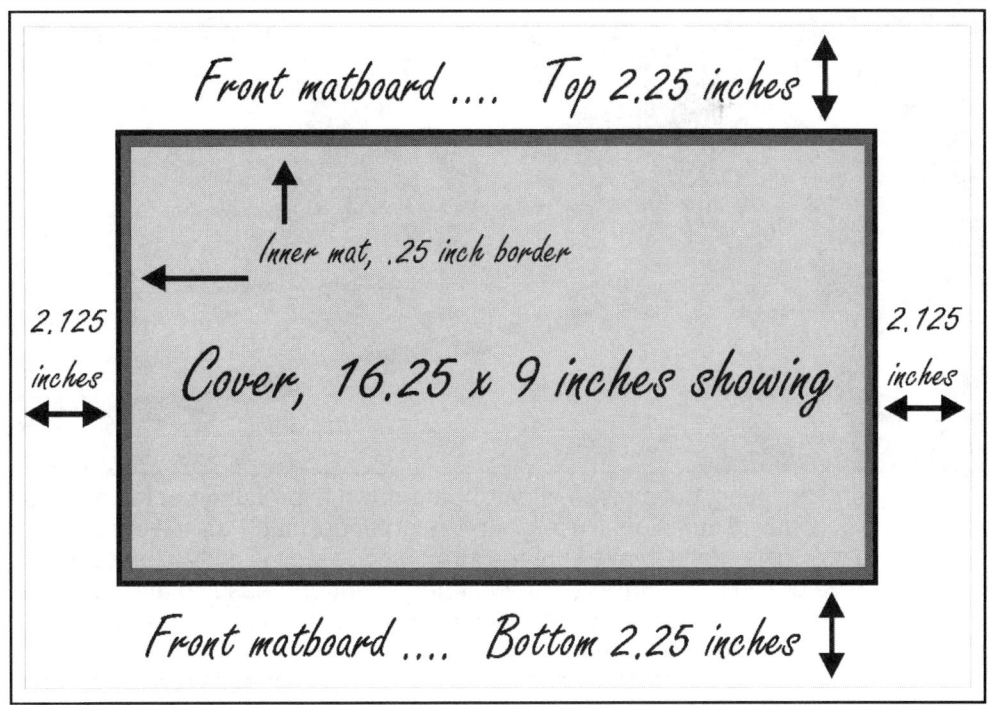

Front matboard .... Top 2.25 inches ↕

↑
Inner mat, .25 inch border
←

2.125
inches ↔

Cover, 16.25 x 9 inches showing

2.125
inches ↔

Front matboard .... Bottom 2.25 inches ↕

My cover matting project planned out with all dimensions for cutting.

dimensions would not fall on full inch increments, and that's how frames are sold. I certainly did not want to be put in the position of having to fiddle about trying to cut a metal frame to fit. So, by doing a bit of simple calculation, I found by making the front mat margin two and a quarter inches top and bottom and two and an eighth left and right, I would have overall dimensions of 21 by 14 inches, for which inexpensive standard frame components are available.

Ready to commit mayhem on matboard, I marked up the outer dimensions (see photo at top of opposite page). You'll want to use a pencil and make all your measurements on the back of the matboard so that no marks will show on the finished job. This is the easy part of matting. In this case, the outer dimensions were 21 x 14 inches. This should be your exact cut for the front matboard and the backing board. Since the edges of the inner liner do not show, you can be sloppy on

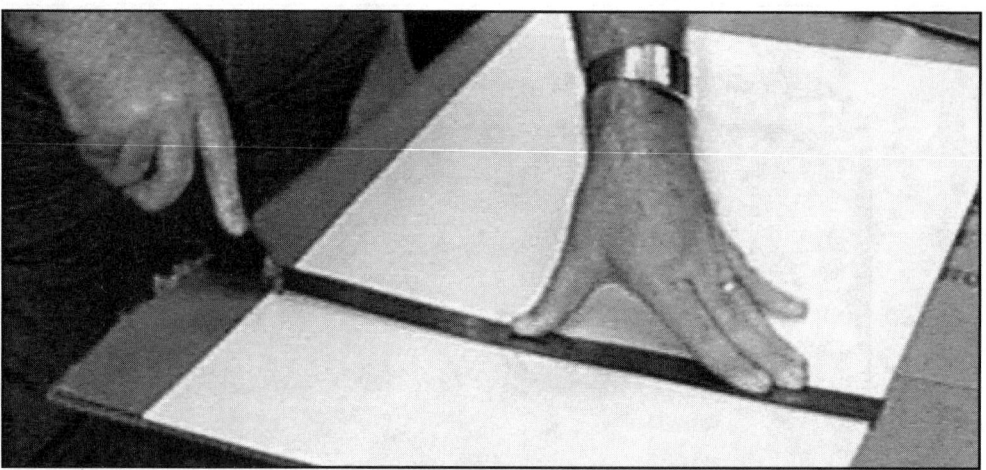

Before cutting anything, put a piece of cardboard down to protect your tabletop. To cut boards to outer dimensions, use your straightedge (such as the metal ruler above) and your utility knife. Make sure the straightedge stays tightly in place, score the line you've drawn a few times (you don't need a lot of pressure) and you'll get a nice even cut. Should there be any minor unevenness, use sandpaper or your emory board to smooth the edges.

it and, often, you might find a scrap of matboard from a previous project that will fit the bill and save you a few bucks.

Keep a large piece of cardboard around, such as a flattened delivery carton, and place that down to protect your table before doing any cutting. Use your straightedge (such as the metal ruler shown in the photograph above) and your utility knife with the retractable blade. Make sure the straightedge stays firmly in place by holding it down tightly. Score the line you've drawn a few times (you don't need a lot of pressure) and you'll get a nice even cut. Should there be any minor unevenness, use sandpaper or your emory board to smooth the edges, removing any tags of uncut material, bumps, and so forth. This outer edge is what fits into the frame so you'll want it as square as possible. Again, cut the front matboard, backing board, and the inner liner. And always have a sharp blade in all your cutting devices.

Now we cut our holes in the mats, beginning with the front mat first. In our example (as shown on the previous page) we want two and a quarter inch margins on top and two and one-eighth for the sides. We draw pencil lines to mark those margins on the back of the front matboard.

Most mat cutters cut mats at a bevel of 45 degrees. This shows off the matboard edges in the finished job and makes a pleasing dimensional effect. Alto's and Logan's mat cutters are designed to implement this bevel properly if you cut from the back of the boards (where your dimension lines show conveniently). Some older cutters, however, require you to cut from the front for the proper bevel. Watch out for those, they are a pain to use. Again, we recommend the Alto.

To cut the inner hole of the front mat (as we are doing below), we use the mat cutter. Most cutters consist of a straight edge with a movable cutting tool containing a razor blade which is slid along the straight edge. Be as precise as possible to hit your corners exactly. An under run will result in the corners tearing and being uneven; an overrun leaves unsightly cut marks on the front of the mat. Cut one side, rotate the mat and cut the next side, and so forth. When all

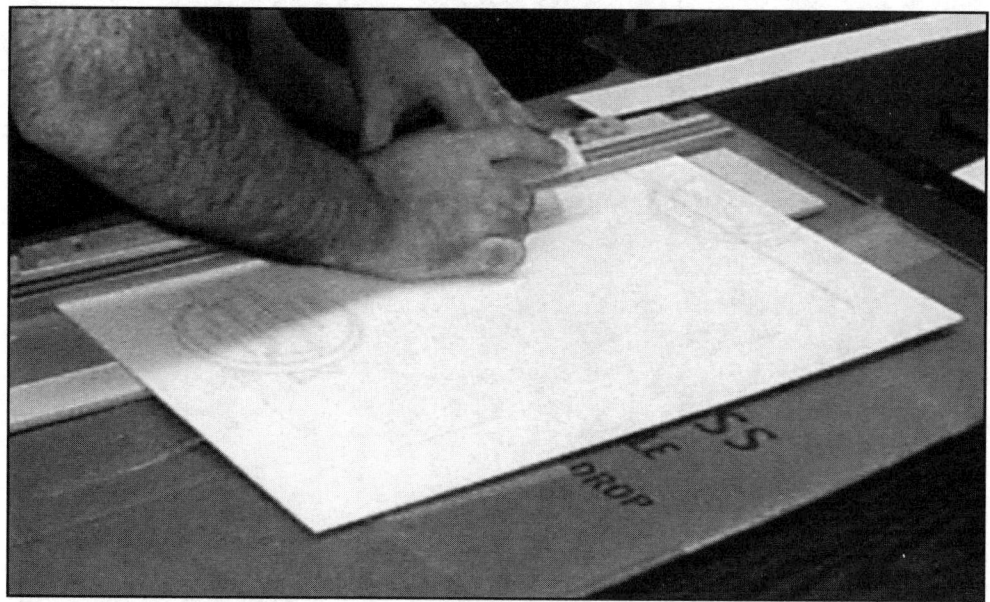

Using an Alto mat cutter to cut the display opening in the front mat.

four sides are cut, pick the mat up and turn it over. The center should plop out easily. The center, by the way, is referred to as the *fallout*. Save this fallout, we have a very important use for it in double matting.

Okay, now for the secret that makes double matting a breeze! Take the fallout and place it *back into* your front mat. Because the edges are beveled at a 45-degree angle, it will fit easily and stay in place as you turn the mat over and put it on the tabletop with the back side up. Place a piece of double-sided tape in the center of the fallout. Only one small strip is needed as this is not a permanent bond. Place more strips of double-sided tape around on the other part of the front matboard. This is the outer margin of your matting project and more tape should be used as this portion will be a permanent bond.

Now (see photograph below) place your inner liner, face

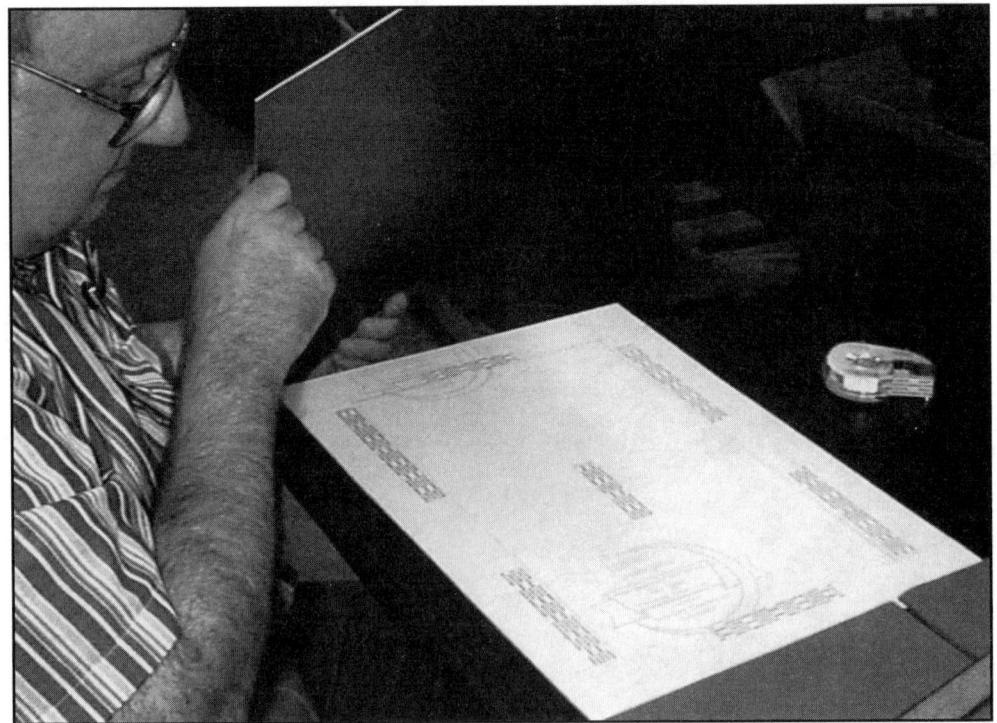

Place inner liner board on back of front board with fallout still in place.

down, on top of the front mat and fallout, making sure that it sticks to the inner and outer components of the mat; i.e. the center or fallout and the mat that will become your margins. Mark the dimensions for your cut on the inner liner mat (now the one on top. Remember we decided we want it to only show a one quarter of an inch border. You can make your own border as thick or thin as you like but this thickness is about right for this project (in other words, I like it).

The margins you are cutting for the inner liner's hole are determined by the front mat's margins (in the case of our example, 2.25 on top and bottom and 2.125 on the sides) *plus* .25 inches! It results in a hole that is .25 inches smaller in all dimensions thnt the hole in the front, which is a wondrous thing as we shall see in just a moment.

Take the taped together mats with your dimensions on the back of the inner mat and cut it on all four sides (below).

Once all four sides of the inner mat are cut, turn it over and you'll find (just like magic!) that the fallout from the front mat comes out with the fallout to the inner mat neatly attached by that one strip of tape you put in the center. Save those fallouts to be used in smaller projects and put them aside. You are left your completed double mat (see below)

The completed double-matted project. All it needs now is a frame.

with a nice, neat, quarter inch border (in our case) of gold. We can now attach the backing board with the artwork, and our project is ready for the frame! Be sure to use nonacidic tape in assembling your mat.

Above all, never be reluctant to experiment while matting. Remember, matboard is only paper! You can always start over.

Framing

Once the matting is done, we put it in the frame. The diagram below shows a complete package (for a single mat). As mentioned before, you can use a mounting board to place the artwork on in addition to the backing board. The word *glaze*, of course, refers to glass.

Beginning from the bottom of the illustration below, you

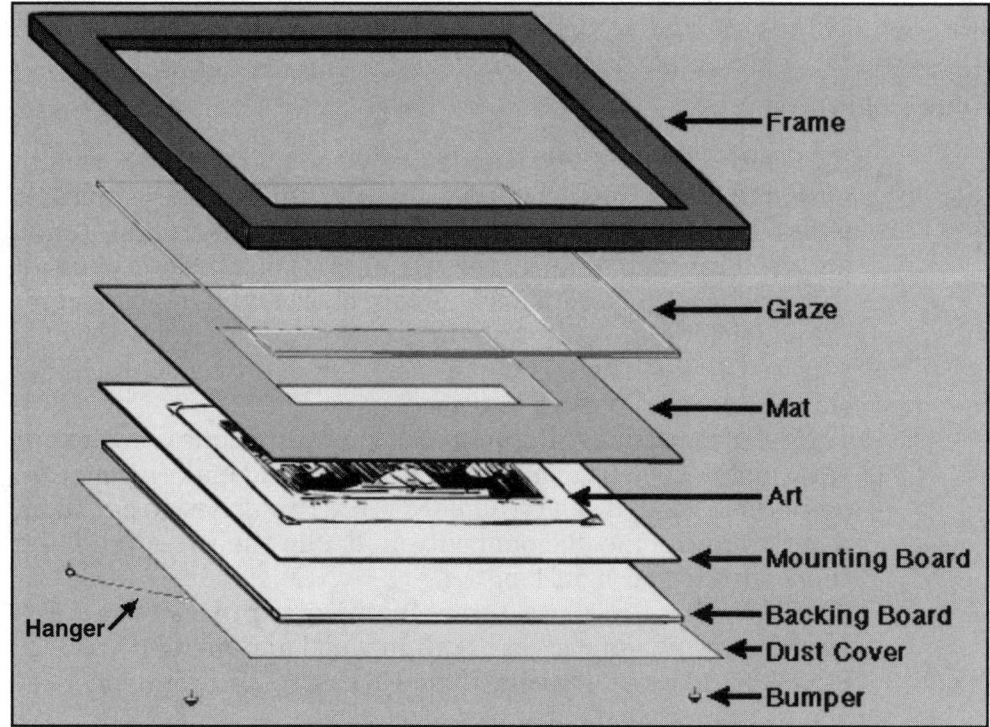

A <u>totally</u> complete matting and framing job (art courtesy Alto's EZ Mat).

need a wire hanger. Next, bumpers are small knobs of felt or rubber used to keep the framed piece from damaging the wall and to keep it out so that air can circulate behind. Bumpers are available at most craft stores and even your local hardware store normally carries a goodly selection of these little peel off, stick on doodads that are useful for so many applications.

A *dust cover* is simply a properly sized sheet of paper glued to the back of the frame to form an airtight seal that keeps dust and moisture from getting inside. Both of these items and the mounting board for artwork are optional. For a really valuable piece, I do recommend you do the job right and build your matted and framed piece as shown on the previous page.

Glass or *glaze* can be obtained many places. Check your yellow pages for places that sell glass and will cut it to your specs. When you buy a piece of glass, always ask that the shop grind its edges smooth so that you won't cut your hands and, even then, it's not a bad idea to wear a pair of rubber gloves while inserting the glass into your frame (especially for very large pieces).

Types of Frames

Frames come in two basic types wood and metal (normally aluminum). Of those two types, you've find an incredible—it will seem infinite—choice of styles, types, finishes, decorations, etc. etc. I refuse to take up the rest of this book in describing all the artistic ways in which frames are chosen and implemented. This article was meant only to give you a starting point but, suffice it to say, there is much scope for realizing your artistic side merely in choosing frames.

Me? I tend to go with simple aluminum frames finished in "gun metal." Seems to match most decors and make my matted pieces look good. And all you need is a screw driver to put them together and some diagonal cutters to clip the wires you hang them with to the right lengths.

Check out Presto at **www.framingsupplies.com** for a vasty array of frame styles, both in wood and metal. Or call 1-828-693-1333 and request their catalog. Tell them you read about it in this book! Thanks.

Places that sell custom frames are referred to as *chop shops*

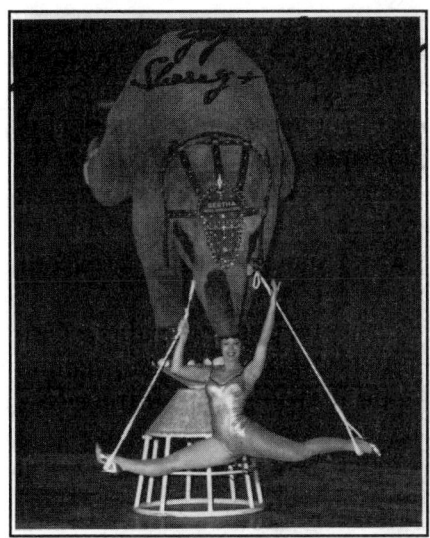

Some Examples of Items to Mat & Frame: Above, an autographed 8x10 of a 1950s circus performer (the lady, not the elephant). This item has little worth for the signature alone, but matting and framing enhances its value considerably. Upper right, if you have a friend who is a celebrity (like my buddy actor/producer John Denos), or a celebrity personalizes a picture to you, they look great hanging on your wall. Also signed items from people you admire are good, giving you continuing inspiration such as my signed photograph (right) of 90-plus-year-old science fiction writer Curt Sidomak. Still active, I want to be as sharp and productive as he when I'm that old. In addition to his several novels, Curt also wrote the classic horror movie "The Beast With Five Fingers," starring the spooky Peter Lorre.

Of course, photographs with a lot of personal meaning are prime candidates for matting and framing. Here Ralph Roberts (me) and George Sanders—along with Helen Sanders, founders of the Sanders price guides—make a rare appearence in suits! George was like a second father to me.

or *chop service*. This is a term that means that you order the frame molding cut (mitered) by the shop or service, but not assembled. You order what you require to fit your glass, or mat, or art size. If you order a frame 16 by 20 inches, for example, you would receive two pieces of molding 16 and one-eighth inches long and two pieces of molding 20 and one-eighth inches long that would fit your glass, or mat, or art size of 16 by 20 inches. The allowance of one-eighth inch is an industry standard. Please note that this is not the outside dimension of your completed piece. The outside dimensions would depend on the width of the molding chosen. It refers rather to the outer dimensions of your matted piece before it goes into the frame.

Tools Needed for Framing

As with matting, the tools and materials you'll need for constucting frames are few, inexpensive, and easy to obtain.

Elmer's® (or similiar) wood glue: Used for making secure joins of wood frames.

Glazier's push points: Small metal pieces that hold glass in place in a wood frame. Obtain these at the same place you buy your glass.

Kraft paper: Plain old brown wrapping paper, it makes excellent dust shields for the back of your framed masterpieces.

Screw eyes and 12 guage braided wire: Any hardware store has this stuff. The eyes screw into wood frames and the wire is threaded through for hanging purposes. On metal frames, be sure to ask for the little hangers that slide into the grooves on the back instead of screw in.

Glass cleaner and paper towels: I've never picked up a clean piece of glass yet from a glass shop. Clean it.

Screwdriver (flathead): That's all you need to assemble metal frames!

Diagonal cutters (wire cutters): For cutting the braided wire above to length. You'll see many cheap ones but buy a good one. It cuts wire easier and the metal does not pit.

Safe Places to Hang or Store Framed Pieces

The following are some rules suggested by the Library of Congress on what to do with your piece after it is matted and framed.

- Avoid hanging or storing anything in the basement, attic, or any other place with extremes in temperature and humidity. A stable, cool, dry environment is best.

- Avoid hanging pieces on outside walls, but if you must, request that a moisture barrier be placed in the mat package.

- Avoid hanging objects in direct sunlight or any other intense light source. Control exposure to ultraviolet light through glazing or placement away from a UV source. Occasionally rotate framed objects to cut down on the duration of light exposure.

- Avoid hanging framed objects directly above working fire places or radiators.

Doing It Right

For the really good stuff you mat and frame; items such as a signed Civil War letter or any other piece that will be in demand for hundreds of years to come, do it right. That means using archival quality materials that will last for the long term.

A great source of information about proper techniques for museum-quality matting and framing is the website of the Library of Congress at **http://lcweb.loc.gov/preserv/care/ mat.html**.

Yes, matting and framing is easy, you'll save lots of money doing it yourself, and you'll get a great sense of accomplishment!

Ralph Roberts is the author of over 80 books and thousands of articles, and is both coauthor and publisher of the Sanders price guides. An avid collector of paper documents—both autographed and otherwise—he has addressed manuscript preservation in several books and many articles. Now he is learning to mat and frame them properly. Next, so he says, is a study of bookbinding. Ralph lives with wife Pat in the beautiful Western North Carolina mountains. E-mail: **ralph@abooks.com**.

Chapter 10

Autopens and Other False Signatures

by Ralph Roberts

Anyone can sign John Wayne's name on a photograph, and many do. A few years ago, we attended a Western show. One of the dealers had a box of signed photos, with several by the immortal red-blooded he-man star neatly grouped. Unfortunately, even a novice could see that these had been scribbled by different hands—at least one far too feminine to be the Duke's. None, by the way, were even close to authentic.

Authenticity, then, is of prime concern to the collector. One reason why books like our own autograph price guide and other books which contain facsimiles are so popular is because of this concern. Using this edition of the **The Sanders Price Guide to Autographs** (or any of the previous four editions for that matter), for example, you could simply turn to the facsimile and compare Wayne's signature to the one on the photograph. One that matches is worth $400 or so. Otherwise, the correct value is zip, nada, nothing since there is little market for the ham-fisted forgeries by obscure but crooked flea market dealers. Should that market ever open up, there sure would be a wealth of material out there.

Honest Mistakes

Nor are out and out forgeries the only thing to be alert about. Historical coincidence is another. There have been a great many men throughout the centuries named John Tyler, but only one was President of the United States. None of the others have a great deal of value, although they are certainly authentic signatures of a person named *John Tyler*.

An even better example is the autograph of the two Winston Churchills. Sir Winston, of course, was the leader of the British Empire during War War II, the very epitome of a cigar-chomping English bulldog. Sir Winston was born in 1874, however *another* Winston Churchill, an American, was born in 1871, and his life paralleled that of the British Churchill.

Winston Churchill, the American was, in his time, a popular author of historical novels about the political and economic issues of his day. He had a wide following and one of his most memorable characters, Jethro Tull, has been perpetuated in the name of a modern day Rock group.

Both Churchills were writers and both wrote about political topics. There are numerous autographed books by both currently extant. The difference in value is about $20 or so for Churchill the American as opposed to $500 or more for Churchill the Englishman. Both autographs are authentic, you just have to research which is which.

In other words, the more knowledge that you have, the less likely you are to be taken in by an "autograph of mistake." You can never know too much, or have too large a reference library.

Secretarial

It has been common practice for very busy people to have their secretaries answer and *sign* routine mail. This is especially true in the movie industry, where even back in the twenties the studios sometimes maintained banks of people who did nothing but sign stars' names on photographs and letters.

A secretarial autograph of John Wayne is worth about the same as that perpetrated by our crooked flea market dealer above—nothing. The answer, of course, is to consult a facsimile reference such as the ones in this book and the others that we offer, and compare the piece against a known authentic signature.

Secretarial autographs are not attempts at out and out forgeries. The name of the famous personage is usually simply signed in whatever hand the secretary may possess. Thus, they are normally easy to detect by comparison.

Expert Help

To this point, we've talked about forgeries that are obvious to any collector (assuming he or she has access to known-authentic comparison facsimiles like those in our price guide). There are and always have been, however, forgers of considerable talent throughout the ages who can fool even experts some of the time. Museums have paintings by unknown forgers hanging on their walls, purporting to be Old Masters. Occasionally, one of these is unmasked, bring much embarrassment to the museum's curator.

The same holds true in the autograph field. *This* is the reason for getting a lifetime guarantee on pieces you buy from an autograph dealer. Legitimate dealers will gladly provide this—which means, should the piece be proven to be a forgery three years from now, you get your money back. Such guarantees place pressure on the dealer to consult with experts and make sure that autographed items are authentic. *Ask* the dealer who he does business with, and what their methods of authentication are.

Major league forgeries require painstaking and extremely thorough examination by experts to expose. Special equipment and a knowledge of characteristics of forged and genuine writing are needed. Correct methods of comparing handwriting must be used. Knowledge of papers prevalent during different historical periods and other such data is a must.

Kenneth W. Rendell—writing in *Autograph and Manuscripts*, Scribner's, 1978—details the equipment and procedures for detecting forgeries. A microscope of variable power (10x-100x), with a special holder for documents, is one of the most important instruments in the authentication expert's arsenal. Considerable time should be spent in closely comparing samples of writing.

Obviously, such time-consuming and knowledge-dependent techniques are beyond (dare we say) the *scope* of most of us. If there is any doubt at all about a piece, seek out a recognized authentication expert.

Autopens

Writing a famous person, especially politicians, and thus receiving a personally signed letter in return is quite easy. Only, chances are, the signature was done by a *machine* called an *Autopen* or, increasingly, by some other method of facsimile reproduction including laser printers. These copies of real signatures are worth nothing compared to an actual autograph.

Even if a real person signed the piece, it might not be the celebrity you think it is. Such signatures signed by others are called *secretarial* signatures.

I emphasize that: facsimiles and secretarials are worthless.

Some of the autograph magazines and celebrity address guides encourage you to spend your time writing off and asking for free autographs. Sometimes what you get is authentic, but often not! For a notable whose autograph is worth money, you are far better off buying one through a reputable dealer where you can get a COA (Certificate of Authenticity) or some other guarantee, all of which good dealers are pleased to supply.

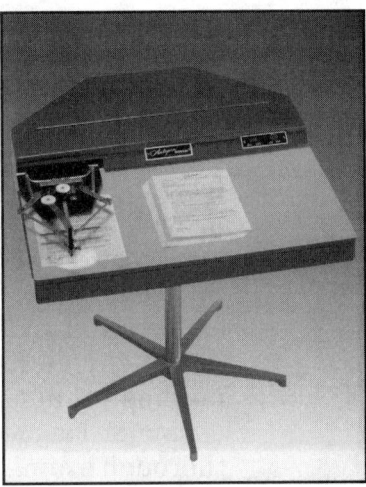

The Autopen Model 80 is the current model autopen. For more information, visit the company's internet web site at **www.damilic.com/autopen**.

In the case of politicians, the closer to election time it is, the more likely you are to receive a "personally" signed letter. Take President Clinton as an example. The White House mailbag brings in hundreds, even thousands of letters a day. There is no possible way the President could actually read all his mail, much less dictate and sign all the replies that go out in his name. Machines do it. The note that comes back to you may look like it was typed by a secretary and then signed by the Chief Executive, but the technological marvels of a word processing program on a computer and an Autopen really generated the letter.

All presidents, from John F. Kennedy on, have relied extensively on this method to satisfy the enormous demands for their autographs. Congressmen, Senators, Cabinet officers, and (more recently) Supreme Court Justices have taken to this technology with a vengeance. In a way, since our tax dollars buy these devices, the American taxpayer is subsidizing *forgery*. We poor taxpayers get tons of letters every year from our elected representatives purporting to be actually signed by that personage him or herself—but... no, they're not. And if the old saw about a politician's word being worthless, his or her facsimile signature brings even less!

"Within four or five square blocks (in downtown Washington), you've got more people who need them than anyplace else in the world," Robert DeShazo said in an article by Lynne Cheney published in the *Washingtonian* Magazine several years ago. DeShazo, at that time, was president of the International Autopen Company, which remains the major manufacturer of automatic signature machines in the United States to this day.

Using a mechanical device to duplicate signatures in specific and writing in general goes back many hundreds of years. Those who, as myself, have had the wondrous fortune to visit Thomas Jefferson's home Monticello (near Charlottesville, Virginia) have seen one of these on display there. Invented by John Isaac Hawkins in and patented in 1803, it was called the *Polygraph* (not to be confused with the modern usage of the word for lie detectors). Jefferson jumped at this device as it relieved at least some of the drudgery of writing. He used it extensively for over 20 years so some of those "original" Jefferson documents in museums and other high end autograph collections could very well be from this very early type of Autopen!

The Polygraph was the 18th century equivalent of the Xerox machine. He used it to make copies. As he wrote with one pen, another (which was mechanically attached to the first) created an exact copy. It was moderately simple mechanically and works as well today as it did back then. Jefferson, as evidenced by this and the other wondrous devices in his palatial home, was an avid gadgeteer. If he was alive today, his office would no doubt boast a thousand watt per channel state of the art stereo and a personal computer system that could do everything but brush his teeth (and maybe that too!).

That supreme 19th century showman, P.T. Barnum, went even further. He had a machine that could sign his signature in his absence—one of the first true Autopens. With a "sucker" being born every minute, Barnum evidently felt he needed help in corresponding with them.

Still, despite the machines existing, no president felt the need for one until John F. Kennedy took office in 1961. This does not mean that earlier presidential autographs are all in the actual hand of the that president. Many were signed by secretaries and fall under the classification of *secretarial*. Refer back to page 146 for more information on secretarial signatures.

President Kennedy and his staff, naturally, did not go around telling autograph collectors that a machine was doing much of his work for him, but certain astute collectors soon became suspicious. The giveaway being that many of his signatures, when two are held up to a light, can be *exactly* superimposed on each other. The odds against anyone signing their name that precisely every time are astronomic. We humans are simply not that precise.

Noted expert—the late, great Charles Hamilton, who has meant so much to the world of autograph collecting—warned on the "Today" show during the Kennedy administration of the possible "grave consequences" of presidential Autopen usage. Pierre Salinger, Kennedy's press secretary, immediately denied that such a device was in the White House. He was wrong.

Hamilton, however, followed his television appearance by demonstrating that there were not one but seven patterns being used by the machine to duplicate JFK signatures. Several of them were "John Kennedy," but there was also a "Jack Kennedy" to be used on letters to his friends.

Lyndon Johnson, who was too busy pulling his beagle's ears (for which some of us will never forgive him), took to the

Autopen even more enthusiastically. The late Jennifer Casoni—an autograph dealer in Alexandria, Virginia—even maintained that Johnson used the Autopen to sign his vice-presidential oath of office!

Richard Nixon continued the tradition. Casoni, in her book *Best Wishes, Richard Nixon*, identified nine "Richard Nixon" patterns and three "R.N." patterns. The Nixon White House, as with previous administrations, was reluctant to admit the use of this automatic signing device.

President Gerald Ford gets credit for honesty in this respect. He was the first president to own up to Autopen usage. In fact, to the surprise of the autograph collecting world, requests for autographs were often replied to with an Autopen signature *and* a letter stating that it was such. In fact, the combination of these two have some small value just for their historical precedent of presidential honesty.

Two examples of Bill Clinton Autopens, courtesy of John Reznikoff and Stuart Lutz of University Archives.

Jimmy Carter, he of the large grin, also used the Autopen extensively. These are relatively easy to detect, when compared against known patterns. But Carter also made extensive use of the "secretarial" signature, which irritates collectors a good deal more than the more obvious Autopen. President Carter, in retirement, has become a much more cooperative signer—especially in person, when contacted on the streets of Plains, Georgia, or at Emory University, where he lectures.

Herman Darvick, a leading autograph expert and auction gallery owner, said that Susan Clough, a Carter secretary, "forged his name beautifully." While many presidents have countenanced this, Carter's usage of it has been very frustrating to collectors, turning up in places where it shouldn't have.

"I saw a picture," Darvick said, "signed by Begin and Sadat, which was sent to the White House for Carter's signature. Susan Clough signed it for him. The Autopen would have been better—at least it would have been his real signature, even if a machine produced it."

The Reagan White House was as unanxious to discuss the Autopen as it was to talk about what Ollie North did or did not do. Still, experts agree that approximately a dozen patterns were used to produce President Reagan's signature. There is a "Ronald Reagan," a "Ron," a "Ronnie," and a "Dutch." There is also an Autopen pattern of "Ronald Reagan" and "Nancy Reagan" together, given away by the fact that both

Two examples of Ronald Reagan Autopens, courtesy of John Reznikoff and Stuart Lutz of University Archives.

signatures are on the exact same level, a physical impossibility in a normal signing by two individuals. My mother received one of those on her 80th birthday. I did not have the heart to tell her it was an Autopen (i.e. in essence, a forgery).

Robert DeShazo, president of the International Autopen Company when we interviewed him, had been manufacturing these devices since 1942. We spoke with him in researching this subject initially a few years ago, and he kindly gave us insight into the use of Autopens from the viewpoint of the public figure.

The average person, Mr. DeShazo explained, has no comprehension of the vast amount of mail received by prominent public figures, and thus little understanding or acceptance of the need for the machines his company provides. Since personal response to each and every letter is physically impossible, it is far better for an Autopen response to be generated than for the correspondent to be simply ignored.

Located in Rockville, Maryland—DeShazo's company ships Autopens all over the world. However, the company's proximity to Washington, D.C., is no accident.

"Almost every member of the Senate has one," DeShazo said. The House of Representatives is well stocked with Autopens

George—as here with Senator and presidential candidate Eugene McCarthy—gave us a lifetime of in-person autograph authenticity for the Sanders guides.

FALSE SIGNATURES   155

also, though DeShazo added that sometimes four or five members might share one machine. In all, he estimated that over 500 Autopens are in use in Washington alone, to the disgust of autograph collectors but the relief of public officials facing literal mountains of correspondence.

International Autopen currently has the Autopen Model 80 on the market (as it has been for over 10 years). This device resembles a small desk with metal arms and springs on the left side of its surface (see photo on page 148). A pen is screwed into the end of a metal arm. The operator places letters or books or whatever beneath the pen. The machine produces about 300 signatures per hour. Since a standard ink pen is used, the signature looks realistic to the uninitiated layman.

Inside the desk-like structure of the Autopen 80 is the revolving matrix which guides the pen. This matrix looks something like a large boomerang. It is cut according to the sample signature supplied by the customer. The matrix is easily changed to produce another version of the signature, or that of another person.

International Autopen has dominated the automatic signing market for many years. Competition has surfaced from time to time. A complex electronic device called the Signa-Signer was one, but the simpler Autopen continues to be the machine of choice at the moment.

The new laser printer technology—especially color lasers—is the latest challenger, being able to produce a signature that looks very close to a handwritten one. With this device attached to a personal computer and a desktop publishing program, letters can be generated that incorporate signatures in a one step process. In fact, there might very soon come a time when an Autopen signature will be considered a "personal" touch—the great one's minion sending you the "autograph" at least having taken the time to put it in a machine.

Tips for Detecting False Signatures

Determining whether or not an autograph in your possession, or one under consideration for purchase, is genuine or an

Autopen takes a modicum of detective work. *Comparison* is the hot tip here. That's why so many hundreds of authentic signatures are included in this price guide.

It is also a good idea, in the case of celebrity signatures done since the advent of the Autopen (i.e. within the last 30 years at least), to have some known Autopen examples as a guide. There are several books available that are worthwhile. A couple may be found at the UACC's web site (**www.uacc.org**). One—available to anyone, member or not—is *The Study of Machine Signed Signatures* by Paul Carr for $8.95. Details for ordering are on **www.uacc.org/premium.htm**. (If you don't have the internet by now, get it—it is the greatest daily research source since the invention of sliced bread!)

A second book available at the above website is *The Robot That Helped Make A President* by the legendary autograph expert Charles Hamilton. (Because of limited quantities, sale of this book is limited to UACC members.)

A key to using such references is to realize that the examples do not have to superimpose exactly 100% to be an Autopen pattern. If the paper was moved while the Autopen was signing, either deliberately or through mechanical slippage, minor variations can be induced. Still, putting a suspected piece over a known Autopen and moving them around while holding them up to a strong light will cause parts of the signatures to match.

No one can sign their name exactly alike twice in a row, so even if just sections of the two signatures match, it is almost certainly Autopen.

There are ways you can really be sure that a signature was done on the Autopen. The best is to match it to a known Autopen example. Secondly is if you have two signatures that match exactly. Again, it's a physical impossibility for any person to sign their name precisely the same way twice, hence any two signatures that superimpose exactly are Autopen or some other means of mechanical or electronic reproduction.

Kirsten Schaulin has a very handy tip about detecting autopens (and a lot of other good information about autographs) on her webpage at **www.iglou.com/schaulkr**. Kirstin says "Autopens always have perfectly even pressure throughout the signature." This is obvious when you think about it; the Autopen is a machine whereas a human being has a hard time maintaining an exactly even pressure as his or her hand moves across the paper, the angle of their wrist changes, etc.

The Autopen and laser printers, etc., are a fact of life for the autograph collector. Knowledge is your only real protection. Seeing a current celebrity actually signing the piece in person the only real guard against it being an Autopen or similar device. Or dealing with a reputable dealer who can knowledgeably attest to the piece's authenticity, or provide provenance such as a photograph of a book being signed by a famous author for the person now selling it. Be careful out there!

Pat and Ralph Roberts at their wedding in 1994, the first marriage for both. George Sanders (right) was our best man and we miss him terribly since his passing in 1998.

The
SANDERS
Price Guide to

AUTOGRAPHS

Fifth Edition

Section 3:

GEORGE SANDERS
1924-1998

Being a tribute to George and a reprint of some of his best writings on that subject he loved so dearly, autographs!

BONUS 1950s HOLLYWOOD HISTORICAL PHOTOGRAPH

This picture we found while going through some old photographs from the Hollywood years of George Sanders is too good not to publish. That's actress Rhonda Fleming laying a big kiss on George. He did have a great life!

Chapter 11

GEORGE SANDERS 1924-1998
IN MEMORIAM

He was a nationally recognized expert on signatures and handwriting, author, movie actor, news commentator, columnist, public speaker, teacher, radio and television emcee, businessman, rancher, actor, talk show host, award-winning disc jockey and, through it all, one of the premier autograph collectors in the world but, above all, wanted to be known for what he truly was, an American patriot.

To all of our great loss in the autograph hobby, George R. Sanders of Enka, North Carolina passed away suddenly August 26, 1998, in Marietta, Ohio while on vacation. He was 74.

Sanders—not to be confused with the other movie actor of the same name—was actually the better known celebrity during the 1950s and 60s in Hollywood. George was constantly on radio and television in Los Angeles during those years as an announcer, talk show host, major movie premiere master of ceremonies, and the star of many hundreds of commercials.

"You're the George Sanders I

George chats with the legendary movie director Alfred Hitchcock during a Hollywood movie premiere.

should have married," Zsa Zsa Gabor, ex-wife of the "other" George Sanders, once told him.

Sanders' face was everywhere in those days, especially in the greater Los Angeles area. While he was forced to accept billing as "Greg Sanders" in the over twenty movies he had parts in because of the "other" Sanders, he won a court case in Hollywood establishing "George Sanders" as his broadcast name because he was the more recognizable of the two.

Leaving Hollywood in the late 1960s, Sanders spent several years as a broadcast celebrity, newsman, and station owner in Portland, Oregon. He and his wife Helen and the rest of his family then moved to New Zealand.

Because of his expertise in broadcasting, Sanders was quickly pressed into service by the government of New Zealand. For five years he worked with Radio New Zealand, ending up as Acting Director General of all broadcast operations in that country.

Retiring from yet another highly successful career, Sanders and his family moved back to the United States twenty years ago, choosing the Asheville, North Carolina area as their home. Settling in the small, picturesque village of Enka, just outside of Asheville, George and Helen engaged in their lifelong hobby of autograph collecting, unwittingly starting George's final career, the one for which he is best known today–autographs!

Sanders had begun his autograph collecting career early. As a youngster during the 1930s in his hometown of Detroit, he worked at the famous radio station WXYZ. There, among other shows, he provided all the child voices (both male and female) on the now classic nationally broadcast radio drama, "The Lone Ranger." This gave him access to many

George in 1939 (age 15) interviews famous boxer Jake "Raging Bull" La Motta on the air.

other celebrities of the day—some of whom he interviewed on the air—and he began collecting their autographs.

In his decades as a newsman and talk show host, in fact for well over 50 years, Sanders amassed what was indisputably one of the world's leading autograph collections, consisting of many tens of thousands of signatures. Nor was this collection restricted to living luminaries—every president of the United States, Queen Elizabeth I, Robert E. Lee, Abraham Lincoln, Napoleon, Greta Garbo, Chief Sitting Bull, and thousands more came into the holdings of George and Helen.

More About George Sanders

George's demanding life led him to meet and know political and civil rights leaders, artists, statesmen, athletes, and celebrities from every walk of life—the famous and the infamous. Harry S. Truman, John F. Kennedy, Richard Nixon (a friend of 40 years standing), Martin Luther King, Robert Kennedy, Ronald and Nancy Reagan, Cecil B. DeMille, Clark Gable, Katharine Hepburn (George conducted her first exclusive interview ever recorded at that point in time and later aired on NBC's "Monitor"), Ty Cobb, John Wayne, Ted Williams, Jack Nicklaus, Jimmy Hoffa—these are only a few of the movers and shakers who have given Sanders exclusive interviews on such talk shows as his long-running nationally syndicated radio and television program, "Sanders Meanders" (1948-1960).

One of his television shows, "Success Story," was nominated for an Emmy for two years running in the 1950s. By a nationwide poll he was selected disc jockey of the year in 1950 (a youthful Elizabeth Taylor presented George with his trophy as "King of the Disk Jockeys"). He was also coanchor of the nationally syndicated "Ted Husing Sports Show" (1958-1962) and hosted several Hollywood TV game shows. His long experience as a broadcast station executive here in the United States also resulted in Sanders being tapped to be Assistant, then Acting Director-General of Broadcasting in New Zealand, a position he held for several years.

As a newscaster, TV anchor for Richfield (now Arco) news, and an actor himself in over 20 motion pictures and on television—he has appeared on "Wild Bill Hickok" with Guy Madison and Andy Devine, and also on "December Bride" with Spring Byington and Harry Morgan—it was only natural that Sanders should start collecting the signatures of the hundreds of celebrities with whom he came in contact. This interest of George and his wife Helen in autographs was soon expanded into one of the nation's finest private collections of historical documents, letters, manuscripts, and signed photographs. He also served as a regional director of the UACC (Universal Autograph Collector's Club), and still held that position when he passed away.

Sanders' experience in writing was also extensive. These hundreds of credits include his regular columns (*In the Spotlight*) in the White Newspaper Syndicate (25 cities, 1939-1941), the Clarke Newspapers from 1963-69, as well as *Home Magazine* (1965-69), *College Humor*, *Country Song Roundup* and *Melodyland* (Contributing Editor), *Western Life*, *Coronet*, *Dog World*, *Terrier News*, Los Angeles *Herald-Express* , *Radio-TV Life*, Detroit *News*, *Esquire*, and many others. He also taught Communications at Portland State University, and Lewis and Clark College for several years.

After retiring from broadcasting for the final time and moving to North Carolina, the Sanders—George and Helen—became internationally famous as significant autograph collectors, buying and selling rare and valuable signatures. In 1986—in partnership with author Ralph Roberts—they began producing the undisputed "bible" of autograph collectors everywhere, the award-winning Sanders Price Guides to Autographs—widely recognized as the world's leading authority on the value of signatures.

George Sanders leaves behind his wife Helen, sons George M. "Sandy" and Stephen, daughter Susan, several granddaughters, and a legion of friends in all walks of life. He will be sorely missed but his work lives on. One of those works is the Sanders Price Guides to Autographs. Helen Sanders is editor-in-chief now of the guides. Ralph Roberts and his company, Alexander Books, remains the publisher. You'll see several books in the next few years with the Sanders name on them, all inspired by George's lifetime work and achievement in the field of autographs.

A Farewell Salute to George Sanders

George Sanders was larger than life. He had it all: looks, brains, wealth, fame, charisma, grace and a beautiful wife and family. He excelled at everything he undertook and he had several successful careers. He was a man who can only be described in superlatives. He chose to devote his considerable talents to the autograph hobby which, as a result, will never be the same. **The Sanders Price Guide to Autographs**, written by he and his wife, Helen, instantly became the Bible of autograph collecting and revolutionized the hobby.

George promoted integrity and cooperation among autograph dealers, organizations and collectors. He was loved and respected by all. We salute George Sanders, and his long and productive life. He will be missed but never forgotten. His many contributions will live on in the annals of autograph collecting.

Mike Minor
Larry Vrzalik
Lone Star Autographs

Michael Minor   Larry F. Vrzalik

Goodbye, George

It was our very great privilege to be able to call George Sanders a friend. We discovered a number of years ago that we lived only 20 minutes from the Sanders and that we shared a great passion for autographs. George and Helen very graciously welcomed us into their home on numerous occasions, and we will always treasure the memory of stimulating conversation on a wide range of subjects (yes, even on religion and politics), often into the wee hours of the morning. George was a fount of knowledge about autographs and a spellbinding teller of tales from his vast experience in Hollywood and all over the world. Not only will he be greatly missed in the international autograph world, he will be especially missed in this corner of North Carolina.

—Michael and Patrice Masters

My Remembrance of Two Great Men
by Chuck McKeen

In the incredibly short period of 18 days in the summer of 1998, my life was changed forever.

On August 8, 1998, my dad died. Eighteen days later a dear friend and mentor followed him.

My dad's name was Robert Blanck. He was my stepfather, but I never knew him as anything but dad. He died three years to the date after my mother, Marion. Like mom, he was buried three days later, on the date Pam and I were married.

On August 26, my very dear friend George Sanders joined mom and dad.

Dad and George were two of the three most influential men in my life. The third of that group, Father Norman Aldred of Oregon, still lives. To the three of them I owe pretty much everything. They made me what I am, in pretty much every way. My love for all three has become ever stronger over the years.

All three were cut pretty much from the same cloth. Dad and George were WWII veterans. Both stood the test of combat, and were not found wanting. Each came out of the war with physical damage because of a willingness to stand up for the country and the people they loved.

Each of these men was very willing to do battle for what he believed. That special brand of courage and determination that was steeled in war stood both well in the 53 years that followed combat. Both were successful men, and both believed strongly in the virtues and the need for hard work.

They had so many similarities. Dad and George both absolutely loved their homes. They both had exactly what they wanted for life. They both LIVED. They had fun. They enjoyed the time they had.

Both of these guys were a joy to be with—full of stories that kept everyone laughing, entranced, amazed. They were unique men, made so by the lives they lived. They were a by-product of the Great Depression. Each was forged by the knowledge that they had lived through that horrible period of time and each believed that if it had happened once it could happen again.

Then these men stood the test of war, and again, each believed that this was not a time they cared to see again in their lives, although both knew that war is such a human quality that it is almost as great a certainty as exists in this world.

They came home, they married, they raised families, and they worked. Then they died. Both unexpectedly. Both leaving great voids in the lives of friends and family they left behind.

As a final coincidence, both died when hearts that had been tested in so many ways, finally, simply, wore out.

I lost my dad, who showed by example an unbelievable courage that I have never seen matched in my life. He had three amputations in his last years, because of the scourge of diabetes, but he never faltered in his ability to enjoy life, and to live it on his terms.

I lost my friend and mentor, who shared my love of broadcasting and my love of sports and my love of autographs. He made me a national figure in this hobby of autographs, and he never stopped promoting me. He would turn aside national publicity for himself, and have reporters of various publications call me for information on the hobby. He had the faith in me to make me a part of his many books, and in this last publication we worked on together, he made me a coauthor.

In the end, both died facing forward, like the combat soldiers they were. They didn't run from God, but embraced Him.

I am certain that mom and dad were waiting for George when he left this world. I don't know what to make of this, but the day after I found out George had died, my brother Dennis Blanck called me from Minnesota. He had been cleaning out dad's piano bench, and had found an article that either mom or dad had clipped from an early 1950s country music magazine.

The article was written by George Sanders. So I know that dad shook his hand when George entered that new life, and I know that mom gave him a hug. And I know they are sharing some laughs over me.

One other thing I know. As a first order of business in heaven, George went over and asked God for an autograph.

So, goodbye for now to these fine and honorable men. My most sincere wish is that when my time here is over, that I will be allowed to join them and mom and my grandparents and other friends and relatives in the presence of God.

They have left lives that should serve as beacons for us all,because these were good men. They weren't perfect men. They never claimed to be, but I'll stand up for either of them any time, anywhere. It was my privilege to have Bob Blanck for a father and George Sanders for a friend.

It was always a pleasant break in my workday to hear George's voice on the other end of the line. He was a regular customer ordering items from my catalog for a good many years. With that distinctive voice of his, you always knew it was George on the other end of the line. One thing he said to me years ago that has always stuck in my mind is that when you are writing about autograph collecting never, ever say anything negative about the hobby. There's too much good to write about, and I've always followed that advice. He was a good man.

—*Jim Stinson, Jim Stinson Sports Collectibles*

That's George (above) kneeling in front of baseball legends (l to r) Ty Cobb, Fred Haney, and George Sisler. George attended many functions in Hollywood and elsewhere as a broadcast celebrity and always got autographs. Inset, a facsimile of a Ty Cobb sig. Right, George, summer 1998.

Chapter 12

Autograph Dealers

by George Sanders

This chapter is directed at anyone who foolishly believes that a truly fine autograph collection can be acquired without drawing from the huge inventories of proven, respected, longtime dealers or reputable auction houses. Obviously, it would be great if the collector could grab especially rare signatures, signed photographs and other memorabilia with just in-person forays and through the mail pleas, but unfortunately John Wayne, Robert Kennedy, Bing Crosby, Greta Garbo, Frank Sinatra, Harry Truman, Elvis, and countless other celebrity immortals just aren't signing anymore.

Finding a Dealer

If you are sincere in your desire to collect the greatest of all time autographs it is mandatory that you eventually turn to the offerings of a professional dealer. Your choice of a dealer or a gaggle of dealers with whom you feel secure will come only when you have thoroughly investigated the various candidates who wish to receive your money.

These are some of the qualities you should look for in the dealerships of your choice. First and foremost, they must readily agree, in writing, to totally guarantee the authenticity of every signature or autographed item they sell you. If they can't or won't offer you such a warranty, pass them by as they should be peddling worthless oil leases, dubious stock tips or be employed as racetrack touts. There is no place in this hobby for such questionable, even dishonest, behavior. If the dealer is not certain of his or her material why should it be offered to a customer?

No collector in their right mind should ever agree to hand over hard-earned money for any unauthenticated material. There are no exceptions to that rule. In short, buying any autograph "as is" can most assuredly be a reckless pursuit, particularly with lazy or careless auction houses that stipulate such an irresponsible condition.

Why should you be so cautious? With the hobby growing in record leaps and sometimes startling bounds, unscrupulous forgers, fast-buck manipulators and sleazy con men and, yes, women have begun to worm their way into the marketplace with bogus autographs and highly questionable memorabilia. You obviously require the expertise of specialists who have the experience to tell a phony and absolutely bogus signature from the "write stuff."

With rare exceptions, I have found in my 50 years of collecting and over 30 years of PURCHASING autograph material that most full-time dealers are highly knowledgeable, courteous, interesting, peculiarly candid, and enormously interested in the hobby they represent. They sell with charming grace and buy with all the toughness of a river pirate. Some have become lifelong friends whose personal lives have intertwined with our own. Most are not eligible for sainthood but I trust them completely.

There are even a few blatant thieves whose light-fingered talents keep honest dealers tensely alert at public autograph shows, as well as in the privacy of their respective offices or galleries. Such felons then slither around shows offering their stolen goods to unsuspecting collectors. If you are approached at shows by "wandering" peddlers who somehow "forgot" to rent a booth, give them a wide berth and none of your cash. You can't afford their suspicious bargains unless you enjoy visits from the F.B.I. or postal authorities.

Customers of thieves are treated like the "fences" they've become and you certainly won't enjoy returning your ill-gotten material nor the loss of your investment. In other words, sometimes a "real bargain" is a real bummer!

You wouldn't purchase a diamond ring or a rare coin from some obscure dealer or a fast-talking stranger on the street. If an autograph dealer refuses to guarantee all material and offer to repay your investment in full should the item prove to be bogus or stolen, do not deal with that person. Good dealers make worthwhile suggestions and search out special items that will make your collection more valuable.

Dealer Catalogs

All major autograph dealers offer excellent catalogues; nearly every week I discover some signature, signed photo or document that I never dreamed would become available to me. Also, I find worthwhile bargains because I thoroughly enjoy shopping through the various catalogues offered by more than a hundred dealers in the United States, Canada and overseas. Even wise dealers make mistakes and frequently underprice an item that has little interest or value for them but has been largely unobtainable for the collector who wants or needs it.

Be extremely cautious in how you haggle or bargain with dealers. If you're too penurious or demanding in dealing, you will be punished in subtle ways. If they find you to be cheap, difficult in manner, overly critical of material, you will find that your copy of their catalogue is mailed to you on a much later date than their preferred customers. That means every other collector has pawed over the dealer's material long before you ever had an opportunity to see or buy it. In brief, you saved a few dollars earlier but now you are never going to see his rare good stuff. Asking for discounts on rarities is like asking a dealer if he or she would consider selling one of their children at any price.

Don't waste a dealer's time with tales of how you acquired some precious autograph through the mail or by outwitting some other dealer. They could care less and you have only warned them that you have a big mouth that might embarrass them someday. All dealers know each other. There are no secrets in the world of autographs and excessive collector bragging does not add to the real value of your collection. Some dealers like each other and will only warn the dealer you duped that you are a fast-talking wise guy. Just be polite, informed and keep your triumphs to yourself. A few dealers have very poor telephone manners and you will dread dealing with them, but if they've got something you need, you'll ignore their attitude problems and go for the prize. Some dealers have such bad manners and ugly dispositions that even if they have a much-needed piece, you do as we do and pray that they'll apply for Chapter 11 in your lifetime!

In-Person Autographs Are Nice, But...

Please don't delude yourself that you can ever own a truly valuable collection by only acquiring whatever autographs you can get for postage charges and by begging from sports celebrities in person. I've done both. I have collected thousands of "in-person" autographs for free because I was a professional broadcaster and journalist with easy access to sports figures and public figures from every walk of life. However, my contemporary collection of such wonderful material does not match the value of my cash investments in this fast-growing hobby.

In-person collecting is fun, filled with the excitement of the hunt and the ultimate joy of personally contacting one of your favorite athletes. Alas, collectors cannot contact the dead, and it is the dead who have become the most sought-after in the autograph world. The man who paid over $23,000 for "Shoeless" Joe Jackson's signature has topped us all and if we want a signature like his, we won't find it in a bargain basement or grossly underpriced in some fool's catalogue.

Face the facts, it's not the living we really covet, it's all those super stars who've gone to the Great Autograph Album in the sky. This is where accredited dealers become skilled mediums for seances that bring the writings of Washington, Lincoln, Einstein, Hemingway, Catherine the Great, Horatio Nelson, Thomas Wolfe, Greta Garbo (even when alive practically impossible to obtain), Billy the Kid, Charles Lindbergh,

George, oldest son Sandy, and Helen Sanders in the studios of KGBS in Los Angeles in 1951. George, at that time, was the nation's highest rated disc jockey.

and Marilyn Monroe into your appreciative hands and thus into your treasured collection of proven historically important luminaries.

Don't sell yourself or your collection short by failing to have the confidence of intelligent investment, and don't attempt to build a valuable collection without the learned skills of an honest dealer or auction house.

Dealers Come in All Sizes

Dealers come in all sizes and descriptions. They may have the warm drawl of the deep South, the comfortable, humorous speech of the Southwest, the prim, often cool enunciations of the Northeast, the oft harsh accents of the Bronx, Brooklyn or Manhattan, the terse twang of the Midwest or the enthusiastic, press agentry patter of Hollywood and LaLa Land not including San Francisco where sophistication is a way of life.

There are cynical curmudgeons, scholarly gentlemen, there are ever-so-pleasant and equally learned sportswomen, there are entertaining humorists, there are always good-friends-to-be. Try not to become captivated by just one dealer, even though you may feel quite secure in dealing only with that "special" one.

Catalogues of sports autographs, like their various publishers, have their own personalities, so do not dismiss a list run off from a copier because you think it may contain less desirable or more common sports material. On the other hand, do not be wary of a slick, profusely illustrated, luxuriously presented catalogue because you've assumed its autographs will be too expensive. You'll find superb buys in both.

Don't be tentative or shy about contacting and buying from autograph dealers. They are a necessary addition to your life if you sincerely intend to become a serious collector with an investment potential. In time you will discover several dealers who are just right for you and your bank account, and the union of interests that ensues will be entirely rewarding to you both.

Chapter 13

Big Business is Big Business in Autographs

Collecting Business and Industry Leaders, Financiers, Tycoons, and Creators of Trademarks

by George Sanders

A wise observer once exclaimed, "The business of America is business." To give that seemingly crass statement some meaningful support, the former Secretary of Defense, Charles E. Wilson—employed in Eisenhower's cabinet and who also just happened to be a former president of the internationally prestigious General Motors Corporation—once had the temerity to shout at reporters, "What's good for General Motors is good for America!"

In short, the well-rewarded leaders of industry in the U.S. not only lend their money-making skills and special technical knowledge to our nation's prime source of income but also have had their own family names become household words.

Growing Up With Industrialists

In the 1930s, as a youngster growing up in "The Motor City," when that Michigan metropolis was the industrial capitol of the world, I personally felt the power, influence and unbelievable wealth of some of those business clans. While attending the Jesuit prep school, The University of Detroit High School, I studied, played and partied with the sons and daughters of some of the largest names in big business.

I played polo and football with Jack Ivory (his father founded the John F. Ivory Trucking Company); participated on the debating team with two sons of the founders of the Fisher Body

James A. Farley—FDR's Postmaster General and later president of The Coca-Cola Company—chats with George, who is wisely drinking a Coke.

Corporation; dated pretty Bonna Briggs, a daughter of the famed Briggs Body Corporation that manufactured auto bodies for Chrysler; attended classes with and dated lovely Louise Martin whose father was a vice president of the Ford Motor Car Company and an early colleague of Henry Ford; received my first kiss from Betty Hill, the stunning blonde daughter of the head of the S.S. Kresge chain of stores, now part of K-Mart; raced around town in the flashy convertible of Billy Mistele whose father owned the largest coal company in the Midwest; and, in those days, many of my friends thought I was related to the wonderful Fred Sanders Stores where the chocolate soda was invented. I wasn't. It was the middle of the Great Depression and my father was fortunate to be the best store-to-store salesman the Wesson Oil & Snowdrift Company ever had on the streets of Detroit. There were no riches at our house but we were far from poor.

It was my obvious good fortune to be a frequent guest in the mansions of some of the most advertised names in the nation and I learned early to respect the financial clout these people exerted on the world. Even in those days I had no qualms about asking for autographed photographs of the parents of my friends. It was the beginning of an autograph collection that is now one of the finest of its kind.

My youthful interest in these powerhouse individuals never waned. For good or evil, I recognized that these "big names" gave tremendous financial support to needy or sometimes just greedy politicians, selected U.S. Presidents in "smoke-filled" rooms, donated millions of dollars to their favorite universities, contributed fortunes to hospital facilities and medical research foundations and certainly created the jobs this nation thrives upon. I sensed, even then, that these tycoons were bearing more important names with considerably greater effect on our daily lives than mere movie stars or much-muscled athletes. More importantly, I knew from my personal acquisitions that they were indeed collectible. Only the great crusade against a disgusting tyrant named Hitler put a temporary halt to my hobby.

A Television "Success Story"

Following World War II, I emigrated to the then glorious environs of an almost smogless Southern California to work as a radio broadcaster. When commercial television was born in Los Angeles around 1949, I was lucky enough to get in on the ground floor.

Being glib by nature, live television did not frighten or dismay. Because I could "wing it" with or without a

Teleprompter (we called them "idiot sheets" in those days) I was constantly in demand whether I was good or not. Nobody cared just as long as you kept on babbling and didn't allow any silences longer than two or three seconds. Dead air, not stupidity was the bane of live TV.

In 1950 I was asked by the late Bob Purcell of Los Angeles Times Television (KTTV) in Hollywood to host a very expensively produced industrial documentary titled "Success Story" sponsored by the old Richfield Oil Company. From February 2, 1951 through May 15, 1953, under the direction of former child star Philippe DeLacy, crusty Joe Conn and dictatorial Ed Roden, it was my task to attempt to at least sound well-informed about industry in general.

Sometimes it was a pleasure to serve as the gabby master of ceremonies as our live cameras, with their endless cables, poked their lenses into every nook and cranny of California's major industries. Sometimes it was not-so-pleasant, but, for those days our financial rewards seemed splendid and being the father of three hungry Pasadena children, I simply kept talking. Despite my own shortcomings, the program was nominated for an Emmy twice in the first three years on the air and was actually a special school assignment every Friday night for the State's bored students.

In this industrially oriented TV role, I hobnobbed with such biggies as kindly Henry J. Kaiser, whose plants made steel, cars, boats and gypsum; Bill Fox of Union Pacific Railroad (who has been a lifelong family friend and served as a role-model for our eldest son who is now an executive with that same railroad); friendly W.P. Fuller of paint fame who had to be one of the nicest "tycoons" I ever brushed past with a camera; stern Donald W. Douglas, Sr. and his wonderfully "unstern" son, Donald, Jr. whom I knew socially for many years; personable W.J. Voit whose sporting equipment still bears his name. Mr. Voit was well-loved at our house because he ordered his assistants to deliver sporting goods treasures to our kids for many Christmases. The trade-name Voit replaced the trade-name Santa at the Sanders residence.

While performing on "Success Story" we also worked with

the Packard-Bell families, who seemed closely knit and comfortable with one another; unyielding and unfriendly Milo Bekins of moving van fame; charming Bob Cannon who gave the modern world the Cannon electric plug; lovely and shapely Rose Marie Reid of swimsuit design fame; generous Conrad Hilton who lent his name to some of the world's finest hotels as well as to Zsa Zsa Gabor. Anyone who didn't like Conrad Hilton had a serious personality problem. He was a fun guy until the day he left this Earth to open a hostelry in Heaven. I obviously loved working and playing with him as he never acted like a "big-shot." We also took our KTTV cameras to the unimposing factory of Mrs Ruth Handler of Mattel Toys before she and her husband had created "Barbie" dolls. If you are a collector, you can well imagine how much I value the thoughtful inscriptions and signatures these people wrote in my many leather-bound guest books.

Business Leaders are People, Too

More than autographs were our rewards during the "Success Story" TV phase of our lives and careers. Helen and I were still in our twenties with a growing family and we needed all the help, wisdom and encouragement we could acquire. Many of these business giants gave us more than their autographs.

One of the most pleasant and thoughtful gentlemen we ever worked with on that show was big, friendly Robert "Bob" McCulloch, whose chain saws and outboard motors still bear his name. His employees adored him because he was the greatest boss on Earth with business ethics that were worthy of imitating. He became my role model and whenever I sought advice from him in later years, when I became an executive in broadcasting, McCulloch was there for me. In 20 years as a radio or TV CEO, my companies enjoyed good labor relations, we never had a strike or walkout, and our employees shared our financial successes. From Bob I got much more than an industrial autograph.

There was another tycoon who gave me more than his John Hancock on "Success Story" and his name was C.F. Braun. This stern, structured, brilliant businessman operated a huge internationally famous corporation with ordered finesse. He autographed books he had written and they are still in my library of signed first editions. From those books and from the many quiet, intelligent conversations I had with Mr. Braun in subsequent years, he became my business mentor and his teachings made us financially secure at an early age. Braun wasn't just another engineering giant, he was an extraordinary man who taught me that running a business, like life itself, must be disciplined.

Some industrialists, or their wealthy offspring, aren't that rewarding. The late Harry Sinclair, Jr., whose father founded the Sinclair Oil Co., now a part of the Richfield Corporation, was forever whining about his infamous sire. As you historians may recall, it was the elder Sinclair who was illegally involved in the corrupt Teapot Dome scandal during the Harding administration. It seemed to me that young Harry (he was then old enough to be my father) was forever carping about Daddy's acts and apparently totally oblivious to the fact that he certainly was enjoying a life of wealth and position that his father had handed to him on a platinum platter. Seldom seen without a drink in his hand and a patronizing manner that was hardly endearing, I avoided him whenever possible and that was difficult because he was attached to our show through his association with Richfield. Fortunately, our acquaintanceship did bring my autograph

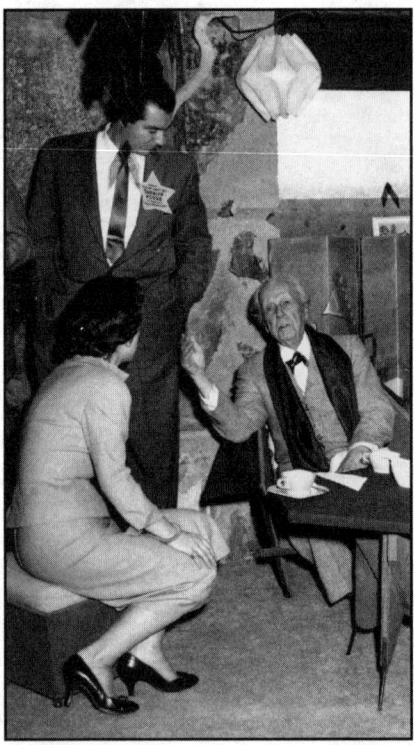

Top, photo of George with architect Frank Lloyd Wright and Wright's granddaughter, Oscar-winning actress Anne Baxter.

collection some interesting items as Sinclair gave me some of his father's letters when I left the TV show.

In any case, let's talk about a few more good guys we met. The late Paul Helms, famous founder of California's Helms Bakeries and the important Helms Sports Foundation was a most exceptional person. He was thoughtfully kind and filled with genuine enthusiasm for all things pertaining to the sports world. His handsome son, Paul, Jr., is just as fine a man as his father. Robert Merritt, Sr. and D.P. O'Keefe were the founders of the O'Keefe & Merritt gas and electrical appliance company that bore their names and I remember them quite well as two of the very best people I ever worked with on television.

There were many others, too numerous to list here, but they all seemed flattered and pleased to sign my ever-present autograph books and I never left home without them. Not one august industrial personality ever refused to sign or made me feel uncomfortable for requesting his or her signature. The same certainly cannot be said for celebrities in other walks of life who are frequently evasive, rude or belligerent. It's a pleasure collecting famous names in the business world and they are valuable.

The Rewards of Collecting Big Business

You will discover that most great industrial leaders have highly efficient executive secretaries who will see to it that your polite requests for autographs will be filled with a courteous cover letter accompanied frequently by a signed photograph. I believe the secretaries are duly impressed with your sincere interest in their famous bosses and are usually the most cooperative aides your collection will ever have. Try it, you'll like it!

In other words, there are many well-known business leaders like Victor Kiam, Lee Iacocca, Donald Trump, Sam Walton, H. Ross Perot and others who may respond and their signatures have value, but, once you've become a serious collector in this facet of autograph collecting, you'll want to expand your horizons.

Soon the contemporary autographs will not be enough for you and that's when it really becomes an exciting hobby. You must ultimately turn to professional autograph dealers who feature the material you will need. Now you are seeking historically important industrial names for your collection and such materials available only from the pages of autograph dealers' catalogs. You'll be searching for and acquiring such great industrial names as Elizabeth Arden, Max Factor and Helena Rubenstein, who paint the ladies; Sherwin-Williams and Glidden, who paint the world; the Astors, who painted the town and gave us Astoria, Oregon, the Waldorf Astoria Hotel and a classy name that has been overused by innkeepers everywhere; Dr. L.H. Baekeland, who gave us Bakelite, the forerunner to the plastic world in which we live; P.T. Barnum, who gave us a three-ring circus and the knowledge that a sucker is born every minute of the day; August Belmont, who gave his name and money to a posh New York racetrack; Clarence Birdseye, whose name flies in every supermarket in the frozen food departments; H. and R. Block, who try heroically to eliminate our income tax problems; David D. Buick, whose name has graced many a hood ornament; likewise, Henry Ford, Clement Studebaker, Charles Duryea, Walter P. Chrysler and other car makers to be mentioned later; rotund beer barons like Jacob Ruppert, August A. Busch plus suds-makers Pabst, Miller, Coors and Hamm who give us happy times and hangovers.

For those of us lacking willpower there are Mr. Hershey and Mr. Cadbury, who give us the best tasting chocolate calories available; Asa G. Candler, who gave us effervescent Coca Cola instead of Coca Candler; Andrew Carnegie, who gave us steel mills and public libraries; CoCo Chanel, who created enchanting aromas and styles fit for any sweet-smelling girl; Charles Crocker and A.P. Gianinni, who gave us banks and reluctant loans; Robert Dollar and Samuel Cunard, who gave us ocean liners that stayed afloat and only one Titanic; George Eastman gave us Kodaks and billions of forgettable snapshots; the DuPonts, who gave us chemicals, some that were good for us and some that were just noxious; Sanford Dole, who gave us prickly pineapple in a can; H.J. Heinz, who gave us 57 varieties of

The truly legendary War World I ace and longtime head of Eastern Airlines Eddie Rickenbacker with George Sanders.

canned goods plus a contemporary U.S. Senator; John Deere and Massey-Ferguson, who gave our farmers tractors to repair; William G. & James C. Fargo joined Henry Wells so they could give us Wells-Fargo stagecoaches for John Wayne to ride and Indians to chase. They also gave us American Express so we could have some plastic cards we weren't to leave home without.

The Goodyears, Goodrichs, Fisks, Dunlops and Firestones, who gave us vulcanized rubber for our wheels; Alfred C. Fuller who sent his brush salesmen from door-to-door; Malcomb Forbes, whose financial magazine counts and names the millionaires amongst us; Edsel Ford, whose name was emblazoned on the most infamous automotive lemon of all time; Elaine Ford, who gave us models not cars; George Gallup, who counted our votes in his polls; Elbert H. Gary, whose name and steel mills graced a smoke-glutted town in Indiana.

J. Paul Getty, who gave us oil and a one-earred grandson; the Macys and Gimbels, who faced each other daily in New York City as they peddled department store wares at competitive prices; F.W. Woolworth, J.C. Penney, W.T. Grant and Mr. Newberry who gave us trinkets, tin toys, tidbits and terrific variety in their hundreds of retail stores; Robert H. Ingersoll gave us the dollar watch while George Gruen gave us costlier watches and Seth Thomas gave us clocks. Are you getting the picture? Your selection of famous autographs in this field is seemingly endless.

Here are some more to add to your collection: The Hearsts gave us newspapers and gossip (sometimes even terrible gossip about themselves); Adolph Ochs gave us the *New York Times* and only news that's fit to print; Guinness gave us booze from Scotland and England as if Jim Beam and Jack Daniels were not distilling enough of a supply here in America; Joyce C. Hall gave us Hallmark Cards and the very best playhouse on TV; Duncan Hines gave us a cake mix that millionaire Roy H. Park peddled from door-to-door until he'd earned enough money to buy the trademark and become one of the richest men in the U.S.; Lord Lever and his pompous brothers gave us kitchen fixings; Nelson Bunker Hunt gave bogus silver prices while his brother, Lamar Hunt, gave Kansas City a helluva pro football team.

Howard Johnson gave us thousands of motel rooms scattered all over the road maps; W.K. Kellogg gave us crispy, crunchy breakfast food and so did Mr. Post with his Toasties; Joseph P. Kennedy gave us a U.S. President and three U.S. Senators; Atwater Kent gave us our early radios; Phil Knight gave us Nike shoes to jog in; Calvin Klein gave us style but so did Oleg Cassini, Don Loper, Oscar de la Renta, Bob Mackie, Hubert de Givenchy and Edith Head; Sam Goldwyn, Louis B. Mayer, the Warner brothers, D.W. Griffith, Mack Sennett,

The fried chicken king, Colonel Harlan Sanders autographed this photo to George.

Hal Roach and Carl Laemmle gave us the magic of movies and great places in which to eat Orville Redenbacher's popcorn.

Such dealers in death as Mr. Remington and Mr. Browning gave us rifles to hunt with while Samuel Colt gave us six-shooters for shooting bad guys in the old wild west and Alfred Krupp gave us cannon to shoot up the whole wide world; Allan Lockheed, Glenn Martin, Glenn Curtiss, William P. Lear, McDonnell & Douglas, John K. Northrup, Mr. Cessna, Mr. DeHavilland and Sir Thomas Sopwith gave us aircraft to soar in; Sir Thomas Lipton gave us hot tea and soup to warm our tummies while his yachts tried to win the America's Cup.

Louis K. Liggett gave us drug stores with sundries; Herman Lay fried potato chips for us to munch; Marcus Loew gave us ritzy movie theatres to dream in; P. Lorrillard gave us snuff to sniff while George Washington Hill wrapped tobacco in burnable paper and called them Lucky Strikes to puff on; E.R. Squibb gave us pills to pop; Tommy Manville gave us asbestos (now we wish his grandfather hadn't as it now has to be removed from schools) and an overabundant supply of his ex-wives; and Fred Maytag gave us appliances that put his servicemen on permanent retirement, including actor Jesse White.

The mention of a Hollywood performer like Jesse White reminds me that some of the faces of the actors and actresses who become almost as familiar as the trademark they represent are also valuable collectibles like Madge (alias Jan Miner) for Palmolive dishwashing detergent or Virginia Christine (alias Mrs. Olson) pushing coffee, (I don't think Juan Valdez is available), a phony British actress called Rula Lenske, whose real name escapes me, peddled hair products, and of course, the singing raisins, but I'm told they positively will not sign anything and are hiding out in bowls of rice pudding.

Let us not forget that bearded King Gillette gave us safety razors with which to trim our beards but could never sell his razors to the Smith Brothers who were too busy sucking on cough drops and profits. Cyrus McCormick gave us reapers with which to trim our crops; Robert Fulton had a thing about steamboats that was more than folly and Eli Whitney put his name on a cotton gin while Mr. Gilbey just gave us a gin; J.P.

Morgan, Jim Fisk, "Beta Million" Gates, the Rothschilds, the Rockefellers, the Mellons, the Morganthaus, Sloans, Sages, Flaglers, Goulds and the infamous Mr. Charles Keating all messed with our money.

Working with another kind of dough, Pillsbury gave us flour and Mr. Burpee gave us flowers; John Ringling and his brothers plus John Ringling North brought the big top to our neighborhoods with none of Barnum's puffery and better acrobats; Perle Mesta was the hostess with the mostest (immortalized on the Broadway stage by raucous Ethel Merman) thanks to her daddy's belching steel mills in Pittsburgh; Pinkerton gave us private eyes and armored cars but Mr. Brink's trucks were more mobile; Mary Quant gave us something to look at.

A.C. Roebuck got a partner named Sears while Montgomery Ward went solo with a name that only sounded like he had a partner; Charles S. Rolls joined Mr. Royce to give us a car most of us couldn't afford while Ransom E. Olds gave us a car even our fathers could afford; Richard McDonald and his late brother put American hamburgers in our daily diet and then watched Ray Kroc make their name the most recognizable commercial entity in the world including Moscow. Every name you have just read in the above litany, and hundreds more, are actually in my own autograph collection of business leaders with their letters, documents, signed photographs and signatures. They are exciting people who have made a real impact on our daily lives and are definitely historically important.

The Big Picture of Big Business

By now, you have the big picture regarding big business. The best known names in the entire world are both interesting and excitingly collectible. Unlike collecting U.S. Presidents or rare scientists or Signers of the Declaration of Independence or scarce artists, these familiar names are all readily available in dealers' stocks.

As you can see, the ultimate extent of such a collection is nearly unlimited in scope. Thus, you are not going to be disappointed nor frustrated by only high-priced material being offered or by a rarity factor that cannot be overcome by your humble budget. If your budget is neither humble nor limited, you are about to embark on an investment that is really worth it's salt. Yes, Mr. Morton whose salt pours when it rains, is also in my collection.

Most U.S. dealers highlight industrialists in their respective catalogs and frequently display such autographic wares at public autograph shows throughout the nation. Overseas dealers also trade in such items as I have recently bought Porsche, Renault and Citroen from French dealers and Tattersall, Harrods and Selfridge from our British friends. Hence, you have availability, lower cost, immediate name recognition, material worthy of creative framing or material that furnishes attractive display pages in your loose-leaf collectors' books. This is an area of collectibles that has just recently become a secure investment worthy of your time, your interest, and your cash.

This 1960 billboard shows George Sanders (far left) and other broadcast celebrities.

Chapter 14

How to Reach the Stars

by George Sanders

Since the challenging hobby of autograph collecting began several centuries ago, collectors have been devising ingenious methods of acquiring the precious signatures, letters, manuscripts or documents of the world's most famous or infamous celebrities. Gaining in-person access to some rather elusive, intentionally difficult, professionally-shielded-from-the-general-public luminaries is one of the most frustrating aspects of this avocation.

In-Person Autographs

Obviously, the most instantly rewarding procedure is to be where your idol is going to be and to simply join the other autograph seekers with their pens-in-hand and autograph books, index cards or photographs ready to be politely offered to the celebrated one so that he or she can quickly sign in person!

Autograph collectors know almost instinctively that the stars appear in public places to entertain. Such stars perform in concert halls, auditoriums, sports arenas, hotel or casino dining rooms, theaters of every size in every large community in the world, plus radio and television studios, motion picture sound stages and even at spacious convention centers.

There are literally thousands of opportunities in which the aspiring collector can personally request an autograph. Most of the celebrities respond graciously and thoughtfully to the eager collectors who crowd around them at nearly every public appearance.

Some in-person autograph collectors are almost uncanny in uncovering the public whereabouts of the stars. They locate them when the celebrities are on vacation, dining out, on buying sprees in exclusive shops and malls, honeymooning, visiting friends, attending movie premieres or other star-studded shows.

If you are to participate in such in-person signature acquisitions you had best begin to study local newspapers and watch your hometown television news or gossip programs to become aware of the comings and goings of such celebrities in your own community. Famous people are usually not static as their careers keep them forever on the move. Every sizable town in America is visited, at one time or another, by the rich, the famous, the successful, the political, the learned, the sought after. Prepare yourself for the possibility of contacting some special person right in your home town by being constantly alert and vigilant as you make yourself aware of their potential visits to your area.

A Little Creativity

[**Editor's Note**: *Yes, this "guard" was George!*]

One clever collector of our wide acquaintance discovered an ingenious method to gain spectacular in-person signatures where the stars couldn't ever refuse him or escape his proffered autograph book. When this U.S. millionaire collector retired from a lengthy broadcasting career in 1977, like so many comfortable retirees, he realized that suddenly he had considerable spare time on his hands. Having been a highly successful executive in both radio and television, he knew exactly where to go to add to his already huge autograph collection without his friends discovering his eccentric, novel and temporary career.

He patiently watched the newspapers until he spied the help-wanted advertisement in the Los Angeles *Times* he'd been waiting to see. Our autograph hound applied for and was hired as a security guard at the NBC studios in Burbank, California.

Within a week, resplendent in his dark blue uniform complete with brass badge and Sam Browne leather belt, plus the ever-present dark sunglasses, he was stationed at the main guard gate. Every celebrity who appeared at NBC on "The Johnny Carson Show," news programs, or other nighttime guest appearances from December 15, 1977 to February 15, 1978 was stopped by our amateur guard and while seated in their respective vehicles, barred by an automatic electric gate, which he controlled from the small guardhouse, were politely requested to sign his thick, leatherbound autograph book.

Assuming this was some new NBC security regulation to be strictly obeyed before being permitted to enter, each and every star signed without the slightest hesitation. In just 60 days he collected over 250 signatures of stars including 35 Academy Award winners (James Stewart, Anne Baxter, Jack Lemmon, Anthony Quinn, Bette Davis, Burt Lancaster, John Wayne, Ingrid Bergman, and so forth), rock and roll stars including Ringo Starr and Bruce Springsteen, sports stars, political leaders including a former actor named Ronald Reagan and many hard-to-get people-in-the-news.

A few years later, he sold the albums he had filled at the NBC gate for several thousand dollars making him the highest-paid short term security guard who ever lived! Incidentally, our highly creative gate guard's career was shortened when the "Tonight Show" host, Johnny Carson complained to NBC authorities that his flashy Mercedes coupe had been stopped at the entrance twice and that he had been literally "forced" to sign an "entry book" before being permitted to enter the main gate.

On one of Carson's forced stops, he muttered to the phantom guard, "What the hell do you do, pull out a gun and shoot 'em if they don't stop and sign?" Johnny's complaint was well-timed however as our retiree was planning on leaving his post for a lengthy vacation in the Greek Islands.

More Creativity

Speaking of "creative" autograph collecting, we are truly impressed with the research and all-out effort of autograph dealer Jerry Granat of Hewlett, New York. Granat initiated a very lengthy written correspondence with Adolf Hitler's infamous architect, Albert Speer.

Following months of highly provocative questioning by Granat, Speer agreed to meet with him in Europe. Within a few weeks, Ellen and Jerry Granat were dining with this one-time Nazi leader in Munich. He answered most of their questions regarding his knowledge, or lack of it, regarding the Holocaust, World War II and his participation in Hitler's hierarchy. Needless to say, the Granat's own a fabulous collection of Albert Speer's writings. They enjoyed a fantastic personal experience because of this exciting hobby of autograph collecting! Ironically, Granat was able to convince Speer to contribute one thousand dollars to be donated to the United Jewish Appeal.

The Best Places for In-Person Autographs

In 1981, autograph dealer/auctioneer Herman Darvick wrote that "the best cities for collecting autographs in person are New York, Los Angeles and Washington, D.C." To that list we would now add San Francisco, Atlanta, Miami, Seattle, Phoenix, and all other large cities that have developed huge convention complexes. Internationally, we believe London, Geneva, Rome, Paris and the French Riviera offer the most famous in-person faces.

The Right Equipment

If you do decide to become an in-person autograph collector be certain to carry the necessary equipment. Obviously, you should always have a small supply of 3x5 cards or a compact autograph book plus several workable pens. As the famous credit card company advertises: "Never leave home without them." One never knows when someone famous or worthwhile, preferably both, will cross your particular path.

Always, without exception, request the autograph you seek in your most courteous tones and with the best of good manners. Don't tug at the celebrity's clothes, don't push or shove, don't assume that their signature on your piece of paper or on the pages of your book is something the celebrity owes you.

Willingness to Sign

It is our experience that if you are exceedingly polite, the celebrity responds in kind and is frequently grateful for your attention. There will be a few exceptions like the boorish Sean

A very young George with a true jazz nobleman, the great Count Basie.

Penn, the haughty Joanne Woodward or the totally inaccessible Greta Garbo—who frequently rewarded autograph seekers with a healthy clout to the side of the head with her hefty handbag when she walked on Manhattan sidewalks.

Until recent years, Miss Garbo was not only amazingly evasive but handled that always-present handbag with all the athletic prowess of Steffi Graf. It has been documented by the walking wounded that Garbo's forehand with the aforementioned purse sent several collectors sprawling, ducking and fleeing whenever they blocked her passage.

Actor Paul Newman was certainly justified in finally deciding that the rudeness of unthinking autograph hounds was too much for him to bear. As the Academy Award-winning actor tells it:

"I was standing at a urinal in a public restroom, and this guy next to me sticks a pen and index card in my face and asks for my autograph! I didn't know which hand to use."

That witless request and breach of courtesy was the contributing factor in causing Newman, who is really a very nice guy, to determine never to sign in public again. A vow he has kept religiously for many years. Likewise, Marlon Brando, Frank Sinatra and Cary Grant told us in personal interviews that it was the rude behavior of some "autograph pests" that made them finally say, "No autographs, ever!"

Please understand that because of terrorists, thieves, kooks, and even cold-blooded assassins, many celebrated people are carefully protected by a phalanx of security guards or secret service. These specially-trained security forces are paid handsomely to surround, obscure from public view, and generally ward off any potential dangers of human contact with their respective celebrities.

You will discover that few of these large professional escorts will relent and permit any autograph seekers to knife through the crowd and reach the star. Can we blame them for such tight security when one considers the assassinations, in such crowds, of Robert F. Kennedy and John Lennon as well as the attempts on the lives of Presidents Ronald Reagan, Gerald Ford and Governor George Wallace of Alabama. Without exception, all of

"Well... cancel my other appointments, Rochester. George is here." One of the funniest comedians of all time talks with George Sanders.

the personalities just mentioned were once delighted to sign autographs while strolling through crowds in public places.

Dangerous times and mean streets have changed the availability to the collector of such people. When little-known Hollywood actresses are murdered or maimed by psychopaths you can expect security to tighten around all of your favorite personalities. It is a pity but your chances of persuading a Secret Service agent that the President of the United States should sign your book or photograph is asking for a special privilege that could cost the agent his or her job for negligence in properly performing their duties.

Only those people wearing proper official badges of identification can ever convince the Secret Service to relax their rules just a little bit. Until America's streets are safe once again, it is better to forgo the autograph today, lest a life be lost tomorrow with lazy, flawed, or careless security.

Obtaining Autographs by Mail

Despite what has been said above, it is best to acquire all such autographs in person because of their obvious authenticity, but, countless collectors like to remind us that they happen to live in remote areas of America and find it much easier to write clever letters requesting autograph material. Such activity has become a cottage industry for many dealers who frequently disguise themselves to the signer as being solely collectors.

In any case, thousands of collectors from all over the world dutifully mail out their photographs, programs, index cards, album leaves, typescripts, First Day Covers, sketches, baseballs and other memorabilia to be signed. Hundreds of contemporary celebrities agree to sign and then return the various pre-postage-paid envelopes or packages to the respective collectors.

It is wise to spend considerable time composing a really unique but brief form letter that can be sent to the people you are hoping will return your precious material. Some of the earlier "How to Collect Autographs" books offered examples of simple requests and the forms that such missives should take. Unfortunately, there are now millions of collectors mailing out such trite, little messages and the stars and their secretaries weary of receiving them.

You must be creative and thoughtful. Think of new ways to attract their attention and make them really want to cooperate with you and be delighted to add their pen scratchings to your particular collection.

An Artful Method of Obtaining Autographs

It goes without saying that some autograph collectors who amass collections by mail are more talented than others.

Canadian artist Jack Ellison, who is employed by a large Toronto ad agency, draws an original portrait of each personality he seeks. Using a secret technique, he draws the sketch from a favorite photograph of the celebrity and then mails the original Ellison sketch, which he asks be autographed and returned to him.

A copy of that original sketch is given to the celebrity for his or her own personal collection of memorabilia. Because the stars are receiving a stunning drawing of one of their own favorite poses, they have been extremely responsive. Hence, artist Ellison enjoys an 80% success ratio in recovering his signed art work.

He is not the first professional artist to use such a ploy as New York cartoonist Jack Rosen and the brilliant artist M.H. Herrin, whose magnificent pencil portraits of the world's most powerful and famous people graced *Time*'s covers for many years, also sent their originals to be autographed and made a copy for each signer to keep.

Persistence Pays

Another collector-dealer of our acquaintance in the Pacific Northwest, Charles "Chuck" McKeen, has mailed out as many as 500 pieces to be signed per day, thanks to the marvels of the computer. In the past seven years, McKeen has spent over $7,000 per year in postage alone. However, his mail return of sports stars, film and stage personalities, and general people-in-the-news types, is staggeringly successful and his sales from other dealers, who buy his extra copies, has given him a handsome profit for years without leaving home. Most of today's professional autograph dealers began their careers with just such mailings. Why not you?

McKeen has come up with other novel notions. He asked glamorous movie stars to place their lip prints on 3x5 index cards and then add their signatures. He was amazed at how many "mailed" kisses he received.

Chuck also had sports stars outline with a pen or pencil their hands on paper or heavy cardboard and then signed beneath the hand print. The jocks thought it was such a great idea that not only did many cooperate but also congratulated McKeen for his innovation. Hall of Fame Golfer, Gene Sarazan even drew arrows to various points of his hands where unusual swellings indicated severe arthritis.

But Don't Get Too Creative

Sometimes, "creative thinking" gets out of control with unfortunate results. Let us tell you about the nefarious Philadelphia collector who wrote a most untruthful message to many foreign Heads of State proclaiming the birth of his firstborn son whom he was purportedly naming after each and every one of the regal or republican heads.

All went well for years as this scheming character received beautiful signed photographs from various presidents, monarchs, prime ministers, sultans and other assorted world leaders. Each of the Heads of State apparently believed that this magical child bore their first and sometimes their second name as well.

Then there was a special United Nations gathering of dignitaries in New York City a few years ago. The cunning letter writer and his neighbors were astonished to find a huge motorcade complete with accompanying security guards and the ever-present press corps, all marching up to his front door. With the bright TV lights focused on his entrance, the suitably embarrassed autograph collector timidly opened his door.

Much to his surprise, there stood the toothy, unshaven

leader of the PLO who had come to visit little "Yassir Arafat, Jr.!" Of course, the "babe," now age 15, naturally had never been given such a name and everyone involved was more than mildly sheepish. The real Yasir pushed his way back to the limousine at curbside muttering Arabic invectives directed at "ze phony infidels." The man from the Middle East who wears the checkered towel around his usually unkempt head has never returned to Philadelphia and may never again believe another letter writer from America who is seeking an autograph.

Actually, it is not necessary to be dishonest in requesting material from world leaders. There are many whose secretaries will see to it that your letter is seriously considered and frequently replied to with a signature on an official card created for just such requests. Sometimes the collector is even blessed with a polite signed letter accompanying a formal and handsomely autographed photograph. The exception is the British Royal Family whose secretarial minions will reply by formal mail that "their Royal Majesties simply do not communicate or autograph anything for anyone with whom they are not personally acquainted."

Addresses

Some readers may wonder how one acquires correct addresses of famous people. Most celebrities do not wish to have their home addresses published for obvious reasons, but you can still find those addresses.

The very best source is available in most public libraries. It is titled *Who's Who in America*, published by Marquis. Following each person's brief biography you will find their business and home addresses. Most celebrities, by the way, prefer that you address your requests to their offices if they have them.

This multivolume collection of famous Americans carries thousands of correct names and addresses that should keep your typewriter or word processor active for some time. As we indicate elsewhere in the book you are reading, it is the responsibility of the autograph seeker to include all return postage whenever you forward material to be signed. Enclose a self-addressed and stamped envelope that is large enough to properly transport the signed piece or pieces back to your home or office.

However, our personal experience with most Hollywood stars tells us that most of the contemporary addresses route your requests to the offices of press agents, personal managers, studio public relations directors and secretaries plus cadres of hangers-on who are permitted to flagrantly serve as signers of thousands of various-sized photographs and cards. There are literally scores of glossy black and white or color photographs being represented as having been signed in person when actually the star signs practically nothing and leaves the tiring chore to underpaid underlings.

As an example, when Michael J. Fox of "Family Ties" fame was receiving thousands of pieces of mail per day at his studio, he had very little time available to peruse such correspondence or ever be expected to reply personally to any of it. Think about it. He was receiving more daily mail than the President of the United States!

Fox worked on his popular TV series from dawn to dusk, six days a week, and had to memorize his lines when he was at home. Add to that, some small semblance of a personal life plus necessary public appearances and when does the naive autograph collector imagine that Fox could find time to personally communicate with the millions of fans who have purchased a home address that is supposedly accepting tons of his mail daily? Surely not Michael J. Fox's home. Likewise, the average Congressman in Washington, D.C. receives approximately five thousand pieces of mail each month. That's why there are more autopens in our nation's capitol than anywhere else on Earth.

Beware of Publicity Departments

When Helen and I worked in Hollywood, from 1945 to 1960, we spent considerable time cooperating with the publicity departments of M-G-M, 20th Century-Fox, Columbia, R-K-O,

Actress Grace Kelly—later, Princess Grace of Monaco—shares some microphone time with George Sanders during a gala event in Hollywood.

Warner Brothers, and Paramount, where one of our business partners in a nationally syndicated radio show was also a studio departmental head.

During that time at Paramount, we regularly saw, in person, a paid staff of female secretaries "forging" signatures on the attractive 8x10 inch glossy publicity photos of Marlon Brando, Ingrid Bergman, Charlton Heston, Bing Crosby and many, many others. This we saw with our own eyes! It has been an established Hollywood practice since the 1920s.

Yet, we still have uninformed peddlers of such worthless trash attempting to convince us that such material is collectible. In reality, it is valuable only as Hollywood memorabilia because the forged or "secretarial" signatures are worthless oddities. Hence, as in all things purchasable, buyer beware!

President John F. Kennedy gave several interviews to newsman George Sanders.

Chapter 15

Marilyn Monroe: Her Final Autograph

by George Sanders

Did she commit suicide? Or was she murdered?
Her final signature may be a clue!

As almost everyone is well aware, Marilyn Monroe has become a Hollywood icon—a screen legend among legends, but also an enigma within a mysterious puzzle of historic proportions. It happens only to those few beautiful ladies who enjoy liaisons with the rich, the famous, the politically powerful. Her personal dreams as a young girl became realities larger than life as a woman.

A Lonely Starlet

When we knew her she was just another lonely starlet attempting to find her way to stardom amongst the cruel, cynical power-brokers who used her like an inflatable doll. In the late forties, Marilyn would often stroll into our family's Los Angeles restaurant and cocktail lounge (for 30 years it was George Sanders' Lark on Third Street and Catalina) as her refuge from the dullness of her life and residency at the Studio Club apartment in Hollywood.

Wearing a camel-hair coat and a colorless scarf tied under her chin, she'd slide gracefully into a red-leathered booth and quietly sip a cup of coffee until our busy tiny mother, Grace Sanders, would find time to join her for some aimless chatter about life in the world of filmmaking. Marilyn seemed to enjoy those chats because she sensed that our mom was genuinely interested in any successes Monroe might report.

Frequently, we'd have a singer-pianist like Jess Stacy (even Liberace auditioned for a job at The Lark) or a loud Dixieland band like Kid Ory or Joe Darensbourg on the bandstand. Marilyn would show only mild interest in the music or dancing. Never requested a song and I know that I didn't dance with her. She seemed to need a modicum of serene companionship dusted with a few kind words of encouragement. She ignored the over zealous, male or female, and seemed content to simply spend her time with the "innkeepers."

"I Was Just Too Adult"

One night, following the broadcast of our "Sanders Meanders" syndicated radio show, I sat with her for several hours and found her to be surprisingly open and totally non glamourous. There was none of that gushy breathiness in her voice or sensuous twisting of her ample figure. The sexy affectations that ultimately were to become her trademarks simply were not on display in my company. She seemed weary, unattached, an unassuming woman seeking some straight talk about anything not pertaining to life in the fast track. We even discussed her feelings regarding religion which seemed fuzzy at best and surprisingly unsophisticated at worst.

Marilyn reluctantly discussed her school days at nearby Emerson Junior High in L.A. and Van Nuys High School out in the Valley where she said, "I was just too adult for the other girls. I filled out my sweaters and walked my walk until the boys all whistled and yelled. They were not ever happy days for me." She continued, "I was only 16 when I found out I was a bastard child and that news didn't make me too popular in school." It seemed there was nothing she wouldn't talk about. "I wasn't always sexy in school. In fact, when I first started junior high school, I was so skinny and sexless that I was called 'Norma Jean, the Human Bean,' and even played a boy's part in my first school play and it wasn't any fun."

George Sanders and coauthor/publisher Ralph Roberts hold George's framed Marilyn Monroe check, nicely set off by photos of Marilyn. This check—a more routine one—is worth $5,000. Her last check, as we shall shortly see, is worth a whole lot more due to its significance.

By 1952—when this photograph (right) was taken of Marilyn and actress Jane Russell placing their handprints in concrete at the famous Grauman's Chinese theater—Marilyn Monroe was on top of the world. Her film career was zooming upwards, millions of men dreamed of her, and the world, so it seemed, was hers merely for the asking.

Final Visit

Later, when she made her fortune portraying breathless, naive, dumb broads, we remembered Monroe as being much smarter than her roles. As a fast-rising star, she'd saunter into the King's Restaurant on Santa Monica Boulevard where we did a disc jockey stint for George Jay or Larry Finley. She didn't come in to be interviewed but rather to rekindle those warm chats we'd had much earlier at The Lark. It wasn't possible because her sudden stardom had changed our perspective. She was now only attainable for the very powerful.

Our final visit with *la* Monroe came in the 1950s when she agreed to serve as a batgirl in a Celebrity charity softball game. She refused to don the standard uniform (shorts and a team T-shirt) that the other female stars like Jane Russell, Marilyn Maxwell, Mona Freeman, Rhonda Fleming, Yvonne DeCarlo, Ava Gardner, Elizabeth Taylor, and Shelley Winters were happily wearing.

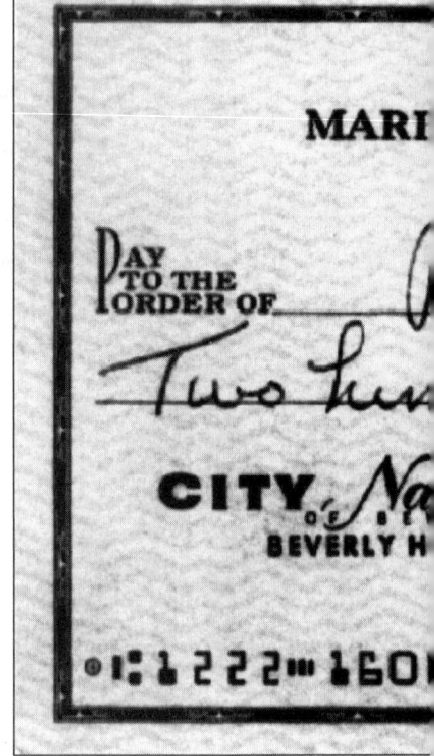

Marilyn popped out of the players' dugout on my arm attired in a sparkling, shocking pink, skintight dress that would have looked fine anywhere but on the pitchers' mound of a Hollywood baseball diamond. (We were playing at the old Gilmore Stadium that was torn down so that CBS TV City could rest upon that hallowed pitchers' mound). Marilyn's ghost may still be searching for the long-gone dugout she once graced so spectacularly.

In any case, like some kind of glowing gypsy moth, she flitted from the center of the playing field to the sidelines oblivious to the glares she was receiving from the more cooperative, properly uniformed starlets and stars on that field. It was Van Nuys High School all over again. The scampering cameramen were of course delighted as Marilyn obligingly bowed low to exhibit voluminous cleavage

Marilyn Monroe's last autograph was on this check (valued at $65,000.00 by the owner). It was written on August 4th, 1962. A few hours later, she was dead (just after midnight on August 5th). Would a woman enthusiastically shopping for and buying furniture for her new house commit suicide? It seems unlikely. She was still working, still a beautiful, voluptuous lady living the dream life.

surpassed only by her engaging toothy smile. No curve could be concealed in that costume and she looked so out of place, even in Hollywood!

Marilyn's Last Check

All of these memories came flooding back to us when a new friend in Dallas, Texas, autograph collector and sometime dealer Danny Cox telephoned to inform us that he had access to a very special Marilyn Monroe artifact owned by Ron Reedy, a CPA from Gainesville, Texas.

It has been reproduced on these pages and as you can see, it is a personal bank check made out to the Pilgrim Modern Furniture Company in Santa Monica for $228.80 worth of household furnishings plus a letter from her auditor that reads: "Dear Bryon, Hope that this suffices--the bank stamp is pale red and does not affect the signature at all. This undeniably is the last check and last time she signed her name as NO other checks were written that day-- Because I had access to her account as auditor, I obviously would have pulled the only checks written that day (August 4, 1962) and there was only this one."

It is a matter of record that on August 4, 1962, according to the officials who investigated her death, she chatted with actor Peter Lawford and asked him for the telephone number of his wife, Pat Kennedy Lawford, in Hyannisport, Massachusetts. Marilyn talked on the phone with Joe DiMaggio's son (by his first marriage to actress Dorothy Arnold) about his broken engagement. She had dinner with her press agent in her new home at 12305 Fifth Helena Drive in LA's Brentwood suburb. Can we assume that the new furniture was for this new home?

At that informal dinner with her press agent, Pat Newcomb, she said she wanted to go to a movie the next day, a Sunday. Sometime on this Saturday, August 4th, she wrote the check you see here. A few hours later, shortly after midnight on August 5th she was dead.

What woman buys furniture and commits suicide on nearly the same day? Could this check be a clue adding a little bit of truth to the theories that Marilyn was killed? We think it might. If true, how very appropriate it would be that her still highly sought-after autograph is what finally brings her killers to justice or, at least, sheds light on the mystery and helps repair her personal honor.

The Marilyn Monroe we knew was never that mercurial and despite her early low self-esteem, not that desperate. Life wasn't always kind to her but she certainly loved every moment of her life as a movie star. She had no reason to end her life; certainly not before her furniture was delivered!

The SANDERS Price Guide to

AUTOGRAPHS

Fifth Edition

Section 4:

ORGANIZATIONS

Being a guide to some of the many fine organizations for autograph collectors and dealers.

Autograph Organizations

Organizations and associations for autograph collectors and dealers are a wonderful adjunct to our glorious hobby. We include some of the better ones in this section. If we've missed your club and you would like it included in our future publications, please send the particulars to us at **Alexander Books**, 65 Macedonia Road, Alexander NC 28701 USA. We'll be delighted to do so.

We must be frank at this point and say that not all is perfect in the autograph world. There is a bit of sniping going on between rival clubs and associations, some dealers, and even competing autograph price guides. (Okay, but we still have the best<g>!) But, as Rodney King advocates, let's all try to get along better together, folks. The organizations below are all good ones. Pick the one or ones you like best—belonging to them will help you and the hobby.

—Ralph Roberts
    Member: I.A.C.C., Manuscript Society, and U.A.C.C.

Chapter 16

I.A.C.C. / I.A.D.A.

by Stephen Koschal, Executive Director

THE INTERNATIONAL AUTOGRAPH COLLECTORS CLUB AND DEALERS ALLIANCE

With a vigor and commitment to excellence, the International Autograph Collectors Club (IACC/DA) has endeavored to heighten awareness of the autograph field in general, and to make much needed improvements. Both plans have met with extraordinary reception. By mixing equally education and enjoyment, we have gained an ever increasing momentum and respect within the autograph community, and to a large degree in other fields as well. It is this rich tapestry of commumity which has been, and will be, our legacy and donation to the preservation of the autograph world.

We were the first organization to combine a collectors club and dealer alliance under the same flag. An international non-profit organization, we are unique as we are exclusively devoted to the collecting of autographs. Some of our membership benefits include:

Our bi-monthly publication *Eyes, Ears & Voice Of The Hobby,* filled with fresh and timely news concerning all things autographic. It will be a valued addition to your permanent reference library.

Our Gerald R. Ford study personally praised by President Ford is available at the Ford Library to be used by scholars and collectors. A complimentary copy of the Ford and our landmark RFK signature study was sent to each member.

Complimentary educational courses conducted at each of our five regional Autograph Extravaganzas. Each member will receive a Certificate of Completion signed by the instructor, who will be one of the most knowledgeable in his or her field. Past speakers include Christophe Jaeckel, Steve Koschal, Kenneth Laurence, Joseph Maddalena and Kenneth Rendell.

IACC/DA innovations include creation of the IACC/DA International Scholarship Fund for collectors in economically depressed areas who can't afford to join a club, and the first autograph authentication service by an organization.

Access to our library of only the finest quality autograph reference materials. Used by researchers, librarians and institution, as well as the finest autograph professionals in the world.

Complimentary educational and autograph catalogues from our roster of 140+ internationally acclaimed professionals who have earned their credentials. Additionally we publish our yearly dealers directory sent to all members which is called by many *"The* Phone Book of Professional Autograph Dealers."

You are invited to share in this rich tradition by becoming a member. Each of our dealer members is happy to consult with you and guide you in the proper direction at no charge. Whether you are developing a new specialty, or continuing a time honored one, you can be assured of prompt and fair service, quality material at competitive prices all from dealers who must adhere to the strictest ethical codes of conduct in the industry.

The 1999 dues to share in this tradition are:

$17.50   Domestic Membership
$25.00   International Membership
$250.00   Lifetime Membership

Separate applications available to autograph dealers.

The IACC/DA may be reached at:

4575 Sheridan Street.
Suite 111, Dept. SPG
Hollywood. FL 33425

Chapter 17

The Manuscript Society

by David R. Smith

The Manuscript Society was founded in 1948 as the National Society of Autograph Collectors, and has grown to an international membership of well over 1,500 members including dealers, private collectors, scholars, authors, and caretakers of public collections, such as librarians, archivists, and curators. There are also many institutional members, such as historical societies, museums, special libraries, and academic libraries.

The Society publishes a quarterly journal, *Manuscripts*, and a newsletter, which are sent to each member without charge. *Manuscripts* has an established reputation for excellent articles reflecting the diverse interests of the autograph field. Issues also have special departments giving news and views on the principal areas of historical and literary collecting, on new and important discoveries and acquisitions, and on auction results. Also featured in *Manuscripts* are dealer and auctioneer advertisements which publicize sources of autographs and related items.

The newsletter features news about the Society and its members. Scholars seeking manuscript material are permitted to place their notices in a special section, and announcements of proposed editions of collected papers also may be made. Warnings of stolen material which may come into the market are faithfully published, as an aid to the victims and a deterrent to thieves.

The Society's chief activity is a three-day annual meeting, held in a community offering good manuscript resources for viewing. The programs feature tours, exhibitions, panel discussions, speakers of note, and social occasions for fellowship and interchange of ideas. Major cities have alternated with smaller communities as the locales for these meetings, in order to provide a varied view of the manuscript riches available throughout the United States.

A comprehensive monograph, entitled *Autographs and Manuscripts: A Collector's Manual*, was published under the auspices of The Manuscript Society by Charles Scribner's Sons in 1978. Its long definitive articles on many aspects of collecting, arranging, and preserving manuscript material, all of them written by experts in their fields, have caused the book to be hailed as a classic treatment of the subject. In 1984, Greenwood Press published *Manuscripts: The First Twenty Years*, an anthology of fifty memorable articles from the Society's journal. Another book—*History in Your Hand: Fifty Years of The Manuscript Society by John M. Taylor*—is now available.

The Manuscript Society welcomes new members. The annual individual membership fee is $35. Contributing memberships are $70, sustaining memberships are $100, and life memberships are $1,000. Memberships are on a calendar year basis—new members joining after July 1 of each year may pay half the annual rate. All moneys go to support the publication program, to aid in the defense of individuals against government agencies in replevin suits, and to maintain the expenses of management of Society affairs.

Additional information about the society may be obtained on their website at **www.manuscript.org**.

To join, the society, contact:

David R. Smith,
Executive Director
THE MANUSCRIPT SOCIETY
350 N. Niagara Street, Dept. SPG
Burbank, CA 91505-3648

Chapter 18

P.A.D.A.

The Professional Autograph Dealers Association, Inc. (P.A.D.A.) was organized in 1995 by many of the nation's leading dealers in historic autograph material. Concerned by the proliferation of new "dealers" lacking expertise, experience, integrity, and fiscal responsibility, PADA's purpose is to raise the standards of the autograph profession by requiring members to adhere to a strict code of ethics when conducting business with collectors, institutions, the general public, and other colleagues.

PADA seeks to encourage interest in and appreciation of the field of autograph collecting. It strives to promote high standards of business ethics, professionalism, and service in the trade. PADA aims to establish a marketplace for autographs in which collectors can buy and sell with confidence, and receive accurate and informed advice from its members.

Membership in PADA is *limited* to dealers who have demonstrated expertise and integrity in buying and selling autographs. All applicants for membership in PADA are carefully screened, and all members must adhere to PADA's strict code of ethics, including its complete guarantee of authenticity. As a result, whether you are buying, selling, or seeking an appraisal of autographs, PADA is your guarantee of quality, service, and integrity.

In addition to a track record of integrity, all members must provide a life-time guarantee of authenticity on the material they sell. Prospective members undergo a rigorous screening process, during which their business history is carefully reviewed and comments by current PADA members are solicited.

PADA members are in all parts of the United States. It is anticipated that as the organization grows, foreign dealers will also join. The present membership includes many leading dealers whose specialties include American and world history, science, literature, music, art, and the performing arts. Dealers who handle primarily contemporary sports and entertainment personalities are ineligible for membership in PADA.

PADA dealers represent a significant market for purchasing autographs, whether single items or entire collections. They can buy autographs outright, offering you a fair price and immediate payment. If you prefer, a PADA dealer can act as your agent for selling material or can take items on consignment, after fully discussing the terms with you. A PADA dealer can also suggest other options for selling your autographs or donating them to an institution.

Believing that PADA fills a strong need in the autograph community, the organization anticipates rapid growth, both in membership and stature. Current plans include trade shows, supporting an internet website, and publications designed to increase knowledge of autographs for collectors and dealers.

For additional information about PADA, check out our extensive website at **www.padaweb.org** or write or phone.

Professional Autograph Dealers Association

P.O. Box 1729-S
Murray Hill Station
New York, NY 10156
1-888-338-4338

Chapter 19

THE U.A.C.C.

(Universal Autograph Collectors Club)

by Bob Erickson, UACC President

The Universal Autograph Collectors Club (U.A.C.C.) is the world's largest organization for autograph collectors with over 2,000 members in the United States, Canada, and more than 25 other countries. Founded in 1965, the U.A.C.C. is a nonprofit educational organization whose purpose is to inform members and the public about all aspects of autograph collecting through its publications, shows, and seminars.

By joining the U.A.C.C., you will receive our renowned 64-page bimonthly journal, *The Pen and Quill,* which features articles and news on autographs in all areas, including U.S. presidents, authors, scientists, aviators, astronauts, royalty, entertainers, athletes, military leaders, Nobel Prize winners, and explorers, to name a few. Studies of authentic, secretarial, Autopen, rubber-stamped, facsimile, and forged signatures help collectors to make informed decisions when purchasing autographic material. Celebrity addresses are published in each issue to assist collectors who enjoy writing for autographs. The U.A.C.C. also sponsors annual literary awards in addition to paying for articles published in *The Pen and Quill.*

You may also have your name and address published as a new member in *The Pen and Quill.* By so doing, you will receive free autograph catalogues from our dealer members and auction houses. Or you can place a free classified ad in *The Pen and Quill* to list your wants, sell your extra material, or just communicate with other members about your common interests.

All members are required to abide by a strict Code of Ethics and violations of that Code are enforced by the U.A.C.C. Ethics Board. By dealing with other U.A.C.C. members, you can be assured that the Ethics Board will assist you in any dispute involving another member who has violated the Code of Ethics. Members who refuse to abide by an Ethics Board decision are subject to sanctions, including expulsion, with notice to members published in *The Pen and Quill*.

The U.A.C.C. also offers its members the opportunity to purchase uncommon autographic material and reference works at affordable prices through the "U.A.C.C. Warehouse" page in *The Pen and Quill*.

The U.A.C.C. sponsors autograph shows in major U.S. cities and London, England featuring educational displays, autograph dealers who abide by the U.A.C.C. Code of Ethics, and celebrity guests. Seminars are occasionally held in conjunction with the shows to educate our members and the public on all aspects of collection and preservation, and identification of non-authentic (bogus or forged) material.

George Sanders, when he was U.A.C.C. Regional Director, with current Treasurer Al Wittnebert.

Finally, the U.A.C.C. sponsors mail auctions through *The Pen and Quill* as well as an annual live floor auction near Washington, DC. These auctions are another avenue to assist our members who buy and sell autographs.

To learn more about the U.A.C.C., send your request for a brochure and membership application to **U.A.C.C., Dept. SPG, PO Box 6181, Washington, DC 20044-6181**. You can also get membership information and an application by visiting our Internet web site at **http://www.uacc.org**. We hope you will join our universe of fellow collectors soon.

The

SANDERS
Price Guide to

AUTOGRAPHS

Fifth Edition

Section 5:

PRICES

Being an explanation of how to best use this price guide and some tens of thousands of prices—by far more than any other autograph price guide!

The immortal big band leader and golden trombonist, Glenn Miller, poses with young CBS radio network band announcer George Sanders prior to World War II. It was a springlike time in the late 30s, with the Great Depression over and things seeming returning to normal. But the fight against Nazi tyranny was just around the corner. Miller would tragically lose his life in the war and George would do his part—a fantastic highly secret contribution and sacrifice to the war effort and for America that we hope to detail in a later book. Above all, the late George Sanders was a patriot!

Chapter 20

How to Use This Price Guide

by Helen Sanders

With some changes, this chapter (of necessity) will be, as in the past, somewhat of a reprise of a similar chapter in the previous editions of our autograph price guides. As before, uncountable hours have gone into the preparation of this book and we have made every effort to be as thorough as possible so that we can bring to you figures that—in our expert opinion—realistically reflect market changes, if any. We urge you to read it despite the fact it may be repetitive and boring, so that you may better understand what we are presenting to you and how to benefit from it.

About Pricing

Over the years one would think that this book should have become easier and easier to compile. This is not the case. We add names, take out names, correct names and replace names with other names. There are names that were inserted in our first edition that we have never seen again. Were they really people? Oh, yes, but they are the people who were encountered only once. It was, perhaps, an early Colonial American history figure whose letter or document came from an old trunk in a musty attic and was saved from the Waste Management truck by some observant friend, neighbor or relative who was curious enough to read its contents and conclude it should be saved for posterity. It was then rescued by an alert autograph dealer who identified the signer in *Appleton's*, placed it in his catalogue, priced it and sold it to a lover of American history and we never saw the name again. What about the price? The price today is the same as it was when originally placed in the price guide. Is that fair? Isn't it worth more today than when it was first listed? Probably. But how do you arrive at a fair price for a one-of-a-kind item that has only been offered once? Maybe you could offer it at the inflation rate over the 10 years it has been listed?

I think not. I think that the next owner of a similar piece signed by the same Colonial American should have a right to name his own price, be it lower or higher than the original price stated. That is why this is called a price guide. Your GUIDE is whatever the price is in the book and you are encouraged to sell your piece at whatever you feel is fair value, just as you are encouraged to offer whatever you feel is fair value when purchasing an item. The prices are the result of gathering hundreds and hundreds of prices of similar items signed by the same person and offered in the best and most trustworthy catalogues from all over the world, averaging them and, where appropriate, overlaying that so-called average with expert opinion; and then presenting them to you. What I am trying to say once again is "there is no single price for a signature, letter, document, autograph letter signed or signed photograph." What you are viewing in this book is equivalent to the fingerprints of the thousands of people represented herein and just like fingerprints there are no two alike. Therefore, while the prices are based on extensive market research, they are also approximate values, involving matters of my professional taste and opinion.

In recent years, you have seen much duplication of material offered in catalogs; dozens of Washingtons, Edisons, Einsteins as well as unlimited supplies of current actors, actresses. You might then say to yourself that there is no rarity here, maybe I'll wait. I can pick one up any old time. You have probably seen so many things in such quantity this past year that you feel these offerings to be superfluous and certainly redundant.

What you must consider is the fact that the autograph market is growing so fast that these so-called redundant pieces are quickly absorbed into the marketplace and may not be seen again for another generation or two or even three.

Because Someone's Gone Missing

This particular edition has certainly been the most difficult to compile for me personally. How can I express the loss of my mate of over 50 years, the father of our three children, my travel-all-over-the-world companion, my laughing companion, my go-to-the-movies companion, my gin rummy pal, my watch baseball-football-tennis friend, my read-it-to-each-other game, my share-it-with-each-other partner. How can you not miss the loss of someone who made a happy world for you for over 50 years. George is gone! I hope to another happy world, but I can *tell* you he's gone, although I still have a hard time *believing* it. Too many things remain. Too many pieces of paper. Too many presidents hung on the wall— An empty chair behind his desk. No one to fix breakfast for. Too many memories! Sorry! I tend to get maudlin.

No it wasn't easy to do this book because someone is missing.

Unfortunately, somewhere out there in "autograph land" was somebody else telling anybody who would listen to him that *he* was going to "fill the shoes." That George had asked him to "fill the shoes."

My response to that? My Editor? NO!!! George's Editor? NO!!! Ralph's Editor? NO!!! *Ad Infinitum*. Said, not in anger. None of the rumors spread by that person are true. Said, in sorrow.

As we have repeated over the years this is not an exact science and as we have discovered via our scanners, there are 256 shades of gray. Those differentials are there for you to use. Content and condition are only two of those 256 shades of gray for you to use as your guide for buying or selling autographic material. The figures presented to you within the confines of this book are there to guide you! *Ergo*: You may safely buy or sell on each side of the price and, let's face it, we have a small group of dealers who specialize in absolutely exquisite material! You will pay more for this material because it is worth more! I sincerely hope that sometime during your collecting career you will be able to acquire such a piece. You will not be sorry!

In the case of one-of-a-kind material that is rare, the price you see is the only price found and it will not become an average until other pieces are found. If you are fortunate enough to come across a one-of-a-kind treasure you will at least have some idea of its value and a starting point.

We have found that some dealers (and even buyers and sellers) oppose a single price given for an item within a category. Please realize, however, what great latitude you have within that given amount. On either side of a $500 price for both buyers and sellers you have the options that are built in because you are given a so-called average price. Therefore, if you have a piece that is better, prettier, cleaner, or more desirable in any way, it is going to sell for more than average. The opposite is true if whatever is offered is less desirable. The price latitude can again be increased or decreased according to the clientele to which the material is offered as well as the guarantee that may or may not be included.

I apologize for the repetition but it is necessary for all of the readers of this book to understand the way prices are derived. The prices used in this book are for similar types of pieces, in similar condition, signed in ink with a full signature of at least the last name and one initial; gathered from all geographical areas of this country and overseas. I must say again—there are no two alike!! Therefore, if there is a price published for a specific person in a particular category of, let's say, $500.00, that is your GUIDE because you can rest assured that in order to get an AVERAGE of $500.00 there had to be higher and lower figures to arrive at this amount. In providing a single number to cover these variables, the authors express their judgement what values for similar items in fine condition should be. The number produced—by definition—is approximate.

The exception to pricing may well be in the area of contemporary movie and television personalities. Because of the fact that 8x10 inch photographs are in plentiful supply due to technological improvements in duplication, there is no lack of supply and the dealer prices them quite close to whatever his cost was and his proximity to a supply of genuine signatures. As long as the celebrity is still alive and the supply of photographs and 3x5 cards is more or less infinite, the price will be directly proportional to the celebrity's popularity or the hype dedicated to his/her newest endeavor. Blockbuster hits can bring about a sudden demand for a certain personality's signature/photograph that escalates prices until the demand is filled at which time there will be deflation until the next personality's blockbuster hits the market. It's pretty much like the stock market.

Classic stars are, of course, not subject to these fluctuations. The Clark Gables, Vivian Leighs, John Waynes, Charlie Chaplins, Greta Garbos, Judy Garlands and Marilyn Monroes etc. are accepted as genuine 'classics' and demand classic prices. Even their supporting players have found a place in this category.

Because autographs are not a manufactured item, there is no Manufacturer's List Price or Fair Traded Price or a discount off of either one. Also, this is not a commodities product or a listed stock on the Dow or the Nasdaq. It is also nothing that is quoted at so much an ounce that can be purchased on an international exchange. Therefore we have to study the prices that ARE available in retail catalogues, private offerings and, in the case of singular pieces, reliable auction prices. We also confer with certain dealers whose products we know to be authentic. We weigh these and other factors to determine the price for each piece within its category. Therefore, as written in previous paragraphs, the prices in this guide represent opinions of what we believe to be the average price for a fine item offered by an informed dealer to an informed buyer.

The sale of a particular item can be higher if the signature of the celebrity has local or personal interest, if the item has exceptional content or if the item is in short supply due to a sudden surge of interest. A collector might also be in need of something specific to complete a topical collection or a set and, of course, rarity, most assuredly, will send a piece well over book value.

Conversely, sales are often made *under* book value due to overstocking, a change in popularity, lack of current interest and shrewd bargaining. We still reflect average prices and your judgment is still needed in deciding whether items in question are of more or less value than the average price. In the Entertainment category, the more common, less popular celebrities fall into lower priced material as a whole with signatures going for $5.00 to $10.00 or $15-$20 and Signed Photographs for $15-$25.

As a reprise for this rather wandering explanation of *Prices:* Although the individual pieces together are <u>similar</u>, the prices for them can be very<u>dissimilar</u> because of the personal assessments and appraisals given by the individual sellers. Even the locale of the various dealers and their financial condition at the time of their offering can make a considerable difference. The important thing to remember is that because of the tremendous growth of interest in autographs since the publication of the 4th edition, the valuations in your fifth edition are going to give you a wider price range in which to work than ever before, even though the current price quoted may be the unchanged or slightly lower. There have been higher highs and lower lows. Use this information to your own advantage.

There are, as always, exceptions to averages. If, after going through all the pricing material available to us, we have found only <u>one</u> price to report then that is the price you will see. Such is the case when there is a new listing and when there is great rarity. Also the prices that change due to private sales or on a trade bases are not recorded due to lack of first hand knowledge.

Condition

Just as it is in the collecting of coins, stamps, antiques, vintage cars and any collectible, condition is only one of the important considerations in autograph collecting. The prices quoted in this guide are for autographs in fine condition. Extra-fine letters, documents, cut signatures and so forth demand a higher price. Tattered, foxed, stained, wrinkled pieces decrease the value. So, within the price averages that you are given you must also consider the condition.

Pricing Categories

Although there are more than four price categories in autographs, we have chosen the four most important ones for this guide. They well cover the vast majority of autograph items you will encounter, and exceptions may be interpolated from these prices. Following are the definitions we shall use:

Signature(SIG). This is the price that a signature is worth—that is, just the actual signature itself on a card, cut out of a letter, a page from an autograph album; may or may not be accompanied by date and/or place, etc.

Letter or Document Signed (LS/DS). An example of more recent pieces might be a typed letter or document signed by a celebrity. During the nineteenth century, before the invention of the typewriter, it was common for secretaries, clerks or relatives to prepare handwritten letters or documents for signatures.

Autograph Letter Signed (ALS). Generally the most important category except in the entertainment field where a signed photograph seems to take priority. This is a letter (or document) completely written in the hand of and signed by the important personage.

Signed Photograph (SP). This can also include signed portrait engravings, woodcuts, photo reproductions, caricatures. Signed original cartoon drawings are designated with an asterisk (*) after the cartoonist's name and are found in the SP column. Reproductions of works of art and signed by the artist are shown in the Comment column.

(SPc..Signed Postcard) or sometimes (SP Pc) Are usually found in the Comment column.

(AMUSQS. *Autograph Musical Quotation Signed... Sometimes* AMQS *when room does not permit in Comment column)*

Major Autograph Categories

The current format for autograph categories may please or upset you. We have maintained a column to identify the category of each entry. In many cases the person is notable in more than one classification. We have identified him/her or them with the category in which the person(s) is most commonly known or collected. In addition, we have given you a "Comment" column to further enhance the information.

In some cases we have included prices in the "Comment" column for special material that could not be included in the averages because they were outside the normal trading range or for material that is not listed as a Category. Unfortunately, because of the size of the column and the amount of information contained in it we have had to abbreviate much of what it contains.

It has become increasingly more and more difficult to manage the LS/DS column due to its inclusion of two different categories. We hoped to divide it in this edition so that we could more clearly delineate the prices but found it impossible to do at this time due to other pressing matters. It is a future plan.

A Final Word

Every effort has been made to provide you with an authoritative, well-researched accounting of current prices as is humanly and electronically possible. We have retrieved thousands and thousands of figures, tabulated them, averaged them, and entered them into what has become our permanent database, applying our expert interpolation to the entire process. We wish that it could have been possible to retrieve all this information from someone else's database so that it might have been presented to you at least six months earlier along with the new names, new prices, dates and comments which we now send to you. Alas, we have to do our own original work and research.

The raw numbers have come from every corner of our country as well as from Great Britain, France, Germany, Switzerland, Scandinavia and Canada. Signed original autograph manuscripts and signed books with values over and above the signature are not included. The comment column contains (whenever applicable) prices for items over and above those carried in the averages as well as musical quotations signed. These all reflect a special added value.

Please note that *some* presidential entries have both presidential and non-presidential records. We have found, however, that in many cases the values do not fluctuate greatly between the two.

Some Civil War letters and documents etc., have both war and non-war prices. As before, in the case of extreme rarity in any category we have reported the prices available to us.

We have presented to you "The Market As We See It." We have not created this market; therefore you may find incongruities whereby an Autograph Letter Signed is priced lower than a Letter/Document Signed and sometimes Signed Photographs are significantly more valuable in a specific category because of a particular group interest. I repeat, we have not created this market but we have given you an unbiased list of collectible autograph material.

If a price was not changed, it most likely indicates there has been no current sale or the change either up or down was too minor to record so it was left unaltered. In some instances of rare material NRPA indicates that because of its rarity there was "NO RECENT PRICE AVAILABLE".

Please do not think these figures are reflections of a particular autograph personality's ability, intelligence, greatness, popularity or beauty. The valuations are based on material from all over the world and are given to you so that you can make knowledgeable judgments regarding purchases or sales. They are approximative statements of opinion (except for single price itmes) by the Sanders Guide authors and editors, based on actual transactions.We sometimes have great long lists of celebrities of one category or another sent to us accompanied by an indignant letter questioning why these people are not listed in our book. To this we must answer that unless you send documentation as to what you paid and/or what you are selling these pieces for we cannot just put them in the price guide and make up a price. As I said before, we do not create the prices, but we do interpret them and report them.

The prices given in this book are retail prices—that is, the price you *would pay* for a given item. If you are going to sell to a dealer, a legitimate offer to you would be about half of the fair retail value taking into consideration the price range that we have already discussed. This is not much different than selling any collectible to a dealer, be it a work of art, jewelry, or an oriental rug. Since the dealer may have to hold the piece for an indeterminate number of months or years before selling it plus whatever his costs may be in its sale, this is a fair markup. You may, of course, bargain and haggle.

Because of the vastness and the ad infinitum concept of this publication and the electronic contribution that makes it possible, there may be errors. For this we apologize and continually update our database as we find these errors or when they are called to our attention.

We sincerely hope you will find this book helpful to you. Remember, this is not an encyclopedia but we have added dates and other information that could be helpful to you. We hope, also, that you find our price guide an enjoyable tool to use and one that is of great benefit to you. As always, we welcome your suggestions on improving our autograph price guides and we welcome you specialists in your particular fields who have special information and prices that you might want to share with other collectors.

Please send your comments to us at:

Helen Sanders
Autograph House
P.O. Box 658
Enka, NC 28728
828-667-9835

e-mail:**sanderspg@ioa.com**
website:**www.autograph-book.com**

ADOPT
A
HIGHWAY

AUTOGRAPH HOUSE
HELEN AND GEORGE
SANDERS

ROADSIDE
CLEANUP
AHEAD

Helen and George Sanders doing one of George's dear-to-heart projects—cleanup!

The
SANDERS
Price Guide to
AUTOGRAPHS

Fifth Edition

Explanations of Headings

NAME	Name of a person or group
DATE	Birth and/or death dates
CATEGORY	Artist, entertainer, writer, etc.
SIG	Signature
DS/LS	A signed letter or other document.
ALS	Autograph Letter Signed, i.e. written entirely in the hand of the celebrity
SP	Signed photograph
*	Signed art instead of photograph
(WD)	War Date

Chapter 21

Prices

Editor's Note: *The prices here are general autograph prices; i.e. all categories except sports-related. For Sports names, please refer to* **The Sanders Price Guide to Sports Autographs** *(3rd edition, 1999). Order at 1-800-472-0438.*

A

NAME	DATE	CATEGORY	SIG	LS/DS	ALS	SP	COMMENTS
Aadland, Beverly		Entertainment	6	15		13	Errol Flynn's paramour & Last Companion
AAlton, Alvar		Architect	110	250		125	Finnish Architect-Designer
Aames, Willie		Entertainment	10	20		24	Actor. Eight Is Not Enough Co-Star
Abba		Entertainment	42			78	Swedish Superstar Pop Group (4)
Abba, Marta		Entertainment	15		40	72	It. Actress
Abbado, Claudio		Entertainment	15			50	Symph. & Opera Conductor
Abbe, Cleveland	1838-1916	Science	15		50	35	Co-Founder US Weather Service 1869
Abbey, Edwin Austin		Artist	15	30	50		Am.Portraitist, Illustrator
Abbot, Charles Greeley		Science	12	50		29	Am. Astrophysicist
Abbott & Costello		Entertainment	567	955		1155	Radio, Film, TV Comedy Team. SP p/c $700
Abbott, Bessie		Entertainment	25			45	Opera
Abbott, Bud	1895-1974	Entertainment	212	348	265	450	Radio, Film, TV Comedian
Abbott, George	1887-1995	Entertainment	25		54	92	Producer/Director/Playwright
Abbott, Henry Larcom	1831-1927	Civil War	30	45	82		Union Gen. Sig/Rank $45
Abbott, Henry Livermore	1842-64	Civil War	108	210			Union Gen. Sig/Rank $125. Killed at Wilderness
Abbott, John		Entertainment	6			12	
Abbott, John S.C.		Author	12		40		
Abbott, Lyman	1835-1922	Clergy	25	45	75	45	Congregational Minister-Author
Abdnor, James		Congress	5	15		10	Senator SD
Abdul, Paula		Entertainment	18		50	60	Singer-Dancer
Abel, I.W.		Labor	10	25	40	25	Pres. United Steel Workers
Abel, Walter	1898-1987	Entertainment	15	32	30	63	Vint. Char. Actor-Leading Man
Abercrombie, John J (WD)		Civil War	55	102	188		Union Gen. ALS '64 $525
Abercrombie, John J.	1798-1877	Civil War	52	105	130		Union Gen. ALS '64 $525
Aberdeen, Lord, 4th Earl	1784-1860	Head of State	35	45	97		Br. Prime Minister
Abernathy, Ralph D.	1926-90	Clergy	38	75	125	67	Civil Rights Leader. Deputy to Martin Luther King
Abernathy, Thomas Gerstle		Congress	5	10		10	Congressman MS
Abernethy, John	1764-1831	Science	45	65	185		Br. Surgeon. Devised External Iliac Artery Surgery
Abraham, F. Murray		Entertainment	11	22	35	34	AA Winner. Amadeus
Abrahamson, James		Military	10			30	

NAME	DATE	CATEGORY	SIG	LS/DS	ALS	SP	COMMENTS
Abrams, Creighton W.	1912-74	Military	20	30	45	70	Gen. WW II Tank Commander
Abrams, Elliott		Diplomat	10	20		25	State Dept.
Abruzzo, Ben A.		Aviation	32			80	
Abt, Franz		Composer	75		200		
Abzug, Bella		Politician	14	15	46	20	Lawyer, Congresswoman NY.Deceased
AC/DC		Entertainment	45	100		115	Rock Group. Signed by All. Color Poster S $150
Acheson, Dean	1893-1971	Cabinet	25	82	95	93	Sec'y State for Truman. Implemented Marshall Plan
Acheson, George R.		Military	5		20	15	
Acland, Arthur Wm.	1805-1877						SEE Hood, Arth.W.
Acosta, Bert		Aviation	40	60	135	95	
Acquanetta, Burna		Entertainment	10			35	Actress. Pin-up $45
Acton, Loren		Astronaut	8		35	25	
Acuff, Roy		Country Music	16		35	42	Grand Ole Opry Star. Deceased
Adair, Allen		Military	20		55	65	Br. Gen. Operation Mkt. Garden
Adair, John		Governor	40	125	185		Early Gov. KY
Adair, Red		Celebrity	20	35	55	30	Oil Well Fires
Adam 12 (Cast Of)		Entertainment	20			45	Kent McCord, Martin Milner
Adam, Adolphe-Charles	1803-1856	Composer	40	125	297	108	Opera & Ballet (Giselle). O Holy Night
Adamic, Louis		Author	15	58	110	45	Am. Novelist. Born Yugoslavia
Adamowski, Timothee		Composer	10			25	AMusQS $45
Adams, Suzanne		Entertainment	50			290	Opera. Great Coloratura Soprano. SP Pc $150
Adams, Abigail		First Lady	563	1825	5125		
Adams, Alva		Governor	5		15	10	Gov. CO
Adams, Andrew		Rev. War	115	388	440		Continental Congress
Adams, Ansel	1902-84	Artist	125	351	475	288	Photographer, TLS/Content $450
Adams, Brooke		Entertainment	6	8	16	15	Actress. Pin-up $40
Adams, Bryan		Entertainment	20			50	Rock
Adams, Charles Francis	1807-86	Author-Diplomat	40	150	195		Civil War Ambassador to Eng. Pres. U.P. RR
Adams, Clara		Aviation	45			70	Pioneer Zeppelin Flyer. 1st
Adams, Daniel W.	1821-72	Civil War	165	295	825		CSA Gen. Sig/Rank $250, War Dte. DS $400
Adams, Dawnn		Entertainment	4			15	Actress
Adams, Don		Entertainment	6	8	14	28	Actor.Get Smart. Voice Artist
Adams, Edie		Entertainment	5	10	20	17	Singer-Actress/Ernie Kovac's Widow
Adams, Edwin	1834-77	Entertainment	15			45	Vintage Stage Actor
Adams, Gerry		Head of State	60	75			Leader Sinn Fein, IRA
Adams, Hannah	1755-1831	Author			350		Historian.May be 1st Fem. Am. Professional Writer
Adams, Harriet		Author	35	45	65		
Adams, Henry Brooks	1838-1918	Author	110	395	450		Am. Historian, Philosopher, Critic
Adams, J. Q. and J. Monroe		Presidents		2467			Signed by Both
Adams, James S.		Business	10	35	45	25	
Adams, Joe E.		Entertainment	5			25	Comedian
Adams, Joey		Entertainment	4	8		10	Comedian
Adams, Joey Lauren		Entertainment	6			30	Actress. Pin-Up $48
Adams, John	1735-1826	President	1696	6660	12050		AMsS $33,350, FF $2500,as Pres.$3200. LS $15000
Adams, John	1778-1854	Congress	25		40		Early MOC. NY

NAME	DATE	CATEGORY	SIG	LS/DS	ALS	SP	COMMENTS
Adams, John	1825-64	Civil War	235	640			CSA Gen. KIA (WD) DS $2350, S $400-$495
Adams, John Couch	1812-92	Astronomer	32	45	130		Discoverer of Neptune
Adams, John Q. & Monroe, James		Presidents		2650			Signed By Both Presidents
Adams, John Quincy	1767-1848	President	367	1265	1829		Engr.S $2990-$12,500.ALS/Cont.$25,000. FF $450
Adams, Julie		Entertainment	8	20		20	Actress. Westerns, Horror Sci-Fi SP $30
Adams, Louisa Catherine	1775-1852	First Lady	325	475	1138		Wife of John Q. Adams. Only Foreign Born 1st Lady
Adams, Mason		Entertainment	8			15	Character Actor. Films, TV, Radio. Familiar Voice
Adams, Maud (current)		Entertainment	8	8	16	25	Actress. Pin-up $40
Adams, Maude	1872-1953	Entertainment	42		85	125	Am. Stage Actress. 'Peter Pan'
Adams, Nick		Entertainment	175	285		362	Actor. The Rebel. Died Young
Adams, Samuel	1722-1803	Rev. War	695	1930	3933		Signer Decl. of Indepen.AMsS $9500
Adams, Sherman		Governor	20	75	110	45	Eisenhower Asst., Gov. NH
Adams, Stanley		Composer	15	25	45	25	Lyricist
Adams, Suzanne		Entertainment	60			295	Opera. Great Coloratura Soprano. SP Pc S $150
Adams, William T. (Oliver Optic)	1822-97	Author	20	25	60	55	Various Popular Series Books For Boys
Adams, William Wirt (WD)		Civil War	365		1368		CSA General
Adams, William Wirt	1819-88	Civil War	275	505	618		CSA Gen.
Adamson, James C.		Astronaut	5			20	
Adamson, William C.		Congress	7	20		30	19th Cent. Congressman GA
Addams, Charles*		Cartoonist	68			425	Addams Family
Addams, Dawn		Entertainment	5			15	Actress
Addams, Jane	1860-1935	Am. Social Worker	65	312	278	322	Social Reformer, Nobel Peace
Addington, Henry	1757-1844	Head of State	35	75	125		Sidmouth, 1st Viscount. Prime Minister. Eng.
Addinsell, Richard	1940-77	Composer	12	30	150	35	Br.' Warsaw Concerto'
Addis, Don*		Cartoonist	10			35	
Addison, Joseph	1672-1719	Author	93	200	340		Br. Poet, Essayist, Playwright
Ade, George	1866-1944	Author	25	75	150	65	Am. Humorist, Dramatist. AQS $50
Adelaide, Queen England	1792-1849	Royalty	45		135		Queen of William IV. Adelaide, Australia Namesake
Adenauer, Konrad (der Alte)		Head of State	38	200	188	177	1st Chan. Fed. Rep. of Germany
Ader, Rose		Entertainment	28			85	Opera
Adjani, Isabelle		Entertainment	20			75	Opera
Adler, Alfred	1870-1937	Science	110	560	1255	195	Psychiatrist. ALS/Content $2,000
Adler, Buddy		Entertainment	10			25	Film Producer
Adler, Felix B.		Entertainment	20			45	Professional Clown
Adler, Larry	1914-	Entertainment	20			35	Harmonica Virtuoso. AMusQS $75
Adler, Luther	1903-1984	Entertainment	10	20	25	30	Vintage Actor-Stage & Film
Adler, Max		Business	15		40	35	Pres.Sears, Roebuck. Philanthropy
Adler, Richard		Composer	15	30	55	35	AMusQS $35-$135
Adler, Stella		Entertainment	20		25	30	Drama Teacher & Coach
Adoree, Renee		Entertainment	30	45		80	Vintage Film Star. Early Talkies.
Adrian, Edgar Lord	1889-1977	Science	30	45	135	65	Nobel Physiology
Adrian, Iris		Entertainment	9	15	15	22	Character Actress. 30's-40's Deceased
Aerosmith (All)		Entertainment	75	250		171	Rock Superstars
Affleck, Ben		Entertainment	15			60	Actor Good Will Hunting
Aga Khan III, Sultan	1877-1957	Royalty	95	300	275		Sultan Sir Mohammed Shah.

NAME	DATE	CATEGORY	SIG	LS/DS	ALS	SP	COMMENTS
Aga Khan IV		Royalty	15	40	85	35	
Agar, John		Entertainment	4	10	13	22	Actor. Westerns. Shirley Temple's 1st Husband
Agassiz, Alexander	1835-1910	Science	20		45		Son of Louis. Naturalist
Agassiz, Jean Louis	1807-73	Science	85	145	289	631	Swiss-Am. Zoologist, Biologist
Agnew, Spiro	1918-96	Vice President	35	150	210	77	VP-Resigned. Special Bumper Sticker S. $150
Agnus, Felix	1839-1925	Civil War	30	55			165th NY. Union Gen'l. War Date ALS $250
Aguinaldo, Emilio		Head of State	100	140	172	140	Filipino Leader Against Spain
Agutter, Jenny		Entertainment	5	6	12	25	British Emmy Winner. Pin-up $55
Aherne, Brian	1902-86	Entertainment	15	15	23	48	British Leading Man. Films from 1924
Ahidjo, Ahmadou		Head of State	15		120	40	(Cameroon)
Ahlfors, Lars V., Dr.		Science	10	25		25	
Aiello, Danny		Entertainment	8	16	25	28	Pleasant Character Actor. Stage-Films-TV
Aiken, Alfred L.	1870-1946	Banker	10		25		Pres. Several Banks. Helped Organize Fed. Reserve
Aiken, Conrad	1889-1973	Author	30	93	155	45	Am.Novelist, Poet. Pulitzer
Aiken, George D.		Senate	20	25		30	Senator & Gov. VT
Aiken, John W.		Political	20			30	Socialist Pres. Cand.1936
Aiken, Susan		Entertainment	5	6	9	18	Miss America
Aiken, William		Governor	10	15	30	20	Gov. & Congressman SC
Ailey, Alvin	1931-90	Entertainment	100			150	Am. Dancer, Choreogr. Founder Am. Dance Theatre
Ainger, Alfred		Clergy	10	15	30	25	
Airy, George B.	1801-92	Science	42	130	265		Br. Royal Astronomer
Aitken, Robert	1734-1802	Printer	87	180	360		!st English Bible Printed in Am
Aitken, Robert Grant		Science	12	20	45		Astronomer
Aitken, Robert Ingersoll		Artist	30	75	170		Am. Sculptor Military Statues
Akbar, Taufik		Astronaut	5			20	Indonesia
Akers Peter		Clergy	35	45	60		
Akers, Elizabeth		Author	5		20	15	
Akers, Tom		Astronaut	10			18	
Akhmatova, Anna	1888-1966	Author					Russian Lyric Poet. Russia's Greatest. AMS $2800
Akihito & Machiko (Both)		Royalty	440				Emperor & Empress of Japan
Akihito, Emperor of Japan		Royalty	475	540	650	350	
Akin, Susan		Entertainment	5	6	9	18	Miss America
Akin, Warren	1811-77	Civil War	50	78	98		CSA Congress. Whig Candidate for Gov. GA
Akins, Claude		Entertainment	9	12	18	25	Character Actor. Deceased
Akins, Zoe		Author	10	25	50	20	Poet, Playwright. Pulitzer
Akroyd, Dan		Entertainment	10	55	35	45	Comedian-Actor
Al Fayed, Mohammed		Business	40	95			Billionaire Owner of Harrod's. Father of Dodi
Al-Said, Sultan		Astronaut	10			35	Saudi Arabia
Alabama (signed by all 4)		Country Music	30			85	
Alard, Nelly		Entertainment	4			10	
Albanese, Licia		Entertainment	35	45	60	75	It. Soprano. Opera, Concert
Albani, Emma, Dame	1847-1930	Entertainment	55	60	118	190	Canadian Soprano. Opera. AMusQS $40, SP Pc $85
Albee, Edward	1928-	Author	15	112	95	82	Am. Dramatist. Pulitzer. Virginia Wolfe
Alberghetti, Anna Maria		Entertainment	10			40	Singer-Actress. Pin-Up $35
Albert I (Belgium)		Royalty	25	115	165	50	

NAME	DATE	CATEGORY	SIG	LS/DS	ALS	SP	COMMENTS
Albert III (Rainier-Monaco)		Royalty	95	200	435	135	
Albert Victor, Duke of Athlone		Royalty	150		1250	550	Eldest Son Edward VII
Albert, Carl		Congress	10	15	20	25	Speaker of the House. OK
Albert, Don		Entertainment	25			50	Trumpet & Bandleader
Albert, Eddie		Entertainment	9	35	38	27	Actor.Green Acres. 100's Versatile Roles
Albert, Edward		Entertainment	10			20	Actor Son of Eddie
Albert, Marv		Entertainment	5	5	8	12	TV Host. Sports Ann'cer
Albert, Prince (Victoria)	1819-61	Royalty	165	406	472		Consort of Queen Victoria
Albert, Stephen		Entertainment	20			35	Pulitzer, AMusQS $75
Albertson, Frank		Entertainment	15	20		30	
Albertson, Jack	1910-81	Entertainment	25	30	46	46	Actor. Oscar Winner
Albertson, Joseph A.		Business	8	10	20	20	Fndr. Large Am. Grocery Chain
Albom, Mitch		Author	4	6	8	8	Tuesdays With Morrie
Albright, Charles (C.W.)		Congress	15	20	35		Union Col. CW, Congressman PA
Albright, Lola		Entertainment	10	10	20	20	Early TV Series Star
Albright, Madeleine		Statesman	20			40	1st woman Secretary of State
Albritton, Louise		Entertainment	15	15	30	30	Promising Actress. Early Death
Albury, Charles Donald, Capt.		Aviation	20	45	60	55	
Alcock, J. & Brown A..W.		Aviation	465			985	Signed by Both Pioneer Aviators
Alcock, John William	1892-1919	Aviation	295	495	685	600	Pioneer Aviator/A.W. Brown
Alcorn, James Lusk	1816-94	Civil War	82	145	315		CSA Gen. U.S. Sen. & Postwar Gov. MS
Alcott, Amos Bronson		Author	40	85	135		Social, Civil, Education Reform
Alcott, Louisa May	1832-88	Author	210	290	445		1 pg AMsS $3500
Alda, Alan		Entertainment	12	15	30	28	TV-Film Star. M*A*S*H SP $40
Alda, Frances	1883-1952	Entertainment	65			85	Opera. New Zealand Born Soprano
Alda, Robert	1914-86	Entertainment	10	15		25	Stage-TV-Film Actor. Father of Alan
Aldasoro, Eduardo		Aviation	15		55	40	
Aldasoro, J. Pablo		Aviation	15		55	35	
Aldington, Richard	1892-1962	Author	25	125	170	35	Br. Poet, Novelist,Biographer
Aldred, Joel		Aviation-WWII	18	38	50	65	Canadian ACE WW II
Aldred, Norman		Entertainment	12	25	48	55	Radio Personality
Aldred, Stephanie		Entertainment	5			20	Actress
Aldrich, Bess Streeter	1881-1954	Author	5	15	35	40	Am. Novelist,Short Story Writer
Aldrich, Louis	1843-1901	Entertainment	15			50	Vintage Actor
Aldrich, Nelson W.		Senate	10	15		20	Senator NY
Aldrich, Thomas Bailey	1836-1907	Author	35			225	Novels, Poetry, Editor
Aldridge, Kay	1917-95	Entertainment	6			30	40's Serial Star. Perils of Nyoka
Aldrin, Edwin 'Buzz'		Astronaut	80	247	300	277	2nd Moonwalker. Important TLS $1000-$2000
Aleichem, Shalom	1859-1916	Author			3100		Rus.Born Jewish Writer-Humorist
Aler, John		Entertainment	10			32	
Alexander I (Rus)	1777-1825	Royalty	308	1301	895		Czar or Russia. Helped defeat Napolean
Alexander II (Rus)	1818-88	Royalty	225	760	1428		Assassinated
Alexander III (Pope)		Clergy		45000			Very Rare
Alexander III (Rus)	1845-94	Royalty		525	688		Czar of Russia. Cabinet SP/Czarina $2500
Alexander, Albert, Sir		Statesman	20				Br.M.P

NAME	DATE	CATEGORY	SIG	LS/DS	ALS	SP	COMMENTS
Alexander, Barton S.	1819-78	Civil War	55	75	95		Union Gen. War Dte. S $90, DS $125
Alexander, Ben		Entertainment	55			195	Jack Webb Sidekick Dragnet. Deceased
Alexander, Cecil Frances		Clergy	10	20	25	35	
Alexander, Clifford, Jr.	1933-	Cabinet	10		25	25	Sec'y Army under Carter. Chmn. EEOC
Alexander, Edward P.	1835-1910	Civil War	268	700	1062		CSA General.
Alexander, Edward Porter (WD)		Civil War	550	925	3075		CSA General. War Dte. ALS/Cont. $6500
Alexander, George		Entertainment	5	8	15	15	
Alexander, Harold R.L., Sir	1891-1969	Military	75	90	163	110	Alexander of Tunis, WW II
Alexander, Henry		Business	3	7	15	10	
Alexander, J. B.		Governor	10			20	Guam
Alexander, Jane		Entertainment	7	10	14	20	Actress, Stage-Film-TV. Arts Activist
Alexander, Jason		Entertainment	20	50		50	Multi-Talented Actor-Singer. 'Seinfeld'. Emmy
Alexander, John		Entertainment	20			40	Played T. Roosevelt. 'Arsenic & Old Lace'
Alexander, Joshua Wallis		Cabinet	15	40		25	Sec'y Commerce, Congress MO
Alexander, Lamar		Governor	12			20	Gov. TN. 2X Pres. Candidate
Alexander, Robert		Rev. War	30	65			
Alexander, William (Lord Stirling)		Military-Rev. War	250	725	1388		Gen. in Continental Army
Alexander, William, Archbishop		Clergy	20	30	40	35	
Alexanderson, Ernst F. W.		Science	60	115	195		Father of Television
Alexandra (Edw VII)	1844-1925	Royalty	125		302	430	Dan. Queen of Edw.VII (Eng.)Coronation SP $1500
Alexandra (Nich. II Rus.)	1872-1918	Royalty	150				Empress Russ. ALS/Content $5,000. Assassinated
Alexis, Kim		Entertainment	12			28	Actress. Pin-Up $40
Alfano, Franco		Composer					AMusQS $285, AMusQS $120 (3 bars mus.)
Alfieri, Carlo		Entertainment	10		35	35	Opera
Alfono, Heradio		Aviation	15			35	
Alfonso II	1533-97	Royalty		2750			Alfonso d'Este, Duke Ferrara.
Alfonso V	1396-1458	Royalty		3250			Aragon, Naples & Sicily. Magnanimo
Alfonso XIII (Sp)	1886-1941	Royalty	140	500	625	500	
Alfonso, Kristian		Entertainment	5			15	Pin-up $25
Alford, Henry		Clergy	5	20	30	25	
Alfred, Prince		Royalty	25	35	75		2nd Son of Queen Victoria
Alfven, Hannes		Science	20	30	45	30	Nobel Physics
Alger, Horatio	1832-99	Author	135	215	340	245	Popular Books For Boys
Alger, Russell Alexander	1836-1907	Civil War, Cabinet	50	60	85	92	Union Gen., Gov. MI, Sec'y War
Algren, Nelson		Author	25	60	185	50	Am. Novelist. Naturalistic Novels
Ali Khan, R. (Prince)		Royalty	15		90	45	
Alice in Chains		Entertainment	35			95	Music. 4 Member Rock Group
Alice, Mary		Entertainment	8			16	Afr-Am Actress. Sparkle
Alice, Princess		Royalty	15		65		2nd Daughter of Queen Victoria
Alicia, Ana		Entertainment	5		15	15	
All in the Family (Cast)		Entertainment	45			125	4 Leading Characters
Allan, Buddy		Country Music	4			10	Singer. Buck Owens' son
Allen, Adrienne		Entertainment	5	10		2015	
Allen, Amos L.	1837-1911	Congress	10			40	Repr. ME
Allen, Andrew		Astronaut	7	10		20	

NAME	DATE	CATEGORY	SIG	LS/DS	ALS	SP	COMMENTS
Allen, Barbara Jo(Vera Vague)		Entertainment	22			35	Comedienne AKA Vera Vague. Radio-Films-Early TV
Allen, Betty		Entertainment	10			22	Afr-Am Dancer, Teacher, Choreographer
Allen, Charles L.		Clergy	10	35	50	35	
Allen, Debbie		Entertainment	10		20	25	Actress-Dancer-Singer-Choreographer-Dir.-Producer
Allen, Deborah		Country Music	4			15	Singer-Songwriter
Allen, Elizabeth	1908-	Entertainment	20		15	35	Br. Actress. Leading Lady.Berkely Square
Allen, Ethan	1738-89	Military-Rev. War	650	1850	3200		Col. Green Mounain Boys. ALS/Cont. $21,000
Allen, Frank A., Jr.		Military	10	25	45		
Allen, Fred		Entertainment	50	65	110	100	Popular Radio Comedian/Portland Hoffa
Allen, Ginger Lynn		Model	5			25	Pin-up $35
Allen, Gracie	1902-64	Entertainment	120	80		225	Usually Signed with Husband, George Burns
Allen, Grant		Author	5	15	30	10	
Allen, Henry J.		Congress	5	20			Senator, Kansas
Allen, Henry T.		Military	25	70	125	50	General WW I
Allen, Henry Watkins(WD)		Civil War	235	395	915		CSA Gen. 1820-66
Allen, Horatio	1802-90	Business-Engineer	65		115		Designed & Ran 1st Locomotive on Am. RR.
Allen, Ira (Brother of Ethan)		Military-Rev. War					Rev. War Date LS $15,000
Allen, Irwin		Entertainment	12			35	Director Disaster Films. Deceased
Allen, Joan		Entertainment	6			40	Actress. Oscar Nominee. Pleasantville
Allen, Joseph P.		Astronaut	10			25	
Allen, Karen		Entertainment	5	8	14	18	Actress, Raiders of Lost Ark SP $35
Allen, Macon B.	1816-94	Legal	195	865			Paved Way for All Blacks To Become Lawyers
Allen, Marty		Entertainment	10	4	12	16	Bushy Haired Comedian
Allen, Paul		Business	8			25	Microsoft Co-Founder
Allen, Peter		Composer	35			125	
Allen, Rex		Entertainment	8	10	15	22	Singer-Actor. Western Star
Allen, Robert (WD)		Civil War	44	60	95		Union Gen. (1811-86)
Allen, Robert F.		Business	5			10	Pres., CEO Carrier Corp.
Allen, Roderick R.		Military	10	20	35		
Allen, Rosalie		Country Music	10			45	Singer. 'The Prairie Star'
Allen, Steve		Entertainment	10	15	15	20	Composer, Pianist,TV-Radio Host
Allen, Tim		Entertainment	17			63	Comic Star of Home Improvement
Allen, Valerie		Entertainment	4			10	Actress. 2nd Leads, 50's Films
Allen, Viola		Entertainment	15		35	25	Vintage Stage Star 1898
Allen, William M.		Business	15	40	55	30	
Allen, William Wirt	1835-94	Civil War	195	375			CSA Gen., War Dte DS $510, ALS $1,275, LS $775
Allen, Woody	1935-	Entertainment	34	21	35	34	Actor, Comedian, Playwright, AA Director
Allenby, Edmund	1861-1936	Military	66	95	225	348	1st Viscount. Br.Fld Marshal, ALS/Cont.$750
Allende Gossens, Salvador		Head of State	35	113	285	70	1st Marxist Pres. Chile
Alley, Kirstie		Entertainment	7	10	12	30	Actress-Comedian. Pin-Up $45
Allgood, Sara		Entertainment	10		35	50	Vintage Screen Character Actress
Allingham, Margery	1904-66	Author	40	65	150	70	Br. Mystery Writer
Allison, Fran		Entertainment	20	30	45	75	Early TV Children's Show.Kukla,Fran & Ollie
Allison, May		Entertainment	15			40	
Allison, Mose		Composer	15			30	Jazz Pianist-Vocalist

NAME	DATE	CATEGORY	SIG	LS/DS	ALS	SP	COMMENTS
Allison, W.B.		Senate	5	15	25	15	Senator IA
Allizard, Adolphe		Entertainment	12		35	45	Opera. Bass
Allman, Greg		Entertainment	20			65	Rock Star. Allman Brothers
Allred, Gloria		Entertainment	10			30	Feminist Att'y. Brown vs O.J. Simpson
Allston, Washington	1779-1843	Artist	275	400	862		Pioneered Romantic Landscapes. Author
Allyson, June	1917-	Entertainment	6	9	14	26	MGM Star. 2nd Career in TV Commercials
Alma-Tadema, Lawrence		Artist	20	65	135		Br. Painter of Roman Scenes
Almond, Edw. M.		Military	12	35	50		
Almonte, Juan Nepomuceno	1804-69	Military	50	200	305		Mex. General, Politician
Almy, John J.		Civil War					Union Adm. ALS/Content $1900
Alonzo, Maria Conchita		Entertainment	10	15	25	23	Actress. Pin-Up $40
Alpert, Herb		Entertainment	9	15		30	Big Band Leader-Trumpet. Tijuana Brass
Alphand, Nicole H.		Celebrity	6			10	
Alsop, Joseph		Author	5	15	25	10	Journalist, Synd. Columnist
Alsop, Stewart		Author	10	25	35	15	Journalist, Synd. Columnist
Alt, Carol		Entertainment	8	12	18	25	Actress. Pin-up $45
Altchewsky, Ivan		Entertainment				250	Opera (Rare)
Altgeld, John P.		Governor	10	40			Gov. IL
Altieri, Albert (Johnny)		Celebrity	4			10	Philip Morris Trademark
Altman, Benjamin	1840-1913	Merchant	45	125			Altman's NY Dry-Goods Co. Philanthropist. Art
Altman, Robert		Entertainment	5	8	18	25	Movie Director
Alvarez, Luis W., Dr.		Science	15	35	85	30	Nobel Physics
Alvarez, Roma		Entertainment	3	3	6	10	
Alvary, Lorenzo		Entertainment	10	12	25	25	
Alvord, Benjamin	1813-84	Civil War	25	54	75		Union General. Mex. War Vet., Civ.War in OR Terr.
Aly Khan, Prince		Royalty	75				
Alyn, Kirk	1910-	Entertainment	12	18	30	32	Original Superman in Movie Serials
Amara, Lucine		Entertainment	15		55	45	Opera
Amato, Pasquale		Entertainment	25			125	It. Baritone. Opera
Ambler, Eric Clifford		Author	50	150			Br.Novelist
Ambrose, Bert	1896-1971	Entertainment	15			45	Notable Br. Bandleader
Ameche, Don	1908-93	Entertainment	22	35	45	58	Versatile Oscar Winner. Deceased
Ameche, Jim	1914-83	Entertainment	10	25		30	Look-alike brother. Radio's Jack Armstrong........
Ameling, Elly		Entertainment	15			70	Famed Lieder Singer
Ament, Jeff		Entertainment	6			38	Music. Guitar Pearl Jam
American President, The		Entertainment				135	Bening, Douglas (cast of)
Ames, Adelbert	1835-1933	Civil War	68	80	200		Union Gen., MOH Bull Run.Last Surviving Gen'l.
Ames, Ed	1927-	Entertainment	8	16		20	Singer-Actor of Ames Bros. Group
Ames, Fisher	1758-1808	Statesman	110		500		Organized Federalist Party
Ames, Leon		Entertainment	10	12	15	30	Life With Father etc. Star. TV-Films. Deceased
Ames, Nancy		Entertainment	4	6	8	12	Singer-Actress
Ames, Oakes	1804-73	Financier	100	410	1900		Founder Union Pac. RR. Rare RR DS $2250
Ames, Oliver		Business.	135	1350	2500		Union Pacific RR. Rare RR DS $2550
Amherst, Jeffrey, Lord	1717-97	Rev. War	455	1075	1433		Gov. Gen. Br. No. Amer. Br.Gen.
Amick, Madchin		Entertainment	4			18	Actress

NAME	DATE	CATEGORY	SIG	LS/DS	ALS	SP	COMMENTS
Amin Dada, Idi		Heads of State	50	275		425	Dictator of Uganda
Amis, Kingsley		Author	15	30	65	25	
Amis, Suzy		Entertainment	4			18	
Ammen, Daniel	1820-1898	Civil War	35	68	95	175	Union General
Ammen, Jacob	1806-94	Civil War	20	40	75		Union Gen.
Amos & Andy (Corell & Gosden)		Entertainment	233	150		250	Signed by Both
Amos, Tori		Entertainment	10			60	Actress. Pin-Up $85
Amos, Wally 'Famous'		Business	4	10	20	10	Afro-Am. Cookie King
Amparan, Belen		Entertainment	10			35	Opera
Ampere, Andre Marie	1775-1836	Science	175	420	1500		Fr. Physicist, Mathematician
Amsden, Ben		Aviation	12	22	38	35	Navy ACE WW II
Amsterdam, Morey		Entertainment	8			30	Comedian-Actor. Dick Van Dyke Show Deceased
Amundsen, Roald	1872-1928	Explorer	95	210	450	405	Norwegian Polar Explorer
Ancerl, Karel		Entertainment	3	6	8	6	
Ancona, Mario		Entertainment			65	150	Singer. London Premiere Pagliacci 1893
Ancona, Sydenham E.		Senate/ Congress	15		45		Civil War Congressman PA
Anders, Luana		Entertainment	17	20		30	Actress. Song of the South, Deceased
Anders, Merry		Entertainment	5			10	
Anders, Pamela		Entertainment	20			35	
Anders, Peter		Entertainment	25			75	Opera
Anders, William A.		Astronaut	40			95	
Andersen, Hans Christian	1805-75	Authors	350	650	1452	1818	AQS on CDV $1450
Anderson, Bloody Bill		Civil War					Lt. Quantrill's Raiders. Rare CDV in death $2500
Anderson, 'Bronco Billy'		Entertainment	105	175	200	375	
Anderson, Barbara	1945-	Entertainment	10	15		30	Actress. TV on Ironside
Anderson, Bill		Country Music	4			12	Whisperin' Bill
Anderson, Brad*		Cartoonist	15		35	25	Marmaduke
Anderson, C.E. Bud		Aviation	12	28	45	40	WW II ACE
Anderson, Carl David		Science	20	35		70	Nobel Physics 1936
Anderson, Carl T.*		Cartoonist	15	45		60	'Henry'
Anderson, Clifford		Civil War	70	130	95		CSA Congress
Anderson, Clinton		Cabinet	15	20		25	Sec'y Agriculture. Senator NM
Anderson, Dusty		Entertainment	10			25	Actress, Artist. Top 40's Model. Films from '44
Anderson, Eddie Rochester	1905-77	Entertainment	48		210	208	Actor-Comedian Rochester/ Jack Benny. GWTW
Anderson, Elizabeth G.,Dr.	1836-1917	Science	55	175	175		1st Eng. Hospital for Women
Anderson, George Burgwyn	1831-62	Civil War	255	450			CSA Gen. War Dte DS $625. Wounded Antietam-Died
Anderson, George T. Tige	1824-1901	Civil War	140	155	470	295	CSA Gen. War Dte. Sig/Rank $395
Anderson, George W.		Military	10	30	40	25	
Anderson, Gillian		Entertainment	14			61	X Files. SP With Duchevny $85-$95
Anderson, Harry		Entertainment	15	28		37	Actor-Comedian-Magician. Night Court SP $30
Anderson, Henry James		Educator	12				
Anderson, Jack		Author	3	7	15	15	Outspoken Syndicated Newspaper Columnist
Anderson, James Patton	1822-72	Civil War	80	285	375		CSA Gen.,ALS/Content $475
Anderson, John		Country Music	4			15	Black Sheep #1
Anderson, John B.		Military	5	10	20		

NAME	DATE	CATEGORY	SIG	LS/DS	ALS	SP	COMMENTS
Anderson, John Jr.		Governor	12	15		15	Governor KS
Anderson, Joseph	1757-1837	Rev. War	68	235	390		Early Senator TN
Anderson, Joseph R.(WD)		Civil War	380	705	880		CSA General
Anderson, Joseph Reid	1813-92	Civil War	85	225	385		CSA Gen.
Anderson, Judith, Dame		Entertainment	25	35	45	56	Powerful Legitimate Theatre & Film Actress
Anderson, June		Entertainment	5			25	Opera
Anderson, Ken	1909-93	Entertainment	10			35	Disney Animator, Art Director, Architect from 1934
Anderson, Laurie		Entertainment	8	15		20	
Anderson, Leroy		Composer	25	75	195	45	AMusMsS $325
Anderson, Les 'Carrot-top'		Country Music	10	12		15	Top Instrumentalist With Spade Cooley
Anderson, Loni	1946-	Entertainment	8	12	18	26	Actress. Pin-Up $38
Anderson, Louie		Entertainment	5			20	Stand-up & TV Comic
Anderson, Lynn		Country Music	4			18	Country Singer Superstar
Anderson, Marian	1902-93	Entertainment	114	190	238	350	1st Afro-Am Singer to Perform at Met. '58
Anderson, Martin B.		Clergy	8	15	25		
Anderson, Mary (American)		Entertainment	15	40		100	Actress
Anderson, Mary (English)		Entertainment	10	20	30	30	
Anderson, Maxwell		Author	30	70	135	50	Am. Dramatist. Pulitzer. Winterset.
Anderson, Melissa Sue		Entertainment	8			29	Actress. Little House on the Prairie SP $35
Anderson, Michael, Jr.		Entertainment	8			20	Producer
Anderson, O.A.		Aviation	10	25	40	30	General
Anderson, Pamela Lee		Entertainment	10			46	Actress. SP Nude $75
Anderson, Philip W.		Science	45		95	50	Nobel Physics
Anderson, Poul		Author	10	35	45		Sci-Fi. Award Winner
Anderson, Richard	1926-	Entertainment	5		15	15	Actor. 2nd Leads. Versatile Supporting Player
Anderson, Richard Dean		Entertainment	6	9	18	35	Actor. McGyver Star
Anderson, Richard Heron (War Dte.)		Civil War	255	610			CSA Gen. Ft. Sumpter Vet.
Anderson, Richard Heron	1821-79	Civil War	105	145	250		CSA Gen., Present at Ft. Sumpter Bombardment
Anderson, Robert	1805-71	Civil War	120	388	873	2075	Cmdr.Ft. Sumter,Wardte ALS$3500-$17,250
Anderson, Robert	1917-	Author	10	20	45	25	Playwright, Screenwriter. 'Tea and Sympathy'
Anderson, Robert B.		Cabinet	10	17	35	20	Sec'y Treasury
Anderson, Robert H. (War Date		Civil War	215	410			CSA General
Anderson, Robert H.	1835-88	Civil War	115	345	350		CSA Gen.
Anderson, Roy A.		Business	5	15	20	10	
Anderson, Samuel		Military	40	130	220		Early Congressman PA 1827
Anderson, Samuel E.		Military	5	10	20		
Anderson, Samuel R.	1804-83	Civil War	125	300	560		CSA Gen. Sig/Rank $200, War Dte. ALS $1500
Anderson, Sherwood	1876-1941	Author	35	95	153	45	Novelist, Journalist, Poet
Anderson, Terry		Journalist	10			25	Radio Host. Longest held Am. Hostage Lebanon
Anderson, Tim		Entrtainment	5			20	Actor
Anderson, W.R.		Military	15	35		50	Cmdr. N/S Nautilus
Anderson, Willie Y.		Aviation	10	25	35	30	WW II ACE
Andes, Keith	1910-	Entertainment	5			10	Actor.Radio-Stage-Films. Leads & Supporting Roles
Andre, John	1750-80	Rev. War	1200	3500	7875		Br. Officer. Hanged as Spy
Andreotti, Guilio		Head of State	10	20	35	20	It. Journalist, Prime Minister

NAME	DATE	CATEGORY	SIG	LS/DS	ALS	SP	COMMENTS
Andress, Ursula		Entertainment	12	16	22	35	Actress. Voluptuous Pin-Up $45
Andrew, A. Piatt		Senate/Congress	5	10		10	MOC MA
Andrew, John A.	1818-83	Governor	45	65	120		Civil War Gov. MA
Andrews Sisters (All Three)		Entertainment	150			500	40's Close Harmony Trio. Radio, Records, Films
Andrews, Arkansas Slim		Entertainment	4		10	10	
Andrews, Chris. C.	1829-1922	Civil War	35	70	195		Union Gen. ALS '64 $265
Andrews, Dana	1909-92	Entertainment	12	35		47	Actor.Popular 40's Leading Man. Laura
Andrews, Edward	1914-85	Entertainment	15			50	Character Actor of Stage, Film, TV
Andrews, George Leonard	1828-99	Civil War	35	55	90		Union Gen. Sig/Rank $50, War Dte. DS $95
Andrews, Harry	1911-	Entertainment	10			30	Br.Character Actor.Key Supporting Part.
Andrews, Julie	1935-	Entertainment	18	24	25	58	SP Sound of Music $125. Mary Poppins $50
Andrews, Landaff W.	1803-87	Congress	10		20		MOC KY
Andrews, Maxine	1918-95	Entertainment	15	20	20	25	Singer. (One of Andrews Sisters)
Andrews, Patti	1920-	Entertainment	10			25	Lead Singer of Andrews Sisters
Andrews, Roy Chapman	1884-1960	Science	75		135	125	Naturalist, Explorer, Author
Andrews, V.C.		Author	4			10	Novelist
Andrews, William Frederick		Business	4	10		10	CEO Scoville, Inc.
Andriola, Alfred*		Cartoonist	5			30	Kerry Drake
Andros, Edmund, Sir		Rev. War			7500		Only Reported Amount Shown
Andrus, Cecil D.		Cabinet	5	10	35	15	Sec'y Interior
Anduran, Lucienne		Entertainment	10			35	Fr. Operatic Mezzo-Sopr.
Anfinsen, Christian		Science	15	25	45	20	Nobel Chemistry
Angel, Heather		Entertainment	8	12	18	42	Br. Leading Lady of 30's-40's
Angel, Vanessa		Entertainment	5			15	Actress TV's Wierd Science
Angeli, Pier	1932-71	Entertainment	76		195	188	Actress. Died Very Young. Rare Autograph
Angelici, Marthe		Entertainment	20			75	Corsican Lyric Sopr.
Angell, Norman, Sir		Author	25	60	95	65	Nobel Peace Prize
Angelou, Maya		Author	25	40	35	35	Black Am. Poet
Angelyne		Celebrity	10			20	
Anglesea, Marquis of		Military	15	35	60		
Angus, Joseph		Clergy	10	20	25		
Animals, The (5)		Entertainment	50			150	Rock HOF
Aniston, Jennifer		Entertainment	18			51	Actress. Friends etc.
Anka, Paul		Composer	12	20		25	
Ankers, Evelyn		Entertainment	15	30	60	40	
Ann-Margret		Entertainment	8	10	18	32	Actress. AA. Pin-Up $65
Anna Ivanovna (Rus)		Royalty	265	825	2250		Czarina of Russia. Niece of Peter the Great
Annabella	1909-97	Entertainment	18	17	28	37	Fr. Actress. Major European Star. M. Tyrone Power
Annaloro, Antonio		Entertainment	10		35	40	It. Tenor, Opera
Anne, Princess		Royalty	95	250		140	Daughter of Elizabeth II
Anne, Queen (Eng)	1665-1714	Royalty	365	2155	2200		Queen of Great Britain & Ireland
Annenberg, Walter H.		Business	10	25	40	35	Publisher
Annesley, H.N.		Law Enforcement	5	10		15	Northern Ireland
Annseau, Fernand		Entertainment	20			75	Opera
Anouilh, Jean		Author	40	100	220	45	Fr. Dramatist, Screenwriter

NAME	DATE	CATEGORY	SIG	LS/DS	ALS	SP	COMMENTS
Ansara, Michael		Entertainment	6	8	15	22	actor
Anselmi, Giuseppe		Entertainment	45			162	Opera. Idolized Handsome Tenor Star
Anselmo, Tony		Entertainment	10				Actor-Animator. Voice of Donald Duck after 1980
Ansermet, Ernest	1883-1969	Entertainment	100			200	Swiss Conductor. SPc $75
Ant, Adam		Entertainment	30			75	Punk Rock
Anthonly, Robert N.		Nobel	15	25		25	Nobel
Anthony, Henry B.		Congress	10	15	35		Editor, Gov., Senator RI
Anthony, HRH		Royalty	30	100			King of Saxony
Anthony, Lysette		Entertainment	5			20	Actress. Pin-Up $45
Anthony, Ray		Entertainment	6	10	13	12	Big Band Leader
Anthony, Robert N.		Science	10			20	Nobel
Anthony, Susan B.	1820-1906	Woman Suffrage	306	1025	2070	1300	Reformer, Women's Rights. ALS/Cont $3500
Antokolski, Mark Matveyevich		Artist	30	65	155		Russ. Sculp. 1843-1902
Anton, Susan		Entertainment	6	8	10	24	Actress
Antonelli, Laura		Entertainment	16	18		298	Actress. Pin-Up $75-Uncommon
Antonioni, Michelangelo		Entertainment	15			88	Film Director
Anwar, Gabrielle	1969-	Entertainment	15			42	Br. Actress. Pin-Up $65
Aoti, Rocky		Business	6	15	30	15	Benihana Japanese Resaurants
Apollinaire, Guillaume	1880-1918	Author	140	400	1575		Avant Garde Poet, Art Critic
Apollo 10		Astronauts		450			Young, Cernan, Stafford. Recovery Postal Cover
Apollo 11		Astronaut	835	1250		1235	(Armstrong-Aldrin-Collins)Recovery Cover $750
Apollo 12		Astronaut	350			1150	Bean, Conrad, Gordon
Apollo 13 (Cast Of Movie)		Entertainment				250	Bacon, Hanks, Paxton
Apollo 14		Astronaut					Mitchell & Roosa.Apollo 14 Philatelic Cover S $175
Apollo 15		Astronaut		450		350	Scott, Worden, Irwin. FDC S $250
Apollo 16		Astronaut				295	Young, Mattingly, Duke. Launch SPc $400
Apollo 17		Astronauts				375	Schmidt, Cernan, Evans
Apollo 7		Astronauts		350			1st US 3 Man Flight.Eisele,Cunningham,Schirra FDC
Apollo 8		Astronauts				550	Lovell, Anders, Borman
Apollo 9		Astronaut	225				Entire Crew (3) $225
Apollo I		Astronauts				3000	Signed by All Three
Apollo II		Astronauts	315			688	Signed by All Three. Anders-Lovell-Borman
Apollo XIII (Crew Of)		Astronauts				1400	FDC Signed All 3 $395
Apollo/Soyuz Mission		Astronaut	175			400	All 5
Apollonia		Entertainment	20			42	Purple Rain
Apple, Fiona		Entertainment	10			60	Rock Star. Pin-Up $65
Appleby, Ray		Entertainment	3	3	5	5	
Applegate, Christina		Entertainment	15	32		52	Actress-Model. Pin-Up $65
Appleton, Daniel	1785-1849	Publisher	12				Appleton's Cyclopaedia
Appleton, Edward, Sir		Science	25	35		55	Nobel Physics
Apt, Jay		Astronaut	6	15		25	
Aquino, Corazon		Head of State	20			45	Pres. Philippines
Arquette, David		Entertainment	5			20	Actor. Scream SP $35
Arafat, Yassir		Head of State	72	195		138	PLO Leader. Nobel Peace Prize
Aragones, Sergio		Entertainment	5			18	Comic Book Art

NAME	DATE	CATEGORY	SIG	LS/DS	ALS	SP	COMMENTS
Aragones, Sergio		Cartoonist	10			25	Long association with Mad Magazine
Araiza, Francesco		Entertainment	5			30	Opera, Concert, Mexican Tenor
Arambula, Roman*		Cartoonist	40			200	Mickey Mouse
Arangi-Lombardi, Giannina		Entertainment				200	Opera.
Araujo, Arturo		Head of State	15	40		30	Salvador
Arber, Werner		Science	20	35		30	Nobel Medicine
Arbos, E. Fernandez		Composer	20				AmusQS $350
Arbuckle, Maclyn		Entertainment	15	15	30	25	
Arbuckle, Roscoe 'Fatty'	1887-1933	Entertainment	425			925	Comic-Actor. Involved In Major Scandal
Archbold, John		Financier	650	1900	2000		A Founder Standard Oil. TLS Std.Oil Lttrhd. $4400
Archer, Anne		Entertainment	8	12	15	30	Actress. Pin-Up $60-Uncommon
Archer, James J.		Civil War	200	375	825		CSA Gen.
Archer, Jeffrey		Author	5	15		15	Novelist
Archer, Jules		Author	7			10	
Archer, William S.	1789-1855	Congress	12				Sen. & Repr. VA
Archi, Attila		Entertainment	10	15	40	45	Opera
Archipenko, Alexander	1887-1964	Artist	90		400		Rus. Painter-Sculptor
Arden, Elizabeth		Business	30	65	145	40	Founder & Owner Eliz. Arden Co.
Arden, Eve		Entertainment	15	25	40	45	Actress. Our Miss Brooks
Arden, Nicke		Entertainment	3	3	5	5	
Arena, Angelina		Entertainment	5		30	25	Australian Soprano
Arens, Moshe		Diplomat-Author		80		20	Israeli
Argentia, Imperia	1889-1962	Entertainment	25			45	Argentine Dancer-Actress. Star 30's Span.Spk Films
Argento, Dominick		Composer	10	30	65	20	Pulitzer, AMusQS $175
Argyll, 8th Duke.	1823-1900	Statesman	20	45			Geo. Dougl. Campbell. P.M.Gen'l, Sec'y State India
Argyll, 9th Duke.	1845-1914	Head of State	30	40	55		John D. Campbell. Gov-General Canada
Arias Sanchez, Oscar		Head of State	35		65	50	Nobel Peace, Pres.Costa Rica
Arias, Harmodio		Head of State	25	50		30	
Arie, Raffaele		Entertainment	5			25	Bulgarian Basso
Ariyoshi, George R.		Governor	15			25	Governor Hawaii
Arkell, Bartlett		Business	5	27	45	15	
Arkell, W.J. (Judge Publ)		Business	5	15	30	10	
Arkin, Adam		Entertainment	4			12	Actor. Chicago HopeSP $22
Arkin, Alan		Entertainment	5	8		22	Character Actor
Arledge. John		Entertainment	5			20	2nd Leads 40's
Arlen, Harold	1905-86	Composer	140	175		210	Over the Rainbow. AMusQS up to $1,600
Arlen, Richard		Entertainment	25	30	70	65	Early Talkies Star of Wings
Arletty		Entertainment	25			75	Fr. Actress
Arliss, Florence		Entertainment	15	30	40	35	
Arliss, George	1868-1946	Entertainment	85		112	100	Br. Actor. Early Academy Award for Disraeli
Armani, Giorgio		Designer	10			35	
Armendariz, Pedro		Entertainment	30	35	45	65	
Armetta, Henry		Entertainment	25	30	50	65	
Armey, Dick		Congress	5	70		45	Majority Leader
Armistead, Lewis Addison		Civil War	600				CSA Gen., Last recorded sale

NAME	DATE	CATEGORY	SIG	LS/DS	ALS	SP	COMMENTS
Armour, Philip D.		Business	300	1238	1750	375	Meat Packing. Armour & Co.
Arms, Russ(ell)		Entertainment	3	5	7	12	Singer-Actor. Radio's Your Hit Parade
Armstead, Henry Hugh		Artist	10	20	35		Br. Sculptor. Albert Memorial
Armstrong, Bess		Entertainment	5			30	actress
Armstrong, Edw. R., Dr.		Science	30	75	150		Inventor Seadrome
Armstrong, Edwin H.		Science	75	250			Invented FM Broadcasting System
Armstrong, Frank Crawford		Civil War	290	365			CSA Gen.
Armstrong, Garner Ted		Religion	3			10	Evangelist
Armstrong, Harry	1879-1951	Composer	85		195		'Sweet Adeline' AMusQS $365-$650
Armstrong, John	1758-1843	Cabinet	45	125	872		Sec'y War. Cont. Congr., War of 1812
Armstrong, Louis	1900-71	Entertainment	200	406	710	422	Satchmo. Immortal. Jazz Trumpet. SP p/c $350
Armstrong, Martin		Author	5	10	15	10	
Armstrong, Neil A.	1930-	Astronaut	175	436	700	560	1st Moonwalker. Special SP $995-$1100-$2100
Armstrong, Robert		Entertainment	55	60	75	350	Actor King Kong
Armstrong, Robert		Military	175	725			Gen. TN Vols, Indian Fighter. Jackson aide-de-camp
Armstrong, Samuel Chapman		Civil War	55	120	350		Union Off. Cmdr. Black Regiment
Armstrong, William, Dr.		Science	20	50	110	40	Inventor
Arnaud, Yvonne	1892-1958	Entertainment	15			40	Fr. Film, Stage actress & pianist. Active in Eng.
Arnaz, Desi	1915-86	Entertainment	50	92	133	158	Actor-Singer-Prod. DS (Last Will & Testament) $750
Arnaz, Desi, Jr.		Entertainment	4			15	Rock Group. Dino, Desi, Billy
Arnaz, Luci		Entertainment	4	8	10	16	Actress Daughter of Lucy & Desi
Arness, James		Entertainment	16	12	18	58	Actor. Gunsmoke
Arnett, Peter		TV News	5			10	CNN News
Arngrim, Alison		Entertainment	6	8	15	10	
Arnheim, Gus		Bandleader				45	
Arno, Peter		Cartoonist	15	30	75	25	Drew for The New Yorker
Arno, Sig		Entertainment	10			25	
Arnold, Archibald		Military	20	62	102		
Arnold, Benedict	1741-1801	Rev. War	1300	2828	6300		Am. Army Officer. Traitor
Arnold, Eddy		Country Music	8			28	Country Music Hall of Fame
Arnold, Edward		Entertainment	30	40		90	Longtime Versatile Character Actor
Arnold, Edwin, Sir	1832-1904	Author	50	90	150	80	Br. Poet, Journalist
Arnold, Fredric		Aviation	20	35		50	ACE, WWII P-38
Arnold, Henry 'Hap'	1886-1950	Military	45	355	450	350	Air Force Gen. WW II
Arnold, Leslie P.		Aviation	10	295		30	Pioneer Pilot. '24 Round the World Flight
Arnold, Lewis Golding		Civil War	55	90	205		Union Gen.
Arnold, Matthew	1822-88	Author	175		850		Br. Poet, Critic
Arnold, Richard		Civil War	40	95			Union Gen.
Arnold, Tom		Entertainment	5			31	Comic Actor
Arnot, William		Clergy	10	20	25		
Arnt, Charles		Entertainment	10			25	
Arntzen, Heinrich		Aviation		60			Br. Ace WW I
Aronson, Judi		Entertainment	5			20	Actress. Pin-Up $45
Arp, Jean		Artist	75		275		Fr. DaDa Artist, Sculptor
Arquette, Alexis		Entertainment	15				

NAME	DATE	CATEGORY	SIG	LS/DS	ALS	SP	COMMENTS
Arquette, Cliff		Entertainment	16	20		50	Charlie Weaver
Arquette, David		Entertainment	5			20	Actor. Scream SP $35
Arquette, Patricia		Entertainment	8			35	Actress. Pin-up $50-$75
Arquette, Rosanna		Entertainment	15	15		36	Actress. Pin-Up $45
Arrau, Claudio		Entertainment		45		135	Chilean Pianist. 3x5 SP $120
Arrhenuis, Svante A.	1859-1927	Science	95	295	725		Nobel Chemistry 1903
Arrington, A. H.		Civil War	75	130			CSA Congress
Arriola, Gus*		Cartoonist	5			25	Gordo
Arrow, Kenneth J.		Economist	35	55			Nobel Economics
Arthur, Beatrice	1926-	Entertainment	9	12	22	22	Stage-Screen-TV Actress. Maude, Golden Girls
Arthur, Chester A. (As Pres.)		President	335	650	3258		WH Card S $450-$500
Arthur, Chester A.	1829-86	President	258	958	1265	625	ALS as Actg Pres $2,500. LS '62 $650
Arthur, Chester A.& Ellen Arthur		Pres. & 1st Lady		2500			Rare as Pair
Arthur, Duke of Connought		Head of State	10	18	25		Prime Minister
Arthur, Ellen Lewis		First Lady	600	1000	1200		
Arthur, George K.		Entertainer	6		15	10	Comedian, Producer
Arthur, Jean	1905-91	Entertainment	110	150	325	203	Somewhat reclusive. Retired Early. Shane Last
Arthur, Julia		Entertainment	15			25	Pioneer Film Star
Arthur, Timothy Shay		Temperance Author	20	45			Am. 10 Nights In A Barroom
Artot, Desiree		Entertainment	35		150	70	Opera, Concert
Arvin, Newton		Author	18	40	85		
Asboth, Alexander S.	1811-68	Civil War	60	190	178		Union Gen. ALS '64 $330
Asbury, Francis, Bishop		Clergy	175	290	625		
Asgeirsson, Asgeir	1894-	Head of State	25				4x Premier of Iceland
Ash, Mary Kay							SEE Kay, Mary
Ash, Roy L.		Business	10	20	50	35	
Ashby, Hal		Entertainment	8	8	15	15	
Ashby, Turner (WD)		Civil War	440	785	2792		CSA General
Ashby, Turner	1828-62	Civil War	358	625	1250	750	CSA Gen.
Ashcroft, Dame Peggy		Entertainment	20	25	35	65	
Ashcroft, Richard		Entertainment	8			40	Music. Lead Singer The Verve
Ashe, John		Rev. War	75	225	450		NC General
Ashe, William Shepperd		Senate/Congress	35	90			CW Blockade Runner
Ashford and Simpson		Entertainment	15			40	
Ashley, Alfred	1835-1913	Author	15			50	Br. Poet Laureate after Tennyson
Ashley, Edward		Entertainment	15			35	
Ashley, Elizabeth		Entertainment	6	8	15	18	Actress. Pin-UP $32
Ashley, John		Entertainment	5			15	
Ashley, William		Celebrity	200	750			Pioneer. Route for Oregon Trail
Ashurst, Henry	1874-1962	Congress	25			75	First Arizona senator
Ashworth, Ernie		Country Music	10			25	Talk Back Trembling Lips
Asimov, Isaac	1920-92	Author	45	160		100	Rus-Am Biochemist.Sci-Fi Writer
Askew, Reubin		Governor	12			15	Governor FL
Asner, Ed		Entertainment	4		12	14	Actor. Lou Grant
Aspin, Les		Cabinet	5			20	Clinton Sec'y Defense

NAME	DATE	CATEGORY	SIG	LS/DS	ALS	SP	COMMENTS
Asquith, Herbert H.	1852-1928	Head of State	35	75	135	150	Prime Minister. Earl of Oxford
Assad, Hafez		Head of State	15	40	105	65	
Assante, Armand		Entertainment	5	8	15	27	Actor. Leading Man
Astaire, Adele		Entertainment	30			75	Dancer Sister of Fred Astaire
Astaire, Fred	1899-1987	Entertainment	81	238	135	268	Dancing Star. Actor-Singer. SP/G.Rogers $775-$1750
Asther, Nils	1897-19??	Entertainment	25	35	65	160	
Astin, John		Entertainment	6	8	12	25	
Astley, Rick		Entertainment	4			10	Singer
Aston, Francis W.		Science	35	80	155		Nobel Chemistry 1922
Astor, Brooke		Author	5	15		10	
Astor, John J.	1886-1971	Publisher	15	40	65	35	1st Baron of Hever.Politician.Owner of 'The Times'
Astor, John Jacob	1763-1848	Business	433	1888	5675		Fur Trader-Capitalist, Financier. LS/Cont. $9500
Astor, John Jacob III		Business	300	850	1050		Grandson of Founder
Astor, John Jacob IV		Business	600	1900	2400		Died On the Titanic. RARE
Astor, John Jacob Jr.		Business	300	750	950	325	Union Gen., Financier
Astor, John Jacob Mrs.		Business	35	100	195		
Astor, Mary		Entertainment	35	70		135	A A
Astor, Nancy (Viscountess)	1879-1964	Celebrity	40	120	95	40	1st Woman To Sit As Br. M.P. American-Born
Astor, Vincent		Business	8	20	45	20	
Astor, Waldorf	1879-1952	Politics	15	35	80	55	Br. M.P., Publisher Observer
Astor, William Backhouse	1792-1875	Business	375	838	1500		Administered Astor Estate. Son of Founder
Astor, William Waldorf		Business	65	200	350		Journalist-Capitalist-Financier
Astronauts (Deceased)		Astronaut				1500	Chaffee, White, Grissom (All)
Asturias, Miquel Angel		Author	50	135	285		Guatamala. Nobel Literature
Atcher, Bob		Country Western	7			25	National Barn Dance Star
Atchison, David Rice	1807-66	President for 1 Day	350	900	975		Pres.for a day.ALS/Cont $4500
Ates, Roscoe		Entertainment	25	30	60	65	
Athenagoras, Archbishop		Clergy	25	40	55	50	
Atherton, Chas. G.	1804-53	Congress	20	30			Senator NH
Atherton, Gertrude		Author	30	55	150	75	Am. Novelist
Athlone, Earl, Prince Alex.of Teck		Head of State	15	25	40		Governor-General of Canada
Atholl, Katharine, Duch. of	1874-1960	Political	65				Br. Anti-Nazi.1st Woman Cabinet Member
Atkins, Chet		Country Music	5	14		22	Guitar Legend
Atkins, Christopher		Entertainment	6		15	21	Actor. Blue Lagoon. Pin-Up $30
Atkins, Gaius Glenn		Clergy	15	30	45		
Atkins, Smith D.	1835-1913	Civil War	25		150		Union Gen. 2nd Illinois. ALS Re Chickamauga $750
Atkinson, Brooks	1894-1984	Author	15	35		30	Theater Drama Critic, Columnist N.Y. Times
Atkinson, Joseph H.		Military	10	25	30		
Atkinson, Rowan		Entrtainment	5			22	Br. Actor-Comic
Atlantov, Vladimir		Entertainment	20		75	55	Opera. Rus. Tenor
Atlas, Charles		Business	15	30	35	35	Mail Order Phys. Culture
Atlee, Clement	1883-1967	Head of State	40	172			Br. Prime Minister
Attenborough, Richard		Entertainment	20		30	34	AA Br. Actor-Director
Attenborough, Sir David		Science	20	70			
Atterbury, William W.	1866-1935	Military	15	50			Gen. WW I, Pres. Penn. RR

NAME	DATE	CATEGORY	SIG	LS/DS	ALS	SP	COMMENTS
Attlee, Clement	1883-1967	Head of State	48	180	250	75	Prime Minister. 1st Earl
Atwill, Lionel		Entertainment	100			250	
Auber, Daniel Francois	1782-1871	Composer	110		160		Father of Fr.Opera, AMusQS $350
Auberjonois, Rene		Entertainment	6	8	14	25	Char. Actor Star Trek, Deep Space Nine
Aubert, Lenore		Entertainment	5	8	15	20	
Aubrey, M. E.		Clergy	10	15	20		
Aubry, Cecile		Entertainment	15			20	Fr. Actress
Auchincloss, Janet L.		Business	3	5	10	5	
Auchincloss, Louis		Author	15	35	75	30	U.S. Novelist, Short Story
Auchinleck, Claude J.E., Sir		Military	45	75		95	Br. Fld. Marshal WW II
Auckland, Baron (Geo.Eden)		Head of State	40	50	100		Gov-Gen India
Audemars, Edmund		Aviation	27			48	
Auden, W(ystan) H(ugh)	1907-93	Author	88	388	414	700	Br.-Am. Poet, Pulitzer
Audran, Edmond		Composer	45	85	175		Fr. Operettas
Audran, Marius		Entertainment	12		75		Opera. Tenor
Audubon, John J.	1785-1851	Artist	785	2200	3400		Ornithologist, Naturalist. Birds of America
Auel, Jean M.		Author	6	10	25	25	Novelist
Auer, Leopold		Entertainment	25	200		40	Hungarian Violinist
Auer, Mischa		Entertainment	30	30	45	60	
Auger, Arleen		Entertainment	25			55	Opera. Am Soprano
Auger, Christopher C.		Civil War	50	125	170		Union General
Augereau, P.F.C. de Castiglione		Military	100	350	525		Marshal of Napoleon
Augsburg, Alex. S.,Prince	1663-1737	Royalty		328			Prince Bishop of Augsburg Count Palatine of Rhine
Augusta, Queen of Prussia		Royalty		135			Consort William I. Empress of Ger.
Augustus I, Duke of Saxony	1526-1586	Royalty	2000				
Augustus III		Royalty	145	425	345		King Poland
Auld, Georgie		Entertainment	5	6	15	10	
Aumont, Jean Pierre	1909-	Entertainment	40	45		95	
Aurand, Henry S.		Military	5	10	20	15	
Auric, Georges	1899-1983	Composer	85				Fr. Member The Six. AMusQS $250-$395
Auriol, Jacqueline		Aviation	15	35	70	45	
Auriol, Vincent	1884-1966	Head of State	45	60	85		1st Pres. 4th Republ. France
Ausensi, Maurel		Entertainment	15			50	Opera, Sp. Baritone
Auslander, Joseph		Author	25	125		50	Poet. Harvard Lecturer Poetry
Aust, Abner		Aviation	10			20	US Ace
Austen, Jane	1775-1817	Author	625	2250	7500		Br.Novelist.Pride & Prejudice.Addr. Panel $1995
Austin, Bobby		Country Music	10			20	
Austin, Charlotte		Entertainment	4			15	
Austin, Horace		Governor	10			15	Governor MN
Austin, Karen		Entertainment	10		12	15	
Austin, Moses	1761-1821	Pioneer	425	1800	3372		Orig. Founder of TX. Mine Owner, Merchant
Austin, Stephen F.	1793-1836	Texas Colonizer	800	1875	6500		Historical DS $6500,$7500
Austin, Teri		Entertainment	5	8	10	10	
Austin, Warren R.		Senate	5	10		20	Senator VT
Autry, Gene	1907-98	Entertainment	25	75	75	138	Singing Cowboy, Businessman.

NAME	DATE	CATEGORY	SIG	LS/DS	ALS	SP	COMMENTS
Avallone, Michael		Author	5	15		10	
Avalon, Al		Entertainment	5			20	TV and film
Avalon, Frankie		Entertainment	6	10	15	24	Singer-Actor. Beach Party SP $30
Avebury, John Lubbock		Science	20		150		1834-1913. Naturalist.Paleolithic
Avedon, Richard		Artist	40	275	95	170	Photographer. Book S $375
Average White Band		Entertainment	15			25	Rock
Averell, William W.	1832-1900	Civil War	65	160	195		Union Gen. ALS '62 $360
Avery, James		Entertainment	4			15	
Avery, John, Jr.		Rev. War	40	77			
Avery, Margaret		Entertainment	3	3	6	10	
Avery, Milton	1893-1965	Artist	35	225		45	Am. Figure Painter 30-40's. Later Landscapes
Avery, Sewell L.		Business	35	55	105	40	CEO Montgomery Ward
Avery, Tex*		Cartoonist	25			400	Animator. (*Original Cell)
Avery, William W.		Civil War	75	140			CSA Congress
Avildsen, John G.		Entertainment	5			20	Film Director
Awdry, Wilbert, Rev.		Clergy-Author	50		175		Railway Series of Children's Books
Axelrod, Julius		Science	35	60	95	35	Nobel Medicine
Axtell, George		Aviation	12	25	45	35	Marine ACE
Axton, Hoyt		Country Music	5	12		20	Singer-Songwriter
Ayckbourn, Alan		Author	10	15	30	25	Br. Prolific Playwright
Aykroyd, Dan		Entertainment	8	12	15	26	Comic Actor.Saturday Night Live.Ghostbusters
Ayres, Agnes		Entertainment	60	75	150	125	Silent Film Star
Ayres, Lew		Entertainment	8	28	22	25	Actor. Oscar Winner. Original Dr. Kildare
Ayres, Romeyn B. (WD)		Civil War	70	135	440		Union Gen.
Ayres, Romeyn Beck	1825-88	Civil War	45	75	110		Union Gen.
Ayub Khan, General		Head of State	20	35	75	100	Afghan Prince. General
Aznavour, Charles		Entertainment	10			35	

B

NAME	DATE	CATEGORY	SIG	LS/DS	ALS	SP	COMMENTS
B52's		Entertainment	40			75	Rock Group
Babbage, Charles	1792-1871	Science-Math.	88	245	796		Br. Pioneer of Modern Computers. Inventor
Babbitt, Bruce		Cabinet	10	20		15	Gov. AZ
Babbitt, Harry		Entertainment	10			20	Band Vocalist, Radio
Babbitt, Milton		Composer	25		70	30	AMusQS $150
Babcock, Alfred, Dr.	1805-71	Congress					Repr. NY
Babcock, Barbara		Entertainment	4	4	9	10	
Babcock, Joseph W.		Senate/Congress	5		30		Congressman WI
Babcock, Orville E. (WD)		Civil War	40	160	255		Union Gen.LS as Grant ADC $385
Babcock, Orville E.	1845-84	Civil War	30	75	168		Union Gen.
Babcock, Tim		Governor	12	20	25	15	Governor MT
Babcock, Verne C.		Aviation	16			40	
Babilee', Jean		Entertainment	30	45		70	Ballet

NAME	DATE	CATEGORY	SIG	LS/DS	ALS	SP	COMMENTS
Babille, Jean		Entertainment	10			25	Fr. Choreographer, Dancer-Actor 50's
Babson, Roger	1875-1967	Economist	75				Predicted 1919 Crash. Founded Babson Coll.
Baby Peggy		Entertainment	5	6	15	15	
Babyfacte		Entertainment	6			42	Young Singer-Songwriter
Bacall, Lauren	1924-	Entertainment	20	55	60	38	Sophisticated, Throaty. Successful on Stage & Film
Bacardi Maso, Facundo	1815-86	Business					Founder Bacardi Rum & Emilio B. 2 DS $1250
Baccaloni, Salvatore		Entertainment	20	25	40	45	Opera, Concert, Films
Bach, Barbara		Entertainment	10	12	15	25	
Bach, Catherine		Entertainment	6	8	15	20	
Bach, Johann Sebastian		Composer	2500	22670	35000		Conservative Estimates
Bach, Richard		Author	25	100	175		
Bach, Sebastian		Entertainment	20			50	Rock
Bacharach, Burt		Composer	13	25	40	25	
Bacharach, Fabian		Artist	50	100	150	75	
Bache, Alexander D.		Science	25	50	110	40	1st Pres. Nat'l Acad. Science
Bache, Harold L.		Business	15	45	110	65	US Stockbroker. J.S.Bache & Co.
Bache, Jules S.		Financier	350	1100	1400		Founder J. S. Bache & Co.
Bacheller, Irving		Author	25	60	65	75	Am. Novelist, Editor
Bachman, Nathan L.		Congress	10				Senator, TN
Back, George, Sir	1796-1878	Explorer	35	105	175		Arctic Navigator
Backhaus, Wilhelm	1884-1969	Entertainment	46		65	100	Ger. Concert Pianist
Backhouse, James		Clergy	20	35	50		
Backstreet Boys (5)			55			155	Rock Group (5)
Backus, Jim		Entertainment	20	35	25	40	Mr. McGoo & Many Others
Baclanova, Olga		Entertainment	10			25	
Bacon, Edmund		Celebrity	10			15	
Bacon, Francis, Sir		Author	1500	3650	10500		Br. Philosopher, Statesman
Bacon, Frank		Entertainment	10	12	20	15	
Bacon, Kevin		Entertainment	9	10	20	40	
Bacon, Leonard		Clergy	10	15	20	25	
Bacon, Lloyd		Entertainment	12			20	Film Director
Bacon, Peggy		Artist	35	65	150		
Bacon, Robert		Senate/Congress	15	25		30	Congressman NY. Military
Bacon, Walter W.		Governor	10		25	15	Governor DE
Baddeley, Hermione		Entertainment	12	15	22	30	
Badeau, Adam (WD)		Civil War	50		275		Union Gen.
Badeau, Adam	1831-95	Civil War	35	88	195		Union General
Baden-Powell, Robert, Sir,	1857-1941	Military	146	395	608	665	Br. Gen., Defender Mafeking, Founder of Boy Scouts
Bader, Douglas, Sir		Aviation	45	130	205	75	Br. Ace
Badger, Charles J.	1853-	Military	20	45	70	40	U.S. Navy Adm.
Badger, George E.	1795-1866	Cabinet	15	62	40		Sec'y Navy, Sen. NC. Jurist
Badger, Oscar C.	1890-1958	Miltary		45		50	Adm. USN WW II
Badham, John		Entertainment	10			20	Film Director
Badham, W.L.		Aviation	25	50	75	55	Bi-plane , WW I
Badler, Jane		Entertainment	5	8	20	25	

NAME	DATE	CATEGORY	SIG	LS/DS	ALS	SP	COMMENTS
Badoglio, Pietro		Head of State	30		135	55	It. Gen.,succeeded Mussolini
Badura-Skoda, Paul		Entertainment	10			65	Pianist. SP Pc $25
Baekeland, L. H. Dr.	1863-1944	Science-Inventor	35	60	140		Invented Bakelite. (Synthetic Resin) 1st Plastic
Baer, Arthur Bugs *	1886-1959	Journalist	10			40	Syndicated Columnist, Cartoonist
Baer, George F.		Business	10	25	45	30	Pres. Reading Railroad
Baer, John		Entertainment	5	6	15	15	Actor.
Baer, Max, Jr.		Entertainment	35	70	85	60	Actor-Son of Boxer.'Beverly Hillbillies', Jethro
Baer, Parley		Entertainment	5	15	22		Familiar Character actor from 50's. Young Lions
Baez, Joan	1941-	Entertainment	10	20		30	Folksinger, Political Activist
Bagian, James P.		Astronaut	5	10		20	
Baglioni, Bruna		Entertainment	10		45	35	Opera
Bagnold, Enid	1889-1981	Author		75	185	75	Novelist, Plays. 'National Velvet', 'Chalk Garden'
Bagot, Charles, Sir	1781-1843	Statesman		45	125		Br. Diplomat.. Gov.-Gen. Canada
Bailey, Buster		Entertainment	30			75	Jazz Clarinet, Sax
Bailey, Carl E.		Governor	10	15			Governor AR
Bailey, F. Lee		Legal	15	25	45	25	Noted Trial Attorney
Bailey, Jack		Entertainment	5			15	Early Radio-TV M.C. 'Breakfast Club'
Bailey, James Anthony	1847-1906	Circus	250	812	1100		Barnum & Bailey Circus
Bailey, Joseph	1825-67	Civil War	95	195	245		Union Gen. ALS '64 $1265
Bailey, Mildred C.		Military	25			70	Brigadier General
Bailey, Pearl	1918-90	Entertainment	16	32	50	50	Singer-Actress
Bailey, Razzie		Country Music	5			20	
Bailey, Temple		Author	30	45	110		
Bailey, Theodorus	1805-77	Civil War	45	85	170		Union Naval Officer. Sig/Rank $70, DS $160
Bailey, Walter R.		Business	10	35	45	20	
Baillie, Joanna	1762-1851	Author	40	65	120		Successful Scottish Dramatist, Poet
Baillie, John		Clergy	35	75	110	50	
Bailly, Jean-Sylvain	1736-93	Astronomer	40	95	160		& Fr. Politician. Guillotined
Bain, Barbara		Entertainment	15	32		40	Actress. 'Mission Impossible'. Original TV Series
Bain, Conrad		Entertainment	5			10	Actor. 'Mork & Mindy' TV Series
Bainbridge, William	1774-1833	Military	150	325	650		US Naval Officer War 1812
Bainter, Fay	1892-1968	Entertainment	58	80	120	125	Actress. Vintage. Stage, Films. AA Winner
Baio, Scott	1961-	Entertainment	8	17		19	Actor. Juvenile 'Happy Days', 'ChaChi'
Bair, Hilbert L.		Aviation	10			45	US Ace. WW I
Baird, Absalom	1824-1905	Civil War	45	85	130		Union Gen. ALS '64 $200. S/Rank $70
Baird, John Logie		Science	150	295	150	600	1st TV Picture of Moving Object
Bairnsfather, Bruce	1888-1959	Cartoonist	15	30	110	25	Br. WW I 'Old Bill' Cartoons
Bakaleinikoff, Constantin	1898-1966	Composer	200				Russion Music Dir. RKO Studios
Baker, Alpheus	1828-91	Civil War	135	400	717		CSA Gen. Sig/Rank $310
Baker, Anita		Entertainment	22			40	Singer
Baker, Art	1898-1966	Entertainment	10	15		20	Early Radio-TV M.C. Master of The Art!
Baker, Benny	1907-94	Entertainment	8		15	25	Chubby, Baby-faced Character Comedian. Actor
Baker, Blanche	1956-	Entertainment	8		15	20	Actress-Daughter of Carroll Baker.
Baker, Bob		Entertainment	50	70		100	Singing Cowboy 1930's
Baker, Bonnie Wee		Entertainment	10			20	Big Band Vocalist With That Wee Small Voice

NAME	DATE	CATEGORY	SIG	LS/DS	ALS	SP	COMMENTS
Baker, Carroll	1931-	Entertainment	15	25	40	25	Actress. AAN 'Baby Doll'. Now Plays Character Roles
Baker, Charles S.		Senate/Congress	5	10		10	Congressman NY.
Baker, Chauncey		Military	10		25	20	General WW I
Baker, Diane	1938-	Entertainment	10			20	Actress. Leading Lady. Now Mature Leads
Baker, Edward D.	1811-61	Civil War	185	508	850		Union Gen. RARE. 2nd Gen. Killed. Sig/Rank $465
Baker, Ellen		Astronaut	5			25	
Baker, George*	1915-75	Cartoonist	40	250		281	'Sad Sack'. Orig. Sketch S $350
Baker, Howard Henry, Jr.		Senate	10		25	25	Senator TN. WH Chief of Staff
Baker, James A., III		Cabinet	10	25		40	Bush Sec'y State
Baker, Janet, Dame		Entertainment	10	15		35	Opera. Br. Mezzo Soprano
Baker, Jehu	1822-1903	Congress	10		25		Repr. IL
Baker, Josephine	1906-75	Entertainment	172	383	350	816	Highest Paid Entertainer in Eur. '20's. SPPc $425
Baker, Kenny		Entertainment	6			38	Actor. 'R2D2'
Baker, Kenny	1912-85	Entertainment	15	15	25	50	Singer-Actor. Jack Benny Show Vocalist. Films
Baker, La Fayette Curry	1826-68	Civil War	155	185	295		Union Gen. Interesting Background! Sig/Rank $325
Baker, Laurence S.	1830-1907	Civil War	135	165	405		CSA Gen. Sig/Rank $205, War Dte. DS $400+
Baker, LaVerne		Entertainment	28			55	Jazz Vocalist
Baker, Lucien		Senate	7		30		Senator KS
Baker, Mark		Entertainment	5	10		30	Opera
Baker, Michael		Astronaut	5			20	
Baker, Newton D.	1837-1937	Cabinet	15	122	100	55	Wilson Sec'y War
Baker, Phil	1896-63	Entertainment	7			25	Early radio comic. Few Films
Baker, Royal N.		Aviation	25		90	50	Air Ace Korea, WW II
Baker, Samuel W., Sir	1821-93	Explorer	40	75	150		Br. Located Sources of Nile
Bakewell, William		Entertainment	15			40	'Gone With The Wind' (Cast Member)
Bakker, Jim		Clergy	20	25	35	40	Built Empire. Convicted & Imprisoned. Now Released
Bako, Brigitte		Entertainment	3			10	Actress. Movies
Bakst, Leon	1866-1924	Artist	95		650		Rus. Painter, Scenic Designer
Bakula, Scott		Entertainment	20			45	'Quantum Leap' etc
Bakunin, Mikhail	1814-76	Anarchist	215		1625		Russian Revolutionist
Balakirev, Mily	1837-1910	Composer			865		Russian
Balanchine, George	1904-83	Entertainment	155		250	287	Ballet-Choreographer
Balbo, Italo	1896-1940	Aviation	125	160	200	195	It. Air Marshal-Pioneer. Valuable Postals Available
Balch, Emily Greene	1867-1961	Sociologist	35	35	60	75	Nobel Economist, Reformer, Pacifist
Balchen, Bernt		Aviation	30	45	75	52	
Balck, Hermann		Military	20			75	Ger. Panzer General
Baldridge, Howard Malcolm		Congress	10	15		15	MOC NE
Baldridge, Malcolm	1922-87	Cabinet	30	145		45	Sec'y Comm. Reagan.
Baldwin, Abraham	1754-1807	Statesman		3375			Signer Constitution, Rare
Baldwin, Alec	1958-	Entertainment	20	75		55	Handsome Leading Man in Current Hit Films
Baldwin, Faith	1893-1978	Author	35		60	45	Popular Novelist & Screenwriter
Baldwin, Henry (SC)	1780-1844	Supreme Court	87	140	230		
Baldwin, James	1924-87	Author	62	426	500	252	Afr-Am. Novelist, Essayist. ALS/Content $975
Baldwin, Judy		Entertainment	4			10	
Baldwin, Raymond E.		Governor	10	20		20	Governor, Senator CT

NAME	DATE	CATEGORY	SIG	LS/DS	ALS	SP	COMMENTS
Baldwin, Roger		Political	20	25			Civil Libertarian. Founder ACLU
Baldwin, Roger Sherman		Senate	35		50		Early Gov.1844, Senator CT 1847
Baldwin, Stanley	1867-1947	Head of State	58	280	125	125	3 Term Br. Prime Minister. Edw. VIII Abdication
Baldwin, Stephen		Entertainment	15			45	Actor
Baldwin, William		Entertainment	15			42	Actor
Baldwin, William E.	1827-64	Civil War	297	685			CSA General. Sig/Rank $420, War Dte. ALS $2975
Balewa, A. T., Sir		Head of State	10	35	85	25	Nigeria
Balfe, Michael William		Composer	22	55	125		
Balfour, Arthur J.	1848-1930	Head of State	68	126	168	90	Br. Prime Minister. 1st Earl.Balfour Declaration
Balfour, Howard		Aviation	25		75		Br. Ace WW I
Balistier, Elliot		Editor	4	15			Liberty Magazine
Ball, Albert	1896-1917	Aviation	125	225	330	275	Brit. RAF ACE WW I. Shot Down 43 Enemy Planes
Ball, Joseph H.		Congress	12			75	Senator
Ball, Lucille (Lucy)	1911-89	Entertainment	113	200		206	5 x 7 SP (Lucy) $125
Ball, Lucille	1911-89	Entertainment	200	484		539	Full Signature.
Ballard, Hank		Entertainment	15			75	Rock Pioneer. Uncommon
Ballard, Kaye		Entertainment	15	25		25	Comedienne-Singer. Standup. Films
Ballard, Robert, Dr.		Science	16	40	85	25	Oceanographer. Found Titanic
Ballentine, John J.		Military	15	35	60		
Ballew, Smith		Entertainment	15	20		40	Actor
Ballinger, Richard A.		Cabinet	10	25	50	25	Sec'y Interior 1909
Ballou, Charles		Military	30	110			General WW I
Balsam, Martin	1919-199?	Entertainment	24	30		48	Actor. AA Winner. Supporting Actor
Baltimore, David, Dr.		Science	15	25	40	35	Nobel Medicine. Controversial Research Scientist
Balzac, Honore' de	1799-1850	Author	600	1250	1792		Fr. Novelist
Bampton, Rose	1909-97	Entertainment	20	35	45	40	Opera, Concert. Metropolitan
Bananarama		Entertainment	32			70	(4)
Bancroft, Anne	1931-	Entertainment	9			30	Actress. Stage-Films. AA. 'Miracle Worker'
Bancroft, Edward	1744-1821	Author			1750		Also Inventor & Spy for British During Am. Rev.
Bancroft, George	1800-91	Cabinet-Author	35	85	125	135	Polk Sec'y Navy, Historian, Diplomat
Bancroft, George	1882-1956	Entertainment	20		45	85	Vintage Actor
Band, The		Entertainment	75			110	Rock HOF. DS $150
Bandaranike, S.W.R.D		Head of State	10	25	45	30	Prime Minister Sri Lanka
Banderas, Antonio		Entertainment	20			54	Latin Actor
Bandy, Moe		Country Music	7			15	Honky Tonk Artist
Bangles, The (All)		Entertainment	40			85	Rock
Bangs, John Kedrick		Author	8	45		20	Humor Editor Harper's Magazine
Banisadr, A.		Head of State	35	45	80	55	Iran. Exiled
Bank, C. D.		Cabinet	10	25			
Bankhead, Tallulah	1902-68	Entertainment	112	115	200	305	Deep Voiced Actress. Orig. Wilding Photo. SP $600
Bankhead, Wm. B.	1874-1940	Congress	10	40			Speaker of the House
Banks, Billy		Entertainment	80			250	Jazz
Banks, Joseph, Sir	1743-1820	Science-Explorer	40	130	533		Br. Naturalist, Botanist. Sailed/Capt.Cook
Banks, Leslie	1890-1952	Entertainment	20			40	Distinguished, Sophisticated Br.Stage-Screen Actor
Banks, Michael A.		Author	4	10	25	10	

NAME	DATE	CATEGORY	SIG	LS/DS	ALS	SP	COMMENTS
Banks, Nathaniel P. (WD)		Civil War	150	498	505		Union Gen.
Banks, Nathaniel P.	1816-1894	Civil War	62	138	148		Gov. MA, MOC, Union Gen.
Banks, Tyra		Entertainment	10			46	Model/actress
Banky, Vilma	1902-91	Entertainment	50	75	200	212	Silent Star. Co-Star with Valentino. Early Vamp
Banner, John	1910-73	Entertainment	75	150		150	Actor. 'Hogan's Heroes' as Sgt. Schultz
Banning, Henry Blackstone		Civil War	30	65			Union Gen., Congressman OH
Banning, Margaret C.		Author	5	12	25	10	
Banting, Frederick G.	1891-1941	Science	600	908	1650	943	Discoverd Insulin with Best. Nobel 1923
Bantock, Granville		Composer	40			125	Br. Composer
Bar-Lev, Chaim		Military	20	65		50	Israeli Military Leader
Bara, Theda	1890-1955	Entertainment	135		300	283	The Vamp. Silent Screen Star.
Baraka, Imamu A.(LeRoi Jones)		Author	35	90	85	45	Afr-Am Playwright, Poet, Novelist, Essayist
Barbara, Agatha		Head of State	10			20	Pres. of Malta
Barbarigo, St. Gregorio L.	1625-97	Clergy		3500			Saint. Canonized 1960
Barbarin, Paul		Entertainment	25		65		Bandleader, Drummer
Barbe-Marbois, Francois de	1745-1837	Napoleon Cabinet	45	75	250		As Napoleon's Min. of Finance-Louisiana Purchase
Barbeau, Adrienne	1945-	Entertainment	5	15		20	Actress
Barbee, John Henry		Entertainment	35				Blues Vocalist
Barbejacque, Prince		Entertainment	4		10	10	
Barber, Rex T.		Aviation	15	35	75	40	Am. ACE WW II, Downed Yamamoto
Barber, Samuel	1910-81	Composer	65	608	395	102	Opera, Songs, String Music. AMusQS/Photo $1250
Barber, William		Military	25			70	Marine MOH Korea
Barbera, Joe*		Cartoonist	40			140	Flintstones, Yogi Bear. (Of Hanna-Barbera)
Barbier, George	1865-1945	Entertainment	10	15		25	Vintage Character Actor
Barbieri, Fedora		Entertainment	25			75	Opera, Concert
Barbirolli, John, Sir	1899-1970	Entertainment	38		60	150	Br. Conductor
Barbour, Dave		Composer	15			40	Jazz Guitar
Barbour, James	1775-1842	Cabinet, Congress	50		155		Sec'y War, Gov. & Senator VA. US Minister Gr.Brit.
Barbour, Philip (SC)	1783-1841	Supreme Court					MOC, Speaker, Pres. VA Constitutional Conv. NRPA
Barbour, William Warren		Senate	10	35		15	Senator NJ
Barclay, Thomas		Rev. War	25	55			Adj.-Gen'l Nova Scotia
Barclay, William		Clergy	40	75	95	75	
Barcroft, Roy		Entertainment	50			150	
Bard, Ralph A.		Cabinet	15	25		25	FDR. Sec'y Navy
Bardeen, John		Science	30	50	105	40	Nobel. Signed Bio Card $55
Bardot, Brigitte		Entertainment	25		45	47	French actress. Internat'l Sex Symbol
Bardshar, F.A.			15	25	45	40	Navy ACE, WW II
Barere de Vieuzac, Bertrand	1755-1841	Fr. Revolution	40	120	150		'The Anacreon of the Guillotine'. Exiled
Baretti, Giuseppe	1719-89	Author	35	80	155		Friend of Burke, Johnson. Italian Critic
Bari, Lynn		Entertainment	5		15	20	Actress. Deep Voiced 'Other Woman' Roles
Baring, Alexander	1774-1848	Banking	130		750		Formalized Webster-Ashburton Treaty
Baring, Francis, Sir	1796-1866	Business	35	50	110		1st Lord of Admiralty. ALS/Cont.$1975
Baring-Gould, Sabine	1834-1929	Author-Divine	25	120	178	65	Onward Christian Soldiers AMS $2400
Barkely, Bob		Aviation	10			25	WW II Ace
Barker, Bob		Entertainment	4	30		15	The Price is Right TV Game Show Host

NAME	DATE	CATEGORY	SIG	LS/DS	ALS	SP	COMMENTS
Barker, Clive		Author	15	25		25	Br. Horror Novelist
Barker, Lex	1919-73	Entertainment	65	138	160	175	Actor. Ex Husband Lana Turner & Ex 'Tarzan'
Barker, William George		Aviation	125	225	350	295	Canadian ACE, WW I
Barkhorn, Gerhard		Aviation	65	185		125	Ger. ACE, #2 Worldwide
Barkin, Ellen	1955-	Entertainment	15			55	Actress
Barkley, Alben W. (V)	1877-1956	Vice President	27	80	175	65	Truman VP. Oldest V.P. & Only One To Marry In Off.
Barks, Carl*		Cartoonist	30			197	Donald Duck, Scrooge
Barksdale, Ethelbert		Civil War	30	50	65		CSA Congress
Barksdale, William (WD)		Civil War	908				CSA General. Wounded Gettysburg 7/2/63.Died 7/3
Barksdale, William	1821-63	Civil War	493		1220		CSA General. KIA Gettysburg '63
Barlow, Francis C.	1834-96	Civil War	55	85	285		Union Gen.
Barlow, Howard		Conductor	40			50	Popular Radio/TV Conductor
Barlow, Jane		Author	5	15	25		
Barlow, Joel		Diplomat	40	120	245		Author, Chaplain Rev. War
Barnabee, Henry Clay		Entertainment	6	15	25	15	Operatic Comedian
Barnaby, Ralph S.		Aviation	27			35	
Barnard, Christian, Dr.		Science	40	125	85	70	Heart Specialist
Barnard, Daniel D.	1797-1861	Congress	12		85		MOC. NY, Minister Prussia
Barnard, Frederick A.P.	1809-89	Educator	75	165	275		Barnard College.For Women's Ed. Pres. Columbia U.
Barnard, George Grey	1863-1938	Artist	25		85		Sculptor. Works in Metr. Mus. Art, The Cloisters
Barnard, John Gross	1815-82	Civil War	35	60	185		Union Gen. Sig/Rank $45, War Dte. ALS $165
Barne, Michael		Celebrity	12	35	90	40	
Barnes, Binnie	1905-	Entertainment	15	12	15	25	Vintage Br. Actress.Leading Lady & Light Comedy
Barnes, Demus		Senate/Congress	5	15	25		Congressman NY. Writer
Barnes, Djuna		Author	45	110	260	85	Am. Novelist-Short Story Writer
Barnes, James	1801-69	Civil War	60	182	185		Union Gen. Very Scarce
Barnes, Joanna		Entertainment	5			15	Actress
Barnes, Joseph K.	1817-83	Civil War	195	450	550		Union Surgeon Gen.Attended Lincoln at Deathbed
Barnes, Julius H.	1873-1939	Business		20		20	Corporation Off'l. Pres. US Chamber of Commerce
Barnes, Priscilla		Entertainment	8		20	20	Actress.
Barnet, Charlie		Entertainment	15			30	Big Band Leader-Tenor Sax
Barnet, Isaac		Political		25			Mayor Cincinnati
Barnett, Ross R.		Governor	10		25	15	Governor MS
Barnette, Vince		Entertainment	15	20	35	45	Vintage Character Actor
Barneveld, Jan Van Olden		Dutch Statesman		2000			Father of Dutch Independence
Barney, Natalie	1876-1972	Author	110	315	412		Am. Poet, Translator, Parisian Hostess
Barnhart, George 'Eddie'		Aviation	20	35		50	
Barnum, Henry A.	1833-92	Civil War	55	95	145		Union Gen. ALS '64 $190, Sig/Rank $70
Barnum, Malvern H.		Military	10		35	25	General WW I
Barnum, Phineas T.	1810-1891	Business-Circus	202	738	911	935	ALS/Content $1,100-1,500-$2,000-$3800
Baronova, Irina		Entertainment	20			58	Rus.-Br. Ballerina
Barr, Candy		Entertainment	10			42	Stripper. Prison for Shooting Husband
Barr, Doug		Entertainment	3	3	6	8	
Barr, Joseph Walker		Cabinet	5	15	30	15	Sec'y Treasury, Congressman IN
Barr, Roseanne		Entertainment	20	25	50	60	

NAME	DATE	CATEGORY	SIG	LS/DS	ALS	SP	COMMENTS
Barras, Paul-Francois-Jean		Fr. Revolution	85	250			Jacobin Club.Exiled From Paris
Barrault, Jean-Louis		Entertainment	40			125	
Barrett, John		Military	20		50		WW I Victoria Cross
Barrett, Lawrence	1838-91	Civil War	20			45	Union Officer, Actor
Barrett, Majel		Entertainment	10			30	Star Trek
Barrett, Rona		Entertainment	6	8	15	15	
Barrett, Wilson	1847-1904	Entertainment	15		90	65	Br. Playwright, Actor, Manager
Barrie, Barbara		Entertainment	10		12	15	Successful Broadway & Film Actress
Barrie, James M., Sir	1860-1937	Author	82	265	344	280	Playwright, Novelist. Peter Pan etc.
Barrie, Mona		Entertainment	15	15	35	30	
Barrie, Wendy		Entertainment	20	25	30	45	
Barrier, Edgar		Entertainment	4	7	10	15	
Barringer, Daniel M.	1806-73	Congress	12				Repr. NC, Minister Spain
Barringer, Rufus	1821-95	Civil War	105	305	470		CSA Gen.
Barrington, Shute		Clergy	10	15	25	20	
Barrios, Justo R.	1835-1885	Head of State	40	112			Pres. Guatemala. Killed in Battle
Barron, Blue		Bandleader	25			10	
Barron, Clarence		Business	25			40	Editor, Publisher Barron's
Barrow, Clyde	1909-34	Criminal			3325	21850	Bonnie & Clyde
Barrow, Edward G.		Business	100	300		150	Gen'l Mgr. NY Yankees
Barrow, John, Sir	1764-1848	Statesman	60	170	325		Explorer, Traveller, Author
Barrow, Robert H.		Military	10	30	50	20	
Barrows, Lewis O.		Governor	12		25	15	Governor ME
Barrows, Sydney Biddle		Celebrity	10			30	Mayflower Madame
Barry, Charles, Sir	1795-1860	Architect	45	55	138		Br. Houses of Parliament, Westminster Palace
Barry, Dan		Astronaut	7			22	
Barry, Dan*		Cartoonist	10			100	Flash Gordon
Barry, Dave		Author	10			20	Creator Dave's World
Barry, Don 'Red'		Entertainment	22	45	35	58	
Barry, Gene		Entertainment	15			25	Actor. Westerns, Straight Leads. Films-TV
Barry, John		Rev. War	1150	2000			Ir. Born US Naval Officer
Barry, John Decatur	1839-67	Civil War	212		490		CSA Gen.
Barry, John Wolfe, Sir		Celebrity	8	15	35	20	
Barry, Marion		Politician	6	8	15	15	Mayor Washington, D.C.
Barry, Sy*		Cartoonist	14			50	'Phantom'
Barry, Thomas		Military	35		150		General WW I
Barry, Wesley		Entertainment	8		25	20	
Barry, Wm. Farquhar	1818-79	Civil War	65	145	205		Union Gen. War Dte. S $85
Barrymore, Diana		Entertainment				42	
Barrymore, Drew	1975-	Entertainment	20			57	Actress.Nude Pin-up $135
Barrymore, Ethel	1898-1954	Entertainment	120	185		200	Stage Star Prior to Films.The Corn is Green etc.
Barrymore, John	1882-1942	Entertainment	192	287	300	505	'The Great Profile'. Academy Award.
Barrymore, Lionel	1878-1954	Entertainment	82	274		202	Member 1st Family of Am. Theatre. Oscar 1931
Barrymore, Maurice	1847-1905	Entertainment	35			90	Founding Member of American Familty of Actors
Bartato, Elisabeth		Entertainment	15			40	Opera

NAME	DATE	CATEGORY	SIG	LS/DS	ALS	SP	COMMENTS
Bartel, Jean	1925-	Entertainment	15			55	Miss America '43, Actress. Set new image.
Barth, John		Author	30	40	85	35	Am. Novelist
Barth, Karl		Clergy	40	95	125	75	
Barthelmess, Richard		Entertainment	20	30	75	70	Vintage Actor.
Bartholdi, Fred. Auguste,	1834-1904	Artist	450	725	550	975	Statue of Liberty Print S $700- $1395
Bartholomew, Freddie		Entertainment	30	35	45	83	Brit. Child Actor of 30's-40's
Bartle, Joyce		Entertainment	5	6	10	10	
Bartlett, Bonnie		Entertainment	5	6	10	10	
Bartlett, Joseph Jackson		Civil War	45	110			Union Gen.
Bartlett, Josiah	1729-95	Rev. War	215	605	908		Signer.ALS/Cont.$3250- $8000, FF $950-$1050
Bartlett, Paul Wayland		Artist	10	15	30		US Sculptor
Bartlett, Robert Abram		Explorer	50	175	125		Cmdr. Ship on Peary Arctic Exp.
Bartlett, Thomas		Clergy	15	20	35		
Bartlett, William F.		Civil War	45	80	170		Union Gen.
Bartoe, John David		Astronaut	7	20		30	
Bartok, Bela	1881-1945	Composer	300	1025	1312	1575	Hung.Pianist-Comp.AmusQS $1800-$2750
Bartok, Eva		Entertainment	5			15	Actress
Bartoli, Cecilia		Entertainment	5			32	It. Mezzo. Opera
Barton, Bruce	1836-1967	Business	10	35	40	30	Advertising Exec.. BBD&O. Writer, Rep. NY
Barton, Clara	1821-1912	Humanitarian	190	775	721	725	Founder & 1st Pres. Am. Red Cross.ALS/Cont.$1250
Barton, Derek H. R., Sir		Science	20	30	40	25	Nobel Chemistry
Barton, James		Entertainment	40			125	
Barton, Seth M. (WD)		Civil War	205		935		CSA General
Barton, Seth Maxwell	1829-1900	Civil War	95	248	308		CSA Gen.
Bartow, Francis Stebbins	1816-61	Civil War	70		360		CSA Congress
Barty, Billy		Entertainment	10	18	20	20	Diminuative Character Actor
Baruch, Bernard M.	1870-1965	Statesman	45	350	512	202	Financier, Pres. Advisor
Baryshnikov, Mikail		Entertainment	62	85	130	161	Rus-Born Ballet Star
Barzun, Jacques		Author	7	12	25	15	
Basehart, Richard		Entertainment	6	10	20	15	
Basie, Wm. 'Count'	1904-84	Composer	72	200		238	Big Band Leader-Pianist
Basinger, Kim		Entertainment	12	55	40	42	Actress. Oscar Winner
Baskett, James		Entertainment	200			600	
Baskin, Leonard	1922-	Artist	25				Sculptor & Graphic Artist
Basov, Nickolay		Science	20	45		30	Rus. Nobel Physicist
Basquette, Lina		Entertainment	15			25	1920's Star
Bassett, Angela		Entertainment	16			58	Singer
Bassett, Charles A.		Astronaut	40			65	
Bassett, Leslie		Composer	15	30	65		Pulitzer,AMusQS $100
Bassett, Richard		Rev. War	375	800			Signer Constitution
Bassi, Amedeo		Entertainment	35			150	Favorite Tenor of Toscanini
Bate, William B. War Date)		Civil War	140		1045		CSA Gen.,Senator, Gov. TN (Listed ALS/Content)
Bate, William Brimage	1826-1905	Civil War-Senate	70	122	175		CSA General-Also Gov. Tenn.
Bateman, Jason		Entertainment	15			25	
Bateman, Justine		Entertainment	15	15	25	30	

NAME	DATE	CATEGORY	SIG	LS/DS	ALS	SP	COMMENTS
Bates, Alan		Entertainment	5			20	Br. Actor
Bates, Arthur Laban		Senate/Congress	5	10		20	Congressman PA
Bates, Blanche		Entertainment	15	25	40	45	
Bates, Clayton 'Peg-Leg'	1907-98	Entertainment	20			45	Famous One-Legged Tap Dancer. Vaud.-TV-Films
Bates, Edward	1793-1869	Cabinet	40	135	365	450	Lincoln Att'y Gen. War Date ALS/Cont. $895
Bates, John C.		Civil War	25		110		Union General
Bates, Katharine Lee	1859-1929	Author	75		288	125	AMsS Am. The Beautiful $6,500. Printed $2000
Bates, Kathy		Entertainment	20			50	Actress. Variety Character Roles. Oscar Winner
Bates, Sanford		Law Enforcement	10	35			Commissioner of Prisons
Bates. Florence		Entertainment	10			25	
Bathazar, Getty		Entertainment	20			45	The Young Riders SP $80
Bathori, Jane	1876-1970	Entertainment			75	125	Opera. Legendary Fr. Soprano
Bathurst, Henry		Clergy	15	25	40	30	
Batista, Fulgencio	1901-73	Head of State	165	350	475	175	Cuban Pres. 1940-44, 1952-59. Dictator
Batiuk, Tom*		Cartoonist	5			25	Funky Winkerbean
Battaglia, Franco		Entertainment	15			50	Opera, Concert
Battaille, Charles	1822-72	Entertainmment	10		50		Opera
Batten, Hugh		Aviation	10	25	40	30	Navy ACE, WW II
Batten, Jean	1909-82	Aviation	45	85		90	Pioneer NZ Aviatrix
Battenberg, Louis	1854-1921	Military	10		50		British Adm of the Fleet 1919
Battle, Cullen Andrews		Civil War	200	405			CSA Gen.
Battle, Kathleen		Entertainment	20	40		52	Opera, Concert
Battu, Marie	1838-88	Entertainment	15		75		Opera. Sang in World Premiere of L'Africaine
Batz, Willhelm		Aviation	35			95	Ger. ACE, #7 Worldwide
Baucus, Bob		Aviation	10	20	35	25	
Baudelaire, Charles-Pierre	1821-67	Author	335	2250	2370		Fr. Modernist Poet, Symbolist, Critic
Baudouin, King (Belg)		Royalty	35	100	250	125	King of Belgium
Baudry, Patrick		Astronaut	12	25		25	
Bauduc, Ray		Entertainment	10			25	Big Band Bassist
Bauer, Harold		Entertainment	38		75	70	Br. Piano Virtuoso
Bauer, Jaime Lyn		Entertainment	6	8	10	15	
Bauer, Michelle		Entertainment	10			125	B-Film Star. Signed Lip Print. 15. SP Nude(below)
Bauer, Steven		Entertainment	6	8	15	20	
Baulieu, Etienne		Science	20		45	40	Inventor RU486 Abortion Pill
Baum, Kurt		Entertainment				40	Operatic Tenor
Baum, L. Frank		Author	500	925	1175		The Wizard of Oz books
Baum, Vicki		Author	20				Novelist. Grand Hotel
Baum, William W., Cardinal		Clergy	35	55	70	50	
Baumer, Steven		Entertainment	10	15	20	25	
Baur, Hans		Aviation	30	45	90	125	Hitler's Personal Pilot
Baur, Harry		Entertainment	30			150	Fr. Star Executed by Nazis
Bauvais, Garcelle		Entertainment				40	Models, Inc.
Bavier, Frances		Entertainment	55	60	95	150	
Bax, Arnold		Composer	70				AMusQS 200
Baxley, Barbara		Entertainment	4	4	10	10	

NAME	DATE	CATEGORY	SIG	LS/DS	ALS	SP	COMMENTS
Baxter, Anne		Entertainment	20	25	40	46	AA
Baxter, Henry		Civil War	35	95	160		Union Gen.
Baxter, James P. III		Author	5	15	30	10	
Baxter, Keith		Entertainment	3	3	6	10	
Baxter, Les		Bandleader	26		40		Arranger, Composer
Baxter, Percival P.		Governor	12		25		Governor ME
Baxter, Warner	1892-1951	Entertainment	95		155	148	Early Leading Man & Oscar Winner
Baxter-Birney, Meredith		Entertainment	6	8	15	15	
Bayard, George D. (WD)		Civil War	295		1222		Union Gen.
Bayard, George Dashiell		Civil War	135	170	558		Union Gen.,
Bayard, John B.	1738-1807	Rev. War	40	165	168		Continental Congress, Rev. War Col.
Bayard, Richard Henry		Senate	20	40	85		Senator DE
Bayard, Thomas F., Sr.		Cabinet	25	35	80		Sec'y State, Senator DE
Bayard, William		Rev. War	85	220	450		
Bayh, Birch		Senate	10	25		20	Senator IN
Bayne, Barbara		Entertainment	20			55	
Bayne, Beverly		Entertainment	9	10	20	20	
Beach Boys (4)		Entertainment	195			425	Alb. Cover. S by 5 Living Members $395. SP $650
Beach, Amy M.	1867-1944	Composer	45		462	200	1st Am. Woman Composer of Note. AMQS $175
Beach, Rex	1877-	Author	20	35	95	35	Am. Novelist
Beacham, Stephanie		Entertainment	10		15	20	Actress
Beadle, George Wells, Dr.		Science	20	30	45	40	Nobel Medicine
Beakley, Wallace M.		Military	5	15	25		
Beal, George Lafayette	1825-96	Civil War	42	112	135	270	Union Gen. ALS '64 $440
Beal, John		Entertainment	15	15	25	25	
Beale, Rich'd Lee T. (WD)		Civil War	150		550		CSA General
Beale, Richard Lee Turberville		Civil War	85	105	225		1819-93. CSA General
Beall, William N.R.(WD)		Civil War	175	325	850	700	CSA General
Beals, Jennifer		Entertainment	20	20	40	45	
Bean, Alan L.		Astronaut	20	200		85	Moonwalker Astro. ADS re Apollo 12 $975
Bean, L.L.	1872-1967	Inventor-Business				300	Unique Business Empire
Bean, Orson	1928-	Entertainment	5			20	Actor-Comedian
Bean, Roy, Judge		Frontier Judge	3950	4500			The Law West of the Pecos
Beane, Hilary		Entertainment	5	10	15	10	
Beard, Charles A.	1874-1948	Author	5	28	65		Am. Historian, Teacher, Political Scientist
Beard, Daniel C.	1850-1941	Author	105	300	352	140	Founder Boy Scouts of America. Author, Teacher
Beard. Stymie		Entertainment	75			175	
Bearden, Romare*	1914-88	Artist	45	225	475	200	Afro-Am. Artist. Principally Blk.-Am. Life Collage
Beardslee, Lester Anthony		Military	20		100		Admiral Spanish American War
Beardsley, Aubrey	1872-98	Artist	175	375	1712	2300	Br. Illustrator. Art Nouveau
Beardsley, Samuel	1790-1860	Congress	10				Repr. NY, Assoc. Judge NY Supr. Ct.
Beastie Boys (3)		Entertainment	40			90	Rock Group (3)
Beatles (all four) on one piece		Entertainment	3098			4715	Set of 4 Separate Sigs. $2,650
Beaton, Cecil	1904-80	Photographer	40	155	202	375	Br. Portraitist. Theatrical Designer
Beatrice, Princess		Royalty	25	125	115	120	Youngest Daughter Q. Victoria

NAME	DATE	CATEGORY	SIG	LS/DS	ALS	SP	COMMENTS
Beatrix, Queen		Royalty	100		450		Netherlands
Beatty, Clyde	1903-1965	Business-Circus	50	95	175	150	Animal Trainer. Circus Performer-Owner
Beatty, David, Adm.	1871-1926	Military	32	75	90	100	Br. Admiral WW I
Beatty, Ned		Entertainment	7	10	15	12	
Beatty, Samuel		Civil War	25	45	70		Union Gen.
Beatty, Warren	1937-	Entertainment	25	119		65	SP as Dick Tracy $45. Oscar 1981 for Reds Dir.
Beatty. John		Civil War	27	55	80		Union General
Beauharnais, Eugene de	1781-1824	Royalty	45	350	430		Son of Josephine, Adopted by Napoleon
Beauharnais, Hortense de	1783-1837	Royalty	50		435		Wife of Louis Bonaparte
Beaumarchais, Caron de	1732-99	Author	150	675			Fr. Playwright. Aided Am. Colonies In Rev. War
Beaumont, Hugh		Entertainment	75			150	
Beauregard, Pierre G.T.		Civil War	390	2250	1812	3500	CSA Gen. Fired on Fort Sumpter (WD)
Beauregard, Pierre G.T.	1818-93	Civil War	385	940	1372	1425	CSA Gen.Stock Cert. S $3950
Beauvais, Garcelle		Entertainment	5			40	Actress, Models, Inc.
Beauvoir, Simone de	1908-86	Author	95		512		Fr. Novelist. Philosopher. Existentialist
Beaux, Cecilia	1863-1942	Artist	55	58	65		Am. Portrait Painter
Beaver, James A.		Civil War-Gov.	30	55	110		Union Gen., Gov. PA
Beaverbrook, Max, Lord							SEE Maxwell, Wm.
Beavers, Louise		Entertainment	60			150	Popular Afr.-Am. Film Actress
Bechet, Sidney	1897-1959	Entertainment	125	550	475	175	Jazz Clarinetist-Saxaphonist
Bechi, Gino		Entertainment	25			55	Opera
Beck, C.C*		Cartoonist	10			100	Captain Marvel
Beck, Dave	1894-1993	Labor Leader	20	50	50	50	Union Exec. Sent to Prison for Union Fraud
Beck, James M.	1861-1936	Congress		25			Repr. PA
Beck, Jeff		Entertainment	20			45	Rock Guitarist
Beck, John		Entertainment	3	3	6	8	
Becker, Barbara		Entertainment	3	3	6	8	
Beckett, Samuel	1906-89	Author	140	748	426	335	Irish Playwright. Nobel Lit. Waiting for Godot
Beckett, Scotty		Entertainment	15			92	Child Actor
Beckinsale, Kate		Entertainment	4			15	
Beckman, Arnold	1900-	Inventor	18				Beckman Instruments. pH testing meter etc.
Beckwith, Edward G.		Civil War	45				Union General
Beckwith, Geo. Sir	1753-1823	Rev. War		390			Br. Gen. in the American War
Beckwith, J. Carroll		Artist	35	80	145		
Becquerel, Edmond	1820-91	Science			2750		Fr. Physicist
Becquerel, Henri	1852-1908	Science	175	450	520		Nobel Curies' Radioactivity
Beddoe, Don		Entertainment	8			20	
Bedelia, Bonnie		Entertainment	3	4	10	10	
Bedford, Brian		Entertainment	5	12	20		Actor
Bedford, Gunning, Jr.		Rev. War	285	700			Signer of Constitution. Scarce
Bedford, Gunning, Sr.		Rev. War	175	325			Cousin of above, Scarce
Bee Gees (3)		Entertainment	40			100	Barry, Robin, Maurice Gibb. Stayin' Alive
Bee, Barnard E.		Civil War	275	725	2798		CSA Gen., Sec'y War Rep. Texas
Bee, Carlos		Senate/Congress	10	20		20	Congressman TX
Bee, Hamilton Prioleau		Civil War	265				CSA General (WD)

NAME	DATE	CATEGORY	SIG	LS/DS	ALS	SP	COMMENTS
Bee, Hamilton Prioleau	1822-97	Civil War	90	168	425		CSA Gen.
Bee, Molly		Country Music	6			20	
Beebe, Charles William	1877-1962	Explorer	30	60	212	75	Bathysphere.Naturalist.Author, Scientist
Beebe, Marshall		Aviation	18	35	55	42	ACE, WW II
Beech, Olive Ann		Aviation	20	45		50	Beechcraft Airplane Mfg.
Beecham, Thomas, Sir	1879-1961	Conductor	68	195		225	Flamboyant Br. Conductor. 3x5 Half-Tone SP $120
Beecher, Henry Ward	1813-87	Clergy	60	120	170	630	Abolition, Temperance Activist, Orator
Beecher, Lyman		Clergy	40	55	65	45	Early Anti Slavery
Beems, Patricia		Entertainment	3	3	6	8	
Beene, Geoffrey		Business	10	25		25	Fashion Designer
Beerbohm, Max, Sir Henry	1872-1956	Author	55	135	225	75	Humorist, Caricaturist
Beerbohm-Tree, Herbert		Entertainment	20			45	Classical Actor
Beery, Noah	1884-1946	Entertainment	78		250	175	
Beery, Noah Jr.		Entertainment	15	20	25	35	
Beery, Wallace	1885-1949	Entertainment	132	243	350	305	Vintage Oscar Winner. The Champ
Beeson, Jack	1921-	Composer	15	30	63	25	AMusQS $35
Beethoven, Ludwig van		Composer	5000	19250	25000		ALS/Content $35,000.Unsigned Envelope IHS $8500
Beggs, James		Astronaut	8			30	
Begin, Menachem	1914-92	Head of State	74	370	245	149	P.M. Israel. Nobel Peace Prize. ALS/Content $1295
Begley, Ed, Jr.		Entertainment	4	7	9	15	
Begley, Ed, Sr.		Entertainment	25	45	70	75	
Behan, Brendan F.		Author	160	400	645		Ir. Author-Playwright
Behrman, S. N.		Author	15	25	60	25	Am. Playwright, Screenplays
Beichel, Rudolph		Science	20			55	Rocket Pioneer/von Braun
Beiderbecke, Bix		Entertainment	5000				Jazz Musician
Beinhorn, Elly		Aviation	10	22	40	30	Ger. Aviation Pioneer
Beith, Ian Hay (John)		Author	10	30	60	20	Br. Novelist, Playwright
Beke, Charles Tilstone		Explorer	20	50	125		Br. Geographer. Nile Source
Bekhterev, Vladimir	1857-1927	Science			2000		Russ. Neuropathologist/Pavlov
Bekhterev, Vladimir	1857-1927	Science		1750	2500		Russ. Neuropathologist/Pavlov
Bekins, Milo		Business	35	45	160	125	Bekins Van & Storage Co.
Bel Geddes, Barbara		Entertainment	10			25	Dallas. NY Drama Critic Award
Bel Geddes, Norman		Artist	20	50	155	35	Scenic Designer Theater
Bela, Magyar		Astronaut	10			25	Hungary
Belafonte, Harry		Entertainment	10	15		30	
Belafonte, Shari		Entertainment	5	6	15	20	
Belasco, David		Entertainment	35	30	70	95	Theatrical Producer
Belaunde, Fernando T.		Head of State	10	20	50	25	
Belcher, Edward, Sir		Military-Navy	15	35	60		Arctic Exped.for J. Franklin
Belcher, Jonathan	1681-1757	Colonial America	210	325	650		Gov. MA, NH, NJ. Instrumental as Fndr. Princeton
Belita		Entertainment	15	25	45	45	
Belknap, George		Civil War	45		60		Union Naval Officer. C.W. Cabinet
Belknap, Reginal R.	1871-1959	Military	50	150			U.S. Admiral. Invented Collapsible Submarine Net
Belknap, Richard R.	1871-1859	Military	50	150			U.S. Adm. Invented Anti-Submarine Net
Belknap, William W.		Civil War, Cabinet	65	158	175		Union General, Sec'y War(Grant) Impeached

NAME	DATE	CATEGORY	SIG	LS/DS	ALS	SP	COMMENTS
Bell, Alexander Graham	1847-1922	Science	350	1567	4025	3040	Inventor of Telephone, Scientist, Educator
Bell, Catherine		Entertainment	6			40	Actress. Pin-Up $55
Bell, Charles H.	1798-1875	Civil War	50	100	145		Union Naval Captain, Admiral
Bell, Charles, Sir	1774-1842	Science	150		475		Scottish Surgeon-Anatomist.Nervous Systm Authority
Bell, Digby		Entertainment	12			20	Vintage Actor
Bell, Eric Temple (John Taine)		Author	30		130	55	Scot., Math Books, Sci-Fi
Bell, Griffin		Cabinet	10			25	Att'y General
Bell, Henry H.	1808-1868	Civil War	60	150			Rear Adm under Farragut
Bell, Herbert A.		Business	15	20	75	50	
Bell, John		Cabinet	95	145			W.H. Harrison, Tyler Sec'y War
Bell, Lauralee		Entertainment	10			20	Soaps Actress
Bell, Peter Hansborough		Governor		195			Gov. TX 1849-53
Bell, Rex		Entertainment	50			125	
Bell, Terrel H.		Cabinet	5	15	26	15	Sec'y Education
Bell, Tyree Harris		Civil War	55	130	215		CSA Gen.
Bell, Vanessa		Artist	100				Br. Artist-Sister of Virginia Woolf
Bellamy Bros.		Country Music	7			20	Howard & David
Bellamy, Edward	1850-1898	Author	25	75	150		Novelist
Bellamy, Elizabeth W.		Author	3	9	18		
Bellamy, Madge		Entertainment	10	15	40	35	
Bellamy, Ralph	1904-91	Entertainment	18	20	28	46	Actor-Leading Man & Character-Films, Stage
Bellanca, Giuseppe M.		Aviation	40	85	160	125	Bellanca Aircraft Designer-Mfg.
Belle, Lulu		Entertainment	10			20	C & W
Beller, Kathleen		Entertainment	6	8	15	15	
Belleri, Marguerite		Entertainment	5		30	25	Metropolitan Opera 1917-20
Bellew, John Chippendall		Clergy	10	20	25	20	
Belli, Melvin		Law	10	15	35	20	Trial Attorney
Belliard, A.D. (Count)	1769-1832	Military	25	55	175		Fr. Gen. under Napoleon
Bellincioni, Gemma		Entertainment	118		195	175	It. Soprano.Sang Premiere of Cavalleria Rusticana
Bellini, Vincenzo	1801-35	Composer	557		5025		It. Opera. Norma, La Sonnambula
Bellmer, Hans	1902-75	Artist	55	160	500		Ger. Surrealist Painter, Engraver, Photographer
Bellmon, Henry Louis		Senate	15	20		20	Senator OK, Gov. OK
Belloc, Hilaire	1870-1953	Author	40	85	150	50	Versatile Novelist, Poet,Critic
Belloc-Lowndes, Marie		Author	15	40	110	30	Br.Author of Historical Works
Bellon, Leoncadia		Entertainment	16			45	Opera, Film
Bellonte, Maurice		Aviation	75	145	270	345	
Bellow, Saul	1915-	Author	45	148	90	50	Nobel Literature 1976. Novelist
Bellows, George	1882-1925	Artist	95	225	375		Urban Scenes, Sports, Landscape
Bellows, Henry W.	1814-82	Clergy	20		55		Founder Antioch College. Unitariarn Clergyman
Bellson, Louis		Entertainment	25		55	70	Jazz Drummer
Bellwood, Pamela		Entertainment	6	9	15	26	
Belmont, August	1816-90	Business	212	875	1275	350	Banker, Diplomat, Belmont Park Stk.Cert. S $2500
Belmont, August, Jr.		Business	45	120			
Belmont, August, Mrs.		Socialite	15	25	40		
Belsham, Thomas		Clergy	15	20	35	30	

NAME	DATE	CATEGORY	SIG	LS/DS	ALS	SP	COMMENTS
Belushi, James		Entertainment		1510	20	30	
Belushi, John	1949-82	Entertainment	250			712	Comedian. Second City, Sat. Nite Live
Bemelmans, Ludwig		Author	45	105	255	50	Writer-Illustrator. Novelist
Ben,t, William Rose	1886-1956	Author	15	35	65	40	Poet, Editor. Pulitzer
Ben-Gurion, David	1886-1973	Head of State	175	1160	1895	458	1st Prime Minister of Israel. LS-ANS/Cont. $5500
Ben-Yehuda, Eliezer		Author	35	175	425		Jewish Scholar
Ben-Zvi, Itzhak	1884-1963	Head of State	135	312	250	100	2nd President Israel
Benacerraf, Baruj		Science	27	55		40	Nobel Medicine-Physiology
Benatar, Pat		Entertainment	20			70	
Benavidez, Roy		Military	10	25	40	20	
Benchley, Peter		Author	15	25	50	20	Sketch of Jaws S $15-$35
Benchley, Robert		Author	40	80	195	75	Am. Drama Critic, Humorist
Bendix, William	1906-64	Entertainment	35	30	60	142	
Benederet, Bea		Entertainment	40			100	
Benedict XV. Pope		Head of State	125		450	550	
Benedict, Dick		Entertainment	15	20	25	30	
Benedict, Julius, Sir		Composer	15			25	Br. Pianist
Benedict, William		Entertainment	25			60	
Beneke, Tex		Entertainment	30			85	Sax for Glenn Miller. Big Band
Benes, Eduard	1884-1948	Head of State	85	90	145	200	P.M. & President Czech.
Benet, Stephen Vincent	1898-1943	Author	80	195	200	150	Poet, Novelist. Pulitzer (2)
Benham, George W. (WD)		Civil War	120	225	389		Union Gen.
Benham, Henry W.	1813-84	Civil War	55	125	150		Union Gen.
Benighi, Roberto		Entertainment	6			38	Actor. Films
Bening, Annette		Entertainment		25	45	43	Actress, Pin-up $65
Benjamin, Judah P.	1811-84	Civil War	290	885	1062		CSA Gen. & Sec'y of State
Benjamin, Judah P.(WD)		Civil War	395	3500	1750		CSA Sec'y of State
Benjamin, Richard		Entertainment	8			42	Actor-Director
Benjamin, William, Jr.		Supreme Court	40	1925		60	
Bennett, Arnold		Author	40	175			Br. Novelist
Bennett, Bruce (Herman Brix)		Entertainment	12	24	30	35	Early Tarzan. Athlete as Herman Brix
Bennett, Constance		Entertainment	30	60	120	81	Glamour Leading Lady of 30's-40's
Bennett, Floyd		Aviation	300	370	750	500	Pilot with Byrd over North Pole
Bennett, James Gordon	1841-1918	Publisher	45	195	150		Financed Stanley-Livingstone African Expedition
Bennett, Joan	1910-1990	Entertainment	16	18	35	66	Actress. Leading Lady Sister of Constance
Bennett, Johnstone		Entertainment	15			35	Actress with Mansfield
Bennett, Julie		Entertainment	3	3	6	10	
Bennett, Richard		Entertainment	15			35	Stage & Silent Films
Bennett, Robert		Legal	15			35	Power Att'y for Pres. Clinton vs Paula Jones
Bennett, Robert Russell		Composer	40		250	95	Great Broadway Composer. Academy Award
Bennett, Samuel F.		Composer	30	75	150		In the Sweet Bye & Bye
Bennett, Spencer Gordon		Entertainment	10			25	
Bennett, Tony	1910	Entertainment	5	12	20	35	Top Recording & Club Singer
Bennett, Wallace F.		Senate	5	10	20	15	Senator UT
Bennett, William J.		Author-Cabinet	20	60	75	55	Book of Virtues.Sec'y Ed.

NAME	DATE	CATEGORY	SIG	LS/DS	ALS	SP	COMMENTS
Bennett, Wm. Andrew		Head of State	4	10	15	10	
Benning, Henry Lewis	1814-75	Civil War	145	275	362		CSA Gen., Statesman. Fort Benning, GA So Named
Benny Show, The Jack		Entertainment	120				6 Principals
Benny, Jack	1894-1974	Entertainment	70	338		211	Great Radio-TV Comedian
Benois, Alexander		Artist	45	195	425		Rus. Designed Sets, Costumes
Benoit, Francois	Circa 1804	Merchant		500			Famous Fur Trader
Benson, Edward Frederic	1867-1940	Author	20	40	112		Satirical, Macabre Novels. Scholar
Benson, Edward W., Archbishop		Clergy	20	35	55	35	
Benson, Egbert		Rev. War	40	75	170		Continental Congress
Benson, Elmer A.		Governor	5	12	20	15	Governor & Senator MN
Benson, Ezra Taft	1899-1994	Cabinet	12	25	55	40	Sec'y Agriculture, Pres. Mormon Church
Benson, Frank Robert, Sir		Entertainment	15	20	35	20	Vintage Br. Actor
Benson, George		Entertainment	15			25	Music
Benson, Jodi		Entertainment	10			35	Actress. Disney Voice
Benson, Richard Meux		Clergy	35	55	65	75	
Benson, Robbie		Entertainment	15		20	25	Juvenile & Adult Actor. Disney Voice Over
Benson, William S.		Military	10	20	35	25	Adm. USN WW I
Bent, James Theodore	1852-97	Explorer	10		35	25	Br. Archaeologist. Greece, Asia Minor, Abyssinia
Benteen, Frederick W.		Civil War		3500		2500	
Bentham, Jeremy	1748-1832	Jurist-Philosopher	120				Br. Writer etc.
Benton, Barbi		Entertainment	5		15	15	
Benton, Robert		Entertainment	10			20	AA Director. 'Kramer vs Kramer', 'Bonnie & Clyde'
Benton, Samuel	1820-64	Civil War	385	675			CSA Gen. Died Battle of Atlanta 1864
Benton, Thomas Hart	1782-1858	Senate/Congress	90	110	205		30-Year Senator From Missouri
Benton, Thomas Hart	1889-1975	Artist	100	250	765		ALS/Content $1,350
Benton, William	1900-73	Senate	10	30	65	20	Publisher, Statesman, Businessman, Sen. CT
Benton, William Plummer	1828-67	Civil War	95	142			Union Gen. Rare
Bentsen, Lloyd		Senate-Cabinet	10	30		20	Senator TX, Sec'y Treas.
Benzell, Mimi		Entertainment	15			35	Opera
Beradino, John	1917-96	Entertainment	25			40	Actor Our Gang comedies, Baseball Player
Berdyaev, Nikolai	1874-1948	Philosopher	75	100	145	175	Russ. Orth. Layman, Marxist. Critic of Both
Berenger, Tom		Entertainment	10			45	Actor
Berenson, Marisa		Entertainment	10	20		25	Model-Actress. Willowy Member International Jet Set
Berenstain, Stan*		Cartoonist	20			75	'Berenstain Bears'
Beresford, Charles, Lord	1846-1919	Military	15	35	112	80	Br. Admiral. Bombardment Alexandria. Khartoum Exped
Berfson, Henri-Louis		Author	30	80	155		
Berg, Alban	1885-1935	Composer	135	660	1450		Austrian. Atonal Music. Orchestral, Songs
Berg, Gertrude		Entertainment	18		25	35	Vintage Actress. Stage & Radio's Longtime Serial
Berg, Moe	1902-72	Celebrity	225				Lawyer, Mathematician, Spy
Berg, Paul		Science	27	35	65	40	Nobel Chemistry
Berg, Peter		Entertainment	6			30	Actor-Director
Berganza, Teresa		Entertainment	9			48	Opera
Bergen, Candice		Entertainment	12	45		45	Actress. Films. Longtime TV Series. Emmy Awards
Bergen, Edgar	1903-78	Entertainment	55	80	125	167	Am. Ventriloquist-Comedian-Actor. Special AA
Bergen, Frances		Entertainment	5			10	

NAME	DATE	CATEGORY	SIG	LS/DS	ALS	SP	COMMENTS
Bergen, Polly	1930-	Entertainment	9	10	18	28	Actress, Singer, Films, TV. Cosmetics Mfg.
Berger, Erna		Entertainment	10			30	Opera
Berger, Gottlob		Military	40	120	200		
Berger, Senta		Entertainment	10	15	35	30	Actress. Leading Lady of Am. & International Films
Bergere, Lee		Entertainment	5			15	
Bergeron, Marion		Beauty Queen	15			75	Miss America 1934
Berggrav, Eivind Josef		Clergy		50			Bishop of Norway. World Council of Churches
Bergh, Henry	1811-88	Reformer	85		400		Founder ASPCA
Bergland, Bob		Cabinet	5	10	20	15	Sec'y Agriculture, Congress MN
Bergman, Ingmar	1918-	Entertainment	32	40	50	175	Swe. Film Director
Bergman, Ingrid	1913-82	Entertainment	119	212	272	302	3x Academy Award Winner. SPc $250-$325
Bergman, Sandahl		Entertainment	10		15	20	
Bergner, Elizabeth	1898-1968	Entertainment	20	35	60	30	Pol-Born Actress. Made Reputation/Max Reinhardt
Bergonzi, Carlo		Entertainment	30			65	Opera
Bergson, Henri	1859-1941	Author	40	125			Philosopher. Nobel Literature 1928. Educator
Berio, Luciano		Composer	20	30	75		
Beriot, Charles Auguste de		Composer	40		175		Violinist Virtuoso. Visual Artist
Berjerac, Jacques		Entertainment	15			30	Fr. Actor of Am. Films.40's-50'2
Berkeley, Busby		Entertainment	100	155	275	295	Dance Choreographer-Director
Berkley, Elizabeth		Entertainment	10			36	'Showgirls' Pin-up $100
Berkowitz, David		Criminal	85	90	250		Son of Sam, Serial Murderer
Berle, Adolph	1895-1971	Economist	15	35			Am. Member of FDR's Original Brain Trust
Berle, Milton		Entertainment	15	40	35	40	Comedian. Successful Vaudeville,Radio,'MR. TV'
Berlier, Jean Baptiste	1843-1911	Science	15	30	45		Fr.Engineer. Paris Underground RR System
Berlier, Theophile, Count		Fr. Revolution	50	150	295		
Berlik, Jan		Entertainment	25			50	Czech. Operatic Tenor
Berlin, Irving	1888-1990	Composer	179	971	1038	1310	AMusQS $2,300. Many TLS's & ALS's Signed Irving
Berlioz, Hector	1803-69	Composer	245	1225	1335		Distinguished Fr. Composer. AMusQS $3,900
Berlitz, Charles		Business	15	25		35	Language Educator
Berman, Eugene	1899-1972	Artist	40	105	195		Rus.-Born Painter-Designer
Berman, Pandro S.	1905-19	Entertainment	20	40		50	Film Producer. 1977 Irving Thalberg Memorial Award
Berman, Shelley		Entertainment	5			10	Comedian
Bernacchi, Antonio		Entertainment			2500		Classical Singer (Castrato) for Handel
Bernadotte, Jean-Baptiste		Royalty	120	415	650		Charles XIV John. Marshal of Nap.
Bernard, Claude	1813-78	Science	145		800		Fr. Fndr. Experimental Medicine
Bernard, Crystal		Entertainment	13			40	Actress. 'Wings'
Bernard, Francis, Sir	1712-79	Colonial Governor	175	522	750		Col.Gov. Mass. Bay Colony
Bernard, John Henry, Archbishop		Clergy	304	45	50	40	
Bernard, Simon	1779-1839	Military	50	125			Fr. Military Eng'r. Nap.at Waterloo. US Gen. 1816
Berndt, Walter*		Cartoonist	10			50	'Smitty'
Bernhard, Sandra		Entertainment	10			15	Comedienne.
Bernhardt, Sarah	1844-1923	Entertainment	133	275	471	850	'The Divine Sarah'. Great French Actress
Bernie, Ben		Entertainment	20		25	25	Big Band Leader-M.C.-Comedian.
Bernsen, Corbin		Entertainment	15	20	40	40	Actor. 'L.A. Law' etc.
Bernstein, Elmer		Composer	25	40	125	50	Am. Composer-Conductor. ALS/Cont $600

NAME	DATE	CATEGORY	SIG	LS/DS	ALS	SP	COMMENTS
Bernstein, Leonard	1918-90	Composer	124	445	575	245	AMusMsS $1,600, $4,500. 3x5 SP $120,AMsS $1450
Bernstorff, John H., Graf von		Diplomat	30		100		German Ambass. To US. Member Ger. Reistag
Berosini, Josephine		Entertainment	5	10	25	30	
Berrien, J. Macpherson	1781-1856	Cabinet	30	55	105		Jackson Att'y General
Berrigan, Daniel, Fr.		Clergy	30		65	40	Controversial Political Priest
Berry, Chuck		Entertainment	50	275		156	Rock. Alb. S $115
Berry, Halle		Entertainment	15			45	Actress
Berry, Hiram G. (WD)		Civil War	475	675			Killed in Action
Berry, Hiram G.	1824-63	Civil War	355	680			Union Gen. Killed in Action
Berry, Jim*		Cartoonist	10			35	Berry's World
Berry, Ken		Entertainment	5		15	15	Actor. F Troop, Mama's Family
Berry, Lucien		Military	15	50		55	General WW I
Berry, Richard	1936-1997	Entertainment	30			60	Composer Louie, Louie
Berry, Sidney M.		Clergy	10	15	25		
Berry, Tom		Governor	5			25	Gov. SD
Berry, William H.		Civil War	20				6th Missouri Survivor
Berryman, Clifford*		Artist	55	75	95	150	'Created The 'Teddy Bear'
Berryman, Clifton K.Jr.*		Cartoonist		45		150	Pulitzer. Political Cartoonist
Berryman, John	1914-72	Author	75	300			'64 Pulitzer for Poetry. Short Stories
Bertelson, Richard L.		Aviation	10	25	38	30	Navy ACE, WW II
Berthier, L. Alexandre	1753-1815	Napoleonic Wars	75	200	425		Marshal of Napoleon
Berthold, Rudolf		Aviation	200	350	650	475	ACE, WW I, The Iron Knight
Berthollet, Claude-Louis, Count	1748-1822	Science	60	150	330		Fr. Chemist. Senator of Napoleon
Bertinelli, Valerie		Entertainment	12		25	25	Actress. TV-Films
Bertolucci, Bernardo	1940-	Entertainment	15			35	Film Director. Last Tango in Paris
Bertrand, Henri G.	1773-1844	Military	70	120	305		Count Bertrand. General. Chamberlain to Napoleon
Berwick, Duke (J.Fitzjames)	1670-1734	Fr. Military	150	400			Gen. of Louis XIV, Marshal Fr.
Berzelius, Jons Jacob	1779-1848	Science	75	165	475		Swe. Chemist. Chemical Symbols
Besant, Annie Wood	1847-1933	Clergy	50	245	398		Br.Radical Free-Thinker.
Besant, Walter	1836-1901	Author	35	125	130	125	Br. Novelist. AMsS $9000
Besch, Bibi		Entertainment	5		15	20	
Beser, Jacob		Aviation	50	100		100	Both Atomic Missions
Bess, Gordon*		Cartoonist	5			25	'Redeye'
Bessell, Ted		Entertainment	10	20		25	Boyfriend in That Girl
Bessemer, Henry, Sir	1813-98	Metallurgist-Inventor	35	60	200	95	Invented Blast Furnace For Producing Steel
Besser, Joe		Entertainment	50			75	One of 'The Three Stooges'
Bessieres, Bertrand		Fr. Revolution	55	100			
Bessieres, Jean-Baptiste	1766-1813	Fr. Military	175	375			Marshal of France under Napoleon
Best, Charles H.	1899-1978	Science	107	188	290	125	Discovered Insulin/Banting
Best, Edna	1900-74	Entertainment	35	42	32	50	Brit. Character Actress. Films & Stage
Best, James	1926-	Entertainment	10		15	20	Actor Dukes of Hazzard
Best, Pete		Entertainment	32			112	Pre Ringo. Beatles Drummer
Best, Willie	1916-62	Entertainment	50			150	Vintage Afro-Am. Film Actor
Bestor, Don		Bandleader	15			30	Jack Benny's 1st Bandleader
Beswick, Martine		Entertainment	5		15	15	

NAME	DATE	CATEGORY	SIG	LS/DS	ALS	SP	COMMENTS
Betham-Edwards, Matilda		Author	5	10	22		
Bethe, Hans, Dr.		Science	35	55		45	Nobel Physics
Bethune, Mary McLeod	1875-1955	Educator	125	325	500	175	Black Teacher, Activist. TLS/Cont. $895
Betjeman, John, Sir	1906-84	Author	40	111	135	50	Br. Poet Laureate
Bettelheim, Bruno		Science	35	65		150	Psychiatrist researched Autism
Bettger, Lyle	1915-	Entertainment	8			20	Actor. Films. 50's. Eventually Western Heavy Roles
Betz, Carl	1920-78	Entertainment	40			75	Actor. 50's. Husband Donna Reed Show
Beugnot, J.C., Count		Fr. Military	85	160			
Beverage, John		Civil War	30	85			Union Gen., Gov. IL
Beveridge, Albert J.	1862-1927	Congress	5	20	35		US Sen., Historian. Organizer of Progressive Party
Bevin, Ernest	1881-1951	Statesman	25	55	125	45	Br. Powerful Union Leader. NATO Treaty
Bewick, Thomas	1753-1828	Artist	105	275	625		Br. Illustrator, Wood Engraver
Bexley, Don Bubba	19xx-97	Entertainment	7	15	30	35	Actor-Comedian Sanford & Son
Bey, Turhan	1920-	Entertainment	15	20	35	30	Actor. Exotic & Mysterious Roles in 40's Films
Bhutto, Zulfikar Ali	1928-79	Head of State	35	102	175	200	Pakistan, Pres. & Prime Minister. Coup. Executed
Biaggi, Mario		Senate/Congress	5	15		15	Congressman NY. NY Police MOH
Bialik, Chaim N.	1873-1934	Author	65	225	425	115	Jewish Poet
Biasini, Piero		Entertainment	10			35	Opera
Bibb, George M.	1772-1859	Cabinet	15		65		US Sen. KY. Sec'y Treasury-Tyler
Bibb, George M.	1776-1859	Cabinet	30	45	80		Early Sec'y Treas.,Senator KY
Bibb, Wm. Wyatt	1781-1820	Governor	25	45			Gov. GA
Bickersteth, Edward H., Bishop		Clergy	15	25	35	35	
Bickford, Charles	1889-1967	Entertainment	30	45	65	100	Actor. Burlesque 1914-Broadway 1919-Films 1929
Biddle, Clement	1740-1814	Rev. War	232	835	1050		Revolutionary Officer, Merchant, War Hero
Biddle, Clement Carroll	1784-1855	Military	25	40	75		Col. of 1st Inf. PA. 1812. Political Science
Biddle, Francis	1886-1968	Cabinet	20	35	75		Att'y General. Judge Intern'l Tribunal-Nurnberg
Biddle, George		Artist	25	85	210		
Biddle, Nicholas	1786-1844	Business	138	510	845		Pres. U.S. Bank, Financier
Biden, Joe		Senate/Congress	5	15		20	Senator DE
Bidwell, Daniel D.	1819-64	Civil War	255		825		Union Gen. ALS '63 $1595
Bidwell, John	1819-1900	Western Pioneer	55	275			Calif. Pioneer, Pres. Candidate-Prohibition Ticket
Biehn, Michael		Entertainment	10		20	35	Actor
Bierce, Ambrose	1842-1914	Author	275	670	590		Journalist,Short Stories. Literary ALS $1250-$2750
Bieri, Ramon		Entertainment	10			35	
Bierstadt, Albert	1830-1902	Artist	140	220	540		Of the Hudson River School. Landscapes
Biery, James S.		Senate/Congress	10	15		25	Congressman PA
Big Bopper		Entertainment	950				Rock.Most Difficult of Three Killed In Plane Crash
Big Man, Chief Max		Native American	30			60	Chief
Bigard, Barney		Entertainment	70			150	Jazz Clarinet, Ten. Sax
Bigelow, Erastus B.	1814-79	Business-Inventor	100	290	595		Power Looms for Carpet Weaving
Bigelow, John	1817-1911	Publisher	5	20	55	25	Editor& Co-Owner NY Evening Post. Diplomat
Bigelow, Poultney	1855-1954	Journalist	5		22		Traveller, Author. Son of John
Bigge, Arthur, Sir		Military	10	30	65		
Biggers, Earl Derr		Author	150	210	382	350	Am. Novelist,Mystery Writer.Created 'Charlie Chan'
Biggs, Asa		Civil War	35	70			CSA Judge, US Senator NC

NAME	DATE	CATEGORY	SIG	LS/DS	ALS	SP	COMMENTS
Biggs, Ronnie		Criminal	25			95	Train Robber. His Book Signed $100
Bikel, Theodore	1924-	Entertainment	5	20		35	Vienna-Born Character Actor-Singer
Bilbo, Theodore G.	1877-1947	Senate	20	30		25	Senator MS, Gov. MS. Demagogue, Racist
Bill, Max	1908-94	Celebrity	10	25	40	35	Swiss Painter & Sculptor. Pc Repro Sculpture S $60
Bill, Tony		Entertainment	10			20	Actor, Film Director, Producer-'The Sting'
Billings, Josh	1818-85	Author	25	80	165	40	American Humorist. (H.W.Shaw)
Billingsley, Barbara		Entertainment	5	10		20	Actress.'Leave It To Beaver'
Billingsley, Peter		Entertainment	4			12	Xmas Story SP $30
Billington, E.		Entertainment	55		250		Opera. Internationally Famous Prima Donna.
Billo, James D.		Aviation	10	25	40	30	Navy ACE, WW II
Billroth, Theodor	1829-94	Science	45	225	295		Ger. Surgeon. Use of Antisepsis
Binci, Mario		Entertainment	15			45	Opera
Bing, Herman	1889-1947	Entertainment	20			40	Actor. Ger. Born. Form Circus Clown, Vaudevilian
Bing, Rudolph	1903-97	Entertainment	15	35	46	35	Longtime Metropolitan Opera Director
Bingham, Amelia		Entertainment	6	10	15	25	
Bingham, Henry		Civil War	85		160		Union Gen., MOH Wilderness
Bingham, John A.		Congress	30	35	90		MOC. OH, Lincoln Judge Adv.
Bingham, Judson David	1831-1909	Civil War	45	140	185		Union General
Bingham, Traci		Entertainment	10			49	Actress. Pin-Up $55
Bingham, William	1752-1804	Rev. War	120	315	340		Continental Congr.Sen.PA. Fndr.1st Bank in Country
Binney, Thomas		Clergy	20	30	45	35	
Binnig, Gerd, Dr.		Science	20	60		45	Nobel Physics
Binns, Edward		Entertainment	5			10	Actor. Familiar Face in Many Supporting Roles
Binoche, Juliette		Entertainment	17			60	Actress. 'English Patient'
Biot, Jean Baptiste	1774-1862	Science	100		575		Fr. Mathematician, Physicist, Astronomer
Birch, Thora		Entertainment	6			45	Talented Young Actress
Bird, Billie		Entertainment	7			15	Character actress
Birdseye, Clarence	1886-1956	Business	100		500	262	Frozen Foods.Prolific Inventor. Over 300 Patents
Birdwood, William R., Sir	1865-1951	Military	45	145			Br. Fld. Marshal, WW I
Birendra, Bir B.		Head of State	10	15		25	Prime Minister Nepal
Birney, David		Entertainment	5		15	10	Actor. Leading Man
Birney, David Bell	1825-64	Civil War	225	295	775		Union Gen. ANS '63 $990. Sig/Rank $365
Birney, William	1819-1907	Civil War	35	80	108		Union General Sig/Rank $80
Bisbee, Horatio, Jr.		Civil War	25	45	105		Union Officer & MOC
Bishop, Barry		Celebrity	7	14			
Bishop, Elizabeth	1911-79	Author	35	125			Am. Poet. Pulitzer Prize '55
Bishop, J. Michael, Dr.		Science	25	40		35	Nobel Medicine
Bishop, Jim		Author	15	35	50	20	Journalist. Best Selling Novels. The Day..... Book
Bishop, Joey	1918-	Entertainment	9		10	20	Comedian member of Sinatra rat pack group
Bishop, Julie		Entertainment	6		15	15	Actress
Bishop, Stephen		Entertainment	5			15	Rock Star
Bishop, Wm. 'Billy'	1894-1956	Aviation	150	225	325	255	ACE, WW I, 72 Kills
Bismark, Prince Otto von	1815-98	Royalty	250	600	745	920	The Iron Chancellor
Bispham, David		Entertainment	60	80	110	120	Opera
Bissell, Clayton L.		Aviation	25	40	100		

NAME	DATE	CATEGORY	SIG	LS/DS	ALS	SP	COMMENTS
Bissell, Emily P.	1861-1948	Humanitarian	125				Introduced U.S Xmas Seals
Bissell, Whit	1919-	Entertainment	10		15	20	Character Actor in Films from Mid-40's
Bissell, William H.		Governor	10	28	60		Governor IL, MOC
Bisset, Jacqueline	1944-	Entertainment	12	20	30	33	Brit. Actress. Leading Roles Since 70's
Bissett, Josie		Entertainment	12			53	Actress, 'Melrose Place'
Bissit, J.E.		Br. Navy	10	25		20	Commander HMS Queen Eliz.
Bitter, Karl Theodore	1867-1915	Artist	25	75	155	100	Am. Sculptor
Bittrich, Wilhelm		Military	27	70	135	60	
Bixby, Bill	1934-93	Entertainment	10	58	40	68	Actor. Premature Death
Bizet, Georges	1838-75	Composer	425	890	1555		Fr. Composer. Carmen, L'Arlesienne Suite
Bjerknes, Jacob A.B.	1887-1975	Science	35				Discovered Origin of Cyclones
Bjoerling, Jussi	1911-60	Entertainment	500	650	1000	925	Great 20th Cent. Swedish Tenor. Died Early
Bjornson, Bjornstjerne	1832-1910	Author	50	65	308		3rd Nobel for Literature
Bjornstad, Alfred		Military	10	20	35		General WW I
Blacher, Boris		Composer	40				Rus-Ger. Classical & Experimental Music
Black, Alexander		Author	5	10	20	10	
Black, Clint		Entertainment	20			50	Country-Western
Black, Eugene R.		Business	5	20	30	15	
Black, Frank, Dr.		Conductor	10			35	NBC Dir. of Music in '40's
Black, Hugo (SC)	1886-1971	Supreme Court	40	120	285	95	Justice 1937-71.Bill of Rights, Constitution Champ
Black, Jeremiah		Cabinet	30	60	115		Att'y General (Buchanan)
Black, John Charles	1835-1915	Civil War	50	125	160		Union General, MOH
Black, Karen		Entertainment	10		15	20	Actress. Memorable in 'Easy Rider','5 Easy Pieces'
Black, Richard B.		Military	10	25	45		
Black, William		Military	20			45	General WW I
Blackburn, John T.		Aviation	15	24	40	35	ACE, WW II
Blackburn, Luke P.		Governor	15	35			Governor KY
Blackett, Patrick M.		Science	20	35	50	30	Nobel Physics. Cosmic Rays
Blackman, Honor		Entertainment	8	15	25	27	Br. Actress. 'James Bond'. Leading Lady
Blackmer, Sidney	1895-1973	Entertainment	10			35	Actor. Stage (Tony Award) Films. Character Actor
Blackmon, Fred L.		Senate/Congress	10	20		15	MOC AL
Blackmore, Richard D.		Author	15	40	95		Br. Novelist. 'Lorna Doone'
Blackmun, Harry A. (SC)		Supreme Court	45	225	270	75	
Blackstone, Harry		Entertainment	150	375	475	200	Magician. Self Sketch Signed $375
Blackstone, Harry, Jr		Entertainment	25			40	Magician
Blackton, J.Stuart & Smith, A. E.		Entertainment		45			Co-Fndrs Vitagraph Films. Inventor
Blackwell, Alice Stone	1857-1950	Reformer	200		195		Woman's Suffrage. Editor
Blackwell, Elizabeth		Medical	125		650		1st Woman to Receive M.D. Degree in Modern Times
Blackwell, Mr.		Business	5	10		15	Fashion Critic
Blackwell, Otis		Composer	25	85	175		
Blaha, John E.		Astronaut	10			20	
Blaine, James G.	1830-93	Cabinet	57	65	208	45	U.S.Sen. ME,Garfield Sec'y St., Pres. Candidate
Blaine, Vivian	1921-95	Entertainment	18		15	25	Actress-Singer. Guys & Doll, State Fair
Blair, Austin	1814-94	Civil War	20		55		CW Governor of MI
Blair, Charles		Aviation	45			60	

NAME	DATE	CATEGORY	SIG	LS/DS	ALS	SP	COMMENTS
Blair, Eric (See Orwell, George)							Pen-name of George Orwell
Blair, Francis P., Jr.	1821-75	Civil War	45	101	145		Union General, U.S.Sen. MO. Sig/Rank $75
Blair, Frank		Journalist	10			35	Radio-TV News Anchor & Correspondent(Deceased)
Blair, Jacob B.		Civil War	25		70		Virginia MOC Who Remained Loyal to Union
Blair, Janet		Entertainment	10		20	25	Actress-Singer. 'My Sister Eileen'.
Blair, John (SC)		Supreme Court	150	775	1200		Signer of Constitution
Blair, John	1802-99	Business	150	750	950		Helped Charter Union Pacific RR.Built 1st 100 Mile
Blair, Linda		Entertainment	8	10	20	26	Young Actress in The Exorcist
Blair, Montgomery		Legal	75	278	545		Counsel to Dred Scott
Blake, Amanda	1927-89	Entertainment	60	128	115	120	Veteran 'Gunsmoke' Actress. Miss Kitty
Blake, Bud*		Cartoonist	5			55	Tiger. S Original Three Panel Strip $125
Blake, Eubie	1883-1983	Composer	80	212	190	175	Songwriter & Ragtime Pianist. AMusQS $385-$650
Blake, Eugene Carson		Clergy	50	95	150	70	
Blake, Madge		Entertainment	100			250	Actress. 'Aunt Harriet' on TV's 'Batman' Series
Blake, Robert (Bobby)		Entertainment	6	15		30	'Our Gang' to 'In Cold Blood' & TV's Baretta'
Blake, William		Artist					Content ALS $30,000
Blakely, Susan		Entertainment	6		15	20	Actress
Blakeslee, Don		Aviation	10	25	40	30	ACE, WW II
Blanc, Louis	1811-82	Author	20	40	100		Fr. Socialist, Journalist, Politician, Historian
Blanc, Mel	1908-89	Entertainment	68	128	135	119	Voice of Bugs Bunny etc.
Blanchard, Albert G.(WD)		Civil War	195	1595			CSA General
Blanchard, Albert G.	1810-91	Civil War	120	205			CSA Gen.
Blanchard, Nina		Entertainment	4			8	
Blanchard, Rachel		Entertainment	7			30	Actress. TV's Clueless. Pin-Up $55
Blanchett, Cate		Entertainment	8			55	Actress. Golden Globe Award
Bland, Richard P.	1835-99	Congress	15				Repr. MO, Defeated by W.J.. Bryan for Pres.
Bland, Schuyler Otis		Senate/Congress	5	15	25		MOC VA
Bland, William T.		Senate/Congress	5	15	20		MOC MO
Blandick, Clara	1880-1962	Entertainment	456			650	Aunt Em in Oz. Rarest of the Oz Signatures
Blane, Ralph		Composer	5			40	AMusMsS 36
Blane, Sally		Entertainment	6	8	15	15	
Blanks, Mary Lynn		Entertainment	3	3	6	6	
Blanton, Leonard Ray		Governor	10			15	Governor TN, MOC TN
Blanton, Thomas L.		Senate/Congress	10	20		20	Senator TX, MOC TX
Blaschka, Rudolph		Artist	10	35	75		Bohemian Artist in Glass
Blasco-Ibanez, Vicente		Author	100			450	Sp. Novelist. Self Exiled
Blaslev, Lisabeth		Entertainment	10			25	Opera
Blass, Bill		Business	10	15		25	Fashion Designer
Blatchford, Samuel (SC)		Supreme Court	58	135	190		Supreme Court in 1882
Blatty, William Peter	1928-	Author	15	32	45	25	The Exorcist, AA . TsS $150
Bledsoe, Tempest		Entertainment	15	35		35	
Bleeth, Yasmine		Entertainment	12			46	Baywatch, Pin-up $60
Blenker, Louis (Ludwig)	1812-63	Civil War	100	210			Union Gen LS '61 $800
Blennerhassett, Harman		Rev. War	115	330	575		Funds, Refuge-Burr Conspiracy
Bleriot, Louis	1872-1936	Aviation	250	500	475	750	1st To Fly English Channel

NAME	DATE	CATEGORY	SIG	LS/DS	ALS	SP	COMMENTS
Bless, Frederick		Aviation	10	22	38	32	ACE, Korea
Bletcher, Billy		Entertainment	50			200	
Blethyn, Brenda		Entertainment	6			42	
Bligh, William, Capt.		Military	775	5900	2500		Br. Adm. Capt. HMS Bounty
Bliss, Arthur, Sir		Composer	25		175		Brit. Opera, Orch. works
Bliss, Cornelius		Cabinet	10	25	55	40	Sec'y Interior
Bliss, George Jr.		Civil War	8	15	25		MOC OH
Bliss, J. S.		Civil War	5	10	20		
Bliss, Tasker H.		Military	15	25	50	25	US Gen.1st Cmdr. War College
Bliss, William Wallace S.		Military	130	968	500		Pvt. Sec'y, Chief of Staff to Gen'l Zachary Taylor
Bliss, Zenas R.		Civil War	35	110	160		Union Officer
Blitzer, Wolf		Journalist	5		15	20	TV News & Special Events. CNN
Blitzstein, Marc		Composer	80	100	250		Opera. Brilliant US Composer
Blixen, Karen (Isak Dinesen)		Author	110	500		200	Danish Novelist Out of Africa
Bloch, Ernest	1880-1959	Composer	80		300	288	Swiss-Am. Composer, Teacher
Bloch, Ernst		Author	55	140	425	90	Ger. Philosopher.
Bloch, Felix		Science	25	40	100	30	Nobel Physics
Bloch, Konrad, Dr.		Science	20	30	45	30	Nobel Medicine
Bloch, Raymond		Composer	10	20	35	10	
Bloch, Robert		Author	20	50	60	20	Novelist. TMsS $450
Block, Henry W.		Business	20	45		65	H & R Block. Founder with Brother
Block, Herb*		Cartoonist	15			100	Herblock-political
Block, John R.		Cabinet	5	10	15	10	
Block, Joseph L.		Business	4	6	9	6	
Block, Martin		Entertainment	5			15	Early radio deejay
Block, Richard		Business	20	35	90	25	H & R Block
Blocker, Dan	1928-72	Entertainment	170			365	Hoss On Long Running 'Bonanza'
Blodget, Samuel Jr.		Rev. War	285	750	1540		Inventor, Soldier, Judge
Bloembergen, Nicolaas Dr.		Science	20	35	40	30	Nobel Physics
Blomberg, Werner Von		Military	30	75	165	125	Ger. Fld. Marshal WW II
Blomfield, Ezekial		Clergy	35	45	60		
Blondell, Joan		Entertainment	35	40	65	67	Oscar Winner
Blondin, Charles	1824-97	Entertainment	30	450	175	60	Tightrope walker Niagara Falls
Blood, Robert O.		Governor	5		25		Governor NH
Blood, Sweat and Tears		Entertainment	35			80	
Bloom, Claire		Entertainment	6	8	15	20	
Bloom, Lindsay		Entertainment	8	9	12	15	
Bloomer, Amelia		Reformer	275	350			Pioneer Dress & Social Reformer
Bloomfield, Joseph		Rev. War	30	95	157		Officer, Attorney, Gov. NJ
Bloomfield-Zeisler, Fannie		Entertainment	25			75	Concert Pianist
Blore, Eric		Entertainment	20	25	65	60	
Blossom Rock		Entertainment	40			75	
Blough, Roger		Business	5	15	25	15	
Blount, James H.		Civil War	25	40			CSA Officer, MOC GA
Blount, William		Senate	320	900			Continental Congr. Senator TN

NAME	DATE	CATEGORY	SIG	LS/DS	ALS	SP	COMMENTS
Blount, Winton M.		Cabinet	5	15	25	10	P.M. General
Bloustein, Edward J.		Celebrity	5	12	20	10	
Blucher, Gebhard L. von		Military	200	550	2200		Pruss. Fld. Marshal vs Napoleon
Blue, Ben	1901-75	Entertainment	26	30	60	55	
Blue, Monte	1880-1963	Entertainment	19	25	45	75	Griffith Great Silent Star
Bluford, Guion S. Jr.		Astronaut	10			28	
Blum, Leon (Fr)		Head of State	25	40	110	35	Pres. France WW II
Blum, Norbert		Statesman	5			10	German Minister & Statesman
Blumberg, Baruch S.		Science	20	30	55	25	Nobel Medicine
Blumenauer, Earl		Congress	5			15	MC from Oregon
Blumenfeld, Felix		Composer		150		300	Russ. Conductor, Teacher
Blumenthal, Jacques		Composer	40		350		And Pianist
Blumenthal, W. Michael		Cabinet	5	10	15	10	
Blunden, Edmund	1896-1974	Poet	55		238		Poet, Critic, Biographer. AMsS $750
Blunt, Asa P.		Military	25		200		General
Blunt, James G., Dr.		Civil War	46	75			Union General
Blunt, John Henry		Clergy	15	25	35	25	
Blyden, Larry		Entertainment	3	3	6	6	
Blyth, Ann		Entertainment	10		15	18	Actress-Singer
Blythe, Betty	1893-1972	Entertainment	35		75	175	Silent Star. Beautiful Vamp of Early Movies
Boardman, Eleanor	1898-1991	Entertainment	15		40	45	Vintage Silent Film Actress. The Squaw Man
Boardman, Russell		Aviation	25	55	95	80	
Bob & Ray		Entertainment	25			50	
Bob, Tim		Entertainment	6			25	Music. Bass Guitar Rage Against the Machine
Bobbitt, John Wayne		Media Celebrity	25			50	Victim of Angry Wife
Bobbitt, Lorena		Media Celebrity					Penis Slasher. NRPA
Bobkins, Addie		Entertainment	5	6	9	8	
Bobko, Karol J.		Astronaut	7			15	
Bochco, Steven		Entertainment	10	15		20	TV Emmy Award Producer
Bochner, Lloyd		Entertainment	4	4	9	15	
Bock, Feodor von		Military	100	295		150	Ger.Gen. WW II. Failed
Bock, Jerry		Composer	40	16	35	80	Fiddler.... AMusQS $250
Bocock, Thomas S.		Civil War	20				CSA Speaker of the House
Bodenschatz, Karl		Aviation	30	75	150	95	
Bodwell, Joseph R.		Governor	8	12		10	Gov. ME
Boe, Nils A.		Governor	10	15			Governor SD
Boerhaave, Herman	1668-1738	Science		2188			Dutch Physician, Medical Educator
Boesch, Ruthilde		Entertainment	5	10		20	Opera
Bogard, Dirk		Entertainment	10		30	25	
Bogart, Humphrey	1899-1957	Entertainment	947	1933	1750	2740	Academy Award. African Queen
Bogdonavich, Peter		Entertainment	10	30		20	Controversial Film Director
Boggs, Charles		Civil War	45	90	115		Union Adm.
Boggs, Hale		Senate/Congress	10	25			MOC LA
Boggs, Lindy (Mrs. H.Boggs)		Congress	10	15		15	MOC LA
Boggs, William R. (WD)		Civil War	170		495		CSA General

NAME	DATE	CATEGORY	SIG	LS/DS	ALS	SP	COMMENTS
Boggs, William R.	1829-1911	Civil War	85	195	315		CSA General
Bogguss, Suzy		Country Music	5			20	Pin-Up $30
Bohay, Heidi		Entertainment	5	6	15	10	
Bohm, Karl		Entertainment	15		75	85	Conductor. Dir. Vienna State Opera
Bohm, Karl	1894-1981	Entertainment	20			45	Austrian Conductor. Leading Strauss Conductor
Bohnen, Carl		Artist	20	35			
Bohr, Aage Niels	1922-	Science	25			55	Nobel Physics 1975
Bohr, Niels H.D.	1885-1962	Science	500	1135		2240	Danish Physicist. Nobel 1922. Development A Bomb
Boisrond-Canal		Haitian Statesman	30	95			
Boito, Arrigo		Composer	45	110	325		& Verdi Librettist. AMusQS $750
Bok, Edward W.		Author-Business	30	55	140	40	Editor, Curtis Publishing, Pulitzer
Bokor, Margit		Entertainment	10			30	Hung. Soprano
Boland, Frederick		Celebrity	5	15	40	10	
Boland, Mary		Entertainment	15	75		70	
Bolcom, William		Composer	15	25	65		Pulitzer, AMusQS $75
Bolden, Charles F. Jr.		Astronaut	6			25	
Boles, John		Entertainment	20	35		40	
Bolet, Jorge		Entertainment	20			120	Pianist
Bolger, James		Head of State	10			20	P.M. New Zealand
Bolger, Ray	1904-87	Entertainment	80	67	325	210	Wizard of OZ. SP as Scarecrow $250-500
Bolger, Ray and Haley, Jack		Entertainment		1500			SP (OZ) $595
Bolingbroke, Henry (St.John)		Author	35	150	398		1st Viscount, Politician, Writer
Bolivar, Simon		Head of State	385	2912	4975		Statesman, Revolutionary Leader
Boll, Heinrich	1917-85	Author	32	30	95	30	Nobel Lit., Novelist, Poet
Bolling, Tiffany		Entertainment	10		15	20	
Bolt, John		Aviation	12	30	50	35	ACE, WW II & Korea
Bolton, Frances Payne		Senate/Congress	10	25			MOC OH
Bolton, Guy		Author	15	100			Playwright
Bolton, James		Inventor	25	75	142		Sewing Machine Inventor
Bolton, Michael		Entertainment	125			150	Singer, Composer
Bolton-Jones, Hugh		Artist	10	25	45		Am. Landscape Painter
Bombeck, Erma		Author	5	18	50	10	Humorous Columnist
Bomford, George		Military Engineer	65	200			Invented Howitzer Bomb Cannon
Bomford, James Voty		Civil War	37	80	116		
Bon Jovi, Jon		Entertainment	10			40	Rock
Bonaduce, Danny		Entertainment	10			25	
Bonaparte, Caroline		Royalty	35	95	275		Marie-Annonciade
Bonaparte, Charles	1851-1921	Cabinet	30	70			Sec'y Navy, Att'y Gen. Gr.Nephew Napol.
Bonaparte, Elisa (Maria Ana)		Royalty	400		500		Oldest Sister of Napoeon
Bonaparte, Eugene Napoleon		Royalty	75	200	435		Adopted by Napoleon
Bonaparte, Jerome Napoleon	1822-91	Royalty	60	150	240		Son of King of Westphalia
Bonaparte, Joseph	1768-1844	Royalty	120	231	343		Elder Brother of Napoleon. King of Two Sicilies
Bonaparte, Letizia		Royalty		1500	2700		Mother of Napoleon
Bonaparte, Louis-Napoleon	1914-97	Royalty	70				Called Le Prince Napoleon from 1926 Till Death
Bonaparte, Lucien	1775-1849	Royalty	50	105	145		Brother. Opposed Nap., Exiled

NAME	DATE	CATEGORY	SIG	LS/DS	ALS	SP	COMMENTS
Bonaparte, Marie Louise		Royalty	195	815	2795		Wife of Napoleon
Bonaparte, Mathilde	1820-1904	Royalty	50		150		Daughter of King Jerome
Bonaparte, Napoleon		Royalty					SEE Napoleon I
Bonar, Horatius		Clergy	15	20	25		
Bonci, Alessandro		Entertainment	35			115	Opera
Bond, Carrie Jacobs		Composer	35	110	170	45	Am. Composer Art Songs
Bond, Charles		Aviation	10	28	40	30	ACE, WW II, Flying Tigers
Bond, Christopher Kit		Senate	5	10		10	Senator MO
Bond, Ford		Entertainment	10			15	Early Network Radio Ann'cer
Bond, Johnny		Country Music	10			20	
Bond, Julian		Politician	10	20	50	20	Afro-Am. Civil Rights Activist. Poet
Bond, Tommy Butch		Entertainment	18			22	Our Gang Comedy. Bad Boy
Bond, Ward	1903-60	Entertainment	88	80	95	179	GWTW, Wagon Train. Serious Western Player
Bond, William C.		Science	45	190	350		Am. Astronomer. Harvard Observ.
Bondi, Beulah		Entertainment	15	15	30	38	
Bondur, Roberta		Astronaut	10			20	Canadian Astro
Boner, Edmond	1500-69	Clergy	650				Appealed to Pope for Henry VIII
Bonerz, Peter		Entertainment	3	3	6	6	
Bonesteel, Charles H.		Military	11	35	58		
Bonet, Lisa	1967-	Entertainment	25			40	Actress
Bong, Richard		Aviation	500	1200	2000	1800	ACE, WW II, Top U.S. Ace
Bongo, Albert B.		Head of State	100			425	President of Gabon. Elected '72, '79,'86,'93
Bonham, Joe 'Bonzo'		Entertainment	75			125	
Bonham, Milledge L.(WD)		Civil War	185	250	428		CSA General
Bonham, Milledge L.	1813-90	Civil War	100	225			CSA General
Bonheur, Rosa	1822-1899	Artist	110	155	325		Fr. Horse Fair & Rural Scenes
Boninsegna, Celestina		Entertainment	150			850	Legendary Soprano. Vintage
Bonjovi, John		Entertainment				40	Rock
Bonnard, Pierre	1867-1947	Artist	115	280	812		Fr.Post-impressionist, Illustrator, Graphic Artist
Bonneville, Benj. L. E. de	1795-1878	Military	225	600	897		Pioneer Explorer NW Territory
Bonney, Barbara		Entertainment	15			35	Opera
Bono, Sonny	?-1998	Entertainment	30			65	Mayor Palm Springs, Congressman. Sonny & Cher
Bonstelle, Jessie		Entertainment	25		40		Stage Actress, Producer, Teacher
Bontemps, Arna		Author	25	175			Am. Novels, Non-Fiction, Poetry
Bonvalot, Gabriel		Celebrity				155	
Bonynge, Richard		Conductor	15			50	Dame Joan Sutherland's Conductor Husband
Book of Love (4)		Entertainment	15			35	Rock Group
Book, Sorrell		Entertainment	5			10	Actress
Boone, Daniel	1734-1820	Rev. War	2000	9300	21500		Am. Pioneer Cumberland Gap
Boone, Debbie		Entertainment	5	15		20	Singer
Boone, Pat		Entertainment	4	15		10	Singer-Actor
Boone, Randy		Entertainment	4			15	Actor. The Virginian Co-Star
Boone, Richard		Entertainment	80	100		135	Actor. 'Palladin'
Boone, Squire		Rev. War			1150		NC Farmer. Father of Daniel
Boorda, Jeremy M.	19xx-96	Military	30		95		Adm. US Navy. Suicide 1996

NAME	DATE	CATEGORY	SIG	LS/DS	ALS	SP	COMMENTS
Boorstin, Daniel J.		Author	25				The Creators
Boosler, Elayne		Entertainment	10		30	25	Stand-up Comedienne
Booth, Adrian		Entertainment	5			20	Vintage Actress
Booth, Ballington		Clergy	25	75	165		Co-Cmdr. Salvation Army
Booth, Bromwell		Clergy	25	50	75		
Booth, Edwin	1833-93	Entertainment	108		288	250	Great 19th Century Actor. Brother of John Wilkes
Booth, Evangeline	1865-1950	Reformer	35	108	345	95	Salvation Army General
Booth, Ewing	1870-1949	Military	20			50	WW I General. Pershing Chief of Staff
Booth, John Wilkes	1838-65	Civil War	1550	3050	4000	4500	Assassin of Lincoln. AMsS $35,000. RARE-ANY FORM
Booth, Junius Brutus, Jr.	1821-83	Entertainment	50	105			Actor Brother of John Wilkes
Booth, Maude	1865-1948	Reformer	45	100	225		Fndr. Vols. of Am. & PTA
Booth, Newell S., Bishop		Clergy	20	35	50	50	
Booth, Newton		Senator	15	25	60		Governor CA, Senator CA
Booth, Shirley	1907-92	Entertainment	30	50		50	Starred on Broadway.Oscar forCome Back Little...
Booth, William	1829-1912	Clergy	95	160	350	175	Founder & Gen'l Salvation Army
Booth, William Bramwell		Clergy	40	75	100	65	Eldest Son & Organizer
Boothe, Powers		Entertainment	5	6	15	15	
Boozer, Brenda		Entertainment	4	5	10	10	
Bor, Tadeusz		Military	15	45	75		
Borah, William E.		Senate	20	30		45	Senator ID
Borch, F.J.		Business	4	10		10	Pres. General Electric
Borchers, Adolf		Aviation	10	15	30	25	
Bordaberry, Juan M		Head of State	7	15	25	10	Uraguay
Bordelon, Guy		Aviation	8	20	35	25	ACE, Korea
Borden, Lizzy		Celebrity			15000		Alleged Ax Murderess
Borden, Olive		Entertainment	30	35	45	150	
Borden, Robert L.	1854-1937	Head of State	35				P.M. Canada 1911-20
Bordogni, Giulio-Marco		Entertainment			40		Opera. Tenor. Teacher
Bordoni, Irene		Entertainment	15	15	35	30	
Boreanaz, David		Entertainment	6			48	Actor Buffy
Borge, Victor	1909-	Entertainment	15	30		35	Pianist-Comedian. Concert Stage & Recordings
Borges, Jorge Luis	1899-1986	Author	75	350			Argentinian.Fiction, Poetry
Borghese, Camillo		Head of State					SEE Paul V, Pope
Borghese, Pauline Bonaparte		Royalty	110		575		Sister of Napoleon
Borgia, Francesco Card'l		Clergy	3200	2200			
Borglum, Gutzon	1867-1941	Artist	225	375	492	545	Creator Mt. Rushmore Sculptures. Sketch S $950
Borglum, Lincoln		Artist	25	60	85		Son of Gutzon. Sculptor
Borglum, Solon		Artist	15		45		
Borgnine, Ernest		Entertainment	6		12	25	Actor. Oscar Winner
Bori, Lucrezia	1887-1960	Entertainment	40	95		90	Opera. Sp. Lyric Soprano. SP 9x13 (Violetta)$200
Boring, Wayne*		Cartoonist	30			400	Superman
Boris III		Royalty	120			185	King & Dictator Bulgaria
Bork, Robert A.		Jurist	5	20		30	
Borkh, Inge		Entertainment	10			25	Opera. Salome
Borland, Carol	1914-97	Entertainment	25			80	Actress. Vintage Horror Films.

NAME	DATE	CATEGORY	SIG	LS/DS	ALS	SP	COMMENTS
Borlaug, Norman, Dr.		Science	20	35	80	30	Nobel Peace Prize
Borman, F. & Lovell, J.		Astronaut	35			75	Signed by Both
Borman, Frank		Astronaut	22	30		115	
Bormann, Martin	1900-45	Military	350	1088	1500	850	Nazi Private Sec'y to Hitler
Born, Max	1882-70	Science	175	375	575		Nobel, Ger.-Br. Physicist
Borne, Hermann von Dem.		Military	20	45	90		
Borno, Louis		Head of State	15	75			Pres. Haiti
Borodin, Alexander		Composer	250	450	1100		Rus. Composer & Prof. Chemistry
Borowski, Felix		Composer	15	40	100	50	
Borso, Umberto		Entertainment	15			45	It. Tenor
Borzage, Frank		Entertainment	40			150	Film Director-Producer
Bosanquet, Helen D.		Author	8	15	22		
Bose, Jagadis, Sir		Science	27	40	150		Indian Physicist
Bose, Lucia	1931-	Entertainment	17			35	Span. Actress. Films from 1950
Boshell, Louise		Entertainment	6	8	15	15	
Bosley, Tom		Entertainment	5	13	20	12	
Bosson, Barbara		Entertainment	5	5	10	20	
Bostic, Earl		Bandleader	15				Jazz Saxaphonist
Bostwick, Barry		Entertainment	6	8	15	20	
Bostwick, George		Aviation	10	25	40	30	ACE, WW II
Boswell, Connie		Entertainment	10	10	25	10	
Boswell, James		Author	750		4545		Biographer of Sam'l Johnson
Bosworth, Hobart	1867-1970	Entertainment	25	30	40	65	Films Actor from 1909-43
Botha, Louis		Head of State	52	110	95		S. Afr. Soldier, Statesman
Botta, Lucca	1882-1917	Entertainment	75			225	Enrico Caruso Protégé. Early Death by Brain Tumor
Bottesini, G.		Entertainment	50				Double-Bass Virtuoso, Conductor. AMusQS 200
Bottolfsen, C.A.		Governor	12		25	15	Governor ID
Bottome, Margaret		Author	15	45	100	25	Lecturer
Bottoms, Joseph		Entertainment	4	4	9	12	
Bottoms, Sam		Entertainment	6	8	15	12	
Bottoms, Timothy		Entertainment	7			15	
Boucher, Voucher		Military	5	25			
Boucicault, Dion		Entertainment	20	35	50	40	19th Cent. Am. Actor-Playwright
Bouck, William C.	1786-1859	Governor	15	25	50		Gov. NY.Supervised Part Construction of Erie Canal
Boudin, Eugene-Louis		Artist	105	280	575		Fr. Sea & Beach Scenes
Boudinot, Elias	1740-1821	Rev. War	240	1980	642		Washington's Att'y Gen. & Close Friend
Boudinot, Elias C.	1835-90	Civil War	95	250	1210		Cherokee Leader. Murdered
Boughton, Rutland	1876-19??	Composer					Opera, Etc. AMusQS $125
Bouguereau, Adolphe Wm.	1825-1895	Artist					Fr. Painter.Mostly Religious & Mythological Themes
Boulanger, Nadia		Composer			115	375	Fr. Conductor, Teacher
Boulard, Georges		Aviation	15		60	35	
Boulez, Pierre		Composer	40			100	Fr. Composer-Conductor-Pianist.AMusQS $325
Boullanger, George	1837-91	Military	100				Gen'l & Politician.Man on Horseback. Suicide
Boulle, Pierre	1912-1994	Author	15		40	115	Bridge Over the River Kwai
Boult, Adrian, Sir		Conductor	18	45	100	75	Esteemed Br. Conductor

NAME	DATE	CATEGORY	SIG	LS/DS	ALS	SP	COMMENTS
Bourbon-Parma, Zita	1892-1989	Royalty				450	Last Austrian Empress
Bourchier, John	1499-1561	Royalty			825		3rd Earl of Bath Lady Jane Grey Trial Commissioner
Bourguiba, Habib		Head of State	15	40	100	25	Pres. Tunisia
Bourke-White, Margaret	1904-71	Artist	100	290	195		Special SP $770. Photo Essays Life Mag.
Bourmont, Louis A.V.	1773-1846	Fr. Military		80	160		General under Napoleon
Bourne, Francis, Cardinal		Clergy	35	45	60	40	
Bourrienne, L.A.F. de		Fr. Revolution	45	60	120		Pvt. Sec'y to Napoleon
Bouton, Chas. Marie		Artist	110	165	400		
Boutwell, George S.	1818-1905	Cabinet	20	45	150	40	Grant Sec'y Treasury. Political Leader. TLS $250
Bow, Clara	1905-1965	Entertainment	145	175	330	495	The It Girl. Silent Film Star
Bowden, Dorris		Entertainment	5			20	
Bowditch, Nathaniel	1773-1838	Science	100	230	610		Astronomer, Mathematician
Bowe, Rosemarie		Entertainment	4	4	9	10	
Bowen, Elizabeth		Author	25	75	170	30	Ir.-Br. Psychological Novelist
Bowen, George F., Sir		Head of State	10	25	35		Governor Australia, New Zealand
Bowen, Ira Sprague		Science	10	25	35	15	Dir. Mt. Wilson-Palomar Obs.
Bowen, John S.	1830-63	Civil War	110	245	450		CSA General.
Bowen, John Stevens (WD)		Civil War	175	260	1265		CSA Gen. Early Prisoner
Bowen, Louise de Koven		Social Reformer	12	20			Pres. Hull House
Bowen, Otis		Cabinet	5	10			Sec'y Health & Human Services
Bowen, Thomas Meed		Civil War	45				Union General, Senator CO
Bower, Antoinette		Entertainment	3	3	6	8	
Bowers, George M.		Senate/Congress	10	20		10	MOC WV
Bowes, Major Edward		Entertainment	12	15	19	25	
Bowie, David		Entertainment	30	95		82	Rock
Bowie, James (Jim)		Military		15000			Co-Cmdr. Alamo. Bowie Knife
Bowie, Sydney J.		Senate/Congress	10	20	35		MOC AL
Bowker, Judi		Entertainment	10	8	15	22	
Bowler, Metcalf		Jurist	50	135	250		Opponent of The Stamp Act 1765
Bowles, Chester		Governor	10	25	85	40	Diplomat, Advertising Exec.
Bowlin, James B.		Senate/Congress	15	30	45		MOC MO
Bowman, Lee		Entertainment	10	20	25	25	
Bowser, Charles	18xx-1998	Entertainment	20			45	Silent Film Character Actor. The Price She Paid
Boxcar Willie		Country Western	6	12		15	Singer
Boxer, Barbara		Congress	5			20	Sen. CA
Boxleitner, Bruce		Entertainment	8	9	19	35	
Boy George		Entertainment	15	30	45	50	
Boyd, Alan S.		Cabinet	4			10	Sec'y Trans., CEO Amtrak
Boyd, Belle		Western Outlaw	1025			9650	Confederate Spy
Boyd, Linn	1800-59	Congress	20	30	55		Repr. KY, Speaker of House
Boyd, Stephen		Entertainment	25	37	70	70	Actor
Boyd, William 'Bill'	1895-1972	Entertainment	225			300	Silent Screen Matinee Idol & 'Hopalong Cassidy'
Boyer, Charles	1897-1978	Entertainment	46	58	75	132	Fr. Actor. Hollywood Screen Lover
Boyer, Jean-Pierre		Head of State	35	125			Pres. Haiti
Boyesen, Hjalmar H.		Author	15	35	70	20	

NAME	DATE	CATEGORY	SIG	LS/DS	ALS	SP	COMMENTS
Boyington, Gregory 'Pappy'	1912-88	Aviation	89	155	215	147	ACE WW II Marine, #4 US, CMH
Boyle, John J.		Artist	5	10	20		
Boyle, Kay	1903-93	Author	25	75	175	40	Am. Short Story Writer, Novels. Expatriot
Boyle, Lara Flynn		Entertainment	20			50	
Boyle, Peter		Entertainment	8	10	15	22	Favorite Character Actor
Boynton, Henry Van Ness		Civil War	45	80	165		Union Officer & MOH winner
Boze, Marie		Entertainment	15			50	Vintage Actress 1879
Brabazon-Moore, John T.		Aviation	25	60	85	50	1st Licensed. WW I Pilot
Bracken, Eddie		Entertainment	5	6	9	10	
Brackett, Charles		Entertainment	20			70	Producer. 2 Oscars as Screenwriter
Bradbury, James W.	1802-1901	Congress	12				Sen. ME
Bradbury, James Ware		Senate/Congress	20	25	40		Senator ME 1847
Bradbury, Norris E.		Science	15		25		
Bradbury, Ray		Author	30	100	275	45	Am. Sci-Fi Writer
Bradford, Augustus W.	1805-81	Civil War		85			Unionist Gov. MD
Bradford, Barbara P.		Author	5			10	
Bradford, William	1729-1808	Senate	125	350	590		Sen. RI 1793
Bradford, William	1755-1856	Cabinet	125	250			G. Washington Att'y Gen'l
Bradlee, Ben		Editor	18	30		45	Ed. Washington Post
Bradley, Bill		Senate/Congress	5	10		20	Sen. NJ., Pro. Basketball
Bradley, Ed		Entertainment	5	15	25	15	TV News. 60 Minutes
Bradley, James		Military	11	35	58		
Bradley, John H.		Military	50	110	175	400	Iwo Jima Flag Raiser FDC $200 S. Only Navy Man
Bradley, Joseph P. (SC)		Supreme Court	55	100	200		
Bradley, Kathleen		Entertainment	4			10	Price is Right Model
Bradley, Omar N.	1893-1981	Military	95	138	400	212	5 Star General WW II. ALS/Cont.$2000, TLS.$1000
Bradley, Owen	1915-98	Entertainment	20			35	Country Music Record Producer. Musician
Bradley, Tom	1917-98	Political	10	62	35	32	Ex Poiceman. Mayor Los Angeles.
Bradna, Olympe		Entertainment	10	75		25	
Bradshaw, Tiny		Bandleader	10				
Bradstreet, John		Colonial	60	140	295		Br. Soldier. Ticonderoga
Brady, Alice	1892-1939	Entertainment	90		95	112	Academy Award Winner
Brady, Charles, Jr.		Astronaut	5			18	
Brady, James B. 'Diamond Jim'		Business	375	1800	1338	500	Financier. TLS $3800. RR DS $6500
Brady, James S.		Celebrity	20	65		35	
Brady, Mathew B.	1823-96	Photographer	340	1050	2300		Presidential & Civil War Photos
Brady, Pat	1914-72	Entertainment	100			250	
Brady, Scott		Entertainment	15			40	Actor. Sometimes Western Heavy/John Wayne
Brady, William A.		Entertainment	256			65	
Braga, Gaetano		Composer				312	Cello Music. 8 Operas
Braga, Sonia		Entertainment	10	15	30	33	Sexy Brazilian Leading Lady
Bragg, Braxton (WD)		Civil War	498		1365	3000	CSA General
Bragg, Braxton	1817-76	Civil War	395	695	823	900	CSA General
Bragg, Edward Stuyvesant	1827-1912	Civil War	55	85	140		Union Gen., Statesman, MOC
Bragg, Thomas	1818-72	Civil War	135	250			CSA Att'y General

NAME	DATE	CATEGORY	SIG	LS/DS	ALS	SP	COMMENTS
Bragg, Wm. Henry, Sir	1862-1942	Science	50	95			Nobel Physics with son Wm. L. in 1915
Bragg, Wm. Lawrence, Sir	1890-1971	Science	50	85			Nobel Physics with father W.H.
Braham, John (Abraham)	1774-1856	Entertainment	25		100		Supreme Br. Opera, Concert Performer
Brahms, Johannes	1833-97	Composer	1000	1350	2831	4350	Major 19th Cent. Composer. AMusQS $2,750-$12,500
Brailowsky, Alexander		Entertainment	50			85	Concert Pianist.. Chopin Specialist
Brainard, David		Explorer	40		125		Arctic Explorer/G.B.Grinnell
Braithwaite, Wm. Stanley		Author	35	120	235	45	
Bramesfeld, Heinrich		Military	15		25	40	Ger. Capt. of See. RK Winner
Branagh, Kenneth		Entertainment	20			55	Br. Actor-Director-Dramatist
Branch, John	1782-1863	Cabinet	30	75	148		Sec'y Navy, Gov. NC, Gov. FL
Branch, Lawrence O.	1820-62	Civil War	200	405			CSA General
Branch, Lawrence O.(WD)		Civil War	470		1075		CSA Gen. KIA 1862, Antietam
Brand, Christopher Q., Sir		Aviation	75	150	300	200	ACE, WW I, Only night Ace
Brand, Harry		Entertainment	5			20	Motion Picture Producer
Brand, Max	1892-1944	Author	50			100	Novelist. 'Destry Rides Again', 'Dr. Kildare'
Brand, Neville	1921-92	Entertainment	75	250		150	Dependable Heavy Through Many Years
Brand, Vance D.		Astronaut	20	55		205	Apollo Soyuz
Brandauer, Klaus Maria	1944-	Entertainment	20		30	45	Austrian Actor-Director. Out of Africa
Brandegee, Augustus		Senate/Congress	15	35	200		MOC. CT. Civil War Member
Brandeis, Louis D. (SC)	1856-1941	Supreme Court	150	482	605	1275	1st Jewish Supr. Ct. Judge. Important ALS $2200
Brandenstein, Daniel		Astronaut	5			15	
Brando, Marlon	1924-	Entertainment	292	600		678	Reclusive Oscar Winning Actor.
Brandon, Henry	1912-90	Entertainment	5			10	Am. Character Actor. Reliable Menace for 30 Years
Brandon, Michael	1945-	Entertainment	8			15	Actor. Leading Man
Brandt, Marianne		Entertainment	25		80	75	Opera
Brandt, Willy	1913-92	Head of State	25	112	210	90	Germ. Chancellor. Nobel Peace Prize
Brandy		Entertainer	20			75	Singer-Actress 'Cinderella'
Brangwyn, Frank	1867-1956	Artist	25		125		Br. Painter-Decorator
Branigan, Laura		Entertainment	10			35	Singer
Branly, Edouard	1844-1940	Science	105	625	442	475	Fr. Physicist. Inventor Radio Wave Detector
Brann, Louis J.		Governor	5	15		10	Gov. ME
Brannan, Charles F.		Cabinet	10	15		15	Sec'y Agriculture
Brant, Joseph (Thayendanegea)	1742-1807	Indian Chief	888		7500		Mohawk Who Fought With British
Branzell, Karin	1891-1974	Entertainment	40			155	Opera. Celebrated in Wagnerian Roles
Braque, Georges	1882-1963	Artist	685	675	1345		Fr. Developed Cubism with Picasso. SB $975
Brattain, Walter		Science	35	50	110	50	Nobel Physics. Transistor
Bratton, John, Dr.	1831-98	Civil War	105	305	420		CSA Gen. Physician. Wounded, Captured
Brauchitsch, Walter von		Military	75	155	225	125	Hitler Fld.Marshall
Braun, Eva	1912-45	WWII Nazi	1000		2750		Hitler's Mistress-Wife
Braun, Wernher von		Science					see Von Braun
Brautigan, Richard		Author	45	150			Counter-Culture Classic
Braxton, Carter	1736-97	Rev. War	275	550	1718		Signer Decl. of Indepen.
Braxton, Toni		Entertainment	7			38	Actress. Pin-Up $65
Brayman, Mason	1813-1895	Civil War	35	90			Union General, Gov. Idaho
Brayton, Charles Ray		Civil War	40	65	100		Union General

NAME	DATE	CATEGORY	SIG	LS/DS	ALS	SP	COMMENTS
Brazzi, Rossano	1916-95	Entertainment	10		25	48	Romantic Italian Actor
Brearley, David	1745-1790	Rev. War	375	800	875		Continental Congress
Breathed, Berke*		Cartoonist	20			175	'Bloom County'
Brecht, Bertolt	1898-1956	Author	400	1750	3100		Important 20th Cent. Ger.-Jewish Playwright, Poet
Breckinridge, John Cabell	1821-75	Civil War & VP US	328	440	910		CSA Gen., Sec'y War. Sig/Rank $525, ALS $1585
Breckinridge, Joseph Cabell	1842-1920	Military	25	40			
Breckinridge, Wm. C.	1837-	Civil War	110	228	275		CSA Officer
Breeding, J. Floyd		Senate/Congress	5	15		10	MOC KS
Breen, Bobby		Entertainment	8	15	30	20	Child Singer. Radio & Films
Breese, Lou		Entertainment	20		45	70	Big band leader
Breese, Vance		Aviation	30	115		40	Aviator & Aircraft Designer
Brefoort, H. B.		Military	15	30			
Bremer, Lucille		Entertainment	10			25	Astaire Dancing Partner MGM Musical
Brendel, El	1890-1964	Entertainment	15	35		42	Stage & Film Comedy Roles
Breneman, Tom		Entertainment	15	15	30	20	Popular Radio Host
Brennan, Eileen		Entertainment	4		10	15	Character Actress. Accident Slowed Career
Brennan, Francis J., Cardinal		Clergy	30	45	55	50	
Brennan, Walter	1894-1974	Entertainment	100	125	262	200	3 Time Oscar Winner
Brennan, William J. (SC)	1913-92	Supreme Court	62	90	155	92	Important 20th Cent. Justice. 1200+ Opinions
Brennecke, Kurt		Military	15	35	60	35	
Brenner, Victor D.	1871-1924	Artist	295	345	675		Designer Lincoln Penny -V.D.B.
Brent, Charles H., Bishop		Clergy	25	40	55	40	
Brent, Evelyn		Entertainment	15			40	Vintage Leading Lady
Brent, George		Entertainment	25	35		60	Vintage Leading Man.
Brent, George Wm.		Civil War	100	210	300		
Brent, Joseph Lancaster	1826-	Civil War	95		396		CSA Colonel. Sig/Rank Brig. Gen. $225
Brent, Robert		Military	35	100	165		
Brereton, Lewis Hyde	1890-1967	Aviation	55	150		300	Am.Cmdr. 1st Allied Airborne Army WW II
Bres, Edward S.		Military	10	30	50		
Breslau, Sophie		Entertainment	35			90	Opera
Breslin, Jimmy		Celebrities	5	15	40	15	Journalist, Novelist
Bresser-Gianoli, Clotilde		Entertainment	20			55	Opera
Breton, Andre	1896-1966	Author	68	175	400		Fr. Poet, Essayist, Critic, Editor.ALS/Cont. $1000
Brett, George H.	1886-	Military		125		45	Air Corps Gen. WW II
Brett, Jeremy	1935-95	Entertainment	20			195	Portrayed Sherlock Holmes. SP Pc $95
Breu, Paul		Aviation	10			25	Ger. Bomber Pilot. RK
Breuer, Marcel		Architect	20	60	125	150	Bauhaus School/Gropius
Brewer, David J. (SC)		Supreme Court	85	123	160		
Brewer, Teresa		Entertainment	5			15	Big Band Singer. Recording Artist
Brewerton, Henry	?-1879	Civil War			125		Union Gen. Corps of Engineers
Brewster, Benjamin		Cabinet	10	35	50		Chester A. Arthur Att'y General.
Brewster, David, Sir	1781-1868	Science	35	55	195		Physicist. Invented Kaleidoscope
Brewster, Kingman Jr		Educator	5	15	25	15	Diplomat
Brewster, Ralph Owen		Senate	10	25	40	30	Senator, MOC ME
Breyer, Stephen		Supreme Court	20			40	

NAME	DATE	CATEGORY	SIG	LS/DS	ALS	SP	COMMENTS
Brezhnev, Leonid I.		Head of State	375	975		400	Soviet Communist Party Leader
Brian, Mary		Entertainment	5	7	15	20	Vintage Actress. Ingenue
Brice, Benjamin W.		Civil War	15	45			Union Paymaster General
Brice, Fanny	1891-1951	Entertainment	102	185	300	328	Vintage Stage, Radio, Films. Top Comedienne-Singer
Brickell, Edie		Entertainment	8			30	
Bricker, John W.		Senate	15	30		20	Gov. Ohio
Brico, Antonia, Dr.		Conductor	15			75	Eccentric Female Conductor
Bridges, Beau		Entertainment	15		30	33	Actor. Like Lloyd and Jeff—Versatile Parts
Bridges, H. Styles		Senate	7	15		10	Senator NH
Bridges, Harry		Labor Leader	70	180		140	Pres. Longshoreman Union. Powerful
Bridges, Jeff		Entertainment	15	28		30	Actor. Versatile Leading Man. Variety of Parts
Bridges, Lloyd	1913-98	Entertainment	28	40		47	Actor. Much loved for TV series Seahunt
Bridges, Robert	1844-1930	Author	15		55		Poet Laureate England
Bridges, Roy D. Jr.		Astronaut	10			25	
Bridges, Todd		Entertainment	15	20		40	Troubled child actor. Different Strokes
Bridgman, Laura D.	1829-89	Celebrity	98		205		1st Blind, Deaf, Mute Systematically Educated
Bridy, Pat*		Cartoonist	10		25		'Rose is Rose'
Briggs, Austin*		Cartoonist	25			200	'Flash Gordon'
Briggs, Charles F.		Author	15	40	125		Editor NY Times
Briggs, Clare A.*	1875-1930	Cartoonist	15			50	'Mr. & Mrs.'
Briggs, Henry	1824-87	Civil War	40		190	65	Union Gen. Wounded 'Seven Pines'. War Dte ALS $340
Briggs, James E.		Military	10	25	50	20	
Briggs, Le Baron Russell	1855-1934	Educator	5		20		Legendary Harvard Professor
Briggs, Roxanne Dawson		Entertainment	15			35	Actress, Star Trek
Brigham, Louis S.		Business	10	35	45	20	
Bright, John	1811-89	Statesman	35	50	155		Radical Br. Orator.(Corn Laws)
Brightman, Sarah		Entertainment	22			50	Star of Andrew Lloyd Weber's Musicals. Ex Wife
Brigitte, Simone		Entertainment	5			20	Model-Actress
Brimley, Wilford		Entertainment	5			20	Character Actor. Films/TV
Brimmer, Andrew F.		Government	10	15		15	Afro-Am. Gov. Fed. Res. Board
Brinegar, Paul		Entertainment	10	15	20	25	
Brinkley, Christie		Entertainment	10	25	5	69	Model
Brinkley, David		Journalist	10			25	TV News Anchor-Commentator
Brinson, Samuel Mitchell		Senate/Congress	10	20	45		MOC NC
Brisbane, Arthur		Author	15	35	100	30	Influential Editorial Writer
Brisbin, James	1837-92	Civil War	35		110		Cmdr. Afr-Am. Cavalry. Abolitionist. ALS/Cont. $775
Brisebois, Danielle		Entertainment	4			9	Actress
Brissette, Tiffany		Entertainment	5			10	Child Actress
Brisson, Carl		Entertainment	15	15	25	20	Danish Actor. Stage-Screen
Bristol, Henry Platt		Business	275	850	1075		Founder Bristol-Myers
Bristol, Mark		Military	20	25		25	Admiral WW I
Bristow, Benjamin Helm	1832-96	Cabinet	25	65	120		Civil War Commanded 25th KY
Britt, Mai		Entertainment	10			25	Actress
Britt, Maurice L., Capt.	1912-84	Military	25	35			WW II Hero CMH & Football Star
Brittany, Morgan		Entertainment	10	15	25	25	Actress

NAME	DATE	CATEGORY	SIG	LS/DS	ALS	SP	COMMENTS
Britten, Benjamin	1913-76	Composer	158	390	488	288	Br. Conductor. Peter Grimes. AMusQS $990-$1600
Britton, Pamela		Entertainment	10			15	Actress
Britton, Barbara		Entertainment	9		15	25	Actress-Model. Leading Lady.
Britton, Sherry		Entertainment	5			10	
Brix, Herman		Entertainment	10	12	15	20	SEE Bruce Bennett
Broadhead, James Overton		Law	25		65		Att'y Friend of Lincoln
Broca, Paul	1824-1880	Science	125		981		Fr. Pathologist, Surgeon, Anthropologist
Broccoli, Cubby		Entertainment	10	20		25	Film director
Brochler, Jan		Entertainment	10			35	Opera, Dutch Baritone
Brock, Thomas, Sir	1847-1922	Artist	10		35		Brit. Sculptor. Statues of Longfellow, Q. Victoria
Brock, William		Clergy	15	25	40	25	
Brock, William G. Sen.		Business	20	70	125	40	
Brod, Max	1884-1968	Author	90		675		Czech-born Austrian Writer. Biographer. Kafka Ed.
Broderick, Helen		Entertainment	25			70	Vintage Character Actress.
Broderick, Matthew		Entertainment	12	22	20	38	Actor. Films-TV-Stage
Brodhead, Daniel	1736-1809	Rev. War	200	650			Legendary Am.Officer.Talented Negotiator.Renegade
Brodhead, James E.		Entertainment	5		15	15	
Brodhead, Richard		Senator	15	35	75		Senator from PA
Brodie, Benjamin C.Sir	1783-1880	Science	35	65	95		Br. Orthopedic Surgeon
Brodie, Steve	1856-1901	Entertainment	100				World Champion. Jumped off Brooklyn Bridge
Brodie, Steve	1919-93	Entertainment	5			25	Actor. Major Film Player in Major Productions
Brody, Lane		Entertainment	4			10	
Broglie, Duke A-C-L-V		Statesman	135	270	540		Fr. Politician. Author
Broglie, Louis Victor de	1892-1987	Science	62	200	342	595	Nobel Physics. Theory of Quantum Mechanics
Brokow, Tom		Journalist	15			65	TV News Anchor-Commentator-Author
Brolin, James		Entertainment	15	20	30	33	Actor. Marcus Welby, Hotel TV Series
Bromberg, J. Edward		Entertainment	30			65	Character Actor. Major Films
Bromfield, John		Entertainment	10			25	Handsome Leading Man. Films
Bromfield, Louis	1896-1950	Author	35	125	175	65	Am. Novelist. Pulitzer. Mrs. Parkington
Bronk, Detlev W.	1897-1975	Science	15	25	40	25	Pres.Nat'l Adademy of Sci. Physiologist, Neurology
Bronson, Betty		Entertainment	35			75	Vintage
Bronson, Charles	1921-	Entertainment	25	50		46	Major Action Star 70's. Watch for Secretarials.
Bronson, David	1800-63	Congress	25				Repr. ME, Collector of Customs
Bronte, Charlotte		Author			8250		Br. Novelist. Jane Eyre
Brook, Alexander		Artist	25	40	75		
Brook, Clive	1887-1974	Entertainment	45	55	75	95	Br.Actor. 1st Talky 'Sherlock Holmes'
Brooke, Alan, Fld Marshal, Sir		Military	40	110	205	87	Cmdr. Br.II Corps WW II, Dunkirk
Brooke, Edward W.	1919-	Senate	10	15		25	Afr.-Am. Rep. Senator MA
Brooke, Hillary		Entertainment	10	15	25	25	Actress. Blonde-Sophisticated Other Woman
Brooke, John Rutter	1838-1926	Civil War	60	85	195		Union Gen. Sig/Rank. Wounded at Gettysburg
Brooke, Rupert	1887-1915	Author	540	575	1890		Br. Poet. Died in WW at 28
Brooke-Popham, Robert		Military	30	65	95	50	Br. Air Chief Marshal WW II
Brookhart, Smith W.		Senate	10	15		15	Senator IA
Brooks & Dunn		Country Music	8			45	Kic and Ronnie
Brooks, A. Raymond		Aviation	35	60	85	75	Bi-Plane ACE, WW I

NAME	DATE	CATEGORY	SIG	LS/DS	ALS	SP	COMMENTS
Brooks, Albert		Entertainment	10			10	Actor
Brooks, Angie		Stateswoman	15				Pres. U.N. Assembly
Brooks, Arthur		Aviation	15		30	35	
Brooks, Avery		Entertainment	20			63	Star Trek
Brooks, Dick*		Cartoonist	5			35	Jackson Twins
Brooks, Foster		Entertainment	5		15	10	Character Actor. Everybody's Favorite 'Drunk'
Brooks, Fred Emerson		Author	10	15	35		Poet
Brooks, Garth		Country Western	20			55	Country Singer. Mega Grammy Winner
Brooks, Gwendolyn	1917-	Author	20	40		25	Afro-Am. Poet. Pulitzer. FDC S $35
Brooks, James L.		Entertainment	10			20	
Brooks, John		Military	55	125	275		Am. Revolution Gen., Gov. MA
Brooks, Leslie		Entertainment	10		15	15	Actress-Dancer.
Brooks, Louise	1906-1985	Entertainment	165	532	425	595	One of the Screen's Great Beauties. Rare
Brooks, Mel		Entertainment	10	32	25	21	Actor-Comic- Director AA
Brooks, Peter H.		Clergy	15	25	35		
Brooks, Phillips	1835-93	Clergy-Author	60	120	130	75	Episcopal Bishop. 'O Little Town of Bethlehem'.
Brooks, Rand		Entertainment	15		40	45	'GWTW' Chas. Hamilton. Scarlett's 1st Husband
Brooks, Randi		Entertainment	5			15	
Brooks, Richard		Entertainment	20	30		60	AA Film Director
Brooks, Shirley	1816-74	Author	15		50		Humorist, Editor of 'Punch'
Brooks, Wm. Thos. H.	1821-70	Civil War	45	80	125		Union Gen. ALS '64 $245
Broom, Jacob		Rev. War	350	900	2000		Continental Congress
Broomall, John M.		Senate/Congress	10	15	40		MOC DE 1863. CW Officer
Brophy, Ed		Entertainment	25			40	Character Actor. Rotund Cigar-Smoking
Brophy, Kevin		Entertainment	4			10	
Brophy, Theodore F.		Business	4			10	CEO GTE
Brosnan, Pierce		Entertainment	25	40	45	55	Newest James Bond. SP $65
Brothers, Joyce		Science	5		25	15	Early TV Psychiatrist. Frequent Consulting Guest
Brough, Candi & Randi		Entertainment	10			25	
Brough, Fanny		Entertainment	4			10	Vintage Actress
Brough, Lionel		Entertainment	4			10	Vintage Actor
Brougham, Henry, Lord	1778-1868	Statesman	82	115	250		Designed One Horse Brougham. Author,Scholar
Brougham, John	1814-80	Entertainment	20			45	Am. Actor-Playwright-Mgr. London Assurance:
Broughton, Joseph M.		Senate/Congress	5	12		10	Senator/MOC NC
Broun, Heywood	1888-1939	Author	10	35	70	20	Journalist, Novelist, Columnist
Browder, Earl	1891-1973	Political	15	35	65	25	US Communist Party Leader
Brown, A. Roy		Aviation WW I	288				Can. Ace. Downed Richtofen
Brown, Aaron V.	1795-1859	Cabinet	45	125			PMG, Repr.& Sen. TN
Brown, Albert Gallatin		Governor	45	60	95		CSA Senator, Gov. Miss.
Brown, Alice		Author	15	35	100	25	Prolific Novelist, Poet
Brown, Arthur Whitten	1886-1948	Aviation	292	410	575	575	Alcock & Brown 1st Nonstop Flight Over Atlantic
Brown, Benjamin Gratz	1826-85	Congress	15		25		Sen. MO
Brown, Blair		Entertainment	10			20	Actress.
Brown, Bo		Cartoonist	5			20	Magazine Cartoonist
Brown, Bothwell		Entertainment	10	15	25	25	Vintage Actor

NAME	DATE	CATEGORY	SIG	LS/DS	ALS	SP	COMMENTS
Brown, Charles		Entertainment	15			50	Blues Singer. Rock/Roll HOF
Brown, Charles Brockden	1771-1810	Author	975		6500		Father of the American Novel
Brown, Clarence		Entertainment	10			25	
Brown, Curtis, Jr.		Astronaut	8			25	
Brown, David		Astronaut	6			20	
Brown, David		Entertainment	10			20	Producer. Oscar Winner
Brown, Down Town Julie		Entertainment	5			15	TV Host-Singer
Brown, Edmund G. 'Jerry'		Governor	10	25		15	Governor CA, Pres. Candidate. Mayor Oakland, CA
Brown, Edmund G. 'Pat'	1905-96	Governor	20	25		25	Governor CA. Liberal Civil Rights Champion
Brown, Edward N.		Business	12			15	RR Exec.
Brown, Ford Madox	1821-93	Artist	45		105		Br. Historical Painter
Brown, Ford Madox	1821-93	Artist	45		105		Br. Historical Painter
Brown, George		Military	25				
Brown, George Stan		Entertainment	6			15	Afr.-Am Actor
Brown, Harold, Dr.		Science-Cabinet	10	20		15	Sec'y Defense
Brown, Harry Joe		Entertainment	20	40	65	25	Film Producer, Director
Brown, Helen Gurley		Author	5	10	20	10	Editor, Publisher
Brown, Henry B. (SC)		Supreme Court	62	175	250		
Brown, Henry W.		Aviation	12	25	45	30	ACE, WW II
Brown, Herbert C., Dr.		Science	25	30	45	35	Nobel Chemistry
Brown, Jacob	1775-1828	Military	50	135	295		Important Gen'l War of 1812
Brown, James		Entertainment	30			65	Rock. Alb. S $70
Brown, James		Entertainment	5			20	Actor
Brown, Jim Ed		Country Music	5			15	
Brown, Joe E.	1892-1973	Entertainment	30	50	45	91	Vintage Film Comedian
Brown, John	1800-1859	Civil War	775	2112	8500	2550	Fanatical Abolitionist-Hung for treason
Brown, John Calvin	1827-89	Civil War	125	205	350		CSA Gen. Sig/Rank $240. Gov. TN 1871-75
Brown, John George		Artist	10	30	45		
Brown, John Y.		Business	10	25	51	20	
Brown, Johnny Mack		Entertainment	50	75		125	Cowboy Actor
Brown, Joseph Emerson		Civil War	45	60	85		Civil War Gov. Georgia
Brown, Les		Entertainment	15			35	Big Band Leader. Many Years/Bob Hope. Radio
Brown, Lt. John		Rev. War	72	175	400		
Brown, Lytle	1872-1951	Military	35			95	U.S. Army Gen'l. Sp-Am.War. Battle San Juan Hill
Brown, Mark N.		Astronaut	6			23	
Brown, Marty		Country Music	4			15	Traditional Country Sound
Brown, Moses		Rev. War	45		265		Naval Commander
Brown, Nicholas	1729-91	Rev. War	35	110	195		Businessman. Supplied Army. Brown University
Brown, Norma		Military	10	20	30	15	
Brown, Norman		Entertainment	4			10	
Brown, Phil		Entertainment	5			20	Actor. Star Wars. Uncle Owen
Brown, Phyllis George		Entertainment	5		20	15	
Brown, Prentiss M.		Senate	10	25		15	Senator MI
Brown, Preston		Military	20	35		45	General WW I. Chief of Staff
Brown, Reno		Entertainment	15			50	Actress. Early Westerns

NAME	DATE	CATEGORY	SIG	LS/DS	ALS	SP	COMMENTS
Brown, Robert		Military	20		75	125	General WW I
Brown, Robert	1773-1858	Science	135		775		Scot. Botanist. Living Cells Nucleus
Brown, Ron	19xx-96	Cabinet	20	40		60	Sec'y Commerce Clinton Cabinet. Tragic Plane Crash
Brown, Ruth		Entertainment	20			45	Rock & Roll HOF
Brown, Sam J.		Aviation	20	40	55	45	ACE, WW II
Brown, T. Graham		Country Music	5			18	Country/Soul/Rock Sound
Brown, Tom		Entertainment	10	15	25	25	Actor. Many Youthful Parts
Brown, William Wallace		Congress	10	15	30		Repr. PA. CW Officer
Brown-Sequard, Chas. E.	1817-94	Science			482		Fr. Physician. Father of Endocrinology
Browne, Charles Farrar							SEE Ward, Artemus
Browne, Chris*		Cartoonist	20			75	'Hagar'
Browne, Coral		Entertainment	10	15	20	25	
Browne, Dik*		Cartoonist	20			60	Hi & Lois, Hagar
Browne, Hablot Knight		Artist	25	90	150		Watercolor. Illustrator of Dickens
Browne, Jackson		Entertainment	20	35	55		Rock
Browne, Leslie		Entertainment	5			10	
Brownell, Herbert Jr.	1904-96	Cabinet	15	20		80	Att'y Gen., Eisenhower Adm. Time Cover S. 35
Browning, Eliz. Barrett		Author	325	1085	2750	2500	Br. Poet
Browning, George		Business	195	580			Browning Arms Mfg.
Browning, John B.		Business	50	160		75	Pres. Browning Arms Co.
Browning, John Moses	1855-1926	Inventor-Business	195	1200	575		Inventor-Designer of Fire Arms. Browning Automatic
Browning, Orville H.	1806-81	Cabinet	25	125			Sec'y of Interior, Sen. IL
Browning, Ricou		Entertainment	12			35	Creature, Olympic Swimmer
Browning, Robert	1812-89	Author	269	470	865	1150	Br. Poet. AMsS $3250, $3400. AQS $1075
Browning, Tod		Entertainment	75			250	
Brownlee, John		Entertainment	10		45	30	Opera, Australian/Am. Baritone
Brubeck, Dave		Entertainment	15	35	45	50	Jazz Great. Pianist, Composer
Bruce, Andrew D.	1894-	Military	35	175		90	Gen. 77th Infantry Div. So. Pacific. WW II
Bruce, Blanche K.	1841-98	Senator	267	500			Born a Slave. 1st Afro-Am. Full Term Senator. RARE
Bruce, Carol		Entertainment	8			30	Blues-Jazz Vocalist. Content ALS $95
Bruce, David		Entertainment	10			20	
Bruce, Ed		Country Music	5			15	Singer/Songwriter
Bruce, Lenny	1926-66	Entertainment	650	575	1150	1075	Comedian ALS/Typescript Archive $5750
Bruce, Nigel	1895-1953	Entertainment	150	175	300	388	Noted for Dr. Watson. Caricature S $250
Bruce, Thos. (7th Earl Elgin)	1766-1841	Diplomat	50	190	340		Conveyed Elgin Marbles. Greece to British Museum
Bruce, Virginia		Entertainment	15				Actress. Late 30's-40's Sophisticated Leading Lady
Bruce, Wallace		Author	35		120		
Bruce, Wm. Cabell	1860-1946	Congress	5	15	30	10	Sen. MD, Author
Bruch, Max	1838-1920	Composer	95	200	362	110	Ger. Opera, AMusQS $950-$1,100-$2,500
Bruckner, Josef Anton	1824-96	Composer	1600	2750	5500	2500	Aus. 10 Symphonies.
Brummel, Geo. B. 'Beau'	1778-1840	Dandy	95	220	850		Br. Man of Fashion, Friend of Prince Regent
Brummer, Renate		Astronaut	10			25	Germany
Bruna Rasa, Lina		Entertainment	65			300	Opera. Great Verismo Soprano. Mascagni Favorite
Brune, G.M.A.	1763-1815	Napoleonic Wars	85	350	450		Marshal of Nap. Assassinated
Brunel, Marc Isambard, Sir	1806-59	Science	75	182	348		Fr.-Br. Inventor, Engineer

NAME	DATE	CATEGORY	SIG	LS/DS	ALS	SP	COMMENTS
Bruning, Heinrich	1885-1971	Head of State			100	425	Ger. Chancellor. Fled to U.S. '34
Brunner, Emil		Clergy	45	75	110	50	
Bruscantini, Sesto		Entertainment	15			45	Opera
Bruson, Renato		Entertainment	10			30	Opera
Bry, Ellen		Entertainment	5			10	Actress
Bryan, Charles W.		Governor	12	25			Governor NE
Bryan, George		Rev. War	120	350	750		Jurist. Proposed Abolition 1777
Bryan, Goode	1811-85	Civil War	155		450		CSA Gen. Sig/Rank $300. Poor Health, Resigned '64
Bryan, Jane		Entertainment	5	10	20	15	Actress. 40's Warner Bros. Leading Lady
Bryan, William E.		Aviation	14	22	42	32	ACE, WW II
Bryan, William Jennings	1860-1925	Cabinet	125	375	504	535	Pres. Nominee 3 Times. Sec'y State. TLS/Cont.$1150
Bryant, Alys McKey		Aviation	35	60	140	75	
Bryant, Anita		Entertainment	5	50	10	10	Controversial Singer
Bryant, Ed		Congress	5			15	Tennessee
Bryant, William Cullen	1794-1878	Author	65	325	502	750	Am. Poet, ALS/Content $1,750
Brynner, Yul	1915-85	Entertainment	50	55	75	146	Academy Award for King & I 1952
Buber, Martin		Clergy	75	175	250	90	
Buchan, John, Lord	1875-1940	Author	25	236			Gov. Gen. Canada, Novelist
Buchanan, Edgar	1902-79	Entertainment	30	40	55	75	Jovial-Rugged AM. Character Actor. 1939-71
Buchanan, Franklin	1800-74	Civil War	160	372	495		CSA Admiral
Buchanan, James	1791-1868	President	377	1117	1104	750	Special SP $12,500, FF $350-$450
Buchanan, James M.		Economics	35	45	85	40	Nobel Economics
Buchanan, Patrick		Political	12	15		40	Political Commentator. Presidential Candidate
Bucher, Lloyd M.		Military	32	90	150	90	Captured Capt. of USS Pueblo
Buchli, James F.		Astronaut	5	15		25	
Buchman, Franklin		Clergy	20	35	65		
Buchwald, Art		Author	10	15	25	15	Syndicated Humor Columnist
Buck, Clayton Douglass		Senate	11	15	25	20	Senator-Governor DE
Buck, Dudley	1839-1909	Composer	10				Organist
Buck, Frank	1884-1950	Big Game Hunter	50	80	198	105	Bring 'Em Back Alive.Author, Lecturer
Buck, Paul H.		Author	4	10	15	5	
Buck, Pearl S.	1892-1973	Author	40	122	195	50	Am. Novelist. Nobel, Pulitzer
Buckingham, Catharinus P.	1808-88	Civil War	30		95		Union Gen. LS '62 $745
Buckingham, George V.	1592-1628	Royalty	100		700		1st Duke of..
Buckingham, George V.	1628-87	Royalty			700		2nd Duke of Buckingham, Politician
Buckingham, William A.		Governor	40	70	128		Civil War Gov. CT. & US Sen.
Buckland, Ralph P. (WD)		Civil War	130		250		Union Gen.
Buckle, Henry Thomas		Author	5	10	25		
Buckley, James		Senate/Congress	6	15		10	
Buckley, William F., Jr.		Author	7	15	45	20	National Revue, Conservative Journalist
Buckner, Simon Bolivar (WD)	Civil War	450	2500	4608			CSA General
Buckner, Simon Bolivar	1823-1914	Civil War	212	332	375	295	CSA Gen.
Buckstone, John B.	1802-79	Entertainment	15		25	35	Br. Actor, Comedian, Playwright
Budd, Julie		Entertainment	3	3	6	6	
Buell, Don Carlos	1818-98	Civil War	90	155	250	150	Union Gen. ADS '62 $400

NAME	DATE	CATEGORY	SIG	LS/DS	ALS	SP	COMMENTS
Buell, Nathaniel		Rev. War	25	225			His Reg't Secured Ft Ticonderoga. Lt. Col.
Buffalo Bill Jr.		Entertainment	25			50	
Buffett, Jimmy		Entertainment	10			35	Rock
Buffington, Thomas Mitchell		Old West	350	550			Chief of Cherokee Nations
Buford, Abraham		Civil War	125	234	789		CSA Gen. 1990 Price Averages
Buford, John	1826-63	Civil War	300	2090			Union Gen.Sig/Rank $400 (1993)
Buford, Napoleon Bonaparte		Civil War	65	145	375		Union Gen. ALS '62 $320
Bugliosi, Vince		Legal	16				Manson Trial Att'y
Buhari, Mohammed		Head of State	15	50	130	25	
Buick, David D.		Business	170	675	885	275	Buick Motor Co.
Bujold, Genevieve		Entertainment	6	8	15	20	
Bukowski, Charles		Author	70				Am. Avant-Garde Writer. BS $750, AMsS $950
Bulfinch, Charles		Architect	130	375	850		Fanueil Hall, Completed Construction of Capitol
Bulfinch, Thomas		Author	20	45	100		Bulfinch's Mythology
Bulkley, John D.		Military	20	65		35	Adm. USN WW II
Bull II, William		Governor	55	80			Governor SC
Bull, John S.		Astronaut	15			25	
Bull, Ole B.		Composer	15		125	125	Nor. Violin Virtuoso
Bull, William, II		Governor	60		240		Governor SC 1760
Bullard, Robert Lee		Military	20	75	130	100	General WW I
Bullard, William		Military	15	35			Admiral WW I
Buller, Redvers, Sir		Military	40	110	250	45	Cmdr-in-Chief South Africa
Bullet Boys (4)		Entertainment	10			40	
Bullitt, William P.		Diplomat	10	20		25	Ambassador To USSR
Bulloch, Terrence		Aviation	20			35	Br. Aviator WWII
Bullock, Sandra		Entertainment	15			65	Actress. Popular Star. Pin-up SP $95
Bullock, Seth		Lawman	200	750			Stock Cert. Signed $975
Bullock, Walter		Author	3	4	7	5	
Bulow, Bernhard H.M.K. von		Head of State	15	35	90	40	Prussian Imperial Chancellor
Bultmann, Rudolph		Clergy	70	90	165	80	
Bulwer, Elizabeth		Author			25		
Bulwer, Wm. Henry Lytton	1801-72	Diplomat	15	40	75		Clayton-Bulwer Treaty. US & Eng
Bulwer-Lytton, Edward		Author	60	220	460		
Bumbry, Grace		Entertainment	10	20		55	Opera. SP 5x7 $30
Bumpers, Dale		Governor	12	15		20	Senator AR
Bunce, Francis M.		Military	25	55	125	65	Admiral Spanish-American War
Bunche, Ralph J.	1904-71	Diplomat	55	101	225	117	Afro-Am. Diplomat. Nobel Peace Prize
Bundy, McGeorge		Law	15	35	45	18	Director FBI
Bundy, Omar		Military	35	90		55	General WW I
Bundy, Ted		Criminal			1000		Infamous Convicted Mass Murderer
Bunner, Henry C.	1855-96	Journalist	70	82	135		Editor Puck Magazine. Story-writer
Bunning, Jim		Political	7			22	Congress from KY
Bunny, John		Entertainment	100	130	160	200	Vintage Film Comedian
Bunsen, Christian K.J., Baron		Diplomat	15	45	115		Prussian Theologian, Scholar
Bunsen, Robert W.	1811-99	Science	175	485	1006	1380	Ger. Chemist, Bunsen Burner

NAME	DATE	CATEGORY	SIG	LS/DS	ALS	SP	COMMENTS
Bunting, Mary		Celebrity	10	28		15	
Bunting, William M.		Clergy	45	100	150		
Buntline, Ned (Pseud)	1823-86	Author	140	185	370	835	(E.Z.C. Judson) Novelist, Adventurer, Dime Novels.
Buono, Victor		Entertainment	30			100	
Burbank, Luther	1849-1926	Science	108	258	295	165	Pioneer, Experimental Botanist. Original Plants-Veg
Burder, George		Clergy	10	15	20	15	
Burdette, Robert J.		Author	20	55	135	40	
Burge, V.L.		Aviation	18			35	
Burger, Warren E. (SC)		Supreme Court	50	175	195	75	Chief Justice
Burgess, Anthony	1917-	Author	40	55		150	Br. Novelist. Clockwork Orange
Burgess, Thomas, Bishop		Clergy	15	25	35		
Burgess, Thornton W.		Author	30	100	225		Peter Rabbit
Burghley, Wm. Cecil, Lord	1520-93	Statesman		585			Elizabeth I, Tudor Statesman. LS/Essex $1550
Burghoff, Gary	1940-	Entertainment	10	35		40	Actor. 'Radar' on Long Running Mash
Burgoyne, John	1722-92	Rev. War	1100	2850	3388		Br. Gen. vs Am. Colonies
Burke, Arleigh	1901-1996	Military	35	55	110	100	Adm. USN WW II
Burke, Billie (Ziegfield)	1885-1970	Entertainment	150	352	185	265	Wizard of Oz. Four Figures as Glinda the Good
Burke, Delta		Entertainment	10	20	25	20	Actress. Designing Women
Burke, Edmund		Senate/Congress	5	12	20		U.S. MOC NH
Burke, Edmund	1729-97	Author			2450		Irish Born Br. Statesman, Author, Orator
Burke, Edward A.		Political	45	35		150	Dominated LA Politics 1880's. Embezzled over $1M
Burke, Paul		Entertainment	5	6	15	15	
Burke, Selma		Artist	10	20	75	15	
Burke, Yvonne B.		Congress	10			20	Afro-Am 3 Term Repr CA
Burleigh, Harry Thacker		Composer	25		150		Singer. Spingarn Med. AMusQS $200-$300
Burleigh, Walter A.	1820-96	Congress	10				Delegate from Dakota Terr.
Burleson, Albert S.		Cabinet	10	25	35		P.M. General, MOC TX
Burleson, Omar Truman		Senate/Congress	5	15		10	MOC TX
Burmester, Willy		Entertainment	90		275		Ger. Violinist. AMusQS $350
Burne-Jones, Edward	1833-98	Artist	125	235	452		Pre-Raphaelite Painter, Designer
Burnet, David G.	1788-1870	Head of State	275	635	1200		1st Pres. Republic TX
Burnet, William	1688-1728	Colonial	145	465			Br. Gov. NY & NJ
Burnett, Carol	1933-	Entertainment	9	17	20	35	Comedienne. TV multi award winner
Burnett, Frances Hodgson	1849-1924	Author	58	145	285		Little Lord Fauntleroy
Burnett, Leo		Business	5	10	25	10	Advertising
Burnett, Peter H.		Governor	200		550		California Pioneer & 1st Gov.
Burnette, Smiley		Entertainment	40	50		75	
Burney, Cecil, Sir		Military	15	35			Br. Adm. WW I
Burnham, Hiram		Civil War	60	195			Union Gen.
Burns & Allen		Entertainment	203			410	George Burns & Gracie Allen
Burns, Bob		Entertainment	25	25	45	45	Bazooka
Burns, Edmund		Entertainment	30			75	Silent Screen Star
Burns, Edward		Entertainment	8			42	Actor. Saving Private Ryan
Burns, Geo. & Gracie Allen		Entertainment	275	375		375	
Burns, George	1896-1996	Entertainment	25	65	50	51	Vaudeville-Radio-TV-Film Comedian

NAME	DATE	CATEGORY	SIG	LS/DS	ALS	SP	COMMENTS
Burns, James MacGregor		Author	20	30			Educator, Political Science
Burns, John	1791-1872	Civil War	350			1250	Vet. War 1812. Vol. Gettysburg
Burns, John A.		Governor	12	15		20	Hawaii
Burns, Ken		Entertainment	5			15	Documentary Film Maker
Burns, Robert	1759-96	Author	500	1450	3650		Scottish Poet
Burns, William Chalmers		Clergy	25	40	50	35	
Burns, William J.		Business	35		175		Chief FBI 1921-24, Det. Agency
Burns, William Wallace		Civil War	35	75	95	150	Union General
Burnside, Ambrose E. (WD)		Civil War	145	390	570	760	Union Gen. ALS $2,500
Burnside, Ambrose E.	1824-81	Civil War	134	250	325	650	ALS war date $2,500
Burpee, David		Business	25	35	70	35	Burpee Seed Co.
Burpee, Jonathan		Business	10	25	50	20	Burpee Seed Co.
Burr, Aaron (V)	1756-1836	Vice President	330	1072	1423		ALS's/Content $7,000-12,000+.Rev.War ALS $5800
Burr, Raymond	1917-93	Entertainment	20	38		65	
Burritt, Elihu	1810-79	Author-Linguist	20		120		Pacifist. Known as Learned Blacksmith.AQS $150
Burroughs, Edgar Rice	1875-1950	Author	250	850	675	625	Tarzan. TLS/Cont. $1900. DS (Check) $200
Burroughs, John		Governor	10		25	15	Governor NM
Burroughs, John	1837-1921	Author	50	100	200	525	Am. Naturalist, Philosopher
Burroughs, Sherman Everett		Senate/Congress	5	15	25	10	MOC NH
Burroughs, William	1914-97	Author	75	350			Am. Writer. Influence Beat Writers of 50's
Burrows, Abe		Author	10	15		25	Playwright, Pulitzer
Burrows, J. C.		Senate	10		25		Senator MI
Bursch, Daniel		Astronaut	7			18	
Burstyn, Ellen		Entertainment	8		15	28	Versatile Leading Lady-Character Leads
Bursum, Holm Olaf		Senate	5	15	25		Senator NM
Burton, Charlotte		Entertainment	8	10	12	15	
Burton, Harold H. (SC)	1888-1964	Supreme Court	33	170	325	90	
Burton, Isabel, Lady		Author	25	85	180		
Burton, LeVar		Entertainment	7	10		18	Actor. 'Roots' etc.
Burton, Richard		Entertainment	100	172		245	Actor. Important DS $950
Burton, Richard F., Sir	1821-90	Explorer	162	285	1672		Orientalist, Linguist, Author
Burton, Theodore E.		Senate/Congress	7	10	30		Senator, MOC OH
Burton, Tim		Entertainment	15			45	Film Director, Actor
Busby, George Henry		Governor	10	15			Governor GA
Buscalia, Leo		Author	15	25	40	25	Educator, Author, Lecturer
Busch, Adolphus	1839-1913	Business	300	3500	4000		Founder Anheuser-Busch.TLS $5800
Busch, August A.		Business	250	1850	2500		Anheuser-Busch Brewery
Busch, Fritz		Entertainment	45		135	250	Ger. Conductor
Busch, Niven		Author	12		25	25	Dramatist, Screenwriter
Busch, Wilhelm	1832-1908	Artist			1400		Painter & Poet.
Busell, Darcey		Entertainment	15			40	Ballet
Busey, Gary	1944-	Entertainment	8	18		29	Actor. Versatile leading man & heavy
Bush		Entertainment	45			150	Music. 4 Member Rock Group
Bush, Barbara		First Lady	59	125		95	Christmas Cd. Signed by Both $600
Bush, George (As Pres.)		President	160	665	1865	300	WH Cd. S $500,President'l Cd. $950.SP Oath $1295

NAME	DATE	CATEGORY	SIG	LS/DS	ALS	SP	COMMENTS
Bush, George	1924-	President	125	241	817	572	Signed Vice Presidential Card $195
Bush, George W.		Business	20			40	Baseball Exec. TX Gov., Presidential Candidate
Bush, Irving T.		Business		35			Owned Largest Shipping Terminal
Bush, Owen		Entertainment	5			10	Character Actor
Bush, Prescott		Senate	25	75		90	Senator CT Father, Grandfather of George & Geo.W.
Bush, Vannevar	1890-1974	Science	60	180	255	125	Pioneer In Analog Computers.Atom Bomb
Bushkin, Joe		Entertainment	6	8	10	12	
Bushman, Francis X.	1883-1966	Entertainment	40	75	110	100	Silent Star of Ben Hur etc.
Bushmiller, Ernie*		Cartoonist	20			125	Nancy
Bushnell, David	1742?	Science	250	750	1250		Invented 1st Submarine
Bushnell, Horace	1802-76	Clergy	25	35	45		New Engl.Congregational Minister
Bushyhead, D.W.		Celebrity	200		1500		
Busoni, Ferruccio	1899-1924	Composer	120		370	425	It-born Pianist, AMusQS $175-$450-$650
Busse, Henry		Entertainment	20			50	Big Band Leader
Bustamante, Jose Luis		Celebrity	9	35	60		
Butcher, Susan		Ididorod	5	10		15	Dog Breeder
Bute, John Stuart		Royalty	85	130			Earl of Bute
Butenandt, Adolf F.J.		Science	20	30	45	25	Nobel Chemistry
Buthelezi, Gatsha Mangosuthu		Head of State	20			35	Chief of Zulu Nation
Butler, B.F.	1795-1858	Cabinet			150		PMG for Jackson
Butler, Benjamin F.	1818-93	Civil War	185	295	230		Union Gen., LS '62 $2750. DS '63 $700
Butler, Carl & Pearl		Country Music	15			30	
Butler, Daws		Entertainment	15	15	20	40	
Butler, Dean		Entertainment	5	8	12	15	
Butler, Ellis Parker	1869-1937	Author	10	60	92	40	Pigs is Pigs
Butler, John		Clergy	10	15	20	20	
Butler, John		Rev. War	75	185	375		Am. Loyalist.Butler's Rangers
Butler, Matthew C. (WD)		Civil War	155	345	675		CSA General
Butler, Matthew C.	1836-1909	Civil War	90	170	285		CSA General, US Sen. SC
Butler, Nicholas Murray		Educator	15	35	90	30	Nobel Peace Prize. Educator
Butler, Pierce (SC)	1866-1939	Supreme Court	40	90	242	45	Jurist 1922-39
Butler, Pierce	1744-1822	Rev. War	60	180	385		Signer of Constitution
Butler, Samuel	1835-1902	Author	20	60	125		Br. Author, Artist, Musician
Butler, Smedley D.		Military	15	35	75	35	Marine Corps Gen/2 CMH
Butler, Thomas S.		Senate/Congress	5	15			MOC PA
Butler, Walter	1752-81	Rev. War		550	675		Captured,escaped. Butler's Rangers
Butler, William Orlando		Military	45	210			Hero Battle of New Orleans
Butler, Yancy		Entertainment	10			25	Actress. Mann & Machine, Hard Target, Drop Zone
Butler, Zebulon		Military	70	200			Col. Rev. War
Butt Rumford, Clara		Entertainment	35			150	Opera
Buttafuco, Joey		Celebrity	12				
Butterfield, Billy		Entertainment	25			45	Jazz Trumpet, Bandleader
Butterfield, Daniel (WD)		Civil War	150	260	315	450	Union General .Composed TAPS
Butterfield, Daniel	1831-1901	Civil War	85	675	335		Union Gen. Composed Taps
Butterworth, Charles		Entertainment	20		40		Character Actor, Comedy

NAME	DATE	CATEGORY	SIG	LS/DS	ALS	SP	COMMENTS
Buttlar-Brandenfels, F.H.		Military	5	15	25	15	
Buttons, Red	1919-	Entertainment	15	18	15	40	Academy Award in Sayonara
Buttram, Pat		Entertainment	20	95		45	Gene Autry Movie Sidekick
Buttrick, George A.		Clergy	25	45	75	45	
Butts, Alfred M.		Inventor	35	50			Scrabble
Butz, Earl L.		Cabinet	6	18	30	15	Sec'y Agriculture
Buzzi, Ruth		Entertainment	3	6	10	15	
Byers, Samuel Hawkins		Author	25	40	60		Union Soldier-Author
Byington, Spring		Entertainment	20			55	
Byner, John		Entertainment	3	3	6	8	
Byng, Geo. Viscount Torrington		Military	25	75			Br. Adm. Destroyed Sp. Fleet 1719
Byrd, Charlie		Entertainment	15			25	Jazz Guitar
Byrd, Harry F. Byrd, Sr.		Governor	25				Gov. VA
Byrd, Harry F., Jr.		Senate	10	25		25	Senator VA
Byrd, Jerry		Country Music	10			20	
Byrd, Ralph		Entertainment	100	150		350	
Byrd, Richard E.	1888-1957	Aviation-Explorer	60	247	560	348	Adm. USN, Polar Expl. TLS/Cont. $575
Byrd, Robert C.		Senate	15	30	100	25	Senator WV
Byrds, The (Entire Group)		Entertainment					Rock. Alb S $120
Byrne, Bobby		Entertainment	20			70	Big band leader
Byrne, Gabriel		Entertainment	4			15	Actor, Films
Byrne, Jane		Politician	5	10	28	10	Mayor
Byrnes, Edd		Entertainment	5			15	
Byrnes, James F. (SC)		Supreme Court	30	125	235	55	
Byrns, Joseph Wellington		Senate/Congress	15	25		20	MOC TN
Byron, Arthur		Entertainment	15	15	20	35	
Byron, Geo. Gordon, Lord	1788-1824	Author	1585	2750	7125		Influential, Romantic Br. Poet
Byron, Jean		Entertainment	5			15	

C

NAME	DATE	CATEGORY	SIG	LS/DS	ALS	SP	COMMENTS
Caan, James		Entertainment	8	7	15	22	Godfather SP $30
Cabana, Robert D.		Astronaut	6			20	
Cabell, Earle		Mayor	10				Dallas JFK Assassination TLS $475
Cabell, James Branch	1879-1958	Author	30	120	165		Novels Attacked for Immorality
Cabell, William L.	1827-1911	Civil War	175	417			CSA General
Cable, George Washington	1844-1925	Author	40	55	158	50	CSA Soldier, Short Story Writer
Cabot, Bruce	1904-72	Entertainment	50	55	90	150	John Wayne Sidekick
Cabot, George	1751-1823	Congress		45	100		Sen. MA. Ratified US Constitution
Cabot, Sebastian		Entertainment	25	30	90	75	
Caceres, Andreas A.		Head of State	10	25	65	20	Peru
Cadbury, George		Business	35		170	50	Cadbury Chocolate Mfg.
Cadbury, Richard		Business	30	45	160	50	Cadbury Chocolate Mfg.

NAME	DATE	CATEGORY	SIG	LS/DS	ALS	SP	COMMENTS
Cade, Robert, Dr.		Business	10	15		10	Inventor of Gatorade
Cadman, Chas. Wakefield		Composer	60	200	350	100	AMusQS $195
Cadman, S. Parkes		Clergy	20	35	50	35	
Cadmus, Paul		Artist	35	110	120		Repro. S $75
Cadwalader, George	1803-79	Civil War	50	110	168		Union Gen. LS '63 385
Cadwalader, Lambert		Rev. War	55	140	335		Continental Congress
Cady, Daniel		Congress	20	35	50		MOC NY 1815
Caesar, Irving	1895-1996	Composer	25	55	125	60	Lyricist (Tea for Two) Collaborator/Gershwin etc.
Caesar, Sid	1922-	Entertainment	5	8	18	37	Comedian. Classic early TV
Cage, John M.	1912-92	Composer	75	95	195	165	AMusQS $125-$250. AMsS $3750
Cage, Nicholas	1964-	Entertainment	21	102		46	AA Actor
Cagney, James	1899-1987	Entertainment	113	120	88	232	AA Actor. Dancer, Singer
Cagney, Jeanne		Entertainment				20	Jimmy Cagney's Actress Sister
Cahier, Madame Charles		Entertainment	25			90	Early Opera
Cahn, Sammy	1913-93	Composer	15	76	125	60	AMusQS $250
Cain, Dean		Entertainment	10			42	Superman
Cain, James		Author	40	55	90		Novelist. Hard Boiled Fiction
Caine, John T.	1829-1911	Congressman				50	Democratic Rep. From Utah. Newspaper Editor
Caine, Michael	1933-	Entertainment	9	12	24	47	Brit. AA winning actor.
Caine, Thos. Hall, Sir	1853-1931	Author	20	45	74	25	Br. Novelist, Dramatist
Calandral, Joe		Entertainment	6			25	Music. Bass Guitar Monster Magnet
Calavano, Phil		Entertainment	6			25	Music. Monster Magnet
Calder, A. Stirling	1870-1945	Artist			65		Sculptor. Father of Alexander Calder
Calder, Alexander (Sandy)	1898-1976	Artist	125	225	867	150	Sculptor, Mobiles. ALS/Cont. $1000, $1500, $1800
Calder, William M.	1869-1945	Congress		20			Sen.NY
Calderio, Frank		Astronaut	5			20	
Calderon, A. W. Gen.		Head of State	5	15	35	10	
Caldwell, Erskine	1903-86	Author	40	150	205	75	Tobacco Road, God's Little Acre
Caldwell, George A.	1814-66	Congress	10				Repr. KY, Officer Mexican War
Caldwell, John Curtis		Civil War	35	75		95	Union Gen.
Caldwell, Sarah		Conductor	15			20	1st Woman Conductor NY Met.
Caldwell, Taylor		Author	35	150	225	50	Novelist
Caldwell, Zoe		Entertainment	5	25	15	15	
Calhern, Louis		Entertainment	30	25	45	45	Eminent Stage-Film Actor
Calhoun, Alice		Entertainment	15	15	35	30	
Calhoun, Eleanor		Entertainment	3	3	6	8	
Calhoun, John C.	1782-1850	Vice President	207	560	475	375	Andrew Jackson VP. Statesman, Sec'y War
Calhoun, Rory		Entertainment	6	28	11	16	Handsome Cowboy, Leading Man
Calhoun, William Barron		Congress	10	15	35		Repr. MA 1835
Calhoun, William M.		Senate/Congress	5	10			
Calkin, Dick*		Cartoonist	75			500	Buck Rogers
Callaghan, James	1912-	Head of State	35	75	140	50	Br. Prime Minister
Callahan, Laurence K.		Aviation	10	20	45	30	
Callas, Charlie		Entertainment	3	5	8	12	
Callas, Maria Meneghini	1923-77	Entertainment	400	762	875	1378	Opera, Concert. Small format SP $525-850-950-1075

NAME	DATE	CATEGORY	SIG	LS/DS	ALS	SP	COMMENTS
Calleia, Frank		Entertainment	19	25	45	45	
Calleia, Joseph		Entertainment	25			55	
Calley, William		Military	20	35	45	40	My Lai, Viet Nam
Calloway, Cab	1907-95	Entertainment	40	55	70	188	Afro-Am. Big Band Leader. Jazz Musician
Calve, Emma		Entertainment	55	90	105	500	Opera
Calvert, Louis		Entertainment	5	6	15	15	
Calvert, Phyllis		Entertainment	5	15		15	
Calvet, Corinne	1925-	Entertainment	8	12		19	Fr. Actress. 50's Genre. Pin-Up $28
Calvin, John		Clergy	5500	7500	10000		
Calvin, Melvin, Dr.		Science	25	35	55	20	Nobel Chemistry
Camacho, Manuel Avila		Head of State	35		80	20	Pres. Mexico
Camargo, Alberto		Head of State	10	18	35	20	Columbia
Cambaceres, J.J.R.(Parma)		Napoleonic Wars	115	200			Prince & Duke
Cambell, James		Cabinet	35	80	120		Pierce P.M. General
Cambern, Donn		Entertainment	10			20	Actor Mayberry
Cambon, Jules		Diplomat	20	25	35		Fr. Ambassador to US
Cambridge, G.O.		Clergy	10	20	25		
Cambridge, Godfrey		Entertainment	25	20		60	Afr-Am Comedian, Activist
Cameron, Betsy		Author	5	10	20	10	
Cameron, George	1861-1944	Military	20		45		General WW I
Cameron, James D.	1833-1918	Cabinet	30	35	45		Senator PA. Sec'y War
Cameron, Kenneth		Astronaut	5			15	
Cameron, Kirk		Entertainment	8	15		20	Growing Pains Star
Cameron, Matt		Entertainment	6			25	Music. Drummer Soundgarden
Cameron, Robert A.	1828-94	Civil War	35	75			Union Gen. ALS '62 $175
Cameron, Rod	1910-83	Entertainment	15			50	Actor. Rugged Star of Westerns & B Films
Cameron, Simon (WD)		Cabinet	130	195	265	300	
Cameron, Simon	1800-89	Cabinet	106	135	220	295	Lincoln Sec'y War, Financier
Cammaerts, Emile		Author	10	20	40	15	Belgian Poet-Writer
Camp, Colleen		Entertainment	6	10	14	18	Pin-Up $35
Campanella, Joseph		Entertainment	3	3	6	6	
Campanini, Italo		Entertainment	65	80	175		
Campbell, Archibald		Rev. War	95	275			Br. General.
Campbell, Archie		Country Music	8			25	
Campbell, Beatrice Stella	1865-1940	Entertainment	25	40	45	105	Mrs. Patrick Campbell. Actress
Campbell, Charles Thomas		Civil War	35	80	110		Union General
Campbell, Colin, Sir	1792-1863	Military	16	45	75		Br. Gen. Vs U.S., War 1812
Campbell, Douglas		Aviation	38	65	80	125	ACE, WW I, Bi-plane Ace
Campbell, E. Simms*		Cartoonist	20			150	1st Black Mag. Cartoonist
Campbell, Ernest T.		Clergy	20	30	40	30	
Campbell, G.J.(8th Duke Argyll)		Statesman	25	60	130		Author. Br. Cabinet
Campbell, George W.	1769-1848	Cabinet	55	160	310		Sec'y Treas. Senator TN 1803
Campbell, Glen		Entertainment	5	25	15	20	Singer-Guitarist. Wichita Lineman Alb. S $30
Campbell, Jack M.		Governor	10	20			Governor NM
Campbell, James E.		Governor	15	25	30		Governor OH, MOC

NAME	DATE	CATEGORY	SIG	LS/DS	ALS	SP	COMMENTS
Campbell, John		Rev. War	62	175	290		Br. General
Campbell, John A. (SC)		Supreme Court	100	500	375		
Campbell, John Hull	1800-68	Congress	6				Repr. PA
Campbell, Malcolm	1885-1948	Sportsman	50	225			Br Auto. & Hydroplane racer-designer
Campbell, Mary		Entertainment			50		Miss America 1922-23
Campbell, Naomi		Model	12	10	12	35	Semi-Nude Col. SP $80. Pin-Up $55
Campbell, Neve		Entertainment	15			52	Actress. Scream, Party of Five SP $65
Campbell, Patrick, Mrs.	1865-1940	Entertainment	35	60			Vintage Stage Actress (Beatrice)
Campbell, Philip P.	1862-1944	Congress	12				Kansas
Campbell, R. L.		Military	5	15	20	10	
Campbell, William (Bill)		Entertainment	5	5		12	SP As Rocketeer $35. Star Trek SP $20
Campbell, William B.		Civil War	40	55	95		Union Gen., Congress TN
Campbell-Bannerman, Henry	1836-1908	Head of State	19	45	95		Br. Prime Minister
Campora, Giuseppe		Entertainment	10			40	It. Tenor, Opera
Camus, Albert	1913-1960	Author	75	308	911		Nobel. Poet, Philosopher. AMsS (Poem) $595
Canary, David		Entertainment	8			15	Actor
Canby, Edward R.	1817-73	Civil War	65	292	370		Union Gen. ALS '64 $330
Cander, John		Composer		40			Pop Music
Candler, Asa Griggs		Business	475	1275		595	Founder of Coca Cola
Candler, Warren Akin		Clergy	25	35	50		
Candlish, Robert Smith		Clergy	10	15	25	35	
Candy, John	1950-94	Entertainment	41	25	50	87	Comedian. Died Prematurely
Canetti, Elia		Author	65	225	350		Bulg.-Br.Nobel Literature
Canfield, Dorothy (Fisher)	1879-1958	Author	50	65	300		Am. Novelist, Essayist.
Canham, Erwin		Journalist	10	20			Christian Science Monitor
Caniff, Milton*	1907-88	Cartoonists	25	85	138	175	Terry & the Pirates & Steve Canyon
Caniglia, Maria		Entertainment	15			88	Opera. Dramatic Sopr.
Cannell, Stephen J.		Entertainment	6	10		10	TV Producer
Canning, Charles John	1812-62	Head of State	35		65	50	Governor-General & 1st Viceroy of India
Canning, Effie I.		Author	45		300		
Canning, George	1770-1827	Head of State	48	130	145		Prime Minister. Served only 3 Months .
Cannon, Annie Jump	1863-1941	Science			100		Great Woman Astronomer
Cannon, Dyan		Entertainment	5	7	12	18	Pin-Up $35-$45
Cannon, Frank J.		Senate	5			10	Senator UT
Cannon, George Q.		Senate/Congress	50	140	200		Utah's 1st Congressman
Cannon, Howard W.		Senator	5	10	25	15	Senator NV
Cannon, John K.		Military	10	30	50		
Cannon, Jos. G.'Uncle Joe'		Congress	20	40	95	40	Speaker of the House
Cannon, Martha H., Dr.		Science	25	30	60	30	
Canova, Antonio	1757-1822	Artist	85	250	612		It. Sculptor. Classical Revival
Canova, Diana		Entertainment	3	3	6	10	Pin-Up $22
Canova, Judy		Entertainment	12	15	22	30	Singer-Comedienne. Deceased
Cantinflas	1911-95	Entertainment	33			87	
Cantor, Eddie	1892-1964	Entertainment	79	155		182	Early Comedian,Singer.Vaudeville,Films,Radio
Cantrell, Jerry		Entertainment	6			25	Music. Guitar, Vocals Alice in Chains

NAME	DATE	CATEGORY	SIG	LS/DS	ALS	SP	COMMENTS
Cantrell, Lana		Entertainment	3	3	6	10	
Canutt, Yakima		Entertainment	12	18	25	42	AA. Legendary Stuntman & Dir.
Canyon, Christy		Entertainment				35	Porn Queen
Capers, Ellison (WD)		Civil War	130		630		CSA General
Capers, Ellison	1837-1903	Civil War	75				CSA General
Capers, Virginia		Entertainment	3	3	6	6	
Caperton, William		Military	20			50	Adm. WW I
Capka, Carol		Entertainment	3	3	6	6	
Caplin, Mortimer		Celebrity	5	5	10	10	
Capon, Robert F.		Clergy	10	15	20	15	
Capone, Al		Criminal	2850	10750		3800	Gangster. Special DS $15,000
Capote, Truman	1924-84	Author	112	340	1079	242	Novelist, Short Story Writer
Capp, Al*		Cartoonist	85	275		250	Li'l Abner
Capper, Arthur		Senate	12	25		30	Senator KS
Capra, Frank	1897-1991	Entertainment	25	155		98	AA Film Director.TLS Ltr/Poem $450
Capshaw, Kate		Entertainment	6	10	35	42	Actress
Captain & Tennile		Entertainment	7	15	15	15	
Capucine		Entertainment	10			49	Sultry Ital. Leading Lady of 50's
Capucine		Entertainment	25	30	70	65	
Caraway, Hattie	1878-1950	Congress	25	55	35	40	1st Woman US Senator, AR
Carberry, John J., Cardinal		Clergy	50	65	80	50	
Cardigan, 7th Earl Brudenell		Military	75	175	250	130	Br.Gen. Charge of Light Brigade
Cardinale, Claudia		Entertainment	20			35	It. International Star. Pin-Up $45
Cardozo, Benjamin N. (SC)	1870-1938	Supreme Court	150	350	665	840	
Carere, Christine		Entertainment	5			20	Actress
Carey, Drew	1958-	Entertainment	12			48	Comedian-Actor
Carey, Harry Jr.		Entertainment	6	9	15	22	
Carey, Harry Sr.		Entertainment	100	110	175	250	
Carey, Hugh L.		Governor	10	15		15	Governor NY
Carey, MacDonald		Entertainment	7	7	9	18	Days of Our Lives Star. 50's-70's Movies
Carey, Mariah		Entertainment	10	65		55	Singer. Pin-Up $60
Carey, Michele		Entertainment	5	6	15	25	
Carey, Ron		Entertainment	5	6	10	10	
Cargill, Henson		Country Music	4			18	Skip a Rope #1
Carias Andino, Tiburcio		Head of State	40	125		45	Pres. Honduras
Carl XIV Johan	1763-1844	Royalty	150	580			King Sweden
Carl XV	1826-72	Royalty	125	425			King of Sweden & Nor. from 1859
Carl XVI Gustaf	1946-	Royalty	55	150			King Sweden
Carl, Marion		Aviation	15	25	48	75	ACE, WW II, 1st Marine Ace. Murdered
Carle, Frankie		Entertainment	12			42	Big Band Leader
Carleton, Guy, Sir (Baron)	1724-1808	Military-Rev. War	250	645	800		Br. Commander-in-Chief
Carleton, James H.	1814-73	Civil War	30		110		Union Gen. LS '63 $825
Carleton, Will	1845-1912	Author	15	50	150	25	Ir. Novelist
Carlin, George		Entertainment	6	10	12	18	Standup Comedian
Carlin, Lynn		Entertainment	3	3	6	6	

NAME	DATE	CATEGORY	SIG	LS/DS	ALS	SP	COMMENTS
Carlisle, 7th Earl	1802-64	Author-Politician	20	45	115		George W.F. Howard. Poet,Orator,Viceroy of Ireland
Carlisle, Belinda		Entertainment	8	12	18	40	Go-Gos Lead Singer
Carlisle, John Griffin		Senate-Cabinet	15	25	35	30	Speaker. Sen. KY,Sec'y Treas.
Carlisle, Kitty		Entertainment	5	7	12	13	What's My Line Regular. Vintage SP $30
Carlisle, Mary	1912-	Entertainment	10	15	25	30	Actress
Carlo Alberto	1798-1849	Royalty	45	150	375		King of Sardinia
Carlotta (Marie-Charlotte-Amalie)		Royalty	340	770	1700		Empress of Mex. Became Insane
Carlsen, Capt. Kurt		Celebrity	20	55	125	45	
Carlson, Frank		Governor-Senate	10	18	25	15	Governor, Senator KS
Carlson, Fred		Collectibles	3			10	Lunch Box King
Carlson, Richard		Entertainment	15			30	Film Leading Man. 40's-50's
Carlton, Guy	1724-1808	Rev. War		1500			Br. Gen.
Carlyle, Russ		Entertainment	5			15	Bandleader
Carlyle, Thomas	1795-1881	Author	90	422	450	95	Br. Philosopher, Social Critic, Essayist. AQS $300
Carman, Tex J.		Country Music	10			20	
Carmen, Jean		Entertainment	4	4	9	10	
Carmer, Carl		Author	20	45	175		
Carmichael, Hoagy	1899-1981	Composer	50	200		200	Stardust. AMusQS $250, $320, $375
Carmichael, Oliver C.		Educator	20	35		25	Pres. Univ. Alabama
Carnarvon, Henry 4th Earl		Statesman	15	35	80		Created Fed. Dominion Canada
Carne, Judy		Entertainment	6	8	15	22	Br. Comedienne. Pin-Up $35
Carnegie, Andrew	1835-1919	Industrialist	222	1030	1425	895	Philanthropist.TLS/Cont.$9800,Stock Cert. S $24000
Carnegie, Dale	1888-1955	Author	45	35		50	Teacher.How To Win Friends & Influence People
Carnes, Kim		Entertainment	4			20	Singer
Carney, Art	1918-	Entertainment	12	26	15	28	'Norton' on The Honeymooners.Oscar Winner
Carney, Robert B.		Military	12	20	35	48	Eisenhower CNO
Carnot, Lazare N.M.		Fr. Revolution	90	250	325		Min. of War. Exiled
Carnot, Marie Francois Sadi	1837-94	Head of State		450	190		Pres. France 1887-1894. Assassinated
Carnovsky, Morris		Entertainment	15		40	45	Character Actor
Carol I	1839-1914	Royalty					King Roumania & Queen Elizabeth. 2 SP's $1250
Carol, Cindy	1945-	Entertainment	5			25	Actress. Played Gidget
Carol, Sue (Ladd)		Entertainment	10	14	18	28	Silent Screen. Wife & Agent of Alan Ladd
Caroline (Monaco)		Royalty	25			80	Princess. Daughter of Grace
Caroline	1768-1821	Royalty	95	150	342		Estranged Queen George IV England
Caroline	1776-1841	Royalty		90	175		2nd Queen of Maximilian I (Bavaria)
Caroline of Anspach		Royalty	335	450	1000		Queen of George II (Eng.)
Caron, George R.	1919-95	Aviation	28	40	118	95	Enola Gay Tail gunner WW II.
Caron, Leslie	1931-	Entertainment	12	30		35	Fr. Dancer-Actress. Pin-Up $40
Carosio, Margherita		Entertainment	15			85	Opera
Carpenter, Carleton		Entertainment	5	6	10	10	
Carpenter, Francis Bicknell	1830-90	Artist	50				Emancipation Proclamation Engraving DS $3500
Carpenter, John		Entertainment	10			25	Film Director-Writer
Carpenter, Joseph Estlin		Clergy	40	50	60	75	
Carpenter, Karen		Entertainment	75			150	Singer. Tragic Young Death
Carpenter, Karen & Richard		Entertainment		485			Early Death for Karen

NAME	DATE	CATEGORY	SIG	LS/DS	ALS	SP	COMMENTS
Carpenter, Mary-Chapin		Entertainment	5			30	Award Winning Country Singer-Composer
Carpenter, Matthew H.		Senate/Congress	10	15	30	35	Senator WI
Carpenter, Richard		Entertainment	5		9	15	Performer-Songwriter
Carpenter, Scott	1925-	Astronaut	50	75	125	95	Mercury 7 Astro
Carpenter, W. Boyd, Bishop		Clergy	10	20	30		
Carpenter, William B.		Explorer	10	35	60		Br. Physiologist
Carpenter, William S.		Military	12	15	40	28	Viet Nam Hero
Carpenters, The		Entertainment	150			375	Richard and Karen
Carr, Darleen		Entertainment	3	3	6	8	Pin-Up $25
Carr, Eugene Asa	1830-1910	Civil War	35	162	200	220	Union Gen. CMH, ALS '63 $2200.Indian Fighter
Carr, Gerald P.		Astronaut	5			15	
Carr, Jane		Entertainment	5			15	Actress
Carr, Jerry		Astronaut	6			22	
Carr, Tommy		Entertainment	20			35	
Carr, Vicki		Entertainment	3	3	6	10	Singer, Recording Artist. Award Winner
Carradine, David		Entertainment	7	20		24	Actor. Kung Fu SP $28
Carradine, John		Entertainment	65	125	150	150	Versatile Actor. Many Characters. Many Films
Carradine, Keith		Entertainment	5			18	Stage, Screen, TV Star
Carradine, Robert		Entertainment	6			18	14 Page DS $150. Revenge Of Nerds SP $22
Carranza, Venustiano		Head of State	52	205	400		Revolutionary Pres.Mex.Murdered
Carrel, Dr. Alexis		Science	75	220	300	85	Nobel Medicine
Carreno, Terresa		Composer	25		118	90	Venez. Conductor- Pianist-Singer. Gottschalk Pupil
Carrera, Barbara		Entertainment	6	8	15	18	Pin-Up SP $45
Carreras, Jose		Entertainment	25	40		65	Operatic Tenor
Carrere, Christine		Entertainment	5			15	Fr. Actress
Carrey, Jim		Entertainment	32			66	Comedian-Actor
Carrigain, Philip		Law	20	50			Surveyed NH, Named Granite St.
Carrillo, Leo	1880-1961	Entertainment	65			175	TLS/Content $150. Pancho
Carroll, Charles	1737-1832	Rev. War	275	679	858		Signer. Important Rev. War ALS $8500
Carroll, Daniel		Rev. War	175	685	710		Continental Congress
Carroll, Diahann	1935-	Entertainment	6	9	14	28	Singer-Actress. Pin-Up $45
Carroll, Earl		Entertainment	85	105	210	190	
Carroll, Georgia		Entertainment	5			15	Pin-Up SP $28
Carroll, Gladys Hasty	1904-	Author	15				US Novelist
Carroll, John		Entertainment	8	15		20	Singing-Strutting Leading Man.
Carroll, John Lee		Governor	10		30		Governor MD
Carroll, Julian M.		Governor	10		35		Governor KY
Carroll, Leo G.		Entertainment	30			55	Br. Actor. Topper, U.N.C.L.E.
Carroll, Lewis							SEE Dodgson, C)
Carroll, Lisa Hart		Entertainment	6	8	15	19	
Carroll, Madeleine		Entertainment	35	150		84	Beautiful Brit. Star of 30's-40's
Carroll, Mickey		Entertainment	10			30	Wizard of Oz Munchkin
Carroll, Nancy		Entertainment	10	15	20	35	
Carroll, William		Military	25		90		Gen. TN Militia, Gov. TN 1821
Carroll, William H.		Civil War	60	145			CSA Gen.

NAME	DATE	CATEGORY	SIG	LS/DS	ALS	SP	COMMENTS
Carryl, Guy Wetmore		Author	4	15	25		
Cars, The		Entertainment	50			85	
Carson, Christopher 'Kit'	1809-68	Frontiersman	3650			2750	Union Gen'l, Scout, Indian Agt., Trapper, Explorer
Carson, Jack		Entertainment	15			50	
Carson, John		Military	10			35	General WW I
Carson, Johnny		Entertainment	8	20	35	35	Comedian. Tonight Show Host. SPc $25
Carson, Leonard 'Kit'		Aviation	12	25	42	35	ACE, WW II
Carson, Rachel	1907-1964	Author-Science	75	205	318	275	ALS/Cont. $1,650. 1st Ed. 'Silent Spring' S $1,000
Carson, Sunset		Entertainment	20	25		45	
Carter, Ann S.		Aviation	25	40		45	1st Woman Helicopter Pilot
Carter, Ben		Entertainment	100			250	
Carter, Benny	1907-	Entertainment	40	60	100	90	Jazz. Alto Sax, Trumpet. Arranger
Carter, Betty		Entertainment	15			35	Lionel Hampton Vocalist
Carter, Billy		Celebrity	4	10	15	10	Pres. Carter's Brother
Carter, Boake		Radio	5	20	35	15	Radio Commentator-Vintage
Carter, Carlene		Country Music	5			25	Grammy Nominee
Carter, Chris		Entertainment	5	15	25	30	Creator X Files
Carter, Dixie		Entertainment	5		20	15	Actress. TV Star. Designing Women
Carter, Elliott		Composer	32	175	202		Pulitzer Prize. 'The Minotaur'
Carter, Helen		Country Music	10			20	
Carter, Helena Bonham		Entertainment	13			47	Br. Actress. Frequent Oscar Nominee. Pin-UP $45
Carter, Hodding		Consultant	4	8	12	10	White House Aide
Carter, Howard	1874-1939	Archaeologist	1295		1600		Egyptologist, King Tut's Tomb Discoverer RARE!!
Carter, Janis		Entertainment	4	4	9	9	
Carter, Jimmy & Rosalyn		Pres. & 1st Lady	100			295	
Carter, Jimmy (As Pres.)		President		564			
Carter, Jimmy	1924-	President	100	357	1030	190	Pres. TLS/Content $3,000. Books S.$65-75-200
Carter, Leslie, Mrs.		Entertainment	20	75	90	70	Vintage Stage & Early Films
Carter, Lillian		Celebrity	12	25		15	Pres. Carter's Mother
Carter, Lynda		Entertainment	8		15	35	Actress. Wonder Woman. Pin-Up SP $25
Carter, Manly L.Sonny	1947-91	Astronaut	25	75		150	Space Shuttle Discovery.Killed '91 in air crash.
Carter, Mother Maybelle		Country Music	40			80	
Carter, Nell		Entertainment	5			15	
Carter, Robert		American Colonial		1400			
Carter, Rosalynn		First Lady	75	90	130	40	
Carter, Thomas H.		Senate	10		35	25	Senator MT. 1st Repr.from State
Carter, Tony		Entertainment	4	4	9	10	
Carter, Wilf		Country Music	10			20	
Carteret, George	1610-80	Military		1600			Br. Naval Off'r. Founded State of New Jersey
Carteri, Rosanna		Entertainment	10			30	
Cartland, Barbara, Dame		Author	10	28	70	75	Br. Novelist. Over 500 Romantic Novels
Cartright, Joy		Entertainment	3			15	
Cartwright, Angela		Entertainment	5		15	15	Lost in Space TV Script S $40
Cartwright, Lionel		Country Music	4			18	Leap of Faith #1
Cartwright, Nancy		Entertainment	5			15	Voice of Bart Simpson. Signs as Bart

NAME	DATE	CATEGORY	SIG	LS/DS	ALS	SP	COMMENTS
Cartwright, Veronica		Entertainment	8			22	Child Actress Now Grown. Older Sister of Angela
Carty, John J.		Science-Business	60	150	275	150	Telephone Pioneer. AT&T
Caruso, Anthony		Entertainment	25	29	70	52	
Caruso, David	1958-	Entertainment	10	35		30	Actor. NYPD Blue
Caruso, Enrico	1873-1921	Entertainment	244	550	1088	968	Caricature Self-Portr. S $625-1450-2550
Caruso, Enrico, Jr.		Entertainment				25	Actor Son Of Caruso Sr.
Caruthers, Robert L.	1800-82	Congress	12				Repr. TN, CW Gov. TN
Carvel, Elbert M.		Governor	10	15			Governor DE
Carver, Geo. Washington	1864-1943	Science	200	1095	950	3495	Hall of Fame, Botanist, Educator. Internat'l Fame
Carvey, Dana		Entertainment	8			28	Comedian-Actor. Sat. Night Live
Carville, Edward P.		Gov-Senate	12	15	40	20	Senator, Governor NV
Cary, Annie Louise		Entertainment	35			150	Opera. 1st Famous American Mezzo.
Cary, Jeremiah E.	1803-88	Congress	10				Repr. NY
Cary, Phoebe		Author	10	15			Am. Poet/Sister Alice
Cary, Samuel Fenton		Senate/Congress	10		30	25	MOC OH
Casadesus, Robert, Dr.		Composer	45		100	100	Fr. Concert Pianist-Composer
Casals, Pablo	1876-1973	Entertainment	101	150	318	338	Spanish Cellist, Conductor, Composer. AMusQS $350
Casanovo, Giacomo		Author	150	580	915		Adventurer, Gambler, Spy
Case, A. Ludlow	1813-88	Civil War	35	75			Admiral. North Atlantic Fleet
Case, Clifford P.		Senate/Congress	5	15		10	Senator, MOC NJ
Case, Francis H.		Senate/Congress	10	25		15	Senator, MOC IA
Case, Jerome I.		Business	30	60	155		Case Tractors & Farm Implements
Case, Kenny		Entertainment			35		Tenor of 4 Ink Spots
Case, Norman S.		Governor	10	25			Governor RI
Case. A. Ludlow	1813-88	Civil War	50	95			Adm. North Atlantic Fleet
Casella, Alfredo		Composer	35	130	250		Pianist, Conductor
Casellato, Renzo		Entertainment	20			50	Opera. Tenor
Caselotti, Adriana		Entertainment	5	15	35	55	Voice of Snow White
Casement, Jack		Civil War	45	170			Union Gen.
Casey, Bernie		Entertainment	5			18	Movie-TV-Artist
Casey, James S.		Civil War	30	125			1st Lt. Won CMH in Battle vs Crazy Horse
Casey, Silas	1807-82	Civil War	50	105	165		Union Gen. ALS '63 $550
Cash, Johnny		Country Music	10	25	40	75	12x14 Calender SP $95. DS for Saratoga Fair $95
Cash, Johnny & June Carter		Country Music	15			35	Husband/Wife Legends
Cash, June Carter		Country Music	6			15	Singer. Carter Family
Cash, Kellye		Celebrity	8		12	12	
Cash, Rosanne		Entertainment	5	6	15	20	Pin-Up SP $25
Cash, Tommy		Country Music	5			10	
Casimir-Perier, Jean Paul P.	1847-1907	Head of State			150		Pres. France 1894-95
Casper (Cast of)		Entertainment				100	Four Cast Members
Casper, John H.		Astronaut	8		95	20	
Cass, Lewis	1782-1866	Cabinet	50	110	152		Jackson Sec'y War, Senator MI
Cass, Peggy		Entertainment	5			10	
Cassatt, Mary		Artist	225	475	975		ALS/Content $4,500, $5,000
Cassavetes, John		Entertainment	20		25	50	Actor, Film Director

NAME	DATE	CATEGORY	SIG	LS/DS	ALS	SP	COMMENTS
Cassidy, David		Entertainment	5			15	
Cassidy, Jack		Entertainment	25			55	
Cassidy, Joanna		Entertainment	5	6	15	18	Actress. Pin-Up $35
Cassidy, Shaun		Entertainment	10			35	
Cassidy, Ted		Entertainment	175	225	325	775	
Cassin, Jimmy		Composer	10	40			Songwriter
Cassin, Rene		Statesman	30	75	175	45	Founder UNESCO, Nobel Peace
Cassini, Oleg		Business	12	25	40	45	Fashion Designer
Casson, Mel*		Cartoonist	10			20	Redeye
Castagna, Bruna		Entertainment	20			100	Opera. SP 4x5 $40
Castanzo, Jack		Entertainment	10			30	Jazz Musician
Castelnuovo-Tedesco, M.		Composer			300	125	Versatile Comp.All Fields.AMuQs $125-$325
Castle, Irene		Entertainment	50		75	75	
Castle, Irene & Castle, Vernon		Entertainment	100			425	Dance Couple
Castle, Lee		Entertainment	5	6	15	15	
Castle, Peggy		Entertainment	10			25	
Castle, Vernon		Entertainment	50			150	
Castle, William		Entertainment	40			100	
Castlereagh, R. Stewart, Visct.	1769-1822	Statesman	25	142	250		Minister War vs Napol. Suicide
Castro, Emilio		Clergy	25	30	35	35	
Castro, Fidel	1927-	Head of State	850	925	1350	1335	Communist Premier of Cuba
Castro, Raul		Military				125	Younger Brother of Fidel
Castro, Raul H.		Governor	5			12	Governor AZ
Cates, Clifton B.		Military	10	25	55	20	
Cates, Phoebe		Entertainment	10		15	51	Actress. Pin-Up SP $35-45-60
Catesby, Robert	1573-1605	Fugitive		1065			Involved in Guy Fawkes Gunpowder Conspiracy
Cathcart, Wm. Schaw Sir		Rev. War	65	125			Cmdr.British Legionin America
Cather, Willa	1873-1947	Author	280	432	600	150	Novelist.ALS/Cont $2,250
Catherine I (Rus)		Royalty	520	2000	4500		
Catherine II (The Great)	1729-1796	Royalty	615	1513	3100		Empress Russia from 1762-96.
Catherwood, Mary		Author	10	15	20		
Catlett, Mary Jo		Entertainment	4			18	Actress. Pin-Up $35
Catlett, Walter		Entertainment	10	15	25	25	
Catlin, George	1796-1872	Artist-Author	100	310	1000		Travel Books.Indian Scenes
Catlin, Isaac		Civil War	50	95	330		Union Gen., CMH
Catt, Carrie Chapman	1859-1947	Women's Rights	75	208	250		Suffragette Leader. Feminist.
Catton, Bruce		Author	30	150	125	30	Historian, Editor. Pulitzer
Caulfield, Joan	1922-91	Entertainment	15			40	Actress. Pretty 40's Ingenue. Pin-Up SP $35
Cavalieri Muratore, Lina		Entertainment	50			220	Opera
Cavallaro, Carmen		Entertainment	15			35	Big Band Leader-Pianist
Cavanagh, Paul		Entertainment	7			20	
Cavanaugh, Hobart		Entertainment	15	18	20	35	
Cavell, Edith	1865-1915	Science	225	375	1600		Br. Nurse. Allied Heroine. Court Martialed. Shot
Cavett, Dick		Entertainment	4	8	12	14	Late Nite TV Host. Writer
Cavour, Camillo, Count	1810-61	Head of State		425			Architect of Italy's Unification. P.M.

NAME	DATE	CATEGORY	SIG	LS/DS	ALS	SP	COMMENTS
Cayce, Edgar		Author	70	225			Am. Rural Healer, Seer
Cayvan, Georgia		Entertainment	6	8	15	15	
Ceausecu, Nicolae		Head of State	40	335		120	Pres. Romania. Assassinated
Cech, Thomas R., Dr.		Science	20	35		25	Nobel Chemistry
Cecil, Edg. Algernon, Lord	1864-1958	Diplomat	35	45	185		Statesman. Pres. League of Nations. Nobel Peace
Celeste		Entertainment				34	Porn Queen
Celine, Louis Ferd. (Destouches)	1894-1961	Author	175		912		Fr. Physician, Novelist
Celler, Emanuel		Senate/Congress	5	20		10	MOC NY
Cellini, Benvenuto		Artist	1000	4800	13500		Florentine Goldsmith, Sculptor
Cello, Aldo		Business	3	9	10	10	TV Ad vertising
Cenker, Robert		Astronaut	5			15	
Cerf, Bennett	1898-1971	Author	15	20	30	15	Random House Editor, Author, Game Show Guest
Cermak, Anton J.		Politician	15	40	95	125	Assassinated Mayor of Chicago
Cernan, Eugene A.		Astronaut	22	40	75	112	Moonwalker Astro.
Cervantes, Miguel de		Author	10000	15000			Sp.Novelist,Poet.Don Quixote
Cesky, Charles J.		Aviation	10	22	38	28	ACE, WW II
Cetywago, King of Zulu		Afr. Leader	375				
Cezanne, Paul	1839-1906	Artist	1150	2300	7833		Fr. Impressionist to Cubism
Chabas, Paul Emile		Artist	35	60	135		
Chabert, Lacey		Entertainment	5			48	Child Actress
Chabot, Phillipe de Brion, Comte		Military	1750				1480-1543. Fr.Cmdr.In Chief
Chabrier, Alexis Emmanuel		Composer	70	255	408		Fr. Opera, Orchestral, Piano
Chadwick, James, Sir		Science	80	215	450		Nobel Phys. Discovered Neutron
Chadwick, June		Entertainment	5			20	Brit. Actress. Riptide etc.
Chaffee, Adna R.		Civil War	35	80	115		Union General
Chaffee, Roger		Astronaut	200		445	400	Died Aboard Apollol I, 1-27-67
Chagall, Marc	1887-1985	Artist	280	400	1235	1285	Color Repro S $225-295-395-650-1095
Chaka Kahn		Entertainment	8			28	Singer
Chakiris, George		Entertainment	10	15	25	25	
Chalia, Rosalia		Entertainment	25	40	65		
Chaliapin, Feodor	1873-1938	Entertainment	120	278	500	550	Opera. Rus. Basso. SPc $450
Chalker, Jack		Author	10	20	40	10	
Chalmers, James R. (WD)		Civil War	250				CSA General
Chalmers, James R.	1831-98	Civil War	130	377			CSA General
Chalmers, Thomas	1780-1847	Clergy	55	69	90	75	Theologian, Philanthropist
Chalon, Alfred E.	1780-1860	Artist	200		375		Portr.Of Q.Victoria Appearing on 1st Postage Stmp
Chamberlain, Austen, Sir	1863-1937	Statesman	30	85	100	100	Br. Politician. Nobel Peace Prize 1925
Chamberlain, Daniel		Governor	50	125			Carpetbag Gov. SC
Chamberlain, Joseph A.	1836-1914	Br. Politician	60	85	85	90	Statesman, Nobel Peace Prize. Colonial Sec'y
Chamberlain, Joshua L.	1828-1914	Civil War	625	1330	1862		ALS Re Gettysburg $3500.Union Officer. Gov. ME
Chamberlain, Neville	1869-1940	Head of State	90	510	400	165	Prime Minister Eng.
Chamberlain, Owen, Dr		Science	25	35	75	30	Nobel Physics
Chamberlain, Richard		Entertainment	12	15		27	Handsome Actor. Dr. Kildare & Many Mini Series
Chamberlain, S.J.		Military	10	30	50		
Chamberlaine, William		Military	10		35	20	General WW I

NAME	DATE	CATEGORY	SIG	LS/DS	ALS	SP	COMMENTS
Chamberlin, Clarence		Aviation	50	250	385	275	Record Non-Stop Flight NY-Ger.
Chamberlin, Jimmy		Entertainment	6			25	Music. Drummer Smashing Pumpkins
Chambers Brothers (All)		Entertainment	50			200	Rock Group
Chambers, Marilyn		Entertainment	7	15	22	25	Adult Film Star of 70's. Pin-Up SP $50
Chambers, Robert Wm.		Author-Artist	10	15	20		Novelist.Life Mag Illustrator
Chambers, Whittaker		Journalist	15	50	150	25	Charged Alger Hiss as Communist
Chaminade, Cecile	1857-1944	Composer	85	195	300	232	AMusQS $125
Champion, Gower		Entertainment	20	30		45	Successful Film-Stage Choreographer-Dancer
Champion, Gower & Marge		Entertainment	30			85	Dance Partner Legends
Champion, Marge		Entertainment	5	9	12	15	Dancer-Actress.
Champollion, Jean-Francois	1790-1832	Archaeologist			2695		Fr. Translator of Egyptian Hieroglyphics 1st Time.
Chan, Genie*		Cartoonist	10			35	Conan
Chan, Jackie		Entertainment				75	Karate-Judo Films
Chancellor, John	1927-96	Journalist	15			95	Radio-TV News & Commentator
Chandler, A.B. 'Happy'		Senate-Gov.	15	35		50	Sen., Gov. KY.Baseball Comm.
Chandler, Christopher		Celebrity	6		40		
Chandler, Dorothy 'Buff'		Business	8	20	45	25	Buffums Dept. Stores
Chandler, George		Entertainment	5			25	Character Actor
Chandler, Helen		Entertainment	30			75	
Chandler, Jeff	1918-61	Entertainment	54	75	150	140	Major Radio-Film Star. Early Death
Chandler, Joseph Ripley		Congress	15		35		Repr. PA 1843. Editor US Gazette
Chandler, Lane		Entertainment	20			40	
Chandler, Norman		Business	15	35	75	30	L.A. Times
Chandler, Otis		Business	20	45	95	40	Founder L.A. Times
Chandler, Raymond		Author	190	540	975		Novelist. Detective Fiction
Chandler, William E.		Cabinet-Senate	20	38	65		Senator NH, Sec'y Navy
Chandler, Zachariah		Cabinet-Senate	25	35	50		Senator NH, Sec'y Int.,Att'y Gen'l
Chandrasekhar, Subrahmanyan		Science	30	110	225		Nobel, Astrophysicist
Chandu the Magician		Entertainment	5	7	25	20	
Chanel, Coco		Business	50	110	235	85	Fashion Designer, Perfumer
Chaney, Lon, Jr.	1906-73	Entertainment	340	557	500	707	
Chaney, Lon, Sr.	1881-1930	Entertainment	1150			1688	Man of a 1000 Faces. SP in Character $2000 & up
Chang		Entertainment	15			45	Chinese Giant
Chang, Franklin R.		Astronaut	5			15	
Chang, Min-Chu	1909-91	Science	50		145		Discoverer of In Vitro Fertilization
Channing, Carol		Entertainment	4			18	Unique Broadway Musical Star. Hello Dolly
Channing, Stockard		Entertainment	5		10	15	Actress. SP Grease $22
Channing, William Ellery		Clergy-Author	40	70	120		
Channing, William Henry		Clergy	35	45	65	50	
Chaparral, John and Paul		Country Music	20			40	
Chapin, Harry		Composer	100	125		295	Singer-Songwriter
Chaplin, Charles, Sir	1889-1977	Entertainment	353	620	450	926	Legendary Film Comedian. BS (Auto-Bio)$550
Chaplin, Geraldine		Entertainment	9	12		25	Actress-Daughter of Charlie. Pin-Up $35
Chaplin, Lita Grey	1908-95	Entertainment	20	25	45	25	
Chaplin, Sydney		Entertainment	15		35	30	

NAME	DATE	CATEGORY	SIG	LS/DS	ALS	SP	COMMENTS
Chapman, Ben, Jr.		Entertainment	15			25	Actor. 'Creature From Black Lagoon' SP $75
Chapman, Graham		Entertainment	15	20	25	30	
Chapman, Leonard, Jr.		Military	15	30		55	USMC General, WW II
Chapman, Marguerite		Entertainment	10			20	Pin-Up SP $25
Chapman, Mark David		Criminal	75	155			Murdered John Lennon
Chapman, Oscar L.		Cabinet	15	20	30	35	Sec'y Interior 1849
Chapman, Philip K.		Astronaut	6			20	
Chappell, Clovis G.		Clergy	20	25	30	30	
Chappell, William	1809-1888	Business	20	45	110	35	Music Publisher
Chaptal, Jean Antoine, Count		Napoleonic	135	200			Chemist.Min.Agri., Interior
Charbonneau, Patricia		Entertainment	4			15	Actress. Pin-Up $28
Charcot, Jean Martin	1825-93	Science	95	225	733		Fr. Neurologist & Prof. Of Pathological Anatomy
Charcot, Jean-Baptiste	1867-1936	Explorer		100	135		Headed 2 Arctic Expeditions. Drowned/38 of his men
Charisse, Cyd		Entertainment	5	6	15	25	Dancing Star of Films. Pin-Up SP $40
Charlemagne		Royalty	75000				Price Estimate Only
Charles & Diana		Royalty		2500		3450	Prince & Princess of Windsor
Charles Albert (Sardinia)		Royalty			225		Count of Savoy
Charles Edw. Stuart	1720-88	Royalty	110	362	1440		The Young Pretender; Jacobite Claiment
Charles Emmanuel I		Royalty		400			King Sardinia
Charles Emmanuel I	1562-1630	Royalty	595	900			The Great
Charles I (Eng)	1600-49	Royalty	700	2488	4000		Important DS (1642) $4500
Charles II (Eng)	1630-85	Royalty	735	1852	2825		King Eng & Ireland. Merry Monarch
Charles II (Sp)		Royalty	275	395			
Charles IV (Eng)		Royalty	245	1100			
Charles IV (Sp)	1748-1819	Royalty	185	795	762		Don Carlos. King of Sp. Forced to Abdicate
Charles IX (Fr)	1560-74	Royalty	295	1428	1700		
Charles V (Charles I {Sp})		Royalty	550	2100	5000		(Charles I & Juana DS $1500)
Charles VI (Charles III {Sp})		Royalty	375	1562			Holy Roman Emperor 1711-1740
Charles X (Fr)	1757-1836	Royalty	150	600	725		King of France.
Charles XIV John (Swe)		Royalty	145	550	880		See also Bernadotte
Charles XV (Swe-Nor)		Royalty	45	140	320		
Charles, Ernest		Composer	20	80		45	
Charles, Josh		Entertainment	5			20	Actor Sports Night
Charles, Prince of Wales	1948-	Royalty	775	842	1500	862	Philip Arthur George
Charles, Ray		Entertainment		200			Blind Afro-Am. Singer-Musician
Charles, Suzette		Entertainment	5	6	15	20	Miss American 1984
Charlotte Sophia	1741-1818	Royalty	145	275	452		Queen of George III (Eng)
Charlotte, Grand Duchess		Royalty	25	75	180	55	Luxembourg
Charo		Entertainment	3	3	6	10	
Charpentier, Gustave	1860-1956	Composer	100	250	300	305	AMusQS $150-$450-$625-$750
Charteris, Leslie		Author	20	55	135	85	The Saint. FDC S $75
Charvet, David		Entertainment	12			45	Actor 'Baywatch'
Chase, Charley		Entertainment	20			150	Vintage Film Comedian
Chase, Chevy		Entertainment	6	7	15	30	Actor-Comedian. SP Xmas Vacation $38
Chase, Ilka		Entertainment	12	15	20	25	Author

NAME	DATE	CATEGORY	SIG	LS/DS	ALS	SP	COMMENTS
Chase, Mary Ellen		Author	25	70	150	35	Educator, Essayist, Novelist
Chase, Salmon P. (SC)	1808-1873	Supreme Court	108	250	500	300	Chief Justice Supr. Ct., Lincoln's Sec'y Treas.
Chase, Samuel	1741-1811	Rev. War	275	815	1925		Signer Decl. of Indepen.
Chase, William C.		Military	6	20	35		
Chase, William Merritt	1849-1916	Artist	95				US Painter of Western Scenes
Chateaubriand, Francois R. de	1768-1848	Author	120	305	525		Fr. Novelist, Diplomat. Fndr. Fr. Romantic Movement
Chatterton, Ruth		Entertainment	15			55	
Chauncey, Isaac	1772-1840	Military	25	95	105		Am. Naval Off. Tripoli, War 1812
Chausson, Ernest		Composer	50	145	345		Fr. Opera, Symphonies
Chauvel, Henry, Sir		Military	25	75			Aussie General WW I
Chavez, Carlos		Composer	15	35	70	40	Mexican Conductor-Composer
Chavez, Cesar E.	1927-93	Labor	40	250		182	Migrant Labor Organizer. Social Activist
Chavez, Dennis		Senate	10	25		25	Sen NM. 1st Hispanic MOC & Senator
Chavez, George A.		Aviation	45	60	175	65	
Chawla, Kalpana		Astronaut	6			20	
Chayefsky, Paddy (Sidney)		Author	75	200	188	125	Plays, TV Dramas, Screenplays
Cheap Trick		Entertainment	35			40	DS by Rick Nielsen Repr. For Band $50
Cheatham, Benj. Franklin	1820-86	Civil War	225	400			CSA General
Cheatham, Benjamin F.(WD)		Civil War	390		652		CSA General
Checker, Chubby		Entertainment	10	20	25	34	Rock
Cheech & Chong		Entertainment	12			45	Raunchy Comic Duo
Cheek, John		Entertainment	10			25	Opera
Cheers (Cast) (6)		Entertainment				335	
Cheever, Charles A., Dr.		Science	40	100		75	
Cheever, George B.	1814-90	Clergy	10		30		Author
Cheever, John	1912-81	Author	45	125	220	88	Subtle, Ironic Novels. Pulitzer 1979
Chekhov, Anton	1860-1904	Author	560	1815	5000		Rus. Dramatist. Novelist, Physician
Chen, Joan		Entertainment	15			60	Model-Actress
Chen, Tina		Composer	10	10		15	
Cheney, Richard		Cabinet	10			25	Sec'y Defense
Cheney, Sherwood		Military	5		25		General WW I
Chennault, Anna	1925-	Celebrity	15	25	50	30	Aviation Exec., Writer, Lecturer. Wife of the Gen'l.
Chennault, Claire L.	1890-1958	Aviation	550		675	638	Flying Tigers. USAAF Gen.
Cher		Entertainment	9	32	24	50	AA Winning Actress. Pin-Up SP $80
Cherkassky, Shura		Entertainment	20			60	Opera
Chernov, Vladimir		Entertainment	10			30	Opera, Rus. Baritone
Cherry, Don	1924-96	Entertainment	5			30	Singer. Popular Decca Recording Artist
Cherry, R. Gregg		Governor	5	15		10	Governor NC
Cherubini, Luigi	1760-1842	Composer	175	352	660		It. 29 Operas, 15 Masses
Chesebrough, Amos	1709-60	Colonial Am.		275			Lt.Col. 8th Reg. French-Ind. War
Chesebrough, George M.		Science		750			
Chesebrough, Robert		Business	15	30	50		Vaseline Products. Chesebrough Mfg. Co.
Cheshire, Leonard		Military	15	50	65	40	Br. RAF
Chesnutt, Mark		Country Music	4			22	Consistent Top 10 Artist
Chester, Bob		Entertainment	20			40	Big Band Leader

NAME	DATE	CATEGORY	SIG	LS/DS	ALS	SP	COMMENTS
Chester, Colby M.		Business	10			55	CEO General Foods
Chester, John		Rev. War	35	80			Continental Army. Judge
Chesterfield, Fourth Earl of							SEE Stanhope, P.D.
Chesterton, (G)ilbert (K)eith		Author	48	305	325	190	'Father Brown, Detective'
Chestnut, James		Civil War	250				CSA Gen.
Chevalier, Albert	1861-1923	Composer	6	25	40	25	Br. Actor,Singer,Humorist
Chevalier, Maurice	1888-1972	Entertainment	52		150	122	Fr. Film & Vaudeville Actor-Singer. Gigi
Chevrolet, Louis	1879-1941	Business	850	4858			Chevrolet Auto Mfg. & Glen Martin Aircraft
Chew, Virginia	1905-87	Entertainment	5		25		Char.Actress. Longtime Broadway. Sometime Films
Chiao, Leroy		Astronaut	7			20	
Chiari, Walter	1924-92	Entertainment	20			45	Comic Italian Actor. Internationally recognized.
Chicago		Entertainment	35			95	
Chichester, Francis, Sir		Celebrity	35	100	165	75	Adventurer,Aviator, Sailed Gypsy Moth IV
Chickering, Thos.E.	1824-71	Civil War-Business	70	90	175		Union Gen. Chickering Piano
Chierel, Micheline		Entertainment	10			30	Actress
Child, Julia		Celebrity Chef	5	12	22	15	TV Chef. Cookbook Author
Child, Lydia Maria		Author	30	90	155		Abolitionist, Reformer, Editor
Childress, Alvin		Entertainment	50			125	
Childs, George Wm.		Publisher	10	15	20		
Chiles, Lawton Mainor, Jr.		Senate	10	15	20	15	Senator FL
Chiles, Lois		Entertainment	5	6	15	22	Actress
Chilton, Kevin P.		Astronaut	4			15	
Chilton, Robert Hall (WD)		Civil War	395	3125			CSA General
Chilton, Robert Hall	1815-79	Civil War	185				CSA General
Chilton, Samuel	1804-67	Congress	50	145			MOC VA. John Brown's Att'y
Chirac, Jacques		Head of State	25	75	185	35	Fr. Prime MInister, Mayor Paris
Chirico, Giorgio de	1888-1978	Artist			765		Major Italian Surrealist
Chisholm, Shirley A.	1924-	Senate/Congress	25			100	1st Afro-Am. Congresswoman
Chittenden, Thos. C.	1788-1866	Congress	10				MOC NY
Chlumsky, Anna		Entertainment	6			45	Young Actress
Choate, Joseph H.	1832-1917	Diplomat	15	60	125	45	Prosecuted Tweed Ring
Choate, Rufus	1799-1859	Senate	20	35	60		Boston Statesman,Orator, NY Sen
Choiseul, Leo. C. de, Cardinal		Clergy	100	165			
Chokachi, David		Entertainment	6			35	Actor. Baywatch
Chong, Rae Dawn		Entertainment	5	8	15	35	Actress. Pin-Up $65
Chong, Thomas		Entertainment	5			30	Comedian-Actor
Chong, Tommy		Entertainment	8			15	Cheech & Chong
Chopin, Frederic		Composer	1200	3500	8000		ALS/Cont.$16,500, ALS/Cont.$22,000
Chou En-Lai		Head of State	1155	4000	10000	2500	Chinese Communist Premier
Chouteau, Rene Auguste	1749-1829	Rev. War	350	1000	1515		American Pioneer. Fur Trader. Fndr. St. Louis
Chretien, Jean-Loup		Astronaut	10			20	France
Christian IX (Den)	1818-1906	Royalty	90	250			King of Denmark 1863-1906
Christian VII (Den & Nor)	1749-1808	Royalty	125	325	625		King of Denmark
Christian, Claudia		Entertainment	8			45	Actress. Pin-Up $65
Christian, George B.		Senate	5	20		10	Senator OH

NAME	DATE	CATEGORY	SIG	LS/DS	ALS	SP	COMMENTS
Christian, Prince	1831-1917	Royalty	45		150		Prince Schleswig-Holstein... Victoria's Son-in-Law
Christians, Mady		Entertainment	25	30	65	52	Star from Golden Years of American Theatre
Christie, Agatha	1891-1976	Author	260	730		925	Classic Detective Novels
Christie, Julie	1940-	Entertainment	28	15	28	55	Brit. Actress Oscar Winner.Pin-Up SP $45
Christina, Queen (Swe)		Royalty	250	1675	2400		
Christine, Virginia		Entertainment	6		15	25	
Christo*		Artist	5	15	20	85	Sculptor in Fabric
Christophe, Henry	1767-1820	Head of State	1325	1500			Haitian Revolutionary, Sovereign.
Christopher, Dennis		Entertainment	3	4	6	6	
Christopher, Warren		Cabinet	15	35		25	Sec'y State
Christopher, William		Entertainment	5		15	15	
Christy, Eileen		Entertainment	5			25	Vintage Actress
Christy, Howard Chandler	1873-1952	Artist	60	125	350	490	Illustrator, Portraitist. Books
Christy, June		Entertainment	10			20	Stan Kenton Vocalist. Recording Star
Chrysler, Walter P.	1875-1940	Business	425	900	1175	1077	Founder Chrysler Motors.TLS $3500
Chrysler, Walter P. Jr.		Business	75	275	350	150	Walter's Son & Financier
Chun Doo-Hwan		Head of State	25		50		
Chung, Connie		TV News	5	10	20	15	TV News Anchor
Chung, Kyung-Wha		Entertainment	10			65	Contemporary Violin Sensation
Chung, Myung Whun		Conductor				75	Controversial Korean Maestro
Church, Benjamin	1734-38	Rev. War	205	530	1010		Am. Physician & Spy
Church, Frank		Congress	5	15		25	Senator ID
Church, Frederick E.	1826-1900	Artist	150	425	1190		Am.Dramatic Landscapes
Church, Frederick S.		Artist	40	65	120		ALS/Sketch $500, ANS/Sketch $225
Church, R.W.		Clergy	20	35	50		
Churchill, Clementine S.	1885-1977	First Lady, Br.	74	200	265	160	Wife of Winston S.
Churchill, Jennie (Jerome)	1854-1921	Celebrity	15	100	305	95	W.S. Churchill's American Born Mother
Churchill, John	1650-1722	Military	1100	785			1st Duke of Marlborough
Churchill, Mary		Celebrity	5		25		
Churchill, Randolph, Lord	1849-95	Br. Statesman	45	90	225		Father of Winston S.
Churchill, Sarah		Entertainment	20	45	30	35	Actress-Daughter of Winston S.
Churchill, Thomas J.	1824-1905	Civil War	75	80	200		CSA Gen., Gov. AR
Churchill, Thomas James		Civil War	195				CSA General (WD)
Churchill, Winston	1871-1947	Author	15	35	60	35	Historical Novelist
Churchill, Winston S.	1874-1965	Head of State	862	2430	3025	3250	WW II P.M.,Author,Artist. 3x5 SP $1500.Chk.S $3200
Ciannelli, Eduardo		Entertainment	20			45	Actor
Ciano, Galeazzo, Conte		Royalty	65	295			Son-in-Law of Mussolini
Cicognani, A.G., Cardinal		Clergy	35	50	75	60	
Cigna, Gina		Entertainment	50	70		65	Opera
Cilea, Francesco		Composer	100			500	It. Composer of Adriana Lecouvreur
Cimaro, Pietro		Entertainment	10	25	50		It. Conductor
Cimino, Michael		Entertainment	8	15	22	32	Film Director
Ciny, Alain	1908-	Entertainment	20			45	Fr. Character Actor La Dolce Vita etc.
Cisneros, Henry	1947-	Cabinet	10			20	Sec'y HUD. Major Problems with FBI
Citroen, Andre-Gustave,	1878-1935	Business	85	419		700	Engineer-Industrialist. Citroen Auto Mfg.

NAME	DATE	CATEGORY	SIG	LS/DS	ALS	SP	COMMENTS
Civiletti, Benjamin		Cabinet	5	10	20	10	
Clair, Rene'	1898-1981	Entertainment	115	145	320		Fr. Film Maker, Actor, Writer
Clairborne, Liz		Business	10			20	Clothing Designer
Claire, Ina		Entertainment	15		35	35	Vintage Leading Lady. Stage-Films
Claire, Marion		Entertainment	10			25	Am. Soprano
Clamorgan, Jacques		Explorer-Trader		750			Missouri Co. 1795. Precursor of Louis & Clark
Clancey, Tom		Author	15	25		20	Am. Novelist
Clanton, Jimmy		Entertainment	20			25	Rock
Clanton, N.H.		Celebrity	1100				
Clapton, Eric		Entertainment	30			102	Rock. August Alb. S $110. Grammy Winner
Clark, Abraham	1726-94	Rev. War	320	800	4500		Signer Decl. of Indepen.
Clark, Barzilla W.		Governor	5	12	20		Governor ID
Clark, Bruce C.		Military	6	20	35	15	
Clark, Buddy		Entertainment	10			25	40's Singer
Clark, Candy		Entertainment	4		7	15	Pin-Up $35
Clark, Carol Higgins		Author	5	15		20	All Around the Town
Clark, Charles	1811-77	Civil War	142	335	412		CSA General, CW Gov. of Miss.
Clark, Clarence D.		Senate	10		35	15	Senator WY
Clark, Cottonseed		Country Music	15			30	Singer
Clark, Dane	1913-98	Entertainment	18			35	Actor noted for Tough Guy roles From 1942
Clark, Dick		Entertainment	6	14	15	22	American Bandstand Host
Clark, Edward	1815-80	Civil War		195			CSA Gen. 8th Gov. TX
Clark, Francis E.		Clergy	10	15	25	20	
Clark, Frank		Senate/Congress	5	15		10	Congressman FL
Clark, Fred	1914-68	Entertainment	25			50	Am. Character-Comedian Actor 1947-68
Clark, Gene		Entertainment	40			195	Deceased Byrds Original
Clark, George Rogers	1752-1818	Rev. War	675	2450	4250		General, Frontier Leader
Clark, James B. Champ	1850-1921	Congress	60		145	95	Speaker of the House. MO
Clark, James, Sir		Medical	15	35	85		Phys.to Queen Victoria & Albert
Clark, John Bullock, Sr.(WD)		Civil War					CSA Gen. ALS/Content $8250
Clark, Kenneth B.	1914-	Activist	20			55	Psychologist-Writer. Brown vs Board of Education
Clark, Laurel Blair		Astronaut	8			25	
Clark, Louis Gaylord		Author	20	35	122		Editor Knickerbocker Magazine
Clark, Marguerite	1883-1940	Entertainment	25			70	Stage.Film Rival Mary Pickford
Clark, Mark W.	1896-1984	Military	35	179	275	83	Gen. WW II 5th Army. FDC S $50
Clark, Mary		Military	5	8	15	15	
Clark, Mary Higgens		Author		38		20	Suspense Novels
Clark, Myron H.		Governor	10	20	35	15	Governor NY
Clark, Petula		Entertainment	8			22	Br. Singer-Actress
Clark, Ramsay		Cabinet	15	35	60	20	Att'y Gen.
Clark, Roy		Country Music	5	30		15	Singer-Guitarist-Comedian. Hee Haw
Clark, Susan		Entertainment	5	9	12	18	Actress. Pin-Up SP $25
Clark, Terri		Entertainment	5			20	Singer-Country
Clark, Tom C. (SC)	1889-1977	Supreme Court	40	110	145	125	And U.S. Attorney General
Clark, Walter J.		Aviation	10	22	38	28	ACE, WW II

NAME	DATE	CATEGORY	SIG	LS/DS	ALS	SP	COMMENTS
Clark, William	1770-1838	Explorer	375	2825	2150		Lewis & Clark Expedition.Gov. MO Territory
Clark, William A.		Senate	35	135	195		Railroad & Mining Magnate
Clarke, Adam		Clergy	75	145	350		
Clarke, Annie		Entertainment	15	15	25	25	
Clarke, Arthur C.		Author	15	35	75	40	2001
Clarke, Charles G.		Entertainment	6			10	Director
Clarke, Charles G.		Entertainment	6			15	Film Director
Clarke, Charles Mansfield		Medical	20	65	140		Br. Obstetrician
Clarke, George		Colonial Gov. N.Y	85	350			
Clarke, Henri J.G. Duc de		Napoleonic Wars	50	275	345		Marshal of Napoleon
Clarke, James Freeman		Clergy	30	50	75	60	
Clarke, James McClure		Senate/Congress	5			10	MOC NC
Clarke, Mae		Entertainment	28			65	Vintage Actress. Scene/James Cagney & Grapefruit
Clarke, Robert		Entertainment	20			50	
Clarke, Thomas		Rev. War	165	550			
Clarkson, Mathew	1758-1825	Military-Rev. War	45	95	175		Rev. Soldier, Philanthropist
Clarkson, Thomas	1760-1846	Reformer	35		100		Br. Devoted Entire Life to Abolition of Slavery
Clary, Alice		Author	15	25		15	
Clary, B. A.		Military	5	15	20	10	
Clary, Robert		Entertainment	4	5	9	13	Diminuative Fr.Actor. Hogan's Heroes
Clavell, James		Author	10	25	55	15	Novelist
Clay, Cassius Marcellus		Civil War	80	220	450		Union Gen., Senate, Abolition.
Clay, Henry	1777-1852	Cabinet	145	816	1079	350	Sec'y State, ALS Auct. $9,300, LS/Cont. $1500
Clay, Lucius D.	1897-1978	Military	35	208	150	105	Gen. WW II. US Military Gov. Berlin Blockade
Clay, William L., Sr.	1931-	Senate/Congress	10			27	Afro-Am. Congressman MO. Civil Rights Activist
Clayburgh, Jill	1945-	Entertainment	6	15	15	28	Actress. Twice Nominated for Oscar. Pin-UP $38
Clayton, Henry D.		Senate/Congress	5	10			MOC AL
Clayton, Jan		Entertainment	12		15	30	Actress-Singer. Mother on Lassie
Clayton, John M.		Cabinet	30	65	140		Taylor Sec'y State
Clayton, Joshua	1744-1798	Rev. War	220	425			1st Gov. DE. Senator DE
Clayton, Powell		Senate/Congress	10	25			Senator AR
Clayton, S. J.		Senate/Congress	5	10			
Clear Sky, Chief		Native American	20			50	Iroquois Chief
Cleave, Mary		Astronaut	10			25	
Cleaveland, Moses		Rev. War	170	850			Cleveland, Ohio Namesake
Cleburne, Patrick R.		Civil War	1050	1650			CSA General
Cleese, John	1939	Entertainment	9	25		36	Monty Python etc. Comedian. Difficult Sig.
Clem, John L. Johnny	1851-1937	Civil War	150	185	220	2760	Union Drummer Boy, Chicamauga
Clemenceau, Georges	1841-1929	Head of State	100	140	185		Physician, Statesman, Journalist. AMsS $835
Clemens, Clarence		Entertainment					
Clemens, Orion (Brother of Sam)		Old West	125		160		Sec'y of Nevada Territory 1861
Clemens, S. as Mark Twain	1835-1910	Author	912	1500	4750	4250	ALS/Content $19,500. P/C SP $2475. AQS $7500
Clemens, S.L. and Twain, Mark		Author	1062	1995	6000		Both Signatures
Clemens, Samuel L.	1835-1910	Author	705	1725	2456	4732	ALS Content $19,000
Clement IX, Pope	1600-69	Clergy		1310			Guilio Rospigliosi

NAME	DATE	CATEGORY	SIG	LS/DS	ALS	SP	COMMENTS
Clement VIII, Pope		Head of State	550	1300			
Clement, Martin Withington		Business	3	8	16	6	Pres. CEO Pennsylvania RR
Clementi, Muzio	1752-1832	Composer			2000		Pianist. Remembered for Musical Combat/Mozart
Clements, Stanley Stash		Entertainment	10			20	
Clervoy, Jean-Francois		Astronaut	5			25	France
Cleveland, Carleton A.		Business	10	35	45	20	
Cleveland, Charles		Clergy	20	25	45		
Cleveland, Frances F.	1864-1947	First Lady	89	123	208	262	ALS As 1st Lady $300
Cleveland, Grover & Francis F. Cleveland		President ,1st Lady	418				
Cleveland, Grover (As Pres.)		President	329	546	750	625	WH Card S $350, SP/1st Cabinet $1200
Cleveland, Grover	1837-1908	President	272	519	898	745	ALS/Content $1,250-$3,000-$3,500
Clewes, Henry		Business	25	45			Banker
Cliburn, Van		Entertainment	25	58		95	Am. Pianist
Clifford, Clark M.	1906-98	Cabinet	20	25	42	35	Sec'y Defense. Advisor to Truman Thru Carter
Clifford, John Henry		Governor	10	55	95		
Clifford, Nathan (SC)	1803-81	Supreme Court	75	175	240	150	Att'y Gen., Ambassador
Clifford, Rich		Astronaut	7			22	
Clift, Montgomery	1920-66	Entertainment	242			700	4 Oscar Nominations. Reclusive Non-Conformist
Clifton, Joseph C.		Aviation	15	35	60	40	
Cline, Patsy		Country Music	475			1450	Early Death
Clingan, William	?-1790	Rev. War	50	185			Delegate Cont.Congress.Early Signer Articles Conf.
Clinger, Debora		Entertainment	3	5		8	Pin-Up $25
Clingman, Thomas Lanier	1812-97	Civil War	95	295	358		CSA General
Clinton, De Witt	1769-1828	Statesman	78	298	390		Promoted Erie Canal. Mayor NYC. Pres. Candidate
Clinton, George	1739-1812	V.P.-Military	135	368	1327		Cont'l Congr.,Gen'l, Gov. NY. ALS/Cont. $7,000
Clinton, Henry, Sir	1730-95	Military-Rev. War	425	1125	2200		Br. Commander Am. Rev. Blamed for Loss
Clinton, James		Military-Rev. War	200	490			General Rev. War
Clinton, James G.	1804-49	Congress	15		35		Repr. NY
Clinton, Roger		Entertainment	25				Singer-Brother of President Clinton
Clinton, William 'Bill'		President		699	1250	282	42nd President. TLS/AN $1500. Pres. SP $895
Clinton, William J. (Bill) (As Pres.)		President	150	1162		450	42nd U.S. President. Impeached?
Clive, Colin		Entertainment	270			555	
Clive, E.E.		Entertainment	20			50	
Clive, Robert		Military	250	600	1200		Baron Clive of Plassey
Cloggers, Stoney Mtn.		Country Music	30			60	
Clokey, Art*		Cartoonist	20			150	Gumby. SP $35-45
Clooney, Geo./A. Edwards		Entertainment				80	Scene E.R. SP
Clooney, George		Entertainment	18	125		55	Actor-Director. Movies/TV. Check S $125
Clooney, Rosemary		Entertainment	5	6	15	15	
Close, Glenn		Entertainment	13	17	25	37	Actress. Oscar Winner. Pin-Up $45
Clostermann, Pierre		Military	55	85	125	75	
Clover, Richardson		Military	35	125			USN Admiral
Clovio, Giorgio Guilio	1498-1578	Artist	650	1400	2000		It. Miniaturist
Clunes, Alec	1912-70	Entertainment	5	20		30	Brit. Stage, Film Actor. Director-Producer
Clyde, Andy		Entertainment	50			150	Vintage Comedian

NAME	DATE	CATEGORY	SIG	LS/DS	ALS	SP	COMMENTS
Clyde, June		Entertainment	8	9	15	20	
Clymer, George	1739-1813	Rev. War	175	608	1550		Statesman. Signer Decl. of Indepen. FF $900
Coase, Ronald		Economist	20	35		25	Nobel Economics
Coates, Eric		Composer	25	55	85	130	
Coates, Phyllis		Entertainment	10			20	
Coats, Bob		Aviation	10	22	38	30	ACE, WW II
Coats, Michael L.		Astronaut	5			15	
Cobain, Kurt		Entertainment				185	Rock
Cobb, Calvin H.		Military	15	40	75		
Cobb, Howell (WD)		Civil War	225			950	CSA General
Cobb, Howell	1815-68	Civil War	115	225	490		Speaker, Sec'y Treas.,CSA Gen., Gov. GA
Cobb, Irvin S.	1876-1944	Author	25	75	150	95	Journalist-Humorist-Playwright
Cobb, Jerrie		Aviation	5	10	19	21	
Cobb, Lee J.		Entertainment	35	50	75	130	Fine Character Actor of Films & Stage
Cobb, Sylvanus	1823-87	Author	12			40	
Cobb, Thos. Reade R. (WD)		Civil War	1250		2500		CSA Gen. KIA '62
Cobb, Thos. Reade R.	1823-62	Civil War	500	1950	2495		CSA Gen. KIA '62
Cobham, Alan J., Sir	1894-1973	Aviation	40	110	220	62	Br. Aviation Pioneer. Pioneered Aerial Photography
Cobham, Gov. Gen. NZ		Head of State	5	8	15	10	New Zealand
Cobo, Albert E.		Celebrity	10	15	45	15	Detroit's Cobo Hall
Coburn, Charles	1877-1961	Entertainment	45	90	155	138	AA Winner. Monacle-wearing Character Actor
Coburn, James		Entertainment	10	12	22	35	Actor. Our Man Flint. Academy Award '99
Coca, Imogene		Entertainment	9			25	Comedienne & TV Pioneer
Cochran, Eddie	1938-60	Entertainment	220			595	Star of Early Rock. Died at 22
Cochran, Jacqueline		Aviation	45	175		150	Speed record holder
Cochran, John L. 'Johnny'		Legal	15			25	O.J. Simpson Trial Lawyer
Cochran, Robert L.		Governor	12	20	30	15	Governor NE
Cochran, Steve		Entertainment	15	15	30	28	
Cochrane, Basil, Sir		Military	15	25	30		
Cochrane, John	1813-98	Civil War	30	45	100		Union Gen. ALS '62 $345
Cochrane, Ralph		Military	5	15	25	20	NRPA
Cockburn, George, Sir		Military	40	100	140		Br. Admiral War 1812
Cockcroft, John Douglas, Sir		Science	60	110	245	75	Nobel Physics
Cocke, Philip St. George (WD)		Civil War			5500		CSA Gen. Suicide '61
Cocke, Philip St. George	1809-61	Civil War	475				CSA Gen. Committed Suicide 1821
Cocker, Joe		Entertainment	12			35	Rock Star
Cockerell, Christopher, Sir	1910-	Inventor	35		90		Inventor of Hovercraft
Cockrell, Francis Marion	1834-1915	Civil War	70	125	200		CSA General, US Sen. MO
Cockrell, Ken		Astronaut	6			20	
Coco, James	1928-87	Entertainment	15	20	40	35	Nomination Letter For Oscar From Academy $225
Cocteau, Jean	1889-1963	Author-Artist	200	225	625	650	Novelist, Playwright.Orig.Sketch S $500,$795, $900
Coda, Eraldo		Entertainment	5			25	Opera
Cody, Buck		Entertainment	3	3	6	6	
Cody, Iron Eyes	1907-	Entertainment	30	45		60	Long Time Indian Star. Film & TV
Cody, John P., Cardinal		Clergy	25	35	50	45	

NAME	DATE	CATEGORY	SIG	LS/DS	ALS	SP	COMMENTS
Cody, Lew		Entertainment	15	20	25	35	
Cody, Louisa		Celebrity		425			Wife of Wm. F. (Buffalo Bill) Cody
Cody, William F. & Buffalo Bill		Celebrity	1012	1750	2150	3165	Signed both Ways. ALS/Content $9300
Cody, William F.	1846-1917	Celebrity	750	2634	1650	1550	CW Scout, Pony Expr.,Showman, CMH
Coffin, Charles Carleton	1823-1896	Civil War-Author	92				Only Journalist to Cover Entire War
Coffin, Henry Sloane		Clergy	25	35	40	50	
Coffin, Howard C.		Manufacturer	30				Pioneer Auto Manufacturer
Coffin, Isaac, Sir	1759-1839	Military	20		75		Boston Born Br. Naval Officer
Coffin, John	1756-1838	Rev. War	175	500			Loyalist General
Coffin, Tris		Entertainment	20			35	
Coffin, William Sloane	1924-	Clergy	10	18		25	Political Activist. Tried with Dr. Spock
Coffyn, Frank		Aviation	40	65		95	
Coggan, Donald, Archbishop		Clergy	35	45	50	50	
Coghlan, Frank, Jr.		Entertainment	7			18	GWTW
Coghlan, Joseph B.		Military	25			60	Adm USN-Spanish American War
Cogswell, William	1838-1895	Civil War	15	35			Repr. MA
Cohan, Alexander		Entertainment					
Cohan, George M.	1878-1942	Composer	110	155	288	319	Actor,Playwright,Director,Singer SP-Fam.Portr.$895
Cohen, Octavus Roy		Author	15	30	45	25	Novels, Screenplays, Radio
Cohen, Stanley, Dr.		Science	20	35		25	Nobel Medicine
Cohen, Wilbur J.		Cabinet	5	14	22	10	Sec'y HEW
Cohen, William S.		Cabinet	10		25	40	Senator ME, MOC ME, Sec. Defense
Cohn, Harry		Business	35	85	165	65	Co-Founder Columbia Pictures
Cohn, Jack		Business	25	70	140	55	Co-Founder Columbia Pictures
Cohn, Roy		Lawyer	15	25	40	20	Legal Aide Sen. McCarthy
Coit, James Brolles		Civil War	25		125		Union General
Coke, Edward, Sir	1552-1634	Law		2162	3500		Eminent Eng. Jurist. Lord Chief Justice
Coke, Richard	1829-97	Civil War	25		60		CSA Officer. Gov. TX, Senator
Coke, Thomas, Bishop		Clergy	250	350	750		
Coker, Jack		Entertainment	6	8	15	20	
Colbert, Claudette	1903-94	Entertainment	32	112		84	Chic Fr.-Am. Leading lady from 30's on
Colby, Bainbridge	1869-1950	Cabinet	10	30	55		Sec'y State Under Wilson
Colby, Leonard		Military	40	90			General. Indian Fighter
Colden, Cadwallader		Rev. War	100	240			Am. Colonialist
Cole, Cornelius		Senate/Congress	15	25	40		MOC CA 1863, Senator CA
Cole, Edward N.		Business	5	12	30	10	Pres. General Motors
Cole, Michael	1945-	Entertainment	4	30	10	18	Actor Mod Squad
Cole, Nat King	1919-65	Entertainment	160	300		308	Am. Jazz Pianist, Singer
Cole, Natalie		Entertainment	9			25	Singer Pin-Up $50
Cole, Sterling		Congress/Senate	5	10			Congressman NY
Cole, Timothy		Artist	35		135		Wood Engraver.
Coleman, Booth		Entertainment	10			40	Planet of the Apes
Coleman, Cy		Composer	25			30	Arranger
Coleman, Dabney		Entertainment	5	6	15	15	Actor
Coleman, Gary		Entertainment	5	7	12	15	

NAME	DATE	CATEGORY	SIG	LS/DS	ALS	SP	COMMENTS
Coleman, George		Entertainment	7			40	Jazz Sax
Coleman, Nancy		Entertainment	6	8	15	10	
Colenso, John W., Bishop		Clergy	20	25	35		
Coleridge, John Duke		Celebrity	6	12	25		
Coleridge, Samuel Taylor	1772-1834	Author	325	575	1250		Br. Lyrical Poet, Literary Critic. AMsS $7,500
Coleridge-Taylor, Samuel	1875-1912	Composer	35	70	160	45	Choral, Musical Theatre, Songs. AMusQS $200
Coles, Charles Honi	1911-92	Entertainment	60			95	Legendary Tap Dancer-Choreographer. Tony Award
Colette, Sidonie-Gabrielle	1873-1954	Author	65	315	408	805	Fr. Novelist , Journalist, Critic. 15 Pg. DS $750
Colfax, Schuyler	1823-85	Vice President	100	135	497	250	Speaker of House, Grant VP
Colgate. James C.		Business	10	25	50	40	Colgate University. Donor
Colgrass, Michael		Composer	20	35	85		Pulitzer, AMusQS $100
Collamer, Jacob		Cabinet	20	55	80		Taylor P.M. General
Collier, Constance	1878-1955	Entertainment	25		30	75	Vintage Br. Actress
Collier, James W.		Senate/Congress	5	15		10	MOC MS
Collier, Peter F.		Business	14	35	70		
Collinge, Patricia		Entertainment	6	8	15	19	
Collingwood, Charles		Journalist	5	35	62	15	News Analyst, War Correspondent,TV Moderator
Collins, Cardiss	1932-	Congress	10	15		12	Longtime Dem. MOC MO
Collins, Eileen		Astronaut	7			25	
Collins, J. Lawton		Military	15	50	80	35	General WW II
Collins, Jackie		Author	10	15	28	20	Novelist. Her Novel Signed/Dust Jacket $ 25
Collins, Joan		Entertainment	15	23	30	26	Pin-Up SP $30
Collins, Judy		Entertainment	5	10	15	30	Singer
Collins, LeRoy		Governor	5	10		14	Governor FL
Collins, Lottie		Entertainment	15	15	25	25	
Collins, Michael		Astronaut	60	177	262	214	Piloted Comm. Module 1st Moon Landing. Apollo XI
Collins, Phil		Entertainment	8			35	Singer
Collins, Ray		Entertainment	50	60	150	175	
Collins, Susan		Congress	5			15	Senator-Maine
Collins, Wilkie	1824-89	Author	100	310	560	1380	Br. Novelist. Regarded as 1st Br.Det. Story Writer
Collis, Charles		Civil War	25		60		Union Gen., CMH
Collishaw, Raymond		Aviation	75	175	375	225	Brit. ACE, WW I
Collyer Clayton Bud	1908-69	Entertainment	20			45	Actor. Radio, Early TV. Popular Game Show Host
Collyer, Robert, Dr.	1823-1912	Clergy	35	60	112		Unitarian. Lecturer. Author
Colman, Booth		Entertainment	4			15	Actor
Colman, Ronald	1891-1958	Entertainment	55	60	142	150	Suave, Sophisticated, Br. Leading Man Oscar Winner
Colman, Samuel	1832-1920	Artist	20		95		Landscapes. Fndr, 1st Pres. Am. Watercolor Soc.
Colombo, Scipio		Entertainment	10			30	Opera
Colonna, Jerry	1903-86	Entertainment	15		22	32	Buggy-Eyed Comedian Radio/Stage/Screen
Color Me Badd		Entertainment	25			55	Rock (Entire Group)
Colquitt, Alfred H.	1824-94	Civil War	125	310	480	275	CSA Gen., US Sen. & Gov. GA. Sig/Rank $295
Colson, Charles W. 'Chuck'		Clergy	20	50	75	35	Convicted Watergate Figure
Colston, Raleigh E.	1825-96	Civil War	225	400			CSA Gen.
Colt, Samuel	1814-1862	Business-Inventor	500	2190	3975		Founder Colt Firearms
Colter, Jessie		Country Music	4			22	Wife of Waylon Jennings

NAME	DATE	CATEGORY	SIG	LS/DS	ALS	SP	COMMENTS
Coltrane, John		Entertainment					Great Jazz Saxophonist. NRPA
Coltrane, Robbie		Entertainment	7			38	Br. Character Actor Mystery Series Star
Colum, Padraic		Author	38	150		45	Irish Poet & Playwright
Columbo, Franco		Entertainment	5			25	Actor-Body Builder
Columbo, Russ	1908-34	Entertainment	50	90	200	165	Talented Crooner. Rival of Crosby.Shotgun Accident
Columbus, Chris		Entertainment	4			12	Screen Writer
Combs, Holly Marie		Entertainment	8			42	Actress. Pin-Up $55
Comden, Betty & Green, A.		Composers	20	45		50	Collaborators. Broadway Musicals
Comiskey, Charles A.	1859-1931	Business	400				Fndr.,Owner Pres. Chicago White Sox
Commager, Henry Steele		Civil War	25	60	125		Union General
Command Performance (5)		Entertainment	20			50	
Commodores		Entertainment	25			60	
Como, Perry	1912-	Entertainment	8	12	18	38	Singer. Radio,Recording,TV 1948-1963
Compson, Betty	1897-1974	Entertainment	15	30	60	70	Actress. Films-1915-1948
Compton, Arthur H.	1892-1962	Science	90	205	275	100	Nobel Physics. Atomic Bomb
Compton, Fay	1894-1978	Entertainment	30			45	Br. Actress. Starred in Barrie Plays...'Peter Pan'
Compton, Joyce		Entertainment	8	9	19	15	
Compton, Karl T.	1887-1954	Science	90	200		110	Physicist, Pres. M.I.T.
Compton-Burnett, Ivy		Author	40	85	175		Wrote Brilliant Original Comic Novels Family Life
Conant, A. Roger		Aviation	12	25	40	32	ACE, WW II, Marine Ace
Conant, James Bryant		Diplomat	10	15	30	20	Educator, US Ambassador
Conati, Lorenzo		Entertainment	20			65	Opera
Conchita, Maria		Entertainment	4			10	
Conde', Louis II	1621-1686	Military		750			One of France's Most Celebrated Generals
Condon, Eddie		Composer	40			60	Guitarist
Condon, Richard		Author	5	15	35	10	
Cone, Fairfax M.		Business	10	35	45	20	Foote,Cone & Belding, Adv.
Cone, Hutchinson		Military	25	35			Admiral WW I
Confalonieri, Carlo, Cardinal		Clergy	50	75	90	65	
Conforti, Gino		Entertainment	3	3	6	6	
Congreve, William	1670-1729	Author	190	575	1050		Br. Drama. Restoration Comedy
Congreve, William, Sir.2nd Bart		Science	45	125	235		Artillerist, Invented Rocket
Coningham, Sir Arthur		Aviation	35	60			Cmdr. RAF 1st Tactical
Conklin, Chester	1888-1971	Entertainment	112	125	220	95	Silent Film Comedian with Chaplin & W.C. Fields
Conkling, Roscoe		Senate	20	25		25	MOC, Senate NY Political Boss
Conlee, John		Entertainment	4			10	
Conley, Eugene		Entertainment	20	30		50	Opera
Conley, Joe		Entertainment	3	3	6	8	
Connally, John B.		Cabinet	25	60	95	45	Gov. TX, Sec'y Treasury
Connally, Tom	1877-1963	Senate	20	25		70	Senator TX. Gov. TX
Connelly, Jennifer		Entertainment	10			36	Pin-Up $75
Connelly, Marc	1890-1980	Author	20	75	75	35	Am. Dramatist. Pulitzer
Connelly, Matthew J.		White House Staff	10	25	35	15	Pres. Truman Aide
Conner, James	1829-1883	Civil War	90	210	270		CSA General. 1st Bull Run, Seven Pines
Conner, Nadine		Entertainment	10			33	Am. Opera, Radio, Records

NAME	DATE	CATEGORY	SIG	LS/DS	ALS	SP	COMMENTS
Connery, Sean		Entertainment	53	299		132	Best Known for James Bond etc. Bond SP $200
Conness, John	1821-1909	Senate	45	85			Civil War Senator CA
Connick, Harry, Jr.		Entertainment	13	30		38	Big Band Leader-Singer-Pianist-Actor
Conniff, Ray	1916-	Entertainment	18	35	68	38	Composer, Conductor
Connolly, Walter		Entertainment	70		90	85	
Connor, Harry P.		Aviation	15	30	45	50	
Connor, James	1829-1883	Civil War	85	215	285		CSA General
Connor, John T.		Cabinet	7	20	35	20	Sec'y Commerce
Connor, Patrick Edward		Civil War	35	58			Union General
Connors, Chuck	1921-92	Entertainment	20	35		55	Former Pro Baseball. The Rifleman TV Series
Connors, Mike		Entertainment	6			14	Actor. Mannix
Connors, Norman		Entertainment	4			10	
Connors, Patti		Entertainment	3	3	6	6	
Conover, Harry		Business	10	17	25	15	Top Modeling Agency
Conquest, Ida		Entertainment	15	15	25	30	
Conrad, Charles Magill	1804-78	Cabinet	45	55	190		Sec'y War
Conrad, Charles, Jr.	1930-1999	Astronaut	50	285		148	3rd Moonwalker. Died 7/8/99 in Motorcycle Accident
Conrad, Gerhard		Aviation	10	25	45	25	
Conrad, Joseph	1857-1924	Author	322	1125	1450	1250	Br. Novelist. Lord Jim etc.
Conrad, Michael		Entertainment	14	18	20	22	Actor. Hill St. Blues SP $35
Conrad, Robert		Entertainment	7	10		30	Actor. Wild Wild West SP $40
Conrad, William	1920-94	Entertainment	20	25		45	Actor
Conried, Hans		Entertainment	15	20	40	40	
Conroy, Kevin		Entertainment	3	3	6	6	
Conroy, Pat		Author					Signed 1st Ed. $125-$200
Consigny, Eugene F.		Banker		20			
Constable, Archibald	1774-1827	Publisher	30				Encyclopaedia Britannica
Constable, John	1776-1837	Artist	260	905	2400		Br. Landscapes, Rural Life
Constantine I,	1868-1923	Royalty	95			425	King of Greece. Twice Abdicated. Plebicite Restored
Constantino, Florencio		Entertainment	75			365	Opera
Conte, John		Entertainment	4	5	9	12	
Conte, Richard		Entertainment	7	10	15	15	
Conti, Bill		Composer	10			32	
Conti, Joseph		Entertainment	4			10	
Contino, Dick		Entertainment	3			8	Accordianist
Convy, Bert		Entertainment	10			20	Broadway, TV Star
Conway, Henry Seymour	1721-95	Military	25	60	135		Br. Fld. Marshal. MsDs $250
Conway, Martin F.	1827-82	Congress	10				Repr. KS, U.S. Consul France
Conway, Rose A.		Cabinet	3	5	10	5	
Conway, Thomas		Rev. War	65	105	250		Maj. Gen. Rev. War
Conway, Tim		Entertainment	5	15	15	18	Comedian-Actor McHale's Navy SP $25
Conway, Tom		Entertainment	50			128	The Saint
Conwell, Russell H.	1843-1925	Clergy	35	45	40		Baptist Fndr. & 1st Pres. Temple Univ.
Cony, Samuel		Governor	30	45	60		Civil War Gov. ME
Conyers, John	1929-	Senate/Congress	10	15		25	Afro-Am. Congressman MI

NAME	DATE	CATEGORY	SIG	LS/DS	ALS	SP	COMMENTS
Coogan, Jackie	1914-84	Entertainment	20		35	88	Actor. Major Child Star. Uncle Fester Addams Fam
Coogan, Richard		Entertainment	5	6	15	15	
Cook, Ann T.	1927-	Model	10			25	Original Model For Gerber Baby Products
Cook, Elisha Jr.	1902-95	Entertainment	15	25	35	82	
Cook, Eliza		Author			75		Poet
Cook, Everett R.		Aviation	10	30		50	ACE WW I
Cook, Francis Augustus		Military	75		55	30	Spanish American War
Cook, Frederick Albert, Dr.		Explorer	75	145	175	150	Claimed 1st at North Pole
Cook, James, Capt.		Br.Naval Explorer	4025	8850	27000		Captain Cook
Cook, Joseph, Sir		Politician	10	20	40		Australian Statesman
Cook, Kyle		Entertainment	6			25	Music. Lead Guitar Matchbox 20
Cook, Philip	1817-94	Civil War	175	320	395		CSA Gen.
Cook, Rachel Leigh		Entertainment	8			48	Actress. Young Star
Cook, Robin		Author	5			10	Novelist
Cook, Thomas		Business	35	110	545		Founder British Tourist Company
Cook, Tommy		Entertainment	15			30	Child Actor
Cook, Walter V.		Aviation	8	20	38	28	ACE, WW II
Cooke, Alistair, Sir		Author	20	95	140	75	TV Host. Masterpiece Theatre
Cooke, Jack Kent		Business	10	22		15	
Cooke, Jay	1821-1905	Business	375	1494	2167	225	Banker, Financier of Union in Civil War
Cooke, Nicholas		Rev. War		1100			Rev. War Gov. Rhode Island
Cooke, Philip St. George		Civil War	50				Union Gen. ALS/Cont.$935
Cooke, Sam		Entertainment	232	675		500	Rock
Cooke, Terence J., Cardinal		Clergy	60	75	100	95	
Cool, Harry		Entertainment	4	4		6	
Cooley, Denton A., Dr.	1920-	Science	15	35	90	32	Heart Transplant Surgeon
Cooley, Lyman E.		Science	10		35		Civil Engineer
Cooley, Spade		Country Music	15			35	King of Western Swing
Coolidge, Calvin & Entire Cabinet		President	295				
Coolidge, Calvin (As Pres.)		President	187	560	3750	608	WH Card S $200-345. ALS/Content $6450
Coolidge, Calvin	1872-1933	President	180	443	856	435	Autogr. Speech Signed $6000
Coolidge, Grace	1879-1957	First Lady	109	175	138	165	FF $55-$80
Coolidge, John		Celebrity	40	65			Father Of Pres. Coolidge
Coolidge, Rita		Entertainment	12	20		25	
Coolidge, T. Jefferson		Statesman	4	10	20		
Coolidge, William David, Dr.		Science	45	85	165	125	Dir. Research G.E., Inventor
Coombs, Patricia		Artist	10	20	35	15	
Cooper, Alfred Duff		Statesman	10	25	60	15	1st Viscount Norwich. Author
Cooper, Alice		Entertainment	25		35	90	Rock. School's Out Alb. S $50
Cooper, Emil		Composer	30	180	80	70	Rus.Internat'l Conductor-Violinist
Cooper, Gary	1901-61	Entertainment	212	341	338	504	3x5 SP $325. Orig.Spurr PH SPI $600. 2 Oscars
Cooper, Gladys, Dame		Entertainment	40	35	65	55	Br. Stage & Film Actress
Cooper, Gordon		Astronaut	25	72		85	Mercury 7 Astro.
Cooper, Jackie	1921-	Entertainment	20	21	35	32	Child-Mature Actor, Director.Little Rascal SP$40
Cooper, James Fennimore	1789-1851	Author	90	185	1188		Am. Novelist. ALS/Cont.$1,750

NAME	DATE	CATEGORY	SIG	LS/DS	ALS	SP	COMMENTS
Cooper, Jeanne		Entertainment	8			15	Actress. Soap Star
Cooper, John Sherman		Senate/Congress	10	25			Senator KY, Statesman, Diplomat
Cooper, Leon N., Dr.		Science	20	35	60	30	Nobel Physics
Cooper, Leroy, Jr.		Astronaut	40				Apollo VII (Early Sig.)
Cooper, Merian C.		Entertainment	100			250	King Kong, Four Feathers
Cooper, Michael 'Ibo'		Entertainment	6			25	Music. Calvinet, Organ Lenny Kravitz
Cooper, Miriam		Entertainment	35			75	
Cooper, Peter	1791-1883	Industrialist	134	400	703	262	Am. Inventor, 1st Steam Locomotive. Philanthropist
Cooper, Prentice		Governor	10	16			Governor TN
Cooper, Rick		Entertainment	5			10	Actor
Cooper, Samuel (WD)		Civil War	165		1860		CSA Gen.Special Content ALS $6325
Cooper, Samuel	1798-1876	Civil War	125	271	445		CSA Ranking Gen.
Cooper, Thos. Sidney		Artist	10	20	35		
Coors, W. K.		Business	20	60	95	50	Coors Brewery
Coots, J. Fred		Composer	35	55	160	50	Santa Claus is....AMusQS $150-$195-$1200
Coots, J.Fred & H. Gillespie		Composer					Santa Claus Is Coming to Town Sht.Mus. S $495
Copas, Cowboy		Country Music	100			225	
Copeland, C.C.		Clergy	30	80	225		
Copeland, L. du Pont		Business	20		50		
Copeland, Royal S., Dr.		Senate	15	70			Senator NY. Author
Copeland, William John		Clergy	20	25	35		
Copland, Aaron	1900-90	Composer	80	275	300	238	Major 20th Cent. Am. Composer.AMusQS $300-$800
Copley, John Singleton	1738-1815	Artist	350	2612	6688		Outstanding Am. Portraitist
Copley, Teri		Entertainment	6			20	Pin-Up SP $40
Copmpanari, Giuseppe		Entertainment	35			125	Opera
Copp,e, Fran‡ois E.	1842-1908	Author	15	45	45		Fr. Poet, Novelist, Dramatist
Coppens, Willy (Baron de H)		Aviation	20	40	125	50	
Copperfield, David		Entertainment	8	15		35	Illusionist
Coppola, Francis Ford	1939-	Entertainment	20	58		40	Oscar Winning Film Director.Screenwriter
Coquelin, Benoit-Constant	1841-1909	Entertainment	25	60	55	155	Fr. Actor-Manager, 'Cyrano'
Coquelin, Ernest-Alex.-H.(Cadet)		Entertainment	15	30	50		Comedie-Francaise. Author
Corbett, Boston		Civil War	965		1800		Shot John Wilkes Booth
Corbett, Henry Winslow		Senate/Congress	10	15	25	20	Senator OR
Corbett, Michael		Entertainment	4			10	Actor Young and the Restless
Corbin, Henry Clarke		Civil War	50		115		Union General
Corbucci, Sergio	1927-90	Entertainment	45			275	Known as Director of Spaghetti-Westerns
Corbusier, Le	1887-1965	Architect	115	575	1048	575	Jeanneret, Charles Edouard. Also Painter, Writer
Corby, Ellen		Entertainment	12			30	Character Actress. Grandma Walton
Corcoran, Kevin		Entertainment	5			20	Actor. 60's Disney Star
Corcoran, Michael (WD)		Civil War			1723		Union Gen. RARE
Corcoran, Noreen		Entertainment	5			20	Actress. Batchelor Father
Corcoran, William W.		Business	20	50			Banker, Philanthropist
Cord, Alex		Entertainment	8			12	
Corden, Henry		Entertainment	25	55		40	Fred Flintstone (Voice)
Corea, Chick		Entertainment	15			35	

NAME	DATE	CATEGORY	SIG	LS/DS	ALS	SP	COMMENTS
Corelli, Franco		Entertainment	25	35	100	110	Opera
Corelli, Marie	1855-1924	Author	38	55	115	70	Eng. Romantic Novelist. (Mary Mackay)
Corena, Fernando		Entertainment	20			45	Opera
Corey, Elias		Science	20	35		30	Nobel Chemistry
Corey, Jeff		Entertainment	5			15	
Corey, Wendell		Entertainment	35	45	80	75	
Corgan, Billy		Entertainment	20			65	Music. Lead Singer Smashing Pumpkins
Cori, Carl F.		Science	20	35	50	25	Nobel Medicine. (Insulin)Phil. Cover S. $150
Corio, Ann		Entertainment	15		20	35	Noted Exotic Dancer, Stripper. Films From '40's
Corlett, Irene		Entertainment	3	3	6	6	
Cormack, Allan M.		Science	20	35	50	25	Nobel Medicine
Corman, Roger		Entertainment	5			20	
Cornbury, Edward Hyde, Lord		Colonial Gov.	200	450			1st Colonial Gov. NJ, Gov. NY
Corneliano, Mario N. di		Clergy	35	45	60	50	
Cornelius, Peter (Carl August)		Composer	55		325		Opera, Choral Works, Song Cycle
Cornell, Chris		Entertainment	12			40	Music. Lead Singer Soundgarden
Cornell, Ezekiel		Military	60	200			Brig. Gen. American Rev.
Cornell, Ezra		Business	30	80	165	75	Financed Western Union Telegr.
Cornell, Joseph	1903-1972	Artist	135	1200	700		Am. Surrealist Sculptor
Cornell, Katharine	1898-1974	Entertainment	20	35	75	77	Superb Am. Leading Stage Actress
Cornell, Lydia		Entertainment	5		10	20	Pin-Up SP $38
Corner, George W.		Science	75	150		100	
Cornfeld, Bernard		Business	10	20	55	35	
Cornforth, John W., Sir		Science	15	35	45	20	Br. Nobel Laureate in Chemistry
Corning, Erastus	1794-1872	Business	70	175	295		1st Pres. NY Central Railroad
Cornwallis, Charles E.	1738-1805	Rev. War	200	400	1241		Br. General Am. Revolution
Cornwell, Patricia		Author	4	7	9	15	Southern Cross
Corot, J.B. Camille	1796-1875	Artist	225	490	1081	3000	Barbizon School. Impressionist, Landscape Painter
Corrigan, Douglas	1907-95	Aviation	38	60	120	145	Wrong Way Corrigan
Corrigan, Mairead/B. William		Irish Activists	35	70	100	50	Nobel Peace Prize 1976
Corrigan, Michael A.		Clergy	10		30	20	Bishop
Corrigan, Ray Crash		Entertainment	40			150	
Corsaut, Aneta	1933-95	Entertainment	25			90	Actress Andy Griffith Show
Corse, John Murray		Civil War	35	245	80		Union General
Corse, Montgomery D.	1816-95	Civil War	120		325		CSA General
Corson, Fred P., Bishop		Clergy	20	30	50	45	
Cortelyou, George B.	1862-1940	Cabinet	50	162	220		Served two Presidents.
Cortes, Hernando (Cortez)	1485-1574	Explorer		44300			Sp. Conqueror of Mex.
Cortez, Ricardo		Entertainment	25			40	
Cortina, Juan N.		Military		1500			Mexican Gen'l. Rio Grande Bandit During Civil War
Cortot, Alfred	1877-1962	Entertainment	78			225	Pianist
Corwin, Thomas		Cabinet	30	55	125		Fillmore Sec'y Treasury
Cosby, Bill	1937-	Entertainment	11	10	30	43	Comedian-Actor-Producer. Authentic Sigs. RARE
Cosby, George B.		Civil War	60	130	200		CSA General
Cosby, N. Gordon		Clergy	20	30	45		

NAME	DATE	CATEGORY	SIG	LS/DS	ALS	SP	COMMENTS
Cosell, Howard		Entertainment	15			65	Radio-TV Sports News
Cosgrave, William T.	1880-1965	Head of State	70	150	275	225	Sinn Fe'in Easter Uprising.
Coslow, Sam		Composer-Author	50	200	300	350	Academy Award 1943
Cosmonauts (Russian)		Cosmonauts				5000	
Titov,Gagarin,Tereshkova,Belyayev,Nikolayev,Popvch							
Cosmovici, C. B.		Astronaut	12			25	
Cossotto, Fioranza		Entertainment	10			30	Opera
Cossutta, Carlos		Entertainment	5			35	Opera
Costa Lo Giudice, Silvio		Entertainment	40			100	Opera
Costa, Mary		Entertainment	6			25	Singer. Opera-Light Opera
Costa, Michael, Sir		Composer	15	40	95	25	Br. Conductor.Opera, Ballet
Costa-Gavras, Constantin		Entertainment	15			35	A A
Costa-Gavras, Constantin		Entertainment	20			40	Film Director
Costas, Bob		TV Host	5			10	TV Host & Sports Commentator
Coste, Dieudonne & Bellonte, M.		Aviation	210			365	
Coste, Dieudonne	1898-1973	Aviation	125	255	385	235	Fr. Aviator. 1st Non-Stop Flight Paris-NY 1930
Costello, Delores (Barrymore)		Entertainment	28	35	65	60	
Costello, Elvis		Entertainment	12			48	Rock Entertainer
Costello, Lou	1906-59	Entertainment	212	350		400	Radio, Film, TV Comedian
Costner, Kevin		Entertainment	33			52	AA Actor-Director-Producer
Coswell, Henry T.		Aviation	55	105	150		1st Balloon ascent 1844
Cotrubas, Ileana		Entertainment	5			30	Opera
Cotsworth, Staats		Entertainment	8			15	
Cotten, Joseph	1905-94	Entertainment	22	15	30	37	Actor. Orson Welles' Group. Citizen Kane SP $40
Cotton, Carolina		Country Music	15			30	
Coty, Francois		Business	100	325	475		Fr.Industrialist. Mfg. Of Coty Perfume & Cosmetics
Cou,, Emile	1857-1926	Science	175		500		Fr. Psychotherapist, Hypnotism
Couch, Darius Nash		Civil War	65	80	145		Union General
Couch, Orville		Country Western	10			35	Music. 50's Recording Artist
Couch, Virgil		Urban Designer	10	20	15		Dir. National Civil Defense
Cougar, John		Entertainment	10			35	
Coughlin, Charles E.	1891-1979	Clergy	40	50	70		Activist Catholic Priest & Radio Evangelist
Coulouris, George		Entertainment	10			25	Character Actor
Coulter, Jessie		Country Music	6			15	
Coulter, Richard		Civil War	42	75	95		Union Bvt. General
Courbet, Jean D. Gustave	1819-77	Artist	225	600	1090		Leader of Realist School
Couric, Katie		TV Host	5			16	Host Today
Court, Hazel		Entertainment	6			30	Pin-Up $28
Courtney, Inez		Entertainment	15			35	
Courts, Ray		Entertainment	3			8	Show Promoter
Cousins, Norman		Author	10	25	40	15	Saturday Review Editor, Author
Cousins, Ralph P.	1891-1964	Aviation		165		95	Army Gen'l.Developed Radio Beam. Aviation Pioneer
Cousins, William E., Archbishop		Clergy	20	35	45	35	
Cousteau, Jacques		Science-Author	50		275	128	Underwater Explorer, Films
Cousteau, Jim (Son of Jacques)		Science	25			150	Underwater Explorer (Deceased)

NAME	DATE	CATEGORY	SIG	LS/DS	ALS	SP	COMMENTS
Couter, John B.		Military	15	47			
Couve de Murville, Maurice		Statesman	5	15	25	25	Fr. Premier, Foreign Minister DeGaulle Cabinet.
Couzens, James		Senate/Congress	10	30		15	Senator MI
Covarrubias, Miguel		Artist	150	325			Mex. Book & Magazine Illustr.
Covey, Richard O.		Astronaut	6			22	
Cowan, Edgar		Senate	15	25	35		Civil War Senator PA
Cowan, Jerome		Entertainment	10			35	
Coward, Noel, Sir	1899-1973	Author-Composer	142	301	295	383	Playwright, Actor, Producer. AMusQS $275
Cowl, Jane		Entertainment	22		35	45	
Cowles, Gardner		Business	12		25	15	Publisher Des Moines Register
Cox Family, The		Entertainment	25			45	Bluegrass
Cox, Archibald		Cabinet	15	170		25	Att'y Gen.,1st Watergate Spec. Prosecutor
Cox, Courtney	1964-	Entertainment	20			59	Actress Friends
Cox, George H.		Author	5	15	30		Br. Historical Writer
Cox, Jacob D.	1828-1900	Civil War	25		95		Union Gen., Sec'y Interior, Gov. OH
Cox, James M.		Governor	15	60	75	25	Pres. Candidate,MOC,Gov. OH
Cox, Kenyon	1856-1919	Artist	30	55			Am. Mural Painter & Figural Compositions
Cox, Nikki		Entertainment	15			55	Actress. Pin-Up $65
Cox, Palmer*	1840-1924	Artist	103	140	300	225	Author Children's Books, Illustrator Brownies
Cox, Samuel S.	1824-89	Congress	125		180		Civil War Repr. OH
Cox, Wally		Entertainment	25		70	75	Actor-Comedian Mr. Peepers
Cox, William R.	1832-1919	Civil War	75	110	295		CSA Gen. Sig/Rank $295, War Dte. DS $350
Coxe, Tenche		Rev. War	45	100	170		Continental Congress
Coxey, Jacob S.		Reformer	20	55	140	30	Led Coxey's Army to Wash. D.C
Coyote, Peter		Entertainment	10			35	
Crabbe, Buster	1909-83	Entertainment	21		40	82	Actor.Flash Gordon or Tarzan SP $85-$125
Crabtree, Lotta (Charlotte)		Entertainment	25	70	125	130	Am. Musical Comedy Actress
Craddock, Crash		Country Music	5	8	20	18	
Craig, Edward Gordon	1872-1966	Entertainment	15	40	155	190	Br. Stage Designer, Actor
Craig, James		Entertainment	15			35	Actor
Craig, James	1817-88	Civil War	45	80	110		Union General. ALS War Dte.$175, DS $134
Craig, James Henry, Sir	1748-1812	Military	75	185	200		Br. Gen. Wounded at Bunker Hill. Gov. Gen. Canada
Craig, Jenny		TV Personality	4			10	Talk Show Host. Diet Expert.
Craig, Malin	1875-1945	Military	10	25	35	30	General. Cuba, Boxer Rebellion, France WW I
Craig, Yvonne		Entertainment	6	20		27	Pin-Up SP $30, Batgirl $30
Craigavon, James C.	1871-1940	Head of State	20		35		1st P.M. Northern Ireland
Crain, Jeanne		Entertainment	15	20		45	Actress. Oscar Nominee Pinky. Pin-Up SP $50
Cram, Donald J., Dr.		Science	20	35		30	Nobel Chemistry
Cramer, Floyd		Country Music	20			33	Pianist
Cramer, Grant		Entertainment	6	8	15	15	
Cranch, Christopher P.	1813-92	Artist	5		25	35	
Crane Frank		Clergy	15	20	35		
Crane, Bob		Entertainment	150			200	Murdered TV Star Hogans Heroes
Crane, Charles Henry		Civil War	25	175	210		Union General.Surgeon
Crane, Cheryl		Celebrity	30			40	Killed Mother's Friend

NAME	DATE	CATEGORY	SIG	LS/DS	ALS	SP	COMMENTS
Crane, Daniel (Scandal)		Congress	5		25	20	MOC IL
Crane, Frank		Clergy	15	25	45		
Crane, Fred		Entertainment	15			35	
Crane, Hart		Author	130	600	1500	350	Am. Poet, The Bridge
Crane, Henry Hitt		Clergy	25	30	50	35	
Crane, John		Military	100	250			Gen. Rev. War
Crane, Richard		Entertainment	20			45	
Crane, Roy*		Cartoonists	30			200	Wash Tubbs, B. Sawyer
Crane, Stephen		Author	370	1100	4350		Died at 28. Red Badge of......
Crane, Walter	1845-1915	Artist - Poet	50	140	275		Br. Painter-Illustrator-Designer. ALS/Cont. $600
Crane, William H.	1845-1928	Entertainment	30	45	90	55	Vintage Actor
Crane, William M.	1784-1846	Military	15				War 1812 Navy
Crane, Winthrop M.		Senate-Business	10	25		35	Crane Stationery, Gov., Sen. MA
Cranston, Alan		Senate	15	20		22	Senator CA
Cranston, Henry Young	1789-1864	Congress	10				Repr. RI
Crass, Franz		Entertainment	5			25	Opera
Craven, Frank		Entertainment	20			55	Vintage Film & Stage Actor
Craven, Wes		Entertainment	10			25	Director
Cravens, Jordan E.		Civil War	25		80		CSA Officer, MOC AR
Crawford, Broderick	1911-86	Entertainment	35	105		90	Character Actor. Bad Guy Image
Crawford, Christina		Author	6	10	20	15	Daughter of Joan Crawford
Crawford, Cindy		Model	8			52	Model-Actress. Pin-Up SP $75
Crawford, Francis M.	1854-1909	Author	12	15	25		Am. Novelist
Crawford, Geo. W.	1798-1872	Cabinet		40	95		Sec'y War. Gov. GA Secessionist
Crawford, J. W. Capt. Jack	1847-1917	Military-Author	35		250		Indian Wars Scout. The Poet Scout
Crawford, Joan	1908-77	Entertainment	45	114	175	190	AA Major Star. Pin-Up SP $200
Crawford, Johnny		Entertainment	7			20	Actor. Remembered for The Rifleman SP $25
Crawford, Michael		Entertainment	20		35	70	
Crawford, Robert		Composer	25				Air Force Song AMusQS $275
Crawford, Samuel W.		Civil War	48	85	210		Union Gen.
Crawford, William H.	1772-1834	Cabinet	40	155	150		Madison Sec'y War. ALS/Cont. $1500
Crawford-Frost, Wm. A.		Business	15	25	70	20	
Cream		Entertainment	50			175	Rock
Creatore, Giuseppe		Entertainment	30			120	Bandleader
Creed		Entertainment	32			75	Music. 4 Member Rock Group
Creedence Clearwater Revival		Entertainment	75			225	Rock
Creeley, Robert	1926-	Contemp. Poet	5	12		10	Am. Poet. The Charm-1st Ed. S $150
Cregar, Laird	1916-44	Entertainment	115	120	250	318	300 lb. Character Actor. Died at 28
Creighton, John O.		Astronaut	5			15	
Creighton, Johnston B. (WD)		Civil War	65	350			Union Adm.
Creighton, Mandell		Clergy	10	15	20		
Cremer, Peter Erich		Military	75		120		
Crenna, Richard		Entertainment	4	6	15	15	Versatile Film-TV Actor
Cresap, Mark		Business	4	6	15	7	
Crespin, R,gine		Entertainment	10			60	Opera

NAME	DATE	CATEGORY	SIG	LS/DS	ALS	SP	COMMENTS
Crestani, Lucia		Entertainment	30			120	Opera
Creston, Paul		Composer	10			125	
Creswell, John A. J.		Cabinet	20	25	40		Senator MD,CW MOC. P.M. Gen.
Crews, John R.		Military	10			20	Award CMH, WWII
Crews, Laura Hope	1880-1942	Entertainment	195			350	Aunt Pittypat-Gone With the Wind
Crewson, Wendy		Entertainment	4			15	Actress. Films
Crichton, Michael		Author	14	150		55	Jurassic Park, etc.
Crick, Francis, Dr.		Science	50	112			Nobel in Medicine, Structure of DNA. FDC $75
Crier, Katherine		TV News	5			10	TV Commentary, Special Analysis
Crimi, Giulio	1885-1939	Entertainment	40			125	Opera. Puccini Tenor Role Creator
Crimson Tide (Cast Of)		Entertainment				130	Gene Hackman
Crippen, Hawley Harvey		Criminal		415	500		Murdered Wife.Executed in Eng.
Crippen, Robert L.		Astronaut	7			115	Shuttle Orbiter 102 Crew
Cripps, R. Stafford, Sir	1889-1952	Statesman	30	90	210		Br.Economist, King's Counsel
Crisp, Charles Frederick		Senate/Congress	20		35		CSA Officer,' Speaker of House
Crisp, Charles Robert		Senate/Congress	12	20		15	MOC GA
Crisp, Donald		Entertainment	50	60	90	150	
Cristal, Linda		Entertainment	8	12	22	22	Pin-Up SP $32
Cristalli, Italo		Entertainment	60				Opera. Great Tenor. SP Pc as Faust $150 Rare
Crittenden, John J.	1787-1863	Cabinet	25	60	125		Sen.,MOC KY, Att'y General
Crittenden, Thomas L. (WD)		Civil War	85			2500	Union Gen.
Crittenden, Thomas L.	1819-93	Civil War	50	135	255	250	Union Gen. Served also in Mex. War
Croce, Benedetto		Author-Philos.	25	35	80		It.Statesman, Critic, Historian
Croce, Jim		Entertainment	275				Rock
Crocker, Charles		Business	475	2800	3850		Am.Financier. Pres. S.P. RR
Crockett, David	1786-1836	Military	6000	9250	34250		Am. Frontiersman.Died at Alamo
Crockett, Samuel R.		Author	7	15	35		Scot.Abandoned Ministry
Croft, Dwayne		Entertainment	5			25	Opera
Croghan, George		Colonial America	195	420	850		Trader,Indian Agt,Treaty Maker
Croker, Richard Boss		Politician	20	45	80		Tammany Hall Leader
Croly, George		Clergy	15	25	40		
Crompton, Richmal	1890-1969	Author	48	62	132	85	(Lamburn) Novelist 'Just William' Series
Cromwell, James		Entertainment	10			40	SP Col./Babe $70
Cromwell, Oliver	1599-1658	Head of State	1200	6293	10225		Named Lord Protector Eng.
Cromwell, Richard		Entertainment	7	9	20	15	
Cronenberg, David		Entertainment	10			25	Film Director
Cronin, A. J.	1896-1981	Author	25	70	170	35	Br. Physician-Novelist. The Citadel
Cronin, James W.		Science	15	25	35	20	Nobel Physics
Cronkite, Walter		TV News	10	20	32	25	TV News Anchor, Commentator
Cronyn, Hume		Entertainment	10	18	25	28	Cronyn & Jessica Tandy SP $100-$145
Crook and Chase		Entertainment	5			10	Lorianne & Charlie
Crook, George	1818-90	Civil War	112	438	375	400	Union Gen. Sig/Rank $385
Crookes, William, Sir	1832-1919	Science	142	125	240		Br.Phys., Chem., Nobel. Thallium
Crooks, Richard		Entertainment	20	35	45	50	Opera. American Tenor
Crosby, Bing	1901-77	Entertainment	65	300	395	174	Am. Singer-Actor. Academy Award. AMusQS $75

NAME	DATE	CATEGORY	SIG	LS/DS	ALS	SP	COMMENTS
Crosby, Bob		Entertainment	20			35	Big Band Leader-Singer
Crosby, Cathy Lee		Entertainment	8		20	20	Pin-Up SP $30
Crosby, David		Entertainment	12			45	Rock & Roll HOF
Crosby, Gary		Entertainment	5	6		8	Actor Son of Bing
Crosby, Howard		Clergy	15	20	25		
Crosby, J.T.		Aviation	15	25	40	30	ACE, WW II, Navy Ace
Crosby, Kathryn		Entertainment	10	15	25	25	
Crosby, Mary		Entertainment	5		10	15	Actress wife of Bing
Crosby, Norm		Entertainment	5	10	15	10	Actor-Comedian
Crosby, Percy*		Cartoonist	40	90		75	'Skippy' Sign Orig. Sketch $200
Crosby, Stills, Nash & Young		Entertainment	185			350	Super Star Rock Group (All Four)
Crosley, Powel Jr.		Business	20	75	95	35	Crosley Radio Corp.
Crosman, Henrietta		Entertainment	15			35	40 Years on Stage. Silent Films & Talkies
Cross, Christopher		Entertainment	10			20	Composer, Singer
Cross, Marcia		Entertainment	10			35	Actress, Melrose Place
Cross, Wilbur L.		Governor	5	10			Gov. CT
Crosse, Andrew	1784-1855	Science	45		165		Br. Electrical Pioneer/Copper-Zinc Battery
Crossfield, A. Scott		Aviation	15	30	45	55	1st U.S. Test Pilot of X-15
Crossman, George H.		Civil War	20		90	60	General
Crothers, Rachel		Author	10		40	20	Am. Playwright. 'Susan & God'
Crothers, Scatman	1910-86	Entertainment	25	30	45	65	Black Character Actor. Disney Voice
Crouse, Lindsay		Entertainment	15	15	30	30	
Crouse, Russell		Author	10	15	45	50	Playwright. 'Life With Father'
Croves, H. (B.Traven)(Torsvan)		Author	250	800			Ger. Novelist, Actor, Pacifist
Crow, Sheryl		Entertainment	12			53	Rocker, Grammy winner. Pin-Up $70
Crowe, Eyre		Statesman	5		20		British Circa 1923
Crowe, William		Military	15	45		30	Admiral U.S. Navy
Crowley, Leo		Cabinet	5		12	10	Chm. FDIC. 9 Gov't Posts
Crowley, Pat		Entertainment	5		15	15	Promising Actress of 50's Films
Crowninshield, Benj. W.		Cabinet	30	85	185		Sec'y Navy 1814
Croy, Homer	1883-	Author	15	40			Novelist, Writer, Humorist
Crozier, William		Military	35			60	General WW I, Inventor
Cruikshank, Eliza		Celebrity			60		Mrs. George Cruicshank
Cruikshank, George*	1792-1878	Artist	152	115	365	375	Illustrator, Caricaturist, Etcher
Cruise, Tom		Entertainment	40	25	65	88	Leading Man. DSBorn on the 4th....... $495
Crumb, George		Composer	25		375		Pulitzer, AMusQS $200, $320
Crumb, Robert*		Cartoonist	25			265	Underground, Psychedelic Cartoons. Sp. Ed. S $495
Crume, Dillard		Entertainment	5			20	Blues Bassist/Koko Taylor
Crummit, Frank		Entertainment	5			15	Vintage Radio/Julia Sanderson
Cruz-Romo, Gilda		Entertainment	5			30	Opera
Cruzen, Richard H.		Explorer	20		50	75	Adm. Arctic-Antarctic/Byrd
Crystal, Billy		Entertainment	20	25		45	Stand-up Comedian-Actor
Cuberli, Lella		Entertainment	10			35	
Cudahy, Michael F.		Business	25	65	135	50	Meat Packer. Refrigeration
Cuellar, Javier P.		Diplomat	5			15	Sec'y Gen. UN

NAME	DATE	CATEGORY	SIG	LS/DS	ALS	SP	COMMENTS
Cugat, Xavier	1900-90	Entertainment	20		35	72	Big Band Rhumba King. Performed in Films
Cui, Cesar	1835-1918	Composer	95	200	450		And Russian Military Engineer
Cukor, George		Entertainment	25	95		150	Stage and Screen Director
Culbertson, Ely	1891-1955	Author	25	80		150	Invented Culbertson Contract Bridge
Culbertson, Frank L. Jr.		Astronaut	6			20	
Culkin, Kieran		Entertainment	4			18	Actor. Mac's Younger Brother
Culkin, Macaulay		Entertainment	20			48	Child Actor, Now Married
Cullen, Countee		Author	200	410	400		Am. Black Poet. 1st Ed. S $450
Cullom, Shelby M.	1829-1914	Congress	35	60			MOC 1865, Senator, Gov. IL
Cullum, George W.	1809-92	Civil War	35		80		Union Gen. Throughout the Civil War.
Culp, Julia		Entertainment	35			150	Opera
Culp, Robert		Entertainment	9	10	25	25	
Culver, Roland		Entertainment	10	15	25	25	
Culverhouse, Hugh		Business	10		15		
Cumberland, Wm. Aug., Duke	1721-65	Royalty	55	205			Third Son of George II. Army Cmdr. 'Butcher Cumb..'
Cumming, Alfred	1829-1910	Civil War	100	295	330		CSA General
Cummings, e.e.(Edw. Estlin)		Author	200	500	500	695	Am. Poet, Painter
Cummings, Homer	1870-1956	Cabinet	25	40	75	125	FDR Att'y Gen.
Cummings, Robert		Entertainment	15			40	Veteran Leading Man & Light Comedian from 1935
Cunard, Samuel, Sir		Business	90	130	210		Br. Shipowner. Cunard Line
Cunningham, Andrew B.	1883-1963	Military	35	100	200		Br. Adm. S. Afr. & WW I
Cunningham, E.V. (Howard Fast)		Author	20			35	Suspense Novels & Sci-Fi
Cunningham, John W.		Clergy	10	15	20	35	
Cunningham, Merce	1922-	Entertainment	40		200	60	Dancer/Choreogr. Kennedy Award
Cunningham, R. Walter	1932-	Astronaut	10	20	30	65	
Cunningham, Randy Duke		Aviation	12	25	45	38	ACE, Nam, Only Navy Ace
Cuomo, Mario		Governor	15	35		65	Governor NY
Curb, Mike		Entertainment	4			15	Songwriter
Curie, Marie	1867-1934	Science	1050	2576	3400	3325	Fr Physicist-Nobel Prize. Curie Inst. DS $9,500
Curie, Pierre	1859-1906	Science	440	895	3750		Content ALS $9,000
Curless, Dick		Country Music	10			20	
Curley, Michael J., Archbishop		Clergy	45	55	65		
Curley, Pauline		Entertainment	4			20	Vintage Actress
Currie, Donald, Sir		Business	10	20	40		Scot. Shipowner. Castle Line
Currier, Moody		Governor	4			10	Gov. NY
Currier, Nathaniel		Artist	225	800			Currier & Ives, Lithographers
Curry, B.		Civil War	30	70			CSA Officer
Curry, Charles Forrest		Senate/Congress	10	15	35		MOC CA
Curry, George		Military	30	105			1st Territorial Gov. NM
Curry, Jabez L.M.	1825-1903	Civil War			40		CSA Congr. Lt. Col. Cavalry
Curry, John Steuart		Artist	65		370		Orig. Ink Sketch S $750, Murals
Curry, Tim		Entertainment	15			48	Rocky Horror Picture Show
Curtin, Andrew G.		Governor	30	45			Civil War Gov. PA.
Curtin, Jane		Entertainment	10	15	20	25	
Curtin, John (Joseph A.)	1885-1945	Head of State	35				WW II Prime Minister New Zealand

NAME	DATE	CATEGORY	SIG	LS/DS	ALS	SP	COMMENTS
Curtis, Alan		Entertainment	12	15	35	25	
Curtis, Benjamin R. (SC)	1809-74	Supreme Court	35	50	235		Resigned. Protest of Dred Scott.Johnson Def. Att'y
Curtis, Charles	1860-1936	Vice President	55	225	180	95	Native Am. Descent. Hoover VP
Curtis, Cyrus H. K.		Business	35	55	140	95	Curtis Publishing Co.
Curtis, Edward Sheriff	1868-1952	Artist		500		1300	Photographer, Native Americans
Curtis, George Wm.	1824-92	Author	60	130	55		Editor Harper's Weekly.Civil War
Curtis, Jamie Lee		Entertainment	28	45		61	Authentic Pin-Up SP $75 up.Janet Leigh Signs Many
Curtis, Ken	1916-91	Entertainment	25			65	'Festus'. Country Music. 'Son of the Pioneers'
Curtis, Newton M.	1835-1910	Civil War	35	90			Union Gen. ALS '62 $155
Curtis, Robin		Entertainment	10	12	20	20	'Star Trek'
Curtis, Samuel Ryan	1817-66	Civil War	50	80	292		Union Gen'l. Hero of Pea Ridge
Curtis, Tony		Entertainment	18	28	25	40	Early Vintage SP $125
Curtis, Verna Maria		Entertainment	10			30	Am. Soprano
Curtis, Wilfred A.		Aviation	10	25	40	25	
Curtiss, Glenn		Aviation	285	400	650	850	Am. Inventor. Pioneer Aircraft Builder
Curtiz, Michael		Entertainment	30	75		100	Film Director
Curzon, George Nathaniel	1859-1925	Head of State	25		65		1st Marquis, Viceroy & Gov. India 1898-1925
Curzon, Robert (Zouche)		Br. Explorer	10		25		
Cusack, Joan		Entertainment	4			25	Talented Actress-Sister of John Cusack
Cusack, John		Entertainment	15			40	Actor
Cushing, Caleb	1800-79	Cabinet	34	75	75		Pierce Att'y Gen., Diplomat
Cushing, Harvey, Dr.		Science	165	475	675		Specialist in Neurosurgery
Cushing, Peter	1913-94	Entertainment	35		45	70	Brit. Actor.
Cushing, Richard	1895-1970	Clergy	40	95	85	55	Rom. Cath. Cardinal
Cushing, Thomas	1725-1788	Colonial Am.	565	1100			Patriot. Prominent in Col. Congr.
Cushman, Charlotte S.	1816-76	Entertainment	20	35	60	90	19th Century Stage Actress. AM. HOF
Cushman, Robert E.,Jr.	1914-	Military	25			40	Gen. U.S. Marines. Vietnam War
Cushman, Samuel		Senate/Congress	10	20	35		MOC NH 1835
Custer, Elizabeth	1842-1933	Author-Civil War	85	220	551	360	Wife of George A. Custer
Custer, George A. (WD)		Civil War	5450	5215	13000	8625	Union Gen., Indian Fighter
Custer, George A.	1839-76	Civil War	2933	8183	8500		Union Gen. LS/Cont. $15000. Killed Little Big Horn
Custine, Adam Philippe, Count de		Rev. War	100	350			Fr.Gen.Fought in Am. Revolution
Cutcheon, Byron M.	1836-1908	Civil War	30			80	Union Gen., U.S.V.-27th Mich. MOH.
Cutler, Lysander	1807-66	Civil War	90	185	275		Union General
Cutler, Manasseh	1742-1823	Rev. War	425	550			Am.Clergyman, Botanist, Pioneer
Cuvier, Georges, Baron	1769-1832	Science	98	497	365		Fr. Father of Comparative Anatomy. Naturalist
Cuyler, Theodore L.		Author	10	15	35		
Cyrus, Billy Ray		Country Music	25	70		48	Singer
Czerny, Carl		Composer	75	255	460		Master of Liszt. Etudes. Teacher
Czerny, Vincenz		Science	110		900		Ger. Leader Abdominal Surgery
Czerwenka, Oskar		Entertainment	5			25	Opera

NAME	DATE	CATEGORY	SIG	LS/DS	ALS	SP	COMMENTS
D'Abo, Maryan		Entertainment	8			32	Actress. Pin-Up SP $25-55
D'Abo, Olivia		Entertainment	10			30	Actress. Pin-Up $50
D'Albert, Eugene		Composer	130	190		150	Ger. Pianist.Opera. AMusQS $150
D'Albert, Eugene F.C.		Composer	55	75	130		Ger. Opera, Piano Concertos
D'Amato, Alfonse		Senate/Congress	10			45	Senator NY
D'Angelo, Beverly		Entertainment	8			35	Actress. Pin-Up $60
D'Annunzio, Gabriele	1863-1938	Author	75	175	150	450	It. Writer, Pro-Fascist Soldier
D'Arclee', Hariclee'		Entertainment	100				Fr. Soprano
D'Artagnan, Comte de		Military			6500		Capt.Louis XIV Musketeers
D'Arville, Camille		Entertainment	15			45	Actress-Vintage
D'Eon, Charles de Beaumont		Adventurer	100		400		Louis XV's secret agent to Russ
D'Errico, Donna		Entertainment	7			44	Actress. Pin-Up $55
D'Estaing, V. Gistard		Head of State	15	40	100	60	Pres. France
D'Indy, Vincent	1851-1931	Composer	40	125	362	375	Fr.Opera,Orchestral,Vocal Music AMusQS $300
D'Orsay, Alfred, Count	1801-52	Artist	25	65	170		Fr.Wit, Fashion Arbiter, Society Leader
D'Orsay, Fifi		Entertainment	15	20	35	35	Fr. Canadian Actress. Vaudeville & 30's Films
D'Oyly Carte, Rupert		Entertainment	25	70	125	135	Producer of Original Gilbert & Sullivan Operettas
D'Oyly, George		Clergy	15	20	35		
Da Ponte, Lorenzo		Librettist		1500			Don Giovanni, Cosi fan tutte, Marriage of Figaro
Dache, Lilly		Business-Designer	55	75	130	150	Coutourier. Specialty-Hats
Daddi, Francesco		Entertainment	5	8	15		
Dafoe, Allan Roy, Dr.	1883-1943	Science	75		135	225	Delivered Dionne Quintuplets
Dafoe, Willem		Entertainment	6	10		25	Actor
Dagmar		Entertainment	20			35	
Dagover, Lil	1897-19??	Entertainment				195	Vintage Ger. Actress
Daguerre, Louis		Science	150	490	1250		Fr. Inventor Daguerreotype. Photography Pioneer
Dahl, Arlene	1924-	Entertainment	8		15	20	Actress. Pin-Up SP $40
Dahl, Perry		Aviation	10	25	38	28	ACE, WW II
Dahl, Roald		Author	15	160		45	Br. Short Stories, Children's
Dahlberg, Edward		Author	20	162		45	Am. Writer & Critic
Dahlberg, Ken		Aviation	15	30	50	40	ACE, WW II
Dahlgren, John A.	1809-70	Civil War	115	375	908		Adm. Union Navy. Dahlgren Gun. Sig./Rank $220
Dahlgren, Ulric	1824-64	Civil War	275		1375		Union Col. Planned Capture Jeff. Davis. Killed
Dailey, Dan	1914-78	Entertainment	20	25	45	40	Actor-Song & Dance Man. Many 20th Cent. Musicals
Dailey, Janet		Author	5	10		10	
Dailey, Peter F.		Entertainment	5	8	15	15	
Dal Monte, Toti		Entertainment	25			95	Opera. SP Pc $75
Daladier, Edouard		Head of State	30	85	150	50	Premier Fr. Arrested-Liberated
Dalai Lama XIV	1935-	Head of State	75	160	225	163	Exiled Tibetan Religious Leader
Daley, Cass		Entertainment	5			15	Comedienne. Films
Daley, Richard J.		Political	20	40	85	35	Mayor Chicago. Last of Big City Bosses

NAME	DATE	CATEGORY	SIG	LS/DS	ALS	SP	COMMENTS
Daley, Richard M.		Political	5			10	Mayor Chicago & Son of Richard J.
Dali, Salvador	1904-89	Artist	313	738	650	985	Sp. Surrealist Painter. AMsS/Sketches $5900-7500
Dali, Tracey		Entertainment	10			45	Model/actress
Dallapozza, Adolf		Entertainment	5			25	Vienna Operettas
Dallas, Alexander J.	1759-1817	Cabinet	52	175	230		Madison Sec'y Treasury
Dallas, George M.		Vice President	65	200	238		Dallas, Texas Named for Him. Polk VP
Dalmores, Charles		Entertainment	25			85	Opera
Dalton, Abby		Entertainment	4	6	15	18	Actress. Pin-Up $32
Dalton, Charles		Entertainment	5		10	10	
Dalton, Dorothy		Entertainment	20	25	65	60	
Dalton, Emmett	1871-1937	Outlaw	650	2338	3776	2500	Western Train Robber
Dalton, Frank		Lawman	890	3000			U.S.Marshal-Old West
Dalton, John		Science	135	400	750		Br. Chemist & Philosopher
Dalton, Lacy J.		Entertainment	5			25	Singer
Dalton, Timothy		Entertainment	18			50	One time 007. James Bond SP $45
Daltry, Roger		Entertainment	15			45	Rock. 'Who' Lead Singer
Daly, James		Entertainment	7		15	25	Actor. Movie-TV. Father of Tyne Daly. Deceased
Daly, John Charles		Entertainment	7			20	News Commentator.Game Show Host. TV Pioneer
Daly, Tyne	1947-	Entertainment	7	12	18	19	Actress. Cagney & Lacy Star
Dam, Henrik		Science	70			105	Danish Biochemist. Nobel. Phil. Cover S $125
Damita, Lili		Entertainment	32	80	85	75	Fr. Film Star. Mrs. Errol Flynn
Damon, Cathryn		Entertainment	5			20	Actress. Character
Damon, Les		Entertainment	5			20	Radio Actor. Nick Charles in 'Thin Man'
Damon, Matt		Entertainment	20			60	Actor. Good Will Hunting
Damone, Vic		Entertainment	5			14	Top Flight Singer
Damrosch, Walter	1862-1950	Composer-Cond.	50	172	115	350	Pioneer of Symphonic Broadcasts. AMusQS $125
Dana, Bill		Entertainment	25			40	Jose Jiminez. Early 60's Comedian-TV Writer
Dana, Charles A.	1819-97	Publisher-Editor	30	30	75	45	Owner & Editor NY Sun. Civil War Member War Dept.
Dana, James D.		Science	15		45		Scientific Observer Antarctic
Dana, James Jackson		Civil War	40	140			Union General
Dana, Napoleon J.T.	1822-1905	Civil War	45	70			Union Gen. ADS '64 $300
Dana, Richard Henry, Jr.	1815-82	Author	55	200	225		Sailor,Lawyer Prosecutor of Jeff. Davis
Danaher, John A.		Senate/Congress	5	15		10	Senator CT
Dandridge, Dorothy	1923-65	Entertainment	45	55	82	400	Afro-Am. Singer, Actress, Dancer
Dandridge, Ruby		Entertainment	35			90	
Dandy, George B.	1830-1911	Civil War	40	95			Twice Brevetted Union Gen. Georgian
Dane, Karl		Entertainment	10			15	Actor
Dane, Nathan		Rev. War	25	65	130		Continental Congress
Danei, Paul Francis	1694-1775	Clergy		7500			Saint Paul of the Cross 1867
Danenhower, John Wilson		Explorer	20	45	115		De Long Arctic Expedition 1879
Danes, Claire		Entertainment	15			50	Actress
Danforth, John C.		Senate	5			10	Senator MO
Danforth, Thomas	1622-1699	Colonial America	390	470			Deputy Governor MA
Dangerfield, George		Author	5	10	25		
Dangerfield, Rodney		Entertainment	6	12	20	22	Comedian. .... No Respect

NAME	DATE	CATEGORY	SIG	LS/DS	ALS	SP	COMMENTS
Danges, Henry	1870-1948	Entertainment	35			70	Opera. Baritone. Sang in World Prem. Louise
Daniel, John W.		Senate	10	25			Senator VA, Disabled in CW
Daniel, Peter Vivian (SC)	1784-1860	Supreme Court	45	125	475		
Daniel, Price		Senate/Congress	15	40		25	Senator, Gov. TX
Daniell, Henry		Entertainment	50			150	Vintage Villainous Character Actor
Daniels, Bebe		Entertainment	20		65	75	Vintage Actress. Major Star 30's
Daniels, Billy		Entertainment	10			20	Afr-Am. Vocalist. Supper Clubs & Early TV
Daniels, Charlie		Country Music	6			20	
Daniels, Jeff		Entertainment	10			35	Actor.
Daniels, Josephus	1862-1948	Cabinet	25	50	160	125	Sec'y Navy WW I. Diplomat, Journalist, Editor
Daniels, William		Entertainment	5			20	
Daniloff, Nick		Celebrity	20		25	20	
Danilova, Alexandra		Entertainment	20	35	65	80	Rus-Am Ballerina, Teacher
Dankworth, Johnny		Bandleader	5			20	Jazz Musician
Dannay, Frederick	1905-1972	Author	50	160	325		ELLERY QUEEN
Dannenberg, Konrad		Science	20			55	Rocket Pioneer/von Braun
Danner, Blythe		Entertainment	5		15	15	Actress. & Mother of Gwineth Paltrow
Danning, Sybil		Entertainment	8	10	20	25	Actress. Pin-Up $45
Dano, Royal		Entertainment	10		20	25	Vintage Character Actor
Danova, Cesare		Entertainment	5	8	15	20	
Danson, Ted		Entertainment	20			45	Actor. New Hit Becker. Cheers SP $45
Dantine, Helmut		Entertainment	15	15		35	Autrian Actor of 40's-50's. Frequent Nazi Officer
Danton, Georges-Jacques		Fr. Revolution	1080	2800			Guillotined Leader of Revolution
Danton, Ray		Entertainment	8			15	Actor
Danza, Tony		Entertainment	10	15	25	30	Actor. Ex-Boxer. Hit TV Series
Darby, Kim		Entertainment	15			35	Actress. Difficult Autograph. True Grit SP $38
Darcy		Entertainment	6			25	Music. Bass, Vocals Smashing Pumkins
Darcy, Emery		Entertainment	15			40	Met. Heidentenor
Darden, Christopher		Law	18	125		20	O.J.Simpson Prosecuting Att'y
Darin, Bobby	1936-73	Entertainment	120		250	165	Singer-Actor. Mack the Knife Topped Charts d. 37
Darion, Joe		Composer	10			30	Jazz. AMusQS $50
Darlan, Francois	1881-1942	Military			448		Fr. Adm. Vichy. Assassinated
Darling, J.N. 'ding'*		Cartoonist	25			150	Political Cartoonist
Darlington, William	1782-1863	Naturalist-Author	25		155		Many Swiss & US plants named for him
Darnell, Linda	1923-65	Entertainment	45	145		180	Died Tragically in Fire
Darrah, Thomas		Military	35	50		45	General WW I
Darrall, Chester B.		Senate/Congress	20	30	55		MOC LA. Union Surgeon CW
Darrell, Johnny		Country Music	10			20	
Darren, James		Entertainment	8			19	Actor-Singer
Darrieux, Danielle		Entertainment	8			25	Fr. Actress. Film & Stage
Darro, Frankie		Entertainment	50			150	Child Actor. Disney Voice
Darrow, Charles B.	1889-1967	Designer	395	995			Developed Best Seller Monopoly
Darrow, Clarence	1857-1938	Law	438	1500	2425	1600	Scopes Trial(Monkey Trial), Loeb & Leopold etc.
Dart, Justin		Business	50	100	250	75	Drugstore Chain. Art Museum
Dartiguenave, Philippe Sudre		Head of State	40	100			President of Haiti 1915

NAME	DATE	CATEGORY	SIG	LS/DS	ALS	SP	COMMENTS
Darville, Camille		Entertainment	10			20	Actress
Darwell, Jane	1880-1967	Entertainment	122	110	200	200	Vintage Actress. GWTW, Grapes of Wrath Oscar
Darwin, Charles	1809-82	Science	583	1917	3007	9775	Br. Naturalist. Theory of Evolution
Daschle, Thomas		Congress	10			20	Senator, SD
Dassin, Jules		Entertainment	20			45	Film Director
Daubigny, Charles Francois		Artist	95	280	425		Fr. Landscape Painter
Daudet, Alphonse	1840-97	Author	35	80	175		Fr. Stories, Novels, Plays
Daugherty, Harry M.	1860-1941	Cabinet	25	55	125	50	Att'y Gen. Tried for Fraud-Acquitted. (Harding Adm)
Daumier, Honore		Artist	240	630	1470		Fr. Caricaturist & Serious Art
Dauphin, Claude		Entertainment	35			75	Fr. Leading Man
Dausset, Jean, Prof.		Science	20	45		35	Nobel Medicine
Dauvray, Helen		Entertainment	4			8	
Daval, Danny		Entertainment	5		15	15	
Dave, Red River		Country Music	10			20	Country Singer
Davenport, Addington	1670-1736	Rev. War	140	265	500		Am. Colonial Jurist
Davenport, Fanny		Entertainment	20			50	Vintage Actress. 1889
Davenport, Harry		Entertainment	100			250	Veteran Char. Actor. 'GWTW' SP $595
Davenport, Homer C.		Cartoonist	30	60	135		Political Cartoons, Uncle Sam
David		Entertainment	5			25	Music. Drummer Korn
David, Felicien-Cesar	1810-76	Composer	100	500			AMusMsS $650-750
David, Ferdinand		Composer	45		225		Ger. Violinist
David, Hal		Composer	20	30	65	35	
David, Jacques Louis		Artist	175	440	610		Fr. Classical Painter
David, Mack		Composer	20			40	Lyricist
Davidson, Allen Turner		Civil War	25	80	125		CSA Congress. Lawyer, Banker
Davidson, Arthur		Business	1100	5300			Harley-Davidson Motorcycle Founder. DS Stock Cert.
Davidson, Gordon		Business	1500	4500			A Founder of Harley-Davidson. DS Stock Cert.
Davidson, Jim		Entertainment	4			18	Actor. Pacific Blue
Davidson, Jo		Artist	35	75	135	105	Am. Sculptor
Davidson, John		Entertainment	4	6		14	Singer-Actor-Host
Davidson, John W.	1824-81	Civil War					Union Gen. ALS '62 $630
Davidson, Loyal		Military	35	60			
Davidson, Randall T., Archbishop		Clergy	25	35	45		
Davidson, Walter		Business	1200	5500			Harley-Davidson Motorcycle Founder. DS Stock Cert
Davidson, William B.		Entertainment	10			30	Character Actor
Davidson, William H.		Business	1000	3500	4800		Son of Wm. A. & Pres. Harley-Davidson 30's-40's
Davies, Gail		Entertainment	4			10	Singer
Davies, Jeremy		Entertainment	3			6	
Davies, Marion		Entertainment	49	65	105	170	C. Bull Original SP $275
Davies, Peter Maxwell		Composer	40			110	'Songs of a Mad King'. Opera
Davies, Ray (The Kinks)		Entertainment	18			45	Rock Give the People..... S Alb. $55
Davies, Rhys		Author	5	20	35	10	Welch. Novels, Stories
Davies, Ronald N.		Law	25		60	30	Nazi War Trials Jurist
Davies, Thomas F., Bishop		Clergy	30	35	45		
Davies, William		Rev. War	145	792			Sec'y War of VA

NAME	DATE	CATEGORY	SIG	LS/DS	ALS	SP	COMMENTS
Davis, Angela	1944-	Activist	12	18	32	35	Afro-Am. Activist. Wanted Poster/Sig. $250
Davis, Ann B.		Entertainment	8			18	Character Actress. Brady Bunch
Davis, Benjamin O. Jr.		Aviation	15	15	38	45	ACE, WW II, 1st Afro-Am. Military Fighter Pilot
Davis, Bette	1908-89	Entertainment	67	190	290	203	Actress Extraordinaire! Multi Oscar Winner
Davis, Brad		Entertainment	35			75	Actor. Midnight Express. Tragic Young Death
Davis, Charles Henry	1807-77	Civil War	38	80	110		Union Adm. ALS '63 $275
Davis, Clifton		Entertainment	5			18	Actor TV
Davis, Cushman K.		Senate	12	25		30	Senator MN
Davis, David (SC)	1815-86	Supreme Court	75	275	345		Sen. IL. Pres Pro Tem. Executor Lincoln Estate
Davis, Dwight F.	1879-1945	Cabinet	30	95	170	65	Sec'y War. Donor of Davis Cup. Gov-Gen. Philippines
Davis, Ellabelle		Entertainment	10			40	Great Afro-Am Singer
Davis, Ewin L.		Senate/Congress	4	10			MOC TN
Davis, Fay	1872-1945	Entertainment	15		65	50	Actress. 1895 London Hit in 'Prisoner of Zenda'
Davis, Gail		Entertainment	14	18	22	35	Actress. Annie Oakley SP $50
Davis, Geena		Entertainment	14	50		48	DS $65. Semi-Nude Pin-up Col. $85. Oscar Winner
Davis, Henry Greene		Civil War	55	135			Union General
Davis, Henry Minton	1817-65	Congress	15		50		Prevented MD from Joining CSA
Davis, James J.		Cabinet	20	50	95	75	Sec'y Labor, Founder of Moose
Davis, Jan		Astronaut	5			20	
Davis, Jefferson (WD)		Civil War		5017	6317	5500	President CSA. ALS/Cont. $15,900
Davis, Jefferson	1808-89	Civil War	662	2042	2946	3500	CSA Pres. ALS/Content $15,000, LS $55000
Davis, Jefferson C.	1828-79	Civil War	50	80	110		Union Gen. ANS '62 $330, Sig/Rank $75
Davis, Jim		Entertainment	40	40	70	70	Actor. Dallas
Davis, Jim*		Cartoonist	35	68	225	175	'Garfield'. Repro Sketch S $75
Davis, Jimmie		Governor	30	45		60	Singing Gov. of LA, You Are My Sunshine
Davis, Jo		Entertainment	4			10	
Davis, Joan		Entertainment	25			55	
Davis, John	1761-1847	Author	30	175	290		Historian, Comptroller US Treas
Davis, John	1787-1854	Governor	25	50	70		Gov. MA
Davis, John Wm.	1873-1955	Congr.-Diplomat	20	45	75	40	Dem. Pres. Candidate. Defended R. Oppenheimer
Davis, Johnny 'Scat'		Entertainment	10	10	12	15	
Davis, Jonathan		Entertainment	12			48	Music. Lead Singer Korn
Davis, Mack		Country Music	7			15	Singer-Songwriter
Davis, Meyer		Entertainment	15			35	Big Society Band
Davis, Miles	1926-91	Entertainment	188	625		422	Immortal Jazz Trumpet Player-Composer
Davis, Nancy		Entertainment	50			150	
Davis, Nancy (Reagan)		First Lady	80			170	
Davis, Nelson H.	1821-90	Civil War	25	60	78		Union Gen. Chancellorsville
Davis, Noah		Senate/Congress	10	25	60		MOC NY 1869, Jurist
Davis, Ossie	1917-	Entertainment	9			16	Actor. Stage-Screen. Playwright, Political Activis
Davis, Patti (Reagan)		Entertainment	5	7	15	20	Model-Actress-Writer. Pin-Up $50
Davis, Phil*		Cartoonist	30			250	Mandrake the Magician
Davis, Phyllis		Entertainment	6	12	18	20	Pin-Up $45
Davis, Reuben	1813-90	Civil War	50		270		CSA General
Davis, Rich'd Harding		Author	10	25	40	20	Correspondent 6 Wars, Novelist

NAME	DATE	CATEGORY	SIG	LS/DS	ALS	SP	COMMENTS
Davis, Robert		Military	5		25		General WW I
Davis, Rufe		Entertainment	25			55	
Davis, Sammy, Jr.	1925-90	Entertainment	40	50	80	142	Charter Member of Sinatra's Rat Pack. Most Talent
Davis, Varina		CSA First Lady	150	300	600	750	Mrs. Jeff. Davis.ALS/Cont $1600-$6000
Davis, William W.H.	1820-1910	Civil War		55			Led 104th PA
Davison, Bruce		Entertainment	5			10	
Davison, Wild Bill		Entertainment	30			75	Jazz Cornet-Bandleader
Davisson, Clinton Joseph		Science	25	75			Nobel Physics.Bell Laboratories
Davout, Louis Nicolas, Duke		Fr. Revolution	45	210	248		Marshal of Napoleon
Davy, Humphry, Sir	1778-1829	Science	118	322	695		Br.Chemist. ALS/Cont $3750,$8,500,AMsS $2500
Dawber, Pam		Entertainment	8	10		20	Actress. Pin-Up $40
Dawes, Charles G.		Vice President	30	150	295	275	Nobel Peace Prize
Dawes, William	1745-99	Rev. War	3500				Patriot. Rode with Paul Revere
Dawson, George		Clergy	20	35	60		
Dawson, John B.	1798-1845	Congress	10				Repr. LA, Maj. General of Militia
Dawson, John L.		Congress	20		70		Governor Kansas Terr. ,MOC PA
Dawson, Richard		Entertainment	5	20		15	Hogan's Heroes Co-Star
Dawson-Briggs, Roxanne		Entertainment				40	Actress. Star Trek
Day, Chon*		Cartoonist	10	35		50	Brother Sebastian
Day, Dennis		Entertainment	10	14	20	28	Vocalist-Comedian. Jack Benny Radio & TV Shows
Day, Doris		Entertainment	14	32		38	24 Page DS Do Not Disturb $425. Pin-Up SP $30-50
Day, Frank		Celebrity	10		25		
Day, J. Edward		Cabinet	4	5	15	10	P.M. General
Day, Jeremiah		Clergy	15	20	35		
Day, Laraine		Entertainment	7			22	Actress. Pin-Up $28
Day, Linda (George)		Entertainment	5			17	Actress Turned Director. Pin-Up $32
Day, William R. (SC)	1849-1923	Supreme Court	40	90	135	65	Sec'y State
Day-Lewis, Cecil	1904-72	Author	15	50			Br. Poet-Laureate
Day-Lewis, Daniel		Entertainment	22			58	
Dayan, Moshe	1915-1981	Military	188	225	220	295	Israeli General, Politician. Masterminded 3 Wars
Dayan, Yael		Author	5			25	And Daughter of Moshe
Daymond, Gus		Aviation	12	25	55	40	ACE, WW II, Eagle Squadron
Dayne, Taylor		Entertainment	5			35	Rock
Dayton, Elias		Rev. War	90	210	395		General. Continental Congress
Dayton, Jonathan		Rev. War	175	450	657		Continental Congress
Dayton, William L.	1807-67	Senator NJ	25	40	110		John C. Fremont Running Mate
De Acosta, Mercedes		Author	10	25	45		Intimate of Greta Garbo
de Almeida, Antonio		Conductor	10			45	Specialist in Fr. Music
De Beauvoir, Simone		Author	35	95	200		Fr. Writer,Philosopher,Feminist
De Bono, Emilio		Military	75	225		375	It. Fascist Politician & Gen.
De Bray, Xavier B.	1818-95	Civil War	125				CSA Gen. ALS/Cont.$2500
De Corsia, Ted		Entertainment	20	25		40	
de Duve, Christian R.		Science	10			40	Nobel
De Falla, Manuel	1876-1946	Composer	425	1200	1200		Sp. AMusQS $2000
De Forest, Lee, Dr.	1873-1961	Science	400	1575	1658	1350	Invented Vacuum Tube. ALS Scientific Cont. $12,500

NAME	DATE	CATEGORY	SIG	LS/DS	ALS	SP	COMMENTS
De Gaulle, Charles	1890-1969	Head of State	612	1075	1650	2530	Fr. WW II Gen., Pres. Karsh SP $1395
De Havilland, Geoffrey		Aviation	70	140	205	125	De Havilland Aircraft Co.
De Hidalgo, Elvira		Entertainment	45			150	Coloratura Soprano Teacher of Callas
De Kooning, Elaine*		Artist	50			242	Willem's Wife. Artist in her own right.
De Kooning, Willem	1904-97	Artist	150	225	450	375	Dutch Abstract Impressionist. Repro S $285-$550
de la Barra, Francisco Leon		Statesman	132	1225			Mex. Diplomat, Politician, Ambass. US, Prov. Pres.
De La Beckwith, Bryan		Activist	15		95	95	Convicted Murderer of Medgar Evers
De La Cierva, Juan		Aviation	90		295	350	Inventor Autogyro
De La Grange, Anna		Entertainment			80		Opera
De La Mare, Walter	1873-1956	Author	38	197	90	45	Br. Poet.Songs of Childhood. Novelist
De La Pena, George		Entertainment	3	3	6	6	
De La Renta, Oscar		Business	10	15	35	20	Fashion Designer.Elegant Gowns
De la Rocha, Zack		Entertainment	8			42	Music. Lead Singer Rage Against the Machine
De La Rue, Warren	1815-89	Science			200		Br. Astron., Inventor Silver-Chlor. Battery
De Lancey, Stephen		Rev. War	75	180	225		Loyalist. Lawyer. Imprisoned
De Leo, Sarafina		Entertainment				40	Opera
De Link, Derek		Entertainment	3			8	
De Luca, Giuseppe		Entertainment	25	35	95	162	Opera
De Mornay, Rebecca		Entertainment	6	15		35	Pin-up Color $60
De Palma, Brian		Entertainment	10		20	22	Film Director
De Paul, Saint Vincent		Clergy	1100	1600	4500		
De Peyster, John W. Jr.		Civil War	10	20	55		Aide to Gen.Kearny
De Quincey, Thomas		Author	145	310	650		AMs $650-$2,250
De Quincy, Thomas	1785-1859	Author	45				AMs $650
De Reszke, Edouard	1853-1917	Entertainment	68			150	Opera-Vintage. AMusQS $75
De Reszke, Jean	1850-1925	Entertainment	100	120		345	Opera-Vintage. SP/Brother Edouard $425
De Reszke, Marie		Entertainment			125		Opera
De Ridder. Anton		Entertainment	10		45	35	Opera
De Rita, Joe		Entertainment	20			40	Three Stooges SP $55, S Check $125
De Russy, Gustavus A.(WD)		Civil War	50	250	233		Union Gen.
De Sade, Marquis	1740-1814	Author			1850		Fr. Social Deviant. Sadism
De Sade, Marquis	1740-1814	Author	125		1800		Fr. Social Deviant. Abnormal Behavior. Sadism
De Seversky, Alex.	1894-1973	Aviation	90	250	205	238	TLS/Historical Cont. $1,200
De Smet, Pierre	1801-73	Jesuit Missionary	225		800		Missionary to Western Indians
De Toth, Andre'		Entertainment	10			20	Film Director
De Trobriand, Philippe R.(WD)		Civil War	50	325	395		Union Gen.
De Valera, Eamon (Ire)	1882-1975	Head of State	65	125	325	110	Pres. P.M. Cont.TLS $550
De Vere, Aubrey T.		Author	20	60	140		Ir. Poet,Critic,Hymns
De Wilde, Brandon		Entertainment	100			300	
De Windt, Harry	1856-1933	Explorer	30	15	75	50	Br. Explorer
De Witt, Alexander		Senate/Congress	5		20		MOC MA
Deacon, Richard		Entertainment	25			50	
Dean, Billy		Country Music	5			20	
Dean, Donald J.		Military	15	45			WW I Victoria Cross
Dean, Eddie		Country Music	10	10	20	25	

NAME	DATE	CATEGORY	SIG	LS/DS	ALS	SP	COMMENTS
Dean, Gilbert	1819-70	Congress	9				Repr. NY
Dean, James	1931-55	Entertainment	2125	5169	3250	5917	Short Lived Spectacular Career in Films
Dean, Jimmy		Country Music	5			21	Sausages & CW Singer
Dean, John W.		Law	5	15	25	95	Special Counsel to Nixon. Watergate
Dean, Julia		Entertainment	6	8	15	15	
Dean, Maureen		Author	10	35			(Mrs. John Dean)
Dean, Millvina		Titanic Survivor	195				Fatal Shipwreck Lithograph S $250
Dean, Pricilla	1896-1987	Entertainment	20			70	Silent Film Star of early 20's
Dean, William F.	1899-1981	Military	20	35	55	195	Gen. WW II. Hero of Korean War
Deane, Silas	1737-89	Rev. War	230	550	975		Diplomat. Negotiated Treaties. Cont'l Congress
DeAngelis, Jefferson		Entertainment	10				Actor
Dearborn, Henry	1751-1829	Cabinet	130	419	1012		Rev. War Gen'l. Jefferson's Sec'y War.Statesman
Dearborn, Henry A.S.	1783-1851	Senate/Congress	55	175	250		Collector Port Boston 1812-29
Dearden, John, Cardinal		Clergy	30	35	45	40	
Death on the Nile (Cast)		Entertainment				75	Signed by 6
DeBakey, Michael, Dr.	1908-	Science	15	38		33	1st Coronary Artery Bypass Op.
Debar, William J.		Senate	10	15			Senator KY
DeBeaune, Charlotte		Celebrity		525			Mistress of Henry IV
DeBeck, Billy*		Cartoonist	30			260	Barney Google, Snuffy Smith
DeBlanc, Jeff		Aviation	12	28	52	38	ACE, WW II, CMH
DeBray, Xavier B.	1818-95	Civil War	95		248		CSA General
Debre, Michael		Head of State	5	20	50		
DeBroglie, Louis-C-V- Maurice		Science	35	90			Physicist. Pioneer in X-Rays
Debs, Eugene		Labor	70	307	255	135	U.S. Socialist Leader.Organizer
Debussy, Claude	1862-1918	Composer	388	1625	920		Fr. Composer. AMusQS $7,500
DeButts, John D.		Business	10	35	45	20	
Debye, Peter J.W.		Science	55	110	175		NobelChemistry-Discovered Rayon
Decamp, Rosemary		Entertainment	5			40	Am.Radio & Film Star
DeCarlo, Yvonne	1922-	Entertainment	8	12	22	33	Actress Pin-Up $38
DeCasseres. Benjamin		Author	5	15	25		Columnist, Editorials NY Mirror
Decatur, Stephen		Military	1100	3100	5710		American Naval Hero, War 1812
DeCisneros, Eleanora		Entertainment	40			185	Opera
DeCordova, Fred		Entertainment	5	8	15	15	
Dee, Francis		Entertainment	8		18	32	Actress & Wife of Favorite Joel McCrea.Pin-Up $38
Dee, Ruby	1923-	Entertainment	10		15	20	1st Afr.-Am./Major Shakespearean Role Am. Festival
Dee, Sandra		Entertainment	8	10	15	35	Actress. Pin-Up SP $25-50
Deems, 'Cousin'		Country Music	4			15	And His Goat Herders
Deems, Charles Force		Celebrity	5	10	20		
Deere, Allan Christopher		Aviation	15	40	50		N.Z. Ace WWII, 22 confirmed
Deere, John	1804-86	Business	300	3500	1450		Steel Plow.Deere Check $4750
Deering, James		Business	10	25	45	25	
Deering, Olive		Entertainment	15			35	
Dees, Morris		Legal	10			25	Lawyer, Political Activist.Tracks Hate Crimes
Dees, Rick		Country Western	2			5	Singer Radio-TV Host
Defoe, Daniel	1660-1731	Author	1500	7500			Br. Journalist, Novelist

NAME	DATE	CATEGORY	SIG	LS/DS	ALS	SP	COMMENTS
DeFord, Bailey		Country Music	20			75	Early Black Opry Star
DeFore, Don		Entertainment	9			20	Actor. Vintage SP $30
DeFranco, Buddy		Entertainment	12			25	Bandleader, Clarinetist
Degas, Edgar	1834-1917	Artist	250	760	1853		Fr. Impressionist. Ballet Scenes
DeGeneres, Ellen		Entertainment	18			53	Comedienne. TV, Standup
DeHart, John		Rev. War	30	65	140		
DeHaven, Gloria		Entertainment	6	8	5	19	Glamor Actress-Singer-Dancer of MGM Musicals
DeHaven, Robert		Aviation	10	20	40	30	ACE, WW II
DeHavilland, Olivia		Entertainment	40	75	195	52	As Melanie in GWTW, SP $90-$150-$225. AA
Dehmelt, Hans G., Dr.		Science	20	35		30	Nobel Physics
Dehner, John		Entertainment	10		10	15	
Deisenhofer, Johann		Science	27	36		35	Nobel
DeKalb, Johann	1721-80	Rev. War			7500		Arrived/ Lafayette.Ordered to Capture Charleston
Dekker, Albert		Entertainment	6			10	
DeKlerk, F.W.		Head of State	75	150		90	Nobel Peace, Pr.Minister S.A.
DeKoven, Reginald	1859-1920	Composer	25	45	150	100	Versatile American Composer
Del Fuegos, The		Entertainment	20			50	
Del Monaco, Mario	1915-82	Entertainment	50	65	150	208	Opera
Del Rio, Delores	1905-83	Entertainment	30	35	55	75	Actress. Serenely Beautiful Mexican Performer
Del Tredici, David		Composer	15	35	80		Pulitzer, AMusQS $100
Delacroix, F.V. Eugene	1798-1863	Artist	175	385	643		Brilliant Colorist.Great Murals
DeLaCroix, Raven		Entertainment	3	3	6	8	
Delafield, John R.		Military	8				General
Delafield, Richard		Civil War	38	65	95		Union General. Engineer
DeLagnel, Juius A.	1827-1912	Civil War	85		200		CSA General
DeLancie, John		Entertainment				45	Actor. Star Trek
DeLand, Margaret		Author	12	25	75	25	Am. Novelist.Old ChesterTales
Delaney, Kim		Entertainment	8			50	Award Winning Actress NYPD Blue. Pin-Up $55
Delano, Columbus		Cabinet	20				Sec'y Interior, Grant
Delany, Bessie		Author	5			20	Co-Author of Best Selling Memoirs
Delany, Dana		Entertainment	8	22		38	Actress. Pin-Up $55
Delany, Sarah Sadie		Author	5			20	Co-Wrote Best-Selling Memoirs
Delbridge, Del		Entertainment	10			15	Radio Announcer
Delbruck, Max		Science	70		200		Nobel in Medicine
Deledda, Grazia		Author	45	105	320		Nobel Literature 1926
DeLiagre, Alfred		Entertainment	5	7	12	10	
Delibes, Leo		Composer	85	220	270		Light Opera, Ballet
Delius, Frederick	1862-1934	Composer	300	400	770		Br.Orchestral, Concerti, Songs.AMusQS $4000
Dell, Gabriel		Entertainment	15	20	25	35	
Dell, Myrna		Entertainment	5	6	10	10	Pin-Up SP $15
Della Casa, Lisa		Entertainment	10			25	Swiss Soprano. Opera
Della Chiesa, Vivian		Entertainment	5	6	15	15	Soprano
Della Joio, Norman		Composer	35	115	240	55	Pulitzer, AMusQS $50-$175
Dellums, Ronald B.	1935	Senate/Congress	10	15		20	Afro-Am. Congressman CA
Delna, Marie		Entertainment	25			90	Fr. Contralto. Opera

NAME	DATE	CATEGORY	SIG	LS/DS	ALS	SP	COMMENTS
Delon, Alain	1935-	Entertainment	15			35	Fr. Actor, Prod.,Dir.Leading Man Internat'l Films
DeLong, Phillip C.		Aviation	12	25	40	30	ACE, WW II
Delpy, Julie	1969-	Entertainment	20			55	Fr.Actress.Unbearable Lightness of Being. Pin-Up $60
DeLuise, Dom	1933-	Entertainment	5		15	20	Comedian
DeMarco, Antonio		Entertainment	10	25			Producer
DeMarco, Tony		Entertainment		25			Dancer
Demarest, William	1892-1983	Entertainment	14		25	37	Vaudeville Star Turned Character Actor
DeMille, Agnes		Entertainment	55	200		170	Dancer,Innovative Choreographer
DeMille, Cecil B.	1881-1959	Entertainment	100	203	422	265	Director, Producer, Film Giant
DeMille, Katherine		Entertainment	10	12	15	25	
DeMille, William C.		Entertainment	15	45		50	Early Dir.,Playwright,Producer
DeMonvel, Boutes		Artist	25	70	125		
Dempsey, John		Governor	12				Gov. CT
Dempsey, Patrick		Entertainment	10			15	
Dempsey, Stephen W.		Congress	4	25			Repr. NY
Demslow, W.W.*		Cartoonist	50			175	Illustrator Of Wizard Of Oz
Demzn, Lev		Cosmonaut	20	30			
Denby, Edwin	1870-1929	Cabinet	20	50	75	50	Harding Sec'y Navy. Teapot Dome Scadal
Dench, Judi		Entertainment	14			62	Marvelous Br. Actress as Victoria-Elizabeth AA
Deneuve, Catherine	1943-	Entertainment	22	15	35	56	Major Fr. Star. Pin-Up SP $40, 4x6 SP $75
Denfeld, Louis E.		Military	10	25	40	25	Adm.Chief Naval Operations WWII
DeNiro, Robert		Entertainment	11	102	45	89	Serious Actor Film & Stage. Oscar Winner
Denis, Maurice	1870-1943	Artist	95		325		Fr. Religious Painter. Art Theoretician
Denison, Charles S.		Senate	5	10	15		Senator IL
Denison, John H.		Clergy	10	15	25		
Denman, G. Tony		Aviation	15	22	5	30	ACE, WW II, Navy Ace
Denman, Thomas, 3rd Baron		Head of State	10	15	35		Gov. General Australia
Dennehy, Brian		Entertainment	10	28		20	Mature Leading Man-Character Actor Movies/TV
Denning, Richard		Entertainment	5	8	15	15	Handsome Film Leading Man. 40's early 50's
Dennis, Sandy	1937-92	Entertainment	45	45		115	Oscar Winning Actress
Dennison, Jo Carroll		Entertainment	5	6	10	10	Actress
Dennison, William		Cabinet	145		600		Lincoln P.M. Gen. CW Gov. OH
Denos, John		Entertainment	7	10	30	15	TV actor The Young and the Restless
Dent, Elliott		Aviation	12	25	35	30	ACE, WW II
Dent, Frederick T.	1820-92	Civil War	35	68	185		Union Gen.
Dent, S. Hubert		Senate/Congress	5	15		15	MOC AL
Denton, Jeremiah A., Jr.		Military-Congress	15	25	30	25	Admiral WW II, MOC AL
Denver, Bob		Entertainment	10			20	Actor. Gilligan's Island
Denver, James W.	1817-92	Civil War	110	225	700		Denver, Colo... Union Gen.,Lawyer, Gov. KS Terr.
Denver, John	1943-97	Country Music	48	15		142	Singer-Composer. Died in Air Crash 1997
Denza, Luigi	1846-1922	Composer					AMusQS $50-$110
Depardieu, Gerard		Entertainment	10			35	
Depew, Chauncey M.	1834-1928	Financier	100	325	975	475	Orator,NY Centr. RR, U.S. Sen.NY.
Depp, Johnny		Entertainment	11			46	Actor. Chooses Off-Beat Roles
Derain, Andre'	1880-1954	Artist	125	210	342		Postimpression Repro Femme Nu Assise S $285

NAME	DATE	CATEGORY	SIG	LS/DS	ALS	SP	COMMENTS
Derby, Edw. Henry Stanley	1826-93	Statesman	20		50		15th Earl of Derby. Sec'y of the Colonies
Derby, Edward Stanley	1799-1869	Head of State	50	60	102		14th Earl. Br. Prime Minister
Derby, 16th Earl (Fred Stanley)		Head of State	20		45		
Derek & Dominoes (all)		Entertainment	50			150	
Derek, Bo		Entertainment	16	20	25	41	Pin-Up SP $50-60-75
Derek, John & Bo Derek		Entertainment	20			45	Husband & Wife
Derek, John	19xx-98	Entertainment	15	28	35	60	Actor-Photographer. A Truly Beautiful Man.
Deringer, Henry	1786-1868	Arms Mfg.	700		6500		Invented Derringer Pistol
Derleth, August		Author	20	75			
Dern, Bruce		Entertainment	6	8	15	18	Sometimes Good-Guy. Sometimes Bad
Dern, George H.		Cabinet	10	20	35		Sec'y War, Mining Exec.,Gov. UT
Dern, Laura		Entertainment	8	10	25	32	Actress Daughter of Bruce Dern. Pin-Up $55
Derr, Richard		Entertainment	10			25	Actor
Dershowitz, Alan M.		Law	15	20		30	Trial Attorney, Author. Controversial
Desai, M.R.		Head of State	5	15	25		Prime Minister India
Desanto, Sugar Pie		Entertainment	15			35	James Brown Vocalist
Descartes, Rene		Philosopher	950	4035	10000		Mathematician.Analytic Geometry
Deschanel, Paul EugŠne L.	1856-1922	Head of State			100		Pres. France 1920. Resigned
Descher, Sandy		Entertainment				30	Child Actress
DeSilva, Howard		Entertainment	10	12	20	25	
Desmond, Johnny		Entertainment	3	5		8	Singer
Desmond, Shaw	1877-1960	Author	25	75			Irish Playwright. Pioneered Paranormal
Desmond, William		Entertainment	40				Vintage Film Actor
Despretz, C,sar		Science	5		30		Fr. Physician. Inventor Electric Arc Furnace
Dessalines, Jean-Jacques	1750-1806	Revolutionary		2500			Haitian Ruler
Destinn, Emmy	1878-1930	Entertainment	110		225	325	Czech Dramatic Soprano
Detaille, Edwouard	1848-1912	Artist	110		325		Fr. Military & Portr. Painter
DeTreville, Yvonne		Entertainment	20			85	Opera, Light Opera
Deutekom, Cristina		Entertainment	10			35	Dutch Coloratura Soprano. Opera
Deutsch, Emery		Bandleader	5				
Deutsch, Patti		Entertainment	3	3	6	8	
DeVane, William		Entertainment	8	5	10	15	
Devens, Charles, Jr.	1820-91	Military -Cabinet	35	50	122	150	Union Gen.-Att'y Gen.
Devereux, James P.S.		Military	35	70	90	150	Gen. WW II, Congress MD
Devers, Jacob L.		Military	10	20	35	35	General WW II
Devine, Andy	1905-77	Entertainment	40	35	50	113	Comic Sidekick of Roy Rogers etc. Vintage SP $95
DeVito, Danny		Entertainment	7	24	20	32	As The Penguin $75. Get Shorty Script S $50
Devo		Entertainment	30			60	
DeVos, Rich		Business	18			25	Founder Amway
DeVries, William, Dr.		Science	15	25	40	20	
Dew, William, Bishop		Clergy	20	30	45		
Dewar, James		Science	85		375		Prof. Chemistry R.I., London. Liquified Air
Dewey, George	1837-1917	Military	78	190	200	300	Captured Manila. Span.-Am. War. Admiral
Dewey, John		Author	60	155	250	75	Philosopher, Educator, Psychol.
Dewey, Orville		Clergy	15	20	25		

NAME	DATE	CATEGORY	SIG	LS/DS	ALS	SP	COMMENTS
Dewey, Thomas E.	1902-1971	Governor	40	79	165	95	Twice Presidential Candidate,Gov.NY
Dewhurst, Colleen		Entertainment	10		35	40	
DeWitt, Joyce		Entertainment	5	8	15	25	
DeWolf, H.G.		Military	5	15		20	Canadian Adm. WW II
DeWolfe, Billy	1907-74	Entertainment	25	40	45	45	Actor. Prissy Stage-Film Comic
Dexter, Al		Country Western	12			45	Western Singing Star of 40's.Piston Packin' Mama
Dexter, J.M.		Clergy	10	15	20		
Dexter, Timothy	1747-1806	Colonial-Rev.		175	275		Egocentric, Eccentric Merchant.Called Himself Lord
Dey, Susan		Entertainment	7	10	20	30	Actress. Pin-Up $45
DeYoung, Russell		Business	5			10	CEO Goodyear Tire & Rubber Co.
Di Stefano, Giuseppe	1921-	Entertainment	30		65	75	It. TenorOpera
Diaghilev, Sergei	1872-1929	Entertainment	435	975	2250		Russian Ballet Impresario. Developed Ballet Russes
Diamond, David		Composer	25		35		AMusQS $200
Diamond, Neil		Entertainment	12		40	55	Composer-Singer. Difficult to Obtain
Diamond, Selma		Entertainment	30	40	55	75	
Diana, Princess (Eng)	1961-97	Royalty	2000			6832	Princess of Wales. 'Time' SP $6950
Diaz, Armando Vittorio		Military	35	100	175	120	It. General WW I
Diaz, Cameron	1973-	Entertainment	20			68	Actress.There's Something About Mary
Diaz, Porfirio	1830-1915	Head of State	100	259	250	225	Dictatorial Pres.Mex. Fought Against Fr.Occupation
Dibrell, George Gibbs (WD)		Civil War	290				CSA General
Dibrell, George Gibbs	1822-88	Civil War	155	365	317		CSA General, MOC TN
DiCaprio, Leonardo		Entertainment	12			69	Actor.Titanic. Current Heart Throb.(Not Signing)
DiCaprio, Leonardo		Entertainment	20			75	Actor. Titanic
Dick, Fred		Aviation	10	22	40	30	ACE, WW II
Dick, Samuel	1740-1812	Rev. War	50	175	225		Continental Congress NJ. Col. 1st Battalion
Dickens, Charles	1812-70	Author	596	804	2336	3340	Br. Novelist.Christmas Carol, O...Twist
Dickens, Jimmy		Country Music	5			10	
Dickenson, Don M.		Cabinet	15	20	45	20	P.M. General 1888
Dickerson, Mahlon	1770-1853	Cabinet-U.S. Sen.	25	85	150		Jackson Sec'y Navy. Gov. NJ
Dickerson, Nancy		Journalist	3			12	Broadcast News Pioneer
Dickey, James	1923-	Author	15	75	135	55	Am. Poet, Novelist Deliverance. Deceased
Dickinson, Angie		Entertainment	6	14	18	25	Pin-Up SP $40
Dickinson, Anna Eliz.	1842-1932	Author	25	70	142		Abolitionist-Lecturer
Dickinson, Clarence		Entertainment	15			95	Legendary Organist
Dickinson, Clement C.		Senate/Congress	5			15	MOC MO
Dickinson, Daniel S.		Senate/Congress	15	25			Senator from NY
Dickinson, Don M.		Cabinet	10	20			P.M. Gen. 1888
Dickinson, Emily		Author	615	2560	6275		
Dickinson, Jacob M.	1851-1928	Cabinet	25	45	125		Taft Sec'y of War
Dickinson, James S.		Civil War	25	40	75		CSA Congressman
Dickinson, John P.		Rev. War	200	575			Continental Congress. Statesman, Administrator
Dickison, J. J.		Civil War	75	155	195		CSA Cav'ry Off.,Florida's Mosby
Dickman, Joseph		Military	50				General WW I
Dicks, Jacob		Governor	15	25	40		Governor NY
Diddley, Bo	1928-	Entertainment	20			85	R & B Singer-Composer-Guitarist. Rock HOF

NAME	DATE	CATEGORY	SIG	LS/DS	ALS	SP	COMMENTS
Didier-Pouget, W.		Artist	30	65	95		
Diefenbaker, John	1895-1979	Head of State	35	35	110	45	Prime Minister Canada
Diem, Ngo Dinh		Head of State	50				Pres. So. Viet Nam
Diemer, Louis		Composer	25			45	Fr. Pianist. AMusQS $100
Diemer, Walter E.		Business	20		75	90	Inventor Dubble Bubble Gum
Dies, Martin		Senate/Congress	15	50		25	MOC TX. Un-American Activities
Diesel, Rudolf		Science	900		3250		Ger. Mech. Engineer. Diesel Eng
Diesenhofer, Johann, Dr.		Science	20	25		40	Nobel Chemistry
Dieterle, William		Entertainment	30			75	Film Dirctor
Dietrich, Dena		Entertainment	5			10	Mother Nature (Commercial)
Dietrich, Marlene	1901-92	Entertainment	45	98	238	140	Bull Vint. Portrait S $595, TLS/cont $250. SPc $60
Dilke, Charles W. 2d Baronet		Author	10	25	45		Br. Travel Books, Politician
Dillards		Entertainment	25			65	Herb, Dean, Rodney, Merle
Diller, Phyllis		Entertainment	6	9	15	20	Comedienne. Housewife Turned Funny-Girl
Dillinger, John		Criminal					DS - Typed Confession Signed $14,000. RARE
Dillman, Bradford		Entertainment	8	9	15	15	
Dillon, C. Douglas		Cabinet	10	25	30	25	Ambassador, Diplomat
Dillon, Kevin		Entertainment	4			20	
Dillon, Matt		Entertainment	10	15		40	Actor
Dillon, R. Crawford		Clergy	15	45	60		
Dillon, Sidney		Business	500	1850	1950		RR Baron-Union Pacific RR. Jay Gould Aide
Dimitrova, Ghena		Entertainment	10			35	Opera
Dinesen, Isak (Karen Blixen)	1885-1962	Author	100	500		500	Danish. Out of Africa
Dingley, Nelson, Jr.		Congress	10	20	35		Governor, Repr. ME
Dinkins, David	1927-	Political	15			20	1st Afr.Am. Mayor NYC
Dinning Sisters (3)		Entertainment	10			15	Jean, Jayne, Ginger
Dion, Celine		Entertainment	6			45	Singer. Grammy Winner
Dior, Christian		Fashion	110	400		225	Fashion Designer
Dippel, Andreas		Entertainment	35			125	Ger. Tenor. Impresario. Opera
Dire Straits		Entertainment	30			75	
Dirks, Rudolph*	1877-1968	Cartoonist	70		175	400	Katzenjammer Kids
Dirksen, Everett M.	1896-1967	Senate	20	58		50	Senator, MOC IL. Powerful Political Figure
Disney, Roy E.		Business	20	55		30	Brother of Walt. Disney Exec.
Disney, Walt*	1901-1966	Cartoonist	1380	3158		12500	Signed Artist Sketch $4750. Orig.Sketch S $12,000
Disney, Walter 'Walt' Elias		Business	1674	3062	3650	4310	Animated Film Producer
Disraeli, Benjamin,	1804-81	Head of State	160	350	1112		Prime Minister, Novelist, Lord Beaconsfield
Disraeli, Isaac	1766-1848	Author	30	132	165		Br. Man of Letters. Novels
Ditmars, Raymond L.	1876-1942	Science	72				Herpetologist, Zoo Curator, Author
Divine		Entertainment	35			75	Rock. Short-lived Popularity
Divine, M.J., 'Father'(Geo. Baker)		Clergy	150	483	700	225	Communal Religious Soc.,Rejected Matrimony.....
Dix, Dorothea L.	1794-1887	Civil War	115	250	472		Union Superintendent of Nurses. Social Reformer
Dix, Dorothy (Eliz. Gilmer)		Author	15	30	45	25	Am. Journalist, Editor, Advice
Dix, John Adams (WD)		Civil War	115		370		Union Gen.
Dix, John Adams	1798-1879	Civil War-Cabinet	65	182	160	500	Union Gen., Sec'y Treasury
Dix, Morgan		Clergy	25	35	50		Abolitionist

NAME	DATE	CATEGORY	SIG	LS/DS	ALS	SP	COMMENTS
Dix, Richard		Entertainment	25	40	65	68	Vintage Movie Star
Dix, Robert		Entertainment				25	
Dixey, Henry E.	1859-1943	Entertainment	10	20	30	25	1st Success as Adonis
Dixie Chicks		Entertainment	20			95	Hot Country Newcomers
Dixon, Dean		Entertainment	35			175	Conductor. 1st Afro-Am. To Conduct NY Philharmonic
Dixon, Donna		Entertainment	8	10	15	20	Actress. Pin-Up $40
Dixon, Jeane		Celebrity	10			15	Forecasts the Future
Dixon, Julian C.		Senate/Congress	10	15		15	Afro-Am Dem. MOC CA
Dixon, Thomas	1864-1946	Author-Clergy	15	30	75		The Clansman.Social Critic
Dixon, Willie		Entertainment	50			100	Rock HOF. Late Blues Man
Dizengoff, Meir	1861-1936	Celebrity	50	162	350		Early Jewish Settler in Palestine. Founde Tel Aviv
Dmytryk, Edward	1908-	Entertainment	20			40	Film Director. Member Hollywood Ten
Doane, G.W.		Clergy		20	25	35	
Dobbin, James C.	1814-57	Cabinet	30	75	150		Pierce Sec'y Navy
Dobbin, John F.		Aviation	20	40	65	45	ACE, WW II, Marine Ace
Dobehoff, F.L.		Aviation	15	150		75	
Dobie, Charles Cald.		Author	5	10	15	5	
Dobie, J. Frank		Author	20	50	130	75	Folklorist & Western Author
Dobrinyin, Anatole		Head of State	40	130	375	75	U.S.S.R. Political Power
Dobson, Kevin		Entertainment	5	6	15	15	
Dockery, Thomas P.	1833-98	Civil War	95		300		CSA General
Dockery, Thomas P.(WD)		Civil War	275	350			CSA Gen.
Docking, Robert		Governor	5	15	22		Governor KS
Dockstader, Lew		Entertainment	75				
Doctorow, E. L.		Author	15	35	90	30	Am. Novelist. Ragtime
Doda, Carol		Entertainment	6			25	Actress. Pin-Up $40
Dodd, Christopher J.		Senate/Congress	5	15		10	Senator, MOC CT
Dodd, Thomas J.		Senate & Congress	20	40	65	30	Chief of Counsel at Nuremberg
Dodd, William E.		Historian	15	60	75	25	Ambassador to Nazi Germany
Dodderidge, Philip		Clergy	25	35	45		
Dodge, Charles C.	1841-1910	Civil War	40				Union Gen.
Dodge, Grenville M.(WD)		Civil War	75	160	235		Union Gen.,Repr. IA.LS/Cont. $1950
Dodge, Grenville M.	1831-1916	Civil War	225	950	1275	375	Union Gen. Post-War RR Tycoon. Stk.Cert.S $1750
Dodge, Henry	1782-1867	Congress				45	Gov. Wisc.Terr.,1st Sen.,Indian Fighter
Dodge, Jerry		Entertainment	3	3	6	6	
Dodge, Joseph M.		Business	10	25	50		Banker, Built Jap. Economy
Dodge, Mary Abigail	1833-96	Author	12	20	25		Am. Novelist
Dodge, Mary Mapes	1831-1905	Author	25	40	90	50	Children's Books.'Hans Brinker & the Silver Skates
Dodge, William Earl	1805-83	Business	95	482	675		Phelps, Dodge & Co. YMCA Fndr.
Dodge, William G.		Civil War	25	55	85		
Dodgson, Chas. L.(Lewis Carroll)	1832-98	Author	250	725	1708		Alice in Wonderland
Dods, Marcus		Clergy	40	45	60		
Dodson, Jack		Entertainment	15		18	25	Actor. Andy Griffith Show SP $45
Doenitz, Karl	1891-1980	Military	85	388	350	175	Ger. Adm., WW II.TLS/Cont. $7500, FDC S $90
Doerflinger, Joseph		Aviation	10		75	45	

NAME	DATE	CATEGORY	SIG	LS/DS	ALS	SP	COMMENTS
Doering, Arnold		Aviation	10	20	35	25	
Dohanos, Stevan		Illustrator	5	15			
Doherty, Shannon		Entertainment	14			42	Actress.Pinup, SP $50
Dohnanyi, Erno von	1877-1960	Composer	55	135	165		Hung. Conductor. AMQS $350
Dohrn, Bernardine		Criminal					Terrorist. FBI Fingerprint Card S $150
Doi, Takao		Astronaut	15	25		25	
Doig, Andrew Wheeler		Senate/Congress	10	20			MOC NY 1839, Banker, Mining
Doisy, Edward A.		Science	20	45	170	35	Nobel Medicine. Vitamin K
Dolby, Ray		Science	20	35			Inventor Dolby Sound
Dolby, Thomas		Entertainment	20			40	
Dole, Charles F		Clergy	10	15	20		
Dole, Elizabeth		Cabinet	10	20	30	25	Sec'y Labor. Head Red Cross. Presidential Hopeful
Dole, James D.		Business	55	145	235	75	Fdr.Hawaiian Pineapple Industry
Dole, Robert		Senate	25			75	Senator KS. Majority Ldr. Presidential Candidate
Dole, Sanford B.	1844-1926	Business	50	420	390	110	Pres. Repub.HI.1st Pres.Dole Pineapple.Chk.S $325
Dolenz, Ami		Entertainment	6			30	Pin-Up $45
Dolenz, Mickey		Entertainment	10		25	35	'The Monkees'
Dolin, Anton		Entertainment	25	40	95	75	Ballet
Dollar, Robert	1844-1932	Business	20	55	130	50	Founder & Pres. Dollar Steamship Line.
Dolliver, Jonathan P.		Senate & Congress	20	35		25	Senator, MOC IA 1889
Dolukanova, Zara		Entertainment	75				Rare SPc of Great Contralto $250
Domenici, Pete		Senate	5			15	Senator NM
Domerque, Faith		Entertainment	12			40	Actress
Domingo, Placido		Entertainment	20		45	55	Opera, Concert
Dominguez, Oscar	1906-57	Artist	70		250		Sp. Surrealist Artist
Dominick, Fred H.		Senate & Congress	5	15		10	MOC SC 1917-33
Domino, Fats	1928-	Entertainment	17	20	35	45	R&B Singer-Pianist-Comp..Rock Hof. AMusQS $125
Donahue, Al		Entertainment	15			75	Big Band Leader
Donahue, Archie		Aviation	12	25	50	45	ACE, WW II, Ace in one day
Donahue, Elinor		Entertainment	5		15	18	Father Knows Best Actress. Pin-Up SP $20
Donahue, Phil		Entertainment	5			18	Popular TV Talk Show Host-Retired
Donahue, Troy		Entertainment	6	7	15	25	Actor. 60's Warner Bros. Star
Donaldson, Jesse M.		Cabinet	10	20	35	25	1st Postman Becomes P.M. Gen.
Donaldson, Sam		Journalist	10			20	TV News Anchor, Commentator
Donat, Peter	1928-	Entertainment	5		15	15	Canadian Character Actor
Donat, Robert	1905-1958	Entertainment	60	75	100	222	Br. From Shakespeare (30's)to AA 'Goodby Mr Chips'
Donat, Zdislawa		Entertainment	5			25	Opera
Donath, Ludwig	1900-67	Entertainment	5			25	Played Al Jolson's Father. WW II Anti Nazi Films
Doniphan, Alexander William		Military	120	250	475		Fought Mex., Indians, Mormans
Donizetti, Gaetano	1797-1848	Composer	500	800	1850		AMusQS $2,750,AMusMs $3,000. ALS/Cont. $4750
Donlan, Roger		Military	10	25	40	15	
Donlevy, Brian	1899-1972	Entertainment	20			100	Ir.With Pershing vs Pancho Villa.Pilot WW I.ACTOR
Donnell, Jeff	1921-	Entertainment	5		10	10	Columbia Pictures Teen-age Starlet. 2nd Leads
Donnelly, Ruth	1896-	Entertainment	10	15	25	25	Chorine-Stage-Films 1927 & Next 30 Years
Donner, Clive		Entertainment	5			25	Film Director

NAME	DATE	CATEGORY	SIG	LS/DS	ALS	SP	COMMENTS
Donner, Richard		Entertainment	10			20	
Donner, Vyvyan		Editor	5			15	Fashion
Donovan, Hedley		Editor	5		15	10	Time-Life Editor
Donovan, King	1919-87	Entertainment	15			25	Actor. Character- Supporting Roles
Donovan, Raymond J.		Cabinet	8	15	30	15	Sec'y Labor
Donovan, Wm. J. 'Wild Bill'	1883-1959	Military	80	225	325	100	Fighting 69th, OSS-CIA
Doobie Brothers		Entertainment	40			80	Signed by all
Doohan, James 'Scotty'		Entertainment	10		25	33	Star Trek Actor
Dooley, Paul		Entertainment	5		15	15	
Dooley, Thomas A., Dr.	1927-61	Science	125	185	400	125	Jungle Physician, SE Asia. Medical Mission
Doolittle, Hilda	1886-1961	Author	75	205	475		Imagist Poet. Ed. 'The Egoist' Rare
Doolittle, James H.	1896-1993	Aviation	78	165	275	112	Gen. WW II, Test Pilot. Bombed Tokyo. Hero/MOH
Doolittle, James Rood		Senate	15	25	40		Civil War Senator WI
Doolittle, Helen		Celebrity	10	15	40	20	
Doors & Jim Morrison (4)		Entertainment	2000			2750	Rock
Doors, The (3)		Entertainment	100	165		150	Rock Doors Alb. $125
Doran, Ann	1914-	Entertainment	15	15	25	20	Am. Character Actress. Supporting Roles
Dorati, Antal		Conductor	15	25		85	Hung.-born
Dore', Paul Gustave	1833-83	Artist	60	235	508		Fantastic Imagination. Illustrated over 90 Books
Dornan, Robert K.		Congress	4			20	MOC CA.
Dornberger, Walter R.	1895-1980	Science	40	100	120	75	Ger. Rocket Engineer. Bell Aircraft. FDC $225
Dorr, Julia C. R.	1825-1913	Author	4	5	15		Best Known for 10 Volumes of Poetry
Dorr, Thomas	1805-54	Reformer		4500			Politician. Formed Own Party. Led Dorr Rebellion
Dors, Diana	1931-84	Entertainment	20			151	British 'Blonde Bombshell' of 40s.
Dorsey, Jimmy	1905-56	Entertainment	50	150		250	Big Band Leader-Saxophone
Dorsey, Stephen	1842-1916	Business	35		125		RR Promoter. Senator AR. Fraudulent RR Scandal
Dorsey, Tommy	1905-56	Entertainment	75	150		250	Big Band Leader-Trombone
Dortch, William T.		Civil War	25	40	75		CSA Senator NC
Dos Passos, John	1896-1970	Author	20	50	75	30	Am. Novelist. Prolific Writer
Dostoevsky, Fyodor	1821-81	Author	1500	5700	13800		Rus. Novelist. 'Crime & Punishment'
Doty, James	1799-1865	Explorer	50		185		Politician, Land Speculator. C.W. Territorial Gov.
Doubleday, Abner	1819-93	Civil War	462	2200	1550		Union Gen.-Credit for Inventing Baseball
Doubleday, Frank Nelson	1862-1934	Business	65	185	375		Book Publisher
Doucette, John		Entertainment	6		115	20	Familiar Face & Voice. Excellent Supporting Actor
Doucette, Paul		Entertainment	6			25	Music. Drummer Matchbox 20
Dougherty, Dennis, Cardinal		Clergy	35	50	65	40	Card'l & Archbishop of Philadelphia
Douglas, Beverly B.		Civil War	35	50	65		CSA Officer, MOC VA
Douglas, Chas. W.H.	1850-1914	Military	25	70	195		Br. Gen.
Douglas, Donald W. Jr.		Business	25	60		45	Douglas Aircraft
Douglas, Donald W. Sr.	1892-1981	Aviation	150	257	450	360	Pioneer Aircraft Mfg. FDC S by Sr. & Jr. $250
Douglas, Donna	1933-	Entertainment	7	8	10	20	Actress. Ellie Mae in TVs 'Beverly Hillbillies'
Douglas, Eric		Entertainment	9			18	Son of Kirk Douglas
Douglas, Helen Gahagan	1900-80	Congress-E'tainmt	30	55	98	55	MOC CA, Opera, Actress
Douglas, Kirk	1916-	Entertainment	18	38	20	47	Versatile Actor. Lifetime Achievement Award
Douglas, Leon		Country Music	10			20	

NAME	DATE	CATEGORY	SIG	LS/DS	ALS	SP	COMMENTS
Douglas, Lloyd C.	1877-1951	Author	25	45	75	30	Retired Minister. The Robe, Magnificent Obsession
Douglas, Melvyn	1901-81	Entertainment	20	23	30	49	Oscar Winning Film Actor. Tony Award for Stage
Douglas, Michael		Entertainment	20		25	43	Talented Actor-Producer-Dir. Son of Kirk
Douglas, Mike		Entertainment	5	6	10	16	Singer. Early TV Host
Douglas, Paul	1907-59	Entertainment	10	15		35	Pro-Football, Sportscaster, News. '48 'Born Yesterday
Douglas, Paul H.		Senate	10	20		15	Senator IL
Douglas, Paul P.		Aviation	15	25	45	35	ACE, WW II
Douglas, Robert	1909-	Entertainment	10			25	Br. Actor. Leads & Supporting Parts
Douglas, Stephen A.	1813-61	Senate	150	295	625	270	Statesman, Pres. Candidate. Debated vs Lincoln
Douglas, W. Sholto	1893-1969	Military	45			75	Br. Air Marshall. D-Day Coastal Operations
Douglas, William O. (SC)	1898-1980	Supreme Court	70	165		200	Longest Tenure to Date.
Douglas, William Taylor		Clergy	15	20	25		
Douglass, Frederick	1817-95	Abolitionist	283	825	3942	6325	Afro-Am. Author, Lecturer, Editor, Abolitionist
Douglass, Robyn		Entertainment	5			12	Pin-Up $32
Doulton, Henry, Sir	1820-97	Potter-Inventor	25	35	145		Royal Doulton China & Appliances. Art Pottery
Doumer, Paul	1857-1932	Head of State	60		100		Pres. France 1931-32. Assassinated
Doumergue, Gaston	1863-1937	Head of State			195		Pres. France., P.M. France
Dove, Billie		Entertainment	10	15	30	35	30's Movie Star. Vintage SP $55
Dow, Neal	1804-97	Civil War	40	75	375		Union Gen., Temperance Reformer
Dow, Tony		Entertainment	5	6	10	15	Actor. As 'Wally Cleaver' SP $20
Dowden, Edward	1843-1913	Author	10	15	25		Ir. Critic, Editor, Professor, Author
Dowding, Hugh C., Lord	1882-1970	Military	95		535		Br. Air Chief Marshal, Architect 'Battle of Brit'.
Dowling, Eddie	1895-1975	Entertainment	20	25	55	45	Major Broadway Star. 'Harvey'. Tony Winner
Down, Lesley-Anne	1954-	Entertainment	9		15	22	Actress. Leading Lady of Br.-Am. Films. Pin-Up $45
Downey, Morton	1901-85	Entertainment	20	20	20	32	Irish Tenor-Bandleader
Downey, Robert, Jr.	1965-	Entertainment	25			60	Contemporary Actor Plagued by Drug Problems
Downey, Roma		Entertainment	16			50	Actress. Touched By An Angel
Downey, Sheridan	1884-1951	Senate	10	35		20	Dem. Senator CA 1938-50
Downing, Big Al		Entertainment	4			12	
Downing, George, Sir	1623-84	Statesman	650	775			2nd Harvard Grad. Developed Downing St., So Named
Downliners Sect		Entertainment				75	Br. Rock Group (All 5)
Downs, Hugh	1921-	Entertainment	10	20	25	22	TV Co-Host 20/20. Perennial Host
Downs, Johnny	1913-95	Entertainment	35			75	Actor Our Gang. Broadway, Vaudeville, Films
Doyle, Arthur Conan, Sir	1859-1930	Author-Physician	600	975	1844	1765	Br. Novelist. Created Sherlock Holmes
Doyle, Dinty		Journalist	5	20			Columnist
Dozier, James		Military	12	30	45	20	
Dozier, Lamont		Entertainment	6			25	Singer/Songwriter
Dr. Seuss*		Cartoonist	59			348	'Cat In The Hat' etc.
Drabble, Margaret		Author	10	20	50		Br. Novelist, Editor
Dragonette, Jessica	1910-80	Entertainment	15	20	25	50	Soprano. Radio, Stage Star 30s-40s
Dragoni, Maria		Entertainment	10			30	Opera
Drake, Alfred	1914-92	Entertainment	17			32	Singer-Actor. Musical Theatre, Concert
Drake, Betsy	1923-	Entertainment	5			15	Actress & Mrs. Cary Grant (Once upon a Time)
Drake, Frances	1906-97	Entertainment	9	10	15	30	Am. Leading Lady of the 30s
Drake, Francis M.		Governor	10	25			Gov. IA. RR Builder. Fndr. Drake Univ.

NAME	DATE	CATEGORY	SIG	LS/DS	ALS	SP	COMMENTS
Drake, Michele		Entertainment	4			15	Pin-Up SP $20
Drake, Samuel Adams		Civil War	45		75		Union General, Author
Drake, Stan*		Cartoonist	20			100	'Blondie'
Drake, Tom	1918-92	Entertainment	5			10	Actor. The Boy Next Door in Many 40's Films
Draper, Eben S.		Governor	5	12			Governor MA
Draper, Rusty		Country Music	5			15	Singer
Draper, Ruth	1884-1956	Entertainment	10	45	75	50	Am. Monologuist
Draper, William F.		Civil War	25	50			General
Draper, William H.		Clergy	20	35	40		
Drayton, Thomas F.	1808-91	Civil War	65		245		CSA Gen..Sig./Rank $175. RR Stock S $295
Drayton, Gracie*		Cartoonist	20			188	Created Campbell Soup Kids
Drees, Willem		Head of State	20	35	100		Survivor Buchenwald
Dreiser, Theodore	1871-1945	Author	70	200	300	300	'American Tragedy','Sister Carrie'.Magazine Editor
Drescher, Fran		Entertainment	15			57	Actress. 'The Nanny'-TV
Dresser, Louise	1878-1965	Entertainment	30			55	Broadway Musicals. Major Silent & Sound Film Star.
Dressler, Marie	1869-34	Entertainment	130			305	Vintage Actress. 1930 Academy Award Min & Bill.
Drew, Daniel	1797-1879	Business	950	6800			Great Bear of Wall Street Fisk-Jay Gould
Drew, Ellen		Entertainment	6	8	13	15	Actress. 40's—. Pin-Up $32
Drew, John	1853-1927	Entertainment	60	75	185	100	Turn of the Century Stage Star
Drexel, Anthony J.	1826-93	Banker		110			Fndr. Drexel, Morgan & Co. Stock Cert. S $975
Drexel, J. A.		Aviation	40	60	100	65	
Drexel, Joseph W.		Business					Drexel & Co. Phil.,Established 1838. Stock S $1750
Dreyfus, Alfred	1859-1935	Military	145	300	818	1955	Framed for Treason, Sent to Devil's Isle.
Dreyfus, Julia Louis-		Entertainment	17	45		48	Actress, Seinfeld. Emmy Awards
Dreyfuss, Henry		Business		14	20		Self Sketch Henry $25
Dreyfuss, Richard		Entertainment	16		25	45	Talented, Versatile Actor. AA Winner
Dribrell, George G.		Civil War	95	250	300		
Drinan, Robert, Father		Senate/Congress	5			15	Catholic Activist Priest
Drinkwater, John	1882-1937	Author	20	50	125	30	Poet, Playwright. Fndr., Mgr.'Pilgrim Players' '07
Driscoll, Bobby	1937-1968	Entertainment	145			373	AA '49. Best Child Actor.Died. Poverty-Drug Addict
Driver, Minnie		Entertainment	20			55	Actress. 'Good Will Hunting'. Pin-Up $70
Driver, Samuel Rolles		Clergy	85	100	125		
Drouet, Robert		Entertainment	25	30	60	68	
Dru, Joanne	1923-	Entertainment	8			30	Actress. Screen, TV, Stage. Deceased
Druckman, Jacob		Composer	20	50	95		Pulitzer, AMusQS $250
Drum, Hugh A. Lt.Gen		Military	25	55	125	50	General WW I, WW II
Drum, Richard C.	1825-1909	Civil War	30	55	90		Union General Sig/Rank $55, War Dte. DS $100
Drummond, Henry	1851-97	Clergy	50	60	80		Scottish Evangelical Writer-Lecturer.
Drummond, James		Clergy	25	35	50		
Drury, Allen	1919-98	Author	10	30	65	35	Novelist. Best Seller Advise & Consent S $50
Drury, Frank		Aviation	10	25	40	30	ACE, WW II, Marine Ace
Drury, James		Entertainment	10			26	Actor. The Virginian SP $25
Dryer, Fred		Entertainment	10		25	25	Actor TV Series 'Hunter'. Pro Football
Du Barry, Jeanne, Comtesse	1743-93	Royal Mistress	285	960	1200		Louis XV Mistress. Banished, Arrested, Guillotined
Du Chaillu, Paul B.	1831-1903	Explorer	35	80	110	75	Brought 1st Gorillas out of Afr.

NAME	DATE	CATEGORY	SIG	LS/DS	ALS	SP	COMMENTS
Du Maurier, Daphne, Dame		Author	45	140	150	65	Br. Novelist. 'Rebecca'
Du Maurier, George	1834-96	Author	15	45	152		Artist, Novelist. Illustrator of 'Punch'
Du Maurier, Gerald, Sir	1873-1934	Entertainment	20	50		35	Actor-Manager
Du Pont, Alfred I.		Business	20				Banking
Du Pont, Elizabeth H		Business	20	75	110	35	
Du Pont, Henry A.	1838-1926	Civ. War-Business	98	357	750		CW, MOH. RR Pres.
Du Pont, Lammot		Business	20			50	CEO Du Pont Chemical
Du Pont, Pierre S.		Governor	15	35		50	Governor DE, Du Pont Chemical
Du Pont, Pierre-Samuel	1739-1817l	Economist	500	1500	2700		Progenitor of Du Pont Lineage
Du Pont, R.		Aviation	40	110			Am Aviation Exec.
Du Pont, Samuel Francis(WD)		Civil War	150	445	650		1803-1865, Union Adm.
Du Vigneaud, Vincent	1901-78	Science	25	55	150	45	Nobel 1955. Synthesized Penicillin
Duane, James	1733-1797	Rev. War	110	290	750		1st Continental Congress. NY Att'y Gen.
Dubcek, Alexander		Head of State	80	130			Czech. Reformer
DuBois, W. E. B.	1868-1963	Author	300	675		450	Black Rights, Educator-Writer
Dubose, Dudley	1843-83	Civil War	138				CSA Gen., MOC GA. Sig/Rank $325
DuBridge, Lee, Dr.		Science	30	100	145	50	Pres. Cal-Tech
Dubuffet, Jean	1931-85	Artist	150	400	831		Swiss proponent of raw art
Dubuque, Julien	1762-1810	Am. Pioneer	600	2500			Am. Pioneer. 1st White Settler Near Dubuque
Duchamp, Marcel	1887-1968	Artist	125	350	775	1365	Fr. Avante Garde Artist
Duchin, Eddie		Entertainment	25	40		100	Big Band Leader, Pianist Father of Peter
Duchin, Peter		Entertainment	8		15	20	Pianist, Band Leader
Duchovny, David		Entertainment	24			60	X Files With G. Anderson
Duckworth, John T., Sir	1748-1817	Military	55	180			Br. Admiral, Gov. Newfoundland
Ducos, Jean Francois		Fr. Revolution	35	100	205		
Dudayev, Dzhokhar		Head of State	15			45	Pres.. Chechen Republic
Dudenhoeffer, Matt		Entertainment	6			25	Music. Guitars Gravity Kills
Dudicoff, Michael J.		Entertainment	8	15		20	Actor. Martial Arts SP $25
Dudley, Dave	1928-	Country Music	6			15	Singer
Dudley, Joseph	1647-1720	Colonial America	450	895	1500		Col.Gov.MA. Philosopher,Scholar, Divine
Dudley, Paul	1675-1751	Colonial America	115	310			Jurist. Religious Activist
Dudley, Thomas V., Bishop		Clergy	35	50	45	50	
Duer, William	1747-99	Rev. War					War Dte/Cont. $1500
Duesenberg, Frederick S.	1877-1932	Business	550	1350			Champ. Bicyclist. Patented Duesenberg Motor etc.
Duff, Arthur, Sir		Military	15	45	70		Br. Admiral
Duff, Howard	1917-90	Entertainment	14		25	35	Actor. Film & Radio Star.
Duff, James H.		Senate	5	15		10	Governor, Senator PA
Duffer, Candy		Entertainment	20			45	Rock
Duffie, Alfred Napoleon A.	1835-80	Civil War	35	75	90		Union Gen. War Dte. DS $235
Duffy, Brian		Astronaut	5			18	
Duffy, Francis P.		Clergy	15	20	25		
Duffy, Julia		Entertainment	7	10		20	Actress. Bob Newhart Show Co-Star
Duffy, Patrick		Entertainment	6			25	Actor. 'Bobby Ewing' on Dallas SP $30
Dufranne, Hector		Entertainment	20				Opera. Fr. Baritone
Dufy, Raoul	1877-1953	Artist	275	450	776		Fr. Impressionist, Fauvism

NAME	DATE	CATEGORY	SIG	LS/DS	ALS	SP	COMMENTS
Duggan, Andrew	1923-88	Entertainment	15			25	Character Actor. Tall, Stalwart Types
Dukakis, Kitty		Author	4			15	
Dukakis, Michael S.		Governor	10			20	Governor MA. Presidential Cand.
Dukakis, Olympia	1931-	Entertainment	15	25	35	30	Actress. Stage-Films. Character Leads
Dukas, Paul	1865-1935	Composer	55	160	355		French
Duke, Basil Wilson	1838-1916	Civil War	95	175	575		CSA Gen. War Dte ALS/Cont. $3900
Duke, Charles M., Jr.		Astronaut	20	200	125	112	Moonwalker. SP of Earth $50
Duke, Clarence		Celebrity	4	10	25	10	Sports Announcer
Duke, David		Activist	40			95	Ex KKK Grand Wizard. Politically Active
Duke, Patty	1946-	Entertainment	14	20	30	28	Child to Mature Actress. AAMiracle Worker SP $35
Duke, Vernon	1903-69	Composer	20	50	145		AMusQS $175-$400
Dulbecco, Renato		Science	20	35	60		Nobel Physiology-Medicine
Dullea, Keir		Entertainment	8	12	15	20	Actor. Films-Stage. 2001 SP $40
Dulles, Allen W.	1893-1969	Diplomat	30	165	225	75	State Dept., OSS, CIA. Author
Dulles, John Foster	1888-1959	Cabinet	35	188	165	75	Sec'y State, Diplomat, UN
Dumas, Alexandre (Fils)	1824-95	Author	55	110	195	425	Fr. Dramatist, Novelist
Dumas, Alexandre (Pere)	1802-70	Author	110	225	499	825	Fr. Novelist-Playwright. 'Count of Monte Cristo'
Dumbrille, Douglass	1890-1974	Entertainment	40			75	Character Actor. Smooth, Suave Villain
Dummar, Melvin E.		Celebrity	20	30	45		Fraudulent H. Hughes Heir
Duna, Steffi	1913-	Entertainment	10		15	25	Dancer-Actress. Few Dramatic Roles in 30s
Dunagin, Ralph		Cartoonist	5			20	'The Middletons'
Dunaway, Faye	1941-	Entertainment	8	12	20	25	Actress. Leading Lady. Pin-Up $45
Dunbar, Bonnie J.		Astronaut	6			25	
Dunbar, Charles E., Sr.	1888-1959	Law	10	25			Chm. US War Trade Board 1914-18 WW I
Dunbar, Dixie	1915-91	Entertainment	12		20	40	Actress-Dancer.Vaudev'l & Star of 30's Musicals
Dunbar, Paul Lawrence	1872-1906	Author	750				Afro-Am. Poet, Novelist etc. Rare
Duncan, Charles T.		Celebrity	4	10	25	10	
Duncan, Isadora	1878-1927	Entertainment	400	688	1150	1018	Am. Interpretive Dancer. Eccentric Personality
Duncan, James	1811-49	Military	75				Mexican War Hero
Duncan, Johnny	1938-	Country Music	10			20	Guitar-Singer. 3 Years With Buddy Holly
Duncan, Lee (Rin Tin Tin)		Entertainment	100				Dog Trainer & Actor
Duncan, Sandy	1946-	Entertainment	5			20	Actress. TV-Stage-Peter Pan. Disney Voice SP $25
Duncan, Thomas		Civil War	20	50	80		Union General
Duncan, Todd		Entertainment	45	125		112	First Porgy. Rare
Dundas, Henry	1742-1811	Statesman	25	40	90		Br. Sec'y War.Pro War with Am. 1st Viscount
Dunham, Sonny		Entertainment	15			25	Bandleader, Trumpet
Dunlap, John	1747-1812	Rev. War	150	575			1st To Print Decl. of Independence & Daily News.
Dunlap, Robert P.	1794-1859	Congress	15				MOC ME, Gov. ME
Dunlop, John T.		Cabinet	5	10	15	15	Sec'y Labor
Dunn, Artie		Entertainment	10			20	Music. The Three Sons
Dunn, Emma	1875-1966	Entertainment	10			35	Br. Character Actress. Longtime Film 'Housekeeper'
Dunn, Holly		Country Music	10			25	Singer
Dunn, James	1905-67	Entertainment	60		100	125	Leading Man. AA For One Good Roll 'Tree Grows in..'
Dunn, William McKee		Civil War	25	40	70		Union Gen.(Judge, Adv. Gen.'75)
Dunne, Dominick		Author		30		35	Columnist

NAME	DATE	CATEGORY	SIG	LS/DS	ALS	SP	COMMENTS
Dunne, Irene	1901-90	Entertainment	18		30	44	Actress-Singer. Major Star. Vintage SP $70
Dunne, Phillip	1908-92	Author	15	20	35	35	Novelist, Director. Fndr. Screenwriters Guild
Dunne, Stephen		Entertainment				25	
Dunning, Debbie		Entertainment	5			15	Actress. Pin-up 67
Dunnock, Mildred	1904-91	Entertainment	10		35	35	Actress. Broadway & Films. AA Nom. 'Death of a ..'
Dunsany, Edw.J.Plunkett, Lord	1878-1957	Author	50		225	120	Traveller, Hunter, Playwright
Dunst, Kirsten		Entertainment	15			50	Actress
DuPonceau, Pierre		Military	25	60	140		
Duportail, Louis le Begue		Rev. War		750			Fr. Gen. in Continental Army
Dupre', Marcel		Composer	45			188	Celebrated Organist
Durais, C.		Artist	10	20	50		
Duran Duran		Entertainment	50			100	Rock Band (Entire Band)
Durand, Asher Brown	1796-1868	Artist	85	175	385		Hudson River School. Engraver, Painter
Durant, Ariel (Ida)	1898-1981	Author	25	50	115	35	Historian with Husband Will
Durant, Thomas C.	1820-85	Business	350	950	1350		Pioneer Builder & Financer of Railroads
Durant, William 'Will'		Author	30	35	135	45	Historian with Wife Aerial (Ida). Pulitzer
Durant, William Crapo	1861-1947	Business	250	850	1075		Durant Motor Car. GM, Chevrolet
Durante, Jimmy	1893-1980	Entertainment	40	83		73	Comedian.Burlesque,Radio,TV & Films.Schnozz
Durbin, Deanna		Entertainment	20			40	Child Singing Star. Retired Early. Vintage SP $45
Durenberger, David		Senate	5			15	Senator MN
Durer, Albrecht	1471-1578	Artist	3000	8200	21000		Foremost Ger.Renaissance Artist. NRPA
Durham, Bobby		Country Music	10			20	Singer
Durkin, Martin P.		Cabinet	10	25			Sec'y Labor, Eisenhower
Durning, Charles		Entertainment	5	15	15	22	Character Actor
Duroc, Geraud C.M.	1772-1813	Military	25	65	185		Napol. Grand Marshal-Diplomat
Durrell, Lawrence		Author	25	70	190	40	Br-Ir Poet,Playwright,Traveller
Duryea, Charles E.	1861-1938	Science-Business	362	625		2300	Built 1st Am.Gasoline Motor Car
Duryea, Dan	1907-68	Entertainment	15	15	30	45	Character Actor. Star in 40's-50's. Vintage SP $55
Duryee, Abram (WD)		Civil War		150	410		Union Gen. ANS '61 $310
Duryee, Abram	1815-90	Civil War	40		155		Union Gen. Raised Volunteer Reg.Duryee's Zoaves
Duse, Eleanora	1859-1924	Entertainment	200	400	795	833	Great Italian Stage Actress
Dussault, Nancy		Entertainment	5			10	Character Actress
Dussek, Jan L	1760-1812	Composer	35	90	145		Marie Antoinette Patron toThis Pianist-Composer
Dustinn, Emmy	1878-1930	Entertainment	30			170	Opera. Czech Soprano. 'Salome', 'Butterfly'
Dutra, Enrico Gaspar	1855-1974	Head of State	10	20	50	35	Pres. Brazil. General. Outlawed Communist
Duvalier, Francois	1907-71	Head of State	75	650		150	Papa Doc. Haitian President
Duvall, Gabriel (SC)	1752-1844	Supreme Court	60	272	360		
Duvall, Robert		Entertainment	10	15	25	35	AA Actor. Writer-Producer.Godfather SP $45
Duvall, Shelley		Entertainment	8		15	19	Actress. Pin-Up $38
Duve', Christian de, Dr.		Science	20	35		30	Nobel Medicine
Duyckinck, Evart A.		Editor	40		150		Literary World
Dvorak, Ann		Entertainment	10		30	35	Actress. Vintage Leading Lady of 30s
Dvorak, Antonin	1841-1904	Composer	475	895	3333		Czech. Symphonies.AMusQS $4160-$6500
Dwan, Allan	1885-1981	Entertainment	15			35	Veteran Am Director-Ex Writer
Dwight, Theodore	1764-1846	Journalist	35	50	150		Harvard Wits, Hartford Convention

NAME	DATE	CATEGORY	SIG	LS/DS	ALS	SP	COMMENTS
Dwight, Timothy	1752-1817	Author-Clergy	20	55			Pres, Yale. Equal Education of Women. Harvard Wits
Dyer, Edward	1543-1607	Author		1000			Br. Poet and Courtier
Dyer, Eliphlet	1721-1807	Rev. War	50	155	425		Continental Congress. Jurist
Dyer, George C.		Military	15	40	60		Admiral USN
Dyer, Leondidas Carstarphen		Senate/Congress	5			10	MOC MO 1915-1933
Dyer, Nehemiah	1839-1910	Military	25			75	Admiral
Dylan, Bob		Entertainment	175	407	400	625	Songwriter, Poet, Folksinger
Dymally, Mervyn M.		Congress	5			15	Afr-Am. Congressman CA
Dysart, Richard		Entertainment	5	15	20	20	Actor

E

NAME	DATE	CATEGORY	SIG	LS/DS	ALS	SP	COMMENTS
Eadie, Betty J.		Author	5			10	Non-Fiction
Eadie, John		Clergy	10	15	25		Scot. Theologian & Scholar
Eads, James Buchanan		Civil War	105	330	500		Engineer, Shipbuilder for Union
Eagleburger, Lawrence	1930-	Cabinet	15	25		35	Bush Sec'y of State.Dept. Career Diplomat
Eagles		Entertainment	100			225	Rock Alb. S/Frey,Henley,Walsh $185
Eagleston, Glenn		Aviation	20	42	70	45	ACE, WW II
Eagleton, Thomas F.		Senate	10	50		20	Senator MO
Eaker, Ira	1896-	Aviation	20	80	95	145	WW II Air Force Cmdr
Eakins, Thomas	1844-1916	Artist	375		3250		Am. Painter-Sculptor. Master Draftsmanship,Anatomy
Eames, Charles	1907-78	Art	75			250	Am. Architect-Designer. Best Known for Furniture
Eames-Story, Emma, Mme.	1865-1952	Entertainment	35			150	Opera. Am. Soprano
Earhart, Amelia	1898-1937	Aviation	518	1777		1560	TLS/Content $2,495. Her Book S $900-$1100
Earle, George H.		Governor	10	15			Governor PA
Earle, Merie	1889-1984	Entertainment	15			35	Character Actress into her 90's. The Walton's
Earle, Virginia		Entertainment	6		15	15	
Early, Jubal	1816-94	Civil War	495	675	1042		CSA General
Early, Jubal A. (WD)		Civil War	797		2750		CSA General
Earp, Virgil		Lawman	650	4500	7150		US Marshal. S Auction $8,250
Earp, Wyatt B.S.	1848-1929	Lawman	4438		27500		Legendary Gambler, Gunfighter Rare
East, Clyde B.		Aviation	25	35		35	Am. Highest Ranking Reconnaisance Ace.
East, James		Lawman	250	750			Western Cowboy
East, John		Senate	10	20	40	35	Senator NC, Suicide
Eastlake, Charles L., Sir	1836-1906	Artist	50	150	575		Critic, Historical Painter. Sec'y Royal Inst. Br.
Eastland, James O.		Congress	10	20		35	1943-78. Powerful Miss. Senator. Pres. Pro Tem.
Eastman, George	1854-1932	Business	283	2047	3500	1440	Fndr Eastman Kodak. Rare DS $4900
Eastman, John		Artist	40		185		Am. Artist. Portraits & Genre
Eastman, Max	1883-1969	Author	35	85	115		Communust & Editor-Fdr. 'The Masses'
Easton, Florence	1882-1955	Entertainment	45			175	Opera. Br. Soprano.Repertory 100 Roles-4 Languages
Easton, Sheena		Entertainment	15		25	45	Singer
Eastwood, Allison		Entertainment	7			38	Actress. Pin-Up $55
Eastwood, Clint	1930-	Entertainment	31			84	Actor-Producer-Dir. AA. 2'x3' Poster S $100

NAME	DATE	CATEGORY	SIG	LS/DS	ALS	SP	COMMENTS
Eaton, Amos Beebe	1806-77	Civil War	32	55	102		Union General. Seminole & Mex. War.Sig/Rank $50
Eaton, Dorman	1823-99	Reformer	10	25	55		Jurist, Nat'l Civil Service Act
Eaton, John Henry		Cabinet	25	55	110		Senator TN 1818, Sec'y War
Eaton, Joseph H.	1816-96	Civil War					Union Gen. ALS '65 $605
Eaton, Shirley	1936-	Entertainment	10			67	Curvy Blonde Brit. Actress. Goldfinger
Eaton, William	1764-1811	Military-Diplomat	38		88		U.S.Consul Tunis,Tripoli Action
Eban, Abba		Diplomat	15	75	75	65	Israeli Diplomat, Ambass. UN
Ebb, Fred		Composer	15		45	25	AMusQS Ebb & Kander $350
Ebbets, Charles H.		Business	150			190	Orig. Brooklyn Dodgers Field (Ebbets Field)
Eben Emael		Military	30	85	140	60	
Eberhart, Adolph O.		Governor	5	22			Governor MN
Eberhart, Richard		Author	10	20	45	15	Major Poet 20th Cent.,Pulitzer
Eberlein, Gustav	1847-1926	Artist	20			72	Ger. Sculp. Mythological Subj & Bismark etc.
Eberly, Bob		Entertainment	5	15		40	Band Singer, Records
Eberly, Ray		Entertainment	10			60	Singer. Band, Records
Ebert, Roger		Entertainment	13			30	TV Movie Critic
Ebsen, Buddy	1908-	Entertainment	10	20		38	Tall, Lanky Dancer-Actor. 'Beverly Hillbillies'
Eccles, John C.		Science	20	30	40	30	Nobel Medicine
Echols, John (WD)		Civil War	195	722			CSA General
Echols, John	1823-96	Civil War	115	195	375		CSA General
Echols, Leonard Sidney		Senate/Congress	5	15			MOC WV 1919
Eckels, James H.	1858-1907	Statesman	15	50	100		U.S. Comptroller of Currency
Eckener, Hugo von	1868-1954	Aviation	215	525	650	512	Ger. Aeronaut, Built Graf Zeppelin
Eckert, Thomas T. (WD)	1825-	Civil War	475				Union Gen.Telegraph Giant.
Eckstine, Billy		Entertainment	20			50	Vocalist-Trumpet-Bandleader
Ed, Carl		Cartoonist	10			30	'Harold Teen'
Eddington, Arthur Stanley, Sir	1882-1944	Science	25	140	185		Br. Mathematician, Astrophysicist
Eddy, Duane		Entertainment	30			45	Rock Guitarist. HOF
Eddy, Mary Baker	1821-1910	Clergy	1275	2125	3890		Am. Fndr. Christian Science Church
Eddy, Nelson	1901-67	Entertainment	50	175		160	30's-40's Baritone Favorite/Jeanette MacDonald
Eden, Anthony, Sir	1897-1977	Head of State	79	140	190	288	Prime Minister. 1st Earl Avon
Eden, Barbara		Entertainment	10	22	25	36	Pin-Up SP $45
Ederle, Gertrude 'Trudy'		Entertainment	25			60	And Showgirl
Edeson, Robert		Entertainment	20			45	Silent Star. 'Ten Commandments'
Edge, Walter E.		Senate/Congress	15	25		20	Gov.NJ 1917, Senator PA, Ambassador
Edison, Charles	1890-1969	Cabinet	55	95	110	60	Sec'y Navy. Son of Thos. A.
Edison, Thomas Alva	1847-1931	Science	505	1491	2960	2078	Prolific Inventor.Rare DS re Electric Lights $4500
Edmonds, Walter Dumanx	1903-98	Author	5	45	40	25	Drums Along the Mohawk
Edmunds, Geo.Franklin	1828-1919	Congress	10	15	30		Senator VT 1866-91
Edmundson, Henry A.		Civil War	40	55	80		CSA Officer, MOC VA
Edson, Merritt A.	1897-1955	Military	45	125		75	MOH Winner.Marine Cmdr. at Guadalcanal. WW II
Edward & Wallis (See Windsor)		Royalty					Duke and Duchess of Windsor
Edward III	1312-77	Royalty					Doc. Written 1340 $450. Doc.in Name of $1400
Edward IV (England)	1442-83	Royalty	25000				NRPA
Edward VI (Reign of...)		Royalty					Land Grant 1551. $1750

NAME	DATE	CATEGORY	SIG	LS/DS	ALS	SP	COMMENTS
Edward VII (Eng) (As King)	1841-1910	Royalty		588		1495	King From 1901-10
Edward VII (Eng.)	1841-1910	Royalty	110	337	258	625	As Albert Edw., Q.Vict. Eldest Son
Edward VIII (As King)	1894-1972	Royalty	300	1875	1750	1122	
Edward VIII, as Prince of Wales		Royalty	148	467	726	678	Content TLS $1250. SP in Investiture Robes $2050
Edward, Duke of Kent	1767-1820	Royalty	50	120	350		Father of Queen Victoria
Edward, Duke Windsor	1894-1972	Royalty	200	639	1900	655	FDC S $200- $300. Card Signed by Duke &Dchs.$425
Edwards, Anthony		Entertainment	20	50	70	50	Actor. 'ER' See Clooney, G
Edwards, Blake		Entertainment	10	24		22	Film Producer-Director. Pink Panther etc.
Edwards, Clarence		Military	35				General WW I
Edwards, Cliff	1895-1971	Entertainment	45	60	100	125	Singer-Actor Known as Ukelele Ike. 'GWTW'
Edwards, Douglas		Journalist	5		15	15	Radio-TV News
Edwards, Edward Irving		Senate	10	15			Senator, Governor NJ
Edwards, Elaine S.		Senate	7	20		10	Senator LA, 8/1/72-11/13/72
Edwards, Gail J.		Entertainment	5		15	15	
Edwards, George		Congress	10				
Edwards, Gordon		Business	4			10	Business Exec., U.S. Steel
Edwards, James B.		Cabinet	10	15	35	10	Governor SC, Sec'y Energy
Edwards, Joan		Entertainment	5			10	Actress
Edwards, Joe, Jr.		Astronaut	6			20	
Edwards, Jonathan	1703-1758	Clergy-Author	110	350	380		Considered Greatest Theologian of Am.Puritanism
Edwards, Oliver	1835-1904	Civil War	35	70	105		Union General Sig/Rank $65
Edwards, Penny	1919-	Entertainment	5			20	Westerns Leading Lady of 40s
Edwards, Ralph		Entertainment	4		15	15	Radio-TV M.C. 'This Is Your Life' Host-Producer
Edwards, Vince		Entertainment	10			25	Actor. Sincere, Tough Leading Man. 'Dr. Ben Casey'
Egan, Richard	1921-87	Entertainment	5		15	15	Actor.Leading Man. Mainly Action Drama & Westerns
Egan, Will		Entertainment	3			8	
Egan, William A.		Governor	5	12		10	Governor AK
Egbert, H.C.		Military	45			65	Gen. Spanish-Am. War
Egbert, Sherwood		Business	4	15	35	15	
Eggar, Samantha	1939	Entertainment	10			22	Br. Leading Lady. Internat'l Films
Eggert, Nicole		Entertainment	5			30	Actress. 'Baywatch'
Eggerth, Marta	1912-	Entertainment	10			45	Opera. Reigning Star of Filmed Operettas in 40's
Eggleston, Benjamin	1816-88	Congress	12	20	25		MOC OH
Eggleston, Edward	1837-1902	Author	5		30		Am. Regional Classic Novels
Eggleston, Geo. C.	1839-1911	Author	10	25			Editor, Novelist, Civil War & Boy's Books
Eglevsky, Andre'	1917-77	Entertainment	35	55	110	75	Rus-Am Ballet Teacher-Dancer
Ehrlich, Paul, Dr.	1854-1915	Science		1250	1850	1380	Nobel. Diphtheria, Syphillis
Ehrlichman, John	1925-99	Political	20			29	Adv. To Nixon. Key in Watergate Scandal
Eichelberger. Robert L.	1886-1961	Military	40	98	75	75	Gen. WW II. Cmdr I Corps
Eichelbrenner, E. A.		Science	45	95	225		
Eichmann, Karl Adolf	1906-62	Military	275	1500	1250	750	Nazi Leader. ALS/Cont.Offered $50,000-60,000
Eick, Alfred		Military	26		50		
Eiffel, Alexandre-Gustave	1832-1923	Arch.-Engineer	275	1012	1775	1450	ALS/Content $1,750
Eigen, Manfred		Science	20	35	80	40	Nobel Chemistry
Eilers, Sally	1908-78	Entertainment	15	15	30	42	Actress. Low Key Leading Lady 30s

NAME	DATE	CATEGORY	SIG	LS/DS	ALS	SP	COMMENTS
Eilshemius, Louis Michel	1864-1941	Artist	35	65	525		Am. Landscape Expressionist
Einstein, Albert	1879-1955	Science	1133	2477	4844	3067	Nobel-Physics. ALS/Sci. Content $25,000
Eisele, Donn F.		Astronaut	50			85	
Eisenberg, Maurice		Entertainment	5	15		20	Cellist
Eisenhower, Arthur B.		Business	5	15		10	Brother to Ike. Banker
Eisenhower, Barbara		Celebrity	5	15		10	Daughter-in Law to Ike
Eisenhower, David	1948-	Author	15	25		25	Historian & Writer
Eisenhower, Dwight D.(As Pres.)		President	424	852		398	FDC (Eisenhower Inauguration) S $750
Eisenhower, Dwight D.	1890-1969	President	289	909	4073	588	ALS/Content $3,750-$17,500.
Eisenhower, Edgar N.		Law	5	20		15	Brother & Lawyer to Ike
Eisenhower, John S. D.		Military	10	20	35	15	General & Only Son of Ike
Eisenhower, Julie Nixon		Celebrity	5	10	25	20	Daughter & Inlaw. Two Presidents
Eisenhower, Mamie Doud	1896-1979	First Lady	65	106	204	50	White House Card S $65, LS $85. FDC S $65
Eisenhower, Milton		Educator	10	30		20	Brother to D.D.E. Pres. Penn. State U.
Eisenman, Robin G.		Entertainment	5			10	
Eisenstaedt, Alfred		Photographer	15	40		125	Celebrity Photographer
Eisenstein, Sergey	1898-1948	Entertainment			1350		Russ.Stage-Film Dir. Innovative Masterpieces
Eisley, Anthony	1925-	Entertainment	7			12	General Purpose Actor
Eisner, Michael O.		Business	30	70		45	CEO Walt Disney Co.
Eisner, William J.		Business	10	35	45	20	
Eizenstat, Stuart E.		Government	5	10	15	10	White House Staff
Ekberg, Anita	1931-	Entertainment	10			20	Voluptuous Swedish Blonde Actress. 50s-70s
Ekland, Britt		Entertainment	8	12	25	32	Actress.Am. & Internat'l Films. Pin-Up SP $40
Ekwall, William A.		Senate/Congress	5	10		10	MOC OR
El Fadil, Siddig		Entertainment	20			50	Actor. 'Star TrekDeep Space Nine'
Elahi, Ostad		Philosopher	3660		15150		Musician, Judge NRPA
Elam, Jack	1916-	Entertainment	8		15	22	Actor. Wall-eyed Western Character
Elbert, Samuel	1743-1788	Rev. War		110	170		Distinguished Officer. Gov. GA
Elder, Ruth (Camp)		Aviation	100	190	310	350	Pioneer Aviatrix
Elder, Will*		Cartoonist	30			100	Best Known for Little Annie Fanny in Playboy Mag.
Elders, M. Joycelyn		Cabinet	15	30		20	Clinton Surgeon General
Eldridge, Florence	1901-88	Entertainment	10			30	Vintage Stage & Film Leading Lady.Mrs Fred. March
Eldridge, Louise		Reformer	10	15	30		Aunt Louisa AQS $25
Eldridge, Roy		Entertainment	30			65	Jazz Trumpet
Electric Light Orchestra		Entertainment	50			100	
Eleniak, Erika		Entertainment	10			40	Actress-Model. 'Baywatch'. Nude SP $100
Elfman, Jenna		Entertainment	10			54	Actress-Comedian. '99 Golden Globe. Pin-Up $60
Elg, Taina		Entertainment	10			30	Fin. Ballet-Actress/Gene Kelly. Internat'l Films
Elgar, Edward, Sir	1857-1934	Composer	138	462	872	525	Br. Composer. AMusQS $1,500-$2000
Elgart, Les		Entertainment	30			45	Arranger for Top Vocalists. Big Bandleader
Elgin, 7th Earl (T.Bruce)		Diplomat					SEE Bruce, Thomas
Elijah, Muhammad		Celebrity	305			425	Religious Activist
Elion, Gertrude, Dr.		Science	20	65		35	Nobel Medicine. Biochemist-Leukemia-Herpes-AZT
Eliopulos, Marcus		Entertainment	6			25	Music. Guitar Stabbing Westward
Eliot, Charles W.	1834-1926	Educator	15	50	65		Pres. Harvard

NAME	DATE	CATEGORY	SIG	LS/DS	ALS	SP	COMMENTS
Eliot, George (Pseud.)	1819-80	Author	160	535	2667		Br. Novelist. (Mary Ann Lewes [Evans])
Eliot, T(homas) S(tearns)	1888-1965	Author	165	865	1468	770	Br. Poet, Critic, Editor, Nobel. Xmas Card S $375
Eliot, Thos. Dawes	1808-770	Congress	5		15		CW MOC MA
Elisabeth, Queen	1876-1965	Royalty		125		350	Queen of Belgium. Wife of King Albert I
Elizabeth I (Eng.)	1533-1603	Royalty	4750	23460			NRPA
Elizabeth I, Petrovna, (Rus)	1709-62	Royalty	425	1475			Czarina of Russia. Daughter of Peter the Great
Elizabeth II & Philip		Royalty	-	1070		1000	
Elizabeth Petrovna (Eliz. I)	1709-1762	Royalty					Empress of Russia. Created Renaissance Russ. Arts
Elizabeth, II	1926-	Royalty	350	875	1200	775	Queen of Gr. Brit. ALS Age 10 $900
Elizabeth, Queen Mother	1900-	Royalty	85	670	425	1032	Queen of George VI. Check Signed $950
Elkins, Stephen B.		Cabinet	15	25	60	25	Sec'y War, Senator WV
Ellender, Allen J.		Senate	4	5		10	Senator LA
Ellerbee, Linda		Journalist	10	35		15	TV News, Commentator
Ellery, William	1727-1820	Rev. War	175	434	785		Signer Decl. of Indepen.
Ellicott, Andrew	1754-1820	Rev. War	60	185	320		Surveyor, Mathematician
Ellington, Buford		Governor	5	10	20		Governor TN
Ellington, Duke	1899-1974	Composer	200	520		498	Big Band Leader. AMusQS $300-$1,200
Elliott, Cass (Mama)		Entertainment	300	585		400	Rotund, Sweet-Voiced Singer. 'Mamas & Papas'
Elliott, David James		Entertainment	15			50	Actor
Elliott, Maxine		Entertainment	30	40	75	70	
Elliott, R.W.B., Bishop		Clergy	25	35	40	40	
Elliott, Robert B.		Senate/Congress	10	15		15	MOC SC
Elliott, Sam	1944-	Entertainment	20		35	45	Low Key Leading Man 70's to 90's
Elliott, Washington L.	1825-88	Civil War	35				Union Gen. ALS '63 $200
Elliott, Wild Bill	1904-65	Entertainment	50			150	Vintage Cowboy Star from 20s-Late 50s
Ellis, F. H.		Aviation	15	35		30	
Ellis, Havelock	1859-1939	Science	55	380	155	275	Br. Pioneer Advocate Sex Ed.
Ellis, Mary		Entertainment	20			50	Opera & Operetta Star. 1st 'Rose Marie'
Ellis, Robert H.		Military	10	25	45		
Ellison, James	1910-93	Entertainment	15		20	30	Vintage Cowboy. Johnny in Hopalong Cassidy
Ellison, Ralph W.	1914-94	Author	45	225		85	Afr.-Am. Novelist. Invisible Man
Ellsberg, Daniel		Activist	20	35	50	30	Leaked Pentagon Papers
Ellsberg, Edward		Inventor		140	325		Naval Engineer. Underwater Torch
Ellsworth, Ephraim E. (WD)		Civil War			3750		Union Zouave Col. 1st CW Martyr
Ellsworth, Ephriam E.	1837-61	Civil War	698	1875	2500		Union Zouave Col.
Ellsworth, Oliver (SC)	1745-1807	Supreme Court	100	362	467		3rd Chief Justice. Constitutional Conv.
Ellul, Jacques		Clergy	25	30	45		
Elman, Mischa	1891-1967	Entertainment	30	198		80	Rus.-Am. Violinist
Elman, Ziggy		Entertainment	25			75	Trumpet. Played With Major Bands 40's-50's.
Elmendorff, Karl		Entertainment	25			110	Ger. Conductor. 4x6 SP $85
Elmore, E.C.		Civil War	55	105			Treas. CSA. ALS $3,500
Elrod, Jack*		Cartoonist	10			35	'Mark Trail'
Elson, Edward L.R.		Clergy	15	20	25		
Elssler, Fanny	1810-84	Entertainment	250				Austrian Ballerina
Elston, John A.		Congress	5	15			Congressman CA

NAME	DATE	CATEGORY	SIG	LS/DS	ALS	SP	COMMENTS
Eltinge, Julian	1882-1941	Entertainment	25	20	35	40	Female Impersonator, Silent Films
Eluard, Paul (Eugene Grinde)	1895-1952	Author	110	225	375		Fr. Poet. Exponent Surrealism
Elvira		Entertainment	10		19	33	Pin-Up SP $35
Elwes, Cary		Entertainment	8			40	Actor. Robin Hood SP $50
Ely, Joseph Buell		Governor	15	35	70		Gov. MA, Anti New Dealer
Ely, Paul, General		Military	65		140	90	Fr. Cmdr. Indochina. Dienbienphu
Ely, Ron	1938-	Entertainment	15		20	45	Actor. One of Several Tarzans. SP asTarzen $195
Ely, Smith		Congress	15				Mayor NYC, Repr. NY
Elzey, Arnold (Jones)(WD)	1816-71	Civil War	350		1700		CSA General
Emberg, Kelly		Entertainment	10			25	Model. Pin-Up SP $40
Embry, Joan		Zoologist	10			25	San Diego Zoo TV Representative
Emerson, Faye	1917-83	Entertainment	10			52	Film Actress-Early TV Panel Show Member
Emerson, George		Entertainment	8			30	
Emerson, Hope	1897-60	Entertainment	15			35	6'2 Am. Character Actress. Early 30s-60s
Emerson, Lake and Palmer		Entertainment	35	125		125	Rock. Alb. Signed (3) $125
Emerson, Ralph Waldo	1803-82	Author-Clergy	265	300	1082	2530	Essayist, Philosopher, Poet. ALS/Content $3,500
Emery, Ralph		Entertainment	4			8	TV Host
Emma, Queen (Ne, Rooker)	1836-85	Royalty	350				Wife of King Kamehameha IV
Emmett, Daniel D.		Composer	300	425	600		1st Minstral Show. Dixie
Emmons, Ebenezer	1799-1863	Science	25	40	70		Early Prof. of Natural History
Emory, William H.	1811-87	Civil War	65	135	220		Union General. Sig/Rank $90, War Dte. ALS $355
Empey, James W.,Lt.Col.		Aviation		25		35	Ace WW II
Enders, John Franklin, Dr.		Science	25	60	110	45	Nobel Medicine.
Endicott, William C.	1826-1900	Cabinet	25	30	55	40	Sec'y War
Enesco, Georges	1880-1955	Composer	125	275	550	550	AMusQS $475-$850
Enevoldson, Einer		Astronaut	10			20	
Engel, Georgia		Entertainment	15		15	20	Actress. 'Mary Tyler Moore' Show
Engel, Samuel G.	1904-84	Entertainment	10			15	Producer
England, Anthony W.		Astronaut	7			28	
England, Sue		Entertainment	5			20	1940's Moppet
Engle, Frederick		Civil War	45				Union Commodore
Engle, Joe Henry		Astronaut	15			45	Engle & Truly SP $195
Engler, Irvin		Author		25	30		Poet
English, Thos. Dunn	1819-1902	Author-Congress	28	30	45		'Alice Ben Bolt'.Dr.,Lawyer, Poet, MOC NJ
Englund, Robert	1949-	Entertainment	10			28	Horror Movies. Character of Freddy Kruger
Ennis, Skinnay		Bandleader	25			65	Singer, Musician
Enos, Roger	1729-1808	Military	55	175	295		General, Honored VT Citizen
Enright, Richard E.		Law	12	24			Police Commissioner
Enriques, Rene	1933-90	Entertainment	35			60	'Hill Street Blues' Lt. Calletano.Aids Victiim
Ensley, F. Gerald, Bishop		Clergy	20	35	50	25	
Ensor, James Sydney, Baron	1860-1949	Artist	75	190	582		Belg. Painter, Etcher. Bizarre Fantasies, Masks
Ephron, Henry	1912-92	Entertainment	15			25	Screenwriter. Worked with wife, Nora.
Ephron, Nora	1941-	Author	15			25	Novelist-Screenwriter.Daughter of Phoebe & Henry.
Ephron, Phoebe	1914-71	Entertainment	15			25	Screenwriter- Mother of Nora & Wife of Henry
Epp, Franz Xaver von	1868-1947	Military	15	40		75	Gen. WW I. Joined Nazi Party. Sturmabteilung Army

NAME	DATE	CATEGORY	SIG	LS/DS	ALS	SP	COMMENTS
Epstein, Brian		Entertainment	350	1500	825		Beatles Manager & Promoter
Epstein, Jacob, Sir	1880-1959	Artist	150	210	375		Controversial Br.-Am. Sculptor
ER (Cast)		Entertainment	98			275	All 6 Original. (5) $250
Erdrich, Louise		Author	5			10	Novelist. 'The Bingo Palace'
Erhard, Ludwig	1897-1977	Head of State	25	70	170	60	Chancellor W. Germany
Erickson, Leif	1911-86	Entertainment	15			40	Singer-Actor. Many 2nd Leads
Ericsdotter, Siw		Entertainment	25			60	Opera
Ericson, B.A.		Aviation	10	25			Piloted XC-99
Ericson, Eric*		Cartoonist	15			75	Appeared New Yorker Mag. 40's-50's
Ericsson, John	1803-89	Civil War	95	195	470		Designed & Built Monitor
Ernest Augustus II	1771-1851	Royalty			285		1st King of Hanover(1837-51)
Erni, Hans		Artist	65		225		ALS-FDC/sig'd art
Ernouf, Manuel L.J(Baron)		Fr. Revolution	35	85	160		
Ernst, Max	1891-1976	Artist	235	355	775		Surrealist-Dada Movement. Orig. Sketch S $825
Errol, Leon	1881-1951	Entertainment	45			93	Talented Character Actor in Comedy Roles
Erskine, Graves B.		Military	15	35	65	40	Led US Marines at Iwo Jima
Erskine, John	1879-1951	Author	35	125	175		Novelist, Pres. Juilliard, Musician
Erte'		Artist	102	205	400	195	
Ervine, St. John		Author	15	50			Br. Controversial Drama Critic
Erwin, Durward		Country Music	10			20	
Erwin, James		Military	45				General WW I
Erwin, Sam J.		Congress	20	80		25	Sen.NC. Watergate Investigator
Erwin, Stuart	1903-67	Entertainment	20			45	Character Comedian. 20s-60s. Played Mr. Average
Esaki, Leo		Science	20	35	50	45	Nobel Physics
Escobedo, Mariano	1827-1902	Military	50	225			Captured Maximillian
Eshkol, Levi	1895-1969	Head of State	245	238	560	120	Israeli P.M., Fndr. Histadrut
Esnault-Pelterie, Robert	1881-1957	Aviation	75	285			Pioneer Aviator. Invented Aileron. Early Monoplane
Esperian, Kalen		Entertainment	10			30	Opera
Esposito, Jennifer		Entertainment	10			55	
Essame, Hubert		Military	25	40			
Estaing, Charles Hector T. de	1729-94	Rev. War	175	500	750		Fr.Gen-Adm. Pro American Hero
Este, Isabella d'	1474-1539	Royalty			10000		(Mantua) Art Patron, Diplomat. NPRA
Estefan, Gloria		Entertainment	12			45	Dancer-Singer.
Esterhasy, Gunt. A.		Head of State	20	70	175		Austria
Esterhazy, Prince Pal A.	1786-1866	Statesman	25		70		Austro-Hung. Diplomat. Ambassador to Eng.
Estes, Billy Sol		Celebrity	5	20	45	15	Grain Storage Scandal
Estevez, Emilio	1962-	Entertainment	15		35	40	Actor-Son of Martin Sheen. Leading Man
Estil, Benjamin		Congress	15	25			Congressman VA 1825
Estrada, Erik	1948-	Entertainment	5	20		25	Leading Man. Puerto Rican Descent. 'Chips' TV
Etter, Philippe		Head of State	15	50			Switzerland
Etting, Ruth	1896-1978	Entertainment	25			60	Major Vint. Singing Star of 20s
Eubanks, Bob		Entertainment	5		10	12	Personable Game Show Host
Eugenie, Empress(Nap.III)	1826-1920	Royalty	200	305	350		Influenced Nap. Fashion Leader
Euler-Chelpin, Ulf Svante von	1873-1964	Science	20	35	60	40	Nobel Medicine 1929
Eurythmics		Entertainment	40			90	

NAME	DATE	CATEGORY	SIG	LS/DS	ALS	SP	COMMENTS
Eustis, Abraham		Military	65		350		War 1812. Promoted to Br. Gen.
Eustis, William	1753-1825	Cabinet	35	142	185		Madison's Sec'y War, MOC MA 1801
Evans, Clement A. (WD)		Civil War	200	1150	1088		CSA General
Evans, Clement A.	1833-1911	Civil War	105		375		CSA General
Evans, Dale	1912-	Entertainment	20		60	55	Former Band Singer. Leading Lady to Roy Rogers
Evans, Daniel J.		Senate-Gov.	15	18		20	Gov., Senator, Washington
Evans, Edith, Dame	1888-1976	Entertainment	20	30		40	Distinguished Br. Stage Actress. Few Films
Evans, E. R.G.,Lord Mountevans		Explorer	35	95		75	Admiral, Arctic Explorer.Lord Mountevans 1880-1957
Evans, Gene	1922-98	Entertainment	20			45	Versatile Character Actor. My Friend Flicka etc.
Evans, George De Lacy	1787-1870	Military	150	220			Br. Col. Who Burned White House
Evans, Geraint, Sir		Entertainment	10			35	Opera
Evans, Joan	1934-	Entertainment	5	10	15	10	Teenage Roles in Early 50s. Works now in Education
Evans, John V.		Governor	10	15			Governor ID
Evans, Linda	1942-	Entertainment	8	12	20	30	Leading Lady. Successful TV Series 'Dynasty'
Evans, Lt. Col. D. M		Civil War	15	25	40		
Evans, Madge	1909-81	Entertainment	15	22	35	30	Film Debut at 5. Film Star Until 1943. Retiredt
Evans, Marian	1819-80	Author		450	1600		Novelist. Formed Relationship/G.H.Lewes.
Evans, Maurice	1909-89	Entertainment	42	73	85	78	Shakespearean Actor, Producer
Evans, Nathan G. 'Shanks'	1824-68	Civil War	175		922		CSA Gen.
Evans, Nathan George 'Shanks'		Civil War	285	1550	2650		CSA General (WD)
Evans, Nicholas		Author		40			Novelist. 'The Horse Whisperer'
Evans, Oliver	1755-1819	Inventor		1500			Built Am. 1st Self-Propelled Land Vehicle 1787
Evans, Ray		Composer	15	35	45	40	Am. Songwriter. 'Buttons & Bows', 'Que Sera Sera'
Evans, Robley D.	1846-1912	Civil War	35	65	125	175	Capt. USN, 'Fight'n Bob'. Adm. USN. Santiago 1898
Evans, Ronald E.		Astronaut	40			100	
Evans, Walker	1903-75	Photographer	75		270		Am. Photographer. Documented Everyday Life
Evarts, William M.	1818-1901	Cabinet	75	82	167	45	Att'y Gen., Sec'y State, Sen NY
Everest. F.K. 'Pete'		Aviation	15	30	45	35	
Everett, Chad		Entertainment	5	10	15	25	Actor Medical Center & More
Everett, Edward	1794-1865	Sen.-Cab.-Clergy	70	165	158	95	Fillmore Sec'y State, Sen. MA. Statesman, Scholar
Everly Brothers		Entertainment	35			95	Don & Phil. 1st R & R Duo. Influence Later Artists
Everly, Phil		Entertainment	20			30	Singer-Songwriter-Guitarist. 'Everly Brothers'
Evers, Charles		Activist	5	20	40	53	Succeeded Brother Medgar as Sec'y NAACP '63
Evers, Medgar	1925-63	Activist		2800			AM. Civil Rights Leader
Evigan, Greg		Entertainment	3	3	6	10	
Ewell, I.R.L.		Civil War	190	395			
Ewell, Rich'd Stoddert (WD)		Civil War	686		1850		CSA General
Ewell, Rich'd Stoddert	1817-72	Civil War	375	550	1275		CSA General
Ewell, Tom		Entertainment	15		25	34	Elusive Actor. Seven Year Itch
Ewing, James		Military	45	142			Officer Am. Revolution
Ewing, Thomas	1789-1871	Cabinet	40	110	245		Sen. OH,Sec'y Treas. & Interior
Exelmans, Rene' J.I.,	1775-1852	Fr. Revolution	20	35	135		Marshal of France
Exile (4)		Entertainment	20			50	Rock
Exon, J. James		Senator-Gov.	5	10		10	Senator, Governor NE
Eyre, Edward John	1815-1901	Explorer	55		150		Gov. Australia. Eyre Rock

NAME	DATE	CATEGORY	SIG	LS/DS	ALS	SP	COMMENTS
Eythe, William		Entertainment	10	15	20	20	
Eytinge, Rose	1838-1911	Entertainment	25		65	50	19th Cent.Actress/Laura Keene, Booth

F

NAME	DATE	CATEGORY	SIG	LS/DS	ALS	SP	COMMENTS
Fabares, Shelley	1942-	Entertainment	6	20	15	25	Actress. 'Coach'
Faber, John Eberhard	1822-79	Business	140	500	725		Eberhard Faber Pencil Co.. 1st Pencil Mfg. In Am.
Fabian (See Forte', Fabian)		Entertainment					
Fabian, Ava		Entertainment	5			25	Actress. Pin-Up $45
Fabian, John M.		Astronaut	7			20	
Fabio		Model	15			38	Male Model
Fabray, Nanette	1920-	Entertainment	5		15	30	Comedy Actress-Singer. 'Our Gang' as Child
Factor, Max		Business	25	125	175	60	Cosmetic Mfg.
Factor, Max Jr.		Business	10	30	55	45	Cosmetic Mfg.
Fagan, James F.	1828-93	Civil War		1725			CSA Gen.& U.S.Marshal For Indian Terr.
Fagerbakke, Bill		Entertainment	10			35	Actor 'Coach'
Fagoaga, Isidodo		Entertainment	15			50	Opera
Fahey, Jeff		Entertainment	8			35	Actor. Leading Man. 'The Marshal', 'Psycho III'
Fair, James G.		Senate	30	145	110		Mining, Financier, CA Developer
Fairbank, Calvin		Abolitionist	40	85	150		Freed Fugitive Slaves
Fairbanks, Charles W.	1852-1918	Vice President	50	110	367	150	T. Roosevelt VP. US Sen.IN
Fairbanks, Douglas, Jr.		Entertainment	18	62	125	40	Actor-Son of the Famous Father
Fairbanks, Douglas, Sr.	1883-1939	Entertainment	163	50		291	Swashbuckling Silent Film Mega Star.United Artists
Fairbanks, Erastus	1792-1864	Governor	35		80		CW Gov. VT. Mfg. Platform Scales
Fairchild, Charles S.		Cabinet	20	35	55	40	Sec'y Treasury 1887
Fairchild, David G.	1869-1954	Science	5	10	20	15	Am. Botanist. Books on Plants
Fairchild, Lucius	1831-96	Civil War	35	50	80		Union Gen., Gov. WI, Statesman. Sig/Rank $55
Fairchild, Morgan	1950-	Entertainment	10	15	20	32	Actress. Leading Lady. Pin-Up SP $90
Fairchild, Sherman		Business	25	60	115	40	Fairchild Camera & Equipment Co
Faircloth, Henry P.	1880-1956	Author	10	35			Noted US Social Scientist & Writer
Fairfax, George Wm.	1787-	Post Rev. War	75	210	395		Companion of Geo. Washington
Fairfax, Thomas Lord	1691-1782	Colonial America	220	550			Historically Important Family.Settled in North-VA
Fairfield, Charles	1842-1924	Cabinet	25		40		Sec'y Treas. under Cleveland
Fairfield, John	1797-1847	Gov.-Senate	15	20	30		Senator, Gov. ME
Fairholt, Frederick	1814-66	Artist	15		50		Engraver & Antiquarian
Fairless, Benjamin F.		Business	35	95	190	70	CEO US Steel
Faisal, King	1906-75	Royalty	25	50	95	125	Saudi Arabia. Many Benficial Reforms. Assassinated
Faith, Percy		Composer	20			150	Conductor-Arranger For Top Artists
Faithfull, Emily		Reformer	25	45	55		Br.Printer-Publisher Q.Victoria
Falck, Wolfgang		Aviation	20	45	6040		
Falconer, William	1732-1769	Author	60	350			Brit. Poet. Shipwrecked, Universal Marine Dict'y
Falk, Peter	1927-	Entertainment	8		15	28	SP As Columbo $45
Falkenburg, Jinx	1919-	Entertainment	5	6	10	25	Model-Actress

NAME	DATE	CATEGORY	SIG	LS/DS	ALS	SP	COMMENTS
Fall, Albert B.	1861-1944	Cabinet	40	85	150	60	Sec'y Interior.Teapot Dome Scandal
Fall, Leo	1873-1925	Composer				105	Austrian Operetta Composer
Falla, Manuel de	1876-1946	Composer	175	510	700	900	Span. AMusQS $875, $1,000-1200
Fallon, Walter A.		Business	4			10	CEO Eastman Kodak Co.
Falstaff, John, Sir		Military		8000			Model for Shakespeare's Play
Falwell, Jerry		Clergy	15	20	25	35	Far Right-Politically-Theologically.(To Some)
Fancourt, Darell		Entertainment	15			65	D'Oyly Carte Gilbert & Sullivan Baritone Star
Faneuil, Peter		Rev. War	125	225	555		Faneuil Hall, Boston
Fang, Wu Ting, Dr.		Statesman	10			20	Chinese Statesman
Fantin-Latour, Henri	1836-1904	Artist	40	90	170		Fr. Illustrator, Lithographer
Far, Frances		Composer	5	15	30	10	
Faraday, Michael	1791-1867	Science	155	410	960	650	Br. Physicist, Chemist. ALS/Cont.$1800
Farentino, James	1938-	Entertainment	15			25	Actor. Leading Man. Mostly TV
Fargo, Donna		Country Music	8	15		20	Singer-Songwriter
Fargo, James C.		Business	312	988			Wells, Fargo & Co. Am. Express DS $2850
Fargo, William G.	1818-81	Business	368	1423	1250		Wells-Fargo, Am. Express Stock S $7500
Farias, Valentin Gomes	1781-1858	Head of State	205	490			President of Mexico until Defeated by Santa Ana
Farina, Dennis		Entertainment	10	35		24	Busy Mature Leading-Man-Character Actor
Farinelli, Patricia		Model	5			18	Pin-Up SP $20
Farley, Chris	19xx-99	Entertainment	40			85	Short-lived Star of 'Saturday Night Live'
Farley, James A.	1888-1976	Cabinet	20	74	95	38	FDR P.M. General. CEO Coca Cola. Politician
Farley, John Cardinal	1842-1918	Clergy	28			65	Religious Leader & Archbishop of New York
Farman, Henri	1874-1958	Aviation	60	110	175	165	Pioneer Aviator. Airplane Mfg.1st Flight over 1 Km
Farman, Maurice		Aviation	75		190		Pioneer Aviator. License #6. Brother of Henri
Farmer, Art		Entertainment	10			25	Jazz Fluegelhorn-Trumpet
Farmer, Fannie Merritt	1857-1915	Author	190			250	Cookery Expert.'..Boston Cooking School Cook Book'
Farmer, Frances	1914-70	Entertainment	165	195	250	573	Tragic End for Beautiful, Talented Actress
Farmer, James	1920-1999	Activist	20			45	Founder CORE ('42).Led Freedom Riders 60's
Farnham, Ralph	1757-?	Military	150				Rev. War Soldier. Fought at Bunker Hill
Farnol, J. Jeffrey		Author	5	25			British
Farnsworth, Charles		Military	25			65	General WW I
Farnsworth, Daniel W.		Business		15	30		Founder Woolen Mills
Farnsworth, John F.	1820-97	Civil War	45	110	155	450	Union Gen. Sig/Rank $50
Farnsworth, Philo T.	1906-71	Inventor					Invented 1st Television Camera. Rare NRPA
Farnsworth, Richard	1919-	Entertainment	8	10	15	20	Character Actor & Former Stuntman
Farnum, Dustin	1874-1929	Entertainment	50	75	90	150	Silent Star. 'The Squaw Man', 'The Virginian'
Farnum, William	1876-1953	Entertainment	40			195	Vintage Leading Man. Silent Films. 'The Spoilers'
Farouk I	1920-65	Royalty	298				King of Egypt. Inept Ruler. Overthrown By Nasser
Farquhar, John Hanson		Senate/Congress	10	20	30		MOC IN, Capt. Union Army
Farr, Hugh		Entertainment	12			35	Singer-Guitar Member of Sons of the Pioneers
Farr, Jamie		Entertainment	5	8	10	15	MASH cast. Klinger
Farr, Karl		Entertainment	12			35	Singer-Violin. Member Sons of the Pioneers/Hugh
Farragut, David G.	1801-70	Civil War	180	400	583	1150	Union Adm. LS/Cont. $1,300. LS '64 $2500
Farrakhan, Louis		Activist	70			150	Leads Nation of Islam
Farrar, Frederick W.		Clergy	25	35	50	50	

NAME	DATE	CATEGORY	SIG	LS/DS	ALS	SP	COMMENTS
Farrar, Geraldine	1882-1967	Entertainment	65	100	100	105	Opera, Concert. Metropolitan. Legendary Star
Farrell, Charles	1901-1990	Entertainment	15	20	30	42	Top Star of Silents. Leading Man 30's-40's
Farrell, Eileen		Entertainment	10			95	Opera, Concert
Farrell, Glenda	1904-71	Entertainment	25	30		75	Leading Lady-Wisecracking Comedienne 30s
Farrell, Mike	1939-	Entertainment	5		20	22	Actor. Mash and More. Providence
Farrimond, Richard		Astronaut	10			25	
Farrow, Mia	1945-	Entertainment	12	30		30	Actress. SPc $25
Farwell, Chas. B.	1823-1903	Congress	15		20		Senator
Fassbaender, Brigitte		Entertainment	10			25	Ger. Mezzo Soprano,Opera
Fast, Howard	1914-	Author	15	70		25	Historical Novelist, Screenplays. Spartacus
Faster Pussy Cat		Entertainment	25			55	Rock
Fauber, Bernard M.		Business	5	10		10	Pres. K Mart
Faubus, Orval E.		Governor	35		70	50	Gov. AR, Blocked Integration
Faulkner, Charles J., Jr.		Senate	15	25			Sen. WV. Battle of New Market
Faulkner, Chas. J.	1806-84	Congress		40	150		Repr. WV. Authored Fugitive Slave Act
Faulkner, William	1897-1962	Author	350	1500	2500	3600	Nobel Lit.1949, Pulitzer Fiction 1954, 1962
Fauquier, Francis		Colonial America	200	575			Colonial Governor VA
Faure', Felix	1841-99	Head of State	30		125		Pres. France 1895-99
Faure', Gabriel	1845-1924	Composer	250		344	550	Fr. 100's Songs,Chamber Music. Organist
Faure, Jean-Baptiste	1830-1914	Entertainment	35	110			Opera. Bass-Baritone. 'Faust', 'Don Carlos'
Fausto, Cleva		Entertainment	30			65	Opera
Faversham, William	1868-1940	Entertainment	30			55	Created Role 'Jim Carson' in Squaw Man
Fawcett, Edgar	1847-1904	Author	45	110	225	40	Verse, Novels & Plays Satirizing NY High Society
Fawcett, Farrah	1947-	Entertainment	12			50	Actress.'Charlie's Angels'. TV Leads.Pin-Up SP $80
Fawcett, Millicent, Dame	1847-1929	Reformer	30	50	162		Br. Women's Suffrage Leader
Fay, Frank	1894-1961	Entertainment	15	25	45	45	Broadway Leads. Few Films. Barbara Stanwyck Husb.
Faye, Alice	1912-98	Entertainment	10	15	30	30	20th Cent. Fox Musical Star. Films from Late 30s
Faye, Julia	1896-1966	Entertainment	4	6	10	14	Ex Max Sennett Bathing Beauty. Early DeMille Films
Faylen, Frank	1907-1985	Entertainment	30			55	Am. Character Actor from '36. Gangsters, Cops etc.
Fazenda, Louise	1895-1962	Entertainment	25			75	Mack Sennett Silent Film Star. Top Comedienne
Featherston, Winfield Scott	1820-91	Civil War	102	255	305		CSA Gen. Sig/Rank $205
Fegelein, Hermann Otto		Military	500				Ger. SS Gen. WWII
Feiffer, Jules		Cartoonist	10			50	Mag. Cartoonist
Feinhals, Fritz		Entertainment	30			50	Ger. Baritone, Opera
Feinstein, Diane		Senate	5	12	25	20	Senator CA
Feld, Fritz	1900-	Entertainment	8			20	Character-Comedian. Mad or Eccentric Characters
Feldany, Eric		Entertainment	4			10	
Felder, Rodney Dr.		Celebrity	5		15	5	
Feldman, Charles K.	1904-68	Business	10	20	40	15	Fndr. Famous Artists Corp. Prod., Lawyer, Agent
Feldman, Corey		Entertainment	6			35	Actor. The Goonies
Feldman, Marty	1933-83	Entertainment	35	80	150	130	Actor-Comedian. Pop-eyed Brit. Comedian
Feldon, Barbara	1939-	Entertainment	5	15	15	30	Actress. Leading Lady. 'Get Smart'
Feldshuh, Tovah	1952-	Entertainment	5		10	15	Actress. Leading Lady. 1st Noticed in Holocaust-
Feliciano, Jose		Entertainment	5	6		20	Guitar-Vocalist. Blind
Felix, Maria	1915-	Entertainment	10			30	Major Star of Many Mex- Internat'l Films 40's-60's

NAME	DATE	CATEGORY	SIG	LS/DS	ALS	SP	COMMENTS
Fellini, Frederico	1920-93	Entertainment	50	210		131	AA Film Director-Producer
Fellows, Edith		Entertainment	10			23	Teen Singer-Actress of 30's
Fels, Joseph		Business	95	210	490		Fels Naptha Soap
Felt, Harry, Adm.		Military	10	30	50	25	
Felton, Cornelius C.	1807-82	Educator	25	45	135		President Harvard 1860-62.
Felton, Happy		Bandleader	15			35	Big Band
Felton, Rebecca L.	1835-1930	Senate	25	45	150		Sen. GA For 1 Day 11/21-11/22 1st Woman Sen.
Fenn, Sherilyn	1964-	Entertainment	10			34	Actress. Films From '85. 'Twin Peaks' '90. SP $45
Fenneman, George		Entertainment	12			25	Veteran Radio Personality. 'You Bet Your Life'-TV
Fenstermacher, Carol		Author	8			18	Glamour SP $42
Fenton, Ruben E.		Governor	30	50	80		Civil War Gov. NY
Fenwick, B.J., Bishop		Clergy	20	25	30		
Fenwick, Millicent	1910-92	Senate/Congress	18	28		50	MOC NJ. Lampooned in 'Doonsbury'. Pipe Smoker
Feoktistov, Konstantin		Cosmonaut	25			75	Pioneer Russian Cosmonaut
Ferber, Edna	1887-1968	Author	105	430	423		Novelist,Screenplays,Pulitzer'24; 'So Big'; 'Giant
Ferdinand I	1503-1564	Royalty	425	1418			Holy Roman Emperor
Ferdinand I	1793-1875	Royalty	70	245			Emperor of Austria
Ferdinand I	1865-1927	Royalty	70			580	King of Roumania, Prince of Hohenzollern
Ferdinand I, III, IV,	1751-1825	Royalty	5200				King of Naples, Two Sicilies NRPA
Ferdinand II	1578-1637	Royalty	100	450			Holy Roman Emperor from 1619
Ferdinand II, The Catholic		Royalty	450	1700	4385		Spain
Ferdinand V	1452-1516	Royalty		2675			King of Spain. Of Aragon. Patron of Columbus
Ferdinand VII (Sp)	1784-1833	Royalty	125	475			His Reign Disastrous to Spain.
Ferebee, Thomas		Aviation	50	125	250	100	Major. Bombadier of Enola Gay
Ferenczi, Sandor	1873-1933	Science	60	180	350		Hung. Psychoanalyst. Freud Friend
Ferguson, Homer		Congress	5	15		10	Senator MI. Ambass. Philippines
Ferguson, Maynard		Entertainment	10			27	FineTrumpet Player. Bandleader
Ferguson, Miriam A. 'Ma'	1875-1961	Governor	60	150			Governor TX. Replaced Impeached Husband
Ferguson, Samuel W. (WD)		Civil War	275	550	928		CSA General
Ferguson, Samuel W.	1834-1917	Civil War	185	350	860		CSA Gen.
Ferguson, William J.		Entertainment	175	225	425		Actor 'Our American Cousin'
Ferkauf, Eugene		Business	8	10	15	15	
Ferlinghetti, Lawrence		Author	20	75	90	25	Am.Poet, Publisher. Beat Movement
Fermi, Enrico	1901-1954	Science	505	1950	3250		Nobel Phys. 1st Controlled Nuclear Chain Reaction
Fernandel	1903-71	Entertainment	25			135	Actor-Comedian Around the World in 80 Days
Ferrar, Geraldine		Entertainment	35			130	Opera. Famous for Puccini Roles
Ferrara, Franco		Entertainment	45			250	Conductor
Ferrare, Cristina		Entertainment	6	8	15	15	Model. TV Host
Ferrari, Enzo	1898-1988	Business	300	665		724	Luxury Sports Car Auto Mfg.& Race Car Driver
Ferraro, Geraldine		Congress	15	45	55	25	Congresswoman NY., V.P. Candidate
Ferrer, Jose	1912-92	Entertainment	20	25	40	57	AA Actor. 'Cyrano'
Ferrer, Mel	1917-	Entertainment	5			20	Actor. Former Radio Producer-Writer.
Ferrer, Miguel	1955-	Entertainment	4			15	Actor son of Jose
Ferrero, Edward (WD)		Civil War	75	245		300	Union General. Commanded Colored Div. 1863
Ferrero, Edward	1831-99	Civil War	50	145	245		Union General

NAME	DATE	CATEGORY	SIG	LS/DS	ALS	SP	COMMENTS
Ferrier, Kathleen	1912-53	Entertainment	55			195	Opera. Br. Contralto. 'Carmen'
Ferrigno, Lou	1952-	Entertainment	5		10	23	Actor. The Hulk. Muscular Former Mr. Universe
Ferris, Scott		Senate/Congress	12	15		15	MOC OK
Ferry, Orris S.(WD)		Civil War	60	95	165	300	Union Gen., U.S. Sen. NY
Ferry, Thomas White	1827-96	Senate	70	95			Sen. MI,Pres. Pro Tem Senate
Fersen, Hans-Axel, Count de	1755-1810	Rev. War		1250			With Rochambeau at Yorktown. Murdered
Fesch, Joseph, Cardinal	1763-1839	Clergy		220	450		Married Napoleon to Josephine.
Fess, Simeon Davison	1861-1936	Senate/Congress	10	27	45	40	MOC, Senator OH. Chmn. Nat. Rep. Committee
Fessenden, Francis (WD)		Civil War	90	182			Union Gen. Lost Leg at Monett's Bluff
Fessenden, Francis	1839-1906	Civil War	56	102	187		Union Gen.
Fessenden, James D.	1833-82	Civil War		55	80		Union Gen.
Fessenden, William P.	1806-69	Cabinet	45	75	175		Lincoln Sec'y Treasury
Fetchit, Stepin	1892-85	Entertainment	35		55	150	Early Afro-Am. Actor-Comedian. Aka Lincoln Perry
Fetterman, William J.	1833-1866	Civil War		9500			Indian Fighter. With 80 Men. Ambushed & Killed
Feuillere, Edwige	1907-	Entertainment	15			38	Fr. Actress. Leading Member 'Comedie Francaise'
Few, William		Rev. War	200	450	750		Continental Congress.1st GA Sen
Feynman, Richard P.		Science	25	40	85	30	Nobel Physics.
Fibich-Hanusova, Betty		Entertainment			250		Opera. Great Czech Alto
Fiderkiewicz, Alfred J., Dr.		Statesman	40	75			Polish Statesman
Fidler, Jimmy	1900-88	Entertainment	20	25	30	45	Powerful Hollywood Gossip Columnist
Fiedler, Arthur	1894-1979	Entertainment	24	95		50	Conductor Boston Pops
Fiedler, John	1925-	Entertainment	5		10	10	Mild, Spectacled, Character Actor. '12 Angry Men'
Field, Charles E.		Clergy	20	35	45	25	
Field, Cyrus W.	1819-92	Business	178	469	550		Atl.Telegraph Cable, Financier. Elevated RRs NYC
Field, Davis Dudley	1805-94	Legal	25		35		Counsel for J.Gould,J.Fiske. Law Codification.
Field, Eugene	1850-95	Author	110	312	400	200	Children's Poet, Journalist. AMsS $900-$1700
Field, Henry Martyn	1822-1907	Clergy	15		35		Presb. Younger Brother Cyrus, Davis, Stephen Field
Field, Kate		Author	10	15			
Field, Marshall, III	1893-1956	Business	95	160	350		Communications Empire. Major Publisher
Field, Marshall, IV.	1916-1965	Business	30	110	170	75	Pres.,CEO Field Entertprises. Publisher, Editor
Field, Marshall, Sr.	1834-1906	Business	400	1250	1150	650	Marshall Field & Co.
Field, Mary French		Author	5	15	20	15	
Field, Rachel	1894-1942	Author	20	85			Am.Novels,'All This & Heaven Too'.Children's Books
Field, Sally	1946-	Entertainment	10	15	25	30	AA Winning Actress. Pin-Up SP $35
Field, Stephen J. (SC)	1816-99	Supreme Court	75	150	300	225	US Supreme Court Justice Under Lincoln
Field, Todd		Entertainment	3			8	
Field, Virginia	1917-92	Entertainment	5		15	15	Br. Actress. Interesting 2nd Leads
Fielder, James F.		Governor	10	15	25	15	Governor NJ
Fielding, Copley		Artist	5		15		Brit. Watercolorist
Fields, Debbi		Entertainment	4			10	
Fields, Gracie, Dame	1898-1979	Entertainment	20	35	55	78	Br. Singer & Comedienne. Knighted for War Effort
Fields, James T.	1817-81	Author	10	20	45		Publisher
Fields, Lew M.	1879-1946	Entertainment	50				SEE Weber & Fields
Fields, Shep		Entertainment	20			40	Big Band Leader-Songwriter-Singer 30's-40's
Fields, Stanley	1884-1941	Entertainment	15	15	30	35	Vintage Character Actor. Former Boxer, Vaudeville

NAME	DATE	CATEGORY	SIG	LS/DS	ALS	SP	COMMENTS
Fields, W. C.	1879-1946	Entertainment	588	1042	1088	1492	Comedian-Actor Stage & Screen. Check S $1375
Fieldy		Entertainment	5			25	Music. Bass Guitar Korn
Fiennes, Joseph (Finnes)		Entertainment	20			65	Br. Actor. 'Shakespeare In Love'
Fiennes, Ralph		Entertainment	15			51	Br. Actor. 'English Patient' etc.
Fiennes, Ranulph		Explorer	10			30	
Fieseler, Gerhard		Aviation	25	55	85	85	
Fifteen (15)		Entertainment	35			60	Rock
Figner, Medea							SEE Mei-Figner
Figueres, Jose		Head of State	15	45	110	20	
Filacuridi, Nicola		Entertainment	15			45	Opera
Filippeschi, Mario		Entertainment	25			85	Opera
Fillmore, Caroline	18xx-1881	First Lady	600	950	800		2nd Wife
Fillmore, Millard (As Pres.)		President	485	877	2738		FF $400-$475. ALS/Cont. $27,500
Fillmore, Millard	1800-74	President	272	900	1697	10000	FF $375-$400-$475. Historic ALS $3750
Finch, Peter	1916-77	Entertainment	80		110	147	Br. Actor.AA. Early Death. Protégé of L. Olivier
Findlay, William	1768-1846	Governor	45	60	115		Gov. PA 1817, Sen. 1821
Fine, Janine		Entertainment				40	Porn Queen
Fine, Larry	1911-74	Entertainment	110			312	Member (1928) Of Three Stooges Comedy Team
Finegan, Bill (William J.)		Entertainment	20			40	Big Band Leader. (Arranger/Sauter)
Finkel, Fyvush		Entertainment	5			20	Character Actor. 'Picket Fences' Emmy
Finlay, Frank	1926-	Entertainment	5	8	15	15	Br. Stage & Film Actor. Screen From '62. TV '84
Finletter, Thomas	1894-1980	Cabinet	7	15	30	20	Korean War Sec'y Air Force. Ambassador
Finley, Jesse J. (WD)		Civil War					CSA Gen., AMsS $6,600
Finley, Jesse J.	1812-1904	Civil War	85	120	220		CSA Gen. US Sen.
Finley, John		Astronaut	5			15	
Finney, Albert	1936-	Entertainment	10	10	20	25	Br. Actor. 'The Entertainer', 'Tom Jones'
Finney, Charles G.	1792-1875	Clergy	50	75	110		Presb. Revivalist-Evangelist.Withdrew-Pres.Oberlin
Finnie, Linda		Entertainment	10			30	Opera
Finston, Nat W.		Composer-Author	10			20	Conductor-Violinist
Fio-Rito, Ted		Entertainment	15			35	Big Band Leader
Fiorella, Pascal A.		Rev.War Era	20	55	125		
Fiorentino, Linda		Entertainment	18			63	Actress
Firestone, Harvey S.	1868-1938	Business	415	2238	2225	607	Fndr. Firestone Tire & Rubber
Firestone, Jr., Harvey S.		Business	25	50	85	35	Pres. CEO Firestone Tire....
Firestone, Leonard K.		Business	15	40	70	30	
Firley, Douglas		Entertainment	6			25	Music. Keyboards Gravity Kills
First Ladies (Four Repub.)		First Ladies	250			900	Nixon, Ford, Reagan, Bush
First Ladies (Kennedy thru Bush)		First Ladies	750				Six
Fischer, Annie		Entertainment				250	
Fischer, Bobby	1943-	Celebrities	45	98	325	112	Champion Am. Chess Player.BS (Chess) $525
Fischer, Edmond H., Dr.		Science	20	45		30	Nobel Medicine
Fischer, Emil	1838-1914	Entertainment	40		75		Opera. Ger. Bass-Baritone. Excelled as 'Sachs'
Fischer, Harold E.		Aviation	10	25	45	35	ACE, Korea, Double Ace
Fischer, Siegfried		Aviation	10	15	25	15	
Fischer-Dieskau, Dietrich		Entertainment	30			90	Opera

NAME	DATE	CATEGORY	SIG	LS/DS	ALS	SP	COMMENTS
Fish, Hamilton	1808-1893	Cabinet	25	64	90	350	Gov., Senator, U.S. Grant & Hayes Sec'y State
Fish, Nicholas		Rev. War	45	120	245		Aide-de-Camp Gen. Scott
Fish, Preserved		Colonial	45	165			Merchant Banker
Fish, Stuyvesant		Business	300	850			RR Baron, Financier
Fishburne, Laurence	1961-	Entertainment	12			55	Actor. Movies. Soap as Child. Difficult Signature
Fisher, Amy		Criminal	20		115		Shot alleged lover's wife.
Fisher, Anna L.		Astronaut	10			25	
Fisher, Bud* (Harry C.)	1885-1954	Cartoonist	75	95		425	'Mutt & Jeff'. Considered 1st Regular Cartoon Strip
Fisher, Carrie		Entertainment	10	36	40	40	Pin-Up SP $35. Star Wars Authentic SP $60
Fisher, Cindy		Entertainment	4			10	
Fisher, Eddie	1928-	Entertainment	5	25		28	Singer. Dumped wife Debbie Reynolds for E. Taylor
Fisher, Fred J.		Business	90				Mfg. Auto Body. Gen'l Motors. 'Body By Fisher'
Fisher, Freddie		Entertainment	5			15	'Schnickelfritz'
Fisher, Geoffrey F.	1887-1972	Clergy	35			50	Archbishop Canterbury
Fisher, Ham*		Cartoonist	100		225	250	'Joe Palooka'
Fisher, Harrison		Artist	40				Orig. Art as Illustrator. S $700
Fisher, John S.		Governor	10	15	35		Governor PA
Fisher, John, Lord	1841-1920	Military	15	25			Brit. Adm. of the Fleet 1905. Prepared Navy For WW
Fisher, Lawrence P.		Business	90	150	410		Co-Founder Fisher Body (GM)
Fisher, William F.		Astronaut	5			20	
Fisk, Clinton B.	1828-90	Civil War	55	85	110		Union Gen. Founded Fisk Univ.
Fisk, James, Jr.	1834-1872	Business	1000	15000		2500	Rarest of Robber Barons. Stock Cert. S $25,000
Fisk, Minnie Maddern	1866-1932	Entertainment	15			35	Am. Stage Actress. Made 2 Silent Films
Fiske, Bradley	1854-1942	Military	15		45		Admiral WW I. Holds 60 Patents for Navy
Fitch, Val L., Dr.		Science	20	35		30	Nobel Physics
Fitz, Reginald H.	1843-1913	Science	75		310		Physician. Identified Cause of Appendicitis
Fitzgerald, Barry	1888-1961	Entertainment	125	135	195	250	Character Actor. AA; Acquired Stardom 'Going My Way'
FitzGerald, Edward	1809-33	Author	90	250	760		Poet. Translator 'Rubaiyat....'
Fitzgerald, Ella	1918-98	Entertainment	83	102	80	250	Am. First Lady of Jazz DS (Conract) $350
Fitzgerald, F. Scott	1896-1940	Author	412	1635	3000	2250	Novelist, Screenwriter. ALS/Content $5,500
Fitzgerald, Garret		Statesman	10	30			Irish Statesman
Fitzgerald, Geraldine	1912-92	Entertainment	12	22		40	Ir. Actress. 'Wuthering Heights'
Fitzgerald, John		Rev. War	35	90	190		
Fitzgerald, John F. (Honey Fitz)		Political	20	55	95		Mayor Boston. JFK Grandfather
Fitzhugh, Gilbert		Business	4		12	10	
Fitzsimmons, Frank E.		Celebrity	3	8	25	10	
Fitzsimons, Thomas	1741-1811	Revolutionary. War	200	325	575		Constitution Signer, Articles of Confed. ALS $6500
Fitzwater, Marlin		Presidential Aide	5			12	
Fix, Paul	1901-83	Entertainment	40			183	Actor. Good General Purpose Actor. Hundreds Roles
Fixx, Jim		Author-Runner	15	35			
Flack, Roberta		Entertainament	15			40	Rock
Flagg, Fannie		Entertainment	5	10	20	20	Also Author, Playwright
Flagg, James Montgomery	1877-1960	Artist	55	190	265	375	Painter, Illustrator. Self Caricature S. $950
Flagler, D. W.		Military	15	20	25	20	
Flagler, Henry M.	1830-1913	Business	900	2712	6500	1800	Stand. Oil Pioneer. Fndr. So. FL

NAME	DATE	CATEGORY	SIG	LS/DS	ALS	SP	COMMENTS
Flagstad, Kirsten	1895-1962	Entertainment	113		150	250	Nor. Soprano
Flahaut, A.C.J., Count	1785-1870	Fr. Revolution	25		60		Exploits in Gallantry. General, Diplomat, Lover
Flahiff, George B., Cardinal		Clergy	35	40	60	40	
Flake, Floyd H.	1945-	Congress	4	10			Congressman NY
Flakus, Walter		Entertainment	6			25	Music. Keyboards Stabbing Westward
Flammarion, Nicolas-Camille	1842-1925	Science	40	65	165		Fr. Astronomer
Flamsteed, John	1646-1719	Clergy-Science	800	975			Br. 1st Astronomer Royal
Flanagan, Edward, Fr.	1886-1948	Clergy	45	110		195	Boy's Town Founder
Flannery, Sean Patrick		Entertainment	15			44	Actor. The Young Indiana Jones
Flatt, Earl Scruggs & Lester		Country Music	50			125	Bluegrass Pioneers
Flaubert, Gustave	1821-80	Author	175	635	1300		Fr. Novelist. Realist School
Flavin, James	1906-76	Entertainment	4	5	10	10	Ir.-Am. Supporting Actor. Usually Bewildered Cop
Flaxman, John	1755-1826	Artist	55		200		Br. Sculptor & Illustrator. Designs for Wedgewood
Fleetwood Mac		Entertainment	111			238	Signed by All 6
Fleetwood, Mick		Entertainment	30			55	Member Fleetwood Mac
Fleischer, Charles		Entertainment	10			20	Voice of Roger Rabbitt
Fleischer, Leonore		Author	15		40	30	'Shadowlands'
Fleischer, Max*	1883-1972	Cartoonist	150	295			Animator. Creator of 'Betty Boop'
Fleischer, Richard	1916-	Entertainment	5			20	Film Director '46's-'87
Fleischmann, Charles L.		Business	110	450			Fleischmann's Yeast
Fleiss, Heidi		Business	10		30	50	Oldest Biz, Hollywood Madame & Hooker to Stars
Fleming, Alexander, Sir	1881-1955	Science	225	281	1500	850	Scottish Bacteriologist. Nobel for Penicillin
Fleming, Ambrose	1849-1945	Science	175		875		Br. Electr. Engineer. Invented 1st Electron Tube
Fleming, Eric	1924-66	Entertainment	225	250		350	Actor. Original 'Rawhide'-TV
Fleming, Francis		Aviation	10	22	40	30	ACE, WW II
Fleming, Ian	1888-1969	Author	475	900	1100	1400	'James Bond' Novels. 1st Ed. Signed $5,000-
Fleming, John Ambrose, Sir	1849-1945	Science	30	65	150		Br. Electrical Engineer. Many Contributions
Fleming, Rhonda	1922-	Entertainment	9	18	25	41	Actress. Pin-Up SP $65
Fleming, Victor	1883-1949	Entertainment	412	250		600	Veteran AA Film Director.'Gone With The Wind'-'OZ'
Fleming-Sandes, Alfred		Military	10	50			WW I Victoria Cross
Fleta, Miguel	1897-1938	Entertainment	45			250	Opera. Span. Tenor
Fletcher, Bramwell	1904-88	Entertainment	20			45	Br. Actor. Light Leading Man of 30s
Fletcher, Frank Jack		Military	25	60	120	60	
Fletcher, Harvey	1884-1981	Science	225				Stereo Sound 1934
Fletcher, James		NASA	10	20	35		Whistle Blower
Fletcher, James Cooley		Clergy	5			25	Missionary
Fletcher, John Gould	1886-1950	Author	18	35	100		Pulitzer Poet. Identified/Imagist Grp., Fugitives
Fletcher, Louise	1936-	Entertainment	6	10	15	35	Oscar Winning Actress.........Over the Cukoos Nest
Flindt, Flemming		Ballet	25			70	Royal Danish Ballet Star
Flint, Austin	1812-86	Physician	70	215	400		Eminent Physician-Teacher
Flint, Keith		Entertainment	10			45	Music. Lead Singer Prodigy
Flint, Lawrence		Aviation	10	16	35	25	
Flippen, Jay C.	1898-1971	Entertainment	25			60	Actor. Vaudeville Background. Cops, Westerns
Flockhart, Calista		Entertainment	14			52	T.V.'s Ally McBeal. Broad Stage Background
Floege, Ernest		Military			45	70	Commandant Paul.Fr.Resistance

NAME	DATE	CATEGORY	SIG	LS/DS	ALS	SP	COMMENTS
Floren, Myron		Entertainment	4			10	Accordian. Lawrence Welk
Florence, William J., Mrs.		Entertainment	10		25	15	Actress-Malvina Pray. Stage. Appeared With Husband
Florence, William Jermyn	1831-91	Entertainment	15	25	40	75	Actor, Songwriter, Playwright. Appeared With Wife
Flores, Juan Jose	1800-1864	Head of State		775			1st President of Equador
Florey, Howard Walter		Science	25	40	75	35	Nobel Medicine, Penicillin
Florey, Paul J., Dr.	1898-1968	Science	25	35	70	45	Nobel Medicine/Fleming. Penicillin
Florey, Robert		Entertainment	15			35	
Flotow, Frederich von	1812-83	Composer	75	220	450		Ger. Opera, Ballet, Concertos
Flourens, Marie-Jean P.	1794-1867	Science		50	225		Fr. Physiologist
Flower, R.P		Governor	10	15			Governor NY
Flower, Wm. Henry, Sir	1831-99	Science	10	25	50		Br. Zoologist. Dir. Natural Hist. Museum, London
Flowers, Bess	1900-84	Entertainment	6	10	15	20	Over 1,000 films. 'Queen of Hollyw'd Extras'
Flowers, Wayland		Entertainment	15			36	Clever Marionette-Puppet Comedian
Floyd, John Buchanan (WD)		Civil War	285		1850		CSA Gen.(Buchanan's Sec'y War 1857-60)
Floyd, John Buchanan	1806-63	Civil War	185	312	342		Gov. VA. Sec'y War, CSA General
Floyd, William	1734-1821	Rev. War	400	1348	1548		Signer Decl. of Indepen. Maj.Gen. NY Militia
Fluckey, Gene		Military	45		110	90	Top US Submarine Cmdr.
Flunger, Anna		Entertainment	6		15	15	
Fluster, Lafayette		Senate	40				Pres. Pro Tem of Senate
Flynn, Edward J.		Political	5	15	25	15	Democratic Boss NY. 'Boss Flynn'
Flynn, Errol	1909-59	Entertainment	325	744	665	1035	Warner Bros. DS $1,500. Legal DS $850, Chk $550
Flynn, James		Entertainment	4	5	10	10	
Flynn, Joe	1925-74	Entertainment	50	60	110	125	Am. Character-Comedian. TV 'McHale's Navy'
Flynn, Steve		Entertainment	3			8	
Flynt, Larry		Publisher	15	75		50	'Hustler Magazine' Publisher
Foale, Mike		Astronaut	5			20	
Foch, Ferdinand	1851-1929	Military	50	125	285	220	Fr. General WW I, Marshal. Active in Major Battles
Foch, Nina	1924-	Entertainment	8		15	18	Dutch-Born Am. Leading Lady. Assoc. Dir.
Fogelberg, Dan		Entertainment	12			30	
Fogerty, John		Entertainment	15	50		35	Rock
Fohstrom, Alma	1856-1936	Entertainment	125			600	Legendary Coloratura Soprano St. Petersburg
Fokker, Anthony H.	1890-1939	Aviation	200	295	525	500	Am. Aircraft Designer-Builder
Foley, David		Entertainment	6			30	
Foley, Red	1910-68	Country Music	30			85	Top Country Star
Foley, Robert	1941-	Military		20		35	General & Vietnam Medal of Honor Recipient
Folger, Charles J.		Cabinet	10	15	35		Sec'y Treasury Under Arthur
Folger, William M.	1844-1928	Military	45	115			Adm. USN. Comm. Phillipine Squadron 189-1905
Follett, Ken		Author	5	12		15	Br. Mystery Novelist
Folsom, Marion B.		Cabinet	15	25		20	Sec'y HEW. Drafter Soc.Sec.Adm.
Folsom, Nathaniel		Rev. War	125		450		Am. Gen., Continental Congress
Foltz, Frederick		Military			45	100	General WW I
Fonck, Paul-Rene'	1894-1953	Aviation	1000	1900			ACE, Fr. WW I. Top Allied Ace
Fonda, Bridget		Entertainment	20			57	Actress. Col. Pin-up $70, Art Print S $100
Fonda, Henry	1905-1982	Entertainment	68	147		138	AA Actor. Lifetime Achievement Award
Fonda, Jane	1937-	Entertainment	15	88	35	37	AA Winner 'Klute' & 'Coming Home'

NAME	DATE	CATEGORY	SIG	LS/DS	ALS	SP	COMMENTS
Fonda, Jelles		Rev. War	50	155	225		Colonial Leader, Rev. War Officer
Fonda, Peter	1939-	Entertainment	12	29		56	Actor. 'Easy Rider'. AA Nominee-'Yulee's Gold'
Fonda, Ten Eyck H.		Civil War	50		95		Military Telegrapher Hero
Fondren, Debra Jo		Entertainment	5			25	'Playboy' '78 Centerfold of the Year. Pin-Up $50.
Fong, Benson		Entertainment	25			40	
Fong, Hiram L.		Senate	5	10		15	Senator HI
Fonseca, Roberto A.		Head of State	5	16	40	20	
Fontaine, Joan	1917-	Entertainment	12	15	40	28	Oscar winning Actress. Pin-Up SP $45
Fontanne, Lynn	1887-1983	Entertainment	15			40	Stage Actress Wife of Partner Alfred Lunt
Fonteyn, Margot	1919-91	Entertainment	40	55	135	195	Premier Ballerina. Fonteyn & Nureyev SP $250
Foot, Solomon		Congress	15	30	45		Repr. VT 1843, CSA Congress
Foote, Andrew Hull	1806-1863	Civil War	55	125	300		Union Adm ALS '63 $3,500. Mortally Wounded 1863
Foote, Arthur Wm.	1853-1937	Composer	30	85	195		Organist. Church Music, Songs, Cantatas
Foote, H.R.B.		Military	10	20			Br. Maj. Gen. Victoria Cross WW II
Foote, Henry S.		Civil War	25	40	70		US Senator, CSA Congress
Foote, Horton		Author	5		20	15	Playwright, Scriptwriter
Foote, Shelby		Author	15	35			
Foraker, Joseph B.	1846-1917	Senator-Gov.	10	32		20	Gov., Sen. OH. Secretly On Std. Oil Payroll as Sen.
Foran, Dick	1910-79	Entertainment	15	20	35	45	Singer-Actor-Cowboy. 40 Year Career
Foray, June		Entertainment	10			25	Voices for Several Rocky & Bullwinkle Characters
Forbes, Bertie Chas.	1880-1954	Business	45	225	175	65	Founder Forbes Magazine
Forbes, George Wm.	1869-1947	Head of State	25	65			NZ Prime Minister.
Forbes, M. Steve		Publisher	15			30	Twice Presidential Candidate
Forbes, Malcolm S.	1933-91	Business	25	60	162	70	Publisher, Motorcyclist, Balloonist, Collector
Forbes, Ralph	1902-51	Entertainment	15	15	30	25	Br. Stage as Child. Movies From 1921
Forbes-Robertson, John, Sir	1853-1937	Entertainment	25		98	58	Br. Vintage Stage, Films. SPc/Gertrude Elliott $125
Force, Manning F.	1824-99	Civil War	40		128		Union Gen. Shiloh, Vicksburg, Atlanta
Ford, Benson		Business	5	15	30	15	Ford Motor Car
Ford, Betty		First Lady	35	115		50	
Ford, Edsel	1893-1943	Business	250	600		500	Pres. Ford Motor Co.
Ford, Edsel B. II		Business	5	10	20	15	Ford Motor Co.
Ford, Eileen		Business	5	30		10	Ford Modelling Agency
Ford, Elaine		Business	20			30	
Ford, Faith		Entertainment	8			43	Actress. Murphy Brown
Ford, Gerald & Ford, Betty		Pres.-1st Lady				125	FDC S. $250
Ford, Gerald R.		President	80	301	1162	111	Content: ALS $5,500, TLS $1,500. Inaug. FDC $550
Ford, Gerald R. (As Pres.)		President	173	479	1440	181	TLS re Warren Comm. $1500. TLS/Cont. $1795
Ford, Glenn	1916-95	Entertainment	37			65	Versatile Film Leading Man
Ford, Harold	1945-	Congress	5	20		15	Longtime Afr.-Am. Dem. MOC TN
Ford, Harrison		Entertainment	72			136	Versatile Film Leading Man. Star Wars SP $250+
Ford, Henry	1863-1947	Business	958	4167	4667	2600	Pioneer Auto Mfg. Important DS $28,500
Ford, Henry II	1917-87	Business	10	45	55	55	Grandson, Pres. & CEO Ford Motor Co.
Ford, John	1895-1973	Entertainment	150			300	Classic Western Film Director
Ford, John Anson		Business	5	10	20	10	
Ford, John Thompson	1829-94	Theatre Owner	475	600	750		Ford's Theater, Wash. D.C.

NAME	DATE	CATEGORY	SIG	LS/DS	ALS	SP	COMMENTS
Ford, Lita		Entertainment	15			45	Singer
Ford, Michael		Entertainment	5			15	Br. Actor
Ford, Paul	1901-76	Entertainment	15			35	Am. Character Actor. Stage, TV, Films. 'OZ' Voices
Ford, Sewell	1868-1946	Author		15	35		Short Story Writer
Ford, Tennessee Ernie	1919-	Country Music	18			36	'Sixteen Tons', 'Mule Train' etc.
Ford, Wallace	1898-1966	Entertainment	20			50	London Born. Played Strong Characters For 30 Years
Fordney, Joseph W.		Senate/Congress	15		30		MOC MI. Lumber, Banking
Forepaugh, Adam	1831-90	Business-Circus	50		75		Early Circus Owner
Forester. C[ecil] S[cott]	1899-1966	Author	75	260	90	95	Br.Biographer, Drama,Novelist.'Horatio Hornblower'
Forgy, Howell M. !908-83		Military Chaplain					'And Pass the Ammunition' S Book $395
Forman, Milos	1932-	Entertainment	20			52	A A Director. One Flew Over the Cukoo's Nest
Forman, Thomas M.		Rev. War	45	100			
Formes, Karl		Entertainment	5	6	15	15	
Formica, Fern		Entertainment	15	25		30	Munchkin,' Wizard of Oz'
Fornay, John	1817-81	Editor	20		48		Prominent Editor & Dem. Political Figure
Forney, John H.	1829-1902	Civil War	125				CSA Gen. Sig/Rank $275, ALS '62 $975
Forney, John W.	1817-81	Journalist	5		25		Author
Forney, William H.	1823-94	Civil War	95	135	300		CSA Gen., Wounded & Captured Twice. MOC AL
Forrest, Edwin	1806-72	Entertainment	35	90	160	150	Early Great Am. Actor. ALS/Cont. $400
Forrest, Frederick	1936-	Entertainment	4			15	Actor. Leading Man of 70's-80's
Forrest, French (WD)		Civil War	175	660			CSA Naval Commander
Forrest, French	1796-1866	Civil War	100	145	195		CSA Naval Commander
Forrest, Hal*		Cartoonist	25			125	'Tailspin Tommy'
Forrest, Nathan B. (WD)		Civil War	1402		14800		CSA Gen. Legendary Exploits! LS/Cont. $22,500
Forrest, Nathan B.	1821-77	Civil War	650	2050	4700		CSA General
Forrest, Sally	1928-	Entertainment	5			15	Ingenue-Dancer-Leading Lady in Early 50's
Forrest, Steve	1924-	Entertainment	7			15	Actor-Brother of Dana Andrews. Leads-2nd Leads
Forrestal, James	1892-1949	Cabinet	45	95		55	Sec'y Navy. 1st Sec'y Defense. Suicide
Forrester, Pat		Astronaut	6			20	
Forslund, Constance		Entertainment	5		15	15	
Forster, Edw. Morgan	1879-1970	Author	70	308	345		Br. Novelist. Howard's End, Passage to India
Forster, John	1812-76	Author	20	35	85		Br. Historian, Biographer of Dickens, Swift
Forster, Robert	1942-	Entertainment	5			15	Actor
Forsyth, Frederick		Author	10	35	80	20	Br., Master of Spy Novels
Forsyth, James	1842-1915	Civil War	25		60		Admiral. Served/Farragut. Also Span-Am. War
Forsyth, James Wm.	1835-1906	Civil War	55	110	180		Union Gen.,Fought at 'Wounded Knee.ALS/Cont. $250.
Forsyth, John	1780-1841	Cabinet	25	55	150		Sec'y of State (Jackson & Van Buren)Senator
Forsythe, John	1918-	Entertainment	10		20	30	Leading Man. Smoothe, Appealing. 'Dynasty'
Fort, George F.		Governor	15	35	50		Governor NJ 1850
Fort, John Franklin		Governor	5	15			New Jersey
Fort, Luigi		Entertainment	20			50	Opera
Fortas, Abe (SC)	1910-82	Supreme Court	50	150	200		Resigned from Court
Forte', Fabian (Fabian)	1942-	Entertainment	5		25	20	Handsome Rock Singer. Teenage Idol
Forti, Carmen Fiorella		Entertainment	25			60	Opera
Forward, Walter	1786-1852	Cabinet	15	42	72		Sec'y Treasury 1841

NAME	DATE	CATEGORY	SIG	LS/DS	ALS	SP	COMMENTS
Fosbury, Dick		Sportsman	25			45	Eponym for Fosbury Flop (High Jump)
Fosdick, Harry Emerson	1878-1969	Clergy	35	60	90	50	Baptist Minister, Author
Foss, Joe		Aviation	30	75	85	55	ACE, WW II, Medal of Honor
Foss, Sam Walter	1858-1911	Author	5	10	20	15	Editor, Humorist. 'House By The Side of The Road'
Fosse, Bob	1927-1987	Entertainment	35	120	90	60	AA. Choreographer-Film Director
Foster, Abiel	1735-1806	Clergy-Political	120	345			Cont. Congress. 1st MOC NH '89
Foster, Charles	1828-1904	Cabinet	35	55	100		Gov. OH, Sec'y Treas.
Foster, Dianne		Entertainment	5			20	Actress
Foster, Hal*	1892-1982	Cartoonist	100			500	'Tarzan',
Foster, Hal*	1892-1982	Cartoonist	100			600	'Prince Valiant'
Foster, Jodie	1962-	Entertainment	38			98	Actress, Dir., AA Winner. Pin-up $135
Foster, John Gray (WD)		Civil War	55	105	275		Union General
Foster, John Gray	1823-74	Civil War	35	45	70		Union Gen.
Foster, John W.	1836-1917	Cabinet	25		58	165	Sec'y State 1892, Diplomat, CW Union Officer
Foster, Lafayette S.	1806-80	Senate	25	62	98		Civil War Senator CT. ALS As Acting VP $800
Foster, Lawrence		Entertainment	5		10	10	
Foster, Myles B.		Artist	17	40	70		
Foster, Norman	1900-76	Entertainment	15	15	35	45	Actor-Director. Stage & Films from 30's
Foster, Preston	1901-70	Entertainment	28	85		65	Actor. Handsome Leading Man. Over 100 Films
Foster, Stephen	1826-64	Composers	1000	3500	10000		Pop Songs of Day. 'My Old Kentucky Home' NRPA
Foster, Susanna	1924-	Entertainment	15	30		25	Singer-Actress. One Major Prod. 'Phantom of Opera'
Foucauld, Charles E.	1858-1916	Explorer-Clergy	300		875		Fr. Priest & Explorer
Foucault, Leon	1819-68	Science	150		715		Fr. Physicist. Speed of Light. Rotation of Earth
Fouche', Jos. Duc d'Otrante	1759-1820	Fr. Revolution	125	400	680		Politician, Advisor Nap.
Foulois, Benj. D.	1880-1967	Aviation	50			150	General. Pioneer Aviator
Fountain, Pete		Entertainment	10		25	43	Top Jazz-Dixieland Clarinetist
Four Seasons, The (4)		Rock Group				125	60's Rock Group. DS $150
Four Tops		Entertainment	40			95	Rock Singing Group
Fournet, Jean		Entertainment	25			70	Conductor
Fournier, G.		Military	55	85			
Fowler, Gene	1890-1960	Author	20	90		30	Journalist, Biographer, Novelist
Fowler, Henry H.		Cabinet	5	20	35		Sec'y Treas.
Fowler, Jim		Entertainment	4			12	Animal Handler. Seen on 'Tonight Show'
Fowler, William, Dr.		Science	20	30	45	30	Nobel Physics
Fowles, John		Author	30	70	150	35	Br.Novelist.Fr. Lieut's Woman
Fowley, Douglas	1911-	Entertainment	10			30	Vet. Stage-Film Character Actor. Over 200 Films
Fox, Bernard		Entertainment	8			30	Actor. Hogan's Heroes, Bewitched, Titanic
Fox, Charles	1749-1806	Statesman	40	65	212		Br.Reformer, Orator, Libel Bill
Fox, Edward	1937-	Entertainment	5			15	Br. Actor. Blonde-Brother of James. Similar Style
Fox, Fontaine T.*		Cartoonist	35	50		200	'Toonerville Trolley'
Fox, Fred S.		Entertainment	10		45		Actor 'Mayberry'
Fox, James	1939-	Entertainment	5			15	Br. Actor. Leading Man. Similar in Style to Edward
Fox, Matthew		Entertainment	10			45	Actor
Fox, Michael J.	1961-	Entertainment	20	37	40	40	'Back to the Future', TV Series 'Family Ties'
Fox, Samantha		Entertainment	12			53	Pin-Up $55

NAME	DATE	CATEGORY	SIG	LS/DS	ALS	SP	COMMENTS
Fox, Samuel		Clergy	15	20	25	35	
Fox, William	1879-1952	Business	185	550		375	Founder Fox Film Corp.
Foxworth, P. E.		Celebrity	5	15	35		
Foxworth, Robert	1941-	Entertainment	5			10	Actor. Good General Purpose . Mostly TV from '72
Foxworthy, Jeff		Entertainment	7			35	Comedian-Red Neck Routines
Foxx, Redd	1922-91	Entertainment	25	38		55	Comedian. Stand-up & Sit-Com. 'Sanford & Son'
Foy, Eddie, Jr.	1905-83	Entertainment	20	25	40	45	Am. Vaudeville Entertainer. Few 50s-60s Films
Foy, Eddie, Sr.	1854-1928	Entertainment	25			60	Am. Vaudeville Comedian. Few Films
Foy, Maximilian S., Count	1775-1825	Fr. Revolution	25	40	95		Fr. Statesman, General. Waterloo
Fradona, Ramon*		Cartoonist	15			50	'Brenda Starr'
Frakes, Jonathan		Entertainment	15			43	'Star Trek-Next Generation'
Frampton, George, Sir	1860-1928	Artist	20		48		Brit. Sculp. Edith Cavell Mem. Peter Pan
Frampton, Peter		Entertainment	10			30	Rock
France, Anatole (Thibault J.)	1844-1924	Author	50	130	235	300	Fr. Novels, Poetry, Critic. Nobel 1921
Francescatti, Zino		Entertainment	30			200	Violinist. 4x6 SP $150
Franchetti, Alberto, Baron	1860-1942	Composer	35		130	90	Wrote 9 Operas, Chamber Music, Symphony
Franchi, Sergio	1933-90	Entertainment	10			30	Singer
Franciosa, Anthony	1928-	Entertainment	7		12	18	Broadway & Film 'Hatful of Rain'=AA Nomination
Francis I Fr.	1494-1547	Royalty	500	750			France. Special DS $2,750
Francis I	1777-1830	Royalty	40	185			King Two Sicilies
Francis II	1768-1835	Royalty	95	300	425		Last Holy Roman Emperor(Aus)
Francis V	1819-75	Royalty	40	100			Duke of Modena
Francis, Anne	1930-	Entertainment	7		15	24	Film Leading Lady. Radio Children. Soaps
Francis, Arlene	1912-	Entertainment	5		15	10	Gained Popularity as Radio-TV Hostess & Panelist
Francis, Connie	1938-	Entertainment	7		35	25	Singer. Top Vocalist late 50's-early 60's
Francis, David R.		Cabinet	15	30	50	25	Sec'y Interior 1896
Francis, Dick		Author	25	72	80	40	Br. Jockey Turned Mystery Writer
Francis, Genie		Entertainment	5		15	15	Actress. 'General Hospital'
Francis, Kay	1903-68	Entertainment	25	30	70	95	One of Hollywood's Highly Paid Glamour Stars-30's
Franciscus, James	1934-91	Entertainment	10	12	15	20	Am. Leading Man. Films and TV Series
Franck, Cesar	1822-1920	Composer	340	1100	658		AMusMsS $5,000
Francks, Cree		Entertainment	4			12	Actress/Voice Artist
Franco, Francisco	1892-1975	Head of State	175	750	1300	338	Sp. General & Dictator
Frank, August		Military	10	30	45		
Frank, Diana		Entertainment	3			8	
Frank, Hans		Nazi Lawyer	275	500			Nazi Administrator of Poland
Frank, Otto	1889-1980	Celebrity WWII		1500			ANS on Hand Painted Card $2500. Ann Frank
Franken, Rose		Author	10	25	40		Playwright
Frankenheimer, John	1930-	Entertainment	10		30	25	Film Director
Frankfurter, Felix (SC)	1882-1965	Supreme Court	155	904	1298	750	Founder Am. Civil Liberties Un. Special TLS $2900
Franklin, Benjamin	1706-90	Rev. War	4250	10114	21450		MAN FOR ALL SEASONS>>Rev. War Dte. DS $25,000
Franklin, Bonnie		Entertainment	5		15	20	Actress. 'One Day at a Time'
Franklin, Herbert H.	1867-1956	Business	35	125			Pioneer Auto Manufacturer
Franklin, Jane	1792-1875	Author	65		285		Wife of John Franklin, Traveller, Explorer
Franklin, John, Sir	1786-1847	Explorer	125	320	610		Proved NW Passage

NAME	DATE	CATEGORY	SIG	LS/DS	ALS	SP	COMMENTS
Franklin, William	1731-1813	Colonial & Revol.	145	475	865		Brit. Gov. NJ, Illegitimate Son of Benjamin
Franklin, Wm. Buell (WD)		Civil War	125		225	450	Union Gen. AES/3 Gen'ls $825
Franklin, Wm. Buell	1823-1903	Civil War	80	162	202	200	Union Gen.
Frann, Mary	1943-98	Entertainment	10			35	Actress. Newhart
Frantz, Charton C.		Business	10	35	45	20	
Franz Ferdinand	1863-1914	Royalty				1380	Archduke Austria. Assassinated
Franz Josef II, Crown Prince		Royalty	40	75	140	50	Liechtenstein
Franz Joseph I,	1830-1916	Royalty	155	540	875		Emperor of Austria
Franz, Arthur	1920-	Entertainment	10			20	Am. Leading Man & Character Actor; Radio,Stage,TV
Franz, Dennis		Entertainment	12			40	Actor. NYPD Blue DS $95. Emmy
Fraser, Brendan		Entertainment	6			40	Actor. George of the Jungle
Fraser, Douglas A.		Labor	10	15		15	Union President
Fraser, James Earle	1876-1953	Artist	540	662			Am.Sculptor of Buffalo Nickel, Lincoln, St.Gaudens
Fraser, Malcolm		Head of State	10			30	P.M. Australia
Fraser, Peter		Head of State	10	25		20	Prime Minister New Zealand
Frasier (Cast of)		Entertainment	102			250	All Five
Frawley, William	1887-1966	Entertainment	255	408		450	Dour Character Actor.Fred Mertz, Lucy...Chk 475
Frazer, James George	1854-1941	Science	120		650		Scottish Anthropologist-Classicist.Golden Bough
Frazer, John Wesley	1827-1906	Civil War	165	255			CSA General. With no shot fired, surrendered!
Frazer, Joseph W.		Business	275	600			Kaiser-Frazer Auto Mfg.
Frazetta, Frank*		Cartoonist	50			375	'Johnny Comet'
Frazier, Brendon		Entertainment	5			30	Actor
Freddy & The Dreamers (All)		Entertainment	105				
Frederic, Harold		Author	10	35	70		Am. Novelist, Correspondent
Frederick Augustus I,	1750-1827	Royalty		275			The Just, Saxony
Frederick Augustus II	1797-1854	Royalty		175			King Saxony
Frederick I (Wurttemburg)	1754-1816	Royalty	70	95			Duke of Wurttemburg
Frederick II, The Great	1712-86	Royalty	400	931	2185		Prussia
Frederick III	1831-1888	Royalty	70	260	495	500	Queen Victoria's Son-in-Law. Ger. Emperor 99 Days
Frederick IV	1671-1730	Royalty		320	805		Denmark
Frederick IX	1899-1972	Royalty	50	175	350		Denmark
Frederick V	1723-66	Royalty	90	270	500		Denmark
Frederick VI	1768-1839	Royalty	85	270			Denmark
Frederick VII	1808-63	Royalty	45	150			Denmark
Frederick Wm. I	1688-1740	Royalty	145	420			Prussia
Frederick Wm. II	1744-1797	Royalty		250	490		Prussia. Succeded by Uncle Frederick II, The Great
Frederick Wm. III	1770-1840	Royalty	65	275	475		Prussia
Frederick Wm. IV	1795-1861	Royalty	100	425	750		Prussia. Insane
Frederick, Pauline		Journalist	10		25	25	Pioneer TV Reporter. Debut 1949
Frederick, Pauline	1883-1938	Entertainment	20	35		80	Chorus Girl at 19. Silent Cinema Star from 1915
Frederick, Prince of Wales	1707-51	Royalty		110			Son of Geo. II. Father of Geo. III
Fredericks, Fred*		Cartoonist	18		85	50	'Mandrake The Magician'
Fredericks, R.N.		Banker	12				
Freed, Bert	1919-	Entertainment	5		15	15	Am. Character Actor
Freeland, Paul van		Head of State	8		40	20	Prime Minister

NAME	DATE	CATEGORY	SIG	LS/DS	ALS	SP	COMMENTS
Freeman, Kathleen	1919-	Entertainment	10	15		20	Long Time Character Actress. Films - TV
Freeman, Mona	1926-	Entertainment	5		15	18	Ingenue-Leading Lady.
Freeman, Morgan	1937-	Entertainment	15		50	45	Fine Afro-Am Actor. Acadamy Award
Freeman, Orville		Cabinet	7	20	25	10	Sec'y Agriculture. Gov. MN
Freeman, Samuel		Rev. War	15	45	100		Rev. War Patriot
Freeman, Ted		Astronaut	10			48	
Fregeville, C.L.J.Marquis		Fr. Rev. War	20	35	75		
Freleng, Friz*	1906-95	Cartoonist	45	145		239	Animator, Krazy Cat, Bugs Bunny, Daffy Duck etc.
Frelinghuysen, Frederick T.	1817-85	Cabinet	20	60	105	45	Sec'y State, Senator NJ
Frelinghuysen, Joseph S		Senate/Congress	5	15			Senator NJ
Fremont, Jessie Benton	1824-1902	Author	35	80	270		Writer-'Far West Sketches'Wife of John C. Fremont
Fremont, John C. (WD)		Civil War	282	1208	1532		Union Gen. Explorer & Statesman
Fremont, John C.	1813-90	Civil War	225	650	875		Union Gen.-Content ALS $6,500
Fremstad, Olive	1871-1951	Entertainment	95			375	Swe-Am. Soprano. Opera. Europe & Met 1903-1917
French, Daniel Chester	1850-1931	Artist	95	210	284	125	Sculptor, Lincoln Memorial
French, John	1852-1925	Military	50		145		1st Earl Ypres. Field-marshal
French, Samuel Gibbs	1818-1910	Civil War	160	310	375		CSA General
French, Victor		Entertainment	15			40	
French, William H.	1815-81	Civil War	55	125	280		Union General
Freni, Mirella	1935-	Entertainment	10			45	It Soprano. Opera. 'Violetta', 'Mimi', 'Butterfly'
Freron, Louis M.S.	1754-1802	Fr. Revolution	25	45	90		Revolutionary Politician.Conspiracy vs Robespierre
Fresnay, Pierre	1897-1975	Entertainment	10			45	Fr. Actor/Dir. Important Film Personality in 30s
Freud, Anna	1895-1982	Science		570	350		Daughter of Sigmund Freud
Freud, Sigmund	1856-1939	Science	1550	4275	4795	9475	Psychoanalysis. ALS/Content $7,500-$22,500
Frey, Richard		Aviation	25	50	100	65	
Friant, Louis, Count		Fr. Revolution	30	75	150		
Frick, Henry Clay	1849-1919	Business	350	1975	1200		Carnegie Steel. Coke Mfg. Frick Art Museum
Frick, Stephen		Astronaut	6			22	
Fricke, Janie		Entertainment	5			10	Singer
Fricke, Richard I.		Business	10	35	45	20	
Fricker, Brenda	1944-	Entertainment	20	35	35	67	Ir. Character Actress. AA for 'My Left Foot'
Frid, Jonathan		Entertainment	10			50	
Friedan, Bette		Feminist	15		25	20	
Friedgen, A.E.		Business	10	35	45	20	
Friedkin, William	1939-	Entertainment	10	20		25	Director. AA for 'The French Connection' 1971
Friedman, Herbert		Science	15	35	55	20	
Friedman, Jerome I.		Science	20	35		30	Nobel Physics
Friedman, Milton		Economist-Author	20	35		25	Nobel Economics
Friends (Cast Of)		Entertainment	90			250	Cast of 6 (Authentic)
Friganza, Trixie		Entertainment	5			10	Actress. Early Films
Friml, Rudolf	1879-1972	Composer	100	275	325	212	Operettas. Major Stage-Film Hits. AMusS $750
Frisch, Karl von		Science	15	30	40	25	Nobel Medicine
Fritchie, Barbara (Frietschie)		Civil War	12500				Patriotic Heroine of Civil War Incident. NRPA
Frith, William P.	1819-1909	Artist	25	45	115		Crowded Scenes Contemporay Life. 'Derby Day' etc.
Fritsch, Werner von		Military	55	150	210	175	

NAME	DATE	CATEGORY	SIG	LS/DS	ALS	SP	COMMENTS
Frizzell, Lefty	1928-	Country Music	25			65	Singer-Songwriter-Guitarist
Frobe, Gert	1913-88	Entertainment	30			108	Ger. Character Actor
Frohman, Daniel	1851-1940	Entertainment	25		100	75	Dean of Am.Theatrical Producers
Froman, Jane	1907-80	Entertainment	15	15	25	50	Major Singing Star. Suffered Air Crash. Crippled
Fromm, Erich	1900-1980	Science	45	150		75	Am. Ger. Born. Psychoanalist-Social Philosopher
Fromme, Lynette 'Squeaky'		Assassin	50	120	210	60	Charles Manson Follower. Attempted Assassination
Frondizi, Arturo		Head of State	15	35	75	55	President Argentina
Frontenac, Louis, Comte	1620-1698	Statesman			5400		Gov. La Nouvelle France(Canada)
Frontiersmen, The		Country Music	25			55	Populart Singing Group. Films-Records
Frost, A.B.*		Cartoonist	40			188	Illustrator
Frost, Daniel Marsh	1823-1900	Civil War	175	245	450		CSA Gen. Surrounded. Saw 1st Blood. Surrendered
Frost, David		Entertainment	5			15	Br. Interviewer of Major Personalities5
Frost, Edwin B.		Science	10	25	45		Am. Astronomer
Frost, Robert	1874-1963	Author	150	685	2350	735	Poet. Pulitzer 1924,'31,'37,'43
Frost, Sadie		Entertainment	10			35	Br.Actress. Bram Stoker's Dracula etc.
Frost, Terry		Entertainment	10			40	Vintage cowboy actor
Frothingham, Octavius B.	1822-95	Clergy	25	35	50		Am. Unitarian. Desciple of Theodore Parker
Fry, Christopher		Author	30	160	230		Br. Dramatist
Fry, Elizabeth	1780-1845	Clergy-Philanthro	40	125	185		Br. Quaker Philanthropist
Fry, Franklin C.	1900-68	Clergy	20	25	35		Pres. Lutheran Church, World Relief, World Fed.
Fry, James Barnet	1827-94	Civil War	40	65	100		Union Gen. Shiloh, 1st Bull Run....
Fry, Roger	1866-1934	Artist	35		200		Br. Art Critic & Artist. Lecturer
Frye, Dwight	1899-1943	Entertainment	950		1750	2000	Cornered the Market in Crazed Hunchbacks
Frye, Wm. P.		Vice President	15				Acting VP
Fuad I, King-Sultan	1868-1936	Royalty	95	300			King-Sultan of Egypt. Gen'l. Fndr. Egypt. Univ.
Fuchida, Mitsuo		Military-Aviation	300	350	500		Led Attack on Pearl Harbor 1941
Fuchs, Rutger		Military	40	125	195	95	
Fuchs, Vivian E. Sir	1908-	Explorer	27	75	158		Br. Antarctic Explorer-Geologist
Fuentes, Daisy		Entertainment	12			55	
Fukuda, Takeo		Head of State	15		50	30	Prime Minister Japan
Fukui, Kenichi		Science	20	30	45	25	Nobel Chemistry
Fulbright, James W.	1905-95	Congress	20	40	100	55	Senator AR, Fulbright Scholarship
Fulford, Millie Hughes		Astronaut	10			15	
Fulgham, Robert		Author	5			15	
Fulkerson, Abraham	1834-1902	Congress	20	35			CSA Colonel. MOC TN
Fuller, Alfred C.	1885-1973	Business	125		195	175	Fndr. Fuller Brush Co.Pioneered Door to Door Sales
Fuller, Alvan T.		Governor	15	25		20	Governor, MOC MA
Fuller, Buckminster R.	1895-1983	Science	42	85	140	176	Br-Am. Architectural Engin'r, Geodetic Dome
Fuller, Delores		Entertainment	20			50	Actress/Ed Wood
Fuller, Eduard		Author	6	20	40		
Fuller, John G.		Celebrity	10	16			
Fuller, Loie	1862-1928	Entertainment	50	124	200	350	Am. Dancer
Fuller, Margaret	1810-1850	Reformer-Author	140	250	450		Feminist, ALS/Content $2,500
Fuller, Melville W. (SC)	1833-1910	Supreme Court	62	150	275	175	
Fuller, Robert	1934-	Entertainment	5			10	Am. Leading Man. Mostly TV. Many Westerns

NAME	DATE	CATEGORY	SIG	LS/DS	ALS	SP	COMMENTS
Fuller, Sam	1912-	Entertainment	35			80	Film Writer-Director.
Fullerton, Chas. Gordon		Astronaut	10	30	35		
Fullerton, Gordon		Astronaut	5			10	
Fulton, Fitz		Astronaut	10		15	22	
Fulton, Robert	1765-1815	Inventor	325	1181	4240		Submarine, Steamboat. ALS/Content $6500
Fulton, William S.	1795-1844	Congress	16		45		Sen. AR, Gov. AR
Funicello, Annette		Entertainment	10		25	35	Actress of Mickey Mouse Club. Pin-Up SP $40
Funk, Casimer		Science	25	65		30	Biochemist Discovered Thiamin
Funk, Isaac K.	1839-1912	Publisher	35	80	135		Funk & Wagnalls Dictionary
Funk, Larry		Bandleader	10			30	
Funston, Frederick	1865-1917	Military	75	195	300		Cuba, Span.-American War, MOH. Captured Aguinaldo
Furcolo, Foster		Governor	10	25			Governor MA
Furnas, Robert W.		Governor	5	10			Governor NE
Furness, Betty	1916-94	Entertainment	15	20	30	45	Actress. Early TV Hostess & Consumer Advocate
Furness, William H.		Clergy	10	15	20		
Furniss, Harry	1854-1925	Artist		178	360		Br. Illustrator-Caricaturist. Political & Social
Furrer, Reinhard		Astronaut	15			95	Germany
Furstenberg, Betsy von		Entertainment	5	10		20	Fashion Designer
Furtwangler, Wilhelm	1886-1954	Entertainment	400	500	800	773	Controversial Ger. Conductor WW II. SPpc $840
Fuseli, Henry	1741-1825	Artist	250	500			Br.-Swiss Romantic Painter, Author
Futrell, J.M.		Governor	5	12		10	Governor AR
Fyfe, John		Military	15			30	WW II Hero. Submarine Ace

G

NAME	DATE	CATEGORY	SIG	LS/DS	ALS	SP	COMMENTS
Gabet, Sharon		Entertainment	5		15	15	
Gabin, Jean		Entertainment	35			255	Fr. Romantic Leading Actor
Gable, Clark	1901-60	Entertainment	375	452	850	1108	Actor. The King.... Rhett Butler SP $1500
Gable, Kay		Entertainment	8		15	20	
Gabor, Eva		Entertainment	25		30	45	
Gabor, Zsa Zsa		Entertainment	5		15	20	Pin-Up SP $20
Gabreski, Frances J. Gabby		Aviation	35	95	125	110	US ACE, WW II, 5th Leading Fighter Ace.
Gabriel, John Peter	1746-1807	Rev. War					General, Politician, Clergy.MsDS to Franklin $3500
Gabriel, Peter		Entertainment	15			50	Rock
Gabrielle, Monique		Entertainment	15			30	Pin-Up SP $35
Gabrilowitsch, Ossip	1878-1936	Entertainment	90	135	240	115	Rus.-Am. Pianist,Conductor. AMusQS $275
Gacy, John Wayne		Criminal	50	195	225	175	Convicted Serial Killer.Original Paintings $1,000+
Gadsden, James		Diplomat-Business	110	350	625		Gadsden Purchase
Gadski-Tauscher, Johanna		Entertainment	50		50	112	Ger.-Born Wagnerian Soprano
Gaffney, Drew		Astronaut	4			20	
Gagarin, Yuri & Gherman, Titov		Cosmonauts					SP's (2) $1,725
Gagarin, Yuri & Leonov, Alleksei		Cosmonauts				2995	SP/Both Cosmonauts
Gagarin, Yuri	1934-68	Astronaut	412	1269		975	1st Man To Travel In Space.SP Pc $500-$650-$1300

NAME	DATE	CATEGORY	SIG	LS/DS	ALS	SP	COMMENTS
Gage, Lyman J.		Cabinet	15	25	50	45	Sec'y Treasury 1897
Gage, Nicholas		Author	10	25		15	
Gage, Thomas		Rev. War	225	885	950		Br. General. Commander-in-Chief
Gagnon, Ren, A.		Military	25	30		40	Iwo Jima Flag Raising FDC $225
Gail, Max		Entertainment	10		15	20	
Gaines, John P.	1795-1857	Congress	20		35		MOC OR, Soldier, Gov. OR
Gainsborough, Thomas	1727-88	Artist	275	760	1762		Br. Portraitist The Blue Boy. Landscapes
Gajdusek, D. Carleton, Dr.		Science	20	35		35	Nobel Medicine
Galanos, James		Business	12	30	50	25	
Galard, Genevieve de		Celebrity	40			50	
Galbraith, John Ken.		Economist	15	35		25	Author Books Economics
Gale, Zona	1874-1938	Author	10	55	75	20	American Novelist Short Story Writer
Galella, Ron		Photographer	8	12		10	Celebrity Photographer
Galer, Robert E., Jr.		Aviation				50	Gen'l WW II. MOH. Air Ace
Galileo	1564-1642	Science					It. Astr. Extremely Rare.Brings Top Auction Prices
Gall, Bob		Business	4			10	Business Exec.
Gallagher, Megan		Entertainment	8			35	Actress
Gallagher, Peter		Entertainment	4			10	Actor
Galland, Adolf	1912-96	Aviation	40	75	150	135	ACE. Ger. WW II, Luftwaffe Head
Gallatin, Albert	1761-1849	Cabinet	100	447	463		Served both Jefferson & Madison-Sec'y Treas.
Gallatin, Albert E.	1881-1952	Artist					Pencil Sketch $250
Galle, Emile	1846-1904	Artist	100	325	645		Fr. Artist in Glass & Furniture Mfg.
Galli-Curci, Amelita	1889-1963	Entertainment	62	190	340	200	Opera
Gallian, Ketti		Entertainment	8		19	20	
Gallico, Paul W.		Author	15	110		35	Am.Novelist. 'Poseidon Adventure'
Galligan, Zach		Entertainment	4			12	Actor. Gremlins
Gallinger, Jacob Harold	1837-1918	Congress	10	20	35	20	MOC.,Senator NH 1891-1919
Gallo, Ernest & Julio		Business	40	145		65	Award Winning Gallo Winery, Sonoma, CA
Gallo, Gustavo		Entertainment	20			50	Opera
Gallo, Robert, Dr.		Science	20	35		45	Research. Co-Discoverer HIV Virus
Galloway, Joseph	1731-1803	Rev. War		3250			Continental Congr.& Army. Tory Loyalist
Galloway, Marie S., 1st Lt. ANC		Medical	20		95		Nurse. Visited Hawaiian Leper Colony. 40's
Gallup, Benadam		Military	40	150			Colonel French-Indian War.Groton, CT Selectman
Gallup, George, Jr.	1901-84	Pollster	10	95		30	Gallup Poll. TLS/Original Poll re '76 Pres. $295
Galsworthy, John	1867-1933	Author	48	85	160	225	Br. Novelist, Playwright
Galvan, Elias G., Bishop		Clergy	20	25	35	35	
Galvin, Robert		Business	12	17	25	15	
Galway, James		Entertainment	10			40	Irish Flutist. AMusQS $50
Gam, Rita	1928-	Entertainment	5	7	15	15	Actress
Gambee, Charles R.		Civil War	20	55			Col. 53rd Ohio Vol. KIA Resecca
Gambier, James, 1st Baron		Military	35	130			Br. Naval Cmdr. Admiral of the Fleet.
Gamble, Hamilton R.	1798-1864	Civil War	35		195		CW Gov. MO. Cmmdr.-in-Chief MO Militia
Gance, Abel	1889-1981	Entertainment		295	500		Fr. Actor,Dir., Writer. One of Greatest Directors.
Gandhi, Indira	1917-84	Head of State	140	350	350	750	Assassinated P.M. India. TLS/Cont.$600, FDC S $175
Gandhi, Mohandas K.	1869-1948	Political Leader	1150	1325	2550	3650	Spiritual Leader India

NAME	DATE	CATEGORY	SIG	LS/DS	ALS	SP	COMMENTS
Gandhi, Rajiv		Head of State	40		85	150	P.M. of India, Assasinated
Gandier, D.M., Rev.		Clergy	10	20	35		Temperance Advocate
Gann, Ernest K.		Author	10	20	35		
Gannett, Frank E.		Business	20	55	140	35	Newspaper, TV, Radio Empire
Ganz, Rudolph		Conductor	15			60	Swiss/Am. Pianist/Conductor
Garat, Pierre (Fils)		Entertainment	45		120		Tenor Son
Garat, Pierre (Pere)	1762-1823	Entertainment	125		300		1st Great French Tenor
Garber, Jan		Entertainment	15			35	Big Band Leader
Garbo, Greta	1905-91	Entertainment	1575	2925	7225	10583	Major Internat'l Film Star. ALS/Cont.$16,500.
Garcelon, Alonzo		Governor	5	12			Governor ME
Garcia, Andy		Entertainment	15			52	Actor
Garcia, Jerry		Entertainment	60	75		175	Rock. Run For The Roses Alb. S $225
Garcia, Manuel	1805-1906	Entertainment	20		75		Musician & Inventor of the Laryngoscope
Garcia-Robles, Alfonso, Dr.		Diplomat	35		130	60	Nobel Peace Prize, Disarmament
Gardanne, Gaspard A.		Fr. Revolution	40	115	250		
Garde, Betty		Entertainment	5			12	Actress
Garden, Mary	1874-1967	Entertainment	42	45	70	145	Opera. Scottish Born, Am. Soprano
Gardenia, Vincent	1922-92	Entertainment	5			20	Actor
Gardiner, Reginald		Entertainment	10			35	
Gardner, Ava	1922-90	Entertainment	52	78	110	121	Actress. Pin-Up SP $150
Gardner, Dale A.		Astronaut	10			25	
Gardner, Erle Stanley	1889-1970	Author	85	225	275	175	Lawyer & Detective Novelist
Gardner, Franklin (WD)		Civil War	375	500	1510		CSA Gen.
Gardner, Franklin	1823-73	Civil War	225	215	850		CSA General
Gardner, Guy S.		Astronaut	6			20	
Gardner, John L.		Civil War	25		155		Union Gen.
Gardner, John W.		Cabinet	5	30	35	10	Sec'y HEW. Fndr. 'Common Cause'
Gardner, O. Max		Governor	15	20	35	20	Gov. NC. Lawyer, Industrialist
Garfield, James A. (As Pres.)		President	323	8308			Assassinated July 1881. Rare DS 4/15/81 $10,000
Garfield, James A.	1831-81	President	250	713	1507	1900	Union Gen., DS/War Dte $2,500, FF$395
Garfield, James R.	1865-1950	Cabinet	20	35	70	35	Sec'y Interior 1907
Garfield, John	1913-1952	Entertainment	75	95		395	Warner Bros.Star.Died at 39.Born Julius Garfinkle
Garfield, Lucretia R.	1832-1918	First Lady	95	180	145		
Garfunkel, Art		Entertainment	25			38	Singer-Songwriter Frequently/Paul Simon
Gargan, William	1905-79	Entertainment	15	15	30	40	Vintage Leading Man. Films-Broadway. 1929
Garibaldi, Giuseppe	1807-82	Head of State	140	415			It. Nationalist Leader, Soldier, Patriot
Garland, Augustus H.	1832-99	Cabinet & CW	70	145	215		Att'y Gen. & CSA Congress,Gov.
Garland, Beverly		Entertainment	5	10		20	Actress
Garland, Hamlin	1860-1940	Author	30	40	173	85	Pulitzer 1921. Novelist, Essayist
Garland, Judy	1922-69	Entertainment	421	850		953	Actress-Singer. Oz Special DS $950. Chk S $550
Garn, Jake		Senate-Astronaut	15	40		25	Senator UT
Garneau, Marc		Astronaut	9			25	
Garner, Erroll		Entertainment	75			150	Jazz Pianist
Garner, Francoise		Entetainment	10			35	Opera
Garner, James	1928-	Entertainment	10	18	22	42	Actor. Maverick & All Around Versatile Actor

NAME	DATE	CATEGORY	SIG	LS/DS	ALS	SP	COMMENTS
Garner, John Nance	1867-1967	Vice President	60	195	225	175	VP & Speaker. FDR VP
Garner, Peggy Ann		Entertainment	30			75	
Garnett, Francis H.		Author	20	60	125		
Garnett, Richard Brooke	1817-63	Civil War	650	535	615		CSA Gen. RARE. ALS 1861 $6600
Garnett, Tay		Entertainment	10	25		30	Director-Producer
Garnier, Charles	1825-1898	Architect	30		225		Designer Paris Opera House
Garr, Terri		Entertainment	8	28	25	20	Actress
Garrard, Kenner		Civil War	45	75	160		Union Gen. War Date ALS $575
Garrett, Betty		Entertainment	7			18	Film & Stage Comedienne
Garrett, Finis J.		Senate/Congress	10	15	25	20	MOC TN 1905
Garrett, Patrick R. (Pat)	1850-1908	Western Lawman	2700	3683	3750		Killed Billy the Kid. Became Sheriff. Assassinated
Garrett, Thomas		Emancipation	100	250	395		Chief Engineer Underground RR
Garriott, Owen I.		Astronaut	5			20	
Garrison, Jim		Legal	55			150	Deceased Distr. Atty. Investigated Kennedy Assass.
Garrison, Lindley M.	1864-1932	Cabinet	35	85	140	50	Sec'y War 1913
Garrison, Samuel	1945-	Author	5	10	25	15	Antiques and collectibles writer
Garrison, Vermont		Aviation	12	25	45	35	ACE, WW II & Korea
Garrison, Wm. Lloyd	1805-79	Abolitionist	80	120	425	200	Reformer. Abolitionist. ALS/Cont. $1200
Garros, Roland		Aviation	125			425	Fr. ACE. 1st To Fly Mediterranean
Garroway, Dave		Entertainment	10			25	
Garson, Greer	1908-1996	Entertainment	25	83	45	70	Actress. Oscar Winner. DS $650 for Mrs. Miniver
Garth, Jennie		Entertainment	10			42	Actress. Beverly Hills 90210
Gartrell, Lucius J.	1821-91	Civil War	95	285	317		CSA Gen.
Garvey, Marcus	1887-1940	Black Nationalist		1254			Back to Africa Movement. Black Nationalism
Gary, Elbert Henry	1846-1927	Business	175	650	675	250	CEO U.S. Steel, Gary, Ind., TLS on Ltrhd. $985
Gary, James Albert		Cabinet	15	25	40		P.M. Gen. Owned Cotton Mills 1897
Gary, John		Entertainment	20			35	Actor-Singer. Juvenile-Films. TV Personality
Gasdia, Cecilie		Entertainment	10	15	35		35
Gasser, Heber S.		Science	20	35	60	50	Nobel Medicine
Gassman, Vittorio		Entertainment	25			85	
Gately, George		Cartoonist	5			20	Heathcliff
Gates, Bill		Business	20	75		35	Microsoft Genius.
Gates, Daryl		Law Enforcement	15			30	Chief Police of L.A.
Gates, Horatio	1728-1806	Rev. War	250	475	2550		General, Continental Army
Gates, John W.	1855-1911	Business	500	1750			Bet a Million Gates. Steel Wire Baron
Gates, Seth	1800-77	Congress	25	40	80		Anti-Slavery Repr. from NY
Gates, Thomas	1906-83	Cabinet	10	35		35	Sec'y Defense under Eisenhower & Sec'y Navy
Gatlin, Larry & Brothers		Entertainment	10			20	C & W
Gatlin, Richard C.	1809-96	Civil War	90	248			CSA Gen.
Gatling, Richard J.	1818-1903	Inventor-Business	450	1250	2308		Gatling Gun. Gat for Gun. ALS on Lttrhd $9500
Gatti-Casazza, Giulio		Entertainment	50	150	250		It. Impresario. Opera Director
Gatty, Harold		Aviation	75	275	462	175	Australian. Wiley Post Navigator
Gaugin, Paul	1848-1903	Artist	585	1235	6600		Fr. Post-Impressionist. Important ALS $17,500
Gauguin, Paul	1848-1903	Artist			12750		Fr. Post Impressionist
Gaumont, Leon	1864-1946	Entertainment	55	330			Fr. Film Pioneer, Exec., Inventor Sound System

NAME	DATE	CATEGORY	SIG	LS/DS	ALS	SP	COMMENTS
Gautier, Dick		Entertainment	5			12	
Gavarni, Paul		Artist	85		300		
Gavassi, Father Allesandro		Clergy	75	100	150		
Gavaudan, Pierre	1772-1840	Entertainment			135		Opera. Tenor
Gavin, James M.	1907-1993	Military	45	108	275	112	Gen. WW II, Diplomat, Ambassador. TLS/Cont.$495
Gavin, John		Entertainment	5			20	Ambassador to Mexico
Gavin, Leon		Senate/Congress	5	10		10	MOC PA 1943
Gaxton, William		Entertainment	10	15	25	25	
Gay, Enola		Aviation	150			350	Tibbets, Van Kirk, Ferebee
Gay, George A.		Civil War	15	25	45		Nat'l Commander GAR 1934
Gay, Sydney Howard		Author	3	10	20		
Gaye, Marvin		Entertainment	75			125	
Gayheart, Rebecca		Entertainment	13			56	Actress. Pin-Up $75
Gayle, Crystal		Country Music	5			15	
Gayle, John		Governor	10	35			Statesman, Jurist
Gaynor, Adam		Entertainment	5			22	Music. Rhythm Guitar Matchbox 20
Gaynor, Janet	1906-84	Entertainment	22	35	50	78	Actress. First Oscar Winner. Vintage SP $140
Gaynor, Mitzi		Entertainment	10			20	Pin-Up SP $25
Gaynor, William J.		Celebrity	20	55	115	30	
Gazzara, Ben		Entertainment	5			15	
Ge'ricault, Theodore	1791-1824	Artist			3000		Broke Classical Tradition.
Gear, John Henry	1825-1900	Congress	10	20	25		Senator IA 1887
Geary, Anthony 'Tony'		Entertainment	6	8	15	15	
Geary, John W.		Civil War	55	125	275	250	Un.Gen., 1st Mayor San Francisco
Gebel-Williams, Gunther		Entertainment	12			44	Circus animal trainer. Showman/Circus Performer
Gedda, Nicolai		Entertainment	15		35	35	Swe. Tenor, Opera
Geddes, James	1763-1838	Engineer		1100	1350		Erie Canal Advocate, Chief Engineer & Surveyor
Gee, Edwin A., Dr,		Business	5	10		10	CEO International Paper Co.
Geer, Ellen		Entertainment	4			12	Actress
Geer, Will	1902-78	Entertainment	25			55	Actor, Folk Singer. On Stage & Films from 1930-
Geezinslaw, Sam & Dewayne		Country Music	15			30	
Geffrard, Nicholas Fabre		Head of State	35	125			Pres. Haiti
Gehlen, Reinhard		Military	15	40	45		
Geiger, Johannes H.	1882-1945	Science	125	350	750		Ger. Physicist. Geiger Counter
Geisel, Ernesto		Head of State	12	20	25	15	
Geisel, Ted		Author					SEE Dr. Seuss
Gell, William, Dr.		Science	25	40			Br. Archaeologist
Gellar, Sarah Michelle		Entertainment	12			77	Actress. Buffy...... Pin-Up $80
Gelston, David		Rev. War	85	170			
Gemar, Charles Sam		Astronaut	5			20	
Gemini 5 (3 Sigs)		Astronauts					US $1 Bill.Aboard Gem.5 Signed $2595
Gene't, Jean		Author	175	295	450		Fr. LS/Content $1,275
Geneen, Harold S.		Business	5	10	25	10	
Genesis		Entertainment	40			85	
Genet, Edmond Citizen	1763-1834	Fr. Revolution	55	150	850		1st Fr. Minister to U.S.

NAME	DATE	CATEGORY	SIG	LS/DS	ALS	SP	COMMENTS
Genet, Jean	1910-86	Author		950	1575		Fr. Novelist, Dramatist.
Genn, Leo		Entertainment	10	15	25	25	
Gentilini, Amerigo		Entertainment	15			45	Opera
Gentry, Bobbie		Country Music	5			20	Composer Ode to Billy Joe Sheet Mus. S $95
Gentry, Jerauld R.		Astronaut	5	25		15	
George (Prince Denmark)	1653-1708	Royalty		270			Consort of Queen Anne
George I (Eng)	1660-1727	Royalty	220	1667	2700		Created Cabinet System of Gov.
George I (Gr)	1845-1913	Royalty	45	85	130		
George II (Eng)	1683-1760	Royalty	390	654	1708		Last English Monarch to Lead His Troops in Battle
George II (Greece)		Royalty	70	80	128	400	Succeeded his Brother, Constantine to Throne
George III (Eng)	1738-1820	Royalty	216	689	1833		Last King of U.S. Colonies
George IV (Eng)	1762-1830	Royalty	96	604	722		13 pp. Warrant 1815 $3,500
George V (Eng)	1865-1936	Royalty	188	592	631	670	King of England
George V And Queen Mary (Teck)		Royalty	250			855	
George VI (Eng)	1895-1952	Royalty	195	720	298	438	WW II King of England. ALS as Duke York $275
George VI and Queen Elizabeth		Royalty	275	730		2022	
George, Chief Dan		Entertainment	20			45	
George, Christopher		Entertainment	20	25	65	75	
George, Duke of Cambridge	1819-1904	Military	40				Br. Cmdr. Crimean War
George, Gladys		Entertainment	20	25	40	40	
George, Grace		Entertainment	25			60	
George, Harold L.		Military	35	90	170	75	
George, Henry		Economist	30	105	200	35	Author, Reformer, Editor
George, Michael		Entertainment	3			8	
George, Phyllis		Entertainment	5		12	15	Miss America
George, Susan		Entertainment	6	8	15	15	
George, Walter F.	1878-1957	Congress	10	30		30	Senator GA 1922-57
Gerard, James W.		Diplomat	12				Ambassador
Gerard, Francis R.		Aviation	10	22	38	28	ACE, WW II
Gerard, Gil		Entertainment	9	10	20	20	
Gerard, Richard		Composer	50	95	165		AMusQS $235
Gerardy, Jean		Entertainment	125			190	Belg. Violin-Cellist
Gere, Ashlyn		Entertainment					Actress-Model. Nude Pin-up 45
Gere, Richard		Entertainment	30	238	55	107	Actor. (Sometimes Uses paint pen)
Gerhardt, Elena		Entertainment	30			100	Opera, Remembered as Great Lieder Singer
Gerhardt, Mike		Astronaut	5			18	
Gerlache de Gomery, Adrien V.J.		Explorer	85	180	300		Belg. Naval Off'r., Antarctic
Gerland, Alfred		Aviation	15	35	55	40	
German, Edward, Sir	1862-1936	Composer	35	105	175	85	Operettas. AMusQS $200
Gernreich, Rudi		Business	10	15	40	25	Fashion Designer
Geronimo		Apache Chieftain	5332			4500	
Gerri, Toni		Entertainment	4	4	9	9	
Gerry, Elbridge (VP)	1744-1814	Rev. War	275	938	2545		Signer Decl. of Ind. V.P., Gov. MA. FF $600-$750
Gerry, James	1796-1873	Congress	10				Repr. PA, Physician
Gerry, Peter G.	1879-1957	Congress	10	15		20	MOC, Senator RI 1913

NAME	DATE	CATEGORY	SIG	LS/DS	ALS	SP	COMMENTS
Gersel Cemal		Head of State	20	65	170	35	Turkey
Gershwin, George & Gershwin, Ira		Composer	1250	3625			
Gershwin, George	1898-1937	Composer	894	1712	4650	4200	'Rhapsody in Blue', 'Porgy & Bess'…ad infinitum
Gershwin, Ira	1896-1983	Composer	88	160	250	165	Lyricist. FDC S $95, AQS $880
Gerson, Betty Lou		Entertainment	3			20	Major Radio Actress. Voice of Cruella de Vil
Gertz, Jami		Entertainment	7			45	Actress Pin-Up $65
Gervais, John L.	1753-98	Rev. War			100		Continental Congress
Gerville-Reache, Jeanne		Entertainment				275	Opera. Tragic French Mezzo
Gessendorf, Mechthild		Entertainment	10			25	Opera
Getty, Estelle		Entertainment	5	9	20	15	
Getty, George F.		Business		50			Founder Getty Oil Company
Getty, George W.	1819-1901	Civil War	30	50			Union Gen. ALS/Cont. $740
Getty, George Washington (WD)		Civil War	40	95			Union Gen. Div. Cmdr.
Getty, J. Paul	1892-1976	Business	185	455	1455	352	Billionaire Oil Mogul Stk.Cert. S$2400, ALS $2900
Getz, J. Laurence		Senate/Congress	10	200	20		MOC PA 1867. Publisher
Getz, Stan		Entertainment	85			225	Am. Jazz Saxophonist
Ghali, Boutros Boutros		Head of State	10			30	Pres. U.N.
Ghiaurov, Nicolai		Entertainment	10			25	Opera
Gholson, Samuel J.	1808-83	Civil War	95	292	575		CSA Gen.
Ghostley, Alice		Entertainment	5		15	15	Comedienne
Giancana, Antoinette		Celebrity	15			50	'Mafi Princess'
Giannini, A. P.		Business	150	290	500		Bank of America Founder
Gibb, Cynthia		Entertainment	5	6	15	35	Pin-Up SP $20
Gibbon, Edward		Author	300	885	1800		Br. Decline & Fall Roman Empire
Gibbon, John	1827-96	Civil War-Indian Fighter	50	185	330		Union Gen.ALS/Cont. $1760
Gibbon, John (WD)		Civil War	120		870		Union Gen.
Gibbons, Barry		Business	5			20	Founder Burger King
Gibbons, Cedric		Art	95	225	450		Hollywood Art Dir. 11 Awards
Gibbons, Floyd	1887-1939	Aviation-Journalist	62	155	285	155	Pioneer Aviator, Adventurer. Early Radio News
Gibbons, Herbert Adams		Celebrity	10	20	45		
Gibbons, James, Cardinal	1834-1921	Clergy	40	115	130	150	Established Washington Univ.,DC. Religious Leader
Gibbons, Leeza		Entertainment	5			12	Pin-up $20
Gibbs, Addison C.		Governor	10	40			Governor OR
Gibbs, Alfred	1823-68	Civil War	30	80	95		Union Gen. ALS '64 $655
Gibbs, Georgia		Entertainment	15			35	Big Band Vocalist
Gibbs, Marla		Entertainment	6	8	15	10	
Gibran, Kahlil		Author-Artist	125	325	750	150	Syrian Poet, Novelist, Essayist
Gibson, Charles		Entertainment	4			12	TV News, 20/20 Co-Anchor
Gibson, Charles Dana	1867-1944	Artist	60	250	285	240	Illustrator-Gibson Girl
Gibson, Charles H.		Congress	5		15		Repr., Senator MD 1885
Gibson, Debbie		Entertainment	10			25	
Gibson, Edward G.		Astronaut	10			25	
Gibson, George		Military	5	15	25		
Gibson, Henry		Entertainment	5			12	
Gibson, Hoot	1892-1962	Entertainment	170	195		240	Vintage Film Cowboy Star

NAME	DATE	CATEGORY	SIG	LS/DS	ALS	SP	COMMENTS
Gibson, Horatio G.		Civil War	50				General
Gibson, James		Military	75	230	425		Officer War 1812. Wounded, Died
Gibson, Mel		Entertainment	30			111	With Pocahontas Cast SP $130
Gibson, Randall Lee (WD)		Civil War	190		2688		CSA Gen.
Gibson, Randall Lee	1832-92	Civil War	90	360	675		CSA General, US Sen. LA
Gibson, Robert L.		Astronaut	7			25	Hoot
Gibson, William		Author	20		170		Playwright. The Miracle Worker
Giddings, De Witt C.		Senate/Congress	15	25	40		MOC TX. Served in CSA Army
Giddings, Joshua R.	1795-1864	Congress	12				Repr. OH
Gide, Andre'	1869-1951	Author	175	350	465		Fr. Nobel Laureate Lit., Moralist, Philosopher
Gielgud, John, Sir	1904-	Entertainment	20	52		42	Noted British Actor
Gies, Miep		Celebrity	40	112	250		Befriended & Hid Anne Frank's family
Gieseking, Walter	1895-1956	Entertainment	44			118	Fr.-born Concert Pianist
Giesler, Jerry		Law	10	20	40	15	Brilliant Trial Lawyer
Gifford, Francis		Entertainment	5	7	12	10	
Gifford, Kathie Lee		Entertainment	8			25	TV Personality-Singer. Pin-Up SP $35
Gifford, Walter S.		Business-Diplomat	5	15	25	10	Pres. AT&T 1925-48, Chm.-'50
Gigli, Beniamino	1890-1957	Entertainment	127	190	300	345	Opera, Concert. SPc $225-$295
Gil, Brendan		Author	16			20	Writer New Yorker Mag.
Gilbert, A. C.		Business	60	95	175		Inventor Erector Set.
Gilbert, Billy		Entertainment	20	25	45	45	
Gilbert, Cass		Architect	20	60		35	Woolworth Bldg., Supr. Court...
Gilbert, H. E.		Celebrity	5	11	28	8	
Gilbert, John		Entertainment	125	750	275	250	Mega Star of Silent Movies. Romantic Hero
Gilbert, L. Woolfe		Composer	20	50	95	25	
Gilbert, Lynn		Entertainment	3	3	6	10	
Gilbert, Melissa		Entertainment	10	18		35	Actress. Little House on the Prairie her domain
Gilbert, Sara		Entertainment	16			25	Actress Rosanne
Gilbert, William. S., Sir	1836-1911	Composer	165	365	572	675	Gilbert & Sullivan Operettas. Pen Drawing S $3500
Gilbreth, Lillian		Engineer	30		100		1st Woman Engineer
Gilder, Richard Watson		Civil War	125				Editor Century Magazine
Giles, Sandra		Entertainment	5			10	Pinup $30
Giles, William Branch		Senate	30	80	115		Early, influential VA Sen. 1801
Gilford, Jack	1907-90	Entertainment	15		30	35	Character Actor.Film,Stage,TV. Blacklisted 1950's
Gill, Eric		Artist	20	70	150		Br. Sculptor, Engraver
Gill, Vince		Country Music	10			30	
Gillespie, Dizzy	1917-93	Entertainment	50			75	Jazz. Trumpet
Gillett, Frederick H.	1851-1935	Speaker of House	15	35	95		MOC, Senator MA
Gillette, Anita	1936-	Entertainment	5		35	20	Actress. Broadway Leads. TV Series. Films
Gillette, Francis		Senate	20	60			Free-Soiler Senator CT
Gillette, King Camp	1855-1932	Business-Inventor	375	950	3500	500	Gillette Co. Invented Safety Razor
Gillette, William	1855-1937	Entertainment	58	1752	215	150	Portrayed Sherlock Holmes.Actor, Playwright
Gilley, Mickey		Entertainment	8			20	C/W Singer
Gilliam, Terry*		Art-Entertainment	15			250	Clever 'Monty Python' Animator and Director
Gillis, J. H.		Military	5	15	25		

NAME	DATE	CATEGORY	SIG	LS/DS	ALS	SP	COMMENTS
Gillmore, Joseph A.		Governor	35	90			Civil War Gov. NY
Gillmore, Quincy A. (WD)		Civil War	60	145	235		Union Gen. LS '63 $7975
Gillmore, Quincy A.	1825-88	Civil War	35	95	163		Union Gen.
Gilman, John T.	1753-1828	Rev. War		100	140		Cont. Congr.Gov. NH
Gilman, Nicholas		Rev. War	110	285	575		Continental Congress
Gilmer, Jeremy F.	1818-83	Civil War	125		412		CSA Gen.
Gilmer, John H.		Civil War	25		100		CSA Congress from NC
Gilmer, Thomas W.		Cabinet		95	145		Tyler Sec'y Navy
Gilmore, Gary		Celebrity	15	25	35		
Gilmore, James R.	1822-1903	Author	20	60	195		Merchant, Abolitionist, Novelist, Songwriter
Gilmore, Joseph A.	1811-67	Civil War Gov.	35	135			Gov. NH
Gilmore, Laura E.	1832-	Celebrity	5		50		Wife of James R. Noted Medium
Gilmore, Patrick Sarfield	1829-92.	Composer-CW	35	80	180		'...Johnny Comes Marching Home Again'. AMQS $275
Gilmore, Virginia		Entertainment	10	15	30	25	Actress. Pretty Wife of Yul Brynner
Gilmour, Patrick S.	1829-92	Bandleader	5				Bandmaster. Sig/Music $30
Gilpin, Henry D.	1801-60	Cabinet	25	50	75		Van Buren Att'y Gen. 1840, Historian, Author
Gilruth, Robert R.		Astronaut	10			20	
Gimbel Brothers (6)		Business	475				Gimbel Department Stores
Gimbel, Bernard F.		Business	75	375	375	100	Gimbel Bros. Dept. Stores
Gimbel, Ellis A.		Business	90	432			Last of Original Gimbel Bros.
Giminez, Eduardo		Entertainment	10			30	Opera
Ginastera, Alberto		Composer		95	175	100	Opera, Ballet
Gingold, Hermione	1897-1987	Entertainment	10			25	Br. Comedienne. Gigi
Gingrich, Newt		Senate/Congress	10	45		40	MOC GA Since 1973. Speaker of House. Resigned
Ginsberg, Ruth Bader		Supreme Court	40	48		45	Clinton Appointment to S.C.
Ginsburg, Allen	1926-98	Author	40	225	331	115	Beat Poet. Social Activist. TMsS $575, FDC S $50
Giordano, Umberto		Composer	225	400	475	725	Opera Composer. AMusQS $450-$750
Girard, Stephen	1750-1831	Rev. War	125	350	325		Philanthropist, Merchant, Banker
Gisborne, Thomas		Author	30				
Gish, Dorothy		Entertainment	75			132	Actress. Silent Film Star
Gish, Lillian	1896-1993	Entertainment	20	65	75	68	Silent Star. Birth of a Nation
Gissing, George Robert	1857-1903	Author	50	175	345		Br. Novelist.
Gist, States Rights	1831-64	Civil War	450	950	1450		CSA Gen. RARE. ALS '61 $2400
Given, Robin		Entertainment	10			30	Actress. 'Head of the Class'
Givenchy, Hubert de		Business	35	70	95	200	Fr. Fashion Designer
Givens, Edward G. Jr.		Astronaut	10			25	
Givot, George		Entertainment	10			20	Comic. 'Greek Ambassador Good Will'
Glad, Gladys		Entertainment	10			20	Actress. Vintage
Gladden, Adley H.	1810-62	Civil War	510	1192			CSA Gen. ALS '61 $6325. Wounded & Died 1862
Gladden, Washington		Clergy	30	40	55		
Gladstone, William E.	1809-98	Head of State	101	98	252	100	Br. Prime Minister
Glaser, Donald A.		Science	20	35	75	35	Nobel Phys. Invented Bubble Chamber
Glaser, Lillian		Entertainment	10			15	Mrs. DeWolf Hopper
Glaser, Lulu		Entertainment	102		20	20	
Glaser, Paul Michael		Entertainment	5			20	Actor

NAME	DATE	CATEGORY	SIG	LS/DS	ALS	SP	COMMENTS
Glaser, Tompall		Country Music	15			30	'Glaser Bros.& His Outlaw Band'. Harmony Group
Glasgow, Ellen		Author	40	180			Novelist. Pulitzer. VA Life
Glashow, Sheldon Lee, Dr.		Science	20	35		30	Nobel Physics
Glaspell, Susan		Author	25	65	110		Am. Playwright. Pulitzer
Glass, Carter	1858-1946	Cabinet	15	45	60	30	Sec'y Treas., Sen. VA 1902
Glass, Philip	1937-	Composer	30	50		190	Am.Orchestral, Opera, Film,Stage
Glass, Ron		Entertainment	5		25	20	Actor. 'Barney Miller'
Glassman, Alan		Entertainment	5			25	Opera
Glazunov, Alexander		Composer	225	365	675	250	Rus. AMusQS $1,000-$2,750
Gleason, Jackie	1916-87	Entertainment	65	148		158	Am. Comedian-Actor TV-Movies. 'Honeymooners'
Gleason, James		Entertainment	40			75	Grumpy Character Actor of 30's to 50's
Gledhill, Arthur		Business	4			10	Stanley Works
Glen, John	1921-	Senator	35		40	45	Ohio Senator-Astronaut
Glenn, John (As Astronaut)		Astronaut	40	148	450	120	1st To Orbit Earth. FDC 2/20/62 Canaveral $125
Glenn, Scott	1942-	Entertainment	10	15	32	30	Actor. Silence of the Lambs, Nashville
Glennon, John, Cardinal		Clergy	40	50	65	45	
Gless, Sharon		Entertainment	8	22		21	Actress.Long Running TV Series 'Cagney & Lacey'
Gliere, Reinhold	1875-1956	Composer	55		350		Rus. Symphony & Ballet
Globus, Yoram		Entertainment	5			16	Producer
Glossop, Peter		Entertainment	10			30	Opera
Gloucester, Henry Wm.Fred, Duke		Royalty	10	20	50	35	Son of Geo. V., Gov-Gen. Australia
Glover, Danny	1947-	Entertainment	12			30	Versatile Afr-Am Actor/Mel Gibson-'Lethal Weapon..
Glover, John	1732-97	Rev. War	250	610	1125		Gen. Continental Army. 27th Reg. (14th)
Glubb, John, Sir Pasha	1897-1986	Military	25	45	60	125	Br. General. Formed, Commanded,Arab Legion
Gluck, Alma		Entertainment	20	35	45	115	Opera, Concert, Recording
Glueck, Nelson		Archaeologist	10	25	50	20	Uncovered 1500 Ancient Artifact
Glyn, Elinor		Author	20	70	165	45	Br. Novelist, Film Scenarios
Gnys, Wladek		Aviation	40			150	Shot Down 1st Plane in WW II
Goard, Nona		Aviation	10	15	25	15	
Gobbi, Tito	1913-84	Entertainment	20			80	It. Baritone, Opera
Gobel, George	1918-91	Entertainment	10			25	
Godard, Benjamin Louis	1849-95	Composer	75	125	238	150	Fr. Opera 'Jocelyn'. Familiar Berceuse
Godard, Jean Luc	1930-	Entertainment	400				Fr. Film Director, Writer. Scarce
Godard, Louis		Aviation-Balloon	200	575			ALS/Content $6,500
Godard, Magdalena		Entertainment	15			75	Violinist
Goddard, Calvin	1768-1842	Political	15		55		Federalist Congress 1801-05
Goddard, Louis	1829-85	Balloonist		2500	2500		Fr. Aeronaut For The Government
Goddard, Paulette	1911-90	Entertainment	28	45	80	85	Actress
Goddard, Robert H.	1882-1945	Science	370	1800	1450	2990	Am. Physicist. Rocket Pioneer. TLS/Cont. $3500
Godden, Rumer	1907-	Author	15		65		Brit. Novelist. Black Narcissus, The River
Goderich, Fred. John Robinson		Head of State	15	40	95		Viscount Goderich. Br. P.M.
Godey, Louis A.	1804-78	Publisher	40	95	175		Godey's Ladies Book
Godfrey, A. Earl		Aviation	30	60	110	75	
Godfrey, Arthur		Entertainment	15	50	55	25	Radio & Early TV Ukelele Playing-Singing Host
Godfrey, Capt. Johnny		Aviation	50				Ace/29 Victories

NAME	DATE	CATEGORY	SIG	LS/DS	ALS	SP	COMMENTS
Godolphin, Sidney, 1st Earl	1644-1712	Head of State	96	350			P.M. Eng. Lord High Treasurer to Queen Anne
Godoy, Manuel de	1767-1851	Head of State	295				Sp. Politician, Prime Minister
Godt, Eberhard		Military	15		70		
Godunov, Alexander	1949-1995	Entertainment	33			60	Ballet. Russian Star Defected
Godwin, Linda		Astronaut	5			20	
Goebbels, Joseph	1897-1945	Nazi Leader WWII	350	1467	1250	1250	Nazi Minister of Propaganda. Pc SP $800
Goebel, Arthur		Aviation	40			110	Pioneer Aviator
Goering, Hermann W.	1893-1946	Military	450	2045	2435	1338	Nazi Leader. Marshal of the Reich. Suicide
Goethals, George W.	1858-1928	Military-Science	175	585			Panama Canal.TLS/Cont. $1,750
Goethe, Johann W. von	1749-1832	Author	1200	2550	5670		Ger. Poet, Dramatist, Novelist
Goettheim, F.		Business	10	20	45		
Goff, Nathan Jr.		Cabinet	15	25	50		Hayes Sec. of Navy
Gogh, Vincent van		Artist	3500	4500	13000		Dutch Painter. Individual Style
Gogol, Nicholai		Author	625	3350	6500		Father of Rus. Realistic Lit.
Going, Joanna		Entertainment	6			40	Actress Pin-Up $55
Golan, Menahem		Entertainment	5		15	15	Film Producer
Gold, Missy		Entertainment	8			20	'Benson'. Has Matured from Child Actress to Leads
Gold, Tracy		Entertainment	10			25	Actress
Goldberg, Arthur J. (SC)	1908-90	Supreme Court	50	168		108	Resigned From Suprme Ct. To Become Ambass. UN
Goldberg, Reiner		Entertainment	10			30	Opera
Goldberg, Rube*	1883-1970	Cartoonist	50	100		317	'Ike & Mike', 'Boob McNutt'. Pulitzer Prize '48
Goldberg, Stan*		Cartoonist	20			80	'Archie'. Repro Drawing S. $65 (4x6)
Goldberg, Whoopi	1935-	Entertainment	12		30	35	Oscar Winning Actress & Comedian. Authentic RARE
Goldblum, Jeff		Entertainment	10		15	40	Actor. Variety of Interesting Parts-'The Fly'
Golden Eye (Cast Of)		Entertainment	80			150	Brosnan,Scorupco, Janssen
Golden Girls, The (Cast Of)		Entertainment	45			195	All Four
Golden, Charles, Bishop		Clergy	15	25	30	30	
Goldenson, Leonard H.		Business	10		30	20	TV Broadcasting Exec.
Golding, Louis		Author	50	85	125	60	Br. Verse, Stories, Novels
Golding, William	1911-1994	Author	65	225	585	135	Nobel Lit., Lord of the Flies
Goldman, Edwin Franco		Composer	25	50	75		Bandmaster
Goldman, Emma		Anarchist	60	240	510	80	Deported. Author-Editor
Goldman, Michael		Author	5	10	15	10	
Goldman, Nahum		Zionist	15		50		Pres. World Zionist Org.
Goldman, William		Author			125		'Soldier in the Rain', 'Princess Bride'
Goldmark, Peter C.		Science	25		40		Inventor. LP Records
Goldowsky, Boris		Conductor	8			35	Opera Coach. Dir. of own Opera Theatre
Goldsboro, Bobby		Country Western	10			18	Singer
Goldsborough, Louis M.	1805-1907	Civil War	65	135	200		Rear Admiral USN Sig/Rank $95
Goldschmidt, Berthold	1903-	Composer				175	Ger. Works Banned by Nazis WW II
Goldschmidt, Neil E.		Cabinet	4	10	25	15	Sec'y Transportation
Goldschmidt, Richard, Dr.	1890-1958	Science		20	40		World Famous Geneticist
Goldsmith, Jerry		Entertainment	4			10	
Goldwater, Barry	1909-19xx	Congress	10	25		30	Sen. AZ. Presidential Candidate
Goldwin, Tony		Entertainment	3			8	

NAME	DATE	CATEGORY	SIG	LS/DS	ALS	SP	COMMENTS
Goldwyn, Sam		Business	100	124	255	195	Goldwyn Studios
Goldwyn, Sam, Jr.		Entertainment	4			12	Producer
Golino, Valerie		Entertainment	10			38	Actress
Gollob, Gordon		Aviation		165		200	WWII Ger. Air Ace. RK
Golonka, Arlene		Entertainment	4	4	9	15	
Gombell, Minna		Entertainment	25	30	55	55	
Gomes, Carlos	1836-96	Composer	25		175		Brazilian. Opera
Gomes, Francisco		Head of State	15	55	135	25	
Gomez, Aurea		Entertainment	5			20	Opera, Brazilian Soprano
Gomez, Thomas		Entertainment	20			50	
Gompers, Samuel	1850-1924	Labor Leader	122	290	450		Founder & 1st Pres. A.F.of L.
Good, James W.		Cabinet	25	50		30	Hoover Sec'y of War
Gooding, Cuba		Entertainment	12			45	Actor. Jerry McGuire SP $60
Goodman, Al		Bandleader				45	
Goodman, Benny	1909-1986	Entertainment	45	185		164	Big Band Leader-Clarinetist
Goodman, Dody		Entertainment	4	4	9	10	
Goodman, John		Entertainment	15			25	
Goodpaster, Andrew	1915-	Military	15	35	55	25	Gen. WW II. Highly Decorated Combat Officer etc.
Goodridge, Robin		Entertainment	6			25	Music. Drummer Bush
Goodson, Mark		Entertainment	10			30	Producer TV
Goodwin, E. S.		Aviation	3	5	10		
Goodwin, Hugh H.		Military	25	65	126	50	
Goodwin, Nat C.		Entertainment	20			30	Vintage Actor
Goodyear, Charles	1800-60	Inventor	350	1462	6450		Developed Rubber Vulcanization
Goodyear, Charles Jr.		Business	20	60	150	30	Goodyear Tire & Rubber Co.
Gookin, Dan		Author	10		35	20	Dos For Dummiesetc.
Goosens, Eugene, Sir		Composer	20	45	90	85	Br.Conductor. Opera/Orchestral Works
Goossens, Eugene		Entertainment	15			45	
Gorbachev, Mikhail (USSR)		Head of State	150	475	895	656	Instituted Perestroika,Glasnost.Nobel '90 FDC $175
Gorbachev, Raisa		Rus. 1st Lady	50			125	
Gorcey, Leo		Entertainment	90	100		155	
Gordon, Alex., 4th Duke of		Rev. War	20		35		
Gordon, C. Henry		Entertainment	20				Actor
Gordon, Charles G.	1833-85	Military	125	812	1093	600	Chinese Gordon,Gordon Pasha. Killed at Khartoum
Gordon, Charles W.		Clergy	20	25	30		
Gordon, Gale	1905-95	Entertainment	25	20		71	Versatile Radio, TV/LUCY, Film Actor
Gordon, Gavin	1901-83	Entertainment	40				Vintage
Gordon, George H.		Civil War	35	65	95		Union General
Gordon, George W.	1836-1911	Civil War	225	375	388		CSA General
Gordon, Gray		Entertainment	20			50	Big band leader
Gordon, Huntley	1897-1956	Entertainment	20	25		45	Silent Film Star. In over 50 films 1918-40
Gordon, John Brown (WD)		Civil War	185	1200	3750		CSA Gen.
Gordon, John Brown	1832-1904	Civil War	192	215	400		CSA Gen., Gov. & US Sen. GA
Gordon, John F.		Business	4		15	10	
Gordon, Judah Leib	1830-92	Journalist	175		1150		Russ. Born Writer For Jewish Haskalah

NAME	DATE	CATEGORY	SIG	LS/DS	ALS	SP	COMMENTS
Gordon, Mack		Composer	30	60	130	40	Lyricist
Gordon, Richard F. Jr.		Astronaut	15			42	
Gordon, Ruth		Entertainment	15		40	30	AA Rosemary's Baby.Actress, Writer,Director
Gordone, Charles	1927-95	Author	25			40	Afr-Am Pulitzer Prize Winning Playwright
Gore, Albert A., Jr.	1948-	Vice President	375				Vice President
Gore, Albert A., Sr.	1907-	Congress	15	60			Repr- Senator TN 1939-44, 53-71. Father of Gore Jr
Gore, Christopher		Senate	85	205	350		Gov. MA, Senator MA 1813
Gore, Howard W.		Cabinet	4	30			Sec'y Agriculture
Gore, Tipper		2nd Lady	5	12		10	
Gorgas, Josiah (WD)		Civil War	225	1345	725		CSA Gen.
Gorgas, Josiah	1813-83	Civil War	195	380			CSA Gen. War Dte. LS $1200
Gorgas, William C., Dr.		Science	125	412	450		Eradicated Yellow Fever
Gorham, George H.		Senate/Congress	10	20	35		
Gorham, Nathaniel	1738-96	Rev. War	375	425	1683		Pres. Continental Congress
Gorie, Dominic		Astronaut	5			19	
Goritz, Otto	1873-1929	Entertainment	30			65	Operatic Baritone
Gorki, Maxim	1868-1936	Author	400	1525	3141	1108	Rus.Writer emerged from lower classes. Novels
Gorman, Arthur P.	1839-1906	Senate	10	15	22		Senator MD 1881-99
Gorman, Margaret		Entertainment	40			75	1st Miss America 1921
Gorney, Karen Lynn		Entertainment	3	3	6	6	
Gorshin, Frank	1933-	Entertainment	10	15	20	28	Actor, Impressionist. As The Riddler $40 SP
Gossard, Stone		Entertainment	6			25	Music. Vocalist Pearl Jam
Gosse, Aristid V.		Science	30		80		
Gosse, Edmund, Sir	1849-1928	Author	20	35	50	35	Br. Poet, Man of Letters
Gosselaar, Mark Paul		Entertainment	6			50	
Gossett, Louis, Jr.		Entertainment	15	80		70	
Gottfrederson, Floyd*		Cartoonist	100			500	Mickey Mouse Strip Art
Gotti, John		Crime	20			75	Mafia Boss
Gottschalk, Louis Moreau	1829-69	Composer	500	1200	1838	2990	Pianist , AMusQS $1800-$3250-$4500
Goudal, Jetta		Entertainment	10	10	20	40	
Goudsmit, Samuel A.		Science	15	25	40	20	Dutch Born Atomic Physicist
Gough, John B.	1817-86	Clergy	25	45	55	35	Temperance Advocate, Reformer
Gould, Charles L.		Business	10	35	45	20	
Gould, Chester*	1900-85	Cartoonist	50			324	Dick Tracy. Large Tracy Sketch S $500
Gould, Elliott		Entertainment	5	6	15	15	
Gould, George		Business	95	175	250	175	Son of Jay.Lost Inheritance.TLS on RR Lttrhd $1900
Gould, Glenn		Entertainment		950	1925	3250	Eccentric, Legendary Pianist. RARE
Gould, Gordon		Inventor	15	40			Commercial Laser Inventor
Gould, Harold		Entertainment	5	6	15	15	
Gould, Jay	1836-92	Business	262	1032	1812	1200	Financier, Pres. Erie RR. Stk. Cert S $21,000
Gould, John	1804-81	Science	110		700		Br. Ornithologist
Gould, Morton		Composer	20	45	70	40	AMusQS $200
Gould, Robert Simonton		Civil War	25	65	90		CSA Cmdr. Gould's Battalion
Gould, Samuel B.		Celebrity	4	8	20	10	
Gould, Sandra		Entertainment	4			15	Actress, Mrs. Kravitz Bewitched

NAME	DATE	CATEGORY	SIG	LS/DS	ALS	SP	COMMENTS
Goulding, Ray		Entertainment	3	3	6	10	
Goulet, Robert		Entertainment	10			20	Handsome Baritone Broadway, Concert Star
Gounod, Charles	1818-93	Composer	125	325	265	500	AMusQS $650-$2,500. Score Sapho S $985
Gourard, Henri J.E.	1867-1946	Military				75	Fr. Gen. WW I
Gouraud, Henri-Joseph E.		Military	40	150		75	Fr. Gen. WW I
Govan, Daniel C.	1829-1911	Civil War	90		540		CSA Gen.
Gowdy, John		Clergy	15	15	25		
Goya, Francisco		Artist	2200	7900	18750		Sp.Painter,Etcher,Lithographer
Goz, Harry		Entertainment	6	8	15	18	
Grevy, Jules	1807-91	Head of State	40				Pres. France 1879-87
Grabe, Ronald J.		Astronaut	8			25	
Grable, Betty	1916-73	Entertainment	68	100	200	288	GI's WW II #1 Pin-up girl. FDC S $75
Grace and Prince Rainier		Royalty	200	320		368	PC SP $225-350.
Grace de Monaco (Grace Kelly)		Royalty	200	511	462	317	As Princess. SP Pc $250
Grace, Eugene G.		Industrialist	25	65	140	40	Pres.,Chmn. Bethlehem Steel
Grace, William R.		Business	15	30	45	30	Mayor NYC. W.R. Grace & Co.
Gracen, Elizabeth Ward		Entertainment	5			25	Miss America '82, Pin-Up SP $55
Grade, Lew, Lord	1906-98	Entertainment	22			35	Br. Impresario of Entertainment. TV-Film Producer
Grady, Don		Entertainment	5			12	
Graf, Herman		Aviation	35			85	Ger. ACE. #9 Worldwide
Graham, Billy.(Wm. F)		Clergy	25	95		80	World-Wide Evangelist. Vintage Portrait SP $595
Graham, C.J.		Entertainment	4			10	Horror
Graham, Donald		Business	10	25	40	15	
Graham, Elizabeth Candler		Author	5	7	10	15	Books about Coca-Cola
Graham, George	1772-1830	Military-Cabinet	20	50	75		Monroe Sec. War (ad int) Soldier, Statesman
Graham, Heather		Entertainment	10			50	Actress. Pin-Up $75. Shout SP $65
Graham, John	1774-1820	Diplomatist	65	215	430		Aided Jefferson, Madison,Monroe
Graham, Katherine	1917-	Publisher	15	25	60	25	Chm. CEO Washington Post
Graham, M. Gordon		Aviaton	25			50	ACE WW II
Graham, Martha	1895-1986	Entertainment	84	263	385	375	Dancer, Teacher, Choreographer
Graham, Robert		Artist	3			10	Sculptor
Graham, Sheila		Author	25		40	35	Journalist, Gossip Columnist
Graham, Sylvester		Inventor			100		The Graham Cracker
Graham, Virginia	1912-98	Entertainment	20			35	TV Hostess, Commentator, Panelist. Radio Actress
Graham, William A.	1804-75	Cabinet	20	40	65		Fillmore Sec. Navy 1850
Grahame, Gloria		Entertainment	50	100		162	Academy Award. Early Death
Grahame, Kenneth		Author	75	110	195		Br.Writer Wind in the Willows
Grahame-White, Claude	1879-1959	Aviation	60	100	250	125	1st Br. School of Aviation. Pioneer Aviator-Mfg.
Grahm		Entertainment	5			15	
Grainger, Percy		Composer	40	105	215	350	Australian Pianist-Composer. SPc $150
Gramegna, Anna		Entertainment	45			95	Opera
Gramm, Phil		Senate	7			15	Senator TX
Grammer, Kelsey		Entertainment	10			40	TV Series-Frasier
Gran, Tryggve		Celebrity	12	30			
Granados, Enrique		Composer			700		Sp. Pianist. Piano Works, Opera

NAME	DATE	CATEGORY	SIG	LS/DS	ALS	SP	COMMENTS
Grandi, Dino, Count	1895-1988	Diplomat	25	45	90	40	Mussolini Cabinet
Grandval, Marie F.C.		Composer	10		95		Fr. Woman Composer
Grandy, Fred		Entertainment	5	10		10	Congressman IA- Love Boat
Grange, E. R.		Aviation	10	25	45	35	
Granger, Farley		Entertainment	5	7	12	20	
Granger, Francis		Cabinet	10	35	50		Wm. H. Harrison P.M. General
Granger, Gideon	1767-1822	Cabinet	85	200	325		P.M. General 1801
Granger, Gordon		Civil War	45	95	145		Union General
Granger, Robert S.	1816-94	Civil War			65		Union Gen. Captured 1861
Granger, Stewart		Entertainment	20			51	Handsome, Swashbuckling Brit. Film Star
Granit, Ragnar		Science	25	50	120	100	Nobel Medicine
Granlund, Nils T. (NTG)		Entertainment	20			40	Producer Radio, TV, Night Club
Grant, Amy		Entertainment	5	6	15	15	
Grant, Cary	1904-86	Entertainment	220	600		576	Suave, Sophisticated Oscar Winner. Pc SP $450
Grant, Duncan	1885-1978	Artist	100		300		Scot. Impressionist. Bloomsbury Grp.
Grant, Frederick Dent		Military	20				Son Of U.S. Grant
Grant, Gogi		Entertainment	3	5	10	10	
Grant, Hugh		Entertainment	20			55	Br. Actor
Grant, Julia Dent	1826-1902	First Lady	348	375	625		
Grant, Kathryn		Entertainment	8			30	Actress-Widow of Bing Crosby
Grant, Kirby		Entertainment	15		25	35	
Grant, Lee		Entertainment	10	30		30	Oscar winner
Grant, U.S. III		Military	10	30	50		
Grant, Ulysses S. (WD)		President	750	2512	5983	3062	ALS/Spec.Cont. $15000-16000-17500
Grant, Ulysses S.	1822-85	President	607	1670	2797	2424	CDV In Uniform S $3000-$6000. Pres. DS $4500
Grant, William T.	1876-1972	Business	50	155	315	275	1,176 W.T. Grant Stores in 40 States
Granville, Bonita		Entertainment	12	20	20	35	
Grapelli, Stephane		Entertainment	20			85	Unique Jazz Violinist. SPc $60
Grapewin, Charles	1869-1956	Entertainment	175			350	Am. Character Actor. Uncle Henry in ....of Oz
Grass Roots, The		Rock Group				188	60's Group (5) DS by Three $40
Grass, Gunter		Author	40	135	260	130	Ger. Novelist. Nazi Era
Grasse, Francois-Jos., Comte de		Rev. War					Kept Aid From Cornwallis. NRPA
Grasser, Hartmann		Aviation	14	25	50	30	
Grassi, Rinaldo		Entertainment	35	95		85	Opera
Grassle, Karen	1944-	Entertainment	5		10	15	Actress. Little House on the Prairie
Grasso, Ella		Governor	10	35		20	1st Woman Governor CT
Grateful Dead (All)		Entertainment	100			250	Rock HOF
Gratiot, Charles		Military	150	205			War 1812. General 1828
Gratz, Barnard		Rev. War	75	212	400		
Gratz, Rebecca	1781-1869	Philanthropist			2750		Noted Am. Jewish Philanthropist. RARE
Graue, Dave*		Cartoonists	10			65	Alley Oop
Grauman, Sid		Entertainment	30	45	90	75	Owner of Opulent Theaters
Gravatte, Marianne		Entertainment	4	4	9	10	
Gravel, Maurice Mike		Senate	5			20	Senator Alaska
Graveline, Duane E.M.D.		Astronaut	5			20	

NAME	DATE	CATEGORY	SIG	LS/DS	ALS	SP	COMMENTS
Graves, Peter	1925-	Entertainment	15		25	35	Actor. Mission Impossible, Airplane etc.
Graves, Robert	1895-1985	Author	65	175	310	110	Br. Poet, Novelist, Critic
Graves, William		Military	50				General WW I
Gravity Kills		Entertainment	30			65	Music. 4 Member Rock Group
Gray, Alexander	1902-75	Entertainment	15			35	Actor-Singer. Broadway Musical Star. Radio-Films
Gray, Asa	1810-88	Science	35	60	168		Am. Botanist.Darwin Supporter
Gray, Billy		Entertainment	8			20	
Gray, Bowman		Business	7	15	35	15	
Gray, Colin		Aviation	35		90		Top New Zealand ACE
Gray, Colleen		Entertainment	15	25	45	30	
Gray, Delores		Entertainment	40			85	Am. Singer, Dancer
Gray, Elisha	1835-1901	Inventor-Business	250	1800	2400		Founder Western Electric Mfg. Telephone Pioneer
Gray, Erin	1952-	Entertainment	9	10	20	25	Actress-Model
Gray, George	1840-1925	Congress	10		35	30	Senator DE. Jurist. Diplomat
Gray, Gilda	1901-59	Entertainment	40			120	Popularized the Shimmy
Gray, Glen		Entertainment	15			35	Big Band Leader
Gray, Harold*		Cartoonists	100			588	Little Orphan Annie
Gray, Harry Jack		Business	5	10	20	10	CEO United Technologies
Gray, Horace (SC)		Supreme Court	75	75	170	45	1882
Gray, Isaac P.		Governor	10	15			Governor IN
Gray, Jack Stearns		Aviation	150				TLS/Content $950. AVIATRIX
Gray, Linda		Entertainment	6	20	12	20	Dallas. Pin-Up SP $20
Gray, Oscar L.		Senate/Congress	5	15		10	MOC AL 1915
Gray, Thomas	1716-71	Author	950	1888	5100		Br. Poet.Elegy Written in a Country Churchyard
Gray, William	1750-1825	Rev. War	40		100		Merchant, Patriot, Privateer
Gray, William H., III	1941-	Congress	10			20	Afr-Am MOC PA. Pres. United Negro College Fund
Grayco, Helen		Entertainment	3	3	6	12	Vocalist & Wife Spike Jones
Grayson, Cary T.	1878-1938	Medical	95				White House Physician to 3 Presidents
Grayson, Kathryn	1922-	Entertainment	10	22	25	45	Singer-Actress.Starred in Many Lavish MGM Musicals
Greatful Dear, The		Entertainment				725	Am. Rock Group (6)
Greco, Jose		Entertainment	10	15		40	Dance
Greeley, Adolphus W.	1844-1935	Explorer	75	200	204	150	Union Gen., Arctic Explorer.Army Officer. MOH
Greeley, Andrew, Rev.		Clergy	6	15		10	
Greeley, Horace	1811-72	Journalist	65	345	319	825	Go West, Young Man...
Green, Adolph		Composer	10	15		20	Collaborated/Betty Comden
Green, Al		Entertainment	10			20	
Green, Anna Katherine	1846-1935	Author	95	50	65		Pioneer Am. Detective Fiction
Green, Brian Austin		Entertainment	5			22	Beverly Hills 90210
Green, Charles	1785-1870	Aeronaut	40	100	250		Br. Balloonist
Green, Dorothy		Entertainment	5	6	15	15	
Green, Dwight H.		Governor	10	15			Governor IL
Green, Fitzhugh	1888-1947	Military	50	225			USN Cmdr.,Polar Explorer, Co-Author 'We'/Lindbergh
Green, Henrietta (Hetty) H.	1834-1916	Financier	2000	9500			Wall St. Speculator. LS re Stocks $18,800
Green, Herschel		Aviation	12	28	48	35	ACE, WW II, Triple Ace
Green, John(ny)		Composer	25	80	145	35	AMsS $250, $150, $350

NAME	DATE	CATEGORY	SIG	LS/DS	ALS	SP	COMMENTS
Green, Kerri		Entertainment	8			38	Actress. Pin-Up $65
Green, Mitzi	1920-69	Entertainment	8	15	25	20	Actress.Musicals-Stage & Film
Green, Paul		Author		45			Playwright, Lost Colony. Pulitzer
Green, Richard		Entertainment	30			75	
Green, Seth		Entertainment	6			42	Actor. Buffy Co-Star
Green, Theodore	1867-1966	Senate	10		20	15	Gov., Senator RI
Green, Thomas (WD)		Civil War	175	725	3250		CSA Gen. KIA. DS/Rare NM CSA '62 $6500
Green, Thomas	1814-64	Civil War	142	200	275		CSA Gen. KIA
Green, William F.		Labor Leader	40	95	195	125	Pres. A.F.of L.
Greenaway, Kate	1846-1901	Artist	1000	1500			Creator Children's Books. Sketch S $ 450-$1,200+
Greenbaum, Everett	1919-	Entertainment	15			25	TV & Film Writer. Andy Griffith, M A S H etc.
Greene, Carl Franklin	1887-	Aviation	65	150			USAAC Col. Collier Award. 1st Pressure-Cabin Plane
Greene, Frank L.		Senate/Congress	10		20	15	MOC, Senator VT
Greene, George S.		Civil War	30	70			Union Gen.
Greene, Graham	1904-1991	Author	110	340	508	380	Br. Novelist, Dramatist, Critic
Greene, Lorne	1915-87	Entertainment	32	100		106	Actor Bonanza
Greene, Michele		Entertainment	5	8	25	22	
Greene, Nathanael	1742-86	Military-Rev. War	900	2892	3065		Am.Rev. War Gen.ALS/Cont. $4800
Greene, Richard		Entertainment	10			40	Vint.Brit. Actor. Robinhood
Greene, Sarah Pratt Mc.		Author	20				1856-1935
Greene, Shecky		Entertainment	5	6	15	15	
Greenhouse, Kate		Entertainment	3			8	
Greenleaf, John		Clergy	30	50	85		
Greenspan, Alan		Economist	15	30		35	Chairman Fed. Reserve Bd.
Greenstreet, Sidney	1879-1954	Entertainment	240		450	650	Casablanca, Maltese Falcon
Greenwood, Charlotte	1893-1978	Entertainment	25			82	Long-legged Comedienne-Dancer
Greenwood, Edward D.		Science	10	15	35		
Greenwood, G.(Lippincott)		Author	10	30	75	15	
Greenwood, Lee		Country Music	5			10	
Greer, Dabbs (Bill)		Entertainment	10			20	
Greer, Jane		Entertainment	5	6	15	15	
Greer, Pam	1950-	Entertainment	10			30	Actress.Jackie Brown. Black Exploitation Films
Greg K		Entertainment	6			25	Music. Bass Guitar Offspring
Gregg, Andrew	1755-1835	Congress	40	155			Sen., MOC PA ALS/Content $475
Gregg, David M. (WD)		Civil War	105	188	428		Union Gen.
Gregg, David M.	1833-1916	Civil War	40	75	182	175	Union Gen. Distinguished at Gettysburg
Gregg, John	1828-64	Civil War					CSA Gen. KIA. AES '63 $880
Gregg, John R.		Business	65	85	150	90	Inventor Gregg Shorthand System
Gregg, Maxcy (WD)		Civil War	565	4000			CSA Gen. KIA
Gregg, Maxcy	1814-62	Civil War	410	600			CSA Gen. KIA
Gregg, Virginia		Entertainment	10	12	20	25	
Gregor XVI, Pope	1765-1846	Clergy		1200			Roman Catholic Pope 1831-46
Gregory, Bill		Astronaut	7			18	
Gregory, Dick	1932-	Entertainment	10	20	75	25	Comedian-Writer-Social Activist
Gregory, F. H. (WD)		Civil War	60	95	115		Union Naval Captain

NAME	DATE	CATEGORY	SIG	LS/DS	ALS	SP	COMMENTS
Gregory, F.H.		Civil War	20		72		Union Gen.
Gregory, Frederick D.		Astronaut	6			22	
Gregory, James		Entertainment	5	6	15	15	
Gregory, Thomas W.	1861-1933	Cabinet	20			45	US Att'y Gen. Woodrow Wilson
Greico, Richard		Entertainment	10			45	
Grell, Mike*		Cartoonist	10			75	Tarzan
Grenfell, Wilfred T.		Physician-Clergy	35	75	75	130	Medical Missionary, Author
Grenville, George	1712-70	Head of State	250	750			Br. P.M., Author of Stamp Act Vs Am. Colonies
Grenville, Peter	1913-	Entertainment	10		30	20	British Director. Stage & sometime Films.
Grenville, Wm. W., 1st Baron	1759-1834	Head of State	100	285	650		Br. Prime Min. Pro Rom.Cath. Emancipation
Gresham, Walter Q.	1832-95	Cabinet-CW	45	70	100		Union Gen. ALS '62 $310
Gretchaninoff, Alexander T.		Composer	65	180	395		AMsS $350
Grew, Joseph C.		Diplomat	10	25		35	Ambassador Japan 1931-41
Grey, Chas. 2nd Earl of	1764-1845	Head of State	85	98	160		Prime Minister
Grey, George Sir	1799-1882	Diplomat	5	25	55		Br. Statesman
Grey, Jennifer		Entertainment	8			50	Actress
Grey, Joel		Entertainment	6	8	15	20	
Grey, Nan		Entertainment	4	8	12	15	
Grey, Virginia	1917-	Entertainment	10	15	18	30	Actress 30's to early 40's
Grey, Zane	1875-1939	Author	87	140	500	400	Dentist Turned Western Writer
Gridley, Chas. Vernon	1844-98	Military	250	410	895		Cmdr. of Adm. Dewey Flagship
Gridley, Richard	1711-96	Rev. War	170	450	790		Gen.Continental Army, Artillery
Grieg, Edvard	1843-1907	Composer	300	600	1360	1095	19th Cent. Norge. AMusQS $1,800-$2,800-$3,250
Grier, David Allen		Entertainment	3			8	Comic-Actor
Grier, Pam		Entertainment	5	6	15	15	Pin-Up SP $20
Grier, Robert C. (SC)	1794-1870	Supreme Court	80	235	420		
Grierson, Benjamin H.(WD)		Civil War	120	235	545		Union General
Grierson, Benjamin H.	1826-1911	Civil War	45		235		Union Gen.
Griesbach, Franz		Military	20			50	Ger. Infantry General
Griffes, Charles T.		Composer	175	515			Outstanding Am. Composer. ALS/Content $3,000
Griffin, Charles	1826-67	Civil War	75	295			Union Gen., Indian Fighter. Uncommon Sig d.1867
Griffin, Chris		Entertainment	10			25	Jazz Trumpet
Griffin, Cyrus		Rev. War	360	765			Continental Congress
Griffin, Merv		Entertainment	5			15	
Griffin, S. Marvin		Governor	10		30		Governor GA
Griffin, W.E.B.		Author	5			10	Fiction
Griffith, Andy		Entertainment	15	45	30	42	
Griffith, Corinne		Entertainment	35	45	90	100	
Griffith, D(avid) W(ark)	1874-1948	Entertainment	350	675	875	1018	Pioneer Film Producer-Dir.
Griffith, Hugh	1912-80	Entertainment	190	275		450	SP PC $200
Griffith, Melanie		Entertainment	28		55	60	Actress. Versatile Leads
Griffiths, Rachel		Entertainment	6			42	Young Actress
Griggs, John W.		Cabinet	12	45	110		Politician-Jurist, Gov. NJ
Griggs, S. David	1939-89	Astronaut	60	150		140	
Grillo, Joann		Entertainment	4			10	

NAME	DATE	CATEGORY	SIG	LS/DS	ALS	SP	COMMENTS
Grimes, Tammy		Entertainment	4	5	9	15	
Grimm, Jacob		Author	565	1840	3760		Grimm's Fairy Tales
Grimm, Wilhelm		Author	500	1425	3150		Grimm's Fairy Tales
Grinnell, Henry	1799-1874	Financier	45	160			Financed Arctic Expeditions
Grinnell, Josiah	1821-91	Congress	25				Repr. IA, Founder Grinnell, IA & University
Grinnell, Moses H.		Business	25	60	120		MOC NY. Merchant Prince NY
Gris, Juan	1887-1927	Artist	175		1500		Sp Cubist Painter
Grisham, John		Author	20	70		45	The Firm, The Pelican Brief
Grisi, Giulia	1811-69	Entertainment	223		215	190	It. Soprano. Great Diva of her time.
Grismer, Joseph R.	1849-1922	Entertainment	4	15			Actor-Manager
Grissom, Virgil I. 'Gus'	1926-67	Astronaut	275	662		1333	Merc. 7. FDC S $750 (Deceased)
Griswald, O.W.		Military	15	35			
Griswold, John A.		Senate/Congress	10		25		MOC NY 1869
Griswold, Matthew		Senate/Congress	12	20	25		MOC PA 1891
Griswold, Putnam		Entertainment	20			50	Opera
Grizzard, George		Entertainment	5	6	15	15	
Grizzard, Lewis		Author	20				Southern humorist
Grodin, Charles	1935-	Entertainment	8		15	25	Actor, Subtle Comedian, TV Personality
Groener, Harry		Entertainment	4			20	Dear John
Groening, Matt*		Cartoonist	45			325	The Simpsons.
Grofe', Ferde		Composer	100	200	245	125	AMusMsS $1,850, AMusQS $360
Grohl, Dave		Entertainment	15			48	Music. Drums, Vocals Nirvana & Foo Fighters
Gromyko, Andrei A.		Statesman	125	160	295	150	Rus.Diplomat. Ambass. to US
Gronau, Wolfgang von		Aviation	75	135	235	195	
Groom, Victor		Aviation	20	45	75	55	
Groom, Winston		Author	20				Forrest Gump
Gropius, Walter	1883-1969	Architect	125	200	600	425	Co-Founder of the Bauhaus Movement
Gropper, William*	1897-1977	Artist	30	85	200	350	Am. Social Protest Artist. Radical Cartoonist
Gross, Calvin		Celebrity	8	20		15	
Gross, Chaim		Artist	50	85	165		4x6 Repro. Peace S $75
Gross, Clayton K.		Aviation	8	16	28	22	ACE, WW II
Gross, Courtlandt		Business	5	10	15	10	
Gross, Milt*		Cartoonist	20			100	Nize Baby
Gross, Samuel D.	1805-84	Medical			1100		Leading Am. Surgeon Of His Time (Rare)
Grosser, Heinz		Science	15			45	Rocket Pioneer/von Braun
Grossinger, Jennie		Business	23	60	135	35	Grossinger's Hotel, Catskill Mts
Grossmith, George	1874-1935	Entertainment	10			25	Br Musical Comedy, Films, Revues
Grosvenor, Charles H.		Civil War	25	40	55		Union Gen., MOC OH
Grosvenor, Gilbert H.	1875-1966	Business	135	100	195	95	Pres.National Geographic.Editor
Grosz, George	1893-1959	Artist	65	338	275		Expressionist Who Expressed Hatred of Bourgeoisie
Grouchy, Marquis E. de		Napoleonic Wars	100	250			Marshal of Napoleon. Exiled
Grover, Cuvier		Civil War	30	65	85		Union General
Groves, Leslie R.		Military	55	145	220	85	Gen.WW II. Manhattan Project
Grow, Galusha A.	1822-1907	Congress	10	175	145	35	Repr. PA, Speaker of the House
Gruberova, Edita		Entertainment	15			40	Opera. SP 4x6 $25

NAME	DATE	CATEGORY	SIG	LS/DS	ALS	SP	COMMENTS
Gruelle, Johnny		Cartoonist	35			250	Raggedy Ann & Andy
Gruen, George John		Business	30	80	150	55	Chm. Gruen Watch Co.
Gruenther, Alfred M.		Military	35		55	45	Gen. WW II. Pres. Am. Red Cr. Cmdr. NATO
Grumman, Leroy R.		Business	50	145		70	Grumman Aircraft
Grunsfeld, John		Astronaut	5			20	
Guardia, R.A.C.		Head of State	15	50		25	Costa Rica
Guardino, Harry		Entertainment	6	15		20	
Guden, Hllde		Entertainment	25		75	50	Opera
Guderian, Hans		Military	30	55	100	45	
Guderian, Heinz		Military	50	175	285	500	Ger. Panzer Gen. WW II
Gudger, V. Lamar		Senate/Congress	10	30		15	MOC NC
Gudin de la Sablonniere		Fr. Revolution	120	235			
Gudunov, Alexander		Entertainment	15		40	35	Rus. Ballet
Guelfi, Piero		Entertainment	10			25	Opera
Guerin, Jules	1866-	Artist	10		35		Muralls at Lincoln Mem'l, Penn.RR Station
Guest, Edgar A.	1881-1959	Author	25	88	165	50	Am.Journalist-Poet of the People. Syndicated
Guest, Lance		Entertainment	6	8	15	19	
Guest, Winston Mrs.		Business	5	10	15	10	
Guevaro, Ernesto Che		Revolutionary	340	895			Aide to Fidel Castro in Cuba
Gueymard-Lautiers, Pauline	1834-?	Entertainment	30		120		Opera, Fr. Mezzo-Soprano
Guffey, Joseph F.		Senate/Congress	5	10		10	Senator PA
Guggenheim, Daniel	1856-1930	Business	20	198	85	35	Guggenheim Foundation
Guggenheim, Harry F.		Aviation		75			Pres. Guggenheim Fund (Aeronautics)
Guggenheim, Peggy		Business	15	25	70	20	Patron of Arts. Collector
Guggenheim, William		Business	55	125		75	Industrialist, Philanthropist
Guidry, Thomas		Entertainment	3			8	
Guilbert, Yvette		Entertainment	40	65	130	150	
Guild, Curtis Jr.		Governor	12	15			Governor MA
Guild, Nancy		Entertainment	6	8	15	15	
Guildford, Henry, Sir	1489-1532	Royal Household	110	430			Henry VIII. Master of Horse & Comptroller of House
Guilfoyle, Paul		Entertainment	10	15	35	30	
Guillaume, Robert		Entertainment	5	10	18	20	
Guillemin, Roger C.L.		Science	20	55	110	35	Nobel Medicine
Guillotin, Joseph-Ignace		Science	275	1650			Fr. Doctor Supported Guillotin
Guinan, Texas (Mary Louise)		Entertainment	25	70	90	40	Actress, Hostess of Speakeasies
Guiney, Louise Imogen		Author	50		300		Poet-Essayist
Guingand, Francis		Military	15	35	50		Fr. General
Guinier, Lani		Law	10	20		15	Afr-Am Law Professer-Writer
Guinness, Alec, Sir		Entertainment	21	25	30	63	Br. Screen Actor. AA. Premium for Star Wars SP
Guinness, Benjamin L.	1798-1868	Business	30	50	110		Guinness Brewing Co.
Guinness, Edward C.	1847-1927	Business	15	25	45	20	Guinness Brewing Co.
Guion, David W.	1892-19—	Composer	100				Home On The Range. ANS $295
Guisewite, Cathy*		Cartoonists	25			85	Cathy
Guiteau, Charles	1842-82	Assassin	418	850	4500	1475	Shot Pres. Garfield
Gulager, Clu		Entertainment	6		15	20	

NAME	DATE	CATEGORY	SIG	LS/DS	ALS	SP	COMMENTS
Gumbel, Bryant		Entertainment	5			10	
Guns 'N Roses (all)		Entertainment	80			135	
Gunsche, Otto		Military	50		85	55	
Gunther, John	1901-70	Author	20		75		Best Seller Inside Europe etc.
Gur, Mordechai	1900-79	Military	20	75			Israeli Gen. 6 Day War. Spec.AirMail Cov. $69.
Gurie, Sigrid		Entertainment	20	25	60	45	
Gurrag-gchaa, Jugderdemidij		Astronaut	15	50		35	Mongolian Astro.
Gusmeroli, Giovanni		Entertainment	5			15	Opera
Gustavus II Adolphus Swe)		Royalty-Military	350	2250	2355		Saved Protestantism in Germ. Great General
Gustavus III (Swe)	1746-92	Royalty	132	700	985		King of Sweden from 1771
Gustavus IV Adolphus(Swe)		Royalty	150				
Gustavus V (Swe)		Royalty				275	
Guston, Philip	1913-80	Artist			175		Canadian-born Am. Painter
Guthrie, Arlo		Country Music	15	35	15	72	Folk Singer in Tradition of His Father Woody
Guthrie, James	1792-1869	Cabinet-Senate	22	45	80		Pierce Sec'y Treas. Sen. KY
Guthrie, Thomas		Clergy	15	20	25		
Guthrie, Woody		Entertainer	300				Folksinger, Poet, Songwriter
Gutierrez, Sid		Astronaut	6			22	
Guttenberg, Steve		Entertainment	5		30	25	
Guy, Thomas		Celebrity	15	40	105		
Guynemer, Georges		Aviation	225	400	650	500	ACE, WW I. A French Legend
Guyot, Arnold	1807-1884	Science	25	45	195		Geographer, Mapmaker, Educator
Guyot, Pierre		Fr. Revolution	25	55	125		
Guyton-Morveau, L.B.Baron	1737-?	Science	20	50	95		Fr. Chemist
Gwenn, Edmund	1875-1959	Entertainment	75	105	145	175	SP Miracle 34th St. $1,650
Gwin, William M.	1805-1885	Senate/Congress	20	45	60		MOC MS, Senator CA
Gwinnett, Button		Rev. War	115000	165000			Rare Signer Decl. Independence
Gwynne, Anne		Entertainment	6	8	15	15	
Gwynne, Fred		Entertainment	20			45	As Herman Munster $150-$175
Gye, Albani		Entertainment	10			25	

NAME	DATE	CATEGORY	SIG	LS/DS	ALS	SP	COMMENTS
Haab, Robert		Head of State	25	70			Switzerland
Haag, Carl	1820-1915	Artist		30	80		Ger.-Born Br. Court Painter to Victoria
Haakon VII (Nor)		Royalty	120	205			1st King Independent of Sweden
Haakon VII and Maud		Royalty	200			450	King & Queen of Norway
Habberton, John		Author	10	15	25		
Haber, Fritz	1868-1934	Science	275		1335		Chemistry. Nobel Prize 1918
Habersham, John	1754-99	Rev. War	40	115			Cont. Congr. Maj. 1st GA Cont. Reg. A Fndr. UofG
Habersham, Joseph	1751-1815	Rev. War	95	260	540		Continental Army,Cont.Congress
Hack, Shelley		Entertainment	4	7	12	15	Pin-Up SP $20
Hackett, Bobby		Entertainment	20			45	Cornet/Benny Goodman

NAME	DATE	CATEGORY	SIG	LS/DS	ALS	SP	COMMENTS
Hackett, Buddy		Entertainment	5	10	20	25	Comedian
Hackett, James K.		Entertainment	12	15		30	Vintage Actor
Hackett, Joan		Entertainment	10	15	25	35	Talented Actress. Untimely Death
Hackman, Gene		Entertainment	20			55	SP/Denzel Washington $130
Hadfield, Chris		Astronaut	7			25	
Hadley, Jerry		Entertainment	10			24	Concert, Opera
Hadley, Reed		Entertainment	15			30	
Haenschen, Gus		Entertainment	15		25	30	Big Band
Hagar, Sammy		Entertainment	10			25	Rock Singer-Guitarist
Hagegard, Hakan		Entertainment				30	Opera
Hagen, Jean		Entertainment	5			10	
Hagen, Johannes	1847-1930	Science	15	40	100		Austr. Astron. Hagen's Clouds
Hagen, Uta		Entertainment	7	12	20	20	
Haggard, Henry Rider	1856-1925	Author	82	130	275	270	King Solomon's Mines
Haggard, Merle		Country Music	10			38	Singer
Haggerty, Dan		Entertainment	5	6	15	15	
Haggin, James Ben Ali		Business	75	275			Am Financier, Anaconda Copper. Hearst Partner
Hagman, Larry	1931-	Entertainment	8	10	15	31	Actor. I Dream of Jeannie, Dallas
Hagood, Johnson	1829-98	Civil War	103	295	383		CSA Gen. War Date S $200
Hague, Frank		Politician	10	25	40	15	Headed Major Dem. Machine
Hahn, Jessica		Entertainment	4			15	Playboy Cover. Pin-Up SP $20
Hahn, Otto	1879-1968	Science	122	345	242	350	Ger. Nobel Chem. Nuclear Fission. ALS/Cont $2000
Hahn, Reynaldo	1874-1947	Composer	70	160			Venezuelan. Critic, Dir. Paris Opera. AMusQS $285
Haider, Michael		Business	15			40	Pres. Standard Oil NJ
Haig, Alexander M.		Military	20	40	50	37	Gen. WW II, Sec'y State
Haig, Douglas. 1st Earl	1861-1928	Military	35	112	130	65	Br. Gen., Boer War, India, WW I
Haig, Lady Dorothy		Celebrity	4		25		Wife of Sir Douglas Haig
Haight, Edward	1817-85	Congress	10				Repr. NY, Founder NY Bank
Haight, Henry H.		Governor	15				San Francisco's Haight-Asbury Distr.
Haile, William	1797-1837	Congress					Repr. MS
Hailey, Arthur		Author	25	40	65	35	Am. Novelist. Hotel, Airport
Haim, Corey		Entertainment	7			40	Actor
Haines, Connie		Entertainment	20			50	Big Band Vocalist
Haines, Daniel	1801-1877	Governor	30	45	90		Governor NJ
Haines, William	1900-73	Entertainment	15	15	35	40	
Hairston, Jester		Entertainment	10			30	
Haise, Fred W. Jr.	1933-	Astronaut	10			95	
Halaby, Najeeb		Celebrity	10	30		15	
Halban, H.H., Dr.		Science	30	65			Fr. Pioneer Of Uranium Fission
Haldane, John B.S.	1892-1964	Science		125	195		Br. Geneticist & Author
Haldeman, George W.		Aviation	30	55	105	75	
Haldeman, H. R.		Political	10	20	62	15	Nixon-Watergate
Halder, Franz		Military	55	95	160	115	Ger. Gen. Opposed Hitler. Prison!
Hale, Alan Jr.		Entertainment	40	138		100	Actor. 'Gilligans Island'
Hale, Alan Sr.		Entertainment	50	55	95	100	

NAME	DATE	CATEGORY	SIG	LS/DS	ALS	SP	COMMENTS
Hale, Barbara	1921-	Entertainment	10		22	25	Actress. Della Street On Perry Mason
Hale, Edward Everett	1822-1909	Clergy	30	190	255	240	Author Man Without a Country
Hale, Eugene	1836-1918	Senate	10	15	30		MOC 1869-75, Senator ME
Hale, George E.		Science	20	100			Invented Spectroheliograph
Hale, John Parker	1806-1873	Congress	15	45	100		Abolitionist., Senator NH
Hale, Lucretia Peabody		Author					1820-1900
Hale, Monte	1921-	Entertainment	10	10	25	35	Big Time Cowboy Star
Hale, Richard		Entertainment	6	8	15	15	
Hale, Robert		Entertainment	10			30	Opera
Hale, Sarah Josepha B.	1788-1879	Author	65	170	295		Editor. Mary Had A Little Lamb
Halevy, Fromental		Composer	30		125		La Juive
Halevy, Jacques	1799-1862	Composer	45	80	135		Opera. Taught Gounod, Bizet
Halevy, Ludovic		Author	25	70	120		Novels, Libretti For Operas
Haley, Alex	1921-92	Author	50	125	358	150	Roots, Malcom X.ALS/Cont. $2900,FDC S $65
Haley, Bill	1925-81	Entertainment	225	500		550	AND The Comets.S Alb. Pg/5 Orig. Members $375
Haley, Jack	1899-1979	Entertainment	140	170		195	Song & Dance Comedian until Tin Man SP $275
Haley, William J., Sir	1901-87	Business	15		35	40	Dir. Gen'l BBC & Editor of the 'Times'
Halifax, Edw. Frederick L.	1881-1958	Statesman	20	60			1st Earl of...Viceroy of India, U.S. Ambassador
Hall and Oates		Entertainment	20			45	
Hall, Abraham Oakey	1826-98	Politician	15		92		NY Mayor, Tweed Ring, Tammany Hall
Hall, Alvin W.		Celebrity	5	10		35	
Hall, Arsenio		Entertainment	10			25	TV Talk Show Host
Hall, Charles M.		Clergy	10	15	20		
Hall, Christopher		Entertainment	8			32	Music. Lead Singer Stabbing Westward
Hall, David		Governor	10			15	Governor OK
Hall, Deidre		Entertainment	10			35	Soaps
Hall, Ella	1976-1981	Entertainment	20			55	Actress. Universal Silent Star 1910-1920's
Hall, Fawn		Entertainment	10		40	20	Pin-Up SP $30
Hall, Gus		Communist	30	55	150	30	US Communist Party Leader
Hall, Harry		Entertainment	4			10	
Hall, Huntz		Entertainment	10	15	25	40	Actor. Early Dead End Gang Type Films
Hall, Jerry		Entertainment	10			30	Pin-Up SP $35
Hall, Jon	1913-79	Entertainment	32	45	85	45	Bare-chested Hero of Many 40's Films
Hall, Josephine		Entertainment	5		15	15	
Hall, Joyce C.		Business	80	540		155	Hallmark Greeting Cards
Hall, Juanita	1901-1968	Entertainment	65			90	'Bloody Mary' in South Pacific
Hall, Lyman	1724-90	Rev. War	2200	2950	4375		Signer Decl. of Indepen.
Hall, Monty		Entertainment	8		10	20	Game Show Host-TV
Hall, Nathan		Cabinet	25	40	115		Fillmore P.M. General
Hall, Pauline		Entertainment	10			30	Vintage Actress
Hall, Radclyffe		Author		45	135		'Well of Loneliness'
Hall, Robert, Sir	1761-1831	Clergy	25	30	35	35	Br. Baptist Minister. Great Pulpit Orator
Hall, Tom T.		Country Music	5			12	Singer
Hall, William		Civil War	40		100		Union Gen., CW Gov. MO
Hallam, Henry	1777-1859	Author	35	115	180		Br. Historian

NAME	DATE	CATEGORY	SIG	LS/DS	ALS	SP	COMMENTS
Halle, Wilhelmine		Entertainment	6	8	15	15	
Halleck, Fitz-Greene	1790-1867	Poet	30	80	105		Member of Knickerbocker Group
Halleck, Henry Wager (WD)		Civil War	225	895	1625	375	Union Gen.ALS/Cont. $4,500
Halleck, Henry Wager	1815-72	Civil War	115	275	670		Union Gen.
Hallett, Mal		Entertainment	20			35	Big Band Leader
Halliburton, Richard	1900-1939	Explorer-Author	30	200		50	World Traveller, Lecturer
Halop, Billy	1920-76	Entertainment	75	75	120	150	One of Orig. Dead End Kids
Halpern, Seymour		Congress	5			15	MOC NY
Halpine, Charles G.	1829-68	Author	20	35	90		Irish-Born C.W. Col. Life Of Pvt. Miles O'Reilly
Halsell, James, Jr.		Astronaut	10			25	
Halsey, Jeremiah		Colonial Am.		75	175		New London, CT Shipbuilder, Owner. Just. Of Peace
Halsey, Wm. F. 'Bull'	1882-1959	Military	100	300	342	338	Adm. WW II. Top Adm. After Nimitz. SP/Nimitz $995
Halstead, Murat		Editor	5	20	35		Journalist
Halston		Business	15	20	40	30	Designer
Halstrom, Holly		TV Model	5			10	'Price is Right' Model
Hamblen, Stewart		Country Music	15			30	Singer-Songwriter
Hamel, Veronica		Entertainment	5	18	20	20	Actress
Hamer, Frank		Military	110	465			
Hamer, Rusty		Entertainment	35		55	75	Child Actor on 'Danny Thomas Show'
Hamill, Mark		Entertainment	10	20	20	46	Actor Star Wars. DS (Gen'l Hosp.) $95
Hamilton, Alex. Jr.	1786-1875	Military	20	40	135		Officer War 1812, Lawyer
Hamilton, Alexander	1757-1804	Cabinet	1075	3428	4067		1st Sec'y Treas. FF $1600-2000. ALS/Cont. $7500
Hamilton, Andrew J.		Civil War					Union Gen. Offic'l Report '63 $5060
Hamilton, Charles Smith	1822-91	Civil War	35	80	110		Union Gen.ALS/Content $575
Hamilton, Donald		Author	7	15	25	10	
Hamilton, Emma, Lady	1765-1815	Celebrity	188	950	1309		Mistress of Lord Nelson Wife of Sir Wm. Hamilton
Hamilton, Gail		Author					See Dodge, Mary A.
Hamilton, George		Entertainment	5			20	
Hamilton, George Alexander, Sir		Diplomatist	75	540			Archaeologist, Husband Emma H.
Hamilton, Ian, Sir	1853-	Military	15				Brit. General. Led Gallipoli Exp.
Hamilton, James		Colonial Am.	65	160			Colonial Gov. PA
Hamilton, James Alex.	1788-1878	Military	45	140			Officer War 1812
Hamilton, John		Entertainment	15				Character Actor
Hamilton, Josh		Entertainment	6			38	Young Actor
Hamilton, Lee		Congress	5	20		10	Congressman IN
Hamilton, Linda		Entertainment	15			45	Pin-Up SP $50
Hamilton, Margaret	1902-85	Entertainment	112	150		185	SP 'Wicked Witch of West' $300
Hamilton, Neil		Entertainment	25	125	65	100	'Commissioner Gordon' in Batman
Hamilton,Ian, Sir		Military	50				Br. General WW I
Hamlin, Hannibal	1809-91	Vice President	102	178	297		Lincoln VP, US Sen., Gov.ME., MOC. FF$150-$350
Hamlin, Harry		Entertainment	8	15	28	20	
Hamlin, V.T.*		Cartoonist	50			325	Alley Oop
Hamlisch, Marvin		Composer	15		142	42	Conductor. AMusQS $35, $85
Hammarskjold, Dag	1905-61	Head of State	120	565	725		Swedish Sec'y General United Nations. Nobel 1961
Hammer		Entertainment	25			45	Rap

NAME	DATE	CATEGORY	SIG	LS/DS	ALS	SP	COMMENTS
Hammer, Armand		Business	55	355	305	185	Occidental Petroleum. Physician in Soviet Union
Hammerstein, O., II & Kern, J.		Composer		1200			
Hammerstein, Oscar, II	1895-1960	Composer	250	350		295	Lyricist-Librettist. 'Oklahoma', 'Show Boat' etc.
Hammett, Dashiell	1894-1961	Author	450	1792	2350	575	Hard-Boiled Detective Fiction. Maltese Falcon
Hammond, James B.		Inventor	20	100			Typewriter
Hammond, James H.	1807-64	Congress		45	115		US Sen., Gov.SC.Cotton is King
Hammond, Jay S.		Governor	10	15			Governor AK
Hammond, L. Blaine		Astronaut	5			20	
Hammond, William A.		Civil War	50	120	400		Union Gen. /Surgeon Gen.Author
Hampden, Renn D.		Clergy	10	25	30		
Hampden, Walter		Entertainment	20		45	45	
Hampson, Thomas		Entertainment	10			32	Opera
Hampton, Hope		Entertainment	40			70	
Hampton, Lionel	1913-	Entertainment	28			65	Big Band Leader-Vibes. Jazz Legend
Hampton, Wade (WD)		Civil War	300				CSA Gen.
Hampton, Wade	1818-1902	Civil War	270	575	918		CSA General, Gov., US Sen. SC
Hamsun, Knut (Pedersen)	1859-1952	Author	40	85	135	200	Nor. Nobel Lit. Neo-Romantic Novels.AMsS $1850
Hanami, Kohei		Military	80	250			
Hancock, Clarence E.	1885-1948	Congress	5	25			Repr. NY
Hancock, Herbie		Composer	10	25	45	20	
Hancock, John	1737-93	Rev. War	2550	5700	7998		First Signer.ALS/Cont. $12,500,$15,000. FF $3900
Hancock, Winfield Scott (WD)		Civil War	208		1375	675	Union General
Hancock, Winfield Scott	1824-86	Civil War	147	325	449	675	Union Gen.ALS/Cont. $3300. Pres. Candidate
Hand, Edward		Rev. War	185	475	1000		Gen. Cont. Army. Repr. PA 1784
Hand, Learned		Jurist				1500	Tenth Justice. Distinguished Among Am. Jurists
Handel, George Frederick		Composer	1000	5800	22000		
Handelman, Stanley M.		Entertainment	3	3	6	6	
Handler, Ruth		Business	40	75			Founder Mattel Toys
Handy, W. C.	1873-1958	Composer	275	494	575	725	AMusQS $2200, Sheet Music S $795
Hanks, Tom		Entertainment	20			85	Actor.Forrest GumpSP $100, Oscar winner
Hanna & Barbera		Cartoonists	35	90		125	Animators. Signatures/Characters Surrounding $85
Hanna, Bill		Cartoonist	30			85	Flintstones', 'Flintstones' Brochure S $125
Hanna, Marcus A.	1837-1904	Industrialist	25	385	225	35	Sen. OH. Political Power Broker
Hannah, Daryl		Entertainment	15	38	45	54	Actress. Pin-Up SP $75
Hannah, John A.		Educator	7			10	Pres. Michigan State Univ.
Hannigan, Alyson		Entertainment	10			52	Actress. Buffy Co-Star
Hansbrough, Henry C.	1848-1933	Congress	10	15	30		MOC, Senator ND
Hansen, William		Entertainment	6	8	15	15	
Hanson, Beck		Entertainment	8			48	Music. Lead Singer Beck
Hanson, Howard		Composer	15	35	80	120	Pulitzer. Dir.Eastman Sch. Music
Hanson, John		Rev. War	2250				Pres. Continental Congress
Haralson, Hugh A.	1805-54	Congress	10				Repr. GA, Maj. Gen'l State Militia
Harbach, Otto	1873-1963	Entertainment	125	100		175	Playwright,Lyricist, Music Publ
Harbaugh, Gregory J.		Astronaut	5			20	
Harbison, John		Composer	20		75		Pulitzer, AMusQS $150

NAME	DATE	CATEGORY	SIG	LS/DS	ALS	SP	COMMENTS
Harbord, James G.		Military	60	145	185	125	Chief of Staff AEF WW I, RCA
Harburg, E. Y. 'Yip'		Composer	100	175	375		Over the Rainbow
Harcourt, Edward Venables		Clergy	25	30	40		
Hardee, William J.(WD)		Civil War	300	875	1110	950	CSA General
Hardenberg, K.A.von Furst		Statesman	15	60	125		Prussian Politician
Hardie, J. Keir	1856-1915	Politician	75			200	Scottish, Founder of the Labour Party
Hardie, James Allen	1823-76	Civil War	68	170			Union Gen.
Hardie, James Allen (WD)	1823-76	Civil War	80	205	245		Union General
Hardie, Russell		Entertainment	10	15	25	25	
Hardin, Clifford M.		Cabinet	5	10	18	15	Sec'y Agriculture
Hardin, Gus		Entertainment	4			10	Female Singer
Hardin, John Wesley	1853-95	Outlaw	3000	6500			Notorious Gunslinger. Bullet Shot Card S $11,750
Hardin, Ty		Entertainment	6	8	15	19	
Harding, Aaron	1805-67	Congress	35	50			MOC KY.Contacts & Recommendations to Lincoln
Harding, Ann		Entertainment	15	15	35	30	
Harding, Florence Kling		First Lady	100	180		80	White House Card S $85
Harding, Tonya		Celebrity	75				Infamous Ice Skater
Harding, Warren G. (As Pres.)		President		919	1950	960	ALS/Cont.$15000. WH Cd S $400-500
Harding, Warren G.	1865-1923	President	125	504	1400	486	Pre-Nomination Political TLS/Cont $3500
Hardinge, Chas., 1st Baron		Diplomat	10	750	35	25	Br.Viceroy India, Ambass.Russia
Hardinge, Henry, Sir	1785-1856	Military			585		Br. Field Marshal
Hardwicke, Cedric, Sir		Entertainment	35	65	90	95	
Hardy, Oliver	1892-1957	Entertainment	275	1300	500	550	1/2 of Popular Comedy Team
Hardy, Thomas	1840-1928	Author	235	1120	1425	1252	Br. Novelist, Poet, Dramatist
Hardy, Thomas Masterman, Sir		Military	75	310			1769-1839 Br. Adm./Nelson. MsLS re War 1812 $750
Hare, John, Sir		Entertainment	20	30		50	
Hare, WIlliam Hobart		Clergy	35	50	65	50	
Hargis, Billy James		Evangelist	10				Right Wing leader of extremist Christian Crusade
Haring, Keith*	1958-90	Artist	40	55	110	800	Pop Artist-Cartoonist.Works in Major World Museums
Harkins, Paul		Military	15	30	50	30	
Harkness, Georgia		Clergy	35	50	95	65	
Harlan, James A.	1820-	Cabinet	25	55	125		Andrew Johnson Sec'y Interior 1865
Harlan, John Marshall (SC)	1899-1971	Supreme Court	25				Grandson of Same. Served Under Eisenhower
Harlan, John Marshall (SC)	1833-1911	Supreme Court	75	122	17		
Harland, Marion		Author	7	15	20		
Harley, William S.		Business	1500	7500			Co-Fndr. Harley-Davidson Motorcycles
Harlfinger II, Frederick J.		Military	10			25	
Harlow, Jean (Mama)		Entertainment	25	30		45	
Harlow, Jean	1911-37	Entertainment	1042	1400	3000	4100	30's Sex Symbol. Died at 26. Mother Signed Most SP
Harman, Fred*		Cartoonist	25			250	Red Ryder
Harmon, Judson		Cabinet	10	25	40	20	U.S. Att'y Gen., Gov. OH
Harmon, Mark		Entertainment	9	10	20	25	
Harmonica Rascals		Entertainment	10			25	Borah Minovitch and the......
Harned, Virginia		Entertainment	15			35	Vintage Actress, Mrs. Sothern
Harney, William S. (WD)		Civil War	50		330		Union Gen.

NAME	DATE	CATEGORY	SIG	LS/DS	ALS	SP	COMMENTS
Harper, Joseph W.		Celebrity	10	30	80		
Harper, Robert G.		Rev. War	65		150		Gen. Rev. War, Statesman
Harper, Tess		Entertainment	9	10	20	25	
Harper, Valerie		Entertainment	5	6	15	15	
Harper, William	1790-1847	Political	25		95		SC Nullification Leader & Slavery Advocate
Harrel, Scotty		Entertainment	8			15	C & W
Harrell, Costen J., Bishop		Clergy	20	25	40	35	
Harrelson, Woody		Entertainment	15			45	Cheers
Harrer, Heinrich		Author	250				Seven Years In Tibet. Tutor of Dalai Lama
Harridge, Will	1883-1971	Business		125			Pres. Org. Known as American League
Harries, George		Military	20	35	80		General WW I
Harriman, Edw. Henry	1848-1909	Business	250	900			U.S. RR Magnate. S RR Bonds $575+
Harriman, Edward Roland		Business	20	55	120	35	CEO Union Pacific RR. Banker
Harriman, W. Averell	1891-1986	Governor	20	56	100	50	Gov. NY, Statesman, Diplomat, Ambassador etc.
Harrington, Pat		Entertainment	4	5	10	15	
Harris		Cartoonist	5			18	The Better Half
Harris, Arthur T., Sir 'Bomber'	1892-1984	Military	99	125	165	150	Cmdr.-in-Chief RAF WW 99II. Head of Bomber Comm.
Harris, Barbara		Entertainment	5			15	Actress. Stage-Films
Harris, Barbara C.		Clergy	10			20	
Harris, Bernard A., Jr.		Astronaut	10			25	Afro-Am. Astronaut
Harris, Cecil		Aviation	20	25	50	40	ACE, WW II
Harris, Ed		Entertainment	8		15	20	Actor
Harris, EmmyLou		Entertainment	10			35	Country Singer
Harris, Fred R.		Senate/Congress	4	10			Senator OK
Harris, George E.		Senate/Congress	10	15			CSA Officer. MOC NC
Harris, Isham	1818-97	Civil War	50	68			Civil War Gov. TN. ALS '64 $450. US Senator
Harris, Jean		Criminal	35	70			Murdered Dr. Herman Tarnower. ALS/cont. $375
Harris, Jed		Entertainment	5	20			Producer. Theatre
Harris, Joel Chandler	1848-1908	Author	217	415	700		Popular Books on Black Folklore. 'Uncle Remus'
Harris, John	1726-91	Frontier Leader	125	265	775		Founder Harrisburg, PA
Harris, John A.		Senate/Congress	4		15		
Harris, Jonathan		Entertainment	7			18	Actor. Lost in Space
Harris, Julie	1925-	Entertainment	8	10	15	25	Actress. Broadway Tony Winner. Films, TV
Harris, Louis		Pollster	20	35		25	
Harris, Mel		Entertainment	8			35	Actress. '30 Something'
Harris, Neil Patrick		Entertainment	10			35	Young Actor in 'Doogie Howser'
Harris, Patricia Roberts	1924-85	Cabinet	15		40	75	1st Afr-Am Woman To Serve in Cabinet. Authen.RARE
Harris, Paul Percy		Business	25	45		30	Fndr. & Pres.- Emeritus. Rotary
Harris, Phil		Entertainment	22			45	Bandleader-Actor-Singer and Disney Voice-Over
Harris, Richard		Entertainment	15		35	40	Irish-Br. Actor
Harris, Robert		Author	10	50			'Enigma'
Harris, Robert H.		Entertainment	6			10	
Harris, Sam H.		Entertainment	4	25			Producer-Manager
Harris, Thomas		Author	20	55			'Silence of the Lambs'
Harris, Thomas S.		Aviation	15	45		30	ACE WW II, Test Pilot

NAME	DATE	CATEGORY	SIG	LS/DS	ALS	SP	COMMENTS
Harris, William A.	1841-1909	Congress-Civil War	30		45		Repr.& Sen. KS, CW Adj. Gen'l
Harris, William L., Bishop		Clergy	15	25	35		
Harrison, Albertis S. Jr.		Governor	10	20			Governor VA
Harrison, Anna Symmes		First Lady	675	1438	2950		Free Frank $975
Harrison, Benj. & Roosevelt, T.		Presidents					Civ.Serv.Commission S $2250
Harrison, Benj. & Caroline		President, 1st Lady	600				Together on One Piece
Harrison, Benjamin (As Pres.)		President	363	962	1900		Exec. Mansion Card S. $450
Harrison, Benjamin	1726-91	Rev. War	450	956	1825		Signer Decl. of Indepen., Gov. Virginia
Harrison, Benjamin	1833-1901	President	200	470	657	2000	TLS/Cont. $1600-2500. DS-Pres. Warrant $1450
Harrison, Burton, Mrs.		Celebrity	10			35	1890's Socialite
Harrison, Byron Patton 'Pat'		Senate/Congress	5	15		10	MOC, Senator MS
Harrison, Caroline Scott	1832-1892	First Lady	180	250	1100	650	1st Pres. D.A.R. Died in White House/Tuberculosis
Harrison, Carter H.		Mayor	10	35	40		Mayor Chicago 1897
Harrison, George		Entertainment	200	576	450	425	Beatle.Check S $785. DS (Settlement $237,500) $950
Harrison, George P.,Jr.	1841-1922	Civil War	95		283		CSA Gen.
Harrison, George P.,Jr.(WD)		Civil War	150	225			CSA Gen..
Harrison, Gregory		Entertainment	9	15	20	20	Busy Actor
Harrison, Helen		Aviation	40	125			Am Aviatrix
Harrison, Henry B.		Governor	12		20		Governor CT 1885
Harrison, Jenilee		Entertainment	4	4	10	15	Actress 'Three's Company'
Harrison, Linda		Entertainment	10			27	Actress. Planet of the Apes
Harrison, Mary Lord	1858-1948	First Lady	79	130	241	120	Niece of 1st Lady Caroline Scott & Second Wife
Harrison, Noel		Entertainment	8			18	Br. Actor-Son of Rex Harrison
Harrison, Rex, Sir	1908-90	Entertainment	38	55	68	84	Br.Actor. My Fair Lady SP $150. Oscar Winner
Harrison, Richard B.	1865-1935	Entrtainment	25	85		150	Am. Vintage Black Actor. 'The Green Pastures'
Harrison, Robert Hanson		Rev. War	210	400	750		Sec'y to G. Washington
Harrison, William Henry	1773-1841	President	660	1690	3817		President Only 1 Month. ALS/Content $6500+
Harrold, Kathryn		Entertainment	10		14	20	Actress Pin-Up SP $35
Harry, Debbie		Entertainment	25			66	Rock Singer-Actress. 'Blondie'
Harry, Jackee		Entertainment	5			15	
Harryhausen, Ray		Entertainment	10			35	Film Director
Harshaw, Margaret		Entertainment	10		40	65	Opera. U.S. Soprano
Hart, Corey		Entertainment	8		15	22	
Hart, Dolores	1938-	Entertainment	5	25		20	Actress
Hart, Dorothy		Entertainment	15		25	30	
Hart, Gary W.		Senator	8	18		20	Senator CO. One Time Presidential Hopeful
Hart, John		Entertainment	10			25	SP as the Lone Ranger $50
Hart, John	1711-1779	Rev. War	335	550	1300		Signer Decl. of Indepen. Important DS $3490
Hart, Johnny*		Cartoonist	20			175	'B.C.' & 'Wizard Of Id'
Hart, Lorenz	1895-1943	Composer	500	7500			Talented Lyricist for Richard Rodgers. Died Young
Hart, Mary		Entertainment	5		15	15	Pleasing 'Entertainment Tonight' Host.Pin-Up SP$25
Hart, Melissa Joan		Entertainment	12			50	Actress. Sabrina The Teenage Witch
Hart, Moss	1904-61	Author	30	55	120	40	Playwright & Musical Librettist
Hart, Paul		Entertainment	5		15	15	
Hart, Roxanne		Entertainment	10			20	Pinup $30

NAME	DATE	CATEGORY	SIG	LS/DS	ALS	SP	COMMENTS
Hart, Terry J.		Astronaut	8	15		30	
Hart, Thomas C.		Military	40			65	Adm. WW II
Hart, Veronica		Entertainment	8	15	30	35	Pin-Up SP $45
Hart, William S.	1870-1946	Entertainment	142	245	235	482	1st Western Movie Star. Silent Films
Harte, Francis Brett	1836-1902	Author	90	185	283		Diplomat. Author of Frontier Life, AMsS $25,000
Hartford, George L.		Business	40	295	280		Great Atlantic & Pacific Tea Co.Huge Grocery Chain
Hartford, Huntington		Business	20	30	50	25	Arts Patron. Playboy. Huntington Hartford Theatre
Hartford, John		Composer	10	45	70		AMusQS $95
Hartle, Russell	1889-1961	Military	20			35	General. Cmdr. US Forces in Britain early WW II
Hartley, David	1729-1813	Colonial			950		Br. Minister.Anti War/Colonies.Signed Peace Treaty
Hartley, Fred A.		Congress	20		50		Congressman NJ
Hartley, Mariette		Entertainment	5	8	15	15	Actress. Films, TV
Hartley, Nina		Entertainment	15			45	
Hartley, Roland H.		Governor	5	12		10	Governor WA
Hartley, Thomas	1748-1800	Rev. War	105		350		Lt. Col. War Content ALS $6500
Hartline, Haldan K.		Science	25	80	140	35	Nobel Medicine
Hartman, David		Entertainment	10		15	15	Early TV Host 'Good Morning America'
Hartman, Don		Entertainment	10			30	Producer
Hartman, Lisa (Black)		Entertainment	8			24	Pin-Up SP $40
Hartman, Phil	1948-98	Entertainment	45			80	Comedian-Actor. Tragic Early Death
Hartmann, Erich	1922-96	Aviation	45	105	208	395	Ger.Ace WW II. #1 Worldwide/Most Kills
Hartranft, John F.	1830-89	Civil War	80	111	165		Union Gen. Statesman. Gov. PA. ALS/Cont. $1045
Harts, William	1867-1961	Military	10		45		Span.-Am.War.General WW I. Extensive Career
Hartsfield, Henry W. Jr		Astronaut	10	40		20	
Hartsuff, George L.	1830-74	Civil War	55	75	152		Union Gen. S/Rank $75-$95
Hartwell, Alfred S.	1836-1912	Civil War	42	97	120		Union General
Harvey, George B. M.		Journalist-Dipl.	20	70		80	Fostered Woodrow Wilson Nomination
Harvey, Lawrence		Entertainment	90			150	Br. Actor. Early Death
Harvey, Lilian		Entertainment	5		15	22	
Harvey, Marilyn		Entertainment	10			35	Star of The Astounding She Monster
Harvey, Paul		Journalist	10	25		20	Popular Syndicated Columnist-TV Commentator
Harvey, William	1578-1657	Science	750	3750	11000		1st Theory Blood Circulation. (RARE in any form)
Hasbrouck, Robert W.		Military	50	165		75	Am. Gen. WW II
Hasen, Irwin		Cartoonist	5			20	'Dondi'
Haskell, James K.		Entertainment	8	15	30	22	
Haskell, Peter		Entertainment	5			10	Actor
Haskil, Clara		Entertainment	120				Legendary Classical Pianist. RARE
Haskin, Joseph Abel	1818-74	Civil War	50		105		Union General. Sig./Rank $65
Hassam, Childe	1859-1935	Artist	150	350	615		Foremost in Am. Impressionism. Etcher
Hassam, Crown Prince		Royalty	20	45		75	Morocco
Hassan, al Bakr, Ahmad		Head of State	10	35	90	18	Last Price Availble
Hassan, Crown Prince		Royalty	10	15	50	20	No Current Price
Hasselhoff, David		Entertainment	17			44	Baywatch
Hasso, Signe		Entertainment	5			20	Actress
Hastings, Alcee	1936-	Congress	15			35	Afr-Am Dem. MOC FL. As Federal Judge, Impeached.

NAME	DATE	CATEGORY	SIG	LS/DS	ALS	SP	COMMENTS
Hastings, Daniel H.		Governor	10	25			Governor PA
Hastings, Warren	1732-1818	Head of State	70	237	300		1st Gov- Gen. India. Colonial Adm.
Haswell, Charles H.	1809-	Civil War	40	60	90		Union Naval Architect War Dte DS $155-200
Hatch, John Porter	1822-1901	Civil War	40	50	125		Union Gen. CMH. ADS(Gen.Orders '62)$4180
Hatch, Orrin		Senate	10			20	Senator UT
Hatcher, Richard G.	1933-	Political	5	10		25	Afro-Am. Mayor, Gary IN
Hatcher, Teri		Entertainment	10			65	Actress. 'Lois & Clark'-'James Bond'
Hatfield, Hurd		Entertainment	15	22	30	35	Actor. Portrait of Dorian Grey
Hatfield, Lansing		Entertainment	15			95	Opera, Concert, Recital Artist
Hatfield, Mark O.		Senate	10	22		20	Senator OR, Governor Oregon. Long Time 'Dove'
Hathaway, Henry		Entertainment	40			95	Film Director
Hatlo, Jimmy*	1898-1963	Cartoonist	10	45		80	'Little Iodine'
Hatton, Christopher, Sir	1540-91	Statesman		1138			Elizabeth Ist, Lord Chancellor
Hatton, Frank		Cabinet	50	70			Chester A. Arthur PMG
Hatton, Raymond		Entertainment	50			125	Vintage Actor
Hatton, Robert	1826-62	Civil War	350				No Current Prices '99.Killed at Fair Oaks 6/1/1862
Hatton, Rondo		Entertainment	450			1200	
Hauck, Frederick H.		Astronaut	10			25	
Hauer, Rutger		Entertainment	11			40	Actor. Lady Hawke
Haught, Helmut		Aviation	10	15	30	20	
Haupt, Herman	1817-1905	Civil War	40				Union Gen. ALS '62 $440
Hauptman, Herbert A., Dr.		Science	20	35		30	Nobel Chemistry
Hauptmann, Bruno Richard		Kidnapper	425				Convicted Killer Lindbergh Baby
Hauptmann, Gerhart		Author	90	295	575	375	Nobel Prize Literature 1912
Hauser, Dr. Gayelord		Medical	20			35	Healthfood Advocate. Garbo Companion
Hausner, Jerry		Entertainment	5			10	
Havel, Vaclav		Head of State	20			45	Czech. Poet. President
Havemeyer, William F.		Business	125		305		Am. Sugar Refining Dynasty. Mayor NYC
Haven, Annette		Entertainment	9	10	20	25	Pin-Up SP $40
Havens, Beckwith		Aviation	18	40	55	50	
Haver, June		Entertainment	5	10	12	20	40's-50's Blonde 20th Cent. Fox Star.Pin-Up SP $25
Havoc, June		Entertainment	10		20	25	Actress. 'Baby June' Sister of Gypsy Rose Lee
Hawes, Elizabeth		Artist	10	20	35		
Hawke, Ethan		Entertainment	18			48	Actor
Hawke, Robert	1929-	Head of State	20	40	130	30	Prime Minister Australia
Hawker, Harry	1886-1921	Aviation	185				Pioneer Australian Pilot & Airplane Builder. Rare
Hawkins, Anthony Hope, Sir		Author	38	42	85	38	Br.Novelist. Prisoner of Zenda
Hawkins, Coleman		Entertainment	140			250	Jazz Tenor Sax. Band Leader
Hawkins, Jack		Entertainment	45			92	Br. Leading Man & Character Actor. Cancer Victim
Hawkins, John	1830-1914	Civil War	40		140		Union Gen. Sig/Rank $50
Hawkins, Paula		Senate/Congress	5	10		15	Senator FL
Hawkins, Rush C. (WD)		Civil War		245			Union Gen.
Hawkins, William	1770-1819	Governor	35	85			Governor NC. War 1812
Hawks, Frank Monroe	1897-1938	Aviation	85	135	325	272	Pioneer Am. Aviator
Hawks, Howard		Entertainment	98	375		200	Diector-Producer-Studio Head

NAME	DATE	CATEGORY	SIG	LS/DS	ALS	SP	COMMENTS
Hawley, Joseph R.	1826-1905	Civil War	50	95	135		Union Gen., Gov. CT, Sen CT.Hero. Anti Slavery
Hawley, Steven A.		Astronaut	10			20	
Hawn, Goldie		Entertainment	15	48		54	Actress-Comedian. Pin-Up SP$65
Haworth, Jill		Entertainment	5			10	Actress
Hawthorn, Alex. Travis	1825-99	Civil War	182	372	628		CSA General
Hawthorne, Julian	1846-1934	Author	40		225		Son of Nathaniel Hawthorne
Hawthorne, Nathaniel	1804-65	Author	400	1262	1968		Novelist, Short Stories, US Consul
Hay, Bill (Announcer)		Entertainment	10	25		20	Radio
Hay, John H.		Military	5		15		
Hay, John Milton	1838-1905	Cabinet	57	168	238	135	Lincoln Private Sec'y. ALS/Content $950 War Dte
Hay, William Henry		Military	5	15	30		
Hayakawa, Sessue		Entertainment	125			372	Japanese. Major Star in Jap., US & Foreign Films
Haydee, Marcia		Entertainment	10			35	Prima Ballerina in The Turning Point
Hayden, Carl		Senate/Congress	10	25		20	MOC, Senator AZ. 42 Years
Hayden, Charles	1870-1937	Banker	20	45		40	Philanthropist. Hayden Planetarium
Hayden, Mellisa		Entertainment	5		15	15	Actress
Hayden, Nora		Entertainment	5			20	Actress. 60's Star The Angry Red Planet
Hayden, Russell		Entertainment	25			75	Actor. Cowboy Star
Hayden, Sterling	1916-86	Entertainment	25			50	Reclusive Actor
Hayden, Tom		Congress	5			15	MOC CA. Ex-Husband of Jane Fonda
Haydn, Franz Joseph	1732-1809	Composer	2850	15500	24000		Working Draft 4 String Quartets $1.04 Mil.
Haydon, Benj. R.	1786-1846	Artist		115	232		Br. Historical Painter,Author,Teacher
Hayek, Salma		Entertainment	15			55	Actress-'Desperado'
Hayes, George 'Gabby'	1889-1965	Entertainment	138	220		450	Western Star. Grizzly 'Sidekick'
Hayes, Helen	1900-94	Entertainment	20	40	45	62	Was First Lady of American Theatre
Hayes, Ira H., Corporal		Military	400				Iwo Jima Flag Raising FDC $550
Hayes, Isaac		Entertainment	9	40		25	Composer-Singer-Musician Recording Artist
Hayes, Isaac Israel	1832-81	Explorer-Civil War	95	190	275		Arctic Expl. ALS/Cont.$1,500. War Dte. DS $375
Hayes, Joseph	1835-1912	Civil War	65	110	170	195	Union General
Hayes, Lucy Webb		First Lady	230		400	700	Mrs. Rutherford B. Hayes
Hayes, Margaret		Entertainment	9	10		15	Actress
Hayes, Patrick, Cardinal	1867-1938	Clergy	35	45	75	50	Founded Catholic Charities
Hayes, Peter Lind	1915-98	Entertainment	20			32	Comedian, Actor, Singer/Wife Mary Healy
Hayes, Roland	1887-1977	Entertainment	80		175	250	Am. Tenor, Spingarn Medal '25
Hayes, Rutherford B. (As Pres.)		President	373	580	995	1375	ALS/Cont. $7,500, WH Cd. $350-$475
Hayes, Rutherford B.	1822-93	President, CW	221	594	670	2855	Union Gen.Post Pres.-Pro Education ALS $3500
Hayne, Paul Hamilton	1830-86	Author	80		562		ALS/Literary Content $2,500.Laureate of South
Hayne, Robert Young	1791-1839	Congress	75		180		Sen. SC, Gov. SC
Haynes, Linda		Entertainment	5			10	Actress
Hays, Frank A.		Aviation	35	55	95	65	ACE, WW II
Hays, Harry Thompson (WD)		Civil War	312	1205			CSA Gen.
Hays, Harry Thompson	1820-76	Civil War	198	450			CSA General
Hays, Robert		Entertainment	5		12	10	Singer-Actor
Hays, Wayne L.		Senate/Congress	5	20		15	MOC OH
Hays, Will H.	1879-1854	Cabinet	28	45		45	Film Czar. Hays Code. Pres.DS $300. PMG

NAME	DATE	CATEGORY	SIG	LS/DS	ALS	SP	COMMENTS
Hays, William	1819-75	Civil War	45	90	165		Union Gen. ALS '64 $385, Sig/Rank $85
Hayton, Lennie	1908-71	Entertainment	20			75	Pianist, Composer, Musical Dir. MGM 1940-53
Hayward, George		Science	10	20	35	15	
Hayward, Louis		Entertainment	10	15	25	50	Br. Leading Man. Many Historical Films.
Hayward, Susan	1917-75	Entertainment	172	200	488	496	Oscar Winning Actress. Early Death
Haywood, Thomas		Military	5	10	15	15	
Hayworth, Rita	1918-87	Entertainment	150	265	420	471	Glamour Star of the 40's
Hazelwood, John	1726-1800	Rev. War	75	190	370		Commodore Continental Navy
Hazelwood, Joseph		Navy Captain	20			45	Capt. Exxon Valdez-Oil Spill
Hazen, Wm. Babcock	1830-87	Civil War	37	55	110		Union Gen. War Dte. DS $150
Head		Entertainment	5			25	Music. Guitars, Vocals Korn
Head, Edith		Entertainment	25			125	8 Academy Awards. Costume Design.
Headle, Marshall		Aviation	25	70		85	Lockheed Chief Test Pilot
Healey, Robert C.		Author	10	15	25		
Healy, George Peter	1813-94	Artist	125	310	838		Eminent 19th Cent. Portraitist
Healy, Ted		Entertainment	25		40	45	Vaudeville Song & Dance Man. 'Me & My Shadow'
Hearn, Lafcadio	1850-1904	Author	300		1200		Irish-Greek-Am. Writer on Japanese Culture
Hearnes, Warren E.		Governor	4	10		15	Governor MO
Hearst, George	1820-1891	Business-Senate	285		1175		Fathered Newspaper Dynasty.Stk.Cert. S $18,000
Hearst, Patricia		Celebrities	275				Kidnapped daughter of Hearst, Jr.
Hearst, Phoebe A.(Mrs. George)		Business	20	40	90		Philanthropies
Hearst, Wm. Randolph	1863-1951	Business	225	585	785	695	MOC. NY. Powerful Publisher. Pres. Cand. DS $1450
Hearst, Wm. Randolph, Jr.		Business	10	30	45	20	Son of Hearst, Sr. Newspaper Publisher
Heart		Entertainment	38			100	Rock
Heath, Edward	1916-	Head of State	30	90	110	45	Br.Prime Minister
Heath, William	1737-1814	Rev. War	160	740	1500		Gen.Cont'l Army. DS War Dte.$1275,$1400
Heatherton, Joey		Entertainment	9	10	18	20	Actress-Dancer-Singer
Heatherton, Ray		Entertainment	20			70	Big band leader
Heber, Reginald	1783-1826	Clergy	85	100	200		Br. Prelate, Hymn Writer. Holy, Holy, Holy
Hebert, Louis (WD)		Civil War	202	505			CSA Gen.
Hebert, Louis	1820-1901	Civil War	112	258	685		CSA Gen.
Hebert, Paul O.	1818-80	Civil War	110	350	458		CSA General Sig/Rank $200
Heche, Anne		Entertainment	8			38	Actress. Pin-Up $55
Hecht, Ben	1894-1964	Author	25	85		50	AA.Playwright, Novelist, Newsman
Heckart, Eileen	1919-	Entertainment	12	10	15	25	Noted Character Actress of Stage, Film, TV
Heckerling, Amy		Entertainment	5		15	14	
Heckman, Charles A.	1822-96	Civil War	35	105			Union Gen. ALS (Autobiog.)$550, Sig/Rank $50+
Hedin, Sven	1865-1952	Explorer	102	170	203	125	Swe. Asian Explorer, Geographer
Hedison, David		Entertainment	5			12	Actor. 'Voyage to Bottom of the Sea'
Hedl, Walter		Composer	15	55	90		AMusQS $175
Hedman, Robert Duke		Aviation	25	45	75	50	ACE, WW II, Flying Tigers
Hedouville, G.M.T.J,Count		Fr. Revolution	70	125			Fr. Gen. Marshal of Fr.?
Hedren, Tippi		Entertainment	7		22	35	Actress. 'The Birds'
Hedrick, Roger		Aviation	15	25	40	35	ACE, WW II
Heflin, Howell		Senate	5	15	15	10	Senator AL

NAME	DATE	CATEGORY	SIG	LS/DS	ALS	SP	COMMENTS
Heflin, James Thomas		Senate/Congress	10	20		15	MOC, Senator AL
Heflin, Van	1910-71	Entertainment	35	75	95	92	Actor-Oscar Winner. Versatile. Leads to Westerns
Hefner, Christie		Business	5	10	30	20	Publisher Playboy Magazine
Hefner, Hugh		Business	10			22	'Playboy'TLS/Cont.$500.'Toddlin Town'1st prtg $750
Heft, Bob		Designer	20		25		Designed US 50 Star Flag
Hefti, Neal		Composer	15	35	50	40	AMusQS $195. 'Odd Couple' Theme AMusQS $45
Hegel, Geo. Wilhelm F.	1770-1831	Philosopher	850	1475	2050		Ger. Idealist Philosopher/Kant
Heggie, O.P.		Entertainment	350			750	Character Actor
Heidegger, Martin	1889-1976	Philosopher			1400		Ger. Existential Phenomonologist
Heidt, Horace 'Musical Knights'		Entertainment	20			40	Big Band Leader. Sigs 12 Members $45
Heifetz, Jascha	1901-87	Entertainment	145	160		585	Violin Virtuoso.AMusQS $700
Heigle, Katherine		Entertainment				75	Actress
Heimlich, Henry Jay, Dr.		Science	20		45	40	Created Heimlich Maneuver
Heine, Heinrich	1797-1856	Author	570	4000	6500		Ger. Poet, Critic, Essayist
Heinlein, Robert A.		Author	55	165	350		Sci-Fi Fiction
Heinrich, Albert H.		Aviation	35		120		
Heintzelman, Samuel P.(WD)		Civil War	45	145	220		Union Gen.
Heintzelman, Samuel P.	1805-80	Civil War	35	95	150		Union General
Heinz, Henry John	1844-1919	Business	110		800	385	Fndr/Brother& Cousin H&J. Heinz Co. Pickles etc.
Heinz, Henry John II		Business	35				Food Manufacturer
Heinz, Henry John III	1938-92	Congress	15	30		25	Sen. PA. Air Crash Victim. Heir to Heinz Fortune
Heinze, F. Aug.		Business	500	2450			Montana Mining Mogul
Heinze, Karl		Astronaut	35			75	
Heise, Karl G.		Astronaut	10			20	
Heisenberg, Werner, Dr.	1901-76	Science	62	560	650		Nobel Physics,ALS/Cont. $950
Helbig, Joachim		Aviation	10	20	35	25	
Held, Anna	1865-1918	Entertainment	65	80	135	85	Mrs. Florenz Ziegfield.Star Fr.,Am.,Yid'sh Musical
Held, John, Jr.*	1889-1958	Cartoonist	165			385	Illustrator Created The 'Flapper'
Heldmann, Aloys		Aviation		70			Ger. WW I Ace
Heldy, Fanny		Entertainment	40			110	Opera
Helena, Princess		Royalty	15	20	150	65	3rd Daughter Queen Victoria. Fndr. Nursing Home
Helgenberger, Marg		Entertainment	15			35	Pin-Up SP $50
Heller, John R., Dr.		Science	12	20		20	
Heller, Joseph		Author	15	30	45	40	'Catch 22'
Heller, Walter E.		Business	5	15		15	Fndr.,Chm. Walter E. Heller
Heller, Walter W.		Cabinet	5	15	30	15	
Helletsgruber, Luise		Entertainment	25			75	Opera
Hellinger, Mark		Author	35	105	225	40	Columnist, Playwright
Hellman, Lillian	1905-84	Author	40	148		100	Am. Dramatist, 'Little Foxes'
Hellyer, Paul T.		Celebrity	15	30			
Helm, Ben Hardin	1830-83	Civil War	235	363			CSA General. Killed 9/20/63 Battle of Chicamauga
Helm, Briditte	1906-96	Entertainment	25			100	Ger. Actress. 1926 Cult Film Metropolis
Helm, Fay		Entertainment	15			50	Actress
Helmholtz, Hermann L.von	1821-94	Science	195		600		Ger Physicist Biologist.Many Science Contributions
Helmond, Katherine		Entertainment	8		20	20	Actress. Comedy & Straight Leads. TV-Films

NAME	DATE	CATEGORY	SIG	LS/DS	ALS	SP	COMMENTS
Helms, Jesse		Congress	5	15		20	U.S. Senator NC
Helms, Richard		Celebrity	5	15	45	20	
Helms, Susan		Astronaut	8			25	
Helmsley, Leona		Business	10			35	Hotel Magnate
Heloise		Author	5			10	Columnist. Household Tips
Helps, Arthur, Sir	1817-75	Author	10	15	40		Historian Re America
Helton, Percy		Entertainment	20			65	
Hemingway, Ernest	1899-1961	Author	931	2480	4075	2395	Nobel Lit. Pulitzer. Rosen Caric. S $2500
Hemingway, Margaux		Entertainment	40			80	Actress-Daughter E. Hemingway
Hemingway, Mariel		Entertainment	15			50	Actress-Daughter E. Hemingway
Hemingway, Mary		Author	20	45	85		Mrs. Ernest Hemingway
Hempel, Frieda		Entertainment	20			70	Ger. Soprano, Opera
Hemphill, John	1803-1862	Congress	20	75			U.S. Sen. TX. Chief Justice Repub. TX.
Hemsley, Sherman		Entertainment	6		15	20	Actor. 'The Jeffersons'. TV Sitcom
Hemstridge, Natasha		Entertainment	20			72	Br. Actress
Hench, Philip S.		Science	100		520		Nobel Medicine & Physiology. Cortisone, Hormones
Henderson, Archibald		Military	65	195			Marine General War 1812
Henderson, Fletcher		Entertainment	15			35	Bandleader
Henderson, Florence		Entertainment	6			20	Brady Bunch Mom. Singer-Actress-TV Announcer
Henderson, J. Pinckney		Statesman	390	525			Gen. TX Army, Gov. Texas
Henderson, John Brooks	1826-1913	Civil War Senator	25	65			Sen. From MO 1862-69. Frequent Contact/Lincoln
Henderson, Marcia		Entertainment	5			20	
Henderson, Skitch		Composer	16			35	Conductor, Bandleader
Hendon, Bill		Senate/Congress	3			5	Congressman NC
Hendricks, Barbara		Entertainment	10			35	Opera
Hendricks, Thos.A. (V)	1819-85	Vice President	50	200	200	85	Cleveland VP, U.S. Sen. IN
Hendrix, Jimi	1942-1970	Entertainment	892	2328		1788	Leading Acid Rock 60's Singer. Drug Overdose
Hendrix, Wanda		Entertainment	10	15		25	Actress.
Hendry, Gloria		Entertainment	5			10	Afr.-Am. Actress
Heney, Hugh		Explorer	325	750			Scout & Interpretor for Lewis & Clark
Henie, Sonja	1910-69	Entertainment	55	82		170	Gold in Olympic Figure Skating
Henize, Karl G.	1926-93	Astronaut	10			50	
Henley, Don		Entertainment	20			42	Composer, Singer. The Eagles Alb. S $45
Henley, Thos. Jeff.	1810-65	Congress	10		30		MOC IN, San Francisco Postmaster
Henn, Mark		Cartoonist	10			35	Disney Animator. Little Mermain, Beauty & Beast
Henner, Marilu		Entertainment	8		20	25	Actress. 'Taxi' etc. Pin-Up SP $60
Henreid, Paul		Entertainment	32			80	Film Leading Man/Dir. Casablanca
Henri, Robert		Artist	80	175	215		Portr. Painter, Ashcan School
Henricks, Terence T.		Astronaut	5			20	
Henry II		Royalty	295	1050	2500		France
Henry III	1551-89	Royalty	250	688	1325		France
Henry IV (Fr)	1553-1610	Royalty	205	740	2900		And Navarre. Assassinated
Henry IV (Sp)		Royalty		1675			King of Castile The Impotent 1454-1474
Henry V (Fr)		Royalty	40	65	150		Pretender to Throne
Henry VI		Royalty	195	525	1350		England

NAME	DATE	CATEGORY	SIG	LS/DS	ALS	SP	COMMENTS
Henry VII (Eng)		Royalty	875	8138	10000		
Henry VIII	1491-1547	Royalty	2950	12000	17500		England. Father of Queen Mary & Elizabeth I
Henry, Bill		Aviation	10	25	40	30	ACE, WW II, Navy Ace
Henry, Bill		Entertainment	10	15	35	30	Actor
Henry, Buck		Entertainment	12		15	20	Actor. Films. Currently on Broadway.'Iceman Cometh'
Henry, Gloria		Entertainment	5		10	15	Actress
Henry, John	1750-1798	Rev. War	35	135	220		Continental Congress. Sen. MD
Henry, Joseph	1797-1878	Science	75	478	295		1st Electric Motor. 1st Dir. Smithsonian
Henry, Mike		Entertainment	10			35	
Henry, O. (Pseud.) W.S. Porter		Author					SEE William Porter
Henry, Patrick	1736-99	Rev. War	1100	3175	3900		Rev. War Leader, Statesman. ALS $7,800, LS $4500
Henschel, George, Sir	1850-1934	Composer	70			150	Br.-Ger. Conductor, Singer
Henshaw, David	1791-1852	Cabinet	25	55	112		Tyler Sec'y Navy. MA Leader Dem. Party 30 Yrs.
Henson, Jim	1936-90	Entertainment	75	200	175	256	Created the Muppets. DS re Muppets $275
Henson, Matthew A.		Explorer	155	350			Afro-Am. Arctic Expl. Historical Statement $5000
Henstridge, Natasha		Entertainment	12			60	Actress Pin-Up $80
Henze, Hans Werner		Composer	45			165	Ger. Opera, Theater Works
Henze, Karl		Aviation	16	35	70	45	
Hepburn, Audrey	1929-93	Entertainment	100	325	485	380	AA Winner. Belg. Born Actress-Humanitarian
Hepburn, Katharine	1907-	Entertainment	152	292	488	747	AA. 4 Times Oscar Winner. 3x5 SP $650.
Hepworth, Barbara, Dame		Artist	70	190		125	Br. Sculptor. Reclining Figure
Herbeck, Ray		Entertainment	5			15	Big Band Leader-Sax
Herbert, F. Hugh		Author	12	20	30	20	Am. Playwright, Producer
Herbert, Frank		Author	15	20	35	20	Am. Sci-Fi. 'Dune Trilogy'
Herbert, Geo.E. (Carnarvon)	1866-1923	Archaeology	32	45	148		With Carter, King Tut Tomb. 5th Earl
Herbert, Hillary	1834-1919	Cabinet	15	35		30	Sec'y Navy Cleveland. Civil War Confed. Colonel.
Herbert, Hugh	1887-1952	Entertainment	35	45	70	75	Actor. Vaudeville-Stage Star. Over 100 Films
Herbert, P.O.		Civil War	100		375		CSA General
Herbert, Sidney		Entertainment	15	25	30	25	
Herbert, Victor	1859-1924	Composer	95	198	485	450	Operettas..Babes in Toyland etc. AMusQS $275-$475
Herford, Oliver		Cartoonist	10	25			
Hergesheimer, Joseph		Author	25	65	145	30	Am. Psychological Novels
Herget, Wilhelm		Aviation	20		50		
Hering, Constantine		Science	15	25	50		1st Homeopathic School
Herkimer, Nicholas		Rev. War		3700			General of Militia.
Herkomer, Hubert von, Sir		Artist	25	92	140		Br. Portrait Painter
Herman's Hermits		Entertainment	195			275	Popular Brit. Rock Group (5)
Herman, Alexis	1947-	Cabinet	4	20		15	Afro-Am. Sec'y Labor Clinton
Herman, Jerry		Composer	15	40	65	30	AMusQS $85 'Hello Dolly'
Herman, Pee Wee		Entertainment	15			43	
Herman, Woody		Entertainment	20	82		78	Big Band Leader-Clarinetist
Hermann, Bernard	1911-75	Composer		700			Music for Movies, Radio. Conductor CBS
Hermann, Hajo		Aviation	25	50		60	
Hermine, Schonaich-Carolath		Royalty		125		250	Married Emp. Wilhelm II (after 1918 abdication)
Herndon, William H.	1818-91	Legal	160	412	925		Law Partner of Abraham Lincoln

NAME	DATE	CATEGORY	SIG	LS/DS	ALS	SP	COMMENTS
Herne, James A.		Entertainment	15	15	30	28	Actor-Manager
Heron, William	1742-1819	Rev. War		1250			Double Agent for Americans & British.
Herres, Bob		Astronaut	5			16	
Herrick, Myron T.	1854-1929	Diplomat	25	90		45	Ambassador, Gov. OH, Banker.Lindbergh Friend
Herriman, George*		Cartoonist	50			525	'Krazy Kat'
Herring, Clyde L.	1879-1945	Congress	7			10	Senator IA
Herring, John F.	1795-1865	Artist	60		275		Br.Race Horses & Sporting Events
Herring, Thomas	1693-1757	Clergy		125	140		Archbishop York & Canterbury
Herrington, John		Astronaut	6			20	
Herriot, Edouard	1872-1957	Head of State	25	80	175		Premier of Fr., Nazi Prisoner
Herriot, James (Wight)		Author-Vet.	20	40	75	30	'All Creatures Great & Small'
Herrmann, Adelaide & Alexander		Magic	50			75	Magicians
Herrmann, Bernard	1911-75	Composer		875			Film Composer
Herron, Francis J.	1837-1902	Civil War	45	110	160		Union Gen. Wounded, Captured, Exchanged
Herschbach, Dudley, Dr.		Science	25	35		40	Nobel Chemistry
Herschel, John Fred. Wm., Sir		Science	81	170	238	1265	1792-1871. Br. Astronomer, Mathematician
Herschel, William, Sir	1738-1822	Science	150	475	857		Ger.-Born Br.Astronomer, Discovered Uranus
Hersey, John	1914-93	Author	20	75	125	25	'Bell for Adano'. Pulitzer
Hershey, Alfred D., Dr.		Science	20	30	45	30	Nobel Medicine
Hershey, Barbara	1948-	Entertainment	20			35	Actress. 1-Sheet Movie Poster Dealing:... S $65
Hershey, Lewis B.		Military	15			25	Gen., Selective Service Adm.
Hersholt, Jean	1886-1956	Entertainment	20		95	65	Character Actor. Major Star & Humanitarian
Herter, Christian	1895-1966	Cabinet	15	25		45	Sec'y State. Gov. MA. Congressman
Hertz, Alfred		Entertainment	25			120	Conductor
Hertz, Gustav	1857-94	Science	350				Ger. Physicist. Nobel 1925. Rare
Hervey, Irene	1910-98	Entertainment	15			35	Vintage Leading Lady. Films.
Herzberg, Gerhard, Dr.		Science	25	65		35	Nobel Chemistry
Herzl, Theodor	1860-1904	Zionist	188	1950	4250	250	Writer-Journalist. Important DS $6,500-$8,000
Herzner, Hans-Albrecht	1907-42	Military	700				1st Ger. Engaged in Combat WW II
Herzog, Chaim	1918-97	Head of State	35	65	175	65	Pres. Israel. Fndr & Head Military Intell. U.N.
Herzog, Roman	1934-	Head of State	20			60	Pres. Of Germany
Hesburgh, Theodore M., Rev.		Clergy	20	30	75	25	Longtime Pres. Notre Dame
Hess, Myra, Dame	1890-1965	Entertainment	60		105	350	Br. Pianist
Hess, Rudolf	1894-1987	Military-Politici	175	450	825	1048	Nazi WW II. Second to Hitler. Suicide in Spandau
Hess, Victor F.		Science	20	30	55	25	Nobel Physics
Hess, Walter R.		Science	20	30	50	25	Nobel Medicine
Hesse, Hermann	1877-1962	Author	95	565	550	385	Ger. Author, Artist, Poet. Nobel Prize
Hesseman, Howard		Entertainment	5		15	20	Actor. 'WKRP-Cincinnati'
Heston, Charlton		Entertainment	12			30	Major Star. AA. SP As Moses $150
Heth, Henry (WD)		Civil War	300	1562	3500		CSA Gen. Battle of Gettysburg. LS $3000
Heth, Henry	1825-99	Civil War	145	475	812		CSA General
Heuss, Theodor	1884-1963	Head of State	45			95	First Pres. Of German Fed. Republic. 1949-59
Hewes, Joseph	1730-1780	Rev. War	2500	7250	8500		Signer Decl. of Indepen.
Hewes, Joseph & John Penn		Rev. War		25000			Signers Decl. of Indepen.
Hewett, Charlston		Entertainment	4			10	

NAME	DATE	CATEGORY	SIG	LS/DS	ALS	SP	COMMENTS
Hewish, Anthony		Science	20	40	85	30	Nobel Physics. Pulsars
Hewitt, Abram S.	1822-1903	Business	30	60	82		Iron Manufacturer, 1st Open Hearth Furnace
Hewitt, H.K.	1887-1972	Military	20	50	85		Am. Adm'l WW II. Landings at N. Afr., Sicily, S.Fr
Hewitt, Jennifer Love		Entertainment	20			73	Actress
Hewlett, William R.		Business	25	70	145	35	Hewlett-Packard
Hexum, Jon-Erik		Entertainment	60			125	Actor
Heydrich, Reinhard	1904-42	Military	200	2500	1350	600	Specialist in Nazi Terror. Assassinated
Heydt, Louis Jean		Entertainment	35			80	
Heyerdahl, Thor		Explorer	30	50	95	35	Norw. Ethnologist, Adventurer. 'Kon Tiki'
Heyman, Edward		Entertainment	4			10	
Heyman, Edward 'Eddie'		Author	5	10	25	10	
Heyrovsky, Jaroslav	1890-1967	Science				300	Czech. Nobel Chemistry 1959
Heyse, Paul	1830-1914	Author	45	135	300		Ger. Poet, Novelist, Nobel Literature
Heyward, Dorothy		Author	55	325			Co-writer of 'Porgy'
Heyward, DuBose	1885-1940	Author	120	400			'Porgy & Bess'....LS/Cont. $2,250
Heyward, Thomas Jr.	1746-1809	Rev. War	475	1125	1400		Signer Decl. of Indepen.
Heywood, Anne		Entertainment	10			20	Br. Actress
Heywood, Eddie		Entertainment	35			100	Big Band Leader-Piano
Hichens, Robert S.		Author	15	40	150		Br. Novelist.'Garden of Allah'
Hickel, Walter J.		Cabinet	10	15	30	15	Governor Alaska, Sec'y Interior
Hickenlooper, Andrew		Civil War	30	55	80		Union Gen., Military Engineer
Hickenlooper, Bourke B.	1896-1971	Senate	10	5		20	Governor, Senator IA
Hickman, Darryl		Entertainment	10			20	Actor. Child-Juvenile-Adult
Hickman, Dwayne		Entertainment	5			15	Actor. Juvenile-Adult
Hickman, Ron		Inventor	20	50			Black & Decker. Workmate
Hicks, Catherine		Entertainment	8		20	20	Actress
Hicks, Frederick Cocks		Senate/Congress	10	15			MOC NY
Hidalgo, Miguel y Costilla		Clergy	1525				Mexican Revolutionary & Priest
Hieb, Richard		Astronaut	5			15	
Higgens, Edward	1821-75	Civil War	115	250	375		CSA General. Vicksburg, Mobile
Higgins, Andrew Jackson		Business	25		50		Inventor & Bldr. WW II Higgins Landing Boat
Higgins, Charles		Science	15	35			
Higginson, Henry L.		Business	10	20	35		
Higginson, Thos. W.	1823-1911	Civil War-Clergy	95	575	206		Antislavery Writer, Military CW
High Eagle		Old West				1650	Sioux Indian. Survived Battle of Little Big Horn
Hildebrand, Samuel		Civil War		2750			Quantrill Raider-Murderer. The Missouri Bushwacker
Hildegarde		Entertainment	5		18	15	Singer, Pianist, Entertainer
Hill, Ambrose P. (WD)		Civil War	2950	7500	11725		CSA Gen. KIA 1865
Hill, Ambrose Powell	1825-65	Civil War	2000	3850		1350	CSA General KIA
Hill, Annie		Entertainment	5		15	10	
Hill, Archibald V.		Science	25	45		35	Nobel Medicine 1922
Hill, Arthur		Entertainment	5		15	15	Actor
Hill, Benjamin H.	1823-82	Civil War-Senate	65	165	235		Signed CSA Constitution & GA Secession
Hill, Benjamin J.	1825-80	Civil War	115	200	363		CSA Gen. Sig/Rank $175
Hill, Benny		Entertainment	20			30	Br. Comedian

NAME	DATE	CATEGORY	SIG	LS/DS	ALS	SP	COMMENTS
Hill, Dana		Entertainment	5		15	15	
Hill, Daniel H. (WD)		Civil War	600		1865		CSA General
Hill, Daniel Harvey	1821-89	Civil War	350	545	655		CSA General
Hill, David B.		Senate	10	15			Governor NY, Senator
Hill, David Lee Tex		Aviation	15	30	45	35	ACE, WW II, Flying Tigers
Hill, Edwin C.		Commentator	5	15		15	Vintage Radio News-Commentator
Hill, Faith		Entertainment	10			45	C & W Singer
Hill, Frank*		Cartoonist	10			50	
Hill, George Roy		Entertainment	5			25	A A
Hill, George Washington		Business	80	220			American Tobacco Co.,Pres.
Hill, Grace Livingston		Author	25	40	75		Am. Novelist
Hill, Isaac	1789-1851	Senate/Congress	20	35	65		Governor, Senator NY
Hill, James J.	1838-1916	Business	650	2500	3000	950	Railrd. Exec., Financier. Created Great Norther RR
Hill, John F.		Governor	5	15			Governor ME
Hill, Jonathan A.	1831-1905	Civil War	25	35			Union Gen.
Hill, Lauryn		Entertainment	4			18	Singer. Grammy Winner
Hill, Napoleon		Author	75	300			'Think & Grow Rich'. How to Succeed Books
Hill, Rowland	1744-1833	Clergy	50	75	175		Eng. Evangelist. Ordained. Denied Priestly Orders
Hill, Rowland,1st Viscount	1772-1842	Military	35	80	170		Cmdr. in Chief. England. General
Hill, Rowland, Sir	1795-1879	Postal Reformer	145	340	785		Originator of Penny Postage Stamp. England
Hill, Sam		Merchant		175	250		Storekeeper. 1st Postmaster New Salem.
Hill, Teresa		Entertainment	5			40	Actress. Models, Inc.
Hill, Thomas	1818-91	Clergy-Educator	15	20	50		Pres. Harvard, Antioch.
Hill, Tiny		Entertainment	5		15	15	
Hill, Walter		Entertainment	5			20	Film Director
Hill, William		Entertainment	4		8	10	
Hill, Wm. J. Billy		Composer	30				Last Roundup',' Wagon Wheels'. AMusQS $175
Hillary, Edmund, Sir	1919-	Mountaineer	60	150	285	140	1st To Climb Mt. Everest
Hillegas, Michael	1729-1804	Rev. War	225	645			1st U.S. Treasurer 1777. Sugar Refiner, Iron Mfg.
Hillegess, C.K. Cliff		Author	10			25	'Cliff's Notes' Study Helps
Hiller, Arthur		Entertainment	5			15	Film Director
Hiller, Ferdinand	1811-85	Composer	40	85	125		Ger. Conductor, Pianist, Composer Operas etc.
Hiller, Frank, Jr.		Aviation	75	150	330	160	
Hiller, Wendy, Dame	1912-	Entertainment	20		35	30	Br. Actress. AA
Hillerman, John		Entertainment	9	15	20	25	Actor
Hilles, Charles D.		Political	8	25			Chairman G.O.P. 1924
Hilliard, Harriet		Entertainment	20			35	Band Singer& Wife of Ozzie Nelson
Hilliard, Henry W.	1808-92	Civil War	39	80	110		Confederate Commissioner to TN
Hilliard, Robert		Entertainment	20			40	
Hillig, Otto		Aviation	40	85	150	115	
Hillis, Marjorie		Author	5	10	15		
Hillman, Chris		Entertainment	8			38	Byrds Co-Founder
Hills, Carla A.		Cabinet	7	20	35	20	Sec'y HUD
Hilmers, David C.		Astronaut	7			25	
Hilton, Barron		Business	10	15	25	20	Hilton Hotel Chain

NAME	DATE	CATEGORY	SIG	LS/DS	ALS	SP	COMMENTS
Hilton, Conrad	1887-1979	Business	60	132	190	168	Fndr. Hilton Hotel Dynasty
Hilton, James, Sir		Author	35	120	205	45	'Lost Horizon'
Himmler, Heinrich	1900-45	Military	250	1067	1500	775	Nazi Head of the Gestapo
Hinchingbrooke, Alex		Celebrity	10	20	45	15	
Hinckley, John, Jr.		Assassin	35	150	200		Attempt on Pres. Reagan's Life
Hincks, Edward W.	1830-94	Civil War	65	185			Union General
Hincks, Edward W.	1830-94	Civil War	40		110		Union Gen. LS 1861 $350
Hindemith, Paul	1895-1963	Composer	110	295	425	475	Ger. Violinist,Teacher,Critic.SP $350. AMQS $1200
Hindenburg, Paul von	1847-1934	Head of State	152	380	400	575	2nd Pres. Weimar Rep. of Ger. Field Marshal
Hindman, Thomas C. (WD)		Civil War	475	675	1025		CSA General
Hindman, Thomas C.	1818-68	Civil War	325		575		CSA Gen.
Hines, Duncan	1880-1959	Business	105	372		133	Food Critic. Duncan Hines Cake-Cookie Mix etc.
Hines, Earl K. 'Fatha'		Entertainment	125	325		250	Pianist, Composer, Bandleader
Hines, Gregory		Entertainment	10		25	30	Dancer-Actor. Stage, TV, Films
Hines, Herm		Entertainment	10			25	Jazz Sax
Hines, Jerome		Entertainment	18			30	Opera, Concert. Basso
Hines, John E.		Clergy	10	15	15		
Hines, Mimi		Entertainment	5			10	Singer, Comedienne
Hingle, Pat		Entertainment	5		15	15	Actor. Character
Hinshelwood, Cyril Norman, Sir	1897-1967	Science	20	45		35	Nobel Chemistry 1956
Hinton, Walter		Aviation	40	85	130	90	Pilot of NC-4. MOH
Hippel, Hans Joachim von		Aviation	10			35	WW I & II Fighter Pilot. Stunt Flyer
Hirohito		Head of State	2000	8000		12000	Japan
Hirsch, Judd		Entertainment	10		20	25	Versatile Actor-Comedian. 'Taxi'
Hirschfeld, Al*		Caricaturist	50			250	Repro S $90-$250
Hirshfield, Harry*		Cartoonist	15			125	Abie The Agent
Hirshhorn, Joseph H.	1899-1981	Financier		150	225		Art Collector. Donated 4000 works of art
Hirt, Al		Entertainment	10			25	Jazz Trumpet
Hiss, Alger	1904-	Diplomat	40	65	190		Figure in Sensational U.S. Spy Case
Hitchcock, Alfred	1899-1980	Entertainment	240	568	575	700	Self-Caricature S $750-$875-$1250, Chk. $795
Hitchcock, Ethan Allen (WD)		Civil War	68	150	200		Union Gen., Also Author
Hitchcock, Frank H.		Cabinet	15	30	35	30	Sec'y Interior 1898
Hitchcock, Gilbert M.	1859-1934	Congress	10	20		15	Governor NE
Hitchcock, Raymond		Entertainment	20			35	
Hitchcock, Thomas	1900-44	Aviation	120			200	Lafayette Escadrille.Greatest US Polo Player
Hitchings, George, Dr.		Science	20	30	70	35	Nobel Medicine
Hite, June		Research	5	15	25		Hite Research
Hite, Les		Entertainment	75			275	Saxophone. 'Hold Tight'
Hitler, A. & Goering, H.		Head of State		3200			
Hitler, Adolf	1889-1945	Head of State	1500	2616	17000	4785	Special DS $9,500-$18,500
Hittorff, Jacques	1792-1867	Architect	10	25	40		Fr.St. Vincent de Paul Church.
Hitz, John		Celebrity	10	35	90		
Hitzfeld, Otto Maximilian		Military	20			50	Ger. Infantry General
Hix, John*		Cartoonist	15	50		60	Author Strange As It Seems
Ho Chi Minh		Head of State	600	1225	2000	2600	Vietnam

NAME	DATE	CATEGORY	SIG	LS/DS	ALS	SP	COMMENTS
Ho, Don		Entertainment	5	6	10	12	Singer
Hoag, R. C., Major		Astronaut	5			18	
Hoagland, Everett		Entertainment	20			55	Jazz Clarinetist. Bandleader
Hoar, Ebenezer R.	1816-95	Cabinet	25		35		U.S. Att'y Gen 1869, Grant
Hoar, George F.	1826-1904	Senate	20	75			MOC, Senator MA 1877
Hoban, James	1762-	Rev. War	255	675			Architect White House, Wash.D.C
Hobart, Garret A. (V)	1844-99	Vice President	70	200	310	200	VP under McKinley. Banker, Lawyer. Died in Office
Hobart, John Sloss	1738-1805	Senate/Congress	25	40	70		Delegate & Senator NY
Hobart, Rose		Entertainment	5			20	Actress
Hobbes, Halliwell	1877-1962	Entertainment	25			45	Vint. Brit. Character Actor
Hobby, Oveta Culp		Cabinet	15	25	40	30	1st Sec'y HEW
Hobson, Richard P.	1870-1937	Military-Author	95	250			MOH Sp.-AM. War
Hobson, Richmond P.		Military	75	260	385	150	Adm.CMH. Blew up USS Merrimac
Hobson, Valerie		Entertainment	25			60	Br. Vintage Film Star
Hoche, Louis-Lazare	1768-97	Fr. Revolution	205	515			Rose From Corporal to General
Hock, Robt C.		Astronaut	5			15	Skylab
Hockney, David		Artist	58	65	75	95	
Hodes, Art		Entertainment	10			25	Pianist-Bandleader
Hodes, H. I.		Military	5	15	25		
Hodge, Al		Entertainment	25			200	
Hodges, Courtney	1887-1966	Military	25	150		45	Gen. WW II. Cmmdr. 10th, 3rd, & 1st Armies
Hodges, George H.		Governor	12		15		Kansas 1913-15
Hodgkin, Dorothy C.		Science	25		35		Nobel Chemistry
Hodgson, John		Clergy	20	25	35		
Hodiak, John	1914-55	Entertainment	20	25	45	45	Radio Actor until WW II. Leading Roles
Hoe, Richard M.	1812-86	Industrialist	90	310	532		Invented Rotary Press
Hoe, Robert	1839-1909	Business	30	55	95		Improved Hoe Rotary & Art Press
Hoegh, Leo A.		Governor	5			12	Governor IA
Hoest, Bill*		Cartoonist	10		35	40	The Lockhorns
Hoey, Clyde R.		MOC-Sen.-Gov.	8	20		15	MOC, Senator, Governor NC
Hoey, Dennis	1893-1960	Entertainment	75			200	Br. Actor. Character Roles in Br. Films
Hofer, Andreas		Military		3000			Tyrolean Patriot,executed
Hoff, Philip H.		Governor	5	15			Governor VT
Hoffa, James R.		Labor Leader	275	350		400	Teamsters Union (disappeared)
Hoffa, Portland		Entertainment	20				Comedienne, Mrs. Fred Allen. Major Radio Star
Hoffer, Eric		Celebrity	5	10	25	15	Self Made Philosopher
Hoffgen, Marga		Entertainment	10			35	
Hoffman, Abbie	1942-94	Activist	90	175		125	Shortlived Author of Psychedelic 60's
Hoffman, Dustin		Entertainment	27	25	35	52	Oscar winner.The Graduate Orig. Soundtrk S $95
Hoffman, Felicity		Entertainment	5			32	Actress. Sports Night
Hoffman, Harold Giles		Governor	12	30			Governor NJ
Hoffman, Jeffrey A.		Astronaut	6			20	
Hoffman, John Thompson		Governor	10	20	35		Governor NY 1868
Hoffman, Julius		Judge	50			295	Controversial. Presided over Chicago 7
Hoffman, Kurt-Caesar		Military	25			65	

NAME	DATE	CATEGORY	SIG	LS/DS	ALS	SP	COMMENTS
Hoffman, Maud		Entertainment	3	5		10	
Hoffman, Paul G.	1891-1974	Business	10	20	35	20	Auto Mfg.-Studebaker Cars. WW II Dir. Marshal Plan
Hoffmann, Oswald C.J.		Clergy	10	20	25		
Hoffmann, Peter		Entertainment	15			55	Opera
Hoffmann, Roald, Dr.		Science	20	30	45	25	Nobel Chemistry
Hofmann, Albert		Science	75			565	Swiss Chemist. Identified Psychedelic LSD Effects
Hofmann, Josef	1876-1957	Entertainment	50	125	155	160	Pianist, Composer. AmusQS $75-$150-$200
Hofstadter, Robert		Science	20	30	45	25	Nobel Physics
Hogan, Hulk		Entertainment	15			25	Wrestler
Hogan, Paul		Entertainment	10	15	25	25	Australian Actor. 'Dundee'
Hogarth, Burne*		Cartoonist	25			175	Tarzan-2nd Artist
Hogarth, Wm.	1697-1764	Artist	995	1665	3500		Br. Painter-Engraver. The Rakes Progress
Hogeback, Hermann		Aviation	10			40	Ger. Bomber Pilot. RK
Hoiris, Holger		Aviation	40	85	155	95	
Hoke, Robert Frederick	1837-1912	Civil War	105		350		CSA Gen. ALS '62 $625, Sig/Rank $180
Hokinson, Helen*		Cartoonist	20			100	Mag. Cartoonist-'The Ladies'
Holbrook, Hal		Entertainment	10		20	20	Actor. Very Versatile Film-TV Roles. 'Mark Twain'
Holden, Fay		Entertainment	20			50	Actress. Many 'Mother' Roles. 'Andy Hardy' Series
Holden, Joyce		Entertainment	10			25	Singer-Dancer/Donald O'Connor
Holden, William	1918-81	Entertainment	70	110		208	Actor. Oscar Winner for Stalag 17
Hole, Jonathan		Entertainment	4			8	
Holiday, Billie	1915-59	Entertainment	438	930		1517	Legendary Jazz-Blues Singer
Holladay, Ben	1819-87	Business	135	350	925		Indian Trade, Army Contracts, RR-Esprss. Financier
Holland, Dexter		Entertainment	7			30	Music. Lead Singer Offspring
Holland, Edmund M.		Entertainment	15			45	Vintage Stage Actor
Holland, John Philip		Inventor	70	160	345		1st Sub/Internal Combustion Eng
Holland, Josiah Gilbert	1819-81	Author	15	90	75		AKA Timothy Titcomb. Co-founder Scribner's
Holland, Spessard L.	1892-1971	Congress	10	20			Governor, Senator FL
Hollen, Andrea Lee		Military	10	20	35	15	
Holley, Marietta	1836-1926	Author	10	15	35		Am. Humorist
Holley, Robert, Dr.		Science	15	20	35	20	Nobel Chemistry
Holliday, Freederick W.M.	1828-99	Civil War	45	85			CSA Officer, Congress, Gov. VA Sig/Rank $75
Holliday, Judy	1922-65	Entertainment	125			250	Academy Award Winning Actress 'Born Yesterday'
Holliday, Polly		Entertainment	10		15	20	Actress. Wise-Cracking Flo in 'Alice'
Holliman, Earl		Entertainment	5	8	10	15	Actor. Supporting Player & Co-Star From 50's
Holliman, John		Journalist	5			15	TV News Commentator
Hollings, Ernest 'Fritz'		Senate	10			15	Senator SC
Hollins, Geo. Nichols	1799-1878	Civil War	275	465			Commodore CSA Navy. Sig/Rank $375 WD DS $600
Holloway, Stanley	1890-1982	Entertainment	95			110	Br. Character Actor. Oscar Nominee My Fair Lady
Holloway, Sterling	1905-	Entertainment	25			50	Played Country Bumkins, Dim Wits. Disney Voices.
Hollowell, George		Aviation	12	25	38	35	ACE, WW II, Marine Ace
Holly, Buddy	1936-1959	Entertainment	895	912	3250	2575	Rock Singer-Songwriter. Sigs Holly & Crickets $750
Holly, Lauren		Entertainment	12			42	Actress. Col. Pin-up 55
Hollywood Wives (Cast of)		Entertainment				65	Signed by 6
Holm, Celeste		Entertainment	5		15	20	Broadway Singer-Dancer. Film Actress. AA Winner

NAME	DATE	CATEGORY	SIG	LS/DS	ALS	SP	COMMENTS
Holm, Eleanor		Entertainment	10			30	
Holman, Bill		Cartoonist		45			'Smokey Stover'
Holman, Libby		Entertainment	10	35		82	Vintage Torch Singer. TLS/Cont. $150
Holman, William Steele		Senate/Congress	12	20	30		MOC IN 1859
Holmes, Augusta	1847-1903	Composer	10		85		Ir./Fr. Conventional Fr. Romantic Music
Holmes, Burton	1870-1958	Author	15	20	45	30	In 1894 Originated Travelogues
Holmes, Christopher		Astronaut	15	25		25	
Holmes, D. Brainerd		Celebrity	10			25	
Holmes, Herbie		Bandleader	12			20	
Holmes, John Haynes		Clergy	15	20	30		
Holmes, Katie		Entertainment	8			40	Actress. Pin-Up $60, Dawson's Creek SP $75
Holmes, Oliver W., Jr. (SC)	1841-1935	Supreme Court	275	412	1435	650	Thirty Year Supreme Court Veteran
Holmes, Oliver W., Sr.	1809-94	Author-Physician	96	205	631		Poet. HOF, ALS/Content $1,800. AQS $475
Holmes, Robert D.		Governor	5	15		10	Governor OR
Holmes, Theophilus H.	1804-80	Civil War	185	285			CSA Gen. ALS '62 $1100, Sig/Rank $215
Holmquest, Donald L.		Astronaut	10	15		20	
Holshouser, James E.		Governor	5		20	15	Governor NC
Holst, Gustav	1874-1934	Composer	45	175	300		AMusQS $275-$490-$625
Holstrom, E.W. 'Brick'		Military	15	35	70	25	
Holt, Jack		Entertainment	40	60	100	100	Actor. Tight-Lipped Hero of Many Silents & Talkies
Holt, Jennifer		Entertainment	5			10	Actress. Leading Lady To Several Western Heroes
Holt, Joseph (WD)		Civil War	85		405		Union Gen. Lincoln's Judge Advocate
Holt, Joseph	1807-94	Cabinet-Civil War	65	180	260		Lincoln Judge Adv.
Holt, Rush D.		Senate/Congress	5	10			Senator WV 1935
Holt, Tim	1918-73	Entertainment	45			120	Child-Juvenile-Mature. 'Magnificent Ambersons'
Holt, Victoria		Author	5		15	12	
Holten, Samuel	1738-1816	Rev. War	85	195			Patriot, Statesman, Activist. Cont'l Congr.
Holton, Linwood		Governor	7			15	Governor VA
Holyoake, Keith, Sir		Head of State	45	95	125	50	NZ Prime Minister, Gov. General NZ
Holzer, Helmut		Science	20			40	Ger. Rocket Pioneer/von Braun
Home, A. Douglas-		Head of State	45	70	150	135	Br. Prime Minister
Homer, Louise		Entertainment	35			225	Opera. Am Mezzo. SPc $95
Homer, Winslow	1836-1910	Artist	360	480	1262		Remarkable Seascapes, Landscapes
Homesteaders, The		Country Music	25			50	
Homma, Masaharu		Military	75	205	340	180	Jap. Gen. Invasion of Philippines
Homolka, Oscar		Entertainment	25	30	50	55	Imposing Character Actor. Ideal Heavy; AA Nomination
Honda, Soichiro	1904-94	Business					Founder Honda Motors. RARE. No Current Prices
Honegger, Arthur	1892-1955	Composer	45	202	345	150	Eminent & Prolific. Les Six, AMusQS $575-$675
Hood, Alexander Sir	1758-1798	Military	55	135	245		Accompanied Capt. Cook
Hood, Arthur Wm.	1824-1901	Military	20		105		Admiral, 1st Baron Hood of Avalon
Hood, Darla	1931-1979	Entertainment	150			375	Child Actress 'Our Gang' Series
Hood, John Bell	1831-79	Civil War	767	1870	2535	1000	CSA Gen. ALS '62 $18,150, Sig/Rank $1575
Hood, Samuel, Sir	1762-1814	Military	35	85	135		Br. Adm. with Lord Nelson
Hood, Thomas (Elder)	1799-1845	Author	40	140	275		Br. Humorist, Poet
Hood, Thomas, 'Tom' (Younger)		Author	15	30	70		

NAME	DATE	CATEGORY	SIG	LS/DS	ALS	SP	COMMENTS
Hooft, W.A. Visser't		Clergy	15	20	25	20	
Hook, James Clarke		Artist	25	40	85		Brit. Royal Academy
Hooker, John Lee		Entertainment	75			145	Jazz Musician. Blues Legend. Guitar S $2000
Hooker, Joseph (WD)		Civil War	270	615	1110		Union Gen. ALS $4500
Hooker, Joseph M.	1814-79	Civil War	185	442	643		Union Gen. ALS/Content $4,500
Hooker, Richard		Author	35			60	creator of M*A*S*H
Hooks, Benjamin L.	1925-	NAACP	10	15	25	20	NAACP Exec. Director. Civil Rights Leader
Hooks, Kevin		Entertainment	10			20	Afr.-Am. Actor
Hooper, Dennis		Entertainment	20			50	
Hooper, William	1742-90	Rev. War	450	4083	6833		Signer Decl. of Indepen. ADS $3,000
Hooper, William Henry		Congress	10	20	35		MOC UT 1859
Hoosier Hot Shots		Entertainment	40			65	G Ward,Hezzie,K Trietsle,F Kettering. C & W
Hooten, Ernest A.		Science	25	65	140		Am. Anthropologist.Harvard Prof
Hoover, Herbert & Entire Cabinet		President	250				
Hoover, Herbert (As Pres)		President	280	533	3000	432	Historic TLS/Content $7,500, Unique DS $2465
Hoover, Herbert	1874-1964	President	133	446	2825	357	Cont.TLS $1300, $2,500. WH Card S $450
Hoover, J. Edgar	1895-1972	Criminologist	40	155	185	150	Director of F.B.I. for 48 Years
Hoover, Lou Henry		First Lady	50	50	245	425	WH Card S $95-$125-$150
Hope, Bob		Entertainment	30	242		60	Comedian-Actor-Singer. Stage, Radio, TV, Films
Hopekirk, Helen		Author	15		25		
Hopf, Hans		Entertainment	25			65	Opera
Hopkins, Anthony		Entertainment	20			50	Br. Oscar Winner. Silence of the Lambs
Hopkins, Antony		Entertainment	20		32	42	Composer & Broadcaster
Hopkins, Bo		Entertainment	8			20	Actor
Hopkins, Claude		Entertainment	30			60	Pianist-Bandleader-Composer
Hopkins, Esek	1718-1802	Military	180	1200			1st Cmdr-in-Chief Continental Navy
Hopkins, Frederick G., Sir		Science	45	120	200		Nobel Medicine 1929
Hopkins, Harry L.	1890-1946	Cabinet	26	88		40	Sec'y Commerce.Important Advisor-Aide to FDR
Hopkins, James H.	1832-1904	Congress	10		22		MOC. PA, Banker
Hopkins, Johns	1795-1873	Business	175	500			Financier, Philanthropist. ALS/Content $3575
Hopkins, Joseph A.	1915-80	Military		125	200	750	Fabulous Career Re Mt. Suribachi Flag-ALS $1500
Hopkins, Mark	1802-87	Educator	50	195	275		Inspired Teacher, Lecturer
Hopkins, Mark	1813-1878	Business		18500			Rarest of Calif. RR Big Four. Stk. S $35000
Hopkins, Miriam	1902-1972	Entertainment	32	40	70	90	Vintage Leading Lady.Ballet to Chorus Girl to Star
Hopkins, Samuel	1721-1803	Rev. War	90	280	375		Officer Cont'l Army.Theologian
Hopkins, Stephen	1707-85	Rev. War	250	866	1188		Signer. Gov. RI. Important ALS $6500
Hopkinson, Francis	1737-91	Rev. War	272	915	1498		Signer, Author, Composer. Designer Am. Flag
Hopkinson, Joseph	1770-1842	Judge-Author	90	200			MOC PA. 'Hail Columbia'
Hopper, Dennis	1936-	Entertainment	15			65	Actor. Oscar Nominee. Offbeat Films
Hopper, DeWolfe	1858-1935	Entertainment	20	40	55	75	Actor. Recitations.ALS/Casey at the Bat quote $395
Hopper, Hedda	1890-1966	Entertainment	15		35	35	Actress. Gossip Columnist. Famous for her Hats
Hordern, Michael, Sir	1911-	Entertainment	10		20	30	Br. Character Actor
Horenstein, Jascha		Entertainment	60			375	Conductor
Horina, Louise		Entertainment	15			45	Opera
Hormel, Jay C.		Business	45	95		75	George A. Hormel & Co. Meat Packing. New Ambass.

NAME	DATE	CATEGORY	SIG	LS/DS	ALS	SP	COMMENTS
Horn, Alfred A. Trader		Explorer	70	200			Br. Expl. Ivory Coast. African Rubber Trader
Hornberger, H. Richard		Author	20	30	45	25	
Horne, L. Donald		Business	5			10	CEO Mennen Co.
Horne, Lena	1917-	Entertainment	12	25		38	Afro-Am Film Actress & Recording Star
Horne, Marilyn		Entertainment	15			35	Opera, Concert
Horner, H. Mansfield		Business	5			10	Aircraft Exec.
Horner, Henry		Governor	10			20	Governor IL
Hornung, Ernest Wm.	1866-1921	Author	50		175		Brother-in-law A.Conan Doyle. Created Raffles
Horowitz, David		Celebrity	3	7	15	8	
Horowitz, Scott		Astronaut	5			19	
Horowitz, Vladimir	1903-89	Entertainment	177	195		350	Rus-born Am. Piano Virtuoso
Horrocks, Gen. Sir Brian		Military	20		50	40	Cmdr. XIII Corps WW II
Horrocks, June		Entertainment	6			35	Actress
Horsford, Eben N.	1818-74	Science	15	25	70		Am. Analytical Chemist
Horsley, John Calcott		Artist	40		65		Brit. Royal Academy
Horsley, Lee		Entertainment	10			25	Actor. 'Matt Houston'
Horthy, Miklos, Adm.	1868-1957	Head of State	55	190	485	150	Hungarian Admiral & Politician
Horton, Edw. Everett	1886-1970	Entertainment	30		45	55	Actor. Delightful Comedy & Character Leads
Horton, Edward A.		Clergy	15	20	25		
Horton, Peter		Entertainment	15			38	
Horton, Robert		Entertainment	5			15	Actor
Hosmer, Titus	1736-80	Rev. War	40	95	192		Continental Congress. Judge
Hotchkiss, Benjamin J.		Inventor-CW			995		Union Arms Supplier
Hotchkiss, Charles T.	1832-1914	Civil War			85		Union Gen. Atlanta Campaign
Houdini, Harry (E.Weiss)	1874-1926	Entertainment	1000	1817	1880	2128	Am. Magician, Escape Artist
Hough, Lynn Harold		Clergy	15	20	35		
Houghton, Katharine		Entertainment	30			45	Actress. 'Guess Who's Coming to Dinner?'
Hounsfield, Godfrey		Science	20	30	45	25	Nobel Medicine
House, Edw. M.'Colonel'		Diplomat	35	100	310	45	Confidant of Pres. Wilson
Houseman, John		Entertainment	20	30		40	Actor/Director. Stage & Film Writer.
Housman, Alfred Edward	1859-1936	Author	65	225	570		Br. Poet, Classical Scholar
Houssay, Bernando A., Dr.		Science	65	135	250	100	Nobel Medicine 1947. Activist
Houston, David	1938-	Country Music	5			10	Singer-Guitar. 50's, 60's, 70,s
Houston, George		Senate	35	85			Civil War Senator AL
Houston, Sam	1793-1863	Military	683	1735	3093		Pres. Rep. TX, Statesman. ALS/Cont.$6500. FF $850
Houston, Temple		Lawyer-Outlaw	375		1667	750	Son of Sam Houston
Houston, V. S. K.		Senate/Congress	10	25	40		MOC HI 1927
Houston, Whitney	1963-	Entertainment	28			58	Singer-Actress
Houston, William C.	1746-88	Rev. War	55		145		Continental Congress, etc.
Hovey, Alvin P.	1821-91	Civil War	35	80	112		Union Gen., Gov. IN Sig/Rank $95. War Dte.DS $135
Hovhaness, Alan		Composer	70		375		Noted for Orchestral Works
Hovis, Larry		Entertainment	15			35	Actor. 'Hogan's Heroes'
How, William Walsham, Bishop		Clergy	15	20	25		
Howard, Curley (Jerome)	1906-52	Entertainment	475	500	950	1000	Rarest of the Three Stooges
Howard, Edward, Cardinal		Clergy	35	50	75		

NAME	DATE	CATEGORY	SIG	LS/DS	ALS	SP	COMMENTS
Howard, Jacob Merritt	1805-71	Congress	15	30			Civil War MOC & Sen. MI
Howard, James H.		Aviation	20	30	55	45	ACE, WW II, CMH; Flying Tiger
Howard, John	1913-	Entertainment	10	20	40	35	Actor. Bulldog Drummond. Navy Hero WW II
Howard, Ken		Entertainment	5		15	15	Actor. Tall, Blonde Leading Man of 70's Films
Howard, Leslie	1890-1943	Entertainment	265	325		498	GWTW. Br. Secret Serv. WW II. SP Pc $200
Howard, Milford W.	1862-1937	Congress	5			10	MOC AL
Howard, Moe	1895-1975	Entertainment	200	290	625	450	Three Stooges Leader
Howard, Oliver Otis (WD)		Civil War	145		375		Union Gen.
Howard, Oliver Otis	1830-1909	Civil War	110	225	250	300	Union Gen. MOH
Howard, Robert, Sir	1626-98	Author	85	325	475		Br. Restoration Dramatist/Dryden
Howard, Ron		Entertainment	20	40	55	50	Child, Juvenile, Mature Actor and Director
Howard, Shemp	1891-1955	Entertainment	490	475		560	Rarest of Three Stooges Autogr.
Howard, Sidney	1891-1939	Author	50	175	338	75	Am. Playwright. Pulitzer. Screenwriter from 1929
Howard, Trevor	1916-19—	Entertainment	27			113	Brit. Actor. Stage, Films. AA Nominated
Howard, Willie		Entertainment	5		20	15	
Howe, Albion P. (WD)		Civil War	40	125	510		Union General
Howe, Elias	1819-67	Science	200	400	3000		Invented Sewing Machine
Howe, James Wong	1988-1976	Entertainment	40			65	AA Winning Cinematographer. 'Hud', 'Rose Tattoo'
Howe, Julia Ward	1819-1910	Author	85	168	403		Battle Hymn of the Republic. AQS $1,475-$3000
Howe, Louis McHenry		Political	5	20			Secretary to FDR
Howe, Richard, Earl	1726-1799	Rev. War	100	875	580		Br. Adm. Rev. War.LS/Cont.$1500
Howe, Samuel Gridley	1801-76	Humanitarian-Mil.	15	35	95		Philanthropist, Doctor, Clergy, Reformer
Howe, Timothy O.	1816-83	Cabinet	5		30		PMG(Arthur).US Sen. WI. Recommended to Lincoln
Howe, William, Sir	1729-1814	Rev. War	200	850	900		Cmdr-in-Chief Br. Forces in Am. Colonies
Howell, C. Thomas		Entertainment	5		25	20	
Howells, William Dean	1837-1920	Author	35	195	475		Novelist, Critic, Editor
Howes, Barbara		Author	5		20	10	
Howland, Beth		Entertainment	5		15	15	Actress. TV-Beth on 'Alice'
Howley, William	1766-1848	Clergy	25	35	40		Archbishop Canterbury
Howlin, Olin		Entertainment	45			70	Actor. 'GWTW' Collectible
Hoxie, Al		Entertainment	45			60	Actor. Westerns. Silents & Few Talkies
Hoxie, Jack	1885-1965	Entertainment	150				Actor-Cowboy Star in Silents & Early Talkies
Hoyle, Edmond	1671-1769	Author	145	675	785		Card Games. Established Rules
Hoyt, John W.		Governor	50	85			Gov. WY Terr.,1st Pres. U. WY
Hruska, Roman		Senate & Congress	5	15		10	MOC, Senator NE
Hubbard, Chester D.	1814-91	Congress	10	15	30		MOC WV
Hubbard, Elbert	1856-1915	Author	50	195	275	145	Roycrofters. Message to Garcia
Hubbard, Gardiner G.	1822-97	Celebrity	30	55	170		Fndr.& 1st Pres. Nat'l Geographic Society
Hubbard, L. Ron	1911-1986	Author	200	1067			Religious Activist. Scientology, Dianetics
Hubbard, Richard B.		Governor		150			Gov. TX 1876-79
Hubbard, Thomas H.	1838-1915	Civil War	25	40			Union Gen. 30th ME
Hubble, Edwin P.	1889-1953	Science	20	80		65	Am. Astronomer.Hubble Telescope Named For Him
Hubel, David H., Dr.		Science	20	30	45	25	Nobel Medicine
Huber, Oscar, Fr.		Celebrity	20		30		
Hubley, Adam		Rev. War	75	300			Officer Cont. Army. Politician

NAME	DATE	CATEGORY	SIG	LS/DS	ALS	SP	COMMENTS
Hubner, Herbert		Entertainment	25			75	Vintage German opera star
Huddleston, George		Senate/Congress	10	15		15	MOC AL 1915-1937
Hudson, Charles	1795-1881	Congress	10				MOC MA, Author Religious Textbooks
Hudson, George	1800-71	Financier	20	50	175		Controlled 1,000 Miles Railrd. Railway King
Hudson, Rochelle	1914-72	Entertainment	25	30	50	40	Actress. Versatile Leading Lady of 30's Films.
Hudson, Rock	1925-85	Entertainment	71	171	90	203	Actor. Handsome Leading Man. Aids Victim
Hudson, W.H.	1841-1922	Naturalist-Author		135	495		'Green Mansions'
Huemer, Dick*		Cartoonist	15			100	Disney Artist
Huerta, Victoriano	1854-1916	Revolutionary	75	250	625	120	Mex. General, Politician. Provincial Pres. Exiled
Hufstedler, Shirley		Cabinet	5	10	15	15	Sec'y Education
Hug-Messner, Regula		Aviation	15	30	50	35	
Huger, Benjamin (WD)		Civil War	190	750			CSA Gen.
Huger, Benjamin	1805-77	Civil War	100	295	315		CSA General
Huger, Isaac	1743-97	Rev. War	110	240	825		General Continental Army
Huggins, Charles, Dr.		Science	25			35	Nobel Medicine
Huggins, Roy	1914-96	Entertainment	20			30	TV Producer-Writer. Fugitive
Huggins, William, Sir	1824-1910	Science	35	100	225	55	Br. Astron. Stellar Spectroscope
Hughes, Carol		Entertainment	12				Actress
Hughes, Charles E. (SC)	1862-1948	Supreme Court	48	176		290	Chief Justice, Sec'y of State. TLS/Content $750
Hughes, Edwin H., Bishop		Clergy	20	25	40	35	
Hughes, Harold E.	1922-	Congress	5			20	Senator IA
Hughes, Howard	1905-76	Business	1500	2706	6125	2625	Aircraft, Oil Tools. RKO Films. Flight Cov S.$2900
Hughes, Hugh Price		Clergy	15	20	25	20	
Hughes, John	1797-1864	Clergy	25		225		1st Archbishop NY. Laid Cornerstone St. Pat's
Hughes, Langston	1902-67	Author	235	435	895	575	Afro-Am. Poet, Short Story Writer
Hughes, Mary Beth	1919-	Entertainment	5	10	15	15	Actress. Supporting Parts & Leads. 40's to 70's
Hughes, Richard		Military-Rev. War	35	70			Br. Adm. during Rev. War
Hughes, Richard J.		Governor	5	15			Governor NJ
Hughes, Rupert		Author	20	50	95		Poet, Author, Historian
Hughes, Sarah T.		Law	65	98		45	Fed. Judge Swore In L.B. Johnson 1963
Hughes, Thomas	1822-96	Author	42		175		Tom Brown's School Days. Social Reformer
Hugo, Victor	1802-85	Author	257	375	845	1100	Novelist-Politician-Poet
Huidekoper, Henry		Civil War	60				Union Col., 'Bucktails'
Hull, Cordell	1871-1955	Cabinet-Statesman	50	135		112	Nobel Peace, Sec'y State. Father Fed. Income Tax
Hull, Henry	1890-1977	Entertainment	52			95	Veteran Am. Actor
Hull, Isaac	1773-1843	Military	195	570	700		Cmdr. U.S.S. Constitution 1812. Naval Hero 1812
Hull, J.E.		Military	25				General
Hull, Josphine	1884-1957	Entertainment	150		200	275	Celebrated Stage Character Actress. AA Harvey
Hull, Warren	1903-74	Entertainment	25			50	Singer-Actor. Comic-strip Heroes. Radio & TV MC
Hull, William		Military	145	370	770		Rev. War Gen.
Hulse, Tom		Entertainment	10	15	20	30	Actor. 'Amadeus'
Humbard, Rex		Clergy	10	15	15	15	
Humboldt, Alex., Baron von	1769-1859	Science	70	125	350		Ger. Naturalist and Traveller
Hume, Benita	1906-67	Entertainment	15			30	Br. Actress. Stage & Films. Wife of Ronald Colman
Hume, Joseph	1777-1855	Politician	20	32	80		Br. Physician. Radical Politician

NAME	DATE	CATEGORY	SIG	LS/DS	ALS	SP	COMMENTS
Hume, Mary-Margaret		Entertainment	5			12	Pin-Up SP $20
Humes, William Young C.	1830-82	Civil War	140	235	557		CSA General. Sig/Rank $165, War Dte. DS $415
Hummel, Johann Nepomuk	1778-1837	Composer	150	190	725		Hung.-Born Child Prodigy. Piano Virtuoso
Humperdinck, Engelbert		Entertainment	10	10	20	30	Contemporary Vocalist
Humperdinck, Engelbert	1854-1921	Composer	115	225	297	250	AMusQS $450-$675-$950
Humphrey, George M.		Cabinet	10	20			Sec'y Treasury
Humphrey, Hubert H.	1911-78	Vice President	35	136	155	58	V.P. & '68 Presidential Cand., MN Senator
Humphrey, Muriel	1912-98	Congress	10	20		20	Senator MN. Replaced Husband, Hubert as Sen.
Humphreys, Andrews A.	1810-83	Civil War	65	180	310		Union Gen'l Sig/Rank $100
Humphreys, David		Rev. War	55	150	200		ADC Washington. Poet, Diplomat
Hungerford, Cy		Cartoonist	10			30	
Hungerford, Orville	1790-1851	Congress	15	45			MOC NY, W & R Railroad Pres.
Hunnicutt, Arthur	1911-79	Entertainment	15			35	Stage Actor. Film Character Parts From Early 40's
Hunt, (H)aroldson (L)afayette	1889-1974	Business	90	485	580	175	TX Oil King. Arch Conservative
Hunt, E. Howard		Gov't Official	15	25	90	25	21 Yr. Vet./CIA. Watergate
Hunt, Earl, Bishop		Clergy	20	25	35	25	
Hunt, George W. P.		Governor					Governor AZ
Hunt, Helen		Entertainment	25			53	Twister'/B.Paxton $130. 'Good as it Gets'. Oscar
Hunt, Henry Jackson (WD)		Civil War	90	155			Union Gen. ALS/Cont. $770
Hunt, Henry Jackson	1819-89	Civil War	60	80	140		Union Gen. Gettysburg.
Hunt, James B. Jr.		Governor	5	10			Governor NC
Hunt, James Bunker		Business	5	15	35	15	Son of Oil Magnate H.L.Hunt
Hunt, John, Lord	1910-	Political	25	40	75		Leader 1st Successful Everest Expedition 1953
Hunt, Leigh	1784-1859	Author	30		40		Br. Essayist, Poet
Hunt, Linda	1945-	Entertainment	20			65	Tiny AA Winning Character Actress.
Hunt, Marsha	1917-	Entertainment	10	12	20	20	Powers Model. Actress Since mid-30's
Hunt, Nelson Bunker		Business	10	20	40	15	Son of Oil Magnate H.L.Hunt
Hunt, Pee Wee		Entertainment	15			45	Trombone-Vocalist
Hunt, Ward (SC)		Supreme Court	65	80	175		1872
Hunt, Washington		Governor	35		60		MOC 1842, Governor NY 1850
Hunt, William H.		Cabinet	15	30	60	25	Sec'y Navy 1881
Hunt, William Holman	1827-1910	Artist	55	165	388		Br. Pre-Raphaelite Painter
Hunt, WIlliam Morris	1824-79	Artist	50	215	500		American Portraitist
Hunt, Willie P.		Governor	40			100	1st Governor of Arizona
Hunter, David O. (WD)		Civil War	85	220	385		Union Gen.
Hunter, David O.	1802-86	Civil War	60	172	194	250	Union General
Hunter, Holly		Entertainment	20			53	AA Actress. The Piano SP $75
Hunter, Jeff	1925-69	Entertainment	50		100	90	Actor. 'Star Trek' Capt. For Short Time
Hunter, Kim		Entertainment	10		15	25	AA. Stella SP $35. 'Planet of the Apes'
Hunter, R. M. T.	1809-87	Civil War	110	175	222		CSA Sec'y State. US Sen. ALS '63 $360
Hunter, Rachel		Cover Girl	15			35	Super Model. Pin-Up SP $100
Hunter, Robert		Rev. War	220	508	1035		Br. Gen. Colonial Gov. VA,NY
Hunter, Ross	1921-95	Entertainment.	25			35	Actor turned Producer. Pillow Talk etc
Hunter, Tab		Entertainment	10			35	Actor
Hunter, William	1774-1849	Diplomat	55	80	125		Statesman, Senator RI

NAME	DATE	CATEGORY	SIG	LS/DS	ALS	SP	COMMENTS
Huntington, Agnes		Opera	25			150	Am. & Brit. Productions
Huntington, Benjamin	1736-1800	Rev. War	60	175	275		Continental Congress
Huntington, Collis P.	1821-1900	Business	120	490	3000	950	Pioneer Am. Railroad Builder. S RR Pass $9500
Huntington, Daniel		Artist		155	250		Portrait Painter
Huntington, Ebenezer		Rev. War	110	250	380		Statesman, Army General
Huntington, Henry E.		Business	75	125	200		Railroad Magnate. Huntington Library, San Marino,
Huntington, Jabez	1719-86	Rev. War	150	795			Maj.Gen. Militia. Merchant. Yale Grad. Legislature
Huntington, Jabez W.		Senate/Congress	20	30	45		MOC 1829, Senator CT 1840
Huntington, Jedediah	1743-1818	Military	75	140	490		Gen. Am. Continental Army. Collector of Customs
Huntington, Samuel	1731-96	Rev. War	275	1729	1225		Signer Decl. of Indepen. Pres. Cont.Congr. Gov. CT
Huntington, Theo. Hastings	1650-1701	Royalty	75		185		7th Earl. Lord Lt. Leicester & Derby. Treason
Huntley, Chet	1911-74	Journalist	50			195	Longtime TV News Anchorman/David Brinkley
Hunton, Eppa	1822-1908	Civil War	115	295	298		CSA General. Sig/Rank $195
Huppert, Isabelle	1955-	Entertainment	10			31	Actress. Versatile Young Lead Fr. Films of 70's
Hurd, Peter		Artist	85	225	362		Fine Painter. His LBJ Portrait Rejected by LBJ
Hurlbut, Stephen A. (WD)		Civil War	70	135	375		Union Gen., ALS/Cont.$2200
Hurley, Charles F.		Governor	12	25			Governor MA
Hurley, Elizabeth		Entertainment	9			45	Actress-Model. Pin-Up $75
Hurley, Patrick J.	1883-1963	Cabinet	15	45	60	25	Sec'y War, Hoover
Hurrell, George		Photographer	15	50			Hollywood Stars.Orig.16x20 Ltd. Ed. Dietrich $1200
Hurst, Fannie	1889-1968	Author	25	45	150	80	Popular, Sentimental Novels
Hurston, Zora Neale	1901-60	Author	145		750		Am. Writer, Folklorist. Black Culture
Hurt, John		Entertainment	14		25	30	Br. Actor. Offbeat Character Portrayals.
Hurt, Mary Beth		Entertainment	6	8	15	18	Actress
Hurt, William		Entertainment	20	25	50	60	Actor. AA Kiss of the Spider Woman
Hurwitz, Hank, Dr.		Science	20			35	Atomic Scientist
Husa, Karel		Composer	15	30	65		Pulitzer, AMusQS $150
Husak, Gustav		Head of State	30			100	Pres. Czechoslovakia. Communist Hard Liner
Husky, Ferlin		Country Music	10			20	Singer- Comedian. AKA Terry Preston, Simon Crum
Hussein I, King	1935-1999	Royalty	183	165	385	450	King of Jordan. Hussein I & Queen Noor SP $675
Hussey, Olivia		Entertainment	5			15	Actress. Romeo & Juliet. Br. & International Film
Hussey, Ruth		Entertainment	5			15	Actress. 'Philadelphia Story'. Leading Lady in 40'
Huston, Anjelica		Entertainment	8			32	AA Winning Actress. Daughter of John Huston
Huston, John	1906-87	Entertainment	40	117	50	84	AA Film Director-Actor
Huston, Walter	1884-1950	Entertainment	67	75	130	150	AA Winning Actor. ...Treasure of the Sierra Madre
Hutchence, Michael		Entertainment	20			50	
Hutchins, Will		Entertainment	10	15		15	Actor. 'Sugarfoot'
Hutchinson, Frederick Sharpe		Civil War	35		130		Union General
Hutchinson, John W.		Composer	15		50		
Hutchinson, Josephine	1904-	Entertainment	10	15	25	25	Vintage Actress.Child/Mary Pickford.Films from '34
Hutchinson, Thomas	1711-80	Colonial	185	450			Am. Colonial Administrator. Royal Gov. MA. Exiled
Hutton, Betty		Entertainment	10	15		30	Peppy Blond Actress-Singer of 40's Genre
Hutton, Gunilla		Country Music	5			10	
Hutton, Ina Ray		Entertainment	20			45	All-Girl Big Band Leader
Hutton, Jim	1933-79	Entertainment	40	70	110	100	Actor.Tall Likeable Leading Man.Timothy's Father

NAME	DATE	CATEGORY	SIG	LS/DS	ALS	SP	COMMENTS
Hutton, Lauren		Entertainment	9	10	20	22	Model-Actress. Pin-Up SP $25
Hutton, Robert		Entertainment	20	40		90	Actor
Hutton, Timothy		Entertainment	18	20		40	AA Winner
Huxley, Aldous	1894-1963	Author	75	400	574	350	Br. Novelist.Brave New World. TLS/Content $1,200
Huxley, Julian Sorell	1887-1975	Science-Author	30	150	142		Br. Biologist, Educator
Huxley, Leonard	1860-1933	Author	20		75		Biographer, Poet. Son of Julian Huxley
Huxley, Thomas Henry	1825-95	Science	52	150	205		Br. Biologist
Hyams, Leila	1905-77	Entertainment	20	25	50	40	Leading Lady of 20's-30's
Hyde, Arthur W.		Cabinet	7	15	30	15	Sec'y Agriculture 1929
Hyde, Edgar R.		Clergy	10	10	15		
Hyde-White, Wilfrid	1903-91	Entertainment	20	20	35	73	Brit. Character Actor
Hyer, Martha		Entertainment	10		15	25	Actress. Oscar Winner
Hylton, Jack	1892-1965	Entertainment	20			70	Major Br. Bandleader
Hylton, Lord		Politician	7	15	25		Chief Whip Unionist Party
Hyman, Earle		Entertainment	5			10	Afr.-Am Actor
Hymes, Myriam		Entertainment				20	
Hynde, Chrissie		Entertainment	25			40	Rock. 'The Pretenders'
Hyndman, Henry Mayers	1842-1921	Socialist	75		350		Br Marxist-Socialist. Interesting Political Career

I

NAME	DATE	CATEGORY	SIG	LS/DS	ALS	SP	COMMENTS
I Remember Mama (Cast of [5])		Entertainment	125			395	50's Popular TV Program
Iacocca, Lee A.		Business	15	50		35	CEO Ford, Chrysler Motors
Ian, Janis		Entertainment	10	40		20	Singer-Actress
Ibert, Jacques-Francois		Composer	75		325	160	AMusQS $450
Ibsen, Henrik	1828-1906	Author	250	600	1456	1325	Nor. Poet & Dramatist. Peer Gynt, Doll's House
Icart, Louis	1888-1950	Artist	115		875		Fr. Art Deco Painter-Illusrator
Ice T		Entertainment	20			50	Rock. Rapper
Ickes, Harold L.		Cabinet	20	35	65	25	Roosevelt Sec'y Interior
Idol, Billy		Entertainment	10			35	Rock Star
Iglesias, Julio		Entertainment	15			50	Singer. International Latin Favorite
Iha, James		Entertainment	6			25	Music. Guitar Smashing Pumpkins
Ihlefedl, Herbert		Aviation	25	55		60	
Ikeda, Hayato		Head of State	15		65		Japan
Iman		Entertainment	25			55	Model
Imboden, John Dan'l (WD)		Civil War	375	810			CSA Gen. Spec'l ALS $4500
Imboden, John Dan'l	1823-95	Civil War	175	432	288		CSA Gen.
Imbruglia, Natalie		Entertainment	18			55	Rock Star
Immelmann, Max		Aviation	200	425	700	500	ACE, WW II, 1st German Ace
Impellitteri, Vincent		Celebrity	4	12	25	10	
Imus, Don		Entertainment	10			25	Obnoxious talk show host
Ince, Thomas H.		Entertainment	40			125	Film Dir. Civil War Epics
Indiana, Robert		Artist	45	95	170	150	Colorful Contemporary Artist. Sports Specialy

NAME	DATE	CATEGORY	SIG	LS/DS	ALS	SP	COMMENTS
Ingalls, John James	1833-1900	Congress	45	80	162		Senator KS
Ingalls, Laura		Aviation		295			Pioneer. 1st Non-Stop Transcontinental Flight
Ingalls, Rufus (WD)		Civil War	60		525		Union Gen., Explorer
Ingalls, Rufus	1818-93	Civil War	41	105	211		Union General, Explorer
Inge, William		Author	50	120	180		Am. Playwright. Pulitzer
Inge, William R.		Clergy	50	80	150		Br. Prelate. GloomyDean St. Paul's Cath., Writer
Ingels, Marty		Entertainment	8			28	
Ingersoll, Charles J.	1782-1862	Senate/Congress	20	25	50		MOC PA 1813
Ingersoll, Charles R.		Governor	5	15	25		Governor CT
Ingersoll, Jared	1749-1822	Rev. War	75	274	450		Continental Congr.,Constitution Signer
Ingersoll, Robert Green		Civil War	30	60	85	62	Agnostic Lecturer, Orator
Ingersoll, Robert H.		Business	80	175	300	225	Ingersoll $1 Watch
Ingersoll, Royal E.		Military	80	135		175	Adm. & Cmdr. Of Atlantic Fleet WW II
Ingham, Samuel D.	1779-1860	Cabinet	35	120	145		Sec'y Treasury 1829
Ingle, Red		Entertainment	25			80	
Ingle, Robert P.		Business	5	15	25	10	Ingles Grocery Chain
Inglis, James		Business	5	20			Mfg.
Ingraham, Duncan N.(WD)		Civil War	172		1100		Capt.CSA Navy
Ingram, Rex		Entertainment	50			125	Actor
Ingram, Rex	1895-1969	Entertainment	100			300	Vintage Afro-Am. Actor
Ingres, Jean-Auguste-Dominique		Artist	205		1050		Fr. Leader Among Classicists
Ingrid, Victoria, Queen		Royalty	20	40			Queen of Frederick IX (Denmark)
Ink Spots, The (4)		Entertainment	225			280	Vintage Singing Group. (All Four Sigs.)
Inman, Henry	1801-1846	Artist	110	305	650		American Portraitist. ALS/Content $1250
Inman, Jerry		Country Music	10			20	
Innes, Roy	1934-	Activist	15			25	Afr.-Am. Activist. Civil Rights. Pres. CORE
Inness, George	1824-94	Artist	75	225	690		Am. Landscape Painter. ALS/Cont. $950
Inouye, Daniel K.		Senate	5			15	Senator HI
Inskeep, Jonathan		Rev. War	80	175			
Insull, Samuel	1859-1938	Financier	132	975	1300		Pvt. Sec'y Edison. Utilities Baron.TLS/Cont.$685
Ionesco, Eugene	1912-94	Author	40	145	225		Romanian-Fr. Dramatist.Theatre of Absurd. AQS $700
Ireland, Jill		Entertainment	25			60	Actress. Pin-Up SP $75
Ireland, John		Entertainment	10			42	Actor
Ireland, John M.F		Governor	40	150			Gov. TX 1883-87
Ireland, Kathy		Cover Girl	20			48	Pin-Up SP $50-60
Irish, James M.		Military	10	30	50		
Irons, Jack		Entertainment	6			25	Music. Drummer Pearl Jam
Irons, Jeremy		Entertainment	10		25	40	Br. Actor
Irvin, James	1800-62	Congress	18		35		Repr. PA, Merchant, Miller, Miner
Irvine, James	1735-1819	Rev. War	55	130	250		Gen. Militia. Cmdr. Fort Pitt
Irvine, William	1741-1804	Rev. War	75	545	428		Gen., Continental Congress
Irving, Amy		Entertainment	9		20	25	Actress
Irving, Clifford		Author	16	60	124	25	
Irving, Edward	1792-1834	Clergy	100		375		Founder 'Catholic Apostolic Church'
Irving, Henry, Sir	1838-1905	Entertainment	48	65	88	173	Vintage Actor-Manager. LS by Bram Stoker $225

NAME	DATE	CATEGORY	SIG	LS/DS	ALS	SP	COMMENTS
Irving, John		Author	13		30	68	Am.'The World According to Garp'
Irving, Washington	1783-1859	Author	150	360	702		Am. Essayist. Rip Van Winkle
Irwin, David		Celebrity	10	20	45	15	
Irwin, James B.Jim	1930-91	Astronaut	102	217	190	156	7th Moonwalker. Apollo 15
Irwin, May		Entertainment	25		35	45	Vintage Stage Actress. 1st Film Kiss
Irwin, Noble E.	1869-1937	Military	55	150			USN Adm.1st Dir. Naval Aviation, Trans-Atl. Flight
Irwin, Will	1873-1948	Journalist			40		War Correspondent, Author
Isabella I, Of Castile	1451-1504	Royalty	850	2669	6500		Queen Spain. Columbus' Patron
Isabella II	1830-1904	Royalty	175	420	730		Spain. Strife, Intrigue. Abdicated
Isabey, Jean-Baptiste	1767-1855	Artist		115	350		Court Painter to Napoleon & Bourbons
Ish Kabibble (Merwyn Bogue)		Entertainment	15			25	Novelty Singer, Kay Kyser Band
Isherwood, Christopher	1904-86	Author	40	140	265	300	Br.-Am. Novelist, Playwright
Ishiguro, Kazuo		Author	15			40	'Remains of the Day'
Isken, Edward		Aviation	15			35	Ger. Air Ace with 56 Victories
Ismay, Hastings Lionel		Military	25	35	60	45	Churchill Chief-of-Staff WW II
Israels, Jozef	1824-1911	Artist	55	180	350	225	Dutch. Hague School Genre Art. Landscapes
Istomin, Eugene		Entertainment	35			125	Pianist-Classical
Ito, Hirobumi (Prince)	1841-1909	Statesman	55	140			Japan. Prime Minister 1886
Ito, Lance, Judge		Law	30			55	O.J. Simpson Trial Judge
Ito, Marquis		Statesman	25				Japanese Statesman
Ito, Robert		Entertainment	4			10	Actor
Iturbi, Jose		Entertainment	20	75		50	Classical Pianist.Jose & Amparo Iturbi S $30-$95
Iturbide, Augustin de	1783-1824	Revolutionary		875			Self Proclaimed Emperor of Mex.
Ivan IV, The Terrible		Royalty	35000				No Current Price
Iverson, Alfred, Jr.	1829-1911	Civil War	145	300	475		CSA Gen. Sig/Rank $240-$290
Ives, Burl		Entertainment	15	35		40	Folk-Singer Turned Oscar Winning Actor
Ives, Charles E.	1874-1954	Composer	325	1250	2000	425	Tonal Experiments. Pulitzer. Mysterious & Elusive
Ivey, Judith		Entertainment	10			35	Actress
Ivins, Marsha S.		Astronaut	7			25	
Ivogun, Maria		Entertainment	45			175	Opera
Izak, Edouard		Military	20	45			WW II CMH

J

NAME	DATE	CATEGORY	SIG	LS/DS	ALS	SP	COMMENTS
Jabotinsky, Vladimir		Zionist	45	120	310	60	Zionist Leader WW I
Jabs, Hans-Joachim		Aviation	60	150			Famed Nazi Pilot.
Jack, Thomas M.	1831-80	Civil War	60				CSA Col. A.D.C. to A.S. Johnston
Jacks, L.P.		Clergy	15	20	45		
Jackson, Alan		Country Music	18			52	C & W
Jackson, Alfred E.	1807-89	Civil War	140		950		CSA General. Sig/Rank $220, War Dte. ALS $1200
Jackson, Andrew (As Pres.)		President		2591	4183		1767-1845. FF $1200-1650. Exceptional LS $12,500
Jackson, Andrew & Van Buren, M.		Presidents		3800			
Jackson, Andrew	1767-1845	President	606	2476	3433		Addr. Leaf/Free Frank $1,375-$1450

NAME	DATE	CATEGORY	SIG	LS/DS	ALS	SP	COMMENTS
Jackson, Anne		Entertainment	6	8	15	15	Actress. Broadway, Radio, TV, Films
Jackson, Charles T.	1805-80	Science	200				Co-Discoverer of Ether
Jackson, Clairborne F.	1807-62	Civil War		175	220		Civil War Gov. MO
Jackson, Eugene Pineapple		Entertainment	15			25	'Our Gang' Comedies
Jackson, Glenda	1937-	Entertainment	15	20	30	35	Br. Oscar winner, Member of Brit. Parliament
Jackson, Gordon	19xx-96	Entertainment	15		50	55	Scot. 'Hudson' in Upstairs, Downstairs
Jackson, Helen Hunt		Author	15	35	50	35	Am.Novelist, Poet. Ramona
Jackson, Henry M. 'Scoop'		Senate/Congress	5	15		20	MOC, Senator WA
Jackson, Henry R.	1820-98	Civil War	95	195	350		CSA Gen.
Jackson, Howell E. (SC)		Supreme Court	88	200		110	U.S. Senator 1881, Supr.Ct.1893
Jackson, James S. (WD)		Civil War	235		1018		Union Gen. KIA 1862
Jackson, James S.	1823-62	Civil War	170		650		Union Gen. KIA 1862. ALS/Cont. $1375
Jackson, James, Dr.	1777-1867	Science		220	500		1st Am. to Perform Vaccinations
Jackson, Janet		Entertainment	25			75	Rock
Jackson, Jesse	1941-	Clergy	20	65	80	40	Reverend Jesse Jackson. Most Material Secretarial
Jackson, Jesse, Jr.	1965-	Congress	5	15		20	Dem. MOC IL. Civil Rights, Operation PUSH
Jackson, Joe		Entertainment	20			35	Vintage Entertainer
Jackson, John King	1828-66	Civil War					CSA Gen. AES '61 $685. RARE
Jackson, Joshua		Entertainment	6			45	Young Actor
Jackson, Kate		Entertainment	10		32	32	One of Charlie's Angels
Jackson, LaToya		Entertainment	20		38	40	Singing Sister of Michael. Pin-Up SP $150
Jackson, Mahalia	1911-1972	Entertainment	120			442	Gospel Singer. Queen of Gospel Music. SP 8vo $375
Jackson, Maynard		Entertainment	5	10	20	15	Big Band Trumpet
Jackson, Michael		Entertainment	159	800		243	Legendary Pop Music Mega Star.Self Annointed KING
Jackson, Rachel		First Lady	575				Mrs. Andrew Jackson
Jackson, Robert H. (SC)		Supreme Court	50	295		125	Chief Prosecutor at Nuremberg
Jackson, Samuel L.		Entertainment	18			68	Versatile Afr-Am Actor
Jackson, Samuel M.	1833-1907	Civil War	40	80			Union Gen. Wilderness. ALS/Cont. $600
Jackson, T.J. Stonewall	1824-63	Civil War	3000	9070	15000		CSA General
Jackson, T.J. Stonewall(WD)		Civil War	3975	15000	19062		CSA Gen. ALS $47,375
Jackson, Thomas		Clergy	25		40		
Jackson, Victoria		Entertainment	6	15		12	actress-Comedian. Sat. Night Live etc.
Jackson, Wanda		Country Music	10			20	C & W Singer
Jackson, William	1759-1828	Rev. War	120	350	750		Gen. Washington Aide. Diplomat
Jackson, William Henry	1843-1942	Photographer	40	110			Photographed Indians etc. on Union Pac. RR Route
Jackson, Wm. Hicks 'Red'	1835-1903	Civil War	95	237	250		CSA General. War Dte. DS $600
Jackson-Lee, Sheila	1950-	Congress	5			20	Afr-Am MOC TX
Jacob, Francois		Science	20	30	55	30	Nobel Medicine 1965
Jacob, John C.		CORE	10	15		15	Afro-Am. Leader CORE
Jacob, John J.		Governor	12	20			Governor WV
Jacobi, Derek		Entertainment	5			15	
Jacobi, Lou		Entertainment	5			15	Actor
Jacobs, Andy		Congress	4	15			Indiana
Jacobs, Josef		Aviation	30	45	80	55	
Jacobs, Lou		Entertainment	50	100		100	Clown

NAME	DATE	CATEGORY	SIG	LS/DS	ALS	SP	COMMENTS
Jacobs, William W.	1863-1943	Author	250				Br. Horror Story Writer. 'Monkey's Paw'
Jacobsen, Fritz		Aviation	10	20	35	45	Ace WW I
Jacquet, Illinois Jean		Entertainment	30			70	Jazz Sax, Bandleader
Jadlowker, Hermann		Entertainment	95			245	Opera
Jaeckel, Richard (Deceased)		Entertainment	15			25	Familiar Character Actor. Westerns-Tough Guys
Jaeger, James A.		Aviation	10		30		
Jaehnert, Erhard		Aviation	10		25	25	
Jaffe, Sam	1893-1984	Entertainment	25			40	Actor. Stage 1915. Films 30's. Gunga Din. TV 50's
Jagger, Bianca		Entertainment	10			25	
Jagger, Dean	1903-91	Entertainment	15	25	30	35	AA Winner
Jagger, Mick	1943-	Entertainment	55			145	Icon of Rock & Roll
Jahn, Sigmund		Astronaut	15			35	
Jakes, John		Author	15	50	70	50	'Holiday for Havoc'
James I & VI (Eng)		Royalty	800	1962	4475		King of Scotland from 1567—Eng. From 1603
James II (Eng)	1633-1701	Royalty	530	1378	2600		King Eng. 1685-88
James, Daniel, Jr. "Chappie"		Military	20	35	85	45	AF Gen. 1st Black 4 Star Gen.
James, Dennis	1917-97	Entertainment	25			30	1938 TV Pioneer. 1st Game Show Host. Emcee etc.
James, Etta		Entertainment	20			40	Rock
James, Frank	1844-1915	Outlaw	1071	1850	3950		Quantrill Raider. Rode With Him Throughout War
James, Harry	1916-83	Entertainment	20	20	40	55	Big Band Leader-Trumpet SP Pc $30
James, Henry	1811-82	Author	102		682		Theological & Social Scholar
James, Henry	1843-1916	Author	110	360	723		Am. Novelist, Essayist. ALS/Content $5,500
James, Manley		Miitary	10		45		WW I Victoria Cross
James, P.D.		Author	20	65	105		Notable Br. Mystery Writer
James, Sonny		Country Music	10			30	Singer. The Country Gentleman. Hits from 50's on
James, Thomas L.		Cabinet	15	25	45		P.M. General 1881
James, Will		Author	75	250	410	750	Illustrated own Western Novels
James, William	1842-1910	Science	90	350	495	125	Psychologist, Pragmatist, Philosopher
Jan & Dean		Entertainment	20			45	Rock
Janacek, Leos	1854-1928	Composer	140				Czech Composer AMusQS $2000
Janeway, Eliot		Author-Economist	16				
Janis, Conrad		Entertainment	5			15	Actor. 'Mork & Mindy'
Janis, Elsie		Entertainment	25		50	55	Stage, Screen Comedienne. WW I Entertainer
Janney, Leon		Entertainment	35			75	Member Original 'Our Gang' Comedies
Jannings, Emil		Entertainment	150			275	1st Academy Award Winner
Janowitz, Gundula		Entertainment	10			65	Opera
Jansen, Marie		Entertainment	15			40	Opera
Jansons, Mariss		Conductor	10			45	Newly Discovered Latvian Conductor
Janssen, David	1930-80	Entertainment	70	120		166	Actor The Fugitive Original TV Series
Janssen, Werner		Conductor	25			45	Conductor of Many US Leading Orchestras
January, Lois		Entertainment	5			15	
Jaray, Hans		Entertainment	5			20	Classical-Semi Classical Singer. Concert-Films
Jardine, William		Cabinet	10	5	55	20	Sec'y Agriculture 1925
Jardine, William, Sir	1800-74	Author	55		200		Writer, Editor, Naturalist
Jarman, Claude, Jr.		Entertainment	15			35	Oscar winner. 'The Yearling'

NAME	DATE	CATEGORY	SIG	LS/DS	ALS	SP	COMMENTS
Jarman, Maxie		Business	15			55	Jarman Shoes
Jaroff, Serge		Entertainment	15		25	35	Jaroff Ballet & Don Cossack Chorus
Jarreau, Al		Entertainment	20			40	Music
Jarrett, Art		Bandleader	15			30	Big Band
Jarriel, Tom		Journalist	5	10		15	TV News
Jarvik, Robert, Dr.		Science	15	35	60	35	Inventor Artificial Heart
Jarvis, Anna M.		Promoter	65	175			Campaigned for Mother's Day
Jarvis, Gregory B.		Astronaut	100	600		275	
Jarvis, Howard		Reformer-Tax	5	12	30	15	Sponsor Proposition 13. CA Property Tax
Jason, Rick		Entertainment	5			15	Actor
Jason, Sybil		Entertainment	5		15	15	
Jassin, Lloyd		Author	7	11	25	12	Copyright author/attorney, rights expert
Javits, Jacob J.		Congress	10	20		25	MOC 1947, Senator NY 1957
Jawlensky, Aleksey von	1864-1941	Artist			600		Russ. Painter
Jaworski, Leon		Law	15	20	45	20	Dir. Watergate Prosecution Force
Jay, James, Sir	1732-1815	Science	90	275	400		Phys. to G. Washington; Inventor
Jay, John (Grandson)		Diplomat	15	25	40		Active Opposition to Slavery
Jay, John (SC)	1745-1829	Supreme Court	375	2150	2650		Pres. Continental Congr. ALS at Auction $6,600
Jean, Gloria		Entertainment	5		20	25	Child Singer-Actress 30's-40's5
Jean, Norma		Country Music	10			20	
Jeans, James, Sir		Science	12	30	65	20	Br. Physicist, Astron., Author
Jedlichka, Ernest		Entertainment	45			200	Rus-Pol Pianist
Jeffers, Robinson	1887-1962	Author	65	350	450	95	Prize Winning Poet, Dramatist
Jeffers, William M.		Business	25	70	135	50	Pres. Union Pacific RR
Jefferson Airplane (All)		Entertainment	125			300	Rock-The San Francisco Sound
Jefferson, Charles E.		Clergy	20	25	40		
Jefferson, Joe	1829-1905	Entertainment	45	70	107	80	Important Am.19th Century Actor
Jefferson, Martha Wayles		First Lady					Rare. Only 2 Known. No Current Price
Jefferson, Thomas & Madison, James		President	2825	6023	10000		Special Doc. S $30,000, MLS $25,000
Jefferson, Thomas (As Pres.)		President	4000	5667	21750		Free Frank $5,000-$5950
Jefferson, Thomas	1743-1826	President	2687	9557	13094		Content ALS's $101,000-$200,000. FF $3900-$5950
Jefferson, Thomas	1859-1932	Entertainment	20			125	Actor. Stage & Silent Films/D.W. Griffith
Jeffreys, Anne	1923-	Entertainment	10	14	22	25	Actress. Topper etc.
Jellicoe, John R.	1859-1935	Military	35	70	125	167	Br.Adm. WW I, P.M. New Zealand
Jenckes, Joseph	1656-1740	Colonial Am.	90	250	520		Colonial Governor RI
Jenkins, Allen		Entertainment	25			45	Cigar-Chewing Character Actor
Jenkins, Butch		Entertainment	10			25	Freckle-Faced Child Actor
Jenkins, Thornton Alex.	1811-	Civil War	35	95			Chief-of Staff Adm. Farragut Squad. Sig/Rank $65
Jenner, Edward, Dr.	1749-1823	Science	450	850	2977		1st to Use. Smallpox Vaccination
Jenner, William E.	1908-85	Congress	10	20			Senator IN
Jenner, William, Sir	1815-98	Science	35	110	295		Identified Typhus-Typhoid. Phys. to Queen Victoria
Jennings, Al		Celebrity	450		850		
Jennings, Peter		Journalist	5	15	35	15	Broadcast Journalist, Anchor
Jennings, Waylon		Country Music	12			28	Country Singer
Jennison, Ralph D.		Business	10	35	45	20	

NAME	DATE	CATEGORY	SIG	LS/DS	ALS	SP	COMMENTS
Jenrette, John W. Jr.		Congress	5	20		15	MOC. SC
Jenrette, Rita		Entertainment	4		15	15	Pin-Up SP $25
Jensen, Karen		Entertainment	4			10	Actress
Jepson, Helen		Entertainment	15			45	Opera, Concert
Jergens, Adele	1917-	Entertainment	10			20	Actress-Model. Over 50 Mostly B-Films.
Jeritza, Maria	1887-1984	Entertainment	50			95	Opera, Operetta, Films. 1st Met. Turandot
Jernigan, Tamara E.		Astronaut	8			25	
Jernstedt, Ken		Aviation	10	25	40	35	ACE, WW II, Flying Tigers
Jerome, Addison G		Financier	300	975			Stock Market Legend in 1850's
Jerome, Jerome K.	1859-1927	Author	50	70	108		Humorist, Playwright. 'Three Men in a Boat'
Jerome, Wm. Travers, III		Education	20	40		35	Pres. Bowling Green Univ.
Jerusalem, Siegfried		Entertainment	15			45	Opera. Current Leading Wagnerian Tenor.SP 4x6 $25
Jessel, George	1888-1972	Entertainment	30	80		92	Noted Emcee, Comic, Toastmaster
Jessup, Thomas S.	1788-1860	Military	60	138	242		War 1812, Seminole. Gen. LS/Content $950-$1750
Jesup, William H.		Military	5	15	25		
Jeter, Michael		Entertainment	10			25	'Evening Shade'
Jethro Tull		Entertainment	30			75	Band
Jethro, Homer and		Country Music	35			125	Henry Haynes (Guitar), Ken Burns (Mandolin)
Jett, Joan		Entertainment	20			50	Rock. (And the 'Blackhearts')
Jewel		Entertainment	15			68	
Jewell, Isabel		Entertainment	50			95	Longtime Vintage Actress.'Emmy Slattery' GWTW
Jewell, Marshall		Governor-Cabinet	40	75	195		ALS/Cont. $400
Jewett, Sarah Orne	1849-1909	Author	45	200	262		New England Life & Folklore
Jewison, Norman		Entertainment	5			20	Film Director
Jillian, Ann		Entertainment	8		15	22	Actress. Pin-Up SP $25
Jimenez, Enrique A.		Head of State	8		25	15	Panama
Jimenez, Marcos P.		Head of State	10	25	50	20	Venezuela
Joachim, Joseph	1831-1907	Composer	95	150	258	245	Hung. Violinist.AMuQS $250-$575
Jodl, Alfred		Military	150	590	550	250	Chief-of-Staff To Keitel WW II
Joel, Billy		Composer	20			57	Singer, Songwriter
Joel, Manuel	1826-90	Judaica	45	125			Rabbi, Scholar. Defended Moderation vs Radicalism
Joffre, Joseph Jacques Cesaire		Military	65	155	250	225	Marshal of France WW I
Johann, Zita		Entertainment	20			45	Actor. 'The Mummy'
Johannson, Paul		Entertainment	4			20	Actor. Beverly Hills 90210
John II, (King Castile)	1406-1454	Royalty	4700	5133			Patron of Literature & Arts. Father of Q. Isabella
John III (Port.)		Royalty	200	1400			King Portugal 1521-1557. Introduced Inquisition
John of Austria (Don John)	1629-1679	Royalty	150				
John XXIII, Pope	1881-1963	Clergy	645			1715	Angelo Giuseppe Roncalli
John, Augustus E.	1878-1916	Artist	50	135	330		Welch. Portraits, Landscapes
John, Elton		Entertainment	45	178	225	87	Br. Singer-Songwriter
Johns, Glynis		Entertainment	15	15	30	30	Br. Actress. Leading Lady. Later, Character Roles
Johns, Jasper		Artist	20	182		45	Am. Pop Artist. FDC/Leroy Neiman $150
Johnson, Amy (Mollison)		Aviation	188	90	135	288	Br. Aviation Pioneer
Johnson, Amy Jo		Entertainment	5			28	Actress. Pin-Up $48
Johnson, Andrew (As Pres.)		President	474	1766	7500	2750	Impeached, Tried, Not Convicted.FF $775-1450-1500

NAME	DATE	CATEGORY	SIG	LS/DS	ALS	SP	COMMENTS
Johnson, Andrew	1808-75	President	440	1439	5080	2500	ALS/Content $19,500. FF $675-$775-1,400
Johnson, Art		Aviation	10	25	40	30	ACE, WW II, USAAF Ace
Johnson, Ben	?-1998	Entertainment	35	70		60	Oscar winner. Popular Western Star
Johnson, Betty		Entertainment	3			8	
Johnson, Bradley T.(WD)		Civil War	220	1500	970		CSA Gen.
Johnson, Bradley T.	1829-1903	Civil War	108	430	275		CSA Gen., ALS/Content $4,500
Johnson, Brian		Entertainment	8			35	Music. Lead Singer AC/DC
Johnson, Bunk		Entertainment	200			550	Jazz Trumpet
Johnson, Bushrod Rust	1817-80	Civil War	135	325	365		CSA General. Mexican War
Johnson, Cave	1793-1866	Cabinet	50	110	195		P.M.Gen. 1st US Postage Stamps
Johnson, Chic		Entertainment	30			55	1/2 of Zany Comedy Team (Olsen & Johnson)
Johnson, Crockett*		Cartoonist	50			500	Barnaby
Johnson, Don		Entertainment	15			45	Actor. Leading Man. Films, TV 'Miami Vice'
Johnson, Eastman	1824-1906	Artist	40	60	185	300	Am. Portrait & Genre Artist
Johnson, Eddie Bernice	1955-	Congress	5			20	Afr-Am Dem MOC TX
Johnson, Edward		Entertainment	25			75	Distinguished Canadian Tenor
Johnson, Edward	1816-73	Civil War	175	438	350		CSA Gen. Captured Twice.
Johnson, Eliza M.		First Lady	750	1500			
Johnson, Frank*		Cartoonist	5			40	
Johnson, Fred*		Cartoonist	10			45	Moon Mullins
Johnson, Gerald		Aviation	15	30	55	40	ACE, WW II
Johnson, H. Hank		Business	4			15	Pres. Spiegel. Catalog
Johnson, Harold K.		Military	15	35	50	35	WW II. Prisoner. 4 Star Gen.
Johnson, Henry A.		Business	5			15	CEO Spiegel Inc.
Johnson, Herschel	1812-80	Civil War	40	115			Gov. GA, CSA Senator
Johnson, Hiram W.	1866-1945	Congress	22	60		70	Powerful Senator CA
Johnson, Howard B.		Business	80			95	Howard Johnson Inns
Johnson, Howard S.		Business	12	30		25	
Johnson, Hugh S.		Cabinet	15	90	125	35	Gen., Dir. NRA During Depression. FDR
Johnson, James Johnnie	1916-97	Aviation	45	75	135	110	ACE, WW II, Br. RAF Top Ace
Johnson, James K.		Aviation	10	25	40	35	ACE, Korea, Double Ace
Johnson, James Weldon		Author	35	100	225		NAACP,1st Ed.'Black Manhattan' S $695-$795
Johnson, Jesse G.		Military	35	85	170	45	Adm. WW II
Johnson, John H.	1918-	Publisher		50		65	1st Afro-Am Periodicals. 'Ebony', 'Jet'
Johnson, Jonathan Eastman		Artist	35	150			Am. Portrait, Genre Painter
Johnson, Keen		Governor	5	15		10	Governor KY
Johnson, L.B. & Lady Bird		President				600	
Johnson, Lady Bird		First Lady	40	97		113	Vintage FDC Beautification of America S $80
Johnson, Leon W.		Military	10	20	35		
Johnson, LeRoy		Congress	4			10	
Johnson, Louis A.	1891-1966	Cabinet	15	40	60	35	Sec'y Defense 1949 Truman
Johnson, Lyndon B.	1908-73	President	215	358		508	ALS As VP $4500. Rare ANS $950
Johnson, Lyndon B.(As Pres.)		President	165	1174	3250	500	TLS as Pres. $1,250-$4,200/Content
Johnson, Lynn		Cartoonist	27			65	'For Better Or Worst'
Johnson, Lynn-Holly		Entertainment	8		12	20	Actress

NAME	DATE	CATEGORY	SIG	LS/DS	ALS	SP	COMMENTS
Johnson, Martin	1884-1937	Explorer-Photogr.	15	40		55	With Osa, Wild Animal Films. African Explorers
Johnson, Nunnally	1897-1977	Author	20	65		40	Am. Playwright, Screenwriter
Johnson, Oliver		Celebrity	5	15	30		
Johnson, Osa		Explorer-Photogr.	15	20	35	45	With Martin, Wild Animal Films
Johnson, Philip		Architect	25			125	Early Skyscrapers
Johnson, Reverdy	1796-1876	Cabinet	25	95	105		Statesman, Att'y Gen.,US Sen. MD
Johnson, Richard L.		Aviation	15	20	35	25	
Johnson, Richard M.		Vice President	70	200	350	400	Van Buren Vice Pres.
Johnson, Robert S.		Aviation	20	25	45	80	ACE, WW II, #5 US
Johnson, Robert W.		Business	55	190			Fndr. Johnson & Johnson. Important DS $7750
Johnson, Russ		Entertainment	5			15	Actor
Johnson, Samuel C.		Business	5			10	Pres. Johnson's Wax
Johnson, Samuel, Dr.		Author	1740	4080			Lexicographer, Critic
Johnson, Van		Entertainment	14			28	MGM Leading Man in Straight Leads & Musicals
Johnson, William		Military	20		125	35	Maj. Gen'l USA 91st Div. AEF. WW I
Johnson, William	1715-74	Colonial Amer.		2250			Br. Fur Trader. Superintendent Indian Affairs
Johnson, William B.		Business	5			10	CEO Railway Express
Johnson, William Cost		Senate/Congress	10	20	35		MOC MD 1833
Johnson, William Sam'l	1727-1819	Rev. War	130	358	675		Signer U.S. Constitution. Continental Congress
Johnson, Willis, Dr.	1869-1951	Educator	8			15	
Johnston, Albert Sidney	1803-62	Civil War	375	2500	3050	1500	CSA Gen.,TX Sec.War. DS $9500. Sig/Rank $650
Johnston, Frances	1864-1952	Photographer	5	25			1st Famous Female Photographer
Johnston, George D.	1832-1910	Civil War	95	360	382		CSA Gen.
Johnston, Harriet Lane		Acting First Lady	200		625		Buchanan's Niece
Johnston, J. Lawson		Business	15	35	60		
Johnston, Johnny		Aviation	20	45		55	
Johnston, Joseph E. (WD)		Civil War	460	1425	1935	3500	CSA Gen. ALS 12/1861/Content $10,000
Johnston, Joseph E.	1807-91	Civil War	295	645	711	1800	CSA ALS/Cont $3,500-12,000. FF $500
Johnston, Lynn*		Cartoonist	20			75	'For Better or Worse'
Johnston, Mary		Astronauts	5			20	
Johnston, Olin D.		Senate/Congress	5	15			U.S. Senator SC 1945
Johnston, Richard M.		Author	5	10	20		
Jolie, Angelina		Entertainment	10			63	Actress. Pin-Up $70
Joliot, Fred. & Irene Curie Joliot		Science	200				Scientific Nobel Winning Team
Joliot-Curie, Irene	1897-1956	Science	45		205		
Joliot-Curie, Jean Frederic	1900-58	Science		350	500		Fr. Physicist. Nobel '35.Son-in-law Pierre/Marie
Jolley, I. Stanford		Entertainment	20			50	
Jolson, Al	1886-1950	Entertainment	157	406		367	Starred in 1st Talking Picture.SP in Blackface$500
Jones, Allan	1907-82	Entertainment	15	15	35	30	Film & Concert Singer. Many Popular 40's Musicals
Jones, Anne		Country Music	10			20	Singer
Jones, Annisa		Entertainment	150			325	TV Sitcom 'Family Affair'
Jones, Anson	1798-1858	Am. Politician	350		1200		Physician, Pres. Texas Repub.
Jones, Anthony Armstrong		Country Music	10			20	Singer
Jones, Bob		Clergy	15	25	60	25	'Bob Jones University'
Jones, Buck	1889-1942	Entertainment	170	230	300	427	Vintage Film Cowboy. Major Star

NAME	DATE	CATEGORY	SIG	LS/DS	ALS	SP	COMMENTS
Jones, Carolyn		Entertainment	75	98		108	Actress. Morticia on TV's 'Addams Family'
Jones, Casey		Aviation	45	90	175	150	
Jones, Catherine Zeta		Entertainment	12			55	Actress. Pin-Up $70
Jones, Chuck*		Cartoonist	25			175	Animator
Jones, Claude A.		Military	40	65			
Jones, David (Davy)		Entertainment	15			40	'The Monkees'
Jones, David C., Gen.	1879-1958	Military	8			42	Chairman/Chiefs of Staff
Jones, David R. (WD)		Civil War	370	2895			CSA Gen.Died Richmond, VA 1/15/63. Coronary
Jones, David R.	1825-63	Civil War	305	800			CSA Gen. Served/Beauregard & Longstreet
Jones, Dean	1933-	Entertainment	10		25	30	Actor. Numerous Disney Films
Jones, Dick		Entertainment	8			30	
Jones, E. Stanley		Clergy	35	50	75	50	
Jones, Edward F.	1828-1913	Civil War	50	110	155	150	Union Gen. War Dte. DS. $210. Sig/Rank $80
Jones, Ernest	1879-1958	Science	20		75		Br. Psychoanalyst, Biographer of Freud
Jones, George		Entertainment	10			25	C & W
Jones, Grace		Entertainment	18		30	40	Pin-Up SP $75. 007 SP $65
Jones, Grandpa							SEE Louis Jones
Jones, Gwyneth		Entertainment	15			40	Opera
Jones, Henry		Entertainment	5			15	Actor. Character
Jones, Howard		Entertainment	10			20	
Jones, Isham		Entertainment	15			40	Vintage Big Bandleader-Composer
Jones, J. Carey		Military	20	45		35	Admiral WW II
Jones, Jack		Entertainment	10			18	Pop Singer Son of Alan Jones
Jones, James		Author	50	190		60	'From Here To Eternity'
Jones, James Earl	1931-	Entertainment	10			30	Broadway-Films-TV Actor. Darth Vader Voice
Jones, Janet		Entertainment	10		30	30	Singer. Pin-Up SP $30
Jones, Jeffrey		Entertainment	4			20	Comic Bad Guy
Jones, Jennifer		Entertainment	140	200		361	AA Actress. Reluctant Signer
Jones, Jenny		Entertainment	10			20	TV Talk Show Host
Jones, Jesse H.		Cabinet	10	15		15	Sec'y Commerce 1940
Jones, Jim		Clergy	250	375	650	850	
Jones, John Marshall	1820-64	Civil War	225	650			CSA Gen. Sig/Rank $1050, War Dte DS $2850
Jones, John Paul		Entertainment	50			175	Music. Drummer Led Zeppelin
Jones, John Paul	1747-92	Military-Rev. War	5125				Naval Hero.I have not yet begun to fight!
Jones, John Percival		Senate/Congress	10		25		U.S. Senator NV 1873
Jones, L.Q.		Entertainment	5			15	
Jones, Le Roi (See Baraka)		Author					Afr-Am Playwright, Poet, Novelist, Essayist
Jones, Lois Mailou	1905-98	Artist	20		35		Noted Afr-Am Artist
Jones, Louis 'Grandpa'	1913-98	Entertainment	20			35	Grandpa Jones. Country Singer, Banjoist.Hee Haw
Jones, Louis R.		Military	10	30			
Jones, Maj. Gen. David M.		Astronaut	10			25	
Jones, Marcia Mae		Entertainment	5	11	15	20	Child & Juvenile Actress
Jones, Mary H. 'Mother'	1830-1930	Labor	60	195	430		Agitator, Speaker, Organizer NYC Garment Workers
Jones, Paula		Celebrity	8			25	Newsmaker, Clinton Accuser
Jones, Quincy		Composer	15	31	35	30	AMusQS $50

NAME	DATE	CATEGORY	SIG	LS/DS	ALS	SP	COMMENTS
Jones, Rickie Lee		Entertainment	20			40	
Jones, Samuel	1819-87	Civil War	110	400			CSA General
Jones, Samuel (WD)		Civil War	202	615	765		CSA Gen.
Jones, Samuel Porter		Clergy	15	25	35		
Jones, Shirley		Entertainment	10	33		20	Actress. AA Award Winner. 'Partridge Family'
Jones, Simon		Entertainment	6			25	Music. Bass Guitar The Verve
Jones, Spike	1911-65	Entertainment	35			75	Big Band Leader. Novelty added
Jones, Thomas		Astronaut	11			20	
Jones, Thomas V.		Business	15	30		25	
Jones, Tom		Astronaut	6			21	
Jones, Tom		Entertainment	12		25	22	'Top Pop Singer 60's. Comeback in 90's
Jones, Tommy Lee		Entertainment	20			55	Col. SP Batman$60. Film DS $650, $495
Jones, William E. (WD)		Civil War	275	2025	2125		CSA Gen. 'Grumble'. KIA
Jones, William E.	1824-64	Civil War	140	212	525		CSA Gen. 'Grumble'. KIA.
Jong, Erica		Author	10	14	25	15	Best Selling Bawdy Autobiography
Jongkind, Johan	1819-1891	Artist	200	450	860		Dutch. Master of Rendering Light
Jonson, Ben	1572-1637	Author	2850				Br. Playwright, Poet. 'Volpone', 'The Alchemist'
Jope, Bernhard		Aviation	10	25	40	30	
Joplin, Janis	1943-70	Entertainment	750	1050	1433	1400	Blues & Rock Singer. Died of Heroin Overdose at 27
Joplin, Scott		Composer	700	1090	2000		Rag Time Composer
Jordan, Barbara	1936-96	Senate/Congress	15	60		30	Highly Respected Afr-Am.Congresswoman TX
Jordan, Dorothy		Entertainment	15	15	35	30	
Jordan, Hamilton		Gov't Official	5	15	25	20	Chief of Staff Carter Admin.
Jordan, Jim (FibberMcGee)		Entertainment	15	20	35	25	Top Radio Comedy Team 'Fibber McGee & Molly'
Jordan, Louis		Entertainment	25			65	Big Band Leader
Jordan, Thomas (WD)		Civil War	140	335	663		CSA Gen. Mexican War. ALS/Cont. $1195
Jordan, Thomas	1819-95	Civil War	88	252	349		CSA General. Mexican War
Jordan, Vernon	1935-	Political	20			90	Powerful D.C. Fixer. Clinton Friend & Advisor
Jordanaires, The (4)		Entertainment	35			95	Gospel Quartet
Jordon, Richard		Entertainment	10		25	25	
Jorgensen, Christine		Celebrities	28	25	45	32	1st To Undergo Sex Change
Jorn, Carl		Entertainment	30			85	Opera
Jory, Victor	1902-82	Entertainment	48	60		142	Longtime Popular Character Actor. GWTW Collectible
Jose, Richard J.		Entertainment	8			15	Singer
Joseph I	1678-1711	Royalty		562			Holy Roman Emp., King Hungary, King of Romans
Joseph II	1741-1790	Royalty	125	350	875		King Ger. & Holy Roman Empire
Josephine, Empress	1783-1814	Royalty	1038	1510	2685		Fr. (First) Wife of Napoleon
Joslyn, Allyn		Entertainment	17			55	Actor. Comedic Character Roles
Jossefy, Raphael	1853-1915	Entertainment	25			125	Pianist, Pupil of Liszt, Teacher. AMusQS $100
Joswig, Wilhelm		Aviation	10			30	
Jouett, James		Civil War	25	55	125		Union Naval Officer/Farragut
Jouhaux, Benjamin	1879-1954	Reformer	25	60	140	50	Nobel Peace Prize 1951
Jourdan, Jean B., Count		Napoleonic Wars	55	260	305		Marshal of Napoleon
Jourdan, Louis	1919-93	Entertainment	18	25		35	Handsome Fr. Leading Man. 'Gigi'
Journey		Entertainment	48			70	Entire Band Signed

NAME	DATE	CATEGORY	SIG	LS/DS	ALS	SP	COMMENTS
Jowett, Benjamin	1817-93	Scholar	10	25	35		Br. Master of Balliol.Plato & Socrates Translator
Jowett, Charles		Clergy	15	20	25		
Joy, Jimmie		Bandleader	10			20	
Joy, Leatrice	1899-1985	Entertainment	25			35	Silent Film Star. ..Ten Commandments
Joyce, Alice	1890-1955	Entertainment	15	25		60	Silent Star
Joyce, Brenda	1917-	Entertainment	15			25	Actress. Jane in 5 Tarzan Films.
Joyce, Elaine		Entertainment	4			12	
Joyce, James	1882-1941	Author	425	595	4440	6300	Ir. Novelist, Poet, Playwright
Joyce, Richard		Military	40	100	175		
Juan Carlos, de Borbon		Royalty	55	120	245	150	King of Spain. So Designated by Franco in 1975
Juarez, Benito	1806-1872	Head of State	425	1288	1625	1500	Twice Pres. Mexico. Revolutionary
Judah, Theodore D.		Business		18000			Started Central Pac. RR .Rare DS $18,000
Judd, Ashley		Entertainment	15			49	Actress. Almost Nude Pin-up 80
Judd, Naomi & Wynona		Country Music	25			54	Beautiful Mother-Daughter Team
Judd, Norman B.	1815-78	Congress	50		85		MOC. IL, Nominated A. Lincoln. Minister to Berlin
Judd, Walter H.	1898-	Congress	10	15		20	Congressman MN
Judge, Arline		Entertainment	10			17	Much Married Actress. 30's-40's
Judge, Mike*		Cartoonist	10				Printed Repro. S $50
Julia, Raul		Entertainment	28			70	Actor. Premature Death. 'Addams Family'-Gomez
Julian, George W.	1817-99	Congress	15	30	75		Co-Founder Free Soil Party, MOC. IN
Juliana, Queen		Royalty	100	250	710	150	Netherlands
Jumangi (Cast Of)		Entertainment				200	Williams, Hunt, Durst, Pierce
Jump, Gordon		Entertainment	8			20	Character Actor.' WKRP in Cincinnati'
Jung, Carl Gustav	1875-1961	Science	555	2165	3175		Swiss Psychiatrist-Psychologist
Junkers, Hugo		Science	50		355		Ger. Airplane Engineer-Designer
Junot, Andoche		Military	70	235			Fr. Gen., Sec'y to Napoleon. Duc d'Abrante's
Jurgens, Curt		Entertainment	15			45	Scandanavian Actor
Jurgens, Dick		Entertainment	20			45	Big Band Leader
Jusserand, Jean Jules	1855-1932	Author		22	48		Pulitzer Prize. Fr. Diplomat, Author, Scholar
Justice, Bill*		Cartoonist	25			58	'The Chipmunks'. Full Size Color S $250
Justin, A.G.		Civil War	10	25			CW Gov. PA
Juttner, Arthur		Military	10			30	Ger. RK Winner
Juxon, William	1582-1663	Clergy	125	425			Archbshp.Canterbury.Attended Chas. I on Scaffold

K

Kabaiwanska, Raina		Entertainment	10			40	Opera
Kabalevsky, Dmitri		Composer	56	385	235		TMsS/Political Content $675
Kadar, Janos		Head of State	50	130			
Kaelin, Kato		Entertainment	30	65		45	Actor. Houseguest O.J. Simpson Turned Celebrity
Kafka, Franz	1883-1924	Author	850		2250		Ger. Novelist. Visionary Tales. Special ALS $16500
Kahn, Julius	1861-1924	Congress	5	15			Repr. CA 1899
Kahn, Madeline		Entertainment	5	6	15	15	

NAME	DATE	CATEGORY	SIG	LS/DS	ALS	SP	COMMENTS
Kahn, Otto H.	1867-1934	Business	95	50	135	60	Banker, Philanthropist, Arts Patron
Kahn, Yahya		Head of State	30			50	Pakistan
Kahoutek, Lubos		Science	5	15	30	15	Am. Astronomer
Kai-Shek, Chiang & Mme. K.		Head of State				375	
Kai-Shek, Chiang	1887-1975	Head of State	100	220	450	772	Republic of China
Kai-Shek, Mayling Soong Chiang		Author	50	275		120	Madame Chiang
Kaiser, Henry J.	1882-1967	Industrialist	188	1450		312	S.F.Bay Bridge.Grand Coulee Dam etc.
Kalakaua, David	1836-91	Royalty	248	425	775	1600	King Hawaii. Opposition To His Reform = Revolution
Kallen, Kitty		Entertainment		20		25	Big Band Vocalist
Kalmanoff, Martin		Composer	10		25		Numerous Works for Musical Theatre, Opera, etc.
Kaltenborn, H. V.		Radio	5	15	30	15	Radio Commentator
Kaltenbrunner, Ernst		Military	150	500		175	Perpetrator of Nazi Atrocities
Kamburg, Arthur, Dr		Science	10	20			Nobel
Kamehameha II, Liholiho	1797-1824	Royalty	960		3850		King Hawaii
Kamehameha III, Kauikeaouli		Royalty	750	1585			King Hawaii
Kamehameha IV	1824-63	Royalty		2500			King of Hawaii
Kaminsky, Max		Entertainment	10			30	Dixieland Jazz Bandleader
Kamio, Mitsuomi		Military	110		225		
Kamionsky, Oscar		Entertainment				350	Great Jewish Baritone
Kammhuber, Josef		Aviation	20	30	65	35	Ger. Air Defense Gen. WW II. RK
Kanaly, Steve		Entertainment	6	8	15	20	
Kander, John		Composer	10	45	95	25	Composed with Fred Ebb. Cabaret etc.
Kandinski, Vasili	1866-1944	Artist	200	795			Rus. Painter. Cont. TLS $1,500
Kandor, John		Composer					See Ebb, Fred
Kane, Bob*	1916-99	Cartoonist	100			495	'Batman'. SPI $275-$350, Comic Bk. S $100
Kane, Carol		Entertainment	10	15	15	25	
Kane, Elisha Kent	1820-57	Explorer	95	215	450		Grinnell Arctic Expedition
Kane, Helen	1904-1966	Entertainment	25			60	Boop-Boop-a-Doop Girl. Singer of the 20's
Kane, Richard		Military	20			90	
Kane, Thomas L.	1822-83	Civil War	48	105	160		Union Gen.ALS '63 $990
Kangaroo, Captain		Entertainment	5	6	15	25	
Kanin, Garson		Author	10	20	50	45	Playwright, Director, Screen.
Kansas		Entertainment	30			60	
Kant, Immanuel	1724-1804	Author	1005	3950	7375		Ger. Philosopher, Professor
Kantor, MacKinlay	1904-77	Author	15	45	75	30	Am. Novelist. Andersonville, Pulitzer 1956
Kantrowitz, Adrian, Dr.		Science	25	70	145	30	
Kantrowitz, Arthur, Dr.		Science	15		30		
Kaper, Bronislaw		Composer	10	30	55	15	
Kapitza, Peter	1894-1984	Science		375	550		Nobel Prize Physics '78
Kaplan, Gabe		Entertainment	5			15	
Kaplan, Gilbert		Conductor				50	Mahler Specialist
Kapliolani	1834-99	Royalty				1265	Queen Hawaii
Kappel, Frederick R.		Business	3	6	15	8	
Kappel, Gertrude		Entertainment	20			95	Wagnerian Soprano
Kapture, Mitzi		Entertainment	8			35	Actress. Pin-Up $60

NAME	DATE	CATEGORY	SIG	LS/DS	ALS	SP	COMMENTS
Karajan, Herbert von	1908-89	Conductor	55		325	335	Austrian Classical Conductor
Karas, Anton		Composer	25	40	85	100	Third Man Theme AMusQS $350
Karloff, Boris	1887-1969	Entertainment	296	415	500	669	Frankenstein. 3x4 SPI $295
Karman, Theodore von		Industrial	30	60	110	65	Automobile Designer. Karman-Ghia VW
Karns, Roscoe		Entertainment	30			75	
Karpis, Alvin 'Creepy'		Criminal	65	395	300	100	30's Public Enemy #1
Karras, Alex		Entertainment	5	6	15	15	
Karsavina, Tamara		Entertainment	50			362	Rus.-Br. Dancer
Karsh, Yousuf		Photographer	35	95	110	95	Portraits, Royalty, World Famous
Kasavubu, Joseph		Head of State	20	75	185	40	1st Pres. Dem. Repub. of Congo
Kaschmann, Giuseppe		Entertainment	60			325	Internationally Important Baritone Star
Kasem, Casey		Entertainment	5	8		12	Disc Jockey
Kasem, Jean		Entertainment	5	8		15	
Kasha, Al		Composer	15			45	
Kashfi, Anna		Entertainment	10		30	35	
Kassebaum, Nancy Landon		Senate	5	15		15	Senator KS
Kassell, Art		Bandleader	10			65	
Kastler, Alfred, Dr.	1902-84	Science	35	60		75	Nobel Physics '66. Orig'l Holograph Ms $850-$975
Katchinsky, Victorin		Aviation	20			45	
Katz, Bernard, Sir		Science	15	30	45	35	Nobel Medicine 1970
Katzenbach, Nicholas		Cabinet	10	20		15	Att'y General 1965
Katzenberg, Jeffrey		Business	15	25		25	Disney CEO
Katzir, Ephraim		Head of State	10			45	Pres. Israel '70's
Kaufman, Andy		Entertainment	75	150		175	Comedian-Actor. 'Taxi'. Very Early Death
Kaufman, George S.	1889-1961	Author	30	85	175	35	Dramatist, Critic, Director. Pulitzer. TLS/Cont. $275
Kaufmann, Christine	1945-	Entertainment	5			20	Germ. Actress. Pretty 2nd Wife of Tony Curtis
Kaunda, Kenneth		Head of State	40	150	350	122	1st Pres. Zambia
Kavelin, Al		Entertainment	10			20	Big Band Leader
Kawato, Masajiro 'Mike'		Aviation	40	100		150	Ace WW II, Downed Boyington
Kay, Beatrice	1910-81	Entertainment	10	20		22	Talented-Raucous Singer-Actress. Occasional Film
Kay, Dianne		Entertainment	3	3	6	6	
Kay, Herbie		Bandleader	10				
Kay, Mary (Ash)		Business	5	15	30	10	Cosmetics Empire
Kay, Mary Ellen		Entertainment				25	
Kaye, Celia		Entertainment	4	5	10	12	
Kaye, Danny		Entertainment	75			100	
Kaye, Sammy		Entertainment	15			40	Big Band Leader
Kaye, Stubby		Entertainment	10			25	
Kazan, Elia		Entertainment	10	12	20	35	Director, Producer, Author
Keach, Stacy		Entertainment	10	10		22	Actor. Mike Hammer etc.
Kean, Jane		Entertainment	5	6	15	12	
Keane, Bil*		Cartoonists	20	40		60	'The Family Circus'. Orig. Art $800
Keane, Edward		Entertainment	10			25	
Kearny, Philip (WD)		Civil War	375	650	880		Union General KIA
Kearny, Stephen		Military-Governor	85	195	380		War of 1812, 1st Gov. of CA

NAME	DATE	CATEGORY	SIG	LS/DS	ALS	SP	COMMENTS
Keating, Kenneth B.		Senate/Congress	5	15		10	Gen. WW II, MOC Senator 1947-65
Keaton, Buster	1895-1966	Entertainment	210	250		428	Great Film Comedian
Keaton, Diane		Entertainment	15	35		60	AA Winning Actress. DS re Godfather III $175
Keaton, Michael		Entertainment	15			62	As Batman SP $75
Keble, John	1792-1866	Clergy	75	125	298	295	Founder of Oxford Movement
Kedrova, Lila		Entertainment	10		25	40	
Keeble, John		Author	10	30	75		
Keel, Howard		Entertainment	5	6	25	20	He-Man Singer-Actor
Keeler, Ruby	1909-93	Entertainment	25			55	Once Busby Berkley Dancer. Wife of Al Jolson
Keene, Carolyn		Author	5	15	30	10	Publisher Pseud.(5 Authors)
Keene, Charles S.		Entertainment	10			25	
Keene, Tom		Entertainment	25			50	Actor
Kefauver, Estes		Senate	15	40		35	Senator TN
Keifer, Joseph W.		Civil War	25	45	60		Union Gen.& Speaker
Keillor, Garrison		Author	15	25	35	20	Humorist
Keim, Betty Lou		Entertainment	5			12	Actress
Keim, George May	1805-61	Congress	10				Repr. PA, Mayor Reading, PA
Keirstead, Wilfred C.		Clergy	10	15	20	15	
Keisha		Model	5			15	Pin-Up SP $25
Keitel, Harvey		Entertainment	15			60	Elusive Signer
Keitel, Wilhelm	1882-1946	Military	350	745	1500	625	Ger. Fld. Marshal WWII
Keith, Arthur, Sir		Author	10		35		Anthropologist, Origins of Man
Keith, Brian		Entertainment	5	8	15	20	
Keith, David		Entertainment	5	6	15	10	
Keith, George Keith E.	1746-1823t	Military	50	280	175		Br. Admiral. 1746-1823. Viscount
Keith, Ian		Entertainment	15				Vintage Actor
Keith, Rosalind		Entertainment	10			75	
Keith, William,	1680-1749	Rev. War	135		700		Colonial Lt. Governor PA & DE
Kekkonen, Urho		Head of State	15	45			Finland
Kelcey, Herbert		Entertainment	10			20	Vintage Stage Actor
Kelland, Clarence Buddington		Author	20	55	150	30	Am. Novelist, Short Stories
Kellar, Harry		Entertainment	15			35	Vintage Stage Actor
Kellard, Ralph		Entertainment	10			25	
Kellaway, Cecil		Entertainment	25			75	
Keller, Helen & A. Sullivan		Author-Teacher	535			2200	
Keller, Helen	1880-1968	Author	175	575	2175	875	Blind, Deaf, Mute Author. TLS/Cont. $1450
Kellerman, Annette		Entertainment	45		165	175	Aussie Dancer & Swimming Star
Kellerman, Jonathan		Author	4			15	Author of Billy Straight
Kellerman, Sally		Entertainment	10			25	
Kellerman,FC,Duke Valmy		Military	75	285	405		7 Years' War. Marshal of Nap.
Kelley, Clarence	1911-97	Cabinet	20	35		45	Dir. FBI
Kelley, Deforest		Entertainment	10	15	25	35	Star Trek
Kelley, Kitty		Author	12			20	Celebrity Biography
Kelley, Patrick Henry		Senate/Congress	5	10		10	MOC MI 1913
Kelley, Virginia Clinton		President Mother	15	65			Mother of Bill Clinton

NAME	DATE	CATEGORY	SIG	LS/DS	ALS	SP	COMMENTS
Kellogg, Charlotte		Philanthropist	7	20			Mrs. Vernon Kellogg
Kellogg, Frank B.	1856-1937	Cabinet	32	200	95	35	Nobel Peace Prize 1929
Kellogg, John Harvey, Dr.		Food Business	15	175	75		Am. Phys.Health Reformer.Breakfast Cereal
Kellogg, Ray		Entertainment	5			9	Actor
Kellogg, W. K.		Business	110	150	325	200	Fndr. W.K. Kellogg Co.
Kellogg, William P.	1831-1918	Congress	50	100			U.S. Senator 1868, Gov. LA 1873-77
Kelly, Edward J.		Political	10			15	Mayor Chicago
Kelly, Emmett, Sr.	1898-1979	Entertainment	60	150		292	Circus Clown Weary Willie Circus FDC S $125
Kelly, Gene	1912-1996	Entertainment	33			142	AA Dancer, Actor, Choreographer, Director
Kelly, Grace (Actress-Personal)	1928-82	Entertainment	200	325	1273	609	AA, AA
Kelly, Howard A., Dr.		Science	20	35	60	40	Orig. Faculty Johns Hopkins U.
Kelly, Jack		Entertainment	15			45	
Kelly, John H.		Civil War	475	975			CSA Gen., Youngest Killed
Kelly, Moira		Entertainment	20			55	
Kelly, Nancy		Entertainment	10	20		25	
Kelly, Patsy	1910-81	Entertainment	26	30	65	60	Comedienne-Actress. Wisecracking Hal Roach Star
Kelly, Paul		Entertainment	25			55	
Kelly, Paula		Entertainment	5		12	15	Pin-Up SP $18
Kelly, Scott		Astronaut	5			18	
Kelly, Thomas W.		Military	10	20		15	Gen. Desert Storm
Kelly, Walt*		Cartoonists	50	200		425	Pogo
Kelsey, Fred		Entertainment	25				Character Actor
Kelsey, Linda		Entertainment	5	6	15	15	
Kelton, Pert	1907-68	Entertainment	25		45	48	Comedienne. Original Alice in The Honeymooners
Kelvin, William T., Lord	1824-1907	Science	85	195	288	175	Kelvin Scale, Atlantic Cable
Kemble, Edward W.*	1861-1933	Artist-Cartoonist	25			375	Am. Illustrator Huck Finn, etc.
Kemble, Frances A. Fanny		Entertainment	35	75	110		Vintage Br. Actress-Diarist
Kemp, Hal		Entertainment	15			40	Big Band Leader
Kemp, Jack		Cabinet	15			25	Sec'y HUD, Presidential Candidate
Kempenfelt, Richard	1720-1782	Military	120		410		Br.Admiral. Introduced Fr. Tactics & Signal System
Kemper, Jackson, Dr.	1789-1870	Clergy	20		95		Educator
Kemper, James L. (WD)		Civil War	375				CSA Gen. AES $1150 '64. Wounded,Captured,Exchng.
Kemper, James L.	1823-95	Civil War	168	295	420		CSA Gen.
Kemper, John M.		Celebrity	3	7	15	10	
Kendal, Madge, Dame	1848-1935	Entertainment	12		20	35	Shakespearean Actress
Kendall, Amos	1789-1869	Cabinet	75	600	950		Jackson P.M. Gen'l,Journalist. Partner S.F.B.Morse
Kendall, Cy		Entertainment	25			50	Vintage Character Actor
Kendall, David		Legal	3			8	Clinton Attorney
Kendall, Edward C., Dr.		Science	30	55	100	40	Nobel Medicine 1950
Kendall, Henry W.		Science	20	35		30	Nobel Physics 1990
Kendall, Kay	1926-59	Entertainment	50			100	Brit. Actress-Comedienne. Died Leukemia at 32
Kendall, Paul		Military	10	30			
Kendren, John C.		Science	15	20	30	20	
Keneally, Thomas		Author	10			20	'Schindler's List'
Kenellopoulos, Panayotis		Head of State	15	35	90		Greece

NAME	DATE	CATEGORY	SIG	LS/DS	ALS	SP	COMMENTS
Kennan, George F.		Author	15	45			Am.Diplomat, Historian.Pulitzer
Kennedy, Anthony M.		Supreme Court	30			50	
Kennedy, Arthur		Entertainment	30	40	95	75	
Kennedy, Caroline		Celebrity-Author		25			Daughter of JFK
Kennedy, Douglas		Entertainment	4			30	AKA Keith Douglas
Kennedy, Edgar		Entertainment	125			250	
Kennedy, Edward M. 'Ted'		Congress	15	40	75	25	Senator MA 1962
Kennedy, Ethel		Celebrity	15	50	75	35	Mrs. Robert Kennedy
Kennedy, G.A.Studdert		Clergy	20				Br. Poet, Author.Woodbine Willie
Kennedy, George		Entertainment	5	20		45	AA Actor
Kennedy, George C.		Aviation	45			250	
Kennedy, Gerald, Bishop		Clergy	25	40	50	40	
Kennedy, J.& Jacqueline		President, 1st Lady		4200		2200	Engr. WH Vignette S $3500
Kennedy, Jacqueline (As 1st Ldy)		First Lady	825	1425	2315	3050	
Kennedy, Jacqueline	1929-94	First Lady	513	954	1938	1142	Auction 10/95 SP $3,300
Kennedy, Jayne		Entertainment	6	8	15	15	
Kennedy, John F. (As Pres.)		President	1650	2920		3910	TLS/Cont. As Pres. $19,500
Kennedy, John F.	1917-63	President	1333	2760	5604	2983	Young ALS $5750
Kennedy, John F., Jr.		Business	50			75	Magazine Publisher 'George'
Kennedy, John P.		Cabinet	35	50	95		Fillmore Sec'y Navy 1852
Kennedy, Joseph P.	1888-1969	Business	175	525	300	220	Boston Financier, Father of JFK
Kennedy, Joseph Patrick II		Congress	15	800		70	Repr. MA 1987
Kennedy, Madge		Entertainment	10			30	
Kennedy, Martin John		Senate/Congress	5	15			MOC NY 1930-45
Kennedy, Robert F.	1925-68	Cabinet-Congress	397	585	3625	784	Att'y Gen. Brother of JFK. Assassinated.WH Cd.$975
Kennedy, Robert F., Jr.		Author					Signed Book $112
Kennedy, Rose Fitzgerald	1890-1995	Celebrity	98	138	175	110	Kennedy Family Matriarch
Kennedy, Tom		Entertainment	50			125	
Kenney, George		Military	25	60	110	40	USAAF Gen. WW II
Kenny G.		Entertainment	20			75	Saxophonist
Kenny, Bill		Entertainment	25			75	Leader of Ink Spots
Kenny, Elizabeth, Sister	1886-1952	Science	175			275	Pioneer Polio Treatment. Autralian Nurse
Kenny, Nick		Entertainment		20			Singer/Ink Spots
Kensit, Patsy		Entertainment	10			60	Actress
Kent, A. Atwater		Inventor	20	195	90	35	Radio Mfg., Philanthropist
Kent, Edw. Augustus, Duke	1767-1820	Royalty	45	150			Son of Geo. III. Father of Queen Victoria
Kent, J. Ford		Military	90	195			Gen., Took San Juan Hill
Kent, Jack		Cartoonist	10			35	King Aroo
Kent, James	1763-1847	Rev. War	85	200	250		Legal Reporting System
Kent, Rockwell	1882-1971	Artist	45	225	305	75	Am. Landscape, Figure Painting, Illustrator
Kent, Walter		Composer	40	105		75	AMusQS $125-$200-$900 (I'll Be Home for Xmas)
Kent, William	1684-1748	Artist	175	920			Sculptor, Architect, Landscape Gardener. RARE
Kent, William	1864-1928	Congress	5	12		10	Repr. CA 1911
Kenton, Simon	1755-1836	Pioneer	420	1350			Hunter, Trader, Spy, General
Kenton, Stan	1912-79	Entertainment	35			110	Big Band Leader-Pianist

NAME	DATE	CATEGORY	SIG	LS/DS	ALS	SP	COMMENTS
Kenyatta, Jomo		Head of State	125	220	525	150	Prime Min. Kenya
Kenyon, Doris		Entertainment	15	25	45	45	
Kenyon, William S.		Senate/Congress	10	15	35		MOC NY 1859
Kepford, Ira		Aviation	15	30	48	42	ACE, WW II
Kepner, Wm. E.		Military	15	35	60	25	
Keppel, Augustus		Military-Rev. War		375	750		Br. Admiral Who Influenced Br. Naval Strategy
Keppel, Francis		Celebrity	5	15	20	15	
Keppler, Joseph	1838-1894	Publisher	15		45		Founder Puck Magazine
Kerbs, Edwin G., Dr.		Science	20	30	55	35	Nobel Medicine
Kercheval, Ken		Entertainment	5			25	
Kerensky, Alexander	1881-1970	Head of State	250	850	1250	475	Rus. Leader 1917 Revolution. Prime Minister. Fled
Kern, Jerome	1885-1945	Composer	308	650	1850		AMusQS $685-$2,500
Kern, Paul B., Bishop		Clergy	20	25	35	25	
Kernan, Francis		Senate/Congress	10		35		MOC 1863, Senator NY 1875
Kerns, Joanna		Entertainment	5		10	15	
Kerns, Kurt		Entertainment	6			25	Music. Bass & Drums Gravity Kills
Kerouac, Jack	1922-69	Author	500	2250	4000	5500	Beat Generation Rep. Clebr. pd. 5000 for DS
Kerr, Clark		Celebrity	5	10	20	10	
Kerr, Deborah		Entertainment	15	45	30	25	Pin-Up SP $35. Nominated 6 Times for Oscar
Kerr, John		Entertainment	10		25	30	Actor Tea And Sympathy, South Pacific
Kerr, Robert S.		Senate/Congress	5	15		10	Senator, Gov. OK
Kerr, Ruth		Business	25	35	150	100	Owner of Kerr Glass Co.. Queen of Home Canning
Kerrigan, J. Warren		Entertainment	35			75	Vintage Char. Actor. 'Johnny Gallegher' GWTW
Kerry, Robert		Senate	10			20	Senator
Kershaw, Joseph B.	1822-94	Civil War	180	900	1625		CSA Gen. LS '61 $3500, War Dte. Sig $350
Kerwin, Joseph P.		Astronaut	7			25	
Kesey, Ken		Author	64	40	65	35	One Flew Over the Cukoo's Nest
Kesselring, Albrecht	1885-1960	Military	101	525		175	Ger. Field Marshal WW II
Kestnbaum, Meyer		Business	15	30		25	Pres. Hart, Schaffner & Marx
Ketcham, Hank*		Cartoonist	25	75		225	Dennis the Menace. FDC S $50. Indx.Cd $50
Ketcham, John H. (WD)		Civil War	150		325		Union Gen.
Ketcham, John H.	1832-1906	Civil War	60	75			Union Gen. War Dte. S $150, DS $275
Ketelby, Albert W.		Composer	15		75		'In a Persian Market....', 'In a.Monastery Garden'
Kettering, Charles F.		Inventor	100	160	325	125	Engineer. Sloan-Kettering Inst.Kettering Engine
Kevorkian, Jack, Dr.		Science	25		55	75	Euthanasia.Dr. Death.Convicted 2nd Degree Murder
Key, David M.	1824-1900	Cabinet	30	45	90		P.M. General. CSA Officer
Key, Francis Scott	1779-1843	Lawyer-Author	500	600	1200		Special ADS $2,500
Key, Philip Barton	1857-1815	Senate/Congress	10	30	40		MOC MD 1807
Key, Ted*		Cartoonist	10			75	'Hazel'
Keyes, Erasmus D.	1818-95	Civil War	65	125	325		Union General. ALS/Cont. $1500
Keyes, Erasmus, D. (WD)		Civil War	95	255	400		Union Gen.
Keyes, Evelyn		Entertainment	22		40	58	Actress. SP in GWTW Costume $40-100
Keyes, Irwin		Entertainment	4			10	Character Actor
Keyes, Roger J.B. 1st Baron	1872-1945	Military	35		65	75	Br. Adm.Fleet. Boxer Rebellion
Keynes, John Maynard	1883-1946	Economist	75	1083	585	250	Br. Econ. Member'Bloomsbury Group'. TLS/Cont.$1600

NAME	DATE	CATEGORY	SIG	LS/DS	ALS	SP	COMMENTS
Keys, Ancel		Science	5	15	30	10	
Keys, Henry W.		Governor	10	20	35		Governor NH
Keyser, Ralph S.		Military	30	50			
Keyserling, Hermann Graf	1880-1946	Philosopher	15	35	65	50	Ger. Social Philosopher (Spiritual Regeneration)
Khalid, King	1913-1982	Royalty	25	65	175	75	Saudi Arabia
Khama, Seretse, Sir		Head of State	65			250	1st Prime Minister of Botswana
Khambatta, Persis		Entertainment	22			60	Star Trek
Khan, Chaka		Entertainment	20			45	
Khan, Mohammad Ayub		Head of State	30	95			
Khan, Yasmin, Princess		Royalty	10			25	Daughter of Rita Hayworth
Khanh, Nguyen, Gen.		Head of State	20	60	175	45	
Khanieff, Nikhandr S.	1922-54	Entertainment				650	Leading Heroic Tenor at Bolshoi
Khatchaturian, Aram	1903-78	Composer	135		938	650	AMusQS $300, $575, $625, $1275
Khomeini, Ruhollah, Ayatollah		Religious Leader	575				Iranian Moslem Leader
Khorana, Har G., Dr.		Science	15	25	45	25	Nobel Medicine 1968
Khruschchev, Nikita S.	1894-1971	Head of State	300	410	550	1250	Premier Soviet Union
Kiam, Victor		Business	5	25		15	Remington Electric Razor Co.
Kibbee, Guy		Entertainment	20			40	Rotund, Ruddy Faced Comedian Char.Actor 30's
Kidder, Margot		Entertainment	10			30	Actress. Pin-Up SP $30
Kiddoo, Jos. Barr		Civil War	65				Union General
Kidman, Nicole		Entertainment	20			63	Actress
Kiel, Richard		Entertainment	5			15	
Kielmansegg, Graf J.A.		Military	15			35	Gen. German Army
Kienzl, Wilhelm	1857-1941	Composer	15		55		Opera
Kiepura, Jan	1902-1966	Entertainment	42			125	Opera, Concert. Vintage, Trimmed SPc $40-$50
Kilban, B.*		Cartoonist	10	25		100	Cat Cartoons, The New Yorker
Kilbourne, Charles E.		Military	15			75	Am. WW I Soldier. 3d Brig. 2d Div.
Kilbride, Percy	1888-1964	Entertainment	138			350	Wimpy Character Actor. 'Ma & Pa Kettle' Films
Kilby, J. S. Jack		Science	20	35	70	35	Inventor of Micro Chip
Kiley, Richard	?-1999	Entertainment	15		25	30	Fine Stage & Film Actor
Kilgore, Harley, M.		Senate/Congress	5	15		15	Senator WV 1941
Kilgore, Merle		Country Music	10			20	
Kilham, Hannah		Clergy	50	75	100		
Kilian, Victor		Entertainment	10		20	25	Character Actor. Many Dark, Brooding Parts
Killinger, John W.		Senate/Congress	10	15	30		MOC PA 1859
Kilmer, Joyce	1886-1918	Author	225	550			Poet. Trees
Kilmer, Val		Entertainment	28	165		59	Batman SP/Chris O'Donnell $150
Kilpatrick, Hugh J. (WD)		Civil War	200	575	650		Union Gen.
Kilpatrick, Hugh J.	1836-81	Civil War	118	230	400	415	Union Gen. Cavalry. '63 LS $1295
Kimball, Dan		Cabinet	20	35	40	25	Sec'y Navy. Aerojet General
Kimball, J. Golden		Clergy	25	150			Pioneer Mormon Leader
Kimball, John W.		Civil War	50		210		Union Gen.
Kimball, Spencer W.		Clergy	25	25	35	30	Morman Leader
Kimball, Ward		Cartoonist	25			75	Musician-Disney Cartoonist. Firehouse 5 Plus 2
Kimberly, John W., 1st Earl		Statesman	20	30	110		Br.Colon'l Sec'y. Kimberly S.A.

NAME	DATE	CATEGORY	SIG	LS/DS	ALS	SP	COMMENTS
Kimberly, R. Lewis	1836-1913	Civil War	30	45	50		Union General
Kimbrough, Emily		Author	10	20	42	15	Our Hearts Were Young & Gay
Kimmel, Husband E.		Military	350			550	US Adm. Cmdr. At Pearl Harbor
Kindelberger, James H. Dutch		Business	45			75	Pres. No. American Aviation. Test Pilot
Kindermann, K. B.		Aviation	5			15	
Kindler, Hans		Conductor	25			100	Conductor Wash., DC Nat'l Symphony
King, Alan		Entertainment	10			20	Stage, Film, TV, Vegas Top Comedian
King, Andrea		Enntertainment	15			25	Actress. 2nd Leads, Other Woman 40's-50's
King, B.B.		Entertainment	20	102		58	Grammy Winning R & B Singer, Guitarist
King, Ben E.		Composer	12			25	Singer-The Drifters. Stand by Me AMusQS $95
King, Cammie		Entertainment	15		35	35	GWTW Child Actress.
King, Carole		Entertainment	15			25	Rock
King, Charles		Civil War	50		175		Soldier-Civil War Author
King, Charles		Entertainment	20			50	
King, Coretta Scott		Celebrity	32	70	95	30	Mrs. Martin Luther King, Jr. Civil Rights Activist
King, Edward J., Bishop		Clergy	25	35	50		
King, Ernest J.	1878-1956	Military	30	120		125	Fleet Adm. Cmmdr. Chief US Fleet WW II
King, Frank*		Cartoonist	35			165	'Gasoline Alley'
King, Henry		Entertainment	30			75	Film Director
King, Horatio	1811-1897	Cabinet	45	175	275		P.M. General 1861
King, Jack	1903-43	Composer					Pop Songwriter AMusQS $35
King, James	1791-1853	Business	20		65		Financier, RR Pres. Son of VP Rufus King
King, John 'Dusty'		Entertainment	20	30	45	55	
King, John Alsop		Governor	10		35		Gov. NY, a Founder Repub. Party
King, Larry		Entertainment	10	20	35	20	Talk Show Host
King, MacKenzie (Wm. L.)	1874-1950	Head of State	55	55	90	55	Prime Minister Canada WW II
King, Martin Luther, III		Activist	5			30	Civil Rights
King, Martin Luther, Jr.	1929-68	Clergy	1519	3795	2675	3625	Advocate Peaceful Nonviolence. Assassinated
King, Martin Luther. Sr.		Clergy	35	45	60	65	
King, Pee Wee		Entertainment	10			20	C & W. Bandleader-Composer
King, Perry		Entertainment	5			20	
King, Preston	1806-65	Congress	15	45	100		Repr. 1843, Senate NY. Suicide 1865
King, Rodney		Celebrity	10				Afro-Am. L.A. Police Vicitim
King, Rufus	1755-1827	Rev. War	250	475	425		Cont'l Congr. Historical ALS $2500
King, Rufus (WD)		Civil War	75				Union Gen. ALS/Cont.'62 $3200
King, Rufus	1814-76	Civil War	42	100			Union General
King, Stephen		Author	95	125	450	110	Master of Horror and Suspense
King, Thomas Starr	1824-64	Clergy	25	35	95	40	
King, Walter Woolf		Entertainment	15		25	50	Broadway Singing Star. Vagabond King in 30's
King, Wayne		Entertainment	15			25	Big Band Leader.
King, William R.	1786-1853	Vice President	200	340			Pierce VP. Died after 45 days
King, Wm. L. Mackenzie	1874-1950	Head of State	40	262		55	3 Times P.M. Canada
Kingman, Dong		Artist	25	50	100		
Kingsford-Smith, Charles		Aviation	145	275		200	FDC Trans-Tasman Fl. $225
Kingsley, Ben	1943-	Entertainment	10	12	20	31	AA Winning Actor Gandhi

NAME	DATE	CATEGORY	SIG	LS/DS	ALS	SP	COMMENTS
Kingsley, Charles	1819-75	Author-Clergy	45	95	160		Br. Novelist, Clergyman
Kingston, Trio		Entertainment	30			70	Folk Group of 59's
Kingston, William H.		Author	25		100		Br. Boy's Adventure Books
Kinks (5 Current Members)		Entertainment	40			85	Rock. LP Cover S $95
Kinney, Sean		Entertainment	6			25	Music. Drummer Alice in Chains
Kinsey, Alfred, Dr.	1894-1956	Science	140	230	375	295	Am. Sexologist Researcher
Kinskey, Leonid	1903-95	Entertainment	20			35	Russian-Born Character Actor. Casablanca
Kinski, Klaus		Entertainment	35		40	175	Actor-Director
Kinski, Natassja		Entertainment	15	25	45	73	Actress, Nude Pin-Up $110
Kinstler, E.R.*		Cartoonist	10			100	Illustrator
Kintner, Robert		Business	5	10	30	10	
Kip, William I., Bishop		Clergy	50	85	125		
Kipling, Rudyard	1865-1936	Author	222	587	728	1064	Nobel Lit., Novelist, Poet
Kiplinger, Austin		Business	10		45	15	Kiplinger Washington Newsletter
Kipnis, Alexander		Entertainment	35	75		95	Opera. Russ. Bass
Kirby, Fred. M.		Business		2450			Founded Dime Store Chain. Woolworth Partner
Kirby, George		Entertainment	5			15	
Kirby, Jack*		Cartoonist	25			170	'Captain America'
Kirby, Rollin*		Cartoonist	20			90	
Kirk, Andy		Bandleader	15			65	
Kirk, Claude Jr.		Governor	7	15			Governor FL
Kirk, Eddie		Country Music	10			20	Country Singer-Recording Artist
Kirk, Florence		Entertainment	10			30	Opera
Kirk, George		Aviation	12		40	35	ACE, WW II
Kirk, Grayson	1903-97	Educator	20			40	Columbia University President for Many Years
Kirk, Norman T.	1888-	Military		50		55	U.S. Gen. WW II
Kirk, Phyllis		Entertainment	20		95	45	Rising Star in 50's. Cover Life Mag. Illness Struck
Kirk, Tommy		Entertainment	10			20	Juvenile Star
Kirkby-Lunn, Louise		Entertainment	30			95	Opera
Kirkconnell, Clare		Entertainment	4			10	
Kirkham, Ralph W.	1821-93	Civil War	27	55	80		Union General
Kirkland, Lane		Labor	8	15	30	15	Labor Leader. AFL-CIO
Kirkland, Sally		Entertainment	10			20	
Kirkland, Samuel	1741-1808	Missionary		1525	2150		Oneida Indian Missionary. Active during Rev. War
Kirkpatrick, Jean J.		Cabinet	20		35	25	Ambassador U.N. Signature on Special Piece $115
Kirkwood, Joe, Jr.		Entertainment	45		110	100	Radio, Movies And Golfer
Kirkwood, Samuel J.	1813-94	Cabinet	15	25	55	45	Sec'y Interior, Gov, Senator IA
Kirman, Richard, Sr.		Governor	10		30		Governor NV
Kirschlager, Angelika		Entertainment	10			30	Opera. Vienna's New Rising Star
Kirsebom, Vendela		Entertainment	15			50	Model-Actress Batman & Robin
Kirsten, Dorothy	1919-92	Entertainment	20			50	Am. Lyric Soprano, Opera. Record 30 Yrs. At Met.
Kiss (Entire Group)		Entertainment	50			125	Rock. Alb. S $145, $150
Kissinger, Henry A.		Cabinet	20	125		55	Sec'y State, Stateman, Diplomat, Prolific Author
Kistiakowsky, G.B., Dr.		Science	40	135		70	Nobel Chemistry
Kitchener, Horatio H.	1850-1916	Military	85	205	278	210	Ir.-born Br. Field Marshal. 1st Earl, Statesman

NAME	DATE	CATEGORY	SIG	LS/DS	ALS	SP	COMMENTS
Kitt, Eartha	1928-	Entertainment	10			30	Actress-Singer. Pin-Up SP $35
Kittinger, Joe		Aviation	25	45			
Kittredge, Walter		Composer	30		45		Tenting Tonight'...AMQS $300-$1,150
Kitzhaber, John		Governor	3			8	Oregon Gov.
Klass, Alisha		Entertainment	6			40	New Adult Film Star
Kleber, Jean-Baptiste		Fr. Revolution	145	410	855		One of France's Greatest Gen'ls
Klee, Paul	1879-1940	Artist	200	615	1850		Swiss Surrealist Painter
Kleiman, Jon		Entertainment	6			25	Music. Drummer Monster Magnet
Klein, Calvin		Business	10	15	35	25	Fashion-Accessory Designer
Klein, Felix	1849-1925	Science	85		450		Ger. Mathematician.Non-Euclidean Geometry
Klein, Robert		Entertainment	5			15	Actor, Comedian
Klemperer, Otto		Entertainment	73		310	260	German Conductor
Klemperer, Werner	1920-	Entertainment	15	25		25	Actor. Col. Klink on 'Hogan's Heroes'
Kleppe, Thomas S.		Cabinet	5	15	30	10	MOC ND, Sec'y Interior
Klimt, Gustav	1862-1918	Artist	170	575	1112		Austrian. Allegorical Murals
Kline, Kevin		Entertainment	15		45	45	Wanda Cast $120. Oscar Winner
Klose, Margarete	1902-68	Entertainment	15			65	Opera. Ger. Mezzo-Soprano
Kluge, Hans Gunther von		Military	75		250		Ger. Gen'l WW II, Suicide
Klugman, Jack		Entertainment	10			22	Actor. 1/2 of the Odd Couple
Klutznick, Philip M.		Cabinet	5	12		8	Sec'y Commerce
Kmentt, Waldemar		Entertainment	10			65	Opera. Eminent Tenor 3x5 SP $40
Knern, Harold H.*		Cartoonist	25		95	180	Katzenjammer Kids
Knibb, William		Clergy	45	60	75		
Knievel, Evel		Celebrity	10	15	35	45	Daredevil Motorcycle Rider
Knight, Evelyn		Entertainment	10				With the Star Dusters
Knight, Fuzzy		Entertainment	50			150	
Knight, Gladys		Entertainment	15	20	35	40	Rock. DS by Knight & 6 Pips $85
Knight, Goodwin J.		Governor	10	15		15	Governor CA
Knight, John S.		Business	10	35	45	20	Publisher
Knight, John T.		Military	25	75		35	Am. WW I Gen.
Knight, Jordan		Entertainment	10			45	
Knight, June		Entertainment	8	9	20	25	
Knight, Laura, Dame	1877-1970	Artist	60	100	175		Ranked Alongside Britain's Greatest
Knight, Phil		Business	22	35	45	25	Nike Athletic Shoes Etc.
Knight, Shirley		Entertainment	9	10	20	25	
Knight, Ted	1923-86	Entertainment	15	35		35	Actor. Best Remembered in Mary Tyler Moore Show
Knopf, Alfred A.		Business	7	20	35		Knopf Publishing
Knote, Heinrich		Entertainment	20			50	Opera
Knott, Walter		Business	35	70		150	Co-Founder Knott's Berry Farm
Knott, Walter & Cordelia Knott		Business	150			475	Co-Founders Knott's Berry Farm
Knotts, Don		Entertainment	10			25	Self Sketch S $35
Knowland, William F.		Senate	10	20		25	Senator CA, Publisher
Knowles, James S.		Author	10	25	50		
Knowles, John		Author	35			100	Br. Author
Knowles, Patrick		Entertainment	10			25	

NAME	DATE	CATEGORY	SIG	LS/DS	ALS	SP	COMMENTS
Knox, Alexander		Entertainment	10	15	30	30	
Knox, Elyse		Entertainment	10	20	35	40	Actress-Wife Tom Harmon
Knox, Frank	1874-1944	Cabinet	50	115	95	100	Sec'y Navy. TLS/Cont $275
Knox, Henry	1750-1806	Cabinet-Military	150	575	700		Maj. Gen'l. Rev. War Dte. ALS $4,500
Knox, James, Cardinal		Clergy	30	30	35	35	
Knox, Philander C.	1853-1921	Cabinet	12	25	70	30	Att'y Gen., Senator PA
Knudsen, William S.		Business	20	35	85	45	Pres. GM. WW II War Prod. Dir.
Knutson, Harold		Senate/Congress	5	10		10	MOC MN
Kobayashi, Takeji		Author	20		60	45	Proletarian Literary Movement
Koch, Edward I.		Political	10	20	35	15	Mayor NYC
Koch, Edward W.		Entertainment	20			35	Prod-Dir. Manchurian Candidate, Odd Couple
Koch, Heinrich H. Robert		Science		1500	2259	1500	Nobel Bacteriology-Medicine '05
Koch, Howard W.	1916-	Entertainment	20			35	Producer-Dir. of Multiple Film & TV Hits
Koch, Robert, Dr.	1843-1910	Science			1367	2300	Founder Modern Bacteriology
Kodaly, Zoltan	1882-1967	Composer	125	300	685	450	Hung. Composer.Content ALS $1750.AMusQS $1150
Koehl, Herman		Aviation	75			250	1st East-West Crossing Atlantic
Koehler, Armin		Aviation	10	20	35	25	
Koenig, Walter		Entertainment	20		45	65	Actor. Checkov on Star Trek
Kohl, Hannelove		Celebrity	5			10	Mrs. Helmut Kohl
Kohl, Helmut		Heads of State	15	30	65	25	Chancellor Germany
Kohler, Walter J.		Business	10	30			Founder Kohler Corp. Plumbing
Kohlsaat, Herman H.		Editor	3		15		
Kohner, Susan		Entertainment	5			25	Actress. Imitation of Life
Kokoschka, Oskar	1886-1980	Artist	95		450	275	Austrian. PC Repro Painting S $180
Kolff, Willem J., Dr.		Science	15	55		40	Created Artificial Kidney
Kolker, Henry	1874-1947	Entertainment	15		65	35	Actor-Dir-Writer, Noted Stage, Film Char. Actor
Kolleck, Teddy		Political	15	38		35	Mayor of Jerusalem
Kollo, Rene		Entertainment	15			55	Opera
Kollo, Rene		Entertainment	10		35	25	Opera
Kollwitz, Kathe	1867-1945	Artist			362		Ger. Sculptor, Graphic Artist
Komarov, Vladimir M.	1927-67	Astronaut	125			317	Rus. Cosmonaut. 1st To Die During Space Flight
Konetzni, Anny		Entertainment	25			65	Opera
Konya, Sandor		Entertainment				40	Opera. Hung. Tenor
Kook, Abraham Isaac		Clergy	45	145			Palestinian Rabbi
Koontz, Dean	1945-	Author	20	55		65	Novelist. Horror. Signed Books VG+ $25
Koop, C.Everett, Dr.		Military	7	20	50	30	Adm., US Surgeon General
Kopell, Bernie		Entertainment	5			15	Actor. Get Smart, Love Boat
Koppel, Ted		TV News	10	15	30	20	
Korda, Alexander		Entertainment	40	45	90	85	
Koren, Edward*		Cartoonist	10			75	New Yorker Cartoonist
Korman, Harvey		Entertainment	5	6	15	15	
Korn		Entertainment	35			115	Music. 5 Member Rock Group
Kornberg, Arthur		Science	20	30	45	25	Nobel Medicine
Kornby, Arthur		Science	15		20		
Korngold, Erich W.		Composer	75	200	350	95	Opera, Orchestral, Films. Spec'l Score S $985

NAME	DATE	CATEGORY	SIG	LS/DS	ALS	SP	COMMENTS
Korolyov, Sergei	1906-66	Science		1718	2300		Russ. Aeronautical Engineer
Korvin, Charles		Entertainment	10	15		20	
Kosciusko, Thaddeus		Rev. War	300	750	2500		Polish Patriot.
Kosleck, Martin		Entertainment	15			35	
Kossa, Frank R.		Military	7	9	12	10	
Kossuth, Lajos	1802-94	Head of State	120	825	475	155	Hungarian Patriot, Journalist
Kostal, Irwin		Composer	3	10	20	10	
Kostelanetz, Andre	1901-80	Entertainment	15	25	45	25	Conductor
Koster, Henry		Entertainment	15	35		40	Film Director
Kosygin, Aleksei		Head of State	275	1190	875	480	Premier of Soviet Union
Koussevitzky, Serge	1874-1951	Entertainment	65		170		Russ. Conductor.Pioneered Introducing Russ. Opera
Kovack, Nancy (Mehta)		Entertainment	4	4	9	10	
Kovacs, Ernie	1919-62	Entertainment	200			400	First Outrageous TV Comedian
Kovalevskaya, Sophia	1850-91	Science			850		Rus. Mathematician, Novelist
Kovansky, Anatol		Artist	15		40	25	
Kove, Martin		Entertainment	6	8	15	15	
Kovic, Ron		Activist	15	25			Anti Viet Nam Autobio.Born on the 4th of July'
Kowarski, L.		Science	10	25	60		
Kozky, Alex*		Cartoonist	10			20	Apt. 3-G
Kozlovsky, Ivan	1900-	Entertainment				1500	Ukrainian Tenor. RARE
Kraft, Chris		Astronaut	15			25	
Kraft, James L.		Business	30	95	175	50	Founder Kraft Foods Co.
Kragen, Ken		Business	5	10	20	20	Entertainment Business Mgr.
Kraigher, Sergej		Head of State				45	President Yugoslavia
Krakowski, Jane		Entertainment	5			32	Actress. Ally McBeal Co-Star
Kral, Roy		Celebrity	10	25		15	
Kramer, Stanley		Entertainment	15	35		35	Film Producer, Director
Kramer, Stephanie		Entertainment	5			20	
Krantz, Judith		Author	25		40	35	Novelist
Krasner, Milton		Entertainment	20			45	Film Director. AA
Kraus, Alfredo		Entertainment	15			35	Opera. 5x7 Half-Tone Portr. $20
Kraus, Clemens		Entertainment	65			220	Austrian Conductor
Kraus, Robert		Artist	10	25	50	25	
Krause, Charles		Entertainment	5			25	Actor. Sports Night
Krause, Peter		Entertainment	5			25	Actor. Sports Night
Krauss, Werner		Entertainment	250				
Kravitz, Lenny		Entertainment	10			42	Music. Lead Singer Lenny Kravitz
Krebs, Hans Adolf, Sir	1900-81	Science	35	260		70	Ger.-Born Br. Biochemist. Nobel Medicine
Krebs, Nita	1904-92	Entertainment	12	20		25	Actress-Dancer Wizard of Oz. Munchkin
Kregal, Kevin		Astronaut	5			18	
Kreisler, Fritz	1875-1962	Composer	81	170	325	290	Violinist, AMQS $275
Kremer, Andrea		TV News	5			12	ESPN News
Krenek, Ernst	1900-91	Composer	15	35	90	55	Austrian-Am. AMusQS $95-$150-$225
Krenn, Fritz		Entertainment	15			35	Opera
Kreps, Juanita M.		Cabinet	4	10	15	12	Sec'y Commerce

NAME	DATE	CATEGORY	SIG	LS/DS	ALS	SP	COMMENTS
Kresge, S. S.		Business	150	250	305	100	Kresge Stores
Kretschmer, Otto		Military	45	140		185	Highest Scoring U Boat Cmdr.
Kreutzer, Conradin		Composer	125	300	650		Ger. Composer/Conductor
Krige, Alice		Entertainment	4	4	9	10	
Kristel, Sylvia		Entertainment	20			45	
Kristofferson, Kris		Entertainment	10		35	30	
Kristyon, Eldgorn		Head of State	20	35			President of Iceland
Kroc, Mrs. Ray (Joan)		Business	5	15	35	15	McDonalds
Kroc, Ray A.		Business	30	90	150	100	McDonalds
Krock, Arthur		Author	7	20	40	15	Bureau Chief,Columnist NY Times
Kroesen, Fred J.		Military	4	15	20	10	
Krofft, Marty		Entertainment	40	125		50	Puppeteer
Kroft, Steve		TV Journalist	5			24	60 Minutes
Krol, John, Cardinal	1910-96	Clergy	30	40	75	50	Archbishop of Philadelphia 1961-88 & Cardinal '67
Kroll, Gustov		Science	10			30	Rocket Pioneer/von Braun
Kropotkin, Peter A.	1842-1921	Anarchist	30	75	502		Rus. Prince Gave Up Title for Working Class
Krueger, Walter	1881-	Military		100			Sp.-Am.,WW I & Full Gen. WW II
Krug, J. A.		Cabinet	10	20	30	15	Sec'y Interior
Kruger, Kurt		Entertainment	8	9	15	35	
Kruger, Otto	1885-1974	Entertainment	30			75	Distinguished Leading & Character Actor
Kruger, Paul		Head of State	75	350		175	Pres. So. Afr., Kruger Nat'l Pk
Kruger, Stephanus J.P.	1825-1904	Head of State	125	450		660	Krugerrand Named For Him
Krupa, Gene	1909-73	Entertainment	52	195		77	Big Band Leader-Drums
Krupinski, Walter		Aviation	15	30	55	60	Ger. Ace. WW II . RK
Krupp, Alfred		Business	180	450	500		Founder Krupp Works
Krupp, Friedrich Alfred		Business	125	350			Arms Manufacturer
Krylov, Ivan A.		Author	15	40	75	20	Russion Fabulist. Fables
Kschessinska, Matilda M.	1872-1971	Ballet	110		580	535	Prima Ballerina Assoluta Imperial Theatre
Kschessinsky, Joseph	1868-1942	Entertainment	75		250		Actor-Brother of Prima Ballerina Matilda K.
Kuatosov, Mikhail	1745-1813	Military		1750			Rus. Military Leader against Turks
Kubelik, Jan	1880-1940	Composer	40	115	250	225	Czech Violinist, AMQS $200-$575
Kubelik, Rafael		Conductor	15	50		50	
Kubiszewski, Andrew		Entertainment	6			25	Music. Drummer, Vocals Stabbing Westward
Kubitschek, Juscelino		Head of State	10	35	90	25	Brazil
Kubrick, Sidney		Entertainment	5	5	10	15	
Kubrick, Stanley		Entertainment	30	195		80	Film Director.
Kuchel, Thomas	1910-	Congress	5	25			Sen. CA
Kuchta, Gladys		Entertainment	10			30	Opera
Kudrow, Lisa		Entertainment	20			62	Actress. 'Friends'
Kuhlman, Katherine		Clergy	35		50		Radio Evengelist
Kuhn, Joseph E.		Military	30		125		Am. WW I Gen.
Kuhn, Maggie	1905-95	Political	20			35	Political & Social Activist. Fndr Of Grey Panthers
Kullman, Charles		Entertainment	20			50	Popular Operatic Tenor/Met. 20 Yrs. Some Films
Kulp, Nancy		Entertainment	10			25	Comedienne-Actress
Kuncewiczowa, Maria		Author	145		345		Escaped Nazi Ger.

NAME	DATE	CATEGORY	SIG	LS/DS	ALS	SP	COMMENTS
Kung, Hans		Clergy	35	50	75	60	
Kunstler, William	1919-95	Law	25	35	75	40	Defense of Radicals. Attny for Martin Luther King
Kupka, Frantisek	1871-1957	Artist	110	225	387		Czech.Abstract Art, Illustrator
Kuralt, Charles		TV News	8	20	35	15	Commentator
Kurtz, Swoosie		Entertainment	5			26	Actress. Sisters
Kusch, Polykarp, Dr.		Science	20	50		25	Nobel Physics
Kutosov, Mikhail	1745-1813	Military		1550			Rus. Military Leader against Turks
Kuykendall, Andrew J.	1815-91	Congress	10				Repr. IL, Union Officer
Kwan, Nancy		Entertainment	9	16		45	
Ky, Nguyen Cao		Head of State	30	100	250	75	
Kyne, Peter B.		Author	5	15	30	10	Homsey Family Novels
Kyser, Kay		Entertainment	15			30	Big Band Leader

L

NAME	DATE	CATEGORY	SIG	LS/DS	ALS	SP	COMMENTS
L A Guns		Entertainment	15			40	Rock
L A Law (Cast of)		Entertainment				275	10 Sigs.
L'Amour, Louis	1908-88	Author	75	220	490	125	Novels Re The Old West
L'Enfant, Pierre Charles		Aviation	400	850	1500		
La Belle, Patti		Entertainment	15			35	Singer
La Cava, Gregory		Entertainment	20			45	Film Director
La Farge, John	1835-1910	Artist	40	95	312		Am. Landscape & Figure Painter. Author
La Forge, Frank		Composer	15			45	
La Marr, Barbara		Entertainment	300			800	
La Motta, Vikki		Entertainment	10			15	Model-Actress. Wife of Jake La Motta. SP Nude 45
La Revelliere-Lepaux,L.		Fr. Revolution	25	70	145		Politician
La Rocque, Rod		Entertainment	20		45	55	
La Rue, Jack	1903-84	Entertainment	10			35	Actor. Gangster Roles and Heavies
La Verne. Lucille		Entertainment	75			150	
LaBeauf, Sabrina		Entertainment				15	Actress. Bill Cosby Show
Labouisse, Eve Curie		Science		60			Celebrity Daughter of Marie & Pierre Curie
Lacepede, Bernhard de		Science	30	75	145		Fr. Naturalist & Politician
Lachaise, Gaston	1882-1935	Artist		125	325		Fr.-Am. Sculptor
Laciura, Anthony		Entertainment	5			25	Opera
Ladd, Alan	1913-64	Entertainment	70	80		187	Actor. Popular Leading Man of 40's-50's
Ladd, Cheryl		Entertainment	8	22	20	20	TV Star. Charley's Angels. Pin-Up SP $30
Ladd, David		Entertaiinment	10			25	Producer
Ladd, Diane		Entertainment	5	6	15	15	
Ladd, Sue Carol		Entertainment	5	6	15	15	
LaDelle, Jack		Entertainment	3	3	6	6	
Laemmle, Carl		Business	80	268	825	750	Film Pioneer, Founder Universal. SCARCE
Laennec, Rene, T.H.	1781-1826	Science	3000	3500	4550		Fr. Phys., Invented Stethoscope
Lafayette, Marquis de	1757-1834	Rev. War	400	1072	1816		Gilbert Motier. Fr. Statesman.ALS/Cont $4,900-9600

NAME	DATE	CATEGORY	SIG	LS/DS	ALS	SP	COMMENTS
LaFollette, Philip		Governor	15	35		50	Governor WI
LaFollette, Robert Jr.		Senate/Congress	10	25		20	Senator WI
LaFollette, Robert M.		Senate/Congress	35	95		40	Senator WI
LaFontaine, Henri Marie		International Law	10	20	30		Nobel Peace Prize
LaForgue, Jules	1860-87	Author	150				Fr. Symbolist Poet. Died at 27. ALS/Cont. $5500
Lagerkvist, P,r F.		Author	30	70	175	100	Nobel Literature 1951
Lagerlof, Selma	1858-1940	Author	95	305		125	Nobel Literature 1909
Lagge, James		Clergy	20	25	35		
LaGuardia, Fiorello	1882-1947	Congress	42	130	150	162	Great Reform Mayor NYC. MOC NY. Colorful Char.
Lahm, Frank		Aviation	35	75	140	90	
Lahr, Bert	1895-1967	Entertainment	292	340		433	Comedian, Cowardly Lion of OZ
Lahti, Christine		Entertainment	6	8	15	15	
Laidlie, D. A.		Clergy	15	20	25		
Laine, Frankie		Entertainment	7	25		12	Singer. Recording artist of Top Hits
Laine, J.L.J., Viscount		Fr. Revolution	30	85	175		
Laingen, Bruce		State Dept.	5			15	Iran Hostage
Laird, Melvin		Cabinet	7	20	25	15	Sec'y Defense
Laithwaite, Eric R.		Inventor	25	95			Electromagnetic Propulsion & Air Cushion Suspensio
Lake, Arthur	1905-86	Entertainment	50			65	Dagwood Bumstead of Blondie
Lake, Ricki		Entertainment	30			60	TV Hostess
Lake, Simon	1866-1945	Science-Business	100	417	1050	450	Inv. Even-Keel Type Sub. Scientific Drawing $3750
Lake, Veronica	1919-73	Entertainment	175			338	Actress
Laker, Freddie, Sir		Business	5			20	Airline President
Lakes, Gary		Entertainment	10			30	Opera
LaLanne, Jack		Entertainment	10	15		20	TV Body Builder
Lalique, Rene	1860-1929	Artist	150		600		Fr. Jeweler & Decorative Glass Artisan
Lamar, Joseph R. (SC)		Supreme Court	35	95	225		
Lamar, Lucius Q.C. (SC)	1825-93	Supreme Court	82		235		CSA Officer, US Sen.
Lamar, Mirabeau B.	1789-1859	Head of State	95	395			Pres., V.P. & Sec'y State Repub. of TX
LaMarck, Jean Baptiste de		Science	400	950	1000		Forerunner of Darwin
Lamarr, Hedy	1913-	Entertainment	40	75	100	103	40's Beautiful Glamour Girl & Inventor
LaMartine, Alphonse de	1790-1869	Author	90	205	225		Fr. Romantic Poet-Statesman
Lamas, Fernando		Entertainment	20	25	45	45	
Lamas, Lorenzo		Entertainment	9	10	20	25	
Lamb, Caroline, Lady	1785-1828	Celebrity			1395		
Lamb, Charles	1775-1834	Author	155	350	1025		Br. Essayist, Critic. Popularly Known as Elia
Lamb, Gil		Entertainment	8			20	Stage-Film Dancer, Comic
Lambert, Christopher		Entertainment	6			35	Actor. Highlander SP $45
Lambert, Ray		Celebrity	5	14		10	
Lambert, William C.		Aviation	75	135	175	150	ACE, WW I, 2nd Leading Ace
Lamm, Richard D.		Governor	5	26			CO Gov.
Lammers, Hans		Military	95	650			Nazi Official. Hitler Legal Advisor
Lamond, Frederic		Composer	25		82	120	Scot. Pianist & Composer
Lamont, Corliss		Activist	10		25		Author. Indicted for Contempt of Congress
Lamont, Daniel S.		Cabinet	15	25	40		Sec'y War, Journalist, Politician

NAME	DATE	CATEGORY	SIG	LS/DS	ALS	SP	COMMENTS
Lamont, Forrest		Entertainment	25			65	Opera
Lamont, Robert P.		Cabinet	25	60	95		Sec'y Commerce
Lamont, Thomas		White House	15	30	45		Cleveland's Pvt. Sec'y
Lamont, Thomas S.		Business	8	25	40	10	Banker. Morgan Guaranty
Lamour, Dorothy	1914-96	Entertainment	10	25	25	125	Pin-Up SP $35, $55
Lamphier, Thomas G., Jr.		Aviation	40	70	120	125	ACE, WWII, Shot Down Yamamoto
Lampton, Mike		Astronaut	7			15	
Lamson, C.M.		Clergy	10	10	20		
Lana,Cosmo Gordon		Clergy	10	15	25		
Lancaster, Burt	1910-94	Entertainment	47	130		136	Rugged Leading Film Leading Man. Oscar Winner
Lance, Bert		Business	3	5	15	10	Banker
Lanchester, Elsa		Entertainment	50			65	Eccentric English Actres Wife Of Chas. Laughton
Land, E. S.		Military	25	65		35	Adm. Maritime Comm. WW II
Land, Edwin H.	1909-1992	Science-Business	80	225		175	Polaroid Camera Inventor
Landau, Lev	1908-68	Science					Russ. Physicist . '62 Nobel. TMsS $650
Landau, Martin		Entertainment	10			45	AA. As Dracula $75
Lander, Frederick West		Civil War	180	225	475		Union Gen.ALS/Cont.'61 $1375
Landers, Ann		Columnist	8	20	30	10	Advice Column
Landers, Audrey		Entertainment	6	8	15	15	
Landers, Judy		Entertainment	5	6	15	15	Pin-Up SP $25
Landesberg, Steve		Entertainment	5			20	
Landi, Bruno		Entertainment	15			60	Opera
Landi, Elissa		Entertainment	45	30	60	70	Vintage
Landis, Carole	1919-48	Entertainment	100			214	Suicide at 29
Landis, Jessie Royce		Entertainment	25			75	
Landis, John		Entertainment	15			25	Film Director Blues Brothers, Am Werewolf
Landis, Kenesaw Mountain		Jurist	200	450		525	And 1st Baseball Commissioner. HOF
Landon, Alfred M.	1887-1987	Governor	27	95	110	50	Rep. Pres. Candidate vs FDR. Gov. KS
Landon, Melville D.		Journalist	20				(aka Eli Perkins) Columnist
Landon, Michael		Entertainment	100	188		268	Actor-Writer-Dir. Little House…, Bonanza
Landowska, Wanda	1879-1959	Entertainment	155		350	295	Pol-Fr Harpsichordist-Composer
Landrieu, Moon		Cabinet	6		15	10	Sec'y HUD
Landry, Robert B.		Military	15			25	Gen'l. Air Aide to Pres. Truman
Landseer, Charles		Artist	30		75		R.A. & Keeper of Royal Academy
Landseer, Edwin H., Sir	1802-1873	Artist	35	65	260		Extraordinary Landscape-Animal Painter
Landseer, John		Artist	25		125		Father of Edwin H.
Landseer, Thomas		Artist-Engraver	25	40	75		Brother of E.H.
Landsteiner, Karl, Dr		Science	50	90	210		Nobel Medicine
Lane, Abbe		Entertainment	15			20	Vocalist. Mrs.Xavier Cugat. Pin-Up SP $15
Lane, Allan Rocky		Entertainment	65			250	Cowboy-Actor
Lane, Christy		Entertainment	5	6	15	15	Gospel Singer
Lane, Diane		Entertainment	10	15		20	Actress
Lane, Evelyn		Entertainment	10			25	Brit. Actress. Vintage
Lane, Franklin K.		Cabinet	25	40		25	Sec'y Interior
Lane, Harriet		First Lady, Actg.	125	250	688		Actg. 1st Lady, Buchanan. RARE

NAME	DATE	CATEGORY	SIG	LS/DS	ALS	SP	COMMENTS
Lane, James H. (WD)		Civil War-Congress	172	450	540		Special DS $7,500
Lane, James H.	1814-1866	Civil War-Congress	85	135	302		Sen. KS, Union Gen.,Suicide
Lane, James Henry	1833-1907	Civil War	65	200	335	950	CSA General
Lane, Joseph		Governor	40	75	130		Gov. OR Terr.& 1st US Sen.
Lane, Lola		Entertainment	15	15	30	25	
Lane, Nathan		Entertainment	15			55	Stage, Screen Actor-Comedian. Tony Award
Lane, Priscilla		Entertainment	12	15	25	25	
Lane, Rosemary		Entertainment	15	15	35	35	
Lang, Anton		Entertainment	25	25	45	40	Play Christ in the Passion Play.
Lang, Cosmo Gordon		Clergy	25	35	45	35	
Lang, Fritz	1890-1976	Entertainment	154	375		188	Ger. Innovative Film Director
Lang, June		Entertainment	10				Actress
Lang, K D		Country Music	20	20		75	
Lang, Rosa		Entertainment	4	4	9	10	
Lang, Sebastian		Entertainment	19	25	45	45	
Lang, Walter		Entertainment	20			45	Film Director. 40 Year Vet.
Langan, Glenn		Entertainment	8	15	35	25	
Langdon, Harry		Entertainment	100			225	
Langdon, John		Rev. War	210	400	1575		Continental Congr.,Gov. NH, Signer Const'n
Lange, David		Head of State	5	15	30	15	New Zealand
Lange, Hope		Entertainment	10			30	Pin-Up SP $30
Lange, Jessica		Entertainment	14	38		35	AA Actress. King Kong SP $75
Lange, Ted		Entertainment	5			15	
Langella, Frank		Entertainment	15			40	Actor. Films-Stage
Langer, Will		Senate	10	35			Senator ND
Langford, Frances		Entertainment	8			20	Big Band Vocalist-Films
Langley, Samuel P.	1834-1906	Aviation	205	535	462	350	1890's Aeronautical Pioneer, Astronomer
Langlie, Arthur		Governor	12	20		15	Governor Washington
Langmuir, Irving		Science	30	75	145		Nobel Chemistry 1932
Langtry, Lily	1852-1929	Entertainment	215	450	565		Actress & Mistress of Edw. VII. Jersey Lily
Lanier, Sidney	1842-81	Author	300	590	1165		Most Important So. Poet of Time. ALS/Cont $2400
Lannes, Jean		Fr. Revolution	675				Marshal of France
Lansbury, Angela		Entertainment		28			Br. Star of Stage-Screen-TV
Lansing, Robert		Cabinet	40	125			Sec'y State
Lansky, Meyer	1902-83	Gangster	200	1375			Jewish Mob Boss
Lantieri, Rita		Entertainment	5	5		20	Opera
Lantz, Walter*	1900-94	Cartoonist	60	85	125	118	Honorary Academy Award Woody Woodpecker
Lanza, Mario	1921-1959	Entertainment	175			795	Tragic Teno-Cinema Star. Early Death.3x5 SP $375+
LaPlace, P.M.,Marquis de	1749-1827	Science	535				Fr. Astronomer, Mathematician
Lapoype, J.F.C., Baron		Fr. Revolution	20		125		
Larch, John		Entertainment	6	10	15	10	Actor
Larcom, Lucy		Author	15	25	45		
Lardner, Dionysius	1793-1859	Author	45	175	245		Irish writer on Sci. & Math.
Lardner, James L.	1802-91	Civil War	40	95	145		Union Naval Commodore. Sig/Rank $60, DS $170
Lardner, Ring	1885-1933	Author	65	195	310	80	Am. Humorist, Social Satirist

NAME	DATE	CATEGORY	SIG	LS/DS	ALS	SP	COMMENTS
Lardner, Ring Jr.	1915-	Author	10	20	35	15	Screenwriter. 'M.A.S.H.' One of 'Hollywood Ten'.
Laredo, Ruth		Entertainment	15	15	30	35	
Largent, Steve		Congress	5			20	Oklahoma. Star Football Player. MOC OK
Larmouth, Kathy		Entertainment	4	4	9	9	
LaRocca, D.J. Nick		Musician-Composer	50			225	AMusQS $250
LaRosa, Julias		Entertainment	5			10	Singer Arthur Godfey Show
LaRoushe, Lyndon, Jr.		Pres. Candidate	20		35	25	Tax Evader
Larrey, Dominick Baron		Fr. Revolution	45	155	310		
Larroquette, John		Entertainment	10			30	
Larsen-Todsen, Nanny		Entertainmnt	20			65	Opera
Larson, Gary*		Cartoonist	20			100	Far Side
Larson, Leonard, Dr.		Science	5	15	30	10	
LaRue, Lash		Entertainment	5	6	15	25	
Lasker, Mary		Business	5	10	15	10	
Lasky, Jesse L.		Business	40	75	150	75	Pioneer Film Producer
Lasser, Louise		Entertainment	5	20		20	Character Actress-Comedian
Lassiter, William		Military	20	120	145	40	General WW I Under Pershing.TLS/Cont. $250
Laswell, Fred*		Cartoonist	25			150	B.Google & Snuffy Smith
Latham, Hubert		Aviation	25	35	90	75	
Latham, Louise		Entertainment	4			20	Current Character Actress
Lathrop, George P.		Author	20	50	150		Am. Journalist, Writer
Latour-Maubourg,M.V.N.F.		Napoeonic Wars	20		75		Cavalry Gen.
Latourette, Kenneth Scott		Clergy	20	30	45	30	
Latrobe, Benjamin H.	1764-1820	Artist		462	1400		Am. Arch. of the White House
Latrobe, Benjamin Henry		Civil Engineer	85				Important DS re Westward Expansion of U.S. $550
Lattimore, Richard		Author	10	15	25	15	
Lattler, Herman		West	70		165		Pioneer & American Indian Photographer of Note
Laubach, Frank C.		Clergy	35	50	90	60	
Lauck, Chet		Entertainment	10				Radio. Lum & Abner
Lauder, Estee		Business	10			30	Cosmetics
Lauder, Harry, Sir	1870-1950	Entertainment	60	90	145	125	Vintage Scottish Comedian-Singer
Laughton, Charles	1899-1962	Entertainmnt	85	230		258	Brit. Actor. Versatile & Fine. Oscar Winner
Lauper, Cyndi		Entertainment	25	35	85	60	Rock
Laurance, John		Rev. War	15		90		
Laurants, Arthur		Author	5			20	Playwright
Laurel, Stan & Hardy, Oliver		Entertainment	700			1459	SP (PC) $650-$1050, SP 5x7 $850
Laurel, Stan	1890-1965	Entertainment	130	469	525	406	Br.-Am Stage-Screen Comic Actor
Lauren, Dyanna		Entertainment				36	Porn Queen
Lauren, Ralph		Business	10	15	40	25	Fashion Designer.
Laurencin, Marie	1885-1956	Artist	125		450		Fr. Painter & Printmaker
Laurens, Henry	1724-92	Rev. War	1225	2003	1975		Pres. Continental Congress. SC Merchant
Laurie, Piper		Entertainment	6	8	15	20	Pin-Up SP $30
Lausche, Frank J.		Governor	12	20		15	Governor OH
Lauter, Harry		Entertainment	5			15	
Lauterbach, Johann Christoph		Entertainment		95	195		Ger. Violinist

NAME	DATE	CATEGORY	SIG	LS/DS	ALS	SP	COMMENTS
Lavi, Daliah		Entertainment	4			10	Pin-Up SP $10
Lavin, Linda		Entertainment	5	6	15	15	
Lavoisier, Antoine L. de	1743-94	Science	400	3625			Fr. Founder Modern Chemistry
Law, Andrew Bonar		Head of State	30	80	135		Br. Prime Minister
Law, Evander McIvor	1836-1920	Civil War	100	250	568		CSA Gen.
Law, George H.		Clergy	10		15	20	
Law, John	1671-1729	Reformer	150				Scot. Economist. LS/Cont.$5000
Law, John Phillip		Entertainment	5			15	
Law, Ruth		Aviation	30			100	
Lawden, Frank O.		Celebrity	4	12	30		
Lawes, Lewis E.		Law Enforcement	20	40	120	25	Prison Warden. Sing Sing
Lawford, Betty	1910-60	Entertainment	15	25		30	Brit. Actress. '25 Film Debut. ....Sherlock Holmes
Lawford, Peter	1923-84	Entertainment	20			62	Collected as Member of Sinatra's Rat Pack
Lawler, Michael K.	1814-82	Civil War	30	95			Union Gen. ALS '61 $360
Lawless, Lucy		Entertainment	11			64	Xena, Warrior Princess. Pin-Up $65
Lawrence, 1st Baron		Head of State	10	30	75		India
Lawrence, Abbott	1792-1855	Congress	25				MA. Financier. Lawrence MA
Lawrence, Barbara		Entertainment	5			20	
Lawrence, Carol		Entertainment	5	6	15	15	
Lawrence, D(avid) H(erbert)	1885-1930	Author	225	688	2991		Br. Novelist.Lady Chatterley's Lover
Lawrence, David L.		Governor	17	20			Governor PA
Lawrence, Elliot		Entertainment	20			40	Big Band Leader. Multiple Emmys
Lawrence, Ernest O.	1901-58	Science	100	275	400	200	Nobel Physics 1939. Invented Cyclotron.
Lawrence, Gertrude	1902-52	Entertainment	20	50		55	Major Br. Actress. 1st Star of 'King and I'(Stage)
Lawrence, Herbert A., Sir		Military	10	30	50	25	
Lawrence, Jacob	1917-	Artist	15	30		30	Afro-Am. Painter, Educator. Print S $100
Lawrence, John		Colonial Am.	35	90	175		CT Statesman, Rev. War Leader
Lawrence, Marc	1910-	Entertainment	10	15	25	25	Stage Actor.Films-'33. Swarthy Pock Marked Villain
Lawrence, Marjorie		Entertainment	15			90	Australian Opera, Concert Soprano
Lawrence, Rosina	1914-98	Entertainment	20			55	Late Silent & Early Sound Film Star. Our Gang
Lawrence, Sharon		Entertainment	10			25	NYPD Blue
Lawrence, Steve		Entertainment	6	8	10	15	
Lawrence, Thomas, Sir	1769-1830	Artist	150	225	200		Br. Portr. Painter. Pres. Royal Academy
Lawrence, Thos. E.	1888-1935	Author-Soldier	650	1250	4525	2917	Lawrence of Arabia
Lawrence, Tracy		Country Music	5			25	Singer
Lawrence, Vicki		Entertainment	5	6	15	15	
Lawrence, Wendy		Astronaut	8			25	
Lawrence, William	1819-99	Congress	8				Repr. OH, Union Colonel
Lawson, James M.		Clergy	20	25	35	25	
Lawson, Ted		Aviation	15	30		40	
Lawton, Alexander R. (WD)		Civil War	195	718	900		CSA Gen.
Lawton, Alexander R.	1818-96	Civil War	110	350	311		CSA Gen.
Laxalt, Paul		Senate/Congress	4	10		15	Governor, Senator NV
Lay, Herman W.		Business	10	25	50	30	Lay's Potato Chips
Lay, Philidda		Entertainment	3			8	Actress

NAME	DATE	CATEGORY	SIG	LS/DS	ALS	SP	COMMENTS
Layard, Austin Henry, Sir	1817-94	Archaeologist	28	40	450		Br. Diplomat. Excavator of Nineveh
Lazarev, Alexander		Conductor				65	Former Bolshoi Maestro
Lazaro, Hippolito		Entertainment					Opera. Tenor
Lazarus, Emma	1849-87	Author		2300			The New Colossus
Lazarus, Mel*		Cartoonist	5			20	Miss Peach, Momma
Lazarus, S. Ralph		Business	4	7	10	5	Pres.Benrus Watch.Philanthropis
Lazenby, George		Entertainment	10	15	30	58	
Lazzari, Virgillo		Entertainment	15			45	
Lea, Homer		Military	55	175			Predicted US-Jap. War/HI as Key
Leachman, Cloris		Entertainment	9	25	15	20	A A
Leadbetter, Danville		Civil War	150	475			CSA General
Leahy, Patrick		Senate/Congress	5	15		10	Senator VT
Leahy, William Daniel		Military	35	145	105	195	Chief of Staff-FDR & Truman
Leake, J. B.		Civil War	20	55	75		
Leakey, Louis B.		Science	45	125	225	65	Anthropologist, Archaeologist
Leakey, Mary D.		Science	15	25	70	30	Anthropologist, Archaeologist
Leakey, Meave, Dr.		Science	20	60			
Leakey, Richard, Dr.		Science	125				Br. Anthropologist
Lean, David, Sir		Entertainment	45			70	Film Director
Leander, Zarah		Entertainment	35			150	Opera
Lear, Edward	1812-88	Artist	140		809		Br. Painter & Nonsense Poet
Lear, Norman		Business	10	15	45	20	TV Film Producer
Lear, Tobias		Rev. War	75	240	325		Pvt. Secretary to G. Washington
Lear, William P. Sr.		Business	35	125	195	200	Lear Jet Aircraft Founder
Learned, Michael		Entertainment	9	10	20	25	
Leary, Timothy, Dr.	1920-96	Activist-Educator	25	60		40	Drug Cult Leader, Psychologist. Acid Print S $225
Lease, Mary Elizabth		Reformer	15	20	40		Orator, Writer Woman Suffrage
Leavelle, James R.		Legal	20			85	Detective Handcuffed to Oswald when Shot
Leavenworth, Henry		Military	250		750		Frontier Soldier, General
LeBlanc, Matt		Entertainment	20			70	Actor.. Friends
LeBrock, Kelly		Entertainment	10	15		35	Pin-Up SP $40
Lebrun, Albert	1871-1950	Head of State	30	50	125	35	Last Pres. 3rd French Repub.
Lebrun, Chas. F. Duc de	1739-1824	Napoleonic Wars	35	100	150		3rd Consul/Bonaparte
LeCarre, John (David Cornwell)		Author	20	45	75	30	Br. Realistic Spy Novels
Lecuona, Ernesto	1896-1963	Composer	150			635	AMusQS $400-$600
Led Zeppelin (all-org.)		Entertainment	250			700	Alb.Cover Signed $850
Lederer, Francis		Entertainment	10			25	
Lederman, Leon M., Dr.		Science	15	25	50		Nobel Phyics
Ledoux, Harold*		Cartoonist	5			25	Judge Parker
Ledyard, John	?-1771	Colonial America		70			Merchant, Justice of Peace. Progenitor of Line
Ledyard, John	1751-89	Explorer		475			Accompanied Capt. Cook. Wrote Adventures.
Lee, Alfred		Clergy	10	15	35		
Lee, Anna		Entertainment	5			15	
Lee, Bernard		Entertainment	15			25	
Lee, Brandon	1964-93	Entertainment	325	1138		775	Son of Bruce Lee. Tragic Death

NAME	DATE	CATEGORY	SIG	LS/DS	ALS	SP	COMMENTS
Lee, Brenda		Country Music	5			15	
Lee, Bruce	1940-73	Entertainment	567	1040	1275	1012	Legendary Cult Celeb
Lee, Canada		Entertainment	60			188	Afro-Am Actor. McCarthy Era Victim
Lee, Charles	1731-82	Military			3318		Turncoat Gen. Rev. War
Lee, Charles	1758-1815	Cabinet	110	250	550		Washington's Att'y Gen.
Lee, Christopher		Entertainment	20			49	Best Known for Role in Dracula
Lee, Dixie (Mrs Bing Crosby)		Entertainment	10	15	25	25	
Lee, Dr. Tsung-Dao		Science	20	30	45	25	Nobel Physics
Lee, E. Hamilton		Aviation	10	25	50	35	
Lee, Edwin G.		Civil War	165	290	410		CSA Gen.
Lee, Fitzhugh (WD)		Civil War	240		600		CSA Gen.
Lee, Fitzhugh	1835-1905	Civil War	150	258	310	480	CSA General. AQS $595, TLS/Cont. $575
Lee, Francis Lightfoot		Rev. War	660	1050	4250		Signer Decl. of Indepen.
Lee, Geo. Wash. Custis	1832-1913	Civil War	183	590	410		CSA General
Lee, Geo. Wash. Custis (WD)		Civil War	270		2500		CSA Gen.
Lee, Gordon Porky		Entertainment	25			35	Little Rascals
Lee, Gypsy Rose	1913-1970	Entertainment	100	167		565	Burlesque Queen & Sometimes Movie Star
Lee, Harper	1926-	Author	110	350		500	To Kill a Mocking Bird Pulitzer. Elusive Signer
Lee, Heather		Entertainment				35	Porn Queen
Lee, Henry	1756-1818	Rev. War	220	1250	767		Light-Horse Harry. Gen'l Revolution'y War
Lee, Henry, Sir	1533-1611	Knight	125		500		Model Knight to Queen Elizabeth I
Lee, Jason Scott		Entertainment	5			25	Actor. Jungle Book SP $35
Lee, Lila		Entertainment	5	6	15	15	
Lee, Mark C.		Astronaut	7			25	
Lee, Mary Custis		Civil War	135		690	475	Mrs. Robert E. Lee
Lee, Michele		Entertainment	5	6	15	15	
Lee, Peggy		Entertainment	10	22		30	Singer-Composer
Lee, Pinkie	1916-93	Entertainment	15			30	Vaudeville & Early TV Comedian, Kid Shows
Lee, Richard Henry	1732-94	Rev. War	275	2350	4058		Signer Decl. of Indepen.
Lee, Robert E. (WD)		Civil War	3825	14567	23125	7645	As CSA Gen. Auction $23K-$36,000
Lee, Robert E.	1807-70	Military	2967	5619	9056	6875	CSA Cmmdg. Gen. Mex. City 1848 ALS/Cont $25000
Lee, Ruta		Entertainment	4			10	Pin-Up SP $10
Lee, Samuel P.		Civil War	60	210	275		Union Adm.
Lee, Spike		Entertainment	10	25		25	Afro-Am Film Director
Lee, Stephen Dill (WD)		Civil War	250	1800			CSA Gen.
Lee, Stephen Dill	1833-1908	Civil War	120	345	384		CSA Gen.
Lee, Tenghui		Head of State	25			55	President Republic of China (Taiwan)
Lee, Tommy		Entertainment	20			50	Rock
Lee, William H.	1837-91	Civil War	185		630		CSA Gen.,ALS War Date/Cont.. $6050
Lee, William Raymond		Civil War	15	45	70		Union General
Lee, Yuan T., Dr.		Science	20	35	45	30	Nobel Chemistry
Leeb, Wilhelm R. von		Military	20		135		
Leech, John	1817-1864	Artist	70	125	138		Br. Caricaturist-Illustrator. Orig. Piece S $875
Leech, Richard		Entertainment	15			30	Opera
Leeds, Andrea		Entertainment	10			25	

NAME	DATE	CATEGORY	SIG	LS/DS	ALS	SP	COMMENTS
Leeds, Peter	1917-96	Entertainment	5	20			Actor. Appeared in over 8,000 TV shows
Leese, Oliver, Sir		Military	20	50		35	Br. Gen. WW II/Montgomery. 8th Army
Leestma, David C.		Astronaut	5			20	
Lefebvre, F.J., Duke		Fr. Revolution	160	300			Marshal of Napoleon
Lefevre, Edwin		Financial Writer	4	8	15		Panamanian Ambass. to Spain
Leftwich, John W.		Senate/Congress	10	15	30		MOC TN 1866
LeGallienne, Eva		Entertainment	5	25	50	35	
LeGallienne, Richard		Author	35	50	162		Brit. Man of Letters
LeGarde, Tom and Ted		Country Music	10			20	
Leger, Fernand		Artist	80	240	575		Fr. Abstract Painter. AMsS $2750
Leggett, Mortimer Dormer		Civil War	20	40	65		Union General
Legrand, Michel		Composer	5	45	25	20	
Leguizamo, John		Entertainment	6			35	Versatile Movie Performer
LeHand, M. A. (Missy)	1898-1944	Gov't Exec. Aide	20	80	130	40	FDR Personal Sec'y 20 Years
Lehar, Franz	1870-1948	Composer	100	225	590	345	The Merry Widow. AMusQS $225, SP Pc $295
Lehman, Herbert H.	1882-1963	Governor	10	58		25	Gov. NY, Senator NY
Lehmann, Ernst August		Aviation	85		365		Ger. Aeronautical Engineer
Lehmann, Lilli	1848-1929	Entertainment	175		100		Ger. Soprano. 170 Operatic Roles
Lehmann, Lotte	1888-1976	Entertainment	50	75	158	195	Ger. Opera. Magnificent Soprano. SPc $80-$135
Lehmann, Marie		Entertainment	50			175	Ger. Prima Donna. Mother Lilli
Lehr, Lew		Entertainment	15	15	35	30	
Leibman, Ron		Entertainment	5	6	15	15	
Leider, Frida		Entertainment	35			150	Opera. Great Brunhilde
Leiferkus, Sergei		Entertainment	10			25	Opera
Leigh, Janet		Entertainment	5	9	15	20	Pin-Up SP $25
Leigh, Jennifer Jason		Entertainment	15			85	
Leigh, Mandy		Entertainment	3			18	Actress Pin-Up $40
Leigh, Richard		Composer	5	18			
Leigh, Vivien (As Scarlett O'Hara)		Entertainment				1775	SP Pc $750-$1750
Leigh, Vivien	1913-67	Entertainment	414	575	587	824	Brit. Actress. Oscar Winner. SP Pc $575
Leigh, Vivien and Laurence Olivier		Entertainment	300	712		1200	
Leighton, Frederic, Baron	1830-1896	Artist	25	90	150		Pres. Br. Royal Academy. Painter, Sculptor
Leighton, Laura		Entertainment	12			65	Actress. Melrose Place
Leighton, Margaret		Entertainment	15			40	
Leik, Hudson		Entertainment	8			40	Actor. Xena Pin-Up $70
Leinsdorf, Erich		Conductor	15			120	Austro-Amer Conductor
Leisure, David		Entertainment	5			10	
Lejeune, John Archer		Military	35	75	150	75	Commandant US Marine Corps
Leland, Henry M.	1843-1932	Business	875	1783			Contract Creating Lincoln Motor Co. S $1200
Leland, W. C.		Business	20	55	140	40	
Leloir, Luis Frederico		Science	20	40	45	25	Nobel Chemistry
Lelong, Lucien		Designer	25				Fashion, Cosmetics
Lelouch, Claude		Entertainment	9	10	20	25	
LeMaire, Charles		Entertainment	15			25	Director
Lemass, Sean		Head of State	10	25	60	30	Prime Minister Ireland

NAME	DATE	CATEGORY	SIG	LS/DS	ALS	SP	COMMENTS
LeMay, Curtis E.	1906-1990	Military	30	110		75	AF Gen. WW II. 200th Air Force, SAC
Lembeck, Harvey		Entertainment	30			75	
Lembeck, Michael		Entertainment	3	3	6	10	
Lemeshev, Sergei		Entertainment				500	Opera. Russ. Tenor of Soviet Era. RARE
Lemmon, Jack		Entertainment	10	14	50	31	AA. DS $75-$200
Lemnitz, Tiana		Entertainment	40			125	Opera
Lemnitzer, Lyman L.	1899-1988	Military	30	40	90	45	Supreme Allied Commd'r WW II. 7th Inf. Korea
Lemon, Mark	1809-70	Author	15		35		Br. Playwright, Humorist, Co-Founder Punch
Lenin, Vladimir Ilyich (N.Lenin)		Head of State					ALS/Content $29,000
Lennon Sisters, The (4)		Entertainment	20			45	
Lennon, John	1940-1980	Entertainment	600	1770		1498	Assassinated Beatle
Lennon, Julian		Entertainment	20			40	
Lennox, Vera		Entertainment	12			20	Br. Actress
Lenny Kravitz		Entertainment	35			90	Music. Rock Group
Leno, Jay		Entertainment	10			35	Self Caricature S $75
Lenoir, William B.		Astronaut	7			20	
Lenormand, Ren,	1846-1932	Composer	30			175	Songs, String & Piano Music
Lenox, Lucie		Entertainment	15			40	
Lenske, Rula		Entertainment	4	4	9	15	
Lenya, Lotte		Entertainment	20	60		150	Cabaret Singer, Character Actr.
Leonard, Ada		Entertainment	20			70	Big band leader
Leonard, Elmore		Author	15			25	Author of Get Shorty, many other novels
Leonard, George		Jurist	40	100			Colonial Am. Jurist
Leonard, Gloria		Entertainment	5	6	15	15	
Leonard, Jack		Entertainment				25	Singer/Tommy Dorsey Orch.
Leonard, Jack E.		Entertainment	5			10	Comedian
Leonard, Sheldon		Entertainment	5	6	15	15	
Leoncavallo, Ruggiero	1858-1919	Composer	175	448	510	675	AMusQS $750, $850, $925, $1200
Leone, Sergio	1921-89	Entertainment	55			347	Master of Spaghetti Western.Fistful of Dollars
Leone, Tia		Entertainment	8			30	Actress. Pin-Up 45
Leonov & Gagarin							SEE Gagarin
Leonov, Aleksei	1934-	Cosmonaut	120	155		212	Rus. Cosmonaut, 1st Space Walker
Leontif, Wassily, Dr.		Economist	20	35		40	Nobel Economics
Leontovich, Eugenie		Entertainment	15		30	45	
Leopardi, Giacomo		Author	80	350	475		Physically Deformed Italian Poe
Leopold (Prince)		Royalty				512	Duke of Albany. Q.Victoria's 4th Son. Hemophiliac
Leopold I		Royalty		1900			King of Hungary & Bohemia, Holy Roman Emperor
Leopold II		Royalty	65	325	540		Belgium
Leopold III	1901-83	Royalty	80		175		King Belgium. Queen Astrid Tragic Death
Leopold V	1586-1633	Royalty		250			Archduke of Austria 1619-33. Papal Bishopric 1625
Leopold, Nathan F.	1905-71	Criminal	512	310	575	150	Am. Criminal Convicted of Murder. Loeb & Leopold
Lerher, Jim		Journalist	3			12	Broadcast News. Radio/Tv
Lermontov, Mikhail	1814-1841	Author	540	2300	4625		Novelist, Poet. Killed in Duel
Lerner, Alan Jay	1918-96	Composer	45	95	175	175	Am. Lyricist, Librettist/Loewe
Lerner, Max		Author	5	30	40	10	

NAME	DATE	CATEGORY	SIG	LS/DS	ALS	SP	COMMENTS
LeRoy, Hal	1914-85	Entertainment	12			20	Tap Dancer. Director
LeRoy, Mervyn		Entertainment	50	65		75	Top Hollywod Film Director-Prod. Wizard of Oz
Leslie, Frank	1821-80	Publisher	95				Founder Illustrated Newspaper
Leslie, Frank, Mrs.		Publisher	20		75	75	Leslie's Magazine
Leslie, Joan		Entertainment	6	8	15	19	
Leslie, Preston H.		Governor	10	15			Governor KY
Leslie, Thomas J.	1796-1874	Civil War	10		35		Union Gen. Paymaster's Dept. 50 Years
Lesseps, Ferdinand, de	1805-94	Engineer	148	744	462	700	Engineer& Diplomat. Promoted Suez Canal
Lester, Buddy		Entertainment	3	4	10	15	
Lesters, The (5)		Entertainment	10			25	Gospel Singers
Leszczynski, Stanislaus		Royalty	575				Stanislaw I, King of Poland
Letcher, John	1813-84	Civil War	85	250	225		CW Gov. VA, ALS/Cont. $2,500
Letterman, David		Entertainment	20	65		40	Comedian. TV Late Show CBS
Letterman, Jonathan		Civil War	95	175			Med. Services for CW Union Army
Leutze, Emanuel		Artist	75		320		Washington Crossing Delaware
Levant, Oscar		Entertainment	75			95	Pianist, Caustic Humorist, Actor, Author
Levene, Sam		Entertainment	10			20	
Levenson, Sam		Entertainment	10	35		15	Radio, TV Comic
Leventhrope, Collett	1815-89	Civil War	90	165	1150		CSA Gen.
Lever, Asbury		Senate/Congress	5	10		5	MOC SC
Lever, Lord (Wm. Hesketh)		Business	30	100	190	60	Br. Soap Mfg. Lever Brothers
Leverett, John	1662-1724	Colonial	50	130	275		President of Harvard, Judge
Levi, Edward H.		Cabinet	7	25	45	10	Att'y General
Levi-Civita, Tullio	1873-1941	Science	50		250		Italian. Math. Helped Found Differential Calculus
Levi-Montalcini, Rita, Dr.		Science	20	65			Nobel Medicine
Levi-Strauss, Claude	1908-	Science	25				Belg.-Fr. Anthropologist. Legion d'Honneur 1991
Levin, Ira		Author	25	35		30	Rosemary's Baby
Levine, David*		Cartoonist	15			100	Caricaturist
Levine, Irving R.		TV News	4	10		5	Commentator
Levine, Jack		Artist	10	15	35		Color Print Repro $100
Levine, James		Entertainment	7	10	35	25	Conductor
Levinson, Barry		Entertainment	5			20	
Levy, David H.		Science	15			20	Discovered Meteor Crater
Lewellyn, Anthony		Astronaut	5	16		15	
Lewinsky, Monica		Presidential Aid	38			75	Monica's' Story' BS Monica $150. Full Sig. $195
Lewis, (Percy) Wyndham	1882-1957	Artist-Writer	60		356		Br. Painter & Writer
Lewis, Al		Entertainment	10			30	
Lewis, C(live) S(taples)	1898-1963	Author	310	575	1520		Br. Medievalist, Philosopher, Scholar
Lewis, David 'Duffy'		Aviation	15	30	55	40	
Lewis, Drew		Cabinet	10		20	15	Sec'y of Transportation
Lewis, Edwin		Clergy	15	20	30		
Lewis, Emmanuele		Entertainment	6	8	15	15	
Lewis, Francis	1713-1803	Rev. War	375	1600	2500		Signer Decl. of Indepen.
Lewis, Geoffrey		Entertainment	4			10	Actor
Lewis, Gwilym H.		Aviation	20	45	80	55	

NAME	DATE	CATEGORY	SIG	LS/DS	ALS	SP	COMMENTS
Lewis, Huey (And the News)		Entertainment	12			30	Rock. Sports Alb. S by Lewis $30
Lewis, J.C.		Entertainment	12			25	Blues Drummer
Lewis, James		Entertainment	15	15	30	25	
Lewis, Jarma		Entertainment	5			12	Actress
Lewis, Jerry	1926-	Entertainment	9		20	30	Comedian-Actor. Signed Lobby Cards $45
Lewis, Jerry Lee		Country Music	30			70	And Rock. DS re Shindig $225
Lewis, Joe E.		Entertainment	20	30	45	42	Nightclub Comedian
Lewis, John	1940-	Activist	5	15			Civil Rights Leader.Sit-Ins-Freedom Rider. Injured
Lewis, John L.	1880-1969	Labor	40	68	195	105	AFL-CIO Labor Leader. TLS/Cont.$275
Lewis, Juliette	1973-	Entertainment	20			50	Actress
Lewis, Kerrie McCarver		Entertainment	4			8	Mrs. Jerry Lewis
Lewis, Meriwether	1774-1809	Explorer	4500	5500	5738		Lewis & Clark Expedition
Lewis, Monica		Entertainment	10			30	Singer-Actress. Big Band Singer. Records
Lewis, Morgan		Rev. War	50	70	110		Gen.Gates Chief of Staff. Gov.
Lewis, Ramsey		Entertainment	25			50	Pianist-Composer
Lewis, Richard		Entertainment	5			20	Stand-up Comic-Actor
Lewis, Robert Q.	1921-92	Entertainment	10			45	Radio-TV Star. Game Show Host. Actor
Lewis, Shari	19xx-98	Entertainment	10	16	15	48	Comedian-Pupeteer. Deceased
Lewis, Sheldon	1868-1958	Entertainment	30			55	Actor. Title RoleDr. Jekyll & Mr. Hyde 1916 Film
Lewis, Sinclair	1885-1951	Author	100	325	665	300	1st Am. Awarded Nobel for Lit.
Lewis, Ted		Entertainment	20	25		75	Bandleader-Entertainer.Me & My Shadow
Lewis, Vera		Entertainment	50				Character Actress
Lewis, William Arthur, Sir		Science	20	25	40	25	Nobel Economics
Lewis, William H.		Aviation	10	22	40	28	ACE, WW II
Lewishon, Ludwig		Author	20		25		Ger.-Born Author of 31 Books
Lewisohn, Adolph		Business	20	45	65	25	Mining, Investment
Lewitt, Sal		Artist	25			100	
Ley, Bob		TV News	5			10	ESPN News
Ley, Willy		Science	25	75	145	35	Rocker Expert, Sci-Fi Writer
Libby, Willard F.		Science	20	35	55	25	Nobel Chemistry
Liberace	1919-87	Entertainment	50	200		144	Sig/Piano Sketch $75-$95-$125
Liberace, George		Entertainment	8	15		15	Violinist Brother of Lee Liberace
Liberman, Evsei, Prof.		Celebrity	15	35		20	
Lichtenberg, Byron, Dr.		Astronaut	10			20	
Lichtenstein, Roy	1923-98	Artist	35	65	145	62	Repro S $175, $225
Lichty, George	1905-83	Cartoonist	10		25		'Grin and Bear It'
Liddell, Henry George		Clergy	20	35	40	45	
Liddy, G. Gordon		Gov't Official	5	20	50	30	Lawyer, Watergate,Convicted
Lie, Jonas		Author	15	40	60		Nor. Novelist, Dramatist
Lie, Trygve	1896-1968	Head of State	50	150	250	175	Norwegian 1st Sec'y Gen'l U.N. His Bible S $475
Liebenow, William F.		Military	50			295	PT Boat Cmdr. Who Rescued JFK
Lieber, Fritz		Entertainment	35			100	
Liebermann, Max	1847-1935	Artist	75		250		Ger. Impressionist Painter. Orig. Pen Sketch $650
Liebig, Justus von,	1803-73	Science	185		925		Discovered Chloroform.ALS/Content $1,750
Lienart, Archille, Cardinal		Clergy	30	40	50	40	

NAME	DATE	CATEGORY	SIG	LS/DS	ALS	SP	COMMENTS
Lifar, Serge		Entertainment	15			80	Opera
Liggett, Hunter		Military	75	125		35	Am. Gen. WW I
Liggett, Louis Kroh		Business	85	170	350		Liggett's Drug Store Chain
Light, Enoch		Entertainment					Big Bandleader-Violinist
Light, Judith		Entertainment	12	15	25	30	
Lightner, Candy		Celebrity	12	30		20	1st Pres. MADD
Lightner, Winnie		Entertainment	19	25	45	45	
Ligi, Josella		Entertainment	5			25	Opera
Ligonier, John	1678-1770	Military	25				Br. Field Marshall of Queen Anne
Liles, Brooks		Aviation	8	20	38	22	ACE, WW II, USAAF Ace
Lilienthal, David E.		Business	15	30		20	Co-Fndr. I.J. Fox, Furriers
Lilienthal, Otto	1848-96	Inventor	150		2600		Aeronautical Eng'r , Author
Liliuokalani, Lydia K.	1838-1917	Royalty	200	450	955	475	Queen Hawaii. Last Monarch of Hawaii. Deposed
Lillie, Beatrice	1894-1989	Entertainment	25		70	65	Br. Comedienne. WW II Entertainer
Lillie, Gordon W. (Pawnee Bill)	1860-1942	Entertainment	125	1182	1145	400	Buffalo Bill Partner. DS/Cody $3500
Lilly, Eli		Pharmaceuticals			1500		Pioneer Am. Manufacturer.Founder Eli Lilly & Co.
Liman, Arthur		Celebrity	4	12		2000	
Limbaugh, Rush		Radio/TV	20			50	Radio/TV Commentator
Lin, Y. S. Maya		Artist	25	100			Designed Viet Nam Wall
Lincke, Paul		Composer	70	185	325		AMusQS $675, Glow Worm
Lincoln, Abraham (As Pres.)		President	3083	8992	12470	24550	Brady SP $50,000.
Lincoln, Abraham (As Pres.)		President					FF $3500-$6800. ALS 16,000-35000
Lincoln, Abraham	1809-1865	President	3150	7146	9067		ALS '48 $101,500.ALS '64 $288,500.ADS $25,875
Lincoln, Benjamin	1700-	Justice of Peace	45	160			Father of Gen. Lincoln
Lincoln, Benjamin	1733-1810	Cabinet-Military	125	200	888		Gen. Rev. War.Sec'y War
Lincoln, Elmo		Entertainment	475			1500	
Lincoln, Evelyn		Gov't Official	15	25		35	JFK Presidential Sec'y
Lincoln, Joseph		Author	13	20	30		Writer of Cape Cod Stories
Lincoln, Levi	1749-1820	Cabinet	35	85	120		Memb. Continental Congr. Early Att'y General
Lincoln, Mary Todd		First Lady	300	985	6425	3000	FF on Mourning Env. $3700,$3,900, $4600
Lincoln, Robert Todd	1843-1926	Cabinet	80	252	612		Capt. CW. Sec'y War.Minister to Eng. LS/Cont. $750
Lincoln, Rufus		Rev. War		1650			Present at Burgoyne Surrender
Lind, Don L.		Astronaut	6			20	
Lind, Jenny (Goldschmidt)	1820-87	Entertainment	70	175	382	885	Concert, Opera. Called Swedish Nightingale
Lindberg, Charles W.		Military	25	85		40	One of 6 Iwo Jimo Flag Raiser
Lindbergh, Anne Morrow		Author	15	45	150	30	Am. Writer-Poet.
Lindbergh, Charles A.	1902-74	Aviation	580	1220	3125	2550	ALS/Content $7,500. 1st Fl. Cover S $975-$2750
Linden, Eric		Entertainment	25			75	GWTW (Amputation Case)
Linden, Hal		Entertainment	4	20		15	
Linderman, H. R.		Civil War	10		25		Civil War Dir. of U.S. Mint.
Lindfors, Viveca		Entertainment	12			40	
Lindholm, Berit		Entertainment	10			25	Opera
Lindley, Audra		Entertainment	4			10	
Lindsay, E. Lin		Aviation	10	22	38	30	ACE, WW II, USAAF Ace
Lindsay, Howard		Entertainment	10	15	25	25	Theatrical Producer

NAME	DATE	CATEGORY	SIG	LS/DS	ALS	SP	COMMENTS
Lindsay, John		Politician	4	8		10	Lawyer, Author, Mayor NYC
Lindsay, Margaret		Entertainment	15	25	45	50	Leading Lady. 30's-40's
Lindsay, Vachel		Author	50	185	575	125	Poet, Artist, Prairie Troubado
Lindsey, Ben B.		Law	15				Jurist
Lindsey, George		Entertainment	6	8	15	19	
Lindstrom, Pia		Entertainment	3			15	Actress. TV News. Daughter Ingrid Bergman
Linenger, J.M.		Astronaut	8			25	
Liney, John*		Cartoonist				50	Henry
Linkletter, Art		Entertainment	10	25		15	Radio-TV MC. Master of the Interview
Linn, Archibald L.	1802-57	Congress	10				Repr. NY, County Judge
Linn-Baker, Mark		Entertainment	5			15	
Linnaeus, Carolus von	1707-78	Science	925	7500			Carl vonLinne.Swe. Botanist.
Linnehan, Richard		Astronaut	5			20	
Linville, Larry		Entertainment	10			25	
Liotta, Ray		Entertainment	20			58	
Lipchitz, Jacques		Artist	130	210	225		Pol.-Fr.-Am. Cubist Sculptor
Lipfert, Helmut		Aviation	35			70	#15 World Highest ACE. Ger.
Lipkovska, Lydia		Entertainment	75			325	Rus. Soprano
Lipman, Clara		Entertainment	12			20	Stage Actress
Lipmann, Fritz A.		Science	25	45	70	30	Nobel Medicine 1953
Lipovsek, Marjana		Entertainment	10			30	Opera
Lippman, Walter		Author	25	75		30	Journalist, Editor, Pulitzer
Lipps, Lisa		Entertainment	6			35	Adult Star
Lipscomb, William N., Dr.		Science	20	35		30	Nobel Chemistry
Lipsner, B.B.		Aviation	30	65		90	Pioneer Air Mail Pilot
Lipton, Peggy		Entertainment	4	4	9	15	
Lipton, Thomas, Sir	1850-1940	Business	132	455	1350	405	Br. Tea Merchant-Yachtsman
Lisa, Manuel		Celebrity	763				
List, Emanuel		Entertainment	35			95	
List, Eugene		Entertainment	20			75	
Lister, Joseph, Lord	1827-1912	Science	188	435	709		Pioneer of Antiseptic Surgery. 1st Baron
Liston, Robert	1794-1847	Science	15	30	50		Skilled Scottish Surgeon
Listowell, Earl of		Philosopher	20				Viscount Wm. Francis Hare
Liszt, Franz	1811-86	Composer	410	650	1540	1895	Hung.-Born. Pianist. AMuQS $3,800,AMMsS $16,750
Litchfield, Grace D.	1849-1944	Author	5		25		
Litel, John	1892-1964	Entertainment	15	15	35	35	
Lithgow, John		Entertainment	5	6	15	20	Third Rock From the Sun
Litjens, Stefan		Aviation	7	15	25	20	
Little Richard (Penniman)		Entertainment	15	20	45	110	Rock. DS re Lease of Master Recordings $150
Little River Band		Entertainment	25			50	
Little, Cleavon		Entertainment	13			35	
Little, Little Jack		Entertainment	15			35	Big Band Leader
Little, Rich		Entertainment	3			10	
Little, Royal		Business	22		55		
Littlejohn, Abram N.		Clergy	10	20	35		

NAME	DATE	CATEGORY	SIG	LS/DS	ALS	SP	COMMENTS
Littlejohn, Dewitt C.		Civil War	40	85	120		Union General
Litvak, Anatole		Entertainment	20			45	Film Director
Litvinov, Maksim M.		Diplomat	50		95	65	Soviet Foreign Minister
Liu, Lucy		Entertainment	7			42	Actress. Ally McBeal Co-Star
Liu-Li Pei		Entertainment	10			25	Chinese Opera Star
Livermore, Dan'l P.		Clergy	15	20	45		
Livermore, Mary A.	1820-1905	Reformer	40	75	175		Woman Suffrage, Temperance
Liverpool,R.B. J., 2nd Earl		Head of State	72	178	200		Robt. Banks Jenkinson, P.M. 1770-1828
Livingston, Alan		Composer	15	55			
Livingston, Edward P.	1764-1836	Cabinet	30	91	175		Jackson's Sec'y of State 1831
Livingston, Henry B. (SC)		Supreme Court	100	310			
Livingston, Jay		Composer	15	45	100	40	AMusQS $35-$100-$300-$375 (Silver Bells)
Livingston, John H.		Aviation	110			150	Premier Racing Pilot. Entered 139. 79 1st, 43 2nd
Livingston, Margaret		Entertainment	10			25	
Livingston, Mary		Entertainment	15	25	45	40	
Livingston, Peter Van Brugh		Rev. War		275			Patriot, Merchant
Livingston, Philip	1716-1778	Rev. War	290	1120	1175		Signer Decl. of Independ. Etc. NY Merchant
Livingston, Robert		Entertainment	20			85	Known for 30's-40's Western Roles
Livingston, Robert	1742-94	Rev. War	170	350	400		Dir. Bank of the U.S. (1792)
Livingston, Robert R.	1746-1813	Rev. War	195	440	1250		Cont.Congr. Administered Pres. Oath To Washington
Livingston, Robert R., Sr.	1718-75	Law		500			Att'y, Judge. Opposed Stamp Act.
Livingston, William	1723-90	Rev. War	300	888	1750		Continental Congr. Gov. NJ
Livingstone, David	1813-1873	Explorer-Clergy	225	885	1350		Missionary, Explorer of Africa. Author
Llewellyn, Anthony		Astronaut	10			30	
Lloyd, Christopher		Entertainment	10	15	28	30	
Lloyd, Emily		Entertainment	10			40	
Lloyd, Frank AA		Entertainment	20	50			Film Director AA
Lloyd, Harold	1894-1971	Entertainment	156	225		309	Film Comedian-Actor. Silent Into 30's
Lloyd, James	1769-1831	Senate/Congress	30	65	90		Senator MA 1808
Lloyd, Kathleen		Entertainment	4	4	9	15	
Lloyd, Norman		Entertainment	4	4	9	10	
Lloyd-George, David	1863-1945	Head of State	64	372	425	265	Br. Prime Minister WW I, 1st Earl
Lo Giudici, Franco		Entertainment	40			150	Opera
Loan, Nguyen Ngoc		Military	150			375	Gen. Viet Nam
Loasby, Arthur W.		Business	5	20			Wall Street Banker
LoBianco, Tony		Entertainment	6	8	15	15	
Locane, Amy		Entertainment	15			35	Actress. Melrose Place
Locke, D. R.		Journalist					SEE Nasby, Petroleum
Locke, John	1632-1704	Author	700	1950	5000		Br.Philosopher. LS/Cont.$12,500
Locke, Sandra		Entertainment	10		20	25	
Locke, William John		Author	20	35	75	30	Br. Novelist
Lockhart, Gene		Entertainment	20			50	Film Character Actor. 30's, 40's
Lockhart, June		Entertainment	5		20	22	Child Actress to Present. 'Lassie', 'Lost in Space
Lockheed, Alan		Aviation	80	150	300	150	Pioneer Aviator, Plane Designer
Locklear, Heather		Entertainment	10	20	30	51	Actress.

NAME	DATE	CATEGORY	SIG	LS/DS	ALS	SP	COMMENTS
Locklin, Hank		Country Music	10			55	Country Star
Lockwood, Belva A.	1830-1917	Women's Rights	225	325	733		1st Woman to Practice Before Supr. Ct. AQS $360
Lockwood, Chas.W, Capt		Civil War	100				1st MN to Enlist, Last Survivor
Lockwood, Gary		Entertainment	5			20	Actor 2001
Lockwood, Margaret	1916-90	Entertainment	12	20	55	55	Br. Film Actress
Lockyer, Herbert		Clergy	25	35	45		
Lodge, Henry Cabot	1850-1924	Senate	30	160	158	95	MOC 1887, Senator MA 1893. Editor, Lecturer
Lodge, Henry Cabot, Jr.		Senate	20	42	95	25	Ambassador UN, Diplomat, VP Candidate
Lodge, Oliver J., Sir	1851-1940	Science	83	135	225	250	Br. Physicist, Spiritualist
Loeb, William		Business	10	25	55	35	
Loesser, Frank		Composer	120		450		Composer of Top Broadway Hits. Movie Hits
Loew, Marcus		Business	30	40	65	35	
Loewe, Frederick	1901-88	Composer	38	75	145	55	AMusQS $220-650-895. My Fair Lady, Camelot
Loewy, Raymond		Business	35	90	140	75	Designer
Lofting, Hugh	1886-1947	Author	95				& Illustrator Dr. Dolittle Books. S Illustr. $195
Loftus, Cissie (Cecilia)	1876-1943	Entertainment	35	65		175	Br. Actress. Vaudeville, Stage, Musical & Film Star
Logan, Benjamin	1752-1802	Military	350	560	675		Pioneer Hero, Indian Fighter
Logan, Ella		Entertainment	10			25	Pop Singer. Band Vocalist. 'A Tiskit A Taskit....'
Logan, John A. (WD)		Civil War	95	345	1195		Union Gen.
Logan, John A.	1826-86	Civil War	88	282	260		Union Gen., Father Memorial Day. Founder G.A.R.
Logan, Josh(ua)	1908-88	Entertainment	20	40		45	Film & Stage Producer, Writer, Director
Logan, Olive		Author	25	35			
Logan, Thomas M.	1840-1914	Civil War	95	225	422		CSA Gen.
Loggia, Robert		Entertainment	6			20	
Loggins and Messina		Entertainment	25		50	50	
Loggins, Kenny		Entertainment	10	40		25	
Loisy, Alfred		Clergy	20	25	35		
Lollobrigida, Gina		Entertainment	12	15	30	57	Pin-Up SP$35
Lom, Herbert		Entertainment	22			43	Character Actor
Lomax, Lunsford Lindsey		Civil War	100	275	375		CSA General
Lomb, Henry	1828-1908	Science-Business		2600			Ger. Born Am. Optician. Co-Founder Bausch & Lomb
Lombard, Carole	1908-42	Entertainment	350	750	1100	750	Died in Air Crash 1942. DS $750
Lombardo, Guy	1902-77	Entertainment	20	75	120	104	Big Band Leader. Royal Canadians
London, Charmian		Celebrity	40			155	2nd Wife of Jack London
London, George		Entertainment	35			70	Opera, Concert, Met.
London, Jack	1876-1916	Author	215	1319	2350	1400	Am. Novelist, Adventurer. Suicide at 40
London, Julie		Entertainment	10			20	Vocalist-Actress. Recording Artist
London, Tom		Entertainment	50			100	
Long, Armistead L.	1825-91	Civil War	85	100	370		CSA Gen.
Long, Earl K.		Governor	20	30		25	Governor LA,
Long, Huey P.		Senate	85	185		175	Sen., Gov. LA. Assassinated
Long, John D.		Cabinet	12	30	40	20	Sec'y Navy, Governor MA
Long, Johnny		Bandleader	25			50	Big Bandleader. Violinist
Long, Lotus		Entertainment	5			30	Actress-Oriental Dancer
Long, Pierse	1739-89	Rev. War	30	75	180		Continental Congress

NAME	DATE	CATEGORY	SIG	LS/DS	ALS	SP	COMMENTS
Long, Richard		Entertainment	20			50	
Long, Russell	1918-	Senate/Congress	5	20		10	Senator LA. Son of Huey Long
Long, Shelley		Entertainment	12	30	25	35	Actress 'Cheers'. Pin-Up SP $35
Longacre, James B.	1794-1869	Engraver	140	950	400		Chief Engraver of the U.S. Mint
Longet, Claudine		Entertainment	8		35	25	
Longfellow, Henry W.	1807-82	Author	217	390	594	1095	Poet, Harvard Prof. AMsS $2295, AQS $500
Longfellow, Samuel		Clergy	40	50	75	55	
Longfellow, Stephen	1775-1849	Senate/Congress	20	50	145		MOC ME 1823
Longley, Charles T.	1794-1868	Clergy	25				Archbishop Canterbury
Longley, James B.		Governor	9	15			Governor ME
Longstreet, James (WD)		Civil War	850		6517		CSA Gen.
Longstreet, James	1821-1904	Civil War	430	1250	1456	922	CSA General. Important ALS $7500. 1pg ALS $750
Longworth, Alice Roosevelt		Pres. Daughter	20	25	100	40	
Longworth, Nicholas		Congress	15	65	85		Speaker of the House, Son-in-law of T. Roosevelt
Loo, Richard		Entertainment	20			55	
Loomis, Gustavus	1789-1872	Civil War	30	65	105		Union General
Loos, Anita		Author	17	55	75	30	Am. Novelist, Film Scripts
Loos, Walter		Aviation	10	20	35	25	
Loper, Don		Business	5	15	35	10	Fashion Designer
Lopez, Jennifer		Entertainment	12			55	Actress. Pin-Up $65
Lopez, Vincent		Entertainment	20			55	Big Band Leader-Pianist
Lopez-Alegria, Michael		Astronaut	5			20	
Loraine, Robert		Aviation	15		55		
Lorca, Frederico Garcia		Author	440	1240	3150		Sp. Poet, Dramatist
Lord, Daniel, Rev.		Clergy	10			35	
Lord, E.J.		Congress	10		30		Senator CA
Lord, Herbert M.		Military	10	25			
Lord, Jack		Entertainment	30	150		78	Hawaii 5 0. Check S $100
Lord, John Wesley, Bishop		Clergy	20	35	45	45	
Lord, Marjorie		Entertainment	20			30	Danny Thomas Show
Lord, Phillips H.		Entertainment	20		35		Writer-Producer. Radio
Lord, Walter		Author	4		10	10	
Lords, Traci		Entertainment	10	15	30	39	Pin-Up SP $65. Nude $130
Loren, Sophia		Entertainment	15	30		38	Pin-Up SP $50. SP from Two Women $315. AA
Lorengar, Pilar		Entertainment	25			40	Opera
Lorenz, Konrad	1903-1989	Science	62	275			Austrian Biologist
Lorillard, Peter		Business	125	260	475		Tobacco Industry
Lorimar, George C.		Clergy	20				Author
Loring, Gloria		Entertainment	10		15	15	
Loring, Israel		Clergy	25	75	125		
Loring, Lisa		Entertainment	5			15	Actress
Loring, William Wing (WD)		Civil War	180		745		CSA Gen.
Loring, Wm. Wing	1818-86	Civil War	120	255	315	425	CSA General
Lorne, Marion		Entertainment	100			225	Broadway Character Actress-Comedian. TV-Films
Lorre, Peter	1904-64	Entertainment	181	595		448	Hungarian Character Actor. Maltese Falcon etc...

NAME	DATE	CATEGORY	SIG	LS/DS	ALS	SP	COMMENTS
Losch, Tilly		Entertainment	10			65	3x5 SP $35
Losey, Joseph		Entertainment	15			60	Film Director
Losigkeit, Fritz		Aviation	12	15	30	20	
Lossing, Benson		Author	15	30	50		Am.Historian, Engraver
Lott, Felicity		Entertainment	15			30	Opera
Lott, Trent		Congress	12			25	Republican Majority Leader. Sen. MS
Loubet, Emile Francois	1838-1929	Head of State			125		Pres. France 1899-1906
Louge, Mike		Astronaut	8			26	
Loughlin, Lori		Entertainment	5			40	Actress
Louis II of Bavaria	1845-86	Royalty		900			King from 1864
Louis II of Monaco	1870-1949	Royalty	30		180	80	Prince of Monaco
Louis Philippe (Fr)	1773-1850	Royalty	75	215	350		Citizen King. Duc D'Orleans
Louis XI (Fr)		Royalty		3500			Earliest Collectible King of France 1461-1483
Louis XII (Fr)		Royalty	800	1750	4200		King of France
Louis XIII (Fr)		Royalty	750	1475	4000		King of France
Louis XIV (Fr)		Royalty	450	1225	3750		The Sun King
Louis XV	1710-74	Royalty	750	1595	5500		King of France
Louis XVI	1754-93	Royalty	375	1152			King of France. Guillotined
Louis XVIII (Fr)	1755-1824	Royalty	200	466	1680		Louis Stanislas Xavier
Louise Caroline Alberta, Princess		Royalty	25		65	175	4th Daughter of Queen Victoria
Louise Vict.(Alex. Dagmar)	1867-1931	Royalty	20		90	170	Princess Royal. Daughter Edw. VII
Louise, Anita		Entertainment	15			45	Frail Leading Lady. Films 40's-50's
Louise, Tina		Entertainment	9	18		25	Pin-Up SP $30. Gilligans Island
Lounge, John M.		Astronaut	10			20	
Lousma, Jack F.		Astronaut	10	20		35	
Love, Bessie		Entertainment	35		55	70	Vintage Actress
Love, Courtney		Entertainment	6			40	Actress. Pin-Up $55
Love, John A.		Governor	5	12		10	Governor CO
Love, Montagu		Entertainment	20			50	Vintage Character Actor
Love, Mother		Entertainment	4			10	Comedienne
Love-Hewitt, Jennifer		Entertainment	8			45	Actress. Pin-Up $75
Lovecraft, H. P.		Author	220	300	785	550	Reclusive Horror Story Writer
Lovejoy, Frank		Entertainment	25			50	Successful Radio Actor to Leading Roles in Films
Lovejoy, Owen		Clergy-Congress	15	30	45		MOC IL 1857-64
Lovelace, Linda		Entertainment	25			60	Porn Queen
Loveless, Patty		Entertainment	15			35	Singer
Lovell, Bernard Dr.		Science	15	25	40	20	
Lovell, James	1737-1814	Rev. War	50	195	500		Continental Congress, Politician, Patriot
Lovell, James A. Jr.	1928-	Astronaut	35	100		125	Cmmdr. of Aborted Apollo 13.Cont. TLS $375
Lovell, Mansfield (WD)		Civil War	185	560	850		CSA Gen.
Lovell, Mansfield	1822-84	Civil War	100	250	290		CSA Gen.
Loverboy		Entertainment	25			50	Music
Lovett, John	1761-1818	Senate/Congress	40		135		War 1812. ALS/Content $300
Lovett, Lyle		Country Music	20			60	Popular Country Music Singer
Lovett, Robert		Cabinet	5	10	25	10	Sec'y Defense

NAME	DATE	CATEGORY	SIG	LS/DS	ALS	SP	COMMENTS
Lovkay, John		Business	4			10	CEO Hamilton Standard
Lovrenich, Rodger T.		Business	4	9	15	10	Inventor of electronic ignition
Low, Abiel Abbot	1811-	Shipbuilder		110	175		Packet & Clipper Ships. Merchant, Civil War
Low, David, Sir*		Cartoonist	15	45	110	140	NZ-Br Political.'Colonel Blimp'
Low, Frederick F.		Governor	45		175		Gov, MOC CA 1860, Diplomat
Low, G. David		Astronaut	8			20	
Low, Nicholas		Rev. War	105	245	450		Prominent NY, Backed Revolution. Merchant
Low, Seth	1819-1916	Mayor NYC	10	35	45		Merchant, Pres. Columbia Univ.
Lowe, Al		Author	10	12	25	18	Creator of Leisure Suit Larry
Lowe, Ed		Inventor	20			45	Kitty Litter
Lowe, Edmund		Entertainment	25	30	60	45	Handsome Leading-Man 30's-40's Films
Lowe, Hudson, Sir		Military		723	500		Last custodian of Napoleon. Gov. St. Helena
Lowe, Rob		Entertainment	17	35		38	Actor
Lowe, Thaddeus S. C.		Civil War	210	325	500		Aeronaut, Inventor, CW Balloonist
Lowell, Amy	1874-1925	Author	35	125	250		Am. Poet,Critic., Imagist School
Lowell, Carey		Entertainment	5			20	
Lowell, James Russell	1819-91	Author	45	148	213	375	Poet.Hall of Fame, Educator, Editor, Diplomat
Lowell, John H.		Aviation	15	25	40	35	ACE, WW II
Lowell, Joshua A.	1801-74	Congress	10		45		MOC ME, Dem. Presidenial Elector
Lowell, Percival	1855-1916	Science	15	40	65		Am. Astronomer, Author. Brother of A.L. & Amy
Lowell, Robert	1917-77	Author	42	412	185		Am. Poet. (2) Pulitzers 'Lord Weary's Castle'
Lowenstein, Allard		Congress	75			175	Dump Johnson Movement. Assassinated
Lowery, John		Senate/Congress	10	15		15	
Lowery, Robert		Entertainment	75	125		125	Actor. 'Batman' Serial
Lowman, Seymour	1868-1940	Cabinet	5	10			Ass't Sec'y Treas., Lt. Gov. NY
Lown, Bert		Entertainment	10			20	Bandleader. Bye Bye Blues
Lowry, Robert		Governor	10	25			Governor MS
Loy, Myrna	1905-93	Entertainment	24	40	50	61	SP as Nora Charles (Thin Man) $100
Lubbers, Bob*		Cartoonist	10			70	Tarzan
Lubbock, Francis R.	1815-1905	Civil War	150	195	295	350	CSA Governor TX. Aide-de-camp Jeff. Davis
Lubbock, Sir John	1834-1913	Statesman-Author	10	22	42		Br. Banker. Author Science-Fiction Books
Lubin, Arthur		Entertainment	25			65	Film Director
Lubin, Germaine		Entertainment				275	Opera. Legendary Fr. Soprano. RARE
Lubitsch, Ernst	1892-1947	Entertainment	55		275	185	Ger.-Am. Vintage Film Director
Lubke, Heinrich	1885-1972	Head of State	10		30	50	Pres. Ger. Fed. Repub.
Lucas, Clyde		Entertainment	15			25	Bandleader
Lucas, Edward Verrall		Author	3		15	8	
Lucas, George		Entertainment	28		108	89	Film Director. 'Star Wars'
Lucas, John P.		Military	70	150		350	General. Cmdr. 4th Army WW II
Lucca, Pauline		Entertainment	30	70	100		Opera
Lucci, Susan		Entertainment	8	10	15	20	Oft Nominated Soap Star & Finally Winner 1999
Luccock, Halford E.		Clergy	20	35	50	40	
Luce, Clare Boothe		Author	30	125	175	45	Ambassador, Playwright, Congresswoman
Luce, Cyrus G.		Governor	5	15	25		Governor MI
Luce, Henry R.		Publisher	40	115	225	55	Time, Life, Fortune, Sports Illustrated

NAME	DATE	CATEGORY	SIG	LS/DS	ALS	SP	COMMENTS
Luce, Stephen Bleecker	1927-1917	Military	15	35	95	40	Admiral. !st Pres. Naval War College
Lucid, Shannon W.		Astronaut	10			50	Set New Space Record
Luckinbill, Laurence		Entertainment	22		40	50	Actor. Active in Star Trek Films
Luckner, Felix, von	1881-1966	Military	172	252	280	120	The Sea Devil WW II. Sank 14 Allied Ships $195
Luckner, Nicholas		Fr. Revolution	225	675			Marshal of Fr. Guillotined
Lucon, L. J., Cardinal		Clergy	45	55	75	60	
Ludde-Neurath, Walter		Military	15	45		45	Aide-de-camp to Donitz
Ludendorff, Erich von	1865-1937	Military	100	225	300	275	Ger. Gen. WW I, Politician
Ludin, Hanns		Military	130	350			Ger. Gen.-Storm Trooper WW II
Ludlington, Marshall I.		Civil War	65	135	195		Union General
Ludlum, Robert		Author	10	25	35	20	Super Spy novels
Ludwig I	1786-1868	Royalty	65	340	450		King of Bavaria
Ludwig II		Royalty	55	255	470		King of Bavaria
Ludwig, Emil		Author	40	125	200		
Lufbery, Raoul		Aviation	125	350	590	400	ACE, WW I, Lafayette Escadrille
Lufburrow, W.A.		Political	5	25			Southern Racist Leader.
Luft, Lorna		Entertainment	12		10	19	Singer Sister of Liza Minelli. Daughter of Judy
Lugar, Richard G.		Congress	5	25			Sen. IN
Lugosi, Bela	1882-1956	Entertainment	333	1375		1567	Hung-Born. Career Playing Dracula
Luhan, Mabel Dodge		Author			388		
Lujan, Albert		Artist	20		45		
Lukas, Foss		Composer	20			75	Versatile Ger./Am./Composer/Conductor
Lukas, Paul	1895-1971	Entertainment	50			100	AA Winner. 'Watch on the Rhine'
Luke, Frank		Aviation	150	400	600	500	ACE, WW I, MOH, #3 U.S. Ace
Luke, Keye		Entertainment	20			50	#1 Son' in Charlie Chan Films
Luks, George Benjamin	1867-1933	Artist	20	55	200		Member Ashcan School.
Lulu Belle (& Scotty)		Entertainment	10				C & W Music. Popular Duo. 40's-50's
Lum & Abner		Entertainment	40			95	Top Radio Comedy Pr-30's.Chester Lauk-Norris Goff
Lumet, Sidney		Entertainment	15			40	TV Director-Dramatist
Lumholtz, Carl		Celebrity	3	8	20		
Lumiere, Louis	1862-1954	Inventor	175		565	375	Cinematographe Projector
Lumley, Carl		Entertainment	3			8	
Lumley, Joanna		Entertainment	15			22	
Luna, Barbara		Entertainment	5			10	Actress
Lunceford, Jimmie		Entertainment	35			140	Big Band Leader-Arranger
Lund, John		Entertainment	5		15	15	Warner Bros. 40's-50's Leading Man
Lunden, Jason		Entertainment	5			30	Actor
Lunden, Joan		TV Host	10			20	TV Host & Special Assignments MC
Lundgren, Dolph		Entertainment	15			35	Actor. Super Hero & Villain
Lundigan, William		Entertainment	15			30	Handsome Leading Man 40's-50's
Lunn, George R.	1873-1948	Congress	4	15			MOC. NY
Lunney, G.		Astronaut	10			20	
Lunt, Alfred & Fontanne, Lynne		Entertainment	75			125	Popular Stage Couple30's-. DS Idiot's Delight $650
Lupino, Ida	18xx-1995	Entertainment	17	70	75	65	Br-Am Actress, Director
Lupino, Stanley	1893-1942	Entertainment	15			35	Br. Comedian. Father of Ida

NAME	DATE	CATEGORY	SIG	LS/DS	ALS	SP	COMMENTS
Lupton, John		Entertainment	10			20	
Luria, Salvador F.		Science	20	35	55	25	Nobel Medicine
Lurie, Bob		Business	10	25	45	15	
Luse, Harley		Country Music	10			20	
Luther, Hans		Head of State	35	55	85	55	Chancellor Ger., Ambass. US
Luther, Martin		Clergy	12500	30000	46688		LS/Extremely Rare $49,500 (Prices Estimated)
Lutyens, Edw. Landseer, Sir	1869-1944	Architect	20	45			Br. Designed Cenotaph in London. Br. Embassy U.S.
Lutzi, Gertrude		Entertainment	15			30	Opera
Lutzow, Gunther		Aviation	175		445	450	
Lvov, Alexis F.	1798-1870	Composer	100		200		Rus. Commissioned by Czar. Russ. Nat'l Anthem
Lyautey, Louis	1854-1934	Military	20	40	105	40	Marshal of Fr., Statesman
Lyell, Charles, Sir	1797-1875	Science	95		425		Br. Founder of Modern Geology
Lyle, The Great		Entertainment	25			50	Vintage British Magician
Lyman, Abe		Bandleader	15			45	Big Band
Lyman, Charles Edwin		Clergy	15	25	50	30	
Lynch, David		Entertainment	20			50	Movie-TV Director.' Twin Peaks'
Lynch, John R.		Congress		250			Former Slave. MOC MS 1873-77, '82-'83
Lynch, Kelly		Entertainment	10			40	Actress. Pin-Up SP $75
Lynch, Thomas Jr.		Rev. War	5565				Rare Signer Declaration of Independence
Lynde, Paul		Entertainment	14	20	25	18	Comedian from Original TV 'Tic Tac Dough'
Lynen, Feodor		Science	20	40		25	Nobel Medicine
Lynley, Carol		Entertainment	10	18	35	25	Actress. Pin-Up SP $40
Lynn, Porsche		Entertainment	5			20	Porn Queen
Lynn, Diana	1926-71	Entertainment	40			60	Actress. Talented Pianist. 'Bedtime for Bonzo'
Lynn, Ginger		Entertainment	5			20	Adult Film Star of 80's
Lynn, Jeffrey		Entertainment	9	10	20	15	40's Warner Bros. Leading Man
Lynn, Loretta		Country Music	6			15	Country Music
Lynn, Vera, Dame		Entertainment	30			112	Br. WW II Singing Star
Lyon, Ben	1901-79	Entertainment	25			40	Actor. Star Silents-Early Talkies. With RAF WW II
Lyon, Lucius	1800-51	Congress	15		35		Sen. & MOC. MI
Lyon, Mary Mason	1797-1849	Educator	55	165	340		Provided Women's Advanced Edu. Mt. Holyoke Coll.
Lyon, Nathaniel	1818-61	Civil War	350		1895		Union Gen. KIA. RARE
Lyon, Sue		Entertainment	10		22	25	
Lyonne, Natasha		Entertainment	5			25	Actress. Pin-Up $45
Lyons, Edmund, Lord	1790-1858	Military-Diplomat	50		252		Br, Admiral
Lyons, Judson W.		Public Office	30	125			1st Afr-Am Register of Treasury 1898-1906
Lyons, Rich'd B.P., 1st Earl	1817-87	Diplomat	35		125		Br. Minister to US in Civil War.
Lyons, William		Business	40	80	175		
Lytell, Bert		Entertainment	30	45	90	65	Vintage Actor. Stage. Migrated to Films
Lytton, E. George Bulwer	1803-73	Author	25	95	208		Novelist, Poet, Colonial Sec'y. 1st Baron

NAME	DATE	CATEGORY	SIG	LS/DS	ALS	SP	COMMENTS

M

NAME	DATE	CATEGORY	SIG	LS/DS	ALS	SP	COMMENTS
Ma, Yo Yo		Entertainment	35			100	Cellist Superstar
Maas, Melvin G.	1898-1964	Military-Congress	25			125	Marine Corps Gen. WW II. Blinded. MOC MN
Mabley, Jackie Moms		Entertainment	75			200	
MacArthur, Arthur		Military	45	90	155	70	CW Off'r, Sp.-Am. War. General
MacArthur, Charles		Author	15	30	55	25	Playwright Husband Helen Hayes
MacArthur, Douglas	1880-1964	Military	235	493	875	780	5* Gen. WW II.A.E.F. ID Card SP $8625. SP $1500
MacArthur, Douglas II		Diplomat	20			30	Ambassador to Japan. Nephew of the General
MacArthur, James		Entertainment	12		15	30	Actor Son of Helen Hayes. 'Hawaii 5-0'
MacArthur, Jean		Military	15	20	30	20	Mrs. Douglas MacArthur
Macartney, Clarence E.		Clergy	15	20	25	20	
Macartney, George		Head of State	10	35	85		
Macaulay, (Emilie) Rose, Dame		Author	10	20	35		Br. Novelist, Critic, Verse
Macaulay, Thos. B., Lord	1800-59	Author	45	65	102		Historian & Poet. Politician
Macbeth, Florence		Entertainment	20			50	Am. Soprano
MacChesney, Nathan Wm.		Celebrity	10	20	85		
Macchio, Ralph		Entertainment	15			30	Young Actor. 'Karate Kid'
MacCracken, Henry M.		Clergy	20	35	45	30	
MacDonald, Charles H.		Aviation	15	30	52	40	ACE, WW II
MacDonald, Cordelia H.		Entertainment	40	75	120		1st Eva in Uncle Tom's Cabin
MacDonald, George		Clergy	20	30	45		
MacDonald, George	1875-1961	Business	35				Public Utilities
MacDonald, J. Farrell		Entertainment	25			50	Char. Actor.SP as Detective in Maltese Falcon $495
MacDonald, J. Ramsey	1866-1937	Head of State	50	130	175	255	Twice Br. Prime Minister
Macdonald, Jacques E.J.A	1765-1840	Fr. Revolution	75	100	250		Marshal of Napoleon
MacDonald, Jeanette		Entertainment	70	185	225	162	Teamed With Nelson Eddy in Top Movie Hits
MacDonald, John Alexander		Head of State	35	90			Premier 1857, 1st P.M. Canada
MacDonald, Ross		Author	45	145	250		Mystery Writer
MacDonald, Torbet		Congress	10				MA. JFK Roommate & Lifelong Friend
Macdonogh, P. M. W.		Military	6	17	22		
MacDonough, Thomas	1783-1825	Military	95	290	700		Am. Naval Off'r. Tripoli, 1812
MacDougall, Clinton		Civil War	35	60			Union General
MacDowell, Andie		Entertainment	15			40	Col. Pin-Up 65
MacDowell, Edward	1861-1908	Composer	140	290	600	400	Songs, Concertos, Piano Pieces
MacDowell, Melbourne		Entertainment	15			40	Vintage Actor
Macfadden, Bernarr		Business	15	45	96	35	Physical Culturist, Publisher
Macfadyen, Dugald		Clergy	45	45	50	50	
MacGraw, Ali		Entertainment	6	12		20	Actress. Pin-Up SP $25
MacGregor, John 'Rob Roy'	1825-92	Philanthropist	12		50		And Traveller
Machado, Anesia Pinheiro		Aviation	35	55	80	65	
Machiavelli, Niccolo	1469-1527	Author	500	1250	4500		
MacInnes, Helen		Author	5	15	20		Am Best Selling Novelist

NAME	DATE	CATEGORY	SIG	LS/DS	ALS	SP	COMMENTS
Mack, Connie III		Senate	7	10		15	Senator FL
Mack, Helen		Entertainment	10			30	
Mack, Marion		Entertainment	10			35	
Mack, Ted		Entertainment	8			15	
Mackaill, Dorothy		Entertainment	20	30	70	65	Vintage Film Actress
MacKall, William W. (WD)		Civil War	250		1250		CSA Gen.
MacKall, William W.	1917-91	Civil War	110	305			CSA General
MacKay, Charles		Clergy	20	25	35		
Mackay, John William		Business	40	100	215		Founder Postal Telegraph Co.
MacKaye, Percy	1875-1956	Author	40	90	150		Am. Poet, Dramatist
Mackensen, August von		Military	12	25	40	85	Ger. Gen. Fld. Marshal WW I. RK
MacKenzie, Gisele		Entertainment	3	5	6	15	
Mackenzie, Morell, Sir		Science	60	165	350		Larygologist. Misdiagnosed
Mackie, Bob		Business	5	10	25	15	Fashion Designer
MacLachlan, Kyle		Entertainment	10			30	Picket Fences
MacLagan, William D., Bishop		Clergy	15	25	35		
MacLaine, Shirley		Entertainment	15	25	35	37	Pin-Up SP $45
Maclane, Barton		Entertainment	50			125	Vint. Tough Guy. Maltese Falcon etc.
MacLaren, Donald M.		Military	25	40	95	75	
MacLean, Steve		Astronaut	7	15		16	
MacLeay, Lachlan		Astronaut	7			15	
MacLeish, Archibald	1892-1982	Author	30	115	135	40	Am. Poet, Lawyer. 3 Pulitzers
MacLeod, Gavin		Entertainment	6	8	15	20	
Macleod, George F.		Clergy	20	25	30		
MacMahon, Aline		Entertainment	20			60	
MacMahon, Marie E.P.		Head of State	35	110	225		Fr. Soldier, Politician, Marshal
Macmillan, Donald B.	1874-	Explorer	67	75	170		Am. with Peary at North Pole
MacMillan, Harold	1894-1987	Head of State	30	85	262	300	Br. P.M.. Lord Stockton
MacMurray, Fred	1908-91	Entertainment	18	85		52	Major Film-TV Star. 40's-50's-60's etc.
MacNee, Patrick	1922-	Entertainment	15			32	Brit. Actor. John Steed in The Avengers
MacNelly, Jeff*		Cartoonist	30			200	Shoe
Macnelly, Jeff*		Cartoonist	5			100	Shoe
MacNider, Hanford		Military	3	9	15		
Macomb, Alexander	1748-1832	Business		98	115		Fur & Shipping Merchant. Associated/John J. Aster
Macon, Nathaniel	1758-1837	Congress	118	125			Sen. NC, Speaker of House, Rev. War Soldier
Macpherson, Elle		Cover Girl	10			25	Pin-Up SP $40
MacPherson, James B.		Civil War	117	240	335		Union General
MacRae, Gordon		Entertainment	15			30	
MacRae, Meredith		Entertainment	5			15	
MacRae, Sheila		Entertainment	3			12	
MacReady, George		Entertainment	20			40	
Macready, William C.	1793-1873	Entertainment	30		202		Foremost Br. Shakespearean Actor
MacVeagh, Franklin		Cabinet	10	25	60	20	Sec'y Treasury
MacVeagh, Wayne	1833-1917	Cabinet	65		98		Att'y Gen., Diplomat, CW Soldier
Macy, Bill		Entertainment	4			15	

NAME	DATE	CATEGORY	SIG	LS/DS	ALS	SP	COMMENTS
Macy, William J.		Entertainment	6			30	Actor. Pleasantville
Madden, Charles Edw.	1919-	Military	45	120	215	100	Brit. Adm.
Madden, John		Entertainment	4			15	Motion Picture Director
Maddox, Lester		Governor	25	40		30	Georgia Anti-Civil Rights Gov.
Madeira, Jean		Entertainment	18			52	Am. Contralto
Madero, Francisco I.		Head of State		3000			Revolutionary Pres. Mex. 1911-13
Madigan, Amy		Entertainment	10			40	
Madison, Dolley Payne	1768-1849	First Lady	750	1792	2635		Free Frank $750-850-1,200
Madison, Guy		Entertainment	6			25	
Madison, James & Monroe, James		Presidents	550	2145			Unusual DS $4500
Madison, James	1751-1836	President	340	1710	3293	2500	FF $695-$775-$925, ALS/Content. $7500
Madonna (Louise V.Cicone)		Entertainment	148			320	Unconventional Pop Female Star. Nude SP $350
Madriguera, Enric		Entertainment	15			30	Big Band Leader
Madsen, Chris		Pioneer Lawman		2750			Outlaw & Indian Fighter
Madsen, Michael		Entertainment	5			35	Actor
Madsen, Virginia		Entertainment	10			25	Pin-Up SP $35
Maeterlinck, Maurice, Count	1862-1949	Author	35	115	208	425	Nobel Literature.Pelleas and Melisand
Maffett, Debbie Sue		Entertainment	4	5	9	9	
Magee, John A.		Senate/Congress	10		35		MOC NY 1827. Banker, RR
Magee, Patrick		Entertainment	10			35	
Magee, Walter W.	1861-1927	Congress	12	25			Repr. NY
Magg, Alois		Aviation	4	9	16	15	
Magilton, Jerry		Astronaut	4			12	
Magnani, Anna		Entertainment	300			650	
Magnus, Kurt		Science				50	Rocket Pioneer. Peenemuende Team/USSR
Magnus, Sandra		Astronaut	7			25	
Magrath, Andrew G.	1813-93	Civil War	35	60	80		CSA Gov.SC. ALS '61 $150
Magritte, Rene' Francois	1898-1967	Artist	200	580	1007		Belg. Surrealist Painter.
Magruder, John B.	1807-71	Civil War	285	510	535		CSA Gen. Sig/Rank $450
Magsaysay, Ramon		Head of State	20	55	155	35	Pres. Philippines
Maguire, Tobey		Entertainment	7			38	Actor. Pleasantville
Maguire, W.A. Cpt.		Military	25	50	75	60	
Mahan, Alfred Thayer		Military	50	75	100		US Navy Off'r-Historian. CW
Maharis, George		Entertainment	10	25	25	20	Star of TV's Route 66 and Films
Mahen, Robert A.		Business	15	30	70	40	
Mahendra Bir Bikram		Royalty	35	50	135	50	King, Leader Nepal
Mahler, Alma		Author	20		125		Author & Wife Gustav Mahler
Mahler, Gustav	1860-1911	Composer	550	1260	3688	2430	Austrian Composer
Mahone, William	1826-95	Civil War	120	250	375		CSA General, US Senator VA, RR Stock $245
Mahoney, Jock		Entertainment	20	35	55	45	
Mahurin, Walker M. Bud		Aviation	15	35	55	40	ACE, WW II, Legendary Ace
Maiakovski, Vladimir V.		Author	300	795	2200		
Maikl, George		Entertainment	5			20	Opera
Mailer, Norman	1923-80	Author	25	137	193	75	Naked & the Dead Reprint Ed. Signed $50
Maillol, Aristide	1861-1944	Artist	200	460	762		Fr. Sculptor, Painter. Large Graceful Statues

NAME	DATE	CATEGORY	SIG	LS/DS	ALS	SP	COMMENTS
Main, Majorie		Entertainment	105			250	
Maintenon, F., Marquise de		Royalty			975		2nd Wife Louis XIV
Maison, Nicholas J.	1771-1840	Fr. Revolution	35	150	175		General under Napoleon
Maison, Rene'		Entertainment	25			52	Opera
Maitland, Lester J.		Aviation	20		40		
Major, John		Head of State	5			20	Br. Prime Minister
Majorana, Gaetano (Caffarelli)		Entertainment			3200		Legendary Male Soprano (castrato)
Majors, Lee		Entertainment	5	6	15	15	
Makarios III, Mikhail	1913-77	Clergy-Head State	50	65	140	125	Archbishop & Pres. Cyprus
Makarova, Natalia		Entertainment	10			15	Ballet
Mako		Entertainment	6			20	
Malamud, Bernard		Author	25	40	105	30	Am. Novelist, Pulitzer
Malcolm X (Little)	1925-65	Black Leader	200	3950	4272		TLS/Content $10,000-15,000
Malden, Karl		Entertainment	10	35		35	Actor. Important DS $250
Malenkov, Georgi M.	1902-1988	Head of State	160	350	800	250	Union Sov. Russia. Premier
Malet, C. Francois de		Fr. Revolution	120	240			Gen'l. Court-martialed, Shot
Malher, J.P.F.		Fr. Revolution	25	80			
Malik, Charles		Head of State	7	15	35	10	
Malik, Terrence		Entertainment	12			45	Movie Director. Thin Red Line
Malipiero, Gian-Francesco		Composer					Important 20th Cent.Comp.AMuQs $225
Malis, David		Entertainment	10			25	Opera
Malko, Nicolai	1833-1961	Entertainment	75		45	197	Rus. Conductor
Malkovich, John		Entertainment	10			44	Actor
Mallarme', Stephane	1842-98	Author		750	150	1100	Fr. Poet. Symbolist Movement
Malle, Louis	1932-96	Entertainment	35		45	50	Fr. Film Director.My Dinner With Andre etc.
Mallick, Don		Astronaut	5			15	
Mallory, Charles M.		Aviation	10	22	38	30	ACE, WW II
Mallory, Francis	1807-60	Congress	10				Repr. VA, Physician, RR Pres.
Mallory, Stephen R.		Civil War	125	225	240		CSA Sec'y of Navy.
Malmesbury, Ist Earl	1746-1820	Br. Diplomat	15	30	45		James Harris. Minister, Ambass.
Malo, Gina		Entertainment	3	3	6	6	
Malodva, Milada		Entertainment	7	9	20	15	
Malone, Dorothy		Entertainment	40	75		65	
Malone, Dumas		Author	10	30	75	15	
Maloney, Francis T.	1894-1945	Senate/Congress	10	20	40		Senator, MOC CT 1933-45
Malten, Leonard	1950-	Entertainment	10	25		35	Film Critic, Writer, TV Personality
Malten, Therese		Entertainment	35			150	Opera
Malthus, Thomas Robert	1766-1834	Br. Economist	310	1100	1915		Educator, Author
Mamas and the Papas		Entertainment	350	900			(Four)
Mamas and the Papas, The		Entertainment	10			20	(Four) (The NEW)
Mamet, David		Entertainment	10			25	Film Director
Mamoulian, Rouben		Entertainment	15	45		175	Top Film & Stage Director
Man Ray		Artist					SEE Ray, Man
Mana-Zucca (Zuckerman, A.a)		Entertainment	20			100	Singer, Composer, Pianist
Manchester, Melissa		Entertainment	10	15		30	Singer. Concert & Recording Artist

NAME	DATE	CATEGORY	SIG	LS/DS	ALS	SP	COMMENTS
Manchester, William		Author	5	10	20	15	
Mancini, Henry	1924-94	Composer	29	30		64	Conductor-Pianist. AMusQS $85-$250
Mandel, Howie		Entertainment	6	8	15	15	
Mandel, John		Entertainment	5	6	15	10	
Mandel, Marvin		Governor	10	15		22	Governor MD
Mandela, Nelson	1918-	Head of State	80	170		432	Leader African Nat'l Congress
Mandell, Howie		Entertainment	5	8	20	15	
Manderson, Charles		Civil War	70	105	150		Union Gen. , U.S. Sen. NE
Mandoki, Luis		Entertainment	5			22	Movie Director
Mandrell, Barbara		Country Music	6			20	
Manet, Edouard	1832-83	Artist	350	2300	1788		Impressionist School Creator
Maney, George E.	1826-1901	Civil War	145				CSA Gen. ALS '62 $760
Manfrini, Luigi		Entertainment	40			125	Opera
Mangano, Silvana		Entertainment	25	35	60	50	
Mangione, Chuck		Entertainment	5	6	15	15	
Manhattan Transfer		Entertainment	35			80	
Manigault, Arthur M.	1824-86	Civil War	105	288			CSA Gen. ALS '61 $1650
Manilow, Barry		Entertainment	15	45		70	Composer, Vocalist, Pianist
Manke, John		Astronaut	5			15	
Mankiewicz, Joseph L.		Entertainment	20		55	55	AA Film Director
Mankiller, Wilma		Author	5			20	
Manley, N. W.		Head of State	12		25	20	Prime Minister Jamaica
Mann, Daniel		Entertainment	10			35	
Mann, Delbert		Entertainment	20			45	Film Director
Mann, Hank		Entertainment	100				Keystone Kop. Caricature S 250
Mann, Heinrich		Author	35	145	275		Ger. Novelist. Exiled, Interned
Mann, Horace	1796-1859	Educator	35	135	250		Education Reformer, Abolitionist
Mann, Johnny		Bandleader	16				
Mann, Manfred (All)		Entertainment	125				
Mann, Orrin L.		Civil War	20	35	60		Union General
Mann, Thomas	?-1967	Aviation	12	25	48	35	ACE, WW II, Double Ace
Mann, Thomas	1875-1955	Author	210	641	1000	1080	Ger. Novelist, Nobel Prize. Death in Venice
Mann, Thomas Clifton		Celebrity	3			10	
Manne, Shelly		Bandleader				45	Drummer
Mannerheim, c. Gustave, Baron		Head of State		290	850	775	Pres. Finland. Soldier, Patriot
Mannering, Mary		Entertainment	15			25	Vintage Stage Actress
Manners, David		Entertainment	10			35	
Manners-Sutton, Charles		Clergy	25	35	40		
Manning, Daniel		Cabinet	18	35	65		Sec'y Treasury
Manning, Henry E., Cardinal		Clergy	40	60	95	50	
Manning, Irene		Entertainment	6	8	15	10	
Manning, Stephen H.		Civil War	30	55	110		Union General
Manning, Timothy J., Cardinal		Clergy	35	40	50	45	
Manning, William T., Bishop	1856-1947	Clergy	20	32	60	30	Episcopal Bishop of New York. 1924-46
Manoff, Dinah		Entertainment	5			20	

NAME	DATE	CATEGORY	SIG	LS/DS	ALS	SP	COMMENTS
Manone, Wingy		Entertainment	10			50	Jazz Trumpet-Vocalist
Mansfield, Jayne	1933-67	Entertainment	166			423	Blonde Glamour Actress. 5x7 SP $375, SP Pc $375
Mansfield, Joseph K..F.(WD)		Civil War	225		2865		Union Gen.KIA 1862
Mansfield, Joseph K.F.	1803-62	Civil War	148	308	436		Union General
Mansfield, Katherine		Author		290			
Mansfield, Mike		Senate/Congress	10	25	40	15	MOC, Senator MT
Mansfield, Richard		Entertainment	50		175		Vintage Stage Actor, Manager, Producer
Manship, Paul Howard	1885-1955	Artist	40	275	412		Am. Sculptor of Prometheus Fountain
Manson, Charles (Buglioni)		Criminal	75	215	455	175	Murderer, Cult Figure
Manson, Shirley		Entertainment	10			75	Music. Lead Singer Garbage
Manstein, Erich von, General		Military	20	60	95	75	Planned Assault vs France WW II
Mantell, Gideon A	1790-1852	Science	10	25	40		Paleontologist. 4 Dinosaurs
Mantell, Robert B.		Entertainment	12			25	Vintage Shakespearean Actor
Mantelli, Eugenia		Entertainment	25			60	Opera
Mantovani		Entertainment	8	12		20	Conductor-Arranger
Manuel II		Royalty	58	350			King of Portugal at 18. Father Assassinated
Manville, Tommy		Business	20		35		Much Married Asbestos Heir
Manzarek, Ray		Entertainment	15	25			The Doors, bassist
Mao Tse Tung		Head of State	3000				Chinese Communist Leader
Maphis, Joe and Rose Lee		Country Music	10			20	
Mapleson, James H.		Entertainment	75				Opera
Mapplethorpe, Robert	1946-89	Artist	75		350		Controversial Am. Photographer
Mara, Adele		Entertainment	5	8		10	Actress
Maragliano, Luisa		Entertainment	5			15	
Marais, Jean	1913-19xx	Entertainment	10		30	45	Fr. Actor. Stage & Film
Marat, Jean-Paul	1743-93	Fr. Revolution			4500		Politician-Doctor-Author. Murdered
Marbot, J.B.A.M., Marquis	1782-1854	Fr. Revolution	25	70	125		Napoleonic General
Marceau, Marcel		Entertainment	20	70		92	World Renown Mime
Marceau, Sophie		Entertainment	12			42	Actress. Pin-Up $65
Marcellino, Muzzy		Entertainment	10	15	25	25	Big Band. Trumpet
March, Barbara		Entertainment	5			30	Star Trek
March, Fredric	1897-1975	Entertainment	43	80	95	85	Long Respected Stage-Film Actor. AA 'Jekyll-Hyde'
March, Hal	1920-70	Entertainment	5			15	Actor-TV Game Show Host
March, Jane		Entertainment	10			38	Actress. Pin-Up $65
March, P.C.		Military	50	125			Am. WW I Four Star Gen.
March, Peyton E., Gen.		Military	12			45	Served 1888-1921
Marchesi, Mathilde	1821-1913	Entertainment	50		160	175	Ger. Mezzo-Sopr. From Famous Family of Singers
Marcinkus, Paul C., Archbishop		Clergy	45	65	100	50	
Marcks, Gerhard	1889-1981	Artist	45		345		Ger. Sculptor and Designer
Marconi, Guglielmo	1874-1937	Science	284	582	2485	890	It. Physicist-Inventor. Nobel. Father of Radio
Marcos, Ferdinand E.		Head of State	50	135		130	Pres. Philippines
Marcos, Imelda		Head of State	15	35		25	Phillipines
Marcoux, Vanni	1877-1962	Entertainment	20			75	Opera, Buenos Aires. Fr. Bass-Baritone
Marcovicci, Andrea		Entertainment	10			20	
Marcus, Jerry*		Cartoonist	5			35	'Fatkat'

NAME	DATE	CATEGORY	SIG	LS/DS	ALS	SP	COMMENTS
Marcus, Rudolph A., Dr.		Science	20	35		30	Nobel Chemistry
Marcus, Stanley		Business	30	75	160	60	Merchant. Nieman-Marcus
Marcy, Randolph B.	1812-87	Civil War	35		180		Union Gen.
Marcy, Randolph G. (WD)		Civil War	50	85			Union Gen. ALS/Cont. $750
Marcy, William L.	1786-1857	Cabinet	40	175	175		Sec'y War, State. Senator NY
Maren, Jerry		Entertainment	10			25	Actor. Wizard of Oz. Lollipop Kid
Marescot, Armand S.		Fr. Revolution	30	80	170		
Maressyev, Alexei		Aviation	135				Rus. ACE & Soviet Hero
Maret, Hugues B., Duke	1763-1839	Fr. Revolution	82	210	375		Napoleon Confidential Advisor
Marey, Etienne		Science	50		700		Fr. Physiologist. Sphygmograph
Margaret of Austria	1522-86	Royalty	110	285	775		Duchess of Parma. Regent Of Netherlands
Margie*		Cartoonist	20			250	Little Lulu
Margo (Mrs Eddie Albert)	1917-86	Entertainment	20	20	35	30	Mex.-Born Actress-Dancer Lost Horizon
Marguerite De Valois	1553-1615	Royalty		1910			Queen of Fr., 1st Wife of Henry of Navarre
Maria (Castile)		Royalty		2000			Queen of Alfonso V of Aragon
Maria Theresa	1717-80	Royalty	185	680	980		Archduchess, Qn Hung.-Bohemia
Marie Amelie (Queen of Fr.)		Royalty	170	240	458		Queen of Louis Phillippe I
Marie Antoinette (Fr)	1755-93	Royalty	1255	5425			Queen of Louis XVI France
Marie Louise	1791-1847	Royalty	200	762	785		Empress of Fr. 2nd Wife of Napoleon I
Marie of Modena (Queen Gr. Brit.)		Royalty	335	530			Queen of James II
Marie of Naples		Royalty	15		85		Queen of King Louis-Phillipe I
Marie of Romania	1875-1938	Royalty	80	115	240	495	Queen of Romania. Wife of Ferdinand I of Roumania
Marin, Cheech		Entertainment	5			30	Actor-Comedian (Cheech & Chong)
Marin, John		Artist	60	225	550		Am. Watercolorist, Etching
Marinaro, Ed		Entertainment	6	8	15	15	
Marion, Francis	1732-95	Rev. War		6500	8500		The Swamp Fox
Mariscal, Don Ignacio		Statesman	20	35	55		V.P. Mexico
Maritain, Jacques		Clergy	40	45	95	75	
Maritza, Sari		Entertainment	8	9		20	
Markevitch, Igor		Entertainment	30			145	Conductor
Markham, Albert H., Sir		Celebrity	5	20	45		
Markham, Clements, Sir	1830-1916	Geographer	15	25	125		Historian, Pres. Royal Geographical. Soc.
Markham, Edwin		Author	30	125	140	65	The Man With The Hoe
Markham, William		Colonial America	135	450			Colonial Gov. PA
Markova, Alicia		Entertainment	20			50	Ballet
Markowitz, Harry M., Dr.		Economics	20	35	45		Nobel Economics
Marks, Johnny		Composer	35	95	125	50	AMusQS $175. TsS Rudolph..$850.
Marks, William, Jr.	1778-1858	Senate	35	140			PA Senator, ALS/Content $400
Marlborough, Consuelo	1876-1964	Royalty	35	185		920	Vanderbilt Heiress. 9th Duchess
Marlborough, James L.,	1550-1629	Judge	85	325			1st Earl of
Marlborough, Sarah Churchill	1660-1744	Royalty	117	275			Powerful Confidante of Queen Anne. Duchess of
Marlborough, John C., 1st Duke	1650-1722	Military	220	578			Br. General and Statesman
Marley, Bob	1945-81	Entertainment	695			1950	Rock HOF. Reggae King. Held World Popularity
Marlin, Mahlon F.		Business	40	115	225		Pres-Treas. Marlin Firearms Co.
Marlow, Lucy		Entertainment	5	6	15	15	

NAME	DATE	CATEGORY	SIG	LS/DS	ALS	SP	COMMENTS
Marlowe, Hugh		Entertainment	25			50	
Marlowe, Julia		Entertainment	25	35	70	60	Major Stage Star/E.H. Sothern
Marly, Florence		Entertainment	4	4	9	9	
Marmaduke, John S. (WD)		Civil War	167		2400		CSA Gen.
Marmaduke, John S.	1833-87	Civil War	95	300			CSA Gen.
Marmont, A.F.L.V., Duke		Fr. Revolution	45	90			Marshal of Fr., Napoleon A-D-C
Marney, Carlyle		Clergy	20	25	35	35	
Marquand, John P.		Author	40	125	165	45	Am. Novelist. Pulitzer
Marques, Antonio		Entertainnment	35			85	Opera
Marquez, Gabriel		Author	70			245	Nobel. One Hundred Years of Solitude
Marriott, J.		Business	20	35	70	30	Marriott Hotel Chain
Marryat, Frederick	1792-1848	Military-Author	30	100	175		Br. Naval Cmmdr. Novelist
Mars, Forest, Sr.	1908-99	Business					Fndr.,-Owner 'Mars Bars', M & M's' etc. NRPA
Marsala, Joe		Entertainment	20			65	Clarinet, Sax, Composer
Marsalis, Branford		Entertainment	10			25	Conductor, Sax
Marsalis, Wynton		Entertainment	15			30	Trumpet Virtuoso. Classic-Jazz
Marsden, Jason		Entertainment	10			25	The Munsters
Marsh, Jean		Entertainment	7			20	
Marsh, Joan		Entertainment	15	20	40	35	
Marsh, Mae		Entertainment	30	40	75	40	
Marsh, Marion		Entertainment	15			40	
Marsh, Ngaio, Dame		Author	20	35	50	40	New Zealand Mystery Writer
Marshall, Brian		Entertainment	6			25	Music. Bass Guitar Creed
Marshall, Catherine		Author	65	75	150	125	A Man Called Peter, Christy
Marshall, Cathy		TV News	7	20		10	CNN News
Marshall, Christopher		Rev. War	100				Am. Patriot & Diarist
Marshall, E.G.		Entertainment	10			25	
Marshall, George C.	1880-1959	Military-Statesman	150	260	550	450	WW II Chief Staff. Nobel Peace Prize. Statesman
Marshall, George E.		Entertainment	35			75	Film Director. 400+ Films
Marshall, Herbert	1890-1966	Entertainment	10	75		65	Sophisticated Br. Actor
Marshall, Humphrey (WD)		Civil War	270	512			CSA Gen.ALS/Cont $1825
Marshall, Humphrey	1812-72	Civil War	93	195			CSA General
Marshall, John (SC)	1755-1835	Supreme Court	435	2200	4250		Chief Justice
Marshall, John, Sir		Head of State	10	20	35	20	Prime Minister New Zealand
Marshall, Margaret		Entertainment	10			25	Opera
Marshall, Penny		Entertainment	8	32		20	Actress And Film Director
Marshall, Peter		Clergy	75	95	100	125	Senate Chaplain
Marshall, Thomas R. (V)	1854-1925	Vice President	75	175	400	175	Wilson VP
Marshall, Thurgood (SC)	1908-93	Supreme Court	105	300	200	175	1st Afro-Am. Justice
Marshall, Tully		Entertainment	20			50	
Marshall, William		Civil War	25	40	75		Union Gen., Gov. MN
Marshall, William		Entertainment	15			25	Film Director
Marshall, William		Entertainment	8			25	Werewolf
Marshall, William, Sir	1865-1939	Military	35			85	Brit. WW I General. France, Gallipoli, Salonika
Marshall. Catherine		Clergy	25	30	50	30	

NAME	DATE	CATEGORY	SIG	LS/DS	ALS	SP	COMMENTS
Marston, Gilman	1811-90	Civil War	30	80			Union Gen. Legislator. Sen.NH
Marterie, Ralph		Entertainment	10			20	Big Band Leader
Martin, Benny		Country Western	5			18	Western Recording Artist
Martin, Charles H.		Governor	10	25			Governor OR
Martin, Chris Pin		Entertainment	50			100	
Martin, Clarence D.		Governor	5	15		10	Governor WA
Martin, Dean & Lewis, Jerry		Entertainment	125			250	Comedy Team
Martin, Dean	1917-95	Entertainment	28	105	40	93	Actor-Singer-Comedian. Member Sinatra Rat Pack
Martin, Dean Vincent		Entertainment	5	6	15	15	
Martin, Dewey		Entertainment	9			25	Leading Man
Martin, Dick		Entertainment	6	28	5	20	Comedian-Actor. 1/2 Rowan & Martin Team
Martin, Frank	1890-1974	Composer	38		425	110	Prolific Swiss Composer. AMusQS $125
Martin, Freddie		Entertainment	35			65	Big Band Leader-Pianist
Martin, Glenn L.	1886-1955	Aviation	75	175	275	250	Aeronautical Pioneer.Fndr.Airplane Mfg.Co./Wrights
Martin, Hugh		Composer					AMusQS 45
Martin, James Green (WD)		Civil War	182	663			CSA Gen.
Martin, James Green	1819-78	Civil War	95	295			CSA General
Martin, John A.		Governor	12		30		Governor KS
Martin, John C.		Senate/Congress	5	10			MOC IL
Martin, Joseph W. Jr.	1884-1968	Congress	25	35		25	Speaker of the House
Martin, Lori		Entertainment				25	Former Ingenue
Martin, Luther		Rev. War	70	175	360		Continental Congress
Martin, Mary		Entertainment	35	45		50	
Martin, Pamela Sue		Entertainment	7		15	22	Actress. Pin-Up SP $20
Martin, Ricardo		Entertainment	15			45	Opera
Martin, Ross		Entertainment	10	20	40	30	
Martin, Steve		Entertainment	12			60	Comedian-Actor.
Martin, Strother		Entertainment	35	50		80	Character Actor
Martin, Theodore, Sir		Author	5	15	25	10	
Martin, Thomas S.	1847-1919	Congress	12	25			Senator VA 1893. CSA Army
Martin, Tony	1912-	Entertainment	13	22		30	Singer-Actor. 35 Top Hits
Martin, William C., Bishop		Clergy	15	25	30	35	
Martin, William T. (WD)		Civil War	170	440	488		CSA Gen.
Martin, William T.	1823-1910	Civil War	112	295	400		CSA General
Martine, James E.		Congress	5	15		10	Senator NJ
Martineau, Harriet	1802-70	Author	50		75		Brit. Miscellaneous Writer
Martinelli, Giovanni	1885-1969	Entertainment	35	60		125	It.-Am. Great Operatic Dramatic Tenor
Martinez, Luis, Cardinal		Clergy	30	45	55	50	
Martini, Nino		Entertainment	15			45	Opera, Films. Handsome Tenor
Martini, Steve		Author	5	10		10	Novelist
Martino, Al		Entertainment	3	5		8	
Martino, Donald		Composer	20	35	90		Pulitzer, AMusQS $180
Martinson, Leslie		Entertainment	15			25	Director TV & Films Bat Man, PT 109 etc.
Martinu, Bronislaw	1890-1959	Composer					Czech. Composer AMusQS $900-1500
Martiny, Philip		Artist	25	40	80	30	

NAME	DATE	CATEGORY	SIG	LS/DS	ALS	SP	COMMENTS
Marton, Eva		Entertainment	20			50	Opera
Marvel, Ik		Author	10		30		Pseud. Donald G. Mitchell
Marvin, Lee	1924-87	Entertainment	142	175		253	Supporting Actor to Star to Academy Award
Marwood, William		Executioner	75		350		Br. Lord High Executioner
Marx Brothers (3)		Entertainment	1167			2000	Three Full Names
Marx Brothers (4)		Entertainment	1575			2925	4 Full Names Rare
Marx, Arthur		Author	7	15		15	
Marx, Chico		Entertainment	145	170	3325	310	
Marx, Groucho	1890-1977	Entertainment	213	467		392	Comedian. Marx Bros. Leader. S Chk. $425
Marx, Harpo		Entertainment	400				
Marx, Karl	1818-83	Author	540	1500	14750	12650	Ger. Political Philosopher
Marx, Richard		Entertainment	20			50	Singer
Marx, Zeppo	1901-79	Entertainment	72	120		189	
Mary (of Modena)	1658-1718	Royalty	140		750		Queen of James II
Mary (of Teck)	1867-1953	Royalty	120	370	245	415	Queen of George V (Eng.)Mother of Two Kings
Mary Adalaide (Dchs. Teck)		Royalty	35	70	150		
Mary I	1516-58	Royalty	900	3000	7500		Queen England, Bloody Mary
Mary II (Eng)		Royalty	370	2200	3100		Queen William II (NRPA)
Mary of Modena		Royalty					SEE Marie of Modena
Masaryk, Jan		Head of State	95	155	275	550	Pres. Czechoslovakia
Masaryk, Thomas G.	1850-1937	Head of State	100	250	717	638	Czech.Philosopher,1st President
Mascagni, Pietro	1863-1945	Composer	165	375	623	615	'Cavalleria Rusticana'. AMusQS $650-1,250.SPc $225
Mascherini, Enzo		Entertainment	15			50	Opera
Masefield, John	1878-1967	Author	35	70	215	75	Br. Poet Laureate
Mash (Show-Cast of)		Entertainment				495	Eight Main Characters
Masini, Angelo		Entertainment				500	Opera. 19th Cent. Intern'l Star. RARE
Maskelyne, Nevil	1732-1811	Science	85	250	390		Br. Astronomer Royal. Inventor
Mason, Alfred Edw. W.	1865-1948	Author	10	30	45	20	Br. Novelist
Mason, George	1725-92	Rev. War	1775	4500			Am. Planter & Rev. Statesman
Mason, Jackie		Entertainment	5			10	Comedian
Mason, James	1909-84	Entertainment	40	70	80	90	Br. Actor-Film Director
Mason, James M.	1798-1871	Civil War	65	115	200		US Sen.VA, CSA Diplomat/Trent Affair.ALS $700
Mason, Jonathan	1756-1831	Federalist Am.	40		75		Federalist US Sen. MA. Exec. Council. Investor
Mason, LeRoy		Entertainment	50			150	
Mason, Marsha	1942-	Entertainment	8	10		25	Actress. Stage-Films From '66. AA Nom.'Goodby Girl
Mason, Sully		Entertainment	5		15	10	
Mason, Walt		Author	5			20	Poet
Mason, William E.	1850-1921	Congress	12	20		15	MOC, Senator IL
Massen, Osa	1915-	Entertainment	5			10	Dan-Am Actress. Hollywood Films From Late 30's
Massena, Andre, Duke	1758-1817	Fr. Revolution	100	375	450		Fr.Marshal.Greatest of Napoleon's Gen'ls
Massenet, Jules	1842-1912	Composer	65	145	294	322	Manon, Thais. AMusQS $375-$650-$2750-$3500
Massey, Daniel		Entertainment	10			20	Actor
Massey, Eyre		Rev. War	300	1250			Br. Gen'l Serving in N.Am. During Am. Rev.
Massey, Gerald	1828-1907	Author	25	70	95		Br. Poet, Journalist, Editor
Massey, Illona		Entertainment	25		30	40	

NAME	DATE	CATEGORY	SIG	LS/DS	ALS	SP	COMMENTS
Massey, Louise & Curt		Entertainment	25			45	Country Western
Massey, Raymond		Entertainment	33			65	Fine Vintage Canadian Actor. Stage & Screen
Massie, Paul		Entertainment	5	6	15	10	
Massie, Robert		Author		65			The Romanovs
Massine, Leonide		Entertainment	20			105	Ballet Dancer,Choreographer...
Masson, Andre		Artist	40	55	95		
Masters and Johnson		Sex Researchers	20			40	Wm. H. and Virginia
Masters, Edgar Lee	1869-1950	Author	50	150	250	65	Poet, Novelist, Biographer. AMsS $600
Masters, Frankie		Entertainment	5			25	Big Band Leader
Masters, William H. & Virginia		Science	10			35	Sex Research Authors
Masterson, Mary Stuart		Entertainment	10			40	
Masterson, Wm. B. Bat	1853-1921	Lawman	4800		3850		Scout, Sheriff, Gambler
Mastracchio, Richard		Astronaut	5			19	
Mastroantonio, Mary Eliz.		Entertainment	10	15	25	40	
Mastroianni, Marcello		Entertainment	20			45	
Mat,, Rudy		Entertainment	15			55	Top Cinematographer
Mata Hari (M.G. Zelle)	1876-1917	Spy	350	1100	4500	5300	Executed Secret Agent WW I
Matchbox 20		Entertainment	30			85	Music. 5 Member Rock Group
Materna, Amalie		Entertainment	30		120		Greatest Wagnerian Soprano of them all
Mather, Cotton	1663-1728	Rev. War-Clergy	850	1950	4200		Author, Published 382 Books
Mathers, Jerry 'Beaver'		Entertainment	15			45	
Matheson, Tim		Entertainment	10			30	
Mathews, Brander	1852-1929	Author	10		35		Novelist, Essayist, Drama Critic for NY Times
Mathews, George	1739-1812	Rev. War	85	190			Statesman, General
Mathias, Bob		Congress	10	15		20	MOC CA, Olymp. Decathlon Champ.Brief Actor
Mathis, Johnny		Entertainment	9	10	20	25	Alb. Cover S $55
Mathis, Samantha		Entertainment				80	Actress Broken Arrow
Mathiuci, Franca		Entertainment	5			15	
Matisse, Henri	1869-1954	Artist	900	800	1922	3220	Fr. Painter, Sculptor, Fauvist. SP (Pc)$1550
Matlack, Timothy	1730-1829	Rev. War	85	275	450		Continental Congress. Am. Patriot. Franklin Aide
Matlin, Marlee		Entertainment	10		45	40	Pin-Up SP $100. AA
Matoni, Walter		Aviation	10			35	Ger. Ace WW II. RK
Matsushita, Konosuke		Business	25	65	145	40	Japanese Electronic Giant
Mattea, Kathy		Country Music	5			15	
Mattern, Jimmie		Aviation	15	25	60	35	
Matthau, Walter		Entertainment	5		15	25	A A
Matthews, DeLane		Entertainment	10			36	Actress Dave's World
Matthews, Frank Arnold		Clergy	20	25	35	25	
Matthews, Jessie		Entertainment	15			30	Br.Vintage Film Actress
Matthews, Stanley (SC)		Supreme Court	45	150	275		
Mattingly, Thos. Ken		Astronaut	15			115	
Mattson, Conrad		Aviation	8	15	28	22	ACE, WW II
Mature, Victor		Entertainment	9	10	20	40	
Matzenauer, Margaret		Entertainment	25			85	Wagnerian Soprano
Matzky, Gerhard		Military	20	60			Nazi WW II Gen.

NAME	DATE	CATEGORY	SIG	LS/DS	ALS	SP	COMMENTS
Mauborgne, Joseph O.	1881-1971	Military	45	150			USA Gen. Air-to-Ground Transmission. Broke Codes
Maubourg, Lafayette		Celebrity	5	12	20		Nephew
Mauch, Billy		Entertainment	10	15	25	25	
Mauch, Bobby		Entertainment	30			65	
Maugham, W. Somerset	1874-1965	Author	70	320	323	375	Br. Novelist and Playwright
Mauldin, Bill*		Cartoonist	25			250	Willie & Joe
Maupassant, Guy de		Author	275	795	1185		Fr. Master of Short Story
Maura, Antonio		Head of State	110	165			Sp. P.M. Provoked Rif War
Maurey, Pierre		Clergy	10	15	30	25	Pres. Reform Church France
Mauro, Ermanno		Entertainment	15			40	Opera
Maurois, Andre (Emile Herzog)		Author	22	75	120		Fr. Biographer, Novelist
Maury, Dabney H. (WD)		Civil War	142	280	1320	605	CSA General
Maury, Dabney H.	1822-1900	Civil War	85		350		CSA Gen.
Maury, Matthew F.	1806-73	Civil War	100		1032	1550	CSA Naval Cmdr., Hydrographer
Mauser, Paul von	1838-1914	Military	285				Ger. Weapon Mfg./Brother Wilhelm. Mauser Rifle
Mawson, Douglas, Sir		Explorer	50	160	375		Australian Polar Explorer
Max, Peter		Artist	90	350			Am. Contemporary Art.
Maxey, Samuel Bell (WD)		Civil War	245		2500		CSA Gen.
Maxey, Samuel Bell	1825-95	Civil War	125	225	295		CSA General, US Sen. TX
Maxey, Virginia		Entertainment	5			10	
Maxim, Hiram Percy	1896-1936	Science	40	265			Inventor Maxim Gun Silencer etc
Maxim, Hiram Stevens	1840-1916	Science	95	208	475	300	Inventor Maxim Machine Gun. Engineer
Maxim, Hudson	1853-1927	Science	78	125	175	175	Inventor Smokeless Powder & Other Explosives
Maximilian II (Bohemia-Hung.)	1811-64	Royalty	110	415	770		Holy Roman Emperor
Maximilian, Ferdinand	1832-67	Royalty	310	1794	1250		Emperor Mexico
Maxon, R.*		Cartoonist	20			100	Tarzan
Maxwell, Elsa		Columnist	8	25	35	15	Hostess & Professional Party
Maxwell, Lois		Entertainment	10			25	
Maxwell, Marilyn		Entertainment	8	10		35	
Maxwell, Robert		Aviation	12	25	28	22	ACE, WW II
Maxwell, Robert		Publisher	45			120	Died Mysteriously
Maxwell, William (Beaverbrook)		Publisher	25	110	180		Newspaper Proprietor, Statesman
May, Billy		Bandleader	10				Arranger
May, Edna		Entertainment	18		30	32	Vintage Stage & Film. Darling of Brit. Music Hall
Mayall, John		Entertainment	10			30	
Maybank, Burnet R.		Governor	10	18		15	Governor, Senator SC
Maye, Carolyn		Entertainment	10			25	
Mayer, Louis B.		Business	70	363	275	225	MGM Film Studio. Informative TDS $750-$900
Mayer, Maria, Dr.		Science	30	85		50	Nobel Physics
Mayfair, Mitzi		Entertainment	10			10	
Maynard, Ken	1895-1973	Entertainment	118		145	175	Western Film Hero
Maynor, Dorothy		Entertainment	25			275	30's-50's Concert & Recording Career. 5x6 SP $75
Mayo, 6th Earl(Rich.Bourke)		Head of State	10		30		Br. Politician. Viceroy of India
Mayo, Charles H., Dr.	1865-1939	Science	140	290	380	475	Co-Founder Mayo Foundation
Mayo, Charles W., Dr.	1898-1968	Science	65	140	235	350	Surgeon Mayo Clinic. Prof. Surg.

NAME	DATE	CATEGORY	SIG	LS/DS	ALS	SP	COMMENTS
Mayo, Frank	1839-96	Entertainment	12				Actor
Mayo, Henry Thomas		Military	30	45	125	45	Adm. Cmdr. Atlantic Fl. WW I
Mayo, Virginia		Entertainment	8			22	Longtime Warner Bros. Actress. Pin-Up SP $40
Mayo, William J., Dr.	1861-1939	Science	105	290	380	475	Co-Founder Mayo Foundation
Mayron, Melanie		Entertainment	4			15	Actress 30 Something
Maytag, Frederick L.		Business	95	275	600	150	Maytag Electric Appliances
Mazarin, Jules, Cardinal	1602-61	Clergy-Statesman		835			Succeeded Richelieu as Chief Minister Louis XIII
Mazurki, Mike		Entertainment	5	6	15	15	
Mazurski, Paul		Entertainment	5			20	Film Director
Mazzini, Joseph (Giuseppe)	1805-72	Revolutionary	75	155	909		Italian Patriot. Unpublished ALS $2325
Mazzoleni, Ester		Entertainment				11372	Opera. Dalmatian-Ital. Diva
McAdam, John		Inventor		850			McAdamized Roads
McAdoo, William G.	1863-1941	Cabinet	25	75	175	75	Wilson Sec'y Treasury & Son-In-Law. RR Czar
Mcaffee, Johnny		Entertainment	3	3	6	6	
McAllister, Lon		Entertainment	15			30	
McAndrew, James W.		Military	62			35	Am. WW I Gen. Gen'l Staff, Chief of Staff A.E.F.
McArdle, Andrea		Entertainment	5	6	15	15	
McArthur, John	1826-1906	Civil War	30			310	Union Gen.
McArthur, Kim		Playboy Bunny	4			8	Pin-Up SP $10
McArthur, William		Astronaut	7			20	
McAuliffe, Anthony C.	1898-1975	Military	85	175	175	395	WW II Gen'l. Replied Nuts.TLS re A Bomb $300
McAuliffe, Christa		Astronaut	450	1995		1400	Died in Challenger Disaster
McAvoy, May		Entertainment	10			25	Vintage Film Actress
McBain, Diane		Entertainment	5	6	15	10	
McBain, Ed		Author	10	20	50	15	Novelist
McBride, George W.	1854-1911	Congress	5	15			Senator OR
McBride, John	?-1800	Military	30	75			Brit. Adm. 1793
McBride, Jon A.		Astronaut	5	15		30	
McBride, Mary Margaret	1899-1976	Entertainment	5		25	20	Radio Talk Show Host. 30's-40's.Household Name
McCabe, Nick		Entertainment	6			25	Music. Lead Guitar The Verve
McCaffrey, Anne		Author	5			10	Novelist
McCain, John N.		Military	15	35			Admiral WW II
McCain, John S., Jr.(III)		Congress	5	30	45	40	Senator AZ, Vietnam war POW
McCall, Tom		Governor	5	10		15	Governor OR
McCalla, Irish		Entertainment	10		25	25	Pin-Up SP $35
McCallister, Lon		Entertainment	10			30	
McCallum, David		Entertainment	5			25	
McCambridge, Mercedes		Entertainment	40			75	
McCampbell, David S.		Aviation	15	25	45	75	ACE, WW II, Top Navy Ace, MOH
McCandless, Bruce II		Astronaut	10		90	24	
McCann, Chuck		Business	5	15	30	10	
McCarey, Leo		Entertainment	35			65	Academy Award Director, Prod.
McCarthy, Eugene J.		Congress	25	53	50	30	Senator MN. Pres. Candidate. '68 'Peace' Candidate
McCarthy, Jenny		Entertainment	6			32	Actress. Pin-Up $65-$75
McCarthy, Joe	1908-1957	Congress	57	150		95	Senator WI. McCarthyism. Notorious Red-Baiter

NAME	DATE	CATEGORY	SIG	LS/DS	ALS	SP	COMMENTS
McCarthy, Kevin		Entertainment	10			35	Actor.
McCarthy, Mary		Author	45	135		50	Novelist
McCarthy, Michael W.		Business	3	5	10	5	
McCartney, Paul		Entertainment	168	450		428	Beatle. SP 4x6 in. $295. SP Paul & Linda $695
McCaulay, Rose, Dame		Br. Author	20			45	
McCay, Peggy		Entertainment	10			35	Actress. Mayberry
McCay, Winsor*		Cartoonists	50			600	Little Nemo
McClanahan, Rue		Entertainment	10	10		25	
McClaran, John W.	1887-1948	Military	35	125			USN Adm. Round-the-World Bases For 1st Flight
McClellan, George B.(WD)		Civil War	340	428	1790	2100	Union Gen.
McClellan, George B.	1826-85	Civil War	198	275	503		Union Gen.ALS/Cont.'66 $2200. Pres. Candidate
McClellan, John L.	1896-1977	Congress	10	20		25	Repr., Senator AR
McClernand, John A. (WD)		Civil War	70	168	217		Union Gen.
McClernand, John A.	1812-1900	Civil War	45	110	175	600	
McClintic, James V.		Senate/Congress	5	10		7	MOC OK
McClintock, Francis L.	1819-1907	Explorer	65	115	200		Br. Adm., Arctic Navigator. Search for Franklin
McClintock, John		Astronaut	5	15		20	
McClinton, Delbert		Country Music	10			25	Singer-Musician. TX Blues Man
McCloskey, John, Cardinal		Clergy	95	125	250	100	
McCloskey, Lee		Entertainment	5	6	15	15	
McClosky, Pete		Senate/Congress	5	10		10	
McClung, J.T.M.		Senate/Congress	5	15		10	
McClure, Doug		Entertainment	5			30	
McClure, Samuel S.	1887-1949	Editor	12				Publisher
McClurg, Alexander C.		Civil War	50	85			Union General
McColpin, Carroll W.		Military	25	45	75	50	ACE WW II, Maj. Gen.
McComb, Henry S., Col.		Business	250	875			A U.P. RR Founder. Esposed Oakes Ames
McComb, William	1828-1918	Civil War	95	235	350		CSA Gen.
McConaughey, Matthew		Entertainment	10			57	Actor. Films
McConnell, Calvin D., Bishop		Clergy	20	25	30	30	
McConnell, Francis J., Bishop		Clergy	20	25	50	30	
McConnell, James, Bishop		Clergy	20	25	35	30	
McConnell, Joseph, Jr.		Aviation	75	140	175	150	ACE, Korea, Top Korea Ace
McCoo, Marilyn		Entertainment	5	6	15	15	
McCook, Alex. M. D.	1831-1903	Civil War	35	70	115		Union Gen.
McCook, Alex. M.(WD)		Civil War	45		195		Union Gen.
McCook, Anson		Civil War	30	55			Union Gen., MOC
McCook, Henry C.		Clergy	10	10	15		
McCool, William		Astronaut	5			20	
McCormack, John	1884-1945	Entertainment	60	105	220	170	Famed Irish Tenor. Opera & Popular Ballads
McCormack, John W.		Speaker of House	10	25	80		Speaker of the House
McCormack, Patty		Entertainment	5	8	15	15	
McCormic, Mary		Entertainment	20				Opera
McCormick, Anne O'Hare		Author	30	45	110	35	1st Pulitzer Woman Journalist
McCormick, Cyrus H.	1809-84	Science-Business	300	812	1888		Invented, Mfg. the Reaper. ALS/Content $4200

NAME	DATE	CATEGORY	SIG	LS/DS	ALS	SP	COMMENTS
McCormick, Myron		Entertainment	15	25	45	40	
McCormick, Nettie Fowler		Business	25		90		Mrs. Cyrus McCormick
McCormick, Robert R., Col.		Business	35	140	165	60	Editor Chicago Tribune
McCorvey, Norma		Celebrity		150			A.K.A. Jane Roe (Roe vs Wade)
McCown, John Porter (WD)		Civil War	245	1095			CSA Gen.
McCown, John Porter	1815-79	Civil War	95	310			CSA Gen.
McCoy, Charles B.		Business	25		85	10	Pres. DuPont Co.
McCoy, Clyde		Entertainment	6	8	15	15	
McCoy, Frank		Military		25	50		Am. WW I Gen.
McCoy, Tim		Entertainment	50			202	Col. Am. Cowboy Star. Innumerable Westerns
McCoy, Wilson*		Cartoonist	15			75	Phantom
McCrea, Joel		Entertainment	15	95		40	
McCready, Mike		Entertainment	6			25	Music. Guitarist Pearl Jam
McCreery, Richard L., Sir		Military	30	75		40	Br. Gen. WW II/Montgomery. 8th Army
McCudden, James T.B.		Aviation	135	225	350	300	ACE, WW I, RAF
McCullers, Carson	1917-67	Author	60	195	500	75	Am. Novelist. Heart is a Lonely Hunter etc.
McCulley, Michael J.		Astronaut	5			15	
McCulloch, Ben	1811-62	Civil War	155	470	565		CSA Gen. Morman War LS $2300
McCulloch, Henry E.		Civil War	145	350			CSA General
McCulloch, Hugh	1808-95	Cabinet	45	140	135		Lincoln, Johnson, Arthur Sec'y Treas.
McCullough, Colleen		Author	35	105	225	40	Austr. Novelist.Thorn Birds
McCullough, John	1832-85	Entertainment	10			35	Vintage Stage Actor
McCullough, Julie		Entertainment	7			27	Playboy Cover. Pin-Up SP $35
McCutcheon, George Barr	1866-1928	Author	10				
McCutcheon, John T.*	1870-1949	Cartoonist				30	Pulitzer.Political Cartoonist. Chicago Tribune
McDaniel, Hattie	1895-1952	Entertainment	659	1450	2100	1875	AA Gone With the Wind.
McDermont, Galt		Composer	10			25	'Hair'. Good Morning Sunshine AMusQS $95
McDermott, Dylan		Entertainment	20			70	Actor. Hit in The Practice
McDevitt, Ruth		Entertainment	10			20	
McDivitt, James A.		Astronaut	30	58		35	Gemini 4 & Apollo 9 Astro.
McDonal, Michael		Entertainment	5			32	Singer. Lead Singer for Doobie Bros.
McDonald, A. J. (Al)		Astronaut	20			30	NASA Whistleblower
McDonald, M. Nick		Celebrity	15	95		120	Captured Lee Harvey Oswald
McDonald, Marie		Entertainment	35	45	90	85	
McDonald, Richard J.		Business	100	917		225	MacDonald's. Need More Be Said?
McDonald, Skeets		Country Music	10			20	
McDonnell, James S.		Business	20	45	95	35	Founder, McDonnell Aircraft
McDonnell, Mary		Entertainment	20			50	
McDougall, Alexander		Rev. War	90	200	415		Gen. Cont. Army,Cont. Congress
McDowell, Andre		Entertainment	5			30	
McDowell, Irvin (WD)		Civil War	120	235	525	1250	Union Gen.Special DS $400
McDowell, Irvin	1818-85	Civil War	85		462		Union Gen. Mexican War
McDowell, Malcolm		Entertainment	10			38	Br. Actor. US & Eng. Remember Clockwork Orange
McDowell, Roddy	1928-98	Entertainment	20		40	35	Talented Child Actor,Mid Life Actor & Photographer
McDuffie, George	1790-1851	Congress	15				Sen. & Repr. SC

NAME	DATE	CATEGORY	SIG	LS/DS	ALS	SP	COMMENTS
McElmurry, Thomas		Astronaut	5			20	
McElroy, Neil H.		Cabinet	15	35		25	Sec'y Defense. Pres. P & G
McEnery, S.D.	1837-1910	Congress	12	25			Governor LA and Senator
McEntire, Reba		Country Music	15			30	
McEntyre, Joe (New Kids)		Entertainment	10			45	
McFadden, Bernar	1868-1955	Publisher-Physician	20	50			Eccentric Pulisher 'Physical Culture'-'True Story'
McFadden, Gates		Entertainment	5			15	Star Trek
McFadden, Obadiah B.		Senate/Congress	15	30	40		MOC WA 1873
McFarland, Spanky		Entertainment	20			45	Little Rascals Lobby Card S $195
McFarlane, Seth		Entertainment	4			22	Family Guy Creator/Voice
McFerrin, Bobby	1950-	Entertainment	10			23	Singer Don't Worry, Be Happy. 4 Grammys
McGarru. William D.		Aviation	15	30	45	40	ACE, WW II, Flying Tigers
McGavin, Darren		Entertainment	15			37	
McGee, Don		Aviation	25				WW II Am. Ace
McGee, Gale		Senate/Congress	5	15		10	Senator WY
McGill, John		Clergy	90		450		CW Bishop of Richmond
McGillis, Kelly		Entertainment	10		20	35	
McGinley, Phyllis		Author	10	30	45	20	Am Poet. Pulitzer
McGoohan, Patrick		Entertainment	20			45	
McGovern, Elizabeth		Entertainment	5			20	
McGovern, George		Senate	10	45		25	Senator SD, Pres. Hopeful
McGovern, John		Author	25	40			
McGowan, Rose		Entertainment	7			45	Actress. Films. Pin-Up $70
McGranery, James P.		Cabinet	10	15	25		Att'y General
McGrath, J. Howard		Cabinet	5	20	35	15	Att'y General
McGraw, Tim		Country Music	6			28	
McGregor, Ewan		Entertainment	8			55	Actor. Films
McGuffy, William H.		Educator	95	475			McGuffy's Reader
McGugin, Harold C.	1893-1946	Congress	10	25			Repr. KS
McGuigan, James, Cardinal		Clergy	5	10	15	12	
McGuinn, Roger		Entertainment	6			35	Byrds Co-Founder
McGuire Sisters		Entertainment	20			40	Singing Group
McGuire, Barry		Entertainment	5	6		25	New Christy Minstrels
McGuire, Dorothy		Entertainment	15			30	
McGuire, Phyllis		Entertainment	4	15		10	McGuire Sisters
McGuire, Thomas B.		Aviation	150	300	650	450	ACE, WW II, #2 U.S. Ace
McHenry, James	1753-1816	Cabinet-Military	180	285	2275		Signer Constitution, Sec'y War. Sr. Surgeon
McHugh, Frank		Entertainment	20	25	65	60	
McHugh, Jimmy		Composer	25	75			AMusQS $825
McHugh, Joseph		Artist	5			10	
McIlvaine, Abraham R.	1804-63	Congress	10				Repr. PA, Whig Presidential Elector
McIntire, John		Entertainment	20			50	
McIntosh, Lachlan	1725-1806	Rev. War	550	812			Killed Button Gwinnett in Duel
McIntyre, Frank		Military	75	140			Am. WW I Gen.
McIntyre, James F., Archbishop		Clergy	40	65	75	60	

NAME	DATE	CATEGORY	SIG	LS/DS	ALS	SP	COMMENTS
McIntyre, Marvin H.		Cabinet	3	10	15		Sec'y to FDR
McIntyre, O. O.		Author	15	25	40	20	Journalist, Synd. Columnist
McKay, Douglas	1893-1959	Cabinet	15	25		20	Governor OR, Sec'y Interior
McKay, Gardner		Entertainment	6	8	15	20	
McKay, Kelli		Entertainment	15			30	Miss USA 1991
McKean, Thomas	1734-1817	Rev. War	225	502	850		Signer. ADS 1778 $2250
McKee, Thomas H.		Senate/Congress	10	20			
McKeever, Chauncey (WD)		Civil War	40		175		Union Gen.
McKeldin, Theodore R.		Governor	5	17		10	Governor MD
McKellar, Kenneth D.	1869-1957	Congress	10	30			Senator TN
McKellen, Ian		Entertainment	12			35	Actor
McKenna, Joseph (SC)		Supreme Court	35	50	80	40	Att'y General
McKenna, Siobhan		Entertainment	15			35	
McKenzie, Fay		Entertainment	5		15	15	
McKenzie, Jacqueline		Entertainment	3			8	
McKeon, Nancy		Entertainment	4	6		30	
McKeon, Phillip		Entertainment	5			20	
McKern, Leo		Entertainment	15			40	Rumpole
McKinley, Ida S.		First Lady	400	625	975	450	
McKinley, Ray		Entertainment	20			65	Bandleader, Drummer
McKinley, William (As Pres.)		President	342	731	2262	1125	White House Card S $425-$750
McKinley, William	1843-1901	President	224	494	932	1067	Assassinated by Anarchist
McKinly, John		Rev. War	65	180			First Gov. DE, Captured by Br.
McKnight, Kauffer E.	1890-1954	Artist	60		425		Br. Known For Book Illustrations, Poster Designs
McKone, John R.		Military	10	20	40	30	
McKuen, Rod		Author	20	25	35	50	Poet
McLachlan, Sarah		Entertainment	12			45	Actress. Pin-Up SP $75
McLaglin, Andrew V.		Entertainment	10		25		
McLaglin, Victor	1886-1959	Entertainment	165			335	AA The Informer
McLain, Raymond S.		Military	30			45	Gen. WW II
McLains, The		Country Music	20			45	
McLane, Louis		Business	35	142			Am. Statesman.Bank Pres. Pres. Wells Fargo & Co.
McLane, Louis	1786-1857	Cabinet	15	45	60		Jackson Sec'y Treasury
McLane, Robert		Diplomat-Gov.	35	80	135		Gov. MD, U.S. Minister to Jap.
McLaughlin, E.A.		Business	10	35	45	20	
McLaughlin, James C.		Senate/Congress	10	15		15	MOC MI
McLaughlin, Kyle		Entertainment	20			75	
McLaws, Lafayette	1821-97	Civil War	165	347	412		CSA Gen. Sig/Rank $290
McLean, Don		Entertainment	20			45	Rock
McLean, George P.		Senate	10	15	25		Gov., Senator CT
McLean, John (SC)	1785-1861	Supreme Court	55	200	285		Dissented Dred Scott Opinion
McLean, Nathaniel C.		Civil War	60	80	170		Union General
McLeod, Archibald Norman		Fur Trader		2500			Hudson's Bay Co. vs NW Co.
McLeod, Catherine	1921-	Entertainment	8	15	20	20	Actress. Films from 40's
McLintock, Francis Sir		Celebrities	10	30	75		

NAME	DATE	CATEGORY	SIG	LS/DS	ALS	SP	COMMENTS
McLuhan, Marshall		Author		37			
McMahon, Brien	1903-52	Congress	10	40		15	Senator CT
McMahon, Ed		Entertainment	5			15	
McMahon, Horace		Entertainment	20			50	
McManus, George*		Cartoonist	50			247	Bringing Up Father, Panel $1,500
McMichael, Morton		Journalist	45	95			1st Editor Saturday Eve'g Post
McMillan, Edwin M.		Science	20	35	69	30	Nobel Chemistry 1952
McMillan, James	1838-1902	Congress	12	20	35		Senator MI 1889
McMillan, James Winning		Civil War	40				Union General
McMillan, Kenneth		Entertainment	5	6	15	15	
McMillan, Terry		Entertainment	3	4	10	8	
McMonagle, Donald		Astronaut	4			20	
McMorris, Charles H. Adm.		Military	10			35	WW II Naval Commander
McMullen, Clements	1892-	Military	50	150			WW I Aviator, WW II General
McMullen, Richard C.		Governor	5	10			Governor DE
McNair, Howard		Entertainment	400				Actor. Andy Griffith Show
McNair, Leslie J.		Military	35	95	165	80	WW I, General, WW II KIA
McNair, Robert		Governor	5	15		10	Governor SC
McNair, Ronald E.	1950-86	Astronaut	75	150		275	Died in Challenger Crash. Postal Cover $1575
McNally, Stephen		Entertainment	10			20	
McNally, W.		Entertainment	5	6	15	15	
McNamara, Robert S.		Cabinet	15	50		15	Sec'y Defense, Pres. World Bank
McNamara, William		Entertainment	5	8	25	25	
McNamee, Graham		Entertainment	20				Legendary Sports Announcer
McNarney, Joseph T.		Military	20	50			General WW II
McNary, Charles L.	1874-1944	Congress	15	35			Senator OR. McNary Dam
McNaughton, Kenneth		Military	4	9	15	10	
McNee, Patrick		Entertainment	10			25	
McNeil, Claudia		Entertainment	3			8	Actress
McNeil, Robert		Entertainment	5			30	Star Trek
McNeill, Don	1907-96	Entertainment	15	15	25	25	Radio-TV. Hosted Don McNeill's Breakfast Club
McNichol, Kristy		Entertainment	10			30	Pin-Up SP $35
McNutt, Paul V.		Governor	15	30			Governor IN
McPartland, Jimmy		Entertainment	30	55		85	Jazz Trumpet
McPate, Randolph R.		Military	30			95	Commandant of U.S. Marine Corps
McPhatter, Clyde		Entertainment	400		800		Classic Rocker
McPherson, Aimee Semple		Clergy	100	300	495	350	
McPherson, Elle		Entertainment	20			65	Model-Actress
McPherson, Isaac V.		Senate/Congress	5	15			MOC MO
McPherson, James B. (WD)		Civil War	375		2286		Union General KIA 1864
McPherson, John R.	1833-97	Congress	12	20	30		Senator NJ
McPherson, William		Author	15		70		Critic & Author. Pulitzer 1977 for Journalism
McQuade, James (WD)		Civil War	45	85			Union Gen.
McQuade, James	1829-85	Civil War	25	70	178		Union General
McQueen, Butterfly	1911-95	Entertainment	61	88		95	SP as Prissy (GWTW) $125, SP 2x4 $75

NAME	DATE	CATEGORY	SIG	LS/DS	ALS	SP	COMMENTS
McQueen, Steve	1930-80	Entertainment	200	412		375	
McRaney, Gerald		Entertainment	5			25	
McReynolds, James C. (SC)	1862-1946	Supreme Court	35	125	145	100	Wilson Att'y Gen. Justice 1914-41
McShane, Ian		Entertainment	9	10	20	25	
McShann, Jay		Entertainment	50			125	Jazz Pianist, Vocalist, Bandlead
McWade, John		Entertainment	10				Character Actor
McWethy, John		Entertainment	4			20	ABC News
McWhorter, Hamilton		Aviation	12	25	45	35	ACE, WW II
McWilliams, Caroline		Entertainment	4	6	9	9	
Mead, Margaret	1901-78	Science	70	125	170	225	Anthropologist, Lecturer, Author
Meade, Carl J.		Astronaut	5			22	
Meade, George G. (WD)		Civil War	695	945	2524	2500	Union Gen. DS $1750
Meade, George G.	1815-72	Civil War	220	298	729	350	Union Gen. Special ALS Re. Officer's Service $1900
Meadowlarks		Entertainment	3			6	
Meadows, Audrey		Entertainment	15			32	Pin-Up SP $45
Meadows, Jayne		Entertainment	5			10	
Meagher, Thomas F. (WD)		Civil War	122	685	1210		Union Gen.
Meagher, Thomas F.	1823-67	Civil War	45	180	240		Union Gen.
Meaney, Colm		Entertainment	15			30	Star Trek
Means, Abigail		First Lady	125		1250		Aunt Abby. Surrogate First Lady for Pierce
Meany, George		Labor Leader	15	30		90	Pres. AFL-CIO
Meara, Anne		Entertainment	4	4		15	
Meat Loaf		Entertainment	5		25	45	Rock
Mecham, Edwin L.		Senate	5	15		12	Governor, Senator NM
Medawar, Peter B., Sir		Science	20	30	60	25	Nobel Medicine 1960
Meddick, Jim*		Cartoonist	5			35	Robotman
Meddick, Jim*		Cartoonist	5			35	Illustrator of Robotman
Medeiros, Humberto, Cardinal		Clergy	35	50	60	50	
Medici, Cosimo I, de	1519-74	Royalty	375	1320			The Great. Duke of Florence
Medici, Fernando de	1549-1609	Royalty	370	1250	3125		Son of Cosimo I. Gr. Duke
Medici, Giovanni Gastone de	1671-1737	Royalty		375	525		Grand Duke of Tuscany
Medici, Leopoldo de, Cardinal		Clergy	300	385	550		Cardinal. Son of Cosimo II
Medicis, Catherine de		Royalty	270	800	5000		Queen of Henry II of France
Medicis, Francesco de		Royalty	100	200	500		NRPA
Medicis, Marie de	1573-1642	Royalty	350	950	2500		Queen of Henry IV (Fr)
Medill, Joseph		Journalist	125		250		A founder Repub. Party
Medill, William	1802-65	Congress	12				Repr. OH, Gov. OH
Medina, Harold R.		Jurist	10	25		15	
Medina, Patricia		Entertainment	5			25	Brit. Actress
Medjugorje (Jugo) Children of		Religious	300				2 Who Saw Vision Virgin Mary
Medley, Bill		Country Music	6			20	
Meeker, Ralph		Entertainment	25			40	
Meese, Edwin III	1931-	Cabinet	10	35	35	40	Att'y General Reagan. Resigned abruptly
Mehta, Zubin		Conductor	12			50	International Conductor
Mei-Figner, Medea	1859-1952	Entertainment				1200	Opera. It.-Russian Mezzo-Soprano

NAME	DATE	CATEGORY	SIG	LS/DS	ALS	SP	COMMENTS
Meier, Waltraud		Entertainment	15			35	Opera
Meighan, James		Entertainment				20	Radio Actor. The Falcon
Meighan, Tom		Entertainment	35			85	
Meigs, Montgomery C.(WD)		Civil War	45	250	255		Union Gen.
Meigs, Montgomery C.	1816-92	Civil War	55	200	175	250	Union Quartermaster General
Meigs, Return J., Jr.	1764-1824	Military-Cabinet	80	205	360		Monroe P.M. General
Meiklejohn, G.D.		Cabinet	15	40			Ass't Sec'y War
Meinl, Tanaka		Entertainment	30			75	Opera
Meir, Golda	1898-1979	Head of State	150	275	600	350	TLS/Content $1,500-$2,500. FDC S $125
Meitner, Lise	1878-1968	Science	95			160	Austrian Physicist. Uranium Fission. Fermi Award '66
Melachrino, George		Bandleader	14				Arranger
Melba, Nellie, Dame	1859-1931	Entertainment	72	135	200	345	Australian Operatic Soprano
Melbourne, Wm. Lamb, Lord	1779-1848	Head of State	70	85	158		Q. Victoria's 1st Prime Minister
Melchior, Lauritz	1890-1973	Entertainment	65	100		184	Opera Danish Tenor. Wagnerian Roles at Met.
Melis, Carmen		Entertainment	35			85	Opera, Teacher
Mellencamp, John		Entertainment	35			62	Rock. Album Cover S $60-$80
Mellnik, Steve		Military	5	25	35		
Mellon, Andrew W.	1855-1937	Business	238	838	1350	325	Pitts. Millionaire Tycoon. Sec'y Treas. Financier
Melnick, Bruce E.		Astronaut	5			16	
Melton, James		Entertainment	10			55	Am. Concert, Radio & Opera Tenor
Melvill, Thomas	1751-1832	Rev. War	90	250	550		Memb. Boston Tea Party
Melville, George W.		Military	40	105	170		Union Adm.
Melville, Herman	1819-91	Author	500	1820	9800		ALS's/Content $20,000-$40,000
Melville, Viscount	1771-1851	Royalty	55	225			Robert S. Dundas. 1st Lord of Admiralty. Arctic Expl
Memminger, Chris.G.(WD)		Civil War	165	625	600		CSA Sec'y of Treasury
Mencken, Henry L.	1880-1956	Author	95	212	365	450	Satirist, Editor, Essayist, Critic, Journalist
Mendel, Gregor Johann		Science	400	850	2000		Laws of Biological Inheritance
Mendeleyev, Dmitry	1834-1907	Science			1650		Rus. Chem. Developed Periodic Table
Mendelssohn-Bartholdy, F.	1809-47	Composer	600	1233	3134		ALS/Content $6,500
Mendes, Abraham Caulle		Author	15	35	100		Fr. Poet. Plays, Verses, Libretti
Mendez, Arnaldo Tamayo		Astronaut	6			15	
Menendez, Lyle		Criminal	50	175			Convicted Murderer of Parents. S Chk. $150
Mengelberg, Willem	1871-1951	Entertainment				210	Dutch Conductor. AMusQS $250
Mengele, Josef	1911-9?	Science	3695				Auschwitz Dr. Experimented on Inmates. WW II
Menjou, Adolphe	1890-1963	Entertainment	35	35		75	Dapper, Well Dressed Film Actor. 20's into 40's
Menk, Louis W.		Business	5			10	CEO International Harvester
Menken, Helen	1902-66	Entertainment	22		30	30	Stage Star & Occasional Films. Bogart's 1st Wife
Menkes, Sara		Entertainment	20			55	Opera
Mennin, Peter		Composer	10		65		AMusQS $75
Menninger, Karl	1893-1980	Science	35	90	120	75	Menninger Clinic & Foundation
Menninger, Roy		Science	10	25	55	30	
Menninger, William C., Dr.		Science	15	45	82	35	Psychiatrist, Pres. Foundation
Menocal, Mario G.		Head of State	25			40	Pres. Cuba 1913-21
Menon, V. Krisna		Diplomat	20		25		Ambassador Gr. Britain
Menotti, Gian Carlo	1911-	Composer	168	350	382	425	It.-Am. Composer Amahl & the Night Visitors

NAME	DATE	CATEGORY	SIG	LS/DS	ALS	SP	COMMENTS
Menuhin, Yehudi	1916-99	Entertainment	45	90		222	Concert Violinist, Conductor, Child Prodigy
Menzies, Robert, Sir		Head of State	15	55	125	25	Australian Prime Minister
Merbold, Ulf		Astronaut	10	25		25	
Mercadante, Saverio	1795-1870	Composer	150		450		Dir. Royal Conservatory, Naples
Mercer, Archibald		Rev. War					Patriot. Cont. ALS $750
Mercer, Frances		Entertainment	5	8		15	
Mercer, Hugh W.	1808-77	Civil War	90	175			CSA General. War Date Sig. $195
Mercer, John Francis	1759-1821	Rev. War	70		125		Aide-de-Camp Gen Lee
Mercer, Johnny		Composer	50			135	Vocalist, Pianist
Mercer, Mable		Entertainer					Jazz Singer
Mercer, Marian		Entertainment	10			35	
Merchant, Natalie		Entertainment	8			65	Music
Mercier, D. Joseph, Cardinal		Clergy	35	45	75		
Mercouri, Melina		Entertainment	25	30	45	65	
Mercury (4 Astronauts)		Astronaut					Schirra, Glenn, Slayton, Shepard S Phil. Cover $1050
Mercury (6 Astronauts)		Astronaut		1300		1250	No Virgil Grissom. FDC $900
Mercury (7 Astronauts)		Astronaut				3536	All 7 Sigs
Meredith, Burgess		Entertainment	10	32	35	48	Stage Actor before Films.
Meredith, Edwin T.		Cabinet	5	20	30	15	Sec'y Agriculture 1920
Meredith, James H.		Activist	35	90	185	60	Afro-Am. Activist
Meredith, Samuel	1740-1817	Cabinet	90	300	370		Rev. War Gen., 1st US Treasurer. Financier, Patriot
Meredith, Solomon		Civil War	125		450		Union Gen. Iron Brig. of West
Meriam, Ebenezer		Science			225		Meteorologist
Merivale, Philip		Entertainment	7		25	25	Vintage Br. Actor
Meriwether, Lee		Entertainment	5	10	12	15	
Merkel, Una		Entertainment	10			25	
Merli, Francesco		Entertainment	25			75	Opera. Dramatic Tenor
Merli, Gino J.		Military	5	25			WW II Hero CMH
Merlin de Douai, P.A.		Fr. Revolution	40		200		Revolutionary. Min. of Justice
Merman, Ethel	1909-84	Entertainment	30			81	Broadway Musical Star Before Movies
Merriam, Frank F.		Governor	5	15		10	Governor CA
Merrick, David		Entertainment	20	20	70	60	Theatrical Producer
Merrick, Samuel Vaughan		Business	40	175			Financier
Merrill, Aaron, Adm.		Military	10			38	WW II Solomon Islands
Merrill, Dina		Entertainment	6	8	15	15	
Merrill, Frank D.	1903-55	Military	225	850	325		Gen. WW II. Merrill's Marauders
Merrill, Gary	1914-90	Entertainment	15	20	45	35	
Merrill, Henry T.		Aviation	30	45	100	100	
Merrill, Lewis		Civil War	60	175			Union General
Merrill, Richard Dick		Aviation	30	55	105	75	
Merrill, Robert		Entertainment	30			50	Metropolitan Opera Co. Baritone
Merrill, Stuart		Author	30		125		Am. Poet. Wrote in French
Merriman, Nan	1920-	Entertainment	20			75	Opera. U.S. Mezzo-Sop.
Merrimon, Augustus S.	1830-92	Congress	22	35			Senator NC
Merritt, Chris		Entertainment	10			30	Opera

NAME	DATE	CATEGORY	SIG	LS/DS	ALS	SP	COMMENTS
Merritt, Wesley	1834-1910	Civil War	85	305	200		Union Gen., Indian Fighter
Merton, Thomas		Clergy	375	1135			Priest-Writer, Poet
Mesmer, F. Anton, Dr.	1734-1815	Science	115	285	535		Ger. Dr.Mesmerise.DS $3750
Messerschmitt, Wilhelm	1898-1978	Aviation	125	275		395	Ger. Aircraft Designer-Mfg. Messerschmitt
Messiaen, Olivier		Composer	70	200			Fr. Organist. AMusQS $475-$1350
Messick, Dale*		Cartoonist	15			105	Brenda Starr
Messick, Don	1921-97	Entertaiment			30	45	Cartoon Voice of Scoobie Do, Boo Boo Bear etc.
Messmer, Otto*		Cartoonist	55			400	Felix The Cat
Mesta, Perle		Business	25	30	70	35	Washington Hostess
Metallica (4)		Entertainment				90	Rock. Metallica CD Jacket S $85
Metcalf, Laurie		Entertainment	15			30	Actress. Roseanne
Metcalf, Victor H.	1853-1936	Cabinet	20	55	95		Sec'y Navy, Commerce, Labor
Metcalfe, Ralph H.		Senate/Congress	5	15		22	MOC IL
Metchnikoff, Elie		Science	60	95		150	Nobel Physiology 1908
Metternich, Prince C. W. von		Head of State	260	282	480		1869-1954. Austrian Statseman
Metzenbaum, Howard		Senate	10			20	Senator OH
Metzer, Joe		Artist	10				Illustrator. Origianal Sm. Sketch $45
Meusel, Lucille		Entertainment	10			25	Soprano
Mewman, Larry		Aviation	25			75	
Meyer, Albert G., Cardinal		Clergy	35	40	50	40	
Meyer, E. C.		Military	6	10	30	20	
Meyer, George von L.		Cabinet	15	20	35	20	P.M. General 1907
Meyer, John C.		Aviation	35			195	Fighter Ace of WW II
Meyer, Joseph	1894-19—	Composer	75		225		Calif. Here I Come, If You Knew Susie....
Meyerbeer, Giacomo	1791-1864	Composer	170	310	542	300	Ger. Composer of Fr. Operas
Mfume, Kweisi		Congress	10			40	Head of NAACP
Miaskovsky, Nikolai	1881-1950	Composer	125				27 Symphonies
Michael, George		Entertainment	20	30	95	100	
Michaels, Barbara		Author	5		25	15	
Michaels, Bret		Entertainment	10	20	50	45	
Michaels, Dolores		Entertaiment	10				Acctress
Michaels, Lorraine		Playboy Model	4			8	Pin-Up SP $10
Michaels, Marilyn		Entertainment	5		25	20	
Michel, Frank Curtis		Astronaut	5			15	
Michelangelo (Buonarroti)		Artist	2250	10000	25000		NRPA
Michele, Denise		Entertainment	3	3		8	
Michelet, Jules	1798-1874	Author	30		77		Great Historian of Romantic School
Michelson, Albert A.		Science	120		450		Nobel Physics 1907
Michelson, Charles		Political	12	15			Speech Writer New Deal
Michener, James A.	1907-98	Author	60	250	340	115	Am. Novelist. Pulitzer. FDC S $50
Middleton, Arthur		Rev. War	1100	3300	3850		Signer Decl. of Indepen.
Middleton, Charles		Entertainment	75			250	
Middleton, Charles, Sir	1726-1813	Military					Issued Orders for Victory at Trafalgar
Middleton, Henry	1717-84	Rev. War	3000	4500			Pres. of Congress. Special DS $9500
Middleton, Robert		Entertainment	50			150	

NAME	DATE	CATEGORY	SIG	LS/DS	ALS	SP	COMMENTS
Middleton, Thomas Fanshaw		Clergy	30	50	80		
Middleton, Troy H., Gen.		Military	10			40	WW I & WW II
Middleton, Velma		Entertainment	30			70	Jazz Vocalist
Midler, Bette		Entertainment	15			45	Singer-Actress
Midori		Entertainment	15			50	
Mielziner, Jo		Entertainment	15		40	35	Film Director
Mifflin, Thomas	1744-1800	Rev. War	190	490			Rev. War Gen'l. Pres. Continental Congr.
Mifune, Toshiro		Entertainment	20		75	50	Popular Japanese Star
Migenes, Julia		Entertainment	15			35	Opera
Mihalovivi, Marcel		Composer	20			150	Rumanian
Miklas, Wilhelm	1872-1956	Head of State	35				Pres. Austria
Mikoyan, Anastasy I.	1895-1970	Head of State	85			125	Pres. Presidium Supreme Soviet USSR
Mikulski, Barbara		Congress	15			30	Democratic senator Maryland
Milano, Alyssa		Entertainment	20			45	
Milanov, Zinka		Entertainment	20			120	Metropolitan Opera
Milburn, William H.	1823-1903	Clergy	35				Blind Circuit Rider Minister
Milch, Erhard		Aviation	80	250	400	175	WW I, Insp. Gen.Luftwaffe WW II
Miles, Josephine		Author	7	15	25	10	
Miles, Nelson A.	1839-1925	Civil War	130	285	352		Union General, MOH
Miles, Sarah		Entertainment	9	10	25	25	Pin-Up SP $35
Miles, Sylvia		Entertainment	10	20	35	35	
Miles, Vera		Entertainment	6	8	15	20	Pin-Up SP $25
Milestone, Lewis		Entertainment	35			85	Film Director
Milhaud, Darius	1892-1974	Composer	190	222	315	450	Fr. Composer. AMusQS $475-$500. SP Pc $250
Mill, James		Author	65	250	515		Scot.Philosopher,Historian,Econ
Mill, John Stuart	1806-73	Author-Editor	150	400	1503		Br. Economist, Philosopher,Reformer
Mill, William Hodge		Clergy	20	25	30		
Millais, John Everett, Sir	1829-96	Artist	45	90	232		Pre-Raphaelite Painter
Milland, Ray		Entertainment	30	50		70	
Millay, Edna St. Vincent	1892-1950	Author	145	325	1000	1275	Am. Poet, Dramatist. Pulitzer
Miller, Alice Duer		Author	15	25	45		Novelist, Poet
Miller, Ann		Entertainment	15			50	Pin-Up SP $30
Miller, Arjay R.		Business	3	10	25	5	
Miller, Arthur	1915-	Author	60	90	175	75	Playwright. Pulitzer.TMsS & AMsS $3,900
Miller, Caroline		Author	10	20			Pulitzer
Miller, Charles Henry	1842-1922	Artist	25			100	Landscape Painter
Miller, Dennis		Entertainment	8	35		24	Comedian-Actor-Writer. Sat. Nite Live. HBO
Miller, Denny	1935-	Entertainment	5			25	Character actor
Miller, Eddie		Entertainment	20			45	Big Band Tenor Saxophonist
Miller, Frederick C.		Business	12	32	64	25	Miller Beer
Miller, G. William		Cabinet	5	15	25	12	Sec'y Treasury
Miller, Glenn	1904-44	Entertainment	158	683	450	497	Big Band Leader-Trombonist. WW II Casualty
Miller, H.G.		Business	10			15	
Miller, Henry		Entertainment	35			55	Vintage Actor
Miller, Henry John	1869-1926	Entertainment	35	40	75	70	Br.-Am. Leading Man. Henry Miller Theatre

NAME	DATE	CATEGORY	SIG	LS/DS	ALS	SP	COMMENTS
Miller, Henry V.	1891-1980	Author	85	160	441	150	Am.Candid Autobiographical Novels.Tropic of Cancer
Miller, Jacob W.	1800-1862	Congress	12				Sen. NJ
Miller, Joaquin	1839-1913	Author	62		108		Am. Poet, Journalist.Spec. TLS $3500
Miller, John F.		Civil War	35	50	60		Union Gen., U.S. Sen. CA
Miller, Ken		Entertainment	3			20	Child Actor
Miller, Leslie A.		Governor	10	20			Governor WY
Miller, Marilyn		Entertainment	72		240	215	Ziegfield Follies Dancing Star
Miller, Marvin		Entertainment	10			25	
Miller, Mitch		Entertainment	5			15	Conductor, Arranger
Miller, Nathan L.		Governor	15	25		20	Governor NY
Miller, Oskar von	1855-1934	Science	115		325		Ger. Co-Founder of German Edison Co.
Miller, Patsy Ruth		Entertainment	25	35	55	45	
Miller, Penelope Ann		Entertainment	20			50	
Miller, Roger		Country Music	35			60	Composer
Miller, Samuel F. (SC)	1816-90	Supreme Court	95	160	290		Appointed by Lincoln
Miller, Stanley		Science	15	35	65	20	
Miller, Stephen		Civil War	95	195	295		Union General
Miller, Taylor		Entertainment	4	4	9	10	
Miller, Warner	1838-1918	Congress	10	20	35		Repr., Senator NY
Miller, William H. H.		Cabinet	10	30	50	20	Att'y General 1889
Millerande, Alexandre	1859-1943	Head of State	40	45	60	35	Socialist Pres. France 1920-24
Milles, Carl		Artist	30	55	90		Am. Sculptor
Millet, Aime'	1819-91	Artist		30	75		Fr.Sculptor-Painter Works Adorn Paris Public Bldgs
Millet, Francis Davis	1846-1912	Artist	25	45	340		Am. Medal Winning Art. Journalist
Millet, Jean Fran‡ois	1814-75	Artist	200	450	2500		Fr.Religious,Classical,Peasant
Milligan, Edward		Business	5	15			Insurance Exec.
Millikan, John		Military	9	30	50	20	
Millikan, Robert A., Dr.	1868-1953	Science	85	182	425	200	Nobel Physics,Educator,Author
Milliken, William G.		Governor	5	15		10	Governor MI
Millinder, Lucky		Entertainment	40			125	Bandleader
Millman, William	1927-	Military	14			25	Israeli Independence Hero.Am.Vol. Sailor on Exodus
Millo, Aprile		Entertainment	10			35	Opera
Mills Brothers (4)		Entertainment	100			200	
Mills, Darius Ogden	1825-1910	Business	238	875	2750		Merchant,Calif.Banking Giant. Philan. RR DS $1550
Mills, Donna		Entertainment	9	10		30	Producer. Pin-Up SP $25
Mills, Earle W.		Military	12	30			
Mills, Elijah Hunt	1776-1829	Congress	20		50		MOC & Sen. MA.
Mills, Hayley		Entertainment	10		25	35	Pin-Up SP $28
Mills, John, Sir	1908-	Entertainment	20			40	Brit. Oscar Winner.
Mills, Juliette		Entertainment	10			20	
Mills, Madison		Civil War	35				Union Gen. Med.Off'r.. War Dte.ALS $275
Mills, Ogden L.	1884-1937	Cabinet	10	23	45	15	Sec'y Treasury 1932. MOC NY
Mills, Roger Q.		Civil War	25	35	50		CSA Colonel, MOC TX
Mills, Wilbur	1909-	Congress	25			35	Senator AR
Milne, A. A.	1882-1956	Author	162	450	950		Winnie-the-Pooh. Playwright, Poet

NAME	DATE	CATEGORY	SIG	LS/DS	ALS	SP	COMMENTS
Milner, Martin		Entertainment	4	6		15	
Milnes, Rich.M.(Baron Houghton)		Celebrity	5	10	25	10	Man of Letters.Oxford Movement
Milnes, Sherrill		Entertainment	10			25	Opera. Am. Basso
Milosz, Czeslaw, Dr.		Author	45	125		50	Nobel Literature
Milroy, Robert H.	1816-90	Civil War	25	80			Union Gen. LS '61 $220
Milsap, Ronnie		Country Music	5			15	Singer. DS re Grammy Awards $75
Milstein, Nathan	1904-1992	Entertainment	45			150	Rus. Violinist
Miltonberger, Butler		Military	35	60			
Mimieux, Yvette		Entertainment	5	8		21	Pin-Up SP $25
Mincus, Leon		Composer	55			375	Austro-Rus. Many Ballets
Mindil, George W.		Civil War	35		210		Union Gen. MOH
Mindszenty, Jozef, Cardinal		Clergy	50	75	135	95	
Minelli, Liza	1946-	Entertainment	15	25	95	25	Actress-Singer.Movie Poster S $100.'Cabaret' SP 85
Mineo, Sal	1939-76	Entertainment	150			388	Murdered at 37. 2 Oscar Nomination
Miner, Jan		Entertainment	5	6	15	10	
Mingus, Charlie		Entertainment					Jazz Musician-No Price Available
Minh, Duong Van Gen.		Military	15	40	75	40	
Minh, Ho Chi		Head of State	750	1500	2500	1500	Pres. & Founder N. Vietnam
Minich, Peter		Entertainment	5			20	Opera, Light Opera
Mink, Patsy T.		Senate/Congress	5	15		10	MOH HI
Minnelli, Liza		Entertainment	9	10	20	35	Pin-Up SP $35
Minnelli, Vincente	1910-	Entertainment	30			82	AA Film Director Father of Liza Minnelli
Minor, Ruediger, Bishop		Clergy	25	40	45	50	
Minow, Newton N.		Law	12			15	Chairman FCC
Minter, Mary Miles		Entertainment	90	115	230	200	
Minton, Sherman (SC)		Supreme Court	45	192	250	100	
Minton, Yvonne		Entertainment	5			25	Opera
Mintz, Eli	1904-88	Entertainment	10	15	25	15	Yiddish Theatre Veteran Character Actor
Minvielle, Gabriel		Fr. Revolution	850				NRPA
Miollis, S.A.F.		Fr. Revolution	100	215			
Mirabeau, Gabriel H.R	1749-91.	Fr. Revolution	95	275	575		Statesman, Diplomat,Politician
Mirabehin (M. Slade)		Celebrity	25		45		Companion-Follower of Gandhi
Miramon, Miguel (Mex)		Military	20	85	140		Cmdr. Army vs Juarez.
Miranda, Carmen	1913-55	Entertainment	100	185		345	Brazilian-Portuguese Singer-Movie Star. 40's
Miranda, Isa		Entertainment	35			85	Fr. Actress
Mirisch, Walter		Entertainment	6	8	15	20	Motion Picture Producer
Miro, Juan	1893-1983	Artist	200	578	788	310	Repro The Hare S $250,$325
Miroslava		Entertainment	25	30	70	65	
Mirren, Helen		Entertainment	10	20		65	Br. Actress
mischakoff, Mischa		Entertainment	25		85		Legendary Violinist. Toscanini's Concertmaster
Mishima, Yukio	1925-70	Author		575	2500		Dichotomy Between Mind & Soul. Ritual Suicide
Mishima, Yukio	1925-70	Author		575	2500		Dichotomy Between Mind & Body. Ritual Suicide 1970
Mission Impossible (Cast)		Entertainment				195	4 Leads incl. Tom Cruise
Mister, Mister		Entertainment	15			55	
Mistinguett, Madamoiselle		Entertainment	90			272	Moulon Rouge Dancer-Actress

NAME	DATE	CATEGORY	SIG	LS/DS	ALS	SP	COMMENTS
Mistral, Frederic		Author	30	75	130	50	Nobel Literature 1904
Mistral, Gabriela		Author	20	35	60	25	Nobel Lit.'43(Godoy Alcayaga)
Mitchel, Ormsby M.		Science-Civil War	125		475		Union Gen., Astronomy Prof.
Mitchell, Billy (William)	1879-1936	Aviation	300	800	975	1495	Gen. WW I. Pioneer Aerial Bombing. Courtmartialed
Mitchell, Cameron	1918-94	Entertainment	20			40	Actor. Leading Roles in Rugged Parts
Mitchell, Charles E.		Business	20	35	65	25	Chmn. National City Bank
Mitchell, Edgar D.		Astronaut	25	125	150	231	Moonwalker. Apollo 14
Mitchell, Grant		Entertainment	35			80	
Mitchell, James P.		Cabinet	15	25	30		Sec'y Labor
Mitchell, John Grant		Civil War	30	50	140		Union General
Mitchell, John Inscho		Civil War	44	60			Union Gen., MOC PA
Mitchell, John N.	1913-88	Cabinet	25			275	Att'y General.TLS/Cont $200
Mitchell, John W.		Aviation	12	25	42	32	ACE, WW II
Mitchell, Joni		Entertainment	4			15	Singer
Mitchell, Maggie	1832-1918	Entertainment	50			20	Entertained 1st CSA Gov't & Troops
Mitchell, Margaret	1900-49	Author	612	2650	3000		Pulitzer.TLS/Content $15,000
Mitchell, Maria		Science	90	185	375		Considered 1st Woman Astronomer. Mathematician
Mitchell, Martha		Celebrity	35	100		45	Wife Att'y Gen.-Watergate
Mitchell, Ormsby M. (WD)		Civil War			957		Union Gen. Died 1862 RARE
Mitchell, Silas Weir		Science-Civil War	25	95			Civil War Surgeon
Mitchell, Stephen Mix	1743-1835	Rev. War	65	295			Cont'l Congr.Federalist Sen. PA
Mitchell, Thomas	1892-1962	Entertainment	260			525	GWTW
Mitchell, Thomas, Sir		Military	10				Lord Provost Aberdeen
Mitchell, William D.		Cabinet	5	25	30	10	Att'y General
Mitchelson, Marvin		Law	13	25		20	Trial Att'y. Specialty Divorce
Mitchum, Robert	1917-97	Entertainment	20	45		90	Actor. Versatile Leading Man
Mitford, Jessica		Author	15	25	25	20	
Mitropoulous, Dimitri	1896-1960	Composer	45	50	95	135	Greek Conductor
Mitscher, Marc A.		Military	375			450	Adm. WW II (RARE)
Mitterand, Francois		Head of State	15	25	40	20	Pres. France
Mittford, Mary Russell		Author	15	20	40		Br. Poet. Historical Drama
Mix, Tom	1880-1940	Entertainment	75		250	462	Cowboy Star of Hollywood Silent & Early Talkies
Mix, Victoria		Entertainment	8	9	15	10	
Mizell, Wilmer D.		Senate/Congress	5	15			MOC KS, Prof. Baseball Pitcher
Mobley, Mary Ann		Entertainment	5	8	15	12	
Model, Walter		Military			500		NRPA
Modesti, Giuseppe		Entertainment	15			35	Opera
Modigliani, Amedeo		Artist	1200		4500		Content ALS $35,000
Modine, Matthew		Entertainment	6			25	Actor
Modjeske, Helena		Entertainment	15	25	35	30	
Moessbauer, Rudolf, Dr.		Science	20			55	Nobel
Moeur, Benjamin B.		Governor	12	15	25		Governor Arizona
Moffat, Robert		Clergy	50	90	100		
Moffett, W.A., Adm.		Military	15		50	55	MOH. With Adm. Dewey. FDC $90
Moffo, Anna		Entertainment	15			35	Opera, Concert

NAME	DATE	CATEGORY	SIG	LS/DS	ALS	SP	COMMENTS
Mohler, A. L.		Business	8	20	40	15	
Mohnke, WIlhelm		Military	35			150	Ger. Gen. SS
Moholy-Nagy, Laszlo	1895-1946	Artist	80	265			Painter, Designer, Photographer
Mohr, Gerald		Entertainment	35			75	
Mohri, Momoru		Astronaut	12	25		25	
Mojica, Jose		Entertainment	60			225	Opera
Mol, Gretchen		Entertainment	20			65	'Vanity Fair' Cover S $75
Molders, Werner		Aviation	175	275	400	325	ACE, WW II, !st to 100 Kills
Molitor, Gabriel J.J.	1770-1849	Fr. Revolution	75	175	250		Napoleon Gen., Marshal of Fr.
Moll, Kurt		Entertainment	15			35	Opera
Moll, Richard		Entertainment	6	8	15	15	
Mollet, Guy		Head of State	20	40	65		Socialist Premier France
Molnar, Ferenc	1878-1952	Author	72	140	275		Playwright, Novelist, Journalist
Moltke, H. Johann L.von		Military	15	30	60	30	Nephew Helmuth.
Moltke, Helmuth von, Count		Military	100	220	400	295	Prussian Field Marshal
Moltmann, Jurgen		Clergy	50	75	100	80	
Momaday, N. Scott		Author	10	15	25	15	
Momo, Giuseppe		Entertainment	10			35	Opera
Mompou, Frederico		Composer					Reclusive Spanish Composer. AMusQS $495
Monaghan, Tom		Business	10			20	Domino's Pizza
Moncada, Rivera y		Military		4500			1st Military Cmmdr.California
Moncey, Bon-Adrien J. de		Fr. Revolution	45	135	160		Marshal of France
Monck, George	1608-70	Military	95	382			1st Duke Albermarle.Restored Monarchy
Mondale, Walter (V)		Vice President	25	40		45	
Mondell, Franklin W.		Senate/Congress	10	15		15	MOC WY
Mondrian, Piet	1872-1944	Artist	312	675	1542		Dutch.Traditional-Cubism
Monet, Claude	1840-1926	Artist	300	1275	2347	1850	Fr. Impressionist Painter
Money, Hernando De Soto		Senate/Congress	10	25	45		MOC, Senator MS. CSA Army
Money, Ken		Astronaut	5	15		15	
Monk, Thelonious		Entertainment	50			150	Jazz Musician
Monkees, The (4)		Entertainment	75			225	Rock Group. Jones, Nesmith, Dolenz, Tork
Monroe, Bill		Entertainment	45		150		Father of Blue Grass Music
Monroe, Elizabeth		First Lady					Rare 10-12 Known
Monroe, James & Adams, John Q.		President					SEE Adams, John Quincy
Monroe, James & Madison, J.		President		3535			SEE Madison
Monroe, James	1758-1831	President	385	1557	2467		Free Frank $525. ANS $2000.DS(Appointm't)$3000
Monroe, Marilyn (Norman Jean)		Entertainment			15000		Signed Norma Jean
Monroe, Marilyn	1926-1962	Entertainment	1702	2692	7500	5167	ALS/Cont. $15,000. ALS (Thank you Note) $19,000
Monroe, Vaughn		Entertainment	15	25		30	
Monster Magnet		Entertainment	32			80	Music. 5 Member Rock Group
Montagu, Charles	1661-1715	Politician		210			Lord Halifax. Wit, Author. Created Bank of England
Montagu, Edwin Samuel	1879-1924	Politician	15	50	80	35	Br. Statesman
Montagu, John (Earl of Sandwich)		Celebrity	65	205	450		Sandwich Named For Him
Montague, Andrew J.		Congress	5	15	35		Repr., Senator VA
Montal, Lisa		Entertainment	5			20	Actres, Vintage

NAME	DATE	CATEGORY	SIG	LS/DS	ALS	SP	COMMENTS
Montalban, Ricardo		Entertainment	10	15	25	25	SP/Herve Villechaize & Montalban $50
Montalivet, J.P.B. Count		Fr. Revolution	35	100	225		
Montana, Bob*		Cartoonist	40			175	Archie
Montana, Bull		Entertainment	25			50	
Montana, Monte		Entertainment	5			15	
Montana, Patsy		Country Music	15			35	
Montand, Yves		Entertainment	10			35	
Montcalm, Louis J. Marquis de		Military	575	1765	3077		Cmdr. Fr.Troops in North Am.
Montefiore, Moses, Sir	1784-1885	Philanthropist	30	850	275		Br.-Jewish Philan.Sherrif of London
Montell, Lisa		Entertainment				15	Retired Actress-Heiress
Montenegro, Conchita		Entertainment	8	9	19	19	
Montessori, Maria	1870-1952	Educator	295		1050		1st Italian Woman Doctor
Monteux, Pierre		Entertainment	50			68	Conductor
Monteverde, Alfred de		Aviation	25	50	85	55	
Monteverde, George de		Aviation	25	50	85	55	
Montez, Lola	1818-61	Adventuress	200		725		Seductress of Louis I of Bavaria. RARE
Montez, Maria		Entertainment	50	55		100	
Montgolfier, Jacques-E.		Aviation			1800		With Joseph,1st hot air Balloon
Montgolfier, Joseph		Aviation					Special Content ALS $63,000
Montgomery, Bernard Law, Sir	1887-1976	Military	80	550	222	353	1887-1976. Of Alamein. Special DS $2,500
Montgomery, Douglass		Entertainment	10	15	25	25	
Montgomery, Elizabeth	1933-95	Entertainment	35	75		85	Star of TV's Bewitched Pin-Up SP $25
Montgomery, George		Entertainment	10	8	25	20	Western Actor & Talented Furniture Maker
Montgomery, James	1771-1854	Composer	15		195		Scot. Poet-Hymnwriter
Montgomery, James Shera		Clergy	50	65	75		Chaplin U.S. Congress
Montgomery, M., Lady		Celebrity	5	10	20		Mother of Bernard L. Montgomery
Montgomery, Melba		Country Music	10			20	
Montgomery, Robert	1904-81	Entertainment	15	30	60	25	Actor. Young & Mature Leading Man. Films.
Monti, Carlotta		Entertainment	15		75	40	W.C. Fields Paramour
Monti, Nicola		Entertainment	35			85	Opera
Montoya, Carlos		Entertainment	10	15	25	30	Classical Guitarist
Moody Blues (All 5)		Entertainment	145			275	60's Rock Group
Moody, Dwight L.	1837-99	Clergy	62	110	195	125	Evangelist, LS/Content $500
Moody, William H. (SC)	1853-1917	Supreme Court	45	125	175	50	Sec'y Navy, Att'y Gen'l, MOC
Moody, William V.		Author	30	85	125		Poet, Playwright
Moog, Bob		Science	50	70	110	65	Inventor. Synthesizer
Moon, Keith		Entertainment	175	280		380	Rock. 'The Who' Deceased Member
Mooney, Art		Entertainment	10			20	Big Band Leader
Mooney, Edward, Cardinal		Clergy	30	40	55	40	
Mooney, Tom	1883-1942	Labor Activist	25	60	180	275	Bombed Parade. TLS/Cont.$550
Moore, Alfred (SC)	1755-1810	Supreme Court	3000				Rev. War Soldier, NC Planter, Politician—RARE—
Moore, Andrew B.	1806-73	Civil War	45	115	145		CSA Gov. AL.ALS '61 $1485
Moore, Arch A. Jr.		Senate/Congress	5	15			Governor, MOC WV
Moore, Arthur J., Bishop		Clergy	20	25	40	40	
Moore, Barbara, Dr.		Celebrity	5		20		Br. Marathon Walker

NAME	DATE	CATEGORY	SIG	LS/DS	ALS	SP	COMMENTS
Moore, Clayton		Entertainment	10			32	Longtime The Lone Ranger
Moore, Clement C.	1779-1863	Author	245	450	1045		'Twas the Night Before ....' Am. Educator & Poet
Moore, Colleen	1900-88	Entertainment	10	20		38	Silent Screen Major Star/Travelling Doll House
Moore, Constance		Entertainment	8			20	Actress-Singer
Moore, Dan K.		Governor	5	15	30		Governor NC
Moore, Demi		Entertainment	45	140		95	Advanced from Soaps to Highest Paid Actress
Moore, Dick		Entertainment	10			25	Dickey Moore. Child Actor
Moore, Dudley		Entertainment	10			35	Actor-Pianist. Light Comedy Parts
Moore, Edward C.		Clergy	10	20	30		
Moore, Foster*		Cartoonist	15			50	'Napoleon'
Moore, Francis D., Dr.		Science	10	30	55	20	
Moore, Gary		Entertainment	15			25	TV Host-Comedian. Early TV
Moore, George	1852-1933	Author	45	115	125		Irish Novelist
Moore, Grace	1901-47	Entertainment	70	95		173	Met.Opera Star-Films.Died in Plane Crash. SPc $200
Moore, Henry		Artist	58	210	550	105	Br. Sculptor. 'The Thinker'
Moore, Jeremy, Sir		Military	5	15	25	15	General
Moore, Joanna		Entertainment	8			20	Actress
Moore, John Bassett		Law-Jurist	65		250		Internat'l Law.Permanent Court Internat'l Justice.
Moore, John, Sir	1761-1809	Military	60	225	350		Br. General vs Am.'til 1783. KIA 1809
Moore, Julianne		Entertainment	10			40	Actress
Moore, Marianne C.	1887-1972	Author	60	185		75	Am. Poet. Pulitzer
Moore, Mary Tyler		Entertainment	10	32		25	Pin-Up SP $25
Moore, Mary Tyler (Show-Cast of)		Entertainment	135			388	Six Main Characters
Moore, Ray*		Cartoonist	25			175	'Phantom'
Moore, Rich'd Channing		Clergy			160		Episcopal Bishop 1814-41
Moore, Roger		Entertainment	18			51	Followed Connery as 'James Bond'. SP as 007 $65
Moore, Roy D.		Business	10	25		20	Fndr. Newspaper-Radio Chain
Moore, Samuel P.		Civil War	595	725	800		Surgeon General CSA
Moore, Sara Jane		Radical	30	80	200		Attempted Assassination Pres. Ford
Moore, Sydenham		Congress-CW	40	55	90		MOC AL. CSA Officer
Moore, Terry		Entertainment	15		25	35	Pin-Up SP $40
Moore, Thomas	1779-1852	Author	50	105	475		Irish Poet. 'Tis The Last Rose of Summer'
Moore, Thomas O.		Civil War		440			CSA Gen., CW Gov. LA
Moore, Victor	1876-1962	Entertainment	25			55	Vaudeville Headliner. Film Wimpy Comedian
Moore, William		Colonial Am.	90	225			Colonial Am. Statseman-Jurist
Moorehead, Agnes		Entertainment	40			95	Fine Radio-Film Character Actress. 'Bewitched'
Moorer, Thomas		Military	70	145		100	Adm. Survivor-Twice
Moores, Dick*		Cartoonist	10			30	'Gasoline Alley'
Morales, Ramon V.		Head of State	15	35			Ecuador
Moran, Erin		Entertainment		25		35	Actress. Happy Days Cast
Moran, Lois		Entertainment	18			25	Actress.
Moran, Thomas		Artist	92	225	350		Specialized in American West
Moranis, Rick		Entertainment	8			25	
Moranville, H. Blake		Aviation	15	25	40	35	ACE, WW II, Navy Ace
Mordecai, Alfred		Military	15		95		West Point Instructor. General

NAME	DATE	CATEGORY	SIG	LS/DS	ALS	SP	COMMENTS
More, Thomas, Sir		Author	19750				NRPA
Moreau, Gustave	1826-98	Artist	35		200		Important Teacher of Matisse, Rouault
Moreau, Jean-Victor		Fr. Revolution	90	275	300		Fr. General under Napoleon
Morehead, James B.		Aviation	10	22	38	28	ACE, WW II, USAAF Ace
Morehead, John M.		Governor	10	25			Governor NC
Morehouse, A.P.		Governor	10	20		25	Governor MO
Moreland, Mantan		Entertainment	100	125		200	
Morell, George W. (WD)		Civil War	45	95	300		Union Gen.
Morell, George W.	1815-83	Civil War	30		80		Union Gen.
Morello, Tom		Entertainment	6			25	Music. Guitar Rage Against the Machine
Moreno, Anthony		Entertainment	3	3	6	6	
Moreno, Bertha		Entertainment	20			95	Opera
Moreno, Buddy		Bandleader				45	
Moreno, Rita		Entertainment	9	10	25	20	Pin-Up SP $30. AA. West Side Story Script S $50
Morgan, Barbara		Astronaut	5	35		15	
Morgan, Charles L.	1894-1958	Author	25	70	80		Br. Novelist, Dramatist, Critic
Morgan, Dennis		Entertainment	8		15	15	Actor-Singer
Morgan, Edward J.		Entertainment	10	12		25	
Morgan, Edwin Barber		Congress	40	75			NY, 1st Pres. Am.Expr.ALS $485-$985
Morgan, Edwin Denison, Jr.	1811-83	Civil War	40	72	95		Union Gen.,CW Gov.,NY.ALS '62 $200, US Sen.
Morgan, F. Crossley		Clergy	10	15	15	15	
Morgan, Frank	1890-1949	Entertainment	400	583		672	Collected as Wizard of OZ
Morgan, G. Campbell		Clergy	20	30	45		
Morgan, George		Country Music	15			35	
Morgan, George	1743-1810	Rev. War	125	425	675		Indian Agent, Speculator
Morgan, George W.	1820-93	Civil War		150			Union Gen.War Dte.ALS/Cont. $1650
Morgan, Harry		Entertainment	5	10	20	15	
Morgan, Helen	1900-1941	Entertainment	43	175		200	1st Julie in Show Boat. Noted Blues singer
Morgan, Jaye P.		Entertainment	5			15	
Morgan, John Hunt	1825-64	Civil War	800	1998	1750		CSA Gen. Wardte. DS $12,500
Morgan, John P., II		Business	275				Financier, Banker
Morgan, John Pierpont, Jr.	1867-1943	Business	85	185	280	95	Banker,Financier
Morgan, John Pierpont, Sr.	1837-1913	Business	328	1130	2500	1025	Banker, Financier, Philanthropist. Legal DS $2400
Morgan, John Tyler (WD)		Civil War	190	650	1600		CSA Gen.
Morgan, John Tyler	1825-1907	Civil War	125	198	350	240	CSA Gen., US Sen. AL.TLS/Cont. $1250
Morgan, Marion		Entertainment	6			14	Singer
Morgan, Michele		Entertainment	10			25	
Morgan, Ralph		Entertainment	35			65	
Morgan, Russ		Bandleader	20			65	Big Bandleader. Arranger
Morgan, Sydney, Lady		Author	15	35	60		Ir.Author.The Wild Irish Girl
Morgan, Thomas H.		Science	95	200	425	125	Nobel Medicine 1933
Morgan, Thos. Jeff.		Civil War	70	90	125		Union General
Morgan, Wm. H.		Civil War	25	55	75		
Morganna		Entertainment	5	8	20	15	Pin-Up SP $30
Morgenthau, Henry Jr.	1891-1967	Cabinet	35	65	145	60	FDR Sec'y Treasury

NAME	DATE	CATEGORY	SIG	LS/DS	ALS	SP	COMMENTS
Moriarty, Cathy		Entertainment	7			30	Actress. Pin-Up $45
Moriarty, Michael		Entertainment	10			30	
Morini, Erica		Entertainment	20			50	Austrian-born Violinist
Morison, Patricia		Entertainment	15	15	30	25	
Morison, Samuel E.	1887-1976	Author	30	55			Am. Historian. Pulitzer Prize Twice
Morita, Pat		Entertainment	10		25	25	
Morland, Mantan		Entertainment	25			50	
Morley, Christopher	1890-1957	Author	34	97	160	60	Am. Writer, Editor, Novelist
Morley, Robert	1908-92	Entertainment	32	75		80	Noted Br. Actor
Morphis, Joseph L.	1831-1913	Congress	10				Repr. MS, U.S. Marshal
Morrill, Justin Smith	1810-98	Congress	45	60	110		Repr., U.S. Senate VT 1855-98
Morrill, Lot M.		Cabinet	15	30	60		Sec'y Treas., Gov., Senator ME
Morris, Anita		Entertainment	6	8		20	
Morris, B. Wistar		Clergy	10		20		
Morris, Charles		Military	20	60			Commodore USN
Morris, Chester	1901-70	Entertainment	25	40		75	Silent Child Star to Adult '29 Oscar Nominee.
Morris, Clara	1846-1913	Entertainment	12				Vintage Actress
Morris, Edward Joy	1815-81	Congress	10				Repr. PA, Minister Turkey
Morris, Felix J.		Entertainment	15			40	Vintage Stage Actor
Morris, Francis (See L. Morris)	1713-81	Rev. War					Signer Decl. Of Independence
Morris, Gouverneur	1752-1816	Rev. War	190	668	625		Continental Congr., Diplomat
Morris, Greg	1934-96	Entertainment	15			40	Actor. Mission Impossible Original TV Series
Morris, Harrison Smith		Publisher	30	55			Magazine Editor
Morris, Howard		Entertainment	3			15	Comedian-Actor
Morris, James		Entertainment	5			25	Opera
Morris, Lewis	1726-98	Rev. War	675	1025	1662		Signer Decl. of Indepen. DS/Fran. Lewis $3500
Morris, Lewis, Sir		Author	5	10	20		
Morris, Robert & J. Nicholson		Rev. War		1500			Content DS $45,000, Content DS $29,500
Morris, Robert	1734-1806	Rev. War	388	1135	1316		Signer. Important DS $13500-22,000. Financier
Morris, Robert Page W.		Senate/Congress	5	10			MOC MN
Morris, Thomas A. (WD)		Civil War			3520		Union Gen.
Morris, Wayne		Entertainment	25			60	
Morris, William	1834-96	Artist	125	275	675		Br.Poet, Artist, Designer, Printer, Social Reform
Morris, William Walton	1801-65	Civil War	25	55	80		Union Gen. ALS '62 $160
Morrison, Harold		Country Music	10			20	
Morrison, Henry Clay		Clergy	25	35	50	40	
Morrison, Herb		Aviation	40	85	160	100	Announcer of Hindenburg Crash
Morrison, Jim	1943-71	Entertainment	683	2800		1375	Composer. Lead Singer The Doors
Morrison, Robert	1782-1834	Clergy		125	240		English Divine. 1st Missionary to China
Morrison, Samuel E.		Author	12	20			Historian
Morrison, Toni		Author	35	35	130	25	Afro-Am. Nobel Literature
Morrison, Van		Entertainment	18			45	
Morrison, William Ralls		Civil War	25		80		Union Officer, MOC IL
Morrow, Buddy		Bandleader	20			45	
Morrow, Dwight W.		Diplomat	10	35			Lawyer, Banker, Amb. to Mex.

NAME	DATE	CATEGORY	SIG	LS/DS	ALS	SP	COMMENTS
Morrow, Jeff		Entertainment	5	6	15	15	
Morrow, Rob		Entertainment	15			40	
Morrow, Vic	1932-82	Entertainment	100	120			Died in Tragic Helicopter Accident
Morse, Carleton E.		Writer-Producer	20	25		30	One Man's Family Vint. Radio
Morse, Jedediah	1761-1826	Science		75	125		Father of American Geography
Morse, Samuel F. B.	1791-1872	Science-Artist	375	1500	2100	3718	Telegraph, Pioneer Photographer. ALS/Cont. $7500
Morse, Wayne	1900-74	Congress	10	25		55	Senator OR
Mortier, Edouard A.C.J.		Fr. Revolution	35	115	230		Marshal of Fr., Statesman
Mortimer, Charles		Business	5	15	25	10	CEO General Foods
Morton, J. Sterling		Cabinet	25	50	145	75	Father Arbor Day, Sec'y Agri.
Morton, John	1724-77	Rev. War	458	1600	1338		Signer Decl. of Indepen., Continental Congr.
Morton, Levi P. (V)	1824-1920	Vice President	60	168	238	240	Gov. NY. VP. MOC, Minister to Fr.
Morton, Oliver P.		Senate	10	25			Governor, Senator IN
Morton, Peter A.		Business	40	195			Founder Hard Rock Café Chain
Morton, Wm. Thos. Green		Science	170	450	825		1st To Us Ether as Anesthetic
Mosby, John S. (WD)		Civil War		8500	9600		Gray Ghost , Mosby's Rangers
Mosby, John S.	1833-1916	Civil War	443	1800	2173	2650	CSA Off.,'Gray Ghost'. Content ALS $12,500
Moscona, Nicola		Entertainment	25			45	Opera
Moscone, George R.		Celebrity	80		95		
Mosel, Tad		Author	16	20	30	25	Am. Dramatist
Moseley, Corliss Champion !894-		Aviation	65	150			1st Pulitzer Aviation Speed Prize Winner-1920. ETC
Moseley, George Van Horn		Military	30	110			MacArthur's Dep. Chief of Staff
Moser, Edda		Entertainment	5			25	Opera
Moses, Anna Mary R. (Grandma)	1860-1961	Artist	250	500	860	660	ALS/Content $1,500
Moses, George H.		Senate/Congress	7	15	35		Senator NH. Diplomat
Moses, Robert	1888-1981	Public Official	15	40	65		Dominated NY Politics.Father of Interstate Hwy Sys
Mosher, Terry		Celebrity	5		10		
Mosley, Jack*		Cartoonists	25			105	Smilin' Jack
Mosley, Oswald, Sir	1896-1980	Political	30	75	210	140	Founder Br. Union of Fascists
Moss, Kate		Model	4			25	Pin-Up SP 25, Nude 90
Moss, Ralph W.		Senate/Congress	10	15	25		MOC IN 1909
Mossadegh, Muhammad		Head of State	40	75	165		Premier Iran. Nationalized Oil
Mossbauer, Rudolf L.		Science	25	55	90	45	Nobel Physics
Mossdorf, Martin		Aviation				25	Ger. RK Winner. Stuka Pilot
Mostel, Zero	1915-77	Entertainment	30	225		285	Stage, Film Comedy Star
Moszkowski, Moritz	1854-1924	Composer	50		200		Ger. Pianist. AMusQS
Motherwell, Robert	1915-91	Artist	60	442	325		Am. Abstract Expressionist. Pc Repro S$175
Motley Crue (4)		Entertainment	45			185	Rock group
Motley, John Lothrop	1814-77	Author	30	50	118		Am. Historian, Diplomat, Hall of Fame
Mott, Charles S.		Business	25				Pioneer Auto.Exec. A Founder Gen'l Motors
Mott, Frank L.		Journalist	10		35	20	Educator, Pulitzer
Mott, Gershom (WD)		Civil War	50	125			Union Gen.
Mott, Gershom	1822-84	Civil War	25		45		Union Gen.
Mott, John R.		Clergy	30	45	75	100	Nobel Peace Prize
Mott, Lucretia	1793-1880	Women's Rights	70	150	375	250	Reformer, Abolitionist, Suffrage

NAME	DATE	CATEGORY	SIG	LS/DS	ALS	SP	COMMENTS
Mott, Neville F. Dr.		Science	20	35	50	25	Nobel Physics
Moulton, Louise Chandler		Author	25	70	125		1835-1908. Bed Time Stories
Moulton, Samuel W.	1821-1905	Congress	10				Repr. IL
Moulton, William		Rev. War	20	145			
Moultrie, William	1730-1805	Governor-Military	160	392			Rev. War Gen. Fort Moultrie Namesake
Mount, James A.		Governor	30	100			Gov. IN
Mountbatten, Edwina, Lady		Celebrity	10	35			Wife of Louis Mountbatten
Mountbatten, Louis, Lord	1900-79	Military	120	200	315	200	Of Burma. Adm. of Fleet WW II. 1st Earl
Mountevens, Baron (E Evans)		Military	20	45		335	Br. WW I Naval Hero
Moutrie, Alexander		Rev. War	35		200		
Mowbray, Alan		Entertainment	45			75	
Mowbray, H. Siddons		Artist	25	40	70		Murals. J.P. Morgan Library etc
Mower, Joseph A.		Civil War	35	95	115		Union General
Moyers, Bill		Author	5	15	45	15	TV Host
Moynihan, Daniel Patrick		Senate/Congress	10	20		20	Senator NY
Mozart, Wolfgang A.		Composer	2500	8000	30000		
Mubarak, M. Hosni		Head of State	60	110	275	80	President Egypt
Mucha, Alphonse	1860-1939	Artist	78		842		Czech-Born French Painter- Illustrator Art Nouveau
Muck, Karl, Dr.		Conductor	10			50	
Mudd. Roger		News	5	10	30	15	Radio-TV News
Mueller, Frederick H.		Gov't Official	5	15	30		
Mueller, Reuben H., Bishop		Clergy	20	25	35	25	
Mueller-Stahl, Armin		Entertainment	4			12	
Muench, Aloisius J., Cardinal		Clergy	35	50	65	50	
Mugabe, Robert G.		Head of State	20	60	145	40	
Muggeridge, Malcolm		Clergy	30	40	50	40	
Muhammed, Elijah	1897-1975	Muslim Leader	120	312			Leader Black Muslim. Nation of Islam(Elijah Poole
Muhlenberg, John Peter Gabriel		Rev. War	125	260	2400		Gen. Cont. Army.ALS/Cont. $2400
Muhlenberg, Peter S.		Rev. War		25			
Muhlenberg, W. Augustus		Clergy	25	40	60		
Muir, Jean		Entertainment	8	9		20	
Muir, John	1838-1914	Science	450	1450	1975		Scot.-Am. Naturalist, Explorer
Mukai, Chiaki		Astronaut	10	25		27	
Muldaur, Diana		Entertainment	6	8	15	20	
Muldaur, Maria		Entertainment	5			15	
Muldoon, Robert		Head of State	10	20	30	20	Prime Minister New Zealand
Mulgrew, Kate		Entertainment	6		15	23	As 'Janeway' from Voyager $55
Mulhare, Edward		Entertainment	15			40	
Mulheen, R.J.		Business	3	5		8	CEO Boston & Maine RR Corp.
Mull, Martin		Entertainment	5	6		20	
Mullane, Richard M.		Astronaut	5			10	
Muller, Herman J.		Science	20	35	75	25	Nobel Medicine 1946
Muller, Hermann	1876-1931	Statesman	45		200		Ger. Foreign Minister. Chancellor
Mullican, Moon		Country Music	10			20	
Mulligan, Gerry		Entertainment	12			25	Baritone Sax. Arranger-Composer

NAME	DATE	CATEGORY	SIG	LS/DS	ALS	SP	COMMENTS
Mulligan, James A.	1830-1864	Civil War	271				Union Col. KIA; Irish Brig. War Dte.LS $550-$850
Mulligan, Richard		Entertainment	5	5		15	
Mulligan, Robert		Entertainment	5			20	
Mulliken, Robert S., Dr.		Science	38	118	65	35	Nobel Chemistry 1966
Mullin, Willard		Cartoonist	10			30	Sports Cartoonist
Mullowney, Deborah		Entertainment	4	6	10	15	
Mumy, Bill		Entertainment	5	18		15	Child Actor etc.5
Munch, Charles		Entertainment	10			35	Ger. Conductor
Munch, Edvard	1863-1944	Artist	65	350	1118		Nor. Painter-Printmaker
Mundel, Ed		Entertainment	6			25	Music. Lead Guitar Monster Magnet
Mundelein, Geo. Wm., Cardinal		Clergy	65	110	225	90	
Mundt, Karl E.		Senate	10	20		35	MOC, Senator SD, Educator
Munford, Thomas T.	1831-1918	Civil War	110		220		CSA Gen. Sig/Rank $310
Muni, Paul	1895-1965	Entertainment	7595		120	207	Academy Award Story of Louis Pasteur 1936
Munky		Entertainment	5			25	Music. Guitar Korn
Munro, Caroline		Entertainment	5	6	15	15	
Munro, Janet		Entertainment	12			30	Br. Actress. Disney Charmer
Munro, Leslie K., Sir		Diplomat	10	15		25	Pres. UN Assembly
Munro, Peter Jay	1767-1833	Jurist	30	65	155		Nephew of John Jay.
Munsel, Patrice		Entertainment	10	20	50	50	Met. Debut at 18
Munsey, Frank A.		Editor	15		35		Muncey's Magazine
Munson, Ona		Entertainment	225			250	Became Classic as Belle Watling in GWTW
Munster, Earl of		Military	10	25	40		
Munsterberg, Hugo	1863-1916	Science		225		95	Ger-Born Am. Psychologist
Munteanu, Petre		Entertainment	35	110	165		Opera
Muntz, Earl 'Madman'		Business	13	18	25	20	Pioneer TV Advertiser-Owner
Murat, Joachim	1767-1815	Fr. Revolution	135	650	590		Napoleon Marshal, Gov. Paris, King Naples
Murchison, Clint		Business	10	15	25	20	TX Oil Entrepreneur Millionaire
Murchison, Clint, Jr.		Business	5	10	20	12	
Murdoch, Rupert		Business	10	35	55	40	International Newspaper Publ.
Murphy Brown (Show-Cast of)		Entertainment				275	Seven Main Characters
Murphy, Audie	1924-71	Military	100	225	325	412	Western Film Star & WW II MOH Winner
Murphy, Ben		Entertainment	5	6	15	15	
Murphy, Eddie		Entertainment	25			75	
Murphy, Edward, Jr.	1836-1911	Congress	6	12			Senator NY
Murphy, Erin		Entertainment	5			15	Actress. Tabitha
Murphy, Frank (SC)	1890-1949	Supreme Court	70	188	350	160	
Murphy, Franklin		Governor	5	10		10	Governor NJ
Murphy, George L.	1902-	Entertainment	20		35	45	U.S. Senator from CA. Film Song & Dance Man
Murphy, John Cullen*		Cartoonist	5			45	Big Ben Bolt & Prince Valiant
Murphy, Richard		Author	15		25		Screenwriter
Murphy, Turk		Entertainment	20	40		50	Bandleader, Composer, Trombone
Murphy, William P., Dr.		Science	30	75	120	35	Nobel Medicine 1934
Murray, Anne		Entertainment	5	35		25	Singer
Murray, Arthur		Business	10	15	30	15	Ballroom Dance Studios

NAME	DATE	CATEGORY	SIG	LS/DS	ALS	SP	COMMENTS
Murray, Bill		Entertainment	12			30	Saturday Night Live ex-Patriot
Murray, Bob		Aviation	12	24	42	30	ACE, WW II
Murray, Don		Entertainment	5			15	
Murray, Eli		Civil War	30	65			Union Gen., Gov. UT Territory
Murray, George, Bishop		Clergy	25	40	50		
Murray, James A.H..	1837-1915	Lexicographer			225		Oxford English Dictionary
Murray, Jan		Entertainment	4			10	
Murray, Jim		Journalist	5			20	Sports Writer, L.A. Times
Murray, John C., S.J.		Clergy	10	15	35	20	
Murray, Joseph E., Dr.		Science	20	30		25	Nobel Medicine
Murray, Ken	1903-88	Entertainment	15			50	Cigar Smoking Comedian. Radio-TV-Film
Murray, Mae		Entertainment	22	35	50	60	Major Silent Star
Murray, Philip		Labor Leader	35	45	70	50	Pres. CIO, United Steel Workers
Murray, Stuart S.		Military	25	75		45	
Murray, William Vans		Rev. War	25	40	90		Diplomat, Lawyer, MOC MD
Murrow, Edward R.	1908-65	Journalist	130	300		375	..See It Now. Live WW II Reports From London etc
Musante, Tony		Entertainment	4	4		15	
Musgrave, Story, Dr.		Astronaut	10			28	
Muskie, Edmund		Cabinet	10	58	40	60	Sec'y State. V.P. Candidate/H.H. Humphrey
Mussolini, Benito	1883-1945	Head of State	372	609	3250	1262	Fascist Italian Dictator. DS/Emanuelle III $350+
Muybridge, Eadweard		Photographer	150		400		Br.-Am Pioneer Motion Pictures
Muzio, Claudia		Entertainment	200			525	It. Soprano
Myers, Carmel		Entertainment	10				Silent Screen Vamp
Myers, Mike		Entertainment	6			28	Austin Powers SP $45
Myers, Mike and Dana Carvey		Entertainment				75	Wayne's World
Myers, Russell*		Cartoonist	10		25	70	Broom Hilda
Myerson, Bess		Celebrities	10	20		25	Miss America. NYC Official
Myrt and Marge		Entertainment	20			60	Vintage Radio Series

N

NAME	DATE	CATEGORY	SIG	LS/DS	ALS	SP	COMMENTS
N'Sync (5)		Entertainment	55			155	Rock Group (5)
Nabokov, Vladimir	1899-1977	Author	325	1208	2650	1095	Novelist, Critic, Researched Butterflies.Lolita
Nabors, Jim		Entertainment	15	15	15	60	Actor-Comedian-Singer. Gomer Pyle
Nache, Maria Luise		Entertainment	20			45	Opera
Nadar (F. Tournachon)	1820-1910	Artist-Author	85	175	510		Fr. Caricaturist, Photographer,Balloonist
Nader, George		Entertainment	15		45	40	Actor. Fine Performer. Victim of Studio Politics
Nadir Shah, Mohammed	1880-1933	Royalty	65			140	King Afghanistan. Assassinated
Nagaoka, Guishi, Gen.	1858-1933	Military				975	Father of Japanese Aviation
Nagel, Anne	1912-66	Entertainment	25			50	Leading Lady 30's-40's
Nagel, Conrad		Entertainment	20	25	45	70	Stage-Film Leading Man to Character Actor
Nagel, Steven R.		Astronaut	5			18	
Naglee, Henry M.	1815-86	Civil War	30	80			Union Gen. War Dte. DS $375

NAME	DATE	CATEGORY	SIG	LS/DS	ALS	SP	COMMENTS
Nagy, Imre	1896-1958	Head of State	90	188			Communist Premier Hungary. Executed
Naish, J. Carrol		Entertainment	25			85	Familiar Character Actor
Nakasone, Y.		Head of State	25	35	85	35	Japan. FDC S $35
Naldi, Nita		Entertainment	20			35	Silent Movies Star
Nansen, Fridtjof	1861-1930	Explorer	162	508	375	450	Nor. Zoologist, Statesman, Arctic Explorer,Nobel
Napavilova, Zofie		Entertainment	25			65	Opera
Napier, Alan		Entertainment	30			55	Sometimes Menacing Character Actor
Napier, Charles		Entertainment	4	4	9	9	
Napier, Chas. James, Sir		Military	25	60	150		Br. Gen. vs U.S. War 1812
Napier, McVey	1776-1847	Law	10	15	30		Editor 4-7th Encyclo.Britannica
Napier, Robert C., Sir	1810-90	Military	45	35	125		Field Marshal,Gov.Gen. India
Napier, Sir Wm. F.P.		Military	20	40	70		Br. General
Napoleon I	1769-1821	Royalty	670	2611	15000		Important LS $7360, DS $6500, Short ANS $5500
Napoleon II (Duke Reichstadt)		Head of State	260	800	2200		Francois-Charles-Jos. Bonaparte
Napoleon III, Emperor of France		Royalty	88	550	525		1808-73. Louis Napoleon, Nephew of Nap.
Napoleon, Eugene L.J.J.	1856-79	Military				575	Son of Nap.III. KIA at 23
Nasby, Petroleum (D. Locke)		Author	50	75	160		Outstanding Humorist
Nash, Charles W.		Industrialist		500			Am. Mfg. Nash Motors. Leading Independent Auto
Nash, Clarence		Entertainment	100			150	
Nash, Graham		Entertainment	10			25	Rock
Nash, Ogden	1902-71	Author	45	60	150	40	Poet-Humorous, Unorthodox
Nash, Walter		Head of State	15	40	85	20	Prime Minister New Zealand
Nasir-edun Shah Qajar		Royalty	750		3500		King (Shah) Persia
Nasmyth, James	1808-90	Inventor	100		32		Machinist, Engineer. Inv. Steam Hammer
Nasser, Gamal Abdel		Head of State	75	400	350	275	President Egypt
Nast, Thomas*	1840-1902	Cartoonist	123	350		1442	Political Cartoonist. Rep. Elephant & Dem. Donkey
Nat, Yves		Entertainment					Legendary Pianist. AMusQS $65
Nathan, George Jean		Author	10	15	35	15	Powerful Drama Critic, Editor
Nathans, Daniel, Dr.		Science	25	35	45	30	Nobel Medicine
Nation, Carry	1846-1911	Reformer	138	185	215		Temperance Agitator. Went wrecking in KS/Hatchet
Natividad, Kitten		Entertainment				20	Model
Natta, Giulio		Science	25	35	80		Nobel Chemistry 1963
Natwick, Mildred		Entertainment	10			25	
Navarro, Ramon		Actor	35		125	150	Latin Silent Star.
Navatril, Michel		Titanic	195				Survivor
Navon, Yitzhak		Head of State	20			50	Israel
Nazimova, Alla	1879-1945	Entertainment	70			100	Russian Stage & Screen Star
Ne'meth, Maria		Entertainment	20			60	Opera
Neagle, Anna, Dame	1904-86	Entertainment	10	22		35	Beautiful Br. Leading Lady. Stage-Films-Musicals
Neal, Bob		Aviation	20	35	50	40	ACE, WW II, Flying Tigers
Neal, Patricia		Entertainment	6			25	Academy Award
Neal, Tom		Entertainment	10			20	
Neale, Bob		Aviation	22			70	Flying Tiger Ace. WW II
Nebel, Rudolf		Science	40	125			
Neblett, Carol		Entertainment	10			35	Opera. U.S. Soprano

NAME	DATE	CATEGORY	SIG	LS/DS	ALS	SP	COMMENTS
Necker, Jacques	1732-1804	Fr. Revolution	125	268			Fr. Financier & Statesman
Needham, Hal		Entertainment	10			20	Film Director-Stuntman
Neel, Louis Eugene Felix		Science	20	30	40	25	Nobel Physics
Neely, Thomas B., Bishop		Clergy	15	25	35		
Neeson, Liam		Entertainment	32			63	Actor. AA
Neff, Francine I.		Cabinet	5	10	25	10	
Neff, Hildegarde		Entertainment	20			35	Ger. 40's-50's Leading Lady & Author
Neff, Pat Morris		Governor	10	15		15	Governor TX, Pres. of Baylor U.
Negley, James S.	1826-1901	Civil War	40	65	95		Union Gen., MOC. War Dte. ALS $105
Negri, Pola	1894-1987	Entertainment	38	75		105	Ger. Import to Am. Silent Films
Neher, Fred*		Cartoonist	18			73	
Nehring, Walter		Military		75			Ger. Gen. WW II/Rommel. RK
Nehru, B.K.		Diplomat	10	15		20	Ambassador
Nehru, Jawaharlal	1889-1964	Head of State	130	525	700	400	Assassinated. 1st Prime Minister India
Neidlinger, Gustav		Entertainment	15			40	Opera
Neil, Stephen, Bishop		Clergy	10	15	35	20	
Neil, Vince		Entertainment	20			50	Rock
Neill, James		Entertainment	15			35	Vintage Stage Actor
Neill, Noel		Entertainment	10			20	Actress Lois Lane-Superman
Neill, Sam		Entertainment	15			45	Aussie Leading Man
Neilson, Adelaide		Entertainment	20				Vintage Actress
Neiman, LeRoy		Artist	45	175	245	95	Colorful Modern Art. Repro S $125-$275.FDC S 150
Nell, Stephen, Bishop		Clergy	10	15	35		
Nelligan, Kate		Entertainment	5	8	20	22	
Nelson, Bill		Astronaut	8			25	MOC FI
Nelson, Craig T.		Entertainment	10			38	Actor.TV's Long Running 'Coach'
Nelson, David		Entertainment	15			45	Early Family Sitcom. 'Ozzie & Harriett'
Nelson, Ed		Entertainment	10			15	
Nelson, Gaylord		Senate	10	25	40		Gov., Senator WI
Nelson, Gene	1920-96	Entertainment	15			60	Dancer-Actor. Films & Stage
Nelson, George D.		Astronaut	5			15	
Nelson, Harriet Hilliard		Entertainment	25			50	Band Singer-Actress. 'Ozzie & Harriet'
Nelson, Horatio, Lord	1758-1805	Military	813	2795	4570		Br. Adm.Trafalgar Hero. ALS/Right Hand $3600
Nelson, Jimmy		Entertainment	3	3	6	6	
Nelson, John		Cabinet	20	50	95		Tyler Att'y General
Nelson, Knute	1843-1923	Senate	5	15		10	Senator MN
Nelson, Lori		Entertainment	5	6	15	15	Pin-Up SP $15
Nelson, Ozzie		Entertainment	35	50		75	Big Band Leader, Actor
Nelson, Ozzie & Nelson, Harriet		Entertainment		250		295	Contract Signed By Both
Nelson, Rick		Entertainment	138	612	475	340	Nelson Family Teen Idol Star. Plane Crash Death
Nelson, Samuel (SC)	1792-1873	Supreme Court	50	175	225		Appointed by Tyler
Nelson, Thomas Jr.	1738-89	Rev. War	510	2900	3100		Signer.Important ALS $5900
Nelson, Tracy		Entertainment	10			22	Actress-Daughter of Ricky Nelson
Nelson, William L.		Senate/Congress	5	15			MOC MO
Nelson, Willie		Country Music	15			35	Singer-Composer. Alb. S $45

NAME	DATE	CATEGORY	SIG	LS/DS	ALS	SP	COMMENTS
Nelson, Wm. Rockhill	1841-1915	Author	10				Journalist
Nemerov, Howard		Author	10		35	25	3rd Poet Laureate US, Teacher
Nero, Peter		Entertainment	6	8	15	15	Jazz Pianist
Neruda, Pablo	1904-73	Author	450	2600			Latin American Poet-Nobel Prize Winner
Nesbit, Evelyn	1884-1967	Entertainment	50			1265	Girl in the Red Velvet Swing
Nesbit, Wilbur		Author		20	30		
Nesbitt, Cathleen		Entertainment	15			30	
Nesmith, Michael		Entertainment	20			45	Rock
Ness, Eliot		Law Enforcement	174	750		600	
Nesselrode, Carl von		Head of State	75		462		Rus. Count von.....Foreign Minister, Chancellor
Nethersole, Olga		Entertainment	15	40		45	Vintage Stage Actress
Nettleton, Lois		Entertainment	5	6	15	15	
Neubert, Frank		Aviation	25	75			Scored 1st Air Victory 9/1/39
Neumann, Theresa		Religious	65	175	395	150	Confirmed Stigmata Bearer
Neurath, Constantin von	1873-1956	Diplomat	45	80	150	115	Ger.Imprisoned For War Crimes
Nevelson, Louise	1900-88	Artist	50	85	155	200	Russ-Am. Sculptor.Large Abstract Wood Pieces
Neville, Aaron		Entertainment	4			15	Singer Neville Brothers
Neville, Henry		Entertainment	4	4	9	10	
Nevin, Ethelbert		Composer	75	140	450	95	Short Piano Pieces & Songs
Nevins, Allan		Author	12	30			Am.Historian, Editor, Professor
New Kids on the Block		Entertainment	50			175	
New, Harry S.	1858-1937	Cabinet	15	30	50	20	PMG 1923. US Senn, IN
Newberry, Truman H.		Cabinet	15	20	35		Sec'y Navy 1908
Newcomb, Simon	1835-1909	Science	65	195	228		Am. Astronomer, Mathematician
Newell, Frederick B., Bishop		Clergy	20	25	50	30	
Newhart, Bob		Entertainment	6	15	12	15	Comedian. 3 Successful TV Series
Newhouse, Samuel		Business	15	25	60	25	Newspaper-Radio-TV Empire
Newley, Anthony	?-1999	Entertainment	45			60	Talented Composer-Actor-Singer
Newman, Barry		Entertainment	4	6		10	
Newman, Edwin		Celebrity	4	10	20	5	
Newman, James		Astronaut	5			20	
Newman, John Henry, Card'	1801-90	Clergy	112	275	608	395	Leader Oxford Movement. ALS/Cont. $1600-$1800
Newman, Paul		Entertainment	95	175		198	Major Motion Picture Star. Authentic Sigs. Rare
Newman, Randy		Entertainment	10			20	
Newmar, Julie		Entertainment	8	10	20	30	Pin-Up SP $30
Newsom, Tommy		Entertainment	5			20	Tonight Show Bandleader
Newton, Huey P.		Activist	100			350	Afro-Am. Activist
Newton, Isaac, Sir		Science	4750				LS/Cont. $16,500
Newton, John	1822-95	Civil War	30		375		Union General.Ware Dte/ALS 325
Newton, Juice		Entertainment	10			25	Singer
Newton, Robert		Clergy	35	45	45	60	
Newton, Robert		Entertainment	50	65	95	128	Deceased British actor
Newton, Wayne		Entertainment	9	10		35	Singer
Newton-John, Olivia		Entertainment	15			50	Singer-Actress
Ney, Michel, Duc d'...	1769-1815	Fr. Napoleon	125	310	718		Marshal of France

NAME	DATE	CATEGORY	SIG	LS/DS	ALS	SP	COMMENTS
Ney, Richard		Entertainment	15			35	
Ngo Dinn Diem		Head of State	100				Pres. South Vietnam
Ngor, Haing S., Dr.	19xx-1996	Entertainment	30		50	100	Murdered AA winner
Ni'matullah, Hajji		Author	4200		7200		Mystic Scholar. Clergy
Niarchos, Stavro		Business	45	110	190	75	Gr.Millionaire Shipping Magnate
Niblack, Albert P.		Military	50		145		Am. WW I Adm.
Nicholas I	1796-1855	Royalty	175	1059			Emperor of Russia (Iron Czar)
Nicholas II	1868-1918	Royalty		1839	9500	3750	Last Czar of Russia. Executed
Nicholas, Denise		Entertainment	5	5		15	
Nicholas, Prince & King	1841-1921	Royalty	25	60	150		Greece
Nicholls, Francis R. T.	1834-1912	Civil War	70	125	173		CSA General, Gov LA
Nichols, Barbara		Entertainment	10			25	
Nichols, Ebenezer B.		Business	35	195			Major Early TX Entrepreneur. Banker
Nichols, John Anthony		Senate/Congress	5		15		MOC NC
Nichols, Mike		Entertainment	35			100	Film Director
Nichols, Nichelle		Entertainment	15			35	Actress. Star Trek
Nichols, Red		Entertainment	35			60	Jazz Instrumentalist
Nichols, Ruth Roland		Aviation	125	295		250	Holder of Flying Records
Nichols, William A.		Civil War	25	80			General
Nicholson, Jack		Entertainment	22			59	SP as 'Joker' $65-$80. Academy Award Winner
Nicholson, John	1783-1846	Military	30	75	190		Commodore U.S. Navy
Nicholson, Meredith		Author	20	50	125	30	
Nickerson, Francis Stillman		Civil War	25	50	65		Union General
Nicks, Stevie		Entertainment	10			38	
Nicol, Alex		Entertainment	10			25	Actor
Nicolai, Elena		Entertainment	30			85	Opera
Nicolay, John G.	1832-1901	Civil War	40	150	312		Lincoln Personal Sec'y. Author
Nicollet, Joseph N.		Explorer	105	225	345		1st Expedition Headwaters Miss.
Nicollier, Claude		Astronaut	10			30	
Niebuhr, H. Richard	1892-1971	Clergy	35	60	95	50	
Niebuhr, Reinhold		Clergy-Author	55	100	135	85	Am. Major Theologian
Nielsen, Alice	1876-1943	Entertainment	35			150	Opera-Operetta
Nielsen, Asta		Entertainment	20			50	Opera
Nielsen, Brigitte		Entertainment	5			20	Pin-Up SP $30
Nielsen, Carl	1865-1931	Composer	180	450	1025		Danish Composer, Conductor
Nielsen, Gertrude		Entertainment	10			25	
Nielsen, Terry		Entertainment	8	9		15	
Nielson, Leslie		Entertainment	10			25	
Niemack, Horst		Military	20			50	Ger. General Major
Niemoller, Martin	1892-1984	Clergy	60	175	410	200	In Concentration Camp WW II
Niesen, Gertrude		Entertainment	10			15	Singer
Nietzsche, Friedrich		Author	470	775	7765		Ger.Poet, Philosopher, Philology
Nigh, William		Entertainment	10			30	Actor-Director
Nightingale, Florence	1820-1910	Science	475	1350	1045		Br. Nurse, Hospital Reformer, Humanitarian
Nijinsky, Vaslav	1890-1950	Entertainment	440			3250	Ballet

NAME	DATE	CATEGORY	SIG	LS/DS	ALS	SP	COMMENTS
Nikisch, Artur		Conductor	25	65	85	375	Hung. Conductor. AMusQS $100
Nikolayev, Andryan G.		Astronaut	150			185	Russian Cosmonaut
Nillson, Christine	1843-1921	Entertainment	60		125		Swedish Opera Singer
Nilssen, Anna Q.		Entertainment	15	20		45	
Nilsson, Birgit	1918-19??	Entertainment	15			35	Swe. Soprano, Opera
Nilsson, Harry		Entertainment	50			100	
Nimersheim, Jack		Author	5	8	20	20	Campbell Award nominee
Nimitz, Chester W.	1885-1966	Military	120	337	505	1147	5 Star Fleet Adm. WW II. SP (3x5) $250
Nimoy, Leonard		Entertainment	35	122	75	75	Star Trek.
Nin, Anais	1903-77	Author	45	125	250		Fr. Born Am. Author. Content ALS $395
Nina		Model	4			15	Pin-Up SP $20
Nirenberg, Marshall W.		Science	15	25	45	20	Nobel Medicine 1968
Nirvana (3)		Entertainment				318	Rock
Nisbit, Eugenius Aristides		Senate/Congress	20	80	150		MOC GA 1839
Nissen, Greta		Entertainment	10			25	
Nissen, Hans Hermann		Entertainment	25			80	Opera
Niven, David	1909-83	Entertainment	50	92	130	80	AA. Sophisticated Versatile Br. Actor
Nivernais, Louis M. Duc de		Military			725		French Soldier-Diplomat
Nixon, John	1733-1808	Rev. War	125	320			Proclaimed Decl. Ind. 1st Time
Nixon, Marion		Entertainment	15			40	
Nixon, Marni		Entertainment	8			20	Sang for Audrey Hepburn, Susan Hayward
Nixon, Patricia	1912-92	First Lady	50	75	325	195	S WH Card $75-130
Nixon, Richard & Pat Nixon		President-1st Lady	300			595	
Nixon, Richard M. (As Pres.)		President	225	1154	5250	520	TLS/Cont. as VP $2000. DS/cont $4900
Nixon, Richard M.	1913-94	President	217	474	5500	406	Souvenir Resignation Typescript S $2595
Nizer, Louis		Law	25	75	215	35	Noted Trial Attorney
Nkomo, Joshua		Head of State	55	125	275	85	African Nationalist, Zimbabwe
Nobel, Alfred		Science	250	426	1180	450	ALS/Content $3,500
Nobile, Umberto	1885-1978	Aviation	75	195	335	225	It. Aeronautical Arctic Pioneer Engineer
Noble, Edward J.	1881-	Business	95		395		Candy Mfg. Popularized Lifesavers
Noble, James		Entertainment	5	6	15	15	
Noble, John W.	1831-1912	Cabinet	35	50	120	95	Union Gen. CW. Sec'y Interior
Noble, Ray		Bandleader	25				British
Noble, Robert	1861-1939	Military	10		50	35	General. Campaigns from Geronimo to WW I
Noe, Sydney P.		Numismatist	5	15			
Noel, Baptist W.	1798-1873	Clergy	20	35	38		Br. Evangelical Minister
Noel-Baker, Philip		Statesman	30	40	130	25	Nobel Peace Prize
Noguchi, Isamu		Artist	25		65		Am. Sculptor, Designer
Noguchi, Thomas T.		Celebrity	10	30		20	Coroner, Los Angeles
Nolan, Jeanette		Entertainment	5	6	15	15	
Nolan, Kathleen		Entertainment	8			15	
Nolan, Lloyd	1902-85	Entertainment	10	57		50	Actor. Fine Versatile Film Actor
Nolan, Mae E.		Congress	10	18			Repr. CA 1923
Nolin, Gene Lee		Entertainment	20			50	Actress. 'Baywatch'
Nolte, Nick		Entertainment	10	25		40	

NAME	DATE	CATEGORY	SIG	LS/DS	ALS	SP	COMMENTS
Nomura, Kichisaburo		Diplomat	275				Japanese Ambassador 12/7/41
Nono, Luigi	1924-90	Composer	115			175	Opera. Conductor
Noodles		Entertainment	6			25	Music. Guitar Offspring
Noonan, Fred J.	1893-1937	Aviation					Guam-San Francisco Flight Cover S $995
Noonan, Peggy		White House	5	20			Reagan Speech Writer
Noone, Peter		Entertainment	20			50	
Noor, Queen		Head of State	15	40	125	70	Queen of Hussein (Jordan)
Norblad, Albin W.		Congress	15	30		20	Repr. OR. Intelligence Off'r WW II
Norblin, Emile		Entertainment	85			350	Celebrated Cellist
Nordau, Simon Max	1849-1923	Science	50	105	357	60	Hung. Phys.-Writer, AMsS $1750
Nordenskjold, Nils Adolf E.		Explorer	200			340	Navigated North-East Passage
Nordenskjold, Nils Otto		Explorer	215			300	Led Antarctic Exped'n, Rescued
Nordhoff, Charles		Author	20	35	60		Collaborator Mutiny _ _ Bounty
Nordhoff, Heinz, Dr.		Business	25			50	Auto Mfg.-VW
Nordica, Lillian	1859-1914	Entertainment	60			350	Am. Soprano
Nordsieck, Kenneth		Astronaut	6			16	
Norgay, Tenzing		Celebrity	40	110	255	50	Sherpa Guide. Mt. Everest
Noriega, Carlos		Astronaut	6			20	
Noriega, Manuel A.		Head of State	100	100		50	Gen., Notorious Pres. Panama
Norman, Jessye		Entertainment	30			30	Opera. US Soprano
Norman, Lucille	1926-	Entertainment	10			35	Film Actress from 1942
Normand, Mabel		Entertainment	135			385	Silent Screen Comedienne. Talented-Popular
Norris, Chuck		Entertainment	8	10		40	
Norris, Frank	1870-1902	Author	125	275	525		Novelist, War Correspondent
Norris, George W.		Senate/Congress	15	30		40	MOC, Sen. NE. Fathered TVA
Norris, J. Frank Dr.		Clergy	5	15	25	10	Fundamentalist Baptist Pastor
Norris, Kathleen		Author	20	40	65	25	Prolific Am. Novelist
Norstad, Lauris		Military	20	50		40	Gen. WW II
North, Brownlow		Clergy	15	25	40		
North, Frederick, Lord	1732-92	Head of State	95	358	595		Br. P.M. During Am. Revolution. 2nd Earl Guilford
North, Jay		Entertainment	10			28	Child actor, 'Dennis the Menace'
North, John Ringling		Business	40	82		85	Ringling Brothers Circus
North, Luther		Celebrity	28	83	225		NRPA
North, Oliver L.		Military	40	100	165	68	Decorated Marine Col.
North, Sheree		Entertainment	5		15	15	Actress.
North, William	1755-1836	Military	75	185	488		Gen. Cont. Army. US Senator NY
Northbrook, Lord (Thos.G Baring)	1826-1904	Head of State	15	25	55		Br. Statesman, Gov.-Gen. India. 1st Earl
Northrop, John K.	1895-1981	Industrialist	45	125	275	110	Engineer-Designer. Founder Northrop Aircraft etc
Northrup, John H.		Science	45	150		100	Nobel Chemistry 1946
Northumberland, 2nd Duke	1742-1817	Rev. War	50	145	250		Hugh Percy. Br. General Fought vs Am.
Norton, Daniel Sheldon		Senate/Congress	7	10	25		Senator MN 1865
Norton, Edward		Entertainment	7			55	Actor. Film
Norton, Gerald		Military	20			45	Brit. WW II Hero. Victoria Cross
Norton, Mary Teresa		Senate/Congress	10	25		15	MOC NJ 1925-51
Norton, Oliver P.		Civil War	20	30	45		Civil War Gov. IN, U.S. Sen. IN

NAME	DATE	CATEGORY	SIG	LS/DS	ALS	SP	COMMENTS
Norton-Taylor, Judy		Entertainment	10	15		20	Pin-Up SP $25
Norville, Deborah		Journalist	8			15	TV News Anchor
Norvo, Red		Entertainment	15			40	Bandleader, Vibes, Xylophone
Norworth, Jack	1879-1956	Composer	130		372		Take Me Out to the Ball Game
Nott, Eliphalet	1773-1866	Clergy-Inventor	20	80			Pres. Union College 62 Years
Nouira, Hedi (Tunisia)		Head of State	7		15		
Nouri, Michael		Entertainment	7			20	Actor
Nourse, Amos, Dr.		Senate/Congress	35	50			Senator ME 1/16-3/3/1857
Nourse, Joseph	1754-1841	Military	500	1250			DS/Content $2,000
Novaes, Guiomar		Entertainment	30			155	Great Classical Pianist of 20th Century.
Novak, Kim		Entertainment	20	55		49	Actress. Pin-Up SP $50
Novak, Michael		Clergy	15	20	35		
Novak, Vitezslav		Composer	40			150	Czech. Composer
Novarro, Ramon	1899-1968	Entertainment	55		195	110	Mexican Silent Movie Star. Murdered 1968
Novatna, Jarmila		Entertainment	15	45		35	Czech. Soprano
Novello, Ivor		Entertainment	25		80	75	Br.Actor, Composer, Film Star
Novoselic, Krist		Entertainment	10			38	Music. Bass Guitar, Vocals. Nirvana
Nowak, Max		Science	15			45	Rocket Pioneer/von Braun
Noyce, Phillip		Entertainment	10		25	20	Film Director
Noyes, Alfred	1880-1958	Author	25	60	75	40	Br. Poet, Poetic Plays, Stories
Noyes, Edward F.		Governor	10	20		15	Governor OH
Nugent, Elliott		Entertainment	6	10		15	Broadway & Film Actor
Nugent, Ted		Entertainment	12		35	28	Guitarist Amboy Dukes
Nungesser, Charles		Aviation	135	225	290	300	
Nunn, Sam		Senate	15			40	Senator GA
Nureyev, Rudolf	1938-93	Entertainment	90	125	212	288	Kirov Ballet Dancer-Choreographer
Nurmella, Kari		Entertainment	15			35	Opera
Nutt, Clifford C.	1896-	Military	55	150			USA Gen.-Command Pilot.Decorated; Mackay Trophy
Nutter, Mayf		Country Music	10			20	
Nuyen, France		Entertainment	8			15	Actress. Interesting, Short-lived Career
Nye, Bill (Edgar Wilson)		Author	18		85		Humorist
Nye, Gerald P.		Senate	8	35		15	Senator ND
Nye, James W.	1815-76	Senate	75	140	175		Gov. Nevada Terr. 1861. Sen. NE '64
Nyerere, Julius		Head of State	30		85	150	Prime Minister, President Tanzania.

O'Boyle, Patrick A., Cardinal		Clergy	30	45	75	50	
O'Brian, Hugh		Entertainment	5	6	15	15	
O'Brien, Conan		Entertainment	4			10	Late Night TV Host
O'Brien, Cubby		Entertainment	5			15	Mickey Mouse Club
O'Brien, Edmond		Entertainment	20	40		50	A A
O'Brien, George		Entertainment	20			40	

NAME	DATE	CATEGORY	SIG	LS/DS	ALS	SP	COMMENTS
O'Brien, Hugh		Entertainment	6			20	TV Wyatt Earp
O'Brien, James		Business	5	10	15		
O'Brien, Lawrence F.	1917-1990	Cabinet	10	20	40	70	JFK Adviser-Strategist.P.M.Gen.
O'Brien, Margaret		Entertainment	15			35	Sig. As Child $50
O'Brien, Pat		Entertainment	45	125		100	
O'Brien, Virginia		Entertainment	5			10	Singer-Actress-Somber-faced Comedienne
O'Callaghan, Mike		Governor	5	15		10	Governor NV
O'Casey, Sean	1880-1964	Author	125	275	670	315	Irish Playwright.Abbey Theatre.Plough & the Stars
O'Connell, Arthur		Entertainment	30			65	
O'Connell, Charles		Business	10	15	30	15	
O'Connell, Daniel	1775-1847	Statesman-Patriot	75	250	633		Irish Nationalist Leader
O'Connell, Helen		Entertainment	15			25	
O'Connell, Jerry		Entertainment	5			30	Actor. Scream SP $42
O'Connell, William H., Cardinal		Clergy	50	65	75	65	
O'Conner, Flannery		Author	300	925			Am. Author. Died At Age 39
O'Connor, Basil		Celebrity	15	25		35	1st Pres.March Dimes Foundation
O'Connor, Bryan D.		Astronaut	5			20	
O'Connor, Carroll		Entertainment	8	45		20	'Archie Bunker' & Many Well Portrayed Parts
O'Connor, Donald		Entertainment	12			25	Singer-Dancer-Actor.Singin' in the Rain SP $45
O'Connor, Glynnis		Entertainment	5			15	
O'Connor, Sandra Day (SC)		Supreme Court	35	160	200	35	Bush Appointee
O'Connor, Una		Entertainment	40			148	Character Actress
O'Connor, Thos. P.	1848-1929	Author	65	120			Irish Journalist & Nationalist. (Tay Pay)AMsS $325
O'Conor, Charles	1804-84	Law-Politician	60	75	385		1st Catholic Presidential Cand.
O'Conor, Herbert R.		Governor	5	10			Gov. MD
O'Daniel, W. Lee 'Pappy'		Senate/Congress	15	50		45	Governor, Senator TX
O'Day, Anita		Entertainment	20				Big Band-Jazz Vocalist
O'Dell, Doye		Entertainment	5			15	C & W Singer-Actor
O'Donald, Emmett		Aviation	15	30	50	35	
O'Donnell, Chris		Entertainment	10			50	'Robin' in Batman
O'Donnell, Chris & Val Kilmer		Entertainment					Batman SP 150
O'Donnell, Rosie		Entertainment	10			32	Comedienne
O'Driscoll, Martha	1922-89	Entertainment	5			20	40's Film Leading Lady. 30's Pin-up 45
O'Flaherty, Liam		Author	90	325			Ir. Novelist. The Informer
O'Grady, Gail		Entertainment	10				Actress NYPD...Pin-Up 60
O'Hair, Madalyn Murray	1919-	Celebrity	35	45			Atheist, Activist, Mysteriously Disappeared '55
O'Hanlon, George		Entertainment	15				Actor-Comedian
O'Hara, Geoffrey		Composer	20	45		25	AMusQS $65
O'Hara, John		Author	160	500	660		Am. Novelist, Short Stories
O'Hara, John F., Cardinal		Clergy	50	85	100	75	
O'Hara, Mary (Alsop)		Author	20	50	75		Am. Novelist.My Friend Flicka
O'Hara, Maureen		Entertainment	16			30	Irish-Am. Actress. Starred Frequently/John Wayne
O'Herlihy, Dan		Entertainment	7			15	
O'Higgins, Bernardo		Head of State	750				Chile.Soldier,Statesmn,Dictator
O'Higgins, Harvey		Author	10	20	75	15	Am. Journalist, Novelist

NAME	DATE	CATEGORY	SIG	LS/DS	ALS	SP	COMMENTS
O'Keefe, Dennis		Entertainment	5	6	15	15	
O'Keefe, Georgia	1887-1986	Artist	312	725	825	438	Scenes S.W. Desert.TLS/Cont.$3500
O'Keeffe, Adrian		Business	5	15		10	CEO First National Stores
O'Laughlin, Gerald S.		Entertainment	10			20	
O'Leary, Brian		Astronaut	5			15	
O'Mahoney, Joseph	1884-1962	Congress	10	35			Senator WY
O'Malley, J. Pat		Entertainment	25			50	
O'Neal, Frederick		Entertainment	5			15	Afro-Am. Actor
O'Neal, Ralph A.		Military	22	40	85	70	
O'Neal, Ryan		Entertainment	10			35	
O'Neal, Tatum		Entertainment	15			50	A A
O'Neil, Barbara		Entertainment	250			595	
O'Neill, Charles		Military	10	20	45		Adm. USN
O'Neill, Charles	1821-93	Congress	10		40		Repr. PA 1863
O'Neill, Eugene	1888-1953	Author	195	312	375	2185	Playwright. Nobel & 3 Pulitzers
O'Neill, Henry	1891-1964	Entertainment	10			50	Major Vint.. Character Actor
O'Neill, James		Entertainment	20	25	45	45	Vintage Actor
O'Neill, Jennifer		Entertainment	5	6	15	15	
O'Neill, Peggy		Entertainment	5	6	15	15	
O'Neill, Thomas 'Tip'	1912-94	Congress	20	35		45	Speaker of the House. MA MOC
O'Shea, Michael	1906-73	Entertainment	9	35		20	Actor- Films from 30's.Career Ended as Detective
O'Sullivan, Gilbert		Entertainment	25	75			
O'Sullivan, Maureen		Entertainment	15	25	35	59	Irish Actress.Jane to Tarzan.Mia Farrow's Mother
O'Toole, Annette		Entertainment	10			30	
O'Toole, Peter		Entertainment	15			76	Actor.
Oak Ridge Boys, The (4)		Country Music	10			25	Gospel
Oakes, Randi		Entertainment	5			15	
Oakie, Jack		Entertainment	20	95		50	
Oakley, Annie	1860-1926	Markswoman	2285		9950	6150	Am. Markswoman/Buffalo Bill
Oakley, Violet		Artist	35	95			Her The Tragic Muse Famous
Oates, Joyce Carol		Author	18	30	60	30	Am.Novelist,Critic,Poet,Teacher
Oates, Lawrence E. G.	1880-1912	Explorer	100		575		Antarctic Explorer
Oates, Warren		Entertainment	25			50	
Ober, W.O. 'Willy'		Aviation	25		55		
Oberhardt, William		Artist	30	65	135		Portraits.Eisenhower,Hoover....
Oberon, Merle		Entertainment	45			102	Major Star. Of Mysterious Heritage
Oberth, Hermann, Dr.	1894-1989	Science	75	225		262	Hung.Early Rocket Pioneer. Taught von Braun
Oboler, Arch		Entertainment	12		35	25	Writer-Producer of Radio Dramas
Oboukhova, N.		Entertainment	35		400		Opera. Greatest Russ. Contralto of Century
Obratszova, Elena		Entertainment	10			40	Opera. Glamourous Rus. Mezzo
Ocasek, Ric		Entertainment	25			50	Rock
Ochles, Wubbo		Astronaut	10	25		25	
Ochoa, Ellen		Astronaut	6			22	
Ochoa, Severo, Dr.		Science	22	35	85	30	Nobel Physiology & Medicine
Ochs, Adolph S.	1858-1935	Business	150	165		65	Publisher-Founder NY Times

NAME	DATE	CATEGORY	SIG	LS/DS	ALS	SP	COMMENTS
Odell, Benjamin Baker, Jr.		Senate/Congress	10	30	40		MOC 1895, Governor NY 1900
Odell, George C.D.		Author	5	15	30		Educator, Theatre Arts
Odell, Moses F.	1818-66	Congress	10	20	30		Repr. NY 1861
Odets, Clifford		Author	55	90	210	140	Playwright.Golden Boy, etc.
Oe, Kenzburo	1935-	Author	90				Japanese Writer.One of Rarest Living Nobel Winners
Oersted, Hans Christian	1777-1851	Science	2500	4750	750		Discovered Electromagnatism
Oesau, Walter 'Gulle'		Aviation	130		415	275	
Offenbach, Jacques	1819-80	Composer	145	240	618	275	Fr. Composer. Many Operettas. ALS/Content $1,400
Offenhauser, Fred		Engineer	130	395			Automobile, Racing Engine Mfg.
Offspring		Entertainment	28			75	Music. 4 Member Rock Group
Ogden, Aaron		Senator	35	110	225		Am. Rev. War Soldier, Gov. NJ
Ogden, Francis B.	1783-1857	Military	15	68	95		Inventor. Steam Eng. Pioneer
Ogden, Thomas L.	1773-1844	Law	20		45		Law Partner Alex. Hamilton
Ogden, William B.		Political	150	950	925		1st Mayor of Chicago 1837.
Ogle, Samuel		Colonial Am.	65	185			Colonial Gov. MD
Ogle, William		Celebrity	5	10	15	8	
Oglesby, Richard J.	1824-99	Civil War	40	78	105	150	Union Gen., Gov. IL, US Sen. IL
Oglethorpe, James Edward	1696-1785	Colonial Am.		5500			One of the Rarest of Colonial Autographs
Oh, Soon-Teck		Entertainment	5			15	
Ohms, Elizabeth		Entertainment	35			150	Opera
Ohrbach, Jerry		Entertainment	8			20	
Oi, Narimoto		Military	40	125	195		
Oistrakh, David	1908-74	Music				150	Soviet Violinist, Conductor
Oland, Warner	1880-1938	Entertainment	150			275	Most Famous Charlie Chan
Olav V	1903-91	Royalty	45	125			King of Norway
Olcott, Chauncey	1860-1932	Composer	65	90	150	90	My Wild Irish Rose etc.Noted Tenor
Oldenburg, Claes Thure	1929-	Artist	20	35	95	40	Swe. Sculptor. Soft Scuptures. Pc Repro S $125
Older, Charles H.		Aviation	12	30	45	32	ACE, WW II, Flying Tigers
Older, Charles S.		Civil War-Gov.	25	40	55		CW Gov. NJ
Oldman, Gary		Entertainment	10			40	Talented, Versatile Actor. Dracula
Olds, Ransom E.	1864-1950	Business	238	1235			REO & Oldsmobile Motor Cars. Stock Cert. S $975
Olds, Robin		Aviation	15	30	45	32	ACE, WW II, Korea, Nam
Olin, John M.		Business	6	12	20	12	Olin Industries
Olin, Ken		Entertainment	5			10	Actor
Olin, Lena		Entertainment	20			50	
Oliphant, Laurence		Author	10	25	60		Br. Writer. Cape Town, S.A.
Oliphant, Pat		Cartoonist	5			30	
Olitzka, Rosa		Entertainment	35			125	Pol./Ger. Mezzo
Oliver, Andrew		Rev. War	65	185	240		Am. Colonial Politician
Oliver, Edna May		Entertainment	45			120	
Oliver, Henry W., Jr.	1840-1904	Business	45	60			Iron & Steel Tycoon
Oliver, Jane		Entertainment	6			15	
Oliver, Paul A.		Civil War	25	50	75		Credit For Inventing Dynamite
Oliver, Sy		Entertainment	30			75	Trumpet, Composer, Arranger
Olivero, Magda		Entertainment	20			100	Opera

NAME	DATE	CATEGORY	SIG	LS/DS	ALS	SP	COMMENTS
Olivetti, Adriano		Industrialist		400		150	Owner Olivetti Typewriter & Business Machines
Olivetti, Adriano		Industrialist		400		150	Owner Olivetti Typewriter & Business Machines
Olivier, Laurence & Leigh, Vivien		Entertainment					SEE Leigh, Vivien
Olivier, Laurence, Sir	1907-89	Entertainment	61	220		186	Special DS $2,000. AA. FDC S $ 95
Olliphant, Pat		Cartoonist	1230				Political Cartoonist
Olmos, Edward James		Entertainment	8	20		20	Actor
Olmstead, Frederick Law	1822-1903	Architect	90	175	340		Landscape Arch, NY Central Park.US Capitol Grounds
Olney, Richard	1835-1917	Cabinet	15	25	45	30	Att'y General, Sec'y State
Olney, Thomas		Clergy	85	125	250		
Olsen & Johnson		Entertainment	35			75	Hellzapoppin. 30's Comedy Team
Olsen, Ashley		Entertainment	8			25	Actress Full House
Olsen, George		Entertainment	25			120	Big band leader
Olsen, Mary Kate		Entertainment	8			25	Actress Full House
Olsen, Mary Kate & Ashley		Entertainment	15			45	Twin Sister Stars of Full House
Olsen, Merlin		Entertainment	9	10	20	25	
Olsen, Ole		Entertainment	25			50	
Olson, Nancy		Entertainment	6	8	15	15	
Onassis, Aristotle		Business	175	475		225	Gr.Millionaire Shipping Magnate
Onassis, Jacq. Kennedy		Celebrity	350	775	1250	1050	good content letter $10,000
Ondricek, Frantisek		Composer				950	Czech Violinist & Composer
Onizuka, Ellison S.	1946-86	Astronaut	125			175	Postal Cover $150
Ono, Yoko		Entertainment	40		100	75	Jap. Artist, Songwriter. Former John Lennon Wife.
Ontkean, Michael		Entertainment	5	6	15	15	
Opatoshu, David	1918-96	Entertainment	20	35		30	Actor. Many Faceted Character Actor
Opdyke, George	1805-80	Civil War					CW Mayor of NY.Chk.S '62 $900
Opp, Julie		Entertainment	12			25	Opera
Oppenheimer, Rob't, Dr.	1904-67	Science	517	1200		1300	Exec. Dir. Manhattan Project.Father of Atomic Bomb
Opper, Frederick Burr*		Cartoonist	25		75	275	Happy Hooligan
Orbach, Jerry		Entertainment	10			35	Versatile Stage, Film, TV Actor
Orbison, Roy	1936-88	Country Music	115	200		244	Blind Singer-Pianist
Orczy, Emmuska, Baroness	1865-1947	Author	40	125	160	150	Br. Novelist, Playwright. Scarlet Pimpernel etc.
Ord, E.O.C.	1818-83	Civil War	50	145	375	750	Union Gen-Indian Fighter
Orenstein, Leo		Composer				100	Russ.-US Pianist-Composer
Orff, Carl	1895-1982	Composer	25			172	Ger.Opera. Carmina Burana
Orfila, Matthieu		Science			65		Founder of Toxicology
Orgonotzova, Ludmilla		Entertainment	5			25	Opera
Orient, John H., Bishop		Clergy	5	10	15		
Orita, Zenji		Military	50	160	255	100	
Orlando, Vittorio E.	1860-1952	Head of State	65	135	275		It. Prime Minister, Pres. One of Big Four
Ormandy, Eugene		Conductor	40	40	100	85	Hung.-Am. Conductor Philadelphia Symph. Orch.
Ormond, Julia		Entertainment	25			75	Actress
Orne, Azor		Rev. War	100	450			Maj. Gen. Am. Forces
Orpen, William, Sir	1878-1931	Artist	45	120	390	350	Portrait, Genre, War Painter
Orr, Robert L.		Civil War	45	200			MOH Major 61st Pennsylvania Inf.
Orr, William T.		Entertainment	25				Film Director-Producer

NAME	DATE	CATEGORY	SIG	LS/DS	ALS	SP	COMMENTS
Ortega, Katherine D.		Gov't Official	3	8		10	
Orth, Godlove Stein	1817-82	Conngress	20		45		MOC IN. CW Officer. Minister to Austr-Hung
Orwell, George	1903-50	Author		1472			Pen-name of Eric Blair. Rare Signed with Pen-name
Ory, Edward Kid		Entertainment	100			200	Dixieland Bandleader
Osborn, Joan		Entertainment	10			70	Singer
Osborn, Super Dave		Entertainment	12			20	Comic Daredevil
Osborne, Baby Marie		Entertainment	10			20	
Osborne, Henry Z.		Senate/Congress	10	20		15	MOC CA 1917
Osborne, John	1929-94	Author	10	20	40	20	Br. Playwright, Screenwriter
Osborne, Ozzy		Entertainment	20			35	
Osborne, Sidney P.		Governor	10	15		10	Governor AZ
Osborne, Thomas A.		Governor	10	15		10	Governor KS
Osborne, Will	1906-81	Bandleader	20			35	1st Crooner. Bandleader 1924 to Late 50's
Oscar I, Joseph-Francois		Royalty	70	215	425		King Sweden & Norway
Oscar II		Royalty	25	70	145		King Sweden & Norway
Osgood, Charles		TV News	4			15	TV News, Host
Osgood, Samuel		Rev. War	125	385	535		Cont'l Congress, First P.M. Gen.
Osler, William, Dr.	1849-1919	Science	350	800	1583		Can. Phys., Important Medical Historian
Oslin, K.T.		Entertainment	5			20	
Osmena, Sergio		Head of State	65	200			Pres. Philippines 1944-46
Osmond Brothers (3)		Entertainment	10			30	
Osmond, Donny		Entertainment	5	8	15	15	
Osmond, Marie		Entertainment	5	15	20	22	
Osten, Hans Georg von der		Aviation				60	Ger. Ace WW I/Richthofen
Ostenso, Martha		Author	25	45	70		Am. Novelist, Poet
Osterhaus, Peter J.		Civil War	30	70	110		Union Gen.
Osterkamp, Theo		Aviation	35	60	130	70	
Osterman, Kathryn		Entertainment	20			50	Silent Films
Osvoth, Julia		Entertainment	20			45	Opera
Oswald, Lee Harvey	1939-63	Assassin	1825	12500	9800		Murdered John F. Kennedy?
Oswald, Marina (now Porter)		Celebrity	50	125	150	55	Mrs. Lee Harvey Oswald
Oswald, Mark		Entertainment	10			25	Opera
Oswald, Steve		Astronaut	5			20	
Otis, Carre		Model	4				Mrs. Mickey Rourke. Pin-Up 60
Otis, Elita Proctor		Entertainment	10	15	25	25	
Otis, Elwell S.		Civil War	25	40	65		Union Gen.
Otis, Harrison Gray		Civil War	450	1450	2500		Union Gen., CW-Sp. Am. War. Publisher. L.A. Times
Otis, Harrison Gray	1765-1848	Congress	25	68	75		Repr. 1797, Sen. MA 1817 MA
Otis, James	1725-83	Rev. War	180	550	750		Statesman, Eloquent Lawyer
Otis, Johnny		Entertainment	25			40	R & R Producer, Director. HOF
Otis, Samuel A.	1740-1814	Rev. War		100			Continental Congr.
Otto I (Othon I)	1815-67	Royalty	105	365	225		Greece. King of the Hellenes
Otto I (The Great) 9	12-973	Royalty	2150				King of Germany, Holy Rom.Emp.
Oudinot, Charles N. Duc de		Napoleonic Wars	70	150			Marshal of Napoleon
Ouida (Marie Louise de la Ramee)	1839-1905	Author	25	60	118		Br. Novelist. A Dog of Flanders

NAME	DATE	CATEGORY	SIG	LS/DS	ALS	SP	COMMENTS
Ould, Robert	1820-82	Civil War	60	142			CSA Col. POW Exch.ALS '65 $690
Ouspenskaya, Maria		Entertainment	150			375	
Outcault, Richard*		Cartoonist	75			450	Yellow Kid, Buster Brown
Outlaw, Edward C.		Aviation	12	25	40	32	ACE, WW II, Ace in a Day
Overall, Park		Entertainment	5			20	
Overman, Lynn		Entertainment	15			45	30's-40's Film Character Actor
Overmyer, Robert	?-1996	Astronaut	5			95	2nd Space Shuttle Flight
Ovington, Earle		Aviation	45		245	180	Pilot 1st Air Mail Plane
Owanneco, Chief	1645-1710	Mohawk Chief		50000			Last of the Mohicans
Owen, David, Sir		Economist	10	25	40	15	Internat'l Planned Parenthood
Owen, John		Clergy	10	10	15	20	
Owen, Joshua T. (WD)		Civil War	70		225		Union Gen.
Owen, Joshua T.	1821-87	Civil War	32				Union Gen.
Owen, Reginald		Entertainment	25			35	
Owen, Richard, Sir	1804-92	Science	75	130			Anatomist, Zoologist. Inventor of Name 'Dinosaur'
Owen, Robert	1771-1858	Political			250		Br. Utopian Socialist
Owen, Robert Dale	1801-77	Congress-Clergy	20		150		Scottish Born.Repr. IN. Reformer
Owen, Ruth Bryan (Rohde)		Diplomat	45	20		15	1st US Woman Diplomat-MOC FL
Owens, Buck		Aviation	12	28	45	30	ACE, WW II, Marine
Owens, Buck		Country Music	5			15	
Owens, Tex		Country Music	10			20	Wrote Cattle Call
Oxenberg, Catherine		Entertainment	25			40	
Oxnam, G. Bromley, Bishop		Clergy	35	50	95	45	
Oz, Frank		Entertainment	5	20		25	Self Caricature S $50

NAME	DATE	CATEGORY	SIG	LS/DS	ALS	SP	COMMENTS
Paar, Jack		Entertainment	6	8	25	20	
Pabst, Fred		Business	210	638		322	Pabst Brewing Co.
Paca, William	1740-99	Rev. War	690	1500	2800		Signer.LS (WD)$2750
Pacca, Bartolomeo, Cardinal		Clergy	45	300			Sec'y of State to Pope Pius VII
Pacetti, Iva		Entertainment	25			108	Opera
Pache, Jean Nicholas		Fr. Revolution	20	65	145		
Pacino, Al		Entertainment	10			64	Actor
Pack, Denis, Sir		Military	25	80	125		
Packard, David		Business	20	45	90	25	Co-Founder Hewlett-Packard Co.
Packard, James Ward	1863-1928	Business		5800			Founder of Packard Automobile
Packard, Vance		Author	10	20	45	15	Am. Nonfiction Writer
Packwood, Bob		Senate/Congress	10	25		35	Senator OR
Pacula, Joanna		Entertainment	9	10		25	
Paderewski, Ignace J.	1860-1941	Composer-Statesman	183	550	450	385	Pianist, AMusQS$550, $750, $850. Pres. Poland
Padgett, Lemuel P.		Senate/Congress	5	15		10	MOC TN 1901-22
Paduca, Duke of		Country Music	20			40	

NAME	DATE	CATEGORY	SIG	LS/DS	ALS	SP	COMMENTS
Paer, Ferdinando		Composer	40	110	200		Italian Opera Buffo
Paganini, Nicolo	1782-1840	Composer	300	3433	2867		Revolutionized Violin Technique. Violin Virtuoso
Page, Anita		Entertainment	8			15	
Page, Bettie		Celebrity				310	The Gibson Girl Model. Vintage Sketch S
Page, Carroll S.		Senate/Congress	10	25		20	Governor 1890, Senator VT 1908
Page, Geraldine		Entertainment	30			60	A A
Page, Jimmy		Entertainment	15			75	Music. Led Zeppelin
Page, Joanne		Entertainment	5			15	
Page, John	1743-1808	Rev. War		275			Patriot, Activist, Gov. VA
Page, Patti		Entertainment	4			12	
Page, Richard Lucian	1807-1901	Civil War	100	190	542		CSA Gen. Sig/Rank $150
Page, Thomas Nelson	1853-1922	Author	10	20	40		Am. Novelist, Diplomat, Lawyer
Page, William	1811-85	Artist	150		410		Am. Portr.Painter.ALS/Cont. $1150
Page, William Tyler		Congress	20				
Paget, Charles, Sir	1778-1839	Military	25				Brit. Adm. Napoleonic Wars
Paget, Debra		Entertainment	10			45	Actress
Pagliughi, Lina		Entertainment	35			140	Opera
Pahlavi, Mohammed Riza	1919-80	Head of State	135	200	375	375	SP Shah of Iran & Farah Diba Pahlavi $475
Paige, Janis		Entertainment	10			28	Actress. Warner Bros. Musicals & Light Comedy
Paige, Mabel		Entertainment	10			25	Vintage Radio Comedienne-Actress
Paine, John Knowles		Composer	15	40	50		Paine Hall at Harvard
Paine, Robert Treat	1731-1814	Rev. War	275	650	1150		Signer Decl. of Indepen., Cont. Congr.
Paine, Thomas		Rev. War	3200		13500		Am. Philosopher-Author
Paine, William A.		Business		875			Founder Paine-Webber Brokerage House
Pakula, Alan J.		Entertainment	5	10		20	Producer-Director
Pal, George	1908-1980	Entertainment	50			125	Producer-Director. Special Effects Expert. Puppets
Palacio, Ernesto		Entertainment	5			30	Opera
Palade, George E., Dr.		Science	20	35		25	Nobel Medicine 1974
Palance, Jack		Entertainment	20			82	AA Actor
Palet, Jose		Entertainment				220	Opera. Fonotipia Tenor
Paley, Petronia		Entrtainment	5			20	Pretty Afro-Am. Actress. Annie Hall etc.
Paley, William S.		Business	20	30	70	30	Founded CBS in 1928
Palfrey, F.W.		Civil War	25		75		Union Gen.
Palfrey, John G.		Clergy	35	50	75		
Palin, Michael	1943-	Entertainment	15			35	Comedian. Mony Python.Full Circle Book S. $65
Pall, Gloria (Voluptua)		Entertainment	15			35	DS re Voluptua $40
Pallette, Eugene		Entertainment	60			85	Rotund, Gravel Voiced Character actor
Palma, Tomas Estrada	1835-1908	Head of State	20	30	45		1st President Cuba
Palme, Olaf	1927-86	Head of State	45	70	145	150	Premier Sweden. Assassinated '86
Palmer, A. Mitchell		Cabinet	10	25	40	30	MOC PA. Att'y General
Palmer, Alice Freeman	1855-1902	Educator	20	35	50		Pres. Wellesley. Member HOF
Palmer, Betsy		Entertainment	5			12	Actress. Stage-Films. Active Early TV Panelist
Palmer, Chuck		Entertainment	3			8	Promoter
Palmer, Gregg		Entertainment	10			30	Actor. Supporting Roles, 2nd LeadsSince Early 50's
Palmer, Innis N.	1824-1900	Civil War	55				Union Gen. Led Only Cavalry at Bull Run

NAME	DATE	CATEGORY	SIG	LS/DS	ALS	SP	COMMENTS
Palmer, Jimmy		Entertainment	15			40	Bandleader
Palmer, Johanthan	1747-1810	Rev. War					Kept War Diary 1774-75. Orig. Diary $1750
Palmer, John McCauley		Civil War	85	140	225		Union General & Political Figure. US Sen.-Gov. IL
Palmer, Lilli	1912-1986	Entertainment	20			70	Ger. Actress. Charming, Elegant Leading Lady
Palmer, Potter		Business	275	975	1650	475	Palmer House Hotel, Chicago. Stock S $1450
Palmer, Robert		Entertainment	20			45	
Palmerston, Henry J.T., Lord	1784-1865	Head of State	52	232	224		Prime Minister Eng. Ended Crimean War
Paltrow, Gwyneth		Entertainment	20			68	Actress. Shakespeare in Love. AA
Paluzzi, Luciana		Entertainment	5			15	Actress. Leads & 2nd Leads. Italian-Internat'l Pix
Pan, Hermes		Entertainment	30			65	Choreographer. Dance Director. 1933-73. AA
Panerai, Rolando		Entertainment	5			25	Opera
Panetta, Leon		Congress	15			30	NY. White House Chief of Staff
Pangborn, Clyde		Aviation	75	140	250	250	Aviation Pioneer
Pangborn, Franklin	1894-1958	Entertainment	42			65	Comedic Character Actor
Pankhurst, E. Sylvia	1882-1960	Women's Rights	60	145	250	660	Br. Woman Suffrage Advocate. Newspaper Editor
Pankhurst, Emmeline	1858-1928	Women's Rights	40	125	240		Br. Leader of Women's Suffrage
Pankhurst, Christabel, Dame	1880-1958	Women's Rights	25	65	160		Br. Woman Suffrage Advocate
Pannenberg, Wolfhart A.		Clergy	35	85	100	75	
Pantaleoni, Romilda		Entertainment			200		Opera. 1st Desdemona
Pantoliano, Joe		Entertainment	5			15	
Papen, Franz von		Military	75	335	350	150	Vice-Chancellor Under Hitler
Papp, Joseph		Entertainment	30	40		55	Major Theatrical Producer
Paquin, Anna		Entertainment	35			70	New Zealand Child Actress. 'The Piano', AA
Paradis, Vanessa		Entertainment	5			22	Singer-Actress
Parazynski, Scott		Astronaut	6			20	
Paris, Joel B., III		Aviation	15	25	40	35	ACE, WW II
Park, Charles E.		Clergy	15	20	25		
Park, Chung-He		Head of State	20			50	Pres. Korea. Assassinated
Park, Frank		Senate/Congress	5	15	25		MOC GA 1913
Park, Roy H.		Business	10	25	55	20	Owner 'Duncan Hines' & Broadcast Stations
Parke, John Grubb	1827-1900	Civil War	45	150	150		Union General. Sig/Rank $55, DS $115
Parker, Alton B.		Jurist-Pres.Cand.	15	35	75	25	Judge, Pres. Candidate 1904
Parker, Amelia, Mrs.		Celebrity	5	15	25		Alton B. Parker Wife
Parker, Cecilia	1905-93	Entertainment	5			15	Actress. 'Andy Hardy's' Sister
Parker, Charlie	1920-55	Entertainment	400	800		3450	Alto Sax Jazz Musician. 'The Bird'. ANS $1000
Parker, David		Military	15	35	60		
Parker, Dorothy		Author	25	40	95	30	Critic, Poet, Humorist
Parker, Edward P.		Business	65	150			Parker Bros. Pen Co.
Parker, Eleanor		Entertainment	6	8	15	15	Pin-Up SP $20
Parker, Ely Samuel		Civil War	300	195			Seneca Indian Chief, Union Gen.
Parker, Fess	1925-	Entertainment	10		25	32	Actor. Remembered Lovingly as Davy Crockett
Parker, Frank		Military	50	75			Am. WW I Gen,
Parker, Frank		Entertainment	10			35	Jack Benny's 1st Vocalist
Parker, Gilbert	1861-1921	Author	12				
Parker, Graham		Entertainment	20			35	

NAME	DATE	CATEGORY	SIG	LS/DS	ALS	SP	COMMENTS
Parker, Isaac	1768-1830	Law	25		140		MOC MA 1796
Parker, Isaac C.	1838-1896	Law	195	1198			Western Judge. The Hanging Judge
Parker, James	1768-1837	Congress	12				Repr. MA
Parker, James	1776-1868	Congress	12				Repr. NJ (Grandfather of Rich'd W. Parker)
Parker, Jameson		Entertainment	5			20	
Parker, Jean		Entertainment	15		30	30	
Parker, Joel	1816-1888	Governor-CW	15	30	75		Civil War Gov. NJ
Parker, John		Civil War		750			Captured by Commanches
Parker, Mary Louise		Entertainment	12			36	Actress
Parker, Moses		Rev. War					POW ALS $625
Parker, Robert A.		Astronaut	6			20	
Parker, Roy, Jr.		Entertainment	5		15	10	
Parker, Sarah Jessica		Entertainment	20			40	Pin-Up SP $75
Parker, Suzy		Entertainment	6			20	
Parker, Theodore	1810-60	Clergy	50	70	175		Abolitionist, Social Reformer
Parker, Thomas		Rev. War	55	90	145		Off"r Cont. Army. General
Parker, Tom, Colonel		Entertainment	10	70		42	Elvis Presley's Manager-Agent
Parker, Willard		Entertainment	10			25	Actor-Husband Virginia Field
Parker, William, Sir	1781-1866	Military	145		300		Br. Adm. Captured Ports thus Ending 'Opium War'
Parkhurst, Charles H.		Clergy	25	30	60	30	Reformer. Anti Tammany Hall
Parkins, Barbara		Entertainment	6	8	15	20	Pin-Up SP $25
Parkinson, Dian		Playboy Cover	5			15	Pin-Up SP $25
Parkman, Francis	1823-93	Author	25	70	150		Historian. The Oregon Trail
Parks, Bert		Entertainment	10			30	
Parks, Gordon	1912-	Author	20	50	75	40	Learning Tree. Photojournalist-Prod.-Director
Parks, Larry		Entertainment	20			50	
Parks, Rosa L.	1913-	Activist	100	145		214	Civil Rights Activist, Bus Boycott
Parnell, Charles Stewart	1846-91	Statesman	55	145	356		Ir. Nationalist Leader. Fought for Home Rule.
Parr, Ralph		Aviation	12	28	42	32	ACE, Korea, Double Ace
Parran, Thomas		Senate/Congress	5	8	10		MOC MD
Parrish, Anne	1760-1800	Philanthropist					NRPA
Parrish, Anne	1888-1957	Author	15	20	30		Am. Novelist
Parrish, Helen		Entertainment	8			20	
Parrish, Julie		Entertainment	4	4	9	10	
Parrish, Maxfield	1870-1966	Artist	225	408	738	702	Repro S $600. TLS/Cont.$950, S Chk $250
Parry, Charles Hubert H., Sir		Composer	10	25	50		Historian, Dir.Royal Coll.Music
Parry, William E., Sir	1790-1855	Explorer	75	95	225		Br.Adm. Arctic Explorer
Parseval, August von		Aviation	80				Ger. Aeronautical Engineer
Parsons, Albert Ross		Composer	5	10	15	5	
Parsons, Dave		Entertainment	6			25	Music. Bass Guitar Bush
Parsons, Estelle		Entertainment	5	10		20	
Parsons, Louella O.		Entertainment	20	30	75	45	Very Powerful Hearst Entertainment Journalist
Parsons, Mosby M.	1822-65	Civil War	170				CSA Gen.ALS '65 $1650, Sig/Rank $250
Parsons, Samuel Holden	1737-89	Rev. War		400	475		Cont'l.Gen'l. MsLs/Content $1500
Parton, Dolly		Country Music	10			25	

NAME	DATE	CATEGORY	SIG	LS/DS	ALS	SP	COMMENTS
Parton, James	1822-1891	Author	15				
Parton, Stella		Country Music	4			10	
Partridge, Bernard, Sir		Artist			45		Brit. Punch Cartoonist
Partridge, Wm. Ordway		Artist	10	20	50	30	Am.Sculptor. Portrait Busts
Parvis, Taurino		Entertainment	40			110	Opera
Pasch, Moritz		Science	60		95		Ger. Mathemat'n. Pasch's Axiom
Pasero, Tancredi		Entertainment	30			75	Opera
Paskalis, Kostas		Entertainment	15			45	Opera
Pasquarella, Gus		Photographer	55				Photo Hindenburg Burning $1500
Passman, Otto E.		Senate/Congress	5			10	MOC LA
Pasternak, Boris	1890-1960	Author	375	750	2450		Rus.Poet,Novelist.Dr. Zhivago. Nobel Prize 1958
Pasternak, Joe		Entertainment	30	65	100	70	Film Director
Pasteur, Louis	1822-1895	Science	500	900	2292	2732	Fr.Biologist. Pasteurization,Vaccines.AMsS $15,000
Pastor, Tony		Entertainment	10			35	Big Bandleader
Pastore, John A.		Governor	5	10		15	Governor RI
Patat, Frederic		Astronaut	12	25		25	
Patch, Alexander M.		Military	85	225	395	205	Am. General WW II
Pate, MIchael		Entertainment	5			15	
Paterson, John	1744-1808	Rev. War	70	200	325		Berkshire Minute-Men. General
Paterson, William (SC)	1745-1806	Supreme Court					Continental Congress NRPA
Patey, Janet		Entertainment	25		80		
Patinkin, Mandy		Entertainment	20			60	Actor-Singer. Chicago Hope
Patman, J. Wm. Wright		Senate/Congress	5			10	MOC TX 1929
Paton, Alan		Author		150	400		S.Afr.Author,Political Activist
Patrick, Butch		Entertainment	10		25		
Patrick, Dennis		Entertainment	4			10	
Patrick, Gail		Entertainment	9	10	20	15	
Patrick, John		Author	4	15			
Patrick, Marsena R. (WD)		Civil War	45	85	118		Union General
Patrick, Marsena R.	1811-88	Civil War	35	50	90		Union General
Patten, Gilbert (Burt Standish)		Author	30	70	160	50	Fictional Hero Frank Merriwell
Patten, Luana		Entertainment	15			25	
Patterson, Annie W.		Composer					S Bars of Music 50
Patterson, Basil	1926-	Political	10	20		30	Vice-Chm. Dem. National Committee
Patterson, Daniel Tod	1786-1839	Military	45	145	225		Navy Commandant vs Jean Lafitte
Patterson, John		Governor	12	25			Governor AL
Patterson, Melody		Entertainment	5			25	Actress. 'Wrangler Jane' on F Troop
Patterson, Paul L.		Governor	5	10		10	Governor OR
Patterson, Richard North		Author	5			10	Fiction
Patterson, Robert	1792-1881	Civil War	25	55	80		Oldest Commissioned CW Maj.Gen.
Patterson, Robert P.		Cabinet	20	35	45	25	Sec'y War
Patterson, William Allan		Business	3	7	12	5	
Patti, Adelina (Niccolini)	1843-1919	Entertainment	140	185	330	425	Great Operatic Coloratura. (Baroness Ledenbrun)
Patti, Amalia		Entertainment	40		135	150	Opera
Pattison, Robert T.		Governor	10	25		15	Governor PA

NAME	DATE	CATEGORY	SIG	LS/DS	ALS	SP	COMMENTS
Patton, Francis L.		Clergy	15	20	25	20	
Patton, George S.	?-1864	Civil War	255		3200		(Grandfather) KIA in Civil War. ALS 6/26/63 $7500
Patton, George S., III		Military	10	20	45	15	Son Of WW II General
Patton, George S., Jr.	1885-1945	Military	1162	2078	5433	4568	Cmmdr. 3rd Army WW II, Spec'l SIG $2,250
Paul I & Frederica		Royalty	250			250	King & Queen of Greece
Paul I, Albino Luciani.	1912-1978	Clergy		1265			Pope From August-September 1978. 33 Days. RARE
Paul I, Pavel Petrovich	1754-1801	Royalty	230	872	1625		Czar Russ. Son of Cath. Great. Assassinated
Paul II, Pope	1920-	Clergy		400		1065	Karol Wojtyla. 1st Polish Pope
Paul III, Pope		Clergy		1300			
Paul VI, Pope		Clergy	300	475	1100	600	Giovanni Battista Montini
Paul VI, Pope	1897-1978	Clergy		500		865	SP Pope Paul VI & Cardinal Jozef Mindszenty $925
Paul, Adrian		Entertainment	7			42	Actor. Highlander
Paul, Alexandra		Entertainment	4			15	Pin-Up SP $20
Paul, Arthur		Celebrity	5		20	32	
Paul, Les		Entertainment	25	35		75	And Manufacturer of Guitars
Paul, Wolfgang	1913-	Science		30		30	Nobel Physics 1989
Paulding, Hiram	1797-1878	Civil War	30	50	170		Adm. Commanded Navy Yard NY During Civil War
Paulding, James Kirke	1778-1860	Cabinet-Author	35	125	165		Van Buren Sec'y Navy, War
Pauley, Ed		Business	10	45		25	Powerful CA Oil Tycoon. Treas. Dem. Party
Pauley, Jane		TV News	4	10	15	15	
Paulham, Louis		Aviation	40	75	135	80	
Pauling, Linus	1901-94	Science	75	295	410	195	Nobel in Chemistry, Nobel Peace. SP(Pc) $125
Paulsen, Valademar		Science	40	120			
Paulsson, Pat		Entertainment	5	6	15	15	
Paulter, Thomas C.		Celebrity	12	20			
Paulton, Harry		Entertainment	3	3	6	8	
Paulucci, Jeno F.		Business	15	25	35	20	
Pauly, Rose		Entertainment	20			60	Opera. Unequaled as Elektra
Pavarotti, Luciano		Entertainment	30	100	145	95	Opera, Concert
Pavie, Auguste-Jean-Marie		Diplomat	40	145	230		Fr. Explorer. Laos, Mekong
Pavlov, Ivan	1849-1936	Science			3900	7675	Rus. Physiologist.
Pavlova, Anna	1885-1931	Entertainment	271		450	558	Russian Premiere Ballerina. SP Pc $450
Pavon, Jose Maria M. y	1765-1815	Clergy		3250			Revolutionary Mex.Priest. Leader of Rebel Forces
Pawnee Bill (Lillie,G.A.)		Entertainment					SEE Lillie, G.A.
Paxinou, Katina		Entertainment	150		300	275	
Paxton, Bill		Entertainment	10			40	Twister/Helen Hunt SP $130
Paxton, Elisha F. (WD)		Civil War	745	2700			CSA Gen., Stonewall Brigade
Paycheck, Johnny		Country Music	8			25	
Payer, Julius von		Explorer-Artist	90	225		285	Austr-Hung. No.Polar Expedition
Payne, Cril		Celebrity	4	8	15	10	
Payne, Eugene B.		Civil War	25	45	65		Union General
Payne, Freda		Entertainment	10			20	Band of Gold Singer
Payne, Frederick	1903-78	Political	5		25		Mayor, Governor, US Senator from Maine
Payne, Henry C.		Cabinet	15	20	35		P.M. General 1902
Payne, John	1912-91	Entertainment	15	30	55	67	Film Actor

NAME	DATE	CATEGORY	SIG	LS/DS	ALS	SP	COMMENTS
Payne, John Barton		Cabinet	7		15		
Payne, John Howard	1791-1852	Composer	90	250	525		Actor, Author. Home Sweet Home
Payne, T.H. (Act'g)		Cabinet	5	25			
Payne, William H. (WD)		Civil War	170	390			CSA Gen.
Payne, William H.	1930-1904	Civil War	85		345		CSA Gen.
Payne, William W.	1807-1874	Congress	10				Repr. AL, Lawyer, Planter
Pays, Amanda	1959-	Entertainment	4			20	Brit. Actress Max Headroom, The Flash etc
Payton, Gary		Astronaut	8	20		15	
Peabody, Andrew Preston	1781-1883	Clergy	15	20	35	30	Unitarian Theologian, Author
Peabody, Charles, Dr.		Science	10	20	25		
Peabody, Eddie		Entertainment	15	15	35	30	
Peabody, Endicott		Clergy	35	45	60		Fnder. Of Groton School.
Peabody, Endicott Chub	1920-97	Political	5	28	35		Gov. MA. Coll. Football Hall of Fame at Harvard
Peabody, Francis		Celebrity	10	25	85		
Peabody, Francis G.		Clergy	10	10	10	15	
Peabody, George	1795-1869	Business	50	140	475		Merchant, Financier
Peabody, George F.	1852-1938	Banker	35	90	385	150	Merchant, Financier, Philanthropy
Peale, Chas. Wilson	1741-1827	Artist-Rev. War	268	525	920		Officer. Portrait Painter, Engr.
Peale, Norman Vincent	1898-1993	Clergy	23	61	125	45	And Bestselling Author. Marble Collegiate Church
Peale, Rembrandt	1778-1860	Artist	295	480	1625		Am. Portrait & Historical Artist
Peale, Titian	1799-1885	Artist		225	975		ALS/Content $695
Pearce, James Alfred		Senate/Congress	10	30	35		MOC, Senator MD 1835
Pearce, Richard		Entertainment	10	15		20	Film Director
Pearl Jam (Entire Group)		Entertainment	35			115	Rock, Alb. S $125-150
Pearl, Minnie		Country Music	10			35	Grand Ole Opry Star
Pearson, Lester B.	1897-1972	Head of State	35	90	175	45	P.M. Canada, Nobel Peace Pr.
Peary, Harold		Entertainment	20			45	
Peary, Robert E.	1856-1920	Military-Explorer	108	415	505	575	Am. Adm. Arctic Explorer. 1st To Reach North Pole
Pease, Charles E.		Civil War	25				Carried Surrender Letter. ALS 1862 $225
Pease, Elisha M.		Governor		395			Comptroller Repub. TX. Gov. TX
Peck, Gregory		Entertainment	18	80	35	67	Oscar Winning Actor. Straight Leads & Westerns
Peck, Robert Newton		Author	10	15	25		Am. Novelist
Peckham, Rufus W. (SC)		Supreme Court	50	120	195	125	
Peckinpah, Sam		Entertainment	25			50	Director
Peddie, G.		Military	10	25			Gen. WW II
Pederson, Monte		Entertainment	10			30	Opera
Pederzini, Gianna	1900-1988	Entertainment	25			103	Opera. Mezzo-Soprano. 5x7 SP $50
Pedro II de Alcantara	1825-91	Royalty	85	242	305		Emperor Brazil 1831-89
Peel, Robert, Sir	1788-1850	Head of State	45	115	158		Prime Minister Eng. Bobbies Named for Him
Peeples, Nia		Entertainment	15			25	
Peerce, Jan	1904-84	Entertainment	28	40		68	Great Operatic Tenor. Long Career With Met.
Pegler, Westbrook		Author	20	20	35	20	Am. Journalist, Columnist
Pegram, John (WD)		Civil War	895	1795	6650		CSA Gen.
Pegram, John	1832-65	Civil War	650	838	445		CSA Gen.
Pei, I.M.		Architect	35	75	140		Internationally Recognized

NAME	DATE	CATEGORY	SIG	LS/DS	ALS	SP	COMMENTS
Peirce, Benjamin	1809-80	Science	20	30	80		Mathematician, Astronomer
Pelham, Henry	1696-1754	Head of State	45	150	265		Prime Minister
Pelham-Holles, Thomas		Head of State	50	105	170		Brother of Henry. Prime Min.
Pell, John		Historian	10	25			Museum Director
Pell, Stephen H.P.		Historian	10	25			Curator
Pellegrini, Margaret		Entertainment	15	20		35	Munchkin, Wizard of Oz
Pellegrino, Francis		Aviation				112	Pilot 509th Bomb Gp. (Atomic Bomb)
Pelletier, St. Marie Euphraise	1796-1868	Clergy			2500		Saint Canonized 1940
Pelouze, Louis H.		Civil War		175	200		Union Gen. War Dte. DS $350
Pemberton, John C. (WD)		Civil War	210	567	812		CSA Gen. Originator COCA COLA
Pemberton, John C.	1814-81	Civil War	85	408	595	400	CSA Gen. Originated COCA COLA
Pemsel, Max		Military				40	Nazi General
Pena, Elizabeth		Entertainment	10			20	
Pendarvis, Paul		Bandleader	10				
Pender, William Dorsey		Civil War	410				CSA Gen. War Dte. ALS $3,250
Penderecki, Krzysztof		Composer	20		90		Pol. Opera, Religious Music
Pendergast, Thomas J.		Political	17	50	105	35	KS Democratic Political Boss
Pendleton, Alex 'Sandie'		Civil War	205	525	475		CSA Staff Officer-T.J. Jackson
Pendleton, Edmund		Rev. War	350	680	975		Continental Congress
Pendleton, George Hunt	1825-89	Congress	20	35	75		Presidential Candidate. Sen. OH
Pendleton, Nat		Entertainment	30	45	60	45	
Pendleton, Nathanael G.	1793-1861	Congress	10				Repr. OH, Father of G.H. Pendleton
Pendleton, William Nelson		Civil War	320		485	935	CSA Gen., Pre War Clergyman
Penn & Teller		Entertainment	10			25	
Penn, Arthur		Entertainment	10			20	
Penn, John	1729-95	Colonial Am.		1250			Son of William (Religious Reformer)Lt. Gov. PA
Penn, John	1740-88	Rev. War	1525	2250	3700		Signer Decl.of Indepen. Signed Book $7500
Penn, Sean	1962-	Entertainment	10	30	30	40	Actor-Director-Writer.Thin Red Line SP $125
Penn, Thomas	1702-75	Colonial		150			Son of William. Proprietor of PA
Penn, William	1644-1718	Religious Reform	1500	5054	6700		Eng. Quaker Founder PA. AMsS $9,000.
Pennell, Joseph		Artist	55	160	320		Am. Artist, Printmaker
Penner, Joe		Entertainment	20	25	45	45	
Penney, J. C.	1875-1971	Business	68	248	245	232	Founder of J.C. Penney. Informative TLS $1500
Penney, Joe		Entertainment	8		25	20	
Pennington, Ann		Entertainment	25	30	70	70	Ziegfield Star
Pennington, William	1796-1862	Congress	48	70			Gov. PA. Speaker of House
Pennoyer, Sylvester		Governor	10	15			Governor OR
Penny, Little Joe		Country Western	5			15	Music. 50's Western Recording Artist
Pennypacker, Galusha		Civil War	70	165	235		Union General
Pennypacker, Samuel W.		Governor	15	25		30	Jurist, Author, Gov. PA
Penrose, Boies	1860-1921	Congress	12	15			Senator PA. Pres. Pro Tempore
Penske, Thomas H.		Business	10	30		20	
Penzias, Arno, Dr.		Science	15	35	65	25	Nobel Physics
Peppard, George		Entertainment	6	8	15	25	
Pepper, Art		Entertainment	30			75	Bandleader

NAME	DATE	CATEGORY	SIG	LS/DS	ALS	SP	COMMENTS
Pepper, Claude	1900-89	Congress	22	38		25	Champion of the Elderly Sen.FL. Sorely Missed
Pepper, George Wharton		Congress	5	15			Senator PA 1922
Pepperell, William, Sir		Military	95	550	375		Merchant.Gen. in Fr-Indian War
Pepys, Samuel	1633-1703	Author-Diarist	570	1890			Br. Sec'y of the Navy. Revealing Diarist.
Pequet, Henri		Aviation	16		37		
Perceval, Spencer		Head of State	120	250			Only Br. P. M. Assassinated
Percival, John 'Mad Jack'		Military	30	95	145		Am.Navy. War 1812 Exploits
Percy, Charles		Senate/Congress	10	15		25	Senator IL
Percy, Walker	1916-90	Author-Doctor	60	125	235		Am. Novelist
Pereira, William L.		Architect	10	35	75	20	Internationally Recognized Arch
Perelman, S.J.		Author	45		160		Humorist, Film Scripts
Peres, Shimon		Head of State	35	110		145	Israeli Prime Minister. Nobel Peace Prize
Perez, Mariano		Head of State	15	25	85	20	President Colombia
Perez, Rosie		Entertainment	10			45	Actress
Perez, Vincent		Entertainment	25			70	The Crow Star
Perier, Jean		Entertainment	25			75	Fr. Baritone. 45 Year Career
Perignon, D.C. Marquis de		Military	65	180	375		Marshal of Napoleon
Perkins, Anthony	1932-92	Entertainment	20			52	Psycho SP Premium. Aids Victim.
Perkins, Carl	1932-98	Country Music	15		195	40	Singer-Songwriter. Rock 'n Roll HOF. TsS $250
Perkins, Frances		Cabinet	25	70	145	60	1st Woman Cabinet Member. Sec'y Labor
Perkins, George C.	1839-1923	Congress	14	20			Governor, Senator CA 1893
Perkins, Marlin		Zoo Director	12			20	Animal Expert
Perkins, Millie		Entertainment	10			30	
Perkins, Osgood		Entertainment	35			75	
Perkins, Thomas H.		Business	20	45	90		
Perkins, Tony		Entertainment	25			45	
Perlman, Itzhak		Entertainment	20			55	Am. Violinist
Perlman, Rhea		Entertainment	5	6	15	15	Cheers SP $45
Perlman, Ronuy		Entertainment	8	12	40	30	
Peron, Eva (Evita)		Head of State	1500	900			Argentina. Statesman
Peron, Juan & Peron, Eva		Heads of State		750			
Peron, Juan Domingo	1895-1974	Head of State	125	713	525	660	President & Dictator of Argentina
Perot, H. Ross		Business	30	55		100	Presidential Candidate
Perpich, Rudolph G.		Governor	10	15		15	Governor MN
Perrault, Charles	1628-1703	Author		1250	2600		Fr. Poet. Fairy Tales. NRPA
Perrin, Jean	1870-1942	Science	75	375			Nobel Prize '26 Physics.TMsS $1,000
Perrine, Valerie		Entertainment	5	6	15	10	Pin-Up SP $30
Perris, Adriana		Entertainment	5			30	Opera
Perry, Alexander J.		Civil War		25			Union Brvt. Gen., Nephew Commodore Perry
Perry, Antoinette		Entertainment		200			Tony Award
Perry, Lila	1959-	Entertainment	5			25	Afro-Am Child Star. TV Shows of Mid 60's
Perry, Lucas		Entertainment	20			75	
Perry, Madison S.		Governor	15	45			Governor FL
Perry, Matthew		Entertainment	10			60	Friends Actor
Perry, Matthew C.	1794-1858	Military	398	867	1740		Adm. Mexican War. Opened Japan to World Trade

NAME	DATE	CATEGORY	SIG	LS/DS	ALS	SP	COMMENTS
Perry, Nora		Author	3	10	20		Novelist
Perry, Oliver H.		Military	750	1000	1250		
Perry, Ralph Barton		Author	10	20	35		Philosopher, Pulitzer Prize
Perry, Susan		Entertainment	20				Actress
Perryman, Lloyd		Country Music	10			20	
Pershing, John J.	1860-1948	Military	70	238	300	645	Comm.-in-Chief AEF WW I. Important ALS $895
Persichetti, Vincent		Composer	10	25	60	15	
Persoff, Nehemiah		Entertainment	5	6	15	15	
Persons, Wilton B.		Gov't Official	5	15	25	10	Gen. Chief Ass't to Pres. DDE
Pertile, Aureliano	1855-1952	Entertainment	40			137	Opera. Favorite of Toscanini at La Scala
Perulli, Franco		Entertainment	20			50	Opera
Perutz, Max		Science	20	40	75	25	Nobel Chemistry 1962
Pesci, Joe		Entertainment	15			50	A A
Petain, Henri-Phillippe.	1856-1951	Head of State	40	165	265	100	Hero WW I. Treason WW II
Peter & Gordon (Both)		Entertainment	75			125	
Peter I		Royalty	90	225	400		King of Serbs, Croats, Slovenes
Peter I, The Great	1672-1725	Royalty	925	5250			Czar of Russia
Peter, Paul & Mary		Entertainment				35	SP All three/full name $35
Peters, Absalom		Clergy	15	20	35		
Peters, Bernadette		Entertainment	5	6	20	25	Pin-Up SP $35
Peters, Brock		Entertainment	5	6	15	15	
Peters, Jean		Entertainment	50	100	30	85	
Peters, Mike*		Cartoonist	5			45	Mother Grimm
Peters, Richard Jr.	1744-1828	Rev. War	40	95	150		Soldier, Jurist, Continental Cong
Peters, Roberta		Entertainment	10			25	Opera, Concert
Peters, Susan		Entertainment	75	85	95	100	
Petersen, Paul		Entertainment	5			15	
Peterson, Bruce A.		Astronaut	5			20	
Peterson, Chesley		Aviation	15	30	55	40	ACE, WW II, Eagle Squadron
Peterson, Donald H.		Astronaut	6			20	
Peterson, Forrest (RADM)		Astronaut	5			15	
Peterson, Oscar		Entertainment	25			45	Jazz Pianist
Peterson, Roger Tory		Author	20	35		25	
Peterson, Rudolph A.		Business	4	6	15	10	
Petiet, Claude		Fr. Revolution	125	265			
Petion, Alexandre	1770-1818	Head of State	225	292			Haitian General, President Southern Haiti
Petrella, Clara		Entertainment	20			50	Opera
Petrie, Wm. Matthew Flinders, Sir		Archaeologist	125	195			Pyramids At Giza. Paved the Way For Carter et al
Petrillo, James C.		Labor	20	55			Czar of Musician's Union
Petrocelli, Daniel		Law	15			20	Prosecuted O.J. Simpson in Civil Suit for Goldman
Petroff, Paul		Entertainment	30			100	Am. Ballet Dancer-Teacher
Petrova, Olga		Entertainment	35			75	Silent Films
Pettet, Joanna		Entertainment	5	6	15	15	
Pettigrew, James J.	1828-63	Civil War	148	518			CSA Gen.
Pettigrew, James, J. (WD)		Civil War	375				CSA Gen. AES '61 $13,200

NAME	DATE	CATEGORY	SIG	LS/DS	ALS	SP	COMMENTS
Pettit, Charles		Rev. War	70	185	315		Continental Congress
Pettit, Don		Astronaut					
Pettus, Edmund W.		Civil War	85	170	360		CSA Gen.ALS War Dte $3500
Petty, Tom		Entertainment	35			95	
Peugeot, Eugene		Business	50	130	315		Fndr. Peugeot Automobile Co.
Pfeiffer, Michelle		Entertainment	30	100		74	Pin-Up SP $90. Batman SP $95-$125
Pflug, Jo Ann		Entertainment	3	5	15	12	
Phelan, James D.	1864-1930	Congress	10	25	40		Senator CA 1915
Phelps, Austin		Clergy	20	30	40		
Phelps, John Smith		Civil War	25	65	100		Union General, Gov. MO
Phelps, John Wolcott		Military-CW	45	135	200		Raised 1st Negro Troops
Phelps, Noah	1740-1809	Military	50	165			Soldier, Patriot, Spy
Phelps, William Walter	1839-94	Congress	10		25		Repr. NJ
Philbin, Mary	1903-93	Entertainment	25			55	Silent Film Star & Beauty Queen
Philbin, Regis		TV Host	5			10	TV Host
Philbrick, Herbert A.		Celebrity	15	30	60	25	I Led Three Lives Agent
Philip (Duke Edinburgh)		Royalty	110	175	325	350	Prince Consort Elizabeth II
Philip II (Sp)	1527-98	Royalty	300	2234			King of Spain 1556-1598. Huband of Mary Tudor
Philip III (Sp) Philip II (Port)		Royalty	250	750			
Philip IV (Sp),III (Port)		Royalty	150	550	1250		
Philip V (Sp)	1683-1746	Royalty	150	395			Founder Bourbon Dynasty
Philipp, Isadore		Entertainment	20		65		Pianist
Philippe II (Duc d'Orleans)		Royalty		500			Regent of Fr. for Louis XV
Philippi, Alfred		Military	5	15			Ger. Gen. WW II. RK
Phillip, Jack W.		Military	27	80			Captain USN
Phillippe, Ryan		Entertainment	10			55	Promising Young Movie Star
Phillips, Bill		Country Music	10			20	
Phillips, Chynna		Entertainment	30			75	Singer-Actress
Phillips, Irna		Entertainment	10			15	Actress. Today's Children
Phillips, J.B.		Clergy	35	50	95	50	
Phillips, John		Astronaut	6			20	
Phillips, John		Entertainment	15			35	Founder Mamas & the Papas
Phillips, Julianne		Entertainment	25			42	Pin-Up SP 72
Phillips, Lou Diamond		Entertainment	10	15	45	30	
Phillips, Mackenzie		Entertainment	10			35	
Phillips, Michelle		Entertainment	10			35	
Phillips, Phil		Composer	15			35	Singer-Songwriter
Phillips, Robert		Astronaut	6			16	
Phillips, Scott		Entertainment	6			25	Music. Drummer Creed
Phillips, Wendell	1811-84	Reformer	30	50	125	50	Abolitionist, Orator, Civ.Rights
Phillips, William		Rev. War	200	550	825		Br. Major General
Phillips, Wm.		Cabinet	4	15	20		
Phillpotts, Eden (Harrington Hext)		Author	10	35	55		Br.Novelist.Plays,Poems,Mystery
Phillpotts, Henry		Clergy	25	35	40		Under Sec'y
Phipps, Spencer		Colonial	55	175			Br. Colonial Gov. MA

NAME	DATE	CATEGORY	SIG	LS/DS	ALS	SP	COMMENTS
Phoenix, River	1971-93	Entertainment	167			337	Ill-fated actor. Death from overdose!
Physick, Philip Syng		Science		775			Father of Am. Surgery
Piaf, Edith	1915-63	Entertainment	150	385	418	542	Legendary Internat'l Chanteuse
Piaget, Jean	1896-1980	Science		375			Swiss Psychologist
Pianchettini, Pio	1799-1851	Composer					Pianist. ANS Framed/Portrait $3500
Piatigorsky, Gregor	1903-76	Entertainment	120	190	300	275	Rus./Am. Cellist. AMusQS $100
Piazza, Marguerite		Entertainment	10			30	Am. Met Sopr.
Picabia, Francis	1879-1953	Artist			225		Fr. Painter. A Leader of Dadaist Movement
Picard, Emile		Science	70	215	475		Fr. Mathematician
Picasso, Pablo	1881-1973	Artist	700	1474	2412	1898	Signed sketch $4,000-$4500. One Line ALS $1600
Picasso, Paloma		Artist	25		95		Artist-Designer. Daughter
Piccaluga, Nino		Entertainment	30			80	Opera
Piccard, Auguste	1884-1963	Science	45	115	195	115	Sw. Physicist. Bathyscaphe
Piccard, Jacques		Science	15	40	75	20	
Piccard, Jean-Felix		Science	65	195		125	Chemist, Aeronautical Eng.
Piccaver, Alfred		Entertainment	75			225	Br. Tenor, Opera
Piccolomini, Marietta		Entertainment	100	275		275	It. Soprano
Pichegru, Charles		Fr. Revolution	35	115	195		Fr. Gen. Strangled In Prison
Pick, Lewis A.	1890-	Military	35	125		40	Gen. WW II
Pickens, Francis W.		Civil War	40	150	200		CSA Gov SC
Pickens, Jane		Entertainment	25			50	(Pickens Sisters) & Actress/Singer
Pickens, Slim		Entertainment	100			200	
Pickens, T. Boone		Business	20	55		45	Corporate Raider. Controversial
Pickering, John	1737-1805	Rev. War	175	250			Impeached & Convicted by Congr.
Pickering, Thomas		Diplomat	10			20	Ambassador to Russia
Pickering, Timothy	1745-1829	Cabinet-Military	220	508	1480		Rev. War Soldier, Sec'y War, Sec'y State
Pickering, William, Dr.		Science	15	35	60	25	Astronomer.Lowell Observatory
Pickett, Cindy		Entertainment	3	3	6	6	
Pickett, George Edward		Civil War	515	1250	2765		CSA Gen. Sig Offered @ $2,500
Pickford, Jack		Entertainment	50			150	
Pickford, Mary & Buddy Rogers		Entertainment	95			275	
Pickford, Mary	1893-1979	Entertainment	55	200	100	168	Co-Founder United Artists. Major Silent Star. AA
Picon, Molly		Entertainment	35	30		45	Stage & Film Star of Yiddish & Am. Theatre
Pidgeon, Walter	1897-1984	Entertainment	20	40		75	Am. Film Actor
Pied Pipers, The (3)		Entertainment	20			45	Big Band Singing Group
Pierce, Benjamin		Rev. War	60	135	200		Father of Pres., Gov. NH
Pierce, Benjamin	1809-80	Science	20		62		Am. Math.& Astronomy.Harvard Prof.
Pierce, David Hyde		Entertainment	5			30	'Niles' in Frasier
Pierce, Franklin	1804-69	President	400	1090	1999		DS as Pres.$1800 DS/J.Davis $4900, FF $385-595
Pierce, Guy		Entertainment	5			35	
Pierce, James		Entertainment	25			45	Vintage Tarzan
Pierce, Jane M.	1806-63	First Lady	215	500	1367		Wife of Franklin Pierce. Tragic Life
Pierce, N. B.		Civil War	30	60	90		
Pierce, Samuel, Jr.	1922-	Cabinet	25		40	70	Afr-Am Sec'y HUD Under Reagan. Key in HUD Scandal
Pierce, Walter M.		Senate/Congress	3	5	10		MOC OR

NAME	DATE	CATEGORY	SIG	LS/DS	ALS	SP	COMMENTS
Pierce, Web		Country Music	4			10	
Pierne', H.C. Gabriel	1863-1937	Composer	15	50	135		Conductor. AMusQS $250
Pierrepont, Edwards	1817-1892	Cabinet	45	55	92		Grant Att'y General 1875. Prosecution of Surratt
Pierson, Roland		Aviation	10	25	35	30	
Pigni, Renzo		Entertainment	15			35	Opera
Pike, Albert	1809-91	Civil War	95	175	306		CSA Gen. Sig/Rank $180
Pike, Christopher		Author	4		15	10	Novelist
Pike, James A., Bishop	1913-69	Clergy	70	120	262	90	Episcopal Bishop.
Pike, Zebulon	1751-1834	Rev. War	40	75	135		Officer Revolutionary Army
Pike, Zebulon M.	1779-1813	Military	230	685	1250		General. Discovered Pike's Peak
Pilatre De Rozier, Jean Francois		Aeronaut	125		500		Pioneer Balloonist
Pillow, Gideon J.	1806-78	Civil War	115		552		CSA Gen.
Pillow, Gideon J.(WD)		Civil War	168	440	500		CSA General. ALS/Cont. $3,750
Pillsbury, George A.		Business		1759	2400		Founder Pillsbury Flour. ALS on Lttrhd. $3850
Pillsbury, John S.		Business	85	675			Governor MN, Pillsbury Flour
Pillsbury, Parker		Reformer	15	25	60		
Pilsudski, Joseph Klemens		Military	115	320	550	275	Pol. Gen., Statesman, Dictator
Pinay, Antoine (Fr)		Head of State	15	35	50		Fr.
Pinchback, Pinckney		Senate	125	350	495		Early Black Elected Official
Pinchot, Bronson		Entertainment	5			15	
Pinchot, Gifford	1865-1946	Governor	35	100	125		Governor PA, Forester
Pinckney, Charles	1757-1824	Rev. War	375		1500		Continental Congress, MOC, Sen. SC
Pinckney, Charles C.	1746-1825	Rev. War	175	1200	725		General, Diplomat, XYZ Affair
Pinckney, Pauline		Author	5	10	20		
Pinckney, Thomas	1750-1828	Rev. War	200	458			Continental Army, Gov. SC
Pincus, Harry		Artist	10	30	60		
Pine, Phillip		Entertainment	3	3	6	8	
Pinero, Arthur Wing, Sir	1855-1934	Author	20	35	65	60	Br. Dramatist, Actor
Ping, Deng Xiao		Head of State	200		700		China. NRPA
Pingel, Rolf		Aviation	10	15	30	25	
Pingree, Hazen S.		Governor	10	15			Governor MI
Pink Floyd		Entertainment	75			140	
Pinkerton, Allan	1819-84	Am. Detective	275	807	1365	1150	Dir. Union Secret Service Bureau During Civil War
Pinkerton, Robert A.		Business	35	105	220	75	CEO Pinkerton's Inc. Detectives
Pinkerton, William A.							SEE Allan, P.
Pinkney, William	1764-1822	Cabinet	90	225	275		MOC, Senator MD. Att'y Gen. 1811
Pinochet, Augusto		Head of State	30	115	245	50	Chilean Mil. Leader
Pinter, Harold		Author	20			95	Br. Playwright. Small (4x5) SP $50
Pinza, Ezio	1892-1957	Entertainment	70	140		202	It.-Am. Basso, Opera, Films
Pioneers, Sons of the		Country Music	100			395	Spencer, Brady, Nolan, K & H Farr, Perryman
Piper, William Thomasr.		Aviation	175	380			Founder Piper Aircraft Corp.
Pirandello, Luigi	1867-1936	Author	70	175	425	390	Nobel Lit. ALS/Content $2,400
Pirchoff, Nelly		Entertainment	10			30	Opera
Pire, Dominique George		Clergy	55		90	65	
Piscopo, Joe		Entertainment	10			35	

NAME	DATE	CATEGORY	SIG	LS/DS	ALS	SP	COMMENTS
Pissarro, Camille	1830-1903	Artist	200	740	1422		Fr. Impressionist-Pointillist
Piston, Walter	1894-1976	Composer	142	225	475	95	Pulitzer Music 1947 & 1960
Pitkin, William	1694-1769	Colonial Am.	65	475			Soldier, Colonial Judge & Gov. CT
Pitkin, William	1729-89	Colonial Am.	30	100			Jurist, Army Major.,Mfg. Gunpowder. Chf.Just. CT
Pitney, Gene		Entertainment	5			25	
Pitney, Mahlon (SC)		Supreme Court	25	50	145	30	MOC NJ 1895
Pitt, Brad		Entertainment	18			59	Current Versatile Heart Throb
Pitt, Ingrid		Entertainment	3			10	Actress
Pitt, John, Sir	1756-1835	Military	45		95		Gen. Cmdr. Failed Walcheren Exp.
Pitt, William (Elder)	1708-78	Head of State	110	225	1175		The Great Commoner
Pitt, William (Younger)	1759-1815	Head of State	115	374	505		England's Youngest Prime Min.
Pittenger, William	1840-	Clergy	15		25		Military (Civil War)
Pittner, William		Civil War-Clergy	15				
Pitts, Zazu		Entertainment	40			100	
Pius IX, G.M. Mastori		Clergy	175	250	400		G. M. Mastori
Pius IX, Pope		Clergy	40	150	275		
Pius VII, Pope	1876-1958	Clergy		1500		750	
Pius X, Pope	1835-1914	Clergy	500	700	1975	5000	Giuseppe Melchiorre Sarto
Pius XI, Pope		Clergy	350	950	3200	950	A.D. Achille Ratti
Pius XII, Pope		Clergy		2000		775	Eugenio Pacelli
Plainsmen, The		Country Music	25			50	
Planck, Max	1858-1947	Science	128	1225	2167	3750	Nobel Physics 1918. ANS Pc $500
Plancon, Pol		Entertainment			85		Opera
Plant & Page (Both)		Entertainment				155	Rock
Plant, Robert		Entertainment	35			100	
Plato, Dana		Entertainment	5			15	
Platt, Ed		Entertainment	75			160	
Platt, Marc		Entertainment	5			35	Dancer-Choreographer
Platt, Orville H.	1827-1905	Congress	5	15			Senator CT
Platt, Thomas C	1833-1910	Congress	15		33	20	Senator NY
Platters, The (Group of 5)		Entertainment				250	Black Singing Group
Playfair, Lyon, 1st Baron		Science	10	25	40		Br. Chem. Modern Sanitation
Pleasant,Mary E.('Mammy')		Celebrity	400				
Pleasanton, Alfred (WD)		Civil War	122	185	672		Union Gen. Sherman's Chief Cavalry
Pleasanton, Alfred	1824-97	Civil War	30		85		Union Gen.ALS War Dte $1,200
Pleasence, Donald		Entertainment	15			40	
Pleasonton, Alfred	1824-97	Civil War			200		Union Gen'l
Pleshette, Suzanne		Entertainment	6	8	15	15	
Plimpton, George		Author	7	20	25	17	
Plishka, Paul		Entertainment	5			25	Opera
Plitsetskaya, Maya		Entertainment	15			40	Ballet
Plowright, Joan		Entertainment	10			25	
Plummer, Amanda		Entertainment	16			25	Actress
Plummer, Christopher		Entertainment	7	10		28	Actor
Plunkett, Charles P.	1864-1930	Military	45	135			USN Adm. Transatlantic Flight Operations 1919

NAME	DATE	CATEGORY	SIG	LS/DS	ALS	SP	COMMENTS
Plunkett, Edw. John		Author					SEE Lord Dunsany Soldier,Traveler,Big Game Huntr
Pocahontas (Cast Of)		Entertainment				130	Mel Gibson & Two Others
Podesta, Rossana		Entertainment	10			35	International Films. Beautiful Italian Actress.
Podmore, Thomas		Clergy	10	10	15	20	
Poe, Edgar Allan	1809-1849	Author			12100		AMsS $35,000, ALS $39,000
Pogany, Willy		Artist	70	190			Illustrator, Muralist,Designer
Poggi, Gianni		Entertainment	10			25	Opera
Pogue, William R.		Astronaut	6			20	
Poincare', Raymond	1860-1934	Head of State	40	60	100	105	3 Times Prime Minister France
Poindexter, John		Military	40			150	US Adm. Iran-Contra
Poindexter, Joseph B.		Governor	10	15			Governor Hawii, Federal Judge
Poindexter, Miles		Congress	5	15		10	Repr., Senator WA 1909
Poinsett, Joel R.	1779-1851	Cabinet	70	460	375		Sec'y War. Poinsettia Flower
Pointer Sisters		Entertainment	30			60	
Poiret, Paul	1879-1944	Designer	125	525			Fr. Dress Designer
Poitier, Sidney	1924-	Entertainment	13	65		58	1st Afr-Am AA Winning Actor
Poland, Luke P.		Senate/Congress	10	15	30		MOC, Senator VT 1865
Polando, John		Aviation	30	60	110	75	
Polanski, Roman		Entertainment	20			125	Fugitive Director
Polansky, Mark		Astronaut	5			19	
Polaski, Deborah		Entertainment	5			25	Opera
Poli, Afro		Entertainment	10			45	Opera
Police, The		Entertainment	70			275	
Poling, Daniel A.		Clergy	20	30	60	35	
Polk, James K. & Buchanan, J.		President	1275	2328			
Polk, James K. (As Pres.)		President	850	2192	3833		FF $975-$1200
Polk, James K.	1795-1849	President	625	1807	3480		FF $975. Political ALS $5250
Polk, Leonidas (WD)		Civil War	500	685	3125		CSA General
Polk, Leonidas	1806-64	Civil War	338		1695		CSA Gen. KIA. Episcopal Bishp.Fndr.Univ. of South
Polk, Sarah Childress		First Lady	500	600	1050	1375	Banned Dancing & Drinking in WH
Pollack, Sidney		Entertainment	12	30	30	25	AA Director-Actor
Pollard, Michael J.	1939-	Entertainment	8			25	Character Actor. Bonnie & Clyde,Dobie Gillis
Pollard, Snub		Entertainment	50			200	Keystone Cop
Pollen, Tracy		Entertainment	10			35	
Pollock, Channing		Author	30	55	145	45	Am. Playwright, Essayist
Pomeroy, Samuel Clarke	1816-91	Congress	35	50			Civil War Senator KS 1861. 2X Cleared of Bribery
Pometti, Vincenzo		Entertainment	5			15	
Pompadour, Mme J. A,Duchess.		Royalty	135	470	1130		Louis VI Mistress
Pompidou, Georges		Head of State	10	25		20	Premier, President France
Ponchielli, Amilcare		Composer	175		1200		It. Opera. La Gioconda.Ballets
Pond, Enoch		Clergy	15	25	30		
Pond, Julian		Science	50		325		
Ponder, James		Governor	12	20			Governor DE
Poniatowski, Jozef A., Prince	1763-1813	Military	375	2050	2150		Rarest Napoleon Marsh'l
Pons, Juan		Entertainment	5			25	Opera

NAME	DATE	CATEGORY	SIG	LS/DS	ALS	SP	COMMENTS
Pons, Lily	1904-76	Entertainment	50			184	Fr.-Born Am. Coloratura Soprano Met. Star.
Ponselle, Carmela		Entertainment	25				Mezzo Sister of Rosa
Ponselle, Rosa		Entertainment	62		90	275	Acclaimed for Norma. SP in Opera Debut Role $475
Pontchartrain, Louis de		Diplomat	450		2000		Fr. Minister of Marine. Lake Pontchartrain Named
Ponti, Carlo		Entertainment	15	20		30	It. Film Producer
Ponting, Herbert George		Celebrity	25	60	165		
Ponty, Jean-Luc		Entertainment	6	8	15	15	
Pool, Tilaman E.		Aviation	10	22	38	28	ACE, WW II, Navy Ace
Poor, Enoch		Rev. War	175	550	875		General. Patriot, Hero
Poore, Benjamin A.		Military		75		40	Am. WW I Gen.
Pope, A.J.		Aviation	20	35			WW II Am. Ace
Pope, Alexander	1688-1744	Author	833	1850	3297	3500	Br. Poet, Satirist, Critic. Rare
Pope, Alexander	1849-1924	Artist	150	370	600		Am.NY Auction Still Life Sold $475,000 '82
Pope, Generoso Jr.		Business	10	40	50	25	It.-Born Publ. Il Progresso
Pope, James Pinckney	1884-1966	Congress	10	15		20	Senator ID. Dir. TVA
Pope, John	1822-92	Civil War	90	115	288	400	Union Genl. Cmdr. 2nd Bull Runn
Pope, John (WD)		Civil War	155	442			Union Gen.
Pope John Paul II	1920-	Clergy	150			842	Polish Roman Catholic Pope since 1978
Popham, William	1752-1847	Rev. War			375		Aide-de-Camp to Gen. Clinton
Popkin, John S.	1771-185	Clergy		40	75		Greek Scholar & Harvard Prof. of Greek
Popovic, Cojetko		Celebrity	40		270		
Popovich, Pavel		Astronaut	45			175	Rus. Cosmonaut
Popp, Lucia		Entertainment	15			50	Opera
Porizkova, Paulina		Entertainment	25			62	Model-Actress. Pin-Up SP $80
Porsche, Ferdinand	1909-98	Business	70			215	Ger. Auto. Mfg. Son of Designer of VW & Porsche
Porsche, Ferdinand, Dr.		Business	225	383		650	Inventor-Designer VW & Porsche.SP 5x7 $325
Portal, Charles		Aviation	20	40	80	50	
Porter, Cole	1891-1964	Composer	225	932	1135	1205	2x3 SPI $600, AMusQS $1250, S Chk $1050
Porter, David	1780-1843	Military	45	145	250		Am.Naval Off. Fought 3 Wars
Porter, David Dixon	1813-91	Civil War	130	518	550		Union Adm., Mex. War,Civil War
Porter, Don		Entertainment	5	5	10	13	
Porter, Fitz-John	1822-1901	Civil War	45	118	292	750	Union Gen. Special ALS $825-$900
Porter, Gene Stratton		Author	50	145	295	65	Am. Novelist. Freckles
Porter, George, Sir		Science	15	35	60	25	Nobel Chemistry 1967
Porter, Horace	1837-1921	Civil War	45	190	385		Union General-MOH.LS/Cont.$1750
Porter, James D.		Governor	5	20	35		Governor TN
Porter, James M.	1793-1844	Cabinet	20	77	120		Sec'y War 1843, Jurist, RR Pres.
Porter, Jane	1776-1850	Author	100		325		Br. Romance Novelist
Porter, Katherine Anne	1890-1980	Author	75	250	385	150	Am.Ship of Fools, Pulitzer
Porter, Noah		Clergy	30	65	100		Editor
Porter, Peter	1773-1844	Cabinet	65	145	180		Sec'y War J.Q.Adams
Porter, Quincy		Composer	17	45			Dean & Dir.New Eng.Conservatory
Porter, William Sidney (O.Henry)	1862-1910	Author	300	850	1873		Am. Short-Story Writer
Portes-Gil, Emilio		Head of State	35		85		Pres. Mexico
Portland, Third Duke of.	1738-1809	Head of State	45		200		Prime Minister. Wm. H. Cavendish Bentinck

NAME	DATE	CATEGORY	SIG	LS/DS	ALS	SP	COMMENTS
Portman, Eric		Entertainment	35			95	
Portman, Natalie		Entertainment	10			58	Young Actress
Portsmouth, Duchess (Chas II)		Royalty	65	465	625		Louise-Renee' de Keroualle. 1649-1734
Posey, Parker		Entertainment	20			62	
Poshetko, Joseph		Aviation	10	15	25	30	WW II Flying Tiger Ace
Possart, Ernst		Entertainment	15		55	50	Classical Musician
Post, Augustus		Aviation	25	45	55	50	Pioneer Aviator, Balloonist
Post, Emily	1873-1960	Author	95	50	125	35	US Etiquette Authority of Her Time
Post, Marjorie Merriweather		Business	15	35	70	25	Philanthropist, Postum Cereal
Post, Markie		Entertainment	6	8		20	Pin-Up SP $35-50
Post, Wiley	1900-35	Aviation	300	772	650	825	1st Solo Around the World Flight. FFC '31 $595
Poston, Tom		Entertainment	5			20	
Potter, (Helen) Beatrix	1866-1943	Author	120	300	2300	175	Illustr.Own Children's Books. ....Peter Rabbit
Potter, Cora		Entertainment	10	15	30	25	
Potter, Edwar E.	1823-89	Civil War	15		100		Recruited & Led Regiment of Black Soldiers in N.C.
Potts, Annie		Entertainment	10			35	
Poulenc, Francis-Jean	1899-1963	Composer	140	380	550		Member Group of Six. Pianist
Poulson, Norris		Mayor	4	30		10	Mayor L.A.
Poulter, Thomas C.		Explorer	20	40			2nd Arctic Expedition
Pound, Ezra	1885-1972	Author	215	763	1283	895	Poet, Editor, Critic, Translator
Poundstone, Paula		Entertainment	7			15	Standup Comedienne
Povey, Len		Aviation	10	15	25	20	
Povich, Maury		TV Host	10			20	TV Host
Powderly, Terence V.	1849-1924	Labor	45	95		50	Am. Labor Leader
Powell, Adam Clayton	1908-72	Congress	35	138		50	Contoversial Minister, MOC NY. Barred, Reelected
Powell, Colin L.	1937-	Military	35	137		128	Chmn.Joint Chiefs of Staff.FDC Desert Storm S$95
Powell, Dick		Entertainment	35	45	60	65	SingerTurned Popular Actor.SP 11x14 Bachrach $145
Powell, Eleanor	1910-82	Entertainment	10	60	35	56	Popular 40's Film Tap Dancer Musical Star
Powell, Jane		Entertainment	9	10	20	25	Pin-up SP $30
Powell, Jeremiah		Rev. War	75		245		President of Mass. Bay Colony Rev. Times
Powell, John Wesley		Explorer	250				Geologist.Pioneer Expl. West US
Powell, Lewis F.,Jr. (SC)		Supreme Court	40	138		450	In Robes-SP $950
Powell, Maud		Entertainment	20			90	Violinist
Powell, Max		Country Music	10			20	
Powell, Robert		Entertainment	4			10	Actor
Powell, Ross E.		Military	10	15	30		
Powell, Talmage		Author	10	20	45	15	Am. Novelist Mysteries
Powell, Teddy		Entertainment	20			70	Big band leader
Powell, William		Entertainment	30	50		90	Perenially Suave, Sophsticated, Major Star
Power, Paul		Entertainment				20	Character Actor
Power, Tyrone	1913-58	Entertainment	120	130		271	Breathtakingly Handsome Actor late 30's-40's
Powers, Bert		Celebrity	4	10	15	10	White House Aide
Powers, Francis Gary		Aviation	80			100	U2 Downed Pilot Over USSR
Powers, Hiram		Artist	45	160	425	150	19th Cent. Major Sculptor
Powers, John 'Shorty'	1923-80	Celebrity	45	195		50	NASA Spokesman. A-OK

NAME	DATE	CATEGORY	SIG	LS/DS	ALS	SP	COMMENTS
Powers, John Robert		Business	10	20	25	20	Fndr. One of 1st Modelling Agy.
Powers, Mala		Entertainment	5	7		15	
Powers, Preston		Artist	25	65	165		
Powers, Richard							SEE Tom Keene
Powers, Ridgely C.		Governor	10	15	30		Governor MS
Powers, Stephanie		Entertainment	9	10	20	25	Pin-Up SP $25
Pownall, Thomas	1722-1805	Colonial Am.	165	375	630		Lt. Gov. NJ, Gov. MA Bay, SC
Powter, Susan		Author	5			10	Non-Fiction
Powys, John C.	1872-1963	Author	28	60			Novelist, Poet, Critic, Philosopher
Powys, Llewelyn		Author	30	65	115	35	Essayist, Novelist
Powys, Theodore Francis	1875-1953	Author	80		350		Br. Allegorical Novels. AMsS $1980
Poynter, Edward John, Sir		Artist	10	35	75		Pres. Royal Academy
Pozzo de Borgo, Chas. A.		Corsican Diplomat	50		200		Opponent of Napoleon
Prado, Perez		Bandleader	25			85	
Praed, Winthrop M.	1802-1839	Author	50		230		Poet
Pran, Dith		Celebrity	10	20	45	20	Cambodian photographer
Pratt, Francis & Whitney, Amos		Inventor		465			Pratt & Whitney Engine
Pratt, Ruth	1877-1965	Congress	10	30			Repr. NY 1929-33
Pratt, Thomas G.		Congress	5	20	25		Gov. 1845, Senator MD 1849
Preble, George H.		Civil War	20	60	85		Adm. USN.DS/Cont. $250
Precourt, Charlie		Astronaut	7			20	
Preddy. George E.		Aviation	10	30	45	30	
Preger, Kurt		Entertainment	5			20	Opera
Prelog, Vladimir		Science	20	30	45	25	Nobel Chemistry 1975
Premice, Josephine		Entertainment	20			35	Afr.-Am. Actress
Preminger, Otto	1906-86	Entertainment	50			95	Important Film Director
Prentice, John*		Cartoonist	10			40	Rip Kirby
Prentiss, Benjamin	1819-1901	Civil War	30		75		IL Soldier. Mex.& CW. Promoted by Lincoln to Gen'l
Prentiss, Paula		Entertainment	12			20	Pin-Up SP $25
Prescott, Oliver		Rev. War	70	175	465		Suppression of Shay's Rebellion
Prescott, Wm. Hickling		Author	30	60			
PRESIDENTIAL OATH		President		5500			FIVE PRES.(Printed Transcript)
PRESIDENTS		President	1250			2296	4 PRESIDENTS(Reagan-Ford-Carter-Nixon)
PRESIDENTS (5)		President	1417	4400		4900	Ford,Nixon,Bush,Reagan,Carter. WH Engr.S $3700
Presley, Elvis	1935-77	Entertainment	590	1025	2075	1102	ANS/Content $10,000-$13,000. SP (Pc) $750
Presley, Priscilla		Entertainment	20		40	30	Pin-Up SP $35. Legal DS $500
Presley, Vernon		Celebrity	15			60	Father of Elvis Presley
Presser, Jackie		Celebrity	10	25		15	
Preston the Magician		Entertainment	4	6		8	
Preston, Kelly		Entertainment	5			30	
Preston, Robert	1918-87	Entertainment	50			75	Actor-Singer Music Man
Preston, William (WD)		Civil War	157	590	400		CSA Gen.
Preston, William	1816-87	Civil War	145				CSA Gen.
Preston, William Ballard		Cabinet	25	50	110		CSA Gov VA.Wardte SP $3,000
Preston, Wm. C.	1794-1860	Congress	15	35			Sen. SC

NAME	DATE	CATEGORY	SIG	LS/DS	ALS	SP	COMMENTS
Pretenders		Entertainment	12			65	
Pretty Things, The		Entertainment				80	Br. Rock Group (All 5)
Preuss, Georg		Military	20		40		
Previn, Andre		Conductor-Comp.	20	40	80	75	
Previn, Dorey		Composer	5	10	20	10	
Prevost, Eugene-Marcel		Author	10	25	55		Fr. Moralist, Feminist Fiction
Prey, Hermann		Entertainment	10			30	Opera
Price, James H.		Governor	5	15			Governor VA
Price, Leontyne		Entertainment	25		45	55	Am. Soprano, Opera
Price, Margaret		Entertainment	15			45	Opera
Price, Ray		Entertainment	5			15	C & W
Price, Sterling (WD)		Civil War	380		6900		CSA Gen. AES $575
Price, Sterling	1809-67	Civil War	218	395			CSA Gen. Gov. MO
Price, Vincent	1911-93	Entertainment	56	118	130	94	Self Sketch S $90. Egghead SP $125
Pride, Charley	1938-	Country Music	10			20	1st Afr-Am Major Country Music Star
Prien, Guenther		Military	300			750	
Priest, Ivy Baker		Cabinet	10	15	30	20	U.S. Treasurer
Priest, Pat		Entertainment	4			20	Actor. Munsters. 'Marilyn Munster'
Priest, Royce W.		Aviation	10	22	35	30	ACE, WW II, USAAF Ace
Priestley, J. B.	1894-1984	Author	35	105	220	125	Playwright, Novelist, Playwright
Priestley, William O., Sir		Medical	50	120	200		Obstetric Physician
Priestly, Jason		Entertainment	20			50	
Priestly, Joseph	1783-1804	Science	350	1200	2200		Br. Clergyman, Chemist.
Prieur-Duvernois, C.-A., Count		Fr. Revolution	35	125			Fr. Revolutionary
Prigogine, Ilya		Science	20	30	45	25	Nobel Chemistry 1977
Prima, Louis		Entertainment	20			45	Big Band Leader-Trumpeter
Primrose, William		Entertainment	75			250	Great Violinist
Prince		Entertainment	110			200	
Prince, Harold 'Hal'		Entertainment	15	20	30	30	
Prince, Henry		Civil War	30	65	85		Union Gen. Pre War ALS $650
Prince, John Dyneley		Educator	10	25		15	Dean Graduate School NYU
Principal, Victoria		Entertainment	10	10	25	45	
Pringle, Aileen		Entertainment	15	15	35	30	
Prinz, Dianne		Astronaut	4			12	
Prinz, Rosemary		Entertainment	3	4		10	
Prinze, Freddie		Entertainment	45	85		85	Promising Career. Short Life
Prinze, Freddie, Jr.		Entertainment	8			40	
Pritchard, Jeter C.	1857-1921	Congress	10	15			Senator NC 1895
Pritchard, John, Sir		Conductor				45	Opera & Mozart Specialist
Procol Harum		Entertainment	35			65	
Proctor, Edna Dean	1838-	Author	35		80		Am. Poet, Magazine Writer
Proctor, Redfield	1831-1908	Cabinet	12	25	50	30	Gov, Senator VT, Sec'y War
Proctor, Richard Anthony		Science	5	15	35		Br. Astonomer, Science Writer
Profumo, John		Politician	40	65		100	Br. Traitor. Member of Parliament
Profumo, Valerie (Hobson)		Entertainment	10		25	25	Br. Film Star

NAME	DATE	CATEGORY	SIG	LS/DS	ALS	SP	COMMENTS
Prokofieff, Serge	1891-1953	Composer	370	1768	2115	1025	Russ. AMusQS $2500-$2,900-$5,000
Prosky, Robert		Entertainment	5	6	15	15	
Protti, Aldo		Entertainment	5			20	Opera
Prouse, Juliet		Entertainment	10	8	15	40	Pin-Up SP $25-$45
Proust, Marcel	1871-1922	Author	500	875	1550	6000	ALS/Content $3,300, $3,500
Prouty, Jed		Entertainment	30			45	
Provine, Dorothy		Entertainment	5	6		10	
Provost, Jon		Entertainment	18			35	Young Actor. 'Timmy' from Lassie TV Series
Prowse, Dave		Entertainment	10			30	Actor. Darth Vadar $35
Proxmire, William		Senate/Congress	5	10		15	Senator WI
Pryce, Jonathon		Entertainment	5			22	James Bond Bad Guy
Pryor, David		Governor	5	15			Governor AR
Pryor, Richard		Entertainment	9	10	35	25	
Pryor, Roger		Entertainment	15	20		45	
Pryor, Roger A. (WD)		Civil War	175		650		CSA Gen.
Pryor, Roger A.	1828-1919	Civil War	112	260	350		CSA Gen. US MOC. 1859-61
Pucci, Emilio		Business	10	25	40	15	It. Fashion Designer
Puccini, Giacomo	1858-1924	Composer	500	850	1394	1512	AMusQS $1,400-$1950-$4,000. SP(Pc) $875
Puck, Wolfgang		Business	5	10		15	Successful Chef & Owner of 'Spago'
Puelo, Johnny		Entertainment	10			25	
Puente, Tito		Entertainment	10			45	Big Band Leader.
Puett, Clay		Business	25	60		35	
Pulitzer, Joseph	1847-1911	Business	125	350	595		Pulitzer Prize. Editor-Publisher. Rare ALS $4500
Pulitzer, Joseph, Jr.		Business	20	25		30	Editor-Publisher
Pulitzer, Ralph	1879-1939	Business	54		250		Journalist, Pres. Press Publishing NY World
Pulitzer, Roxanne		Celebrity	5	15	35	20	Pin-Up SP $25
Pullenberg, Albert		Science	20			60	Rocket Pioneer/von Braun
Pullman, Bill		Entertainment	12			45	Actor
Pullman, George M.	1831-97	Business-Inventor	383	855		250	Pullman RR Car. ALS on Lttrhd. $9600
Pullman, Hattie Sanger		Philantropist	15	25	30		Mrs. George M. Pullman
Pulsford, Nigel		Entertainment	6			25	Music. Guitar Bush
Puma, Salvatore		Entertainment	5			20	Opera
Punshon, W. Morley		Clergy	25	40	50		
Pupin, Michael, Dr.		Science	90	305	300	225	Physicist-Inventor-Author
Purcell, Edward M., Dr.		Science	20	30	45	25	Nobel Physics 1952
Purcell, Lee		Entertainment	4	5	12	10	
Purcell, Sarah		Entertainment	5	6	15	10	
Purdy, James		Author	15	50			
Purl, Linda		Entertainment	6	8	15	20	
Purvis, Melvin		Lawman	35	200	175	100	FBI. Noted Agent. Hunted Down Most Wanted
Purvis, Robert		Anti-Slavery	15	40	85		Underground Railroad
Pusey, Edward B.	1800-82	Clergy	45	55	110	55	Anglican High Church Leader of Oxford Movement
Pusey, Nathan M.	1907-	Educator	15	45	100	30	President Harvard
Pusey, Pennock		Political	10	15			Government Official
Pushkin, Alexander		Author	825	3250	16200		Rus. Poet, Dramatist,Novelist

NAME	DATE	CATEGORY	SIG	LS/DS	ALS	SP	COMMENTS
Pusser, Buford		Lawman	50	150			Walking Tall Tennessee Sheriff
Putman, Frederick Ward	1839-1915	Science		30	55		Anthropologist-Naturalist. Curator of Top Museums
Putnam, George Haven	1844-1930	Business	90	682			Publishing House. Putnam & Sons
Putnam, George Palmer		Business	15	40	75	30	Book Publisher, Author
Putnam, Israel	1718-90	Rev. War	200	3358	925		Don't Fire Till ...... War Dte. MsLS $3500
Putnam, Rufus		Rev. War	175	405	825		General. Ohio Pioneer
Putney, Mahlon		Celebrity	20	55			
Puzo, Mario	1921-99	Author	20	75	100	45	Am. Novelist. The Godfather
Py, Gilbert		Entertainment	5			25	Opera
Pyle, Denver		Entertainment	4	6	10	20	
Pyle, Ernie		Author	250	400	485	350	Correspondent WWII, Pulitzer. Killed
Pyle, Howard		Artist	170	375	750		Am.Art Nouveau Illustrator-Auth
Pynchon, John	1621-1703	Colonial America			3750		Statesman, Soldier. NRPA

NAME	DATE	CATEGORY	SIG	LS/DS	ALS	SP	COMMENTS
Qaddafi, Muammar el		Head of State	85	225	500	150	Chairman Libyan-Arab Republic
Quackenbush, Stephen P. (WD)		Civil War	35		165		Union Adm.
Quaid, Dennis		Entertainment	20			50	
Quaid, Randy		Entertainment	6	48		20	
Quale, Anthony		Entertainment	20	25	55	45	
Qualen, John		Entertainment	10			20	
Quang, Thich Tri		Head of State	20	45	125	30	NRPA
Quant, Mary		Business	5	10	20	10	Br. Fashion Designer.
Quantrill, Wm. C.		Military	900	3000	4150		CSA Army Guerilla Leader
Quarles, William A.	1825-93	Civil War	78	295			CSA General. Sig. War Dte. $150
Quarry, Robert		Entertainment	10			25	
Quasimodo, Salvatore		Author	25	40	55	30	Nobel Literature 1959
Quay, Matthew Stanley		Senate/Congress	15	75			Senator PA 1887
Quayle, Dan	1947-	Vice President	58	92		61	Sen. IN. Bush VP. Signed White House Card $50
Quayle, Marilyn		2nd Lady	20			60	
Queen, Ellery							SEE Dannay
Queensberry, Wm. Douglas		Celebrity	15	40	95		
Quesada, E.R. 'Pete'		Military	15	35	55	25	
Quesada, Elwood R.		Aviation	16	30	45	30	
Questel, Mae		Entertainment	50				Original Voice of Betty Boop
Quie, Albert Harold		Senate/Congress	5			10	MOC MN
Quigg, Lemuel Ely		Senate/Congress	5	10			MOC NY 1894
Quillan, Eddie		Entertainment	20			45	
Quincy, Josiah	1772-1864	Congress	108	75	150		Repr. MA. Pres. Harvard
Quine, Richard		Entertainment	10			20	Actor turned Director
Quinn, Anthony		Entertainment	15	38		52	AA Winning Mex.-Irish Actor. Zorba
Quinn, Carmel		Entertainment	5			15	

NAME	DATE	CATEGORY	SIG	LS/DS	ALS	SP	COMMENTS
Quinn, Martha		Entertainment	4			10	MTV
Quinn, Robert E.		Governor	10	15			Governor RI
Quinn, William F.		Governor	5	10		15	Governor HI
Quintard, Charles Todd		Clergy	75	95	160		Served Confed. Army as Phys.
Quirk, Michael J.		Aviation	12	25	40	30	ACE, WW II
Quiros, Jean B.		Head of State	45	70			
Quisling, Vidkun		Military	115	220	475	450	Nor. Collaborator
Quitman, John A.	1799-1858	Millitary-Congr.-Gov.	25				General. Gov. & Sen. MS

R

NAME	DATE	CATEGORY	SIG	LS/DS	ALS	SP	COMMENTS
Raab, Julius		Head of State	5	15	35	15	Chancellor Austria
Raabe, Meinhardt		Entertainment	25			50	
Rabaud, Henri	1873-1949	Composer	35			200	Fr. Composer-Conductor. Opera. AMusQS $120
Rabi, Isador I.	1898-1988	Science	42	60	80	40	Nobel Physics 1944. Delopment of Radar, A Bomb
Rabin, Yitzhak	1922-96	Head of State	210	540	775	506	PM Israel, Nobel. Assassinated '96
Rabinowitz, Solomon		Author					SEE Aleichem, S.(Pen Name)
Raboy, Mac*		Cartoonist	10			95	Flash Gordon
Rachin, Alan		Entertainment	5			15	
Rachmaninoff, Sergei	1873-1943	Composer	360	926	1425	1406	AMusQS $2,000, $3950, $4500
Racine, Jean	1639-99	Author	4500				Fr. Dramatist. NRPA
Rackham, Arthur	1867-1939	Artist	60	175	450		Br.Illustrator Children's Books. Water Color
Radford, William	1808-1890	Military		375			CW Naval Off'r. Adm. Mex. War
Radford, William	1814-1870	Congress	10	15	30		Repr. NY
Radhakrishnan, Sarvepalli	1888-1975	Head of State	65	167	380	75	Pres. India, Philosopher,Educator, Author
Radner, Gilda		Entertainment	50	62		225	Am. Comedienne
Rae, Cassidy		Entertainment	5			40	Actress Models, Inc.
Rae, Charlotte		Entertainment	5			15	
Raeder. Erich	1876-1960	Military	75	208	550	125	Ger. Navy Cmdr., Convicted of War Crimes WW II
Raff, Joseph Joachim		Composer	25			150	Ger. Wide Variety Of Music
Rafferty, Frances		Entertainment	4			10	
Raffin, Deborah		Entertainment	10			45	
Rafko, Kaye Lani		Entertainment	8			15	Miss America 1988
Raft, George	1895-1980	Entertainment	45	120		170	11 x 14 Vintage SPI $200
Rage Against the Machine		Entertainment	32			90	Music. Rock Group
Raglan, Fitzroy Somerset, Lord		Military	40	115	150		Crimean War. Raglan Sleeve
Ragsland, Rags		Entertainment	40			75	
Rahman, Abdul		Head of State	10	35	80	15	Malaysia. 1st Ambass. U.S.
Raimondi, Ruggero		Entertainment	20			50	Opera
Rain-in-the-Face		Indian Chief	13000			8260	
Rainer, Luise		Entertainment	15	35	40	50	Austrian Two Time Oscar Winner. Back to Back
Raines, Ella		Entertainment	7			18	
Rainey, Ford		Entertainment	3	5		10	

NAME	DATE	CATEGORY	SIG	LS/DS	ALS	SP	COMMENTS
Rainey, Henry Thomas		Senate/Congress	5	15			MOC IL 1903-21, Speaker
Rainger, Ralph		Composer	20			40	AMusQS $55, $85
Rainier III, Prince		Royalty	70	95	205	125	Monaco
Rains, Claude	1899-1967	Entertainment	113			241	Brit. Character Actor. Casablanca
Rains, James E. (WD)		Civil War		4850			CSA Gen.. KIA. RARE
Rainwater, Leo James		Science	20	30	45	25	Nobel Physics 1975
Rainwater, Marvin		Country Music	15			30	
Raisa, Rosa	1893-1963	Entertainment	30	45		60	Opera. Created Title Role in Turandot
Raitt, Bonnie		Entertainment	5			30	
Raitt, John		Entertainment	5	7	15	15	
Raksin, David		Composer					AMQS $75
Raleigh, Cecil		Entertainment	6	8		10	
Raleigh, Sara		Entertainment	6	8		10	
Rall, Guenther		Military-Aviation	30	75	150	90	#3 ACE, WW II, Ger./275 Kills.
Ralston, Esther		Entertainment	10	15	45	33	Am. Leading Lady 20's-30's
Ralston, Jobyna		Entertainment	25	35	65	50	
Ralston, Vera Hruba		Entertainment	7	15		25	
Ralston, William		Business	55	90	150		Founder Bank of California
Rama VI		Royalty	135				King Siam (Thailand)
Rambeau, Marjorie		Entertainment	20	25	45	45	
Rambo, Dack		Entertainment	15	20		50	
Rambo, Dirk		Entertainment	20			40	
Ramey, Samuel		Entertainment	10			35	Opera
Ramirez, Carlos		Entertainment	8			25	Baritone
Ramone, Johnny		Entertainment	7			32	Romones Rock Group
Ramos, Ramon		Entertainment	10			35	1930's Big Band Leader
Rampling, Charlotte		Entertainment	5			27	Brit. Actress-Model. Pin-up SP $35
Ramsay, William, Sir	1852-1916	Science	150	410	750		Nobel Chemistry 1904
Ramseur, Stephen D.(WD)		Civil War		13000			CSA Gen. RARE
Ramsey, Alexander		Cabinet	20	45	90		CW Gov. MN, Hayes Sec'y War
Ramsey, Michael, Archbishop		Clergy	35	45	50	45	
Ramsey, Norman F., Dr.		Science	15	25		20	Nobel Physics 1989
Rand, Ayn	1905-82	Author	733	2750		800	Objectivist Novels
Rand, Sally	1903-79	Entertainment	25	110		55	Fan Dancer 20's-30's. Pin-Up SP $60-$100
Randall, James R.		Writer-Composer	70				Maryland, My..... MsS $1,900, AMsS $9,500
Randall, Samuel J.		Senate/Congress	7	20			MOC PA 1863-90
Randall, Tony		Entertainment	5	5	15	20	
Randell, Mike		Business	3			5	TV Exec.
Randolph, A. Philip	1889-1979	Labor	65	75			US Black Labor Leader 1925. Train Porter's Strike
Randolph, Beverly		Rev. War	100	325			Early Gov. Virginia 1788
Randolph, Boots		Entertainment	5			15	Country Rockabilly Saxaphonist
Randolph, Charles D.		Showman	75	210	315		Buckskin Bill Assoc./Wm. Cody
Randolph, Edmund J.	1753-1813	Rev. War	200	808	625		Sec'y State, Washington Aide de... ADS/Cont.$1600
Randolph, Geo. Wythe	1818-67	Civil War	268	660	565		CSA Gen. ALS '62 $825
Randolph, John (of Roanoke)		Rev. War	85	265	485		MOC, Senator VA

NAME	DATE	CATEGORY	SIG	LS/DS	ALS	SP	COMMENTS
Randolph, Joyce		Entertainment	5	10		15	Actress. 'Trixie' on The Honeymooners
Randolph, Lillian		Entertainment	100			250	
Randolph, Peyton	1721-75	Am. Revolution	400	2250			1st Pres. Continental Congress
Randolph, Thos. Mann, Jr.	1768-1828	Congress	75	275			Repr. & Gov. VA. Special ALS $2800
Randy & the Rainbows (3)		Entertainment	20			40	Rock
Rangel, Charles B.	1930-	Congress	10			15	Afr-Am MOC NY.Important Advocate for Disadvantaged
Rank, J. Arthur, 1st Baron		Entertainment	25		75	55	Br.Industrialist, Film Magnate
Rank, Otto		Science	200		425		Austrian Psychoanalyst
Rankin, Jeannette	1880-1973	Congress	80	200			Voted against both World Wars
Rankin, Nell		Entertainment	10	20		25	Am. Contralto-Mezzo
Rankin, Robert J.		Aviation	12	25	42	35	ACE, WW II, Ace in a Day
Ransier, Alonzo Jacob		Senate/Congress	75				MOC SC
Ransom, John Crowe		Author	35	85	200		Am. Poet, Critic, Professor
Ransom, Matt W.		Civil War	80	285	320		CSA Gen.
Ransom, Robert, Jr.(WD)		Civil War	220	1250	2850		CSA Gen. (1828-92)
Rapaport, Lester		Artist	10	15	30	15	
Rapee, Erno		Conductor	15			45	Hung.-Am. Radio City Music Hall
Raphael		Artist	3500	9800	25000		
Raphael, Sally Jessy		TV Host	5			23	TV Talk Show Hostess
Rapper, Irving	1898-	Entertainment	15			35	40's Film Director. Now Voyager
Rappold, Marie		Entertainment	30			95	Opera, Concert
Rashad, Phylicia		Entertainment	5			15	
Raskob, John J.		Business	10	20		15	CEO General Motors
Rasmussen, Knud J.V.		Explorer	200		325	150	Danish Arctic Explorer, Author
Rasputin, Gregori E.	1872-1916	Clergy	2000	4500	7250		Rus. Mystic. Influenced Royal Family. Assassinated
Rathbone, Basil	1892-1967	Entertainment	178	325	525	452	Menacing, Leading Man & Sophisticated Villain
Rathbone, Monroe J.		Business	4	8	15	10	Exxon.Important Oil Innovations
Ratner, Payne		Governor	5	15			Governor KS
Ratoff, Gregory		Entertainment	20	65		60	Film Director
Ratzenberger, John		Entertainment	5			15	Cheers SP $35
Raum, Green B.	1829-1909	Civil War	28	65			Union Gen., MOC IL
Rauschenberg, Bob		Artist	50				Color Pc Repro. S $165
Ravel, Maurice	1875-1937	Composer	381	1245	1427	1695	AMusQS $1,675-$3,800-$4,800
Rawdon, Francis	1732-97	Military			475		Br. Gen'l Rev. War.
Rawdon-Hastings, Francis, Lord		Rev. War	25	60	110		Br. Off'r. Bunker Hill
Rawlings, Edward V.		Military	10	20			
Rawlings, Marjorie Kinnan		Author	45	150			Am. Pulitzer. The Yearling
Rawlins, John A.		Civil War	75	160	245		Union Gen., Sec'y War 1869
Rawlinson, Herbert	1886-1853	Entertainment	15	20	45	65	Br. Actor. Starred in dozens of B Westerns,
Rawls, Lou		Entertainment	15	25		35	Singer
Rawson, Edward	1615-1693	Colonial America	125	350	685		Colonial Sec'y.ADS $1500
Ray, Aldo		Entertainment	4	5		15	
Ray, Charles		Entertainment	25	35	65	60	
Ray, Dixie Lee		Governor	15			40	Governor WA
Ray, James Earl		Assassin		212	290		Shot Martin Luther King, Jr.

NAME	DATE	CATEGORY	SIG	LS/DS	ALS	SP	COMMENTS
Ray, Johnny		Entertainment				40	Singer-Actor
Ray, Leah		Entertainment	10			15	
Ray, Man (Rudnitsky)	1890-1976	Artist	262	575			Surrealist Painter, Photographer
Ray, Robert D.		Governor	5			10	Governor IA
Ray, Susan		Country Music	5			10	
Rayburn, Sam	1882-1961	Congress	35	83		75	Speaker of the House, TX. Was Speaker Longest
Raye, Cassidy		Entertainment				40	Models, Inc.
Raye, Collin		Country Music	10			25	
Raye, Martha	1916-94	Entertainment	15	75		33	Pin-Up SP $35
Rayleigh, John W. S.	1842-1919	Science			402		Nobel Physics. 3rd Baron
Raymond, Alex*		Cartoonist	15			75	Rip Kirby, Secret Agent X-9
Raymond, Alex*		Cartoonist	60		95	55	Flash Gordon. Spec. Ltrhd. TLS $225
Raymond, Gene		Entertainment	10	15	25	25	
Raymond, Henry J.		Business	30	75	150		Fndr. New York Times, MOC NY
Raymond, Jim*		Cartoonist	15			75	Blondie
Raymond, John T.	1836-87	Entertainment	20				Vintage Actor
Raymond, Paula		Entertainment	5			15	
Razaf, Andy		Composer	45		225		Lyricist Ain't Misbehavin'
Re'jane, Gabrielle-C. Re'ju		Entertainment	15	70	105		
Read, Albert Cushing		Aviation	40	85	180	115	Adm. Record Flight, WW I & II
Read, Dolly		Entertainment	5	6	15	15	Pin-Up SP $15
Read, George	1733-98	Rev. War	350	605	1275		Signer Decl. of Indepen.
Read, T. Buchanan	1822-72	Artist	17	30	40		Poet. Sheridan's Ride
Readdy, William F.		Astronaut	5			20	
Reade, Charles		Author	30	70	135		Br. Novelist, Dramatist
Reagan, John H.		Civil War	140	525	620		CSA Postmaster Gen.
Reagan, Maureen		Celebrity	5	15	30	15	Political Daughter of President
Reagan, Nancy		1st Lady	65	109	172	92	
Reagan, Ron, Jr.		Entertainment	4			30	Dancer
Reagan, Ronald (As Pres.)		President	385	850	3335	305	R. Reagan & Nancy SP $380-$500.
Reagan, Ronald	1911-	President	278	625	1307	352	Personal Paternal ALS $18,000
Real, Pierre F., Count		Fr. Revolution	15	35	80		
Reale, Antenore		Entertainment	20			55	Opera
Ream, Vinnie		Artist			450		Am. Sculptor
Reason, Rex		Entertainment	10			20	
Reasoner, Harry		TV News	15			40	60 Minutes
Rector, George		Business	20			35	World Famous Chef-Rector's NY
Rector, Henry M.	1816-18??	CSA Governor	190	725			CSA Gov. AR. War Dte. DS $875
Red Hot Chili Peppers (4)		Entertainment	75				Funk Rock Band Under the Bridge
Reddy, Helen		Entertainment		20	20	20	
Redenbacker, Orville	1907-95	Business	10	30		35	Popcorn King. Agricultural Expert (Gourmet Popcorn
Redfield, Billy		Entertainment	4	7		15	
Redfield, William C.	1889-1932	Cabinet	10	45	45	15	Sec'y Commerce 1913
Redford, Robert		Entertainment	55	195		205	Actor-Producer, Director, Writer. MANY SECRETARIALS
Redgrave, Lynn	1943-	Entertainment	8			25	SB 'This is Living' $35. AA Nominations

NAME	DATE	CATEGORY	SIG	LS/DS	ALS	SP	COMMENTS
Redgrave, Michael, Sir	1908-85	Entertainment	24		55	45	Tall, Distinguished Actor. Stage-Films from 30's
Redgrave, Vanessa	1937-	Entertainment	20	35		55	Br. Leading Lady. Numerous AA Nominations
Redman, Don		Entertainment	20			45	Jazz Musician
Redmond, John E.	1856-1918	Politician	5	15	40	15	Ir. Leader of Home Rule
Redon, Odilon	1840-1916	Artist	70		435		Flowers-Phantoms. Also Lithographer & Engraver
Redoute', Pierre Joseph	1759-1840	Artist	200	1550	1392		Belg- Fr. Painter, Lithographer. Known for Flowers
Reed, Alan	1907-77	Entertainment	25			50	Character Actor, Original Fred Flintstone Voice
Reed, Carol, Sir	1906-76	Entertainment	45	500		150	Influential Br. Film Director
Reed, David H.C.		Clergy	20	25	35	30	
Reed, Donna	1921-86	Entertainment	87	150		196	AA Winner. 'It's A Wonderful Life'. Pin-Up SP $180
Reed, Erik		Entertainment	5			10	
Reed, Frances		Entertainment	10			20	
Reed, James Alexander		Senate/Congress	5	15		10	Senator MO 1910
Reed, James F.		Celebrity	1250				NRPA
Reed, Jerry		Entertainment	5			15	Singer-Actor
Reed, John	1887-1920	Author	200	1308	1350	300	Radical Am.Journalist & Revolutionist
Reed, Joseph	1741-85	Rev. War	75	125	550		PA Statesman, Continental Cong.
Reed, Lou		Entertainment	20			50	
Reed, Oliver	1938-	Entertainment	15			65	Br.Actor. Br., Am. & Internat'l Films. Leading Man
Reed, Phillip	1908-	Entertainment	10	20	35	30	Handsome Leading Man & 2nd Lead. From Early 30's
Reed, Rex	1938-	Entertainment	8		15	15	Showbiz Interviewer and Gossip Columnist
Reed, Robert		Entertainment	40	70		68	Actor. 'The Brady Bunch'
Reed, Roland		Entertainment	15			35	Vintage Actor
Reed, Stanley (SC)	1884-1980	Supreme Court	48	185	202		TDS $1500 (Opinion) F.D.R. Court
Reed, Thomas Brackett	1839-1902	Congress	15	35	45		Speaker of the House. ME
Reed, Walter		Entertainment	10			25	Actor
Reed, Walter	1851-1902	Science	400	925	5000	675	Am. Army Surgeon. Proved Mosquito=Yellow Fever
Reedy, George		Cabinet	4			8	
Rees, Roger		Entertainment	4			10	
Rees, Thomas		Business	10	25	45	25	
Reese, Della		Entertainment	15	45		45	Actress-Singer 'Touched By An Angel'
Reeve, Christopher		Entertainment	58		150	122	Actor. Super Man. Badly Injured in Accident.
Reeves, George	1914-59	Entertainment	867	2733	1800	2400	Orig. TV Superman. GWTW Collectible
Reeves, Jim	1923-64	Entertainment	675			1500	Country Singer. Died Tragically in Plane Crash
Reeves, Keanu	1965-	Entertainment	20	70		57	Actor.Graduated from Juvenile Actor to Leading Man
Reeves, Martha		Composer	5			20	Composer-Entertainer
Reeves, Ronna		Entertainment	5			10	Singer
Reeves, Steve	1926-	Entertainment	18			36	Actor-Muscleman. Mr. America, World & Universe
Reeves-Smith, Olive		Entertainment	5	7	15	15	
Refice, Licinio	1855-1954	Composer-Clergy	20			55	Mostly Church Music. 2 Operas. AMusQS $85
Regan, Donald		Cabinet	10	15		30	Sec'y Treasury
Regan, Phil		Entertainment	10			35	Handsome Actor-Singer. Films From 1930's
Reger, Max	1873-1916	Composer	75	250	550		Ger. Composer
Reginald, Lionel		Entertainment	10			20	
Regnault de Saint-Jean etc	1761-1819	Fr. Revolution	35		105		Fr. Politician. Aided Napoleon. Exiled

NAME	DATE	CATEGORY	SIG	LS/DS	ALS	SP	COMMENTS
Rehan, Ada		Entertainment	20			40	Fine Vintage Shakespearean Actress
Rehm, Dan		Aviation	12	25	45	30	ACE, WW II
Rehnquist, William H.(SC)		Supreme Court	65	160	182	138	Chief Justice. Confirmation Ballot S $3900
Reich, Wilhelm	1897-57	Science	120	325	650		Austr. Psychoanalyst. Author.
Reichers, Lou		Aviation	30	45	60	65	
Reid, Albert T.*		Cartoonist	20			112	Political Cartoonist. FDR Genre
Reid, Samuel C.	1783-1861	Military	70	195			Naval Cmdr. War 1812. Designed US Flag
Reid, Tim		Entertainment	5		15	15	Actor
Reid, Wallace	1891-1923	Entertainment	195			650	Actor-Dir-Screenwriter. Died Drug Addict
Reid, Whitelaw	1837-1912	Journalist	30	75		50	Correspondent, Ambassador
Reifel, Benjamin		Senate/Congress	5			10	MOC SD
Reightler, Ken		Astronaut	5			25	
Reik, Theodor	1888-1969	Science	105	218	425		Austrian Psychoanalyst
Reilly, Charles Nelson		Entertainment	5			12	Actor
Reinburg, J. Hunter		Aviation	15	35	50	40	ACE. WW II, Marine Ace
Reinecke, Karl		Composer	55	145	225	250	Ger.Pianist, Conductor, Teacher
Reiner, Carl	1922-	Entertainment	10	28	30	25	Movie-TV Actor-Writer-Director
Reiner, Fritz		Entertainment	50	150		225	Hung. Conductor
Reiner, Rob		Entertainment	10	25		25	Like Father, Carl, Writer-Director-Actor
Reinert, Ernst Wilhelm		Aviation	20			50	Ger. Ace. RK
Reinhardt, Max	1873-1943	Entertainment	105	175	410	358	Austrian Innovative Theatre Dir.
Reinhold, Judge		Entertainment	5			22	Actor. Beverly Hills Cop SP $35
Reinking, Ann	1949-	Entertainment	10	10	20	20	Dancer-Choreographer. Tony. All That Jazz
Reisch, Walter	1900-83	Entertainment	10			20	Screenwriter.AA (Shared) for 'Titanic' Script 1953
Reischauer, Edwin O.		Celebrity	4	5	10	10	
Reiser, Paul		Entertainment	20			48	Actor-Comedian. 'Mad About You'. Emmy
Reiserer, Russell		Aviation	15		40		ACE WW II
Reitsch, Hanna		Aviation	65	165	270	185	Flew 1st Practical HeliCopter.
Reitz, Francis W.		Head of State	50	135			South Africa
Reizen, Mark		Entertainment				750	Opera
Rejane, Gabrielle-Charlotte		Entertainment	35		80	85	Vintage Fr. Tragedienne
Remarque, Erich Maria	1898-1970	Author	40	150	375	75	'All Quiet on the Western Front' etc
Rembrandt van Rijn	1606-69	Artist	2950		3600		Dutch Painter-Etcher NRPA
Remer, Otto		Military	20			70	SS Gen. WW II. RK
Remick, Lee	1935-91	Entertainment	30			65	Perky-Talented-Attractive Actress. Pin-Up SP $75
Remington, Eliphalet, Jr.	1793-1861	Business	350	650			E. Remington & Sons, Guns. Bond S $4500
Remington, Frederic	1861-1909	Artist	575	805	2056	1850	Sculptor,Writer,War Correspond.
Remington, Samuel		Business			1450		Gun Manufacturer. ALS on Lttrhd. $1450
Renaldo, Duncan	1904-80	Entertainment	25		100	188	Actor.Supporting Roles Minor Films.4th 'Cisco Kid'
Renaud, Maurice		Entertainment	35			175	Opera. Important Fr. Baritone
Renaud, Paul		Head of State	50			100	Premier France
Renault, Louis	1877-1944	Jurist	35	95	125		Fndr. Renault Freres. Autos.Nobel Peace Prize 1907
Renay, Liz		Entertainment	20				Actress-Model.Mafia Connection/Mickey Cohen
Renner, Karl, Dr.	1870-1950	Head of State	25	50	105	40	Fndr.,Pres.Austrian Republic
Rennie, John	1761-1821	Engineer			625		Br. Civ. Eng. Built Waterloo Bridge

NAME	DATE	CATEGORY	SIG	LS/DS	ALS	SP	COMMENTS
Rennie, Michael	1909-71	Entertainment	95			185	Tall, Gaunt Leading Man. Br.-Am. Movies.
Reno, Kelly		Entertainment	5			20	Young Actor Star of Black Stallion DS $35
Reno, Marcus A.		Military	950	2750			Battle of Little Big Horn
Renoir, Jean	1894-1979	Entertainment	120	312			Fr. Inovative Film Maker-Son of Impressionist
Renoir, Pierre-Auguste	1841-1909	Artist	275	700	2550	3500	Repro Artwork S $3,000-$5,000
Rent, Cast of		Entertainment	75			120	Tony Award Winning Broadway Musical. 20-25 Sigs.
Renwick, Edward Sabine	1823-1912	Inventor	25	55	195		Inventor Breech-Loader & Modern Poultry Indust
REO Speedwagon		Entertainment	35			65	Rock (Signed by All)
Repplier, Agnes	1855-1950	Author	5	15	35	50	Am.Dean of Essayists. Biographer
Requesens, Luis de Zuniga	1528-76	Military	750				Sp. Soldier. Succeeded Duke of Alba as Gov. NRPA
Resnick, Laura		Author	5	7	15	10	Award winning author in both SF & Romance
Resnick, Mike		Author	12	20	40	15	Hugo & Nebula SF award winner
Resnick, Regina		Entertainment	15			60	Opera
Resnik, Judith A.	1946-86	Astronaut	100	275		225	Postal Cover $125-$175
Respighi, Ottorino	1879-1936	Composer	75	200	550		It.Opera, Orchestral,Choral. AMusQS $550
Reston, John 'Scotty'		Author	15	20	35	25	Journalist, Synd. Columnist
Rethberg, Elisabeth	1894-1976	Entertainment	40			140	Ger-Am Sopr.Opera. Admired by Toscannini-Strauss
Rethers, Harry F.		Military	40				Am. WW I Qtrmaster Gen.
Rethy, Ester		Entertainment	10	15	35	30	Opera, Operetta
Rettig, Tommy	1941-96	Entertainment	10			25	Juvenile Actor. Jeff on Lassie
Reuter, Edzard		Business	40	60	250	150	
Reuther, Walter P.	1907-70	Labor	25	40	95	32	Pres. UAW-CIO. Gained Many Benefits for Union
Revelle, Hamilton		Entertainment	5			10	
Revels, Hiram Rhoades	1822-1901	Clergy-Civil War	500				1st Elected Black U.S. Senator, MS
Revere, Anne	1903-90	Entertainment	25		45	60	Stage-Screen Char. Actress. AA 'National Velvet'
Revere, Paul	1735-1818	Rev. War	1700	5400	13700		ALS $26000,DS Revere & J Hancock $95,000. NRPA
Rexroth, Kenneth	1905-82	Author	10	35	65	20	Am.Columnist, Poet, Avant-Garde
Rey, Alejandro	1930-87	Entertainment	25			45	Actor. Handsome Argentine-Born
Rey, Alvino		Entertainment	20			75	Big Band Leader
Reybold, E.		Military	15	35	55		Gen. WW II. Engineer Corps.
Reymann, Hellmuth		Aviation	30		75		
Reynolds, Albert		Head of State	20			30	P.M. Ireland
Reynolds, Alexander W.	1816-76	Civil War	108	270	323		CSA General. Captured-Exchanged. Sig/Rank $195
Reynolds, Burt	1936-	Entertainment	16	37		28	Actor...'Smokey & The Bandits', 'Boogie Nights'
Reynolds, Craig		Entertainment	10			25	Actor
Reynolds, Daniel H.	1832-1902	Civil War	92		385		CSA Gen. Sig/Rank $125-$160
Reynolds, Debbie	1932-	Entertainment	10		50	25	Still Cute & Charming. Pin-Up SP $25
Reynolds, Donn		Country Music	10			20	Aussie 50's Yodeling Cowboy
Reynolds, Frank		Journalist	9			20	Broadcasting News Pioneer
Reynolds, Gene	1925-	Entertainment	5		15	20	Juvenile Actor. Mature Director
Reynolds, John Fulton	1820-63	Civil War	515	1550			Union Gen. KIA Gettysburg. Sig/Rank $1375
Reynolds, Joseph Jones	1822-99	Civil War	45	110	190		Union General, Indian Fighter. Sig/Rank $75
Reynolds, Joshua, Sir	1723-92	Artist	350	1300	1690		Br. Portraitist, 1st Pres. Royal Academy
Reynolds, Marjorie		Entertainment	20	40		45	Actress. 'Holiday Inn', 'GWTW' Collectible
Reynolds, R.J.		Business	225	750			Founder Tobacco Empire

NAME	DATE	CATEGORY	SIG	LS/DS	ALS	SP	COMMENTS
Reynolds, Richard Samuel		Business	45	110	240	55	Reynolds Metal Co., Aluminum
Reynolds, William		Entertainment	5			15	Actor. TV 'FBI'
Reynolds, William H.	1910-	Entertainment	15			25	Film Editor. AA 'The Sting'. Three AA Nominations
Rezner, Trent		Entertainment	10			45	Music. Lead Singer Nine Inch Nails
Rhea		Entertainment	10	15	30	20	
Rhee, Syngman	1875-1965	Head of State	168	225	955	250	1st Pres. So. Korea
Rhett, Alicia		Entertainment	300				SP N/A. GWTW Collectible. NRPA
Rhett, Robert Barnwell	1800-76	Civil War	152	285	880		CSA Gen. ALS/Content $2,500
Rhett, Robert G., Mrs.		Celebrity	3		10		Blanche Rhett
Rhodes, Billie	189?-19??	Entertainment	15			35	Am. Star of Al Christie Comedies from 1911
Rhodes, Cecil John	1853-1902	Head of State	135	230	438	1175	S.Afr. Fndr. Rhodesia. Rhodes Scholarship Fund
Rhodes, Erik	1906-90	Entertainment	20			45	Am. Comic Actor From Musical Comedy Stage. Films
Rhodes, John J.		Senate/Congress	5	15		10	MOH AZ 1953-83
Rhys-Davies, John		Entertainment	15			38	Br. Actor. 'Indiana Jones' Films
Ribbentrop, Joachim von	1893-1946	Military	160	465	645	325	Hitler Foreign Affairs Advisor. Convicted & Hung
Ribbentrop, Rudolf von		Military	65	95	150		
Ribicoff, Abraham	1910-	Cabinet	10	15	35	20	Gov., Senator CT. Sec'y HEW
Ricardo, David	1772-1823	Statesman	425				Founder Classical School of Political Economy(RARE
Ricci, Christina		Entertainment	20			75	Actress. Addams Family (Movie)
Ricciarelli, Katia		Entertainment	5			25	Opera
Rice, Alexander H.	1818-95	Congress-Gov.	10	15	20		Sen. & Gov.. MA
Rice, Alice C.	1870-1942	Author	70		220		Children's Books. 'Mrs. Wiggs of Cabbage Patch'
Rice, Anne		Author	25			50	Novelist
Rice, Dan (Dan'l McLaren)	1823-1900	Business	50	100	455		Circus Clown & Owner
Rice, Donna		Model	15			30	Hart Stopper. Pin-Up SP $35
Rice, Elmer	1882-1967	Author	80	250		102	Pulitzer Prize. Playwright
Rice, Florence	1907-74	Entertainment	5	10		15	Actress. Pleasing Leading Lady of Late 30's
Rice, Grantland	1881-54	Journalist	25			75	Sportswriter-Sportscaster. One Reel Sports Films
Rice, Henry M.		Senate/Congress	5		15		Senator MN 1858-63
Rice, Merton S.		Clergy	20	20	40		
Rice, Tim		Composer	10	30	65	30	Composer. Disney Films
Rice-Davies, Mandy		Celebrity	5	10	25	20	Involved In Br. Scandal
Rich, Buddy	1917-87	Entertainment	38			140	Big Bandleader-Drummer
Rich, Charlie	1932-95	Entertainment	15			30	Rock/Rockabilly Singer 50'-60's. Country Superstar
Rich, Irene	1891-1988	Entertainment	25			150	Silent Film Star. Few Talkies. Radio Star
Richard II (Anjou-Plantagenet)	1367-1400	Royalty					Writ of Privy Seal in Name of Richard II $2000
Richards, Adriana		Entertainment	10			30	Juvenile Actress in Jurassic Park
Richards, Ann		Governor	7			20	Attractive, Outspoken, Admired Governor TX
Richards, Cliff		Entertainment	15			40	Rock
Richards, Denise		Entertainment	10			55	Actress. Pin-Up $85
Richards, Dickinson W.	1895-1973	Science	25	35	70	30	Nobel Medicine 1956. Perfected Heart Catherization
Richards, J.K. (Act'g)		Cabinet	4	15	25		
Richards, Jeff	1922-89	Entertainment	5			20	Was Young MGM Star
Richards, Keith		Entertainment	25			110	Rock. 'Rolling Stones' Guitarist
Richards, Lloyd	1923-	Entertainment	10			20	Afr-Am Stage Director

NAME	DATE	CATEGORY	SIG	LS/DS	ALS	SP	COMMENTS
Richards, Michael		Entertainment	20			58	Kramer on Seinfeld
Richards, Richard N.		Astronaut	10			35	
Richards, William		Senate/Congress	15		50		Rep. NY 1871
Richardson, Dorothy	1872-1857	Author	35	115	255		Br. Introduced Stream of Consciousness Technique
Richardson, Elliot		Cabinet	7	25	45	20	Att'y Gen. Watergate Period
Richardson, Friend W.		Governor	5		15		Gov. CA 1923-27
Richardson, Ian	1934-	Entertainment	5			15	
Richardson, John P.		Governor	15	25			Governor SC 1840
Richardson, John, Sir	1787-1865	Science-Explorer	20	60	150		Surgeon-Naturalist. Franklin Expedition
Richardson, Miranda	1958-	Entertainment	22			50	Br. Actress. 'Enchanted April', 'The Crying Game'
Richardson, Natasha		Entertainment	15			60	Br. Actress-Daughter of Vanessa Redgrave
Richardson, Patricia		Entertainment	10			35	'Tool Time' Hostess
Richardson, Ralph, Sir	1902-83	Entertainment	20	25	50	45	Distinguished Br. Stage-Film Actor. AA Nominations
Richardson, Robert Vinkler	1820-70	Civil War	535	825			CSA General
Richardson, Tony	1828-91	Entertainment	20			30	Br. Stage & Film Director. AA 'Tom Jones'. Aids
Richardson, William A.	1821-96	Cabinet	18	48	95		Sec'y Treas.1873
Richardson, William Alex.	1811-75	Congress	10		20		Sen. IL
Richelieu, Armand E. du	1766-1822	Head of State	105	240	350		Military, Prime Minister France
Richelieu, Armand-Jean, Card'l	1585-1642	Head of State	275	1177	2150		1585-1642.Statesman & Card'l.Special DS $3,450
Richey, Helen		Aviation	20	50		55	
Richey, Lawrence		Cabinet	4	10			
Richie, Lionel		Composer	10	52		40	Composer-Singer-Arranger
Richman, Charles		Entertainment	10	15	30	25	
Richman, Harry	1895-1972	Entertainment-Avia.	15	50	35	35	And Flew 'Lady Peace' 1st R/T Atlantic Crosssing
Richter, Burton, Dr.		Science	20	45	70	35	Nobel Physics 1976
Richter, Charles, Dr.	1900-85	Science	25	175		65	Devised Richter Scale. Earthquake Measure
Richter, Hans (Janos)	1843-1916	Conductor	150		583		Ger. Conductor. AMusQS $350
Richters, Christine		Playboy Ctrfold	5			15	Pin-Up SP $25
Richthofen, Manfred von	1892-1918	Aviation	5900			7800	ACE, WW I, 'The Red Baron'
Rickard, George L. Tex		Business	350	950		675	Boxing Promoter & Entreprenuer. DS $2,000
Rickenbacker, Edw V.	1890-1973	Aviation	96	309	516	264	ACE, WW I, Auto Race, Exec. TLS/Cont.$1500
Rickles, Don	1926-	Entertainment	5		15	25	Comedian.Vegas-Clubs-TV-Films. Rare Authentic Sigs
Rickover, Hyman G.	1900-1986	Military	100	428	761	300	Rus-Born Am. Admiral. Father of Atomic Sub.
Riddle, George		Country Western	10			35	50's Western Recording Artist
Ride, Sally K.		Astronaut	15	75		40	1st US Woman in Space
Riders in the Sky (3)		Entertainment	5			20	
Ridgeway, Matthew B.	1895-1993	Military	75	195	162	95	Supreme Allied Cmdr. WW II, Korean War
Riefenstahl, Leni	1902-	Photographer	23	42	80	67	Hitler's Photographer
Rieger, Vince		Aviation	12	25	40	30	ACE, WW II, Navy Ace
Riegger, Wallingford	1885-1961	Composer	20	65	125	35	Am. Orchestral, Choral, 12 Tone
Rigal, Delia		Entertainment	15			45	Opera
Rigg, Diana	1938-	Entertainment	20	35	45	95	Br. Leading Lady. Prominence in 'The Avengers'
Riggs, Clinton E.		Inventor	24			40	Created Highway Yield Sign
Riggs, Tommy		Entertainment	5		15	15	Ventriloquist? (And Betty Lou)
Righteous Brothers		Entertainment	45			110	Bill Medley & Bobby Hatfield

NAME	DATE	CATEGORY	SIG	LS/DS	ALS	SP	COMMENTS
Riis, Jacob A.	1849-1914	Author-Reformer	18	50	85		Dan.-Am. Journalist. ALS/Cont. $350
Riley, James Whitcomb	1849-1916	Author	95	175	583	225	The Hoosier Poet. Little Orphant Annie etc.
Riley, Jeannie C.	1945-	Country Music	5			15	Singer. Internat'l Star with 'Harper Valley PTA'
Riley, Larry		Entertainment	5			10	
Rilke, Rainer Maria	1875-1926	Author	145	345	1695		Czech. Lyric Poet-Translator. Highly Influential
Rimes, Leann		Entertainment	15	60		30	Singer. Country-Pop
Rimsky-Korsakov, Nicolai	1844-1908	Composer	525	2000	3317	2125	Rus. AMusQS $4700-$5800-$6500
Rinehart, Mary Roberts	1876-1958	Author	20	80	125	50	Am. Novelist, Playwright. Mysteries-Romances
Ring, Blanche		Entertainment	15			40	Vintage Silent Star
Ringgold, George H.	1814-64	Civil War	20	40	55		Union Paymaster War Dte DS $80
Ringling, Albert C.	1852-1916	Business-Circus	132	425			Ringling Bros. & Barnum & Bailey
Ringling, Charles	1863-1926	Business-Circus	120	453			Ringling Bros. & Barnum & Bailey
Ringling, Henry		Business-Circus	112	400		125	Special DS $1,250
Ringling, John	1866-1936	Business-Circus	145	565	620	700	Ringling Bros(Owner-Performer)& Barnum & Bailey
Ringling, Otto	1858-1911	Business-Circus	230	650			Ringling Bros. & Barnum & Bailey
Ringling, William		Business-Circus	100	325		138	2nd Generation Owner
Ringo, John		Outlaw	2000	6500			Early West. Cowboy Gunslinger
Ringwald, Molly		Entertainment	10	20	40	43	Actress
Rinna, Lisa		Entertainment	6			35	Actress. Pin-Up $48
Rio Rita		Entertainment	15			40	And Her All-Girl NBC Orchestra. 1930's
Ripley, Eleazar W.	1782-1839	Military	68		250		General War 1812
Ripley, George	1802-80	Social Reformer	140	350	780		Critic, Editor, Unitarian Clergy
Ripley, James Wolfe	1794-1870	Civil War	55	185	225		Union General
Ripley, Robert*	1893-1949	Cartoonist	100	105	225	225	'Believe It Or Not' SP $125. 2x2 SP $150
Ripley, Roswell	1823-87	Civil War	170	220	425		CSA Gen. Nephew of Union Gen.
Ripley, Roswell S. (WD)		Civil War	230	2500	1025		CSA Gen.
Risner, James R.		Military	10	25	35	20	
Ritchard, Cyril	1896-1977	Entertainment	20			60	Br. Dancer & Comedian.
Ritchie, Adele		Entertainment	20		50	45	Vintage Musical Theater Star
Ritchie, Albert C.		Governor	10		35		Gov. MD
Ritchie, Neil, Sir		Military	15	35	60	30	General
Ritchie, Steve		Aviation	15	35	45	40	ACE, Nam, Only AF Ace
Ritt, Martin	1919-90	Entertainment	30			65	Film-Stage-Tv Director. Taught at Actor's Studio
Rittenhouse, David	1732-96	Science	850	1150	4500		Am Astronomer, 1st US Telescope
Ritter, John	1948-	Entertainment	8			22	Light Romantic-Comedy Roles. Son of Tex Ritter
Ritter, Tex	1907-74	Country Music	100			232	Major Singing Cowboy Star
Ritter, Thelma	1905-69	Entertainment	45			150	Am Character Actress & Comedienne.
Ritterscheim, Karl		Entertainment	5			25	Opera
Ritz Brothers, The (3)		Entertainment	80			150	Jimmy, Al, Harry. Zany Nightclub Act. A Few Films
Ritz, Jimmy	1903-85	Entertainment	15			40	The Middle Ritz Brother
Rivera, Diego	1886-1957	Artist	295	849	970	1375	Mex. Political-Social Muralist
Rivera, Geraldo		Entertainment	20	42		30	TV Host
Rivers, Joan	1933-	Entertainment	5		25	15	Comedienne. Cabaret, Standup, TV Hostess
Rivers, Larry	1923-	Artist	40	75	250		Forerunner Pop Art Movement
Rives, Amelie		Author			675		

NAME	DATE	CATEGORY	SIG	LS/DS	ALS	SP	COMMENTS
Rivington, James	1724-1802	Rev. War	100	225			Journalist-Publisher-Spy
Rizzo, Frank L.		Political	10	20		25	Mayor Phila. Fmr. Chief of Police
Ro'Al, Zhang		Artist		700			
Roach, Hal, Jr.		Entertainment	5			15	
Roach, Hal, Sr.	1892-1992	Entertainment	100	442		185	AA Film Pioneer. Our Gang Comedy. Silent-Sound
Roarke, Hayden		Entertainment	52			65	Actor. 'Jeannie' Dr, Bellows
Robards, Jason, Jr.	1920-	Entertainment	15	22		30	Am. Stage-Film Actor. AA 'Julia'
Robbins, Frederick C., Dr.		Science	20	30	45	25	Nobel Medicine 1954
Robbins, Gale	1922-80	Entertainment	15	20	35	30	Singer-Leading Lady
Robbins, Harold	1916-	Author	20	100	130	40	Am.Novelist.The Carpetbaggers
Robbins, Jay T.		Aviation	10	25	40	35	ACE, WW II
Robbins, Jerome	1918-	Entertainment	40	75	110	79	Ballet Dancer, Choreographer. AA 'The King & I'
Robbins, John	1808-80	Congress	12		25		Repr. PA, Steel Mfg.
Robbins, Marty	1925-	Country Music	25			60	Country & Pop Singer-Songwriter
Robbins, Reg. L.		Aviation	25			60	Pioneer Aviator
Robbins, Tim	1958-	Entertainment	23			52	Actor-Singer-Songwriter-Screenwriter-Director
Roberti, Margherita		Entertainment	15			30	Am. Soprano
Roberts, Barbara		Governor	7			20	Governor, Oregon
Roberts, Cokie		Journalist	10			20	TV-Radio Journalist
Roberts, David	1896-1964	Artist	40	90	162		Scottish Painter
Roberts, Doris		Entertainment	10	15	15	20	Character-Comedienne. 'Everybody Loves Raymond'
Roberts, Eric	1956-	Entertainment	10			25	Leading Man, 70's. AA Nom. 'Runaway Train'
Roberts, Frederick Sleigh	1832-1914	Military	40	65	125	100	1st Earl. Field Marshal, Kandahar
Roberts, Jack		Country Music	10			20	
Roberts, Jonathan	1771-1854	Senate	60		350		Introduced Important Legislation
Roberts, Julia	1967-	Entertainment	40	235		91	Pretty Woman etc. Major Star at Present
Roberts, Kenneth	1885-1957	Author	25	80	150		Am. Historical Novels. 'Northwest Passage' etc
Roberts, Lee S.		Composer	30	65	150		AMusQS $285
Roberts, Oral		Clergy	18	65	50	45	Am. Evangelist. Oral Roberts Univ. 5x7 SP $25
Roberts, Oran M.		Governor	15		30		Gov. TX 1879-83
Roberts, Owen J. (SC)	1875-1955	Supreme Court	50	150	220	100	Justice 1930-45. Dean U. of Penn. Law School
Roberts, Pat Hutchison		Author	5			10	Cookbook author, Editor
Roberts, Pernell	1930-	Entertainment	40	75		65	Actor. Original 'Bonanza' Brother. 'Trapper John'
Roberts, Ralph		Author	10	20	40	15	1st U.S. book on computer viruses
Roberts, Robin		Journalist	5			10	ESPN News
Roberts, Roy		Entertainment	15			35	
Roberts, Tanya		Entertainment	10			25	Actress. Pin-Up SP $35
Roberts, Tony	1939-	Entertainment	5		15	15	Actor. Successful Investor
Roberts, William P.	1841-1910	Civil War	85	800			CSA Gen.Youngest In CSA Service. Sig/Rank $150
Roberts, Xavier		Business	15	20	35	25	
Robertson, James	1720-88	Rev. War			975		Br. Gen. Fought in Rev. War
Robertson, Alice Mary		Senate/Congress	5		20	25	MOC OK, Self-Taught Creek Indian
Robertson, Beverly H.	1827-1910	Civil War	113	155	320		CSA General. Sig/Rank $185
Robertson, Cliff	1925-	Entertainment	20			35	Am. Leading Man. Stage-Films. AA 'Charley'
Robertson, Dale	1923-	Entertainment	10			35	Am. Actor. Western Star

NAME	DATE	CATEGORY	SIG	LS/DS	ALS	SP	COMMENTS
Robertson, Felix H.	1839-1928	Civil War	85		262		CSA General Sig/Rank $150
Robertson, Morgan		Author	15		60		Sea Stories
Robertson, Pat, Rev.		Clergy	20	25	50	30	Rt. Wing Evangelical, Presidential Hopeful
Robertson, Willard	1886-1948	Entertainment	15			25	Am. Character Actor. Lawyers & Wardens
Robeson, George M.	1834-96	Cabinet	15	62	92		Sec'y Navy 1869. Gov. MA, Def. Lawyer Lizzie Borden
Robeson, Paul	1898-1976	Entertainment	106	205	280	528	Am. Singer, Actor, Athlete, Activist. SPc $175
Robespierre, Maximilien	1758-94	Fr. Revolution	1200	2650	12500		Revolutionist Leader. 'Reign of Terror'. DS $4,275
Robin, Mado		Entertainment	40			225	Opera. Coloratura. Young, Tragic Death
Robinson, Bill 'Bojangles'	1878-1949	Entertainment	90	235	450	458	Afro- American Tap-Dancer, Entertainer. 30's Films
Robinson, C. Roosevelt		Celebrity	5	15	20	15	
Robinson, Dwight P.		Business	5	15	25	15	
Robinson, Edward	1794-1863	Archaeologist		185	395		Biblical Scholar. Explored Palestine-Syria.
Robinson, Edward A.	1869-1935	Author	55	125	215		Am. Poet, 3 Pulitzers
Robinson, Edward G.	1893-1973	Entertainment	55	100		202	Actor Famous for Gangster Roles & Art Collection
Robinson, George D.	1834-96	Governor	10			35	Repr. & Gov. MA
Robinson, John	1761-1828	Rev. War	60	175	340		Soldier, Merchant
Robinson, John C.	1817-97	Civil War	60	185	220		Union Gen., MOH Gettysburg. Sig/Rank $100
Robinson, Joseph T.	1872-1937	Congress	20		25		Sen. Arkansas
Robinson, Lucius		Governor	10	20	40		Governor NY 1876
Robinson, Smokey		Entertainment	25			45	Rock and Country Singer
Robson, Flora, Dame	1902-84	Entertainment	28	25	40	70	Distinguished Br. Stage & Film Actress. 30s-80s
Robson, May	1858-1942	Entertainment	40			75	Australian-Am. Stage Actress. Films 1915-1942
Robson, Stuart		Entertainment	20	25	45	45	Vintage Actor
Rochambeau, Count de	1725-1807	Rev. War	305	2500	825		Fr. Gen. in Am. Revolution
Rochan, Debbie		Entertainment	4			25	Actress. Pin-Up Col. $45
Roche, James M.	1906-	Business	10	15	30	20	Pres. Ford Motor Co., CEO Gen. Motors
Rochefort, Henri, Marquis de	1830-1913	Author	18	30	50		Fr. Journalist. Anti Napoleon III
Rochford, Leonard		Aviation	20	40			Br. Ace WW I
Rock, Blossom (Blake, Marie)	1896-1978	Entertainment	175			225	Sister-Jeanette MacDonald. 'Addams Family' Granny
Rock, John	1890-	Science	25	80			Developed 1st Birth Control Pill
Rockefeller, Abby A.		Business	15	30	52	25	Socialite-Wife of John D., Jr.
Rockefeller, David		Business	15	38	55	25	Banker
Rockefeller, Happy		Business	5	15	25	10	Wife of Nelson Rockefeller
Rockefeller, John D.	1839-1937	Business	400	2109	1983	1525	Standard Oil. Philantropist. DS Oil Contract $9450
Rockefeller, John D., Jr.	1874-1960	Business	35	131	225	75	Rockefeller Ctr. Philanthropist. Son of John D.
Rockefeller, John (Jay) D., IV		Governor	5	15		10	Governor WV. Confidential Political ALS $450
Rockefeller, Laurance		Business	5	15	25	10	Philanthropist
Rockefeller, Nelson A.	1908-79	Vice President	30	74	150	45	Governor NY. Ford's VP. TLS as VP $325
Rockefeller, Winthrop		Governor	10	20		15	Governor AR
Rockwell, George Lincoln		Activist	50	238	200	95	Am. Nazi Party TLS $450. Chk $375. Assassinated
Rockwell, Norman*	1894-1978	Artist	125	243	535	521	Am. Illustrator-Artist. FDC S $125. Print S $295+
Rockwell, Robert		Entertainment	5			20	Actor. Leads & Supporting Actor. 'Our Miss Brooks'
Roddenberry, Gene	1931-91	Entertainment	132	235		225	Creator of Star Trek
Roddey, Philip D. (WD)		Civil War	200	878	2498		CSA Gen.
Roddey, Philip D.	1826-97	Civil War	105	375	415		CSA Gen.

NAME	DATE	CATEGORY	SIG	LS/DS	ALS	SP	COMMENTS
Roden, George		Civil War	30	55	85		
Rodenburg, Carl		Military	15			40	Ger. Gen. Stalingrad. WW II. RK
Roderick, Milton David		Business	5			10	CEO U.S. Steel
Rodes, Robert Emmett (WD)		Civil War	750		8800		CSA Gen. RARE
Rodes, Robert Emmett	1829-64	Civil War	425		1050		CSA General KIA RARE
Rodgers, Geo. Washington	1822-63	Military	40	105	195		Naval Off'r War 1812. Killed in Ft. Wagner Attack
Rodgers, Jimmie	1897-1933	Entertainment	225			500	Legendary Country Music Singer-Composer
Rodgers, John		Aviation	65	125	240	135	
Rodgers, John	1771-1838	Military	80	338			Distinguished US Naval Officer
Rodgers, John	1812-82	Civil War	110	335	470		Un. Naval Commodore,-Explorer
Rodgers, Richard & Hammerstein		Composers	500				Oscar Hammerstein III
Rodgers, Richard & Hart, Lorenz		Composers	675	1350			Rodgers AND HART Very Rare. Hart Died 1943
Rodgers, Richard	1902-79	Composer	95	330		222	Pulitzer. AMusQS $460. FDC S $110
Rodin, Auguste	1840-1917	Artist	222	380	720	1150	Fr. SP of Sculpture $1250-$1700
Rodman, Hugh		Military	55				Adm. USN, Am. WW I
Rodman, Judy		Entertainment	5			15	
Rodney, Caesar	1728-84	Rev. War-Cabinet	495	1123	2075		Signer Decl. of Indepen.
Rodzinski, Artur	1892-1958	Conductor	30	75		75	Pol.-Am. Conductor. 4x5 SP $50
Roe, Edward Payson	1838-88	Author	15	25	35		Novelist, Clergy
Roe, Tommy		Entertainment	25	40		45	Singer
Roebling, John A.	1806-69	Engineer	85	175	325		Mfg 1st US Wire Rope. Designer of Brooklyn Bridge
Roebling, Washington A.	1837-1926	Science	100	225	450		Actual Builder of Brooklyn Bridge
Roebuck, Alva Curtis		Business	175	215		375	Co-Fndr. Sears & Roebuck. Stock Cert. S $1900
Roederer, Pierre C., Count		Fr. Revolution	20	50	95		
Roehm, Ernest		Celebrity	200	540			
Roell, Werner		Aviation	5			20	Ger. RK Winning Stuka Pilot
Roentgen, Wilhelm	1845-1923	Science	604	1300	3158		1st Nobel in Physics. Discovered X Rays
Roethke, Theodore		Author	35	135	275	45	Am. Poet. Pulitzer
Rogallo, Francis M.		Inventor	27		45		Invented Hang Glider.
Rogatchewsky, Joseph		Entertainment	20			85	Ukranian. Lyric/Dramatic Tenor
Roger, Gustav		Entertainment	40		160		Opera. Creator of Important Tenor Roles
Rogers, Charles 'Buddy'	1904-	Entertainment	15	20	35	40	Actor. Light Leads & Support. 20's-30's
Rogers, Andrew Jackson	1828-1900	Congress	10				MOC NJ, Teacher, Lawyer
Rogers, Bernard W.		Military	10	25	50	40	
Rogers, Carroll P.		Business	8	15	35	15	
Rogers, Fred		Entertainment	8	15		32	'Mr. Rogers'
Rogers, Ginger	1911-95	Entertainment	40	135		157	Actress, Dancer. AA 'Kitty Foyle. SP/Astaire $675
Rogers, Jean	1916-91	Entertainment	25			58	40's Adventure Serial Queen. B Movie Leads
Rogers, John		Military	150	350	375		
Rogers, Joseph W.		Aviation	15	30	60	35	
Rogers, Kenny		Entertainment	20	40		40	Singer-Actor-Producer
Rogers, Marianne and Kenny		Country Music	10			35	
Rogers, Mimi	1956-	Entertainment	15			30	Actress. Leading Lady Film & TV
Rogers, Randolph	1825-92	Artist	18		30		Sculptor
Rogers, Richard		Astronaut	6			20	

NAME	DATE	CATEGORY	SIG	LS/DS	ALS	SP	COMMENTS
Rogers, Robert	1731-95	Rev. War	335	1195	3300		Frontier Soldier. 'Rogers Rangers'. Fled to Eng.
Rogers, Roy	1912-98	Entertainment	45	160		101	King of the Cowboys SP/Roy & Dale $135-$195
Rogers, Samuel	1763-1855	Author	15	30	100		Br. Poet. Patron Of The Arts
Rogers, T.S.		Military	75				Am. WW I Rear Adm. U.S.N., U.S.S. Utah
Rogers, Wayne		Entertainment	15			30	Actor. 'Mash'
Rogers, Will	1879-1935	Entertainment	278	475	1030	875	America's Favorite Humorist.Plane Crash/Wiley Post
Rogers, Will Jr.		Senate/Congress	10			25	Congressman CA, Actor
Rogers, William F.	18??-1899	Civil War	22	40	55		Union General
Rogers, William Findlay		Senate/Congress	5		10		MOC NY, Soldier CW
Rogers, William P.		Cabinet	12	20	35	25	Sec'y State
Roget, Peter M., Dr.	1779-1869	Author	75	85	220		Br.Physician & Savant. Roget's Thesaurus
Rohmer, Eric	1920-	Entertainment	40	218			Fr. Director. Literate, Articulate Searching .60's
Rohmer, Sax (A.S.Ward)	1886-1959	Author	75	240	250	100	Br. Mystery Novels. 'Fu Manchu'
Rohrer, Henreich	1933-	Science	20		45		Nobel Physics 1981
Rojo, Gustavo		Entertainment	10			30	On Screen from 1948
Roland de La Platiere,Jean	1734-93	Fr. Revolution	40	95	185		Fr. Statesman. Leader of Gerondists. Suicide
Roland, Gilbert	1905-94	Entertainment	20	21		42	Latin Romantic Leading Man Silent & Sound Films
Roland, Ruth	1893-1937	Entertainment	22	35		42	Silent Serials & One Time Child Star.Baby Ruth
Roldan, Salv. C.		Head of State	10	20	50	15	Columbia
Rolfe, William James		Author	5	10	20	10	
Rolland, Romain	1866-1944	Author	35	85	130	58	Nobel Lit. 1915, AMsS $2,000
Rolle, Esther		Entertainment	10			20	Afr. Am. Actress. Character Leads
Rolling Stones (5)		Entertainment	250			610	Rock Group (5)
Rollins, Edward Henry		Senate	15	22	35		NH RR Tycoon & Bank Executive
Rollins, Sonny		Entertainment	30			55	Jazz Tenor Sax
Rolls, Charles S.	1877-1910	Business	300	375	588		Roll-Royce Motors. Aviator. Flying Record.
Rolph, James		Governor	10		35	20	Governor CA
Roman, Ruth	1924-	Entertainment	10			25	Leading Lady Films from 40's
Romanoff, Michael, 'Prince'	1890-1972	Business	30	65	145	55	Romanoff's Restaurant. Hollywood. (H. Gurgason)
Romanov, Stephanie		Entertainment	10			40	Actress. Models, Inc.
Rombauer, Irma S.		Author	5	15	30	10	'The Joy of Cooking'
Romberg, Sigmund	1887-1951	Composer	112	225	350	225	Hung.-Am. Composed Hit Operettas. AMusQS $650
Rome, Harold		Composer	15	50	100	30	AMusQS $125. Many Pop Hits
Rome, Sydney		Entertainment	5	8	15	15	
Romero, Cesar	1907-93	Entertainment	30	38		70	Actor. Handsome Film Star from '30's. Batman
Romijn, Rebecca		Entertainment	7			40	Actress Pin-Up $65
Rominger, Kent		Astronaut	6			20	
Romjue, Milton Andrew		Senate/Congress	5	12		10	Rep. MO 1917
Rommel, Erwin	1891-1944	Military	667	1517	3325	2800	Ger. Field Marshal WW II. SPc $1500
Romnes, Haakon I.		Business	5	10		10	CEO A T & T
Romney, George	1734-1802	Artist	150	475	600		Signed Original Sketch $1,500
Romney, George W.		Business-Governor	20	30	55	22	Pres. American Motors. Gov. MI., Pres. Candidate
Romulo, Carlos P.	1901-85	Head of State	48	80	95	75	Philippines. Pres.UN, Pulitzer.General WW II
Ronne, Edith M.		Explorer	20	30			Antarctic Land Named Edith Ronne Land
Ronne, Finn	1899-1980	Explorer	25		70		Proved Antarctic a Continent. 'Ronne Ice Shelf'

NAME	DATE	CATEGORY	SIG	LS/DS	ALS	SP	COMMENTS
Ronstadt, Linda		Entertainment	20	38	40	42	Singer. Versatile Vocalist. Pop-Standards-Country
Rooney, Mickey	1920-	Entertainment	25	35		36	Talented Versatile Actor From Young Boy to Old Man
Roosa, Stuart R.		Astronaut	10			25	
Roosevelt, Alice (Longworth)		Pres. Daughter	35	45	275		Author. Daughter of Theodore
Roosevelt, Edith Kermit	1861-1948	First Lady	62	240	275	375	FF $60, $75
Roosevelt, Eleanor (As First Ldy)		First Lady	172	366	1075	800	White House Cd. S $90-$225. TLS/Content $2500
Roosevelt, Eleanor	1884-1962	First Lady	110	394	400	250	Own Persona as UN Delegate & Social Worker
Roosevelt, Franklin D.(As Pres.)		President	425	1662		1054	WH Card $525.ALS/Cont $19,000
Roosevelt, Franklin D.	1882-1945	President	257	897	1650	966	Special Equator-Crossing DS $2950
Roosevelt, Franklin Jr.		Senate/Congress	10			20	MOC NY. Businessman-Farmer
Roosevelt, James		Senate/Congress	10	25	45	20	MOC CA. Marine Corps General
Roosevelt, John A.		1st Family	20	35			FDR Son
Roosevelt, Nicholas J.		Rev. War	25	60	135		Inventor
Roosevelt, Quentin	1897-1918	Military	50		200		Army Air Corps. Shot Down & Killed over Fr. WW I
Roosevelt, Sarah D.	1854-1941	Presidential	75	110	80	50	FDR Mother
Roosevelt, Theodore (As Pres.)		President	492	1476	2500	2278	TLS/Cont.$12,000, WH Cd. $500. SPc $1495
Roosevelt, Theodore	1858-1919	President	275	1159	1388	1228	TLS/Content $1,250-$6500-$9,000
Roosevelt, Theodore II		Celebrity	10	20	45	15	
Roosevelt, Theodore, Jr.	1887-1944	Military-Author	20	50	88	40	WW I & II. Gov. Puerto Rico
Root, Elihu	1845-1937	Cabinet	65	133	165	140	Sec'y War, Sec'y State, Nobel Peace Prize
Root, George F. (G.Wurzel)	1820-95	Composer	50	150	135		Many Popular & Civil War Songs.AMQS $895-$1,195
Root, Jesse		Rev. War	25	75	125		Continental Congress
Roper, Daniel		Cabinet	10	30	50	20	Sec'y Commerce 1933
Rops, Felicien	1833-98	Artist	65	165	477		Belg. Licentious Subjects. Graphic Artist
Rorem, Ned		Composer	20	45	110		Pulitzer1976, AMusQS $175
Rorschach, Hermann	1884-1922	Science	200	3400			Swiss Psychiatrist Developed Ink Blot Test
Rosas, Juan M. de		Head of State	10	25	40		Argentina
Rose Marie		Entertainment	10	20		20	'Dick VanDyke Show', Actress-Singer-Comedienne
Rose, Axl (Guns N' Roses)		Entertainment	25			48	Rock
Rose, Billy		Entertainment	25	90	35	55	Entrepreneur, Producer. Husband of Fanny Brice
Rose, David		Composer	10	20	35	20	Musical Dir. MGM. 'Holiday for Strings'.
Rose, Fred	1897-1954	Country Music	30			60	Country Music HOF. Fndr. Acuff-Rose Publishing Co.
Rose, Juanita		Country Music	10			20	
Rosebery, Archibald P.,5th Earl	1847-1929	Head of State	30	70	145		Br. Prime Minister
Rosecrans, William S.	1819-1902	Civil War	80	270	300		Union Gen.
Rosecrans, William S.(WD)		Civil War	144		1348		Union Gen.
Rosellini, Albert D.		Governor	5	15		10	Governor WA
Rosenberg, Alfred	1893-1946	Military	175	345		450	Nazi Head of Foreign Policy.Hanged as War Criminal
Rosenbloom, 'Slapsie Maxie'		Entertainment	55			120	Heavyweight Boxer-Actor
Rosendahl, Charles E.		Aviation	75	170	225	200	Am. Adm. Premiere U.S. Dirigible Capt.
Rosenman, Samuel I.		Jurist	5	20	55	15	Confidant-Advisor to FDR
Rosenquist, James		Artist	20	55	150		Am. Pop Art. Huge Canvases. Pc Repro. S $85
Rosenthal, Joe		Artist-Photographer	75	275	290	320	Iwo Jima Special 1st Day Issue $450.FDC S $100
Rosenthal, Laurence		Composer	5	10	20	10	
Rosenthal, Moriz		Entertainment	75		105		Pol. Pianist

NAME	DATE	CATEGORY	SIG	LS/DS	ALS	SP	COMMENTS
Rosenwald, Julius	1862-1932	Business	283	1325			Bought out Roebuck (of Sears)DS/Sears Sig.$12500
Rosing, Bodil		Entertainment	10			30	
Ross, Charles J.		Entertainment	5	8	15	15	
Ross, Charlotte		Entertainment	5			10	
Ross, Craig		Entertainment	6			25	Music. Guitar Lenny Kravitz
Ross, David	1755-1800	Rev. War			385		Cont'l Army & MOC MD.
Ross, Dianna	1944-	Entertainment	35	70	150	85	Mega Star Singer-Actress. Of the 'Supremes'
Ross, G.		Military	10	35	55		
Ross, George	1730-79	Rev. War	344	1101	1410		Signer Decl. of Independ. Cont. Congress
Ross, Jerry L.		Astronaut	6			20	
Ross, Joe E.		Entertainment	100			250	Short, Fat American Comedian. Frazzled Character
Ross, John	1790-1866	Am. Indian Chief	312	1260	1842		Chief Cherokee Nation. Coowescoowe
Ross, John, Sir	1777-1856	Explorer	70	180	275		Arctic Expeditions. Author
Ross, Katharine	1942-	Entertainment	15	30		40	Leading Lady. AA Nom. 'The Graduate'.
Ross, Lanny		Entertainment	15		25	25	Vintage Radio Tenor of 30's & 40's
Ross, Lawrence Sullivan	1838-98	Civil War	165	450			CSA General, Texas Governor. In Over 100 Battles
Ross, Lewis W.		Senate/Congress	10	15	30		MOC NY 1863
Ross, Marion		Entertainment	15	25		35	Actress. Happy Days & Many More
Ross, Nellie Tayloe	1876-1977	Governor	35	75	145		1st Woman Governor in U.S., WY
Ross, Robert		Author	5	10	20	10	Mystery Writer. Poe Award
Ross, Ronald, Sir	1857-1932	Science		125	275		Br. Phys. Nobel 1902 for Studies in Malaria
Ross, Samuel	1822-80	Civil War	30	175			Union Gen'l. 20th Conn.
Ross, Sobieski		Senate/Congress	10	15	25		MOC PA 1873
Rossdale, Gavin		Entertainment	12			55	Music. Lead Singer Bush
Rosselini, Isabella	1952-	Entertainment	15			40	Leading Lady Daughter of Ingrid Bergman
Rosser, Thomas L.	1836-1910	Civil War	125	302	550	375	CSA Gen. Sig/Rank $175
Rossetti, Christina	1830-94	Author	45	125	250		Br. Poet. Sister of Dante
Rossetti, Dante Gabriel	1828-82	Artist	130	235	630		Br. Poet & Painter
Rossetti, Wm. M.	1829-1919	Author	75		408		Pre-Raphaelite Art Critic.AQS $300
Rossi, Dick		Aviation	10	25	45	30	ACE, WW II, Flying Tigers
Rossini, Gioacchino	1792-1868	Composer	500	1075	1846	3408	AMusMsS $3900. Spec,Engr.S $4500.AMusQS 3900
Rossmann, Edmund		Aviation	20	30	45	50	Ger. Ace WW II. RK
Rostand, Edmond	1868-1918	Author	70	200	450	860	Fr. Playwright. 'Cyrano de Bergerac'.
Rostenkowski, Dan		Congress	15	25		40	Powerful Rep. IL, Federal Prison Term
Rostropovich, Mstislav		Entertainment	25	75	100	70	Cello Virtuoso, Conductor. 5x7 SP $45
Roth, David Lee		Entertainment	30	75		65	Ex Van Halen Group
Roth, Lillian	1910-80	Entertainment	35	52	85	62	Tragic 20's-30's Vocal Star.Problems with Alchohol
Roth, Philip	1933-	Author	20	118	90	45	Novels. 'Portnoys' Complaint', 'Goodbye Columbus'
Roth, Tim	1961-	Entertainment	20			45	'Pulp Fiction'
Rothafell, S. L. 'Roxy'		Entertainment	15	25	40	45	NY Entrepreneur,Theatre Owner
Rothenstein, William, Sir	1872-1945	Artist-Writer	20	45	75		Off'l Artist WW I & II
Rothschild, Alfred	1843-	Banker	35	90	150		Grandson of Nathan Mayer
Rothschild, Alix de		Banker	70	190	375		
Rothschild, Amschel Mayer	1773-1855	Banker		1000			Eldest Son of Mayer Amschel
Rothschild, Guy de		Banker	15	40	80	85	

NAME	DATE	CATEGORY	SIG	LS/DS	ALS	SP	COMMENTS
Rothschild, Jakob	1792-1868	Banker	125	588			Founded Paris Branch
Rothschild, Karl	1788-1855	Banker	200	575			Founder of Naples Branch
Rothschild, Leopold	1845-	Banker	35	75	150		Grandson of Nathan Mayer
Rothschild, Lionel Nathan	1808-	Banker	25	75	125	45	Son of Nathan Mayer
Rothschild, Mayer Amschel	1743-	Banker	145	400	550		Founder House of Rothschild
Rothschild, Nathan	1840-	Banker	50	150			Eldest son of Lionel
Rothschild, Nathan Mayer	1777-1836	Banker	260	650			Founder London Bank Branch. Banking Empire
Rotia, Rocky		Business	5	15	30	25	
Rotten, Johnny		Entertainment	18	40		48	
Rouault, Georges	1871-1958	Artist	200	475	783	1150	Landscapes,Religious,Clowns....SP (Pc) $840
Rouget de Lisle,Claude-Joseph	1760-1836	Military,Composer	118	295	912		Composed 'La Marseillaise'. Fr. National Anthem
Rountree, Richard		Entertainment	10			30	Opera, Concert
Rourke, Mickey	1950-	Entertainment	20			45	Abrasive, Eccentric Am. Actor.
Rous, F. Peyton, Dr,	1879-1970	Science	20	30	45	25	Am. Pathologist.Nobel Medicine 1966. Tumor Viruses
Roush, Clara		Author	10	15		15	
Rousseau, Jean-Jacques	1712-78	Author	398	1050	2950		Fr. Philosopher, Political
Rousseau, Lovell H.	1818-69	Civil War	45	85			Union Gen. Congress
Rousseau, Theodore	1812-67	Artist	75	175	475		Fr. Leader of Barbizon School
Roussel, Albert-Charles	1869-1937	Composer			610		Leading Fr. Composer after WW I
Roux, Pierre Paul Emile	1853-1933	Science	20	45	90	40	Fr. Bacteriologist with Pasteur. Dir. Pasteur Inst
Rovero, Ornella		Entertainment	15			45	Opera
Rowan, Andrew S.		Military	35	95	165	95	Delivered Message to Garcia
Rowan, Carl	1925-	Journalist	15	35		45	1st Afr-Am Ambass to Finland. Head U.S. Info. Agy.
Rowan, Dan	1922-87	Entertainment	25	35		40	Comedian Partner of Dick Martin. 'Laugh-In'
Rowan, John	1773-1853	Senate/Congress	90	250			Rep. 1807, Senator KY 1825
Rowan, Stephen C.	1808-90	Civil War	40	75	155		Union Naval Commodore
Rowe, Leo S.		Cabinet	5	20	35	10	Ass't Sec'y
Rowe, Misty		Entertainment	8			20	Pin-Up SP $25
Rowland, Adele	1883-1971	Entertainment	10			20	Silent Film Actress
Rowland, David		Colonial America	45	150			Member Stamp Act Congress
Rowlands, Gena	1934-	Entertainment	10		25	25	Actress. Multi AA Nominations
Rowlandson, Thomas	1756-1827	Artist	250	625	900		Br. Portrait Painter-Caricaturist, Illustrator
Rowling, William E.		Head of State	10	15	20	35	Prime Minister New Zealand
Roxas y Acuna, Manuel	1892-1948	Head of State	35	90	230	110	1st Pres. Philippines Republic
Roy and Siegfried		Entertainment				40	Animal Trainers
Roy, Maurice, Cardinal		Clergy	30	30	40	35	
Royce, F. Henry, Sir	1863-1933	Business	350	700	900		Co-Founder Rolls-Royce, Ltd.
Roylance, Pamela		Entertainment	4			10	
Roze, Marie		Entertainment	40			145	Opera
Rozema, David Lee		Clergy	10	15	25	15	
Rozsa, Miklos	1907-	Composer			500		Hung. Known Best for Film Music. AA(3). AAN (6)
Rubattel, Rudolph		Head of State	30	55			Switzerland
Rubens, Alma	1899-1931	Entertainment	65	85	165	175	Actress. Major Film Star Early 20th Cent.
Rubens, Paul A.		Composer	15		60		Br. Musical Comedy. AMusQS $75
Rubens, Peter Paul	1577-1640	Artist	2000	9250	21750		Flem. Baroque Landscapes, Portraits

NAME	DATE	CATEGORY	SIG	LS/DS	ALS	SP	COMMENTS
Rubik, Erno		Science	35	65	85	45	Hung. Mathematician. Remember 'Rubik's Cube'?
Rubin, Jerry		Celebrity	15		35	20	
Rubini, Jan		Entertainment	20			65	
Rubinoff, David	1897-1986	Entertainment	18			45	Rubinoff & His Violin. Eddie Cantor Show Regular
Rubinstein, Anton	1829-94	Composer	90	230	530	445	Pianist. AMusQS $625-$1250 AMsS $4,750
Rubinstein, Artur	1887-1983	Entertainment	50	125	205	383	Pol./Am. Pianist. AMusQS $425
Rubinstein, Helena	1870-1965	Business	72	665		312	Beautician Who Invented the Cosmetics Industry
Rubinstein, Ida		Entertainment	125			500	Rus. Ballerina/Nijinsky
Rubinstein, John	1946-	Entertainment	8		15	18	Actor-Director-Composer. Son of Artur
Rubio, P. Ortiz		Head of State	35			50	Pres. Mex. 1930-32
Ruby, Harry	1895-1974	Composer	30	90	162	50	AMusQS $265
Ruby, Jack	1911-67	Assassin	250	608	3267		Killed Lee Harvey Oswald. AMsS $1300, Chk $450
Rucker, Daniel H.	1812-1910	Civil War	30	65	90	150	Union Col., Bvt. General
Ruckman, John W.		Military	75				Am. Gen.
Rudel, Hans-Ulrich		Aviation	118	295	700	345	Most Highly Decorated Ger. Ace
Rudman, Warren B.		Senator	10			20	Senator NY
Rudner, Rita		Entertainment	5			15	Actress-Standup Comedienne
Rudolf, Archduke (Aus)	1858-89	Royalty			750	985	Dual Suicide at Mayerling/Baroness Marie Vetsera
Rudorffer, Erich		Aviation	40			75	Ger. World's 7th Highest Ace
Ruehl, Mercedes	1954-	Entertainment	25			60	Actress-Stage-Films. AA 'The Fisher King'
Ruff, Charles F.	1817-85	Civil War	30	55	85		Union General
Ruffo, Titta	1887-1953	Entertainment	100		765	410	It. Operatic Bariton
Ruge, Friedrich		Military	68			175	Ger. Vice Adm.
Ruger, Thomas H.	1833-1907	Civil War	30	50	85		Union General
Ruggles, Charles 'Charlie'	1886-1970	Entertainment	40			75	Character Comedian. 100s Films 1928-66
Ruggles, Daniel (WD)		Civil War	162	1051	1302		CSA General
Ruggles, Daniel	1810-97	Civil War	120	295	590		CSA Gen. ALS/Cont. $4900
Ruggles, Wesley	1889-1972	Entertainment	20	25	45	45	Film Dir. Original Keystone Cop. Director 1922-46
Ruick, Barbara	1932-74	Entertainment	5			10	Actress-Daughter of Lorene Tuttle Radio Star
Rukeyser, Louis		Business	5	15	20	15	'Wall Street Week' Host. Investment Guru
Rulter, John (SC)		Supreme Court					No Entry. Rare
Rumpler, Edward		Aviation	20	40	75	50	
Rumsfeld, Donald		Cabinet	10	20	45	15	Sec'y Defense
Runcie, Robert A.K., Archbishop		Clergy	30	40	50	40	
Runco, Mario		Astronaut	8			16	
Rundstedt, Karl R. Gerd von	1875-1953	Military	225	415	370	275	Ger. Fld. Marshal. Cmdr. Armies in Pol., Fr., USSR
Runger, Gertrud		Entertainment	15			50	Opera
Runkel, Louis		Business	5	15		10	
Running Horse, Chief		Native American	5		30		
Running Water, Chief		Native American	75		275		Model For US Indian Head Nickel
Runyon, Damon	1884-1946	Author	160	388	425	210	Short Stories & Sports Writer
Ruppert, Jacob	1867-1939	Business	95	300	415	225	Founder Ruppert Brewing Co.
Rush, Barbara	1927-	Entertainment	8		15	20	Actress. Leading Lady. Pin-Up SP $25
Rush, Benjamin	1745-1813	Rev. War	712		2417		Signer Decl. of Indepen. Prominent Physician
Rush, Geoffrey		Entertainment	15			45	Autralian Oscar Winning Actor.

NAME	DATE	CATEGORY	SIG	LS/DS	ALS	SP	COMMENTS
Rush, Isadore		Entertainment	10			30	Stage
Rush, Richard	1780-1859	Cabinet	76	306	400		Att'y General, Sec'y Treas, Sec'y State.
Rusk, Dean	1904-94	Cabinet	20	57		40	Sec'y State Under JFK
Rusk, Jeremiah M.		Civil War-Cabinet	28	55	120		Union Gen.,Sec'y Agri. 1889
Rusk, Johnny		Country Music	5			15	
Rusk, Thos. Jefferson	1803-57	Military	233	445	700		TX Provisional Gov. & Sec'y War. U.S. Sen. TX
Ruskin, John	1819-1900	Artist-Critic	60	130	407		Br. Painter, Art Critic, Author, Social Reformer
Rusling, James F.	1834-1918	Civil War	15	30	45		Union Gen. Bvt.
Russell, Annie		Entertainment	10		25	25	Vintage Stage
Russell, Bertrand	1872-1970	Author	85	258	528	292	Philosophy, Math., Nobel Prize Lit.
Russell, Bruce*		Cartoonist	25			50	Political Cartoonist, Pulitzer
Russell, Charles		Governor	5	15			Governor NV
Russell, Charles M.	1864-1926	Artist	525	750	4300		Known For Cowboy-West Art. RARE
Russell, David Abel		Congress	10	25	35		Repr.NY 1835
Russell, David Allen	1820-64	Civil War					Union Gen.-Killed at Gettysburg. RARE (No Prices)
Russell, Donald J. M.		Business	5	10	20	10	
Russell, Harold		Entertainment	10	15	25	35	Military Hero, AA Best Years Of Our Lives
Russell, Henry	1874-1936	Entertainment	10	20			Theatrical Mgr. & Singer
Russell, Jane	1921-	Entertainment	12	40		41	Actress Famous for The Outlaw. Pin-Up SP $35
Russell, John	1921-91	Entertainment	20			45	Actor. Western Star in The Lawman
Russell, John, Lord,	1792-1878	Head of State	38	188	125		Br. Prime Minister, 1st Earl
Russell, Johnny		Entertainment	5			15	Singer-Songwriter
Russell, Jonathan	1771-1832	Diplomat	390	800			Treaty of Ghent
Russell, Keri		Entertainment	18			66	TV/'Felicity'. Pin-Up $75
Russell, Kurt	1947-	Entertainment	25			45	Former Child Actor. Successful Leading Man
Russell, Leon		Entertainment	8			38	Legendary Rocker
Russell, Lillian	1861-1922	Entertainment	100	145	300	400	Vintage Musical, Operetta Star
Russell, Mark		Entertainment	5			10	
Russell, Richard B., Jr.	1897-1971	Congress	20	35		35	Gov., Senator GA. Content TLS $300
Russell, Richard M.		Congress	5	10			Rep. MA
Russell, Rosalind	1911-76	Entertainment	48	56		98	Actress. Sophisticated Comedy. AA Nom.(4)
Russell, Sol Smith		Entertainment	20			40	Vintage Comedian
Russell, Theresa	1957-	Entertainment	8	15	30	25	Am. Leading Lady. US Films from 1977
Russell, George W.	1867-1935	Author	40	145		55	Leader Irish Literary Renaissance
Russo, Rene'		Entertainment	10			40	Actress-Model. Ransom
Rust, Albert	1818-70	Civil War	90	180	205		CSA Gen. AES '$155
Rustin, Bayard		Activist	15	35	70	25	Afro-Am Civil Rights Activist
Rutan, Dick		Aviation	15	70		30	
Rutan, Dick & Jeana Yeager		Aviation	75	75		125	Non-Stop Trans-World w.o. Refueling
Rutgers, Henry	1745-1830	Rev. War	95	295	298		Benfactor Rutgers University
Ruth, Babe	1895-1948	Entertainment	1050	1450	3500	4200	Baseball Immortal
Rutherford, Ann	1917-	Entertainment	18	15		50	Pin-Up SP $35. GWTW Collectible. SP$50-75
Rutherford, Ernest	1871-1937	Science	155	448	1088	225	NZ Born Physicist. Nobel Chem. 1908
Rutherford, Kelly		Entertainment	15			60	Actress
Rutherford, Margaret, Dame	1892-1972	Entertainment	50	145	160	362	Brit. Actress. Oscar Winner.Miss MarpleSPc $330

NAME	DATE	CATEGORY	SIG	LS/DS	ALS	SP	COMMENTS
Rutledge, Edward	1739-1800	Rev. War	225	500	2108		Signer
Rutledge, John (SC)	1739-1800	Supreme Court	195	600	1775		Continental Congress.Chief Just. Brother to Edward
Rutledge, Wiley B. (SC)	1894-1949	Supreme Court	35	115	265	50	
Ruttan, Susan		Entertainment	5			15	Actress
Ryan, Irene	1903-73	Entertainment	75			250	Comedienne/PartnerTim
Ryan, James W.	1858-1907	Congress	12				Repr. PA
Ryan, Jeri		Entertainment	14			57	Actress. 'Star Trek'
Ryan, Meg		Entertainment	30			65	Adorable Sleepless In Seattle Star
Ryan, Mitchell		Entertainment	5				Actor
Ryan, Peggy		Entertainment	10	15	35	30	
Ryan, Robert		Entertainment	20	30		60	
Ryan, Sheila		Entertainment	5	6	15	15	
Ryan, T. Claude		Aviation	85	300		225	Ryan Aircraft Mfg.-Designer
Rydell, Bobby		Entertainment	12			22	Rock Singer
Ryder, Albert P.	1847-1917	Artist	90	250	560		Am. Landscapes,Marine,Portraits
Ryder, Winona		Entertainment	20			59	Actress
Ryle, Martin, Sir		Science	35	110	190	45	Nobel Physics 1974

S

NAME	DATE	CATEGORY	SIG	LS/DS	ALS	SP	COMMENTS
Saarinen, G. Eliel		Architect	20	65	150	40	Am. Foremost Arch. Of His Day
Sabatier, Paul		Science	60		180		Fr. Chem. Nobel 1912
Sabatini, Rafael	1875-1950	Author	30	70	105		It. Historical Romance Novels, Dramatist.
Sabin, Albert Bruce, Dr.	1906-93	Science	65	108	150	182	Physician-Virologist. Oral Polio Vaccine
Sabin, Dwight May		Senate/Congress	5	10		10	Rep. MN 1883
Sabin, Florence R.,Dr.	1871-1953	Science	25		145		1st Woman Elected to Nat'l Acad.of Sciences
Sabine, Edward, Sir	1788-1883	Military	45		190		Br. Gen. With Ross & Parry on Arctic Exped.
Sablon, Jean		Entertainment	20	25	45	45	Vintage Fr. Romantic Singer
Sabu (Dastagir)	1924-63	Entertainment	50			126	Overnight Star in 'Elephant Boy'
Sacco, Nicola	1891-1927	Political Radical			3700		With Vanzetti Convicted of Murder
Sacher-Masoch, Leopold von	1836-95	Author	135	275	420		Word Masochism Attributed to Abnormality
Sackett, Frederic	1868-1941	Congress	5	25			Sen. KY. Business. Ambass. Germany
Sackler, Howard		Author	5	15	25	10	
Sacks, Oliver, Dr.		Science	15	45		30	'Awakenings'. Neurologist
Sackville-West, Lionel, Sir		Diplomat	10	25	40		2nd Baron
Sackville-West, Victoria Mary	1892-1962	Author	100	301	425		Br. Poet and Novelist
Sadat, Anwar	1918-81	Head of State	50	145	325	567	Assassinated Pres.of Egypt
Sade		Entertainment	20			38	Vocalist
Sade,D.A.F., Marquis de	1740-1814	Author	402	725	2050		Sadist, Sadistic Attributed.Prison Confinement.
Safer, Morley		Journalist	5	10		15	'60 Minutes' Regular
Safire, William		Author	5			15	Journalist. Newspaper Columnist. TV Guest
Sagan, Carl, Dr.		Science	15	30	55	30	Am. Astronomer, Author. Pulitzer
Sage, Russell	1816-1906	Business	200	950	2400	275	Financier, Speculator/J.Gould. Invented Options

NAME	DATE	CATEGORY	SIG	LS/DS	ALS	SP	COMMENTS
Sagendorf, Bud*	1915-94	Cartoonist	45			250	'Popeye'- after Segar
Sager, Carole Bayer		Composer	5	15	20	15	
Saget, Bob		TV Host	10			20	TV Host & Actor. 'Full House'
Sahl, Mort		Entertainment	5	10		15	Political Humorist
Said, Nuri		Head of State	5	15	35	10	Pr. Minister Iraq
Sailing, John	1847-1959	Civil War	100		395		Last Surviving Certifiable Confed. C.W. Soldier
Saint Hilaire, L.V. Jos.		Fr. Revolution	30	75	155		
Saint James, Susan	1946-	Entertainment	10			30	Am. Leading Lady of 70's.
Saint Laurent, Yves		Business	25	40	70	40	Fashion Designer
Saint Phalle, Niki de	1930-	Artist	80				Fr. Artist. Scarce Autograph
Saint, Eva Marie	1924-	Entertainment	10	15		30	Leading Lady. AA For 'On the Waterfront'
Saint-Cyr, Gouvion		Military	50	175	190		Fr. Marshal, Minister of War
Saint-Exupery, Antoine de	1900-44	Aviation	50	145	225	135	Fr. Aviator.Author Popular Children's Books
Saint-Gaudens, Augustus	1848-1907	Artist	225	335	1562	1150	Known For Monumental Sculptured Projects
Saint-Just, Louis A.L. de	1767-94	Fr. Revolution	375	1235			Guillotined. Fr. Revolutionary
Saint-Saens, Camille	1835-1921	Composer	140	516	432	625	Organist, Opera, AMusQS $450-$650-$825
Saito, Hiroshi		Celebrity	5	15	35	20	
Saito, Makoto, Baron		Head of State	90	205	350		Prime Minister Japan
Sakai, Saburo		Aviation	35			85	3rd Highest Japanese Ace
Sakall, S.Z. 'Cuddles'	1884-1955	Entertainment	150			325	Also: Szakall. Hungarian Character Actor from 1916
Sakharov, Andrei & Elena Bonner		Science	425				Nobel Phys.,Political Activists
Sakharov, Vladmir		Celebrity	20			40	Communist agent
Salalm, Abdus		Science	20	30	55	25	Nobel Physics 1979
Salan, Raoul		Military	20	45	95	50	
Salazar, Jose, Cardinal		Clergy	30	30	35		
Sale, Charles 'Chic'	1885-1937	Entertainment	28	40	65	95	Comedian-Actor
Sales, Soupy		Entertainment	5	15	25	15	Comedian. Early Entry to Children's Programming
Saleza, Albert		Entertainment	40			70	Opera. Tenor
Salinger, J[erome] D[avid]		Author	1575	5075	6500		Novelist Catcher in the Rye. RARE in any Form!
Salinger, Pierre		Journalist-Author	40	45	45	20	Press Sec'y Pres. JFK
Salisbury, Frank O.	1874-1962	Artist	25	75	125		Br. Portr. Painter of FDR as Pres., Geo. V, etc.
Salisbury, Harrison		Author	15			25	Pulitzer Journalist, Editor
Salisbury, Peter		Entertainment	6			25	Music. Drummer The Verve
Salisbury, Robert C.3rd Marquis	1830-1903	Head of State	40	45	80		Prime Minister
Salk, Jonas, Dr.	1914-95	Science	88	233	300	275	Polio Vaccine Booklet S $200
Salling, John		Civil War	15	25	50		Union General
Salmi, Albert		Entertainment	25			40	
Salminen, Sally		Author	15	40	75		
Salt, Jennifer		Entertainment	3			10	
Salt, Titus, Sir	1803-76	Business	5	20	40		Pioneer Wool Industry.Inventor
Salten, Felix	1870-1946	Author	75	100	235		Austrian Author of Bambi
Saltonstall, Leverett	1892-1979	Congress	12	20		15	Senator MA
Salvini, Tomaso		Entertainment	45			175	Tragedian with Booth
Sam the Sham		Entertainment	10			20	Rock
Samaroff-Stokowski, Olga		Entertainment	20			88	Acclaimed Pianist,Teacher,Critic

NAME	DATE	CATEGORY	SIG	LS/DS	ALS	SP	COMMENTS
Sambora, Richie		Entertainment	10			35	
Samms, Emma		Entertainment	6	8		20	Pin-Up SP $35
Sammt, Albert		Aviation	30			65	
Samples, Candy		Entertainment	25			60	
Sampson, Will		Entertainment	35	55	85	100	
Sampson, William T.	1840-1902	Military	70	90	145	90	Am. Adm. Cmdr-in-Chief, Sp.-Am. War
Samuel, Herbert		Statesman	28		150		1st Jew to Govern Palestine Since Romans
Samuelson, Paul A., Dr.		Economics	25	40		35	Nobel Economics
San Giacomo, Laura		Entertainment	15			40	Actress. TV Series Don't Shoot Me
San Juan, Olga		Entertainment	5			10	Singer-Dancer-Actress
San Martin, Jose de	1778-1850	Head of State	500	800	2650		Soldier Hero of Argentina
Sanborn, Franklin B.	1831-	Author-Reformer	5	15	15		Journalist, Editor, Biographer
Sanborn, Katherine A.		Author	5	20	35		
Sand, George	1804-76	Author	100	220	624		Fr. Non-Conformist.ALS/Cont.$3500.(A.A.Dupin)
Sandburg, Carl	1878-1967	Author-Poet	100	319	340	425	Biographer, Journalist. Orig. Pencil Portr. S $750
Sanders, George		Author	5			10	'Autograph Price Guide' Author
Sanders, George	1906-72	Entertainment	90			165	Laid Back Br. Actor. AA Award
Sanders, Gregg		Entertainment	10		25	20	Supporting Actor
Sanders, Harland Col		Business	30	75	150	125	KFC Colonel Sanders
Sanders, Helen		Author	5			10	Autograph Price Guide expert
Sanders, Horace T.	1820-65	Civil War	25	75	180		Union Gen'l.Sig/Rank $50. Wounded-Bled to Death
Sanderson, Julia		Entertainment	10	20	30	30	Vintage Radio Team With Frank Crummit
Sandler, Adam		Entertainment	9			45	Actor. The Wedding Singer, Waterboy
Sandoz, Marie		Author	25	70	170	40	
Sands, Tommy		Entertainment	10			15	
Sandwich,4thEarl(Montagu)		Statesman	125	783	550		The Sandwich Attributed To Him
Sanford, Edw. Terry (SC)		Supreme Court	75	195			
Sanford, Isabel		Entertainment	5	7	15	18	
Sanger, Frederick		Science	20	35	60	25	Nobel Chemistry 1958
Sanger, Margaret	1883-1966	Reformer	65	210	350	105	Birth Control Advocate
Sangster, Margaret E.		Author	30	55	175		Journalist, Poet, Editor
Sangster, William E.		Clergy	25	40	55		Br. Meth. Minister-Author
Sankey, Ira D.		Clergy	65	95	150	100	Singing Evangelist. Associated/Dwight Moody
Sankford, Henry		Clergy	35	50	60		
Sano, Roy L., Bishop		Clergy	20	25	35	25	
Sansom, Art		Cartoonist	5			20	The Born Loser
Santa Anna, Antonio L. de	1794-1876	Head of State	235	1428	1570	585	General,Revolutionary,Pres.Mex.
Santa Cruz, Andres	1792-1865	Head of State	95	245			General. Pres.Bolivia. Exiled
Santa Rosa, Annibale S.,Count		Military	25	70	150		It.Piedmontese Insurgent
Santana		Entertainment	10			30	Singer-Musician
Santander, Francisco de Paula	1792-1837	Head of State			450		Pres. Columbia.
Santayana, George		Author	65	175	350		Poet, Philosopher, Critic
Santelmann, William H.		Entertainment		25			Marine Corps Bandmaster
Santley, Charles, Sir		Entertainment	40			175	Baritone. Debut/1857. Retired/1911
Santos, Joe		Entertainment	5	6	15	15	

NAME	DATE	CATEGORY	SIG	LS/DS	ALS	SP	COMMENTS
Santos-Dumont, A.		Aviation	300	390	580	720	Brazil. Aeronaut. PioneerAirman
Santunione, Orianna		Entertainment	5			20	Opera
Saperstein, Abe M.		Business		375		150	Owner-Coach-Founder Harlem Globetrotters
Sara, Mia		Entertainment	15			50	Actress
Sarandon, Chris		Entertainment	4			15	Actor
Sarandon, Susan		Entertainment	12	22	150	45	AA, Actress. Pin-Up SP $55
Sarasate, Pablo de		Composer	113		250		Violin Virtuoso, AMusQS $275
Sardi, Vincent		Business	4	15	25	10	Fndr. Sardi's Restaurant NYC
Sardou, Victorien	1831-1908	Playwright	20	45	125	150	Fr. Librettist, Bourgeois Drama
Sarett, Lew		Author	75	100			
Sarfatti, Margherita		Author	10	30	50		
Sarg, Tony*	1882-1942	Artist	15			75	Illustrator-Marionette Maker
Sargent, Dick		Entertainment	7			20	
Sargent, John G.		Cabinet	15	30	60	25	Att'y General 1925
Sargent, John Osborne	1811-	Legal	10		65		Lawyer, Author. Political Activist
Sargent, John Singer	1856-1925	Artist	95	250	380		Am. World Famous Portraitist
Sargent, Kenny		Entertainment	20			45	Big Band Singer
Sargent, Winthrop		Rev. War	30	100	240		Cont'l Army, 1st Gov. MS Terr.
Sarnoff, David	1891-1971	Business	100	750	900	150	Broadcasting Pioneer. TLS on RCA Lttrhd. $1450
Sarocco, Suzanne		Entertainment	10			25	Opera
Saroyan, William	1908-81	Author	87	225	285	88	Playwright. Pulitzer The Time of Your Life
Sartain, John	1808-97	Artist-Engraver	25	85	100		Sartain's Union Magazine
Sarton, May		Author	5	15	40		
Sartre, Jean-Paul	1905-80	Author	110	612	698		Leader Existentialist Movement. ALS/Cont. $1350
Sassoon, Beverly		Entertainment	3	3	6	15	
Sassoon, Siegfried	1886-1967	Author	50	225	362		Br. Poet. Anti-War Verses
Sassoon, Vidal		Business	15	20	25	20	Hair Design & Products
Satie, Erik		Composer	210	825	1650		Eccentric, Avant Garde Music
Sato, Eisaku		Head of State	20	55	150	35	Premier Japan. Nobel Peace
Sauckel, Fritz		Military	50	200			Nazi War Criminal. Hanged
Sauer, Emil		Entertainment	15	15	75	30	
Sauguet, Henri		Composer	65		275		Fr. Opera, Ballet AMQS $250
Saulsbury, Grove		Governor	5	15	30		Governor DE
Saumarez, James, Sir,	1757-1836	Military	90	265	600		Br. Adm., Battle of the Nile
Saunders, Alvin		Senate/Congress	15	35	80		Sen.KY, CW Gov. Nebr.Territory
Saunders, Edward Watts		Senate/Congress	10	20			Rep. VA 1906
Saunders, Hugh W.		Aviation	5	10	20	15	
Saunders, John Monk		Entertainment	10	25			ANS 35, writer/director
Saunders, Lori		Entertainment	4			15	
Saunders, Stuart J.		Business	3	7	15	10	
Saunders, Stuart T.	1909-	Business	5			10	CEO Penn-Central RR
Savage, Ann		Entertainment	12	15		35	
Savage, Fred		Entertainment	7			20	
Savage, M. J.		Clergy	15	30	45		
Saval, Dany		Entertainment	5		25	20	Pin-Up SP $25. Fr. Actress

NAME	DATE	CATEGORY	SIG	LS/DS	ALS	SP	COMMENTS
Savalas, George		Entertainment	15			40	
Savalas, Telly	1924-94	Entertainment	15	43		40	Actor. TV's Kojak. Oscar Nominee
Savitch, Jessica		Journalist	20			95	TV-News. Died Young in Car Accident
Savitt, Jan		Bandleader	15			45	
Savles, Thomas F, Bishop		Clergy	30	40			
Savoia, Attilio		Artist	15	40	75		
Sawyer, Charles		Cabinet	5	25	30	10	Sec'y Commerce 1948
Sawyer, Diane		Journalist	5	20		25	TV Broadcast Journalist
Sawyer, Joe		Entertainment	75			200	
Sax, Adolphe		Science	55	180	375		Invented Saxophone & Others
Saxbe, William B.		Cabinet	8	12	20	15	Att'y General 1974
Saxe, John G.		Author	10	30	55	30	
Saxon, John		Entertainment	5			20	
Saxon, Rufus, Jr.		Civil War	25	55	70		Union General
Sayao, Bidu		Entertainment	15			75	Opera Soprano
Sayers, Dorothy	1893-1957	Author	183	467	565	138	Br. Mystery Novelist. Created Lord Peter Wimsey
Saylor, Anna, Mrs.		Socialite	5	10			
Scacchi, Greta		Entertainment	10			35	Actress
Scaggs, Boz		Entertainment	15			35	
Scagliarini, Eleanora		Entertainment	10			40	Opera
Scalchi Lolly		Entertainment	35			75	
Scales, Alfred M.(WD)		Civil War	165	270	345		CSA Gen. Sig $90-110
Scalia, Antonin (SC)		Supreme Court	30	90		55	
Scalia, Jack		Entertainment	10			25	
Scammell, Alexander	1746-81	Rev. War	350		1500		Officer. Wounded Died 1781
Scancarelli, Jim*		Cartoonist	10			45	Gasoline Alley
Scarborough, John		Clergy	10	15	20		
Scarlatti, Alessandro	1660-1725	Composer	725	4150	12000		115 Operas, Over 600 Cantatas
Scarwid, Diana		Entertainment	5		15	20	
Schaal, Richard		Entertainment	3	3	6	8	
Schaal, Wendy		Entertainment	3	3	6	6	
Schacht, Hjalmar		WW II	60	160	300		Nazi Minister WW II
Schafer, Natalie		Entertainment	20			35	
Schaff, Phillip		Clergy	40	55	75	50	
Schaffner, Franklin J.		Entertainment	30			75	
Schaffner, Hans		Head of State	10			20	Pres. Austria
Schall, Thomas D.		Senate/Congress	5	15			Rep., Senator MN 1915
Schallert, William		Entertainment	5	6	15	15	
Schally, Andrew V., Dr.		Science	22	30	45	30	Nobel Medicine 1977
Schanberg, Sydney, H.		Author	10	30	75	15	
Scharwenka, Franz Xavier		Composer	25		75	150	Pianist. Founder of Conservatory
Schary, Dore		Entertainment	15		25	30	Producer, Director, Writer
Schary, Emanuel		Artist	10	25	35		
Schawlow, Arthur L., Dr.		Science	22	30	35	25	Nobel Physics 1981
Scheel, Jeff		Entertainment	8			40	Music. Lead Singer Gravity Kills

NAME	DATE	CATEGORY	SIG	LS/DS	ALS	SP	COMMENTS
Scheer, Reinhard	1863-1928	Military	20	45	95	40	Ger. Adm. Battle of Jutland.
Scheff, Fritzi	1882-1954	Entertainment	20			25	Austr-Am. Soprano. Musical Theatre & Silent Films
Scheidemann, Philippe		Head of State	10	20	50	40	1st Chancellor of Repub. 1919
Scheider, Roy		Entertainment	7	20		20	Actor
Schell, Augustus	1812-84	Business	275	850			Financier & C. Vanderbilt Attorney
Schell, Maria	1926-	Entertainment	5		20	25	International Austrian Film Star 50's
Schell, Maximillian		Entertainment	10	15	35	30	A A
Schell, Richard	1810-79	Business		975			Commodore Vanderbilt's Aide During 'Erie War'
Schenk, Robert C.		Civil War	42	45	70		Union Gen., Rep OH, Ambassador
Scherchen, Hermann		Conductor	20			125	
Scherer, Paul		Clergy	20	25	40	30	
Schick, Bela, Dr.		Science	60	135	225	125	Hung.-Am Pediatrician. Schick Test for TB
Schiele, Egon		Artist		1400			Austrian Expressionist Painter
Schiff, Jacob H.	1847-1920	Business	75	497	265		Banker, Philanthropist. Wall Street Brokerage
Schiffer, Claudia	1972-	Entertainment	18			49	German Model. Pin-Up SP $65
Schifrin, Lalo		Composer	5	55	25	88	Argentine Composer. Film Themes. AMusQS $40
Schildkraut, Joseph		Entertainment	75	150		220	Oscar winner
Schiller, Hans von		Aviation	20		45		
Schilling, David		Aviation	18	38	60	45	ACE, WW II
Schine, G. David		Business	20			40	Hotel Chain Owner
Schiotz, Fredrik A.		Clergy	20	25	35	30	
Schipa, Tito	1889-1965	Entertainment	65			140	Opera. Important Tenor
Schirach, Baldur Von		Ger. Politician	125	515			Nat'l Dir. Hitler Youth Movement
Schirra, Walter M.		Astronaut	20	65	208	75	Mercury 7 Astro.
Schlafly, Phyllis		Political	10	20	35	25	Activist, Feminist
Schlafly, Phyllis, Mrs.		Activist	10			35	
Schlesinger, Arthur Jr.		Author	10	38	50	20	Historian. Special Ass't to JFK. Pulitzer 1946
Schlesinger, James R.		Cabinet	5	10	25	15	Sec'y Defense 1973
Schlesinger, John		Entertainment	5			20	Film Director
Schley, Winfield Scott	1839-1909	Military	131	260	400	375	Am. Naval Officer. Arctic rescue of Greely
Schliemann, Heinrich	1833-90	Archaeologist	245	1600	1665		Discovered Ancient Troy. ALS re Mycenae $5,000
Schmalz, Wilhelm		Military	15	40	75	30	
Schmidt, Friedrich		Astronaut	30				
Schmidt, Helmut		Head of State	15	25	40	20	Ger. Political Leader, Chanc.
Schmidt, Maarten, Dr.		Science	10	25	30	20	
Schmidtmer, Christiane		Entertainment	4			15	Ger. Actress. Pin-Up SP $25
Schmied, Francois-louis	1873-1941	Artist	90		375		Fr. Art Deco Painter - Illustrator
Schmitt, Harrison H.		Astronaut	20		185	100	Apollo 17 Moonwalker
Schmitt-Walter, Karl		Entertainment	10			35	Opera. Baritone. Wide Repertoire
Schnabel, Artur	1881-1951	Entertainment	40	135	220		Austrian Pianist
Schnaut, Gabriella		Entertainment	5			25	Opera
Schneider, John		Entertainment	4	10		15	Singer-Actor
Schneider, Romy		Entertainment	75			130	
Schneider, Wm. C. (SKYLAB)		Astronaut	6			20	
Schochet, Bob*		Cartoonist	5			35	

NAME	DATE	CATEGORY	SIG	LS/DS	ALS	SP	COMMENTS
Schoenberg, Arnold	1874-1951	Composer	300	896		675	Austrian-Born. AMusQS $2,250, $2500
Schoene, Heinrich		Military	125	450		195	Ger. Gen. Storm Trooper
Schoenebeck, Karl August		Aviation	30	65		75	
Schoenert, Rudolf		Aviation	10	20	40	25	
Schoepfel, Gerhard		Aviation	5	15	25	15	
Schofield, John Arthur		Civil War	98		185		Union General
Schofield, John M. (WD)		Civil War	125	155	340		Union General, Sec'y War 1868
Schofield, John M.	1831-1906	Civil War	45	80	150		Union Gen. MOH At Wilson's Creek
Schopenhauer, Arthur		Author	700	17500	5000		Ger. Philosopher
Schorner, Ferdinand		Military	40		120		
Schorr, Daniel		Journalist	10			45	CBS Correspondent Till '76. Nat'l Public Radio Now
Schrader, Paul		Entertainment	5	15		20	Film Director
Schram, Emil		Business	3	10	20	5	
Schramm, Margit		Entertainment	5			15	Opera, Operetta
Schreiber, Avery		Entertainment	3	5	8	12	
Schricker, Henry F.		Governor	5	20		10	Governor IN
Schrieffer, John R.		Science	10	20	35	15	Nobel Physics 1972
Schriver, Edmund		Civil War	40	90	125		Union General
Schroder, Ricky		Entertainment	10			35	
Schroeder, Patricia		Senate/Congress	5	10		15	Rep. CO
Schroeder-Feinen, Ursula		Entertainment	5			30	Opera
Schroer, Werner		Aviation				65	Ger. Ace WW II. RK
Schroeteler, Heinrich		Military				60	Ger. Capt. U-667,U1023. RK
Schubert, Franz	1797-1828	Composer	2200	4567	10000		
Schuk, Walter		Aviation	25	45		85	Ger. 12th Highest ACE
Schulberg, Budd		Author	30	55		15	Novelist, Screenwriter. On The Waterfront
Schuller, Gunther		Music	35			55	Pulitzer '94 in Music. AMusQS $250
Schuller, Robert		Clergy	15	20		25	
Schultz, Theodore William		Agri-Science	10	15	25		Nobel Economics
Schulz, Charles	1922-	Cartoonist	118	180	1800	270	Full Color Lobby Card S $225.Snoopy Sktch S $550
Schulz, Charles*		Cartoonist	100	175	680	395	Peanuts S Orig. Strip $1,500+-
Schulze, William		Science	15			45	Rocket Pioneer/von Braun
Schuman, William	1910-92	Composer	10	30	75	60	Pulitzer (2) & NY Critics Award. AMusQS $275
Schumann, Clara	1819-96	Composer	70	205	495	925	Ger. Pianist-Composer. ALS/Content $3,000
Schumann, Elizabeth		Entertainment	45			140	Opera
Schumann, Robert	1810-56	Composer	800	1100	4000	5000	AMusQS $15,000 (3rd Symph).$22,000(Die Nonne)
Schumann-Heink, Ernestine		Entertainment	45		100	150	Opera, Concert. Contralto
Schurz, Carl	1829-1906	Civil War	45	114	150		Union Gen., U.S.Sen. MO. Advisor to 5 Presidents
Schuschnigg, Kurt von	1897-	Head of State	70	85	225	75	Austrian Chancellor. Deposed & Imprisoned by Nazis
Schuyler, Philip J.	1733-1804	Rev. War	275	575	900		Soldier, Statesman. Rev. War General. Cont'l Congr
Schwab, Charles M.	1862-1939	Industrialist	175	562	1150		Pres. Carnegie,US & Bethlehem Steel/Mil. $ Salary
Schwab, Frank X.		Political	5	20			Mayor Buffalo, NY
Schwantner, Joseph		Composer	10		55	40	Pulitzer, AMusQS $95
Schwartz, Arthur		Composer					Dancing in the Dark AMQS on Ph. $410
Schwartz, Melvin, Dr	1932-	Science	24			30	Nobel Physics 1988

NAME	DATE	CATEGORY	SIG	LS/DS	ALS	SP	COMMENTS
Schwartz, Scott		Entertainment	6			25	Actor. Xmas Story SP $30
Schwartz, Stephen		Composer	55	200			'Godspell'
Schwarzenegger, Arnold		Entertainment	38	35	75	99	Actor-Producer
Schwarzkopf, Elizabeth		Entertainment	15			50	Opera
Schwarzkopf, Norman		Military	30	125		90	Gen. Desert Storm
Schwatka, Frederick		Celebrity	10	20	55		
Schwedtman, Ferd. D.		Science	5	15		10	
Schweickart, Russell L.		Astronaut	15			25	
Schweiker, Richard S.		Senate/Congress	5	10		10	Rep., Senator PA 1961
Schweitzer, Albert, Dr.	1875-1965	Science-Music	180	480	714	745	Nobel. Clergy. 3x4 SP $350-$650. AMusQS $650
Schwellenback, Lewis B.		Cabinet	10	35	70	15	Sec'y Labor 1945
Schwimmer, David		Entertainment	15			60	Actor. Friends
Schwinger, Julian, Dr.		Science	20	30	55	25	Nobel Physics 1965
Schwitters, Kurt	1887-1948	Artist	250	775			Ger. Best Know For His Collages
Sciorra, Annabella		Entertainment	10			30	Actress
Scobee, Dick	1939-89	Astronaut	100	425		175	Challenger Victim. Postal Cover $150
Scofield, Glenni W.		Senate/Congress	10	15	25		Rep. PA 1863
Scofield, Paul	1922-96	Entertainment	25		125	85	Brit. AA Winner. Man for All Seasons etc
Scoggins, Tracy		Entertainment	5	8	25	20	Pin-Up SP $50
Scopes, John T.	1900-70	Educator	200	1800		1495	Defendant In Monkey Trial
Scorsese, Martin		Entertainment	15	55		42	Film Director
Scorupco, Izabella		Entertainment	5				Actress.Golden Eye Pin-Up 55
Scott, Blanch Stuart	1891-1970	Aviation				492	1st Fem. Pilot to Solo
Scott, Charles		Rev. War	90	195	350		General, Indian Fighter,Gov.KY
Scott, Charles Wm. A.		Aviation	25	50	80	50	Br. Won Harmon Trophy
Scott, Cyril Meir		Composer	15	50	105	20	Br. Orchestral, Piano, Chamber
Scott, David C.		Business	5	10		10	CEO Allis-Chalmers
Scott, David R.		Astronaut	25	175		273	Moonwalker. SP 8x10 of Earth $150
Scott, E. Irwin		Business		965	1475		One of Founders of Scott Paper Co.
Scott, Earl		Country Western	10			35	Music. 50's Western Recording Artist
Scott, Eric		Entertainment	4	6		10	
Scott, Fred		Entertainment	18			42	Vintage Cowboy Actor
Scott, George C.		Entertainment	20			85	AA Patton
Scott, Gordon		Entertainment	15			35	
Scott, Gustavus		Rev. War	35	90	140		Lawyer, Patriot (MD)
Scott, Hazel		Entertainment	35	45		130	Piano-Organ
Scott, Hugh		Senate/Congress	5	15		25	Senator PA
Scott, Hugh L.		Military	30	95	250		Am. WW I Gen. 7 Chief of Staff
Scott, Jack		Entertainment	10			25	Rock
Scott, Jerry*		Cartoonist	10			45	Nancy
Scott, John Morin		Rev. War	35	85	150		General, Patriot, Rep.NY
Scott, Lizabeth		Entertainment	8	10		20	Pin-Up SP $25
Scott, Martha		Entertainment	5			20	
Scott, Pippa		Entertainment	6			15	Actress
Scott, Randolph	1903-1987	Entertainment	40	55		104	Actor. Handsome Western Hero

NAME	DATE	CATEGORY	SIG	LS/DS	ALS	SP	COMMENTS
Scott, Raymond		Composer	25	40	65	50	Big Band Leader, Arranger
Scott, Robert Falcon	1868-1912	Explorer	90	255	1167	195	Br. Arctic Expeditions
Scott, Robert Kingston		Civil War	55				Union Gen.,Scoundrel Gov. SC
Scott, Robert Lee, Jr.		Aviation	25	35	60	40	ACE, WW II, God Is My Co-Pilot
Scott, Thomas		Clergy	40	50	75		
Scott, Thomas A.		Business	275	875	1500		Pennsylvania RR Baron
Scott, W. Kerr		Senate	5			25	Gov. NC 1949, Senator NC 1954
Scott, Walter, Sir	1771-1832	Author	135	588	711		Poet, Novelist, Historian
Scott, Willard		Entertainment	4	4		10	
Scott, William R.		Business	5	15			RR Exec.
Scott, Winfield (WD)		Civil War	175	490	682		Union General
Scott, Winfield	1786-1866	Civil War	122	338	600	450	Union Gen., Pres. Candidate
Scott, Zachary		Entertainment	25			50	
Scotti, Antonio		Entertainment	40		100	185	It. Baritone, Opera
Scotto, Renata		Entertainment	15			50	Opera
Scowcroft, Brent		Military	10	30		20	Gen., Statesman,Pres. Advisor
Scranton, Bill		Governor	5	15		15	Gov. PA. Pres. Candidate
Scriabin, Alexander	1872-1915	Composer	650	3500	5000	3200	Rus.Symphonies, etc.AMusQS $3500-$6000
Scribe, Eugene	1791-1861	Author	10	35	60		Fr. Librettist.Meyerbeer,Halevy
Scribner, Charles		Publishing	175	1350			Publishing Giant. Stk. Cert. S $1750
Scrimm, Angus		Entertainment	6			20	Actor
Scripps, William E.		Aviation	15	90		40	
Scudder, Horace E.	1838-1902	Author	10	30	55		Ed.Atlantic Mnthly, Biographer
Scuderi, Sara		Entertainment	35			85	Opera
Scullin, James H.	1876-1953	Head of State	40			70	P.M. Australia
Scully, Thomas		Artist	190	375	650		
Scully-Power, Paul		Astronaut	25			65	
Seaborg, Glenn T.	1912-99	Science	25	105	150	75	Chm. AEC. Nobel Chemistry 1951.Plutonium-A Bomb
Seaforth, Susan		Entertainment	5			20	Pin-Up SP $30
Seale, Bobby	1936-	Activist	25				Political Activist. Co-Fndr. Black Panthers
Seals, Dan		Country Music	5			15	
Searle, Ronald		Cartoonist	20	45	80		Painter, Author. 'St. Trinians School Girls'
Sears, Edmund		Clergy	20	25	35		
Sears, Richard Warren		Business		6500			Sear's Founder. DS Sears Contract $12,500
Seaton, George		Entertainment	35			70	Film Director
Seawell, Molly Elliot		Author	5	15	35	10	
Seawell, William T.		Business	3	10	15	15	
Sebastian, John		Entertainment	15			40	Singer-Songwriter. The Lovin' Spoonful
Sebastini, H.F.B.	1772-1851	Fr. Military		80	150		Gen. under Napoleon, Marshal of Fr.
Seberg, Jean		Entertainment	75			165	Early Suicide
Sechelles, Marie-Jean Herault de		Fr. Revolution			895		Att'y to Louis XVI
Sedaka, Neil		Composer	10			25	Entertainer. AmusQS $35
Seddon, James A. (WD)		Civil War	170	550	2350		CSA Sec'y War Dte. DS $1,000
Seddon, Margaret R.		Astronaut	6			25	
Sedgewick, John		Civil War	135	407			Union General (Uncle John). KIA Spotsylvania

NAME	DATE	CATEGORY	SIG	LS/DS	ALS	SP	COMMENTS
Sedgwick, Catherine M.	1789-1867	Author	10	20	45		Am. Early Novelist. Moral Tales
Sedgwick, John	1813-64	Civil War	200	895			Union Gen. KIA. Twice Breveted
Sedgwick, Kyra		Entertainment	15			75	Actress
See, Elliot M. Jr.		Astronaut	225			250	
Seeburg, Justus Percival		Business	40	120	195		
Seeger, Pete		Composer	20	50	95	40	Folk Singer
Seeley, Blossom		Entertainment	5	6	15	15	
Seeley, Jeannie		Country Music	10			20	
Seelye, Julius Hawtry		Clergy	15	20	25		College Pres., Rep.MA
Segal, Erich		Author	20				Love Story
Segal, George		Artist	25		35		
Segal, George		Entertainment	5		15	25	Actor
Segal, Steven		Entertainment	15			60	Actor. Major Action Films
Segar, Elzie C.*		Cartoonist	125			575	Popeye
Segar, Joseph E.		Senate/Congress	10	20			Rep. VA 1862
Seger, Bob		Entertainment	20			40	
Seger, C.B.		Business	15	45	85	40	
Segovia, Andres		Entertainment	100		475	140	Classical Guitar Virtuoso
Segre, Emilio, Dr.		Science	20	35	50	30	Nobel Physics 1959
Segura, Wiltz P.		Aviation	15	25	40	30	ACE, WW II, USAAF Ace. Flew/Chennault
Segurola, Andres de		Entertainment	45			150	Sp. Bass
Seidel, Toscha		Entertainment	20			75	Noted Rus.-Am. Violinist
Seidelman, Susan		Entertainment	5	10		10	Film Director
Seignolle, Claude		Author	120	175	220		
Seinfeld (Cast)		Entertainment	150			353	Four Main Characters
Seinfeld, Jerry		Entertainment	15			45	
Seipel, Ignas Dr.		Head of State	10	30	80	40	Austrian Prelate & Chancellor
Seka		Entertainment	9	10	20	25	Pin-Up SP $35
Selassie, Haile	1891-1975	Head of State	175	385	730	900	(Tafari Makonnen) Emperor of Ethiopia
Selfridge, Harry G.	1858-1947	Business	15	65	110	35	Founder Selfridge's, London Dept. Store
Selfridge, Thos. O.		Civil War	40	85	120		Union Naval Commander
Sellecca, Connie		Entertainment	10			30	
Selleck, Tom		Entertainment	10	15	30	30	Magnum P.I. TV Star. SP $75
Sellers, David Foote		Military	20	55	95	50	
Sellers, Jim		Entertainment	6			25	Music. Bass Guitar Stabbing Westward
Sellers, Peter	1925-1980	Entertainment	87	155	175	158	British comic actor. Insp. Clouseau SP $200+
Sellers, Winfield S.		Military	15	40	75	40	
Selman, John		Outlaw-Lawman	1200	3000			
Selznick, David O.		Business	105	350		150	Film Producer (GWTW). S Chk $350
Selznick, Irene		Entertainment	10	15		20	Film Executive
Sembrich, Marcella	1858-1935	Entertainment	85		300	228	Opera, Concert. Polish Soprano
Semenov, Nikolai		Science		95		75	Rus. Chem., Physicist. Nobel 1956
Semmelweis, Ignaz	1818-65	Science	500	1200	3200		Hung. Obstetrician.Antisepsis
Semmes, Paul J.	1815-63	Civil War	912	1372	900		CSA Gen. Sig/Rank $1450
Semmes, Raphael	1809-77	Civil War	325	750	2262	1750	CSA Admiral Sig/Rank $475

NAME	DATE	CATEGORY	SIG	LS/DS	ALS	SP	COMMENTS
Semple, James	1798-1866	Congress	15				Sen. IL, Elsa, IL Founder
Sendak, Maurice		Author	20	65			Writer & Illustrator of Many Children's Books
Senechal, Michel		Entertainment	5			25	Opera
Senn, Nicholas		Civil War	35		140		Union Surgeon
Sennett, Mack	1880-1960	Entertainment	288	1012		550	Historic DS $4,500
Sergeant, John		Celebrity	10	20	35		
Sergeant, John	1779-1852	Congress	15	35	55		Rep.PA. ALS/Cont $1600
Sergievsky, Boris		Aviation	75			150	
Serkin, Rudolf	1903-91	Entertainment	40	130	155	162	Austr.-Born Piano Virtuoso, AMusQS $50-$175
Serling, Rod	1924-75	Author-Entertain.	125	250	375	340	Creator Twilight Zone. MGM DS $425
Serpico, Frank		Law	10	20	45	20	Undercover Detective-Hero
Serurier, Jean M.P., Count		Fr. Revolution	50	145	215		Marshal of Napoleon
Service, Robert W.	1874-1958	Author	75		235		Canadian Poet, Author, Versifier
Sessions, Roger		Composer	15	45	165		Pulitzer, AMusQS $250
Sessions, William L.		Government	25	75		30	Dir. FBI
Seton-Thompson, Ernest	1860-1946	Author	75	115	365	75	Co-Fnd. Boy Scouts of Am.Wild Life Stories.Illustr
Seuss, Dr. (Theodore Geisel)*	1904-91	Author	48	300	395	663	Orig. Sketch on FDC S $500-950. Print S $225
Severance, Joan		Entertainment	5			25	Nude Pin-UP S $85
Severeid, Eric	1912-92	Journalist	15			95	TV-Radio Anchor & Sr. Commentator/Cronkite
Severeid, Susanne		Model	4			15	Pin-Up SP $20, Actress
Severinson, Doc		Entertainment	6	8	25	25	Trumpet, Big Band
Sevier, John	1745-1815	Rev. War	625	1875	750		Hero of Battle of King's Mt. Historical DS $3,750
Sewall, David		Rev. War	20	50	110		Jurist, Patriot, Justice Peace
Sewall, Samuel	1652-1730	Colonial America	275	1200	1300		Salem Witchcraft Trials
Sewall, Samuel	1757-1814	Senate/Congress	25		60		Rep. MA 1796.MA Chief Justice
Seward, Frederick Wm.(son of W.H.)		Cabinet	30	55	80		Ass't Sec'y State
Seward, William H.	1801-72	Cabinet	75	245	575	745	Lincoln's Sec'y State. LS/Re Assassination $1,750
Sewell, William J.	1835-1901	Civil War	40	90	130		Union Gen., U.S. Sen. NJ
Sexton, Anne	1928-74	Author	35	300			Am. Poet. 1967 Pulitzer. Suicidal Breakdown '55
Sexton, Walton R.		Military	10	30	45	30	Adm. US Navy. WW II
Seymour, Anne		Entertainment	10			20	
Seymour, George F., Bishop		Clergy	25	25	40		
Seymour, Horatio	1810-1886	Governor	30	60	80		Civil War Gov. NY. Pres. Candidate
Seymour, Jane		Entertainment	15			48	Br. Actress.
Seymour, Stephanie		Entertainment	20			62	Model-Actress
Seymour, Truman	1824-91	Civil War	75	115	190		Union General. At Ft. Sumter When Surrendered
Shackelford, Ted		Entertainment	5			15	
Shackleton, Ernest H., Sir	1874-1922	Explorer	192	400	420	450	Br. Antarctic Explorer
Shaffer, Paul		Entertainment	5			15	
Shaffer, Peter L.		Author	10	20	35	15	
Shafter, William H.	1835-1906	Civil War	15	95	75	35	Union Gen. MOH. Indian Fighter
Shafter, William R.		Civil War	35	55	110	150	Union Gen.
Shaftesbury, A.A.C.7th Earl	1801-85	Reformer	25	80	160		Politician, M.P., Statesman, Social Reformer
Shah, Zahir		Royalty	50				King Afghanistan
Shahn, Ben		Artist	55	150	240	145	Am.Painter-Graphic Artist

NAME	DATE	CATEGORY	SIG	LS/DS	ALS	SP	COMMENTS
Shalamar		Entertainment	12	15	60	50	
Shaler, Alexander		Civil War	35	60	110		Union General
Shalikashvili, John		Military	10	25		20	Chm. Joint Chiefs of Staff
Shamir, Yitzhak		Head of State	25	95	105	75	7th Prime Minister Israel
Shamroy, Leon		Entertainment	20				Director, Cinematographer. AA
Shandling, Gary	1949-	Entertainment	15			35	Comedian. TV Emmy Winner
Shannon, Del		Entertainment	35			80	Country Music
Shannon, Wilson		Governor	25	65	100		Kansas Peacemaker 1870
Shapely, Harlow	1885-1972	Science	20	80			Noted for work on Photometry & Spectroscopy
Shapiro, Harry		Artist	10	25	45		
Shapiro, Karl		Author	10	30	70	20	
Shapiro, Robert		Law		125		37	O.J. Simpson Trial Attorney
Shapley, Alan		Military	10	35	50		
Shapley, Harlow	1885-1972	Science	35	275	150		Astronomer. Dir.Harvard Observ.
Shapp, Milton J.		Governor	10	20			Governor PA
Sharan, Shri Chakradhar		Head of State	15	35		75	Pres. India
Sharett, Moshe (Shertok)	1894-1965	Head of State	50		325		Israeli Prime Minister
Sharif, Omar		Entertainment	15	25	60	52	Egyptian Actor-Champion Tournament Bridge
Sharkey, Ray		Entertainment	7	22		25	
Sharman, Helen		Astronaut		55		45	First British Astronaut in Space Aboard A Soyuz
Sharnova, Sonia		Entertainment	10			25	Am. Contralto
Sharon, Ariel		Military	20	50	90	45	Israeli General, Politician
Sharon, William		Senate-Business	45	110	200		Senator NV, Banker & Financier
Sharp, U. S. Grant		Military	10	25	35	15	
Sharp, William		Artist	15	40	105		
Sharpe, George H.		Civil War	20	45			Union Gen., Diplomat
Sharpe, Karen		Entertainment	4	6		8	
Sharpe, William, Dr.		Economist	22	30		25	Nobel Enconomics 1990
Sharpton, Al, Rev.		Clergy	20			35	
Shatner, William		Entertainment	12			48	Star Trek SP $75
Shaud, Grant		Entertainment	10			30	Murphy Brown
Shaunessy, Charles		Entertainment	5	6	15	15	
Shavelson, Melville		Entertainment	5	10		25	
Shaver, Helen		Entertainment	10			25	
Shaw, Anna Howard	1847-1919	Women's Rights	35	80	175		Physician, Suffragist, Clergy
Shaw, Artie		Entertainment	25			60	Big Band Leader-Clarinetist
Shaw, Bernard		Journalist	10			25	TV Broadcast Journalist
Shaw, Brewster H.		Astronaut	6			15	
Shaw, George Bernard	1856-1950	Author	350	948	1486	1160	Ir. Playwright, Critic. Nobel Prize. FDC $500
Shaw, Irwin		Author	25	70	170	40	Am.Novelist, Short Story Writer
Shaw, Lemuel		Rev. War	15	40	75		Chf.Justice MA Supreme Court
Shaw, Leslie M.	1848-1932	Cabinet	30	35	50		Sec'y Treasury 1902
Shaw, Robert	1916-99	Entertainment	32			122	Conductor Robert Shaw Chorale
Shawn, Dick		Entertainment	40			100	
Shawn, Ted		Entertainment	45			100	Am. Dancer-Choreographer

NAME	DATE	CATEGORY	SIG	LS/DS	ALS	SP	COMMENTS
Shay, John		Entertainment	4	6		10	
Shayne, Robert		Entertainment	10			30	
Shazar, Zalman		Head of State	20			60	Israel
Shea, George Beverly		Clergy	15	20	25	30	Singing Evangelist
Shea, John		Entertainment	4			15	Actor
Shea, William A.		Business	5	20	40	10	
Shear, Rhonda		Entertainment	4			10	TV Personality
Shearer, Moira		Entertainment	50		70	85	Ballet. The Red Shoes
Shearer, Norma	1902-83	Entertainment	84	202		302	AA. Bull Orig. SP $650
Shearing, George		Entertainment	20			45	Jazz Pianist
Sheedy, Ally		Entertainment	6	15		30	
Sheehan, John		Entertainment	10				Character Actor
Sheen, Charlie		Entertainment	10			42	
Sheen, Fulton J.,	1895-1979	Clergy-TV Star	50	70	175	50	Archbishop Rochester, NY. Television Personality
Sheen, Martin		Entertainment	9	45		25	A A
Sheffer, Chris		Entertainment	6	8	15	15	
Sheffield, Johnny		Entertainment	10			29	As Child Played Tarzan's Son
Shehan, Lawrence J., Cardinal		Clergy	35	45	50	60	
Shelby, Isaac	1750-1826	Rev. War	325	350	550		Officer VA Militia. 1st Gov. KY
Shelby, Joseph O. (WD)		Civil War	450				CSA Gen.
Shelby, Joseph O.	1830-97	Civil War	280	1519	1250	1950	CSA General
Sheldon, Charles M.		Clergy	20	35	50	40	
Sheldon, Sidney		Author	5	15	25	15	Am. Novelist
Shelley, Mary Wollstonecraft		Author	475	1050	1412		Frankenstein
Shelley, Percy Bysshe		Author	1060	2500	4375		ALS/Content $14,000
Shelton, Deborah		Entertainment	8	9		20	Pin-Up SP $30, Miss USA
Shepard, Alan B.	1923-	Astronaut	65	500		125	1st Am. In Space. Mercury 7 Astro., Moonwalker
Shepherd, Ben		Entertainment	6			25	Music. Bass, Vocals Soundgarden
Shepherd, Cybill		Entertainment	152	25		50	Pin-Up SP $40
Shepherd, William M.		Astronaut	5			15	
Shepis, Tiffany		Entertainment	5			15	Actress. Pin-Up $22
Sheppard, Dick		Clergy	25	35	50	30	
Sheppard, Morris		Senator/Congress	10	20		15	Rep., Sen. TX. Author 18th Amend.
Shera, Mark		Entertainment	5			20	
Sheridan, Ann		Entertainment	50			120	40's Oomph Girl
Sheridan, Nicollette		Entertainment	15			35	Pin-Up SP $60
Sheridan, Philip H. (WD)		Civil War	261	1500	4500	2175	Union Gen.
Sheridan, Philip H.	1831-88	Civil War	215	580	592	1765	Union Cmdg. Gen.
Sheridan, Richard Brinsley		Author	65	120	370		Ir. Dramatist, Politician. 1751-1816
Sherlock, Nancy		Astronaut	7			20	
Sherman, Forrest P.		Military	20	50	95	50	Adm. WW II. Ch. Naval Operationsl
Sherman, Frederick C.		Military	20	45	70	35	Adm. Cmdr Carrier Lexington
Sherman, George		Entertainment	10			25	
Sherman, James S.	1855-1912	Vice President	75	275	325	230	Taft VP. MOC
Sherman, John	1823-1900	Cabinet-Senate	98	750	315	180	Sherman Anti-Trust Act, Sec'y Treas. RR ALS $1450

NAME	DATE	CATEGORY	SIG	LS/DS	ALS	SP	COMMENTS
Sherman, Richard and Robert		Composer	40	60	100		AMusQS $150
Sherman, Roger	1721-93	Rev. War	205	582	975		Signed All 4 Major Fed. Papers. Only Am. To Do So.
Sherman, Thomas West		Civil War	30	55	85		Union General
Sherman, William T. (WD)		Civil War	435	1750	5950	2000	Content ALS's go up to & incl.$50,000+
Sherman, William T.	1820-91	Civil War	404	512	985	1925	Union Gen.War. Content ALS $7500, $17,500
Sherriff, Robert C.	1896-1975	Author	45		140	80	Playwright, Novelist, Screenwriter
Sherwood, (Mary) Martha	1775-1851	Author	10	15	35		Br. Author Juvenile Tales
Sherwood, Bobby		Entertainment	6	8	15	15	
Sherwood, Isaac R.		Senate/Congress	10	15		20	Rep. OH 1873
Sherwood, Percy		Composer	25			60	Ger. Pianist. AMusQS $75
Sherwood, Robert E.	1896-	Author-Cabinet	30	95	195	50	Am.Plays,Speeches FDR,Pulitzers
Sherwood, Samuel	1779-1862	Cogress	20	35	50		Rep. NY 1813
Shields, Arthur		Entertainment	10			25	Actor-Brother Barry Fitzgerald
Shields, Brooke	1965-	Entertainment	10	12	35	45	Actress. Films & TV. Pin-Up SP $36
Shields, James		Civil War	50	80	115		Union Gen., U.S Sen.IL,MN,MO
Shigeta, James		Entertainment	6	8	15	20	
Shillaber, Benjamin P.	1814-90	Author		50	110		Humorist-Editor
Shimmerman, Armin		Entertainment	15			35	Star Trek
Shinn, Conrad S.		Aviation		35		25	Landed 1st Plane at So.Pole
Shipman, Nina		Entertainment	4			15	Hawaiian Leading Lady
Shippen, Edward		Rev. War	45	95	165		Ch. Justice PA, Statesman
Shipstad, Henrik	1881-1960	Congress	5	20		25	Senator MN 1922
Shiras, George, Jr. (SC)		Supreme Court	90	250	375		
Shire, David		Composer	15			30	Oscar winner
Shire, Talia		Entertainment	15			35	
Shirer, William L.		Author	15	40		25	News Commentator. Berlin Diary S 50
Shirley, Anne		Entertainment	15	15	35	30	
Shirley, William	1693-1771	Colon'l Gov. MA	180	475			Cmdr.-in-Chief, Explorer, Colonial Gov. MA
Shivers, Allan		Governor	12			30	Governor TX
Shockley, William, Dr.		Science	35	150	165	100	Nobel Physics 1956. Transistor
Shoemaker, Eugene M. & Carolyn		Science	45			75	Discovered Meteor Crater
Shoemaker, Lazarus D.		Senate/Congress	10	20		15	Rep. PA 1871
Shoemaker, Vaughn*		Cartoonist	10			75	Pulitzer Prize Editorial Cartoonist.John Q. Public
Shoemaker, William L.		Author	5	8	15		
Shoen, Sam		Business	5	15	35	25	
Shoma, William		Aviation	15	32	50	40	ACE, WW II, CMH
Shoop, Pamela Susan		Entertainment	5	6	15	15	
Shor, Bernard Toots		Business	30	45	75	35	NY Restaurateur.Celebrity Host
Shore, Dinah	1917-94	Entertainment	15	31	100	50	Singer-Actress-TV Host. Golf Sponsor
Shore, Pauley		Entertainment	10				Signed 'In The Army Now' Poster $55
Shore, Roberta		Entertainment	7			25	Actress. Movies-TV Disney Star. The Virginian
Short, Bobby		Entertainment	5			20	Nightclub Pianist-Vocalist
Short, Martin		Entertainment	15			50	
Shortridge, Samuel	1861-1952	Congress	10	20			Senator CA 1920
Shostakovich, Dmitri	1906-75	Composer	468	1150	2167	2000	ALS/Content $3,200, 4000, AMusQS $750-$2500

NAME	DATE	CATEGORY	SIG	LS/DS	ALS	SP	COMMENTS
Shoumatoff, Elizabeth		Artist	35	45	75		Painting FDR Portrait At Time Of Death. Repro S 295
Shoup, David M.	1904-1983	Military	25	40	80	95	MOH Winning Cmdr. 2nd Marines. Commandant
Shoup, Francis, A.	1834-96	Civil War	85		348		CSA Gen. Sig/Rank $120
Shoup, George L.	1836-1904	Congress	12	20	35		1st Gov. ID, Senator ID 1890
Show, Grant		Entertainment	6			32	Actor
Showalter, Max		Entertainment	6	10	15	15	
Shower, Kathy		Entertainment	5				Actress-Model. Nude SP 60
Shrimpton, Jean		Entertainment	5	6	15	10	
Shriner, Herb		Entertainment	4	5		15	
Shriver, Edmund V	1812-99	Civil War	20	40			Union Gen.
Shriver, Eunice Kennedy		Celebrity	15			35	Sister JFK, Wife Sargent Shriver
Shriver, Loren J.		Astronaut	7			28	
Shriver, Maria		Journalist	6			15	Broadcast Journalist
Shriver, Sargent		White House	4	10	25	20	Created Job Corps
Shroyer, Sonny		Entertainment	3			7	
Shrum, Cal		Entertainment	4			25	Cowboy Actor
Shubert, John		Entertainment	5	9		15	
Shubert, Lee	1873-1953	Business	20	70	85	40	Theatrical Mgr.-Producer
Shue, Andrew		Entertainment	8			52	Actor
Shue, Elizabeth	1963-	Entertainment	10			52	Actress. Pin-Up S $75
Shugart, Alan		Inventor	10	20		20	Computer Disk Drive
Shulman, Ellen L.		Astronaut	6			25	
Shulman, Max		Writer	10			20	Creator Dobie Gillis
Shultz, George P.		Cabinet	15	25	55	50	Sec'y State, Labor, Treasury
Shuman, Charles B.		Celebrity	3	7	15	5	
Shuster, W. Morgan		Business	10	15	35	15	Chm.Appleton-Century-Crofts
Sibelius, Jan	1865-1957	Composer	352	900	1625	1142	Fin.Symph. AMusQS $1600-1850-3500, SPc $1115
Sibley, Henry H.	1816-86	Civil War	100	450	438		CSA Gen.,Pioneer, Indian Fighter. Gov MN
Sickles, Daniel E.	1819-1914	Civil War	95	240	200	175	Union General, MOH winner
Sickles, Noel*		Cartoonist	20			175	Scorchy
Siddons, F. Scott, Mrs.		Entertainment	25			50	Vintage Actress
Siddons, Sarah Kemble	1755-1831	Entertainment	175		850		18th-19th Cent. Br. Tragedienne
Sidney, George		Entertainment	15			35	Film Director
Sidney, Robert, Sir	1563-1626	Miltary	150	920			Poet Brother of Sir Philip. Earl of Essex
Sidney, Sylvia		Entertainment	10	15	25	35	Vintage Actress from 30's. Still Active
Siegbahn, Kai Manne		Science	30	55	100	90	Nobel Physics 1981
Siegbahn, Karl Manne G.	1886-1978	Science	35	65	130	100	Nobel Physics 1924
Siegel & Shuster*		Cartoonist	150			900	Superman
Siegel, Don		Entertainment	20	65		40	Film Director
Siegel, Franz		Civil War	40	85	200		Union General
Siegel, Jerry	1915-96	Entertainment	10	25		15	One of Creators. Superman
Siegel, Joel		Journalist	4			10	TV Film Reviewer
Siegfried & Roy		Entertainment	10			20	Animal Trainers
Siegmeister, Elie		Composer	25	85	175	40	
Siems, Margarethe		Entertainment	45			110	Opera

NAME	DATE	CATEGORY	SIG	LS/DS	ALS	SP	COMMENTS
Sienkiewicz, Henryk	1846-1916	Author			350		Polish Writer. Nobel. Quo Vadis
Siepi, Cesare		Entertainment	15			65	Opera. Self-Taught Bass
Sierra, Gregory		Entertainment	4	4	9	9	
Sierra, Margarita		Entertainment	3	3	6	6	
Sigall, Joseph		Artist	100	190	385		Pres. Portraits & Eur. Royalty
Sigel, Franz	1824-1902	Civil War	55	115	210		Union General
Sighele, Mietta		Entertainment	10			30	Opera
Sigler, Kim		Governor	5	15		10	Governor MI
Signac, Paul	1863-1935	Artist	142	170	700		Fr. Watercolor Land & Seascapes. Neo-Impressionist
Signoret, Simone	1921-1985	Entertainment	52			168	Oscar winner
Sigourney, Lydia Howard H.	1791-1865	Author		95	175		Most Famous Lady Writer in Am 1830's. Professional
Sigsbee, Charles D.		Military	35	105	165	75	Capt. USN The Maine
Sihanouk, Norodom, Prince		Head of State	125	95	155	75	Cambodia
Sikes, Cynthia		Entertainment	5			15	Pin-up SP $25
Sikking, James B.		Entertainment	6	8	15	15	
Sikorsky, Igor I.	1889-1972	Aviation	100	268	350	373	Designed & Built 1st Helicopter. Aviation HOF
Silhouette, Etienne de	1709-67	Cabinet		950			Fr. Controller Gen., Financier, Silhouette so Named
Silhouette, Etienne de	1709-67	Financier		950			Fr.Controller Gen. Silhouette Named For Stinginess
Silja, Anja		Entertainment	15			40	Opera
Sill, Susan		Astronaut	7			25	
Silla, Felix		Entertainment	5			15	Actor. Addams Family
Silliman, Benjamin	1816-85	Science	30	65	125		Am.Chemist. Editor. Professor
Silliman, Gold Sellick	1732-90	Rev. War	70	175			Colonel & Brig. General
Sills, Beverly		Entertainment	15		125	33	Am. Soprano
Sills, Milton	1882-1930	Entertainment	30	40	75	80	Leading Man of Silent Films
Siloti, Alexander		Composer	55		225		Pianist, Conductor
Silver, Abba Hillel		Zionist	15	50			Zionist Leader
Silver, Joe	1921-89	Entertainment	10			20	Actor
Silver, Ron		Entertainment	15			40	Actor-Director
Silverheels, Jay		Entertainment	175			500	
Silverman, Fred		Business	3	9	20	10	Broadcasting Executive
Silverman, Jonathan		Entertainment	5			10	
Silverman, Robert		Entertainment	10	15		45	Contemporary Pianist
Silvers, Phil	1912-85	Entertainment	32	60	125	100	Am. Comedian-Actor. Sgt Bilko
Silverstone, Alicia	1976-	Entertainment	10	35		58	Actress. Pin-Up SP $80
Sim, Alastair !900-76		Entertainment		90		150	Br. Actor
Simenon, Georges	1903-89	Author	65	100	275	125	Fr-Belg. Creator Inspector Maigret
Simeon II		Royalty	80				King of Bulgaria 1937
Simeon, Charles		Clergy	45		75		
Simmons, E.H.H.		Business	25	40			Pres. NY Stock Exchange
Simmons, Gene (Kiss)		Entertainment	10			35	Rock. Love Gun Alb. S $85
Simmons, Jean		Entertainment	8		22	35	Pert Brit. Actress. Child to Spartacus etc.
Simmons, Richard		Entertainment	15			40	Actor
Simmons, Richard		Entertainment	5			15	Diet & Aerobics
Simms, Ginny		Entertainment				22	Band Vocalist

NAME	DATE	CATEGORY	SIG	LS/DS	ALS	SP	COMMENTS
Simms, William G.		Author	35	100	250		Lawyer, Pro-Slavery Editor
Simon and Garfunkel		Entertainment	40			100	LP S $110 (Both)
Simon, Carly		Entertainment	20			50	Singer-Composer
Simon, Claude		Author	150				Nobel Literature 1985
Simon, Herbert A.		Science	20	35	50	25	Nobel Economics
Simon, Jules	1814-96	Head of State		45	110		Premier of France. Orator. Prof. Philosophy, Sorbonne
Simon, Neil		Author	45	75	150	75	Playwright, Screenwriter
Simon, Norton		Industrialist	15	35	65	25	Norton Simon, Inc., Philanthropy
Simon, Paul		Composer	20			75	Entertainer
Simon, Paul Martin		Congress	5			10	Repr., Senator IL
Simon, Simone	1911-	Entertainment	20			70	Pouty Fr. Actress
Simon, William E.		Cabinet	5	15	25	20	Sec'y Treasury
Simoneau, Leopold		Entertainment	5			25	Opera
Simpson, Alan		Congress	5	10		15	Senator WY
Simpson, James H.	1813-83	Civil War	30	70			Union Gen.
Simpson, James Y., Sir		Science	35	95	385		Scot. 1st Obstetric Ether Use
Simpson, Louis		Author	20			65	Am. Poet
Simpson, Matthew	1811-84	Clergy	90				Methodist Bishop. Lincoln Eulogy
Simpson, O.J.		Celebrity				150	Accused Murderer-Acquitted
Simpson, Russell		Entertainment	50			120	Grapes of Wrath, Meet John Doe
Simpson, Wallis Warfield		Head of State	110		675		Became Duchess of Windsor
Simpson, William H.	1888-	Military	25	150	400	75	Gen. WW II
Sims, William S.	1858-1936	Military	30	250	115	50	Adm. USN WW I, Pulitzer Author
Sinatra, Frank	1915-98	Entertainment	262	533		921	Actor-Singer AA, MGM DS $875. SP Pc $630
Sinatra, Nancy		Entertainment	5	30	20	15	Pin-Up SP $25
Sinclair, Harry F.		Business	140	175	350	200	Teapot Dome
Sinclair, Upton	1878-1968	Author	58	88	150	125	Am. Writer-Socialist Politician, Novelist
Sinding, Christian A.		Composer	45	120	210		Symphonies, Concertos, Sonatas
Singer, Isaac Bashevis	1904-91	Author	40	200	300	175	Nobel Lit. '78. Polish Passport $1800, US $1000
Singer, Isaac M.	1811-75	Inventor	575		2500		Singer Sewing Machine
Singer, Marc		Entertainment	10	12		30	
Singlaub, John K.		Military	10	20	35	20	General WW II
Singleton, Penny		Entertainment	5	20		25	Blondie (Dagwood & Blondie) Popular 40's Films
Sinise, Gary		Entertainment	15	20	30	70	Oscar winner
Sinopoli, Giuseppe		Conductor	5			35	
Sioli, Franco		Entertainment	5			15	Opera
Siple, Paul A.		Aviation	22	45			Explorer, Geographer
Sirica, John J.	1904-93	Jurist	20	35		50	Watergate Judge. Respected Federal Judge
Sirk, Don		Entertainment	65				Film Director
Siroky, Villiam		Head of State	50				Premier Czech.
Sirtis, Marina		Entertainment	10			35	Actress. Star Trek
Siskel, Gene	1947-99	Entertainment	12			15	Film Critic. Siskel & Ebert
Sisley, Alfred	1839-99	Artist	150	400	1193		Fr. Impressionist. Landscape Painter
Sissle, Noble		Entertainment	25			50	Big Band Leader-Arranger
Sitgreaves, John		Rev. War	30	75	145		Officer. Continental Congress

NAME	DATE	CATEGORY	SIG	LS/DS	ALS	SP	COMMENTS
Sitting Bull (T. Iyotake)		Indian Leader	6817				Sioux Indian Leader
Sitwell, Edith, Dame	1887-1964	Author	70	135	185	660	Br.Poet, Critic, Novelist
Sitwell, Osbert, Sir	1892-1969	Author	35	70	148		Playwright, Novelist
Sixty Minutes (all)		Entertainment	25			45	
Sizoo, Joseph R.		Clergy	20	25	35		
Skaggs, Ricky		Country Music	10			20	
Skala, Lilia		Entertainment	10	15	25	30	
Skelly, William Grove		Business	320				Founder Skelly Oil, Financier
Skelton, Red	1913-97	Entertainment	35	53	40	72	Film-TV Comedian.Sm.Original Clown Painting S $395
Skerrit, Tom		Entertainment	8	18	20	20	Actor. Emmy Awards. DS re Top Gun $150
Skinner, B. F.		Author	20	30	50	75	Behavioral Psychology-Theorist
Skinner, Cornelia Otis	1901-50	Entertainment	10	40	50	28	Actress, Monologuist, Author
Skinner, Cortlandt	1728-99	Military	40	85	155		Born NJ. Loyalist General
Skinner, Otis	1858-1942	Entertainment	53	45	70	65	Vintage Stage Star
Skinner, Samuel K.		Cabinet	10	20			Sec'y Transportation
Skinner, Stella		Artist	25	40	75		
Skipworth, Alison		Entertainment	15	15	30	25	
Skorzeny, Otto	1908-75	Military	245	225	540	500	Nazi SS Officer & Adventurer
Skouras, Spyros	1893-1971	Business	15			175	Fndr-Pres-Chm 20th Century Fox
Skovhus, Boje		Entertainment	10		25		Opera
Slack, Freddie		Bandleader				45	
Slade, Chris		Entertainment	6			25	Music. Drummer AC/DC
Slade, William	1786-1859	Congress	12				Repr. VT, Gov. VT
Slater, Christian	1969-	Entertainment	10			48	Actor
Slater, Helen		Entertainment	8	15	30	50	
Slaughter, Frank G.		Author	8	15	35	10	
Slayton, Donald K. Deke		Astronaut	45	110	100	122	Mercury 7 Astro (Deceased)Flight DS $750
Sledd, Patsy		Country Music	4			12	Pin-Up SP $15
Slezak, Leo	1873-1946	Entertainment	45	60		125	Great Austrian Tenor, Opera. SPc $75
Slezak, Walter		Entertainment	15			35	
Slick, Grace		Entertainment	25			40	
Slidell, John	1793-1871	Civil War	75	450	195		Statesman, CSA Diplomat
Slim, Wm. Joseph, Sir		Military	30	75	120	60	Br. General WW II
Sliwa, Curtis		Celebrity	10			20	Founder of Guardians
Sliwa, Lisa		Celebrity	6	15		10	NY Street Protection Group
Sliwinski, Josef		Entertainment	20		100	75	Pol Pianist
Sloan, Alfred P. Jr.	1875-1966	Business	45	95		65	Sloan-Kettering Inst. CEO GM. Philanthropist
Sloan, John	1779-1856	Cabinet	20	45	95		Fillmore Treasurer of U.S.
Sloan, John	1871-1951	Artist	85	275	612		Am.Painter, Etcher, Illustrator. 'Ashcan School'
Sloane, Everett		Entertainment	30			55	
Sloat, John Drake		Civil War	45	95	130		Union Naval Officer
Slocum, Henry Warner	1827-94	Civil War	75	75	150		Union General, Rep. NY
Slough, John P. (WD)		Civil War	160		950		Union Gen. Killed in Gunfight 1867
Small, John Humphrey		Senate/Congress	5		15		Rep. NC 1899
Smallens, Alexander		Conductor	20			50	World Premiere Porgy & Bess

NAME	DATE	CATEGORY	SIG	LS/DS	ALS	SP	COMMENTS
Smallwood, Norma		Entertainment	20			50	Miss America 1926
Smart, Jean		Entertainment	5			15	
Smashing Pumpkins		Entertainment	45			142	Music. 4 Member Rock Group
Smathers, George A.		Senate/Congress	5		25	15	Rep., Senator FL 1947
Smear, Pat		Entertainment	8			55	Music. Lead Singer Foo Fighters
Smedberg, William	1871-1942	Military		35		40	WW I Gen. Hero of Sp.-Am. War
Smedley, Richard		Entertainment	3	3	6	8	
Smetana, Bedrich		Composer	1500		9000		Czech. Operas, Symphonies etc.
Smiley, Delores		Country Music	10			20	
Smirnoff, Dimitri		Entertainment	30	55	95		Russian Tenor
Smirnoff, Yakov		Entertainment	8			15	
Smith, Adam	1723-1790	Economist	3000				Architect of Br. Political Econ
Smith, Addison T.		Senate/Congress	5	10	15		Rep. ID 1913
Smith, Al*		Cartoonists	15			60	Mutt & Jeff
Smith, Albert E. & Blackton, J. Stuart	SEE Blackton						
Smith, Alexis	1921-93	Entertainment	15	45		35	Warner Bros. Beautiful 40'-50's Leading Lady
Smith, Alfred E.	1873-1944	Governor	50	83	400	105	Presidential Candidate, Gov NY.1st Catholic Nom.
Smith, Anna Nicole		Entertainment	10			45	Model-Actress. Nude Pin-up SP $95
Smith, Armistead B.		Aviation	10	22	38	28	ACE, WW II, Navy Ace
Smith, Ashbel		Civil War	140		615		TX Historical Politician, CSA
Smith, Bernie		Entertainment	6	8	15	15	
Smith, Betty		Author	50	110		65	
Smith, Bob		Congress	5			15	MC from Oregon. Agricultural Comm. Chm.
Smith, C. Aubrey		Entertainment	35			80	
Smith, C.R.	1899-19—	Aviation	25	75		45	American Airlines. Aviation Hall of Fame.Cabinet
Smith, Caleb	1808-64	Cabinet	40	200	365		Lincoln Attorney General
Smith, Carl		Country Music	5			12	
Smith, Charles E.		Cabinet	15		25	20	P.M. General 1898
Smith, Charles M.		Entertainment	10			25	
Smith, Charles M.		Governor	5	15			Governor VT
Smith, Connie		Country Music	5			12	
Smith, Edmund K. (WD)		Civil War	390	975	1420		CSA Gen.
Smith, Edmund Kirby	1824-93	Military	325	645	798		CSA Gen. War Dte. S $390, DS $1105, ALS $1500
Smith, Edmund Kirby	1824-93	Civil War	300		615		CSA General
Smith, Edward K.	1850-1912	Navy			8995		Capt. Of Ill-Fated Titanic
Smith, Elinor		Aviation	45	100	160	130	
Smith, Elizabeth Oakes		Reformer	90	205	385		Early Supporter Woman Suffrage
Smith, Ellison	1864-1944	Congress	5	25			Sen. SC
Smith, Elmo		Governor	10	25			Governor OR
Smith, Elton		Aviation	15	30			World Helicopter Record '52
Smith, Ely	1825-1911	Congress					Rep. NY, Mayor NYC
Smith, F. E.		Celebrity	36				
Smith, Francis Hopkinson	1838-	Artist	15	20	35		Am.Engineer-Artist-Illustrator
Smith, Francis M. Borax		Business	30	65	95		Founder U.S. Borax Co.
Smith, Frank, Bishop		Clergy	15	20	25	25	

NAME	DATE	CATEGORY	SIG	LS/DS	ALS	SP	COMMENTS
Smith, Frederick W.		Business	15	30	55	20	Fndr., Chm. Federal Express
Smith, George Washington		Senate/Congress	5	15			Rep. IL 1889
Smith, Gerrit	1797-1874	Senate/Congress	50		312		Abolitionist, Reformer, Rep.NY, Philanthropist
Smith, Gipsy		Clergy	25	45	75	35	
Smith, Gordon		Congress	5			15	US Senator from Oregon
Smith, Green Clay	1826-95	Civil War	50	75	150		Union Gen., Congress KY
Smith, Gustavus W.(WD)		Civil War	140	355	715		CSA General. LS/Cont. $2500
Smith, H. Allen		Senate/Congress	5	10		10	MOC. CA 1957
Smith, Hamilton		Science	20	30	45	25	Nobel Medicine 1978
Smith, Harry		Journalist	5	10		15	Broadcast Journalist
Smith, Harsen		Business	3	10	25	10	
Smith, Hoke	1855-1931	Cabinet	10	35	70	30	Gov.,Sen. GA, Sec'y Int.1911
Smith, Holland M., Gen'l	1882-1967	Military					Iwo Jima Flag Raising FDC $550. 'Howlin' Mad'
Smith, Howard	1893-1968	Entertainment	25			40	Active Character Actor 40's. Death of a Salesman
Smith, Howard K.		Journalist	15			65	TV CBS News Anchor Opposite Huntley-Brinkley
Smith, Ian		Head of State	10	20	50	30	South Africa?
Smith, Ida B. Wise		Reformer	30	55	95		Temperance Advocate, WCTU
Smith, J. Gregory		Governor	5	15		10	Governor VT
Smith, Jaclyn		Entertainment	9	15	20	25	Actress. A 'Charlie's Angels'. Pin-Up SP $30
Smith, James	1719-1806	Rev. War	235	888	3750		Signer Decl. of Indepen.
Smith, James Y.		Governor	35	60			Civil War Gov. RI
Smith, James, Jr.	1851-1927	Congress	10	15			Senator NJ 1911
Smith, Joe		Entertainment	15			45	
Smith, John	1580-1631	Colonial Am.	2200	11500	29000		NRPA-RARE
Smith, John Pye		Clergy	20	25	35		
Smith, Joseph	1805-44	Religious Leader	775	1775			Founder Morman Church
Smith, Julia Holmes, Dr.		Science	90		425		1st Pres. Women's Med. Assoc.
Smith, Kate		Entertainment	45	195	175	100	Clear, Strong-voiced. Introduced God Bless America
Smith, Keely	1932-	Entertainment	10			30	Band Vocalist for Louis Prima. Jazz Specialist
Smith, Kent	1907-	Entertainment	6			15	Harvard Educated Actor. Atypical Hollywood Lead.
Smith, L. C.		Business	50	135	240		L.C.Smith Typewriters, Business Machines etc.
Smith, Maggie		Entertainment	15	25	30	35	Br. AA Winner.'Prime of Miss Jean Brodie'
Smith, Margaret Chase		Senate/Congress	10	20		20	Columnist, Rep., Sen. ME
Smith, Martha		Entertainment	5			15	
Smith, Martin Luther (WD)		Civil War	130		575		CSA Gen. ALS/Cont.$2750
Smith, Martin Luther	1819-66	Civil War	75	135	240		CSA General
Smith, Matthew		Rev. War	25	75			
Smith, Melancton	1744-98	Rev. War	75	140			Continental Congress
Smith, Melancton	1810-93	Civil War	40	85	120		Un. Adm. Served Under Farragut
Smith, Michael J.		Astronaut	275			375	Died on Challenger. Postal Cover $375
Smith, Nels H.F.		Governor	5	10		15	Governor WY
Smith, R.T.		Aviation	15	30	40	40	ACE, WW II, Flying Tigers
Smith, Richard	1735-1803	Rev. War	50	130	250		Continental Congress
Smith, Robert 'Buffalo Bob'		Entertainment	16	20		90	Howdy Doody. Early TV Personality.
Smith, Robert	1757-1842	Cabinet	55	170	290		Att'y Gen.,Sec'y Navy,Sec'y St.

NAME	DATE	CATEGORY	SIG	LS/DS	ALS	SP	COMMENTS
Smith, Robert H. 'Snuffy'		Aviation	15	30	50	45	ACE, WW II, Flying Tigers
Smith, Rodney Gipsy		Clergy	50	50	85	50	
Smith, Roger		Entertainment	5			20	Actor
Smith, Roy L., Bishop		Clergy	20	30	45	30	
Smith, Samuel F.	1752-1839	Rev. War	75	175	255		Gen'l, Rep., Sen. MD.
Smith, Samuel Francis	1808-95	Clergy-Poet	100	650	478		AQS America $500-$700-$795-$1800,$2,250
Smith, Shelley		Entertainment	5			10	Pin-Up SP $20
Smith, Stanley		Entertainment	9			25	Stage
Smith, Steve		Astronaut	5			20	
Smith, Susan M.		Entertainment	5			10	Playboy Centerfold. Pin-Up SP $15
Smith, Sydney*		Cartoonist	30			150	'The Gumps'
Smith, Thomas A.		Military	95	240			Fort Smith Arkansas. General
Smith, Thomas Church Haskell	1819-97	Civil War	29	55	80		Union General
Smith, Tom E.		Business	5	15	30	20	Pres. Food Lion Grocery Chain
Smith, Truman	1791-1884	Senate-Cabinet	10	25	40		Rep., Sen. CT, Sec'y Interior
Smith, W. Angie, Bishop		Clergy	20	25	35	25	
Smith, W. Wallace		Clergy	40	45	60		
Smith, Walter Bedell		Military	35	50	115	50	Gen. WW II, Ambass., Dir. CIA
Smith, Will		Entertainment	10			50	Independence Day Co-Star
Smith, William		Entertainment	5			10	Actor
Smith, William (WD)		Civil War	220	375			CSA Gen. War Dte. ALS/Cont $3475
Smith, William	1797-1887	Civil War	135	280	295		CSA Gen., Congress, Gov. VA.
Smith, William Farrar	1824-1903	Civil War	45		180		Union Gen. Sig/Rank $65, War Dte. ALS $245
Smith, William S.	1755-1816	Rev. War	50	95	225		Rev. Officer. A Fndr. & Pres. Soc. Of Cincinnati
Smith, William Sidney, Sir	1764-	Military	50		185		Br. Adm. Napoleonic War
Smith, Willie The Lion	1910-67	Entertainment	75			125	Jazz Alto-Baritone Sax, Clarinet
Smithers, Jan		Entertainment	6	8		15	Actress
Smits, Jimmy		Entertainment	10			45	Actor. L..A.Law, NYPD Blue
Smoot, Reed	1862-1941	Congress	25	45		45	Senator UT. 1st Morman Sen.
Smothers Bros. (both)		Entertainment	15	50		40	Tommy and Dick
Smucker, Paul		Business	10			25	Smuckers Jams & Jellies
Smuts, Jan Christian	1870-1950	Head of State	45	130	295	250	Fld. Marshal. Pres. Un. So. Afr
Smythe, Reg*		Cartoonist	20	78		112	Created Andy Capp
Snead, Thomas L.		Civil War					
Snell, George D., Dr.		Science	15	30	45	45	Nobel Medicine 1980
Snipes, Wesley		Entertainment	15			70	
Snodgrass, W.D.		Author	25	75		65	
Snow, Charles Percy, Baron		Author	25	80	170	60	Br. Novelist, Physicist
Snow, Hank		Country Music	25	575		50	RCA Country Music Star
Snyder, Howard		Military	10	25			
Snyder, John W.		Cabinet	15	30		25	Sec'y Treas.
Snyder, Simon		Governor	5	15	35		Governor PA
Soarez, Alana		Entertainment	3	5	10	10	Pin-Up SP $15
Sobinov, Leonid	187x-1934	Entertainment	90			375	Russian Tenor
Sockman, Ralph		Clergy	15	20	25		

NAME	DATE	CATEGORY	SIG	LS/DS	ALS	SP	COMMENTS
Soddy, Frederick, Dr.		Science	60	160	275	125	Nobel Chemistry 1921
Soderstrom, Elisabeth		Entertainment				35	Opera
Soglow, Otto		Cartoonist	20			100	The Little King
Sohn, Lee		Entertainment	4			20	Singer
Sokoloff, Vladimir		Entertainment	25			65	
Soles, P. J.		Entertainment	5			15	
Solomon, Charles		Criminal	60	300			Prohibition-Era Bootlegger. Assassinated '33
Solow, Robert M., Dr.		Economics	22	30		25	Nobel Economics 1987
Solti, Georg, Sir		Entertainment	28	45		85	Conductor. Winner of Multiple Grammys
Solzhenitsyn, Alex.	1918-	Author	100	350	648	185	Sov. Novelist. Nobel Lit. 1970
Somers, Suzanne		Entertainment	6			20	Pin-Up SP 60
Somerset, Lord Fitzroy							SEE Raglan
Somervell, Arthur, Sir		Composer	20	55	85		Br.Oratorios...AMusQS $150
Somervell, Brehon B.	1892-	Military	35	125			Gen. WW II
Sommer, Elke		Entertainment	9	10	20	25	Pin-Up SP $30
Sommers, Joannie		Entertainment	3	5		10	
Somoza, Anastasio		Head of State	20	95			Nicaragua
Sondergaard, Gale		Entertainment	40			75	A A
Sondheim, Stephen	1930-	Composer	45	90	142	140	AMusQS $275- $375
Sonny & Cher		Entertainment	30			100	
Sontag, Henrietta Rossi		Entertainment	70			375	Opera
Sontag, Susan		Author	10	25	45	20	
Soo, Jack		Entertainment	150			55	
Soong, T.V. (Tzu-wen)		Diplomat	35	50			Chinese Financier, Negotiator
Sooter, Rudy		Country Music	10			20	
Soper, Donald O.		Clergy	20	25	30	30	
Sopwith, Thos. O. M., Sir		Aviation	65	115	190	100	Br. Pioneer. ALS/Content $850
Sorbo, Kevin		Entertainment	8			40	Actor. Hercules SP $50
Sorenson, Ted		Author	6			15	JFK Aide
Sorkin, Arleen		Entertainment	4	5		10	Pin-Up SP $20
Sorma, Agnes		Entertainment	25				Opera
Sorrel, Gilbert M. (WD)		Civil War	295	2175			CSA Gen.
Sorrel, Gilbert Moxley	1838-1901	Civil War	165	370	428		CSA General
Sorrvia, Agnes		Entertainment	20			45	Opera
Sorvino, Mira		Entertainment	15			54	AA 1996. Supporting Actress
Sorvino, Paul		Entertainment	15			35	
Sothern, (E)dward (A)skew	1846-1923	Entertainment	30	85	120		Actor. 19th Century Romantic Idol
Sothern, Ann	1909-	Entertainment	15		35	45	Actress. Wisecracking Maizie. 40's Star
Soto, Talisa		Entertainment	10			40	Col. Pin-Up SP 60
Soucek, Appolo, Lt.		Aviation	15	25			World Altitude Records
Souez, Ina		Entertainment		50			Opera. Great Mozart Soprano
Soul Asylum		Entertainment					Rock. No Price Available
Soul, David		Entertainment	5	10	20	15	
Soule, Pierre		Civil War	75	170	285		Sessessionist. US Sen.LA., CSA Gen.
Soult, Nicolas J. de Dieu, Duke		Fr. Military	105	325	388		Nap.Marshal of Fr.,Minister War

NAME	DATE	CATEGORY	SIG	LS/DS	ALS	SP	COMMENTS
Soundgarden		Entertainment	35			95	Music. 4 Member Rock Group
Sousa, John Philip	1854-1932	Composer	155	308	515	690	Bandmaster. AMusQs$400-$690-$795-$1250
Soustelle, Jacques		Head of State	5	15	40	15	
Souter, David H. (SC)		Supreme Court	38			55	
Southampton, 1st Earl of	1505-50	Royalty	75	215	450		Politician. Sec'y to Cromwell
Southampton, Thos. W. 4th Earl	1607-67	Royalty	40	155			Lord Treasurer
Southcott, Joanna		Clergy	45	60	90		Br. Religious Fanatic
Southey, Robert	1774-1843	Author	95	280	450		Br. Poet Laureate 1813
Sovine, Red		Country Music	12			35	
Soyer, Raphael	1899-1987	Artist	20	50	140	100	Signed Repro. $200-$300
Soyinka, Wole (Akinwande O.)		Author	25	80			Nigerian. Nobel Literature 1986
Spaak, Paul-Henri		Head of State	15	30	50	25	Belg. Fndr. EEOC, NATO
Spaatz, Carl Tooey	1891-1974	Military-Aviation	55	142		195	Gen. WW II, AF Commander Strategic Bombing
Spacek, Sissy		Entertainment	10	15		40	A A
Spacey, Kevin		Entertainment	15			70	Actor. AA 1996
Spaight, Richard Dobbs	1758-1802	Rev. War	115	325			Continental Congr., Signer Constitution. Killed Duel
Spain, Fay		Entertainment	10			30	
Spalding, Albert	1888-1953	Composer	30			138	Violinist, AMQS $85-$250
Spalding, J. Walter		Business	25	7	140	55	
Spallanzani, Lazzaro	1729-99	Science	120	400	1042		It. Physiologist. Artificial Insem.
Spani, Hina		Entertainment	20			110	Magnificent spinto Soprano
Sparkman, John	1899-1985	Congress	12			25	Senator AL. VP Candidate
Sparks, Chuncey		Governor	5	20			Governor AL
Sparks, Jared	1789-1866	Author	15	35	70		US Historian, Editor, Publisher, Harvard Pres.
Sparks, Ned		Entertainment	25	30	60	70	
Sparks, William E.		Military	15	30	50		
Sparv, Camilla		Entertainment	8	9	25	20	
Spate, Wolfgang		Aviation			125		Ger. Ace WW II. Test Pilot
Spaulding, Albert		Composer	25	65			
Spaulding, Elbridge Gerry	1809-97	Congress	20	45			MOC NY. Father of the Greenback
Spaulding, R.Z.		Business	15	40	55	25	
Speakes, Larry		Cabinet	4	10	16	10	
Speaks, Oley		Composer	38	90	125		On The Road To Mandalay
Spears, Britney		Entertainment	10			55	1999 #1 Record
Specter, Arlen		Congress	10			30	Sen. PA. Presidential Hopeful
Spector, Phil		Entertainment	75	86		115	Rock HOF
Speed, James	1812-87	Cabinet	50	80	140		Lincoln Att'y Gen. ALS/Cont. $995
Speed, John Gilmer		Author	5	15	25		Journalist. Biographer
Speer, Albert	1905-1981	Architect	45	210	275	222	Hitler's Architect & Nazi Leader. FDC S $55
Speer, Robert Elliott		Clergy	15	20	25		
Speer, Robert Milton		Senate/Congress	5	10	20		Rep. PA 1871
Speidel, Hans		Military	35	90	165	75	Nazi Gen., Rommel Chief-of Staff
Speight, John J.	1885-	Senate/Congress	10	25			Lawyer & Judge at Nurenberg War Crimes Trial
Speir, Dona		Entertainment	5			15	Pin-Up SP $20. Playboy Ctrfold
Speke, John	1827-64	Explorer			2250		Found Lake Tanganyika/Rich. Burton

NAME	DATE	CATEGORY	SIG	LS/DS	ALS	SP	COMMENTS
Spelling, Aaron		Entertainment	6	10		25	Film Producer, Writer
Spelling, Tori		Entertainment	8			52	Actress
Spellman, Francis, Cardinal	1889-1967	Clergy	30	48	95	45	
Spelvin, Georgina		Entertainment	5			40	Porn Queen
Spencer, George Eliphaz		Civil War	35	80	145		Union General, Senator AL 1868
Spencer, Herbert, Sir	1820-1903	Author	50	120	225		Br. Philosopher
Spencer, John C.	1788-1855	Cabinet	25	60	105		Tyler Sec'y War
Spencer, John P. 5th Earl		Politician	10	15	35		Liberal Leader House of Lords
Spencer, Joseph	1714-89	Rev. War	200	650			Am. Maj. Gen'l. Defended NY.
Spencer, Susan		TV News	4			10	CBS News
Spender, Stephen	1909-95	Author	65	418	250	75	Br.Poet, Critic. Protest Poetry
Spenser, Tim		Country Music	15			25	Fndr. Sons of the Pioneers
Sperry, Elmer A.	1860-1930	Science	195	375	550	225	Inventor Gyroscope. Co-Founder 'Sperry-Rand'
Sperry, Roger W.		Science	22	30	35	25	Nobel Medicine 1981
Spielberg, David		Entertainment	5	6	15	200	
Spielberg, Steven		Entertainment	85			150	Producer-Director
Spillane, Mickey		Author	35	62	110	55	Am. Detective Fiction. Created Mike Hammer
Spiner, Brent		Entertainment	15			35	Star Trek
Spinner, Francis E.	1802-90	Cabinet	35	120	100		Treasurer for 4 Presidents. Civil War Treasurer
Spinner, Robert		Entertainment	4			25	Actor Star Trek
Spivak, Charlie		Entertainment	20			50	Big Band Leader-Trumpeter
Spock, Benjamin, Dr.		Science	35	55	120	50	Am. Pediatrician-Psychiatrist.Recanted some ideas.
Spofford, Harriet P.	1835-	Author	10	25	40		Am. Romantic Poet, Novelist
Spong, Hilda		Entertainment	15			40	
Spontini, Gaspare, Count de		Composer	95		385		It. Influenced Wagner Operas
Spooner, John C.	1843-1919	Congress	5	15		10	Senator WI 1885
Spooner, William A.		Clergy	25	35	45		Br. Creator Of The Spoonerism
Sprague, Charles A.		Governor	10	20		15	Governor OR
Sprague, Frank Julian		Science	55	100	165	115	Inventor Ass't To Thos. Edison
Sprague, William	1830-1915	Civil War	75	90	105		Union Gen., CW Gov. RI, Senate
Sprague, William Buell		Clergy	45	70	110		
Spreckels, Claus		Business	95	325		175	Am. Sugar Manufacturer
Spring, Gardiner		Clergy	25	35	45		
Spring, Samuel		Clergy	20	25	35		
Spring, Sherwood C.		Astronaut	6			15	
Spring, Woody		Astronaut	7			25	
Springer, Jerry		Entertainment	6			30	Host of Controversial Talk Show
Springer, Robert C.		Astronaut	7			26	
Springfield, Dusty	1939-99	Entertainment	25			45	Br.Singer
Springfield, Rick		Entertainment	14	40		25	Singer
Springfield, Sherry		Entertainment				50	Actress. E.R.
Springsteen, Bruce		Entertainment	50	75	150	162	Rock 'n Roll Superstar
Sproul, William Henry	1867-1932	Congress	4	10			Repr. KS. Farmer. Oil & Gas Exploration
Spruance, Presley	1785-1863	Congress	12	20	40		Senator DE 1847
Spruance, Raymond A.	1886-1969	Military	25	125	130	60	Am. Adm. Victor at Midway WW II

NAME	DATE	CATEGORY	SIG	LS/DS	ALS	SP	COMMENTS
Spurgeon, Charles H.	1834-1932	Clergy	75	105	242		Br. Evangelist & Baptist Minister
Squibb, Edward R.		Business	80	150	255		Pioneer Mfg. of Pharmaceuticals
Squier, Emma		Author	5	10	15		
Squier, George O.		Military	100				General. Inventor Radio Devices
St. Clair, Arthur	1734-1818	Military-Rev. War	135	315	931		Gen.,Pres. Continental Congr.
St. Cyr, Lili	1917-99	Entertainment	12	15	30	40	Exotic Dancer-Actress. Pin-Up SP $50
St. Denis, Ruth	1878-1968	Entertainment	50	140	250	310	Dancer, Choreographer
St. George, T.R. Ozzie		Author	5			28	Post WW II: C/O Postmaster
St. Jacques, Raymond		Entertainment	15			45	African-American actor
St. James, Susan		Entertainment	10			35	Actress. Kate & Allie, McMillan & Wife
St. John, Al Fuzzy		Entertainment	150			350	
St. John, Isaac M.	1827-880	Civil War	85		330		CSA Gen. Sig/Rank $175
St. John, Jill		Entertainment	8	9	20	20	Pin-Up SP $30
St. Johns, Adela Rogers		Author	10	25	45	15	Star Hearst Reporter. Novelist
St. Laurent, Louis		Head of State	10			50	P. M. Canada
St. Vincent, John Jervis	1735-1823	Military	35	65	160		Br. Adm. Of the Fleet. Earl of Vincent
Stabbing Westward		Entertainment	35			85	Music. 5 Member Rock Group
Stabile, Dick		Entertainment	20			40	Big Band Leader
Stacey Q		Entertainment	5			10	Rock
Stacey, John		Aviation	8	20	30	20	
Stack, Robert		Entertainment	10	32		35	AA. Most Wanted emcee. Untouchables
Stack, Rose Marie Bowe		Entertainment	4	5		9	
Stacpoole, Henry de Vere		Author	15	45	80		Writer, Publicist
Stadlman, Anthony		Aviation	10	20	30	20	
Stael, Anne-Louise, Mme. de	1766-1817	Author	65	185	675		Fr. Writer. Exiled By Napoleon
Stafford, Jo		Entertainment	5			15	40's-50's Top Vocalist
Stafford, Robert T.		Governor	8	15	20		Governor VT
Stafford, Susan		Entertainment	10				Actress
Stafford, Thomas P.		Astronaut	15			65	
Stager, Anson		Civil War	20	60	110		Gen.Supt.Govt.Telegraphs
Stahl, Gerald		Aviation				233	Engineer 509th Bomb Gp. (Enola Gay)
Stahl, Leslie		Journalist	5	15		10	TV. 60 Minutes
Stainback, Ingram M.		Governor					Gov. HI 1942-51
Staley, Layne		Entertainment	8			40	Music. Lead Singer Alice in Chains
Stalin, Joseph	1879-1953	Head of State	1290	6700	9250	2150	USSR Dictator. Rare WW II DS $8900
Stalin, Svetlana		Celebrity	35	105	250	45	Daughter of Stalin
Stallone, Sylvester		Entertainment	15	40	75	62	Actor. As Rocky SP $75
Stamos, John		Entertainment	10			35	
Stamp, Terence		Entertainment	10			25	
Stanbery, Henry		Cabinet	10	20	45		Att'y General 1866
Stander, Lionel		Entertainment	10	15	25	25	
Standing, Guy, Sir		Entertainment	25			55	
Standish, Myles		Colonial America	1885	8800	26400		Mayflower Colonist. NRPA
Stanford, Leland	1824-93	Senate	200	1942	3725	312	RR Pres.,Fndr. Stanford U., Gov. CA. Stk. S $30000
Stanford, R. C.		Governor	6	15		10	Governor AZ

NAME	DATE	CATEGORY	SIG	LS/DS	ALS	SP	COMMENTS
Stang, Arnold		Entertainment	5			15	
Stanhope, Edward		Military	10	20	30		
Stanhope, Hester, Lady	1776-1839	Non-Conformist	15	45	95		Adopted Eastern Ways.Prophetess
Stanhope, Phil. H., 5th Earl		Historian	10	20	25		Lord Mahon. M.P., Author
Stanhope, Phil.H., 7th Earl		Celebrity	7	20	45		
Stanhope, Philip D.	1694-1773	Author-Politician	125	420	625		4th Earl Chesterfield. Statesman,Wit,Letter-Writer
Stanislavski, Konstantin	1863-1938	Entertainment	398		950	1860	Rus. Actor, Dir., Producer. Method Acting Tech.
Stanislaw II Augustus Poniatowski		Royalty	95	375	730		Last King of Poland
Stanley, Arthur		Business	4	6		8	Pres. Stanley Works
Stanley, David Sloane		Civil War	25	65	90		Union Gen. Wardte ALS $750
Stanley, Freelan O.		Inventor	325		1400		Auto. Pioneer. Stanley Steamer
Stanley, Henry M.,Sir	1841-1904	Explorer-Civil War	275	350	612	1148	Anglo-Am.Author, Journalist, CSA Civil War
Stanley, Henry, Capt.		Military	10	25	40		
Stanley, Reed (SC)		Supreme Court	25				
Stanley, Wendell M.		Science	20	25	90	30	Nobel Chemistry 1946
Stans, Maurice H.	1908-98	Cabinet	25	40		40	Nixon Sec'y Commerce. Watergate Scandal
Stansbury, Howard	1806-63	Explorer	20	55	100		Surveyor, Military
Stanton, Benjamin		Senate/Congress	20	45	100		Rep. OH.ALS/Content $250
Stanton, Edwin M.	1814-69	Cabinet	150	275	388	150	ALS War Dte $1,495, Sec'y War
Stanton, Elizabeth Cady	1815-1902	Women's Suffrage	190	348	577		1st Pres.Nat'l Women's Suffrage
Stanton, Frank L.		Author	5	15	25		Am. Journalist, Poet, Publ.
Stanton, Frank, Dr.		Business	15	45	80	30	Pres. CBS
Stanton, Harry Dean		Entertainment	6	8	1	20	
Stanwyck, Barbara	1907-90	Entertainment	40	68		88	Actress. Major Film & TV Star. Pin-Up SP $95
Stapleton, Jean		Entertainment	5	25		28	Actress. Best Known as Edith Bunker
Stapleton, Maureen		Entertainment	8	10		25	
Stapp, John, Col.		Military	5	15	20	10	
Stapp, Olivia		Entertainment	10			35	Opera
Stapp, Scott		Entertainment	8			35	Music. Lead Singer Creed
Star Wars (Cast)		Entertainment				375	SP (7)
Stark, Benjamin	1820-98	Congress		30	70		Sen. OR, A Founder of Portland
Stark, Harold R.		Military	15	40	75	40	Adm.,Cmdr.Eur.Waters WW II
Stark, John	1728-1822	Rev. War	440	625	1565		War Dte LS $2500 Gen. Fr & Indian War, Bunker Hill
Starker, Janos		Entertainment	6	8	15	15	
Starkey, Thomas A., Bishop		Clergy	20	35	40		
Starr, Belle		Outlaw	2500	7625			Early West Bandit Queen
Starr, Blaze		Entertainment	15			50	Pin-Up SP $50. Stripper
Starr, Dixie		Entertainment	20				Western Movies. Mrs. Jack Hovie
Starr, Kay		Entertainment	2			65	Big Band Singer. Vocalist
Starr, Kenneth		Legal	8			38	Special Counsel Re. Clinton Investigation
Starr, Leonard*		Cartoonist	25			160	Little Orphan Annie
Starr, Michael		Entertainment	6			25	Music. Bass Alice in Chains
Starr, Ringo		Entertainment	95	367		170	Beatles' Drummer. Endorsed Check $785
Starrett, Charles Durango	1904-88	Entertainment	25	35		88	Early Cowboy Film Star
Starry, Donald A.		Military	5	6	15	10	

NAME	DATE	CATEGORY	SIG	LS/DS	ALS	SP	COMMENTS
Starzl, Thomas E., Dr.		Science	15	25			Transplant Specialist
Stassen, Harold E.		Governor	10	15	35	20	Governor MN
Stassevitch, Paul		Entertainment	25		60		Influenced a Generation of Violinists
Statler, Ellsworth M.		Business	75	205	375	150	Statler Hotel Chain
Statlers, The		Country Music	25			50	
Stead, Wm. Thomas	1849-1912	Journalist	20	60	140	45	Died On Titanic. AQS $95-$125
Stebbins, George C.		Clergy	45	70	95		
Steber, Eleanor		Entertainment	20			75	Opera, Concert
Stedman, Edmund C.	1833-1908	Author	55	90			Poet, NY Stock Broker, Publ.
Steel, Danielle		Author	10	20		25	Novelist
Steele, Barbara	1938-	Entertainment	20			35	Br. Actress. Leads in Br., Am. & Internat'l Films
Steele, Bob & Twin, Bill	1904-	Entertainment	25	30	45	50	Silent Films at Age 14 to Western Starring Roles
Steele, Frederick	1819-68	Civil War	55	95	185		Un.Gen. War Dte/Content ALS $2500
Steele, Karen		Entertainment	5			15	Actress
Steele, Richard, Sir	1672-1729	Author	200	600	1320		Essays, Drama. 'The Tatler'
Steele, Tommy	1936-	Entertainment	15		25	25	Pop Singer-Actor. Former Merchant Seaman
Steely Dan		Entertainment	25			50	Rock (2)
Steenburgen, Mary		Entertainment	10			35	AA Actress
Stefansson, Vilhjalmur	1879-1962	Explorer	65	165	250	295	Arctic Explorer, Ethnologist
Stefanyshyn-Piper, Heide		Astronaut	10			30	
Steffens, Lincoln	1866-1936	Author	85	100	175		Journalist. Leader Muckrakers
Steger, Will		Celebrity	35	95			Arctic explorer
Stegner, Wallace		Author	20		45		Am. Novelist. Pulitzer
Steichen, Edward J.	1879-1973	Artist	85	310	375	475	Pioneer in Photgraphy as Art Form
Steig, William*		Cartoonist	20		85	100	New Yorker Cartoonist
Steiger, Rod		Entertainment	8	35		30	Oscar winner 'In The Heat of The Night'
Steimle, Edmund A.		Clergy	10	15	20		
Stein, Gertrude	1874-1946	Author	522	535	712	795	Expatriate Am. Writer. Resided Paris From 1903
Stein, Jules		Humanitarian-Bus.	50	200			Founder MCA
Steinbeck, John	1902-68	Author	375	2116	2275	1467	Pulitzer, Nobel Lit., DS $2,500
Steinem, Gloria		Feminist	12	25	45	25	Fndr.,Editor Ms Magazine. Feminist Political Leade
Steinhoff, J. 'Mickey'		Aviation	15	25	50	30	
Steinlen, Theophile	1859-1923	Artist	35	105	250		Fr. Known For Posters, Lithography
Steinmetz, Charles P.	1865-1923	Science	75	150	362		Ger.-born Electrical Engineer. Wizard of G. E.
Steinway, Henry Z.		Business	20	55	85	30	Steinway Piano
Steinwehr, Baron Adolph von	1822-77	Civil War	95	170			Union Gen. Geographer, Cartographer
Steiwer, Frederick	1883-1939	Congress	5		15		Senator OR 1926
Stekel, Wilhelm		Science	65	275			Austrian Psychiatrist
Stella, Antonietta		Entertainment	25			55	Opera
Stempel, Robert		Business	25	60		35	Pres. & CEO of Gen. Motors
Sten, Anna	1908-	Entertainment	15	15	30	35	Russ. Actress. Sam Goldwyn Find. Unpopular
Stendhal (Marie H. Beyle)	1783-1842	Author	350	1020	2315		19th Cent. Fr. Novelist. Served in Napoleon's Army
Stengle, Charles I.		Senate/Congress	5	15	25		Rep. NY 1923
Stennis, John C.		Senate/Congress	10	15			Sen. MS 1947. Pres. Pro Tem.
Stephanie, Princess		Royalty	10			25	Princess of Monaco

NAME	DATE	CATEGORY	SIG	LS/DS	ALS	SP	COMMENTS
Stephanopoulos, George		Government	10	20		25	White House Aide. Author
Stephen, Adam	1730-1791	Rev. War	70	165	320		General. Trenton, Brandywine
Stephens, Alexander H. (WD)		Civil War	275	525	735		V.P. CSA
Stephens, Alexander H.	1812-83	Civil War	214	385	419		US MOC & Gov. GA, VP CSA. FF $190
Stephens, George F.	1859-	Artist	20		65		Sculptor, Lecturer. Single Tax Advocate
Stephens, William D.	1859-1944	Congress	10	30			Governor CA, Senator CA
Stephenson, George	1781-1825	Science	275	425	875		Invented 1st Practical Steam Locomotive
Stephenson, Henry	1871-1956	Entertainment	35			75	Br. Character Actor
Stephenson, Robert	1803-59	Science	90	245	330		Br. Railroad Engineer-Devloper Steam Locomotive
Stepp, Hans		Aviation	5	15	20	20	
Steppenwolf		Entertainment	75	125		150	Rock Group (All)
Sterling, Andrew B.		Composer	20	50	100		
Sterling, Robert	1917-	Entertainment	5			20	Actor. Leading Man. Mostly B Films.2nd Leads in A'
Stern, Henry Aaron		Clergy	20	20	25		
Stern, Isaac		Entertainment	15	35	45	60	Violinist. AMQS $80, ALS/Cont. $110
Sterne, Laurence	1713-68	Author	95	375			Br. Whimsical, Eccentric Humor
Sterrett, Cliff*		Cartoonist	35			225	Polly And Her Pals
Stettinius, Edward R.,Jr.	1900-49	Cabinet	40	138	195	50	FDR, Truman, Sec'y State
Steuben, Friedrich von	1730-94	Rev. War	1325	1800			Prussian Off'r. Cont'l Army. ALS/Content $9,750
Stevens, Albert W., Capt.	1846-1949	Aviation	25	50			Balloonist. Record Holder. Aerial Photographer
Stevens, Andrew		Entertainment	10		20	20	Actor. Leads & 2nd Leads
Stevens, Brinke		Entertainment	5			15	Actress. Scream Queen. Pin-Up SP $20
Stevens, Cat		Entertainment	30	100		65	
Stevens, Clement H. (WD)	1821-64	Civil War	375	3740	2650		CSA Gen. 1821-64. Died of Wounds Rec'd Atlanta
Stevens, Connie	1938-	Entertainment	6		15	15	Perky Actress-Singer.
Stevens, Craig	1918-	Entertainment	10		20	20	Handsome Actor. Routine Leads. TV-'Peter Gunn'
Stevens, Dave		Artist	5			15	Rocketeer Creator
Stevens, Ebenezer		Rev. War	75	195			Memb. Boston Tea Party
Stevens, George	1904-75	Entertainment	30			60	Film Director-Major Productions. AA (2)
Stevens, Inger	1934-70	Entertainment	75			150	Actress.Burlesque-Chorus Girl-TV-Movies-Suicide
Stevens, James F.	1892-1971	Author	125	310			Paul Bunyan Stories
Stevens, John	1748-1838	Rev. War	25	50	110		Officer. Engineer. Perfected Steam Engine
Stevens, John Paul, III (SC)		Supreme Court	48	90		150	
Stevens, K.T.	1919-	Entertainment	5			10	Actress. Leads & 2nd Leads. 40's-50's Films
Stevens, Onslow		Entertainment	30			65	Numerous Film Leads. Ran Afoul of Wm. R. Hearst
Stevens, Ray		Country Music	5			15	Singer. Recording Artist
Stevens, Rise'		Entertainment	30	25		42	Opera, Concert, Films
Stevens, Robert T.		Cabinet	10	25		20	Sec'y Army
Stevens, Stella		Entertainment	5			25	Actress. Pin-Up SP $35.Topless $75
Stevens, Tabitha		Entertainment	10			25	
Stevens, Thaddeus	1792-1868	Senate/Congress	35	110	200		MOC PA 1849-68, Abolitionist
Stevens, Wallace	1879-1955	Author	288	853		2000	20th Cent. Am. Poet, Pulitzer
Stevens, Walter Husted	1827-67	Civil War	275				CSA Gen. Extremely Scarce Signature
Stevens, Warren	1919-	Entertainment	5		15	20	Actor. Familiar Face in Supporting Roles. Films-TV
Stevenson, Adlai E.	1835-1914	Vice President	60	238	402	165	Cleveland Vice Pres., MOC, PM Gen.

NAME	DATE	CATEGORY	SIG	LS/DS	ALS	SP	COMMENTS
Stevenson, Adlai E.	1900-65	Governor	50	117	145	125	Gov. IL, Twice Pres. Candidate
Stevenson, Adlai E., III		Governor	5	10		10	Gov. IL
Stevenson, Andrew	1784-1857	Senate/Congress	15	20	35		MOC VA 1821.Speaker of House. Minister to Gr.Brit.
Stevenson, Carter L. (WD)		Civil War	305	645	995		CSA General. Captured & Exchanged
Stevenson, Carter L.	1817-88	Civil War	120	295	500		CSA Gen. Vicksburg
Stevenson, Coke		Governor	5	15			Governer TX
Stevenson, McLean		Entertainment	35	70		64	Actor. Mash
Stevenson, R. H.		Civil War	10	20	30		
Stevenson, Robert Louis	1850-94	Author	335	1073	2021	4370	Novelist, Poet, Essayist. Treasure Island etc.
Stewart, Alexander P.(WD)		Civil War	275	325	580		CSA Gen.
Stewart, Alexander P.	1821-1908	Civil War	175	295	350		CSA Gen.
Stewart, Alexander T.	1803-76	Business	10	25	45		Am. Merchant, Founded Garden City, L.I.
Stewart, Catherine Mary		Entertainment	5			15	Actress
Stewart, Charles	1778-1869	Military	110	275			Cmdr. USS Constitution War 1812
Stewart, Elaine		Entertainment	5			10	Actress. Pin-Up SP $15
Stewart, James (Jimmy)	1908-97	Entertainment	45	174	225	196	S Harvey Original $350-$800. 15 pg DS $500
Stewart, James C.		Aviation	15	25	40	30	ACE, WW II
Stewart, James S.		Clergy	30	45	60	45	
Stewart, John A.		Business	3	10	25		
Stewart, Lisa		Entertainment	5			15	
Stewart, Martha		Author	5	10		30	Columnist. TV Hostess
Stewart, Nick		Entertainment	8			25	Actor. Brer Bear SP $40
Stewart, Paul	1908-	Entertainment	15			45	Actor-TV Dir., Radio/Orson Welles Mercury Theatre
Stewart, Peggy	1923-	Entertainment	5			10	Swimmer-Rider-Actress. Films at 14. Westerns
Stewart, Potter (SC)	1915-85	Supreme Court	35	65		95	
Stewart, Rex		Entertainment	75	95		150	Cornet
Stewart, Robert L.		Astronaut	6			25	
Stewart, Rod		Entertainment	12	50		65	Rock. Foolish Behavior Alb. S $45
Stewart, Walter	1756-96	Rev. War		225			Am. General. 3rd Penn. Aide de Camp to Gen. Gates
Stewart, William	1827-1909	Senate	25	45	70		Drafted US Mining Law-1872 Sen. NV
Stewart, Wynn		Country Music	10			20	Singer
Steyn, Martinus T.	1857-1916	Head of State	35				Last Pres. Orange Free State
Stiborik, Joe		Aviation	30			50	Enola Gay Radar Operator WW II
Stickney, Dorothy		Entertainment	5	7	20	25	Actress. Stage Leading Lady. Early Films
Stieglitz, Alfred	1864-1946	Artist-Photographer	200	675	810		Revolutionized Camera Technique
Stiers, David Ogden		Entertainment	35			98	Actor. Mash. Reluctant Signer
Stigler, George J.		Economist	20	25	40	25	Nobel Economics 1982
Stiles, Julia		Entertainment	6			35	Actress. Pin-Up $48
Stiles, William H.	1808-65	Congress	20		65		MOC GA, CSA Colonel
Still, William Grant	1895-1978	Composer	120	265	385	250	1st Afro-Am. Symphony Conductor
Stiller, Ben		Entertainment	8			35	Actor. Something About Mary SP $45
Stiller, Jerry		Entertainment	5			22	Comic Actor. 1/2 of Stiller & O'Meara Team
Stills, Stephen		Entertainment	40			75	
Stilwell, Joseph W.	1883-1946	Military	165	200		450	Gen. WW II. 'Vinegar Joe'.
Stimson, Henry L.	1867-1950	Cabinet	40	117	195	50	Sec'y State 1929. Served Several Cabinets

NAME	DATE	CATEGORY	SIG	LS/DS	ALS	SP	COMMENTS
Sting		Entertainment	25			45	Rock
Stirling, Linda		Entertainment	15			35	Actress
Stirling, Wm. Alex., Lord	1726-83	Rev. War	385	950	1950		General Continental Army
Stock, Frederick A.		Composer	20	55	100	45	Dir. Chicago Symphony Orch.
Stock, Harold		Business	10	35	50	20	
Stockdale, James B.		Military	22	30		25	Adm. WW II. Perot Running Mate for V.P.
Stockton, Frank R.	1834-1902	Author	25	98		30	Juvenile Fiction, Novels, Editor
Stockton, Richard	1730-81	Rev. War	500	1275	2625		Member Continental Congr. Signer Decl. of Indepen.
Stockton, Richard	1764-1828	Senate/Congress	20	35	50		MOC, Senator NJ 1796
Stockton, Robert Field	1795-1866	Military	125	375	490		Sen. NJ. Conquered Calif. Named Stockton, CA
Stockwell, Dean	1936-	Entertainment	10			30	Child to Adult Actor. AA Nomination 'Quantum Leap'
Stockwell, Guy		Entertainment	10			25	Actor-Brother to Dean
Stockwell, Harry		Entertainment	50			122	
Stoddard, Richard H.	1825-1903	Author	20	30	45		Poet, Writer, Literary Critic, Novelist
Stoddart, James H.		Entertainment	20			40	Vintage Actor
Stoddert, Benjamin	1751-1813	Rev. War	95	270	430		1st Sec'y Navy 1798
Stoica, Chivu		Head of State	50				Premier Roumania
Stoker, Bram	1847-1912	Author	105	325	462		Ir.Business Advisor-Sec'y Henry Irving. Dracula
Stokes, Carl Burton	1927-9x	Political	25		40	45	1st Afr-Am Mayor of Major Am. City, Cleveland
Stokes, Louis	1925-	Congress	10	20		15	Afro-Am. Repr. OH
Stokes, William		Civil War	75				Union Gen., MOC TN
Stokowski, Leopold	1882-1977	Entertainment	100	142	140	150	Br-Am. Flamboyant Conductor AMusQS $350
Stolle, Bruno		Aviation	5	15	20	15	
Stoloff, Morris	1893-1980	Entertainment	10			30	Musical Dir.-Conductor. AA (3)
Stoltz, Eric		Entertainment	9	10	20	25	
Stolz, Robert	1880-1975	Composer	20	75			Conductor. Composed 65 Operettas
Stolz, Teresa		Entertainment	40	75			ALS/Content $400
Stone Temple Pilots (All)		Entertainment	35			88	Rock Drumhead Signed $150
Stone, Cliffie		Country Music	10			25	Singer, Songwriter, Record Exec.
Stone, Ezra		Entertainment	25	35		50	Vintage Radio's 'Henry Aldrich'
Stone, Fred	1973-1959	Entertainment	20		30	40	Vaudeville Star of 1st The Wizard of OZ on stage
Stone, George E.	1903-67	Entertainment	20			45	Song & Dance-Vaudeville-Stage-Character Roles
Stone, Harlan Fiske (SC)	1872-1946	Supreme Court	100	250	775	225	Chief Justice
Stone, Harold J.		Entertainment	15			30	
Stone, Irving	1903-89	Author	20	75	175	40	Historical Biographical Novels & Successful Films
Stone, John Samuel		Clergy	20		85		
Stone, Lewis	1879-1953	Entertainment	30	40	75	65	Am. Leading Man in Silents. Later Character Actor
Stone, Lucy (Blackwell)	1818-93	Reformer	113	700	340	1500	Suffragist, Women's Rights Pioneer.
Stone, Marcus		Artist		15	30		Illustrated for Chas. Dickens
Stone, Milburn		Entertainment	55	65	100	100	Busy Character Actor Until Full Time GunsmokeDoc
Stone, Oliver	1946-	Entertainment	20			35	Oscar Winning Film Director. Writer, Producer
Stone, Paula		Entertainment	25			40	Western Heroine
Stone, Peter H.		Author	20		70		Playwright. Acad.Award '64, Tony '69, '81,Emmy '63
Stone, Sharon		Entertainment	20	72		58	Pin-Up SP $75-$90
Stone, Thomas	1743-87	Rev. War	590	930	1750		Signer Decl. of Indepen.

NAME	DATE	CATEGORY	SIG	LS/DS	ALS	SP	COMMENTS
Stoneman, George	1822-94	Civil War-Gov.	90	220	305		Union General, Gov. of CA. Sig/Rank $170
Stooges, The Three (3)		Entertainment	1500			3500	Original Stooges. Full Names (First Names SP $695)
Stoopnagle, Colonel Lemuel Q.		Entertainment	15	15	30	30	Vint.Radio (Fred. C. Taylor).' Stoopnagle & Bud'
Stopes, Marie Charlotte	1880-1958	Reformer	85		250		Birth Control Pioneer
Stoppard, Tom	1937-	Author	30	80	155	35	Czech Born. Br. Plays of Verbal Brilliance
Storch, Larry	1923-	Entertainment	5		15	18	Actor-Comedian. 'F Troop'
Storchio, Rosina	1876-45	Entertainment	70			400	It. Soprano. Created Cio-Cio-San in Mme.Butterfly
Stordahl, Axel		Conductor-Arranger	25			65	Arranged for Major Vocalists
Storey, June		Entertainment	10			40	Actress. Western Leading Lady
Storm, Gale		Entertainment	8			20	Star of Early TV Series
Storm, Tempest		Entertainment	10	18	28	25	Pin-Up SP $35. Stripper
Storms, Harrison A.		Business	9		25		
Storrs Richard Salter	1821-1900	Clergy	25	35	50		Congr. Minister-Scholar-Author
Story, John P.		Military	65	125			Am. WW I Gen.
Story, Joseph (SC)	1779-1845	Supreme Court	100	165	300		ALS/Content $2,500
Stott, John		Clergy	15	25	30		
Stoughton, William	1632-1701	Colonial America	450	1200			Gov. MA, Stoughton Hall,Harvard
Stout, Rex	1886-1975	Author	35	110	215	45	Created Detective Nero Wolfe
Stowe, Harriet Beecher	1811-96	Author	217	320	770	1610	Suffragist, Anti-Slavery. AMsS $3,850
Stowe, Madeline		Entertainment	22			75	Pin-Up SP $30-90
Stracciari, Riccardo	1875-1955	Entertainment	42			375	Opera. Baritone/46 Year Career
Strachey, Lytton		Author	70	175	475		Br. Member of Bloomsbury Group
Stradlin, Izzy		Entertainment	15			40	Guns N' Roses
Straight, Beatrice		Entertainment	510		15	20	A A
Strait, Donald G.		Aviation	12	25	40	35	ACE, WW II
Strait, George		Country Music	10			30	
Strait, Horace Burton		Senate/Congress	10	15			Rep. MN 1873, Banker, Agri.
Stranahan, Robert A., Jr.		Business	5			10	CEO Champion Spark Plugs
Strand, Paul	1890-1976	Photographer	30	85	420		Am. Known for Photo Documentaries
Strange, Glenn		Entertainment	50			150	
Strasberg, Lee	1901-82	Entertainment	35	40	55	95	Drama Coach. Hd. Actor's Studio. Actor
Strasberg, Susan	1938-99	Entertainment	16	10	35	35	Actress. Pin-Up SP $30
Strassmann, Fritz	1902-80	Science	75	270			Ger. Chemist/Otto Hahn Worked on Nuclear Fission
Stratas, Teresa		Entertainment	25			50	Opera
Stratemeyer, George F.		Military	30	40		50	
Strathmore, Earl of	1855-1921	Royalty	10		50		Grandfather of Queen Elizabeth II
Stratten, Dorothy		Entertainment	100			250	
Stratton, Chas. S.		Entertainment	250		475	468	Barnum's General Tom Thumb
Stratton, Samuel S.		Senate/Congress	5	10		10	Rep. NY. Navy Intelligence
Stratton, William G.		Gov-Congress	4	10			Rep., Gov. IL
Straub, Robert W.		Governor	5	15			Gov. OR
Straus, Jack I.		Business	4	10	25	10	3rd Generation R.H.Macy Dept...
Straus, Nathan	1848-1931	Business	95	70		55	Owner R.H. Macy Co. Dept Store
Straus, Oscar	1870-1954	Composer	150	240	265	200	The Chocolate Soldier. AMusQS $250
Strause, Charles		Composer	8	15	30	25	

NAME	DATE	CATEGORY	SIG	LS/DS	ALS	SP	COMMENTS
Strauss, Adolf		Military	10	15	35	15	
Strauss, Eduard II	1910-69	Composer	125				Younger Brother of Johann. AMusQS $150.
Strauss, Franz Josef		Head of State	15	45	125	35	
Strauss, Johann	1804-49	Composer	250	445	1775		Aus. Waltzes. Cond. Own Orchest
Strauss, Johann, Jr.	1825-99	Composer	450	1225	900	3950	The Waltz King. AMusQS $3000
Strauss, Levi		Business					1850 Establ'd Levi Strauss & Co
Strauss, Peter		Entertainment	15			45	
Strauss, Richard	1864-1949	Composer	213	498	1144	759	Ger. Conductor. AMusQS $700-$950-$1,600,$2,500
Strauss, Robert		Cabinet	4	12	20	10	
Strauss, Robert		Entertainment	25			45	
Stravinsky, Igor	1882-1971	Composer	246	787	530	974	Russ-Am. AMusQS $975-$1,150-$1,750-$2500
Stravinsky, Sulima		Entertainment	40			120	Pianist
Straw, Ezekiel A.		Governor	5	15			Governor NH
Strawbridge, James Dale		Senate/Congress	5	15			Rep. PA/. CW Brigade Surgeon
Stray Cats		Entertainment	35			100	Rock
Strayhorn, Billy		Entertainment					Jazz Musician-No Price Available
Streep, Meryl		Entertainment	20	30	45	62	Versatile AA Winning Actress
Street, Julian		Author	15			75	
Streett, St. Clair		Aviation	50	165			Alaskan Air Expedition
Streib, Werner		Aviation				60	Ger. Ace WW II. RK
Streich, Rita		Entertainment	10			25	Opera
Streicher, Julius		Journalist	70	135			Nazi Anti-Semitic, Hanged
Streight, Abel		Civil War	50	165			Union Gen. Escaped Libby Prison
Streisand, Barbra		Entertainment	150	499		320	AA. Pin-Up SP $275. Authentic Signatures RARE
Stribling, Thomas S.		Author	12	25	60		Am. Novlist. Pulitzer
Strindberg, August	1849-1912	Author	275		872	1095	Swe.ALS's/Cont. $1,400-$2,200
Stringfield, Sherry		Entertainment				40	Actress ER
Stringham, Silas Horton	1798-1876	Civil War	52	80			Union Adm. Led Atlantic Blockade Fleet
Stritch, Samuel, Cardinal		Clergy	40	45	75	45	
Strode, Woody		Entertainment	50				Actor-Athlete
Stroheim, Eric von	1885-1957	Entertainment	160			508	Austrian. Classic Film Director-Actor
Stromberg, Hunt		Entertainment	10	15		30	Film Producer, Director
Strong, Caleb	1745-1819	Rev. War	65	188	338		1st U.S. Sen. & Gov. MA. Constitutional Convention
Strong, Frederick	1855-1935	Military	20		65	80	Army General. Indian Fighter. Span-Am War
Strong, George C.	1832-1863	Civil War	235	875			Union Gen.Mortally Wounded '63
Strong, Susan		Entertainment	12			20	Vintage Actress
Strong, Vincent	1837-63	Civil War		3295			3rd Brigade. Gen.Defended Little Round Top. Killed
Strong, William (SC)		Supreme Court	80	170	300		
Stroud Twins		Entertainment	18			40	
Stroud, Robert,Birdman of Alcatraz		Celebrity			800		Remarkable 7 pp. ALS $15,000
Strouse, Charles	1928-	Composer	20	125	200	75	Broadway Composer Annie AMusQS $120
Struck, Heinz		Science	10			35	Rocket Pioneer/von Braun/von Braun
Struthers, Sally		Entertainment	4		10	15	
Stryker (4)		Entertainment	10			20	Gospel Singers
Stuart, Alexander H. H.	1807-91	Cabinet	25	60	95		Fillmore Sec'y Interior

NAME	DATE	CATEGORY	SIG	LS/DS	ALS	SP	COMMENTS
Stuart, George R.		Clergy	10	15	20		
Stuart, Gilbert	1755-1828	Artist	200	500	850		Portraitist. Presidents-Royalty
Stuart, Gloria		Entertainment	5			15	
Stuart, J.E.B. (WD)		Civil War	12500	8200	7950		CSA Gen. ALS/Cont. $19000
Stuart, J.E.B.	1833-64	Civil War	3900	5775	12200		CSA Gen.
Stuart, Leslie		Composer	20				Floradora AMusQS $200
Stuart, March B.		Military	30	75			Supt. West Point
Stuart, Marty		Country Music	10			25	
Stuart, Randy		Entertainment	3			10	
Studebaker, Clement		Business	200	500	765		Auto Pioneers.Studebaker Bros.
Studebaker, Jr., Clement		Business	40	105	195	75	Studebaker Bros. Mfg. Co.
Studer, Cheryl		Entertainment	10			35	Opera
Stultz, Wilmer		Aviation	50	135		150	Pioneer Aviator/A. Earhart
Stump, Felix B.		Military	25	80		50	Adm. Capt. Lexington WW II
Sturge, Joseph	1793-1859	Philanthropist	12	20	95		Quaker Pacifist,Reformer,Abolitionist
Sturgeon, Daniel		Senate-Cabinet	25	70	125		Sen. PA 1839, US Treasurer 1853
Sturges, John	1911-92	Entertainment	55			235	Am Dir. Many Action Films Including Great Escape
Sturges, Preston		Entertainment	20			50	Film Director, Producer, Writer
Sturgis, Samuel D.		Civil War	50	105			Union Gen.
Styne, Jule		Composers	25			75	AMusQS $180, $370
Styron, William		Author	20	35	80	75	Sophie's Choice MsS 1p $200
Styx		Entertainment	25			50	
Suchet, David		Entertainment	10			30	Br. Actor. Poirot
Suchet, Louis G.,Duc d'A		Napoleonic Wars	85	215	390		Marshal of Napoleon
Sucre, Antonio de	1795-1830	Military	295	1525			Liberator of Venezuela, General &2 Bolivar's Ass't
Sudarmono, Pratiwi		Astronaut	12	25		25	
Suenens, Leo Joseph, Cardinal		Clergy	45	75	90	65	
Suharto, General		Head of State	15	30	75	35	Indonesia
Sukarno, Achmad	1902-70	Head of State	95				1st President (Later as Dictator) of Indonesia
Sul, Terra		Entertainment	4			10	
Sullavan, Margaret		Entertainment	60	65		173	Retired at 33. Suicide at 49
Sullivan, Anne (Annie)		Educator	100		425		TLS/Content $1,000
Sullivan, Arthur, Sir	1842-1900	Composer	175	400	762	1000	Conductor. AMusQS $1,200
Sullivan, Barry		Entertainment	10	15		25	
Sullivan, Ed	1902-1974	Entertainment	25	45	85	160	Columnist, TV Host. 'Ed Sullivan Show'
Sullivan, Francis L.		Entertainment	10	20		25	
Sullivan, James		Rev. War	50	95	200		Continental Congress, Gov. MA
Sullivan, John	1740-95	Rev. War	150	425	575		Continental Congress, General
Sullivan, Kathleen		Entertainment	10			20	TV Hostess
Sullivan, Kathryn D.		Aviation-Astro.	10	25	45	30	
Sullivan, Pat*		Cartoonist	50			400	Felix The Cat
Sullivan, Peter John		Civil War	55	105	160		Union General
Sullivan, Susan		Entertainment	5	6	20	15	
Sullivan, William	1774-1839	Author	20	40	95		Politician, Gen. Militia, Orato
Sully, Alfred		Civil War	35	80	110	150	Union General

NAME	DATE	CATEGORY	SIG	LS/DS	ALS	SP	COMMENTS
Sully, Thomas	1783-1872	Artist	165	395	442		Lead Portrait Painter of His Day
Sully-Prudhomme, Rene', F.A	1839-1907	Author	40	135	209		Fr. Poet, 1st Nobel Literature
Sulzberger, Art Ochs, Jr.		Business	10	25	30	15	NY Times
Sulzer, William		Congress-Gov.	15	35		25	Rep.,Gov. NY, Impeached 1913
Sumi, Jo		Entertainment	5			35	Opera. Korean Coloratura
Summer, Donna		Entertainment	10	15		20	
Summerall, Charles Pelot		Military	10	20	35	25	Gen., Pres. Citadel 1931-53
Summerfield, Arthur E.		Cabinet	15	20	30	20	P.M. Genera, Modernized Systeml
Summersby, Kay		Military-WWII	95	325		125	D.D. Eisenhower's WW II Aide
Summerville, Slim		Entertainment	35			75	
Sumner, Charles	1811-74	Civil War	88	150	274		Abolitionist. Founder Rep.Party. U.S. Sen.
Sumner, Increase	1746-99	Governor	65	170			Rev. War Jurist & Stateman
Sumner, John B.	1780-1862	Clergy	25				Archbishop Canterbury
Sumter, Thomas		Rev. War	375	1200			Soldier, Rep.,Sen., SC 1789
Sun Yat-Sen	1866-1975	Head of State	700	925	3025	2500	1st Pres. Chinese Republic
Sunday, William A. 'Billy'	1862-1935	Clergy	80	165	275	400	19th Cent. Early Evangelist-Baseball Player
Sung, Kim II		Head of State	50			150	North Viet Nam
Sununu, John		Cabinet	12	15	25	15	Chief of Staff White House
Supertramp		Entertainment	35			75	
Supervia, Conchita	1895-1936	Entertainment	150			688	Spanish Opera Singer. Rare In Authentic SP
Suppe', Franz von		Composer	110	225	450	395	Aus. Opera, Operetta,Choral
Supreme Court (Burger)		Supreme Court				1825	Burger Court. TsS (7) $3950. SB (9) $2600
Supreme Court (Hughes)		Supreme Court				4900	
Supreme Court (Stone)		Supreme Court				3000	All 9 Justices. Roosevelt 1941-42
Supreme Court (Taft)		Supreme Court				5800	Wm. H. Taft Court
Supreme Court (Waite)		Supreme Court	500				Morrison R. Waite Court
Supreme Court (Warren)		Supreme Court		1400		5100	Possibly Most Influential.
Susann, Jacqueline		Author	20	35	45	40	Valley of the Dolls etc.
Susskind, David	1920-87	Entertainment	15			25	Controversial TV Producer
Sutherland, Donald		Entertainment	9	28	20	20	Actor. Mash, Klute
Sutherland, George (SC)	1862-1942	Supreme Court	65	165	350	250	Justice 1922-38. Brit. Born. Opposed FDR
Sutherland, Joan		Entertainment	25		40	40	Magnificent Australian Soprano. Opera, Concert
Sutherland, Keifer		Entertainment	10			45	
Sutro, Adolph H. J.		Business-Engineer	90	165	200		Prussian-Born Mining magnate. Sutro Tunnel
Sutter, John A.	1803-80	CA Pioneer	1190	3400	8875	1955	Sutter's Fort.ALS/Cont. $15,000
Sutton, Grady		Entertainment	8	10		15	
Sutton, John		Entertainment	5			25	Suave Br. Co-Star
Sutton, Willy	1901-80	Criminal	125	3000		250	Bank Robber. Multi Prison Escapes
Suzman, Janet	1939-	Entertainment					So. Afr. Born Actress
Suzman, Janet	1939-	Entertainment	20			25	Oscar Nominated - Nicholas & Alexandra.
Svanholm, Set		Entertainment	15			55	Opera
Svenson, Bo		Entertainment	4	5	9	10	
Swaggart, Jimmy		Clergy	10	30	35	30	Evangelist
Swain, Dominique		Entertainment	8			30	Actress. Lolita SP $50
Swan, James	1754-1830	Rev. War	180	540	575		Finan'l Speculator. Scottish-Born Patriot

NAME	DATE	CATEGORY	SIG	LS/DS	ALS	SP	COMMENTS
Swank, Hilary		Entertainment	6			35	Actress Pin-Up $48
Swann, Thomas		Senate/Congress	5	15			Senator, Gov, MD. Pres. B & O RR
Swanson, Claude A.	1862-1939	Cabinet	18	25	95	20	Sec'y Navy 1933 FDR
Swanson, Gloria	1897-1983	Entertainment	50	340		160	Premium for Sunset Blvd. SP's
Swanson, J.		Civil War	65	135	180		
Swanson, Kristy		Entertainment	15			70	Actress (See Zane, Billy)
Swart, Charles R.	1894-	Head of State	5		20	40	
Swarthout, Gladys		Entertainment	25	75		85	Opera and Film Star. 5x7 SP $50
Swasey, Ambrose		Business	40	90			
Swayne, Noah H. (SC)		Supreme Court	45	115	195		
Swayne, Wager		Civil War	25	45	105		Union General
Swayze, John Cameron		Entertainment	5			10	Radio, TV News & Commercials
Swayze, Patrick		Entertainment	20			46	Actor
Swearingen, John		Business	10	25	40	15	CEO Continental Ill. Corp.
Sweat, Lorenzo DeMedici		Senate/Congress	10	15	25		Rep. ME 1863
Swedenborg, Emanuel	1688-1772	Science	3000	3000			Swe. Science, Philosophy, Religion
Sweeney, Brian		Law Enforcement	4			10	Law Enforcement No. Ireland
Sweeney, Walter C.		Military	5	15	25	15	Gen. Tactical Air Cmd.
Sweet, Blanche	1895-1986	Entertainment	20		30	35	Important Silent Film Star Protégé of D.W.Griffith
Sweet, John H.		Business	5	15		10	CEO US News & World Report
Swenson, Bo		Entertainment	10			30	Actor. Walking Tall
Swenson, Ruth Ann		Entertainment	10			25	Opera
Swett, James E.		Aviation	15	30	50	42	ACE, WW II
Swift, Frederic W.		Civil War	55	135	195		Union General, MOH
Swift, George B.		Political	10	25			Mayor of Chicago
Swift, Harold Higgins		Business	20	50	95	35	Chm. Swift & Co., Meatpackers
Swift, John W.	1750-1819	Rev. War	65	180			Merchant. Soldier
Swift, Jonathan	1667-1745	Author	2500	7300	13230		Satirist, Poet, Clergy, Political
Swigert, John L. Jr.		Astronaut	40	75		125	
Swinburne, Algernon C.	1837-1909	Author	185	295	1008		Br. 19th Cent. Lyric Poet
Swing, Philip D.	1884-1963	Congress	5	25		15	Repr. CA
Swinnerton, Frank		Author	20	55	100		Br. Novelist, Critic
Swinnerton, James*		Cartoonist	35			180	Little Jimmy
Swinton, Ernest D.	1868-1951	Military	45	110	310		British Inventor of Tank
Swit, Loretta		Entertainment	15			28	
Switzer, Carl 'Alfalfa'		Entertainment	588			712	Our Gang Comedies
Swope, Gerard		Business	60				CEO General Electric
Swope, Herbert Bayard	1882-1958	Author	10	125	75	20	Journalist, War Corresp., Pulitz
Swope, James S.		Aviation	15	25	40	30	ACE, WW II
Sykes, Jerome H.		Entertainment	15			30	Light Opera
Sylva, Carmen (Queen of Romania)		Author	50	75			Elizabeth, Queen of Romania
Sylva, Marguerite		Entertainment	15			25	Vintage Actress
Sylvia		Entertainment	5			15	
Symington, Stuart		Cabinet	10		35	25	Sen. MO, Sec'y Air Force
Symmes, John Cleves		Rev. War	110	375	550		Patriot. Continental Congress

NAME	DATE	CATEGORY	SIG	LS/DS	ALS	SP	COMMENTS
Szakall, S. Cuddles		Entertainment	35			155	Character Actor
Szell, George		Entertainment	20			65	Hung. Conductor. AMusQS $125
Szent-Gyorgyi, Albert		Science	35	65	125	50	Nobel Medicine 1937
Szigeti, Joseph	1892-1973	Entertainment	40	75		239	Hung.-Am. Violinist. AMusQS $125
Szilard, Leo	1898-1964	Science	25			45	Nuclear/Phys.TLS/Cont.$2500
Szold, Henrietta	1860-1945	Zionist Leader	140	475	600		Founder, Pres. Hadassah
Szyk, Arthur		Artist	25	65	90		Highly Detailed Portaits, Manuscripts. Miniaturist
Szymanowski, Karol M.		Composer	125	235	505		AMusMsS $1250

T

NAME	DATE	CATEGORY	SIG	LS/DS	ALS	SP	COMMENTS
T Hooft, Visser		Celebrity	3	5	10	10	
T, Mr.		Entertainment	8			36	Actor. Afr-Am. TV Series
Tabb, John Banister	1845-1909	Civil War Clergy	40		200		Rom.Cath. clergy, Poet.CSA
Taber, Robert		Entertainment	6	8	15	15	
Taccani, Giuseppe		Entertainment	35			225	Opera, Noted Tenor
Taft, Charles P.		Publisher	10	15	25	15	Owner-Ed. Cincinnati Times-Star
Taft, Helen Herron	1861-1943	First Lady	100	200	550	975	ALS White House $1,200
Taft, Helen Manning		First Lady	80	185	300	500	Daughter
Taft, Henry Wallace	1859-1945	Lawyer	4	20		15	Politician, Writer Brotherof Pres. Wm.Howard Taft
Taft, Lorado	1860-1936	Artist	55	110	130	155	Influential Am. Sculptor-Author
Taft, Robert A.	1889-1953	Senate/Congress	20	35		25	S caric. $75. US Sen. OH. Taft-Hartley Amendment
Taft, Robert, Jr.	1917-	Senate/Congress	8	20		15	Rep., Senator OH.
Taft, William Howard (As Pres.)		President	215	753	3262	571	White House Card S $325-375. TLS/Content $1800
Taft, William Howard	1857-1930	President	169	441	1130	475	ALS/Cont. As Chief Justice $2200-$4500
Tagliabue, Carlo		Entertainment	45			175	Opera
Tagliavini, Feruccio		Entertainment	35			95	Opera. 4x6 SP $50
Taglioni, Marie	1804-1884	Entertainment	300		935		It. Premier Ballerina
Tagore, Rabindranath, Sir	1861-1941	Author	100	258	350	300	Nobel Prize Lit., Indian Poet
Tait, A.C., Archbishop		Clergy	12	35	50		
Tait, Arthur Fitzwilliam		Artist	28	55	110		Landscape Artist
Taka, Miiko		Entertainment	15			25	Japanese Actress
Takahira, Kogoro, Baron	1854-1926	Diplomat	45				At Treaty Signing of Russo-Jap. War.
Takei, George		Entertainment	15			35	Actor. 'Star Trek'
Talbert, Melvin, Bishop		Clergy	20	25	30	35	
Talbot, Gloria		Entertainment	8			25	Actress
Talbot, Helen		Entertainment	10			25	Actress
Talbot, Lyle	1902-96	Entertainment	8	12	20	20	Vint B Movie Lead. Migrated to Westerns & Sci-Fi
Talbot, Nita		Entertainment	7			20	Actress
Talbot, Wm. Henry Fox	1800-77	Science	295		1250		Br.Inventor of Photogr. Process
Talbott, Harold D.		Cabinet	10	15		20	Sec'y AF
Talcott, Joseph	1669-1741	Colonial America	35	75	170		Colonial Governor CT
Talese, Gay		Author	10	62		20	Am. Novelist

NAME	DATE	CATEGORY	SIG	LS/DS	ALS	SP	COMMENTS
Taliaferro, William B. (WD)		Civil War	188	422			CSA Gen.
Taliaferro, William B.	1822-98	Civil War	95		375		CSA Gen.
Talking Heads		Entertainment	25			70	
Tallchief, Maria		Entertainment	15		35	45	Ballerina
Talley, Marion		Entertainment	15		45	50	Am. Soprano
Talleyrand, Charles Maurice de	1754-1838	Head of State	195	615	950		Grand Chancellor of Napoleon. Important DS $2500
Talmadge, Benjamin	1754-1835	Rev. War	220	475			Served Throughout War. Rep. NY
Talmadge, Constance		Entertainment	45			115	Silent Star. Intolerance.
Talmadge, Eugene		Governor	20	60	95	35	Governor GA
Talmadge, Herman		Senate/Congress	10	25		20	Gov., Senator GA. Senate Watergate Committee
Talmadge, Norma		Entertainment	50			142	Beautiful Silent Screen Star
Talmage, T. Dewitt		Clergy	50	70	95		America Divine, Editor
Talman, William		Entertainment	50	70	150	125	Regular on Original Perry Mason. Cancer Victim
Talvela, Marti		Entertainment	30			75	Opera. Finnish Basso
Tamblyn, Russ		Entertainment	9			20	Actor-Dancer
Tambor, Jeffrey		Entertainment	8			15	
Tamiroff, Akim		Entertainment	30	40	75	70	Russ. Character Actor
Tandy, Jessica	1904-94	Entertainment	22	39	50	60	AA-& Tony Awards. Hume Cronyn & Tandy $100
Taney, Roger B. (SC)	1777-1864	Supreme Court	98	315	1092		Chief Justice., Rendered Dred Scott Decision
Tanner, Henry Ossawa		Artist	270		750		Religious Subjects, Realistic
Tanner, Joe		Astronaut	6			20	
Tanner, John Riley		Governor	12	20			Governor IL
Tanner, Rich., Dr. (Diamond Dick)		Celebrity	450				Companion to Wild Bill Hickok
Tanning, Dorothea	1910-	Artist	35		200		Am. Painter
Tansman, Alexandre		Composer	40	125		240	Composer-Pianist. Operas, Symphonies, Films
Tappan, Arthur	1786-1865	Abolitionist	25	65	125		Merchant, Philanthropist
Tappan, James C.	1825-1906	Civil War	80	135	245		CSA General. S/Rank $145
Tarantino, Quentin		Entertainment	20			50	AA Pulp Fiction Writer-Director
Tarbell, Ida M.	1857-1944	Author	20	45	100	40	Muckraking Journalist re Std.Oil
Tarkington, Booth	1869-1946	Author	40		195	125	Playwright, Novelist. Pulitzer. TLS/Cont $425
Tarleton, Banastre, Sir		Rev. War	135	365	715		Barbaric Br.General. Am. Rev.
Tarnower, Herman Dr.		Medical	15	50	135	25	Murdered Diet Dr.
Tartakov, Joakim		Entertainment			450		Opera. Imperial Russ. Baritone Star. SPc $150
Tartikoff, Brandon		Business	10			30	TV executive
Tashlin, Frank		Entertainment	15			25	Director
Tashman, Lilyan		Entertainment	30	40	75	70	Vintage Actress. Major Star in 30's
Tassigny, J.M.G. de		Military	35	90	140		Fr. Gen.
Tate, Allen	1899-1979	Author	10	30	75		Am. Poet, Critic, Biographer
Tate, Harry	1872-1940	Entertainment	10			50	Brit. Music Hall Comedian. Silent Films
Tate, Henry, Sir, 1st Baronet		Business	40	105	240		Br.Sugar Refiner Philanthropist, Art-Tate Gallery.
Tate, Jackson R.		Military	10		35	30	Adm. WW II.
Tate, Sharon	1943-69	Entertainment	238	300	500	600	Murdered By Manson Gang. Special SP $3600
Tati, Jacques	1908-82	Entertainment	50				Fr. Actor. Monsieur Hulot's Holiday SP(Pc)$415
Tattersall, Richard	1724-95	Business	20	45	105		Rendevous For Sporting-Betting
Tattnall, Joseph		Civil War			715		CSA Naval Capt.

NAME	DATE	CATEGORY	SIG	LS/DS	ALS	SP	COMMENTS
Tatum, Edward L.	1909-75	Science	45	70	125		Nobel 1958. Research in Molecular Genetics
Taube, Henry, Dr.		Science	25	40		30	Nobel Chemistry 1983
Tauber, Richard	1892-1948	Entertainment	50			242	Opera, Austrian-Born, British Tenor
Taufflieb, Gen.		Military	45	120	215	100	
Taurog, Norman		Entertainment	50			150	Film Director
Taussig, Frank William	1859-1940	Economist	10	25			Author. Chm Tariff Bd.
Tawes, J. Millard		Governor	5	15			Governor MD
Tawney, James A.		Congress	7	15	25		Repr. MN 1893
Tayback, Vic		Entertainment	22			45	Character Actor. Films-TV 'Alice'
Taylor, Caleb Newbold	1813-87	Congress	15		35		MOC PA. Visited Lincoln/Recommendations
Taylor, Thomas H. (WD)		Civil War	125	210	550		CSA Gen.
Taylor, Bayard	1825-78	Author	20	70	135		Journalist, Traveller, Diplomat
Taylor, Charles H.		Congress	5	10		15	Congressman NC
Taylor, Deems		Composer	35	80	90	50	Musicologist, Critic, Author
Taylor, Don		Entertainment	20			35	Actor turned Director. Star of 40's-50's Films
Taylor, Dub		Entertainment	15			40	Western Character Actor
Taylor, Elizabeth	1932-	Entertainment	180	412	275	435	AA. MGM Early Contract S $1500
Taylor, Estelle		Entertainment	10	25	45	45	Vintage Actress
Taylor, George	1716-81	Rev. War	1400	3575	7050		Signer. ALS $35,000
Taylor, Glen H.	1904-1984	Congress	10	25		25	Sen. ID, Actor, Singer
Taylor, Graham		Clergy	15	25	35		
Taylor, H. C.		Military	10	25	40		
Taylor, James		Composer	35	100	215	80	Singer-Guitarist
Taylor, James (Afro-Am.)		Entertainment	40			75	
Taylor, James Willis		Senate/Congress	4	10	20		Rep. TN 1919
Taylor, Joan		Entertainment	7			15	Actress. Paramount Contractee. Mostly Westerns
Taylor, John		Celebrity	50	130			
Taylor, John W.		Senate/Congress	204		45		Early MOC. 1813, Speaker
Taylor, Joseph P.	1796-1864	Civil War	65	175			War 1812 & CW Union Gen.
Taylor, Kent		Entertainment	5			15	Popular Handsome B Movie Leading Man
Taylor, Laurette	1884-1946	Entertainment	32		50	200	Major Star of Am. Theatre. SPc $75
Taylor, Margaret		First Lady					Only 1 Known. No Price Avail.
Taylor, Mary		Country Music	10			20	Singer
Taylor, Maxwell D.		Military	25	75	125	65	Gen. WW II
Taylor, Meshach		Entertainment	9			23	Afr-Am Actor. 'Designing Women', 'Dave's World'
Taylor, Nikki		Entertainment	15			63	Actress-Model. Pin-Up $75
Taylor, Richard (WD)		Civil War	390	1222			CSA Gen. Son of Pres. Taylor
Taylor, Richard	1826-79	Civil War	225	755			CSA Gen. Son of Pres. Taylor
Taylor, Richard E., Dr.		Science	20	50			Nobel Physics 1990
Taylor, Robert	1911-69	Entertainment	45	143	125	222	Handsome Am. Actor and Leading Man
Taylor, Robert L.	1850-1912	Congress	10	15		15	Gov., Rep. & Senator TN
Taylor, Rod		Entertainment	4	50		20	Actor
Taylor, Thomas H. (War Dte)		Civil War	118	205	285		CSA General.
Taylor, Thomas H.	1825-1901	Civil War	80	115	275		CSA General
Taylor, Vaughn		Entertainment	20			50	

NAME	DATE	CATEGORY	SIG	LS/DS	ALS	SP	COMMENTS
Taylor, Walter H.		Civil War	45	90			CSA Col. Aide-de-camp R.E. Lee
Taylor, William, Bishop		Clergy		40	50	75	
Taylor, Wm. Levi (Buck)		Celebrity	175				NRPA
Taylor, Zachary (As Pres.)		President	1150	5133	6500		3rd Rarest in Presidentially Signed Items.FF $2750
Taylor, Zachary	1784-1850	President	805	3033	2920		General in Mexican War.ALS/Cont $8500
Taylor-Young, Leigh		Entertainment	5	8	15	15	Actress
Tazewell, Littleton		Senate/Congress	45	135	232		MOC 1800, Sen. 1824, Gov. VA
Tchaikovsky, Piotr I.	1840-93	Composer	2117	3450	4969	5300	Rus. Opera,Symphony,Ballet,Etc.
Tchelitchew, Pavel	1898-1957	Artist	75		500		Russian-born American Painter
Tcherepnin, Alexander		Composer					AMusQS $350
Tchernihovsky, Saul		Author	175		550		Rus-Hebrew Dr., Poet,Translator
Te Kanawa, Kiri, Dame		Entertainment	40	55		75	New Zealand Born. Opera, Concert
Teagarden, Charlie		Entertainment	10			25	Jazz Trumpet
Teagarden, Jack		Entertainment	60	100		125	Big Band Leader-Trombonist
Teal, Ray		Entertainment	50			150	
Teale, Edwin W.	1899-1980	Nauralist			75	30	Photographer, Pulitzer Writer.
Tearle, Conway		Entertainment	15			40	Vintage Br. Actor
Tearle, Godfrey, Sir		Entertainment	20			50	Br. Actor. Vintage
Teasdale, Sara	1894-1933	Author	95	250		100	Poet. Bouts of Depression. Suicide at 39
Teasdale, Veree		Entertainment	20	25	45	45	Vintage Actress 30's-40's. Wife of Adolf Menjou
Tebaldi, Renata		Entertainment	25			100	Opera. Italian Soprano
Tedrow, Irene		Entertainment	4			15	Character Actress 40's-50's. Mother Parts
Teitjens, Therese		Entertainment	50			190	Opera
Telfair, Edward		Rev. War	35	95	150		Continental Congress from GA
Telford, Thomas	1757-1834	Engineer		105	330		Br. Road and Bridge-builder
Teller, Edward, Dr.	1908-94	Science	45	130	210	100	Fermi Award. Father of H-Bomb
Teller, Henry M.	1830-1914	Cabinet	30	25	50	30	Sec'y Interior 1882, Arthur
Telva, Marion		Entertainment	15			40	Opera.. Noted Contralto
Temin, Howard M., Dr.		Science	20	35	55	25	Nobel Medicine 1975
Tempest, Marie		Entertainment	25	35	50	65	
Temple, Frederick	1821-1902	Clergy	22		90		Archbishop Canterbury, Educator, Author
Temple, Shirley (Agar)		Entertainment	61			350	Shirley's First Husband, John
Temple, Shirley (as a child)		Entertainment	250			700	As Child-SPc $400. As Teenager SPI $250. Sig. $100
Temple, Shirley (Black)		Entertainment	20		40	45	SP (Vintage Ph/'87 Sig.) $385
Temple, Wm.		Clergy	40	45	85	65	Archbishop Canterbury
Templeton, Alec		Entertainment	10			50	Br. Blind Jazz Pianist
Templeton, Ben		Cartoonist	5			20	Motley's Crew
Templeton, Faye		Entertainment	25	30	60	65	Musical Career For Over 50 Year
Temptations (All)		Entertainment	40			125	
Ten Broeck, Abraham	1734-1810	Rev. War	100	125	1025		Gen. Judge, Banker
Tennant, F.R.		Clergy	15	20	25		
Tennant, Veronica		Ballet	10			25	National Ballet of Canada
Tennant, Victoria		Entertainment	5	8	25	20	
Tenniel, John, Sir	1820-1914	Artist	70	110	260		Illustr. 'Alice in Wonderland'
Tennille, Toni		Entertainment	5			15	Singer. The Captain & Tennille'

NAME	DATE	CATEGORY	SIG	LS/DS	ALS	SP	COMMENTS
Tennyson, Alfred, Lord	1809-92	Author	215	718	572	1050	Br. Poet Laureate
Tennyson, Jean		Entertainment	10			20	Am. Soprano
Teresa, Mother	1911-1997	Clergy	103	342	794	358	Worked/Poorest of Poor. Nobel Peace Prize 1979
Tereshkova, Valentina		Cosmonaut	200	250		250	1st Woman in Outer Space
Terfel, Bryn		Entertainment	10			35	Welsh Operatic Baritone
Terhune, Alfred Payson	1872-1942	Author	33	75	130	50	Famous Writer of Dog Stories
Terhune, Max	1891-1973	Entertainment	100			250	Western Sidekick in Republic & Monogram Series
Terkel, Studs		Author	10	15	25	15	Columnist, Biographer, TV
Ternina, Milka		Entertainment	20		135		Opera. Croatian Soprano
Terrell, Bob		Author	10			25	Author, Newspaper Columnist
Terriss, Ellaline		Entertainment	15			48	Br. Actress. 19th Century
Terry, Alfred Howe	1827-90	Civil War	110	475	590		Union Gen.,Cmdr. Dakota Terr.Sig/Rank $185,DS $800
Terry, Clark		Entertainment	50				Trumpet, Fluegelhorn
Terry, Ellen, Dame	1847-1928	Entertainment	35	70	135	188	Br. Actress Partner of Henry Irving. SP Pc $145
Terry, Fred	1864-1933	Entertainment	10	15	25	25	Br. Stage & Film Star
Terry, Henry D.	1812-69	Civil War	45	100	160		Union General. Sig/Rank $65
Terry, Luther, Dr.		Celebrity	3	5	10	5	
Terry, Paul*		Cartoonist	50			198	Animator-Mighty Mouse
Terry, Phillip	1909-	Entertainment	5		10	15	Actor. Films from 30's. Leads-2nd Leads in B Films
Terry, Ruth	1920-	Entertainment	10			25	Actress-Singer.Films at 16. Numerous Westerns
Terry, William H.	1814-88	Civil War	85		270		CSA Gen. Sig/Rank $120
Terry, William Richard	1827-97	Civil War	90	195	370		CSA General. Sig/Rank $200, War Dte. DS $625
Tesla, Nikola, Dr.	1856-1943	Science	450	950	1950	1150	Physicist, Electrical Genius. Power Systems
Tetard, J.		Aviation	45	60	170	100	
Tetrazzini, Luisa	1871-1940	Entertainment	50	115	200	225	It.Opera. SPc $300 as 'Lakme'
Tevis, Lloyd		Business		475			Mining & Partner of Geo. Hearst & Haggin
Teyte, Maggie		Entertainment	35			130	Opera
Thacher, James, Dr.	1754-1844	Science-Author	55		300		Rev. War Surgeon
Thackeray, Wm. Makepeace	1811-63	Author	110	375	542		Br. Novelist Vanity Fair
Thaden, Louise McP.		Aviation		295			Altitude, Endurance, Speed Records
Thagard, Norman E.		Astronaut	10			30	
Thalberg, Irving		Entertainment	250	485	585	350	MGM's Boy Genius Producer
Thant, U	1909-74	Head of State	75	195	295	200	UN Sec'y General
Tharp, Sister Rosetta		Entertainment	65			125	Jazz Vocalist-Guitar
Tharp, Twyla		Entertainment	20	25		40	Dancer-Choreographer
Thatcher, Henry Knox		Civil War	55	95	155		Union Naval Commander. Sig/Rank $85
Thatcher, Margaret, Dame		Head of State	45	140	225	150	Prime Minister. Engr. P.M. Card/Addr. $175
Thatcher, Peter		Clergy	75	100	150		
Thaves, Bob		Cartoonist	5			20	'Frank & Ernest'
Thaw, Harry K.		Business	40	95	195	75	Playboy. Shot Sanford White. Major Scandal
Thaw, Russell T.		Aviation	20				Racing Pilot
Thaxter, Celia		Entertainment	20	25	45	45	
Thaxter, Celia	1835-94	Author	20	40	95	150	Am. Poet
Thaxter, Phyllis		Entertainment	10			25	Stage & Film Leading Lady
Thayer, Abbott	1849-1921	Artist	15	35	70		Am. Ideal Figures, Landscapes

NAME	DATE	CATEGORY	SIG	LS/DS	ALS	SP	COMMENTS
Thayer, Celia		Author	5	10	15		Am. Novelist, Screenwriter
Thayer, John Milton	1820-1906	Civil War	45	95	180		Union Gen., Gov. WY Terr.
Thayer, Silvanus	1785-1872	Military	60	140	245		'Father of the Military Academy'
Thayil, Kim		Entertainment	6			25	Music. Lead Guitar Soundgarden
Thebaw		Head of State	145				Burma
Thebom, Blanche		Entertainment	20	35		75	Am. Contralto, Opera, Concert
Theiss, Ursula		Entertainment	10	15	25	25	Ger. Actress. Several Hollywood Films 50's
Theissen, Tiffany Amber		Entertainment	15			50	Actress. Pin-Up $75
Thelen, Bob		Aviation	10	25	40	35	ACE, WW II, Blue Angels
Theron, Charlize		Entertainment	9			48	Pin-Up $85
Thesiger, Ernest		Entertainment	225			650	
Thevenot, Melchisidec	1620-92	Traveler	20		95		French Traveler Family Introduced Coffee to France
Thibodeaux, Keith		Entertainment	20				Child Actor. Played Little Ricky on 'I Love Lucy
Thicke, Alan		Entertainment	10		25	25	Actor-Humorist. 'Growing Pains'
Thielicke, Helmut		Clergy	20	50	65	60	Germ. Evangel. Theologian
Thiers, Louis-Adolphe	1797-1877	Fr. Revolution	35	65	170		1st Pres. 3rd Republic
Thieu, Nguyen Van		Head of State	20	60	150	40	So. Viet Nam
Thinnis, Roy		Entertainment	5	10	20	15	Actor
Thirsk, Bob		Astronaut	5	15		15	
Thomas, Andrew		Astronaut	6			20	
Thomas, B.J.		Entertainment	5			10	Singer-Songwriter
Thomas, Betty		Entertainment	5		15	10	
Thomas, C.-L.-Ambroise	1811-96	Composer	85	335	312	250	Fr. Romantic Composer. Operas,etc. AMusQS $525
Thomas, Charles	1840-78	Military		800			45 Yrs. Service. Union Gen.
Thomas, Clarence (SC)	1948-	Supreme Court	25			35	
Thomas, Danny	1914-91	Entertainment	15	26		47	Comedian. Danny Thomas Show
Thomas, Dave		Business	15	25		35	Founder of Wendy's. TV Spokesman. S Sketch $175
Thomas, Donald		Astronaut	8			25	
Thomas, Dylan	1914-53	Author	510		1917	1500	Welsh Poet, Playwright, Short Stories
Thomas, E. Donnall, Dr.		Science	15	25		30	Nobel Medicine 1990
Thomas, George Henry	1818-70	Civil War	120	395	485		Union Gen.'Rock of Chickamauga'
Thomas, Heather		Entertainment	10	10	30	40	Actress
Thomas, Heck		Western Lawman					Special DS $2500
Thomas, Isaiah	1749-1831	Colonial Printer	135	380	1000		Publ. 1st Eng. Bible in America
Thomas, James, Bishop		Clergy	20	25	35	30	
Thomas, Jess		Entertainment	15			40	Opera
Thomas, John	1724-76	Rev. War	510	855	1750		Am. Physician & Gen. Cont'l Army
Thomas, John Charles	1891-1960	Entertainment	20	45	45	45	Multi Media Am. Baritone
Thomas, Jonathan Taylor	1981-	Entertainment	10			63	Talented Child-Young Actor Home Improvement etc.
Thomas, Kurt		Entertainment	5		15	15	
Thomas, Lorenzo (WD)	1804-75	Civil War	90	180	310		Union General. Seminole, Mexican & Civil Wars
Thomas, Lowell		Entertainment	15		35	125	World Traveller. Top Radio Commentator 30's-40's
Thomas, Marlo		Entertainment	5	25		20	Actress & Daughter of Danny. TV's That Girl
Thomas, Michael Tilson		Conductor	15			50	Am. Conductor
Thomas, Norman	1884-1961	Socialist Leader	35	95	205	55	6 Times Presidential Candidate. Socialist Leader

NAME	DATE	CATEGORY	SIG	LS/DS	ALS	SP	COMMENTS
Thomas, Olive		Entertainment	65	70	150	150	Actress. Jack Pickford Wife. Suicide at 36
Thomas, Philip Evan		Business	5	15	25		
Thomas, Richard		Entertainment	8		20	25	Actor.
Thomas, Rob		Entertainment	7			30	Music. Lead Singer Matchbox 20
Thomas, Robert Bailey		Author	20	45	105		Publisher, Editor 'Farmer's Almanac'
Thomas, Samuel		Civil War	45				Union General
Thomas, Seth E.	1785-1859	Business	125	250	475		Founder Seth Thomas Clock Co.
Thomas, Seth E., Jr.	1816-88	Business	65	175	350		Cont'd Seth Thomas Clock Co.
Thomas, Terry		Entertainment	50		100	150	Br. Comedian-Actor
Thomas, Theodore		Entertainment	15			30	Conductor. NY & Chic. Symph.
Thomasson, William P.	1797-1882	Congress	12	15			MOC KY, Union Officer CW
Thomberg, Kerstin		Entertainment	15			35	
Thompson Twins		Entertainment	30			75	Signed by Both
Thompson, Benj.(Rumford)	1753-1814	Rev. War	275	450	1138		Count von Rumford. Br. Physicist, Inventor, Loyalist
Thompson, Benjamin	1798-1852	Senate/Congress	5	15	25		MOC MA 1845
Thompson, Denman		Entertainment	10			30	Vintage Stage Actor
Thompson, Dorothy	1894-1961	Author	35	55	110	80	Journalist, Correspondent, Columnist, Wit
Thompson, Emma		Entertainment	20			58	Br. Actress-Playwright AA. Pin-Up SP $75
Thompson, Ernest Seton		Author	40	100	95		Wild Life Stories, Naturalist
Thompson, Gordon		Entertainment	8			20	
Thompson, Hank		Country Music	6			15	Singer-Songwriter
Thompson, J. Walter	1847-1928	Business	100	950		90	J. Walter Thompson Adv. Agency. Bond S $2400
Thompson, Jacob	1810-85	Civil War-Cabinet	145	375	1380		Sec'y Interior, CSA Secret Agt.
Thompson, Jim		Governor	5	10		20	Governor IL
Thompson, John P.		Business	15	30	65	20	Pres. Southland Corp.
Thompson, John T.	1860-1940	Inventor-Military	85	300			USA Officer, Inventor Thompson Sub-Machine Gun
Thompson, Lea		Entertainment	10			35	Actress. Back to the Future, Caroline in the City
Thompson, Linda		Entertainment	5			10	Actress. Pin-Up SP $20
Thompson, M.E.		Governor	5	15			Governor GA
Thompson, Marshall		Entertainment	15		25	35	Actor. Juvenile Leads-40's. Mature Leads 50's
Thompson, Merriwether J.(WD)		Civil War	212		3020		MO Militia General. Noted Guerrilla Fighter
Thompson, Merriwether J.	1826-76	Civil War	135	425	465		CSA General
Thompson, Orlo and Marvis		Country Music	20			45	(Both)
Thompson, Richard W.		Cabinet	25	45	70		Sec'y Navy 1809
Thompson, Robert E.		Clergy	10	10	15		
Thompson, Ruth Plumly		Author	450				
Thompson, Smith (SC)	1768-1843	Supreme Court	75	168	192		
Thompson, Sue		Country Music	10			25	Singer
Thompson, Wm. H. Big Bill	1869-1944	Celebrity	125				Gangster Era Mayor. Backed by Al Capone
Thomson, Andrew		Clergy	35	65	75		
Thomson, Charles	1729-1824	Rev. War	715	1740	1500		Wealthy Merch. LS As Sec'y Cont'l Congr.$1,750
Thomson, Elihu	1853-1937	Science	525	1250			Electrical Engineer-Inventor. Over 700 Patents
Thomson, Geo. Paget, Sir	1892-1975	Science	55			100	Nobel Physics 1937
Thomson, Hugh		Artist	25		100		Br. Illustrator
Thomson, James E.		Business	5	15	30	15	Pres. Merrill-Lynch.

NAME	DATE	CATEGORY	SIG	LS/DS	ALS	SP	COMMENTS
Thomson, Virgil	1896-1989	Composer	40	85	117	135	Conductor & Music Critic, AMusQS $125-$225
Thorborg, Kerstin		Entertainment	20			75	Opera
Thorburn, Grant		Colonial Am.	40	95			Grocery, Seed Merchant. Hero
Thoreau, Henry David	1717-1862	Author	1540	3000	7200		Am.Schoolmaster-Naturalist.Retired to 'Walden Pond
Thorndike, Sybil, Dame		Entertainment	30	45		75	Br. Preeminent Actress. Seven Decade Career
Thorne, Chas. Rob't	1814-1893	Entertainment	65	80		120	
Thorne-Smith, Courtney		Entertainment	6			38	Actress. Pin-Up $55
Thornhill, Claude		Bandleader	12			45	Big Band
Thornhill, F. D.		Military	15	25	40		
Thornton, Billie Bob		Entertainment	7			40	Versatile Actor. Writer-Director
Thornton, Charles Tex		Business	5	15	25	15	
Thornton, Dan		Governor	5	15		10	Governor CO
Thornton, Dr. William E.		Astronaut	10			20	
Thornton, Kathryn		Astronaut	10			27	
Thornton, Matthew	1714-1803	Rev. War	525	1550	3212		Signer Decl. of Indepen.
Thornton, William		Astronaut	5			20	
Thornton, William	1759-1828	Rev. War	140	356			Am. Architect. Designed Capitol
Thornton, William A.	1803-66	Civil War	35				Union Gen. '62 DS $95
Thornton, Willie Mae	1926-84	Entertainment	90		275		Am. Jazz-Gospel Singer. Died of Alcoholism
Thorpe, Jeremy		Politician	10	20	45	15	Br. Parliamentarian
Thorpe, Rose Hartwick		Author	10	20	35		Am. 'Curfew Must Not Ring Tonight'
Thorson, Ralph'Papa'		Law	10	25	45	20	Bounty Hunter
Thorvaldsen, Bertel		Artist	105	325			Dan. Sculptor 'Lion of Lucerne'
Thouot, Pierre		Astronaut	6			20	
Three Stooges, The		Entertainment	1500			3500	With Moe, Curly and Larry. Sig.(1st Names) $695
Three Suns, The		Entertainment	15			45	Pop-Jazz Musicians
Throop, Enos T.		Governor	25	55			Governor NY 1829
Thruston, Gates P.	1835-	Civil War	25	30	55		Union General
Thuot, Pierre		Astronaut	5			15	
Thurber, James	1894-1961	Author	105	612	578	110	Am. Humorist & Comic Artist
Thurber, James*		Cartoonist	105			500	New Yorker Illust. & Cartoonist
Thurman, Allen G.	1813-95	Congress	10	30	45		Senator OH
Thurman, Howard		Clergy	35	40	50	50	
Thurman, Uma		Entertainment	12	30		58	Actress. Pin-Up SP $75
Thurmond, J. Strom		Senate/Congress	10	20		15	Senator, Governor SC
Thurston, Howard	1869-1936	Entertainment	80	212	250	225	Thurston The Magician
Thurston, John M.	1847-1916	Congress	1530				Senator NE 1895
Thurston, Lorrin A.	1858-1931	Political	35		55		Pioneer Hawaiian Political Leader
Tibbatts, John W.	1802-52	Congress	10		55		MOC KY, Officer Mexican War
Tibbett, Lawrence	1896-1960	Entertainment	75	80		120	Opera, Concert, Films, Radio
Tibbetts, Paul W.		Aviation	30	128	175	92	Pilot of Enola Gay WW II. General.FDC S $35
Tidball, John C.	1825-1906	Civil War	60	135	175		Union General Bvt.Sig/Rank $75
Tiege, Karl		Artist	80		275		Czech. Surrealist Painter
Tiegs, Cheryl		Entertainment	8			22	Model. Pin-Up SP $25
Tierney, Gene		Entertainment	30	25	50	45	Actress. Laura. Pin-Up SP $50

NAME	DATE	CATEGORY	SIG	LS/DS	ALS	SP	COMMENTS
Tierney, Harry		Composer	40	95	195		AMusQS $350
Tietjens, Therese		Entertainment	40			135	Ger. Soprano . Opera
Tiffany, Charles Lewis	1812-1902	Business	175	500		2125	Founder Tiffany and Co. Jewelry Designer. Artist
Tiffany, Louis Comfort		Artist-Business	175	550			Stained glass artist. Spec. Ed. Book S $3200
Tiffin, Pamela		Entertainment	5		15	15	Actress
Tilden, Samuel J.	1814-86	Governor	75	160	275		Gov. NY, Presidential Cand.
Tilghman, James		Rev. War	25	70	165		Lawyer, Politician
Tilghman, Lloyd (WD)		Civil War	235		1980		CSA Gen. KIA. AES $635
Tilghman, Lloyd	1816-63	Civil War	140	290	502		CSA General. NRPA. KIA
Tilghman, Matthew		Rev. War	200		825		Cont. Congress.ALS/Cont. $2,750
Tilghman, William M.	1755-1827	Law	200	1200	1400		Early Western Sheriff
Tilkin-Servais, Ernest		Entertainment	25			85	Opera
Tilley, Reade		Aviation	10	20	35		Am. Air Ace as Member of Royal Air Force
Tillich, Paul		Clergy	70	95	125	100	
Tillinghast, Charles C. Jr.		Business	10	20	40	15	CEO TWA. Merrill-Lynch
Tillis, Mel		Country Music	5			15	Songwriter-Singer
Tillman, Floyd		Country Music	10			25	Songwriter-Singer-Guitarist-Mandolinist
Tillman, Pitchfork Ben	1847-1918	Congress	25	40	55		Senator SC 1894
Tillotson, Johnny		Country Music	6			20	Singer
Tillstrom, Burr		Entertainment	25			50	
Tilly, Jennifer		Entertainment	8			48	Actress. Pin-Up SP $35-60
Tilly, Meg		Entertainment	10		20	37	Actress. Pin-Up SP $35
Tilton, Charlene		Entertainment	25			40	
Tilton, Martha		Entertainment	12			20	Big Band Singer, Recording Artist
Tilton, Theodore	1835-1907	Journalist			90		Sued Henry Ward Beecher for Adultery
Tilton, Wm. Stowell		Civil War	45	100			
Timberlake, Bob		Artist	15			20	Painter, Designer. Litho S $600+
Timken, Henry	1831-1909	Inventor	85	140	225		Timpken Tapered Roller Bearings
Timken, William Robert		Business	35	95	155	60	Pres. Timken Roller Bearings
Ting, Samuel C. C., Dr.		Science	20	35	50	25	Nobel Physics 1976
Tingey, Thomas		Military	80	165	225		Continental Navy
Tingley, Clyde		Governor	12	20		15	Governor NM 1935
Tinker, Grant C.		Entertainment	8	10		15	TV Film Producer
Tinnell, Carol		Entertainment	15			45	Actress. Pin-Up $55
Tiny Tim		Entertainment	25	35		45	Singer. 'Tiptoe Through The Tulips'
Tiny, Texas		Country Music	10			20	Singer
Tiomkin, Dimitri	1894-1979	Composer	35		175	400	Music Major Movie ProductionsAMusQS $225-$675
Tippett, Michael Sir		Composer	40			150	
Tisch, Laurence A.		Business	15			45	CEO of CBS
Tisserant, Eugene, Cardinal		Clergy	35	45	50	40	
Tissot, James	1836-1902	Artist	75	175	250		Fr. Painter, Engraver, Enameler
Titchener, Paul		Business	10	35	45	20	
Titian (Vecelli, Tiziano)		Artist					Italian Master. NRPA
Tito, Marshal (Josip Broz)	1892-1980	Head of State	95	205	280	250	Yugoslav Statesman. Communist
Titov, Gherman		Astronaut	40			135	

NAME	DATE	CATEGORY	SIG	LS/DS	ALS	SP	COMMENTS
Tobey, Charles W.		Senate/Congress	5	15		10	Governor, Rep., Senator NH
Tobey, Ken		Entertainment	10			25	Actor. Hundreds of Supporting Roles
Tobias, George	1901-	Entertainment	50			150	Actor. Stage, Films-1939-70's.
Tobin, Genevieve	1901-	Entertainment	15		30	35	Actress. Warner Bros. Leads-2nd Leads from 30's
Tobin, James, Dr.		Economist	22	30		25	Nobel Economics 1981
Tobin, Maurice		Cabinet	10	20	30	15	Sec'y Labor 1948, Gov. MA
Tocqueville, Alexis de	1805-59	Author	45	150	350		Fr.Politician,Statesman,Writer
Tod, David		Governor	10	25			Governor OH
Todd, Alexander Robertus, Sir		Science	30	85		40	Nobel Chemistry 1957
Todd, Ann	1909-	Entertainment	20			40	Br. Actress. Internat'l Film Star From 30's
Todd, Charles Scott		Celebrity	5	15	40		
Todd, Henry D., Jr.	1866-	Military	15		35		WW I Genl
Todd, Richard		Entertainment	58			100	Ir. Actor. AA Nomination for Hasty Heart
Todd, Robert		Aviation	15	30	45	25	
Todd, Thelma	1905-35	Entertainment	138	235	350	475	Actress. Mysterious Death at 30
Tognini, Michel		Astronaut	15	25		35	
Togo, Heihachiro, Marquis	1846-1934	Military	110	315	448		Jap. Adm. Sino-Jap. War. Small Format SP $185
Togo, Shigenori		Diplomat	250			400	Jap. Foreign Minister-Statesman
Tojo, Hideki	1884-1948	Military	250	700	1500	1380	PM Jap. Adm. Pearl Harbor.Executed DS/Spec $2400
Toklas, Alice B.	1877-1967	Author	45	185	822		Companion of Gertrude Stein
Tokody, Ilona		Entertainment	5			25	Opera
Tokyo Rose (Iva I. Toguri)		Military	225	330		325	WW II Radio Propagandist
Toledo, Francisco, Cardinal		Clergy	15000				Introduced Inquisition into Peru. NRPA
Toler, Sidney	1874-1947	Entertainment	150			362	2nd Charlie Chan After Warner Oland
Tolkien, John R.R.	1892-1973	Author	400	1705	1847		Br.Writer of Lord of the Ring
Tolstoy, Alexandra, Countess		Author	25		80		
Tolstoy, Leo, Count	1828-1910	Author	1200	1800	2988	2258	Rus. Novelist & Moral Philosopher
Tomagno, Francesco		Conductor	40		250		Opera etc.
Tombaugh, Clyde W.	1906-97	Science	25	135	270	135	Am. Astronomer, Discoverer of Planet Pluto 1930
Tomei, Marissa		Entertainment	20			57	Actress. Oscar Winner
Tomlin, Lily		Entertainment	5	25	15	25	Comedienne. TV. Theatre One Woman Show
Tomlin, Pinky		Bandleader	10			35	Scat Singer
Tompkins, Angel		Entertainment	10	15	20	25	Actress. Pin-Up SP $35
Tompkins, Daniel	1774-1825	Vice Pres.	85	200	200		Monroe VP, Governor NY
Tompson, Alexander K.		Clergy	15	25	35		
Tone, Franchot	1905-68	Entertainment	22		50	73	Am. Leading Man & Later Char. Actor
Tony, Simon		Entertainment	6			25	Music. Guitar, Keyboard The Verve
Toombs, Robert A.	1810-1885	Civil War	135	250	250		CSA General & Sec'y State. Sig/Rank $205
Toomey, Regis	1902-	Entertainment	15	20		45	Actor. Familiar Face With Over 150 Film Credits
Toones, Fred Snowflake		Entertainment	150			300	
Toorop, Jan (Dutch)	1858-1928	Artist	25	100	210	125	Posters, Tiles, Stained Glass. Leader Of Luminists
Topal		Entertainment	10			30	Israeli Actor. Stage, Films. AA Nominated(Fiddler)
Topp, Erich		Military	35		175	95	Ger. U Boat Cmdr. WW II
Topping, Dan		Business	10	15	30	20	Millionaire One Time Owner NY Yankees
Torisu, Kennosuke		Military	60		175	75	

NAME	DATE	CATEGORY	SIG	LS/DS	ALS	SP	COMMENTS
Tork, Peter		Entertainment	15	35		35	Singer-Actor 'The Monkees'
Torme, Mel		Entertainment	20	22		50	Vocalist, Composer. Known as The Velvet Fog
Torn, Rip		Entertainment	15			35	Actor. Major Roles in Major Films-TV. Emmy Award
Torrance, Ernest	1878-1933	Entertainment	75			150	Scot. Silent Films. Ex Opera
Torrence, Ridgely	1875-1950	Author	25	30	85		Am. Poet, Editor, Dramatist
Torres, Raquel	1908-	Entertainment	20			45	Mex. Actress. Several Early Sound Films
Torrey, R.A.		Clergy	20	35	50		
Tors, Ivan	1916-	Entertainment	15			35	Producer-Director-Screenwriter. USAAF-OSS
Toscanini, Arturo	1867-1957	Conductor	264	635	1021	731	AMusQS $750-$950, AMusMs $3,750. SP Pc $625
Tosti, Paolo		Composer	25	60	155		Italian Composer
Toto	1898-1967	Entertainment	65			250	It. Comedy Star. Films From 1936
Totten, Jos. G.	1788-1864	Civil War	20	40	85		Union Gen. Wardte DS $200-$400, Sig/Rank $50
Totter, Audrey		Entertainment	5	15		20	Actress. Radio Dramas, TV Soaps, Films 1939
Toucey, Isaac	1792-1869	Cabinet	25	80	135		Polk Att'y Gen. 1848, Sec'y Navy '57
Toulouse-Lautrec, Henri	1864-1901	Artist	1150	2950	5900		Fr. Parisian Nightlife. Over 300 Lithographs
Toumanova, Tamara		Entertainment	30			110	Rus-Am Ballerina
Tourel, Jennie		Entertainment	20			50	Opera
Tourgee, Albion W.	1838-1905	Author	15	20	45		Lawyer, Judge, Diplomat
Toussaint-L'Ouverture, Pierre	1743-1803	Statesman		1888			Haitian General. Led Haitian Slave Revolt 1791
Tower, John		Senate/Congress	5	15		25	Senator TX
Tower, Zealous B.	1819-1900	Civil War	25	35	60		Union General
Towers, Constance		Entertainment	5		10	10	Actress
Towl, E. Clinton		Business	20		55		
Townes, Charles Hanson		Science	30	40	65		Inventor. Nobel (Laser & Maser)
Townley, James		Clergy	35	50	75		
Townsand, Colleen (Evans)		Entertainment	5			15	Actress. Short Career In Films. 50's-
Townsend, Edward D.	1817-93	Civil War	32	52	68		Union General
Townsend, Francis Everett	1867-1960	Science	40			150	Social Reformer & Physician. Old Age Pension Plan
Townsend, Frederick		Civil War	20	30	52		Union General
Townsend, George A. (Gath)		Author	15		40		War Correspondent
Townsend, Lynn		Business	10	20	35	20	CEO-Pres. Chrysler Corp.
Townsend, M. Clifford		Governor	10	15			Governor IN
Townsend, Pete		Entertainment	30			70	Lead Singer 'The Who'
Townsend, Peter		Military	10	35	50	25	
Townsend, Robert		Entertainment	10	15		20	Film Director
Townsend, Washington		Senate/Congress	10	20			Rep. PA 1969
Toy Story (Cast Of)		Entertainment				275	Hanks, Varney, Potts, Rickles
Toynbee, Arnold	1852-83	Author	25	105	190	80	Br. Economist, Sociologist
Toynbee, Arnold Joseph	1889-1975	Author	20	45	120	30	Br. Historian, Prof., Paris Peace Conf.
Tozzi, Giorgio		Entertainment	20			40	Opera
Trachte, Don*		Cartoonist	25			75	'Henry'
Tracy, Arthur		Entertainment	20			45	'The Street Singer'.
Tracy, Benjamin F.		Cabinet	20	45	70		Sec'y Navy 1889
Tracy, Edward Dorr (WD)		Civil War	300	800			CSA Gen. KIA 5/1/63. AES $1100
Tracy, Lee	1898-1968	Entertainment	10			25	Actor- Broadway '24;Screen '29. Fast-Talking Roles

NAME	DATE	CATEGORY	SIG	LS/DS	ALS	SP	COMMENTS
Tracy, Spencer	1900-67	Entertainment	152	433	375	390	50th Anniv.Movies/K.Hepburn $595. SP 5x7 $275
Train, Arthur		Author	10	15	35		
Train, George Francis	1824-1904	Author-Tycoon	42		300		Wealth from Shipping, Railroads, Streetcars
Trapier, James H.	1815-65	Civil War	130	310	405		CSA Gen. AES '61 $575
Trask, Diana	1940-	Country Music	10			20	Australian Pop-Country Singer. To U.S. in 1959
Trask, Spencer		Business		950			Founder Spenser Trask & Co., Wall Street
Traubel, Helen		Entertainment	50			100	Opera. Am. Soprano. Concerts, Radio, Films
Trautloft, Hannes		Aviation	25			50	Ger. Ace WW II RK
Travalena, Fred		Entertainment	5		15	15	Actor-Comedy
Travanti, Daniel J.		Entertainment	6		15	20	Actor
Traven, Berwick (Torsvan)	1890-1969	Author	265	800	1765		Ger. Novelist, Actor, Pacifist
Travers, Henry	1974-1965	Entertainment	195			350	Mild-Mannered Character Actor. Films- Early 30's
Travers, Pamela L.		Author	25	125			Mary Poppins Books
Travers, Patricia		Entertainment	5			30	Violinist.
Traverso, Giuseppe		Entertainment	15			45	Opera
Travis, Kylie		Entertainment	5			20	Actress. Models, Inc. Pin-Up SP $40
Travis, Merle		Country Music	20			40	Top Multi-Talented Guitarist, Singer, Songwriter.
Travis, Nancy		Entertainment	18			40	Actress
Travis, Randy		Country Music	15	32		40	Singer. Sometimes Actor
Travis, Richard	1913-	Entertainment	5			20	Actor. Became Wealthy Hollyw'd Realtor
Travis, William Barret		Military		5000			Co-Cmdr. Alamo.Texas Frontier. NRPA
Travolta, John		Entertainment	25			64	Get Shorty SP $50-80
Treacher, Arthur	1894-1975	Entertainment	25		40	45	Lawyer-Trained. Became Perrenial Br.Butler in 30's
Treadway, Allen Towner		Senate/Congress	4	15			MOC MA 1913
Treadwell, John		Rev. War	25	60	95		Del. CT. Elected to Cont.Congr.
Treas, Terri		Entertainment	5			10	
Trebek, Alex		Entertainment	10		20	25	Perennial Host of 'Jeopardy' TV Game Show
Trebor, Robert		Entertainment	5			20	Hercules/Xena
Tree, Herbert Beerbohm, Sir	1852-1917	Entertainment	30	85	145	75	Br.Actor-Mgr. Fndr. Royal Academy
Treen, Mary	1907-	Entertainment	5	15	30	25	ActressComedienne. Films from 1934
Treilhard, Jean-Baptiste	1742-1810	Fr.Revolution	25	40	75		Fr. Politician. Important in Drafting Legal Codes
Trelawny, Edward	1792-1881	Author		445	750		Br.Author-Adventurer. Companion of Shelley & Byron
Tremayne, Les		Entertainment	5			20	Top Radio Actor 30's-40's—
Tremonti, Mark		Entertainment	6			25	Music. Guitar, Vocals Creed
Trench, Richard C., Archbishop		Clergy	45	60	95	65	
Trenholm, George A.	1807-76	Civil War	105	175	200		CSA Sec'y Treasury. Sig/Rank $175
Trent, William		Celebrity		600			
Trettner, Henrich 'Heniz		Aviation	20	45		50	
Trevelyan, George Otto, Sir	1838-1928	Author	15	35	75		Br.Historian,Sec'y To Admiralty, Author
Treves, Frederick, Dr.		Science	200		440		Dr. To Elephant Man
Trevor, Claire	1909-	Entertainment	20			48	AA Winning Actress. Key Largo, Stagecoach
Trilling, Lionel	1905-75	Author	10	30	50	25	Am. Lit. Critic. Professor, Essayist
Trimble, Isaac R. (WD)		Civil War	395		1575		CSA General
Trimble, Isaac Ridgeway	1802-88	Civil War	185	900	405		CSA General
Trimble, Lawrence	1825-1904	Congress	15		25		MOC KY

NAME	DATE	CATEGORY	SIG	LS/DS	ALS	SP	COMMENTS
Trinh, Eugene		Astronaut	5			15	
Tripler, Charles E.		Science	75	185			Inventor Liquid Air
Trippe, Juan T.	1899-1981	Aviation	30			55	Fndr. Pan American Airways. Clipper Service
Tripplehorn, Jeanne		Entertainment	15			50	Actress
Trist, Nicholas P.	1800-1874	Diplomat	75	225			Am. Negotiated Treaty of Guadaloupe
Tritt, Travis		Country Music	15			35	Singer
Tritton, William Ashbee, Sir		Science	25	70	125	40	Developed Military Tank
Trollope, Anthony	1815-82	Author	122	264	927		Br. Novelist. 50 Novels
Trollope, Frances	1780-1863	Author	40	115	225		Br. Novelist. Mother of Anthony
Trollope, Thomas A.	1810-92	Author		25	50		Novels, History. Tremendous Output
Trotsky, Leon	1879-1940	Head of State	838	2512	2725	1000	Communist Revolution leader-Assassinated
Trotter, James Monroe	1842-92	Civil War	40	250			
Trotter, Mark C.		Clergy	15		35		
Troubridge, Thomas, Sir		Military	75		250		Br. Admiral, Battle of the Nile
Troup, Bobby	1918-99	Entertainment	20			35	Pianist, Composer, Vocalist-Actor
Troup, Frank W.		Aviation	15			35	WW II Air Ace
Trowbridge, John T.	1827-1916	Author	15		25		
Trower, Robin		Entertainment	15			30	
Troyanos, Tatiana		Entertainment	15			40	Opera
Trudeau, Gary*		Cartoonist	40			250	1st Cartoonist Awarded Pulitzer-Editorial Cartoons
Trudeau, Pierre	1919-	Head of State	25	60	95	80	Prime Minister Canada
Trueblood, D. Elton		Clergy	15	30	45	35	
Truett, George W.		Clergy	15	35	50	35	
Truex, Ernest	1890-1973	Entertainment	20			35	Character Actor From Silent Era into 50's-60's
Truffaut, Francois	1932-84	Entertainment	83	422		402	Fr. Dir. & Critic, ALS/Content $800
Trujillo, Rafael	1891-1961	Head of State	75	95		283	Dominican Republic. Assassinated
Truly, Richard H.		Astronaut	15	75		45	
Truman, Benj. C.	1835-1916	Author	20		45		Soldier-Author
Truman, Bess W.	1885-1982	First Lady	82	90	212	170	S WH Card $85-100-$195. FDC S $75
Truman, Harry (Mt.St.Helens)		Celebrity	5		25	25	Resident of Washington Volcano Eruption
Truman, Harry S. (As Pres.)		President	375	1874	4278	787	TLS/Cont. $4,750, $7,850, $13,200
Truman, Harry S.	1884-1972	President	166	468	2192	416	ALS/Content $14,000
Truman, Margaret (Daniel)		First Family	25	65	80	30	Author-Daughter Of Harry S. Truman
Trumbo, Dalton	1905-76	Author	50	200		75	Blacklisted Screenwriter. AA For 'The Brave One'
Trumbull, Annie E.	1858-1949	Author	15		25		
Trumbull, John	1750-1831	Author-Lawyer	85	250			CT Poet & Lawyer
Trumbull, John	1756-1843	Artist	100	565	2437		ALS/Content $8,000. Engr. by R.Riker S $750
Trumbull, Jonathan	1710-85	Rev. War	290	487	1200		Confidant of G. Washington. ADS Special $1100
Trumbull, Jonathan	1740-1809	Military-Senate	125	300	565		Sec'y Washington's Staff
Trumbull, Lyman		Senate	25	80	140	95	U.S. Senate IL 1855-1873
Trump, Donald J.		Business	12	45	75	42	Millionaire Entrepreneur
Trump, Ivana		Celebrity	10			40	Ex Mrs. Donald Trump
Trump, Marla Maples		Celebrity	15			35	Current Mrs. Donald Trump
Truscott, L.K., Jr.		Military	25	105			TLS/Cont.$225
Truth, Sojourner	1797-1883	Abolitionist					Religious Missionary, RARE in any form. Only 3 Known

NAME	DATE	CATEGORY	SIG	LS/DS	ALS	SP	COMMENTS
Truxton, William Talbot		Civil War	30	55	95		Union Naval Officer. Adm. 1882
Truxtun, Thomas	1755-1822	Rev. War	110	355	675		Cmdr. USS Constellation
Tryggvason, Bjarni		Astronaut	5			20	
Tryon, Tom		Entertainment	10	20	25	20	Actor-Author
Tryon, William	1728-88	Rev. War	145	375	770		Colon'l Gov. NC, Gov. NY
Tschernenko, Konstantin	1911-1985	Head of State	75			375	Pres. Soviet Union 1984-'85
Tshombe, Moise	1919-69	Head of State	55	90	195	112	Prime Min.,Zaire(Congo Rep.)TLS/Cont. $795-1250
Tsiolkovsky, Konstantin	1857-1935	Science			2500		Pioneer Rus. Space Program
Tsongas, Paul E.		Senator	15	35		25	Senator MA, Pres. Hopeful 1992
Tubb, Ernest	1914-	Country Music	15			40	Country Music Hall of Fame
Tubb, Justin	1935-	Country Music	5			15	Singer-Son of Ernest Tubb
Tuchman, Barbara W.		Author	35	125	155	45	2 Time Pulitzer Pr., Historian
Tucker, Forrest	1919-	Entertainment	20	35	40	45	Actor.Husky, Blonde Bully in 40's, Hero in 50's
Tucker, John R. (WD)		Civil War	180	290			CSA Navy Commdr. 1812-83
Tucker, Orrin		Entertainment	15			25	Big Band Leader
Tucker, Richard		Entertainment	30	45		120	Opera
Tucker, Samuel	1747-1883	Rev. War	125	325	675		Am. Naval Hero. Commodore
Tucker, Sophie	1884-1966	Entertainment	32	40	95	67	Burlesque,Vaudeville, 'Last of the Red Hot Mamas'
Tucker, Tanya	1958-	Entertainment	10			20	Country Singer
Tucker, Thomas T.	1745-1848	Rev. War	55	185	175		Soldier, Statesman, Treasurer
Tucker, Tilghman M.		Senate/Congress	20	35	55		Senator 1838, Governor MS 1841
Tucker, Tommy		Entertainment	15			45	Big Bandleader
Tudor, Anthony		Entertainment	35	45		100	Br. Dancer, Choreographer
Tuell, Jack M., Bishop		Clergy	20	25	35	30	
Tufts, Cotton	1734-1815	Rev. War	75	175	262		Highly Esteemed Physician. Patriot
Tufts, Sonny	1911-70	Entertainment	20	25		35	1st Singer, 2nd Actor.Became Laughed-at Alchoholic
Tulford, Nellie Hughes		Astronaut	5			15	
Tully, Alice		Philanthropist	15	30		35	Lincoln Ctre. Tully Hall
Tully, Grace G.		White House	15	25	50	25	Sec'y to FDR
Tully, Tom		Cabinet	5	15	35	15	
Tully, Tom	1908-	Entertainment	25			45	Vet. Of US Navy, Legit. Stage, Radio & Many Films
Tumulty, Joseph P.	1879-1954	White House	15	35	75	40	Important Aide to President Wilson
Tune, Tommy		Entertainment	10		15	25	Dancer, Choreographer. 'Tony' Award Winner
Tunnell, James M.		Senate/Congress	10	30		20	Senator DE 1940
Tunney, John V.		Senate/Congress	5	10		10	MOC, Senator CA
Tupper, Martin F.	1810-89	Inventor	25		50		Brit. Author-Poet. Proverial Philosophy
Turgenev, Ivan	1818-33	Author	295	525	958	1265	Russ. Novelist, Dramatist. AQS $1450
Turkel, Ann		Entertainment	4	6		156	Pin-Up SP $20
Turkel, Studs		Author	10	20	35	20	Columnist. TV Commentator
Turlington, Christy		Entertainment	15			40	Super Model-Actress. Pin-up $50
Turner, Edward	1798-1837	Science	32		175		Scot. Chemist. Atomic Weights of Elements
Turner, Eva, Dame	1892-	Entertainment	40			75	Opera.Vocal Phenomenon
Turner, Frederick J.	1861-1932	Author	55		225		Pulitzer Prize 1932. Historian
Turner, J. M. W.	1775-1851	Artist	225	605	1475		Br. Landscape Painter
Turner, Janine		Entertainment	20			50	Actress. Pin-Up SP $65

NAME	DATE	CATEGORY	SIG	LS/DS	ALS	SP	COMMENTS
Turner, John Wesley	1833-99	Civil War	100	125	300		Union General Sig/Rank $145
Turner, Kathleen		Entertainment	10	40		40	Pin-Up SP $45
Turner, Lana	1920-95	Entertainment	37	73		81	Actress. Glamour StarPin-Up SP $90
Turner, Morrie		Cartoonist	5			20	'Wee Pals'
Turner, Philip		Rev. War	70	135	250		Unrivalled Sugeon During War
Turner, Robert E. Ted		Business	25	317		45	Media Tycoon. Founder CNN etc.
Turner, Roscoe, Col.		Aviation	75	150		100	Pioneer Aviator. Early Race Pilot. Speed Records
Turner, Tina		Entertainment	20		40	45	Rock-Pop Singer
Turpie, David		Senator/Congress	15	25	35		Senator IN 1863
Turpin, Ben	1874-1840	Entertainment	175		300	433	Beloved Cross-Eyed Mack Sennett Comic. Silents
Turreau De Garambouville		Fr. Revolution	20		85		
Turtles		Entertainment	35			75	Signed by All
Tusmayan, Barsag		Entertainment	5			25	Opera
Tussaud, Marie	1760-1850	Artist	200	725			Swiss Modeler in Wax. Madame Tussaud's Exh.
Tuttle, Lurene		Entertainment	5		15	15	Top Radio Dramatic Star. Supporting Roles in Films
Tuttle, Wes & Marilyn		Country Music	15			30	Duet. Turned Evangelist. With Religious Music Only
Tutu, Desmond, Bishop		Clergy	55	100	225	170	Nobel Peace Prize. 4x5 SP $100 (Col)
Tutwiler, Margaret D.		Cabinet	10	15		15	Ass'y Sec'y State
Tuve, Merle Antony	1901-82	Science	35	80	155	50	Neutron, Ionosphere, Radar
Twain, Mark		Author					SEE Clemens
Twain, Mark and Sam. Clemens		Author	1138				Both Signatures
Twain, Shania		Entertainment	12			82	Singer. Pop - Country
Tweed, Shannon		Entertainment	8		20	30	Actress-Model. Pin-Up SP $30, Nude SP$ 80
Tweed, William Marcy	1823-78	Political Giant	120	226	385	980	Boss Tweed. Corrupt Tammany Hall Politician
Twiggs, David E.	1790-1862	Civil War & 1812	195	370	1188		CSA General Sig/Rank $205
Twiggy (Nee: Leslie Hornsby)		Entertainment	15	25	25	35	60's Brit. Fashion Model. Actress
Twining, Nathan F.	1897-1982	Aviation	50	135	185	120	Gen. WW II. Commanded 15th Air Force
Twiss, Peter		Aviation	10	15	30	20	
Twitty, Conway	1933-93	Country Music	30	50		70	Early Rocker turned Country Superstar
Two Guns White Calf	1872-1934	Blackfoot Chief	650		4000	1925	Buffalo Nickel Model. SPPc $795
Tydings, Millard E.	1890-1961	Congress	20	50		30	Rep., Senator MD, Author
Tyler, Asher	1798-1875	Congress	10		35		MOC NY, Founder Elmira Rolling Mill
Tyler, Beverly		Entertainment	5			20	Actress
Tyler, Bonnie		Entertainment	15			30	
Tyler, Daniel	1799-1882	Civil War	35	85	125		Union Gen.
Tyler, Edward Burnett, Sir		Science	15	30	50		!st Prof. Anthropology Oxford
Tyler, Gerald E.		Aviation	10	25	40	30	ACE, WW II
Tyler, John	1790-1862	President	448	1570	2086		As VP. ALS/Content $7,500, FF $550
Tyler, Julia Gardiner		First Lady	195	545		650	Special DS $1,100
Tyler, Liv		Entertainment	18			58	Actress. Pin-Up $85. ...Thing You Do SP $65
Tyler, Moses Coit		Author	5	15	25		Historian. Am. Historical Assoc
Tyler, Robert	1816-77	Military	105		250		President's Son. Mex War. CSA Register
Tyler, Robert C.		Civil War	220	580	850		CSA General. Killed April 16, 1865
Tyler, Royall	1757-1826	Rev. War	25	50	120		Jurist, Author, Playwright
Tyler, T. Texas		Country Music	15			30	Singer. Deck 'O Cards

NAME	DATE	CATEGORY	SIG	LS/DS	ALS	SP	COMMENTS
Tyler, Tom	1903-1954	Entertainment	68			150	Started '24 as Stuntman-Extra. Western Star 1940's
Tyndale, Hector	1921-80	Civil War	30	60	85	175	Union General Sig/Rank $45, War Dte DS $125
Tyndall, John	1820-93	Science	44	200	160		Irish Physicist, Natural Philosopher
Tyner, James N.		Cabinet	10	40	75		P. M. General 1876
Tyner, McCoy		Entertainment	10	20		30	Jazz Pianist-Composer
Tyson, Cicely		Entertainment	10		20	20	Actress.
Tyson, Don		Business	15			25	Pres., Founder, CEO Tyson's Chicken

U

NAME	DATE	CATEGORY	SIG	LS/DS	ALS	SP	COMMENTS
U-2 (All)		Entertainment	185			300	Irish Rock Group
Ubico Casteneda, Jorge		Head of State	25	75			
Udall, Morris K.		Congress	4			10	Repr. AZ
Udet, Ernst	1896-1941	Aviation	225	375	700	550	ACE, WW I, German Ace. 2nd Only To Richthofen
Ueberroth, Peter		Business	10	25	40	10	
Uecker, Bob		Entertainment	5	8	15	15	
Ufford, Edward S.		Clergy	40	50	70		
Uggams, Leslie		Entertainment	5	10	15	20	
Ullman, Liv		Entertainment	6	8	20	35	Sw. Film Actress
Ullman, Tracey		Entertainment	20			50	
Ulmanis, Karlis		Head of State	90				1st Pres. Latvia. Fate Unknown
Ulmar, Geraldine		Entertainment	6	8	15	15	
Umberto I (It)		Royalty	50	150	375		King Italy
Umeki, Miyoshi		Entertainment	235			450	
Umstead, William B.		Governor	5	15	20		Governor NC
Underwood, J. T.		Inventor	25	100	200		Underwood Typewriter
Underwood, Oscar W.		Senate/Congress	4	10		10	Rep., Senator AL
Undset, Sigrid	1882-1949	Author				325	Nor. Nobel Prize Winner
Unger, Jim		Cartoonist	15	20		25	Henry
Ungher, Caroline	1803-77	Entertainment			150		Opera. Great Contralto
Unreal, Minerva		Entertainment	25			60	
Unruh, Howard B.		Celebrity	80				
Untermeyer, Louis	1885-1971	Author	20	50	90	25	Am. Poet,Critic,Satirist,Biogr.
Updike, John	1932-	Author	25	108	150	45	Am. Novelist, Poet, Short Story Writer
Upham, Charles	1802-75	Clergy	30		95		Unitarian Minister, Author, Whig Congressman
Upham, Charles	1908-	Military	100	250			One of Only 3 Men to Win Victoria Cross Twice
Upjohn, E. Gifford, Dr.		Business	125	450			Founder Upjohn Pharmaceuticals
Upshaw, Dawn		Entertainment	10			25	Opera
Upshaw, William D.		Senate/Congress	5	15		10	Rep. GA 1919, Evangelist
Upshur, Abel Parker	1790-1844	Cabinet	30	95	110		Tyler Sec'y Navy, State
Upton, Emory		Civil War	25	55	85		Union Gen. Wardte DS $465
Urbanowicz, Witold A.		Aviation	35	70	125	60	Pol. ACE, WW II
Ure, Mary		Entertainment	5	10	20	20	

NAME	DATE	CATEGORY	SIG	LS/DS	ALS	SP	COMMENTS
Urey, Harold C.	1893-1981	Science	78	550	433		Nobel in Chemistry 1934. Disc. Heavy Hydrogen
Urich, Robert	1946-	Entertainment	10	15	25	28	Handsomely Rugged Actor. Spencer
Uris, Leon		Author	20	65	125	65	Am. Novelist. Battle Cry, Exodus
Urso, Camilla		Entertainment	25			40	Fr. Violinist
Ursuleac, Viorica		Entertainment	30			85	Great Strauss Singer & WW II Heroine
Urvanowicz, Witold A.		Aviation	20	45	75	50	ACE, WW II, Polish Ace
Usher, John P.		Cabinet	40	110	195		Sec'y Interior 1863-65
Ussishkin, Menachem	1863-1941	Statesman	175		625		Rus-Zionist Leader. A Founder Hebrew Univ.
Ustinov, Peter		Entertainment	25	125		72	And Playwright, Author, Actor. AA
Utley, Garrick		Journalist	10			35	TV Reporter & Commentator
Utrillo, Maurice	1833-1955	Artist	475	585	650	200	Fr. Montmartre, Paris Scenes

V

NAME	DATE	CATEGORY	SIG	LS/DS	ALS	SP	COMMENTS
Vaccaro, Brenda		Entertainment	4	6	15	10	
Vaccaro, Tracy		Entertainment	5			15	Pin-Up SP $30
Vacio, Natividad		Entertainment	3	3	6	6	
Vadim, Roger		Entertainment	20			50	
Vague, Vera		Entertainment	25				SEE Barbara Jo Allen. Comedienne
Vai, Steve		Entertainment	15			35	Rock
Valdengo, Giuseppe		Entertainment	15			40	Opera
Vale, Virginia		Entertainment	15				Actress
Valens, Richie		Entertainment	688	725		1100	
Valenti, Jack	1921-	Entertainment	10	15		18	Pres. Motion Picture Assoc. Special Ass't LBJ
Valentine, Karen		Entertainment	4	6	10	15	
Valentine, Lewis		Law	35	105		50	Legend'y NY Police Commissioner
Valentino, Rudolph	1895-1926	Entertainment	925	1275	1550	1750	Major Silent Film Star. Early Death Created Legend
Valery, Paul A.	1871-1945	Author	45	105	170		Fr. Noted Poet, Philosopher
Valette, A.J.M.		Fr. Revolution	15		75		
Valetti, Cesare		Entertainment	20			50	Opera
Vallandigham, Clement L.	1820-71	Civil War	125		348		Civil War 'Copperhead' (Peace Democrat)
Vallee, Rudy		Entertainment	15	35	45	35	Am. Singer (Crooner).Radio-TV Personality
Vallejo, Mariano Guadalupe		Military	140	450			Early CA Off'l & Military Leadr
Valli, Frankie		Entertainment	15			45	Singer
Valli, Virginia		Entertainment				40	Films From 1915-1931
Vallone, Raf		Entertainment	5	6	15	15	
Van Allan, Richard		Entertainment	5			25	Opera
Van Allen, James		Science	45	135	260	72	Nobel Physics. Rocket Research. Van Allen Belt
Van Ark, Joan		Entertainment	5	8	15	15	
Van Buren, Abigail		Journalist	10	18	30	20	Am. Syndicated Columnist
Van Buren, Angelica		First Lady					NRPA
Van Buren, Hannah		First Lady					No Known Examples
Van Buren, James D.		Gov't Official	5	15			Son of Pres. Van Buren

NAME	DATE	CATEGORY	SIG	LS/DS	ALS	SP	COMMENTS
Van Buren, Martin (As Pres.)		President		1285	4000		Free Frank $350-$475
Van Buren, Martin	1782-1862	President	305	1786	1694		FF $450-$475
Van Buren, Raeburn*		Cartoonist	10			50	Abbie & Slats
Van Cleef, Lee		Entertainment	25			45	
Van Dam, Rip	1662-1736	Colonial America	60	175	360		Merchant,Politics,Col. Gov. NY
Van Damme, Jean-Claude		Entertainment	20			55	Actor. Action with an Accent
Van Den Berg, Lodewik, Dr.		Astronaut	5			16	
Van Der Beek, James		Entertainment	8			45	Young Movie/TV Star
Van der Rohe, Ludwig Mies	1886-1969	Architect	120	350			Ger.-Am. Exponent Of Glass & Steel Architecture
Van Devanter, Willis (SC)	1859-1941	Supreme Court	40	125	200	75	Justice 1910-37
Van Dine, S.S. (W.H.Wright)		Author	45	100	190	225	Created Philo Vance
Van Dongen, Kees		Artist	30	45	120		Fauvist Painter, Portraitist
Van Doren, Carl		Author	15	45	60	20	Pulitzer in Biography
Van Doren, Mamie		Entertainment	15		35	25	Pin-Up SP $35-$45. 49'-50's Sex Symbol
Van Doren, Mark	1894-1973	Author	15	57	60	30	Critic, Editor, Pulitzer Poetry
Van Dorn, Earl (WD)		Civil War	350		5775		CSA Gen. Assassinated
Van Dorn, Earl	1820-63	Civil War	250		718		CSA Gen. Assassinated
Van Dresser, Marcia		Entertainment	15			40	Vintage Actress
Van Druten, John W.		Author	10	20	35	15	Playwright, Novelist
Van Dusen, Henry P.		Clergy	15	15	25	20	
Van Dyck, M. Ernest		Entertainment	15	25		40	Tenor
Van Dyke, Dick		Entertainment	8		15	25	
Van Dyke, Henry	1852-1933	Clergy-Author	20	55	100		Minister To Netherlands-Luxem.
Van Dyke, Jerry		Entertainment	5			20	
Van Dyke, Leroy	1919-	Country Music	5			15	Songwriter. 'The Auctioneer', 'Walk on By'
Van Dyke, Nicholas	1738-89	Rev. War	110	275	625		Statesman, Continental Congress
Van Fleet, James, Gen.	1892-1992	Military	28	75	95	125	Gen. WW II. US 8th Army, Korea
Van Fleet, Jo		Entertainment	15	20	45	40	A A
Van Halen (All)(4)		Entertainment	45			150	Rock LP Cover S $85, Women & .....1st S $150
Van Halen (all-original)		Entertainment	88			160	Rock
Van Halen, Alex		Entertainment	20	95		50	
Van Halen, Eddie		Entertainment	25	78		58	Rock. 1982 Check Signed $200
Van Heusen, James (Jimmy)		Composer	60	90	175	100	AMusQS $250
Van Hoften, James D.		Astronaut	6			20	
Van Horn, Burt		Senate/Congress	10	20			Rep. NY 1861, Manufacturer
Van Horne, David		Rev. War	10		75		
Van Kirk, Theodore		Aviation	50	130		95	
Van Loon, Hendrik Willem		Author	18	30	125	40	Historian, Journalist, Lecturer, Illustrator
Van Ness, Cornelius P.		Governor	15	35	60		Jurist, Gov. VT, Minister Sp.
Van Nuys, Frederick	1874-1944	Congress	10			25	Senator IN 1932
Van Patten, Dick		Entertainment	5	6	15	15	
Van Patten, Joyce		Entertainment	4	4	10	15	
Van Peebles, Mario		Entertainment	20			45	Actor-Director
Van Rensselaer, Henry		Civil War	225				Rep. NY 1841, Union General
Van Schaick, Goose		Rev. War			2900		General Rev. War. Served Honorably Thru The War

NAME	DATE	CATEGORY	SIG	LS/DS	ALS	SP	COMMENTS
Van Sloon, Edward		Entertainment	125			250	
Van Stade, Frederica		Entertainment	15			45	Opera
Van Sweringen, Otis P.		Business	15	40	90	35	RR Exec-Developer Shaker Height
Van Valkenburgh, Debbie		Entertainment	6	8	15	15	
Van Vechten, Carl		Author	40	80	220	45	Am. Novelist, Staff NY Times
Van Vleck, John H., Dr.		Science	30	45	75		Nobel Physics 1977
Van Vliet, Stewart	1815-1901	Civil War	45		295		Union Gen.,Indian Fighter
Van Vooren, Monique		Entertainment	4	6	10	15	Pin-Up SP $25
Van Wagoner, Murray D.		Governor	5	20		15	Governor MI
Van Wyck, Charles Henry		Civil War	40	70	90		Union General, Senator NE
Van Zandt, Philip		Entertainment	50			150	
Van Zant, Ronnie		Entertainment	25			100	
Van Zealand, Paul, Viscount		Head of State	15			35	Premier Belgium, Foreign Min.
Van, Bobby		Entertainment	5			20	Dancer
Van, Gloria		Entertainment	5	6	15	15	
Van, Isabelle		Entertainment	5			10	Dancer
Van, Jackie		Entertainment	5			15	Dancer
Vance, A.T., Capt.		Aviation	15	25			Record Polar Flight
Vance, Cyrus		Cabinet	10	20	35	25	Sec'y State, Sec'y Army
Vance, Jack		Author	15	25	50	25	Hugo & Nebula winning SF writer
Vance, Louis Joseph		Author	15	35	90		Am. Novelist
Vance, Robert Brank	1828-99	Civil War	125	150	305		CSA Gen., Sig/Rank $145
Vance, Vivian	1913-79	Entertainment	162	200		250	Actress. Lucy's TV Sidekick. Lucy SP $450
Vance, Zebulon Baird	1830-94	Civil War	175		950		CSA Gov. & Sen. Of NC, Opposed J.Davis
Vandamme, Dominique Rene		Napoleonic Wars	50	150	210		Battle of Waterloo
Vandenberg, Arthur H.	1884-1951	Congress	20	70		25	Senator MI, Pres. Pro Tem.
Vandenberg, Hoyt S.		Military-Aviation	25	150		100	
Vander Pyl, Jean		Entertainment	10			15	Voice Wilma-Pebbles Flintstone
Vanderbilt, Alfred Gwynn		Business	15	35	65	25	
Vanderbilt, Amy		Author	10	25	40	35	Columnist, Authority on Manners
Vanderbilt, Cornelius	1794-1877	Business	550	2600	3738	2880	'Commodore'. Financier of Railroads & Steamships
Vanderbilt, Cornelius	1843-99	Business	250	825	1750	450	Grandson of 'Commodore'. RRs, Breakers
Vanderbilt, Cornelius, Jr.	1898-1974	Journalist	25	75	125	40	
Vanderbilt, George Washington	1862-1914	Business	250	750	1100	325	Grandson of 'Commodore'. Biltmore House
Vanderbilt, Gloria		Business	25	45	80	35	Fashion Designer. Artist. Litho S $125
Vanderbilt, Harold S.	1884-1970	Business	168				Philanthropist-Businessman
Vanderbilt, Jacob H.	1807-93	Business	500	1900	2950		Brother of 'Commodore'. RRs & Steamships
Vanderbilt, William H.	1821-85	Business	300	975	1950	362	'Commodore' Son. Philanthropist. Giant RR Empire
Vanderbilt, William H., Jr.		Business	45	120	250	75	Governor RI
Vanderbilt, William K.	1849-1920	Business	250	650	1500	375	'Commodore' Gr. Son.RR Exec.,Financier-Yachtsman
Vandergrift, Alexander A.	1887-1973	Military	45	100	175	395	1st Marine Div. Gen. WW II. MOH at Guadalcanal
Vanderlyn, John	1775-1852	Artist	250	275	750		Am. Pres. Portraits, Capitol
Vane, John R., Dr.		Science	20	30	50	25	Nobel Medicine 1982
Vaness, Carol		Entertainment	10			35	Opera
Vanili, Milli		Entertainment	10			50	

NAME	DATE	CATEGORY	SIG	LS/DS	ALS	SP	COMMENTS
Vanilla Ice		Entertainment	20			40	Rock
Vanity		Entertainment	4	7		15	Pin-Up SP $25
Vanzetti, Bartolomeo		Political Radical	600	1800	6500		Convicted Murderer, Electrocuted
Varese, Edgard	1883-1965	Composer	185	400	675		Fr.-Am. Music Pioneer
Varga, Francis		Celebrity	30				
Vargas, Alberto		Artist	135	345	575		Repro Varga Girl S $325-$450
Vargas, Getuilio		Head of State	50	150		75	Revolutionary Pres. Brazil.
Varick, Richard		Rev. War	75	200	290		Soldier, Washington's Sec'y
Varmus, Harold E., Dr.		Science	25	60		35	Nobel Medicine 1989
Varnay, Astrid		Entertainment	10			65	Opera
Varney, Jim		Entertainment	7			20	
Vasarely, Victor	1908-	Artist	55	130			Hungarian. Op Art Repro S $75-$150-$275
Vasquez, Roberta		Playboy Ctrfold	4			10	Pin-Up SP $20. Actress
Vassar, Matthew		Business	200	2000			Founder Vassar College. ALS/Cont. $3400
Vaubois, J.F.G.		Fr. Revolution	5	15	40		
Vaughan, Alfred J., Jr..	1830-99	Civil War	75		400		CSA Gen. Sig/Rank $150
Vaughan, Robert		Clergy	10	10	10		
Vaughan, Sarah	1924-90	Entertainment	40	100	210	208	Am. Jazz Vocalist-Pianist
Vaughan-Williams, Ralph, Sir	1872-1958	Composer	102	265	498	175	Established Br. Nat'l Musical Style. SP Pc $450
Vaughn, George A.		Aviation	35	55	95	65	ACE, WW II
Vaughn, Herbert, Cardinal		Clergy	30	50	90	75	
Vaughn, John C. (WD)		Civil War	195	325	2500		CSA Gen.
Vaughn, John C.	1824-75	Civil War	90				CSA Gen.
Vaughn, Robert	1932-	Entertainment	6	10		35	Actor. Signed Man From Uncle Comic Book $50
Vaughn, Vince		Entertainment	8			46	Replaces Anthony Perkins as New 'Norman Bates'
Vaughn, William S.		Business	4	10		10	Pres. Eastman Kodak
Vaux, Roberts	1786-1836	Philanthropist	110		522		Prison Reform, Houses of Refuge
Veach, Charles L.		Astronaut	5			15	
Vedder, Eddie (Eddy)		Entertainment	12			70	Music. Lead Singer Pearl Jam
Vedder, Elihu		Artist	50	135	225		Drew From Dreams & Fantasy
Vedral, Joyce L.		Author	5			10	Non-Fiction
Vedrines, Jules		Aviation	200	395	650	265	
Vee, Bobby		Entertainment	8			20	Singer/14 Top 40 Hits 1960-68
Veidt, Conrad	1893-1950	Entertainment	85	90	130	310	
Veit, Stan		Author	5	10	20	20	Computer Shopper, PC historian
Vejvoda, Jarmir	1902-	Composer	70				The Beer Barrel Polka AMusQS $195
Velez, Lupe		Entertainment	85	95	175	188	Fiery Latin 20th Cent. Fox Musical Star. Suicide
Veloz & Yolanda		Entertainment	15			35	30-40's Ballroom Dance Team
Venable, Evelyn		Entertainment	15	20	40	35	
Venable, William Webb		Senate/Congress	5	15		10	Rep. MS 1916, Judge
Vendela		Entertainment	20			39	Model-Actress
Vendome, L.J., Duke de	1654-1712	Fr. Military	150	450			Marshal of France
Ventura, Charlie		Entertainment	40			150	Am. Bandleader-Saxophonist
Venuta, Benay		Entertainment	7			15	
Vera, Ellen		Entertainment	20			45	Dancer, Films. Pin-Up SP $50

NAME	DATE	CATEGORY	SIG	LS/DS	ALS	SP	COMMENTS
Verdi, Giuseppe	1813-1901	Composer	1175	1750	5245	4098	AMusQS $4750, $5,000, $5,700, $7,500, $12,500
Verdin, James, Lt.Cdr.		Aviation	10	25			US Navy Pilot. Record Holder
Verdon, Gwen	1925-	Entertainment	5		15	15	Dancer-Actress-Singer, Top Broadway Star, Films
Verdugo, Elena		Entertainment	8			15	Actress
Verdy, Violette		Entertainment	10			30	Opera
Vereen, Ben	1946-	Entertainment	8	20		20	Dancer, Singer, Actor
Vereshchagin, Vassili V.	1842-1904	Artist	35		150	500	Paintings of Russian Wars
Vergennes, C. G.,Le Comte de		Statesman	175	375			Fr. Ambass. Supported Am. Rev.
Verlaine, Paul	1844-96	Author	175	470	850		Fr. Symbolist Poet
Vermehren, Werner		Aviation	15	35	55	58	Ger. Capt. WW I Zepps..
Verne, Jules	1828-1905	Authors	185	655	1060	1725	Fr. Sci-Fi Novelist 'Around the World in 80 Days'
Vernier, Theodore, Count		Fr. Revolution	35	100			
Verve, The		Entertainment	40			125	Music. 5 Member Rock Group
Vessey, John W.		Military	10			30	
Vetch, Samuel	1668-1732	Colonial America	90	225	450		Colonial Governor
Vetri, Victoria		Entertainment	4			10	Pin-Up SP $20
Veverka, Jaroslav		Entertainment	20			45	Opera
Vezzani, Cesare		Entertainment	45			150	Opera. Corsican Dramatic Tenor
Viardot, Pauline		Entertainment	30		175	100	Fine Singer from Manual Garcia Musical Family
Vickers, Jon		Entertainment	15			55	Opera. Dramatic Tenor
Vickers, Martha	1925-1971	Entertainment	4			10	Model-Actress. Routine Feminine Leads
Victor Amadeus III	1726-96	Royalty	95	295			King Sardinia
Victor Emmanuel I,	1759-1824	Royalty	70	250			King of Sardinia
Victor Emmanuel II (It)	1820-78	Royalty	70	188	475	100	
Victor Emmanuel III & B.Mussolini		Royalty, Hd of St		150			Fine DS by both $850-$1050
Victor Emmanuel III	1869-1947	Royalty	100	550			King Italy 1900-46
Victor, Claude Perrin	1766-1841	Fr. Military	125		148		Marshal of Napoleon
Victor, Henry	1898-1945	Entertainment	65			200	Br. Tall Leading Man of Br. Silent Movies.
Victoria, Duchess of Kent		Royalty	45		125		Mother of Queen Victoria
Victoria, Empress (Fred. III, Ger)	1840-1901	Royalty	85		488		Imperial Presentation Frame & SP $3700
Victoria, Mary Louisa		Royalty	40	110	175		
Victoria, Queen	1819-1901	Royalty	175	517	773	1385	Great Britain etc.DS by Victoria & Albert $575
Vidal, Gore	1925-	Author	10	20	35	20	Am. Novelist, Playwright, Critic, Screenplays
Vidor, Florence	1895-1977	Entertainment	40	45	65	60	Silent Film Star. Wife of Director King Vidor
Vidor, King	1894-1982	Entertainment	30	75		89	AA Film Director. LS/Cont. $250
Vieira, Meredith		TV News	4			15	Commentator
Viele, Egbert L.	1825-1902	Civil War	30	45	60	100	Union Gen'l, Eng'r. Sig/Rank $40, WarDte DS $150
Vigneaud, Vincent du		Science	10	25	45		
Vigran, Herb		Entertainment	10	15		20	Actor. Vintage Character Actor
Vila, Bob		Entertainment	5			15	TV Tool Show. 'This Old House' Host
Vila, George R.		Business	7	20	32	15	CEO Uniroyal Tire
Vilas, Jack		Aviation	6	16			
Vilas, William F.		Cabinet	30	30	45	35	P.M. Gen., Sec'y Interior 1888. Cleveland Cabinet
Viljoen, Benjamin		Celebrity	5	15	40	15	
Viljoenk, B.J.		Military	35		145		

NAME	DATE	CATEGORY	SIG	LS/DS	ALS	SP	COMMENTS
Villa, Francesco (Pancho)	1878-1923	Military	762	1500	3050	3680	Mexican Guerilla Leader, Revolutionary
Villa-Lobos, Heitor	1887-1959	Composer	100	262	525	333	Brazilian. AMusQS $500, AMusMsS $550-$1,000
Villalpando, Catalina Vasquez		Cabinet	15			30	US Treasurer
Villechaize, Herve		Entertainment	30			50	Diminutive Actor. 'Fantasy Island', Tattoo
Villepique, John B.	1830-62	Civil War	265		690		CSA Gen. Sig/Rank $350-$395 Rare
Villiers, Alan J.		Author	10		25		Australian. Maritime, Adventure, History
Villiers, Frederic		Artist	10	20	50	40	
Villon, Jacques (Psued)	1875-1963	Artist	65		300		(Pseud. Gaston Duchamp)Brother Marcel Duchamp
Vinay, Ramon		Entertainment	70			200	Opera. Sang Otello Internationally
Vincent, Gene		Entertainment	175			295	Rock
Vincent, Jan-Michael	1944-	Entertainment	10		15	20	Actor. Leading Man of the 70's
Vincent, June		Entertainment	5			20	Actress. Secondary Leads & Supporting Roles
Vincent, Romo		Entertainment	5	10	20	15	Actor. Character, Supporting Player
Vincent, Stenio Joseph	1874-1959	Head of State	125				Pres. Haiti. Lawyer, Diplomat
Vincent, Thomas M.	1832-1909	Civil War	30	55	100		Union General, Bvt. Sig/Rank $55
Vinci, Leonardo da		Artist	5500	13000	34000		NRPA-RARE
Vinson, Carl	1883-1991	Congress	20	40		70	Rep. GA 1914
Vinson, Frederick M. (SC)	1890-1953	Supreme Court	95	230	425	325	Chief Justice, Cabinet, Rep. KY
Vinson, Helen	1907-	Entertainment	15	20	40	35	Actress. Sophisticated Leading Lady Of 30's-40's
Vinton, Bobby		Composer	5	10		15	AMusQS $40
Vinton, David	1803-73	Civil War	125	325			Union Gen., 1st P.O.W.
Vinton, Will		Celebrity	12	25			
Virchow, Rudolf	1821-1902	Science	212		1188		Founder Cellular Pathology
Virtanen, A. I.	1895-1973	Science	30	85	145	55	Nobel Chemistry 1945
Vishinsky, Andrei		Head of State	70	230	370	120	Rus.1st Deputy Foreign Minister
Visitor, Nana		Entertainment	15			35	Actress. 'Star Trek' SP $45
Vittor, Frank		Artist	40		165		
Vivian, Richard H. Sir		Rev. War	45	125	255		
Vlaminck, Maurice de	1876-1958	Artist	125	235	458	325	Fr. Fauvist Painter
Voelker, John D.		Author	5	10	15	15	
Vogl, Heinrich		Entertainment	75		285		Important Early Wagnerian Tenor
Voight, Deborah		Entertainment	5			25	Opera
Voight, Jon		Entertainment	12		30	40	Oscar Winning Actor.
Voisin, Gabriel	1880-1973	Aviation	65	135	225	125	Fr. Airplane Mfg. & Pioneer Experimentor
Vokes, Christopher		Military	15	30	40	25	
Vokes, Rosina		Entertainment	10		20	15	
Volcker, Paul A.		Cabinet	5		10	15	Chm. Federal Reserve
Voliva, Wilbur G.	1870-1942	Clergy	30		50		
Volk, Leonard W.	1828-95	Artist	55	350	475		Sculptor. Famed for Lincoln Works, etc.
Volkov, Vladislav	1935-71	Cosmonaut	100			225	Russ. Astronaut Soyuz 7. Killed in Soyuz 11
Voll, John J.		Aviation	18	40	65	45	ACE, WW II
Volstead, Andrew J.	1860-1947	Congress	70	210	250		MOC MN 1903. Volstead Act
Volta, Alessandro	1745-1827	Science	400	2500	2917		It. Volt, Electrical Unit, For Him
Voltaire, Francois M.	1694-1778	Author	400	1926	3500		Fr. Writer-Philosopher-Satirist
Volz, Nedra		Entertainment	4			10	

NAME	DATE	CATEGORY	SIG	LS/DS	ALS	SP	COMMENTS
Von Behr, Henrich, Baron		Military	10			30	
von Braun, Magnus		Science	15			40	Rocket Pioneer/Brother Wernher
Von Braun, Wernher	1912-77	Science	170	570	638	485	Ger-Am Rocket Pioneer. Planned Apollo Program
Von Bulow, Claus		Celebrity	15	25		20	Danish Count. Accused Murderer
Von Bulow, Hans		Entertainment	20		145		Germ. Conductor, Pianist. ALS/Content $500
Von D'niken, Erich		Author	15	30	75	30	Sci-Fi
Von Debizka, Hedwig		Entertainment	40			150	Opera
Von der Chevaerie, Kurt		Military	10			40	
Von Edelsheim, Macmilian		Military	20			45	Panzer General
Von Einem, Gottfried		Composer	40			200	Eminent Austrian Composer
Von Gazen, Waldemar		Military	20			50	Panzer General
Von Gronau, Wolfgang		Aviation	102			338	Ger. ACE, WW I
Von Hesse-Nassau, Adolph		Royalty	100	300			1st Duke of Luxembourg
Von Karajan, Herbert		Entertainment				300	
Von Kleist, Paul		Military	50	85		100	Ger. WW II Tank Commander
Von Kretchmer, Otto		Military	35	90			Top Ger. U Boat Cmdr. WW II
von Manteuffel, Edwin F.	1809-85	Military	75	595	420		Prussian Fld. Marshal WW I
von Manteuffel, Hasso	1897-1978	Military	45	295	190	350	WW II Ger. Tank Commander-Panzer Divisions
Von Oy, Jenna		Entertainment	5			15	Blossom
Von Papen, Franz	1879-1969	Military	95	200	395	175	Ger. Acquitted Major War Crimes
Von Paulus, Friedrich	1890-1957	Military	165	600			Ger. WW II Field Marshal. Cmdr. 6th Army
Von Sauken, Dietrich		Military	25			75	Panzer General
Von Stade, Frederica		Entertainment	15			35	Opera
Von Sternberg, Joseph	1894-1969	Entertainment	100	115		75	Film Director. A Legend!
Von Stroheim, Erich	1885-1957	Entertainment	150			595	Vintage Film Dir-Actor & Tragic Hollywood Figure
Von Sydow, Max	1929-	Entertainment	10	30		20	Swe. Character Actor
Von Tilzer, Albert		Composer	40	110	200	55	Founder ASCAP
Von Trapp, Maria, Baroness		Celebrity	68	150	250	75	Sound of Music Fame. FDC $125
Von Zell, Harry		Entertainment	10	15	25	25	Radio Announcer-Comedian-Jack Benny Sidekick
Vonnegut, Kurt, Jr.		Author	20	108	105	50	Am. Black-Humor Novels.
Voorhees, Daniel W.		Senate/Congress	15	40			Rep., Senator IN 1861
Voronoff, Serge	1866-1951	Science	35		205		Rus.Physicist. Used Animal Glands for Rejuvenation
Vorster, Balthazar J		Head of State	25	70	165	50	Prime Minister South Afr.
Voss, James		Astronaut	6			20	
Voss, Janice		Astronaut	5			22	
Vosseller, Aurelius B.		Military	35	95			
Voysey, Charles	1828-1912	Clergy	35	50	75		Founder of the Theistic Church.
Vraciu, Alex		Aviation	15	25	50	35	ACE, WW II
Vuillard, Edouard	1868-1940	Artist	140	290	367		Fr.Painter,Printmaker, Illustrator, Decorator

NAME	DATE	CATEGORY	SIG	LS/DS	ALS	SP	COMMENTS
Wachtel, Theodor		Entertainment	70		195		Opera. 19th Cent. Ger. Tenor
Wade, Benjamin Franklin	1800-1878	Congress	40	95	160		Senator OH 1851-69

NAME	DATE	CATEGORY	SIG	LS/DS	ALS	SP	COMMENTS
Wade, Leigh		Aviation	30	100	100	50	Pilot '24 Round The World
Wade, Keptha H.		Business		875			Telegraph & RR Pioneer. Big 3 Telegraph 1860's
Wadopian, Eliot		Entertainment	10			25	Bassist. Paul Winter Consort. Grammy
Wadsworth, James S.	1807-64	Civil War	50	95	235		Union Gen. KIA Battle of the Wilderness. Rare
Wadsworth, James W., Jr.	1877-1952	Congress	12	30			Senator NY
Wadsworth, Jeremiah	1743-1804	Rev. War	145	332	585		Commissary Gen'l. Continental Army. CT. Merchant
Wadsworth, Peleg		Rev. War	105	315			General, Aide Artemas Ward
Waesche, R.R.		Military	20	50			US Coast Guard Commandant
Wagener, David D.	1792-1860	Congress	12		45		MOC PA, Founder Easton Bank
Waggin, Patti		Entertainment	3	3	6	10	
Wagner, Cosima	1837-1930	Celebrity	85	450	425	950	Wife of Rich'd. Daughter of Liszt. ALS/Cont. $1850
Wagner, Jane		Author	10	15		20	Playwright. Emmy & Peabody Awards
Wagner, Lindsay		Entertainment	5	18	15	20	Actress.'Six Million Dollar Woman'.Film & TV Leads
Wagner, Natasha Gregson		Entertainment	8			45	Actress-Daughter Natalie Wood
Wagner, Richard	1813-83	Composer	1300	1865	2763	3325	Ger. ALS/Content $5,000, $5,500, $8500
Wagner, Robert		Entertainment	15	25		30	Still Handsome Film-TV Leading Man. 'Hart to Hart'
Wagner, Robert F.	1877-1953	Senate/Congress	30	120	225	40	Senate NY 1926, Wagner Act
Wagoner, Porter	1930-	Country Music	10			25	Major Country Star.Duets/Norma Jean & Dolly Parton
Wahl, Ken		Entertainment	15			55	Actor
Wahl, Lutz		Military	30		75		Am. Gen. WW I
Wahlberg, Mark		Entertainment	20			67	Actor Boogie Nights
Waigel, Theo, Dr.		Ger. Government	4	10		15	Ger. Government Official
Wainwright, Charles S.	1826-1905	Civil War	30	75			Union General
Wainwright, James		Entertainment	5			15	Actor
Wainwright, Johathan	1864-1945	Military	20		32		MOC NY, Capt. NY Vols. Span-Am War
Wainwright, Jonathan M.	1883-1953	Military	118	250	315	218	Am. Gen. WW II. MOH. Death March.SP/Mac. $995
Waite, H. Roy		Aviation	15	25	40		
Waite, Morrison R. (SC)	1816-88	Supreme Court	40	95		75	ALS as Chief Justice Supreme Court $435
Waite, Ralph		Entertainment	5	10	15	25	Actor. 'Walton's Mountain'
Waite, Terry		Hostage	30		40	35	Also Hostage Negotiator
Wakely, Jimmy	1914-	Country Music	30			100	Major Country Star During 40's & Early 50's
Wakeman, Rick		Entertainment	15			30	
Waksman, Selman A.	1888-1978	Science	45	75	95	60	Nobel Medicine 1952
Walburn, Raymond		Entertainment	10		40	35	Vintage Buggy-Eyed Comedic Character Actor
Walcott, Charlels F.	1836-87	Civil War	20		55		Union Gen. Final Campaign
Walcott, Fred C.	1869-1949	Congress	10	30			Senator CT 1929. Mfg., Banker
Walcutt, Charles C.	1838-98	Civil War	30	70	85		Union General Sig/Rank $45, War Dte DS$175
Wald, George		Science	15	30	50	25	Nobel Medicine 1967
Wald, Jerry		Bandleader	10			40	Big Band
Wald, Lillian D.	1867-1940	Reformer	30	90	175	50	1st City School Nurse Service
Walden, Greg		Congress	5			15	MOC from Oregon
Waldheim, Kurt	1918-	Head of State	35	70	150	45	P. M. Austria. Sec'y Gen'l U.N. WW II War Criminal
Waldo, Anna Lee		Author	15			20	
Waldo, Janet		Entertainment	4			15	Major Radio Actress. Judy Jetson Voice
Waldron, Hicks B.		Business	5			10	CEO Heublein Inc.

NAME	DATE	CATEGORY	SIG	LS/DS	ALS	SP	COMMENTS
Walesa, Lech		Head of State	25	65		102	Nobel Peace Pr., Pres. Poland. FDC S $30
Walgreen, Charles Rudolph	1873-1939	Business	35	70	145		Pharmacist Fndr. of Walgreen Drugs
Walken, Christopher		Entertainment	15		45	42	Actor. 'Deer Hunter'
Walker, Alice	1944-	Author	23			45	Novelist. Color Purple etc.
Walker, Benjamin		Rev. War	105	315			Rev. Army Officer. Rep. NY
Walker, Bree		Journalist	5			10	TV News
Walker, Charles		Astronaut	5			15	
Walker, Clint		Entertainment	33	48	100	62	Top Western Actor-Cowboy
Walker, David M.		Astronaut	5			30	
Walker, Francis Amasa	1840-97	Civil War	45	105	145		Union Gen. Rose From Private.Sig/Rank $75
Walker, Frank C.		Cabinet	5	15		10	P.M. General 1940
Walker, Fred L.		Military	10	35	50		
Walker, Gilbert C.		Governor	15	20	25		Gov. VA 1869, Rep. VA 1875
Walker, James	1794-1874	Clergy	15	25	44		Pres. Harvard
Walker, James J.Jimmie	1881-1946	Politician	25	80	125	45	Flamboyant Mayor NYC. Corruption Charges
Walker, Jerry Jeff		Entertainment	10	15	30	35	
Walker, Jimmy		Entertainment	5			15	Afr.-Am. Actor-Comedian. 'Good Times'
Walker, John Brisben		Journalist	10	30			Editor 'Cosmopolitan Magazine'
Walker, John George		Civil War	95	185	255		CSA General. Sig/Rank $195
Walker, Leroy Pope (WD)		Civil War	265	440	640		CSA Gen.-1st CS Sec'y of War $845
Walker, Leroy Pope	1837-84	Civil War	150	210			CSA General. 1st CS Secretary of War
Walker, Mary E.	1832-1919	Civil War	295		575	4370	Union Nurse & Surgeon, MOH,ALS/Cont.$10,000
Walker, Meriwether L.		Military	40		125		Am. WW I Gen. Panama Canal Zone Gov.
Walker, Mort*		Cartoonist	15			80	'Beetle Bailey'
Walker, Nancy	1921-92	Entertainment	20			30	Comedienne-Actress. Broadway, Films
Walker, Paul		Entertainment	5			38	Actor. Co-Star Varsity Blues
Walker, Percy	1812-80	Congress	15	35			MOC AL, Medicine, Soldier
Walker, Reuben L.	1827-90	Civil War	80		285		CSA Gen. Comdr. Artillery in 64 Battles
Walker, Robert J.	1801-69	Cabinet	25	75	175		Polk Sec'y Treasury. Largely Created US Dept. Int.
Walker, Robert Jarvis C.		Senate/Congress	12	20			MOC PA. 1881.
Walker, Robert, Jr.		Entertainment	10			25	Actor son of Rob't Walker & Jennifer Jones
Walker, Robert, Sr.	1918-51	Entertainment	50		150	155	Actor Leading-Man-Husband of Jennifer Jones
Walker, T. Bone		Entertainment	30			85	Jazz Guitar-Vocalist
Walker, Walton H.		Military	30	55	9550		General. Killed in Korea 1950
Walker, William S.	1822-99	Civil War	85		305		CSA Gen. Sig/Rank $150-$200
Walker, Wm Henry T.	1816-64	Civil War	145	350	575		CSA Gen. KIA
Walker, Wm. Henry T.(WD)		Civil War	205	1350	1742		CSA Gen. KIA 1864
Wallace, (Wm. Roy) Dewitt	1889-1981	Publisher	30			85	Founder Readers Digest
Wallace, Alfred R.	1823-1913	Science	75	160	366		Developed Theory of Evolution Same Time As Darwin
Wallace, Dee		Entertainment	5		15	18	Actress. E.T. DS $125
Wallace, Dillon		Author	5	15	30	10	
Wallace, Edgar	1875-1932	Author	75	270	345	370	Popular Thriller Writer
Wallace, George C.		Governor	20			95	4 Term AL Governor. Pres. Candidate
Wallace, Henry A.	1888-1965	Vice President	45	119	212	100	FDR V.P., Sec'y Agr., Sec'y Commerce
Wallace, Henry C.	1866-1924	Cabinet	15	25	50	20	Sec'y Agriculture 1921

NAME	DATE	CATEGORY	SIG	LS/DS	ALS	SP	COMMENTS
Wallace, Irving		Author	20	125	200	75	Am. Novelist
Wallace, Jean	1923-	Entertainment	10	5	20	25	Blonde Leading Lady From Early 40's
Wallace, John		Civil War	100	300			Black Leader 1860's
Wallace, Lewis 'Lew'	1827-1904	Civil War, Author	150	300	448		Union Gen.-Statesman-Author Ben Hur
Wallace, Lila Acheson		Business	10	25	35	20	
Wallace, Lurleen B.		Governor	20	75		25	Governor AL. Replaced Husband
Wallace, Marjorie		Entertainment	4			20	Miss USA, Actress
Wallace, Mike		Journalist	10		25	25	News Journalist. '60 Minutes'
Wallace, William H.	1827-1901	Civil War	85	258			CSA Gen. Sig/Rank $210, War Dte DS $425
Wallach, Eli		Entertainment	5		22	20	Stage-Film Character Actor
Wallburg, Donnie		Entertainment	10			45	Marky Mark
Wallenberg, Knut	1853-1938	Financier	60	155			Swe. Enskilda Bank, Statesman
Wallenda, Debbie		Entertainment	20			40	Trapeze Artist. 'Flying Wallendas'
Wallenda, Karl	1905-1978	Entertainment	100			450	Trapeze Artist.'Flying Wallendas'.Killed High Wire
Wallenstein, Alfred, Dr.		Conductor	20			75	Am. Cellist/Conductor
Waller, Littleton		Military	100				Marine General 1880-1920
Waller, Robert James		Author	5			10	Novelist
Waller, Thomas 'Fats'	1904-43	Composer	262	362	775	983	Jazz Pianist. AMusQS $900. Rare
Waller, Thomas M.		Governor	15	25	40		Governor CT 1883
Walley, Deborah		Entertainment	5	10	15	30	Actress
Wallington, Jimmy	1907-72	Entertainment	15	25		20	Radio, TV Announcer-Actor Burns & Allen Show
Wallis, Barnes, Sir		Aviation	30	75			Br. Aircraft Designer. Inventor
Wallis, Hal	1898-1986	Entertainment	15	42		40	Major Film Producer & Exec.
Wallis, Ruth		Entertainment	10			25	
Wallis, Shani		Entertainment	5		10	10	
Wallmann, Jeff		Author	5	10	15	10	
Walmsley, John		Entertainment	5			10	Actor
Walpole, Horace	1717-97	Author	150	450	1160		Br. Wit, Letter Writer (2700), Novelist
Walpole, Hugh Seymour, Sir	1884-1941	Author	30	105	120		Novelist, Playwright, Biographer
Walpole, Robert, Sir	1676-1745	Head of State	96	212	575		First Recognized Prime Minister of England
Walpole, Spencer H.		Celebrity	5	15	25		
Walsh, Blanche		Entertainment	15			35	Vintage Actress
Walsh, David I.	1872-1947	Congress	10	15			Governor MA 1914, Senator 1919
Walsh, John		Entertainment	5			10	Fox TV Host
Walsh, Kenneth		Aviation	15	25	50	35	ACE, WW II, CMH
Walsh, M. Emmet		Entertainment	5		15	15	Character Actor
Walsh, Raoul	1887-1980	Entertainment	35			75	Film Director-Actor From 1912. Dir. 1914-1964
Walsh, Thomas J.	1859-1933	Cabinet	15	40		25	Senator MT 1912. FDR Att'y Gen.
Walston, Ray		Entertainment	10	9		25	Actor. Vet. Character Comedian Stage, TV, Films
Walt, Lewis W.		Military	20			75	Korea. Sr. Marine General Vietnam
Walter, Bruno	1876-1962	Conductor	62		150	375	Ger. Conductor. AmusQS $200. SP Pc $100-$275
Walter, Gustav		Entertainment	65		160		Wagnerian Tenor, Famous Lieder Singer
Walter, Jessica	1940-	Entertainment	6		15	18	Actress. Stage Trained. Film Leads
Walters, Barbara	1931-	Entertainment	10	35		25	TV Anchor, Specials Interview Hostess
Walters, Julie		Entertainment	5		15	15	

NAME	DATE	CATEGORY	SIG	LS/DS	ALS	SP	COMMENTS
Walters, Vernon A.		Military	5		10		
Walthall, Edward C. (WD)		Civil War	190	1020			CSA Gen.
Walthall, Edward C.	1831-98	Civil War	105	210	348		CSA Gen.
Walthall, Henry B.	1878-1936	Entertainment	30		55	65	Stage Actor. Joined Griffith for 'Birth of a Nation
Walton, Ernest T.S., Dr.		Science	75				Nobel Physics 1951
Walton, George	1741-1804	Rev. War	390	1088	1518		Signer, Cont'l Congr, Gov. GA. ADS/Content $2,500
Walton, Gladys		Entertainment	5		15	15	
Walton, Jayne		Entertainment	5			10	
Walton, Sam M.		Business	68	145		85	Founder Wal-Mart. Deceased
Walton, William, Sir	1902-83	Composer	70	90	195	150	AMusQS $375-$500-$700
Walz, Carl		Astronaut	5			20	
Wambaugh, Joseph		Author	12	25	40	20	Am. Novelist re Law Enforcement
Wanamaker, John	1838-1922	Business-Cabinet	55	155	805	225	Dept. Store Pioneer of Money Back Guarantee Fame
Wanamaker, Zoe		Entertainment	4			25	Actress. Stage
Wang, Cheng-T'ing		Diplomat	20	60	90		Chin. Political Leader, Ambass.
Wang, Taylor		Astronaut	7			20	
Wanger, Walter	1894-1968	Entertainment	30	150		45	Am. Film Producer. Served Time For Shooting Agent
Wapner, Jos. A., Judge		Jurist	5			15	TV Judge
War		Entertainment	35			70	Rock Group (All)
Warburton, Irvine 'Cotton'		Entertainment	30		45		AA Film Editor, Football Star
Ward, A. S.							See Rohmer, Sax
Ward, Aaron		Military	15	35	50		General, War 1812, MOC NY 1825
Ward, Artemas	1727-1800	Rev. War	375	1575			Rev. War Commander
Ward, Artemas	1834-67	Author	20	35	60		(Pseud. Of C.F. Browne)Humorist. Vanity Fair Staff
Ward, Burt		Entertainment	15			28	Actor. TV Bat Man's Robin
Ward, David		Entertainment	10			35	Opera
Ward, Genevieve		Entertainment	4			10	
Ward, Henry	1732-97	Rev. War	150	430	870		Colon'l Congr. Pro Independence
Ward, Henry A.	1835-	Merchant	40		150		1st White Child Born on Site of Chicago
Ward, J.H. Hobart	1823-1903	Civil War	35	60	105		Union General. Sig/Rank $50
Ward, John Q. Adams	1830-1910	Artist	25	80	118	45	Am. Sculptor
Ward, Joseph, Sir		Head of State	15	25	60		PM New Zealand
Ward, Marcus L.		Congress	15	25			MOC NJ 1873
Ward, Mary A. (Mrs. Humphrey)		Author	10	30	60		Br. Moral, Reforming Novels
Ward, Rachel		Entertainment	9	10	20	25	Aus. Actress. Pin-Up SP $30
Ward, Richard	1689-1763	Colonial Am.	25	40			Colon'l Gov. RI
Ward, Samuel	1725-1776	Am. Revolution		625	775		Patriot,Farmer,Merchant,Colon'l Legislator
Ward, Sela		Entertainment	12			30	Actress
Warden, Jack		Entertainment	6		15	15	Durable Character Actor
Wardlaw, Ralph W.		Clergy	30	35	45		
Ware, Eugene F.	1841-1911	Author-Lawyer	15	30			
Ware, Henry	1764-1845	Clergy	15	25	55		Led Unitarian Separation
Ware, Linda		Entertainment	4	5		15	40's Teen Singing Star in Films
Warfield, David	1866-	Entertainment	35	40	75	75	Am. Stage Actor for Belasco Prod.
Warfield, Marsha		Entertainment	5			20	Actress. 'Night Court'

NAME	DATE	CATEGORY	SIG	LS/DS	ALS	SP	COMMENTS
Warfield, William		Entertainment	10		20	40	Afr-Am Singer-Actor. 'Ol' Man River' Baritone
Warhol, Andy	1930-87	Artist	328	455	575	467	Am. Pop Artist. Celebrity Repros S $450-$2,000
Waring, Fred		Entertainment	15	45	50	30	Big,Big Band & Chorus. Waring Blender
Warner, A.P.(Borg-Warner)		Business	45	145		75	Fndr.Stewart-Warner.Speedometer
Warner, Adoniram J.		Civil War	35		115		Union Gen., MOC OH 1879
Warner, Charles Dudley	1829-1900	Author	20	65	115		Am. Man of Letters, Editor, Essays
Warner, H.B.	1876-1958	Entertainment	25			65	Br.Actor.Am. Films 1914. Christ in 'King of Kings'
Warner, Harry M.		Business	95	245	395	150	Fndr. Warner Bros.(One oF Four)
Warner, Jack L.	1891-1978	Business	80	217	300	150	Fndr. Warner Bros.(1 of Four)DS re MGM $900
Warner, James		Aviation	25		40		
Warner, John W.		Senate-Cabinet	10	15		20	Sec'y Navy 1972, Senator VA
Warner, Malcolm Jamal		Entertainment	10	30		25	Actor. 'Cosby Show'
Warner, Seth	1743-84	Rev. War	200	1200	1200		Officer.Leader/ Ethan Allen. Fndr.Green Mt. Boys
Warnow, Mark		Entertainment	10			25	Big Band Leader
Warrant		Entertainment	45			72	Rock Group (All)
Warren Commission		Kennedy Assass.				975	Photograph of Entire Comm. Signed
Warren, Chas. Marquis	1912-	Author	10		25	30	Screenwriter, Prod, Dir, Novelist. Films & TV
Warren, Earl (SC)	1891-1974	Supreme Court	82	225	225	250	Chief Justice, Governor CA
Warren, Francis	1844-1929	Congress	80	100	150		CW MOH, Gov.,Senator WY
Warren, Gouverneur (WD)		Civil War	190	525			Union General
Warren, Gouverneur K.	1830-82	Civil War	90	195	380		Union Gen., ALS/Cont. $1,250
Warren, Harry	1893-1981	Composer	30	120		45	Over 300 Songs. 3 Oscars. AMusQS $275-$450
Warren, James	1726-1808	Rev. War	130	275	540		Patriot, Merchant, Colon'l Assembly
Warren, Jennifer		Entertainment	5		10	15	Actress
Warren, Joseph	1741-1775	Rev. War	6875				Physician, Gen'l, Active Patriot. KIA. NRPA
Warren, Joseph, Sr.		Colonial America	45	135	175		
Warren, Lavinia	1841-1919	Entertainment	60			295	Mrs.Tom Thumb, Charles Stratton
Warren, Leonard		Entertainment	75			175	Opera. Am. Baritone
Warren, Leslie Ann		Entertainment	10	20		30	Actress
Warren, Michael		Entertainment	5		10	15	
Warren, Robert Penn	1905-89	Author	35	100	135	85	Am. Poet, Novelist. Pulitzers 1st US Poet Laureate
Warren, Russell	1783-1860	Architect	25		165		RI Designer of Many Early Banks, Churches
Warren, William	1812-88	Entertainment	5		25		Am. Character Actor
Warrick, Ruth	1915-	Entertainment	9		20	25	40's Leading Lady. 'Citizen Kane'. Singer, Soaps
Warsitz, Erich		Aviation	15	35	65	40	
Warwick, Countess Evelyn F.		Celebrity	35	125			Mistress of Edward VII
Warwick, Robert R.	1587-1658	Parlementarian		475			2nd Earl. Gov. Eng. Plantation Owners in America
Washburn, Bryant	1889-1963	Entertainment	5		15	20	Actor. Star of Silents. Character Actor Till 40's
Washburn, Cadwallader C.	1818-82	Civil War	52	100		95	Union Gen., Gov. WI 1855. War Dte. DS $225
Washburn, Israel, Jr.		Governor	30	80	135		Civil War Gov. ME
Washburn, W. D.		Senate/Congress	4	15			MOC MN 1879, Senator 1889
Washburne, Elihu B.	1816-87	Cabinet	20	40	75		Sec'y State 1869, Minister Fr.
Washington, Booker T.	1856-1915	Author-Educator	364	532	630	1495	Afro-Am.Built Tuskegee into Great Institution
Washington, Bushrod (SC)	1762-1829	Supreme Court	115	350	795		
Washington, Denzel		Entertainment	20	40		50	AA Actor

NAME	DATE	CATEGORY	SIG	LS/DS	ALS	SP	COMMENTS
Washington, Dinah	1924-63	Entertainment	125			200	Extraordinary Vocalist. Late 40's to Early 60's
Washington, George	1732-99	President	4683	15166	23458		G.Washington & T.Jefferson DS $12,000-$20,000
Washington, George Augustine		Presidential Relative			900		
Washington, George C.		Senate/Congress	15	35	55		MOC MD 1827
Washington, Harold		Senate/Congress	5	15	35	15	MOC IL 1981, Mayor Chicago 1983
Washington, John A.		Civil War	140		788		CSA Lt.Col.,G. Washington Nephew. Killed 1861
Washington, Martha		First Lady					RARE. Sig. $8500
Washington, Ned		Composer	45			100	
Washington, William	1752-1810	Military	65	165	315		Patriot. General
Wassel, Corydon M., Dr.		Military	45	85	150	50	Med. Missionary China. WW II Hero
Wasserman, Dale		Composer	15		35	30	'Man of LaMancha'
Wassermann, August von	1866-1925	Science	360				Ger. Bacteriologist. Blood Test for Syphilis. RARE
Watanabe, Gedde		Entertainment	9	10	20	25	
Waterhouse, Benjamin	1754-1846	Science	255	765	2750		Pioneer in Small Pox Vaccination
Waterhouse, J. W.		Artist	12		50		
Waterhouse, Richard	1832-76	Civil War	150	320	550		CSA General. War Dte.ALS $1050
Waterloo, Stanley		Author	10	20	35		
Waterman, F.D.		Business	75	195			Waterman Pen
Waterman, W.		Aviation	15		25		
Waters, Ethel	1896-1977	Entertainment	50	115	130	172	Prominent Black Actress-Singer. Stage-Films
Waters, Muddy		Entertainment	110	188		248	Jazz Musician
Waterston, Robert Classie		Clergy	10	15	30		
Waterston, Sam	1940-	Entertainment	12			30	Stage & Screen Leading Man. TV's 'Law & Order'
Watkins, Henry George Gino		Explorer	125		450		Youngest Arctic Expl. Died at 25
Watkinson, William L.		Clergy	15	20	35		
Watson, Emily		Entertainment	10			45	Actress. Pin-Up $55
Watson, Harold F.		Aviation	10	30	45	25	
Watson, J. Crittenden		Civil War	25	60	105		Union Commodore
Watson, James D., Dr.		Science	35	70	60	85	Nobel Medicine 1962. Genetics, DNA
Watson, James E.	1863-1948	Congress				195	Senator IN. Majority Leader
Watson, John	1850-1907	Clergy	15		35		Presbyterian Minister-Author
Watson, Minor		Entertainment	5			15	Fine Stage-Film Character Actor
Watson, R.J. Doc		Aviation	10	22	38	30	ACE, WW II, USAAF Ace
Watson, Thomas A.	1854-1934	Science	65	275	315	1850	Ass't To A.G.Bell.Teleph. Pioneer
Watson, Thomas E.	1856-1922	Congress	15	35			US Sen. GA, 1904 President'l Cand.
Watson, Thomas J., Jr.		Business	100	562	1250	175	Developed IBM. Chmn. in Productive Growth Years
Watson, Thomas J., Sr.	1874-1956	Business	65	145		125	Founder IBM
Watt, James		Cabinet	7	10	20	20	Controversial Sec'y Interior 1981
Watt, James	1736-1819	Science	400	895	2250		Scottish Inventor. Steam Engine
Watt, James, Jr.	1769-1848	Science	45	85	185		Marine Engineer. Son of Inventor
Watterson, Bill*		Cartoonists	25			165	Calvin & Hobbes
Watterson, Henry	1840-1921	Journalist-Congress	15	50	90	95	CSA Army. Editor, Pulitzer
Watts, Charlie		Entertainment	45			75	Rock Alb. Signed by Charlie $115
Watts, George Frederick	1817-1904	Artist	75	150	255		Br. Painter & Sculptor
Watts, Thomas H.	1819-92	Civil War	45		460		CSA Att'y Gen.,Gov. AL. Sig/Rank $60, War DS $270

NAME	DATE	CATEGORY	SIG	LS/DS	ALS	SP	COMMENTS
Waugh, Evelyn	1903-66	Author	58	195	687	67	Brideshead Revisited. ALS/Cont.$1350
Wavell, Archibald, Sir	1883-1950	Military	55	235	175	65	Br. Field Marshal, Viceroy India
Wayans, Damon		Entertainment	7			42	
Wayans, Keenen Ivory		Entertainment	7			42	Actor. In Living Color
Wayne, Anthony	1745-96	Rev. War Military	625	1750	2950		Mad Anthony ...ADS $4500
Wayne, Carol		Entertainment		55	130	150	
Wayne, David	1914-96	Entertainment	15	30	45	45	Broadway Since '38. Wide Variety Films Roles-40's
Wayne, Henry C. (WD)		Civil War	175	420			CSA Gen.
Wayne, Henry C.	1815-83	Civil War	95	200	325	250	CSA General
Wayne, James M. (SC)	1790-1867	Supreme Court	85	200	350		
Wayne, John	1907-79	Entertainment	412	824	850	899	DS Wayne & John Ford $1,500-2500. FDC S $450+
Wayne, Pat		Entertainment	10			20	Actor-Son of John
Wazniak, Steve		Business	15			70	Cofounder of Apple Computer
Weare, Meshech	1713-86	Rev. War	50	250			Pres. of New Hampshire Council DS $2500
Weatherhead, Leslie D.		Clergy	30	35	60	40	
Weathers, Carl		Entertainment	6		15	20	
Weaver, Dennis	1924-	Entertainment	9	15	15	25	Actor. Supporting Roles From Early 50's. TV Star
Weaver, Doodles		Entertainment	15			30	Rather Eccentric Comedy Act. Films, Night Clubs
Weaver, Erasmus		Military	35		125		Am. WW I Gen.
Weaver, James B.	1833-1912	Civil War	30		140		Union Gen., Pres. Candidate
Weaver, Robert C.		Cabinet	20	45		30	1st Afro-Am. Cabinet Member. Sec'y HUD
Weaver, Sigourney		Entertainment	12			42	Actor. Pin-Up SP $45-$60. 'Alien' SP $65
Weaver, Walter Reed	1885-1944	Military	45	150			Extensive Aviation Career
Webb, Alexander S.	1835-1911	Civil War	25	142	255		Union General. Sig/Rank $140. War Dte DS $255
Webb, Beatrice Potter	1858-1943	Reformer	45	125			Member Fabian Society. SP Pc/ Matthew Webb $375
Webb, Charles Henry		Author	5	15	30		
Webb, Clifton	1891-1966	Entertainment	35			65	Dancer-Actor. Silents in 20's-To Villain in Laura
Webb, Del		Business	5	15	25	25	'Desert Inn Casino', Las Vegas
Webb, Jack	1920-82	Entertainment	40	94	110	185	Radio-TV Actor. Dragnet SP $125
Webb, James E.		Astronaut	10			25	Admiral
Webb, Jimmy		Composer	20	35		65	Singer-Songwriter
Webb, Matthew	1848-83	Channel Swimmer			250		'Captain Webb'. 1st Man to Swim English Channel
Webb, Richard		Entertainment	15			35	'Capt. Midnight'
Webb, Samuel B.		Rev. War	105	400	645		Fndr. Soc. of Cincinnati
Webb, Sidney	1859-1947	Reformer	15		192	175	Br Economist, Fabian Society. SP Pc/Beatrice $375
Webb, U.S.		Political	6		25		California Official
Webb, W.R. 'Spider'		Aviation	15	30	45	35	ACE, WW II, Ace in a Day
Webber, Andrew Lloyd	1948-	Composer	82	250		250	Br. Musical Theatre. Cats, Phantom of the Opera
Webber, Robert		Entertainment	15	20		35	Actor. Versatile Lead, 2nd Lead & Character
Weber (Joe) & Fields (Lew)		Entertainment	85			175	Pioneer Vaudeville Comedians
Weber, Joe	1867-1942	Entertainment	25	35		45	Vintage Comedian/Lew Fields
Weber, Karl Maria von	1786-1826	Composer	375	1035	1320		9 Operas. Leader Ger. Romantic & Nationalist Music
Webster, Ben		Entertainment	125				Tenor Sax-Arranger
Webster, Daniel	1782-1852	Cabinet-Senate	136	827	783	540	NH Statesman, LS/Cont.$1750. LS as Sec'y St. 8500
Webster, H.T.*		Cartoonist	20	45		125	'The Timid Soul'. 'Caspar Milquetoast'

NAME	DATE	CATEGORY	SIG	LS/DS	ALS	SP	COMMENTS
Webster, Jean	1876-1916	Author	15	45	135		Am. Novelist. 'Daddy-Long-Legs'
Webster, Noah	1758-1843	Author	600	795	1432		Am.Lexicographer,Editor.Dictionary Of Eng.Language
Webster, Paul Francis		Composer	20	50	70	45	
Webster, William		Cabinet	10			40	Director FBI
Wedekind, Erika		Entertainment	10		50		Opera. Legendary 19th Cent. Soprano
Wedell, Jimmie		Aviation	12	30	40	35	
Wedemeyer, Albert C.	1897-1985	Military	30	200		150	Gen. WW II. Cmdr. US Forces China Theatre
Wedgwood, John H., Sir		Business	15	25	40	35	Decorative Ceramics.One of World's Major Producers
Wedgwood, Josiah	1730-95	Potter	450		1980		Fndr. World Famous Wedgwood Pottery. Rare Sig.
Weed, Marian		Entertainment	15			50	Opera
Weed, Thurlow	1797-1882	Politician	15	30	62		Influential Political Leader NY, Journalist
Weede, Robert		Entertainment	10			35	Opera, Concert, Operetta
Weedon, George		Rev. War	450		1900		Gen'l Cont'l Army. ALS/Content $2500
Weeks, Anson		Entertainment	15			45	Dancin' with Anson. Big Bandleader
Weeks, John W.	1860-1926	Cabinet	15	35	70		Sec'y War 1921. US Sen. MA
Weeks, Sinclair	1893-1972	Cabinet	5	15	35	20	Sec'y Commerce 1953. US Senator
Weems, Ted		Bandleader	20	20	62	45	Big Band Leader-Trombone. Vocalist-Perry Como
Weicker, Lowell Jr.		Congress	10	20		15	Repr.CT 1969, Senator 1971. Watergate Committee
Weidler, Virginia	1927-68	Entertainment	12		20	25	Popular Child & Juvenile Actress
Weidman, Jerome		Author	5	10	20	10	
Weikl, Bernd		Entertainment	5			20	Opera
Weill, Kurt	1900-50	Composer	250	862	1717	412	Ger.-Am. Opera, Ballet, Musical Comedy, Films
Weinberg, Steven, Dr.		Science	25	35		30	Nobel Physics 1979
Weinberger, Casper		Cabinet	10		30	40	Sec'y HEW, Sec'y Defense, Sec'y State
Weingartner, Felix von	1863-1942	Composer	90	125	180	150	Austrian Conductor & Writer on Music
Weir, Benjamin M.		Celebrity	12	15	25	20	
Weir, Julian Alden		Artist	40	135	250		Early Am. Impressionist
Weir, Peter		Entertainment	5			25	Movie Director
Weir, Robert Walter	1803-89	Artist	50	135	265		Prof. Drawing At West Point. Taught R.E. Lee
Weisbart, David		Entertainment	15			25	Director-Producer
Weiser, Jan Conrad	1696-1760	Indian Agent	290	950	1600		Helped Form Iroquois-Eng. Alliance Against French
Weisiger, David A.	1818-99	Civil War	80	265			CSA Gen. ALS/Cont. $1045, Sig/Rank $175
Weiss, John	1818-79	Clergy	10	15	28		Unitarian Author, Abolitionist
Weiss, Michael T.		Entertainment	9			52	Actor. The Pretender
Weissmuller, Johnny	1904-79	Entertainment	124	338		376	SPI As Tarzan $325-$695. Olympic Gold Swimmer
Weitz, Paul J.		Astronaut	10			25	
Weitzel, Godfrey (WD)		Civil War	45	110	235		Union Gen. 1835-84
Weiz, Paul		Astronaut	8			20	
Weizman, Vera		First Lady	25	80		35	Widow of 1st Pres. Israel
Weizmann, Chaim	1874-1952	Head of State	445	1700	2335	895	1st Pres. Israel
Weizmann, Ezer		Head of State	25	65			Israeli AF Gen. Pres. of Israel
Welby, Amelia		Author	450		2900		Poet. Appreciated by E.A.Poe
Welch Herbert, Bishop		Clergy	15	25	30	35	
Welch, Raquel		Entertainment	10	40	30	46	Actress. Pin-Up SP $75. '72 Life Mag. S $85
Welch, Robert A.		Business	25	40	82	35	Batchelor Oil Multi-Millionaire

NAME	DATE	CATEGORY	SIG	LS/DS	ALS	SP	COMMENTS
Weld, Tuesday	1943-	Entertainment	10	15	30	25	Child Model-Actress. Unfortunate Start. Talent Won
Welden, Ben		Entertainment	10			25	Actor
Weldon, Felix de		Artist	60	85			Iwo Jima Memorial Statue
Welensky, Roy, Sir		Head of State	20	55	115		
Welk, Lawrence		Entertainment	10	50	35	25	Big Bandleader-TV Variety Show. 50's Most Popular
Weller, Peter		Entertainment	10	15	25	20	Actor
Weller, Thomas H., Dr.		Science	25	35	50	30	Nobel Medicine 1954
Welles, Gideon	1802-78	Cabinet-CW	125	260	300	675	Lincoln Sec'y of Navy, LS War Dte $775-$850
Welles, Orson	1915-85	Entertainment	114	458		510	AA. Actor-Dir.-Prod-Writer. Special DS $650
Welles, Sumner	1892-1961	Diplomat	25	75	150	55	State Dept.,Ambassador
Wellington, 1st Duke of	1769-1852	Head of State	180	414	404		Arthur Wellesley,Prime Minister-Military ALS $1750
Wellington, George Louis	1852-1927	Congress	12	20			MOC 1895, Senator MD
Wellman, Manly Wade		Author	35	100		60	North Carolina Literary Figure
Wellman, Walter	1858-1934	Aviation-Journalist	60	145	230	75	Aviator-Explorer. Derigible Time Distance Record
Wells, B. H.		Military	30	75			Am. WW I Gen.
Wells, Carolyn		Author	10	25	40	15	Sketches, Parodies,Detective
Wells, Carveth		Author	20	45	110	25	Explorer, Author, Lecturer
Wells, Dawn		Entertainment	5	10	20	20	Actress. Mary Ann. Pin-Up $35
Wells, H(erbert) G(eorge)	1866-1946	Author	150	295	488	1035	Br. Sci-Fi Novelist, ALS/Cont.$6000
Wells, Henry & Fargo, James		Business	850	1375			Wells-Fargo, American Express
Wells, Henry & Fargo, William G.		Business		1475			Wells-Fargo. American Express Stk. Cert. S $800
Wells, Henry	1805-78	Business	275	750	1450		Wells-Fargo, Founder American Express
Wells, James M.		Governor	15	40			Governor LA 1865
Wells, Junior		Entertainment	4			10	
Wells, Kitty	1918-	Country Music	10			30	Onetime 'Queen of Country Music'. Country HOF
Welty, Eudora		Author	35	100	225	100	Am.Short Stories, Novelist.
Welty, Ron		Entertainment	6			25	Music. Drummer Offspring
Wenck, Walter		Military	25	60	120	55	
Wendelin, Rudolph*		Cartoonist	32			125	'Smokey the Bear'. FDC $250
Wendorf, E.G. Wendy		Aviation	10	25	40	30	ACE, WW II, Navy Ace
Wendt, George		Entertainment	15	35		35	Actor. 'Cheers'. Successful TV Adv. Personality
Wenrich, Percy		Composer	55	125			AMusQS $175, $350
Wentworth, Benning	1696-1770	Colonial America	95	270	550		Col. Gov. NH. Bennington, VT
Wentworth, John	1737-1820	Rev. War	95	250	340		Gov. Vermont. Loyalist. Forced to FleeTo Canada
Wentworth, Joshua	1742-1809	Rev. War		320	975		Soldier,State Sen. NH, Declined Cont'l Congr.Appt.
Wentz, Carol		Entertainment	7	12	30	30	Actress. Pin-Up $75
Werfel, Franz	1890-1945	Author	100			350	Aus.40 Days of Musa Dagh,Song of Bernadette
Wermuth, Arthur W.		Military	20	35	50	35	WW II Hero
Werner, Oskar	1922-	Entertainment	25		45	60	Intelligent,Sensitive Actor. AA Nom.Ship of Fools'
Werrenrath, Reinald	1883-	Opera	15		23	50	Am. Baritone. Met.Debut 1919
Wert, Richard L.		Military	5	15	25	20	
Wesley, Charles	1707-88	Clergy	188		1035		Methodist Divine. Authored Several Thousand Hymns
Wesley, John	1704-91	Clergy	438	650	2000		Methodist Fndr, ALS/Cont.$3000
Wesley, Samuel	1663-1735	Clergy					Father of John & Charles Wesley. AQS $580
Wessell, Vivian		Entertainment	10		40	35	

NAME	DATE	CATEGORY	SIG	LS/DS	ALS	SP	COMMENTS
Wesselowsky, Alessandro		Entertainment	40			160	Opera
Wesson, Daniel B.	1825-1906	Inventor	488		875		Inventor, Mfg., Gunsmith (Smith & Wesson)
West, Adam		Entertainment	10	25		34	Actor. Batman TV Series
West, Benjamin	1738-1820	Artist	240	880	1683		Am. Born Historical Painter
West, Dottie	1932-	Country Music	15			40	Singer. Many Awards, a Few Movies, 400 Songs
West, F.H.		Civil War	40	110			Union Gen. War Dte LS $250
West, Jessamyn		Author	12	30	35	20	Popular Novelist
West, Joseph R.	1822-98	Civil War	40	85	120		Union Gen.
West, Mae	1892-1980	Entertainment	73	136	300	215	Provocative Seductress. S Chk $175
West, Morris L.		Author	15	45	80	30	'Shoes Of The Fisherman'
West, Rebecca, Dame	1892-1983	Author	20	45	102	50	Br. Novelist, Critic, Historian
West, Richard L.		Aviation	10			30	ACE WW II
West, Roy O.		Cabinet	25	40			Sec'y Interior 1928
Westall, William		Artist	15	40	95		
Westheimer, Ruth, Dr.		Medical	5		25	20	Sex Therapist. Radio-TV Personality
Westinghouse, George	1846-1914	Business	125	648	788	350	Fndr. Westinghouse Corp. Over 400 Patents
Westman, Nidia	1902-70	Entertainment	15	15	35	30	1st as Child Stage Actress. From '32 Comic Support
Westminster, 2nd Earl		Royalty	15	50			Robert Grosvenor
Westmore, Wally		Entertainment	15			50	Hollywood Makeup Director
Westmoreland, Wm. C.	1914-93	Military	22	66	75	70	Gen. WW II, Korean & Viet Nam War
Weston, Agnes, Dame		Celebrity	6	20	40	25	
Weston, Edward	1850-1936	Business	40	125	315	75	Weston Electrical Instruments.
Weston, Edward	1886-1958	Artist	35				Am. Western Photographer. ALS/Cont. $600
Weston, Paul	1912-96	Entertainment	18			35	Composer-Arranger-Conductor-Pianist For Top Stars
Westover, Russ*	1887-1966	Cartoonist	25		45	75	'Tillie The Toiler'
Wetherbee, James D.		Astronaut	6			20	
Wettig, Patricia		Entertainment	6			35	Award Winning Actress- TV
Weyer, Kurt		Military	15			60	
Weygand, Maxime	1867-1965	Military	40	75	150	150	Fr. Gen. Foch's Chief of Staff. WW I, WW II
Weyman, Stanley J.	1855-1928	Author	25	35	75		Brit. Novelist
Whalen, Grover		NYC Official	10	30		15	Merchant-NYC Official Greeter
Whalen, Michael	1902-74	Entertainment	10	15	20	30	Leading Man of Many 'B' Movies. 30's-40's
Wharton, Edith N.	1862-1937	Author	205	475	1600		Pulitzer, 'Age of Innocence', 'Ethan Frome'
Wharton, Gabriel C.	1824-1906	Civil War	80		185		CSA Gen. DS '64 $470, Sig/Rank $125
Wharton, John A.	1828-65	Civil War	150	450	1100		CSA Gen.Killed in Feud 4/6/1865. ALS WarDte $1,950
Wharton, Thomas	1735-1778	Rev. War	132	1068	1482		Gov. PA, Patriot. Pres. PA 1777. Wealthy Merchant
Wheatley, Melvin E., Bishop		Clergy	20	25	35	30	
Wheaton, Nathaniel S.	1792-1862	Clergy	10		36		Founder Trinity College, Hartford, Washington Coll
Wheaton, Will		Entertainment	20			45	Actor. 'Star Trek', Westley
Wheatstone, Charles, Sir	1802-1875	Science	100	320	565		Br. Physicist, Inventor
Wheeler, Bert	1895-1968	Entertainment	25			75	Comedy Team Wheeler & Woolsey. Vaudeville, Films
Wheeler, Burton K.	1882-1975	Congress	25	70		35	Senator MT 1922. Progressive Party V.P. Candidate
Wheeler, Charles B.		Military	35	125			Am. WW I Gen.
Wheeler, Earle G.		Military	15			50	
Wheeler, Ellie		Entertainment	10	15	25	25	

NAME	DATE	CATEGORY	SIG	LS/DS	ALS	SP	COMMENTS
Wheeler, Joseph (WD)		Civil War	295	1375	1525		CSA Gen.
Wheeler, Joseph	1836-1906	Civil War	120	241	245	950	CSA Gen. Fightin Joe
Wheeler, Lyle	1905-	Entertainment	15			30	Film Art Director. AA Gone With the Wind & 3 More
Wheeler, William A.	1819-87	Vice President	75	225	295		Hayes VP
Whelan, Arleen	1916-	Entertainment	10		25	20	Actress. Redheaded Leading Lady. Late 30's-50's
Whelchel, Lisa		Entertainment	8			18	Actress. 'Facts of Life'
Wherry, William M.		Civil War	25	55			Union Gen. MOH
Whewell, William	1794-1866	Science		90			1st to Measure Tides in S. Pac. To Learn of Forces
Whipple, Abraham	1733-1819	Rev. War	250	750			Fired 1st Gun of Rev. on Water
Whipple, Amiel Weeks	1816-1863	Civil War	115	235	350		Astronomer, Surveyor, Union Gen
Whipple, Edwin Percy	1819-86	Author	15		30		Essayist, Critic, Lecturer
Whipple, Fred L.	1906-	Author-Science	10	25		18	Astronomer. Rocket Research
Whipple, George H.	1878-1976	Science	45	75	150		Nobel Medicine 1934
Whipple, Henry B.	1822-1901	Clergy	50	100	200		Episcopal Bishop. Reforms re Cruelty to Indians
Whipple, William	1730-85	Rev. War	622	1250	4200		Signer Decl. of Ind.
Whipple, William D.	1826-1902	Civil War	25	40	58		Union Gen'l. Sherman Aide-de-Camp. Sig/Rank $40
Whirry, Shannon		Entertainment	8			25	Actress. 'Exit'
Whisner, William T.		Aviation	20	45	75	50	ACE, WW II
Whistler, James McNeill	1834-1903	Artist	300	525	807		Am. Painter, Etcher. Lived Abroad Never to Return
Whitaker, Johnnie		Entertainment	10			25	Actor
White, Alice	1907-	Entertainment	25	45		75	Vintage Actress. Late Silents & Early Sound Films
White, Andrew Dickson	1832-1918	Educator-Diplomat	20	75	85	50	Co-Fndr. Cornell University
White, Anthony Walton	1750-1803	Rev. War	55	165	250		Washington Aide-de-Camp. General
White, Betty		Entertainment	9	15	20	20	'Golden Girls', 'Mary Tyler Moore Show'. Emmy Wins
White, Byron R. (SC)		Supreme Court	60	125	180	65	
White, E.B.		Author	30	118			'Charlotte's Web'
White, Edw. H. & McDivitt, J.		Astronauts				1325	SP After Pickup Gem. 4. $595
White, Edward D. (SC)	1845-1921	Supreme Court	60	192	225	135	Chief Justice
White, Edward H. II	1930-67	Astronaut	325	325	585	685	1st Am. To Walk In Space
White, George		Entertainment	60	75	575	100	Founder-Producer 'George White's Scandals'
White, George Stuart	1835-1912	Military	40		65		Br. Fld. Marshal. Ladysmith Seige
White, Horace	1865-1943	Governor	10	25			Gov. NY
White, Horace	1834-	Journalist	25		75		Editor NY Evening Post. Corresponded/Lincoln
White, Hugh		Governor	5	20		15	Governor MS 1936
White, I.D.		Military	10			25	
White, Jacqueline		Entertainment	5			15	Actress
White, Jesse	1919-	Entertainment	25	40		40	Character Actor. TV 'Maytag' Spokesman
White, Jim		Explorer	40		175		Discover Carlsbad Caverns
White, Josh		Entertainment	60			225	Am. Folk Singer
White, Julius	1816-90	Civil War	30	55	125		Union General
White, Lee 'Lasses'		Entertainment	25				Minstrel
White, Paul Dudley, Dr.		Science	45	110		80	Heart Specialist
White, Pearl		Entertainment	150		290	285	Queen of the Silent Serials
White, Robert, Maj.		Aviation	10	25		30	'60 Speed & Altitude Records
White, Sanford	1853-1906	Architect	100	268	790	150	Murdered By Harry K. Thaw. TLS/Content $1,600-5,500

NAME	DATE	CATEGORY	SIG	LS/DS	ALS	SP	COMMENTS
White, Stewart E.	1873-1946	Author	10	20	40	30	Am. Western Adventure Stories
White, Theodore		Author	9	15	25	20	Detailed Presidential Campaigns
White, Vanna		Entertainment	5	25		20	TV Personality. Pin-Up SP $25.'Wheel of Fortune'
White, Vanna & Pat Sajak		Entertainment	15			30	'Wheel of Fortune'
White, Wallace H., Jr.	1877-1952	Congress	5	15			MOC ME 1917, Senator 1930
White, William	1748-1836	Clergy	130	265	250		1st Protestant Episcopal Bishop
White, William Allen	1868-1944	Author	25	120	85	60	Pulitzer Journalist. 'Sage of Emporia'
White, Windsor T.		Business	110		550		Pioneer Auto-Truck Mfg.
Whitehouse, James	1833-	Artist	25		75		Tiffany Designer-Engraver of Many Major Pieces
Whitelaw, Billie	1932-	Entertainment	15			30	Br. Actress.Stage 50s. Leading Lady TV, Films 60s
Whiteman, Paul	1890-1967	Entertainment	60	140	168	193	King of Jazz. Introduced Gershwin Rhaposdy in Blue
Whitestone, Heather		Entertainment	15			40	Miss America 1995. Hearing impaired
Whiting, Jack		Entertainment	5		10	10	Actor
Whiting, John D.		Diplomat	5		20		Jerusalem
Whiting, Margaret		Entertainment	10			15	Pop Vocalist
Whiting, Richard		Composer	50		135	100	Top Pop & Standards. AMusQS $150
Whiting, William Henry	1824-65	Civil War	200				CSA General ALS '65 $935-1500.
Whitlam, Gough		Head of State	10			20	Prime Minister Australia
Whitley, Ray	1901-	Country Music	10			35	Singing Cowboy. Movies from '38. Major Sidekick
Whitman, Charles S.		Governor	10	25		15	Governor NY 1915
Whitman, Slim	1924-	Country Music	5			15	Singer. Slips in a Yodel or Two. London Palladium
Whitman, Walt	1819-92	Author	1028	2500	3000	3108	Am. Poet. Self-Educated.Leaves of Grass
Whitmore, James	1921-	Entertainment	5		15	15	Actor. Excellent Character Actor
Whitney, Adeline D.	1824-1906	Author	20		35		
Whitney, Asa	1797-1872	Merchant	30		100		Promoter of Transcontinental RR
Whitney, C.V.		Business	15	35	70	25	
Whitney, Casper		Publisher	10	25	35		Publisher
Whitney, Courtney		Military	15	40	75	35	General WW II. MacArthur Aide
Whitney, Eli	1765-1825	Science	650	3042	3250		Am. Inventor Cotton Gin
Whitney, Grace Lee		Entertainment	15	30	35	28	Actress. 'Star Trek'
Whitney, Josiah D.	1819-96	Science	65		275		CA State Geologist. Mt. Whitney in His Honor
Whitney, Richard		Business	35	50			Pres. NY Stock Exchange
Whitney, William Collins	1841-1904	Cabinet	25	45	65	35	Financier, Cleveland Sec'y Navy
Whitson, Peggy		Astronaut	7			25	
Whittaker, Charles E.(SC)	1901-73	Supreme Court	50	75	175	85	
Whitten-Brown, Arthur, Sir		Aviation	250	375			Pioneer Aviator/John Alcock
Whittier, John Greenleaf	1807-92	Author	55	350	406		Quaker Poet.Abolitionist
Whittle, Frank, Sir		Aviation	20	50		45	Invented jet engine
Whittle, Josephine		Entertainment	5		15	15	
Whittlesey, Elisha	1783-1863	Statesman	20		55		Founder of Whig Party
Whitty, Dame May	1865-1948	Entertainment	35	45	85	75	Grand Old Brit. Character Actress. 2x Nominated AA
Who, The (All 4)		Entertainment	412			710	Rock. DS $2050
Whorf, Richard	1906-66	Entertainment	10			20	Actor-Producer-Director
Wickard, Claude		Cabinet	15	25			Sec'y Agriculture 1940
Wicke, Lloyd C., Bishop		Clergy	15	25	35	30	

NAME	DATE	CATEGORY	SIG	LS/DS	ALS	SP	COMMENTS
Wicker, Irene		Entertainment	10			25	Vintage Radio's 'Singing Lady'
Wickersham, George W.	1858-1936	Cabinet	15	45	75	45	Taft Att'y Gen. 1909
Wickes, Mary	1916-	Entertainment	18			30	Lanky, Gawky, Character Comedienne. Films 40s-70s
Wickham, William C. (WD)		Civil War	275	395			CSA Gen.
Wickham, William C.	1820-88	Civil War	85	265			CSA Gen.
Wickliffe, Charles A.		Cabinet	30	60	95		P.M. Gen. 1841
Widmark, Richard	1914-	Entertainment	10		25	65	Actor. Leading Man & Heavy.
Widor, Charles Marie		Composer	30		165		Fr. Organist, Teacher
Wieck, Dorothea	1908-	Entertainment	15	15	35	30	Max Reinhardt Protégé. German Star. 2 Am. Films
Wieghorst, Olaf		Artist	60	225	350	180	Dean of Western Art
Wiemann, Ernst		Entertainment	5			20	Opera
Wien, Noel		Aviation	25	55	105	65	
Wiere Brothers		Entertainment	15			25	
Wiesel, Elie		Author	20	45	55	25	Nobel Peace Prize 1986. Holocaust Authority
Wiesel, Torsten S., Dr.		Science	22	30	45	25	Nobel Medicine 1981
Wiesenthal, Simon		Activist	20	45	90	35	Famed Nazi Hunter. FDC S $25
Wiest, Diane		Entertainment	20		35	45	Actress. Versatile AA Winner
Wigfall, Louis T.	1816-74	Civil War	140	212	395		CSA Gen. CSA Senator. Sig/Rank $210
Wiggin, Kate Douglas	1856-1923	Author	110		195	110	Author of Popular Children's Books.
Wigglesworth, Edward	1804-76	Editor	5		30		Harvard Law Grad. Mercantile Business. Charities
Wigglesworth, Frank		Composer					AMusQS $100
Wigglesworth, Richard B		Congress	5	10			MOC MA 1928, Diplomat
Wigner, Eugene P. Dr.		Science	30	40	70	30	Nobel Physics 1963. Atomic Nuclei. Typescript S $150
Wihan, Hanus		Entertainment	30		120		Czech Viol-Cellist. AMusQs $85
Wilberforce, Samuel, Bishop	1805-73	Clergy	30	45	60		'Soapy' Wilberforce. Evolution Controversy/T.Huxley
Wilberforce, William	1759-1833	Abolitionist	50	145	300		Br. Anti-Slavery Politician, Philanthropist
Wilbur, Curtis D.		Cabinet	10	25	35	25	Sec'y Navy 1924
Wilbur, Ray Lyman		Cabinet	15	25	55	20	Sec'y Interior 1929
Wilbur, Richard		Author	5		35	10	U.S. Poet Laureate. Pulitzer. LS/Cont. $135
Wilbur, W.H.		Military	5	15	25	10	
Wilburn Bros.		Country Western	10			35	Teddy & Doyle
Wilcott, Terry		Astronaut	5			10	
Wilcox, Cadmus M. (WD)		Civil War	245	400			CSA Gen.
Wilcox, Cadmus M.	1824-90	Civil War	100	195	320		CSA Gen.
Wilcox, Ella Wheeler	1850-1919	Author	20	35	100		Journalist, Poet, Essayist, Daily Syndicated Poem
Wilcoxon, Henry	1905-	Entertainment	20		35	45	Actor. Important Roles/ DeMille. Supporting in Bs
Wilcutt, Terry		Astronaut	5			20	
Wild Choir		Entertainment	15			35	Rock
Wild, Edward A.	1825-91	Civil War	70	150	220		Union General Sig/Rank $95, War Dte DS $175
Wild, Jack		Entertainment	5			15	Actor. The Artful Dodger in Oliver
Wilde, Cornel	1915-89	Entertainment	10	22	40	31	Handsome Leading Man. Played Variety of Roles
Wilde, Oscar	1856-1900	Author	758	1550	3903	2215	Ir.-Born Eng. Poet, Playwright, Wit
Wilde, Percival		Author	20	55	110		Playwright, Novelist
Wilder, Billy	1906-	Entertainment	20	50		57	Multiple AA Film Dir. Producer. Content DS $285
Wilder, Gene	1935-	Entertainment	10	33		30	Actor-Comedian. 'Young Frankenstein'

NAME	DATE	CATEGORY	SIG	LS/DS	ALS	SP	COMMENTS
Wilder, Marshall P.		Entertainment	15	20	30	35	Vintage Reciter, Imitator.
Wilder, Thornton	1897-1975	Author	70	200	333	200	Playwright, Novelist.3 Pulitzers, ALS/Content $675
Wilding, Michael	1912-79	Entertainment	30			55	Br. Actor. Ex Leading-Man Husband Eliz. Taylor
Wilentz, David T.		Celebrity	25				
Wiley, Alexander	1884-1967	Congress	15	40			Senator WI 1938
Wiley, Harvey W., Dr.	1844-1930	Science	80	195			Created FDA.Chemist Investigated Food Adulteration
Wilhelm I (Ger)	1787-1888	Royalty	80	350	362		King of Prussia, Emperor Ger.
Wilhelm II (Kaiser)(Ger)	1859-1941	Royalty	170	395	510	295	Official DS $8500. Last Emperor of Ger.
Wilhelm, August		Military	125			500	Ger. Gen'l. Storm Trooper
Wilhelmina, Queen	1880-1962	Royalty	110		400		Netherlands. Abdicated in Favor of Juliana
Wilhelmj, August		Entertainment	25			75	Ger. Violinist
Wilk, Brad		Entertainment	6			25	Music. Drummer Rage Against the Machine
Wilke, Robert J.		Entertainment	10			25	
Wilkerson, Guy		Entertainment	25			65	
Wilkes, Charles	1798-1877	Civil War	50	105	200		Union Adm.,Explorer.Sig/Rank $70, War Dte. DS $180
Wilkes, Earle		Military	10			50	
Wilkie, David, Sir	1785-1841	Artist	60	88	137		Br.Genre Paintings, Portraits
Wilkins, Geo. Hubert,Sir	1888-1958	Explorer	30	50	110	55	Led Arctic & Antarctic Exped.
Wilkins, Hans		Aviation	10	25	45	30	
Wilkins, Roy		Activist	15	35	70	25	Sr. Statesman of Civil Rights
Wilkins, T. H.		Science	15	25	40	20	
Wilkinson, Geoffrey		Science	15	25	40	25	Nobel Chemistry 1985
Wilkinson, James	1757-1825	Rev. War	125	342	430		General, Implicated In Aaron Burr Conspiracy
Wilkinson, June		Entertainment	6	10	18	20	Actress.Pin-Up SP $30
Wilkinson, Raven		Dance	4			12	Ballerina
Wilks, Matthew		Clergy	15		25	50	
Willard, Charles		Aviation	15			35	
Willard, Edward S.		Entertainment	15		35	30	Vintage
Willard, Frances E.	1839-98	Temperance	50	82	230		Pres. W.C.T.U. Prof. At Northwestern U.
Willard, Frank*		Cartoonist	35			182	'Moon Mullins'
Willard, Fred		Entertainment	5		12	15	Actor
Willard, John		Entertainment	10			25	Playwright
Willcox, Orlando B.	1823-1907	Civil War	40	90	165		Union Gen. Sig/Rank $60
Willebrands, John, Cardinal		Clergy	30	45	65	40	
Willem VI & I,	1772-1848	Royalty		692			Prince of Orange, King Netherlands
Willett, Marinus	1740-1830	Rev. War	75	150	250		Officer Cont. Army.Mayor NYC
William II, Germany	1859-1941	Royalty		265	335		King from 1888-1918. Political During Reign
William III (Eng)	1650-1702	Royalty	605	1609	2500		Wm. III & Mary II DS $2195. Jointly Ruled
William IV (Eng)	1765-1837	Royalty	128	425	449		The Sailor King, DS $995
William, 4th Duke of Devonshire		Head of State	75	185	355		Prime Minister 1756
William, Warren	1894-1948	Entertainment	10	15	40	45	Am. Film Leading Man & Character Actor
Williams, Alford J., Jr.		Aviation	30	45	95	125	
Williams, Andy		Entertainment	20	35		40	Major 50's-70's Pop Singer. TV, Records, Vegas
Williams, Barry		Entertainment	10	40		35	Actor. 'Brady Bunch'
Williams, Bart		Entertainment	5			15	

NAME	DATE	CATEGORY	SIG	LS/DS	ALS	SP	COMMENTS
Williams, Ben Ames	1889-1953	Author	15	25	40	25	Am. Novelist
Williams, Bill	1916-	Entertainment	10	15		25	Nice Guy Leading Man-Husband of Barbara Hale
Williams, Billy Dee	1937-	Entertainment	10	25		25	Stage-Film-Tv Leading Man. 'Empire Strikes Back'
Williams, Brian		Journalist	4			9	Broadcast News TV
Williams, Cindy		Entertainment	5		15	20	Actress. 'American Graffiti', 'Laverne & Shirley'
Williams, Cliff		Entertainment	6			25	Music. Bass Guitar AC/DC
Williams, Clifton C.		Astronaut	6			25	
Williams, Donald E.		Astronaut	6			20	
Williams, Edward B.		Law	5	15	40	15	Top Criminal Lawyer
Williams, Edward M.		Business	35	90	155		
Williams, Edy		Entertainment	5			20	Actress.Pin-Up SP $30
Williams, Eleazer	1787-1858	Clergy	45	115	1600		Am.Missionary. Louis XVII-Lost Dauphin? Author
Williams, Esther	1923-	Entertainment	8			21	Actress-Swimmer-Part-Time Model. Major Star
Williams, G. Mennan	1911-	Political	5	20		35	5 Times MI Gov., Ambass. Philippines. Soapy
Williams, Geoffrey		Science	10	20	35	20	
Williams, George H.		Cabinet	10	25	40		Att'y Gen. 1872, Senator OR
Williams, Gluyas*	1888-19xx	Cartoonist	10		45	75	New Yorker Cartoonist
Williams, Grant		Entertainment	45			125	Actor
Williams, Griff		Bandleader	25				Big Band
Williams, Guinn Big Boy	1899-1962	Entertainment	75			150	Actor. Starred in Many Westerns.
Williams, Gus		Entertainment	10			25	Showman
Williams, Guy	1924-89	Entertainment	130	200		375	Actor. 'Lost in Space', 'Zorro'. SP as Zorro $695
Williams, Hal		Entertainment	5			15	Afro-Am Actor
Williams, Hank	1923-53	Country Music	712	1200		1250	Major Country Singing Star
Williams, Hank Jr.		Country Music	20	30		38	
Williams, Harrison A., Jr.	1919-	Congress	15	35		20	Rep. 1953, Senator NJ
Williams, J.R.*		Cartoonist	18	25		85	'Way Out West'
Williams, JoBeth		Entertainment	10	30		25	Actress. Poltergeist etc.
Williams, Joe		Entertainment	15			40	Jazz Vocalist
Williams, John		Composer	20	65	75	75	Conductor. AMusQS $225, $100
Williams, John Sharp		Congress	10	20		20	MOC MS 1893, Senator 1910
Williams, Jonathan		Author	5	15	25		
Williams, Mary Alice		Journalist	10			20	TV News Journalist
Williams, Mason		Entertainment	10			20	Singer-Guitar Soloist-Composer
Williams, Michelle		Entertainment	12			52	Actress. Pin-Up $60
Williams, Montel		Entertainment	4			15	Talk Show Host-TV
Williams, Otho	1749-1800	Rev. War	140	420	735		Officer. Fought/Gates & Greene
Williams, Paul		Composer	5		15	20	Actor-Singer
Williams, Robin		Entertainment	17			45	Actor-Comedian. AA
Williams, Roger		Entertainment	5		20	35	Pianist-Arranger
Williams, Seth	1822-66	Civil War	30	70	95		Union Gen. War Dte. LS $175, Sig/Rank $55
Williams, Tennessee (Thos L.)	1914-83	Author	152	475	600	395	Pulitzer. Cat on a Hot Tin Roof &Streetcar....
Williams, Tex		Country Music	10			20	Big Band-Singer-Leader
Williams, Treat		Entertainment	5	15	25	20	Actor
Williams, Van		Entertainment	25			43	TV's Green Hornet

NAME	DATE	CATEGORY	SIG	LS/DS	ALS	SP	COMMENTS
Williams, Vanessa		Entertainment	20			50	Miss America, Pin-Up SP $ 55
Williams, Vaughan R.	1872-1958	Composer					SEE Vaughan-Williams
Williams, William	1731-1811	Rev. War	275	505	753		Signer Decl. of Indepen. Statesman
Williams, William Carlos	1883-1963	Author	275	500	1500	300	Am. Poet, Novelist, Physician
Williams, Willie, Chief		Law Enforcement	5			25	Los Angeles Chief of Police
Williamson, Fred		Entertainment	8			20	Afro-Am. Actor
Williamson, Hugh		Rev. War		2000			Continental Congress. Physician, Scientist. Rare
Williamson, James A.	1829-1902	Law	5		20		
Williamson, Marianne		Author	5			10	Non-Fiction
Williiams, Roger Q.		Aviation	10		20		'29 Record Non-Stop Flight
Willing, Foy	1915-	Country Music	10			25	And-The Riders of the Purple Sage
Willing, Thomas		Rev. War	75	250			Banker, Continental Congress
Willis, Bruce		Entertainment	25	125		70	Actor. Mega Action & Straight Leads
Willis, Nathaniel P.	1806-67	Author	20	40	118		Major Editor Poetry Mags. Playwright, Critic
Willis, Richard S.		Clergy	20	25	35		
Willkie, Wendell	1892-1944	Politician	25	75		125	Pres. Candidate
Wills, Bob	1905-75	Country Music	75			200	Bob Wills and His Texas Playboys
Wills, Chill	1903-78	Entertainment	55			85	Actor. Character Actor. Many Western & Other Genre
Willson, Meredith		Composer	25	80	205	80	'The Music Man'
Willys, John North		Business	60	110	245	90	Auto Pioneer, Diplomat. (Originally Willys Jeep)
Wilmer, Richard Hooker, Bishop		Clergy	8	25	40		
Wilmot, David	1814-68	Congress	85	230			Repr. & Senator PA.' Wilmot Proviso'
Wilson, August		Author	10	30	45	20	Dramatist, Dir., Pulitzer, Tony
Wilson, Brian		Entertainment	68			90	Singer-Songwriter-Record Producer Beach Boys
Wilson, Bridget		Entertainment	8			30	Actress. 'Mortal Combat'. Pin-Up 45
Wilson, Charles Edward	1886-1972	Business	20	75			Pres. General Electric
Wilson, Charles Erwin	1890-1961	Business-Cabinet	20	35	70	30	Pres. GM., Sec'y Defense 1953
Wilson, Demond		Entertainment	10			35	Actor. 'Sanford & Son'
Wilson, Dennis		Entertainment	62			132	'Beach Boys'95
Wilson, Don		Entertainment	5			25	Jack Benny Announcer & Sidekick
Wilson, Dooley	1894-1953	Entertainment	432			900	Supporting Player 'Casablanca'
Wilson, E. Willis		Governor	12	25			Governor WV 1885
Wilson, Earl		Journalist	10	15	25	15	Powerful Synd. Columnist
Wilson, Edith Bolling	1872-1961	First Lady	90	213	332	190	ALS as 1st Lady $500-750
Wilson, Edmund	1895-1972	Author	25	85	130		Am. Critic. ALS/Content $650
Wilson, Edmund Beecher	1856-1939	Author-Science	350	450			Am. Biologist. Morphology, Cytology, Heredity
Wilson, Ellen Louise		First Lady	100	345	590		1st Wife - Pres. Wilson
Wilson, Flip	?-1999	Entertainment	20	50		50	Afr-Am. Comedian. 'Flip Wilson Show'. Geraldine
Wilson, Francis	1854-1935	Entertainment	12		15	25	Vintage Actor
Wilson, Gahan*		Cartoonist	20		125	50	Mag. Cartoonist for Playboy, New Yorker etc.
Wilson, George W. Lt.		Celebrity	15	35	120		
Wilson, Harold, Sir	1916-95	Head of State	38	105	146	60	Br. Prime Minister
Wilson, Henry	1812-75	Vice President	74	150	238		Grant VP. Died in Office. Started Career as Cobbler
Wilson, Jackie		Entertainment	175	285		275	Singer
Wilson, James (SC)	1742-98	Supreme Court	725	1212	1933		Scottish Born Signer. ALS/Content $4,000. SB $2250

NAME	DATE	CATEGORY	SIG	LS/DS	ALS	SP	COMMENTS
Wilson, James	1835-1920	Cabinet	25	50	95		Sec'y Agriculture 1897
Wilson, James G.	1833-1914	Civil War	60		260		Union Gen. Led 4th U.S. Colored Cavalry
Wilson, James H.	1837-1925	Civil War	90	180	395		Union Gen. Cavalry. Captured Jefferson Davis
Wilson, John Lockwood	1850-1912	Congress	15	30	40		MOC 1889, Senator WA 1895
Wilson, Joseph R.		Celebrity	40		175		Father of Woodrow Wilson
Wilson, Julie		Entertainment	10			35	
Wilson, Kemmons		Business	20	60	80	70	Founder Holiday Inn Chain Hotels-Motels
Wilson, Lois	1896-	Entertainment	15	15	35	40	Starred in Many Paramount Silents. Talkies to 1949
Wilson, Marie	1916-72	Entertainment	25	35	65	60	'My Friend Irma' Early TV. Years Wiith Ken Murray
Wilson, Mary		Entertainment	10			20	Rock, 'The Supremes'
Wilson, Peta		Entertainment	7			32	Actress. Pin-Up $55
Wilson, Pete		Governor	10	20		20	Governor CA
Wilson, Robert, Dr.		Science	15	25	35	25	Nobel Physics 1978
Wilson, Sloan		Author	15	35	58	25	'Man in the Grey Flannel Suit'
Wilson, Stephanie		Entertainment	8			25	
Wilson, Teddy	1912-86	Entertainment	40		75	95	Pianist-Arranger. Big Band
Wilson, Tom*		Cartoonist	20			50	'Ziggy'
Wilson, William B.	1862-1934	Cabinet	10	25	50	40	Organized United Mine Workers. Sec'y Labor 1913
Wilson, W. & Roosevelt, F.D.		President		1500			DS
Wilson, Woodrow (As Pres.)		President	375	885		620	
Wilson, Woodrow	1856-1924	President	156	797	1501	760	
Wiman, Dwight Deere		Business	15	25			John Deere Farm Implements
Winans, Ross		Inventor	85	250			Railroad Equipment
Winant, John	1889-1947	Governor	25			40	Gov. NH, WW II Ambassador to Britain. Suicide
Winchell, Paul		Entertainment	10	25	35	78	Talented Ventriloquist
Winchell, Walter	1897-1972	Journalist	30	38	45	35	Powerful Radio-Newspaper Columnist
Winchester, Oliver F.	1810-80	Industrialist	338	3250	1500		Winchester Repeating Arms, Inc. LS on Lttrhd $5850
Winchester, Wm.P.Sir, 1st Marquis	1485-1572	Elizabethan	275	955			Elizabeth I. Lord Treasurer Eng.
Winder, Charles S.(WD)	1829-62	Civil War			6335		CSA Gen. KIA LS/DS pre $595
Winder, John Henry (WD)		Civil War	140	1012	565		CSA Gen. Commandant Libby & Andersonville
Winder, Levin		Rev. War-Gov.	15		55		Gov. MD 1812
Windgassen, Wolfgang		Entertainment	15			45	Opera
Windom, William		Cabinet	20	35	60	40	Sec'y Treasury 1881
Windom, William		Entertainment	5		10	20	Actor. Character
Windsor, Claire	1897-72	Entertainment	10	15		25	Blonde-Blue-eyed 20's Silent Star.
Windsor, Duke & Duchess of		Royalty	445			825	Edward & Wallis
Windsor, Marie	1922-	Entertainment	5		15	15	Actress. Many 2nd Leads & Westerns. Pin-Up SP $30
Windsor, Wallis, Duchess of		Royalty	130	312	510	312	1896-1986. Content ALS $775, FDC S $150
Winfield, Paul		Entertainment	5	15		20	Afr.-Am. Actor
Winfrey, Oprah		Entertainment	18			42	Actress-TV Host. Award Winner. Producer
Wing, Toby		Entertainment	10	15	25	25	Vintage Film Actress
Wingate, Francis R., Sir	1861-1953	Military	35	75	140	75	Gen. Succeeded Kitchener. Gov.-Gen. Of Sudan
Winger, Debra		Entertainment	10	32	42	35	Actress. Pin-Up SP $40
Winkler, Betty		Entertainment	5		15	15	Top Radio Performer-40's
Winkler, Henry	1945-	Entertainment	5	15	20	20	Actor. The Fonz on 'Happy Days'

NAME	DATE	CATEGORY	SIG	LS/DS	ALS	SP	COMMENTS
Winkler, K.C.		Entertainment	4			10	Pin-Up SP $20
Winner, Septimus	1827-1902	Composer	92	205	350		Wrote Many Pop Songs. AMusQS $495-$1,000
Winninger, Charles	1884-1969	Entertainment	25		50	60	Much Seen Character Actor 30's-50's. Cap'n Andy
Winningham, Mare		Entertainment	10			25	Actress. AA Nominee
Winship, Blanton	1809-94	Politician	40			125	Orator, Philanthropist
Winship, Blanton	1869-1947	Military	40			125	General. Sp-Am & Phil.Insurrection. Billy Mitchell
Winslet, Kate		Entertainment	14			67	Br. Actress. Titanic Pin-Up $85
Winslow, Edward	1699-1753	Colonial America	225	675			Silversmith.Government Official
Winslow, Edward	1714-84	Rev. War	25	50	90		Loyalist. Port Plymouth Collector
Winslow, John	1753-1819	Rev. War	20	65	110		Soldier, Hero, Patriot, General
Winslow, John Ancrum	1811-73	Military	95	275	385		Union Naval Cmmdr. Sank CSA Raider 'Alabama'
Winslow, John F.		Civil War	65	162	225		Builder of the 'Monitor'
Winsor, Kathleen		Author	15	35	90	30	Novelist 'Forever Amber'
Winter Consort, Paul		Entertainment	50			125	Enviromental Music, Grammy
Winter, William	1836-1913	Author	20	30	34		Drama Critic, Poet, Biographer
Winters, Jonathan		Entertainment	10	15	22	25	Comedian. Standup-TV-Films
Winters, Roland	1904-19—	Entertainment	30	45	85	110	Actor Charlie Chan. Third And Last
Winters, Shelley		Entertainment	8		25	30	Actress. Oscar Winner. Early Pin-Up SP $35
Winthrop, John	1714-1779	Rev. War	200	685			Physicist-Astron.Science Leader
Winthrop, John, The Younger	1638-1707	Colonial America	800	1900	4750		Col. Gov. CT. NRPA
Winthrop, Robert C.	1809-94	Congress	25	65	55		Served out Daniel Webster's Term. Speaker
Winthrop, Theodore	1828-61	Author	75		450		Soldier. Killed CW. Heroic CW Death. AMsS $950
Winthrop, Thomas L.	1760-1841	Rev. War	35	55	100		Merchant. Widely Esteemed
Winwood, Estelle	1883-19—	Entertainment	25	35		45	Br. Character Actress. Often Eccentric Parts
Wire, Calvin C.		Aviation	10		30	25	ACE, WW II
Wirt, William	1772-1834	Cabinet	40	100	155		Att'y General 1817. Author
Wirtz, Willard		Cabinet	5	10	20	15	Sec'y Labor 1962
Wirz, Henry Hartmann		Civil War	450	3850	4950		CSA Comdr. Andersonville. HUNG for WAR CRIMES
Wisch, Theodor		Military	110		165		NRPA
Wise, Henry A. (WD)		Civil War	192		377		CSA Gen.
Wise, Henry A.	1806-76	Civil War	95	220	290		CSA General. Gov.,Senator VA
Wise, Robert	1914-19—	Entertainment	15	38		30	Film Dir. 2 AA.Sound of Music & West Side Story
Wise, Stephen S.	1874-1949	Clergy	32	60	145	88	Important Jewish-German. Content TLS $1100
Wiseman, L.H.		Clergy	10	15	25	20	
Wiseman, Nicholas	1802-65	Clergy	25	45	74		Br. Cardinal of Catholic Church. Author
Wisliceny, Gunther-Ehrhardt		Military	25			55	Ger. SS-Panzer Div. RK
Wisoff. Peter		Astronaut	5			20	
Wister, Owen	1860-1938	Author	50	150	350	75	Am. Novelist, The Virginian
Withers, Jane		Entertainment	10		25	25	Shirley Temple Sidekick
Withers, Robert W	1835-96.	Civil War	32	45	75		CSA Colonel, US Sen. VA. War Dte.S $70, DS $105
Witherspoon, Jimmy		Entertainment	14			30	Jazz Musician
Witherspoon, John	1723-94	Rev. War-Clergy	675	2250	5750		Signer Decl. of Indepen.Active Clergy When Signed
Witherspoon, Reese		Entertainment	10			53	Actress. Pin-Up $75
Witt, Alicia		Entertainment	10			38	Actress. Pin-Up $65
Wittber, Bill		Aviation	20	50	75	80	

NAME	DATE	CATEGORY	SIG	LS/DS	ALS	SP	COMMENTS
Witte, Serge (1st Prem Rus)	1849-1915	Head of State	25	50	95	340	1st Constitutional Russian Prime Minister. SP Rare
Wittig, Georg F.K.		Science	25	50		40	Nobel Chemistry 1979
Wixell, Ingvar		Entertainment	20			45	Opera
Wodehouse, P. G.	1881-1875	Author	153	607	631	550	Br. Novelist Creator of Jeeves. FDC S $175
Woggon, Elmer*		Cartoonist	5			35	'Big Chief Wahoo'
Woidick, Franz		Aviation	15	25	45	35	
Wolcott, Derek		Author	15	25		25	Poet. Nobel Literature
Wolcott, Edward O.	1848-1905	Congress	10	25			Senator CO 1889
Wolcott, Oliver	1726-97	Rev. War	258	433	1875		Signer Decl. of Ind. Gov. CT. FF Addr. Leaf $875
Wolcott, Oliver, Jr.	1760-1833	Cabinet	65	221	355		Washington & Adams Sec'y Treas.FF $350
Wolf, David		Astronaut	8			25	
Wolf, Gary		Entertainment	5			15	Voice of Roger Rabbitt
Wolf, George (Wolfe)	1777-1840	Governor	35	90	185		Gov. PA 1829, Statesman
Wolf, Hugo	1860-1903	Composer	175		1500		Austrian. RARE ALS/Cont.$3500
Wolf, Scott		Entertainment	8			42	Actor. Party of Five
Wolfe, Ian	1896-	Entertainment	10			25	Stage Vet. Hollywood Films Mid-30s.Shady Charact's
Wolfe, James	1727-59	Military	1550		8250		Br. Gen. French & Indian War
Wolfe, Thomas	1900-38	Author	485	2000	2895		Early Death For Gifted Writer Look Homeward Angel
Wolfe, Tom		Author	15	40	70	35	Am. Novelist
Wolfe-Barry, John, Sir	1836-1918	Civil Engineer	15	30	45		London Electr. RR, Docks, Bridges
Wolff, Amalie		Entertainment	15		30	25	
Wolff, Joseph		Clergy	35	40	50		
Wolff, Karl		Military	175	550			Ger. Gen. SS
Woll, Matthew		Labor	10	30	80		Lux.-Am. Labor Leader
Wolper, David	1928-	Entertainment	12		20	20	Film Producer, Executive
Wolseley, Garnet J.,Viscount	1833-1913	Military	25	100	105	50	Br. Field Marshal; Crimean War.Led Nile Expedition
Wolsey, Thomas	1475-1530	Statesman		7800			Influential Cardinal, Statesman. Very Active
Wonder, George*		Cartoonist	20			95	'Terry & The Pirates'
Wonder, Stevie		Entertainment				192	Blind Pianist-Composer. Thumbprint Subs for Sig.
Wonders, Whitney		Entertainment	10			35	Porn Queen
Wong, Anna May	1907-61	Entertainment	81	150	165	185	1st Major Chinese Film Star
Woo, John		Entertainment	10			35	Actor. Face Off SP $65
Wood, Edward F.L.	1881-1959	Statesman	15	35	50	25	Diplomat, Ambassador to U.S.
Wood, Evelyn, Sir.		Military	20		55		Br. Fld. Marshal (Boer War)
Wood, F. Derwent		Artist	10	25	60		
Wood, Fernando	1812-81	Civil War	28	65	90		Civil War Mayor NYC.Tammany MOC.Copperhead
Wood, Garfield 'Gar'		Science	60		80	75	Boat Designer, Builder, Racer
Wood, Grant	1891-1942	Artist	150	338	575		'American Gothic'
Wood, Haydn	1882-1959	Composer	20	55	85	32	AMusQS $100-$150
Wood, Henry J.	1869-1944	Composer	35	60		60	Br. Conductor. Founder of the Proms
Wood, James	1750-1813	Rev. War	50	82	132		House of Burgesses; Gov. VA
Wood, Lana		Entertainment	12	35		20	Actress. 'James Bond'. Pin-Up SP $35
Wood, Leonard, Dr.	1860-1927	Military	30	45	82	250	Gen'l T. Roosevelt's Rough Riders.
Wood, Murray		Entertainment	20	80		85	Actor. Munchkin. Wizard of OZ
Wood, Natalie	1938-81	Entertainment	145			410	Am. Child & Top Adult Actress. SP/R. Wagner $310

NAME	DATE	CATEGORY	SIG	LS/DS	ALS	SP	COMMENTS
Wood, Nigel		Astronaut	8			25	
Wood, Peggy	1892-1978	Entertainment	20	35		35	Theatre & TV Award Winner. I Remember Mama
Wood, Robert		Astronaut	7			18	
Wood, Robert E.		Military	20	70		25	Business (Sears), Gen. WW II
Wood, Robert W.	1868-1955	Science	10	25		20	Physicist. Manhattan Project
Wood, Sam	1883-1949	Entertainment	40			90	Dir.-Producer.Goodby Mr. Chips, Night at Opera
Wood, Sterling Alex. M. (WD)		Civil War	150	465	452		1823-91.CSA General. Wounded. Resigned 1863
Wood, Thomas J.	1823-1906	Civil War	45	125	168		Union Gen. Sig/Rank $60
Wood, Thomas Waterman	1823-	Artist	10	20	55		Pres. Am. Water-Color Society
Woodbury, Levi (SC)	1789-1851	Supreme Court	65	208	270		Gov., Sen., Sec'y Navy & Treas. (Busy Politician)
Woodcock, Amos Walter, Gen.		Military	10	20		25	War Crimes Prosecution Staff. WW II
Woodfill, Samuel		Military	10	30	50	25	Major WW I, MOH Winner
Woodford, Stewart L.	1835-1913	Civil War	43	100	200		Union Gen., Led 103rd Colored Troops. Gov. NY
Woodhouse, Henry		Financier-Explorer	65	265			Turned Forger
Woodhull, Victoria C.	1838-1927	Reformer	115	240	510		1870's Feminist. Legalized Prostitution.
Woodring, Henry H.	1890-1967	Cabinet	25	45	70	35	FDR Sec'y War. TLS/Cont. $300
Woodruff, Wilford	1807-98	Religion	25	65	130		Morman Religious Leader. In 1st Group to Salt Lake
Woods, Charles Robert	1827-85	Civil War	40	60	85		Union General. Sig/Rank $55-$75
Woods, Donald	1904-	Entertainment	15		30	30	Actor. Leading Man 30's-40's. Mostly Stage 50's on
Woods, James		Entertainment	15		30	40	Actor. Versatile Leads. Controversial Personality
Woods, Phil		Entertainment	15			45	Jazz Alto Sax-Clarinet
Woods, Rose Mary		White House	15		35	75	Nixon Sec'y. Watergate
Woods, William B. (SC)	1824-87	Supreme Court	40	85	190	125	
Woodward, Bob		Author,Journalist	10	25	40	25	Uncovered Watergate/C.Bernstein
Woodward, Edward		Entertainment	10	15	25	20	Br. Actor. Active in TV Series'
Woodward, George W.	1809-75	Congress	15		25		MOC PA, Attorney, Judge
Woodward, Joanne		Entertainment	20	60		32	Oscar Winning Actress. Authentic Sigs Are RARE
Woodward, Marjorie		Entertainment	4		10	15	Actress. 40's Glamour Girl
Woodward, Robert Burns	1917-79	Science	20	40	78	35	Nobel Chemistry 1965
Woodworth, Samuel		Author-Composer	45	140	350		Wrote 'The Old Oaken Bucket'
Wool, John E.	1784-1869	Civil War	100	210	375		Union Gen., 1812 Vet.. ALS '65 $950. ALS'47 $2000
Wooley, Sheb	1921-19—	Country Music	12			26	Very Versatile Actor-Singer. Co-Star Rawhide
Woolf, Virginia	1882-1944	Author	378	1550	3350	4500	Br. Novelist, Essayist
Woollcott, Alexander		Journalist	30	95		150	Drama Critic,Actor Essayist. Algonquin Round Table
Woolley, Mary E.	1863-1947	Educator	40	80	215		1st Woman Grad. Brown U. Pres. Mt. Holyoke
Woolley, Monty	1888-1963	Entertainment	25	35		50	Character Actor Star of Man Who Came To Dinner
Woolrich, Cornell		Author	150	550			Am. Writer of Detective Fiction
Woolsey, Theodore D.	1801-89	Educator		38	75		Pres. Yale 186-1871
Woolson, Albert	1846-1956	Civil War	75		295		Last Surviving Union Soldier
Woolworth, Charles S.		Business	250	1250			F.W. Woolworth's Brother-Partner.Stk.Proxy S $1650
Woolworth, Frank W.	1852-1919	Business	450	3250	1550		Fndr. F.W. Woolworth Co.TLS/Cont $9500
Woorinen, Charles		Composer	10	20		40	Pulitzer, AMusQS $100
Wooster, David	1710-77	Rev. War	235	875	2638		General; Continental Army. Mortally Wounded
Wopat, Tom		Entertainment	10			20	Actor. 'Dukes of Hazzard'
Worden, Al M.		Astronaut	15			22	SP of Earth $50

NAME	DATE	CATEGORY	SIG	LS/DS	ALS	SP	COMMENTS
Worden, Hank		Entertainment	10			20	
Worden, John L.	1818-97	Civil War	142	195	412		Union Navy, Comdr. Monitor. War Dte. S $180
Wordsworth, Christopher		Clergy	20	30	35	35	
Wordsworth, William	1770-1850	Author	413	1137	1902		Br. Romantic Poet Laureate. AQS $2500
Work, Hubert		Cabinet	15	40	110	35	Sec'y Interior 1923
Worley, Jo Ann		Entertainment	5			15	Laugh In Comedienne
Worth, Irene		Entertainment	10			25	Actress
Worth, William J.	1794-1849	Military	30	75	125		General; Mexican War
Wouk, Herman		Author	30	85	175	100	Am. Novelist; Caine Mutiny Pulitzer
Woulfe, Michael		Fashion Designer	5			30	Film
Wozniak, Steve		Inventor	50		295		Co-Inventor of 1st Apple Computer
Wray, Fay	1907-1998	Entertainment	45			90	1st King Kong Heroine. King Kong SP $150
Wren, Christopher	1632-1723	Architect-Science	1550	5488	4500		St. Paul's Cathedral, London. Last Recorded Prices
Wright, Bobby	1942-	Country Music	7			15	Actor-Singer. 'McHale's Navy'
Wright, C.S.		Celebrity	15	35			
Wright, Cobina Sr. & Jr.		Entertainment	5			10	Socialite-Actresses of the 40's
Wright, Edyth		Entertainment	15			25	Band Vocalist
Wright, Frank Lloyd	1867-1959	Architect	900	1725	4350	2070	ALS/Content $4,000, $4,750
Wright, Harold Bell	1872-1944	Author	10	20	35	25	Am. Novelist & Minister. 'Shepherd of the Hills'
Wright, Henry C.	1797-1870	Reformer	10	20	35		Anti-Slavery Reformer-Lecturer
Wright, Horatio G.	1820-99	Civil War	40	175	250		Union General. Sig/Rank $65
Wright, Jerauld		Military	10	35		30	
Wright, Jim (James Claude)		Senate/Congress	10	30		20	Rep. TX 1955, Speaker
Wright, John J., Cardinal	1909-79	Clergy	40	75	90	65	
Wright, Luke E.	1846-1922	Cabinet	15	45	90	35	Sec'y War 1908, Ambass. Japan
Wright, Marcus J.	1831-1922	Civil War	125	180	320		CSA Gen. Sig/Rank $175-$250, '64 ALS $550
Wright, Orville & Wright, Wilbur		Aviation		8500		12500	First Flight Pioneers
Wright, Orville	1871-1948	Aviation	595	1312	2625	2371	TLS/Historical Content $15,000, S Chk $795
Wright, Richard	1908-60	Author	90	225		375	Afro-Am. Wrote of Suffering, Prejudice
Wright, Robin		Entertainment	10			35	
Wright, Silas, Jr.	1795-1847	Senate/Congress	20		75		Gen'l,Statesman, Gov. & Sen. NY
Wright, Teresa	1918-	Entertainment	30			60	AA for 'Mrs. Miniver'
Wright, Turbutt	1741-1783	Rev. War	35	60	95		Continental Congress
Wright, Wilbur	1867-1912	Aviation	825	2865	10250	5450	Historic SP $12,500, TLS $15,000
Wright, William		Military	25		125		Am. WW I General
Wrigley, Philip K.	1894-1977	Business	80	120	200	125	Wrigley Gum; Chicago Cubs
Wrigley, William, Jr.	1861-1932	Business	165	350	387	315	Founder Wrigley Gum Mfg.
Wunderlich, Fritz		Entertainment	75			500	Opera
Wunsche, Max		Military	50			125	Hitler's Adj. WW II
Wyant, Alexander Helwig	1836-92	Artist	85		350		Of Hudson River School. Landscapes.ALS/Cont.$750
Wyatt, Jane	1911-	Entertainment	5			20	Actress. Broadway. Film Leading Lady From 1934
Wyatt, Wendell		Congress	5	10		15	MOC OR 1964
Wyden, Ron		Congress	5			15	US Senator from Oregon
Wyeth, Andrew	1917-	Artist	225	450	955	1025	Eminent Am. Painter.
Wyeth, Henriette		Artist	75	225			Artist in Her Own Right. Sister of Andrew Wyeth
Wyeth, Jamie		Artist	150	445	400	325	Orig. Ink Sketch Pig $550-$950-$1275 Signed
Wyeth, John A.		Medical Author	65		250		Noted Surgeon
Wyeth, N. C.	1882-1945	Artist	155	470	1308	875	Am.Painter-Illustrator of Classic Children's Books
Wyler, Gretchen		Entertainment	5			15	Actress

NAME	DATE	CATEGORY	SIG	LS/DS	ALS	SP	COMMENTS
Wyler, William	1902-81	Entertainment	30			100	3 Best Picture Acad. Awards
Wylie, Elinor	1885-1928	Author	60	95	285		Am. Poet, Novelist
Wylie, Philip	1902-71	Author	15	30	95		Iconoclastic Author. 'Generation of Vipers'
Wylie, Robert	1839-1877	Artist	45	150			
Wyllys, Samuel	1739-1823	Rev. War	15	65	45		Military. Sec'y State of CT
Wyman, Bill		Entertainment	40		495	75	Rolling Stones Bass Guiitar
Wyman, Jane		Entertainment	14	100		52	AA Actress. Pin-up S $40+
Wyman, Willard G.		Military	15	25	40	25	4 Star General WW II
Wymore, Patrice		Entertainment	5		15	15	Actress-Model-Singer. Married Errol Flynn 1950
Wyndham, Charles, Sir	1837-1919	Entertainment	15	32	45	58	Br. Actor-Mgr, Physician, Civil War Surgeon
Wyndham, Mary, Lady		Entertainment	5		10	18	
Wyndorf, Dave		Entertainment	18			35	Music. Lead Singer Monster Magnet
Wynette, Tammy	1942-98	Country Music	15			45	Singer-Actress. Queen of Country. 50 Albums
Wynn, Ed	1886-1966	Entertainment	50	92	100	125	Vaudeville Comic. Ziegfield Follies Spec'l DS $350
Wynn, Keenan	1916-86	Entertainment	25	30		45	Actor-Son of Ed Wynn. Dependable Supporting Actor
Wynter, Dana	1930-	Entertainment	5			15	Br. Actress. Elegant, Reserved Leading Lady
Wynyard, Dianna	1906-64	Entertainment	5		15	25	Br. Charming, Graceful Leading Lady 30's-40's
Wysong, Forrest R.		Aviation	10	15	30	20	
Wyszynski, Stefan, Cardinal	1901-81	Clergy	50	65	100	75	Defied Communist Government
Wythe, George	1726-1806	Rev. War	500	1240	3075		Signer. ALS/War Dte. $7,500. Historic DS $7900

X

NAME	DATE	CATEGORY	SIG	LS/DS	ALS	SP	COMMENTS
Xenakis, Iannis	1922-	Composer	75			175	Greek Composer
Xenia, Alexandrova	1875-1960	Head of State	75		412		Russia. Grand Duchess. Sister of Nicholas II

Y

NAME	DATE	CATEGORY	SIG	LS/DS	ALS	SP	COMMENTS
Yadin, Yigael		Science		55		85	War Hero. World Famous Archaelogist
Yale, Brian		Entertainment	5			22	Music. Bass Guitar Matchbox 20
Yale, Elihu	1648-1721	Statesman			5000		Am-Born Eng. Gov. E. India Co.& Benefactor of Yale
Yalow, Rosalyn S.		Science	15	25	40	20	Nobel Medicine 1972
Yamaer, George		Celebrity	10	20	80	15	
Yamamoto, Isoroku, Adm.		Military	150	295	625	475	Pearl Harbor Attack, 12/7/1941
Yamanashi, Hanzo		Military	95	265			
Yamasaki, Minoru		Celebrity	10	25	60	20	
Yamashiro, Katsumari		Military	100			300	
Yamashita, Tomoyuki		Military	115	275	500	275	Jap. General. Hanged
Yang, Chen N.		Science	15	20	35	20	Nobel Physics 1957
Yang, Y. C.		Diplomat	10			20	Ambassador to Republic of Korea
Yankovic, Frank		Entertainment	4	4	9	10	
Yardbirds		Entertainment	325				The Set
Yarnell, Harry E.		Military	15	35		20	Adm. Fleet Commander
Yarnell, Lorine		Entertainment	3	3	6	6	Shields & Yarnell

NAME	DATE	CATEGORY	SIG	LS/DS	ALS	SP	COMMENTS
Yarrow, Ernest A.		Clergy	15	20	25		
Yates, Edmund	1831-94	Author	15	25	105		Br. Journalist-Novelist, Editor
Yates, Peter W.	1747-1826	Rev. War	30	120	175		Continental Congress
Yates, Richard	1815-73	Civil War	42	120	22512		Civil War Governor IL 1861
Yaw, Ellen Beach		Entertainment	30			200	Am. Soprano
Yeager, Chuck	1923-	Aviation	45	50	85	95	Ace, WW II, Pioneer, Test Pilot, Broke Sound
Yeager, Jeana		Aviation	15				
Yeager, Jeana & Dick Rutan		Aviaton	75	75		125	Voyager
Yearwood, Trisha		Country Music	10			25	Singer
Yeates, Jasper	1745-1817	Rev. War	15	35	60		Jurist
Yeats, Jack Butler		Artist	25	60	150		Brother of Wm. Butler Yeats
Yeats, Wm. Butler	1865-1939	Author	175	600	900		Nobel Poet, Dramatist; Abbey Theatre
Yeltsin, Boris		Head of State	750	1350		635	Russia
Yen, C.K.		Head of State	50	175			Pres. Republic China
Yerby, Frank G.		Author	35	80	165	40	Afro-Am. Novelist
Yerkes, Charles T.		Business	35	100			Capitalist. TLS/Content $450
Yes		Entertainment	45			85	Rock DS $125. Signed by all 5 1984
Yogananda, Paramhansa		Religious (Yoga)			495		
Yokum, Dwight		Country Music	10			25	
Yon, Pietro A.	1886-1943	Composer					Ital-Am. Gesu Bambino AMusQS $195
Yorgesson, Yogi		Country Music	10			20	
York, Alvin, Sgt.	1887-1964	Military	275	308	575	425	MOH WW I
York, Dick		Entertainment	25			50	
York, Michael		Entertainment	8	10	20	20	
York, Susanna		Entertainment	6	8	15	20	
Yorty, Sam	1909-98	Political	15	20		15	MOC. CA, Mayor L.A.Unsuccessful Pres. Candidate
Youmans, Vincent		Composer	55	165	255	150	Tea for Two. MusMsS $800
Young, Alan	1919-	Entertainment	10	25		30	Early TV Comedian.Mr Ed etc.Alan Young Show
Young, Andrew		Political	10	20	35	25	Afro-Am. Mayor Atlanta
Young, Angus		Entertainment	6			25	Music. Lead Guitar AC/DC
Young, Ann Elizabeth		Celebrity	125				One of Brigham Young's Plural Wives
Young, Art*		Cartoonist	20			125	Political Cartoonist
Young, Brigham	1801-1877	Clergy	495	1638	4450	2775	Morman Leader. Rare DS $8500
Young, Burt		Entertainment	6			20	
Young, Charles Augustus		Science	35	140	225		Am. Astronomer, Author
Young, Chic*	1901-73	Cartoonist	35	80		200	5 Original Pieces S for WW II Cartoons. $2000
Young, Clara Kimball		Entertainment	45			75	Vintage Stage Actress
Young, Coleman		Political	5	15		20	Afro-Am. Mayor of Detroit
Young, David H.		Aviation	10	25		30	
Young, Dean		Cartoonist	25				'Dagwood'. Orig. Strip $275
Young, Faron		Country Music	10			30	Deceased
Young, Gig		Entertainment	30	38	70	67	Oscar Winner
Young, Henry E.		Civil War	25	45	70		CSA Major, Judge Advocate
Young, John		Astronaut	30	250		101	Moonwalker. Apollo 16, Shuttle Cmdr.
Young, John		Senate/Congress	15	25	45		Rep. NY 1836
Young, Lester		Entertainment	70	75	145	150	Jazz, Tenor Saxophone
Young, Loretta		Entertainment	20		35	61	Beloved Actress of 30's-40's-50's AA & Emmy
Young, Lyman*		Cartoonist	10			50	Tim Tyler's Luck
Young, Malcolm		Entertainment	6			25	Music. Rhythm Guitar AC/DC

NAME	DATE	CATEGORY	SIG	LS/DS	ALS	SP	COMMENTS
Young, Neil		Entertainment	15			45	Rolling Stones
Young, Owen D.	1874-1962	Business	15	25	50	20	CEO Gen. Electr.,Financier, Law, Advisor to Pres.
Young, Pierce M.B.	1836-96	Civil War	195		300		CSA Gen. S War Dte. $155, DS $350
Young, Robert		Entertainment	15	39	5	45	Actor. Films-TV Father Knows Best,Marcus Welby
Young, Roland		Entertainment	50			75	Droll Br. Actor. Remembered for Topper
Young, Samuel B.M.		Civil War	30	55	80		Union General Bvt.
Young, Sean		Entertainment	15	50		35	Actress. Pin-Up SP $35-70
Young, Thomas L.	1832-88	Congress	35				General, Gov OH
Young, Trummy		Entertainment	15			45	Jazz Musician
Young, Whitney		Activist	5	20	45	15	Am. Civil Rights Leader. Author
Youngdahl, Luther		Governor	5	15		10	Governor MN 1947
Younger, Bob		Outlaw	2500				Fought/Quantrill.Died in Prison
Younger, Cole (Thos. Coleman)		Civil War	2700				Served/Quantrill; Bank Robber
Youngman, Henny	1906-98	Entertainment	20	25		32	Club & TV Comedian. Take My Wife....Please!
Ysaye, Eugene		Composer	115			225	Belg. Violin Virtuoso,Conductor. AMusQS $120
Yudenich, Nikolay N.		Military	95			175	Rus. Gen. Russo-Jap.& WW I
Yukawa, Hideki		Science	35	45	70		Nobel Physics 1949
Yulee, David Levy	1810-1886	Civil War	45		140		CSA Congress
Yun, Isang	1917-	Composer		80		150	Korean Born. Kidnapped by S. Korean Agents
Yung, Carl Gustav	1875-1961	Science	375	1570			Swiss Founder Analytical Psychology.
Yung, Victor Sen		Entertainment	35			65	
Yunge, Traudl		Military	15			55	Hitler's Pers'l Sec'y End of WW II
Yurka, Blanche	1886-1974	Entertainment	30		75	45	Hamlet/Barrymore
Yutang, Lin (Lin Yutang)		Author	50	165			Chin. Novels,Philosophy,Plays

Z

Zabach, Florian		Entertainment	5			20	
Zabeleta, Nicanor		Entertainment	40			150	Opera
Zablocki, Clement John		Senate/Congress	5			20	Rep. WI 1949
Zabriskie, Andrew C.		Business	35		140		Capitalist, Financier
Zackerly		Entertainment	3			10	TV Horror Host
Zadora, Pia		Entertainment	5			15	Pin-Up SP $20
Zaharoff, Basil	1850-1936	Manufacturer				1495	Mystery Munitions Mfg. A Cause of WW I
Zahn, Timothy		Author	10			35	Star Wars Trilogy
Zais, Melvin		Military	10	20	35	15	
Zajic, Dolora		Entertainment	5			25	Opera
Zamboni, Maria		Entertainment	40			200	Opera
Zancanaro, Giorgio		Entertainment	10			30	Opera
Zandonai, Riccardo	1883-1944	Composer		60		195	Opera
Zane, Billy		Entertainment	15			55	'Phantom' Cast of $100+. 'Titanic'
Zangwill, Israel	1864-1926	Author	40	110	125	60	Br. Playwright, Novelist, Poet, Journalist
Zanuck, Darryl F.	1902-79	Entertainment	50	300		75	Producer. Co-Founder 20th Century Fox
Zanuck, Richard Darryl		Entertainment	8		20	25	Film Producer, Exec.
Zapata, Emiliano	1879-1919	Revolutionary	500	2217	1625		Mex. Guerilla Leader
Zappa, Frank	1940-93	Entertainment	25	200		195	Composer, Guitarist
Zapruder, Abraham		Celebrity	40				Filmed JFK Assassination in 8mm

NAME	DATE	CATEGORY	SIG	LS/DS	ALS	SP	COMMENTS
Zavodszky, Zoltan		Entertainment	30			85	Opera
Zeani, Virginia		Entertainment	15			45	Opera
Zeeman, Pieter	1865-1943	Science	200		975		Nobel for Physics 1902. Dutch Physicist
Zefferelli, Franco		Entertainment	12			35	Film Director
Zelenski, Wladyslaw		Composer	50		150		Polish Music Teacher
Zellerbach, James D		Business	15	40	85	35	US Ambassador, Industrialist
Zeman, Jacklyn		Author-Actress	5	8	5	10	Pin-Up $20
Zemekis, Robert		Entertainment	5	15		20	Film Director
Zemke, Hubert Hub		Aviation	15	35	65	40	ACE, WW II, Triple Ace
Zemlinsky, Alexander		Composer	90	265			Aus. Conductor
Zenatello, Giovanni		Entertainment	45		65	125	Opera
Zeppelin, Ferdinand, Graf von	1838-1917	Aviation	275	830	1500	1035	Inventor Dirigible Air Ship
Zerbe, Anthony		Entertainment	10		25	25	
Zetland, Earl, Thos. Lawrence		Freemason	60				Master of the Freemasons NRPA
Zetterling, Mai		Entertainment	15			35	Actress
Zhukov, Georgi K.		Military	85	617	500	325	Rus. Marshal. Soviet Hero WW II
Ziegfeld, Florenz	1869-1931	Entertainment	245	562	638	550	Am. Vaud. Prod. Famous Follies, ALS/Content $950
Ziegler, George M.	1834-1912	Civil War	40	55	75		Union General, Bvt.
Ziegler, Karl		Science	45	85	100	55	Nobel Chemistry 1969
Ziegler, Ronald L.		White House	5	95	25	15	White House Aide. Nixon Press Sec'y
Ziegler, Vincent C.		Business	5			10	CEO Gillette Safety Razor Co.
Ziering, Ian		Entertainment	5			25	Actor. Beverly Hills 90210
Zimbalist, Efrem, Jr.		Entertainment	5	8		20	Popular Actor. Leading Man Films. Early TV Leads
Zimbalist, Efrem, Sr.		Entertainment	45			265	Violinist, Composer
Zimbalist, Stephanie		Entertainment	6	10		20	Actress. Pin-Up SP $30
Zimmer, Norma		Entertainment	3	5		10	Early TV Vocalist for Lawrence Welk
Zindel, Paul		Author	10	20		25	Playwright
Zinnemann, Fred		Entertainment	20		35	60	AA Film Director
Ziolkowski, Korczak		Artist	15	35	65	40	
Zmed, Adrian		Entertainment	5	6	15	15	
Zog I		Royalty	40			85	King Albania
Zola, Emile	1840-1902	Author	165	350	658	2070	Fr. Novelist & Social Reformer
Zollicoffer, Felix K. (WD)		Civil War	575	1750			CSA Gen. KIA
Zollicoffer, Felix K.	1812-62	Civil War	300	350	845		CSA General
Zombie, Rob		Entertainment	10			50	White Zombie Lead Singer
Zorina, Vera		Entertainment	20			35	Ballerina, Films, Stage
Zuazo, Hernan Siles		Head of State	10	15	25	15	
Zucco, George		Entertainment	85			250	
Zucherman, Pinchas		Entertainment	10			75	Violinist. 5x7 SP $40
Zukoffsky, Louis		Author	25		80	50	Am. Poet
Zukor, Adolph	1873-1976	Entertainment	50	145	200	120	Founder Paramount. Pioneer Film Producer
Zuloaga, Ignacio		Artist	25	75			Sp. Painter
Zumwalt, Elmo R., Jr.	1920-	Military	15	120	125	55	Bud. Adm. WW II
Zweig, Arnold		Author	25	65		50	Ger. Novelist, Playwright
Zweig, Stefan		Author	30	90	195	45	Aus. Psychoanalytical Biogr.
Zweigert, Eugen, Lt.		Aviation	100			300	Ger. ACE WW II
Zwicky, Fritz		Science	20	35		45	Am. Astronomer. Jet Propulsion
Zworykin, Vladimir		Science	65	260	230	95	Am. Inventor TV System. Father of Am. TV

The SANDERS Price Guide to AUTOGRAPHS

Fifth Edition

Section 6:

FACSIMILES

Being depictions of authentic autographs for your handy comparison as to authenticity.

Ronald Reagan happily signs for George Sanders. George's long stint in broadcasting and the entertainment business means that he was able to meet and personally obtain the autographs of thousands of celebrities. This "in-person" knowledge is the basis of the authentic facsimiles in this book.

Chapter 22

Facsimiles

Anyone can sign John Wayne's name, and many do! A person of low morals might invest $2 in an 8x10 glossy of Wayne, sign it as Wayne, and sell it at a collectibles show for $35 or $40. If this unprincipled thief got a good deal on an assortment of Hollywood stars, he might come away with several hundred dollars from the pockets of unsuspecting autograph collectors. The trash they've bought is, of course, worthless!

Our best advice is to buy autographs only from reputable dealers (such as the ones advertising in this book). Yet, we all dream of finding that signed Greta Garbo photograph at the flea market for $5. It's good to dream but, how do you know what's authentic and what's just so much ink on paper? The answer is having known authentic examples of signatures available. These are called *facsimile signatures*. They are simply copies of real signatures of the celebrity. Compare your "find" to a known good sig and, if it matches, you're much more likely to have an authentic autograph!

The following pages are a good start to developing your own reference library of facsimiles. This book presents you with several thousand facsimiles known to be good. While our attorney screams if we try to say anything absolute (i.e. we make no warranties either express or implied), the sigs in this book are good to the best of our knowledge.

Use this book as a start in amassing a reference library of facsimiles. Enlarge the library with other facsimile books (we have a few of those in the works ourselves) and by keeping (*never* throwing away!) all the dealer catalogs you can find. Please write the dealers advertising in these pages, many of them put out most useful and interesting catalogs, chock full of facsimiles. Then when you come across a questionable signature, a few minutes of browsing through your facsimile library can answer the question of authenticity by simple comparison with a known good example.

Which is not to say all of this is easy. Over the course of years, a person's signature changes with age and through other factors such as injury or just the technology of writing instruments. You'll want to accumulate, wherever possible, the facsimiles of an individual's autograph at differing ages.

There is no such thing as having too many facsimiles!

We hope these that follow prove helpful.

We were all young once! Here a 31-year-old Angela Lansbury (long before "Murder She Wrote") autographed a special copy of the movie premiere program of Paramount's "High Society" during George Sanders's 1956 broadcast around the world on the Armed Forces Television and Radio Network from Hollywood.

A

[signature] Bud Abbott

Bud Abbott

[signature] Red Adair

Red Adair

[signature] California 1948, Photograph by ANSEL ADAMS

Ansel Adams

[signature] J. Adams

President John Adams

[signature] J. Q. Adams

President John Quincy Adams

[signature]

Maude Adams

[signature]

Charles Addams

[signature] Jane Addams

Jane Addams

[signature]

Richard Adler

[signature] L^s Agassiz

Louis Agassiz

[signature] Spiro T. Agnew, Governor of Maryland

Vice President Spiro T. Agnew

[signature]

Edward Albee

[signature] Jack Albertson

Jack Albertson

[signature] APOLLO 11

Buzz Aldrin

[signature] Yours truly, Horatio Alger

Horatio Alger

[signature] FRED ALLEN

Fred Allen

[signature]

Roald Amundsen

Wally "Famous" Amos

General Robert Anderson

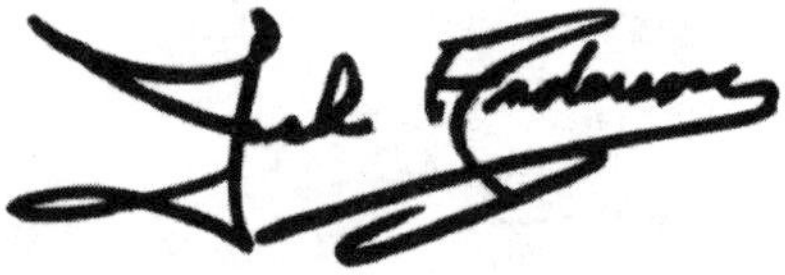

Jack Anderson

Marian Anderson

Maxwell Anderson

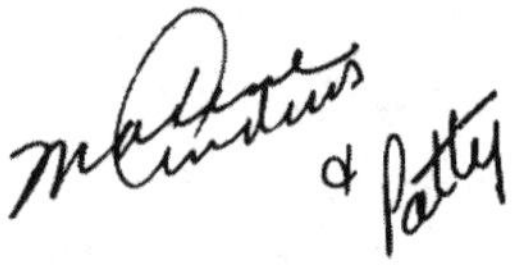

Maxine & Patty Andrews

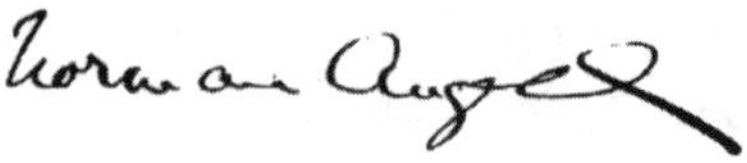

Norman Angell

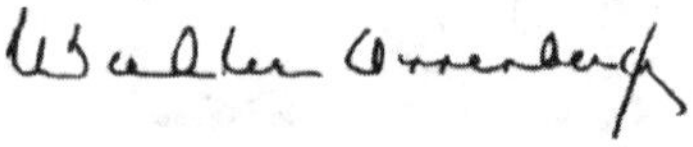

Walter H. Annenberg

Roscoe "Fatty" Arbuckle

Sir William Armstrong

President Chester A. Arthur

Isaac Asimov

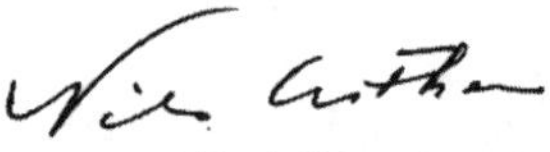

Nils Asther

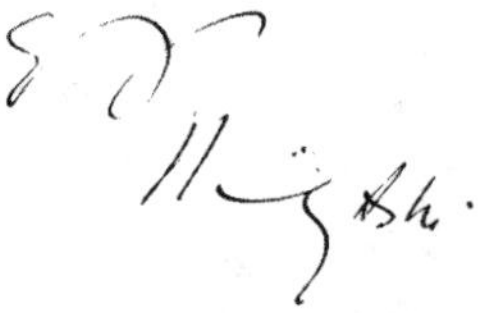

Lady Astor

Waldorf Astor

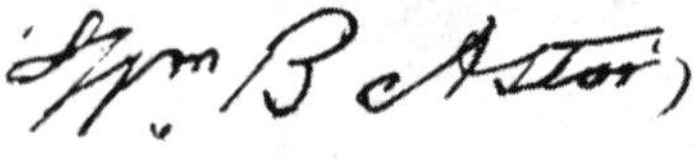

William Backhouse Astor

President David R. Atchison

Clement Attlee

Jacqueline Auriol

Gene Autry

B

Leo Hendriik Baekeland

F. Lee Bailey

Theodorus Bailey

Bernt Balchen

James Baldwin

Stanley Baldwin

Tallulah Bankhead

Michael A. Banks

John Bardeen

Vice President Alben William Barkley

Christian Barnard

P. T. Barnum

J. M. Barrie

Mona Barrie

Ethel Barrymore

Lionel Barrymore

Frederic Auguste Bartholdi

Freddie Bartholomew

Clara Barton

Bernard M. Baruch

P. G. T. Beauregard

Noah N. Beery

Menachem Begin

S. N. Behrman

Alexander Graham Bell

Ralph Bellamy

Saul Bellow

Peter Benchley

Your obedient servant,

Stephen Vincent Benet

Joan Bennett

Jack Benny

Ezra Taft Benson

Most sincerely,

Gertrude Berg

Gertrude Berg

Elizabeth Bergner

Irving Berlin

Sarah Bernhardt

Father Daniel Berrigan

Ken Berry

Josh Billings

Clarence Birdeye

Jussi Bjoerling

Hugo L. Black

Patrick M. S. Blackett

Harry A. Blackmun

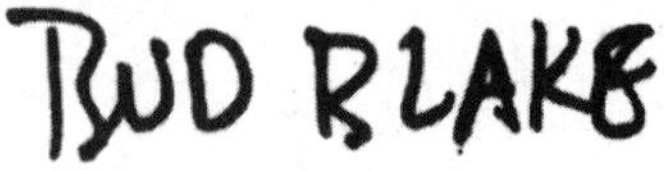

Bud Blake

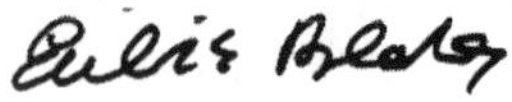

Bud Blake

Eubie Blake

Eubie Blake

"P-P-P- Porky Pig"
Mel Blanc

Mel Blanc

Z.R. Bliss

Major General Zenas Bliss

Herb Block

Herb Block

Guion S. Bluford Jr.

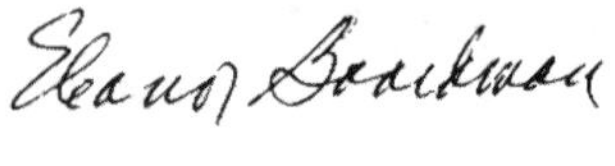

Guion S. Bluford Jr.

Eleanor Boardman

Eleanor Boardman

Niels Bohr

Niels Bohr

Ray Bolger

Ray Bolger

Louis Napoleon Bonaparte

Louis Napoleon Bonaparte

Julian Bond

Julian Bond

Pat Boone

Pat Boone

Edwin Booth

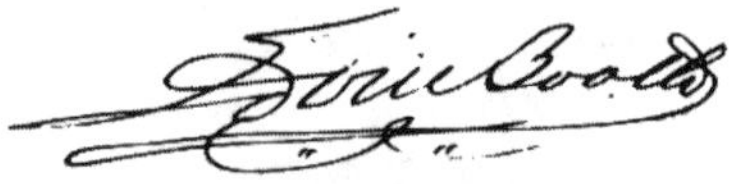

Edwin Booth

Evangeline Booth

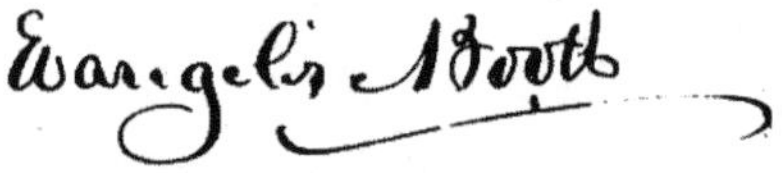

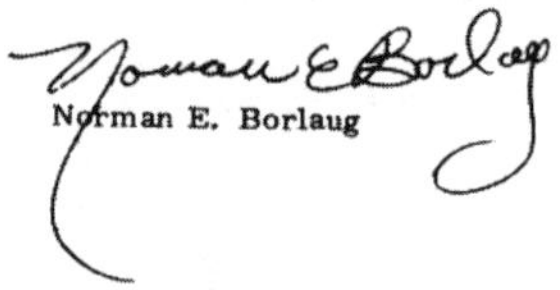

Evangeline Booth

Norman E. Borlaug

Norman E. Borlaug

Frank Borman

Frank Borman

Major Edward Bowes

Bill "Hopalong Cassidy" Boyd

Ray Bradbury

General of the Army

Omar Bradley

Louis D. Brandeis

Dan Brandenstein

Willy Brandt

Karl Branting

Bertolt Brecht

John Cabell Breckinridge

Justice William J. Brennan, Jr.

Leonid I. Brezhnev

David Brinkley

W. E. Brock

Clive Brook

Rand Brooks

Joe E. Brown

Johnny Mack Brown

Dik Browne

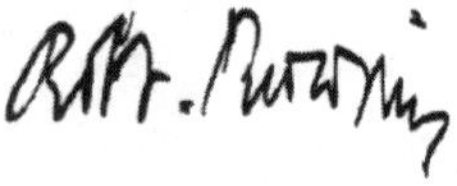

Robert Browning

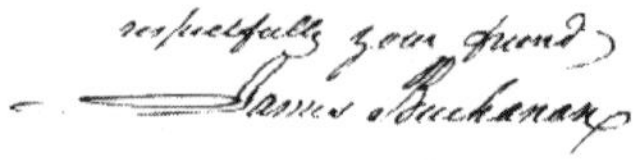

President James Buchanan

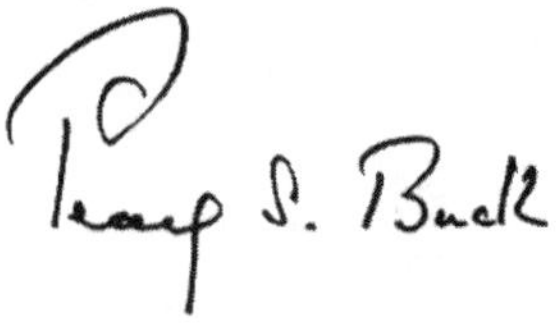

Pearl S. Buck

General D. C. Buell

David D. Buick

Ned Buntline

Luther Burbank

Justice Warren E. Burger

Billie Burke

William John Burns

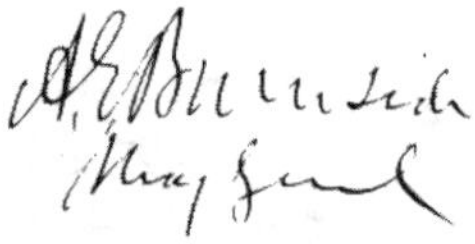

General Ambrose E. Burnside

David Burpee

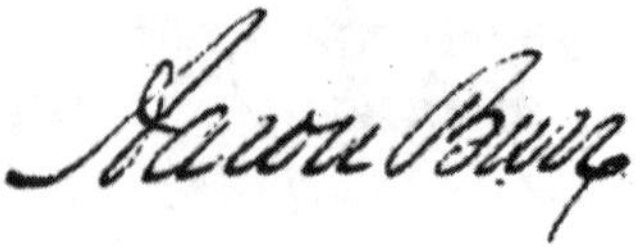

Aaron Burr

President George Bush

Vannever Bush

Francis Bushman

Major General Benjamin F. Butler

C

James Branch Cabell

James Cagney

Sammy Cahn

Erskine Caldwell

John Caldwell Calhoun

Melvin Calvin

Rod Cameron

Albert Camus

Milton Caniff

Yakima Canutt

Truman Capote

Al Capp

Dr. Alexis Carrel

Mary Carlisle

Sunset Carson

King Juan Carlos

President Jimmy Carter

Hoagy Carmichael

Enrico Caruso

Andrew Carnegie

George Washington Carver

Dale Carnegie

Pablo Casals

Scott Carpenter

Kellye Cash

John Carradine

Catherine II (The Great)

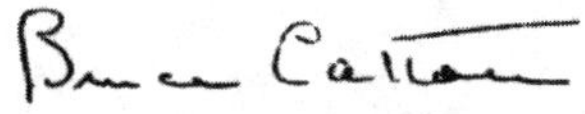

Bruce Catton

Walter P. Chrysler

Whittaker Chambers

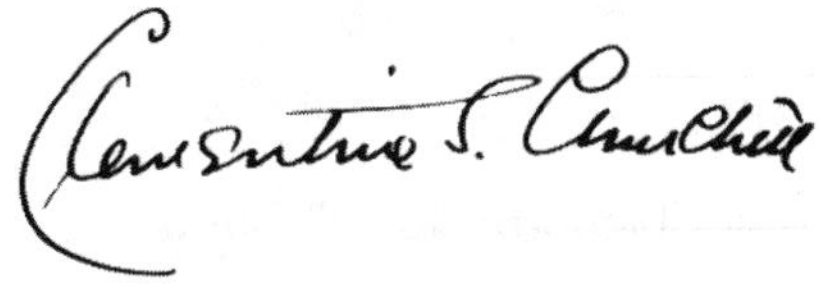

Lady Clementine Churchill

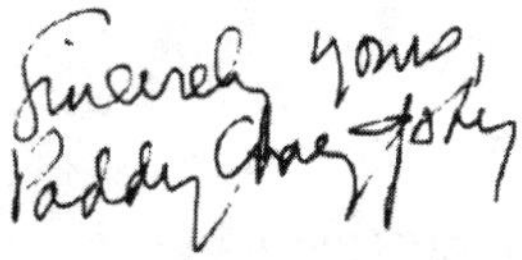

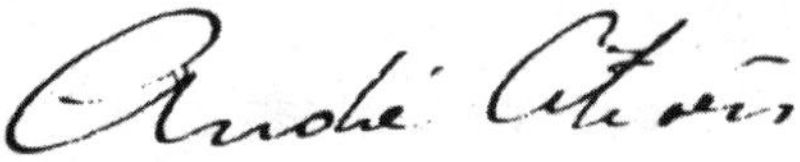

Coco Chanel

Andre Citroen

John Charles XIV

Joe Clark

Cesar Chavez

Mae Clarke

Paddy Chayefsky

President Grover Cleveland

Gilbert Keith Chesterton

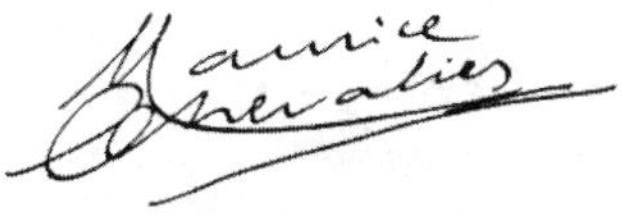

President Bill Clinton

Maurice Chevalier

Dewitt Clinton

Irvin S. Cobb

Major General Howell Cobb

Jacqueline Cochran

William F. "Buffalo Bill" Cody

Ronald Coleman

Vice President Schuyler Colfax

P. T. Collins

Jerry Colonna

Jerry Colonna

Jackie Coogan

President Calvin Coolidge

Peter Cooper

General Samuel Cooper

Aaron Copeland

Jean Baptiste Camille Coret

"Wrong Way" Corrigan

Jacques Cousteau

Joan Crawford

Michael Crichton

Dr. A. J. Cronin

Bing Crosby

E. E. Cummings

Sir Samuel Cunard

Charles Curtis

Harvey W. Cushing

Richard Cardinal Cushing

D

Idi Amin Dada

Richard J. Daley

Vice President George M. Dallas

Charles Darwin

Marion Davies

Richard Harding Davis

Sir Humphry Davy

Charles G. Dawes

Dr. Lee de Forest

Charles de Gaulle

Geoffrey de Havilland

Alexander P. de Seversky

Dr. William DeVries

Dr. Michael DeBakey

John Deere

Delores Del Rio

Cecil B. de Mille

Thomas Dewey

Charles Dickens

Benjamin Disraeli

Dorothea Dix

James D. Dole

Abner Doubleday

Cordially yours,

Donald W. Douglas

Lloyd C. Douglas

William O. Douglas

Sir Arthur Conan Doyle

W. E. B. DuBois

Pierre S. duPont.

Pierre S. Du Pont

Love 'n kisses,

JIMMY DURANTE

Jimmy Durante

E

Amelia Earhart

Jubal Early

George Eastman

Kevin Eastman

Abba Eban

Hugo Eckener

Mary Baker Eddy

Sir Anthony Eden

Thomas A. Edison

Albert Einstein

Dwight D. Eisenhower

Julie Nixon Eisenhower

Mamie Doud Eisenhower

T. S. Eliot

Queen Elizabeth II

Ralph Waldo Emerson

Charles Evers

F

John Eberhard Faber

Vice President Charles Fairbanks

Michael Faraday

Diane Feinstein

Edna Ferber

Cyrus W. Field

Eugene Field

Marshall Field, Jr.

President Millard Fillmore

James Montgomery Flagg

Father Flanagan

Sir Alexander Fleming

Errol Flynn

Anthony Fokker

Henry Fonda

Malcolm Forbes

Benson Ford

Edsel B. Ford

President Gerald R. Ford

Henry Ford II

Henry Ford

E. M. Forster

Justice Felix Frankfurter

King Frederick VII

John Charles Fremont

Milton Friedman

David Frost

R. Buckminster Fuller

G

John Galsworthy

Indira Gandhi

Mahatma Gandhi

Greta Garbo

Ava Gardner

Erle Stanley Gardner

President James A. Garfield

Guiseppe Garibaldi

Vice President John Nance Garner

William Lloyd Garrison

Richard Gatling

King George I

Henry George

Elbridge Gerry

Ira Gershwin

J. Paul Getty

Charles Dana Gibson

A. C. Gilbert

John Gilbert

Allen Ginsberg

Lillian Gish

John A. Glenn, Jr.

Paulette Goddard

Arthur Godfrey

George W. Goethals

William Golding

Samuel Goldwyn

Samuel Gompers

Benny Goodman

Charles Goodyear, Jr.

Mikhail S. Gorbachev

Chester Gould

Betty Grable

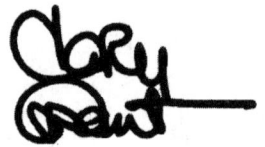

Cary Grant

Ulysses S. Grant

Dave Graue

Horace Greeley

John Green

Zane Grey

Zane Grey

issued by the METROPOLITAN LIFE INSU
David Wark Griffith

David W. Griffith

Gus Grissom

Gus Grissom

Gilbert Grosvenor

Gilbert Grosvenor

Edgar Guest

Edgar Guest

Very sincerely yours,
Daniel Guggenheim

Daniel Guggenheim

Peggy Guggenheim

Paggy Guggenheim

Charles Guiteau

Charles Guiteau

H. Rider Haggard

H. Rider Haggard

Josephine Hall

Josephine Hall

Armand Hammer

Dr. Armand Hammer

Sincerely,
Oscar Hammerstein

Oscar Hammerstein

E. Y. Harburg

E. Y. "Yip" Harburg

Warren G. Harding
Defendant

President Warren G. Harding

Oliver Hardy

Oliver Hardy

Thomas Hardy.

Thomas Hardy

W. Averell Harriman

Prince Hassam

Joel Chandler Harris

Brig General Joseph R. Hawley

President Benjamin Harrison

Helen Hayes

President William Henry Harrison

President Rutherford B. Hayes

Johnny Hart

Susan Hayward

Moss Hart

William Randolph Hearst

William S. Harts

Edward Heath

Paul Harvey

Christie Hefner

Joseph Heller

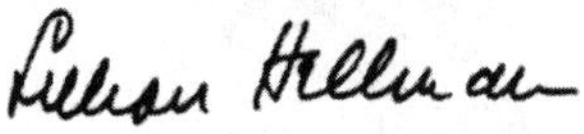

Lillian Hellman

Henry III (old age)

Henry III (young)

Katharine Hepburn

Frank Herbert

Victor Herbert

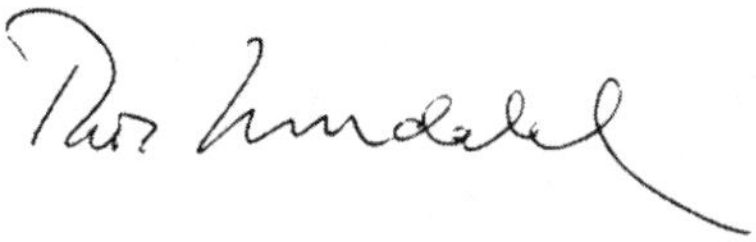

Thor Heyerdahl

Sir Edmund Hillary

Alfred Hitchcock

Vice president Garret A. Hobart

William Holder

Oliver Wendell Holmes

Winslow Homer

Herbert Hoover

J. Edgar Hoover

Hedda Hopper

Harry Houdini

Major General Oliver Otis Howard

Julia Ward Howe

Victor Hugo

Hubert H. Humphrey

King Hussein

Will Hutchins

Aldous Huxley

I

Lee Iacocca

Henrik Ibsen

James B. Irwin

J

Andrew Jackson

Jesse Jackson

Andrew Johnson

Lyndon Baines Johnson

Richard Mentor Johnson

Quincy Jones

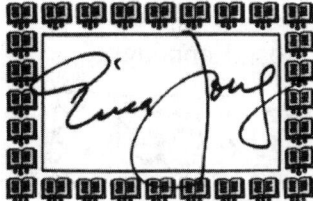

Erica Jong

Janis Joplin

Jim Jordan "Fibber McGee"

C. G. Jung

K

Henry J. Kaiser

Chiang Kai-Shek

Madame Chiang Kai-Shek

Bob Kane

Boris Karloff

Bill Keane

Major General Philip Kearny

Buster Keaton

Carolyn Keene

Helen Keller

W. K. Kellogg

Emmett Kelly, Sr.

Grace Kelly

Arthur Kennedy

Ethel Kennedy

John F. Kennedy

Joseph P. Kennedy

Rose Kennedy

Hank Ketcham

Cammie King

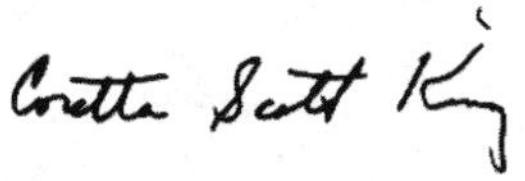

Coretta Scott King

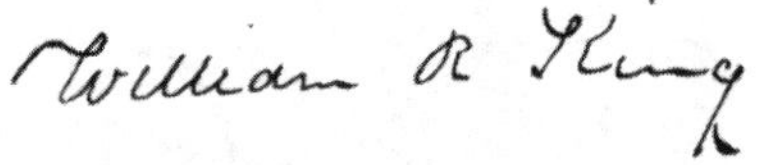

William R. King

Lane Kirkland

Calvin Klein

Werner Klemperer

Evel Knievel

Henry Thatcher Knox

Edward I Koch

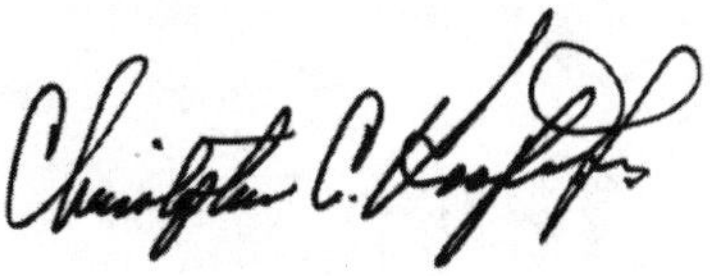

Christopher Kraft

Eugene Kranz

Paul Kruger

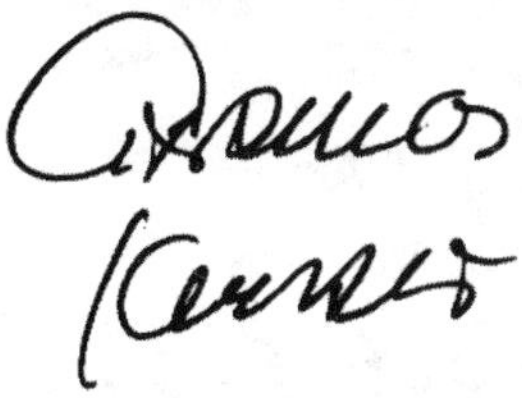

Charles Kuralt

L

Alan Ladd

Fiorello LaGuardia

Simon Lake

Veronica Lake

Dorothy Lamour

Louis L'Amour

Bert Lance

Edwin Land

Ann Landers

Carole Landis

Alf Landon

Samuel Pierpont Langley

Lillie Langtry

Walter Lantz

Ring Lardner

Lash LaRue

Stan Laurel

Yves Saint Laurent

Ernest Lawrence

Gertrude Lawrence

Mary D. Leakey

Norman Lear

John leCarre

Anna Lee

Gypsy Rose Lee

Robert E. Lee

Dr. Willy Ley

Liberace

Trygve Lie

Beatrice Lillie

Abraham Lincoln

Robert Todd Lincoln

Jenny Lind

Charles Lindbergh

Joseph Lister

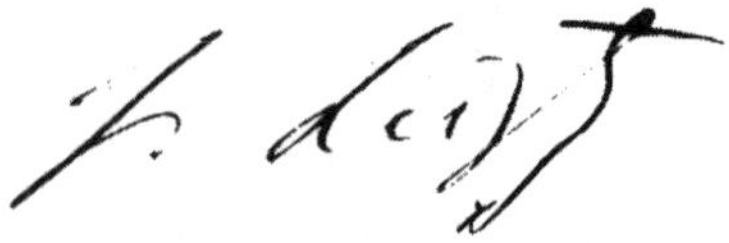

Franz Liszt

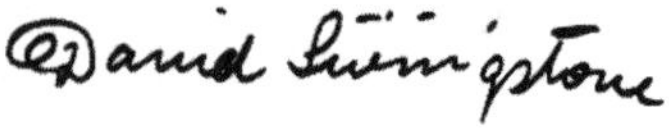

David Livingstone

Harold Lloyd

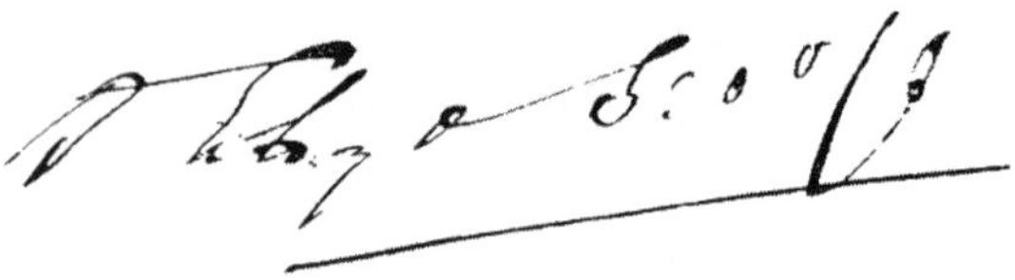

David Lloyd-George

Allan Lockheed

Gina Lollobrigida

Alice Roosevelt Longworth

King Louis VIII

King Louis Philippe

Bernard Lovell

James Russell Lowell

Clare Booth Luce

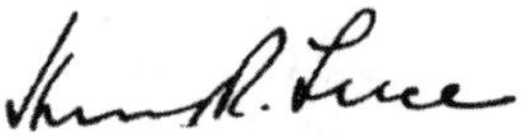

Henry R. Luce

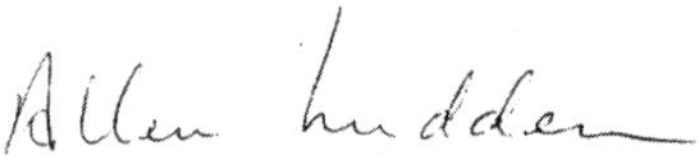

Allen Ludden

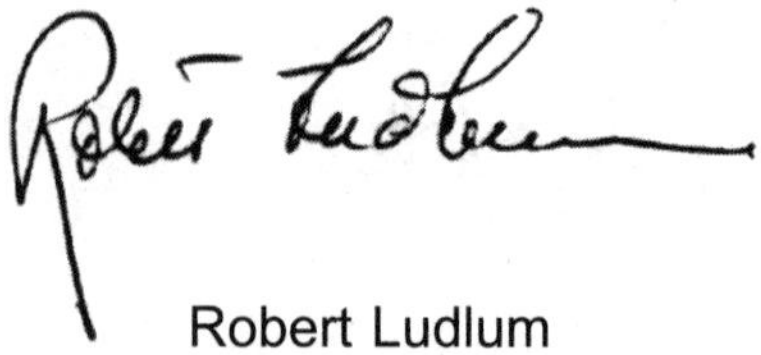

Robert Ludlum

M

Marion Mack

Ted Mack

Archibald MacLeish

Dolley Madison

President James Madison

Ramon Magaysay

Norman Mailer

Bernard Malamud

Henry Mancini

Edouard Manet

Horace Mann

Thomas Mann

Mantovani

Gugelielmo Marconi

Ferdinand Marcos

Johnny Marks

Justice Thurgood Marshall

Glenn L. Martin

Groucho Marx

Harpo Marx

Zeppo Marx

Raymond Massey

Henri Matisse

W. Somerset Maugham

Hiram Percy Maxim

Louis B. Mayer

Dr. Charles W. Mayo

Dr. William Mayo

Frederick L. Maytag

General George McClellan

Cyrus McCormick

Colonel Tim McCoy

President William McKinley

Aimee Semple McPherson

Margaret Mead

General George Meade

George Meany

Adolphe Menjou

Burgess Meredith

Ethel Merman

Ray Milland

Arthur Miller

Henry Miller

Newton Minow

Ed Mitchell

Tom Mix

Walter F. Mondale

President James Monroe

Robert Moog

Christopher Morley

Samuel F. B. Morse

Major John "the Gray Ghost" Mosby

Grandma Moses

R.G. Mugabe

Rupert Murdock

Edward R. Murrow

Story Musgrove

Russell Myers

N

Napoleon

Ogden Nash

Poli Neri

Edwin Newman

Brigitte Nielsen

President Richard Nixon

John Ringling North

Lord North

Alfred Noyes

O

Hermann Oberth

Edmond O'Brien

Sandra Day O'Connor

Clifford Odets

Ransom E. Olds

Eugene O'Neill

Robert Oppenheimer

Baroness Orczy

P

David Packard

William S. Paley

John Dos Passos

Lester B. Pearson

Sir Robert Peel

J.C. Penney

George Plimpton

Svetlana Peters

President James K. Polk

Eugene Peugeot

Lily Pons

Slim Pickens

Admiral David Porter

Mary Pickford

Cole Porter

President Franklin Pierce

Katherine Anne Porter

J.S. Pillsbury

Marina Oswald Porter

ZaSu Pitts

Emily Post

Ezra Pound

Dick Powell

Lewis Powell

Tyrone Power

Francis Gary Powers

Otto Preminger

Jackie Presser

Robert Preston

Andre Previn

John Profumo

Joseph Pulitzer

Melvin Purvis

Mario Puzo

Ernie Pyle

Howard Pyle

Q

Col. Muammar el-Qaddfi

Dan Quayle

Ellery Queen

Vidkun Quisling

R

Prince Ranier

Sally Rand

James Earl Ray

Ronald Reagan

William Rehnquist

Renek

Duncan Renaldo

Pierre Auguste Renoir

Judith A. Resnick

James B. Reston

Robert Reud

Walter Reuther

Richard Reynolds

Captain Eddie Rickenbacker

Leni Riefenstahl

James Whitcomb Riley

Robert Ripley

Jason Robards

Kenneth Roberts

Oral Roberts

Ralph Roberts

Happy Rockefeller

John D. Rockefeller, Jr.

Nelson Aldritch Rockefeller

Norman Rockwell

Richard Rodgers

August Rodin

Ginger Rogers

Charles S. Rolls

Sigmund Romberg

Stu Roosa

Franklin Roosevelt

Theodore Roosevelt

General William S. Rosecrans

Jerry Rubin

Arthur Rubenstein

Helena Rubenstein

Charlie Ruggles

Damon Runyon

Bertrand Russell

Lillian Russell

Dick Rutan

S

Rafael Sabatini

Dr. Albert B. Sabin

Pierre Salinger

Dr. Jonas Salk

George Sand

Carl Sandberg

David Sarnoff

Vidal Sassoon

Arthur Schlesinger

Charles Schulz

Charles Schwab

Randolph Scott

Sir Walter Scott

General Winfield Scott

Glenn Seaborg

Jean Seberg

Pete Seeger

Andres Segovia

David O. Selznick

Mack Sennett

Rod Serling

Dr. Seuss

Sir Ernest Shackleton

George Bernard Shaw

Alan B. Shepard Jr.

Ann Sheridan

General Philip Sheridan

General W. T. Sherman

William Shockley

Maria Shriver

B. T. Skinner

Phil Silvers

Alfred P. Sloan

Georges Simenon

Alfred Smith

Neil Simon

Kate Smith

Frank Sinatra

Kingford Smith

Harry F. Sinclair

Sir Thomas Sopwith

Upton Sinclair

Ann Souther

Isaac B. Singer

John Philip Sousa

Francis Cardinal Spellman

Elmer A. Sperry

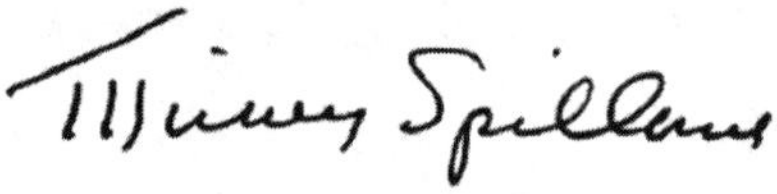

Mickey Spillane

Dr. Benjamin Spock

Edward Robinson Squibb

Lili St. Cyr

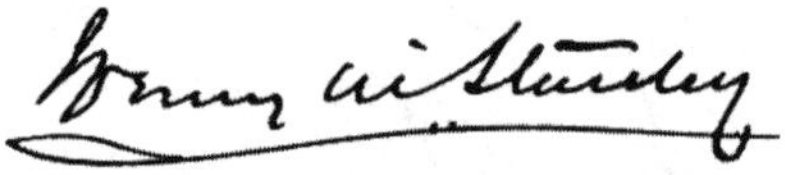

Sir Henry Stanley

Frank Stanton

Harold Stassen

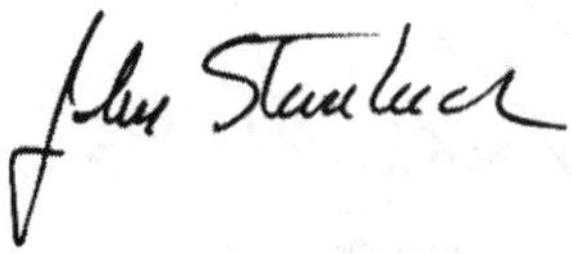

John Steinbeck

Charles P. Steinmetz

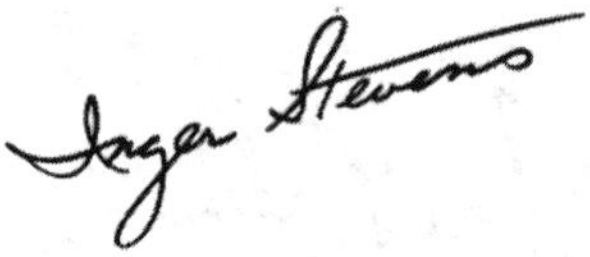

Inger Stevens

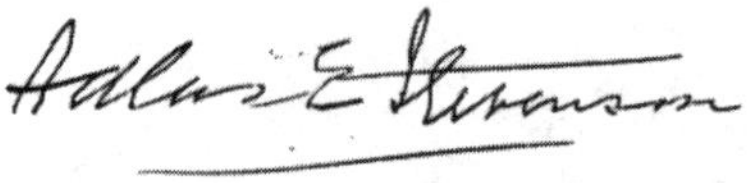

Adlai E. Stevenson

James Stewart

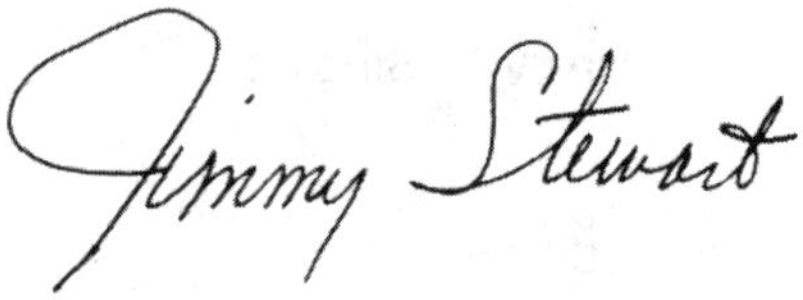

Jimmy Stewart

Tempest Storm

Sincerely,

Rex Stout

Igor Stravinsky

Ed Sullivan

Arthur Sullivan

T

William Howard Taft

Booth Tarkington

Zachary Taylor

Edward Teller

God bless you

Mother Teresa

Valentina Tereshkova

Studs Terkel

Nikola Tesla

Margaret Thatcher

Jeremy Thorpe

Étrangères
Yougoslavie,

Tito

Arnold J. Toynbee

George A. Trenholm

Gary Trudeau

Pierre Trudeau

Harry S. Truman

Donald Trump

Forest Tucker

Ted Turner

U

John Updike

Leon Uris

V

Rudy Vallee

James Van Allen

Martin Van Buren

S. S. Van Dine

Carl Van Doren

Mark Van Doren

Amy Vanderbilt

W

Cornelius Vanderbilt

George W. Vanderbilt

Jules Verne

Queen Victoria

Wernher von Braun

Erich Von Daniken

Alexander von Humboldt

Maria Von Trapp

Terry Waite

Kurt Waldheim

Lech Walesa

Agard Henry Wallace

Irving Wallace

Barbara Walters

Andy Warhol

Robert Penn Warren

Jessamyn West

George Washington

George Westinghouse

Harold Washington

James McNeil Whistler

Byron White

Thomas Watson

Edward H. White

James Watt

Theodore H. White

John Wayne

Walt Whitman

Charlie Weaver "Cliff Arquette"

Daniel Webster

Eli Whitney

Charles E. Whitaker

John Greenleaf Whittaker

Oscar Wilde

Thornton Wilder

Sincerely yours,

Wendell Wilkie

King WIlliam IV

Ben Ames Williams

Esther WIlliams

John Williams

Mason Williams

Paul Williams

Tennessee Williams

Meredith Willson

Henry Wilson

Woodrow Wilson

Walter Winchell

Owen Wister

Thomas Wolfe

Grant Wood

Natalie Wood

Orville Wright

Andrew Wyeth

Y

Charles E. "Chuck" Yeager

Jeana Yeager

Frank Yerby

Sgt. Alvin E. York

Brigham Young

Z

Ferdinand von Zeppelin

The
SANDERS
Price Guide to

AUTOGRAPHS

Fifth Edition

Section 7:

DEALERS

Being a guide to some recommended dealers in autographs and historic documents.

Chapter 23

Autograph Dealers

This section contains a <u>Buyer's Guide</u> representing many of the major dealers in the autograph world. While inclusion here does not *per se* mean we endorse a particular dealer over one not participating in this guide, it <u>does</u> mean we believe the dealers here to be reputable experts in their various areas of expertise. And—on the other hand—just because a dealer elected not to participate does not necessarily mean that he or she should be avoided.

However, we hasten to point out that the kind folks who *are* in this book deserve a great vote of thanks (and even a little business, perhaps) from all of us, authors and readers alike. They made this huge book practical and allowed us to both add much more than otherwise would have been possible, and to keep the retail price down to a most reasonable $24.95. Believe us, the printing bill on this tome is immense—please at least say a hearty "thank you" to our wonderful advertisers.

Index to Dealers

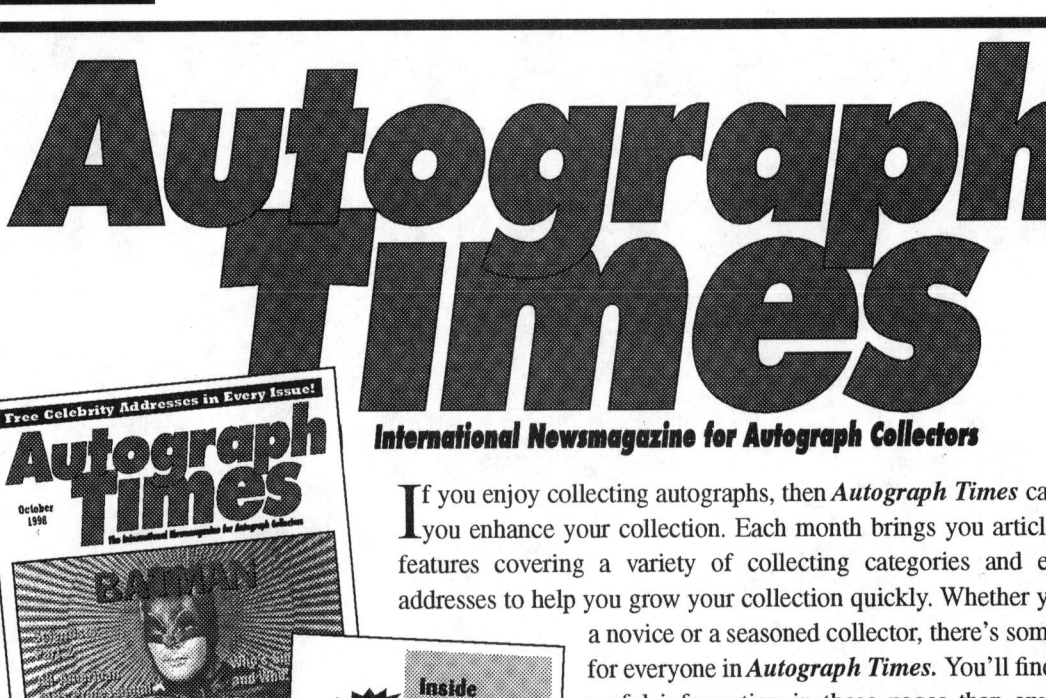

The Professional Autograph Dealers Association™

The source for autograph dealers who are

- ✐ experienced and knowledgeable
- ✐ dedicated to customer service
- ✐ committed to a strict code of ethics

Whether you are buying, selling, or appraising autographs, PADA assures you of quality, courtesy, and integrity

For a free brochure and membership directory, write to

Professional Autograph Dealers Association
P.O. Box 1729–S, Murray Hill Station
New York, NY 10156

Visit our web site: http://www.padaweb.org

For the only guarantee you will ever need, look for our logo

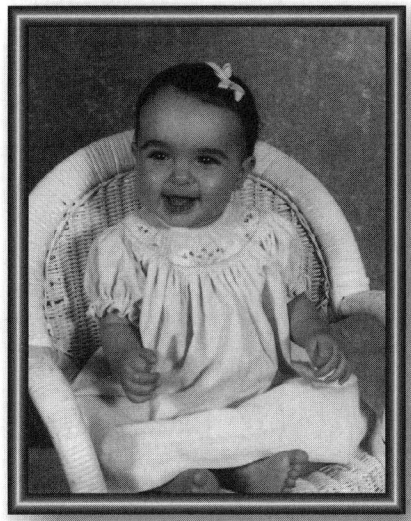

I.A.C.C.
I.A.D.A.

INTERNATIONAL AUTOGRAPH COLLECTORS CLUB
INTERNATIONAL AUTOGRAPH DEALERS ALLIANCE

With a vigor and commitment to excellence, the International Autograph Collectors Club (IACC/DA) has endeavored to heighten awareness of the autograph field in general, and to make much needed improvements. Both plans have met with extraordinary reception. By mixing equally education and enjoyment, we have gained an ever increasing momentum and respect within the autograph community, and to a large degree in other fields as well. It is this rich tapestry of commumity which has been, and will be, our legacy and donation to the preservation of the autograph world, and we were the first organization to combine a collectors club and dealer alliance under the same flag. An international non-profit organization, we are unique as we are exclusively devoted to the collecting of autographs. You are invited to share in this rich tradition by becoming a member. Each of our dealer members is happy to consult with you and guide you in the proper direction at no charge. Whether you are developing a new specialty, or continuing a time honored one,

you can be assured of prompt and fair service, quality material at competitive prices all from dealers who must adhere to the strictest ethical codes of conduct in the industry.

The 1999 dues to share in this tradition are:

$17.50	Domestic Membership
$25.00	International Membership
$250.00	Lifetime Membership

Separate applications available to autograph dealers.

The IACC/DA may be reached at:

4575 Sheridan Street.
Suite 111, Dept. SPG
Hollywood. FL 33425

The Manuscript Society

The Manuscript Society was founded in 1948 as the National Society of Autograph Collectors, and has grown to an international membership of well over 1,500 members including dealers, private collectors, scholars, authors, and caretakers of public collections, such as librarians, archivists, and curators. There are also many institutional members, such as historical societies, museums, special libraries, and academic libraries.

The Manuscript Society welcomes new members. The annual individual membership fee is $35. Contributing memberships are $70, sustaining memberships are $100, and life memberships are $1,000. Memberships are on a calendar year basis—new members joining after July 1 of each year may pay half the annual rate. All moneys go to support the publication program, to aid in the defense of individuals against government agencies in replevin suits, and to maintain the expenses of management of Society affairs.

Additional information about the society may be obtained on their website at **www.manuscript.org**.

To join, the society, contact:

David R. Smith,
Executive Director
THE MANUSCRIPT SOCIETY
350 N. Niagara Street
Burbank, CA 91505-3648

WANTED

Autographs and Documents

TOLL FREE
1-800-906-KEYA
(1-800-906-5392)

Buy-Sell-Appraisals-Consultants
PARIS • LONDON • BONN • ROME • NEW YORK CITY

To receive a **catalog** call **212-366-9742** or E-mail **Key15@aol.com**
www.keyagallery.com

- One of the Worlds Largest Selections of original Authentic Autographs, letters and Documents of the Most Famous People in History, From a Cuneiform Document of a Babylonian King 2000 B.C., To a Handwritten Letter by Abraham Lincoln.
- America's Largest Inventory of 19th Century Photographs of Famous Historical People
- Very Large Selection of Civil War, Lincoln, and Slavery Documents, Relics & Memorabilia

KEYA GALLERY
110 West 25th Street, Gallery 304A, New York NY 10001

UNIVERSAL AUTOGRAPH COLLECTORS CLUB

an invitation to join the U.A.C.C.

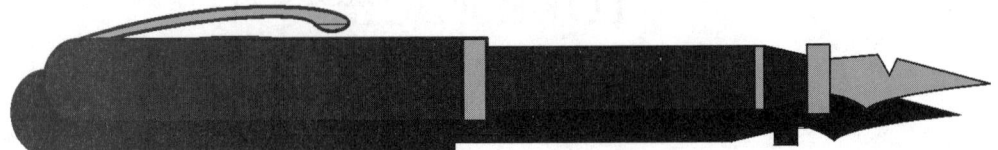

The Universal Autograph Collectors Club, Inc. is a federally approved nonprofit organization dedicated to the **education** of the autograph collector. Founded in 1965, the **U.A.C.C.** is known as "**The Collectors Advocate**." The organization sponsors shows worldwide and publishes its journal the *Pen and Quill* bi-monthly. The U.A.C.C. is an organization for collectors, run by collectors.

The U.A.C.C. sponsors autograph shows in major U.S. cities and London, England featuring educational displays, autograph dealers who abide by the U.A.C.C. Code of Ethics, and celebrity guests. Seminars are occasionally held in conjunction with the shows to educate our members and the public on all aspects of collection and preservation, and identification of non-authentic (bogus or forged) material.

Finally, the U.A.C.C. sponsors mail auctions through *The Pen and Quill* as well as an annual live floor auction near Washington, DC. These auctions are another avenue to assist our members who buy and sell autographs.

To learn more about the U.A.C.C., send your request for a brochure and membership application to the address below. You can also get membership information and an application by visiting our Internet web site at **http://www.uacc.org**. We hope you will join our universe of fellow collectors soon.

For membership information, please write:

UACC
Dept. SPG
P.O. Box 6181
Washington, DC 20044-6181

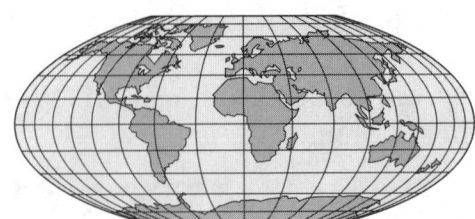

Check out our website at: **http://www.uacc.org**

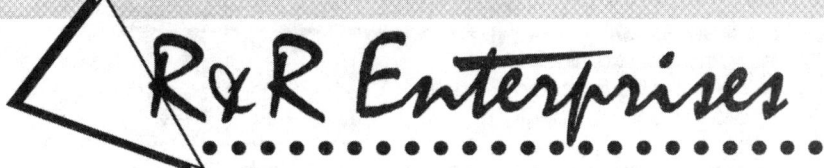

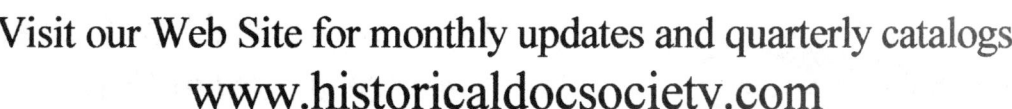

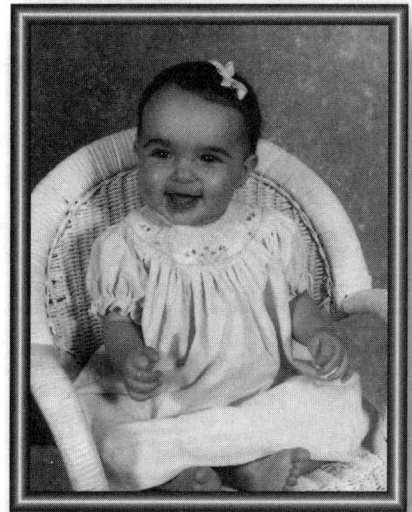

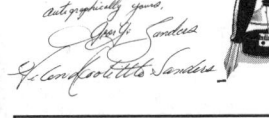